Murray's
HANDBOOK FOR SCOTLAND
(1894)

Also published by David & Charles

MURRAY'S HANDBOOK FOR DEVON AND CORNWALL (1859)

Murray's
HANDBOOK FOR SCOTLAND (1894)

A reprint of the 1894 edition
of *Handbook for Travellers in Scotland*

DAVID & CHARLES REPRINTS

ISBN 0 7153 5317 8

This book was originally published in 1894
by John Murray, London
Reprinted by the present publishers in 1971

NOTE

To achieve some economy the large scale maps of the districts, the town plans and the index map referred to on page v of the Preface, and also on page xiv, have been omitted from this reprint. However, the general atlas of the country is reproduced, and will be found as a supplement at the end of the book.

Printed in Great Britain by
Latimer Trend & Company Limited Whitstable
for David & Charles (Publishers) Limited
South Devon House Newton Abbot Devon

PUBLISHER'S NOTE

This guide, a travelling companion of mine whenever I have visited Scotland during the past 25 years, gives a vivid if relatively brief portrait of the country at a fascinating period of its development for tourists. Much of the Highlands had already become a national British showpiece; visitors had a wide choice of accommodation at Pitlochry and Strathpeffer ('engage rooms beforehand' – something you need seldom do at that particular resort today) and the more adventurous were even expected to reach Cape Wrath, perhaps swimming their horses over the Kyle at low water to avoid the walk there and back ('a good day's work').

But some areas even in the Highlands and certainly on the islands were entirely untouched by tourism, though anywhere in Scotland might be visited by one of that band of travellers anxious to improve their knowledge on every aspect of the country's life and work – and as interested in the deepening of the Clyde (Glasgow then accepted the largest vessels afloat) and in manufacturing processes and the ramifications of railway competition as in Queen's View. Catering for such people, this is a remarkably well-balanced picture of Scotland, with a far greater wealth of details on many aspects such as mines and shipping than are to be found in most later works. Much of it is also most interestingly written; many a time have I been persuaded to make a diversion having been influenced by its pages – though one of its attractions is that odd sentences and asides can be as compelling as much longer passages. It is a veritable mine of information and suggestion, and must have been well worth its 9s (an expensive price for any book in the last century) when it was published. I hope it will justify today's inevitably far higher price and bring enjoyment to many modern tourists.

David St John Thomas

HANDBOOK FOR SCOTLAND

HANDBOOK FOR TRAVELLERS

IN

SCOTLAND

SIXTH EDITION

WITH TRAVELLING MAPS AND PLANS

LONDON
JOHN MURRAY, ALBEMARLE STREET
EDINBURGH: OLIVER & BOYD
1894

PREFACE

THE great changes which have taken place in Scotland during the last few years, in the extension of railways, and the greater facilities for travelling, even to the most remote parts of the country, have made it necessary to recast, and in a great measure to re-write this handbook.

The larger part of the work of revision is the result of the editor's personal acquaintance with the places described, supplemented by information derived from the most trustworthy sources.

The editor has taken pains to point out the best centres for excursions, and to give the tourist who is desirous of exploring the surrounding country such careful, detailed information as shall enable him to do so without a guide. In addition, the book is provided with special large-scale maps for these districts, showing the contours of the mountains, coloured in different tints to indicate at a glance their altitudes. Besides these there are numerous plans of towns, a key map (inside the cover of the book), showing all the routes and giving the pages where the most important places are described, and a general atlas of the country, made to correspond with the sections of the handbook.

Another new feature of this edition is the index and directory, in which are incorporated the names of all hotels and particulars regarding them, as well as information relating to shops, coaches, steamers, telegraph offices, and such other matters as are liable to change, and require frequent revision.

The editor takes this opportunity to express his sense of obligation to the many persons who have been good enough to supply him with official statistics, local information, and valuable suggestions.

Great pains have been taken to keep this edition free from inaccuracies, but owing to the nature of the book, which is replete with detailed information, it is hardly possible but that a few errors and omissions should occur, and the editor would esteem it a favour if readers would enable him to remedy such defects by sending him notice of them, to the care of Mr. Murray, 50 Albemarle Street.

Finally, the editor desires to call especial attention to the size of the book, which, though it contains more than 500 *pages, has been compressed to its present small dimensions by being printed on thin paper, made specially for the purpose, with the object of making it as handy and portable as possible for the tourist.*

CONTENTS

SECTION I.

THE SOUTH OF SCOTLAND—LAND OF SCOTT—EDINBURGH—VALE OF TWEED—FALLS OF CLYDE—LAND OF BURNS

ROUTES.

_ The *Names of Places* are printed in *Italics* in those Routes in which the *Places* are *described*.

SECTION II.

WESTERN MIDLANDS—GLASGOW—HAMILTON—LOCH LOMOND—STIRLING—LOCH KATRINE—THE TROSSACHS—CALLANDER AND OBAN RLY.

ROUTES.

SECTION III.

EASTERN MIDLANDS AND CENTRAL HIGHLANDS—FORTH BRIDGE—FIFE—ST. ANDREWS—TAY BRIDGE—KINROSS—CLACKMANNAN—PERTHSHIRE—HIGHLAND RLY.

ROUTES.

SECTION IV.

NORTH-EAST OF SCOTLAND—DUNDEE—FORFARSHIRE—ABERDEENSHIRE —DEESIDE—BRAEMAR—BANFFSHIRE—ELGIN

SECTION V.

WEST COAST (SOUTHERN PORTION)—ESTUARY OF THE CLYDE—BUTE—KYLES OF BUTE—ARRAN—LOCH FYNE—CAMPBELTOWN—ISLAY AND JURA.

ROUTES.

SECTION VI.

WEST COAST (CENTRAL PORTION)—WEST HIGHLAND RAILWAY (GLASGOW TO FORT-WILLIAM)—ARDRISHAIG—CRINAN CANAL—OBAN—MULL—STAFFA—IONA—LOCH LINNHE—GLEN COE—FORT-WILLIAM—BEN NEVIS—CALEDONIAN CANAL.

ROUTES.

SECTION VII.

NORTH-WEST HIGHLANDS—INVERNESS—GLEN AFFRIC—DINGWALL—STRATHPEFFER—ULLAPOOL—LOCH MAREE—GAIRLOCH—STROME FERRY—LOCH DUICH—SKYE—OUTER HEBRIDES.

ROUTES.

SECTION VIII.

NORTH OF SCOTLAND—BLACK ISLE—CROMARTY—SUTHERLAND—LOCH INVER—CAITHNESS—JOHN O' GROAT'S—CAPE WRATH

ROUTES.

SECTION IX.

THE ORKNEY AND SHETLAND ISLANDS.

ROUTES.

LIST OF MAPS AND PLANS

ABBREVIATIONS.—Br. = Bridge; Cas. = Castle; Ch. = Church; (Estab. = Established; Epis. = Episcopal; U.P. = United Presbyterian; R.C. = Roman Catholic); Ho. = House; Junc. = Junction; Lo. = (Shooting) Lodge; m. = mile; Mt. = Mountain; Mont. = Monument; Rly. = Railway; Rte. = Route; St. = Street; Stat. = Station; N.S.E.W. = Points of the compass; l. = left; rt. = right; C.R. = Caledonian Railway; G. & S.W.R. = Glasgow and South-Western Railway; G.N.S.R. = Great North of Scotland Railway; H.R. = Highland Railway; N.B.R. = North British Railway.

✲ After a place-name refers to the Index for further information.

† Indicates a pier or landing-place for steamers.

An asterisk * or asterisks ** before a place-name indicate that it is specially worthy of attention.

GENERAL INTRODUCTION

I. General Information as to Ways of reaching Scotland—Railways, Steamers, Coaches, Hotels, and Posting.

Since the days when Pennant (1772) made his slow but comprehensive journey to the West Coast and the Hebrides—when Dr. Johnson (1773) travelled with ill-suppressed sneers and disgust to the Isle of Skye—or when, in later days, the persevering Macculloch (1811) examined every little inlet on that dangerous coast in the very frailest of conveyances—a perfect revolution has been effected in Scotland in favour of the tourist. In place of the rugged fastnesses which guarded the romantic scenery of the Highlands, we have, generally speaking, good roads and swift conveyances on them. Even the once dreary solitudes of Sutherland and Caithness are, for practical purposes, as well off for roads as many an English county. At all the important points good hotels, sometimes rising to the magnitude of palaces, have been erected, while, where possible, railways and steamers convey travellers into the very heart of the mountains.

Principal ways of reaching Scotland.

[A] By Steamer.

(1) From Hermitage Wharf, *London* (London and Edin. Shipping Co.) to *Leith* (Rly., tramway, or cab to Edin., 2 m.) 3 times a week, in about 30 hrs. Fares, 22s. and 16s.; Ret., available for 12 months, 34s. and 24s. 6d.

(2) From Irongate Wharf, *London* (General Steam Navigation Co.) to *Granton* (Rly. to Edin. 2 m.) twice a week (in summer) in about 30 hrs. Fares, 22s. and 16s.; Ret. 34s. and 24s. 6d.

(3) From New Dundee Wharf, *London* (Dundee, Perth, and London Shipping Co.) to *Dundee*, twice a week, in about 32 hrs. Fares, 22s. 6d. and 15s.; Ret. (3 months) 35s. and 22s. 6d. (14 days in summer, single fare).

(4) From Aberdeen Steam Navigation Co.'s Wharf, *London* to *Aberdeen*, twice a week, in about 36 hrs. Fares, 30s. and 15s.; Ret. (6 months) 45s. and 25s.

(5) From St. Katherine's Dock, *London* (Clyde Shipping Co.) to *Greenock* and *Glasgow*, three times a week. Fares, 30s. and 12s. 6d.; Ret. 50s. and 18s. 9d.

(6) From Carron Wharf, *London* (Carron Line) to *Grangemouth* (through trains to Glasgow), three times a week, in about 30 hours. Fares to Glasgow, 26s., 24s., and 17s. 6d.; Ret. 39s., 35s., and 26s. 6d.

(7) From *Liverpool* to *Greenock* or *Glasgow*, daily. Fare, 12s. 6d.; Ret. (2 months) 20s.; (10 days) 15s.

(8) From *Liverpool* to *Oban*, *Skye*, *Stornoway*, *Orkney*, *Aberdeen*, and *Leith*, once or twice a week. Apply M. Langlands and Sons, Liverpool.

[B] BY RAILWAY.

(1) **East Coast Route** from King's Cross, *via* York, Newcastle, and Berwick to *Edinburgh* (397 m.) in 8½ hrs. [Rte. 1]; to Glasgow [Rte. 19] in 10 hrs.; to Perth [Rte. 34] in 10 hrs.; to Dundee [Rte. 30] in 10½ hrs.; to Aberdeen [Rte. 48] in 12¼ hrs.; and to Inverness [Rte. 42] in 15 hrs.

(2) **West Coast Route** from Euston, *via* Preston, Carlisle, and Carstairs to *Edinburgh* (401 m.) in 8½ hrs. [Rtes. 2 and 9]; to Glasgow [Rte. 2] in 8¾ hrs.; to Perth in 9¾ hrs.; Dundee 10¾ hrs., and Aberdeen 12¼ hrs. [Rtes. 2, 25, 38, 46, and 47]; and to Inverness [Rte. 42] 15 hrs.

By (1) and (2), besides the morning and night trains, there are afternoon trains from London, reaching Edinburgh or Glasgow about 11 P.M. and (in summer) Perth shortly after midnight.

(3) **Midland Route** from St. Pancras, *via* Normanton to Carlisle; thence by N. British Rly. **Waverley Rte.** to *Edinburgh* [Rte. 3] (404 m.) in 9¾ hrs.; or by Glasgow and S.W. Rly. to *Glasgow* [Rte. 12] in 9¼ hrs., and *Greenock* 10 hrs.

Railway Communication has developed enormously of late years both in number of lines and in rate of speed. The centre of Scotland is a network of railways. Lines penetrate to the S.W. corner of the country, and to within 20 miles of John o' Groat's House in the extreme N.E.; they traverse some of the finest scenery on their way to Oban or Fort-William; they thread their way through the heart of the Highlands to Inverness and the North; and, since the opening of the Forth Bridge in 1890, Aberdeen can be reached from Edinburgh in three hours and a half. If in some parts of the country trains are fewer in number and slower than the traveller would wish, little remains to be desired as to through communication between the leading centres. The tourist who leaves London at night breakfasts at Perth and can sleep in a hotel at Fort-William, Stornoway, or Orkney; or, having lunched at 2 o'clock in London, he can reach Edinburgh, Glasgow, or Perth the same day. There are six leading railway companies in Scotland with, in many instances, running powers over each other's lines.

The **North British Rly. Co.**, keeping largely to the *East Coast*, has the lines from Berwick-on-Tweed *via* Dunbar to Edinburgh, and from Carlisle by the *Waverley Route* (with various branches) to Edinburgh, thence by the Forth Bridge to Fife and Perth, and by the Tay Bridge to Dundee and Aberdeen. It has the local lines to the E. and S.E. of Edinburgh, lines from Edinburgh to and around Glasgow, to the Clyde, Loch Lomond, and Stirling, and throughout Fife. The attractive West Highland line, opened in 1894, by the head of Loch Lomond and across the dreary Moor of Rannoch to Fort-William, is worked by the N. Brit. Rly. Co.

The **Caledonian Rly. Co.** has the *central* lines from Carlisle by Carstairs to Edinburgh, Glasgow, Stirling, Perth, and Aberdeen, with branches to Dumfries, Peebles, Lanark, Dundee, etc. It has local lines to the W. of Edinburgh, lines from Edinburgh to and around Glasgow, most important lines from Glasgow to Gourock, Wemyss Bay, and Ardrossan for the Clyde traffic, and the favourite tourist line from Stirling *via* Callander to Oban.

The **Glasgow and South-Western Rly. Co.** has, as its name implies, lines to the S.W. of the great commercial capital, including those from Carlisle *via* Dumfries to Glasgow, with a branch from Dumfries to Castle-Douglas and Kirkcudbright, from Glasgow to Ayr, Girvan, and Stranraer, and from Glasgow to Greenock, Ardrossan, and Largs, for the Clyde traffic.

The **Highland Rly. Co.** has the all-important line for tourists and sportsmen which runs from Perth to Inverness and the extreme N. of Scotland, with branches to Aberfeldy, Keith, Strathpeffer, and Strome Ferry.

The **Great North of Scotland Rly. Co.** has no line W. of Elgin, but supplies the lines of Aberdeenshire (including that by Deeside to Ballater) and of Banffshire. It has a branch from Elgin to the Highland Rly. at Boat of Garten, which traverses the picturesque Strathspey.

The **Portpatrick and Wigtownshire Rly. Co.** has the comparatively short line from Castle-Douglas to Stranraer and Portpatrick, with a branch from Newton-Stewart to Wigtown and Whithorn.

Steamers on the E. coast sail from London to Leith or Granton (for Edinburgh), and to Dundee and Aberdeen. From Leith there is communication two or three times a week with Aberdeen, Wick, Thurso, Orkney, and Shetland. On the W. coast steamers from Bristol and Liverpool sail to Glasgow, and from Liverpool—once or twice a week—to Oban, Skye, Stornoway, Orkney, and round the N. of Scotland to Leith.

An ever-increasing fleet of river-steamers, to the various watering-places on the Clyde, sail daily from the Broomielaw, Glasgow, or may be found at Craigendoran, Greenock, Gourock, Wemyss Bay, or Ardrossan, after taking express trains to these different stations. The "Ivanhoe" conveys tourists daily by the Kyles of Bute to Arran, and the "Lord of the Isles" sails through the Kyles to Inveraray. These comfortable steamers are only surpassed by Mr. David Macbrayne's floating palaces—the "Iona" and "Columba"—which ply daily in summer to Ardrishaig, whence Oban is reached by the Crinan Canal and steamer on the other side. His powerful "Claymore" and "Clansman" sail round the Mull of Kintyre and up the W. coast to Oban,—where they may be joined,—Skye, and Stornoway; while his swift steamers, starting from Oban, sail daily to Mull, and (in the season) to Staffa and Iona, to Fort-William, for the Caledonian Canal boat to Inverness, and three times a week to Skye and Gairloch. Daily throughout the year a steamer plies from Strome Ferry to Skye and Stornoway; also from Oban daily to Lochmaddy and three times a week to other ports in the Outer Hebrides. Other steamers sail between Glasgow and the Western Isles, but are more specially arranged for goods traffic.

Steamers ply across the Forth between Granton and Burntisland several times daily, and almost hourly (in summer) between Leith and Aberdour, frequently calling at South Queensferry beyond the Forth Bridge. Steamers also sail daily (in summer) from Leith, tide permitting, to Alloa and Stirling; while Excursions once or twice a week are made to North Berwick, May Island, Elie, and St. Andrews.

On the Tay a steamer sails daily, according to tide, between Dundee and Perth; and on all the larger Scottish inland lochs steamers ply in connection with trains or coaches.

Coaches are to be found on all the leading tourist routes, and their place is generally supplied in the less-frequented parts of the country by mail-carts capable of accommodating from two to six passengers.

Hotels are abundant, and vary from the lofty and splendidly furnished hotel to the little wayside inn. In all the large towns and the principal "trysting-places," particularly on the west coast, the hotel accommodation is admirable, and if it is rather expensive, as it doubtless is in some places, it must be remembered that for eight months in the year the hotel, with all its outlay, is practically tenantless; and even the success during the other four months depends on the good graces of the weather. In many places, too, the cost of transit for necessaries and provisions is a large item in the hotel-keeper's expenses.

As tourists in the height of the season are gregarious, and follow the beaten track, the traveller, particularly if with a party, is recommended to time his arrival at certain places as early as possible, and to secure beds and rooms beforehand, as he will otherwise find that even sofas are not always to be obtained. This precaution applies still more to some of the more solitary districts of Ross and Sutherland, as the inns are limited in size, and are frequently monopolised by sportsmen.

Hydropathic Establishments are to be found in many of the leading tourist centres, *e.g.* Moffat, Peebles, Melrose, Rothesay, Bridge of Allan, Dunblane, Callander, Crieff, Pitlochrie, Forres, etc. Visitors are accommodated at rates varying from 8s. 6d. a day, or £2 : 2s. a week, upwards, inclusive of meals, which are provided in common for all the guests. Spirituous liquors are not generally kept. Most of these establishments have excellent recreation grounds attached to them.

Although the principal centres are well supplied with hotels, there is often a want of wayside inns, and in some districts in the Highlands, and even in the Lowlands, the pedestrian may have to walk 20 m. or 30 m. without reaching one. Many of the Lowland hotels—chiefly patronised by commercial travellers—if plain, are clean and comfortable, with good simple fare at moderate rates. There is *Telegraphic Communication* with all the principal places, with most of the islands, and with many an out-of-the-way spot.

Posting.—On all the high roads, travellers not availing themselves of public coaches may travel, as comfortably and as cheaply (or dearly) as in England, with post-horses.

The charges are generally 1s. a mile for 1 horse, 3d. a mile for driver—half fare returning. For 2 horses 1s. 6d. a mile, 4d a mile for driver, but for a whole day's work the driver ought not to get more than 5s. In some districts the post-masters exact 1s. 9d. a mile.

The carriages for hire—generally called "machines"—are tolerable, and are to be had at most of the hotels and inns. The more common are waggonettes—some of large size, holding eight or ten persons. It is well to order carriages beforehand by telegram (pay for a reply), as in the tourist season the supply may fall far short of the demand.

II. Hints for Tourists, Sportsmen, Cyclists, and Pedestrians.

All tourists should provide themselves with *Murray's Time Table*, published monthly, price 3d.—the Bradshaw of Scotland, but a very much simpler compilation. The following are also useful :—"Summer Tours in Scotland," price 3d., issued annually by the Caledonian Rly. Co., with maps attached, the N.B. Rly. Co.'s "Tourist Arrangements," and, if the W. coast is to be visited, Macbrayne's "Summer Tours in Scotland," issued annually, price 6d.—apply 119 Hope Street, Glasgow. *Bartholomew's excellent maps* (2 miles to the inch—orographically coloured—reduced from the Ordnance Survey, covering the whole of Scotland in 29 sheets—2s. each)—to be had of all large booksellers or direct from the Geographical Institute, Edinburgh—are recommended to all intelligent travellers ; they are indispensable for cyclists and will meet the wants of all pedestrians, except mountaineers, who should get the Ordnance Survey map—1 mile to the inch—for the district in which they propose to climb.

The "Sportsman's Guide," published monthly, May–October, price 1s.—with time-tables and map—furnishes anglers and sportsmen with special information as to lochs and rivers, while by the ordinary traveller its lists of the proprietors of the different shootings and fishings, and their tenants, will be found interesting. "Nauticus in Scotland ; a Tricycle Tour of 2462 miles," published by Messrs. Simpkin and Marshall, and the "Handbook of the Cyclist Touring Club," are recommended to those who meditate a "cruise on wheels."

Even Alpine climbers need not despise several of the Scottish mountains, and will find particularly ticklish rock work on the Coolins in Skye. Few of the mountains, however, are dangerous unless in mist. A *compass* should be always carried, a good *field glass* is desirable and at times useful, and a *comforter* of *Shetland wool*, which takes little room in pocket or bag—to be worn as a waistcoat or protection for the throat—is strongly recommended. A fair supply of provisions and a flask of Scotch whisky are among the indispensables. A mackintosh, excellent for steamers and coaches, may be dispensed with by the hardy pedestrian, provided he has a change of clothes awaiting him at the end of his walk. The "Mountaineering Journal," published three times a year since 1890, price 1s., contains descriptions of most of the leading mountain expeditions, and several excellent photographs.

It is well for all tourists to remember that, even in the middle of summer, nights among the hills or on the east coast, when an easterly "*haar*" (as a damp mist is called in Scotland) comes driving up from the sea, make some additional warm clothing essential, while it is not quite *comme il faut* to walk about large towns like Edinburgh and Glasgow in a costume that would be suitable enough for a hillside or a moor. They should recollect, too, that the Scottish middle and lower classes are not, as a rule, given to joking, except with their own dry, sententious humour, and that they very rarely understand what is commonly called "chaff." It is better to bear this in mind, as it may account for many an apparently surly manner or gruff reply.

Finally, every tourist should visit Scottish scenery prepared for every kind of weather, and gifted with a considerable stock of patience. Sometimes on the very day, or hour, when he is preparing to turn back, disheartened at the weather, it clears up, and reveals views unparalleled for atmospheric effects.

The traveller in the west of Scotland, among the lochs and rivers, is subjected to an intolerable insect plague of "midges,"—small gnats, scarcely visible, but covering the face with painful and enduring punctures. Prince Charlie, in his year of hiding, 1746, was nearly driven distracted by them. Ammonia is very efficacious in removing the pain of the stings; and tobacco smoke, or a little paraffin oil rubbed on any exposed part of the skin, is a good preventive of the attacks of these assailants. Turpentine is said to be an antidote, but the cure is almost as bad as the disease.

III. ANTIQUITIES AND ARCHITECTURE.

Scotland has a large field open to antiquarian exploration, and the wonder is how few attempts have been made to examine and describe it systematically. It may not be amiss to give a short list of the principal works in this branch, so that the tourist who is interested in the subject may consult them. They include Pennant's "Tour in Scotland"; the publications of the Bannatyne and Spalding Clubs (the latter of which is particularly full on inscribed stones); "Transactions of the Royal Society of Antiquaries of Scotland"; the "Cambridge Camden Society's Papers," which contain a learned series on the "Argyllshire Ecclesiastical Antiquities" by Mr. Howson; Grose's "Antiquities"; Billings' "Baronial and Ecclesiastical Antiquities," a magnificent and exhaustive work; "Castellated Domestic Architecture of Scotland," from 12th to 18th century, by D. Macgibbon and T. Ross; "Pre-Historic Annals of Scotland," by Daniel Wilson; "The Sculptured Stones of Scotland," by John Stuart, 2 vols. 4to. (Spalding Club), 1856 and 1867. The works of the late Cosmo Innes—"Scotland in the Middle Ages: its History and Social Progress" (1860), and "History of the Northern Parts of Britain,"—abound in valuable and trustworthy information. Reeves' "Life of Adamnan" contains the best account of Iona and St. Columba. "Scotland in Early Christian Times," by Dr. Joseph Anderson, Keeper of the National Museum of Antiquities, Edinburgh, 2 vols. (1881); and "Scotland in Pagan Times," by the same author, are standard works. "Scottish Land-Names," by Sir Herbert Maxwell, Bt. (1894), is an interesting and pleasantly-written volume on thoroughly scientific lines. In "The Orkneys and Shetland," by J. R. Tudor, will be found a full and interesting account of those islands. These, together with Skene's "Celtic Scotland" and Burton's "History of Scotland," are perhaps the most important and the most accessible sources of information. Of late years much attention has been directed to

(1) **Pre-historic Remains**, which, in the districts on the coast, and more especially towards the north, appear to be unusually abundant.

i. **Lake Dwellings** and **Mounds**.—Operations for draining have revealed in the bed of the Loch of Dowalton, Wigtownshire, and in other lochs in Galloway, Ayrshire, Argyllshire, and Inverness-shire, traces of the lake-dwellings so common in Switzerland; and researches in Caithness and Orkney have discovered large numbers of mounds containing kists and relics of inhumation. Mr. Laing says:—

"The rocky coasts and commanding heights are not more thickly studded with the strongholds of Scandinavian pirates and mediæval barons, than are the shores and straths with large conical mounds, showing traces of concentric walls, which are in all probability the ruins of burghs or circular towers. In addition there are numerous chambered cairns and Picts' houses, and barrows or sepulchral tumuli of various forms and dimensions. There are also many traces of hut-circles, and other pre-historic dwellings, of a humbler class than the circular burgh;

and numerous shell-middens, or refuse heaps of the food of the ancient inhabitants, are found in connection with their dwellings."

ii. **The Brochs** (also written Burghs and Broughs) or **Picts' Houses**, as some call them, are involved in much obscurity as to date, some archæologists attributing them to Celts, others to Scandinavians. The probability is that they were anterior to either of them, notwithstanding the smoothness and regularity of the buildings themselves, which would seem to point to the work of a more civilised people, and that they were used by the different races of inhabitants, who found them ready to hand, for dwelling, storing, or burying purposes. Scandinavian authorities declare that nothing like them was ever found in those countries. Wilson, in his "Pre-Historic Scotland," considers them to be long prior to the earliest recorded Scandinavian invasion; and Dr. Petrie discovered in a broch in the parish of Birsay, in Orkney, contents of a similar character to those in the mounds. They are chiefly found in the N. of Scotland, beyond the Great Glen or line of the Caledonian Canal. The most perfect type is the Tower of Mousa, on an islet in Shetland. From this example, and others less perfect, they appear to have been cylinders of masonry tapering upwards into a truncated cone, or waisted like a dice-box. The walls are composed of an outer and inner concentric shell of untrimmed stones—evenly set, but without mortar. This rude masonry is bound together by four or five courses of slabs of slate placed crosswise, so as to leave in the thickness of the wall a gallery or inclined plane winding up to the top like a corkscrew, and lighted by small openings or slits in the inside. The rest of the wall is filled up with loose stones, and it may measure in thickness from 10 to 15 feet. The towers vary in height from 25 to 40 feet, and in diameter from 30 to 50 feet. They were not roofed, but the inner slits open into a circular court.

A low door on the ground level led into this and communicated with the winding galleries or cells, which in some instances are so low and narrow (3 feet) that it is difficult to understand how any but a race of pigmies could have traversed them. Sir Walter Scott compares the Tower of Mousa to a ruined pigeon-house. More than 400 examples—more or less ruined—are known of these towers in the N. and N.W. of Scotland and in the Isles. They are thus distributed—in Shetland, 75; Orkney, 70; Caithness, 79; Sutherland, 60; Long Island, 38; Skye, 30, etc. (See Dr. Joseph Anderson's "Scotland in Pagan Times.")

iii. **Circles**, which, although not very abundant, show more or less evidences of size and importance, were probably the great centres of religious and legislative ceremonies. A curious feature in connection with these remains is, that the largest circles are usually found in the islands, such as Stenness in Orkney, Callernish in Lewis, and Tormore in Arran, which seems to point to the conclusion that these "trysting-places" were generally established where they could overlook large bodies of water. It is worth noticing that the Cromlech in Wales and Ireland is almost always placed in a similar position.

(2) Early Historic Remains.

i. Amongst the very earliest of these we should be disposed to class the **Round Towers**, which, though common enough in Ireland, are represented by but three specimens in Scotland—(*a*) On the island of Egilsay, Orkney; (*b*) at Brechin, in Forfarshire; (*c*) at Abernethy, in Perthshire. Of these the first two are attached to the remains of a church. The third is detached but stands in a churchyard. Their uses, as described by the late Dr. Petrie in his erudite work on "Irish Round Towers," seem to have been those of providing places of safety and defence for the ecclesiastical buildings and treasures in their neighbourhood, as well as of the population gathered around. Their date varies from the 8th to the 12th century, and it seems probable that those of Scotland are of the later class.

ii. **Memorial Stones** are of two sorts—the plain slab used to commemorate some interment or some event, and generally known as a "stele." Sometimes, however, they are used for purposes of demarcation, as in the Welsh "maenhir." The inscribed stone varies very much in its character, from the simple name which it was intended to commemorate, to the most elaborate ornamentation and device of sculpture (see p. 245).

iii. **Crosses** likewise exhibit a great diversity of character, from the plain cross to the sculptured. But very few are now left in Scotland, and these cannot vie in comparison with those of Ireland. The most perfect are those of Iona, Campbeltown, and Inveraray.

iv. Of **Dykes and Roads** there are likewise very few remains, what there are being limited to the south. They include the Catrail or Picts' Dyke across the Cheviots, and the Devil's Dyke in Dumfriesshire, both early British works. Of a later date is the Roman wall of Antoninus, extending from the Forth to the Clyde, also the Roman road from Nithsdale to Elvanfoot, and that from Ardoch to Perth.

v. The **Camps** are nearly all Roman. The number of Roman camps is very great, greater it is said than in all the rest of Europe, and denotes the arduous nature of the struggle with the natives, and its long duration. They stretch as far N. as Aberdeen and Inverness-shire, but are most numerous in the comparatively flat districts, at the foot of the Grampians—Strathearn, Strathmore, and Strathallan. Ardoch camp near Greenloaning Station is the most perfect, not only in Scotland, but in the British Isles. Among British Forts the best specimens are Dun-da-lamh near Laggan in Inverness-shire, and those on the Caterthuns near Brechin. Other examples are to be found in Peeblesshire.

While on the subject of defences we must not omit mention of those singular *vitrified forts* which are ascribed to the Danes. Dunjardil in Glen Nevis (easily accessible), Knockfarril near Dingwall, Craig Phadrick near Inverness, Tap o' Noth in Aberdeenshire, and Dunskeig in Kintyre, are the best-preserved and most interesting examples. It will not escape notice that they generally occupy projecting and isolated heights, suited for *beacons* or bale-fires, which in ancient times served the purpose of telegrams to give notice of foreign invasion. The action of fire on the stone heaps upon which the fires were lighted may in course of ages have caused the vitrification of these stone heaps. Some antiquaries believe these so-called forts to have been merely enclosures for cattle.

(3) **Ecclesiastical Remains** in Scotland cannot well be judged by the same rules that apply to similar remains in England.

"Though so near a neighbour, and so mixed up with England in all the relations of war and peace, the Scotch never borrowed willingly from the English, but, owing probably to the Celtic element in the population, all their affinities and predilections were for continental nations, and especially for France. So completely is this the case that there is scarcely a single building in the country that would not look anomalous and out of place in England; and though it is true that the edifices are not entirely French in design, the whole taste and character of them is continental, though wrought out in a bolder and generally in a simpler and ruder fashion than the corresponding examples in other countries."—FERGUSSON.

The consequence is, that, in addition to the foreign admixture of style, the very date of the various styles in Scotland is long subsequent to the prevalence of the same style farther south.

Thus, in the 12th century (reign of David I.), when the pointed arch was in use in the South, we find the round arch in full vigour in the North; and when the Scotch adopted the E.E. lancet window, they were so pleased with it that they did not give it up, but continued to use it long after the Dec. and even the Perp. styles prevailed in England. The styles of the several periods are accordingly not so definitely marked off from each other in Scotland as in England, a great mixture of styles being often observable, *e.g.* the round-headed arch is often found in early pointed buildings with mouldings of that date. In this respect they resemble some foreign examples, and may owe their peculiarity, perhaps, to the influence of French architects. To these there are some exceptions, for Dunfermline reminds one of Durham, and features of Arbroath may be traced to Canterbury. Scotland, however, possesses glorious examples of Gothic art. Besides the Cathedral of Glasgow, a national monument which alone will repay a pilgrimage, and Rosslyn Chapel,—an anomalous curiosity of the 15th century, so unlike other contemporary buildings that a Spanish or Portuguese origin has been attributed to it, though, after all, it may owe its peculiarities to the freaks of a native genius—there are the four abbeys of Tweedside, Melrose, Dryburgh, Kelso, and Jedburgh. In the secluded dales of the Nith and of Galloway are the three less-known but always charming ruined abbeys of Lincluden, Sweetheart, and Dundrennan; the artistic ruins of Crossraguel in Ayrshire, and on the remote N.E. sea coast, St. Andrews, Arbroath, Elgin, and Pluscardine, are all highly interesting to English architects and antiquaries, and all furnish admirable subjects for the artist's pencil.

The real decorated features are very scarce, and what does remain of the Dec. style of architecture is associated with the Flamboyant character prevalent on the Continent.

Of Perp. churches, Melrose is almost the only example; and even this, Mr. Fergusson observes, is more of a foreign than of English type. Remarkable features in many of the ecclesiastical buildings in Scotland are the bold and perfect vaults or crypts, which often retain beautiful specimens of moulding, although the vaulting itself, as compared with those in England, is poor and weak.

It has been too readily assumed that these fine buildings owe their present state of ruin to John Knox and the hammer of his fanatic followers. In the instances of Perth and St. Andrews he must indeed bear the blame; but in the case of the Border abbeys, the injury was inflicted by the English soldiers of Henry VIII. and Elizabeth, during those savage invasions or forays led by Hertford, Bowes, Sussex, and others.

(4) **Castles, Towers, and Mansions.** — "Scotland is, generally speaking, very deficient in objects of civil or domestic architecture belonging to the Middle Ages;" nor are there any *Norman* castles in Scotland. The earliest and largest feudal fortresses seem to date from the Edwardian era, and many of them were actually built by the English. Such may have been the origin of Dirleton, Doune, and Castle Urquhart. "Of her palaces, Holyrood has been almost rebuilt in the reign of Charles II., and Edinburgh Castle entirely remodelled. Stirling still retains some fragments of ancient art, and Falkland passes into rich and fantastic Renaissance."

Of *Towers* there are numerous examples, almost all of the same rude and simple type of Border or Peel towers, in which strength and the greatest capability of defence, with a small number in garrison, seem to have been the desiderata. A chain of these towers runs along the Borders. The house of every one who had farm produce or live stock to protect, was a *Peel Tower* or Bastel. The terrific invasions of borderers and mosstroopers, lifting cattle, spoiling crops, burning barns and homesteads, compelled the land-owner to construct a refuge for his family and retainers. On the ground floor was a byre or a dungeon; above, a room for servants; and still higher, the dwelling-room of the family; a corkscrew stair led to the top, and the bottom was closed by an iron door or gate.

The wealthier nobles lived in *Castles* consisting of a tower broader and loftier, surrounded by an enclosing wall for defending the out-buildings, forming a court, into which cattle could be driven.

Such castles are Borthwick, Crichton, Hermitage (stronghold of the Douglases), Craigmillar, Castle Campbell, and Caerlaverock, etc., which are very fine and extensive, showing that they were not merely limited to purposes of warfare, but served also as places of residence.

Of *Mansions*, many of them still inhabited, there are many noble examples, presenting a singular style, which is very peculiar to Scotland, and strongly indicates the French tendency. As the architectural features are described under each example, it will not be necessary to enter here into greater detail.

IV. Geology.

The professional Geologist will find much interesting information in the "Transactions of the Royal Geological Society" and in those of the Geological Society of Scotland, including several contributions by Sir Archibald Geikie and his brother Professor

James Geikie (author of the "Great Ice Age"). He will do well to procure, if possible, the Ordnance Sheet (1 inch to the mile) of the district he wishes to study, but only some of the sheets are as yet published. No one, however, has done more to popularise the Geology of Scotland than Sir Archibald Geikie, and every one who takes any interest whatever in this science should read his "Scenery of Scotland" (2nd ed., 1887, 12s. 6d.), and should get Bartholomew's "Geological Map of Scotland," accompanied with a Memoir by Sir A. Geikie, 7s. 6d.

V. Explanation of Gaelic Words and Highland Names of Places.

The following list of Gaelic roots in current use for the naming of places in the Highlands is only a very small fraction of what might readily be given. Persons who wish to study Gaelic place-names will find great aid in Joyce's "Orig. and Hist. of Irish Names of Places" (Dublin, 1871-72). Excellent lists of place-names are found in "Place Names of Scotland," by James B. Johnston, B.D. (David Douglas, 1892), and in "Scottish Land Names," by Sir Herbert Maxwell, Bart. (W. Blackwood and Sons, 1894). In order to understand certain changes to which a Gaelic root is subject in flexion, and in the formation of compound words, some peculiarities of the language require to be known.

Modern Scottish Gaelic may be defined as a member of the Goidelic branch of the Celtic stock of the Aryan family of languages. The Gaelic of the Isle of Man and that of Ireland are but different dialects of the one and the same language. Prichard, in his work, "The Eastern Origin of the Celtic Nations proved by a Comparison of their Dialects with the Sanscrit, Greek, Latin, and Teutonic Languages" (Quaritch, London, 1831), first directed the attention of the learned world to the place of the Celtic tongues in the science of comparative philology. It was, however, the German scholar Zeuss who first satisfactorily established the exact position of the Celtic languages in the Aryan family. The old belief that Gaelic was closely connected with Hebrew is discarded by Celtic scholars. The number of Gaelic words which are found to resemble Latin is striking. It is found that the relationship between those two languages is closer than between any other two of the Aryan family. The language which ranks next to Latin in this relationship is Moeso-Gothic, the oldest known representative of our English speech. Words such as the Gaelic *tigh* (a house) =

Latin *tectum; beann* (a peak) = *pinna; each* (a horse) = *equus; loch* = *lacus; fear* (a man) = *vir; faith* (a prophet) = *vates*, strike the most casual observer. There are hundreds of words in Gaelic of cognate origin with Latin and Gothic words, that is, both come from a common source older than either Latin, Gothic, or Gaelic, and hundreds more in Gaelic are so altered in form that it is sometimes difficult to say whether they are of cognate origin, or are "loan-words" from Latin.

The method of varying roots by flexional syllables added to their termination, so familiar to the classical scholar, is used also in Gaelic, but to a limited extent. The attrition to which Gaelic words have been subjected for ages before they became fixed in writing, accounts for the fragmentary and rubbed-down look of these words when they are compared with those of the classic languages. Our Anglo-Saxon speech underwent a similar process, as compared with German, before it came to be fixed in literature. Hence the larger number of flexions in German than there is in its sister speech, English. The case of *Taynuilt* [Tay = Tigh = House (by the brook)], a well-known station between Oban and Loch Awe, illustrates an inflexional change which is peculiar to Gaelic, viz. that the relation of one word to another is indicated by inflection, not merely at the end of the word, but at its beginning; *uilt* here is the genitive case of *allt*, a brook, and means "of the brook"; the *n* is but the consonant of the definite article *an* = the, adhering to *uilt*, just as in English "for the nonce" = *for then once*, i.e. *for this once*, in which the article "the" has its old accusative form *then*. But what requires much more attention from every person who is anxious to understand the significance of Gaelic names is the remarkable change in the form of words which habitually takes place by what is technically called *aspiration*, shown by adding *h* to the letter to be aspirated. Thus *b* aspirated becomes *bh* pronounced *v*, and *ph*, similar to the English *f*. Thus *f*, if still further aspirated as *fh*, disappears; so with *d* and *t* aspirated. Thus *th*, if in the middle of a word, disappears. The letters *c* and *g* aspirate into *ch* and *gh*. To know the cases in which this aspiration takes place forms, to a Saxon ear, one of the great practical difficulties of the language. The general principle on which it proceeds is doubtless a regard to euphony, but it will be enough to state here that the initial consonant of an adjective is aspirated only when it is in concord with a feminine substantive. Thus we say *Skerryvore*, properly "skerrvore," because *sgeir* is feminine, and hence *mòr*, "great," becomes *mhòr*. In "Lismore" (Gael. *lios*, a "fortress," now a "garden," and mòr, "great"), the *lios* is masculine, hence mòr is not aspirated. In the same way *breac*, "spotted" or "brindled," becomes *vrackie* with *Ben*, as in "Ben Vrackie," because *beann* is feminine; and again when *fad-a*, "long," is affixed to "Ben," the *fh* disappears, *e.g. Ben Fhada* in Ross-shire is pronounced *Ben Ad-a*, hence Eng. *Ben Attow*. By another singular phonetic rule, in words beginning with *s*, if preceded by *t*, the *s* becomes lost in the *t* sound, as *saor*, "a carpenter," but *Mac-an t-saoir* becomes "Macintyre"; so *sàl*, genitive *sàil* or *sàile*, "the sea," when joined with *ceann*, "head" or "end," becomes *Kintail* (*Ceann an t-sàile*). In the corresponding case of "Kinsale," in the south of Ireland, the article *an t-* does not come in (*Ceann sàile* = end of sea), and thus the *s* remains unchanged.

The laws which regulate the form of a word from Latin in its derivative languages are active within the Gaelic language. Thus *pater*, *mater*, *frater*, become in French *père*, *mère*, and *frère*, with the disappearance of the *t*; so in Gaelic, *Athair*, *mathair*, *brathair*, father, mother, and brother, are pronounced *a'air*, *ma'air*, *bra'air*. The change of the Latin *femina* into Spanish *hembra*, a woman, is an illustration of the disappearance of the aspirated *f*, so frequent in Gaelic. Doubtless the Celtic races in ancient France and Spain determined largely the forms which Latin took, as we find it spoken by their descendants.

Those who wish to pursue the study of Gaelic—a language full of interest not only to the philologist but to the students of history and poetry—should not allow themselves to be deterred by any considerations of extraordinary difficulty imagined to belong to that language. No doubt two-thirds of the vocabulary may prove altogether new, even to a good linguist; but, in other respects, Gaelic is no more difficult than any other European language. Its peculiar liquid and nasal sounds, which contribute so much to its euphony, will be found mostly in French, German, Italian, or Spanish; its *ch*, equivalent to the German *ch*, is easily learned, and the frequent mute consonantal combinations in which it delights (as in the English *might*, *sigh*) fall under a common rubric which the ear will learn to acknowledge. For Gaelic pronunciation "Macalpine's Pocket Dictionary" will be found useful for acquiring a certain limited vocabulary to start with. No expedient will be more profitable than the study of topographical etymology, to which the subjoined list may be looked on as giving an introduction. Many hundreds of descriptive Celtic roots are stereotyped in the place-names of Scotland and Ireland, and the amount of curious and interesting information that naturally springs out of this topographical study will surprise and delight those who have not been accustomed to connect philology with any special associations of intellectual enjoyment.

It is not to be supposed that all place-names in Scotland will yield up their meaning as easily as those in this list. Within Gaelic-land, the names of divisions of the country, such as Perth, Nairn, Atholl, Elgin, Arran, Bute, Badenoch, Lochaber; the names of large rivers, such as the Tay, Spey, Findhorn, Conan, Lossie, Oykell, and many others; of hills like Bens Nevis, Wyvis, and Ledi; of islands such as Lewis, Skye, Mull, and Islay, are all obscure, and are in themselves a strong testimony that these names have been handed down to us from a pre-Celtic race, whose language cannot be as yet related to any known language. Again, the predominance of Norse names, examples of which are given below, over the Hebrides and the Northern and Western sea-boards of Scotland, testifies not only to the Scandinavian origin of the place-names, but to the Norse origin of the inhabitants of these coasts and islands, a fact which has been long accepted on historical and ethnological grounds.

To Gaelic-speaking people *Scotland* is known by its ancient name *Alba; Edinburgh* is *Dunedin; Falkirk, An Eaglais-Bhreac* (The Mottled Church); *Beauly, A Mhanachuinn* (The Priory); *Tain, Bail-a-Dhuaich* (St. Duthac's town); *Dingwall, Innerffeoran* (The Mouth of the Peffray); *Helmsdale, Bunallai* (The end of the Ullai river); *Rothesay, Bail-a-Bhoid* (The town of Bute); *Campbeltown, Ceannloch,* or Kinloch (The Head of the Loch); and *Cromarty, Crombaidh* (The Winding Bay). Among districts, *Applecross* is *A Chomraich* (The Sanctuary); *Sutherland, Catthaobh* (pron. Cattu); *Caithness, Gallthaobh* (pron. Gallu); among arms of the sea, The *Pentland Firth* is *An Caol Arcach* (Kyle of Orkney); The *Minch, An Cuan* (sea) or *An Linne* (watery expanse) *Leoghasach* (of Lewis); among headlands, *Cape Wrath* is *Am Parbh* or *An Carbh* (Norse, *Hvarf* = The turning-point); among islands *St. Kilda* is *Hirt* (pron. Hirst); and so with many other place-names which are all better known to Highlanders by their Gaelic names. The same remark holds good with regard to the outer world: *Ireland* is *Erin; England* is *Sasunn; Norway* is *Lochlin; Italy, An Eaduilt; France* is *A-Fhrainc; Spain* is *A-Spaìn; Sweden, An t-Suain;* and The *Baltic, A Muir-as-Ear* (The East Sea). These are but a few of the more prominent Celtic "peaks of a submerged world" which dates back far beyond mediæval times.

ABER (see Inver)	Mouth of or confluence	Abertarf	At the mouth of the Tarff.
Achadh	A field	Ach-na-cloich	Field of stones.
Aird—Ard	A height—high	The Aird	Heights of Inverness.
Allt	A brook	Taynuilt	The house by the brook.
Abhuinn	A river	Avondow	The Black River.
-an	Diminutives of (masc.) words	Ben Lochan	Mountain of the little loch.
Aluinn	Beautiful	Loch Aline	The lovely loch.
Aros	A dwelling	Aros	The dwelling.
Airidh	A shealing	Fiunary	The fair shealing.
Á (Norse)	Water	Laxay (river)	Salmon water.
BA or Bo	A cow	Bealach-nam-bo	Mountain pass of the cattle.
Borg (Norse)	A fortress	Dunbhuirgh (in Lewis)	The Dun of the fortress (Dun is Gaelic = fortress), hence we have here a "doublet" = a similar name added to a native name through ignorance of its meaning.
Baile	An enclosed place, a town	Balnakill	Church or cell town.
Ban	White, fair	Banchory	The fair hollow.
Barr	A projecting point or head	Barrhead	(A "doublet.")
Beath	A birch tree	Dalbeath	Birch Dell.
Bealach	A mountain pass	Ballochbuie	The Yellow Pass.
Beag	Little	Glenbeg	The little valley.
Beann	A mountain	Ben More	The great mountain.
Blar	A plain	Blair Atholl	The plain in Atholl.
Bruach	A bank, slope, brae	Tighnabruaich	The house on the brae.
Boireann (obsolete)	A great slope	Glenburnie	The glen of great slopes.
Breac	Spotted, brindled	Ben Vrackie	The brindled hill.
CAM or CAMBUS	Crooked, curved	Cambusmore	The great curve.
Carn	A cairn or heap of stones	Cairngorm	Blue cairn.
Car	A turn or winding	Carron	The winding river.
Cathair	A fortress, a town	Keir	The fortress.
Caolas	A strait, a firth	Ballachulish	The town by the strait.
		Kyles of Bute	The Straits of Bute.
Ceann	Head, or end	Kintail	End of the sea.
Cille, Cill	A church, or cella	Kilbride	The church of St. Bridget.
Cro	A fold	Glencroe	Valley of the fold.
Clach (Cloich)	A stone	Clachnacudainn	Stone of the tub (at Inverness).
Cluain	A meadow	Cluny	The meadow.
Cnoc	A hill or knoll	Knockbain	The white knoll.
Coille	Wood	Schiehallion	The mountain (Sith) and (chaoillin) of the wood.
		Dunkeld	The fortress of the wood.
Creag	A rock or cliff	Craigentinny	The rock of the fire.
Cruach	A rick or stack	Ben Cruachan	The Ben of the stacks.
Cul	The back, behind	Culross	The place lying behind the peninsula or the forest.
DAIL	A field	Dalnaspidal	Field of the hospital.
Dalr (Norse)	A valley	Glendale	(A doublet.)
Darach	An oak	Craigendarach	Rock of the oaks.
Dearg	Red	Ben Dearg	Red Ben.
Dour	Water	Aberdour	At the mouth of the water.
Drochaid	A bridge	Drumnadrochit	The bridge of the ridge.
Druim	A back or ridge	Drumalban	The ridge of Scotland—The Grampians.
Dubh	Black, dark	Ben Muich-dhui	The ben of the black sow.
Dun	A hill fortress	Dun-keld. See *Coille*.	The fortress of the wood.

EADAR	Between	Eddrachillis	Between the two straits.
Eaglais	A church	Ecclefechan	The church of St. Feochan.
Eas	A waterfall, or ravine	Dalness	The valley of the waterfall.
Eilean	An island	Ellen's Isle	(A doublet.)
Ey (Norse)	An island	Pabbay	The pape's (Culdee priest) island.

A place termination for islands numerous in the Hebrides, etc., as Jura, Gigha, Raasay, Skalpay, Canna, etc.

FADA	Long	Inchfad	Long island.
Fail	A rock or cliff	Dunphail	The fortress on the cliff (ravines of the Divie).
Fell (Norse)	A wild hill-top	Goat-fell, (*Gaoth* = wind)	The wind-swept hill.
Fiord (Norse)	A sea loch	Loch Seaforth	(A doublet = sea fiord.)

Found over the Norse occupied region as -art, -ard, -ord, and -orth.

Faiche	A green field (Scotch Fauch -ich -ie, numerous)	Faichfields	(A doublet.)
Fead	A whistle or blast	Tighnafead	House of the blasts.
Fionn	White, shining	Fionn-a-gabhar	The white goat, corrupted into "Vinegar" Hill.
GARBH	Rough	Garvalt	Rough stream.
Gart	An enclosed place	Gartmore	Great field.
Gearr	Short	Gairloch	The short loch.
Gleann	A narrow valley	Glenure	Glen of the yew trees.
Gobha	A blacksmith	Balgownie	The blacksmith's town.
Gorm	Blue or green	Tullochgorum	The green upland.
Grian	The sun	Greenock	The sunny hill.
Gil (Norse)	A ravine	Auchengil	Field of the ravine.
Giubhsach	The fir wood	Kingussie	Head of the fir wood.
How (Norse, haugr)	A burial mound	Howmore	The Great Mound.
INNIS (INCH)	An island	Inchgarvie	The rough island.
Inver, Gaelic equivalent of Aber (which see)		Inveresk	At the mouth of the Esk.
LAG	A hollow	Laggan	A little hollow.
Larach	Site of an old ruin	Crianlarich	Little old ruin.
Leac	A flagstone	Auchinleck (pron. Auffleck)	Field of flagstones.
Leana	A plain	Leny	A plain.
Lios	A fortress, now a garden	Lismore	The great garden.
Lón	A marshy meadow	Tighanlone	House of the meadow.
Learg	A hill-side or slope	Largs	The slopes.
Linne	A pool	Corra linn	The caldron pool.
Loch	A lake or sea loch	Loch Maddy	The loch of the dogs.
Lub	A bend or loop	Loch Lubnaig	The loch of the bend.
MACHAR	A plain by the sea	The Machar of Iona, Uist, Lewis, etc.	
Magh	A plain	Moy	The plain.
Maol	A bald headland	Mull of Kintyre	The bald headland of Kintyre (Land's End).
Muli (Norse)	A projecting headland	Moull Head in Orkney	The headland.
Monadh	An upland moor	Monadh liath	The gray upland.
Mòr	Great	Ben More	The great Ben.
Muc	A sow	Glenmuick	The glen of the sow.
		Ben Muich-dhui	Ben of the black sow.
OB-AN (Norse, hope = bay)	The little bay	Oban (Gaelic = an t-Oban)	The little hope or bay.

PIT (prob. Pictish and equivalent to Gael. *Baile*=a place or town)		Pitlochrie (Gael. name Balachloichrie)	The place of stones.
Poll	A pool	Polbeath	Pool of the birches.
Port (Latin)	A harbour	Portree	King's harbour, named after visit of James V.
RAINEACH	A fern	Rannoch Moor	Moor of ferns.
Rath	A fort	Raith, near Kirkcaldy	The fortress.
Reidh	Smooth	Achray	The smooth field.
Ross	A peninsula or a forest	Ross-shire	The shire of peninsulas or of forests.
Rudha (ru, rhu, or row)	A point	Row (pron. ru)	The point.
Riabhach	Brindled	Braeriach	The brindled brae.
SETR (Norse)	Seat (found in place-names as -sta, -say, -s)	Shader	The seat or settlement.
Sgeir	A sea rock	Skerryvore	The great sea rock.
Sgor or Scuir (Norse)	The sheared rock or Scaur	Scuir-na-gillean	The Scaur or ridge of the young men.
Strath, (akin to Latin *stratus*=strewn, or spread out)		A broad valley	Strathmore, the great strath.
TIGH	A house	Taynuilt (Tigh-an-allt).	The house by the stream.
Tir	Land	Kintyre	Land's End.
Tobar	A well	Tobermory	St. Mary's Well.
Tom	A hillock	Tomintoul	The hillock of the barn, *Sabhuil*.
Torr	A heap	Torloisk	Burnt Hill, after beacon fires.
Tulloch	An upland place	Tullochgorum	The green upland place.
UACHDAR	Upper	Ochtertyre	Upper land.
Uamh	A cave	Uam Var	The great cave.
		Loch-nan-Uamh	Loch of the caves.
VIK (Norse, a bay or creek), places ending in -aig, -och, -ag, -ig—*e.g.* Uig, Nigg (an uig), Wick, etc.			The bay, or creek.

The boundary line dividing the Gaelic-speaking from the Saxon-speaking population is a very irregular one, but may be roughly laid down thus:—Leaving Kintyre and Arran to the Gaelic, the linguistic boundary line begins at Etterick Bay, thence runs across Bute to Kames Castle, thence taking in a strip of the Argyllshire coast by Toward, Innellan, and Dunoon, it reaches a point on the Dumbartonshire coast near the head of Loch Long; thence by Glen Douglas to Loch Lomond and across to Rowardennan, and so by Gartmore and the Pass of Menteith to the Teith between Callander and Doune. From the Braes of Doune it strikes N. past Comrie to the head of Glen Turret, and by Glen Almond to Strath Braan, Birnam Hill, and Dunkeld; thence across the moors, Strath Ardle, and Glenshee to Mount Blair, crossing the Dee about 6 m. above Balmoral, thence down the Dee to a point between Balmoral and Ballater, whence it lies across Strathdon and along the S. shed of Glenlivet to the Spey between Cromdale and Ballindalloch; thence by the Knock of Moray to the Findhorn at Coulmony, thence across the Nairn to the Loch of the Clans, and so to the Moray Firth about 3 m. W. of the town of Nairn.

Throughout the district lying N. and W. of this boundary the Gaelic language prevails, with the exception of the bit of coast from Fortrose to Cromarty, the N.E. portion of Caithness, and the Orkneys and Shetland.

VI. Some of the most Interesting Mountains, their Heights and Situations.[1]

Name.	Page.	Situation.	Most easily ascended from.	Height. Feet.
Ben Nevis	365	Inverness-shire	Fort-William	4404
Ben Muich-dhui	284, 228	Aberdeenshire and Banffshire	Braemar or Aviemore	4296
Braeriach	228	Aberdeenshire and Inverness-shire	Aviemore	4248
Cairn Toul	227, 228	Aberdeenshire	Kincraig or Aviemore	4241
Cairn Gorm	228	Banffshire and Inverness-shire	Aviemore	4084
Ben Lawers	238	Perthshire	Lawers Inn	3984
Ben More	170	Perthshire	Crianlarich	3843
Lochnagar	282, 278	Aberdeenshire	Braemar or Ballater	3786
Ben Alder	224	Inverness-shire	Dalwhinnie	3757
Ben Lui	171	Perthshire and Argyllshire	Dalmally	3708
Ben Cruachan	173, 174	Argyllshire	Loch Awe Hotel or Taynuilt	3689
Ben-y-Gloe	223	Perthshire	Blair Atholl	3671
Schiehallion	240	Perthshire	Kinloch-Rannoch	3547
Scour Ouran	385	Ross-shire	Glen Shiel Inn	3505
Glas Maol	285	Forfarshire	Spital of Glenshee	3502
Leagach	383	Ross-shire	Kinlochewe	3456
Ben Wyvis	381	Ross-shire	Strathpeffer	3429
Ben Attow	385	Inverness-shire and Ross-shire	Glen Shiel Inn	3383
Buchaille Etive	364	Argyllshire	Kingshouse Inn	3345
Ben Eige (Eay)	383	Ross-shire	Kinlochewe	3309
Ben More (Assynt)	413	Sutherland	Inchnadamph or Lochinver	3273
Slioch	383	Ross-shire	Kinlochewe	3260
Ben Voirlich	210	Perthshire	Lochearnhead or St. Fillans	3224
Ben Lomond	153	Stirlingshire	Rowardennan	3192
Ben More (Mull)	356	Argyllshire	Salen (Mull)	3185
Scuir-na-Gillean	392	Inverness-shire	Sligachan (Skye)	3167
Driesh	369	Forfarshire	Kirkton of Clova	3105

[1] For exhaustive tabulated lists of all the Scottish Peaks over 3000 feet, compiled by H. T. Munro, Esq. of Lindteris, see Sept. No., 1891, of the "Mountaineering Journal."

Name.	Page.	Situation.	Most easily ascended from.	Height. Feet.
Mount Keen	273	Aberdeenshire and Forfarshire	Ballater	3077
Ben Chonzie	213, 209	Perthshire	Crieff or Comrie	3048
Blaven (Skye)	386	Inverness-shire	Torrin or Sligachan	3042
Ben Hope	423	Sutherland	Heilim Inn	3040
Ben Ledi	162	Perthshire	Callander	2875
Goatfell	325	Arran	Brodick	2866
Morven	277	Aberdeenshire	Ballater	2862
Merrick	108	Kirkcudbrightshire	Newton-Stewart	2764
Ben Vrackie	220	Perthshire	Pitlochrie	2757
Ben Rinnes	309	Banffshire	Aberlour	2755
Broad Law	90	Peeblesshire and Selkirkshire	Crook Inn	2754
Hartfell	15	Dumfriesshire	Moffat	2651
Cairnsmore of Carsphairn	107	Kirkcudbrightshire	Carsphairn	2612
Paps of Jura	343	Argyllshire	Port Askaig (Islay) or Craighouse Inn (Jura)	2571
Farragon	235	Perthshire	Aberfeldy or Grandtully	2559
Dun-da-Gu (Mull)	355	Argyllshire	Craignure (Mull)	2512
Ben Venue	164	Perthshire	Trossachs Hotel	2393
Buck of Cabrach	301	Aberdeenshire and Banffshire	Lumsden or Glenkindie Inn	2368
Ben Cleuch (Ochils)	199	Clackmannanshire	Alva	2363
Storr Rock (Skye)	389	Inverness-shire	Portree	2360
Tinto	16	Lanarkshire	Symington or Abington	2335
Morven	417	Caithness	Berriedale	2313
Queensberry	15	Dumfriesshire	Beattock	2285
Loch Fell	15	Dumfriesshire	Moffat	2256
Blackhope Scar (Moorfoots)	78	Midlothian	Eddleston	2136
Scald Law (Pentlands)	66	Midlothian	Penicuik or Balerno	1898
Earl's Seat (Campsie Fells)	155	Stirlingshire	Strathblane	1894
Criffel	99	Kirkcudbrightshire	New Abbey	1866
Bennachie	300	Aberdeenshire	Oyne	1733
West Lomond	181	Fife	Mawcarse	1713
Ronas Hill	439	Shetland	Hillswick	1475
East Lomond	181	Fife	Falkland	1471
Eildon	23	Roxburghshire	Melrose	1385
Birnam Hill	218	Perthshire	Birnam	1324
Dunsinane	197	Perthshire	Perth	1012
Neilston Pad	324	Renfrewshire	Neilston	854
Arthur's Seat	61	Midlothian	Edinburgh	823
Wideford Hill	430	Orkney	Kirkwall	740

HANDBOOK FOR SCOTLAND.

Additions and Corrections, 1895.

GENERAL INTRODUCTION.

Additional Information.

Principal ways of reaching Scotland.

[A] By Steamer.

(4*a*) From St. Katherine's Dock, *London* (Clyde Shipping Co.) to *Greenock* and *Glasgow*, three times a week. Fares, 30s. and 12s. 6d.; Ret. 50s. and 18s. 9d.

(4*b*) From Carron Wharf, *London* (Carron Line) to *Grangemouth* (through trains to Glasgow), three times a week, in about 30 hours. Fares to Glasgow, 26s., 24s., and 17s. 6d.; Ret. 39s., 35s., and 26s. 6d.

Corrections.

Page 22, col. 2, line 24.—*For* "Alton" *read* "Allan."

Page 99, col. 2, line 22.—The "ugly kirk" of 1731 was removed when the present church was erected, 1877.

Page 158, col. 1, line 26.—*For* 1646 *read* 1746.

Page 198, col. 1 }
Page 203, col. 1 } Coaches from Culross now meet the train at Kincardine Stat.

Page 207, col. 2, line 1.—*Gleneagles* was built in 1624 out of the stones of the former mansion (now in ruins) by Sir John Haldane of Gleneagles.

Page 226, col. 1, last paragraph.—The road to the Pass of Corrieyairack leaves the Fort-William road fully 1 m. west of Laggan Br., crosses the Mashie, and keeps up the *rt.* bank of the Spey, which it crosses at Garve Br., 4 m. before Meallgarbha, which is 12 m. from Laggan. The sixteen zigzags are on the *S.* side of the Pass, but several of them can scarcely now be traced.

Page 227, col. 1, line 3.—The coach does not now run beyond Inverlair Stat., which has been re-named Tulloch.

Page 252, col. 1, line 11.—After "highest pt." add "of this part of the range. The highest pt. of the Sidlaw range is *Craigowl*, 1493 ft., 10 m. N.E."

Page 253, col. 1, line 10.—*For* "12" *read* "3."

Page 269, col. 2.—Small print 4th line after of Glenmuick text should run thus—"the ruins of a shooting lodge 7 m. from Clova. Halfway up, the Esk has to be crossed by a footbridge. The site of Bachnagairn amongst the rocks at the head of the glen . . . amidst firs is very grand."

Page 347, col. 1.—No Stat. has yet (1895) been made at Whistlefield.

Page 349, col. 1.—Inverlair Stat. has been re-named Tulloch.

Page 379, col. 1, 15th line from foot.—After "ft." insert "after the Cairnwell (p. 285) and the road to Loch Builg (p. 282) both 2200 ft."

HANDBOOK FOR SCOTLAND.

SECTION I.

THE SOUTH OF SCOTLAND—LAND OF SCOTT—EDINBURGH—VALE OF TWEED—FALLS OF CLYDE—LAND OF BURNS.

§ 1. GENERAL INFORMATION.

THE Highlands of Scotland ought by no means to engross the exclusive attention and admiration of travellers. The South of Scotland, miscalled the Lowlands, since it is for the most part a mass of mountains or round-backed hills intersected by valleys and plains, is full of picturesque beauty and "wildness, which just stops short of sublimity." Though inferior to the Grampian ranges in elevation and romantic outline, it surpasses the North of Scotland in historic association, in legends, local poetry, and in the romance which the works of Scott and the pathos of the songs and poems of Burns have thrown over many of the scenes, causing it to be called the Land of Scott and Burns. It also excels the Highlands in the number and picturesqueness of its ancient buildings, its ruined abbeys and castles, and especially in that long chain of fort-like towers—Peels or Bastels—which the insecure state of the Borders from the earliest times to the 16th century made to be the necessary form of a country gentleman's house.

The traveller, imbued with the recollection of the "Lay of the Last Minstrel," "The Abbot," etc., may repair to Melrose or Kelso, either directly from England or making the excursion from Edinburgh. He will there find himself in the most beautiful part of the valley of the Tweed, under the shadow of that picturesque and eerie knot of hills, "The Eildons." He may spend hours among the exquisite ruins of Melrose, Kelso, and Jedburgh. He will go as a pilgrim to the shrines of Dryburgh (where rest the remains of Sir Walter and his family), and to Abbotsford, not forgetting the Peel Tower of Smailholm, where Sir Walter spent his childhood. The view from Kelso Bridge over the Tweed and Teviot, and the park of Floors, may tempt the traveller to tarry and explore the Valleys of Tweed, Teviot, Yarrow, Ettrick, and many others.

If he enter Scotland by Berwick, there is the grand coast scenery of St. Abb's Head and Fast Castle, where the Lammermuirs drop down into the sea in strangely-contorted cliffs (interesting to the geologist), or he may thread the Defile of the Pease Burn, and traverse the Battlefield of Dunbar, the turning-point of Cromwell's career. Diverging to North Berwick—resorted to for bathing and golf—he will have before him the sparkling shores of the Firth of Forth, with its rocky islets, the mysterious Bass Rock, and the conical Law, and in autumn may admire the golden crops of the Lothians, where agriculture, aided by steam, asserts her just claims to be esteemed a science. The attractions of Edinburgh and its environs are fully described in Route 4.

Nor need the stranger be at a loss if he enter Scotland by the S.W. at the head of the Solway. Here he is near the scenery of "Redgauntlet" and "Guy Mannering." If he halt at Dumfries he should visit Burns's Grave, and the very picturesque Abbeys of Lincluden (1½ m. up the Nith) and Sweetheart (7½ m. down the Nith), under the shadow of Criffel, or may visit the triangular Castle of Caerlaverock, 8 m. S. of Dumfries, near the margin of the Solway.

Proceeding W. by Castle-Douglas to Stranraer, he will traverse some of the finest and wildest scenery in the S. of Scotland, and may turn aside to visit St. Mary's Isle, Kirkcudbright, near which, in Dundrennan Abbey, Queen Mary spent her last night in Scotland. At Anwoth, close to Gatehouse-on-Fleet, Archbishop Usher visited the saintly Rutherford; at Wigtown the Covenanting Martyrs were drowned; and at Whithorn St. Ninian, one of the earliest of Christian missionaries to this country, built the first stone church in Scotland.

There is good rock and cliff scenery in the bays which indent the shores of Galloway, as the combined Counties of Kirkcudbright and Wigtown are called, and round the Mull of Galloway, the most southern point of Scotland.

From Stranraer the traveller should by all means visit the noble woods and pine-tree groves of Castle Kennedy, and if possible take the charming drive N. along the coast by Loch Ryan and Glen App to Ballantrae and Girvan.

The chief associations with Burns are to be found at Ayr, Mauchline, and Dumfries. At Ayr, especially, half a day may well be spent visiting Burns's Cottage, Alloway Kirk, Brig o' Doon, etc.

Arrived at this point, the Alpine Peaks and serrated ridges of Arran will tempt the traveller across the firth from Ardrossan; and, if he love grand scenery, he will be amply rewarded. But this and the Firth of Clyde belong to Section V.

Near Lanark, between Ayr and Edinburgh, are the Falls of Clyde, the nearest approach in Britain (*longo intervallo*) to those of the Rhine, and close to Lanark are the very picturesque *Dene* of the Mouse Water and the Cartland Crags. Above it the upper waters of the Clyde have claims to arrest the traveller's steps, especially the wild, easily accessible, but little-known Passes from the Clyde to the Nith. The orchards and country houses on the Clyde below Lanark, passed on the road to Hamilton, are described in Section II., in which reference to the "Black Country" will also be found.

§ 2. PRINCIPAL CENTRES.

1. **Edinburgh** for its immediate Environs.
   The Forth Bridge, Roslin, Hawthornden can be visited by road or rail. Melrose, Dryburgh, and Abbotsford can easily be visited in one day by rail, as can also North Berwick, Lanark and the Falls of Clyde, Linlithgow, Dunfermline, Lochleven, and Falkland. Cf. Sects. II. and III.
2. **Melrose** for its Abbey, the lower part of the Tweed, Abbotsford, Dryburgh, Kelso, Jedburgh, and Hawick (Teviotdale).
3. **Selkirk** for the Yarrow and the Ettrick.
4. **Peebles** for the upper part of the Tweed and the Manor.
5. **Moffat** for innumerable expeditions into the S.E. part of "The Border Country."
6. **Dumfries** for the Nith and the Solway.
7. **Newton-Stewart** for the fine scenery of Galloway.
8. **Ayr** for Burns's Country.

ROUTES.

ROUTE 1.

Berwick-on-Tweed to Edinburgh by Reston (Coldingham), Dunbar, and Drem. N.B.R. (East Coast Rte.).

About 12 trains daily to Edinburgh 57½ m. in 1¼ to 2½ hrs. Through carriages N. by this Rte. and on by the *Forth* and *Tay Bridges* to Dundee, 116¾ m. in 3 hrs. 20 min., and to Aberdeen, 188 m. in 5¼ hrs. [Rtes. 30 and 48]; also by Forth Bridge and Glen Farg to Perth, 105¼ m. in 2½–3½ hrs., and Inverness, 249¼ m. in 8½–10 hrs. [Rtes. 34 and 42].

The traveller from the S. cannot fail to be struck with the first view of Scotland after passing Tweedmouth. The rly. is carried high up on the hills bounding the valley of the Tweed, so that you look down upon the river, its junction with the sea, and the town on its N. bank. The rly. clears the valley, still maintaining its elevation, by Robert Stephenson's noble *Viaduct*, commonly called the Royal Border Bridge, of 28 arches in a curve, 126 ft. high, and nearly ½ mile long (cost £120,000), leading into

Berwick Stat. [*Branch* to Coldstream, Kelso, etc., Rte. 8], occupying the site of the ancient historic *Castle*, which it has nearly erased, only a few fragments of walls and towers remaining on the steep slope running down towards the Tweed. The view from the edge over the river and viaduct is striking.

Berwick-on-Tweed ✲ is now included in England, but formerly belonged to Scotland, and was from its position on the frontier for ages the most important fortress in the N., the object of constant struggles between the two nations, and the scene of great events. The most remarkable of these were the sieges by Edward I., 1296, when the slaughter of 8000 citizens, and the burning alive in the Town Hall of a handful of Flemish merchants who held it, followed the surrender of the town; and that by Edward III., in 1333, when the battle of Halidon Hill drove Berwick to capitulate. A strong garrison was maintained at all times, and the Captain of Berwick was always a man of mark and reputation. A Minstrel Ballad recounts to the praise of Harry Hotspur (Percy) that he "kept" Berwick. The town was surrounded by a fortified wall in Elizabeth's reign, and again by a smaller bastioned *Rampart* in the 17th cent. This wall is in very good preservation, and affords a promenade. The chief gates are the *Scotch Gate* on the N.W. side, the *Cow Port* on the E. side, and the *English Gate* near the bridge. It is disappointing to find that on this historic spot so little remains of antiquity with which to associate so many memories. The *Bell Tower*, 3 stories high, still stands on the line of the old fortifications; on it a beacon was lighted to give notice when marauding parties crossed the Border; and the curfew is still rung every night at eight. A *Bridge* was thrown across the Tweed here as early as 1271.

Although there is nothing striking in Berwick, it is a thriving town, with ironworks and other manufactories, is the seat of considerable salmon-fisheries, which have always been a fruitful source of trade and are still worth £4000 a year, and possesses a harbour, protected on the N. side by a stone *Pier* ¾ mile long. A dock has also been constructed at a cost of £50,000. In the broad main street is the *Town Hall*, with a belfry that serves for the adjoining ch. built of stone taken from the Castle by Col. Fenwick, an officer of Cromwell, and governor of Berwick, 1652. It is an example of Puritan architecture, without tower or ornament: within is Col. Fenwick's monument.

[EXCURSIONS:—

(1) To **Norham Cas.** and **Flodden** (Rte. 8).

(2) To **Lindisfarne** or **Holy Island** (10 m. S.) reached on foot at low tide from Beal or Goswick. [See "Handbook to Northumberland."]

(3) **Halidon Hill** (537 ft.) 2 m. N.W. where, in 1333, the Scottish army, under the Regent Archibald Douglas, endeavouring to raise the siege of Berwick, attacked the English posted in a strong position W. of the town, and were signally defeated, with the loss of 14,000 men, including the Earls of Lennox, Ross, Carrick, Sutherland, Atholl, and Menteith, and the Regent himself. Thus did the English avenge the fatal day of Bannockburn.]

The rly. to Edinburgh is carried

for a considerable distance near the edge of the cliffs, affording a good sea view, and an occasional peep into rugged gullies.

4 m. l. are the ruins of *Lamberton Kirk*, where in 1502 the foundation of the union of the two kingdoms was laid by the marriage-contract of Margaret, daughter of Henry VII., with James IV. The ceremony was performed the same year at Holyrood. In former days the man at the toll-bar of Lamberton performed the same good offices to runaway couples as did the smith at Gretna Green on the W. (see p. 94).

5½ m. **Burnmouth Stat.** In the old ch., of which the transept, built in the 12th cent., is still standing, a treaty was signed between England and Scotland in 1384 ; and another in the castle, after its capture by the Earl of Surrey in 1497.

[*Branch* N. to the fishing town of **Eyemouth** ✲ 3 m., formerly celebrated for its contraband trade, charmingly placed on a little bay at the mouth of the Eye Water, formed by a point known as Cromwell's Fort and the Nest End rocks. The mouth of this bay was the scene of a memorable disaster, 14th October 1881, when almost the whole of the fishing-fleet was destroyed, while putting out to sea, by a sudden and terrific gale, and 191 fishermen were drowned. Adjoining the village is *Netherbyres* (A. Gibson, Esq.), in whose grounds is a tension bridge built by Sir Samuel Brown, the designer of the Union Bridge (p. 87).

Gunsgreen House was built by a smuggler, and adapted to the exigencies of his profession.]

The rly. now trends inland, traversing **The Merse** (p. 81).

7¼ m. **Ayton Stat.** ✲ Rt. is *Ayton Castle* (A. H. Mitchell Innes, Esq.), built 1851, in the Scotch style, of red sandstone, in a commanding position, and occupying the site of an old castle mentioned in Ford's drama of "Perkin Warbeck."

11¼ m. **Reston Stat.**

[*Branch* S.W. to Duns and St. Boswells (Rte. 7)].

[From **Reston**[1] ✲, a long village, a hilly road leads to (3½ m. rt.) * **Coldingham,** crossing on the way the Eye Water, the Ale Water, and the Abbey Burn. Notice about 1½ m. from the village (l.) some gateposts formed of whales' jaws. Coldingham (the Urbs Coludi of Bede), a large village, with an elegant Market Cross, is celebrated for its *Priory.*

It is said that Edwin, King of the Northumbrians (617-633), wishing to marry Ebba, a nun, she fled hither, and was miraculously saved by the rising of the waters. To show her gratitude she founded the nunnery of Coldingham, became its first abbess, was canonised, and gave her name to St. Abb's Head. In 886 the nunnery was attacked by the Danes, and the inmates, to avoid the ruthless attentions of the barbarians, cut off their noses and lips in self-defence, whereupon the intruders burnt the building, the abbess, and the nuns. Upon the site was founded a Benedictine priory by the Scottish King Edgar in 1098, which eventually became so rich as to be the cause of the civil war that cost James III. his life. It was taken and much injured by Lord Hertford (1545), and again by Cromwell (1650), who blew up a great part of the ch. The tower, which was 90 feet high, fell, 1775. The building has since been partially restored and fitted up as a parish ch. During some repairs which took place at the beginning of the cent. the skeleton of a woman was found built up in the wall in an upright position, supposed to be that of a nun who had broken her vows. This discovery has been turned to much account in the 2nd canto of "Marmion."

The building which remains, a most interesting fragment of the earliest Pointed style, is a chancel without aisles. The N. and E. walls inside support a triforium gallery with detached shafts. The visitor should notice externally the Romanesque arcades and string-courses surmounted by lancet windows at the E. end of the building, and internally the exquisite E. Pointed arcade with foliaged columns that forms a gallery round the wall. There are also

---

1 Omnibus from St. Abb's and Coldingham meets trains twice daily in summer.

traces of the monastic offices, together with some tombs of priors, and many carved fragments.

1 m. N.E. on the shore is **St. Abb's** ✲, a picturesque little village with a golf course, under the lee of *St. Abb's Head* (1½ m. N.), one of the most noted promontories on the E. coast on which is a most important *Lighthouse*. On its E. side are the remains of *St. Abb's Kirk*. The cliff scenery here is scarcely to be surpassed in Scotland for grandeur, and has a peculiar attraction for geologists on account of the plications of the Silurian strata.

4 m. W. of St. Abb's Head is **Fast Castle**, supposed to be the original of "*Wolf's Crag*," in the "Bride of Lammermoor." It was once a fortress of the Home family, and subsequently belonged to Logan of Restalrig, one of the Gowrie conspirators, who intended (1600) to confine James VI. here. Logan's body was exhumed after death, tried for high treason, and found guilty, but was subsequently buried in the crypt of Restalrig Ch. (p. 66). His property was forfeited and his family declared infamous. It can be reached by the cliffs or, to within 1 m., by carriage road from Coldingham 5 m. S.E. The train might be joined at Cockburnspath (below) after another grand cliff walk of about 7 m. from Fast Castle, with views N.W. of the Bass Rock, the Isle of May, and the Fife coast.]

From Reston the line enters the defiles and broken ground to the E. of the Lammermuir Hills. Berwickshire is divided into 3 districts—the **Merse** to the E., **Lammermuir** to the N.W., and **Lauderdale** (see p. 34) to the S.W. *Lammermuir*, which is now crossed, is wild and hilly, and devoted almost entirely to pasturage. The rly. ascends the narrow valley of the Eye, and through woods and rock cuttings surmounts the summit near

16¼ m. **Grant's House Stat.**, situated among hills. After traversing a short tunnel, the *Pease Deane*, or dell, is crossed by the railway, and (rt.) a little lower down, by the old London Road, at *Pease Bridge*, a viaduct of 4 arches, 127 ft. above the Pease Burn. It was built in 1786, and is 100 yards long. The scenery of the deep, narrow, wooded and ferny dingle of the *Pease Burn*, crossed by the colossal bridge, is extremely picturesque.

This defile was the object of contention before the battle of Dunbar (1650), Gen. Leslie gathering toward the hills, labouring to make a perfect interposition between Cromwell and Berwick.

"And having in this posture a great advantage, through his better knowledge of the country, he effected it by sending a considerable party to the strait pass at Copperspath (Cockburnspath) where one man to hinder is better than twelve to make way."—*Cromwell's Despatch*.

The railway is carried through much rock cutting to

21 m. **Cocksburnpath Stat.** ✲ (pron. Co'path), in the open, not far from the sea, of which a few pretty peeps are caught. The village is pleasantly situated at the base of the Lammermuirs; l. is an old tower, a fortress of the Homes, of rough masonry, with a circular staircase in its S.W. angle, overlooking a deep glen.

[Fast Castle is 7 m. from this stat. (above).]

Just beyond Cocksburnpath the rly. crosses the pretty wooded dell of the Dunglass Burn by a viaduct connecting Berwickshire and East Lothian, and passes (l.) *Dunglass* (Sir Basil Hall, Bt.), a modern building, erected upon the site of an old castle of the same name, which belonged to the Earls of Home, and still gives the 2nd title to that family. In the beautiful grounds is a ruined, but nearly perfect, very elegant Gothic church, founded

1450 by Sir Alex. Home, consisting of choir, nave, transepts, and central tower.

24 m. **Innerwick Stat.** l. are the remains of *Innerwick* and *Thornton Towers*, both destroyed by the English in the invasion of 1547. Beyond them is the village, and 2 m. S. *Cocklaw Hill*, 1046 ft.

At 27 m. the rly. crosses a small stream, the *Broxburn*. This spot is historical as the field of the *Battle of Dunbar*, 3rd Sept. 1650. Oliver Cromwell had his headquarters in the pretty park of *Broxmouth House* (a modest mansion of the Duke of Roxburghe) rt. in whose ground is a mound from which Cromwell reconnoitred his enemy's strong position.

His army was posted between this and Belhaven, with its back to Dunbar and the sea. His antagonist, David Leslie, with the Scottish army, occupied high ground (Doon Hill 582 ft.) along the right bank of the Broxburn, which flows in a gully like a deep ditch. His position was impregnable, and he effectually barred with his army Cromwell's access to Cockburnspath, and closed the roads to England. Cromwell was hemmed in, and his army was diminished by famine and disease. At this moment Leslie, moved, it is said, by the urgent pressing of the Covenanting clergy at headquarters, came down from his vantage ground and pushed forward his right wing to occupy the flat open space near the mouth of Broxburn glen. Cromwell and Ireton at once perceived this, and began the attack; sending forward Generals Monk, Fleetwood, Lambert, and Whalley, with a large force of cavalry, they charged through Leslie's right wing, drove it in disorder back upon the infantry, which, not having space to deploy between the gully of the Broxburn and the hills, was broken, disordered, and routed; 3000 of the Scotch army were slain, 10,000 made prisoners, and the possession of Edinburgh and Leith soon after were Cromwell's gains from this astounding victory.

28¼ m. Dunbar Stat. ✲

"A small town, standing high and windy, looking over its herring boats, over its grim old castle, now much honeycombed, on one of these projecting rock promontories with which the shore and the Firth of Forth is nicked and vandyked; a beautiful sea and grim niched barrier of whinstone sheltering it from the chafings and tumblings of the German Ocean."—CARLYLE, *Cromwell*, ii. 198.

It is a lifeless town and small seaport, and consists mainly of one long street, at the end of which is *Dunbar House* (once the residence of the Earl of Lauderdale), now a barrack. Behind it are the ruins of *Dunbar Castle*, now reduced to a few shapeless masses of masonry, on a red sandstone rock, hollowed by the waves into an arch. Close under the castle is the entrance to the new harbour, between two scarped rocks. In the history of Scotland Dunbar was an important fortress and outlet to the sea.

It was captured by Edward I. 1296. Its most celebrated defence was by Black Agnes, Countess of March, daughter of Randolph, Earl of Moray, and grandniece of Robert Bruce, 1339. The Earl of Salisbury, after trying every means to reduce it, was compelled to raise the siege, upon which the town was made a royal burgh by David II. Edward II. fled hither after Bannockburn (1314), and embarked here for Berwick.

The governorship was conferred (1566) on the Earl of Bothwell by Q. Mary, who was carried off from Edinburgh by him and an armed band under his orders, to this castle, 22nd April 1567, after the murder of Darnley, and only three weeks before her marriage with Bothwell. Accompanied by Darnley, she had taken refuge here after the murder of Rizzio; and hither again she fled, in the disguise of a page, with Bothwell, after the interruption of their honeymoon at Borthwick Castle. A few days afterwards she surrendered at Carberry Hill, and Dunbar Castle was destroyed by the Regent Moray.

In the neighbourhood of Dunbar were fought two great and decisive *Battles*. 1st, in 1296, Edward I. defeated John Baliol; and 2ndly, in 1650, Cromwell defeated Gen. Leslie. (See above.)

Notwithstanding its antiquity there are no buildings of any age or beauty in the town. The *Parish Church*, rebuilt 1821, whose tall red tower is seen from the Stat., contains a huge marble monument to George Home, Earl of Dunbar, Treasurer of Scotland under James VI., 1593. His effigy, under an arch, is supported by armed knights on either side.

Great efforts have been made to establish a safe and commodious harbour, for Dunbar is an important rendezvous for the herring-fishers of this district, and the coast is very dangerous from sunken rocks. For this purpose the harbour has been deepened at a cost of £35,000.

Adjoining Dunbar (l.) is *Lochend*, a seat of Sir G. Warrender, Bt., rebuilt since destroyed by fire in 1860, and 2 m. S. is the village of *Spott*, with *Spott Ho.* (Miss Watt) at the foot of Doon Hill (p. 7). 1 m. beyond is *The Chesters* (*Castra*), a circular British fort.

The rly. now passes through one of the finest farming districts in Great Britain. Every farmyard has its own steam engine, whose chimney marks its site, rising over a level sea of yellow grain in autumn. Near Dunbar appear in view rt. *N. Berwick Law*, and the *Bass Rock*.

29 m. rt. is **Belhaven**, a small fishing village, from which Lord Belhaven takes his title (see p. 17). The rly. now turns inland, and soon crosses the high-road at the Biel Water, having l. *Belton* (G. J. B. Hay, Esq.), the grounds of which are celebrated for their firs; and higher up the stream, *Biel* (Mr. and Mrs. Hamilton Ogilvy), surrounded by charming pleasure-grounds. *Biel* was the birthplace of the poet Dunbar (1460).

The house contains some fine pictures by *Van Dyck*, including Wm. Earl of Lanark, King Charles I., Prince Rupert and Prince Maurice, a fine portrait of the 2nd Marquis of Hamilton by *Van Somer*, Mrs. Hamilton Nisbet by *Gainsborough*, The Flight into Egypt by *Murillo*, some excellent *Raeburns*, and an extensive collection of pictures of the *Italian*, *Flemish*, and *Dutch* schools. Here, too, is kept the famous Biel Prayer Book which has acquired the credit of bringing good luck, and has in consequence been used at the following marriages:—George III., 1761; Duke of Kent, 1818; Princess Augusta, 1764; Princess Charlotte, 1816; Duke of Gloucester, 1816; Princess Elizabeth, 1818; Duke of Cambridge, 1818; Duke of Clarence (Wm. IV.), 1818; Prince of Wales, 1863; Duke of Edinburgh, 1874; Duke of Connaught, 1879, etc.

Farther to S.W. is *Whittinghame* (Rt. Hon. A. J. Balfour, Esq., M.P.) where Darnley's murder is said to have been planned.

34 m. **East Linton Stat.** ✲, a large village, the postal name of which, like the parish, is *Prestonkirk*, on the river Tyne, here crossed by a red stone bridge. On right, close to the rly., is *Phantassie*, where Rennie the engineer was born (1761); 1 m. N. is *Smeaton House* (Sir T. Buchan-Hepburn, Bt.). 2½ m. N.E. beautifully situated on the banks of the river, and surrounded by plantations, is *Tyninghame House*,[1] the seat of the Earl of Haddington (cf. p. 72). In the house are some good portraits by *Sir J. Reynolds*, *Raeburn*, etc., and "The Gamblers," by *Q. Matsys*. Binning Woods, once among the finest in Scotland, were lamentably injured by the Tay Bridge gale, Dec. 1879, and by the hurricane in Oct. 1881, when the fishing fleet of Eyemouth perished (p. 5). The district is celebrated for its holly, the roads being lined with holly hedges in some places 15 ft. high.

l. 2 m. above Linton, on the right bank of the Tyne, are the ruins of *Hailes Castle*, where Queen Mary lived with Bothwell, and where George Wishart was imprisoned (1546). Near it is the dome-shaped hill of felsite, called **Traprain Law**, 724 ft., which is a conspicuous feature in the landscape. The line trends N. to

36½ m. **East Fortune Stat.** There are several seats in the vicinity—*e.g.* 1 m. l. *Gilmerton* (Sir Alex. Kinloch, Bt.); 2 m. E. *Newbyth* (Sir David Baird, Bt.), and 1 m. N. *Rockville*, beyond which lie *Sheriffhall*, and *Balgone* (Sir G. Grant Suttie, Bt.), in the beautiful grounds of which is a picturesque lake overhung by cliffs.

[1] Grounds open on Saturday afternoons in summer.

Close to Gilmerton lies **Athelstaneford** village in a district famous for its fox covers. There an obelisk has been erected in memory of Blair (1700-46), the author of "The Grave," who was minister of the parish and was succeeded by John Home, afterwards compelled to retire from the living on account of having written the tragedy of "Douglas" (1756).

39¾ m. **Drem. Stat.** [*Branch* to North Berwick 4¾ m. N. (p. 70)].

See Rte. 5 for the continuation of the line from Drem to

57½ m. **EDINBURGH**✲ (p. 36).

ROUTE 2.

Carlisle to Edinburgh, Glasgow, and the North by Lockerbie (for Lochmaben and Dumfries), Beattock (for Moffat), Symington (for Peebles), Carstairs Junc. (for Edinburgh and Lanark), and Law Junc. (for the North). Cal. Rly.

Abt. 10 trains daily to Edinburgh (102 m.) in 2-5 hrs., and to Glasgow (102¼ m.) in 2¼-4¾ hrs. Abt. 7 trains daily to Perth (150¾ m.) in 3¼-4½ hrs., and to Aberdeen (240½ m.) in 5½-8 hrs.

Quitting the Citadel Stat. at Carlisle, the line skirts the walls of the old city, with the cathedral and castle (on the right), crosses the river Eden, and soon after passes under the North British Rly., arriving at

5 m. **Rockcliffe Stat.**

7 m. **Floriston Stat.** Beyond the line crosses the River Esk (see Rte. 3), and then enters a tract of Border Country which was called the *Debateable Land.* It extends to the river *Sark*, and is about 8 m. long by 4 broad, and was for many years held only by the worst set of Border robbers. In 1552 a boundary-line was agreed upon by the sovereigns of the two kingdoms (see p. 81); but the habits of the people were little improved till the union of the crowns.

On the l. is **Solway Firth,** recipient of the Eden, Esk, Annan, and Nith. The tide comes in at certain seasons with extraordinary rapidity, forming what is known as the Bore, in which the waves are frequently 3 ft. or 4 ft. high. Strangers to the coast should be careful of this danger, remembering the caution given by Herries of Birrenswark to Darsie Latimer, that "he who dreams on the bed of the Solway will wake up in the next world." The estuary has been bridged across, lower down, by the Solway Junc. Rly.

On right is *Solway Moss*, memorable for the defeat of the Scots in 1542. A body of 10,000 men had entered England; but the leaders, quarrelling amongst themselves, were surprised by a small English force and routed, leaving 200 noblemen and gentlemen in the enemy's hands. James V. died of grief in consequence (see p. 182).

8½ m. **Gretna Stat.**

[*Junc.* for (1) G. and S.-W. Rly. line W. to Annan and Dumfries (Rte. 12).
(2) N.B.R. line E. to Longtown (p. 18).
For *Gretna Green* see p. 94.]

Just beyond the stat. the *Sark*, which is here the *Boundary* between England and Scotland, is crossed.

13 m. **Kirkpatrick Stat.** On l. is the village of *Kirkpatrick-Fleming*, situated near the banks of Kirtle Water, together with *Mossknow* (W. M. Graham, Esq.) and *The Cove*. At 15 m. (l.) is *Bonshaw Tower*, the seat of the late R. N. Irving, Esq. (d. 1894), picturesquely situated overhanging the river.

16¾ m. **Kirtle Bridge Stat.** [Branch to Annan 5½ m. S. (p. 94)].

About 2 m. rt. on the estate of *Springkell*, formerly a seat of the Heron Maxwells, is the ruined ch. of *Kirkconnell*, the churchyard of which is the scene of the pathetic ballad of "Fair Helen of Kirkconnell Lee."

The daughter of the Laird of Kirkconnell loved and was beloved by Adam Fleming of Kirkconnell, but was promised in marriage by her family to Bell of Ecclefechan. The favoured swain was in the habit of meeting her in the churchyard, which so excited the jealousy of the rival that he one evening took up his station, armed with a gun, for the purpose of watching them. Unable to contain himself with rage, he fired, when the fair Helen received the bullet intended for her lover. A fierce combat ensued, in which the murderer was cut to pieces. Fleming went abroad, but returned hither to die. The graves of the unfortunate couple are still to be seen here.

The country through which the tourist is passing is now well wooded, but

"It is said to have been cleared of wood by Act of Parliament in the time of James VI., in order to destroy the retreat of the moss-troopers, a pest this part of the country was infamous for—in fact, the whole of the borders then was, as Lindesay expresses, no other thing but theft, reiff, and slaughter."—*Pennant.*

A fine view is obtained on l. over **Annandale**, as the train approaches

20 m. **Ecclefechan Stat.**, 1 m. N.W. of Ecclefechan, a small clean town near the banks of the Mein Water, which 1½ m. S. falls into the Annan. It derives its name, Ecclesia Fechani, from St. Fechan, an Irish saint of the 7th cent. "The Lass of Ecclefechan" is one of Burns's songs. Thomas Carlyle was born here, 4th Dec. 1795, son of a small farmer. The small stone house, extending over a gateway in the centre of the town, has been secured for the collection of Carlyle relics. The principal room is fitted up with furniture brought from his study at Chelsea, and contains numerous most interesting memorials of "The Sage." He was buried on 10th Feb. 1881 in the churchyard, adjoining which is a handsome red sandstone U.P. Church. Mrs. Carlyle is buried at Haddington.

[The antiquary or geologist should pay a visit to the hill of *Burnswark* (or Birrenswark), nearly 3 m. to the N., an igneous escarpment of carboniferous age, 920 ft. high. It is strongly d fended by 3 Roman camps, the largest of which looks S., and encloses an area 900 ft. in length by 600 in breadth. The summit commands a fine view of Lochmaben, Queensberry Hill, Hartfell, the Solway Firth, Criffel, Annan, Carlisle, and the Cumberland Lake Hills, and has several forts, probably British. Horsley considers Burnswark to be the work of Agricola. A Roman road may be traced at the S.E. foot of the hill, and several altars and coins have been dug up in the vicinity. 1¾ m. E. near *Middlebie* is another Roman Camp.

2½ m. S.W. of Ecclefechan across the Annan is *Hoddam Castle* (Edw. Brook, Esq.), a castellated house, built between 1437-84, by John Lord Herries, a powerful Border baron. Sir Walter Scott was a frequent visitor, and here became acquainted with many of the scenes described in "Guy Mannering" and "Redgauntlet." On the hill above, conspicuous from the rly., is a beacon tower called *Trailtrow*, or more commonly "Repentance," either because it was built of stone taken from a church, or, according to the ballad "Lord Herries' Complaint," because of remorse felt by a Lord Herries, who, returning in his ship with a large booty gained in England, threw some of his prisoners overboard in a storm to lighten the vessel. Over the door is carved the word "Repentance," between a dove and a serpent.]

At 24 m. before crossing the *Water of Milk* the traveller obtains a beautiful though transient view l. including *Castlemilk* (Sir Robt. Jardine, Bt.).

The scenery of the Water of Milk, which rises in the fells bordering on Eskdale, is very pretty, and can be explored conveniently from

25¾ m. **Lockerbie Stat.** ✲ [*Branch* W. to *Dumfries* and *Stranraer* (p. 11).] Lockerbie is celebrated for its sheep and cattle fairs, the one in August being the largest lamb fair in Scotland. There is a handsome *Town Library* of Mediæval architecture, and a *Jubilee Hall.* Near Lockerbie are the ruins of a

Castle of the Johnstones, one of the most powerful families in this part of Scotland. A "Lockerbie lick" is still proverbial from the slaughter inflicted by them on the Maxwells (1593). "Maxwell's Thorn" on the W. side of the Dryfe marks the spot where Lord Maxwell, Warden of the W. Marches fell, and where he was, according to tradition, killed by the wife of Johnstone of Kirkton with the great key of the castle.

1 m. E. is *Murrayfield* (Miss Beattie). 5 m. S.W. is *Rammerscales* (Major Macdonald) up a very steep avenue and commanding a wide view. The grounds are celebrated for their beautiful silver firs and larch, one of the latter, cut for the Caledonian Rly., measuring 106 ft. of solid timber.

EXCURSIONS :—

(1) E. up the *Water of Milk* to *Langholm* 16 m. (p. 19).

(2) N.E. up the *Corrie Water* to *Hutton Ch.* and *Gillesbie Ho.* (Col. Rogerson) on the *Dryfe Water* (8½ m.); thence down the Dryfe to Lockerbie 14½ m., or over the moor —a fine drive—to *Wamphray Glen* [p. 14] (4½ m.), Wamphray Stat. (2 m.), and Lockerbie (9 m.) 24 m.

(3) N.W. to *Raehills Ho.* and *Glen* 9 m. (see p. 14).

[Branch W. to **Dumfries** (14 m.) and **Stranraer.** This line crosses the Annan, skirts l. the *Castle Loch* (below) with rt. *Halleaths Ho.* (A. J. S. Johnstone, Esq.) and *Loch* to

4 m. **Lochmaben Stat.** ✲, a royal and parl. burgh with a modern *Town Hall* (1878) and a *Statue of Robert Bruce* (Hutchison, 1879).

Lochmaben, when seen from a height, appears to be almost an island, as it is surrounded by 6 lochs which abound with pike, perch, roach, bream, eels, and trout.

The largest, about ¾ m. square, is *Castle Loch* to the S. In it alone the far-famed *Vendace* (*Coregonus Willoughbii*, Yarrell) is found. Tradition adds that it was introduced here by Queen Mary, but more probably it was brought hither by the monks of some neighbouring convent for the benefit of their table. It is delicious eating, resembling smelt; it is best in July. It defies the angler, resisting all sorts of baits, and is caught only with nets by the members of the *Vendace Club*, who meet here annually. Upon a peninsula at the S. end of this loch are the scanty remains of a once almost impregnable *Castle* belonging to the Bruces, in which, if not at Turnberry Cas. (p. 117), Robert Bruce was born 1274, and which he made his headquarters in the War of Independence against England. Some say, however, that this castle was built by him and superseded an older building upon *Castle Hill* on the W. shore of the loch. It consisted of 3 courts, enclosed by massive walls 12 ft. thick, and by a triple fosse. The faces of the walls have been plundered of the stone, and little is left but shapeless masses of rubble. The property now belongs to the Earl of Mansfield, and includes 4 villages in the neighbourhood, held by the "Kindly Tenants of Lochmaben," as they are called. This is a sort of copyhold tenure acknowledging no feudal superior, and is supposed to have originated in a grant of land by Robert Bruce to his servants, when superannuated. This tenure was confirmed by the Court of Session on an appeal in 1824.

8 m. **Shielhill Stat.**, a hamlet on the banks of the Water of Ae. 1½ m. rt. is *Kirkmichael Ho.* (J. S. Lyon, Esq.).

10 m. **Amisfield Stat.**, ¾ m. (rt.) is *Amisfield Ho.* (W. R. Walton, Esq.), and beyond, *Glenae Ho.* (R. S. Dalzell, Esq.).

Having passed l. Tinwald village we reach

12 m. **Locharbriggs Stat.**, and

14 m. **Dumfries** ✲ (p. 95). For line W. to Stranraer see Rte. 13. For line S.E. to Carlisle, and N.W. to Glasgow, see Rte. 12.]

Soon after quitting Lockerbie the rly. crosses the Dryfe Water, reaching

28¾ m. **Nethercleuch Stat.** 3 m. W. across the Annan is *Corncockle Quarry*, yielding the finest red sandstone for building in Scotland, and numerous fossils. In it the late Rev. Mr. Hunter of Ruthwell found tracks of an immense extinct tortoise, which has been named *Chelichnys Titan*.

At 30 m. l. is *Jardine Hall*, which contains a collection of fossil footprints of reptiles from *Corncockle.*

Across the river is *Spedlin's Tower*, once the residence of the Jardines of Applegarth, a massive quadrangular structure, with circular turrets at the angles. Over the gateway is the date 1605, probably the year when it was last repaired.

32 m. **Dinwoodie Stat.** 1 m. l. are Johnstone Bridge over the Annan —a picturesque spot, close to which is a mill—and the *Johnstone Ch.*, where the Hope Johnstones of Annandale are buried.

34½ m. **Wamphray Stat.** 2 m. rt. up the hill is the Ch. of *Wamphray*, picturesquely situated beside *Wamphray Glen* (p. 14). Here is the scene of the ballad "The Lads of Wamphray." The line soon crosses the Annan.

At 38½ m. a splendid view up **Moffatdale** is obtained. Then *Kirkpatrick Juxta Ch.* and *Craigielands* (James Smith, Esq.) are passed l. before

40 m. **Beattock Stat.** ✲

[A *Branch* line (opened 1883) goes rt., crosses the Evan Water, passes rt. *Lochhouse Tower*, a square peel belonging to the Johnstones of Corehouse, and crosses the Annan to

2 m. **MOFFAT Stat.** ✲ This clean thriving little town, 345 ft. above sea-level, is a favourite resort and a capital centre for innumerable expeditions to some of the finest mountains and glens of the Borders.

Its history can be traced back beyond the days of the Knights Templar, who had a chapel here, but it owes its modern celebrity in the first instance to a sulphur well 1½ m. distant. Now, however, its many other attractions, its bracing air and its great variety of walks and drives, draw large numbers of visitors who never taste the waters.

There are handsome *Estab.*, *Free*, and *U.P. Churches*, an *Epis. Ch.* and a *R.C. Chap.*, banks and good shops. The *High St.*, the centre of which in former days was occupied by the Bowling Green, surrounded by a yew hedge, and now spoilt by a rough-hewn sandstone drinking fountain surmounted by a ram, is probably the broadest in Scotland. Adjoining its W. side is the quaint and plain-looking *Moffat Ho.* and its grounds, belonging to J. J. Hope Johnstone, Esq., the chief landowner in this neighbourhood.

EXCURSIONS :—

(1) To the N. rises the wooded **Gallow Hill** (832 ft.) with grassy paths round and over it.

(2) The **Mineral Well**, approached by the *Well Road*, lined with summer residences, and a long steady ascent, passing rt. *Heathery Haugh Ho.* and *Archbank*, stands 1½ m. N.E. (600 ft.), overlooking a pretty dell. *Coaches* daily at 7.30 A.M.

The water tastes like rotten eggs, but not so strongly as at Harrogate.

Pedestrians will do well to ascend the hill behind (964 ft.) for a pleasant view, easily obtained by keeping to the rt. shoulder, and in returning from the Well may reach the Gallow Hill by turning off rt. at Archbank, or may take the Old Well Road by turning off rt. at Heathery Haugh.

(3) To the **Beld Crag Glen** 4 m. S.E. by the *Old* Carlisle Road, cross-

ing (2 m.) the Moffat Water with l. *Dumcrieff Ho.* (Lord Rollo) and from the top of the hill beyond viewing rt. the *Meeting of the Waters*, where the Moffat and the Evan join and swell the smaller but central Annan which gives its name to **Annandale.**

At 3½ m. a road through a gate strikes l. in ¼ m. to a stile where carriages turn. Cross the stile, descend steeply, turn l. at the foot of the hill, and when the glen forks follow the stream to the rt. The banks are profusely covered with ferns. A *bald* crag (which gives its name to the glen), with trickling water and strange "devil's hoof" marks at its base, is passed l. before the rustic bridge and ravine at the top are reached. From the stile the pedestrian should not return to the road but proceed rt. through *Brakenside* farmyard and over the hill to Dumcrieff.

(4) The **"Garple,"** a fairy-like glen with an iron Spa near its head, lies 1 m. N. of Beattock Stat. on the W. side of the rly.

Carriages cross the Evan and the rly. behind what was once Beattock Hotel—an important stage in the days of the Glasgow and Carlisle Coach—to the foot of the "Crooked Road." Thence the path strikes rt., enters the 2nd wood (after crossing, with the rly., a curious tunnel made by the water of the glen before it joins the Evan), and ascends beside the stream. At the top is a summer house above and a rustic bridge below between an upper and lower waterfall. The carriage having driven 3 m. round is quite close—near the top of a hill crowned with old *Auchen Castle*, a stronghold of Randolph Earl of Moray, Bruce's nephew and trusty lieutenant, which commands a fine view. New *Auchen Castle* (Wm. Younger, Esq.) is passed l. as we descend to the bridges over the rly. and river at "Egypt." Across the Glasgow road a delightful path leads over *Coates Hill* direct (2 m.) to Moffat. The round is abt. 7 m. for pedestrians, reduced to 5 m. by taking train to Beattock. With a carriage only 1½ m. have to be walked.

(5) N.E. to the **Grey Mare's Tail** (10 m.), (**Loch Skene**) and **St. Mary's Loch**, 15 m.

This is considered the principal expedition in the neighbourhood. [*Coaches*, Tues., Thurs., and Sat. (fare 3s., ret. 5s.) in connection with coaches to Selkirk, 34 m.] The drawback is that return must be made the same way. As the coach climbs *Hunterheck* hill (1 m.), one of the best views of Moffat is obtained looking back. Descending to the Moffat Water a glimpse of *Dumcrieff Ho.* is caught rt. Beyond the 2nd milestone we cross the stream and pass through the woods of which Burns wrote—

"Sweet fa's the eve on Craigieburn."

Craigieburn Ho. l. is invisible. "Burns's Cottage," on the site of the one in which the poet is said to have written "O Willie brew'd a peck o' maut," is passed rt. before the 3rd milestone, at which a view of **Moffatdale** for 8 m. opens up, with *Bodesbeck Law* (2173 ft.), associated with Hogg's "Brownie of Bodesbeck," prominent on the rt.

At 4 m. a glimpse is caught (rt.) of the *Craigmichan Scaurs*, 2 m. up the Selcoth Burn, one of the strangest places in the S. of Scotland, and peculiarly interesting to the geologist. Thence *Loch Fell* [see (10)] may be reached rt., or l. the *Ettrick Valley* (p. 33).

At *Capplegill* (5½ m.) l. the *Blackshope Burn* comes down from Hartfell [see (11)] through a wild glen, a refuge of the Covenanters, bounded rt. by the curious double-peaked narrow-ridged *Saddleyoke* (2412 ft.); and rt. a cart track leads over Bodesbeck Law to the upper waters of the Ettrick (p. 33).

At 7 m. *Carrifran*, another wild glen, is crossed l., and at 10 m. we reach the ravine l. in which the *Grey Mare's Tail* is situated. This is one of the highest waterfalls in Scotland, being over 200 ft. high. A path, steep and rocky in one place, leads to the very foot of the fall

"Where, deep deep down, and far within,
Toils with the rocks the roaring linn;
Then, issuing forth one foamy wave,
And wheeling round the Giant's Grave,
White as the snowy charger's tail,
Drives down the pass of Moffatdale."
Marmion, Introd. to Canto ii.

The *Giant's Grave* is a long tumulus, between the road and the foot of the cataract.

The source of the stream is "Dark

Loch Skene," a wild and solitary loch (¾ m. long by ¼ m. broad), situated under *Loch Craig Head* (2625 ft.), fully 1 m. beyond the waterfall and abt. 1700 ft. above sea-level. Robert Chalmers first announced, 1845, that it had been produced by the moraine of a glacier which once filled the deep recesses in these mountains.

[Those in private carriages (including ladies) should, if good walkers, ascend the very steep but not dangerous hillside to the l. of the Fall, follow the stream to Loch Skene (1 hr.) and thence by a peaty path, not easy to follow though marked by small cairns, which strikes off E. a few yards down the stream, cross the bogs (2 m.) by Dobb's Linn to Birkhill (1 hr.) [below] and there rejoin the carriages.]

Having crossed the Tail Burn the coach climbs for a mile to 11 m. *Birkhill* ✲ (1080 ft.), a shepherd's cottage where the horses are watered, close to the watershed between the Moffat and the Yarrow and on the boundary between Dumfriesshire and Selkirkshire. l. is *Dobb's Linn,* a hiding-place of the Covenanters, where Halbert Dobson and David Dun, according to an old rhyme, put the De'il to flight with the aid of the Bible, and interesting to geologists on account of its graptolites. The whole of Moffatdale lies upon the Lower Silurian system. The road descends the Yarrow and passes (14 m.) l. *Chapelhope,* the haunts and home of Hogg's "Brownie."

[Here a path turns rt. up *Riskinhope* burn, where James Renwick, the last of the Covenanter martyrs (1688), preached almost his last sermon, over to Ettrick Ch. 4 m. (p. 33).]

We now keep along the banks of the *Loch of the Lowes* to

15 m. "Lone St. Mary's silent lake."

At the S.W. end is **"Tibbie Shiels" Inn** ✲, long kept by Tibbie Shiels (Mrs. Richardson) [1781-1878], where Hogg [1770-1835] and Wilson ("Christopher North") [1785-1854] spent their "Noctes Ambrosianæ." On the hillside l. is a statue to Hogg, representing the "Ettrick Shepherd" seated.

[A hilly road ascending to 1350 ft. leads E. to Tushielaw Inn ✱ (6 m.) in Ettrickdale (p. 32).]

At 16 m. l. on a charming situation overlooking the loch is *Rodono Hotel* ✲.

For *St. Mary's Kirk* and road down Yarrow Vale to Selkirk see p. 31.

(6) S. to **Raehills** (J. J. Hope Johnstone, Esq.). The *Ho.* (not shown), built by the 3rd Earl of Hopetoun 1786, stands well, surrounded by fine parks. The *Glen* is below St. Ann's Bridge on the Dumfries road—8 m.

[Wooden foot-bridges, respectively ½ m. up and ¾ m. down the *Kinnel Water,* make a pleasant round.]

We pass rt. (2½ m.) *Craigielands Ho.* (3½ m.) *Marchbank Wood Ho.* (with a grand view l. up Moffatdale), beyond which the Lochmaben road l. should be taken so as to visit, by a detour of 1 m., the ruins of *Lochwood Tower* in a wood of some of the most venerable *oaks* in Scotland. It was long the principal seat of the Johnstones, and so protected by surrounding bogs, that James VI. declared "whoever built Lochwood was a knave at heart." The Maxwells burnt it in 1592 and suffered terribly in consequence the following year at Dryfe Sands. Return direct or by *Johnstone Ch.* (p. 12) and Wamphray.

(7) S. by the *Old* Carlisle road passing l. Beld Crag Wood (above) to **Wamphray Ch.** and **Glen**—8 m.

Drive 1 m. farther to *Laverhay Farm.* Thence pedestrians should take the track up Wamphray Water to foot of Loch Fell (5 m.) [see (10)] —then l. and down the Cornal Burn to Moffat 11 m.

(8) N.W. to the **Devil's Beef Tub,** 5½ m. on the new Edinburgh road—one of Telford's great engineering

works. We cross the Annan above the town, l. is *Chapel* farm with scanty remains of the Chapel of the Knights Templar. In 5 m. we ascend 950 ft., enjoying splendid views back over Moffat to *Birrenswark* (p. 10) and Skiddaw. To the rt. is a large semicircular hollow, the head of Annandale, and an excellent hiding-place for stolen cattle—hence its name. Maclaren, a rebel, escaped from his guards in 1746 by rolling heads over heels into the Tub, then enveloped in mist—an incident introduced into "Redgauntlet." Beyond is the watershed where

"Tweed, Annan, Clyde,
Rise out o' ane hillside;
Tweed ran, Annan wan,
And Clyde fa' down and brake its neck
ower Corra Linn."

Down Tweedside are *Talla Linn*, *Broad Law*, and the *Crook Inn* ✲ 16 m. (p. 90).

(9) 2½ m. along new Edinburgh road, over "**Greenhill Steps**" to the Glasgow road (6 m.), returning by Beattock—15 m. A fine moorland drive.

(10) E. **Ascent** of **Loch Fell** (2256 ft.) with the most *central* hill view in the neighbourhood—7 m.

Ponies have been ridden to the very top. The track goes up the Cornal burn, which it crosses, and keeps l. over the watershed to the Wamphray Water, crossed (6 m.) before the climb begins. Return may be made (even with ponies, but boggy) down the Wamphray Water [see (7)]. From the top there is a grand view N. of the Moffatdale Hills (11), E. over the bleak Eskdale Muir, and S. into England. Pedestrians may go on into Eskdale (p. 20) or return by the *Craigmichan Scaurs* (exceedingly interesting, especially to the geologist) and Selcoth Burn to the Selkirk road at 4th milestone from Moffat.

(11) N.E. **Ascent** of **White Coomb** (2695 ft.) and **Hartfell** (2651 ft.) the *highest* hills in the neighbourhood. Best pedestrian expedition.

Take coach to the Grey Mare's Tail. Ascend to Loch Skene [see (5)]. Thence S. up *White Coomb* and over the hills (boggy) to *Hartfell*, which stands out unmistakably. Descend by *Auchencat Burn* and *Hartfell Mineral Spa* to the old Edinburgh road at *Granton Ho.* (A. M. Jardine, Esq.), 3 m. from Moffat, where carriages can be met; or keep along the hill-tops, descending by Moffat Well. Walking all the way from the coach will take abt. 7 hrs. For Hartfell alone ascend from Granton and descend to the Well, 5 hrs.

(12) S.W. **Ascent** of **Queensberry Hill** (2285 ft.)

Drive by the *Crooked Road* behind Beattock to *Kinnelhead* (6 m.), one of the most famous sheep-breeding farms in the S. of Scotland. Thence cross over to and ascend the *Lochan Burn* to its source in the side of the hill. The top (2 hrs.) affords view into Nithsdale, but the surrounding country is uninteresting.

(13) For a grand circular driving tour to **Leadhills** and **Nithsdale** see Elvanfoot (below).]

Leaving Beattock the hills draw in and the whole character of the scenery becomes wilder. The rly. ascends the Evan valley, through much rock cutting, up the "Beattock Bank," which, it was once thought, would require a stationary engine at the top, now ascended by express trains at over 40 miles an hour. l. we pass *Auchen Castle* (Wm. Younger, Esq.); rt. runs the Glasgow and Carlisle road, one of Telford's grandest engineering works. Beyond it may be traced the parallel line of the old Roman road. The train crosses into Lanarkshire on its way to the summit (1028 ft.)—reached in 10 m.—and descends into Clydesdale. The Clyde, swelled by its greater tributaries the *Daer* and the *Powtrail* (l.), is crossed before

52¾ m. **Elvanfoot Stat.** where another trib. the *Elvan* comes in.

[5 m. l. up the Elvan is the mining village of **Leadhills** ✲ (1350 ft.), where Allan Ramsay, author of "The Gentle Shepherd," was born 1686. Beyond over the watershed is **Wanlockhead** (1380 ft.), also a mining village. These are the *two highest villages in Scotland*, and their mines have produced more lead than any in Scotland, and a considerable quantity of silver, from 1511 down to the present time. *Gold* is found in the streams of the district, and from this supply in 1526 part of the Scottish coinage was minted; and 42 oz. obtained for a crown for the King, and 35 oz. for one for the Queen.

A carriage may be ordered from Leadhills to be at Elvanfoot Stat. for the magnificent drive up the Powtrail Burn, through the *Dalveen Pass*, and down the Carron to Carron Bridge Stat. (p. 101) 12½ m. Thence up Nithsdale passing l. *Drumlanrig Castle* (p. 100) to *Enterkin Foot* 17 m., where horses can be baited (rt. is the celebrated narrow pass to Leadhills, described by Defoe and Dr. John Brown, in which a body of dragoons had ignominiously to surrender their prisoners to Covenanters holding the heights). 4 m. farther up the Nith we turn rt. up the *Menoch Water* and *Pass* to Wanlockhead, Leadhills (29 m.), and Elvanfoot 34 m., having traversed the two finest passes in the Lowlands, and seen some excellent river scenery.]

55¼ m. **Crawford Stat.** having a fragment of *Tower Lindsay*, an old ruined seat of the Lindsays, Earls of Crawford. The Camps and Midlock Waters here fall in rt. The Clyde is crossed just beyond the stat. The *Glen Gonner Water* comes in l. *Abington Ho.* (Sir E. A. Colebrooke, Bt.) is picturesquely situated on the Clyde (l.) before

57¾ m. **Abington Stat.** ✲ The river is again crossed before

63¼ m. **Lamington Stat.** ¾ m. rt. is *Lamington House* (Lord Lamington), a gabled mansion. In the hall is the chair of Wallace. The heiress of Lamington married Sir Wm. Wallace, and this property was inherited by his daughter. Burns went to church here on one occasion, and was so little pleased that he left on the seat an epigram, called "The Kirk of Lamington":—

"As cauld a wind as ever blew;
A caulder kirk, and in't but few;
As cauld a minister's e'er spak;
Ye'll a' be het ere I come back."

The *Church* retains the "jougs," or pillory-collar (see p. 62), and the stool of repentance.

On rt., near the river, is the ruined tower of Lamington.

On left rises the isolated and picturesque outline of **Tinto Hill**, a mass of flesh-coloured felsite, 2335 ft. high, from the top of which, on a clear day, a view may be seen from Goatfell in Arran on the W., to the Bass Rock on the E.

"Be a lassie ne'er so black,
Gin she hae the penny siller,
Set her up on Tinto's tap,
The wind will blaw a man till her."

To carry a stone to the top of Tinto was in old times a common form of penance. On the E. side of the hill are the ruins of *Fatlips Castle*, an ancient seat of the Lockharts. A fine view (rt.) of the hills at the head of Tweeddale is obtained as we approach

66¾ m. **Symington Junc.** [*Branch* rt. *via* Biggar to Peebles 19 m. Rte. 10] said to have taken its name from Simon Locard, who had a grant of the land from Malcolm IV.

68½ m. **Thankerton Stat.**, which gives his title to Lord Watson, who was born (1828) in the Manse of Covington, a hamlet 1¼ m. farther (rt.), with a large ruined tower near it, built 1442 by the Lindsays of Covington, and conspicuous from the rly. The hill rising directly up from the opposite bank of the Clyde is *Quothquhan Law*, 1097 ft.

Once more crossing the Clyde, which then flows l. to *The Falls* and *Lanark*, we reach

73½ m. **Carstairs Junc. Stat.** ✲

[Branch (1) E. to *Dolphinton* 11 m. (p. 78). (2) N.E. *via* Midcalder to *Edinburgh* 27½ m. (Rte. 9). (3) S.W. to *Lanark* (4¾ m.) and *Ayr* (51¼ m.) (Rte. 11).]

This place is supposed to be the ancient Corn-Caer, a Roman settlement, and capital of the Damnii, a native tribe. Roman remains, including a bath, have been found in the parish.

Between the stat. and the Clyde is *Carstairs House* (Joseph Monteith, Esq.). The house is a fair specimen of modern Tudor architecture, and contains some good paintings by Guido, Morales, Raeburn, etc. Carstairs is 5 m. distant from Lanark and the Falls of the Clyde (Rte. 11).

On quitting Carstairs the river Mouse is crossed, which lower down enters the Clyde through the chasm of the *Cartland Crags* (p. 93).

$76\frac{1}{4}$ m. **Cleghorn Junc. Stat.** [*Branch* to Ayr *via* Lanark, Douglas, and Muirkirk (Rte. 11)]. Beyond l. is *Cleghorn* (Wm. E. Lockhart, Esq.) on the Mouse Water; in the park is a Roman camp. A little to the l. before reaching

$80\frac{3}{4}$ m. **Braidwood Stat.** where there are limestone quarries, is *The Lee* (Sir Simon Lockhart, Bart.), a castellated mansion, renovated by Gillespie Graham. It contains interesting portraits of Claverhouse and Cromwell. Under the latter served Sir William Lockhart, eminent as diplomatist and general, who was a match for Cardinal Richelieu, and took Dunkirk from Spain and France. Here is kept the famous Lee Penny, upon which the story of the "Talisman" is founded, and which was brought from the East by Sir Simon Lockhart in the time of Robert the Bruce.

"The water in which it is dipped operates as a styptic, as a febrifuge, and possesses several other properties as a medicinal talisman. Of late its powers have been chiefly restricted to the cure of persons bitten by mad dogs; and as the illness in such cases frequently arises from imagination, there can be no reason for doubting that water which has been poured on the Lee Penny furnishes a congenial cure."—Introduction to "Talisman."

In reality the Lee Penny is a groat (probably of Edward III.) in which is set a cornelian or sard stone, constituting the real Talisman. The use of it was authorised and confirmed by a synod of the Kirk of Scotland, while condemning all other amulets. In the Park is the *Pease Tree*, a very aged oak.

Crossing the gorge called Jock's Gill we reach

28 m. **Carluke Stat.** for *Milton Lockhart* and *Maudslie Cas.*, both lying W. on the Clyde (p. 148).

The tourist will now perceive by the altered character of the scenery that he has reached the great manufacturing district of the *Lanarkshire Coalfield*, and that the charming braes and woods of the Clyde have given place to monotonous and dark hills, with the foreground occupied by blazing furnaces and dingy-looking collieries.

84 m. **Law Junc. Stat.**, a mining place which has sprung up since 1877.

[Line to Stirling and the North branches rt. through the heart of the *Black Country* (p. 18) to

1 m. **Overtown Stat.**, *i.e. Oretown*, with Garrion Bridge over the Clyde, on the Edinburgh and Ayr road (p. 148), and the village of Dalserf $1\frac{1}{2}$ m. S.

$2\frac{1}{4}$ m. **Wishaw Central Stat.**, surrounded by coal-pits, by which the town is partly undermined. $1\frac{1}{2}$ m. N.E. are the *Coltness Iron Works*, 1 m. N. *Coltness Ho.* (J. Houldsworth, Esq.), and $1\frac{1}{2}$ m. N.W. *Wishaw Ho.*, the seat of Lord Belhaven, in a park of great beauty.

$5\frac{3}{4}$ m. **Holytown Stat.** [Line rt. to Edinburgh—Rte. 21].

7 m. **Mossend Stat.** with important *Iron Works.*

$9\frac{1}{2}$ m. **Whifflet Stat.**

$10\frac{1}{2}$ m. **Coatbridge Stat.** [*Branch* W. to Glasgow by *Baillieston* and

Rutherglen (p. 146); and E. (from *Sunnyside Stat.*) to Edinburgh (Rte. 20)]. A large mining town, the Capital of the Black Country, and the centre of a group of blazing *Iron Furnaces*, surrounded by a network of rlys. on the *Monkland Canal*. It is a desolate, black district—of smoke, coal, and ashes, —treeless, sunless, the verdure of Nature's surface scarified and loaded with rubbish heaps. Yet it deserves to be seen as a busy and crowded hive of human industry.

The handsome *Gothic Church*, with octagon spire, was built by J. Baird, Esq., the iron-master, 1874.

We pass *Gartsherrie Ho.* (G. F. R. Colt, Esq.) and *Iron Works* (W. Baird and Co., Lim.) to

11½ m. **Gartsherrie Stat.** [Line l. to Glasgow by *Gartcosh*, etc. (p. 156)]. At

12½ m. **Glenboig Stat.**, with large *Brick Fields*, the line from Glasgow to the North is joined (Rte. 25).]

86½ m. **Wishaw South Stat.**

88¼ m. **Flemington Stat.** l. is *Dalzell Ho.* (Lord Hamilton), on the Clyde; the house includes the former mansion and a Keep 700 years old. The *Gardens* have been improved from suggestions by Mr. Ruskin.

89½ m. **Motherwell Stat.** ✲ [*Branch* N. (1) to Holytown, (2) to Mossend and Coatbridge, and (3) S. to Hamilton]. The town, of modern growth, owes its sudden prosperity to the mineral wealth around it. It possesses several churches, including a handsome R.C. Ch., erected 1882 (Messrs. Pugin, archt.). A viaduct over the wooded glen of the *S. Calder* is crossed to

92¾ m. **Fallside Stat.** [*Line* l. to *Bothwell* (Rte. 22)].

93¾ m. **Uddingston Stat.** [*Line* to Edin. (Rte. 21)].

95¾ m. **Newton Stat.** See p. 146 for line between this and

102¼ m. **Glasgow Central Stat.**

For **GLASGOW** ✲ see p. 132.

ROUTE 3.

Carlisle to Edinburgh, by Liddesdale, Hawick, Newtown St. Boswells (Dryburgh), Melrose (Abbotsford), and Galashiels (Selkirk).

98¼ m. 5 trains daily, in 2½ to 4¾ hrs.

This line of rly., belonging to the N. British Rly. Co., is usually known as the **Waverley Route**, from its passing through the district associated with Sir Walter Scott and his writings. The portion of the rly. between Carlisle and Hawick is essentially a Border line, and was made in 1854.

Quitting **Carlisle** we pass (rt.) the Cathedral and Castle, cross the river Eden, and, at a high level the Caledonian Rly., traverse the plain between the Eden and the Esk, and pass **Harker** and **Lyneside** stations to

9½ m. **Longtown Stat.** [*Branch* (l.) to Gretna Junc., whence W. to Dumfries (Rte. 12) and N. by Cal. Rly. main line (Rte. 2).], an ancient Border town in Cumberland, on the left bank of the Esk, a considerable stream which is here crossed. A market has been held here since Henry III.'s time and it is somewhat celebrated for its supply of cranberries, which are sent to London during the season in large quantities. There is not much to be seen except the old parish ch. of *Arthuret*, of the early part of the 17th cent., which is outside the town.

$11\frac{3}{4}$ m. **Scotch Dyke Stat.** On the opposite side of the Esk are the woods and mansion of *Netherby*, from which "Young Lochinvar" carried off his bride, the seat of Sir F. U. Graham, Bt.

From the nature of the alluvial flats that bound the Solway Firth and its tributaries, a fine distant view is obtained of the hills in the neighbourhood of Langholm and Eskdale. The Esk is again crossed below its junction with the Liddel. The scenery improves rapidly, and becomes very picturesque at

14 m. **Riddings Junc. Stat.** The view of the village and church of *Canobie* (l.) is charming.

[*Branch* to $1\frac{1}{4}$ m. **Canobie Stat.**; $2\frac{3}{4}$ **Gilnockie Stat.**; and 7 m. **Langholm Stat.**

The drive by the banks of the Esk to *Langholm* (7 m.) is far prettier than the journey by the railway, which keeps the high ground on the l. bank of the river, so as to accommodate the collieries in Canobie parish. These collieries are situated upon the middle series of coal-measures, overlaid by Permian strata, sections of which may be seen at Riddings Junc., Penton, Carwinlay Burn, and Canobie Stat. The banks of the Esk in this neighbourhood are steep and precipitous; one rock in particular is named *Gilnockie's Garden*, and is said to have been a favourite haunt of Johnnie Armstrong, the famous Border riever and captain of Mosstroopers, whose stronghold, the *Tower of Hollows*, a square Peel, 70 ft. high, is about 2 m. from Canobie.

Langholm ✲ is a thriving Border town (with a suburb called *New Langholm*) on the old high road between Carlisle and Berwick, where the Ewes Water falls into the Esk. It is an industrious place, famous for its sheep fairs and woollen manufactures; and possesses a library, to which Telford the engineer bequeathed £1000. The scenery of the hills around is picturesque, although they have the rounded monotonous form characteristic of S. Scotland. On White Hill to the E. of the town is a *Monument* in memory of Sir John Malcolm (1769-1833), Governor of Bombay, visible even from the Waverley Line. He was one of ten sons of an Eskdale farmer, born at *Burnfoot*, $3\frac{1}{2}$ m. N.W. of Langholm. To his brother, Admiral Sir Pulteney Malcolm, there is a statue in the Market-place. Two other brothers contributed to render the name illustrious and to do honour to their native valley. In the immediate neighbourhood are *Langholm Lodge*, a seat of the Duke of Buccleuch, the Border tower of Langholm, and slight remains of *Wauchope Castle*, situated on the water of the same name. The headquarters of the Esk and Liddel Fisheries' Association, which issues tickets to anglers at fixed rates, and gives all information, are at Langholm.

The neighbourhood of Langholm is intimately associated with the memory of Johnnie Armstrong, the Border hero, who in the days of James V. levied blackmail as far as Newcastle. As old Lindsay of Pitscottie tells us, "He rode ever with 24 able gentlemen well horsed; yet he never molested any Scottishman." The king, under the pretext of a hunting party, made an expedition against Armstrong, enticed him over to *Caerlanrig* (about 15 m. N.), and hanged him and 36 of his accomplices there, notwithstanding many tempting offers made by the culprits to procure a respite.

6 m. N.W. of Langholm is the solitary hamlet of *Westerkirk*, the birthplace of Telford, 1757, whose father was a shepherd on the banks of the Megget.

There are fine drives—

(1) N. up the *Ewes Water* and down the *Teviot* to Hawick (p. 22), 22 m.

(2) N.W. up the Esk beyond Burnfoot and Westerkirk to *Eskdalemuir* Ch. and hamlet (13 m.); thence (*a*) over the watershed and down the *Tima Water* to *Thirlestane Cas.* and *Tushielaw Inn* in Ettrickdale, 27 m. (p. 33); or (*b*) (on foot) by old drove road over *Loch Fell* (p. 15) to Moffat, 26 m.

(3) W. by Paddock Hole and the *Water of Milk* to Lockerbie (p. 10), 16 m.]

From Riddings the main line keeps high ground, overlooking the *Liddel*, which for 7 m. above this divides England from Scotland (see p. 81). Its serpentine reaches are embowered in woods, while an occasional homestead on the banks above gives relief to the otherwise bleak-looking country at the foot of the moorland ranges.

17 m. **Penton Stat.** At *Penton Linns* is a wild and rapid reach of the river, which flows through a narrow channel between the rocks.

21 m. **Kershopefoot Stat.** Here we enter Scotland, the scenery on the right closes in, and the gray table-lands that skirt the Cheviots begin to show themselves, varied by an occasional "burn" that joins the Liddel through a tangled ravine. The Liddel is crossed before reaching

24 m. **Newcastleton Stat.,** a Liddesdale town of two streets, founded 1793, in a more convenient spot than *Old Castleton* of which only the church (see below) remains.

The line rises rapidly up **Liddesdale**, the country of Dandie Dinmont, the scenery of which is admirably portrayed in "Guy Mannering."

[1½ m. S. of Newcastleton is *Mangerton Tower*, on the left bank of the Liddel, another of the Armstrong Border residences; and on the opposite hill once dwelt Jock o' the Side, a nephew of the Laird of Mangerton, and, according to Sir Richard Maitland, of very doubtful reputation:

"He is well kenn'd, Johne of the Syde,
A greater thief did never ryde;
He never tires
For to break byres,
O'er mure and mires
Ower gude ane guide."

In a raid by the Liddesdale men Jock o' the Side was taken prisoner; but was rescued by his cousins of Mangerton, known as the Laird's Jock and the Laird's Wat.

Near the roadside, at *Milnholm*, is a stone *Cross*, with a sword and some letters inscribed on it. The cross marks the spot where the body of one of the owners of Mangerton, who was barbarously murdered by Lord Soulis, was rested on its way to interment.]

1½ m. to the N. of Newcastleton the Hermitage Water joins the Liddel. The railway crosses it and keeps the high ground on the right bank of the Liddel, passing rt. the *Ch. of Old Castleton*, and, beyond, the site of *Liddel Castle*, built by Randolph de Soulis in the 12th cent.

29 m. **Steele Road Stat.**

[3 m. N.W. is **Hermitage Castle** on *Hermitage Water*, one of the most interesting historic edifices on the Border, the grand stronghold of the Douglases, and called by Burton the oldest baronial building in Scotland.

Descending to the valley through which the Hermitage Water passes, the tourist can get the key at the gamekeeper's house. Cross the bridge, and take the road to the right. At the next bridge take the road to the left. Hermitage stands in a dreary open plain, and was protected on one side by the stream and on the other by a fosse. The exterior, which is perfect, consists of 4 rectangular towers, one of which, on the S.W., is much larger than the others. These towers are connected on the N. and S. sides by a lofty curtain at their interior angles, on the E. and W. by a corresponding lower curtain, while the exterior angles are also connected by an arch which serves to support the lofty corbelled parapet that crowns the whole building. It is believed to have been built, 1244, by Walter Comyn, Earl of Menteith, and became the great stronghold of the powerful Comyns. One of this family, "The Wizard" (Lord Soulis), so irritated his vassals by his cruelty, that they rebelled against him, and actually boiled him to death—the idea of this punishment having been put into their heads by King Robert Bruce, who peevishly said, when complained to, "Boil him if you please, but let me hear no more of him." The building of such a menacing stronghold so near the English frontier was one of the grievances of King Henry III., which served as a pretext for invading Scotland, 1244. Having been taken by the English in the reign of David II., it was recovered from them by the prowess of William Douglas, called the Knight of Liddesdale, the natural son of the good Lord James. It was to this place that he carried off Sir Alexander Ramsay, and left him to die of starvation, the unfortunate man supporting life for seventeen days by some corn which fell from a granary above, through chinks in the floor, into his dungeon. The Douglas family was so powerful that no notice was taken of this atrocious act. Queen Mary, accompanied by Murray, visited Bothwell here, October 1566 (p. 82).

The Pedestrian may make his way from Hermitage across the hills to Hawick, about 15 m.

To the E. between Whitterhope Burn and Roughley Burn, and sloping down to the Hermitage Water, is *Nine Stane Rig*, 943 ft. high, 4 m. long, and 1 m. broad, on which it is said that Lord Soulis was boiled. There is an Old Stone Circle on it, once of 9 stones, now of 5, 2 of which are pointed out as having supported the caldron. Lord Soulis was suspected of witchcraft (see the ballad by John Leyden, Scott's "Minstrelsy", where a full account of the story is given):

"Lord Soulis he sat in Hermitage Castle,
And beside him Old Redcap sly."]

After leaving Liddesdale the country becomes very desolate as the rly. ascends to

$32\frac{1}{2}$ m. **Riccarton Junc.**

[*Branch* S.E. to *Reedsmouth* (for Morpeth), *Hexham*, and *Newcastle.*]

The summit level is gained in a tunnel under Limekiln Edge, a part of the ridge of hills where the Pictish Ditch or **Catrail** was carried from *Peel Fell* on the Border to *Borthwick Water*, on the N.W., and from thence into the neighbourhood of Galashiels. It consisted of a double fosse and vallum, supported by a number of intermediate forts, and was constructed by the Romanised Britons dwelling on the Tweed, as a protection against the Anglian invasions. After passing through the tunnel the Catrail is well seen (l.) under the curiously shaped hill called *Maiden Paps* (1677 ft.). With a rapid descent down the Hawick side of the Fells, the rly. enters the valley of the *Slitrig*, passing

$38\frac{1}{2}$ m. **Shankend Stat.**

$41\frac{1}{2}$ m. **Stobs Stat.** beyond *Stobs Castle* rt. the picturesque seat of Sir Wm. Eliott, Bt., whose ancestor, Sir Gilbert, was created a knight by King Charles I., 1643.

$45\frac{1}{2}$ m. **Hawick Stat.** ✲, at the junction of the Slitrig with the Teviot, a thriving town and parl. burgh. If population decided its rank, it would be the capital of Roxburghshire, for Jedburgh has not a quarter of its inhabitants. It is an uninteresting town. The manufactures principally consist of woollens, yarns, stockings, etc. The manners and customs of the inhabitants have considerably improved since 1831, when they assisted in stoning, hooting, and even spitting on Sir W. Scott in his old age at Jedburgh.

The streets are regular, and the town has benefited by the carrying out of a good system of drainage in 1876. The *Episcopal Ch.*, from designs by G. G. Scott, is a fine Gothic building. The parish ch., surmounted by a tall square tower, was the scene of the capture of Sir Alexander Ramsay by Sir Wm. Douglas, who confined him in Hermitage Castle, and there starved him (above).

The only objects of antiquity in the town are the *Moot Hill*, a tumulus about 300 ft. in circumference and 30 ft. in height, the old place of meeting of the Court of the Manor, and the *Tower Inn*, once the residence of the Barons of Drumlanrig, which still shows traces of its former strength. It was the only house not burned down by Sussex in 1570.

[EXCURSIONS :—

(1) *Down the Teviot* and across the *Rule Water* to **Jedburgh** 11 m. (p. 82). At 2 m. (rt.) is Cavers Ch. behind which lies *Cavers House* (E. P. Douglas, Esq.), a large square building, erected about 1400 by Sir A. Douglas, and containing the banner carried before Douglas at the battle of Otterburn.

At 5 m. we pass through *Denholm*, the birthplace of John Leyden (1775-1811), who was successively a clergyman, a doctor, and a professor of Eastern languages. He was a great friend of Sir W. Scott, and contributed to the "Minstrelsy of the Scottish Border." An obelisk has been erected to his memory. Conspicuous from Denholm is the eminence of *Ruberslaw* (1392 ft.) (p. 83).

Some crags on the summit are called "Peden's Pulpit," from the fact that Alexander Peden, the Covenanter, used to preach from them.

1½ m. beyond, we turn off rt. Left, across the Teviot, is *Minto Ho.* (Earl of Minto) [Grounds open every week day], with *Minto Crags* to the W.

(2) *Up the Teviot* to **Branxholm** 3 m. At 2 m. is *Goldielands*, a well-preserved Border fortress of the clan of Scott, the last of whom was, for "March treason," hanged over his own gateway. At this point the Teviot is joined by the Borthwick Water; 1 m. beyond is *Branksome* (or *Branxholm*) Tower, an ancient possession, from the middle of the 15th cent., of the Scotts, Barons of Buccleuch, but chiefly known as the principal scene of Sir Walter Scott's "Lay of the Last Minstrel"—

"Nine-and-twenty knights of fame
Hung their shields in Branksome Hall;
They were all knights of mettle true,
Kinsmen to the bold Buccleuch."

Its present aspect is that of a modern house, and it is the residence of the Duke's chamberlain. Some years ago, on the return of the late Duke of Buccleuch from Malta, whither he had gone for the benefit of his health, a dinner was given him in a pavilion erected at Branksome by 1000 of his tenantry, of whom about 300 were hereditary, *i.e.* who from father to son had possessed their farms since the days of the first Buccleuch.

The older part of the building consists of a square tower, ending in an overhanging story with a billet moulding. The rest of it seems to have been begun by Sir Walter Scott in 1571, and completed by his wife, Margaret Douglas.

The *Silver Teviot* rises from the slopes of the ridge of hills that form the northern boundary of Eskdale, and receives in its course to Hawick (rt.) the *Alton* and (l.) the *Borthwick Water*, besides some minor streams.

[The old coaching road leads up the *Teviot* and down the *Ewes Water* to *Langholm* (p. 19), 22 m. from Hawick.]

In returning from Branksome the tourist should drive l. up the *Borthwick Water* 2 m. to *Harden Burn*, and walk ½ m. up its l. bank, on which is *Harden Castle*, the ancient seat of the Scotts of Harden, now represented by Lord Polwarth. Mary Scott dau. of John Scott of Dryhope (p. 32), "The Flower of Yarrow," married (1576) the notorious "Auld Wat" of Harden. His custom was to subsist on the spoils of his freebooting until the serving up of a clean pair of spurs on a dish signified the emptiness of the larder and the necessity of a fresh adventure. The house is devoid of all architectural interest, but the situation is very romantic.]

Quitting the valley of the Teviot in 3 m.,—rt. *Teviot Bank* (Mrs. E. H. Maxwell Blair),—the rly. reaches

49½ m. **Hassendean Stat.**, a corruption of Hazeldean, once belonging to a family of Scotts. The old ch. of Hassendean was demolished in 1690. On the rt. the scenery is very picturesque with the *Minto Crags* (905 ft.), east of which is Minto Ho. (above).

The traveller now gains a distant view (l.) of the triple heads of the *Eildon Hills*, which form the leading feature in the scenery of the district. After passing

53 m. **Belses Stat.** the train crosses the *Ale Water*, a picturesquely-wooded trout-stream which joins the Teviot near Ancrum.

58 m. **Newtown St. Boswells Junc.** ✲

[*Branches* — i. Through Earlston and Duns, to Reston (Rte. 7).

ii. To Roxburgh Junc. (for Jedburgh) and Kelso, where the line forms a connection with the N. Eastern Rly. to Berwick (Rte. 8).]

The situation of *Newtown St. Boswells*, so called after St. Boisil, prior of Melrose in the 7th cent., at the foot of the *Eildon Hills*, is very pretty. In feudal times this village contained 16 *Bastel houses*, which were destroyed by the English in the 16th cent. E. of the village are the hunting stables of the Duke of Buccleuch. On St. Boswells Green a great *Sheep Fair* is held in July, which attracts flockmasters and wool merchants from all parts. Overlooking the village, at a considerable height, is *Eildon Hall*, a seat of the Duke of Buccleuch. The **Eildon Hills,** from their singular isolation and triple cones (respectively 1216, 1385, and 1327 ft. in height), at once strike the attention of the traveller; in addition to which, great interest has always attached to them from the tradition of the magic charm of "the words which cleft Eildon Hills in three."

"Michael Scott was once on a time much embarrassed by an evil spirit, for whom he was under the necessity of finding constant employment. He commanded him to build a *cauld*, or damhead, over the Tweed at Kelso; it was accomplished in one night, and still does honour to the infernal architect's engineering skill. Michael next ordered that Eildon Hill, which was then a uniform cone, should be divided into three. Another night was sufficient to part its summit, as we now see it. At length the enchanter conquered the indefatigable demon by employing him to make ropes out of sand."—SCOTT.

These hills are also connected with the prophecies and sayings of Thomas of Ercildoune, usually known as "Thomas the Rhymer,"[1] who was supposed to have been carried captive by the Queen of Elfland and detained for more than 3 years in the enchanted country within the hills. From the summit is a beautiful view extending over the counties of Roxburgh and Selkirk. The antiquary will find on the northern cone a *Camp* defended by earthen ramparts.

As a Roman station it was known by the name of Trimontium. Much of the interpretation of the Roman military movements depended on the identification of "Trimontium," usually placed on the N. side of the Solway. Gen. Roy remarked that everything harmonised with the supposition that Trimontium was Old Melrose, under the Eildon Hills, and he gives in his "Military Antiquities" a view of the hills from the place where the Roman road crosses the Cheviots on the way to the fortress.

[EXCURSIONS from St. Boswells:—

(1) 1¼ m. E. of the stat. are the ruins of ** **Dryburgh Abbey.**

Follow the highroad to *St. Boswells Green* for ½ m. and then turn l. down a lane leading to the Tweed, which is crossed by a suspension foot-bridge.

Carriages can approach the Abbey going round by Mertoun Bridge (about 4½ m.), or by the ford beside the foot-bridge if the river is not in flood.

Adjoining the modern mansion of the Erskines is the ancient Abbey of Dryburgh,[2] of which there are still considerable remains, surrounded by

[1] His real name was Learmonth of Ercildoune or Earlston (p. 79), and he lived in the latter end of the 13th cent.

[2] Charge for admission 6d. each person; apply at the lodge.

yew-trees nearly as ancient: it is charmingly situated on a semicircular piece of land, round which the Tweed sweeps broad and swift. It never was of great size or wealth, but almost every part of the monastic buildings is still represented by a fragment.

It was founded in 1150 by Hugh de Morville, Lord of Lauderdale (or, as some say, by his master, David I.), and was peopled by White Canons from Alnwick. In 1322 the Abbey was burnt by Edward II., but was rebuilt soon after. In 1544 the English, under Sir Geo. Bowes and Sir Brian Layton, again burnt it, and in all probability it was never rebuilt.

Of the cruciform *Church*, which was 190 ft. long by 75 broad, there are left only part of the outer walls, and the bases of the piers, the N. transept, with its E. aisle, the western entrance, and the original chapel of St. Moden. The N. transept *aisle*, known as *St. Mary's*, is the burying-place of the Erskines; and here, too, are buried Sir Walter Scott (d. 1832), his wife, his son, and his son-in-law, John Lockhart, as also his ancestors, the Haliburtons of Newmains. This chapel opens into the choir by 2 pointed arches, above which are quatrefoil openings,

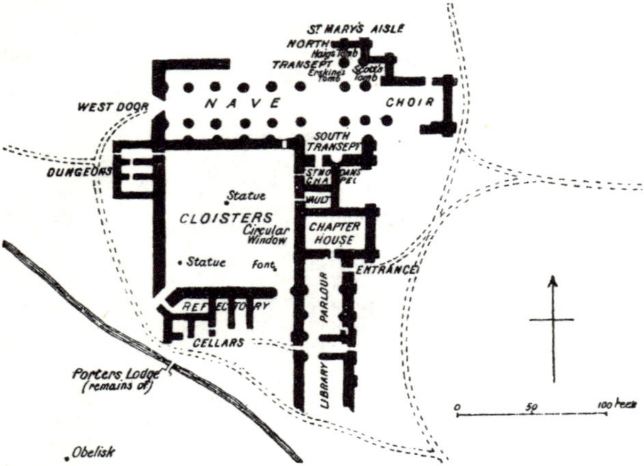

and a triforium gallery. On the S. side of the Church and at a lower level is the quadrangle of the cloisters, which is bounded S. by the Refectory and E. by the Chapter-house, on a still lower level.

The *Chapter-house*, which is still entire, is a very plain long building, with a simple vaulted roof, entered by a beautiful portal and originally surrounded by an arcade of pointed arches, only part of which now remains. Adjoining it is the Abbot's parlour, with a large fireplace. The arms of the last Abbot, James Stewart, are carried over the staircase leading to what is called a dungeon, but probably was a store-cellar. St. Moden's Chapel, the burial-place of the Buchan family, intervenes between the chapter-house and transept. The two end walls of the *Refectory* are left, and its gable is still decorated with an elegant rose window. Close to the Chapter-house window is a yew-tree reputed to be 700 years old.

At the dissolution of religious

houses the Dryburgh estates were granted by James VI. to John, Earl of Mar. He gave them to his 2nd son, from whom they descended, after being sold and repurchased, to the family of the Earl of Buchan, and *Dryburgh Abbey Ho.*, in whose grounds the ruins stand, now belongs to G. O. H. E. Biber-Erskine, Esq., a member of that family. Also adjoining is *Dryburgh Ho.* (Misses Baillie).

On a neighbouring hill, overlooking the Tweed, is an atrocious red sandstone effigy, put up by a former Earl of Buchan as an effigy of Wallace. That hero suffers much from the clumsy worship of his Scottish admirers.

The tourist, instead of returning to Newtown St. Boswells, may keep along the N. bank of the Tweed to Melrose (see p. 28).

(2) By **Ancrum Moor** to **Jedburgh,** 10 m.

In 1 m. we pass *St. Boswells Green*, celebrated for its July fair.

Off the road l. between St. Boswells Green and the Tweed is St. Boswells village, or Lessudden, with Lessudden Ho. (R. Scott, Esq.), an old Border house, "the small but stately and venerable abode of the Lairds of Raeburn." From behind the village, at *Braeheads*, the tourist obtains a lovely view of Dryburgh Abbey.

In front the **Waterloo Monument** (p. 82) will be observed on the top of *Peniel Heugh*, on which there are a couple of camps.

4 m. **Ancrum Moor** (also called *Lilliard's Edge*), where in 1545 the Earls of Arran and Angus and Norman Leslie defeated 3000 English under Lord Evers and Sir Brian Layton, as they were returning laden with plunder from a devastating inroad. The timely appearance on the field of Walter Scott of Buccleuch, with a chosen body of retainers, decided the fortune of the day. Both Evers and Layton were killed, and the English were routed with great slaughter and loss of booty.

l. 6 m. from St. Boswells, nearly on the battlefield, on the N. bank of the Ale, is *Ancrum House* (Sir Wm. Scott, Bart.), destroyed by fire 1873, rebuilt in Scotch baronial style 1875, beyond which a road strikes rt. crossing the Ale to **Ancrum** Village (with old *Cross*), and, farther on, *Ancrum Ch.* and *Kirklands* (Adml. Hon. C. Eliott). In the steep sandstone banks of the Ale above Ancrum are several caves. One of them was a favourite retreat of Thomson the poet. From Ancrum another road keeps up the l. bank of the Teviot to Hawick, passing *Chesters* (T. Ogilvie, Esq.), and *Minto Ho.* (E. of Minto).

Passing l. *Mounteviot*, the seat of the Marquis of Lothian, our road crosses (7 m.), the Teviot, which it descends [up (rt.) leads to Hawick in 11 m.] for a mile and then turns rt. to **Jedburgh** 10 m. (p. 82).

[From the bridge, the pedestrian keeping straight on can cross the hill direct to Jedburgh in 2 m.].]

From Newtown St. Boswells the line takes a curve, following the contour of the valley of the Tweed, and leaves on right *Old Melrose*, the site of the original abbey of St. Aidan of Lindisfarne. The situation is peculiar, the river surrounding it as at Dryburgh.

61 m. **MELROSE Stat.** ✲ has nothing attractive in its streets or buildings, but it is surrounded by neat villas, is charmingly situated at the foot of the Eildon Hills, and overlooks the Tweed. In the Market-place is a stone cross, dated 1642, and bearing the arms of Scotland. Melrose is celebrated for

"the most beautiful not only of the Scottish second pointed churches, but of all the northern fanes of whatever age. The splendour of middle-age romance which

Scott has thrown around the place has almost obliterated its older and holier renown, when it was described by Bede as the home of the meek Eata, the prophetic Boisil, the austere Cuthbert; when, with Coldingham, and Abercorn, and Tyninghame, it was the lamp of that Anglo-Saxon Lothian, which, deriving its own faith from Iona, sped the glad gift to many an English province, and even sent a missionary across the seas to become the apostle of the Austrasian tribes on the Meuse, the Waal, and the Rhine."—*Quarterly Review.*

3 minutes' walk from the station, descending the hill, is the entrance to the ** **Abbey Church** of St. Mary at its W. end (admission, 4d. each person).

The building which we now see standing in such venerable ruin is the third abbey—the first having been the famed Culdee monastery at Old Melrose (see *ante*), on the decay of which King David I. built a second in 1136, and filled it with Cistercian monks from Rievaulx. Melrose lay on the highway of English invasion, and, in consequence, the abbey was wrecked over and over again, notably in 1322 by the troops of Edward II.

King Robert the Bruce at once set to work to repair the damage, and devoted £2000 (a large sum in those days) to this purpose. It was again wrecked at the fruitless invasion of Scotland by Richard II. 1385, when the English entered Scotland on the eastern side, and the Scots entered England on the west, each army afraid of the other, and intent only on plunder and destruction. But a small portion is older than the 15th cent., say about 1400. It is interesting to find in the S. transept monumental tablets recording the name of the architect or master-mason, one John Murdo or Morreau, by whom probably it was rebuilt. One of them reads thus—

John Murdo sum tym callit was I
And born in Parysse certainly
And had in kepying all Mason werk
Of Santandroys the hye Kyrk
Of Glasgu, Melros, and Paslay
Of Nyddysdayl and of Galway
Pray to God and Mary baith
And sweet St. John keep this holy Kirk
frae Skaith.

Much of the work now standing is probably his, though much altered by the restorations which subsequent injuries rendered necessary. In 1545 the abbey was plundered by the English under Evers and Layton, and soon afterwards it received more serious damage from the Earl of Hertford. Its next enemies were the Reformers, and since then it has been plundered considerably for the sake of the materials. In 1566 Mary bestowed the Abbey and its property upon Bothwell. At his proscription it reverted to the Crown, and, after passing through many different hands, is now the property of the Duke of Buccleuch, and well cared for.

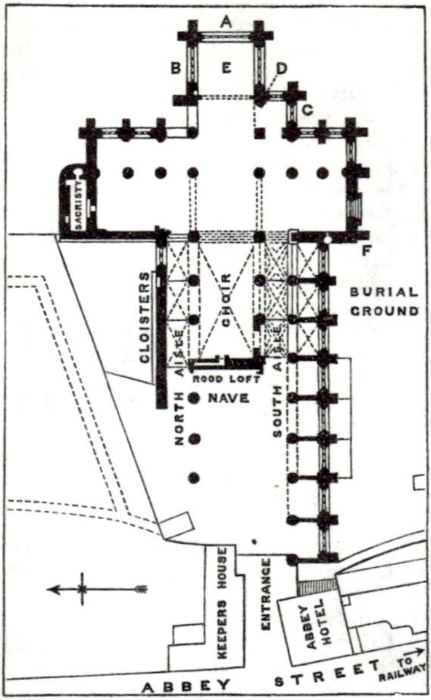

WEST END ENTRANCE FROM THE TOWN.

PLAN OF MELROSE ABBEY.

A E. Window, Bruce's heart.
B Douglas Burial Chapel.
C Michael Scott, the Wizard.
D Lord Evers. E King Alexander II.
F Murdo's (the architect) Monument.

The cruciform Ch., 258 ft. long, comprises a presbytery the width of the central aisle; an aisled choir of 6 bays, extending 3 bays westward beyond a central tower as far as the low stone choir-screen of later date; a nave extending over 5 bays; and transepts with E. aisles. The W. front is entirely gone. Along the

S. side of the nave extends a row of 8 chapels separated by buttress walls, and between these chapels and the central aisle runs a S. aisle, richly groined, of which 3 bays remain. The N. corresponding aisle is peculiarly narrow, and has no chapels. At the E. end of it is a fine late pointed arch. Every part of the ch. will repay careful study. The remains of stone vaulting are very elaborate, and the bosses and capitals of columns display in their intricate and delicate foliage, especially in the leaves of curly kale, the proverbial skill and fancy of the Scotch masons. The N. transept, strongly impressed with the Early English character, would appear to be the oldest part of the church.

The portion of the choir W. of the central tower is completely spoiled by some heavy piers and arches which were put up in 1618, when the abbey was fitted up for a time as a Presbyterian ch., and which obscure the elegant pointed arches of the original structure. The S. aisle chapels, each of which serves as the burial-place of some family, were a 15th cent. addition. The tracery of the windows of these chapels is flamboyant, of a French type.

In the *S. Transept* is a decorated *Window*, the finest in the abbey. It is 24 ft. high and 16 broad, divided into 5 lights, and ornamented above with flowing tracery of much elegance. It ought to be viewed from the outside, in combination with the door and panelled walls and buttresses.

We turn now to the E. end.

In many places the dec. framework of windows remains with perp. shafts and tracery inserted. The E. window (of 5 lights, divided into 2 rows by a transom) and the E. end adjoining, date probably from the reign of James IV., who married Margaret, daughter of Henry VII. Sir W. Scott's description of this window is very poetical and accurate, except in the doubtful use of the word "oriel."

"The moon on the east oriel shone
Through slender shafts of shapely stone,
By foliaged tracery combined;
Thou wouldst have thought some fairy's hand
'Twixt poplars straight the osier wand,
In many a freakish knot had twined;
Then framed a spell, when the work was done,
And changed the willow-wreaths to stone."—*Lay of the Last Minstrel.*

In the presbytery, directly in front of it, lies (it is said) the heart of Robert Bruce, which Douglas attempted in vain to carry to the Holy Land. A slab of dark marble, spotted with mountain-limestone corals, is pointed out as covering the grave of Alexander II. [p. 352] (1249). Against the opposite wall is the grave of James, 2nd Earl of Douglas, slain at Otterburn, 1388; also of Sir William Douglas, the Knight of Liddesdale. There is also the tomb of Lord Evers, who was killed at the battle of Ancrum Moor, 1544, after plundering the Abbey; and close to it the supposed tomb of *Michael Scott the Wizard*, but others assert it to be the tomb of Sir Brian Layton, colleague of Evers, and slain along with him.

On the N. of the nave is all that is left of *The Cloisters*, including a very rich circular-headed doorway of dec. style—the one through which William of Deloraine passed into the ch. This and an elegant arcading attached to the transept wall constitute one of the beauties of the Abbey. In the churchyard outside is the grave of Sir David Brewster. Tom Purdie, Sir W. Scott's favourite keeper, is also buried here. The stone marking his grave was erected by Sir Walter.

A suspension footbridge, toll ½d., joins Melrose with *Gattonside* on the l. bank of the Tweed, close to which village is *Allerly*, the residence of Sir D. Brewster, who d. there, 1868.

[**Excursions**:—(1) To *Dryburgh*, 4½ m. by Newtown St. Boswells, or 6 m. by Bemerside; (2) *Smailholm*, 8 m. and *Kelso*, 14 m.; (3) *Abbotsford* 2½ m., and *Selkirk*, 7½ m.

(1) The first-named road to Dryburgh is much easier but not nearly so fine as that crossing the Tweed about 2½ m. below Melrose, beside the rly. viaduct, and immediately after (at Leader Foot), the *Leader*, a river which, rising in the Lammermuir Hills and flowing past the towns of Lauder and Earlston, here joins the Tweed. After crossing this stream the road to Dryburgh turns off rt. (the straight road leading to Smailholm), passing *Gladswood* (Miss Julia Meiklam), at the gate of which is a fine view called "Sir Walter's View." But a still finer prospect is obtained from the top of the hill of the Tweed, winding round a peninsula just below, emerging here from a patch of wood, there disappearing into another, while at some distance, on the opposite side of the valley, rise the Eildon Hills. On the peninsula stands *Old Melrose*, and higher up the river is *Ravenswood* (Capt. Fairfax). Descending the hill we pass *Bemerside*, seat of the family of Haig, who have held it for more than 700 years, according to a prophecy of Thomas the Rhymer—

"Betide, betide, whate'er betide,
Haig shall be Haig of Bemerside."

6 m. *Dryburgh Abbey* (p. 23).

(2) To **Smailholm** and **Kelso**. This road crosses Leader Bridge, keeps straight on, and speedily ascends high ground to the village of

8 m. *Smailholm*, 1¼ m. to the S. of which, overlooking a very extensive tract of country, stands *Smailholm Tower*, the scene of Sir Walter Scott's ballad "The Eve of St. John." It belonged formerly, like all this district, to the Pringles, but is now the property of Lord Polwarth. Sir Walter's grandfather —"the thatched mansion's gray-hair'd sire"—lived at Sandyknowe, a farmhouse close by, where the poet spent part of his childhood. The Tower is a lofty but plain building, in a very ruinous state. The scene and its associations are described in the Introd. to the 3rd Canto of "Marmion."

Even were the associations not so interesting, the view from Smailholm would be a sufficient inducement to visit it, "as it takes in a district in which every field has its battle and every rivulet its song."

From Smailholm the road gradually falls to

14 m. Kelso ✲ (p. 84).

(3) It is a very pretty drive to Selkirk (7½ m.) past Abbotsford (2½ m.) along the valleys of Tweed and Ettrick. To *Bowhill* and *Newark Castle* is 4 m. farther.

Leaving Melrose W. the village of Darnick is passed on the left, with *Darnick Tower*, a Border Peel or "Strength," the ancient residence of the Lairds of Darnick, and containing a museum of Border antiquities. Sir Walter Scott obtained the nickname of the "Duke of Darnick," from his excessive fondness for the place. In the distance l. across the rly. are *Huntlyburn* (Lady H. Kerr), and *Chiefswood*, the latter a pleasant little cottage, in which Mr. and Mrs. Lockhart lived during the lifetime of Sir Walter, and where he himself was accustomed to spend many a holiday after the fatigues of authorship.

The road turns l. away from the river, that to the rt. leading to Melrose Bridge and Galashiels. In 2½ m. we reach the entrance to

Abbotsford[1] (Hon. Mrs. Maxwell Scott) which is by a small postern in the wall.

[Pedestrians can save ½ m. by keeping

[1] *Admittance* (1s. each) every lawful day from 1st May to 30th Sept. from 10 A.M to 5 P.M.

to the S. of Darnick and descending by a path upon Abbotsford.]

The many-turreted house is ill-placed, close under the road, on a slope descending to the Tweed, but is interesting not only for its founder's sake, but as an historic museum of (chiefly) national relics.[1] The position of the present house was occupied by a small farm-house when Sir Walter bought the property in 1811. He changed the name of "Clarty Hole" to that of Abbotsford, built a new house—the W. wing of the present mansion, which he completed later—and made many additions to the place, priding himself especially on having planted almost every tree in the grounds.

Visitors enter by a small side door, and, having inscribed their names, are conducted to the *Study* in which the poet wrote, and which is little changed since his time. Opening from this is a small octagonal closet, in which is a bust of Sir Walter taken after death. The *Library* was preserved as the best Memorial by the friends who wished after his death to do the poet honour, and has become an heirloom in the family. Sir Walter by his will charged it with a legacy of £5000 to his younger children, which was defrayed by the subscription, thus preventing a sale. Over the fireplace hangs Sir W. Allan's portrait of Sir Walter's son. The *Dining-room*, in which he died, is not shown to the public, but contains family portraits of Sir Walter's father and mother in their youth, and of Sir Walter's great-grandfather, called "Beardie," who was a partisan of the Stuarts, and refused to shave till their restoration. In the *Drawing-room* are portraits of Sir Walter by *Raeburn*, of Cromwell, of Hogarth by himself, etc. In a cabinet table in the bay window are various relics, *e.g.* Queen Mary's seal, Balfour of Burleigh's egg snuff-box, Charles Stuart's quaigh, a purse made by Flora Macdonald, Napoleon's pen and writing-case, Burns's toddy-tumbler, miniature of Sir Walter as a boy—his knife and fork and snuff-box, several miniatures, etc. In a recess at the end of the room stands *Chantrey's* noble bust, considered to be the best likeness of Scott.

Among the other portraits are those of Dryden, James VI., etc.

A curious but not attractive picture is one of Queen Mary's head, taken an hour after her execution.

The *Armoury* contains weapons of every age in the history of Scotland. Here, too, are the keys of the old Edinburgh Tolbooth, a good portrait of Prince Charlie, the pistols of Napoleon and of Claverhouse, James IV.'s armour, swords used by a German executioner, thumbikins, Montrose's sword, Rob Roy's gun, claymores of the '45, etc. The panelling of the *Entrance Hall* was brought from the old kirk of Dunfermline, and the fire grate belonged to Archbishop Sharpe. Round the cornice are the armorial bearings of the families who kept the Scottish Border, and here are preserved the last suit of clothes worn by Sir Walter, some ancient armour, and two cuirasses from Waterloo. The doorway is embellished with fossil stags' horns. Outside the visitor should observe the door of the Old Tolbooth of Edinburgh built up into the W. end of the house.

Now several staring residences, —"Castles of *Glower-o'er-'em*,"— planted on the banks of the Tweed, opposite Abbotsford, somewhat mar the privacy of the house.

The Abbotsford estate comprises 1237 acres.

Abbotsford Ferry Stat. (p. 30) is within 1 m. of the house. The site of the Battle of Melrose (1526) is

[1] See "Abbotsford: The Personal Relics and Antiquarian Treasures of Sir Walter Scott." Described by the Hon. Mary Monica Maxwell Scott of Abbotsford, and illustrated by Wm. Gibb (A. & C. Black, 1893).

on rising ground to the l. of the visitors' gate.

For *Selkirk* and *Bowhill*, see below.

(4) A charming ramble may be made up the Huntlyburn, which flows through the *Rhymer's Glen*,[1] so called because Thomas of Ercildoune is supposed to have met the Queen of the Fays in it. Keep over *Bowden Moor* W. to *Cauldshields Hill*, and haunted *Loch*, around which are numerous examples of Sir Walter's taste as a planter.

(5) Equally pretty are the banks of the *Allan Water*, which joins the Tweed on its l. bank, 2 m. above Melrose near the Pavilion, and 2 m. up which is the "Glen Dearg" of the "Monastery."]

On leaving Melrose we see rt. *Darnick Village* (see p. 28), and the Waverley Hydro. Estab., and, across the river, the *Pavilion* (Gen. Henry), before the rly. crosses the Tweed, which here makes almost a right angle, near the village of *Bridgend*, the locale of the scene in the "Monastery" where Father Philip met the White Lady of Avenel at the Ford.

65 m. **Galashiels Stat.**

[Branches (1) S. to Selkirk (below).
(2) W. to Innerleithen and Peebles, and thence N. to Edinburgh (Rte. 6).]

Galashiels✲, celebrated for its woollen manufacture of tweeds and tartans, has drawn to itself all the trade of the district. The town is situated on both sides of the Gala Water, which is sadly polluted by the numerous factories. *Gala House* is the seat of John Scott, Esq.

About 1 m. to the S. the antiquary will find traces of the *Catrail* or Picts' Work Ditch (cf. p. 21) which runs from Mossilee S. to Rink Hill (638 ft.) and the Tweed. On this hill is a fort, strongly defended, and commanding the valley of the Tweed to its junction with the Gala. There are also a number of ancient Caledonian fortifications on Cauldshields Hill (1176 ft.) above Abbotsford.

At *Clovenfords*, 3½ m. W. of Galashiels on the Peebles Line, are Wm. Thomson's *Grape Gardens and Forcing Houses*, heated by 5 miles of iron piping, sending up to London in winter nearly ½ ton of grapes weekly.

[Branch to Selkirk 6¼ m.—11 trains daily in 20 min.

See Map, p. 23.

The line to Selkirk leaves the main line 1¼ m. S. of Galashiels, and following l. bank of Tweed, affords an excellent view l. of *Abbotsford* (p. 28).

2¾ m. **Abbotsford Ferry Stat.**—1 m. beyond the house. It then crosses the Tweed just below its junction with the Ettrick, and keeps up the rt. bank of the latter stream to

4¼ m. **Lindean Stat.**, and

6¼ m. **SELKIRK Stat.** ✲ The town is perched on the top of a hill overlooking Ettrick Water, 2 m. below its junc. with the Yarrow. The town hall has a lofty spire and in front are statues of Sir Walter Scott, by Ritchie, and of Mungo Park, the African traveller, born at *Foulshiels* (p. 31). The town possesses large woollen manufactories for "tweeds" on the river, and is famed for its cakes called "bannocks."

It used to be celebrated for its shoemaking; hence the old verses—

"Up wi' the sutors of Selkirk,
And doon wi' the Earl of Home."

The sutors distinguished themselves at the battle of Flodden, 1513:

"Selkirk, famed in days of yore
For sutors, but for heroes more . . .
And on red Flodden's dreadful day,
When other pow'rful clans gave way,
The burly sutors firmly stood,
And dyed the field with Southron blood . . .

[1] The public are not generally admitted, but leave may be obtained to visit the glen.

Though gall'd by darts, by horses trod on,
They bore their standard off from Flodden,
Which still, on that returning day,
We bear aloft in proud array!"

HOGG'S *Russiade.*

After the battle the town was burnt by the English. The old ceremony of admittance to the dignity of burgess of the town involves the penalty of sucking a brush of bristles such as shoemakers use, dipped in wine, attached to the seal of the Corporation. This is called "licking the birse." A banner, said to be that taken at Flodden, is still preserved by the Corporation, and is borne by the Convener of Trades. Adjoining the town is *The Haining* (Mrs. Pringle Pattison).

After Abbotsford (p. 28) the principal excursions are up the Valleys of Yarrow and Ettrick, of which the former is the more interesting on account of its scenery, its associations, its ballads, and Wordsworth's 3 poems. There are *Coaches* (Tues., Thurs., and Sat.) up Yarrow to **St. Mary's Loch** (19 m.) in connection with others from and to Moffat (p. 12). One of them occasionally makes the tour of the two valleys, 39½ m.

We cross the Ettrick, and turn l. up the l. bank of the Yarrow, passing 3 m. (rt.) *Philiphaugh* (W. S. Steel, Esq.). The house is Old English, with flights of terraces in front. Here, Sept. 13, 1645, encamped upon the haugh, or flat land, Montrose was defeated by Gen. Leslie and his army of "Covenanting cuirassiers," and lost all that his previous victories had gained.

"On *Slain Man's Lee* is a green mound raised above the slaughtered Royalists."
—SCOTT.

The *General's Bridge* (which visitors are allowed to cross to reach *Newark Cas.* [below]), built by Gen. Mackay, leads to **Bowhill**, a residence of the Duke of Buccleuch, situated between the Ettrick and Yarrow. Here is *Raeburn's* whole-length portrait of Walter Scott as a young man, with his dog Camp,—a replica of which is at Abbotsford—one of the best likenesses of him; also *Kneller's* Duke and Duchess of Monmouth.

4½ m. rt. is *Foulshiels*, at the foot of a hill of the same name (1454 ft.), the birthplace of Mungo Park (1771). Left across the Yarrow is

Newark Castle, where the Duchess of Buccleuch is represented as listening to the "Lay of the Last Minstrel," who

"Pass'd where Newark's stately tower
Looks out from Yarrow's birchen bower."

Newark was originally a royal hunting seat, and held by the Scotts, who were hereditary rangers of Ettrick Forest. When the forest was broken up the castle was granted to the Scotts for ever. It is a massive square tower of the early part of the 15th cent., and the arms and supporters of James I. are still preserved on its W. side. In its courtyard Gen. Leslie shot the prisoners of Montrose's army taken at Philiphaugh.

Beyond, the river is twice crossed. Rt. is *Broadmeadows* (H. M. Lang, Esq.), a modern house beautifully placed; l. is another approach to Bowhill.

At 6 m. (rt.) on the banks of the Hangingshaw Burn, is *Hangingshaw*, the property of Johnstone of Alva. A few fragments of wall alone are left of the old castle of the "outlaw Murray," the subject of an interesting ballad *temp.* James V.

The scenery now changes; the road emerges from the woods, and, though it still runs alongside the Yarrow, the banks are bare, the hills rise naked and cheerless, and the contrast with the scenery already passed recalls Wordsworth's phrase of "pastoral melancholy."

9 m. **Yarrow Church** (with a curious sun-dial upon it) and *Manse*.

[A road here crosses the river and leads over the hill to *Kirkhope* on Ettrick (p. 33) 3 m.]

The Yarrow[1] has always been famous in song, from the ballad preserved in the "Border Minstrelsy" of "The Dowie Dens (=sad hollows) of Yarrow," downwards. Some upright stones on the hillside near the Church (one of which has a Latin inscription) are said to commemorate the fight there referred to, but really date back, according to Prof. Rhys, to the 5th or 6th cent. Hamilton of Bangour (1704-54) wrote "The Braes of Yarrow," beginning

"Busk ye, busk ye, my bonny bonny bride,"

while Wordsworth, Scott, Hogg, Shairp, Veitch, and many others have sung under the "Power of Yarrow."

11 m. **Yarrow Feus**—a number of cottages affording tempting summer quarters.

13 m. *Gordon Arms Inn* ✡, whence a road is given off (rt.) to Traquair and Innerleithen, 9 m. (p. 79). This is a good angling station for the middle waters of Ettrick and Yarrow. On rt. is the farm of *Mount Benger*, of which James Hogg, the Ettrick Shepherd, was for a time tenant; l. a road leads past (½ m.) the farm of *Altrive Lake*, where Hogg died 1835, to *Tushielaw Inn* (below) in Ettrick 6½ m.

14 m. we cross the *Douglas Burn*, leaving on right the Craig of Douglas. 2 m. up the glen, and overhanging the stream, are the remains of *Blackhouse Tower*, which seems to have been a square building, with a circular turret at one angle. It was the retreat and stronghold of Sir James Douglas, the friend of Bruce. This was the scene of the exploit of Lord Wm. Douglas and Lady Margaret, as told in the "Douglas Tragedy."

At the farm of Blackhouse Scott found his future amanuensis and friend William Laidlaw, author of "Lucy's Flitting," and by him was introduced to Hogg who had for ten years been one of his father's men.

15½ m. (rt.) are the ruins of *Dryhope Tower*, supposed to have been the birthplace of Mary Scott, the Flower of Yarrow, who was wooed by many Border chiefs and won (1576) by Scott of Harden (p. 22). It stands at the N.E. end of

"Lone St. Mary's silent lake";

which is 3 m. long by less than ½ m. broad—poetically described in the Introd. to Canto ii. of "Marmion."

16¼ m. up on the hillside are the ruins of *St. Mary's Kirk* and its ancient churchyard

"Where the Shepherds of Yarrow are sleeping."

At 17¼ m. we cross the *Megget Water*, spoken of in the "Noctes Ambrosianæ" as "a very famous fishing ground." A road leads up it to *Henderland* (¾ m.), the ruins of an old stronghold of one Perys Cockburn, a celebrated freebooter, who, like Adam Scott, Johnny Armstrong, and others, was hanged by James V. (1529) in his own castle-yard. It is to this execution that the pathetic "Lament of the Border Widow" refers. *Obs.* the *Lady's Seat* by the cascade on a trib. of the Megget.

At 18 m. is *Rodono Hotel* ✡, charmingly situated overlooking the loch, at whose S.W. end is

19 m. "*Tibbie Shiels*" *Inn* ✡ (see p. 14).

For Road to Moffat, 15 m., see p. 13.

A road turns E. between St. Mary's Loch and the Loch of the Lowes, ascending steeply in

2 m. to 1350 ft., passes l. the road to the Gordon Arms by Altrive Lake (above) and descends to *Tushielaw Ho.* (Col. Anderson) and *Inn* ✡ in Ettrick, 6 m., where 4 roads meet.

A road S.E. crosses the Ettrick, ascends the *Rankleburn*, passing (3

[1] See "Reminiscences of Yarrow," by Rev. James Russell, D.D. (1886), and "Yarrow, its Poets and Poetry," by Rev. R. Borland (1890)—both Ministers of Yarrow.

m.) **Buccleuch** farm, beside the site of a castle from which the Duke takes his title, and descends, crossing the Ale Water, down the *Borthwick Water*, to Hawick, 16 m. (p. 22).

Another road keeps up the l. bank of the Ettrick, passing (¼ m.) rt. *Tushielaw Castle*, which stands on a ledge of the hill overlooking the meeting of the Rankleburn and Ettrick. It is a singular situation, and seems to have been chosen for the extensive prospect of the valley which it commands both E. and W. It was the finest castle in this neighbourhood, and its last inhabitant was Adam Scott, who was known in his own country as the "King of the Border," and everywhere else as the "King of Thieves." James V., having executed Cockburn of Henderland, marched across by the road (still called the King's Road) to Tushielaw, stormed and plundered the castle, hanged Scott on an elm (still shown in the courtyard), and carried his head to Edinburgh. The father of the "Flower of Yarrow" was Laird of Tushielaw.

The whole of this district was at one time densely covered with timber;

"Ettrick Forest is a fair forest,
In it grows many a seemly tree;
The hart, the hind, the doe, the roe,
And of all wild beasts great plentie";

but the only remains of *Ettrick Forest* is a quantity of stunted wood between Cracra Bank and the slopes at the mouth of Rankleburn.

2 m. rt. are the ruins of Thirlestane Castle, and the modern house of Lord Napier. *Thirlestane Castle* is memorable as the residence of John Scott, who, when the Scottish nobility, in 1542, refused to support James V. in an invasion of England, offered with his retinue to follow the king whithersoever he chose to go. James rewarded his loyalty by granting him as a crest a bunch of spears, with the motto, "Ready, aye ready."

On the other side of the river is the old tower of *Gamescleuch*.

1 m. beyond, a road strikes l. up the *Tima Water* to Eskdalemuir 12 m. and Langholm 26 m. (p. 19).

Beyond Ettrick school an inscription upon a wall marks the site of the cottage where Hogg was born 1770. He was working at *Ettrickhouse* across the valley when Scott found him 1801; and he was buried (1835) in the ch.-yd. of *Ettrick Ch.* (4 m. from Tushielaw) close by. There also lie Thomas Boston, author of "The Fourfold State," and minister of the parish, d. 1732; the 8th Lord Napier, who d. in China 1834, and Tibbie Shiels (1781-1878). The road continues up the valley, crossing (6 m.) the *Back Burn* haunted from time immemorial both by fairies and by the ghost of a wandering minstrel cruelly murdered there, who sleeps in a lone grave at a small distance from the bridge. Its source is in *Androwhinnie Hill* (2220 ft.) which commands a view of Loch Skene and the Grey Mare's Tail (p. 13). At 10 m. [1 m. short of *Potburn Farm*, behind which rise *Ettrick Pen* (2269 ft.), *Wind Fell* (2180 ft.), and *Capel Fell* (2223 ft.), and 3 m. beyond which are the *Sources of the Ettrick* and *Craigmichan Scaurs* (p. 13)] a road rt., unused, rough, and finally hardly made, crosses Bodesbeck Law in 3½ m. to Capplegill in Moffatdale (p. 13), 5½ m. from Moffat.

The road to Selkirk from Tushielaw descends the Ettrick, passing, 3 m. rt., *Deloraine*, a name familiar to all readers of the "Lay of the Last Minstrel." It gave the title of earl to Henry Scott, third son of the Duke of Monmouth, but the peerage is now extinct.

A lovely bit of river with steep sides and rapids is enjoyed at *Kirkhope* (whence a road l. leads to Yarrow Ch. 3 m.) before we reach the hamlet of **Ettrickbridge**, 8 m.—a pretty spot—where the river is crossed.

At 10½ m. (rt.), perched on the top

of a steep bank, overlooking the river, is *Oakwood Tower*, supposed to have been the scene where the

"Three lords were birling at the wine,"

in "The Dowie Dens of Yarrow." It was at one time inhabited by Michael Scott, the wizard.

At 12 m. l. the Ettrick and the Yarrow unite at a place called Carelhaugh, corrupted into *Carterhaugh*, the scene of Hogg's "Pilgrims of the Sea," and of the ballad "Tamlane," in the "Border Minstrelsy"; beyond is Bowhill.

At 14½ m. Selkirk is again reached after a round of 39½ m.]

From Galashiels the line to Edinburgh runs up the valley of the *Gala*, celebrated in an old song touched up by Burns,

"Braw, braw lads of Gala Water."

This stream is crossed again and again. To the l. are the **Moorfoot Hills** rising to 2000 ft.; on the rt. the outliers of the **Lammermuirs** which rise to 1700 ft.

At 67 m. l. is *Torwoodlee* (J. T. Pringle, Esq.). The family of Pringle suffered for their adhesion to the Covenant in the time of Charles II. The traveller now soon enters the county of Edinburgh or Midlothian.

68½ m. **Bowland Stat.**, near to which on left is *Bowland* (W. Ramsay, Esq.). On the banks of the Lugate, which flows into the Gala on the left, are the remains of two Border towers. rt. is *Torsonce Ho.*

71½ m. **Stow Stat.**, a clean-looking place with a fine church and spire.

[Coach 4 times daily to **Lauder** ✲, 6 m. N.E., an uninteresting little town, but the only royal burgh in Berwickshire. Lauder was the scene of one of those deeds of ferocity which abound in Scottish history. In 1482 James III. halted here with his army, on his way to invade England. His nobles, disgusted with the favour shown to Cochrane, the king's architect and minister, seized him, and without trial or process hung him over the bridge in the king's sight. Archibald Douglas, Earl of Angus, who was the first to lay hands on him, was called from this "Bell the Cat." Adjoining Lauder is *Thirlestane Castle* (the Earl of Lauderdale), a spacious house of the date of Charles II. 1672, including a tower built by Edward I., in a fine park. The ch. was removed to make way for it. It contains family portraits of Secretary Maitland, of the Duke of Lauderdale Charles II.'s Minister, etc.]

75 m. **Fountainhall Stat.**, S. of which (rt.) is *Burnhouse*, and 1½ m. N. (rt.) *Crookston* (both J. Borthwick, Esq.).

1½ m. l. on the banks of the Heriot Water, which flows in before

79 m. **Heriot Stat.**, is *Borthwick Hall* (D. J. Macfie, Esq.), near which is a camp, in good preservation, overlooking Corsehope Burn.

At 80½ m. the rly. attains the summit-level 900 ft.

82 m. **Tynehead Stat.**, a good starting-point for rambles over the *Lammermuirs*, which extend N.E. to the sea; or S. over the *Moorfoots*, through which a pleasing old coaching road leads to Innerleithen, 18 m.

Beyond, the railway embankment traverses a shallow valley in which the new-born *Tyne* flows. About ¾ m. rt. is **Crichton Castle**, and about ¼ m. l. the commanding ruin of *Borthwick Castle*.

* **Crichton Castle**, now a mere shell, was built at different times. "The oldest part is a narrow keep or tower, such as formed the mansion of a lesser Scotch baron," and belongs to the 14th cent. The E. front of the court is raised upon a very peculiar open Venetian arcade, decorated with entablatures bearing anchors of the 16th cent. "All the stones of this front are cut into diamond facets, the angular projections of which have an uncommonly rich appearance." The mouldings of the windows and other parts are profusely de-

corated with a variety of carvings. "The castle belonged originally to the Chancellor Sir William Crichton," who had a struggle for supremacy with the Douglases in the reign of James II., and from whom it was taken and dismantled in 1445 by John Forrester of Corstorphine. The ornamental part of the castle is evidently of a date subsequent to this. "In 1483 it was garrisoned by Lord Crichton against King James III. . . . Few ruins in Scotland display so well the style and beauty of ancient castle architecture" (Scott's *Notes to Marmion*). Here Marmion is supposed to have been detained by Sir David Lindesay before he was allowed to see the Scottish host encamped on the Borough Moor. A short distance E. of the castle are the remains of a small cruciform Church, probably founded about 1449, but never completed.

"Crichton! though now thy miry court
But pens the lazy steer and sheep,
Thy turrets rude and totter'd Keep
Have been the minstrel's loved resort."
Marmion, Canto IV.

The ruined * **Borthwick Castle**, a massive, gloomy, double tower, built by Sir Wm. Borthwick, 1430—the largest Peel tower on the Border,—110 ft. high, nearly square, with a recess on the W. side, stands on a tongue of rock flanked on two sides by ravines, whose streams feed the Gore Water.

The tower, which rises out of an enclosing wall, is turreted, and was entered by a drawbridge. It had 6 stories, 2 of which still retain vaulted roofs; but they are fast decaying. In the basement is the dungeon and well-tower; on the 1st floor are the great hall, with dec. ornaments over the grand fireplace, the kitchen, and buttery-hatch, and the withdrawing-room (Queen Mary's). On the 2nd floor are a smaller hall and the chapel, with an E. recess, piscina, etc. The 3rd floor was one large apartment, probably for the retainers. The castle walls are 12 to 14 ft. thick. Hither fled Queen Mary and Bothwell, 7th June 1567, about a month after their marriage, on the alarm of the Confederate Lords gathering their force against them. But they were scarce safe within the walls when Lords Morton and Hume, with a hostile array, appeared before them. Under these circumstances Bothwell first got clear away, and afterwards Mary (in the disguise of a page) fled to Dunbar. One of the rooms is still traditionally called the Queen's Room. In November 1650 Cromwell, annoyed by a horde of moss-trooping marauders, who had taken post in Borthwick, sent a missive to Lord Borthwick, that, if he did not "walk away, and deliver his house," he would "bend his cannon against him," a threat which was at first disregarded; but, after a brief bombardment, the castle was surrendered. The marks of Cromwell's cannon-shot are still visible on the E. front.

The parish ch., surmounted by a spire, on a level with the castle, was rebuilt in 1865, is dedicated to St. Kentigern, and has an apsidal chancel. The manse of Borthwick was the birthplace of Robertson the historian, 1721.

85½ m. **Fushie Bridge Stat.**

86¼ m. **Gorebridge Stat.**, close to which are the ruins of *Newbyres Castle*, and the powder-mills of Stobs. 2 m. rt. of the stat. is a Roman Camp.

2 m. l. is *Arniston*, the seat of Robert Dundas, Esq., whose ancestors were highly distinguished in the 17th and 18th cents. 1 m. farther S., on the banks of the South Esk, which here flows through a most picturesque ravine, is the small ruined ch. of *Temple*, once a possession of the Knights Templar, and 1 m. beyond that is *Rosebery*, a very plain house with fine trees, which gives his title to the Earl. In its neighbourhood are some of the Edinburgh water-supply Reservoirs.

The rly., which has for some little distance been traversing limestone strata, now enters the Midlothian coalfield, as is evident by the appearance of collieries. Following the valley of the South Esk, we pass *Dalhousie Castle* (the Earl of Dalhousie), an old Scotch castle, changed into a mansion of no great beauty, but situated in the midst of lovely scenery; and *Cockpen*, the ownership of which conferred on the possessor of Dalhousie the title of "The Laird of Cockpen," whose wooing has been made famous by the song of that name.

89 m. **Dalhousie Stat.** A fine entrance, called King David's Gate, leads into **Newbattle Abbey** (Marquis of Lothian), one of the most interest-

ing mansions in the S. of Scotland, situated in a park traversed for more than 2 miles by the South Esk, and approached also by lodge gates close to Eskbank and to Dalkeith.[1] The house, a modern battlemented building, occupies the site of a Cistercian Abbey, founded in 1140 by David I., of which the foundations remain near the house, and a fine *Crypt* is included in it. The abbot at the time of the Reformation—one Mark Kerr—by opportunely changing his religion secured the abbey lands to himself and his family. Round the house are magnificent trees. *Obs.* the finest beech in Britain, 100 ft. high, 120 ft. round, the bole measures 33 ft. in girth; also some huge sycamores, and a cypress 60 ft. high.

The interior of the house, generously shown to strangers, will delight every lover of art and student of history by its collection of paintings. The library is also a very valuable one. Much of the woodwork of the house is the work of local carvers, and the wood itself was grown on the estate. The carving, etc., displays the most refined taste.

Obs. among the paintings—*Anton. More:* Lord Mark Kerr and Lady Helen Leslie. *Holbein:* Henry VIII., Margaret Tudor, and Sir Thos. More. *Alb. Dürer:* Virgin and Child (one of the few Dürers in Britain). *Ghirlandajo:* St. George in Armour. In dining-room, adorned with 2 wreaths carved by *Grinling Gibbons*, portraits of Hawkins, Drake, and Cavendish. *Van Dyck:* Charles I., the 3 heads; Henry, P. of Wales; Princes Maurice, as a boy, and Rupert; Marquis Cattaneo, a Genoese; Duchesse de Croye; Charles I., on white horse, under the arch; Henrietta Maria. *Sir J. Reynolds:* Charles, D. of Rutland; Lady Eliz. Fortescue; same Lady and Infant by *Angelica Kauffmann*. *Van Somers:* Charlotte de la Tremouille. James I., in red stockings, by *Jamesone*. *Luca Signorelli:* Two Saints, *Kneller:* Marshal Schomberg on horse. *Titian:* Holy Family; A Bearded Old Man. *Bonifazio:* Return of the Prodigal. Clever paintings of the Dutch School; and, in the boudoir, a Virgin with folded hands—*Raphael.* Virgin and Child —*Perugino.* Female head—*Guido.*

[1] The Grounds are open Weds. and Sats.

Robert Leighton the divine was pastor of Newbattle from 1641-51—the happiest years of his life.

90 m. **Eskbank Stat.** From Eskbank Stat. to Edinburgh, see Rte. 6.

95¼ m. **Portobello Stat.** (p. 66).

98¼ m. **Edinburgh**, see Rte. 4.

ROUTE 4.

EDINBURGH ★.

Situation.—Edinburgh occupies a natural situation unsurpassed for beauty by any of the Capitals of Europe, except, perhaps, by Athens and Constantinople. Its appellation of "the Modern Athens" is not merely a general comparison.

"There are several points of view on the elevated grounds from which the resemblance is complete. From Torphin in particular, one of the low heads of the Pentlands, immediately above Colinton, the landscape is exactly that of the vicinity of Athens, as viewed from the bottom of Mount Anchesmus. Close upon the right, Brilessus is represented by the hill of Braid; before us, in the dark and abrupt mass of the Castle, rises the Acropolis; the hill Lycabettus, joined to that of Areopagus, appears in the Calton; in the Firth of Forth we behold the Ægean Sea; in Inchkeith, Ægina; in Leith, the Piræus; and the hills of the Peloponnesus are precisely those of the opposite coast of Fife."—Williams.

Arthur's Seat (823 ft.)—named after "the blameless king," who, historically in the 6th cent. and in the S. of Scotland,

"fought and in 12 great battles overcame"—

with its majestic lion-like form, flanked by the ramparts of Salisbury Crags, guards the city on the E. To the W. is Corstorphine Hill; to the S. Blackford Hill and the Braid Hills with the Pentland range beyond, and to the N. the Firth of Forth.

The two Towns.—It must be borne in mind that no two towns, although far further apart, could be more distinct and different than the Old and New Town of Edinburgh. The latter, with its magnificent Princes St.—a wide boulevard having handsome clubs, hotels, and shops on the N. side, trees and gardens on the S. —is a town of broad streets and spacious squares, but it dates only from the end of the 18th cent., the plans being prepared by James Craig, archt., nephew of the poet Thomson, in 1767. It derives its chief interest from the views of the Castle Rock and adjoining slopes which it commands. The Old Town, which has a history of more than a thousand years, is built upon a long sloping ridge; the High Street and Canongate extending along its whole length from Holyrood Palace at the foot to the Castle at its upper end.

The High Street and Canongate are bordered by tall houses, some of them 9 stories high—each story or "flat" a hive of population—and off them open scores of steep narrow "closes," "wynds," or alleys, and dingy courts.

In the valley between the two towns are gardens (open to the public)—once the Nor' (North) Loch—through which the N.B. Rly. runs. The towns are connected at the E. end of Princes St. by the high viaduct of the North Bridge (1772), farther W. by the Waverley Bridge, and in the middle by the artificial raised causeway of "*The Mound*," made with earth dug from the foundations of the New Town houses.

Historical Notes.—In the 7th cent. a military station was formed on the Castle Hill by Edwin, the first Christian King of Northumbria, whose dominions extended to the Forth (d. 633), and the town which grew up under its protection was called by his name. In the 10th cent. this English town was taken by the Scots under their king Indulph. David I., in a charter, calls it "Burgo meo de Edwinesburg," from which it may be gathered that it was made a royal burgh before his time, probably by Malcolm Canmore. The early history of the city is in reality the history of the Castle (p. 38). It was at first a Border fortress, too near the frontier to be the capital of the kingdom, and it did not become so until the middle of the 15th cent., when the murder of James I. (1437), disgusted the court with Perth.

King James II. erected the first *City Wall* (1450), a fragment of which is said to remain in the *Wellhouse Tower* within Princes St. Gardens at the foot of the Castle Rock (N. side), and the line of which towards the Grassmarket is marked by a slab on the married soldiers' quarters on the S. side of the Castle. King James III., grateful for the interest shown in his behalf when he was at variance with his nobles, erected the city into a Sheriffdom within itself, and presented to the incorporated trades a banner or standard, round which they rallied, and which was contemptuously styled by James VI. "the Blue Blanket." It is still preserved in the Trades' Maiden Hospital. After Flodden (1513) the *City Wall* was extended so as to protect the important suburb of the Cowgate, and in 1618 a final extension was made, of which a considerable portion may be seen in the *Vennel*, S. of the Grassmarket and W. of Heriot's Hospital. The city gradually increased in wealth and importance till 1544, when it was seriously injured by the English under the Earl of Hertford. This wanton destruction, followed by a century of civil and religious discord, with many will account for the poverty of its ancient architecture and the absence of buildings of any great age.

Of old public buildings, except the Castle and St. Giles's Cathedral, there are none; and no older date than that of James V. (1513-1542) is claimed for any part of Holyrood

Palace, and that only for two of the towers. There are only a few houses upon which may be seen a date prior to the accession of James VI. to the English throne (1603). This event gave an impulse to building all over the country. The further history of the town may be gleaned from the notices of the different places and buildings given below.

Under the Improvement (Chambers's) Act of 1867, much has been done to widen the streets of the Old Town and to benefit the health of its inhabitants, but many of the most interesting "closes" and houses have been removed in the process. Of late years the city has spread rapidly to the N. and W., but specially to the S. No city is richer in Educational and Charitable Institutions, whose buildings are also among its principal ornaments. R. L. Stevenson[1] suggests that it got its homely name of "*Auld Reekie*" from the Fife folk impressed with the smoke of its tall houses.

The following routes will exhaust most of the sights.

OLD TOWN.

(1) Castle by High Street and Canongate to Holyrood.

The tourist should first ascend the Mound from Princes St. direct to the Castle, where he will best get his "bearings" for exploring the city and its surroundings. Passing l. the *Royal Institution* and the *National Gallery* (p. 56) he sees l., in an imposing position, the **Bank of Scotland** (incorporated by Act of the Scottish Parliament, 1695), surmounted by a dome. It was built 1805 at an expense of £75,000, but underwent a thorough renovation 1869-75 (Bryce, archt.). The backs of some of the tallest houses in the High St. confront him as he proceeds. To the rt. of them are the *Savings Bank*, the *Free Church College* (founded soon after the "Disruption" of the Church, 1843), with *Church* and *Assembly Hall*, erected 1858-9. The Hall occupies on its S. side the site of the Palace of Mary of Guise, mother of Mary Queen of Scots. Farther rt. above the garden slopes is a striking group of gabled and turreted buildings, plastered with various colours (S. Mitchell and S. H. Capper, archts.), erected 1893-94 by Prof. Geddes of Dundee for better-class "flats" and a Students' Settlement. Incorporated into them is *Ramsay Lodge*, where the poet Allan Ramsay spent his last years and d. 1758. The visitor should keep rt. (sending his carriage round) up Ramsay Lane—not forgetting the view back—past l. the *Soldiers' and Sailors' Home*, and rt. the *Reservoir*, through which the water from the Pentland Hills is supplied to a portion of the city, to the

Castle Esplanade or parade-ground, with a statue of Field-Marshal Frederick, Duke of York (1827), a monumental *Cross* to the officers and men of the 78th Highlanders who fell in the Indian Mutiny, and a monument to Col. Mackenzie of the 92nd Highlanders (1811-73).

The W. end of the old town ridge, where it attains a height of 445 ft. above the sea, drops suddenly down in rocky precipices on 3 sides, which formed an unassailable position for an ancient fortress. On this ground of vantage stands

** **The Castle.**[1] — Here Malcolm Canmore left Queen Margaret when he and his sons last invaded Eng-

[1] The tourist should read his "Picturesque Notes"; the antiquarian should purchase from W. & A. K. Johnston, 16 S. St. Andrew St., Gordon of Rothiemay's Map of Edinburgh, 1647, price 1s. 6d.; and from the same firm the geologist should get Sir Arch. Geikie's "Geology of Edinburgh" (with map), price 1s. 6d.

[1] Admission free daily till sundown: Sundays after 3 p.m. Guides, 6d. each person, or 1s. 6d. for a party. *Crown Room*, etc., 10-4; winter 11-3 daily; Sundays excepted.

land (1093), and here, on hearing the news of his death, she herself fell sick and died. The Castle being besieged by a claimant to the throne, her body was stealthily conveyed down the cliffs to the W. The Castle was one of the 5 fortresses surrendered to Henry II. by the Treaty of Falaise 1174. In 1296 it was taken by Edward I., and held by the English, till in 1312 it was retaken by some of Bruce's followers, who climbed up the southern face, previously deemed inaccessible. It was dismantled by Bruce, given back to the English by Edward Baliol, and re-fortified in 1337 by Edward III. In 1341 it was recovered by stratagem by Sir Wm. Douglas. In 1573 Kirkaldy of Grange held the fortress with the greatest difficulty for 33 days in favour of Mary Queen of Scots, against the Regent Morton and his English auxiliaries under Sir Wm. Drury. The garrison then insisted on a capitulation, in spite of Kirkaldy, who would have persisted to the last gasp, foreseeing the death that awaited him. During this siege the Castle suffered greatly. In 1650, after the battle of Dunbar, Cromwell took the place after 12 days' siege. He made a feint of blowing up the rock, having brought with him Derbyshire miners for that purpose. The mere threat of these extemporised sappers and miners effected his object. He wrote to the Speaker Lenthall, "I need not speak of the strength of the place, which, if it had not come in as it did, would have cost very much blood to have attained, if at all to be attained." In 1745 it refused to open its gates to Prince Charles Edward Stuart, who was unable either to reduce or blockade it.[1]

The entrance is across the moat, now dry, and through the outer gateway, erected 1888, up to a 2nd vaulted archway called *The Portcullis Gate.* Over it is the *Constable's Tower*, called later the *Argyll Tower*, the old State prison which was built by David II. 1369, was dismantled in the siege of 1573, and has been restored by the late Mr. Wm. Nelson, publisher. Here the 1st Marquis of Argyll was confined before his execution (1661): hence his son, the 9th Earl of Argyll, escaped in the disguise of a page (1683); and hither he was brought back to be executed after his unsuccessful invasion of the W. coast (1685). Above the prison apartment is the *Constable Hall.* Passing rt. the *Argyll Battery* and beyond it the *Armoury and Officers' Quarters*, the road winds l. through another gateway to a platform on which stands *Mons Meg* in front of *Queen Margaret's Chapel.*

This platform commands a magnificent view over the New Town—E. down the Forth, N. to the Lomonds in Fife, the Forth Bridge, and the Ochils, W. to Ben Ledi and Ben Lomond.

Mons Meg is a gigantic piece of artillery of long iron bars hooped together, said to have been made at Mons, in Hainault, in 1486; another tradition asserts that it was forged at Castle-Douglas in Galloway, by a blacksmith named M'Kim and his 3 sons who presented it to James II. at the siege of Thrieve Castle (1455) (p. 106), and received in return the lands of Mollance—hence "Mollance Meg."

It was employed at the siege of Norham Castle in 1497, and burst in 1682, when firing a salute in honour of the Duke of York, although Claverhouse is represented as saying in 1689—

> "Let Mons Meg and her marrows speak
> twa words or three,
> For the love of the bonnets of bonny
> Dundee."

In 1754 it was removed to the Tower of London, but was restored to Edinburgh in 1829, at the request of Sir W. Scott.

[1] For some interesting reminiscences of the Castle rock in the early part of the 19th cent., see Borrow's *Lavengro*.

Queen Margaret's Chapel is certainly the oldest building in Edinburgh, and perhaps the oldest ecclesiastical structure in Scotland. If used by the Queen as an Oratory, and not merely erected in her honour by her son, it must date from before 1093.

It is of very contracted dimensions, 16 ft. 6 in. long by 10 ft. 6 in. wide within the nave. The chancel arch separating the nave from the E. semicircular apse has good zigzag mouldings, and lozenge patterns on it. The chapel was restored in 1853 (and again in 1887), after having been long neglected, and latterly used as a powder magazine.

Beyond the platform just described is the *Half-Moon Battery* (erected after 1573), from which royal salutes are fired, and from which a time-gun is discharged daily (Sundays excepted) at 1 P.M. (Greenwich time), by a clock controlled from the Observatory on the Calton Hill. A large hoisted ball is simultaneously dropped on the top of the Nelson Monument there. Behind this battery is a quadrangle on the S. side of which is the **"Great Hall"** or "*Parliament Hall*," and on the E. side the *Old Palace*. The Hall (84 ft. by 33 ft. with an open timber roof 45 ft. high) was built in 1424, was used for State receptions, and occasionally as the meeting-place of the Estates of the realm, and was last occupied when the Earl of Leven entertained Cromwell there in 1648. For 200 years it was practically lost sight of, being subdivided into stories for use as the Military Hospital. It has been carefully restored at the expense of the late Mr. Wm. Nelson (H. J. Blanc, archt.), has been suitably embellished with armour on the walls, and was handed over to the Princess Louise as representing the Crown in October 1892.

The Palace probably dates from the 15th cent., with additions made in 1566 and 1615. In the S.E. corner are **Queen Mary's Apartments,** in the smaller room of which, on the ground floor, James VI. was born on the 19th June 1566. Over the doorway are the initials H. and M., those of his father and mother; and in the ceiling are his own and his mother's, surmounted by a crown. Up a stair on the E. side is the **Crown Room,** a bomb-proof vault in which the *Regalia* are kept within an iron cage. They were deposited here in an old chest, with much formality, on the 7th March 1707, and here they were found on the 4th Feb. 1818.[1] The fact of their not having been seen for upwards of 100 years had raised suspicions that they had been removed to England, or perhaps stolen. They consist of a crown, sceptre, sword of state, and treasurer's rod of office. The crown, at least the double circlet or diadem, is supposed to be as old as the days of Robert Bruce, but was ornamented with concentric arches of gold in the reign of James V. The last time it was used was for the coronation of Charles II., before the battle of Worcester. The sceptre, which was made in the time of James V., is embellished with figures of the Virgin Mary, St. James, and St. Andrew. The sword was a present from Pope Julius II. to James IV. (1507), and is a piece of rich Italian work; its scabbard is ornamented with silver-gilt oak-leaves and acorns. Besides the Regalia, the following objects, bequeathed to George IV. by the Cardinal Duke of York, the last of the Stuarts, are exhibited. The *Golden Collar* and *George* of the *Order of the Garter*, presented by Queen Elizabeth to James VI.; the badge of the Thistle, also the property of James VI., a ring given by him to Charles I., and a miniature of Princess Louisa of

[1] An account of their disinterment is to be found in Lockhart's "Life of Scott," Sir Walter Scott having been one of the Commissioners appointed for the purpose.

Stolberg, wife of Prince Charles Edward.

Leaving the Castle and its Esplanade we pass E. down Castle Hill, once the abode of the noblest of the aristocracy, but all their interesting houses have disappeared through fires or so-called improvements. To the rt. is the *Assembly Hall of the Ch. of Scotland,* built in 1844, by Gillespie Graham, at a cost of £16,000, a very handsome Church in its outward aspect, of the Dec. Gothic style of architecture, (enlarged 1894), where the General Assembly, or Supreme Court of the Church, meets for a fortnight every May. At its E. end is a noble tower and spire rising to a height of 240 ft., and forming a very prominent object in all the views of Edinburgh. The hall is also used as the *Tolbooth Parish Ch.*, and occupies the site of an old weigh-house.

From this a narrow steep winding alley—now greatly changed and turned into a flight of steps—called the *West Bow* led S. down to the **Grassmarket** (p. 51), the place of public execution from 1666-1784: hence the rhyme—

"Up the Lawnmarket—down the West Bow,
Up the long ladder, and down the little tow."

In the West Bow once lived Lord Ruthven, who took a prominent part in the murder of Rizzio, and Major Weir, a criminal and reputed magician, who was burnt with his sister in 1670. From 1602-1720 the first *Assembly Rooms* were here.

The section of High Street below Castle Hill is known as the **Lawnmarket,** because it used to be crowded with stalls and booths for the sale of *linen* goods. Down to the beginning of the 19th century it was nearly shut in at the two ends by projecting buildings, and had no lateral carriage communications until 1825-30.

Left is **James's Court,** where stood the house of David Hume, afterwards of James Boswell, burnt down in 1857. Here Boswell entertained Paoli in 1771, and Johnson in 1773. Opposite (rt.) is **Riddle's Close,** a double court, and one of the most interesting remaining. In the outer part Hume began his Hist. of England 1751; in the inner one, in a splendid suite of apartments, now fitted up as a University Students' Settlement (well worthy of a visit) Bailie MacMorran, afterwards shot while quelling a High School Boys' riot, entertained James VI., his Queen, and other royal guests, 1593. On the same side (rt.) is *Brodie's Close,* where lived the hypocritical Deacon Brodie, Convener of the Trades and night burglar, who was hanged in 1788 by a "drop" invented by himself. Adjoining, but now swept away, was *Old Bank Close,* where the Bank of Scotland did business from 1700 to 1805.

Oppos. (l.) is **Lady Stair's Close,** once the principal thoroughfare to the New Town. Here Lady Eleanor Campbell (granddau. of the E. of Loudoun), whose history as Lady Primrose is the basis of Sir W. Scott's story of "My Aunt Margaret's Mirror," lived (after the death of her 2nd husband the 2nd Earl of Stair), the leader of Edinburgh society, and d. 1759. Her house bears the date 1622, the initials W. G. and G. S.—(Sir W. Gray d. 1648 and his wife Geida Smith) —and the text, "Feare the Lord and depart from evill." In the house to the E. of the close (rebuilt with gabled front 1894) Burns lodged, 1786.

To the S. **George IV. Bridge,** erected 1825-36, spans the Cowgate. Before the bridge (rt.) are the offices of the *Highland and Agricultural Society of Scotland*, a most useful institution, dating from 1784, and the **Free Public Library** in the French Renaissance style of

Francis I. (Washington Browne, archt.), the gift of Mr. Andrew Carnegie of Pittsburg, U.S.A., a Scotsman by birth. It cost £50,000, was opened June 1890, and has (1894) 50,300 books for lending, and 29,300 for reference. It occupies the site of the "Hope House" built (1616) by Sir Thomas Hope, King's Advocate, and "ancestor of all the considerable men of this name now in Scotland." Left are the *Parliament House* (p. 45), with the handsome turreted uppermost story of the S.S.C. Library (p. 46), overlooking the Cowgate, very prominent, and the **Sheriff Court Buildings.**

Right of the bridge on the S. side of the Cowgate is the *Magdalen Chapel* (p. 52).

We now proceed down the High Street proper, passing (rt.)

The **County Buildings,** erected 1816-19, on the model of the Erechtheum at Athens. In the sq. in front is a bronze *Statue* of the late (5th) *Duke of Buccleuch* (1806-1884) with panels exhibiting scenes from his own or his family's history. Immediately to the E. of it, traced out with stones, is the **"Heart of Midlothian,"** marking the site of the old *Tolbooth*, or Toll-house for receiving the city duties. Built about 1466, it became the meeting-place of Parliament and of the Court of Session upon its institution (1532). It subsequently became a mere prison, the lower story being let out as shops. Upon a platform projecting on the side next the Lawnmarket were exposed, at different times, the heads of the Regent Morton (1581), the Marquis of Montrose (1650), and the Marquis of Argyll (1661), and here, after 1784, public executions took place. The Tolbooth was pulled down in 1817. Its old doorway may still be seen at Abbotsford, built into the wall, and the keys hang in the armoury of the same mansion. It was separated by a narrow passage from the

** **Church of St. Giles,**[1] a cruciform building with slightly projecting transepts originally of great architectural beauty, but at various times so mutilated—both intentionally and unintentionally—as to be almost unrecognisable, has at length been admirably restored, so far as regards the interior. The exterior has been so lamentably spoilt by previous "restorations" that nearly all traces of the original have disappeared with the exception of the Choir, which remains as it was, and the square central Tower. This is surmounted by light flying buttresses, springing from the sides and angles of the parapet, forming an arched imperial Crown ; while, resting upon the keystone of the whole, a short and graceful spire springs from among a cluster of pinnacles to the height of 160 feet from the ground.

HISTORY.—Some kind of ch. seems to have existed here as early as the 9th cent. The present edifice was erected by degrees, at periods ranging from the beginning of the 12th cent. to the middle of the 15th. In 1466 it became the seat of a collegiate foundation. At the introduction of the Reformed worship into Scotland the thirty-six altars of the ch., together with the rood-loft, were removed, and the statue of St. Giles was carried off by a Protestant mob, and thrown into the Nor' Loch. Soon after, the ch. was pillaged and "purified," but the whole building continued to be used for divine service by John Knox,

[1] See "St. Giles', Edinburgh—Church, College, and Cathedral," by J. Cameron Lees, D.D., Minister of St. Giles', Dean of the Chapel-Royal of Scotland and of the Order of the Thistle.

Admission every week day (except Sat.), 10–3 : 3d. Mondays free.

Services—Daily on week days (in side Chapel) 3.30 ; Sunday 9.30 (Military Service), 11.30, and 6.30.

who was minister of St. Giles's 1559-1572. In 1571 the tower was fortified by Kirkaldy of Grange, who held it against the Regent Morton. James VI. took leave of the citizens of Edinburgh in St. Giles's when about to depart to ascend the English throne (1603). He promised to defend the Presbyterian faith, and to pay his Scottish subjects a visit every three years at farthest. He went away, re-established Scottish Episcopacy, and it was fourteen years before he set foot in Scotland again.

It was in the following reign, however, that St. Giles's became the scene of the most momentous events connected with the religious history of Scotland. A bishopric of Edinburgh was established in 1634, and St. Giles's Ch. became the Cathedral of the diocese. From the very

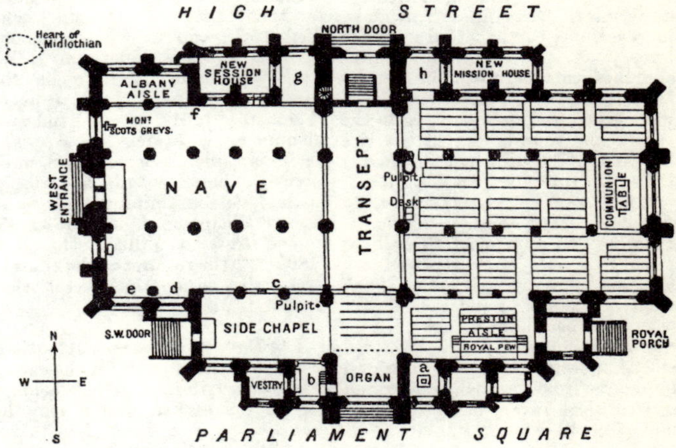

PLAN OF ST. GILES'S CATHEDRAL.

a. Chepman or Montrose Aisle.
b. Moray Aisle.
c. Jenny Geddes's Tablet.
d. Service Books.
e. Font.
f. Brass to "Black Watch."
g. Hammermen's Aisle.
h. Chambers's Aisle.

pulpit whence Knox had thundered against popery and prelacy the new liturgy prepared by Laud was being read for the first time, July 1637, when Jenny Geddes, incensed at the innovation, took up the cutty stool on which she had been sitting, and threw it at the head of Dean Hannay the officiating minister. The (traditional) stool is still preserved in the Antiquarian Museum. The church has undergone strange vicissitudes, having been "at various times a grammar school, the courts of justice, the town-clerk's office, a prison, and the storehouse of the machinery of the gallows." From 1639 to 1817 it contained four separate places of worship, and a police office, while a number of small shops called "krames" were built against the exterior walls of the ch., and half the breadth of the High St. on the N. side was occupied by "*Luckenbooths*" (=locked-shops) which were tenanted chiefly by booksellers and jewellers. During that time the fabric was subjected to the most ruthless mutilation. A so-called restoration took place in 1829, when the part W. of the central tower was almost entirely rebuilt by an architect thoroughly ignorant of Gothic, many of the ancient side chapels were demolished, and the whole exterior sobered down into a heavy, dull, and uninteresting uniformity. The fine E. window, however, was partly copied from the tracery of the original. Three churches remained until the restoration of St. Giles's, which, begun 1872, was carried out mainly owing to the energy and munificence of the late Dr. Wm. Chambers (Lord Provost 1865-69), who died in May 1883, just before the work was successfully completed (Hay, archt.). The partitions have been removed, the injured pillars restored and replaced ; a handsome carved pulpit of Caen stone, an organ, reredos, and oak pews have been added ; the unity of the whole church has been restored and a handsome doorway surmounted by figures from Scottish secular and ecclesiastical history has been made under the W. window.

On the N. wall of St. Giles is a monument to Napier of Merchiston (1550-1617), the inventor of logarithms.

INTERIOR.—The lofty middle-pointed **Choir** is in a masculine style of Gothic. Its two easternmost bays, with fluted columns, are of later date than the rest. The vaulted stone roof, diagonally groined with bosses at the intersections of the ribs, merits notice.

The part of the choir called the *Preston Aisle*, E. of the S. transept, erected by the citizens in gratitude to Sir Wm. Preston for presenting them (1454) with an arm-bone of the patron saint ! is the "gem of St. Giles's." On its E. wall is a bronze relief of Dean Stanley, with a brass tablet to the 13th Earl of Dalhousie (1847-87) below ; also a handsome *Mural Monument* to the Rt. Hon. John Inglis of Glencorse (1810-91), Lord Justice-General of Scotland and Chancellor of Edinburgh University. Against the S. wall is the *Royal Pew* occupied by the Lord High Commissioner when he attends service during the sitting of the General Assembly ; and in the S.W. corner is the *Chepman Aisle* founded by that "Scottish Caxton" who died 1532, and in whose memory there is a brass tablet on its W. wall. Beneath its floor lie the collected remains of the Marquis of "Montrose 1661," whose handsome monument is against its E. wall. There is a fine window in its S. wall.

In the choir E. of the N. transept is an *Aisle* containing a *Window* to Robert Chambers (Jun.), 1832-88, and a *Brass* to William Chambers (1800-83), the restorer of the church. The choir also contains several other memorial windows.

The **Nave** now deserves attention. It is about the same size as the choir ; traces of a triforium gallery belonging to the earlier church may be seen.

In it W. of the S. transept is a side *Chapel* with an elegant little wooden canopied *Pulpit* presented by J. R. Findlay, Esq., to commemorate the resumption (1884) of daily service "after an interval of 200 years." At the entrance to this chapel from the nave, an inscription on the floor by the late Lord Justice-General Inglis says that

> "Constant oral tradition affirms that near this spot a brave Scotch woman Janet Geddes on the 23 July 1637 struck the first blow in the great struggle for freedom of conscience which after a conflict of half a century ended in the establishment of civil and religious liberty."

In the S.E. corner of this chapel Regent Moray is buried in what is called "*The Moray Aisle.*" His monument, erected 1864, contains Buchanan's Latin epitaph of 1570, and a window, designed by Sir Noel Paton, represents his murder, and Knox preaching his funeral sermon.

In the S.W. corner of the nave is a *Font* in Caen stone—a kneeling angel holding a shell—a copy by Rhind of Thorwaldsen's font in the Frue Kirke, Copenhagen. Close by is a case containing the *Service-books*—9 in number—which have been used in this church.

In the N.W. corner is the *Albany Aisle*, supposed to have been erected by the Duke of Albany and the Earl of Douglas in expiation of the murder of the Duke of Rothesay 1402. Near it are several regimental monuments, especially a very fine *Brass* to the memory of those of the 42nd ("Black Watch") who died in Egypt in 1882, and a handsome *Cross* to those of the Scots Greys who fell in the Soudan 1885.

The old flags of the Scottish regiments are hung above the pillars of the nave. Upon the central pillars are *Memorial Brasses* to Gavin Douglas (Bp. of Dunkeld), Provost 1501, who "d. in exile at London 1522," Craig (1512-1600), colleague and successor of Knox, Hannay (Dean 1634-39), Archbp. Leighton (Principal of the University 1653-62), Henderson (minister 1639-46), and Carstares, 1649-1715, Principal of the University. W. of the N. transept is the *Hammermen's Aisle*.

The space to the S. of St. Giles's, now called *Parliament Square*, was originally the cemetery of the ch. A square stone, inscribed "I. K. 1572," let into the pavement, nearly opposite the S. transept, marks the *Grave* of *John Knox*. Boswell happened to ask where Knox was buried. Johnson burst out, "I hope on a highway." It is singular that his wish should be fulfilled. In the middle stands an equestrian statue of Charles II., erected 1685, made of bronzed lead, and cast in Holland.

The ****Parliament House**, the building on the S. side of this square, which was completed in 1640, was burned down 1824, and is replaced by a modern Italian pile, for the use of the Courts of Justice. The *Parliament Hall*, in which the Scottish legislature used to sit before the Union, the only part saved of the old edifice, presents an animated scene during session (Oct. 15–Mar. 20 and May 12–July 20 —Mondays excepted), crowded with advocates in wig and gown, solicitors, and clients waiting for cases to be called. It is a Gothic hall, 122 ft. long by 49 ft. broad. Its best feature is the open timber roof, which rests on brackets ornamented with boldly-sculptured heads, and is formed of dark oaken tie and hammer beams, with cross-braces. At the S. extremity, where formerly stood the royal throne, is a large painted window, manufactured at the Royal Factory at Munich (1868) from designs of Kaulbach, representing the Institution of the Court of Session by James V. (1532). The Scottish Parliament, it must be remembered, consisted only of one house, and till the 17th cent. there was ample room for it in the Tolbooth. At the N. end is a white marble statue of the 1st Viscount Melville (1742-1811) by *Chantrey*; and next to him on the right is Lord Chief Baron Dundas of Arniston (1758-1819) in a sitting attitude, also by *Chantrey*. First against the E. wall is Henry Cockburn (1779-1854) in his robes of Solicitor-General; next Duncan Forbes of Culloden (1685-1747) by *Roubillac*. Read the inscription. It was owing chiefly to Forbes's great influence in Scotland, and to his unswerving fidelity to the Hanoverian cause, that the Rebellion of 1745 was so soon suppressed. He is represented in his official robes, giving his decision and explaining the grounds: the right hand is raised. The forcible attitude reminds one of that of the husband in the Nightingale Monument, Westminster Abbey. (For a panegyric upon Forbes, see Thomson's "Autumn.") Next to him is Lord President Boyle (1772-1853), and, beyond the doorway, Lord Jeffrey (1773-1850), both by *Steell*. Then comes Lord President Blair (1741-1811), by *Chantrey*, erected by the county of Midlothian, for which he was member. The hall also contains a great many fine busts and portraits (by Raeburn, Macnee, Reid, etc.) of judges and other eminent lawyers with their names attached.[1]

In this hall 4 grand banquets have been given: 1st to Gen. Monk, in 1652; 2nd, to the Duke of York (afterwards James VII.), in 1680; 3rd, to George IV., in 1822; and 4th, the Jubilee banquet in 1887. The Scottish Parliament sat here for the last time, 25th March 1707.

The *Court of Session* is composed of 13 judges who are divided into the Outer and Inner House. The Courts at the S. end of the Hall are occupied by the Outer House, or Lords Ordinary, 5 in number, who sit singly, those on the E. side by the Inner House. The Inner House is composed of the First and Second Divisions (of equal authority)—4 judges in each—presided over respectively by the Lord President and the Lord Justice-Clerk, who hear appeals from the Lords Ordinary and Sheriffs of Counties. The judges of the Court of Session also form the *High Court of Justiciary*, the Supreme Criminal Court of Scotland, in which causes are conducted by a Public Prosecutor, the Lord Advocate, or one of his deputes. It sits (in a Court at the E. end of the Parliament House) every alternate Monday during Session, and the judges hold circuits 2-6 times a year throughout the country. The number of the jury is 15, a majority is sufficient to decide, and their verdict may be "Guilty," or "Not Guilty," or "Not Proven," which also finally liberates the prisoner.

[1] See "Handbook to the Parliament House," prepared by J. B. Paul, Esq., Treasurer to the Faculty of Advocates—to be had in the vestibule (6d.).

Adjoining and below the Hall is the **Advocates' Library.**

At the top of the stair is the Earl Marshal of Scotland's Standard carried at the battle of Flodden 1513.

The *Advocates' Library* is the largest in Scotland, and the only one there enjoying, like the British Museum, etc., the privilege under the Copyright Act of receiving a copy of every book published in Great Britain, Ireland, and the Colonies. It was founded in 1682 when Sir George Mackenzie ("Bloody Mackenzie") was Dean of the Faculty of Advocates. In 1692 it had 3140 vols.; it now (1894) has about 370,000 vols., besides 3000 vols. of MSS. 8000-9000 vols. are added annually, requiring 1300 ft. of shelving for their accommodation.

It contains valuable collections of MSS. of the Scriptures, the Classics, Genealogy and Heraldry, Early Scottish Poetry, Ancient English Poems and Romances, Icelandic Sagas, etc. etc., as well as a MS. copy of the *Vulgate* of the 12th cent. brought from the abbey of Dunfermline, fourteen Letters from Mary Queen of Scots to her mother, Letters from James VI. and Charles I. and the original MS. of "Waverley."

Among the books are a *Mazarin Bible* printed at Maintz by Gutenberg and Faust (1450-55)—the first Bible printed with movable metal types,—a vol. of Scottish Poetry printed by Chepman and Miller, 1508, etc. There is a copy of the King's Confession, 1580, and of the Solemn Covenant, 1638, with the nobles' signatures appended. Strangers are admitted to part of the library without introduction, and can obtain leave from the Librarian to consult any books or MSS. in which they are interested.

The *Writers to the Signet* have an excellent library[1] at the N. end of the Parliament House with a large handsome hall above; while the *Solicitors before the Supreme Courts* in 1891 erected a fine new suite

[1] Admission by Member's Card.

of rooms[1] for their library to the S. of the 2nd Div. Court Room (J. B. Dunn, archt.).

In the E. corner of Parliament Square is the **Police Court** and **Offices.** The Edinburgh Police Force was established in 1807 ; the protection of the citizens having previously been entrusted to the "Town Guard," originally raised in 1682.

Between St. Giles's and the Police Office the **City Cross,** an old shaft of one stone 20 ft. high, surmounted by a unicorn, stands upon a small octagon tower (erected 1885 by Rt. Hon. W. E. Gladstone, M.P. for Midlothian, with a Latin inscription by himself), similar to that which formerly stood in the High St., on a spot close by, marked by a circle of stones in the causeway and of whose removal in 1756 Scott wrote—

> "Dun-Edin's Cross, a pillar'd stone,
> Rose on a turret octagon ;
> (But now is razed that monument,
> Whence royal edict rang,
> And voice of Scotland's law was sent
> In glorious trumpet clang.
> Oh ! be his tomb as lead to lead,
> Upon its dull destroyer's head !—
> A minstrel's malison is said)."
> *Marmion.*

Royal Proclamations are now again made by the heralds from this tower. Beside the Cross public executions took place until 1666.

On the opposite side of the street is Writers' Court in which was *Clerihugh's Tavern* where Dandie Dinmont found Counsellor Pleydell at "High Jinks," and to the E. of it in a square called the *Royal Exchange*, entered by an archway, are the **Municipal Buildings** where the Town Council meet. In size and plainness they form a marked contrast to the palatial buildings in Glasgow, but the *Council Chamber*, although small, is a striking room, well designed, with pillars, a handsome mantelpiece, and portraits of the leading Lord Provosts. At the top of the building there is a most interesting little *Museum* containing many relics connected with civic and national history. On the staircase leading to it are several inscribed lintels belonging to old houses taken down in the course of carrying out the scheme of city improvement. Visitors are admitted upon presentation of their cards.

1. is *Cockburn Street*, a modern thoroughfare leading to the "Scotsman" offices and to Waverley Bridge and Station.

rt. The **Tron Church** (built 1637-63) received its name from a public "tron," or weighing beam, which stood close by, and to which the keepers of false weights were nailed by the ears. The side of the church facing the street is the oldest part : a curious old wooden steeple was burnt in 1824, when the present stone steeple was erected. Outside this church the populace assemble to "bring in" each New Year.

l. The **North Bridge** (built 1763, widened 1874, and about to be rebuilt 1894) leads to the New Town. Beyond, near the corner, stood the barber's shop kept by Allan Ramsay the poet.

rt. The *South Bridge* leads over the Cowgate to the University, Industrial Museum, etc. (p. 53).

l. In *Carrubber's Close* stood the house of Archbishop Spottiswood (1565-1639).

Beyond, projecting into the street, is ***John Knox's House**[1] (admission daily from 10 to 4, 6d.). The house is irregularly shaped, and has an external staircase. The interior is divided into small, dark, and low rooms. On the outside, just above the ground floor, is the inscription, "Lufe · God · abufe · al · and·yi · nychbour · [as] · yi · self."

A carved stone figure with uplifted hands passed for Knox in a pulpit preaching, until the repairs in 1850

1 Admission by Member's Card.

1 Whether Knox really lived here has been disputed. See "Proceedings of Society of Antiquaries of Scotland, 1890-91."

made manifest that the effigy represented "Moses receiving the Law on Sinai," God being represented by a golden disc, inscribed "Θεός, Deus, God." This house became Knox's manse in 1559 (when he was appointed minister of St. Giles's), and in it he narrowly escaped assassination from a shot fired at him through the window; here also he died in 1572. Some of the panelling of the walls has been brought from other old houses.

l. *Jeffrey Street*, a wide airy street opened through masses of dense old buildings, on the line of Leith Wynd from the High Street to below the North Bridge. Halfdown (l.) is a commonplace church, into one side of which has been incorporated that elegant fragment of late Gothic, *Trinity College Church*, founded 1462 by Mary of Gueldres, widow of King James II. It consists of two bays, and an apse pierced by 3 tall lancet windows, with a fine groined roof, and though pulled down, 1845, to make way for the N. British Railway, was preserved stone by stone, and every stone numbered for future reconstruction. This is the only part worth looking at, and it has been pushed out of sight, round a corner, by its modern neighbour, "a meaningless annexe."

Opposite Jeffrey St. is *St. Mary St.*, leading to the Cowgate. A tablet on its E. side marks the site of the *White Horse Inn* in Boyd's Close, where Dr. Johnson put up (1773) before his tour to the Hebrides.

At the contraction of the street here stood the **Nether Bow** or Lower gate of the City—which was originally of very moderate dimensions, including neither the Castle, nor Castle Hill, nor the Canongate. The Nether Bow was removed in 1764, in consequence of, though not till many years after, the Porteous Riot. From this point to Holyrood the street is called the **Canongate**, having originally belonged to the Abbey, then tenanted by "Canons regular." From its proximity to Holyrood Palace this portion of the city contained the houses of many of the most powerful members of the Scottish nobility.

rt. **Moray House,** now a Normal School connected with the Free Church, was built by the Countess of Home in 1628, and bears the initials M. H. in various places, besides a lozenge with the lions rampant, the arms of the Home family. The entrance gate is ornamented on each side by a pointed pinnacle. It passed to the Countess of Moray 1645, and beneath the large window is a balcony, in which the Marquis of Argyll, during the festivities connected with the marriage of his son to the Countess's daughter (1650), and other guests stood to see Montrose bound and carried in a cart through the city to the Old Tolbooth. The house was taken possession of by Cromwell for his abode on his first visit to Edinburgh, 1648, and again in 1650. In its gardens the Treaty of Union 1707 was arranged, if not actually signed.

l. **Canongate Tolbooth,** with its clock projecting over the entrance, was built in 1591 as a jail and court-house. Over the door is inscribed "Pro patriâ et posteris," and on one side are the arms of Holyrood Abbey, a stag's head with a cross between the antlers, and the motto, "Sic itur ad astra." The building is now used as a register and revenue office. The old *Cross*, which formerly stood in the centre of the street, has long since disappeared, and been replaced by a more modern one in front of the Canongate Ch. which was built 1688, and stands back from the street. In its ch.-yd. are buried Adam Smith (d. 1790), Dugald Stewart (d. 1828), and the poet Fergusson (d. 1774, aged 24), to whom Burns erected a headstone.

Across the street (rt.) is "*The Speaking House*," the only timber-fronted house remaining, with 4 Latin aphorisms on its face. It was built 1570, and belonged to the Earl of Huntly. In a court behind is an interesting lintel with date 1633, surmounted by the motto "Vigilantibus," and a cock and trumpet. The finials of the gables above represent the Rose, the Thistle, and the Shamrock.

Lower down (rt.) is **Queensberry House**, once a very handsome building, in the style of a French château. It is now used as a house of refuge. The poet Gay lived here during the latter part of his life in the capacity of secretary to the Duchess of Queensberry. The house was dismantled in 1801 by the then Duke of Queensberry, who was usually known by the appellation of "Old Q."

l. The picturesque **White Horse Close**—restored—deserves a visit. It was a famous Inn in the 17th and 18th cent., where journeys between Edinburgh and London usually began and ended. Here Captain Waverley stayed: but it is now tenanted by a number of poor families.

Opposite what was once the Water-gate, the radiated pavement marks the site of the "Girth Cross," or the bounds of the former Sanctuary of Holyrood for Debtors.[1] The road now opens out into the space before Holyrood.

Left, in a shrubbery, is a curious little turreted lodge called *Queen Mary's Bath-room*, by means of which Rizzio's murderers escaped, and in the roof of which their (?) weapons were found abt. 1800. In front of the palace stands a *Fountain* of quaint design—a copy of the one at Linlithgow Palace—erected by the late Prince Consort.

** **Holyrood Abbey and Palace.**[1]

Holyrood Abbey, i.e. the Abbey of the Holy Cross, owes its origin to the rescue of King David I. while hunting in the neighbouring forest of Drumsheugh, from the horns of a stag at bay, by the apparition of a luminous cross in the sky, which put the animal to flight. The king founded the abbey in 1128, to commemorate his miraculous deliverance, endowing it richly with revenues. Doubtless David had the design of depositing here the Holy Rood or fragment of the true Cross brought by his mother, St. Margaret, from Waltham Abbey.

The existing *Church* or *Royal Chapel*, on the N. side of the Palace, is of later date, and consists of the nave only; the choir and transept have disappeared. In the old choir were married all the Scottish kings since James I.; and in front of the E. window (restored *temp.* Charles I.) Queen Mary married Darnley.

The finest portion of the Ch. is the W. front, which has been elbowed and intruded on by the Palace. Here is a small, but richly arcaded, N.W. Tower, and near it a doorway, composed of six shafts and orders of mouldings, with foliage exquisitely undercut, but now blackened with smoke. The nave consists of eight bays with aisles. One circular arch remains on the S. aisle, a fragment of the original building of David I.; the remainder is of the First Pointed style, and belongs to the latter part of the 12th cent. The ch. suffered considerably during the Reformation, when the mob plundered and burnt it, and also when the English, under Lord Hertford, burnt the Palace, in

1 Until imprisonment for debt was abolished, the precincts of Holyrood used to afford sanctuary to insolvent debtors, a privilege granted by David I. in his original charter. The limits of this sanctuary included the grounds to the E. of the Palace, Salisbury Crags, and Arthur's Seat, a circuit of at least 4 miles.

1 Admission daily (Sundays excepted), 11 A.M. to 6 P.M.—Winter 11 A.M. to 4 P.M.—Tues., Thurs., and Sat. gratis, other days 6d.; but during the residence of the Queen, or the Lord High Commissioner, there is no admittance.

their invasion of 1544. In 1547 the abbey was suppressed. In 1633 the building was repaired, and sumptuously fitted up by Charles I., and at the Restoration was converted into a Chapel Royal, having previously been the parish ch. of the Canongate. The vault at S.E. end was used as the royal sepulchre, and in it were buried David II., James II., James V., and his wife Magdalen; the murdered Rizzio was buried in the chapel by the express orders of Queen Mary; and here, on Feb. 11, 1567, were secretly interred the remains of Lord Darnley, two days after his mysterious murder. The body of Mary of Gueldres was removed hither from Trinity Ch. when it was pulled down. In the middle of the 18th cent. a plan for repairing the chapel was eventually carried out (1758); but so heavy a roof was put on, that in 1768 it fell in. Everything portable was then stolen, including the skull of Darnley. The ruins are now sadly defaced by time.

The *Palace of Holyrood* was begun by King James IV., and completed by his successor James V., Sir James Hamilton of Trimarty, who had been employed on the Palaces of Linlithgow, Falkland, and Stirling, being the architect. This palace was burned by the English under the Earl of Hertford, 1544, and again by the soldiers of Cromwell, 1650, the only part which escaped being the wings and towers at the N.W. angle, which were occupied by *Queen Mary* from the time of her return from France, 1561, and which possess a great but painful historic interest in consequence.

The Historical Apartments.—A door on the N. side of the Inner Court, l. of the main entrance, leads to the Picture Gallery, and the apartments of Darnley and Queen Mary. The rooms upon the first floor were those of Darnley. They communicated by a private stair, in the thickness of the wall, with those of Queen Mary's apartments on the second floor. These consist of an audience-chamber, containing an old bedstead and some dingy furniture, a bedroom with another old tattered bed, said to be that of the queen, and two small cabinets within the angle towers.

In one of these cabinets or boudoirs, entered from the bedroom, Mary and a small party were at supper, March 9, 1566, when Darnley and Ruthven, followed by other conspirators, entered for the purpose of seizing Rizzio, an accomplished Italian secretary and skilful musician, who had gained the Queen's confidence and roused the jealousy of the Presbyterian lords and ministers of the Kirk. Suspecting their purpose, Rizzio threw himself behind the queen, and caught hold of her dress, but was stabbed by George Douglas, leaning over the queen's shoulder, while her miserable husband held her fast in his arms, and the ruffian Ker of Fawdonside held a pistol at her breast, she being at the time seven months gone with child! Rizzio, having been dragged out into the outer room, was despatched by fifty-six wounds, and his body with Darnley's dagger left sticking in it, was thrown down the private staircase, the head of which is in the bedroom close to the door of the boudoir.

The present palace was in great part rebuilt, 1671-79, after a design by Sir William Bruce, and was a copy of the Château de Chantilly, the residence of the family of Condé. The royal apartments are on the S. and E. sides. They have been inhabited by James VII. when Duke of York, by Prince Chas. Edw. in 1745, and by the Duke of Cumberland, 1746; by Louis XVIII.; by Charles X. of France, both before his elevation to, and after his displacement from the throne; and by George IV. in 1822. H.M. Queen Victoria has occasionally spent a night or two here on her way to Balmoral, but it is now pretty well deserted by royalty, as expressed by Hamilton of Bangour, who called it "a virtuous palace where no monarch dwells." It is the official residence of the Lord High Commissioner of the Church of Scotland for a fortnight in May during the session of the General Assembly.

The *Picture Gallery*, in which the Representative Peers of Scotland are elected, is 150 feet in length, 27 in breadth, and 18 in height. The walls are hung with portraits of 106 Scottish kings, who, as Sir Walter Scott observes, "if they ever existed, lived several hundred years before the invention of painting in oil." Elsewhere he inquires "the reason why the kings should each and every one be painted with a nose like the knocker of a door?" One De Witt was the painter (1684-86). At the farther end are four pictures of considerable historic and artistic value: 1. Represents James III. and his son; 2. his wife, Margaret of Denmark; 3. the Holy Trinity; 4. Sir Edward Boncle or Bonkil, Provost of Trinity College Church, where the last two (with another, since lost) formed the altar-piece. These pictures, which are of the school of Van Eyck, and in admirable preservation, were carried to Hampton Court at the Union, and removed hither, 1862, by permission of the Queen.

The description in "Waverley" of the court held at Holyrood by the Young Chevalier in 1745 is familiar to most English readers.

S. of Holyrood are the Queen's Park and Arthur's Seat. See p. 61.

W. up the *South Back Canongate* are numerous *Breweries*, including that of Messrs. Younger, celebrated for its "Edinburgh Ale."

The tourist should now proceed N. under the N.B. Rly. and then W. along the Regent Road. He will pass (l.) **Burns's Monument**, erected in 1830. The body of it is circular, surrounded by 12 columns. The cupola is a copy of the monument of Lysicrates at Athens. It contains some relics of Burns. Adm. 2d.

rt. is the **Royal High School**, built in 1825-29. It was founded in the 12th cent., and remodelled 1598 (cf. p. 54). The actual building, a happy adaptation (Hamilton, archt.) of the Temple of Theseus in Athens, comprises a centre, 2 wings, and 2 lodges, extending 277 ft. in front, and was erected at a cost of £30,000. The number of pupils is about 350.

W. of the High School stands the **Prison**, a castellated building in a prominent situation, overhanging the North British Railway; and adjoining it, on the S. side of Waterloo Place, lies the *Old Calton Burying-Ground*, in which there are a tower-like monument to David Hume (1711-76) and a lofty *Obelisk* to the five premature Radical Reformers, transported for sedition 1818, and now styled martyrs to the cause of popular freedom. Public appreciation of their efforts was rather tardy, for the monument was not raised till 1845. rt. is the **Calton Hill** (p. 55).

---

(2) Grassmarket — Greyfriars Churchyard—University—Heriot's Hospital.

From the W. end of Princes St. proceed S.E. behind St. Cuthbert's Ch. by *King's Stables Road* to the **Grassmarket**, where a weekly market, now chiefly of horses, has been held since 1477. A *Cross* in the causeway marks the place of public execution (1666-1784), where most of the Covenanters suffered—hence the saying of the D. of Rothes, "Let him glorify God in the Grassmarket"—and where the mob hanged Captain Porteous of the City Guard (1736), as described in the "Heart of Midlothian." The **Corn Exchange** erected 1849, and used for large political meetings, etc., is on the S. side. In the *West Port*, the approach to the Grassmarket from the S.W., lived the notorious Burke and Hare (1828).

E. from the Grassmarket runs the **Cowgate,** built in 1500, and then a fashionable suburb, but now one of the poorest localities, abounding in Irish. In a house at its head Lord Brougham was born, Sept. 19, 1778. A few yds. down (rt.) is * **Magdalen Chapel** (now within Medical Mission Premises), with a large carved and inscribed lintel. This is one of the oldest and most interesting buildings left in Edinburgh. Originally a portion of an ancient Maison Dieu, but having fallen into decay, it was restored (1503) at the expense of one Michael Macquhan and Janet Rhynd his wife, whose tomb is within, and by them left in trust to the Corporation of Hammermen. John Craig, the colleague of John Knox, preached here; here in 1578 the first General Assembly of the Ch. of Scotland was held; and here were deposited (1661) the beheaded remains of the Marq. of Argyll prior to their removal to Kilmun. The windows, with the arms of Scotland, of Mary of Guise (Queen Regent), and of the restorers, are almost the only specimens of pre-Reformation stained glass in Scotland. In the interior panelling of the chapel are the coats of arms of Mary of Guise, of many benefactors, and of the 22 corporations who united to form the body of Hammermen—the guardians of the "Blue Blanket," or sacred banner of the Trades, on the unfurling of which every true burgess was bound to answer to the summons.

Passing behind the Chapel up *Candlemakers' Row* we reach rt. **The Greyfriars Churches** (*Old and New*) **and Burying Ground,** from which an excellent view may be obtained of the Castle and S. side of the Old Town. The whole of this ground was formerly a garden belonging to the monastery of the Greyfriars, founded by James I.

Old and New Greyfriars Churches form one long line of building, the E. portion, termed *Old Greyfriars*, originally erected in 1612, being partially destroyed in 1718, and totally burnt in 1845. The present building contains some good stained glass. Principal Robertson, the eminent historian, was minister here in 1762. New Greyfriars Ch., built in 1721, contains nothing worthy of note. On the tomb of Boswell of Auchinleck, opposite the S. door of the ch., was signed in March 1638 "The Covenant,"[1] which obtained for the popular party the name of Covenanters.

In the churchyard were penned and guarded for 5 months the 1200 prisoners taken at Bothwell Brig (1679), no prison being large enough to hold them.

Observe in N.E. corner of the ch.-yd. the *Martyrs' Monument* and S.W. the tomb of Principal Robertson (d. 1793), grand-uncle of Lord Brougham, historian of Scotland and of America, and the leader of the Kirk for 20 years. Here also are the graves of Allan Ramsay, poet (d. 1758); George Heriot, 1563-1624; Colin Maclaurin, 1698-1746; Hugh Blair (d. 1800); Mackenzie (d. 1831), "The Man of Feeling"; Dr. M'Crie (d. 1835), biographer of John Knox; Geo. Buchanan (d. 1582), the historian, whose only memorial is an iron plate erected by a working man; Joseph Black, chemist (d. 1799), etc.

"In this venerable cemetery, which contains the dust of all the contending factions of Scottish history—where the monument of the Covenanters recounts their praises almost within sight of the Grassmarket where they died; where rest the noblest leaders both of the moderate and of the stricter party, there rises, S. side, another stately monument, at once the glory and the shame of Scottish liberals. It is the ponderous centre tomb, bolted and barred, of Sir George Mackenzie, King's Advocate under James II., and as such prosecutor of the Covenanters. He it is of whom Davie

1 For the difference between this "Covenant" and the subsequent "Solemn League and Covenant" (1643) see an article by the late Lord Justice-General Inglis entitled "Montrose and the Covenant of 1638" in *Blackwood's Magazine*, Nov. 1887.

Deans has said, that 'he will be kenned by the name of Bluidy Mackenzie so long as there's a Scots tongue to speak the word.'" DEAN STANLEY'S *Church of Scotland.*

It was popularly believed that his corpse would not remain quiet in the grave.

Almost opposite the gate is the broad **Chambers St.**, called after and with a statue (by Rhind) to *Wm. Chambers, LL.D.* (1800-83), Lord Provost (1865-69), and restorer of St. Giles's.

On the N. side are **Heriot-Watt College**, with a monument to James Watt, where over 3000 students receive, in day and evening classes, thorough scientific and technical instruction at moderate rates; also the *School of Medicine*, a *Medical College for Women*, and a Church of Scotland *Normal Training College.*

At the E. end in *College Wynd*, now swept away, Sir W. Scott was b., 15th Aug. 1771. On its S. side is the **Museum of Science and Art.**[1] a handsome edifice of stone, iron, and glass, after the fashion of the Museum at South Kensington. The first stone of it was laid by the Prince Consort on the 23rd Oct. 1861. It is Venetian in character, from designs by the late Capt. Fowke. The E. wing is devoted to the Natural History Collection (removed from the College). Suspended from the roof is a perfect skeleton of a Greenland whale (*Physalis antiquarum*), 79 ft. long, an animal almost extinct; also specimens of the gorilla from the Gaboon, of the yak from the Karakorum Mountains, etc. The minerals, fossils, etc., including the collection formed by Hugh Miller, are very good. The Geology of Scotland is illustrated in the most complete and instructive manner by specimens, sections, etc., collected and arranged by officers of the Geological Survey. On the ground floor is a very interesting series of models of Scottish *Lighthouses*, including the Bell Rock, Skerryvore, and Dhu Heartach, 15 m. W. of Iona—all marvels of constructive ingenuity. The galleries are occupied with works of art of all times and countries, with raw materials fitted for manufacturing processes, and a collection of Indian and Chinese curiosities. The contents of the Highland and Agricultural Society's Museum have been removed hither.

1 Open Wed. 10-4, and Fri. and Sat. 10-4 and 6-10, *free;* Mon. Tues. and Thurs. 10-4, 6d.

To the E. are the **Old University Buildings** (in which the Divinity, Arts, and Law Classes are taught), a massive pile entered from the South Bridge by a triple archway. The *University* was founded in 1582 by James VI., and is now justly celebrated for the excellence of its medical school, which is hardly surpassed by any other in Europe. The building was pulled down in 1789, and the present front, styled by Fergusson "a truthful and well-balanced design," is Robert Adam's best work. The quadrangle was finished by Playfair. It has a statue of Sir D. Brewster. A dome, surmounted by a figure of "Youth," by J. Hutchison, was, through the munificence of the late R. Cox, Esq., added to the front in 1887.

The N.E. corner covers the site of the *Kirk o' Field*, where Darnley was blown up, 10th Feb. 1567.

"The aggregate annual value of the Fellowships and Scholarships (all founded since 1858) is about £6550. Besides there are 202 bursaries in the Faculty of Arts, 40 in Divinity, 8 in Law, and 19 in Medicine." There are about 44 professors and lecturers (besides assistants), and about 3220 students, of whom fully one-half are enrolled in the Faculty of Medicine. The University Session begins in November and ends in April; but there is another for law and medical students from May to July. The *Library Hall* is a handsome room 198 ft. by 50. "The collection of books numbers about 180,000 vols. besides 3000 vols. of MSS. There is also a Theological Library containing 10,000 vols."

Visitors should apply to the Janitor to see the rooms of the *Speculative* (*Debating*) *Society* in the N.E. corner, which contain oil paintings of Scott and Horner, and numerous portraits of former members. It was founded in 1764. Scott was once Treasurer, and his books may be seen, while most of the leading men in Edinburgh —Brougham, Jeffrey, Wilson, Hamilton, etc., have belonged to it.

[For the New Buildings, see below.]

E. of the College is the *Old Infirmary*, now the **City Hospital** for infectious diseases. The *High School*, where Sir W. Scott, etc., were educated, stood beside it until 1829.

A little S., in Nicolson St., is the Grecian portico of the **Royal College of Surgeons**, by Playfair, one of his best works. Its *Museum*—containing an excellent anatomical and pathological collection—is open to the public.

Passing W. through College St. we reach the **New University Buildings**, in which the Medical Classes are taught, erected in 1878 (R. R. Anderson, archt.). At the E. end Mr. Wm. M'Ewan, M.P., is erecting (1894) an imposing **University Hall** (R. Rowand Anderson, archt.) for graduation ceremonials, etc. Behind are the *University Music Class-Room* (in Park Place), erected in 1860, with an organ of European celebrity, and the *University Students' Union* or Club, a handsome building opened 1889 (Sydney Mitchell, archt.).

To the S. is **George Square**, an old-fashioned square, where Sir W. Scott's parents lived (No. 25), and in which is *George Watson's Ladies' College*.

W. across the broad Meadow Walk is the magnificent **Royal Infirmary**, erected 1870-78, in the Scottish Baronial style, on the "pavilion system" of separate blocks, connected by galleries (Bryce, architect), at a cost of £380,000. This Infirmary is divided into the Surgical and Medical departments, which are altogether capable of accommodating nearly 700 patients. In the hall is a bust by Nollekens of Geo. Drummond (1772), 7 times Lord Provost of Edinburgh; and busts of Lord Provost Boyd and Mr. Bryce.

It overlooks the **Meadows**, a sort of enclosed park (with one carriage drive and several walks through it), which, with **Bruntsfield Links** to the S.W., formed a part of the Borough Muir, where, in 1336, Guy, Count of Namur, with reinforcements for the army of Edward III., then at Perth, was encountered and defeated by the Earl of Moray. Upon that ground, too, James IV. reviewed his forces (1513) before marching to Flodden (cf. p. 62).

N. of the Infirmary, and adjoining Greyfriars Ch.-yd., stands **Heriot's Hospital**, an institution similar to Christ's Hospital, London, and the handsomest and most original old building in Edinburgh.

It may be seen daily, except Saturday and Sunday, 12 to 3, by order from the office of the Treasurer, 20 York Place. There is no fee.

This hospital, the oldest and richest in Edinburgh, was founded by George Heriot,[1] goldsmith and banker to James VI., who, dying in 1624, left property amounting to £23,625 to the Town Council of Edinburgh, to build an hospital for the maintenance and education of poor and fatherless boys, the sons of freemen in the city. The income of the Trust now far exceeds its original capital, as a very large part of the New Town stands on ground bought with its funds. The building was begun in 1628, and finished in 1650, at a cost of £30,000. It was designed by William Aytoun[2] (though long attributed to Inigo Jones). Its architecture, a mixture of Palladian and Gothic, is very original, and deserves inspection. Of its 200 windows, the enrichment of no two are exactly alike. When Cromwell took possession of the city after the battle of Dunbar he placed his sick and wounded here, and it continued to be used as a military hospital till 1659, when General Monk removed the patients, and it was then opened according to the intentions of the founder. It is a square building, with towers at the corners, each tower rising a story above the main building, and surmounted by 4 small projecting turrets. A picturesque gateway leads into a quadrangle 94 ft. each way, very like an

[1] For a description of "Jingling Geordie," we refer our readers to Scott's "Fortunes of Nigel."

[2] Burton's "Hist. of Scotland," vii. p. 366, *note*.

Oxford college. Above the inner entrance is a statue of the founder. The Gothic *Chapel*, restored 1836, contains some painted windows, and is fitted up with dark oak. Besides this are shown the dining-room, reading-rooms, containing portraits of ex-officials, etc. A separate building in similar style was built to the W. for an *Examination Hall* (1894), at a cost of about £9000 (Gow, archt.) In 1885 the application of the funds was varied. They are now applied to give "modern," scientific, and technical instruction at the Hospital, a day school, with 120 foundations, 60 scholarships, and 40 bursaries, and to keep up the Heriot-Watt College (p. 53).

The Hospital is bounded on the W. by a portion of the **City Wall** of 1618.

On the S. side of Lauriston Place is *George Watson's College for Boys*, erected 1818 (Burn, archt.), at a cost of £12,250.

The founder was a merchant's clerk, and afterwards accountant to the Bank of Scotland, who d. 1723. His endowment of £12,000, of which the revenue is now over £1700, helps to maintain this College (with 60 foundationers) and a Ladies' College (p. 54). They are under the excellent management of the Merchant Company, as are *James Gillespie's Schools* for *Boys and Girls* (on Bruntsfield Links), endowed 1796.

Passing l. **Chalmers Hospital,** "for the sick and hurt," opened 1864, upon an endowment of £30,000 left by George Chalmers, plumber (d. 1836), and rt. the *Cattle Market*, we approach by Lady Lawson St., *Castle Terrace*, with the U.P. Church *Synod Hall* and *College*, and the *School Board Offices*, behind which is the *Lyceum Theatre*, and beyond reach the W. end of Princes St.

NEW TOWN.

(3) **Princes Street.**

At its E. end rises the **Calton Hill,** an easily accessible elevation with interesting views. On the summit is *Nelson's Monument*[1] (1815), which has been likened to a butter-churn or a telescope. A large Time-ball, controlled from the neighbouring *Observatory*, falls down the flagstaff on the top daily at 1 P.M., simultaneously with the firing of the gun at the Castle.

[1] Admission to the top, 3d.

To the N.E. stands the most prominent object, the *National Monument*, raised to those who fell in the Peninsula and the Waterloo campaign—a building intended to have been a restoration of the Parthenon in its perfect state, but which is a much nearer copy of the temple of Minerva as it stands at present. It was commenced in 1822, but, as each column cost £1000, when it arrived at its present state no more funds were forthcoming. To the N.W. is an *Observatory*, built in 1818 in the form of a Greek cross. Between them is a rectangular heavy cenotaph to *Professor Playfair* (1748-1819). On the S.W. is the monument to *Dugald Stewart* (1753-1828), copied from that of Lysicrates at Athens, commonly called the "Lanthorn of Demosthenes."

To the S. are the *Royal High School* and the *Prison*, see p. 51.

Proceeding W. along *Waterloo Place*, with the *Inland Revenue Offices* (l.), at the corner of *North Bridge* (l.) is the **General Post-Office,** a lofty, handsome Italian edifice, the first stone of which was laid by the late Prince Consort, 23rd Oct. 1861, his last appearance at any public ceremony.

From this point *Leith St.* leads N.E. into Leith Walk, where an earthwork was erected against Cromwell; it was afterwards converted into a "Walk," and finally opened out into the present roadway.

rt. is the **General Register House,** a fine building, with a central cupola, designed by Robert Adam, 1772. It is the Public Record Office of Scotland, in which all public documents relating to Scotland are kept. Strangers are admitted to see some of the valuable *State Papers*, Autographs, Letters of Queen Mary, etc. Adjoining is the **New Register House**, for the registration of births, deaths, and marriages, and also of all deeds conveying or charging landed property in Scotland. In front stands an equestrian *Statue of the Duke of Wellington*, by Steell, erected in 1852.

Keeping along Princes St. we pass rt. *St. Andrew Street*, leading into St. Andrew Square (p. 58).

l. Between North Bridge and Waverley Bridge is the **Waverley Market**, for fruit and vegetables. Popular Concerts are held here on Saturday evenings.

l. **Waverley Bridge**—down from which is the *North British Railway Station*—gives access to the Old Town.

l. W. of the Waverley Bridge is a *Statue* of *David Livingstone*, by Mrs. D. O. Hill, erected 1876, and beyond it rises the **Scott Monument**, a graceful Gothic cross or spire, with pinnacles, resting on 4 Pointed arches, the piers of which are strengthened by 4 outer piers, forming lancet arches, and serving to buttress up the whole structure. It thus forms a canopy of open arches to enclose the statue. It was erected in 1840-44, from the designs of George Kemp, an architect previously unknown to fame, who did not live to see his plans completed. He was an intense admirer of Melrose Abbey, and has endeavoured in this monument to combine all the characteristics and proportions of that building. Thus the monument may be said to consist of a pile of arches, gradually decreasing in size till the whole terminates in a single pinnacle. An interior staircase (admission 2d.) conducts to the top, which is 200 ft. from the ground, and commands an excellent view. Above the principal arches, and in various parts of the structure, are niches, filled with statues, representing the most prominent characters in Sir Walter's poems and novels. Beneath the main arches is placed a statue of Sir Walter Scott and his dog Maida, by Steell, a first-rate work of art.

The uppermost house on the right in *St. David Street* (rt.) was the last residence of David Hume, who died in it, 1776. W. of the Scott Monument are *Statues* of *Adam Black*, by Hutchison, and of *Professor Wilson*, in bronze, by Steell—a very good likeness, and a fine work of art.

l. At the foot of the *Mound* is the **Royal Institution** (Playfair, archt.), of which the N. side was completed in 1836. It is an oblong building, of the Grecian Doric style. It contains the Rooms of the *Royal Society* of Edinburgh, a *Sculpture Gallery* (open daily 10-4; Wed. and Fri. 6d.; other week-days *free*), an *Art School*, and a *School of Applied Art*, for acquiring "knowledge of Art Design as applied to industries."

To the south of the Royal Institution stands the **National Gallery**,[1] erected 1850-58, after Playfair's design.

It contains good examples of British artists—*W. Aikman*, His own Portrait; *David Allan*, The Origin of Painting; *S. Bough*, Volunteer Review, 1860; *H. Cameron*, Going to the Hay; *Sir W. F. Douglas*, The Spell; *J. Drummond*, The Porteous Mob; *Duncan*, Bran, a Scottish Deerhound; *W. Dyce*, Francesca da Rimini; *W. Etty*, The Story of Judith (3 pictures), Benaiah, *The Combat; *J. Faed*, Annie's Tryst; *Gainsborough*, **Hon. Mrs. Graham, wife of General Sir Thomas G. (perhaps the gem of the collection); *A. Geddes*, Summer; *Sir J. Watson Gordon*, Lord Murray, Sir W. Scott; *J. Graham Gilbert*, The Bandit's Bride; *Sir G. Harvey*, Quitting the Manse, Covenanters' Communion; *R. Herdman*, After the Battle; *W. B. Johnstone*, Murder of Rizzio; Sir *E. Landseer*, Rent Day in the

[1] Admission, Mon., Tues., Wed., Sat., 10-4 (in summer 10-5); Sat. evening, 7-9, free; Thurs., Fri., 10-4, 6d.; catalogues, 6d.

Wilderness (bequeathed by Sir R. Murchison); *H. Macculloch*, Inverlochy Castle, Lowland River; *A. Nasmyth*, Robert Burns (bequeathed by the poet's son), Stirling Castle; *E. Nicol*, Day after the Fair; *Sir Noel Paton*, Oberon and Titania (2 pictures); *Waller H. Paton*, Lamlash Bay; *J. Phillip*, Spanish boys playing at bull-fighting, Portraits of Mr. and Mrs. W. B. Johnstone; *T. Phillips*, Sir D. Wilkie; *Sir H. Raeburn*, Mrs. Hamilton, Mrs. R. Scott Moncrieff, Dr. Adam, F. Horner, Lord Newton, Lady Miller; *Allan Ramsay*, J. J. Rousseau, David Hume; *Sir G. Reid*, P.*R.S.A.*, Dornoch; *Sir J. Reynolds*, Edmund Burke, Sir Thomas Miller; *D. Roberts*, Rome at Sunset; *Sir D. Wilkie*, Artist's Sister, John Knox administering the Sacrament; *H. W. Williams*, Burns's Cottage.

Of foreign painters the best specimens are—*Bassano*, 2 Portraits; *Boucher*, Mme. de Pompadour; *Giorgione*, *An Archer; *Greuze*, Girl and Dead Canary, Boy with Lesson-Book, Girl with Broken Jar; *Guido-Reni*, Ecce Homo, Venus attired by the Graces; *Francis Hals*, 2 Portraits; *Hobbema*, Landscape; *Murillo*, Boy Drinking; *Rembrandt*, **Hendrikje Stoffels, purchased for £5500 and presented by W. M'Ewan, Esq., M.P.; *Jacob Ruysdael*, Flemish Landscape; *Sustermans*, Marq. Spinola (fine colour); *Teniers*, *Dutch Boors Drinking, Peasants Playing at Skittles; *Ten-Oever*, *Figures Bathing; *Tiepolo*, *Finding of Moses, Antony and Cleopatra; *Titian*, St. Catherine Presenting Flowers to the Infant Saviour, Ariadne in Naxos; *W. Vandevelde*, Sea Fight; *Vandyck*, **Martyrdom of St. Sebastian, Portrait of a Man in Armour, *The Lomellini Family, a fine work, including 5 full-length portraits, etc.; *Veronese*, *Mars and Venus, Venus and Adonis; *Watteau*, French Pastoral, Fête Champêtre. Toy Windmill. *Observe*, also, *Michel Angelo's* 3 wax models; *Chantrey's* bust of Francis Horner, several busts by *Steell;* busts of Lord Brougham and David Wilkie, by *Samuel Joseph;* "Hebe," by *W. Calder Marshall, R.A.*

For other celebrated portraits see National Portrait Gallery, p. 58.

The east side of this building is used as the exhibition rooms of the Royal Scottish Academy, which is open from February to May. There is also a Life School in connection.

rt. is *The New Club*, 85 Princes St. Among its members are the chief nobility and gentry of Scotland.

Oppos. l. in the W. Princes St. Gardens is a marble *Statue* by Steell of *Allan Ramsay* the poet. In these gardens, which have been open to the public since 1876, a military *band* plays once a week in summer. The walks through them under the black rock of the Castle are charming, leading past the remains of the Wellhouse Tower, possibly erected 1361 [cf. p. 37].

rt. are the *Liberal Club* (No. 109), the *Conservative Club* (No. 112), and the *University Club* (No. 127), an excellent club founded 1867. Opposite l. is a *Statue* (seated) *of Sir J. Y. Simpson;* and W. of it an Iona Cross to the memory of *Dean Ramsay* (1793-1872), author of "Reminiscences of Scottish Life and Character," and incumbent of the adjoining *St. John's Epis. Ch.*, built 1818. Its style of architecture is Florid Gothic, with details after the model of St. George's Chapel, Windsor. In 1882 a chancel was added.

Just behind is *St. Cuthbert's Parish Church* (rebuilt 1894, Hippolyte Blanc, archt.), retaining a steeple of 1775. In the S.W. corner of its churchyard is the grave of Thomas de Quincey, "The Opium Eater" (d. 1859).

At the W. end of Princes St. is the **Caledonian Rly. Stat.** (1893-4) with a façade of red sandstone to the E.

(4) **Charlotte Square — George Street—St. Andrew Square—Queen Street.**

By turning N. at the west end of Princes Street we enter **Charlotte Sq.**, a handsome residential square (numerous doctors) on whose W. side is the ponderous **St. George's Ch.** (with a handsome dome), erected 1810-1814 (R. Reid, archt.) at a cost of £33,194. In the centre of the gardens is the national *Monument to the Prince Consort* (by Steell) —an equestrian statue of the Prince, surrounded by figures of the various classes of the community, the aristocracy, the intellectual and teaching class, the working and agricultural class, etc., all in attitudes testifying respect to the Prince's merits. It was unveiled by the Queen, 17th August 1876.

Passing E. along **George St.** a very handsome wide street, at Castle St. is a *Statue of Dr. Chalmers,* also by Steell—a very characteristic likeness. A few yds. l. down *Castle St.* on the E. side is "poor No. 39," *Sir W. Scott's Dwelling-house*, 1800-1826. On quitting it he wrote: "It has sheltered me from the prime of life to its decline."

At *Frederick St.* is a *Statue of Pitt* by Chantrey, and beyond rt. is the **Music Hall** (1843)—containing the principal Concert-Room and the Assembly Rooms—and l. (No. 45) the shop of Mr. Blackwood, the publisher of the "Magazine," and the resort in times past of Prof. Wilson, Lockhart, Hogg, Moir, and many other distinguished writers whose portraits adorn the saloon behind.

At *Hanover St.* is a *Statue of George IV.* by Chantrey, then rt. is the *Commercial Bank*, and l. **St. Andrew's Parish Ch.** (marked by a tall spire), out of which the Free Church seceders marched on 18th May 1843. At the E. end of George St. is a statue of *Bucephalus* by Steell, in **St. Andrew Sq.**, now occupied by shops and large offices. In the centre of the square is a fluted column surmounted by a *Statue* of the 1st *Viscount Melville* (1740-1811), who was impeached by the House of Commons, but acquitted. The statue is 14 ft. high, and the whole is 150 ft. from the ground. It was erected 1828, and cost £8000. On the E. side are the *National Bank*, the *British Linen Co.'s Bank* (a rich front with large figures), and the *Royal Bank*, with a statue of the 4th Earl of Hopetoun. In the N.W. corner is the small but handsome *Stock Exchange*.

North St. Andrew St. leads from the square to the E. end of **Queen St.** where stands the **National Portrait Gallery,** "dedicated" (1890) by J. R. Findlay, Esq., of Aberlour, proprietor of the *Scotsman*, "to the illustration of Scottish History." It cost £40,000, and its donor gave another £10,000 towards its endowment. It is 3 stories high, in the Gothic style of the 13th cent., and of red Corsehill sandstone (R. R. Anderson, archt.).

At the W. end of the ground floor are the rooms of the *Scottish Geographical Society*, and above are the *Portrait Galleries.*[1]

The portraits—a splendid collection—are not only most interesting historically, but include such works of art as *W. Aikman's* John Gay; *Sir W. Beechey's* Sir D. Wilkie; *Thomas Duncan's* Lord Colonsay; *Sir H. Raeburn's* Prof. Wilson and Neil Gow; *Colvin Smith's* Gen. Sir R. Abercromby; *Flaxman's* Statue of Burns; *S. Joseph's* bust of Henry Mackenzie; and a large collection of portrait medallions by James and Wm. Tassie; also a water-colour on ivory of Burns, done at Dumfries the year of his death, etc. There are some fine portraits of his ancestors lent by the D. of Hamilton, and on

[1] Admission Thurs. and Fri., 10-4, 6d.; other week-days, 10-5 free; in winter, 10-4.

the uppermost story drawings of Old Edinburgh, engraved portraits, and a large collection of classical busts.

The eastern half of this building is given up to the very interesting ***Scottish National Museum of Antiquities,**[1] not only a depository of historic relics and objects of value, but, from its excellent arrangement and copious catalogue (price 1s.), a school of instruction in relation to the primitive civilisation of North Britain. Not to dwell on the Egyptian antiquities, the like of which may be seen elsewhere, except to point out a "funereal canopy" in the form of a temple, we pass on to the *Antiquities found in Scotland*, illustrating what are called the Stone, Bronze, and Iron periods. *Observe*, a vast assemblage of stone and bronze axes, and other primitive implements; whorls of spindles used for hand-spinning; querns or hand-mills for grinding corn, which continued in use to the end of the 17th cent. in the north; 3-legged bronze pots for cooking; burnt and glazed stones from *Vitrified Forts;* arms, utensils, ornaments, and other relics found in Picts' houses, brochs, weems (or underground dwellings); relics from Scottish lake-dwellings; from Carlinwark and Dowalton Lochs; *personal ornaments* of gold and silver —armlets, torques, chains, and Celtic brooches; do., found at Sandwick, Orkney, along with *Anglo-Saxon* and *Cufic Coins* of the Caliphs of Bagdad, 10th cent.; Casts of *Sculptured stone monuments and crosses*, including that of Ruthwell (Dumfriesshire), Campbeltown (Argyllshire), and other parts of Scotland; *Memorial Inscriptions* from various parts of Scotland—in Ogham characters from Shetland, Aberdeenshire, etc.; Pictish, from St. Vigeans, Forfarshire; Latin, from Kirkliston (Midlothian), and Kirkmadrine (Wigtownshire); and Scandinavian Runes, from Maeshowe (Orkney), and the Isle of Man; monuments, altars, and inscriptions found on the line of the Roman Wall between Forth and Clyde—a *Sculptured Tablet*, 9 ft. long, representing on one side a sacrifice (Suovetaurilia), on the other Roman Cavalry trampling down the Caledonians, dedicated to the Emperor Antoninus Pius by the 2nd Legion, stating that they had built 4652 paces of the wall; bronze patellæ or saucepans; a Roman oculist's stamp; the *Quigrich* or Pastoral Staff of St. Fillan, of Celtic workmanship and great age, belonging to the Abbey of Glen Dochart; ancient cannon and firearms; *Robert Burns's Pistols*, used by him as an exciseman; a bronze *Battle-axe* found at Bannockburn; Lochaber axes; Flags borne by the Covenanters at Bothwell Brig, etc.; Relics found in the grave of Robert Bruce at Dunfermline in 1818, and a cast of his skull; the *Pulpit* from which John Knox preached; the folding *Stool* which Jenny Geddes threw at the head of the Dean of St. Giles's when he began to read the Liturgy; Relics from the old Tolbooth—fetterlock, girdle, etc.; *The Stool of Repentance*, from Old Greyfriars Church, etc.; the sackcloth gown worn by penitents while standing on the stool, from West Calder; *The Jougs*, a sort of iron collar, from Galashiels Church; various charms against witchcraft; *The Maiden*, an early form of the guillotine, in use during the 16th and 17th cents. — the Regent Morton, erroneously said to have been its inventor, 1581, and the Marquis of Argyll, 1661, were beheaded by it; a brass collar of a Scotch convict condemned for theft and gifted by the Justiciaries as a perpetual serf, as late perhaps as 1701; *Relics of Prince Charles Stuart*—miniatures of him and his family, his ribbon of the Garter, his bagpipes; the sea-chest and carved cocoa-nut cup which belonged to

1 Admission 10-4, Tues., Wed., and Sat. (free); Thur. and Fri. (6d. each).

Alexander Selkirk—the original of Robinson Crusoe, cast away on Juan Fernandez—they came from Largo, his birthplace. This collection of historic and antiquarian relics is well worth the stranger's notice.

Proceeding W. along Queen St. we pass l. the *Philosophical Institution* (estab. 1832), the *Royal College of Physicians* with imposing front, the *United Service Club*, the *Church of Scotland's Offices* (Nos. 21 and 22), and the *Edinburgh Ladies' College* (Nos. 70–73), founded 1695 by the Merchant Co., who manage it. It is now a Day School (with 41 foundations and numerous bursaries) providing superior education for girls of the middle class. Queen St. now consists chiefly of offices, but (rt.) across the gardens are *Abercromby Place* and *Heriot Row*, a favourite residential line of houses. At the W. end of Queen St. below Charlotte Sq. is a *Monument to Catherine Sinclair* (1800-64). Down *Forres St.* (rt.) is **Moray Place,** a spacious circle of fine large houses—in No. 24 Francis Jeffrey lived and died. These names, with those of the neighbouring *Darnaway St.*, *Great Stuart St.*, and *Randolph Cres.*, remind us that the Earl of Moray is superior of this property.

---

(5) **The West End.**

From the W. end of Princes St. we proceed down *Queensferry St.*, W. along the wide *Melville St.* (near which l. is *Free St. George's Ch.*, with a fine clock chime), past a monument to Viscount Melville, to

***St. Mary's Episcopal Cathedral,** probably the largest and grandest Gothic church erected in Great Britain since the Reformation. The undertaking was due in the first instance to a large sum bequeathed for the purpose by two Misses Walker of Coates; the cost of the building amounted to over £110,000. Sir G. G. Scott, the architect, died before the completion of the Cathedral, which was commenced in 1874, and consecrated in 1879. It is a fine example of an Early Pointed cross church, the design having been based on a careful study of ecclesiastical buildings in Scotland and the N. of England. The total length is 260 ft., and the height of the central spire 280 ft. The W. front, which is much admired, is flanked by two towers, which are to be surmounted in due course by smaller spires, as at Lichfield. The interior consists of nave and choir, with aisles and transept, the nave having 7 bays and the choir 4. The nave and transept have waggon-shaped roofs of oak. The details and embellishments throughout are very elaborate and handsome. The *Reredos* was the gift of the ladies of Scotland, and is the work of Miss Grant. The tower contains a peal of 10 bells, cast by Taylor of Loughborough. N. of the building is *East Coates House*, formerly the home of the benefactresses of the Cathedral, now the Choir School. Farther W. is the *Episcopal Training College*, and beyond that

Donaldson's Hospital,[1] the largest and best-situated building of the kind in Edinburgh, and the masterpiece of the architect Playfair. Donaldson was a printer, who died in 1830, and left £200,000 for the education and maintenance of 300 boys and girls. 115 of the children are deaf mutes.

Turning N. by *Douglas Cres.*, and crossing the Water of Leith by *Belford Bridge* (1887) and keeping l. we pass rt. the beautiful *Dean Cemetery* (1845), in which many men of note are buried—*e.g.* Lords Jeffrey, Cockburn, Rutherfurd, both Mackenzies, and Fraser (the last monument a unique piece of art), "Christopher North," Alison the historian, Patrick

[1] Admission on Tuesdays and Fridays, 2.30 to 5, by order from the Treasurer, 61 Castle Street.

Nasmyth (a handsome monument showing the steam-hammer), Russel, editor of the *Scotsman* (a tall obelisk), etc. etc.;—adjoining the cemetery on S.W. is the *Orphan Hospital* (founded 1733), erected 1833 (Hamilton, archt.), which provides a home for fatherless children who attend the public schools. W. of it is *John Watson's Hospital* (1825-28, Burn, archt.), founded in 1759 by a writer to the signet. Here 100 destitute fatherless children of the better class —under 14—are maintained.

We return to Princes St. by the Queensferry Road and see l. (½ m.) **Fettes College**, a good specimen of architecture, imitating successfully the domestic Gothic of Scotland, with a tower and spire over the central archway, projecting oriels, and bartizan turrets. Behind are a Middle Pointed *Hall* and *Chapel*; the whole is of the finest masonry; the capitals, string-courses, window-frames, foliage, and masques are carved with the most perfect finish.

The building, which was opened in 1870, is from the design of the late *David Bryce*, and cost about £150,000, the funds having been bequeathed (in 1836) by Sir William Fettes, a rich banker, to found an educational institution. It is a public school for the education of boys of the upper classes, 50 being foundationers. The system adopted is from the best parts of the schemes of Eton, Winchester, and Rugby, to furnish at a moderate cost an education fit for sons of gentlemen.

A little to the W. of it is *St. Cuthbert's Poorhouse.* To the E. of it is a **Public Park**, with handsome stone *Gateways*, S. of which is the *Academy Cricket Field*, one of the finest in Scotland. From *Comely Bank*, in front of Fettes College, a *Cable Tramway* runs to Princes St. through the suburb of **Stockbridge**.

We pass rt. *Daniel Stewart's Hospital* (founded 1814), of Elizabethan architecture (1849-53)—now another boys' day school managed by the Merchant Co.—and *Trinity Epis. Ch.* at the end of the **Dean Bridge**, which crosses the *Water of Leith* at a height of 106 ft. above its bed. It was built in 1832, one of Telford's best designs, consisting of four arches, each of 96 ft. span. On the rt. bank below and seen l. from the bridge is a Doric temple, raised above *St. Bernard's Mineral Well* in 1789, and containing a statue of Hygeia. The design was by Nasmyth, an imitation of the Sibyl's Temple at Tivoli. It was tastefully restored at a cost of £5000 by the late Mr. W. Nelson 1887, who erected a new Statue of the Goddess in marble by D. W. Stevenson, R.S.A.

rt. lies the quaint *Water of Leith village*, with a modern "Court" of model workmen's houses erected by J. R. Findlay, Esq.

ENVIRONS, DRIVES, AND WALKS.

See Map, p. 66.

(6) The Queen's Drive, Arthur's Seat, and the South Side.

The suburban circular rly. from Wav. Stat. by *Portobello, Duddingston, Newington, Blackford Hill, Morningside, Gorgie,* and *Haymarket*, or *vice versa*, every ½ hr., takes conveniently to the S. side.

Enter the *Queen's Park* at Holyrood and drive E. Observe rt. the path known as the *Radical Road*—given to the unemployed to make in 1819—under the bold trap Cliffs of *Salisbury Crags* (origin of name uncertain). Close by is an elegant Gothic vault called *St. Margaret's Well* (dating from James IV.'s days, and brought from Restalrig [p. 66], 1860), behind which is the *Hunter's Bog*, now a rifle range. l. is the Parade Ground and rt. *St. Margaret's Loch* overlooked by *St. Anthony's Chapel*, to the W. of which runs the path up *Arthur's Seat* (p. 38), the geology[1] of which showing sand-

[1] See p. 38, note.

stone, etc., strata of Lower Carboniferous age, and volcanic eruptions of different dates, is exceedingly interesting but complicated. Near this stood "Muschat's Cairn." The road ascends to *Dunsappie Loch*, from which the hill may most easily be climbed by pedestrians. Below l. is the pretty village of *Duddingston*, at the gate of whose Norman Ch. (where John Thomson, 1778-1840, the landscape painter, was minister) is an excellent example of a "loupin'-on stane" ascended by steps. Here, too, hang the *jougs*—an iron pillory collar, from an old Celtic word cognate to the Latin *jugum*, and in all probability the "jug" that in thieves' slang signifies prison. *Duddingston Loch* is a favourite resort of skaters and curlers. E. of it is *Duddingston Ho.* (D. of Abercorn) in a well-wooded park (1768), and W. is the interesting mansion of *Prestonfield* built 1687 (Sir W. Bruce, archt., cf. pp. 50, 192). From this point the road, passing above the porphyritic cliffs of "Samson's Ribs," descends to St. Leonard's gate, beyond which is St. Leonard's Hill with *Jeanie Deans's Cottage.* This whole locality is replete with associations of "The Heart of Midlothian." Passing through this gate we have l. *St. Leonard's Ho.* (Mrs. T. Nelson) and beyond, *Salisbury Green* (Mrs. W. Nelson); rt. Messrs. Bartholomew's *Geographical Institute Works* and the extensive *Printing Works* of Messrs. T. Nelson and Sons. Proceeding W. by *Salisbury Place*, in which is the **Longmore Hospital** for Incurables, we enter *Grange Road*, behind which rt. is *The Sciennes*, so called after Catherine of Siena, a Convent in whose honour lies 1 m. W. Passing through "*The Grange*," with a Cemetery, where Chalmers, Guthrie, Hugh Miller, Duff (the Indian Missionary), Wm. Nelson, etc., are buried, we reach the pleasant suburb of **Morningside**, with numerous fine villas in grounds. A stone built into the wall beside the Parish Ch. is said to be the *Bore Stone* which supported the standard while the army was mustering here before Flodden. ¼ m. W. is *Merchiston Cas.*, the birthplace of Napier, the inventor of logarithms (1550-1617).

---

(7) **North Side.—Leith, Newhaven, Trinity, and Granton.**

Suburban Rly. to Trinity, Newhaven, and Leith from Cal. Rly. Stat. (20 min.) is recommended for its views of Edinburgh. There are also trains from Waverley Stat. to Leith and to Trinity and Granton Pier. Tram cars along Princes St. to Leith and Newhaven, and cable cars from Mound to Golden Acre, thence omnibus to Trinity and Newhaven or Granton.

LEITH✲, a Parl. Burgh, and by pop. the 5th largest town in Scotland, lies 2 m. N.E. of Edinburgh, of which it has been the Port since the days of Robert Bruce. It has witnessed the landing of many a royal personage. In 1561 Mary Queen of Scots was received with great ceremony on her return from France; and George IV. landed here in 1822, an event which is well described in Sir Walter Scott's Life. In 1544 Leith was sacked by the English under Lord Hertford. In 1560 the French raised here a fortress, in which they planted a strong garrison to maintain the authority of the Guises in Scotland. Queen Elizabeth despatched a fleet to expel them from Leith. It carries on a very great trade in corn and timber from the Baltic, besides wine from France and Spain, and esparto (for paper) from Oran and Algeria. The Wine trade has had its chief seat here from earliest history, arising in great measure from its connection with France, and the more recent development of Scotch Whisky-blending has now assumed vast proportions, especially for export. There are large manufactures of cordage, sailcloth, soap, oil-cake, etc. Besides these, there are shipbuilding yards, engineering works, and one of the largest *Flour Mills* in the country, that of A. and R. Tod.

Leith is also celebrated for the ability with which its *Institutions* are conducted. The *Sailors' Home and Sailors' Rest*, the *Infirmary*, *Trinity House*, and *Industrial Schools* are all model buildings and well worthy of inspection.

The number of *Steamers* belonging to Leith is very large—trading to American, Baltic, Mediterranean, and Eastern Ports. Passenger steamers sail to Aberdeen, Orkney, and Shetland, to London, to Norway, Hamburg, Copenhagen, Holland, etc. The Galloway Steam Packet Co. have a fleet of swift steamers which in summer sail to Aberdour, S. Queensferry, Alloa, Stirling, Elie, etc.

The old harbour, the estuary of the black and foul Water of Leith ("quasi *Lethe*," quoth Dr. Johnson, "because Scotchmen embarking here forget their own country"), divides the town into S. and N. Leith. Opening from it to the W. are the *Wet Docks* (opened 1806 and 1817), and the *Victoria Dock* (opened 1852); to the E. are the *Prince of Wales Graving Dock*, and the *Albert* and *Edinburgh Docks*, excavated out of the east sands, all due to the enterprise of the Leith Dock Commission. The *Albert* (opened 1869) has a water area of 11 acres, and the *Edinburgh Dock* (opened 1881) has an area of nearly 17 acres. On its quays may be seen Sir William Armstrong's Scientific Hydraulic Cranes for raising cargoes. The entrance from the sea to the Docks and Harbour is between two *Piers* 1000 yards long. Near the mouth of the Harbour a *Martello Tower* rises out of the sea. *Leith Fort*, to the W., is now of no strength as a defence—little more than an Artillery Barrack. Of the three citadels built by Cromwell for keeping the Scots in order, only an archway remains.

Leith was the cradle of the *Gladstone* family. There is a *Church* here founded by them. On *Leith Links*, S.E. of the town, Charles I. was playing golf when news of the Irish Rebellion (1641) was brought him.

To the W. of Leith is **Newhaven** ✲, celebrated for its fishing and its fish-dinners. An interesting stone with naval devices surmounted by the thistle and date 1588, is built into the wall of *Main St.* near the Harbour. The fishwives of the village are noted for their peculiar costume, and may be seen in all parts of Edinburgh selling fish, the produce of their husbands' or fathers' labour. Their high reputation for morality (see Chas. Reade's novel *Christie Johnstone*), though exaggerated, is not wholly undeserved. The Newhaven fishers are of Jutland origin, and are singularly conservative in their household customs. They rarely marry outside of their own race; the men are celebrated for their skilful seamanship and hardy daring; the women are noted for their keenness in driving a bargain (*vide* "The Antiquary"). The sytem of *Steam Trawling* is, however, effecting a silent revolution in their trade and habits.

Between Newhaven and Granton lies **Trinity**, a favourite suburb, with a *Chain Pier* (opened when Geo. IV. visited Edin. 1822) used by bathers.

Farther W. is **Granton** ✲, the point at which the Earl of Hertford disembarked his troops when he invaded Scotland in 1544. The excellent *Pier*, built entirely at the expense of the late Duke of Buccleuch, was begun in Nov. 1835, and cost £150,000. It is 1700 ft. in length and from 80 to 160 ft. in breadth, and has the great advantage of being accessible at any state of the tide, and sheltered on three sides by a Breakwater. The Victoria jetty, where the Queen landed and re-embarked in Sept. 1842, is on the W. side, and extends 90 ft. From this pier (on which is the rly. stat.) is the *steam ferry* to Burntisland, almost superseded by the Forth Bridge.

[There is a pleasant walk from Granton along the S. shore of the Firth to *Cramond* (p. 65), and thence back to Edinburgh, or across the river Almond into Dalmeny Park Grounds.]

From Granton return should be made by *Inverleith Row* (along which cable tramcars run), stopping by all means to visit on the way (rt.) the **Royal Botanic Garden** and extensive **Arboretum** beyond [free admission daily], which are remarkable for the excellent way they are managed, the beauty of their walks, the order of their arrangement, their fine trees, and for the pictorial *Views* of Edinburgh which they command. The *Rock Garden* of Alpine flowers demonstrates how such plants may be cultivated with perfect success. The *Palm-houses* and foreign *Fernery* are not surpassed even by Kew. In the Arboretum is *Inverleith Ho.*, now the official residence of the Prof. of Botany, who is Keeper of the Gardens.

Across Inverleith Row is *Warriston Cemetery* where are buried Sir James Simpson, Adam Black, and other distinguished citizens of Edinburgh.

---

(9) **Craigmillar Cas., Braid Hills, Blackford Hill**, etc.

Craigmillar Cas., 3 m. S.E. of Edinburgh, behind Arthur's Seat, is seen crowning a sloping hill; it is both a picturesque object and interesting as a favourite residence of Mary Queen of Scots.

It is ½ m. from Duddingston Rly. Stat. or 1 m. from the tramway terminus.

It consists of the usual square Border-tower, to the east side of which wings and a tall curtain wall, flanked by round towers, have been added in front. In the central tower are 2 great vaulted halls, and, adjoining the tower, a vaulted room called Queen Mary's Chamber. The staircase was added in 16th cent., but the open well of the older stair gapes beside it. It belonged originally to the Prestons, from whom it passed, 1760, to Sir John Gilmour, and is still in possession of his descendants. The view of Edinburgh and the country around is very striking. Craigmillar was used as a prison for John, Earl of Mar, brother to James III., in 1477, and here he is said to have been bled to death. According to Drummond of Hawthornden, however, he was seized with a severe fever, and either bled too freely, or in a fit of delirium tore off the bandages. The castle was occupied by James V. during his minority, and Mary lived here for several months after the death of Rizzio, 1566. At a secret meeting held here between her and Murray, Lethington, and Bothwell, it was proposed to rid "her of her ungrateful husband" by a *divorcement*; but she refused to listen, and protested against any step by which "spot might be laid on her honour"; nevertheless a bond was signed here, 1567, to secure his death, by Argyll, Huntly, Maitland, and Bothwell. To this place also she was brought a prisoner after the battle of Carberry.

Niddry House, 1 m. N.E. of Craigmillar, is the seat of Col. Wauchope, Mr. Gladstone's opponent in the Midlothian Campaign of 1892.

A charming road with varied views leads W. in 4½ m. from Craigmillar past **Liberton** (*Leper's Town*) village with *Parish Ch.*—a conspicuous landmark from Edinburgh—and large *Industrial School*, and through "the furzy hills of Braid" to *Morningside* (p. 62).

The **Braid Hills** (l.) with *Golf Course* and *Ride*, and **Blackford Hill** (rt.), the view from which Scott has so well described in "Marmion," and upon which a new **Observatory** (for the astronomical appliances from Dunecht presented to Edinburgh by the Earl of Crawford) is being (1894) erected, are both public parks and splendid recreation grounds for the citizens of Edinburgh.

---

(9) To **Cramond Bridge, Dalmeny**, and **Forth Bridge**, 8 m.

[Coach from Princes St. almost hourly, fare 1s., return 1s. 6d. For trains to Dalmeny and Forth Bridge, see p. 178.]

For the Dean Bridge and first mile of Queensferry Road, see p. 61.

1½ m. rt. is *Craigleith Quarry*

(with rly. stat. l.), whence came the stones for building large part of the New Town of Edinburgh. The stone is a sandstone of the carboniferous period, and is remarkable for its fossil trees, one of which, lying in a slanting position, and upwards of 60 feet in length, may now be seen in the Royal Botanic Gardens, Edinburgh.

Just beyond l. is *Ravelston Ho.* (Miss Murray Gartshore), only seen from the road to the S., and beyond is *Blackhall* village.

At 2 m. *Craigcrook*, formerly the residence of Lord Jeffrey, beautifully situated under the N. side of Corstorphine Hill, lies ½ m. left.

[At 3 m. a road strikes rt. in 1¾ m. passing l. *Barnton Estate* (Sir James Maitland, Bt.), now being feued, to which there is a rly. (1894) from Cal. stat., and rt. *Davidson's Mains* village, *Lauriston Cas.* (T. M. Crawford, Esq.), and *Cramond Ho.* (Col. J. C. Craigie Halkett) to **Cramond**,[1] pleasingly situated at the mouth of the *Almond Water*. *Cramond Island* ¾ m. N. can be reached on foot at low tide.]

At 4¾ m. *Cammo Ho.* or *New Saughton*, lies ½ m. l., the *Almond Water* is crossed (1 m. above its mouth) by **Cramond Bridge**[2] and Linlithgowshire is entered. It was on the predecessor of the *Old Bridge* (rt.), which itself bears date 1619, although frequently "repaired by both shires," that James V., attacked while wandering in disguise, was rescued by Jock Howieson the miller, who furnished him with water and a towel to cleanse his face from the blood. He was rewarded with the property on condition that he or his successors should be ready to present a basin and ewer for the king to wash his hands whenever he should come to Holyrood or cross the Bridge of Cramond. In 1822 the descendant of this man (Howieson Craufurd) fulfilled the condition to George IV. with a silver basin and ewer still extant.

Across the bridge l. is *Craigiehall* (J. C. Hope Vere, Esq.), and rt. the entrance to **Dalmeny Park**[1] (Earl of Rosebery).

The house is modern. It is ornamented with fine woods and many noble trees growing close down to the Firth of Forth. On the shore stands *Barnbougle Castle*, a magnificent structure (1881-2), in which are incorporated the remains of an ancient castle. It is intended chiefly as a place for entertaining guests, not as a residence. The original castle was sold by the Moubrays in the 17th cent. to Sir Archibald Primrose, and was dismantled by the 3rd Earl of Rosebery in 1760.

At 7 m. the *Village of* **Dalmeny** with a beautiful little **Romanesque Ch.** [p. 178] lies ½ m. l.

Descending the steep "*Hawes Brae*" and passing under the Forth Bridge Viaduct, we reach 8 m. *Hawes Inn*, an ancient hostelry, bearing dates on its back gable of 1588 and 1633, on the outskirts of **S. Queensferry** [p. 202]. Here Jonathan Oldbuck and young Lovell began their friendship, see "The Antiquary."

The **Forth Bridge**, see p. 178, is well seen from the steam launch which sails from here.

---

(10) To **Rosslyn Chapel** and **Castle** and **Hawthornden**, by rail, see pp. 72 and 76. Also Circular Route by *Coach* daily (in summer), from E. end of Princes St.

---

(11) To **Stirling** by Steamer from Leith — daily in summer, if and when the tide permits. This sail, described in Rte. 37, affords excel-

1 Coach 3 times daily from Register Ho. Edinburgh.

2 *Cramond Bridge Stat.* is ¾ m. E.

1 Pedestrians are allowed to walk through when the Earl is not at home; orders for driving from Tods, Murray, and Jamieson, W.S., 66 Queen St.

lent views of the Forth Bridge and of the Windings of the Forth.

---

(12) **The Pentland Hills** afford numerous pedestrian expeditions within moderate compass. The best starting-points are Colinton, Currie, Balerno, and Midcalder Stats. (Rte. 9) on the N.W. side; and Penicuik and Broomlee Stats. (Rte. 6) on the S.E. The principal routes are

(*a*) From *Colinton* by Bonally Ho. or from *Currie* by Currie Moor to *Glencorse Reservoir* (both 3¾ m.); thence rt. by *Loganlee Reservoir* to a charming nook (with a waterfall), erroneously called Habbie's Howe, 6½ m., *Bavelaw Cas.* (p. 88) 8 m., and *Balerno* 11 m.; or l. by Flotterstone Bridge 5¼ m. (7 m. by road from Edinburgh) to *Glencorse Stat.* 7 m.

(*b*) From *Penicuik* by *Penicuik Ho.* and *Coates Farm* to the Biggar Road 2¼ m.; ¼ m. W. ascend the *Pass* between (l.) *Scaldlaw* (1898 ft.)—the highest of the Pentlands—and rt. *Carnethy* (1890 ft.). [From the top (1456 ft.) 3½ m. either of these hills—commanding fine views—may be ascended in ¼ hr.] Descend to the *Loganlee Reservoir* 4 m., where Route (*a*) is joined. *Balerno* is 9 m. *Currie* or *Colinton* 10 m.

(*c*) From *Balerno* by Bavelaw and over the shoulder (1500 ft.) of the *West Kip* to *Nine Mile Burn* ✲ 7 m. and *Penicuik* ✲ 11½ m.

(*d*) From *Balerno* or *Midcalder Stat.* by the "Bore Stane" (1300 ft.) and the head-waters of the N. Esk to *Carlops* ✲ 9½ m.; thence—visiting rt. after ½ m. the real *Habbie's Howe* of the "Gentle Shepherd" in the grounds of Newhall—to Penicuik 15½ m.

(*e*) From *Midcalder Stat.* by the "Cauld Stane Slap" (1430 ft.) to *West Linton* ✲ and *Broomlee Stat.* (p. 78) 13 m.

The Rights of Way Society's signposts mark all these routes. See their publication "The Pentland Hills—their paths and passes" (with a map), 1s. (The distances there are slightly exaggerated.)

ROUTE 5.

Edinburgh to Portobello, Musselburgh, Inveresk, Macmerry, Prestonpans, Longniddry (for Haddington), Drem and North Berwick. N.B.R.

Trains to Portobello (3 m.) every few minutes; to Musselburgh (6 m.) almost hourly in 25 min.; to Macmerry (13½ m.) 2 or 3 times daily in 45 min.; to Haddington (18 m.) 8 times daily in 50 min.; to North Berwick (22½ m.) 8 times daily in 40-60 min. All distances are from Edin.

Leaving the **Waverley Stat.** eastwards, with l. the Prison and rt. the Gasworks, the train passes through a tunnel under the Calton Hill. At its E. end the line to Granton and Leith strikes off l.; rt. a good view is obtained of *Holyrood Palace* and *Arthur's Seat.* Passing the engine sheds at St. Margaret's, we have rt. the Cavalry barracks of *Piershill* and l. *Piershill Stat.* on a loopline and *Restalrig Ch.* a very early ecclesiastical foundation with an interesting history. It was destroyed 1560 as a monument of idolatry; but was partially restored 1836. Among the old remains is a fine octagonal crypt, claimed by the E. of Moray but scandalously neglected and filled up with earth containing coffins. Here Logan, one of the Gowrie conspirators (pp. 6, 70, 195), is buried. In the neighbourhood are the sewer-irrigated *Craigentinny Meadows.* Large clay fields rt. and pottery works l. are seen before reaching

3 m. **Portobello Stat.** a seaside town and second-rate watering-place with *Promenade Pier* (1250 ft. long, erected 1871) and extensive sands crowded in summer with bathing-machines, donkeys, and trippers. Equestrians from Edinburgh greatly enjoy, like Sir Walter Scott, the gallops which these sands afford at low tide. Its eccentric name was given to this town by a sailor who had taken part in the capture

of the American town (1739) and built the first house here. Beyond the stat. the Waverley Route by Eskbank, etc., to Carlisle turns off rt. (Rtes. 6 and 1).

3¾ m. **Joppa Stat.**, now a suburb of Portobello.

4¾ m. **Newhailes Stat.**

[*Branch* N. in 1¼ m., passing l. *Newhailes Ho.*,—a fine old mansion built by Sir D. Dalrymple (Lord Hailes) and still containing his library and many good family portraits,—and crossing the Esk to **Musselburgh**✲, "an old-world, old fashioned, half fishing, half manufacturing town," and a favourite resort of the Edinburgh citizens for the purposes of golf. The town is named from a bed or "broch" of mussels at the mouth of the Esk. This will explain the meaning of an old rhyme, common in this place :—

"Musselburgh was a broch
When Edinbroch was nane,
And Musselburgh shall be a broch,
When Edinbroch is gane."—*R. C.*

On the W., across the Esk, is the village of **Fisherrow**, inhabited chiefly by fishermen and their families, and connected with the town by 2 foot and one driving bridge. Of the former, one is very steep and old, and is believed by some antiquaries to be of Roman origin. The last was built by Rennie, and near it is a monument to Dr. Moir (1798-1851), the "Delta" of Blackwood, who was born at Musselburgh.

Behind the town is *Pinkie Ho.* (Gen. Sir Wm. Hope, Bt.), an interesting and well-preserved old mansion, at one time a country seat of the Abbot of Dunfermline.

A large part of it shows, unaltered, the architecture of the Jacobean era. In front is a fountain, topped by a crown of two crossed arches. The original building was a square tower, to which it seems the rest was added, in 1613, by Alexander Seton, Earl of Dunfermline and Chancellor of Scotland, as an inscription modestly testifies: "Non ad animi sed fortunarum et agelli modum." In the interior are some fine apartments, particularly the painted gallery, which is an arched room 120 ft. in length, and lighted by an oriel window, the roof being covered with paintings and inscriptions. Prince Charlie slept here the night after Prestonpans.

Hard by are the *Links*, headquarters since 1774 of various golf clubs and bordered by residential villas. Here are held the Edinburgh races, and here Cromwell had his camp after the battle of Dunbar, 1650.]

6½ m. **Inveresk Stat.** The parish, with ch. standing on the top of the hill l., includes Musselburgh.

[Before reaching this stat. a line branches rt. to 7½ m. **Smeaton Stat.** with collieries in the neighbourhood, for the benefit of which there is a line to Dalkeith, etc. l. is *Carberry Tower*, the seat of Lord Elphinstone — built 1579 but enlarged and modernised. To the E. is **Carberry Hill** where Mary Queen of Scots after being defeated surrendered (1567) to the rebel lords, by whom she was immediately sent to Lochleven Castle. The line trends E. passing l. *Elphinstone Tower* (14th or 15th cent.) to

11½ m. **Ormiston Stat.** a colliery village, birthplace of Dr. Moffat the African missionary (1795-1883), whose statue has been erected here by public subscription. S. lie (1½ m.) *Ormiston Hall* (Earl of Hopetoun), (2½ m.) *Preston Hall* (H. Callendar Esq.), and (3 m.), *Oxenfoord Castle* (Earl of Stair), in the valley of the Tyne.

12½ m. **Winton Stat.** with collieries. S.E. lie (¾ m.) *Winton Ho.* (Mr. and Mrs. Hamilton Ogilvy)—seat of the Earls of Winton down to their attainder, 1716—a fine old mansion, with elegant round tower and ornamented chimneys, nearly hidden by a modern house of Wyatt's, and (1 m.) *Old Pencaitland Ch.*, and (2½ m.) *Salton Hall* at the junc. of the Tyne and the Humbie, 3 m. up which is *Humbie Ho.* (Lord Polwarth).

13½ m. **Macmerry Stat.** near Tranent (below) with Iron works.]

We pass rt. the site of the *Battle of Pinkie*, 10th Sept. 1547, where the English under the Protector Somerset almost exterminated the Scotch army. Beyond is *Carberry* (above). A road rt. leads to the ruins of *Dolphinston Castle* before we reach

9½ m. **Prestonpans Stat.** (for **Tranent**). Tranent is about 1 m. S.; l. is the village of *Preston*, and ½ m. N., on the shore of the Firth of Forth is Prestonpans. It and Tranent are both dingy places, and depend on the collieries, as they once did on the salt *Pans*, which supplied the E. of Scotland with salt. l. of the station is *Preston Tower*, the sole remnant of an ancient fortalice, supposed to have been an outpost of the Earls of Home. The castle, of which this was the keep, was burned by the Earl of Hertford in 1544, and again by Cromwell in 1650. *Preston Cross*, an interesting erection in the immediate neighbourhood, said to have been acquired by the Chapmen of the Lothians in 1636, is recognised by their descendants still as a centre of merrymaking and interchange of salutations every year on the 1st of July. Beyond the tower is *Preston Grange*, formerly the property of Wm. Grant, Lord Prestongrange, the 2nd Lord of Session of that name. His daughter married Sir George Suttie, in whose family the place still remains. Over the entrance is their motto: "Nothing hazard, nothing have." Rt. close to the stat. is *Bankton House*, occupying the site of the headquarters of Col. Gardiner, who fell at the *Battle of Prestonpans*, fighting against the Highlanders. He was carried into Tranent Manse, died there and is buried in the churchyard. An *Obelisk* to his memory stands (rt.) within an avenue close to the railway. The *Battlefield* where Prince Charles Stuart defeated the royal forces under Sir John Cope, Sept. 21., 1745, lies l. 1 m. after passing the stat. The Highlanders, led across the morass from Tranent by a friendly laird, surprised the royal forces, and by their furious charge decided the battle in 10 min., losing 30 men to 400 killed on the other side. (See *Lord Mahon's* "History of the '45," and "Waverley.")

At 11 m. l. is *Seton*, which gave its name and title to one of the oldest and most distinguished families of the Scottish nobility. A hideous modern house replaces one which was the frequent resort of James VI. and Charles I. Queen Mary repaired hither, 1567, after the murder of Darnley. The party included Bothwell and his supporters. Near the house is a small old ch. in ruins, in which are several monuments to past members of the family. The last Seton, Earl of Winton, was attainted in 1716 (above), and the title has since become merged in that of Eglinton. Of the *Church*, founded in the 14th cent. but never completed beyond the chancel, transepts, tower, and an unfinished spire, there remains the fine 3-sided apse (restored along with the choir, by the late Earl of Wemyss), which contains recumbent effigies of George, 2nd Lord Seton (in armour), who rendered the Church collegiate 1493, and of his wife. The roof is vaulted and ribbed. The architecture is mixed, but principally Dec., and the tracery of the windows is remarkably good.

13 m. **Longniddry Stat.**

[Branch to Haddington (p. 69).]

John Knox was private tutor in the village here 1543-47 and preached in the church.

[Coach twice daily N. passing *Gosford Ho.* (below), **Aberlady** village [3 m.] (in whose bay Napoleon meant to land the French troops!), with *Luffness Ho.* (H. W. Hope, Esq.), and *Golf Links* (private), to **Gullane** ✲ village 5½ m. where there are *Golf Links* (public).

At **Muirfield** (½ m. farther E.) the Hon. Company of Golfers now have their headquarters and private links.]

---

2 m. S. of Longniddry is the village of *Gladsmuir*, at which place Dr. Robertson (1721-93) held the living, and wrote his "History of Scotland." George Heriot's family belonged to this place.

[Branch S. E. in 5 m. to **Haddington Stat.** ✲, a parl. burgh, prettily situated on the Tyne. It gives its name to the county of East Lothian, and is one of the best grain-markets in Scotland. The name is derived from Ada, Countess of Northumberland, mother of Malcolm IV. and William the Lion, who founded a nunnery here 1178, which latter may still be traced in "Nungate," the name of the suburb on the E. bank of the river. On the S. side of the town, in a neatly kept churchyard near the river, stands the *Parish Church*, formerly the nave (of 5 stately bays, restored 1892) of the cross church of the Franciscan Friary. The choir and transepts are in ruins and open to the sky. The *Tower* (90 ft. high) at the crossing, now a mere shell, has its upper story pierced with narrow windows in triplets, whence it was called "*The Lamp of Lothian.*" *Obs.* the W. end—a fine late pointed façade and doorway, crowned by a window of peculiar tracery, and an open parapet above. A chapel shut off from the transept contains the tombs of the Maitland family—one of marble to the Duke of Lauderdale, 1682. In the churchyard is the tomb of Mrs. Carlyle (d. 1866), wife of Thomas Carlyle. Haddington was the birthplace (1812) of Dr. Samuel Smiles, the well-known writer.

The quarter of Haddington beyond the Tyne, called Gifford Gate, was the birthplace of John Knox, 1505. He was educated at the school here. As a memorial to him the Knox Institute was built, 1879, and a statue of the Reformer occupies a niche in the front. A tree has also been planted to mark the site of his birthplace. Near the stat. is a monumental statue of the late Robert Fergusson of Raith.

Near the town are the residences of *Alderston; Amisfield* (Earl of Wemyss), and *Stevenston* (Sir R. C. Sinclair, Bt.)

The most interesting place near this is (1 m. S.) Lethington, or *Lennoxlove* (Lord Blantyre), so called from Frances, Duchess of Lennox, one of the beauties of King Charles II.'s Court. There is a portrait of her in the house by Lely. The house consists of a grand old tower, to which a modern mansion has been added. It stands in the midst of magnificent old trees, the walks—one of which is called "The Politician's Walk," after "Secretary Lethington" — extending to the banks of a small burn. An avenue of old silver firs leads to the house. It was originally a seat of the Maitlands of Lethington. John, Duke of Lauderdale, was born here, 1616. *Coalstoun* (Lady Susan Ramsay) just beyond, on a pretty wooded glen, was inherited by the Ramsays, Lords Dalhousie, who possess the jewel called "The Coalstoun pear."

At **Gifford** [Coach from Haddington 2 or 3 times daily], a picturesque village (5 m. S.), with an old market cross, is a handsome broad avenue of limes leading to the entrance gate of **Yester House**, the seat of the Marquis of Tweeddale. It is reached by a pleasant avenue[1] 1 m. long, and adjoining it is an old chapel, now used as a mausoleum. 1½ m. beyond the house the old castle of *Gifford* or *Yester* stands upon a peninsula between the *Hopes Water* on the W. and the *Newlands Burn* on the E.

1 Permission to drive through may be obtained at the Estate Offices in Gifford.

Sir D. Dalrymple, in his "Annals," relates that Hugh Gifford de Yester died in 1267; that under his castle was a capacious cavern, formed by magical art, and called in the county Bo Hall (= Bogey Hall). The real object of the cavern was to obtain a supply of water from the brook, which ran at a considerably lower level. The story of its magical building is told at length in the 3rd canto of "Marmion."]

At 14 m. l. are the ruins of *Redhouse*, a double tower of the year 1500, and behind it *Gosford House* (Earl of Wemyss) with a Gothic Lodge designed by Mr. Billings and therefore nicknamed "Billingsgate." The top only is visible among the plantations. A new house was built close by, but has never been inhabited, and the old one has been restored. There is a good collection of pictures (not open to the public), by *Teniers, Murillo, N. Poussin, Hogarth, Hobbema*, a landscape, an important work; *Ruysdael*, 4 fine landscapes; *J. Romano*, a procession; *Wm. Vandervelde*, Ships at sea in a Breeze; *Lely*, Portrait of a Lady; *Memling*, Head of St. Sebastian; *S. Rosa*, Rocky Landscape; *Velasquez*, Portrait of a Man.

rt. are the **Garleton Hills** (590 ft.), on which is a British fort called *Chesters* (Castra), and an *Obelisk* raised to the memory of the 4th Earl of Hopetoun (1766-1823), a Peninsular hero.

17¾ m. **Drem Stat.** Just beyond, the main line to Berwick (Rte. 2) is left (rt.), the branch line bending N. to

20½ m. **Dirleton Stat.** with 1 m. rt. *Fenton Tower*. 1 mile to the N.W. is the picturesque village of **Dirleton**✲, with a church bearing date 1661, a large village green, and the ruins of a *Castle* built in the 13th cent., and once the property of the De Vaux family.

The grounds in which it stands belong to *Archerfield Ho.*, the property of Mrs. Hamilton Ogilvy, and are well kept up. The gardens (open on Thursdays) are tastefully laid out, in good keeping with the solemn grandeur of the ruins. The original plan of the building, which stands on a rocky elevation, is nearly square. The side toward the S.E. is a continuous wall of great height, with scarcely an embrasure. At the S. extremity is a round tower, and a second towards the N. Each of these springs from a broad base, and becomes narrower as it rises. The entrance to the castle is under a projecting archway, in front of which are the moat and the vestiges of the masonry upon which the old drawbridge rested. The hall in the upper story is roofless, and the kitchen is at one end of it on the same level. The offices and storerooms are on lower stories, whence supplies were raised to the kitchen by a windlass. In 1298 this castle held out for Wallace against Edward I., who detached Bishop Beck to besiege it. After some resistance it surrendered. It subsequently belonged to the Ruthven family, and was the promised bribe that induced Logan of Restalrig to join the Gowrie Conspiracy (1600).

22½ m. **NORTH BERWICK Stat.** ✲ This is a station for the herring-fishery, pleasantly situated on the Firth of Forth, and the most favourite watering-place for the Edinburgh upper classes. There is an E. and a W. bay and the sands are excellent for sea-bathing, but there are no bathing-machines, only cots (private) on the shore. There are extensive *Links* W. of the town, constantly covered by golf-players. It is a very pleasant summer residence, without the usual fuss of a fashionable watering-place, healthy, with fine sea views of the Bass and other rocky islets, and of the Fife coast in the distance, enlivened by the constant passage of shipping.

On the S. side of the rly. stat. are scant remains of a *Priory* for Cistercian nuns, founded by Duncan 6th Earl of Fife, towards the end of the 12th cent. They consist of part of the refectory, with cellars underneath the kitchen, with its grand old fireplace, and at the E. end a fragment of the chapel is still standing. The ruined archway which formed the entrance is at a little distance. Here it was that the Abbess of St. Hilda stopped while Clara and Marmion went on to Tantallon. (See 5th canto of *Marmion.*)

Near the Harbour is a Celtic Cross, erected by public subscription in memory of Miss Catherine Watson, of Glasgow, aged 19, who saved a boy from drowning, 27th July 1889, at the cost of her own life. A medallion at the base is the work and "loving tribute" of a fellow-student of the Glasgow School of Art.

¾ of an hour's walk to the S. of the town is **North Berwick Law**, a conical hill of felsite 612 ft. high, whence a splendid panorama, including Fife Coast, Arthur's Seat, Pentlands, Dunbar, St. Abb's, Tantallon, and the Bass and Isle of May is obtained on a clear day. The ground to the W. is comparatively flat, so that the prospect reaches from the Pentlands to Ben Lomond. Upon the top are the ruins of a watch-tower, built during the war with France. These "Laws" were probably all used as beacon-hills, and the word seems to be identical with the Derbyshire "Low," derived from the Anglo-Saxon word "Hlæw," a heap, a hill. The cliffs E. of North Berwick consist of volcanic tuffs, like those of Dunbar. The geologist will find no finer sections in the kingdom to illustrate this class of rocks.

From the small hamlet on *Canty Bay* ✲ 2½ m. E. of N. Berwick, a boat or steam launch[1] may be obtained to go to the

Bass Rock, 1½ m. distant, a mass of basalt (350 ft. high) with precipitous sides descending to the sea, and the home of innumerable sea birds.

The landing is slippery, and a little difficult except in very calm weather. A castle upon the island was from early times one of the "strengths" of Scotland, and was used as a prison for English captives in the wars with England, and for some of the Covenanters in 1671. Traces of fortifications and of an old chapel are still to be seen. The island is farmed, the only production being solan geese, which are shot for their feathers.

3 m. E. of N. Berwick, ½ m. beyond Canty Bay, are the ruins of **Tantallon Castle.**

Broad, massive, high, and stretching far,
And held impregnable in war.
On a projecting rock they rose,
And round three sides the ocean flows,
The fourth did battled walls enclose,
 And double mound and fosse.

. . . . . .

Marmion, canto v.

The description there given will be found very accurate. Within a deep natural moat on the S. side was the outer courtyard, one tower of which is still standing. A passage through an archway led into the inner court, where probably were the stables and offices. On the N. side of these was the artificial moat, crossed by a drawbridge, the piers of which are still to be seen on each side of the entrance to the castle. The original gateway has been bricked up, and a small wicket now leads through a narrow passage into the interior. The great tower in the centre is quadrilateral with rounded corners. From it extends to the edge of the rock on each side a solid curtain about 50 ft. high, terminated by lofty towers, each of which enclosed a staircase. The inside of the castle appears to have consisted of three sides of a square. Of the E. wing, which probably contained the chapel, there are no remains except the line of foundations, but of that towards the W. there are portions of banqueting-hall and cellar underneath. The great strength of the place gave rise to the saying, "Ding down Tantallon, and build a brig to the Bass," as feats of equal difficulty. It is not known at what time Tantallon Castle was built. It first belonged to the Earls of Fife, whence it passed to the Menteiths, and at the death of Murdoch Duke of Albany, was forfeited to the crown and conferred upon the Douglas family. After the Earl of Angus had been attainted in 1528, the castle stood a regular siege by James V. Sir Ralph Sadler, the English ambassador, lived here under the Earl of Angus's protection, during his unsuccessful negotiation for mating the infant Mary with Edward VI. The castle was eventually destroyed by Gen. Monk, the Douglas of the day being a Royalist. At the beginning of the 18th cent. the whole of this property was sold to Sir Hew Dalrymple, and is still in possession of his family. The present proprietor has had the well cleared out, the staircase restored, and a gallery made from

[1] 10s. for party of 1-8, 2s. for each additional person.

which a safe and good view may be obtained, and has otherwise done his best to preserve this interesting ruin.

1 m. E. of Tantallon is a dilapidated ruin, which goes by the name of "*Auldhame Church*," and is said to have been St. Baldred's place of abode and death. It was apparently a small monastery, of which the refectory and cellars are alone represented in the ruins. It stands in the grounds of *Seacliffe House* (R. W. Laidlay, Esq.), the entrance to which is passed l. as we drive S. to **Whitekirk** (3 m. from Tantallon), with a fine old (pre-Reformation) Church.

The direct road from N. Berwick to Whitekirk (5 m.) is prettier, passing *Luchie Ho.*, the seat of Sir W. H. Dalrymple, Bt. 2 m. beyond Whitekirk is *Tyninghame Ho.* (see p. 8).

ROUTE 6.

Edinburgh to Millerhill, Roslin, Dalkeith, Eskbank, Lasswade, Hawthornden, Penicuik, Peebles, Innerleithen, and Galashiels. N.B.R.

Edinburgh to Roslin 12 m. (8 m. by road) in 35 min., 6 trains daily.

Edinburgh to Dalkeith or Eskbank 8½ m. in 25 min., almost hourly.

Edinburgh to Lasswade and Polton 11 m. in 35 min., 6 trains daily.

Edinburgh to Peebles 27 m. in 1 hr. 20 min., and Innerleithen 33½ m. in 1 hr. 35 min., 5 trains daily.

The *direct* route to Galashiels is by Rte. 1.

The distances given below are all from Edinburgh.

3 m. **Portobello Stat.** (p. 66), thence the line trends S. away from the East Coast line, passing **New Craighall** mining village, before which the suburban line branches rt. and 1 m. E. of which is *Niddrie Ho.* (Col. Wauchope), to

6¼ m. **Millerhill Stat.** 1½ m. E. is *Edmonstone Ho.* (Sir J. D. Don Wauchope, Bt.)

[*Branch* rt. to **Roslin**,[1] etc. The line passes (rt.) *Drum Ho.* before

8½ m. **Gilmerton Stat.**, near which is a large artificial cavern in the limestone, supposed to have been the original of Wayland Smith's cave in "Kenilworth."

10¼ m. **Loanhead Stat.** (6 m. by road; *Coach* 4 times daily from Edinburgh), a large mining village. 1 m. N.E. of it are *Straiton Oil Works*, and ½ m. further N. is *Burdiehouse*, interesting to the geologist as being the locale of the celebrated fresh-water limestone of the carboniferous group, ably described by Dr. Hibbert, and prolific in estuarine fossils and plants. Among them will be found Palæoniscus, Megalichthys, Gyracanthus, and large beds of Cyprides.

To the rt. is Wishart's monument in Dryden Park, before reaching

12¼ m. (8 m. by road) **Roslin Stat.** ✡ in the village (famous for strawberries), and only ½ m. from the *Chapel* which overlooks Roslin Glen and is quite near Rosslyn Castle.

[Rosslyn Castle Stat. on the Penicuik line (p. 76), and Roslynlee Stat. on the Peebles line (p. 77), are both fully 1 m. off across the valley.]

****Rosslyn Chapel.**[2] It is a common error to speak of this building as merely a chapel. From the first it was designed as a collegiate church, dedicated to St. Matthew, with a provost, 6 prebendaries, and 2 choristers. It was founded, 1450, by William St. Clair, 3rd Earl of Orkney (and subsequently of Caithness), Grand Master of the Masons of Scotland, but was unfinished at his death, 1484, and was carried on by his son Wm. Earl of Caithness. It is merely the choir of a cruciform church, of which the transept was begun but never finished. It is well worth

[1] See Map, p. 66.

[2] Admission, 10-6 daily, except Sunday, 1s. each person. Sunday (Epis. Ch. of Scotland) Services, 12 and 3.30.

while to walk round the outside, to inspect the carvings, flying buttresses, and pinnacles. The Ch. consists of a choir of 5 bays with aisles, and the pier arches are continued behind the altar, so as to form a low Lady Chapel like that of Glasgow Cathedral, the plan of which seems to have been copied here. Two of these arches support the E. window. The roof of this retro-choir is vaulted and groined in 4 bays, and from the central ribs descend great carved pendants, giving a very rich effect. This chapel

"is certainly unclassable as a whole, being unlike any other building in Great Britain of its age; but if its details are minutely examined they will be found to accord most completely, in the ornamental work, with the style then prevalent, though debased by the clumsiness of the parts and their want of proportion to each other."—RICKMAN.

The workmen employed on it by the founders were foreigners, and, from a comparison of this work with others on the Continent, it is probable that the artificers were brought from the N. of Spain. *Fergusson* ("Architecture," vol. ii.) shows that it resembles parts of Burgos, while it has the greatest affinity to the chapel at Belem in Portugal. Still there is in parts a considerable clumsiness and scamping, both in the carving and construction, that would lead us to believe that the foreign artificers left a good deal to incapable pupils. The chapel owes its beauty entirely to the profuseness of its decorations, for the original plan and proportions are far from pleasing.

"It has little pretension to symmetry, and its squat, stumpy outline is a great contrast to the slender grace of Melrose. All the beauties of Roslin are superinduced on the design in the shape of mouldings and incrustations."—BILLINGS.

The length of the chapel internally is only 68 ft., and its breadth 35 ft. The central aisle is 15 ft. wide, 40 ft. high, and has the southern peculiarity of a barrel vault, with only transverse ribs, just as may be seen in the S. of France. Upon this stone vault the roofing slabs are laid, and follow its curves without intervening timber. The aisles are roofed with cross-vaults rising from straight stone transoms, supported by the piers and outer walls, and covered with elaborate bas-reliefs of Scripture subjects rudely carved. The variety of design in each compartment becomes perfectly bewildering. The niches on a line with the clerestory were occupied by statues of the 12 Apostles and the Virgin. On one of the transoms across the aisle are represented the 7 Deadly Sins, and on the opposite side are the Cardinal Virtues. The mouldings on the arch-lintels, behind the altar, portray the Angelic choir playing on various instruments, and include an angel performing on the bagpipes, the Martyrdom of St. Sebastian, etc. At the E. end of the S. aisle is the **'*Prentice Pillar*, ornamented with a spiral festoon of flowers and foliage more elaborately carved than the rest. It received its name from a story (not uncommon) that the 'prentice executed it while the master had gone to Rome for a pattern, and was killed on the return of the latter in a fit of jealousy. The story of the foundation of the chapel is that Sir William St. Clair made a rash bet of his life against the Rosslyn property, that his dogs Help and Hold would run down a stag before it passed a certain brook. The stag was already in the water when the dogs, excited by the desperate cries of their master, made a tremendous spring, and pulled it down before it could mount the opposite bank. An incised slab in the pavement bearing the figure of a knight in armour, attributed to Sir Wm. St. Clair, is evidently of later date. There is a legend (not founded in fact) that the lords of Rosslyn were buried in full armour, and that on the night preceding the death of any of the family the chapel appeared on fire, an illusion which is supposed to arise from the peculiar position of the chapel admitting the rays of the sun point blank through the windows of both sides.

"Blazed battlement and turret high,
Blazed every rose-carved buttress fair;
So blaze they still when fate is nigh
The lordly line of high St. Clair."
SCOTT's Ballad of *Rosabelle*.

In 1881 a baptistery and organ chamber were added at the W. end (And. Kerr, archt.); from them a good view of the whole interior is obtained.

Projecting beyond the E. end of the chapel, on a lower level, is a chamber which the altar and piscina prove to have been used as a chapel, while the fireplace and other secular conveniences show it to have been fitted up for a vestry.

Since 1862 the Chapel has been used for the service of the Scottish Episcopal Church.

Rosslyn Castle (adm. 6d.), on an insulated mound below the Chapel, and near the extreme edge of the precipice overhanging the N. Esk, is reduced to a mere fragment, and a modern house occupies the enclosure. The oldest part dates from its founder Sir Wm. St. Clair, who was killed in Spain fighting against the Moors, 1330. The keep or S.W. tower was built by his grandson, Henry St. Clair, 2nd Earl of Orkney, and it was enlarged by Sir William, 3rd Earl, founder of the Chapel. Destroyed 1544 by the invading forces of Henry VIII., it was restored by Sir Wm. St. Clair, 1580, and his son (see the arms over fireplace in great hall). It was finally battered down and plundered by Gen. Monk (1650). A bridge and solid wall of masonry over a gully formed the approach to it, guarded by a feudal gateway, of which a fragment remains.

Walk down the Glen, and either enter Hawthornden Grounds (p. 76)—gatekeeper usually there in summer, admission 1s.—or follow the Esk to Pólton (p. 76) 3 m.

A little to the N. of Roslin is the *Moor*, where in 1303 the Scotch army under the Regent Comyn fought 3 battles against 3 divisions of the English. It was victorious over 2, and took some prisoners, but was defeated by the 3rd under Sir Robert Neville.

14¼ m. **Glencorse Stat.** close to which is *Greenlaw Military Depot.* ¾ m. N. is *Glencorse Ho.* (A. W. Inglis, Esq.), the seat of the late Lord Justice General of Scotland (d. 1891), and ¼ m. beyond, *The Bush* (Col. R. A. Trotter). 1½ m. W., on the slopes of the Pentlands, is **Rullion Green,** where 900 Covenanters were defeated on 28th November 1666 by Sir Thomas Dalyell of Binns.]

After Millerhill the l ne skirts the grounds l. of Dalkeith Palace and crosses the N. Esk to

8¼ m. **Eskbank Stat.** close to which 6 roads radiate. 1 m. N. is *Dalkeith Palace* (p. 75); ¾ m. S.E. on the S. Esk *Newbattle Abbey* (p. 35); 1 m. W. on the N. Esk *Melville Cas.* the modern seat of Viscount Melville.

[*Branch* between the stat. and the river to

8½ m. **Dalkeith Stat.** ✲ The town is situated on a ridge between the N. and S. Esk rivers, and though in the midst of a colliery district boasts a considerable grain market.

Close to the station is the *West Parish Church* (erected by Duke of Buccleuch 1844), with a tall spire. The main street runs from the station to the Park gate of Dalkeith Palace, about ½ m.; midway (l.) stands the old Parish Ch. of St. Nicholas (1384), in heavy Gothic style, with a stunted tower and spire. It was repaired 1852, except the roofless E. apse, used as the burial chapel of the Douglas and Buccleuch families. Here is the grave of Anne, Duchess of Buccleuch, widow of the Duke of Monmouth (1651-1732), to whom "the last minstrel" sang his "lay."

The *Park*, which has an area of nearly 1000 acres fenced round, abounds in magnificent timber, and avenues, and single trees, but owes its chief charm to the winding course of the N. and S. Esk, which meet within it. Not far from the junction is a picturesque oak wood of great age. Besides the public roads the Park is traversed by miles of paths through woods and gardens.

Close to the Park gates is a neat Gothic *Chapel*, built by the Duke, where the Epis. Ch. of Scotland service is conducted twice on Sundays.

About 200 yards l. a path leads to **Dalkeith Palace**,[1] the chief seat of the Duke of Buccleuch. The old castle of Dalkeith belonged to the Grahams for 200 years till the middle of the 14th cent. Froissart, who stayed here for a considerable time, calls the place D'Alquest, and mentions its capture by Edward III. in 1333; he was the guest of the Earl of Douglas (into whose family it came by marriage with the heiress of the Grahams). The castle and lands seem to have been granted to Douglas, in 1369, on payment of a pair of white gloves or a silver penny to the king at the Feast of Pentecost. It descended to the Regent Morton, who increased its strength and magnificence, until it got the name of the "Lion's Den." It was sold to Francis Scott, 2nd Earl of Buccleuch, in 1642, in whose family it has since remained. Amongst its celebrated residents was General Monk, and it is not improbable that the plan of the Restoration was concocted here. The actual building, erected by Duchess Anne in the early part of the 18th cent., is a heavy imitation of the palace of Loo in the Netherlands, and was the work of Sir John Vanbrugh. The situation, however, is charming, and makes up for any deficiency of architecture. The palace contains a good collection of paintings.

[1] Palace and grounds shown Weds. and Sats. when family absent.

In the entrance-hall—portrait of Duke of Monmouth, *Kneller;* also of George IV., by *Wilkie*—animated in conception, and exhibits great power of colour. Lucy Walters (mother of the Duke of Monmouth), and Nell Gwynne, by *Lely*.

In the next room are some battle-pieces. In 1st dining-room are the Duchess of Monmouth, *Kneller*, and the Earl of Strafford.

In the breakfast-room are Venetian views, probably the work of *Bernardo Bellotto;* Baths of Titus, and Roman Ruins, by *Pannini*—both admirable.

In the old entrance-hall are a clock presented by Louis XIV., and the torso of a female figure found in the grounds. Here are the portraits of Francis, 2nd Earl of Buccleuch, *Dobson;* Lucy Waters, and Mary Scott, "the Flower of Yarrow" (p. 32), by *Lely*.

Drawing-room—Duke and Duchess of Montague, by *Gainsborough*, of true and refined conception; Duke of Buccleuch, and Elizabeth, Duchess of B., and a Boy with a Dog, by *Sir J. Reynolds;* Henrietta Maria, *Vandyck*, a portrait of great delicacy and refinement, but insipid; the Jewish Bride, *Rembrandt* (?), a work of marvellous power and transparency; Stag-hunt, *Wouverman;* Six Saints, two adoring the Cross, by *Andrea del Sarto;* Landscape, by *Claude;* Wooded Landscape, *Ruysdael;* another by *Wynants*. Here are also 2 cabinets given to the Duke of Monmouth by Charles II.

In the small dining-room are six Venetian views by *Canaletti;* a view of Montague House, Whitehall, in the middle of the 18th century.

The staircase is very handsome, and the inlaid oaken floor deserves notice. Portraits of Duke of Monmouth, mounted; Sir Nicholas Carew, Master of the Horse to Henry VIII., by *Holbein*, of animated conception and masterly carrying out.

Dalkeith has had many royal visitors; Charles I. in 1642; George IV. in 1822; and the Queen and the Prince Consort on their first journey to Scotland, 1842.

The pleasure grounds extend for a considerable distance, and contain some fine shrubberies, conifers, etc. The gardens and vineries have a high repute among horticulturists.]

[*Branch* from Eskbank rt. to

9½ m. **Broomieknowe Stat.**

10 m. **Lasswade Stat.** (6 m. by road—*Coach* 4 times daily from Edin.), a busy village seated in a hollow on the banks of the N. Esk, surrounded by chimneys of carpet and other factories, and by numerous villas, is still atractive from its position in a deep glen, over whose steep sides rises the picturesque outline of the Pentlands.

Sir Walter Scott passed some of the happiest years of his life here—soon after his marriage (1798)—in a very small thatched cottage with garden and paddock, amidst the dearest haunts of his boyhood. Lasswade was the type of the "Gandercleugh" of "Tales of my Landlord."

"Sweet are the paths, oh passing sweet,
By Esk's fair streams that run,
O'er airy steeps through copsewoods deeps,
Impervious to the sun."—SCOTT.

Thomas De Quincey resided in this cottage in 1843, although he removed to Edinburgh before his death, 1859.

Around the ruins of the Norman Ch. rest the remains of the families of Melville and Hawthornden, including those of Drummond the poet (d. 1649), to whose memory a *Memorial Stone* with bronze medallion (*Rhind*, sculp.) was erected, Oct. 1893.

11 m. **Polton Stat.** (with Paper Mills), whence a pleasant path up the Esk leads to Rosslyn Cas., Chapel, and Village (3 m.).]

Beyond Eskbank the Peebles line, leaving the Waverley Route (Rte. 1), trends rt. to

9½ m. **Bonnyrigg Stat.**

11¼ m. **Hawthornden Stat.** A short walk brings the visitor to *Hawthornden.* The house (Sir James H. W. Drummond, Bt.) is a modern mansion, grafted on an old fortified Peel-tower, planted on the very edge of a red cliff looking down into the den or glen of the N. Esk, and surrounded by pretty gardens and woods. Beneath the Castle the rock is pierced with a number of caves, said to have been inhabited before people were civilised enough to erect huts. They have no doubt been used as hiding-places. Tradition says that they were once so occupied by Bruce. The soft rock was easily hewn out into chambers, which were inhabited or used for cellars or prisons. They are furnished with a well, also cut in the rock.

Hawthornden has obtained its chief reputation from being built and inhabited by the poet Drummond (1585-1649). The melancholy tone of his poems is said to have arisen from the fact of his betrothed dying on the day before that fixed for the marriage (see *Crail*, p. 189). He was a great friend of Ben Jonson, who walked all the way from London to pay him a visit here.

Visitors having traversed Hawthornden grounds, cross the Esk by a bridge and passing through a gate pursue the path up the fine glen to Roslin (p. 72) 1½ m.—a very pretty walk, though the Esk is polluted by Penicuik Paper-mills. It terminates with a fine view of Rosslyn Castle and Chapel, as the visitor emerges from the glen.

[Beyond Hawthornden is a *Branch* rt. *to Penicuik*, passing

12½ m. **Rosslyn Castle Stat.**, commanding a splendid view rt. of the Castle, the Chapel, and the Glen, but 1 m. from the village (see p. 72). Close at hand are *Gunpowder Mills*, for whose protection from sparks the line passes through an artificial iron tunnel.

The Valley of the Esk beyond this is extremely picturesque, with scarcely room for the rly.

At 13½ m. l. are the slight remains of *Old Woodhouselee Cas.*, once the property of Hamilton of Bothwellhaugh. Its being taken from him, and his wife's brutal expulsion in the middle of the night, by which she was rendered a maniac, led to the murder of the Regent Murray at Linlithgow by the hands of Hamilton (1569). *New Woodhouselee*, residence of the Tytler family, lies 2½ m. N.

14 m. **Auchendinny Stat.**, in a narrow gorge.

14¾ m. **Eskbridge Stat.** thence past *Paper Mills* (A. Cowan & Sons, Lim.), the largest in Scotland, to

15¾ m. **Penicuik Stat.** ✲ (10 m. by road), a pleasantly situated little town on the l. bank of the N. Esk, and at the base of the Pentlands, which may be conveniently visited and crossed from here (see p. 66).

1 m. S.W. is *Penicuik House* (Trs. of Sir G. D. Clerk, Bt.), a handsome Grecian edifice. The Baron of Penicuik was bound by his tenure, when the king came to Edinburgh, to receive him at the *Hare Stone* with 3 blasts of his horn. So Scott says—

"Come, Clerk, and give your bugle breath,
Carle, now the king's come."

The motto of the Clerks is "Free for a blast." The house has some of the ceilings painted by Runciman, the Scotch artist, with subjects from Ossian, and contains an interesting collection of Roman antiquities, and some good pictures: Ascension, and portrait of a Bp. of Ghent, by *Rubens;* Fisher Boy, by *Murillo;* portrait of Allan Ramsay, by *Aikman*, etc. Here is kept the buff coat that Claverhouse wore at the battle of Killiecrankie. In the grounds are an *Obelisk* to the memory of Allan Ramsay the poet (1686-1758), who is much associated with this district, and a *flag tower* conspicuous from a great distance. At the bend of the grounds, and higher up the valley of the Esk, are the ruins of *Brunstane Castle*, formerly a stronghold of the Crichtons.]

Beyond Hawthornden on the Peebles line is

12½ m. **Roslynlee Stat.** 1½ m. from Roslin.

15 m. **Pomathorn Stat.**, serves as an additional stat. to Penicuik, ½ m. rt. *Wellington Reformatory* is passed rt. before reaching

17½ m. **Leadburn Stat.** ✲, 12½ m. by road, standing 862 ft. above sea level, and on the boundary of Peeblesshire.

[*Branch to Dolphinton.*

20½ m. **Lamancha Stat.**

Lamancha Ho. (J. Mackintosh, Esq.), ¾ m. l., built 1663, was so called by an Earl of Dundonald, after some property he possessed in Spain. ¾ m. rt. is *Whim Ho.* (J. M. Thomson, Esq.).

22 m. **Macbiehill Stat.** ½ m. S. is *Macbiehill* (Mrs. Massy-Beresford).

24 m. **Broomlee Stat.** 1 m. S. are *Spittalhaugh*, the handsome modern Gothic residence of Sir J. R. Ferguson, Bt., and *Halmyre Ho.* (C. Gordon, Esq.), 16th cent., an old residence of the Gordon family.

½ m. N. is the village of **West Linton** ✲ once "a burgh of regality" and of considerable importance. The masons and sculptors of Linton were renowned for their skill in carving tombstones. In the village is *Lady Gifford's Well* (re-erected 1861) surmounted by her figure, carved in 1666 by her husband, Laird Gifford, who was celebrated for his skill in stonework. There is also a curious bas-relief built into the wall of one of the houses with the dates 1678 and 1660, the names of James Gifferd and Eupham Veatch, his wife, and figures representing "the six progenitors of James Gifferd, his awne protract and eldes son."

From **Broomlee Stat.** the antiquary will find it to his account to explore the valley of the Lyne (to the S.), which was guarded by numerous forts and camps, the principal of which, viz. Whiteside Hill, Boreland Rings, Drochil Castle, and Hamildean, are in a fair state of preservation. The last occupies the summit of an eminence rising 600 ft. above the bed of the Lyne. At **Rommano,** close to Newlands Ch., is one of those curious series of terraces similar to Purvis Hill, near Innerleithen, rising 14 in number to the height of 250 ft.

N. up the Lyne past *Medwyn Ho.* (Trs. of late Wm. Forbes, Esq.) is the charming *Cauld Stane Slap* pass over the Pentlands to Midcalder Stat. 13 m.—4 hours' walking.

27½ m. **Dolphinton Stat.** 1 m. S.W. (in Lanarkshire) is *Dolphinton Ho.* (J. O. Mackenzie, Esq.,) and 3 m. S. (in Peeblesshire) *Castle Craig* (Sir W. Gibson Carmichael, Bt.) beside *Kirkurd Ch.* and 1 m. E. of *Netherurd Ho.* (Mrs. J. White). 1 m. N.W. is. *Garvald Ho.* (W. A. Woddrop, Esq.) From Dolphinton the Cal. Rly. Co. have a line 11 m. long down the Medwyn Valley *via Dunsyre*, *Newbigging*, and *Bankhead* to **Carstairs Junc.** (p. 16).

Beyond Leadburn (at 20 m.) rt. is a picturesque waterfall called *Cowie's Linn;* and 1½ m. beyond (l.) is *Portmore Ho.* (C. J. Mackenzie, Esq.) behind which are the camp of *Northfield Rings*, of an oval shape, consisting of three walls with sunk ditches, the whole measuring 450 by 370 ft., and Portmore Loch, backed by the **Moorfoot Range** attaining in *Blackhope Scar*, 2136 ft.

23 m. **Eddleston Stat.** rt. are *Darnhall*, an old house in the French château style, the seat of Lord Elibank, and the road to *Lyne Stat.* p. 90). ¾ m. S. (l.) is *Milkieston Rings*, the largest camp in the county, circular, having a detached rampart on the slope of the hill below, and 1 m. farther (rt.) is *Cringletie*, the seat of Major J. Wolfe-Murray.

At the junction of the Eddleston Water with the Tweed is

27 m. **Peebles Stat.** ✲ (22 m. by road)—a pleasant centre—see Rte. 10. The rly. now keeps the l. bank of the Tweed passing rt. *Kerfield* and (across the river) *Kingsmeadows* (both Sir J. A. Hay, Bt.) It then crosses the road and 1 m. beyond passes l. the scant ruins of *Horsburgh Cas.*, the old house of the family of that name, and rt. (across the river) *Kailzie* (W. C. Black, Esq.)

30¼ m. **Cardrona Stat.** 1 m. beyond which on the rt. bank is the old ruined tower and the modern mansion of *Cardrona* (Miss Kerr Williamson), and on the l. bank *Glenormiston Ho.* (M. G. Thorburn, Esq.) above which rises the peaked summit of *Lee Pen* (1647 ft.)

33½ m. **Innerleithen Stat.** ✲ prettily placed at the junc. of the Leithen water with the Tweed, has mineral springs, and is noted as the locale of the scenes in "St. Ronan's Well." Overlooking the stat. on left is *Caerlee Hill Fort*, a large circular British camp, measuring 400 by 350 ft. across. On the opposite side of the Leithen is another, not so large, known as the *Pirn Hill Fort. Pirn Ho.* is the residence of Col. Horsburgh. 1 m. E. of Innerleithen, at *Purvis Hill*, are some remarkable earthen terraces, rising in the form of gigantic steps, about a dozen in number to the height of 450 ft. above the Tweed. Their appearance has given rise to much discussion, some attributing them to geological causes, while archæologists point to the fact that a fort itself is to be found in connection with them, as is also the case at *Romanno* (above).

1 m. up the Leithen is a *Golf Course*, passing which a delightful old coaching road runs through the Moorfoots to *Heriot* (14 m.) or *Tynehead*, 18 m. (p. 34).

1¼ m. S. is *Traquair House* (Hon. Maxwell Stewart), a 17th cent. house added to a tower of much earlier date. There is a handsome *Gateway* flanked by two figures of bears in stone, and a fine avenue. These are the supposed prototypes of the Bradwardine bears in "Waverley." A short distance up the *Quhair Water* are the remains of the "Bush aboon Traquair," the subject of a poem written by Robert Crawford in 1724, beginning

"Hear me, ye nymphs and every swain,
I'll tell how Peggy grieves me!"

and of the late Principal Shairp's exquisite and pathetic poem (1864)

"Will ye gang wi' me and fare
To the bush aboon Traquair?"

The road may be followed up the glen, the scene of Laidlaw's "Lucy's Flittin'," to (5 m.) *The Glen*, the modern mansion of Sir Chas. Tennant, Bt., of Glasgow, designed by the late Mr Bryce in the old Scotch baronial style. The road past *Traquair Ch.* up the *Newhall Burn* leads over to the *Gordon Arms Inn* in Yarrow 9 m. (p. 32). It was by this road "The Ettrick Shepherd" led Wordsworth (1814) when Yarrow was "visited." To the E. of this road lies "**Minchmuir**" (1656 ft.) so charmingly described by Dr. John Brown.

At *Grieston*, 1 m. W. of Traquair, the geologist will find Silurian rocks with graptolites.

The Tweed is crossed before reaching

35 m. **Walkerburn Stat.**, a busy seat of woollen manufactures. 2½ m. farther rt. is *Elibank Tower*, the ruined seat of the Murrays.

39 m. **Thornielee Stat.**, 1½ m. beyond which (rt.) across the Tweed is *Ashiestiel* (Miss Russell), from 1804-12 the residence of Sir W. Scott, where great parts of "the Lay" and of "Marmion," in the introduction to which it is described, were written.

At 41 m. the line turns N. leaving the river, 2 m. down which is *Yair Ho.* (Alex. Pringle, Esq.) beside a bridge with a fine spanned arch over the Tweed 2 m. above its junc. with the Ettrick.

42 m. **Clovenfords Stat.** with the Tweed Vineyards (p. 30).

45½ m. **Galashiels Stat.** ✲, p. 30.

ROUTE 7.

Newtown St. Boswells to Reston Junc. by Greenlaw and Duns.

31 m. 3 or 4 trains daily.

This line connects the Waverley and East Coast sections of the N.B. Rly. (see Rtes. 3 and 1). The scenery is uninteresting. From St. Boswells (p. 23) the train keeps along the Melrose line for 1½ m. then branches rt. and crosses the Tweed near Leaderfoot by a high viaduct of 15 arches, 133 ft. above the river, and runs up the Leader valley passing 3½ m. (rt.) *Cowdenknowes* (Capt. Hope) the subject of an old ballad and of Robert Crawford's (1695-1733) song, "The Broom of the Cowdenknowes."

The Leader is crossed before

4½ m. **Earlston Stat.** ✲ formerly known as Ercildoun, and celebrated as the residence of Thomas the Rhymer, in whose prophecies the whole country side once put implicit faith. His real name was Learmonth. He was born in the reign of Alexander II., was contemporary with Wallace, and died about 1286. To him is attributed the authorship of "Sir Tristram," a metrical tale. It was the general belief that he was carried away by the Queen of the Elfins, into the interior of the Eildon Hills (p. 23).

The *Rhymer's Tower* is to be seen at the W. end of the village, close to the river Leader, an excellent stream for trout-fishing.

1 m. up the river is *Carolside* (Lady Reay), and 6 m. farther **Lauder** (p. 34).

10½ m. **Gordon Stat.** 5 m. to the N.W. is *Spottiswoode*, the seat of Lady Alicia A. Scott Spottiswoode. 6 m. N. is the old Border tower of *Evelaw.* Crossing the Eden we reach

14½ m. **Greenlaw Stat.** ✲, a small town on the banks of the Blackadder, which shares with Duns the position of capital of Berwickshire. 3½ m. N. the geologist will find S. of *Bed-*

shiel farm an excellent example of a "kaim" of great length. *Hume Cas.* (p. 85) is 3 m. S.

18¼ m. **Marchmont Stat.** l. of which is *Marchmont House*, the seat of the late Sir Hugh Hume-Campbell, Bt. (d. 1894).

It contains a fine collection of paintings, including Philip baptizing the Eunuch, *Cuyp;* Forest Scene, *Ruysdael*, "fine and very uncommon in composition"; Corps de Garde, *Teniers;* portrait of Don Livio Odescalchi, *Vandyck;* Forest Scene, *Wynants;* Ships in distress, *Vandervelde.*

In the family burial vault under *Polwarth Ch.*, within the Park, Sir Patrick Hume, an adherent of Argyll in 1685, was concealed for a month in the dark, sleeping on a mattress stealthily conveyed from the house, and fed by his young daughter afterwards the celebrated Lady Grisell Baillie, who repaired to him at midnight with supplies, unknown to any one but her mother. The house meanwhile was frequently searched by the soldiers of James II. Sir Patrick eventually escaped to Holland, but was afterwards restored.

22 m. **Duns Stat.** ✲, the capital of Berwickshire, and after Berwick (which is under English administration) the largest town in the county, claims the honour of being the birthplace (*cir.* 1275) of Duns Scotus, the schoolman. It is certain that Dr. Thos. M'Crie (1772), biographer of John Knox, and Thos. Boston (1676), author of "The Fourfold State," were natives. It is of some importance as a cattle, horse, and sheep market, standing at the foot of the Lammermuir Hills, and at the base of *Duns Law*, a flat-topped hill (700 ft.) which was twice entrenched and held by the Covenanters under Gen. Leslie. From this hill or *Dun* no doubt the town gets its name.

Adjoining the town on the W. are the grounds of *Duns Castle* (R. M. Hay, Esq.), a spacious and handsome building, which includes the old tower built by Randolph Earl of Moray. 2 m. S.E. is *Wedderburn Cas.* (Col. D. Milne Home), a stately mansion of Grecian architecture; 1 m. beyond is *Kimmerghame Ho.* (J. L. Campbell Swinton, Esq.) a handsome modern mansion, Bryce, archt.: while 2 m. S. of Duns is *Nisbet Ho.* (Lord Sinclair). *Langton Ho.* (Trs. of late Hon. R. Baillie Hamilton) 2 m. W., also by Bryce and begun by the late Marquis of Breadalbane, contains paintings by *Ruysdael, Backhuysen, Cuyp*, etc.; portraits by *Sir J. Reynolds* (Eliz. Gunning), *Jamesone*, and *Raeburn* (the Laird of Macnab), etc.

"On the N. side of Cockburn Law, about 4 m. N. from Duns, and about a mile E. from Abbey St. Bathans, are the interesting remains of an ancient building of unhewn and uncemented stones called *Edinshall.* It is circular in shape, and about 90 ft. in diameter: the wall varies in thickness from 15 to 20 ft. It is surrounded by ditches and ramparts of earth and stone, and there are trenches round the top of the hill on which it stands."—OLIVER.

Duns is a good fishing station for the upper waters of the *Whiteadder*, which flows about 3 m. to the N. Near its source and 11 m. N.W. of Duns is *Priestlaw*, where a convent once stood, and where the *Faseney Water* flows over some rock sections of great interest to the geologist, as showing the manner in which the granite and greywacke shale of the Lammermuirs are related to each other.

Passing 24 m. (l.) *Manderston Ho.* (Sir James Miller, Bt.) the train reaches

25½ m. **Edrom Stat.**, which is probably a corruption of Adderham, from adder or ader = *awedur* (Cam. Brit.) = running water, and *ham* (Ang.-Sax.) = a home or village. 3 m. N.E. is *Broomhouse*, a modern castellated building, erected on the site of the old fortress, burnt by the English under Lord Evers (1545). 1 m. S. is *Blackadder Ho.* (Sir G. L. H. Boswell).

The *Whiteadder* is crossed at

27 m. **Chirnside Stat.** The village is 1 m. E., and contains a fine old ch. of the 15th cent. in good repair. Close to it is *Ninewells House* (J. A. Ross Hume, Esq.), the family residence of Hume the historian.

31 m. **Reston Junction**✲, see p. 5.

From Reston to Berwick is 11¼ m. and to Edinburgh 46¼ m. (Rte. 1).

ROUTE 8.

Newtown St. Boswells Junc. to Berwick-on-Tweed by Roxburgh (for Jedburgh), Kelso, and Coldstream (Flodden).

35½ m. 5 trains daily.

This is the only line to Jedburgh and Kelso, but for most tourists the direct line to Berwick is by the East Coast (Rte. 1). There is generally an awkward halt at Kelso, whence the line W. is North Brit., that E. being North Eastern.

This line to Berwick follows the right bank of the Tweed all the way, but the beauties of that river are not seen from the rly.

It is only for the last 20 m. of its course that the Tweed forms the boundary between Scotland and England, which is a line running not E. and W. but nearly N.E. and S.W.—up the Tweed, along the Cheviots, down the Kershope Burn and the Liddelwater, then W. and down the Sark to the Solway. During these 20 m. the Tweed flows along the part of Berwickshire called **"The Merse,"** perhaps a corruption of "Meres" in allusion to the time when it was under water, or = March = The Border. It is one of the most fertile districts in Scotland.

Quitting **Newtown St. Boswells** (p. 23) the line curves E. to

3 m. **Maxton Stat.** The village is on the left, and on the opposite bank of the Tweed are the noble groves of *Mertoun*, the seat of Lord Polwarth. At *Maxton* is the seat of Sir Wm. Fairfax, Bt., and beside the river is *Littledean Tower*, a fortress belonging to the Kerrs of Nenthorn. Across the river, in the far distance, conspicuous for very many miles, is *Smailholm Tower* (p. 28).

5½ m. **Rutherford Stat.** On the opposite bank of the Tweed is *Makerstoun House*, the beautiful seat of Hugh Scott, Esq. On the rt. the *Waterloo Monument* (p. 82) soon comes into view.

The scenery hereabout is highly romantic, especially at a spot called *Trow Crags*, where the trap rocks rising out of the Tweed approach so closely to each other as to afford a daring passage across. In consequence of accidents, however, one of the steps was blown up.

As the train approaches

9 m. **Roxburgh Junc. Stat.** Beautiful glimpses are caught of the valley below, backed in the distance by the woods and grounds of *Floors Castle* (Duke of Roxburghe) [p. 85]. The village of *Roxburgh* is prettily placed, and in the churchyard is the gravestone of Edie Ochiltree, the bedesman of the "Antiquary," whose real name was Andrew Gemmel. The *Castle* and site of the *old town* are 2 m. N., and are more conveniently visited from Kelso (p. 84).

[*Branch* to **Jedburgh**, 7 m., keeping at first up l. bank of the Teviot.

½ m. l., on the opposite bank of the Teviot, is *Sunlaws*, the Elizabethan residence of R. Scott Kerr, Esq. The banks of the river here are steep and rocky, and are perforated with caverns, as is also the case in the neighbourhood at Grahamslaw, on the banks of the Kale Water.

1¾ m. **Kirkbank Stat.**, near which is a ruined tower. 1 m. E. the Teviot is crossed by a chain bridge to *Kalemouth* and *Eckford* Ch., at the door of which still hangs an iron pillory collar, known as the "jougs" (see p. 62).

4¼ m. **Nisbet Stat.** To the right,

on *Penielheugh* commanding a fine view, is the **Waterloo Monument.**

"To the Duke of Wellington and the British army William Kerr, vi. Marquis of Lothian, and his tenantry dedicate this monument, xxx June MDCCCXV." The lat. and long. and height of the base above sea level (774 ft.) are also given. The stair to the top is not open to the public.

The line crosses the Teviot—rt. lies *Mounteviot* (Marq. of Lothian) —to

5½ m. **Jedfoot Bridge Stat.**, where the line quits the vale of Teviot to ascend that of the Jed. rt. (out of sight) is *Bonjedward Ho.* (Marq. of Lothian), honourably mentioned in "The Raid of the Reidswire," a Border ballad, relating to an affray in 1575 between the Scotch and English:—

"Bonjeddart bauldy made him boune
Wi' a' the Trumbills, strong and stout;
The Rutherfords, with grit renown,
Convoy'd the town of Jedburgh out."

Very prettily situated, in a glen surrounded by wooded hills, lies

7¼ m. **JEDBURGH Stat.** ✲, the county town of Roxburghshire. It is watered by the Jed, and has an air of antiquity. The royal castle stood upon the site of the gaol (no longer used). It was one of the 5 strongholds surrendered by the Treaty of Falaise in 1174 to England as security for the ransom of William the Lion, and after its restoration became a favourite residence of the Scottish monarchs till the English wars, when (in 1409) it was destroyed as being more serviceable to the English than the Scotch.

In an old bastel-house still standing in Queen Street, Queen Mary lived for some time, but not of her own accord. She had come hither in 1566 to hold the assizes, when she heard that Bothwell had been wounded in a personal encounter with John Elliott, of Park, a notorious Border freebooter, and that he was lying sick at Hermitage Castle, 20 m. distant. She immediately set off on horseback to see him, returned the same day, and was, in consequence of the fatigue, seized with a fever. A morass into which her horse sank, and from which she was with difficulty extricated, is still called "The Queen's Myre."

The Court of Justiciary for the Borders was held here from early times. Its process must have been summary: hence the phrase "Jeddart justice," equivalent to what is now called "Lynch law"—hanging a man first and trying him after.

Facing the Market Place is a 17th cent. *Gatehouse*, containing the town clock and bells.

The grand old ***Abbey**[1] was founded by David I., early in the 12th cent., for Canons Regular, brought from the Abbey of St. Quentin at Beauvais.

The *Abbey Church*, in general character, resembles Kelso, especially in its W. front. In plan it is different: it has a very long nave (130 ft.) of 9 bays with aisles, one of the finest examples of the Romanesque in Scotland, and is remarkable for the mixture of Round and Pointed styles. The main arches are pointed, supporting a triforium of semicircular arches, each enclosing 2 pointed arches. Above is a clerestory of pointed arches, alternately high and low, through which a gallery is carried. The tower, over 100 ft. high, is supported on circular arches. The choir consists of only 2 bays; its massive cylinder piers are carried up to include the triforium in a semicircular arch, embracing 2 smaller arches. The ruins have been put in order by the Marquis of Lothian, under the supervision of Dr. R. Anderson, archt. Some of the more characteristic fragments, including the S. door have been restored.

The visitor should notice the very fine Norm. mouldings of the great W. door, and also the doorway forming the S. entrance from the cloisters,

1 Custodier's Ho. at W. end, fee 6d. each.

which is elaborately decorated. As the mouldings show signs of decay the Marq. of Lothian has had a facsimile erected at the W. Near this door in the S. aisle, but marked by no monument, is the grave of Lord Chancellor Campbell (d. 1861) and his wife, Lady Stratheden. The N. transept (not generally shown), which is the burying-place of the Kerrs, is a fine specimen of Dec., and the window contains geometrical tracery. It contains a recumbent effigy by Watts of the late (8th) Marq. of Lothian, who d. 1870.

"The Abbey churches of Kelso and Jedburgh, as we now find them, belong either to the very end of the 12th or beginning of the 13th cent. They display all the rude magnificence of the Norm. period, used in this instance not experimentally as was too often the case in England, but as a well-understood style, whose features were fully perfected. The whole was used with a Doric simplicity and boldness which is very remarkable. Sometimes, it must be confessed, this independence of constraint is carried a little too far, as in the pier arches at Jedburgh, where they are thrown across between the circular pillars without any subordinate shaft or apparent support. Here the excessive strength of the arch in great measure redeems it."—FERGUSSON.

The visitor should ascend the tower for the sake of the view of the town and its environs. Conspicuous to N.E. is *Hartrigge Ho.* (Lord Stratheden and Campbell), approached by a fine avenue. It was purchased by Lord Chancellor Campbell.

A *Parish Church* was built 1873-1875 by the Marq. of Lothian, at an expense of £16,000 (Wyatt, archt.) to leave the abbey, previously partly used, unmodernised.

The other buildings in the town are the *County Hall*, the *Episcopal Church*, and the *School*. Sir David Brewster was born in the Canongate (1781), and Mrs. Somerville (1780-1872), the learned elucidator of La Place, and authoress of various celebrated works, in a house now swept away, which stood in the Abbey Garden. The Rev. Dr. Somerville, her father-in-law, author of the "Hist. of Queen Anne," was fifty years minister of Jedburgh. Thomson the poet received his early education here.

EXCURSIONS :—

(1) To **St. Boswells** by *Ancrum*, etc., 10 m. (p. 25).

(2) To **Hawick** by *Denholm*, 11 m. (p. 22).

2 m. S.W. on this road (l.) is *Dunian Hill* (1095 ft.), and farther on across the *Rule* l. *Ruber's Law* (1392 ft.) A weather rhyme says—

" When Ruberslaw puts on its hat,
And Dunion on its hood,
All the old wives of Rule Water
May expect a flood."

(3) **Up the Jed valley,** with ancient caves in the red sandstone cliffs, to the **Cheviots.** On the outskirts of the town is a famous old oak, known as the *Capon Tree.*

At 2 m. rt is *Linthaughlee Burn*, a romantic little dell where the Scots, under Lord James Douglas, are said to have gained a victory over the English in 1317, and l. is *Fernieherst Castle* (Major Paton), in the 15th cent. a strong fortress and a picturesque specimen of Border architecture. It was for centuries a stronghold of one branch of the family of Kerr, and its history is full of the varying incidents of Border warfare. In the beautifully wooded grounds are some noble trees.

At 6 m. the Jed, which rises farther W., is crossed, and 1 m. beyond l. is *Edgerstone* (W. E. O. Rutherfurd, Esq.) The road ascends steeply and at 10 m. (1405 ft.) crosses the shoulder of **Carter Fell** into England—an extensive view back. The return to Jedburgh from this point may be varied (slightly longer) by descending N.W. by the headwaters of the Jed to *Southdean Ch.* (5 m.)—close to which is a *fort*, and 2 m. W. *Wolfelee* (Trs. of late J. T. S. Elliot, Esq.)—*Chesters Village*, *Rule Water*, and *Swinnie Moor*.]

Leaving Roxburgh Stat. the line crosses the wooded vale of the Teviot on a high viaduct. l. is *Springwood Park* (Sir G. B. Douglas, Bt.) and across the Tweed *Floors Castle*.

11½ m. **Kelso Station**, on the top of a hill, ½ m. from the town across the river. In crossing the Tweed by a very handsome *Bridge* (built by Rennie) of 5 arches, each of 72 ft. span, a bright and beautiful view is obtained.

KELSO ✲ is beautifully situated on the left bank of the Tweed, opposite its confluence with the Teviot. It is a busy town, and has a fine open market-square, in which a Court-house has been erected, from whose tower ring the chimes, and at nightfall the *Curfew*. A monthly cattle-fair is held here. Close to the Bridge is

**The Abbey*, one of the earliest completed by David I. It was founded in 1128, and in it he buried his eldest son Henry, who died in 1152.

The monks, who were of the Tironensian order, were moved here from Selkirk. The abbots of Kelso at one time claimed the precedence in the Scottish hierarchy, though the abbey itself was never of any great size. The ruined cruciform *Church* is a fine example of later Romanesque architecture. Of the W. front only half remains, with half of its grand, deeply-moulded doorway. The entrance to the N. transept, surmounted by a reticulated gable, is also fine. The choir alone has aisles, and its main circular arches are surmounted by 2 tiers of triforium galleries. An elegant intersecting arcade runs round the wall at the ground level. The nave and transepts are aisleless, and project only 23 ft. from the central tower. The main feature is the central tower. It was supported by 4 magnificent arches of Early Pointed character; 2 of these are still standing, and are 45 ft. high. The present state of dilapidation of this abbey is due to the ferocious marauding English army under the Earl of Hertford, 1545, who on entering the town found the abbey garrisoned as a fortress, and the tower held by 100 men, including 12 monks. It was battered with guns and the breach assaulted, a party of Spanish mercenaries leading the way, and all found within it were put to the sword. After this it was razed and defaced. During the 18th cent. part of the *Ch.* was roofed over to serve for divine service, the other part being used as a jail!

The property of the abbey was granted shortly after the Reformation to the Kerrs of Cessford, and still remains in that family (now represented by the Duke of Roxburghe).

No place has suffered more by fire than Kelso. It was repeatedly burnt by the English during the Border wars, once by accident in the latter part of the 17th cent., and again in the middle of the 18th.

The Kelso people have a great reputation for business habits, but used to be considered slack in their observance of the duties of religion and hospitality—

"The Kelso men slank all away,
They liked not much to hymn nor pray,
Nor like they 't much unto this day."
SCOTT.

and a "Kelso convoy" implies that the host accompanies his parting guest no farther than the door. It was one of the first provincial towns in Scotland to adopt the printing-press, and Ballantyne here brought out the earliest edition of Sir W. Scott's "Border Minstrelsy."

Kelso possesses a good *Library*, a **Museum* (open free Mon., Wed., and Fri.) and a public park called *Shedden Park* on the E. side of the town, presented in 1852 by Mrs. Robertson of Ednam House.

An unusual number of pleasant residences are to be found in the neighbourhood of Kelso, *e.g. Floors Cas.* (below); 2½ m. N. *Newton Don* (C. B. Balfour, Esq.), in whose grounds the pretty fall called *Stichill Linn* is produced by the river Eden; and from which *Nenthorn Ho.* (F. L. Roy, Esq.) is 2 m. W., and *Stichill Ho.* (Trs. of late G. A. Baird, Esq.), a grand modern house with a tower 100 ft. high, 1½ m. N. *Hendersyde Park* (Sir R. J. Waldie Griffith, Bt.), lying 1½ m. N.E., contains a good library as well as some interesting pictures and antiquities (Cards of admission procurable in Kelso).

Rosebank, a small house on the l. bank of Tweed just below the town, was a favourite sojourn of Sir W. Scott when a boy. It belonged to his uncle, at whose death it was bequeathed to him. He formed a seat out of the boughs of an elm overhanging the river, where he used to sit with a gun at his side to shoot gulls or herons, and a book of ballads in his hand.

[EXCURSIONS :—

(1) **Floors Castle**[1] (Duke of Roxburghe). The lodge is at the top of Roxburgh Street, and is distant about 1 m. from the Market Place.

The castle, with a magnificent façade and placed opposite the junc. of the Teviot with the Tweed, was built by Sir John Vanbrugh in 1718, but was transformed by the architect Playfair to its present shape. In the park James II. was killed in 1460, by the bursting of a cannon, when besieging Roxburgh Castle. A holly-tree is said to mark the spot where the accident occurred. The Gardens are among the most beautiful and best kept in Scotland. The Terraces command a noble view. The estate comprises 50,000 acres.

(2) 1¼ m. W., reached by crossing both Tweed Bridge and Teviot Bridge, are the scanty remains of **Roxburgh Castle**, on a ridge between the 2 rivers. It was, down to 1460, a royal residence and Border fortress, but so often in English hands that it was finally captured and razed by the Scotch after the death of James II. before its walls. There was a large town close by it, containing a mint and 3 churches; but this has long since disappeared. The fragment of the gateway and of the S. wall, though of massive masonry, scarce deserve a visit:

> "Roxburgh! how fallen, since first in
> Gothic pride,
> Thy frowning battlements the war
> defied!"—LEYDEN.

For the present village see p. 81.

(3) It is a very pretty walk to **Ednam**, a village lying 2½ m. N. beyond the race-course. An *Obelisk* has been erected to the memory of the poet Thomson (1700-48), author of the "Seasons," who was born at the manse here, and educated at the Grammar School at Jedburgh.

(4) Few will now be tempted to make an excursion, Cheviot-ways, to **Yetholm**, a village 8 m. S.E., once celebrated for being the headquarters of the gipsy tribe, and the residence of their king. It is a humble village on the banks of the *Bowmont Water*, which divides it into Kirk-Yetholm, the gipsy resort, and Town Yetholm. It is only 1½ m. from the English Border. Modern locomotion and supervision of highways have done much to diminish the importance of the Romany tribes, and they exist here more in name than fact. The regal family of the Faas is extinct.

Those who are fond of romantic scenery should explore the *Bowmont* to its source, by which **The Cheviot** (2676 ft.), about 8 m. distant from Yetholm, may be reached. The return from Yetholm may be made by *Linton Church* (5 m. W.), which is on an eminence. On S. wall is a carving of a man on horseback, thrusting a long spear into the mouth of a dragon. To Kelso 11 m.

(5) **Hume Castle**, 5½ m. N., a picturesque ruin beyond Newton Don and Stichill, and commanding a fine view, was once the stronghold of the Earls of Home. It was besieged by Cromwell, who summoned the governor, one Cockburn, to surrender. The governor bravely responded in the child's rhyme:

1 Admission to grounds on Weds., apply for order to Bank of Scotland, Kelso.

"I, Willie Wastle,
Stand fast in this castle,
And all the dogs in the town
Shall not drive Willie Wastle down;"

but he was very quickly compelled to submit notwithstanding.]

Beyond Kelso *Hendersyde Park* (p. 84) is seen l. across the Tweed, nearly opposite

14 m. **Sprouston Stat.** *Hume Cas.* (p. 85) is a conspicuous object to N.E. before reaching

16½ m. **Carham Stat.**, where the rly. enters England.

18½ m. **Sunilaws Stat.** Between the rly. and the Tweed is *Wark Castle* (Lady Waterford), one of the strongest and most celebrated of the Border fortresses.

It was given by Edward III. as a marriage present to the Earl of Salisbury, and defended by his handsome and virtuous countess against King David II. Edward arrived to relieve it after the Scots had raised the siege, and fell in love with its beautiful defender. The story is told at some length by Froissart.

The *Church* of Wark is well restored and adorned with paintings by Lady Waterford.

The rly. crosses a viaduct at Learmouth and close to the village of *Cornhill* ✲ (rt.), reaches

22 m. **Coldstream Stat.**✲, 1½ m. distant from the town (l.) across the river. Here General Monk in 1660 raised a regiment, which has ever since been known as the "Coldstream Guards." It is a pleasant, well-built town, with a conspicuous monument in memory of Chas. Marjoribanks, a former county member, but with very little to detain the visitor. Adjoining the town W. is *Lees* (G. E. Marjoribanks, Esq.); 1 m. E. is *Lennel Ho.* (Earl of Haddington), where Patrick Brydone, author of "Travels in Sicily and Malta," lived for many years, and 1 m. N. is *The Hirsel* (below). In consequence of Coldstream being just upon the Border it competed with Gretna Green (p. 94) as a scene of runaway matches.

Here Brougham, afterwards Lord Chancellor, was married, 1819, and there Lord Chanc. Erskine; while John Scott, afterwards Lord Chanc. Eldon, when 21, was similarly married at Blackshiels. Close to the town is the ford, the first of much consequence from Tweedmouth upward, constantly passed by English and Scottish armies on forays and invasions of their neighbours' territory. Here Edward I. passed in 1296. In the old inn nobles and princes stayed for days, waiting the subsidence of the waters of the Tweed, which is now crossed by a handsome *Bridge* of 5 arches, built by Smeaton, 1766.

The field of **Flodden** is about 3 m. S.E. of Cornhill, on the left bank of the river Till: the Wooler road passing through it. The battle was fought on the 9th Sept. 1513. It is graphically described in the last canto of "Marmion."

The Scots were utterly routed, and left 10,000 dead on the field, amongst whom were the King, his illegitimate son the Archbishop of St. Andrews, 2 bishops, 2 abbots, 12 earls, 13 barons, and upwards of 50 gentlemen of distinction. Scarcely a family of note in Scotland but was in mourning in consequence. The loss of the English out of an army of 26,000 men—half that of the Scots—was about 500 of all ranks. The loss of this battle was mainly due to the infatuation of James IV., who, as a point of honour, allowed the English vanguard to cross the Till at *Twizel Bridge* (p. 87) near its junction with the Tweed, unmolested, and to marshal their whole line between him and his own country.

A hillock near Branxton church is said to be the spot where King James's followers fought around him to the last.

[There is a road from Coldstream to Duns, 9½ m. (p. 80), passing 1 m. (l.) *The Hirsel*, the seat of the Earl of Home, and 4½ m. (rt.) *Swinton House*, the property of the family of the Swintons, justly celebrated in the military annals of

Scotland. One of them in the French service unhorsed the Duke of Clarence at the battle of Beaugé:

"And Swinton laid the lance in rest,
That tamed of yore the sparkling crest
Of Clarence's Plantagenet."]

---

25 m. **Twizel Stat.** rt. is **Twizel Castle,** to the ruins of which a large mansion was attached by the late Sir Francis Blake, but never occupied. It is magnificently situated on the brow of a steep precipice, overlooking the deep and sluggish river Till, 1 m. above its junction with the Tweed, and here spanned by the **Bridge** of a single arch, which was crossed by the Earl of Surrey just before the battle of Flodden (p. 86), where James ought to have disputed the passage. On l., across the Tweed, we pass *Milne Graden* (Miss Milne Home) and *Ladykirk House*, the seat of the late David Robertson, who for two days possessed the title of Lord Marjoribanks. To it succeeds the village of **Ladykirk,** the *Church* of which was built 1500, and dedicated to the Virgin by James IV. in gratitude for his rescue from peril while crossing the swollen waters of the Tweed, at the ford near this. It consists of nave, transepts, and chancel, with an apse, in the Perp. and third Pointed style, with a simple barrel roof.

27½ m. **Norham Stat.** l. between the rail and the river is **Norham Castle,** the opening scene in "Marmion"—

"Day set on Norham's castled steep,
And Tweed's fair river, broad and deep."

The extent of its remains, as well as its historical importance, show it to have been a place of magnificence as well as strength. The castle stands on an eminence overhanging the water, and is built of a soft red freestone.

The ruins consist now of a large shattered *keep*, with vaults beneath and fragments of other edifices, enclosed within an earthen rampart of wide circuit and deep ditches.

In 1121 there was a fortress here. It was repeatedly taken and retaken during the wars between England and Scotland. In 1154 it was almost rebuilt by Hugh Pudsey, Bishop of Durham, who added the huge keep which still stands. Henry II., in 1174, took the castle from the bishop, and committed it to the keeping of William de Neville, after which it was generally garrisoned by the King, and considered a royal fortress. Hither came all the claimants to the Scottish crown to plead their cause before Edward I. (1291), and here John Baliol swore fealty to him. It was taken by the Scots before the battle of Flodden, with Wark, Etal, and Ford. After the Reformation it passed through various hands, including Sir Robert Carey afterwards Earl of Monmouth, who sold it to George Home, Earl of Dunbar.

Norham Ch. is a very interesting Norman edifice well restored. In the churchyard is the grave and effigy of the Rev. Dr. Gilly, who devoted so much attention to the Vaudois, and was rector here. From Norham down the bank of the river, a pleasant footpath extends to the village of **Horncliffe,** near which a glen strikes off, terminating at a picturesque mill and encrusting spring. 1 m. S. of Horncliffe is

30 m. **Velvet Hall Stat.,** and 1 m. N. the *Union Suspension Bridge*, built by Sir Sam. Brown in 1820, the first of the sort in the British Islands. Below the bridge on the l. bank is *Paxton Ho.*, the seat of Col. D. Milne Home, which contains a gallery of good paintings. Between this and Tweedmouth the *Whiteadder*, which, rising in the Lammermuirs, flows across the Merse, enters the Tweed. As the train approaches

34 m. **Tweedmouth Stat.,** the traveller obtains on the left an attractive view of Berwick, with the lofty viaduct built by Stephenson, connecting it with this suburb, and reaching right across the valley of

the Tweed. It consists of 28 arches, 126 ft. in height, and is 2000 ft. in length.

35½ m. **Berwick-upon-Tweed** ✲, See p. 4.

ROUTE 9.

Edinburgh to Carstairs Junc. by Midcalder. Cal. Rly.

27½ m., about 9 trains daily in 40-70 min.

This line leaves Princes St. Stat.

At ½ m. *Branch* strikes rt. to *Cramond Br.* (p. 65) and *Leith* (p. 62).

1¼ m. **Merchiston Stat.**, for S.W. suburbs. Views l. of Arthur's Seat, Braid Hills, and Pentlands. Conspicuous on a ridge in the foreground is *Morningside* (*Private*) *Lunatic Asylum*, occupying the site of the house of J. Hill Burton, the Historian of Scotland.

2¼ m. **Slateford Stat.**, beyond which the rly. and the Union Canal are carried over the Water of Leith by a magnificent viaduct. The village is in the valley below.

[At 2½ m. a branch loop line l. ascends the contracted Water of Leith valley to

3¾ m. **Colinton Stat.** 1 m. S. lie *Dreghorn Cas.* (Mrs. Macfie) and *Bonally House*, formerly the seat of Lord Cockburn, at the foot of the Pentlands. Behind the latter a pleasant track leads over to Glencorse Reservoir (p. 66).

4¾ m. **Juniper Green Stat.**

6 m. **Currie Stat.**, also a good starting point for walks over the Pentlands (p. 66).

Lennox Tower (in the grounds of Lymphoy), formerly the property of the Lennox family, is passed l. before

7¼ m. **Balerno Stat.** l. is *Malleny* (E. of Rosebery) and the village, beyond which are paper mills and a track leading by Threipmuir Reservoir to *Bavelaw Cas.* 3 m., an ancient hunting seat, and thence over the Pentlands (p. 66).

At 8½ m. the main line is rejoined.]

---

3 m. **Kingsknowe Stat.**

At 4½ m. l. is the quaint old *Baberton Ho.*, with a short but fine avenue, for a time the residence of Charles X. of France.

5½ m. **Curriehill Stat.** ½ m. rt. is *Riccarton Ho.* (Sir J. H. Gibson Craig, Bt.), with one of the most extensive and beautiful *Pinetums* in Scotland.

Beyond, l. is *Curriehill Ho.*, which occupies the site of the old castle of the Skenes of Currie, and gave their title to two Judges of the Court of Session. Rt. are the extensive grounds of *Dalmahoy*, the seat of the Earl of Morton. Amongst its curiosities are the keys of Lochleven Castle, which were thrown into the lake when Mary Queen of Scots escaped. Seven sets of these keys, in different Scottish houses, contend for authentication! The park has fine timber, and the picturesque precipices of Dalmahoy Crags to the S. add a feature to the view.

At 7½ m. the Currie line (above) falls in l. *Hatton*, a quaint house with flanking towers, plastered, built by the Lauderdales about Charles II.'s time, with terraced garden, and the modern *Linburn* (R. E. Scott, Esq.) are seen rt. before reaching

10 m. **Midcalder Stat.** l. is *Kirknewton Ch. and Manse*, beyond which are Kirknewton village and *Meadowbank Ho.* (J. A. Maconochie Wellwood, Esq.). 1½ m. N.W. is *Midcalder Village*, and beside it *Calder House* (Lord Torphichen) beautifully situated on the bank of the Murieston Water, near its confluence with the Almond. Part of it is very old, and in a room here the Holy Communion was first administered after the Protestant

fashion by Knox. Midcalder Ch. (13th cent.) Middle Pointed Gothic, consisting of choir and W. tower, has been restored and enlarged.

The aspect of this district has been greatly changed since 1865, by the discovery of certain shales which yield a considerable supply of mineral oil. Pits and oil-works now dot the country all round Mid- and West-Calder, contributing sadly to mar the scenery and pollute the rivers.

Beyond the stat. l. is *Ormiston Ho.* (W. Wilkie, Esq.)

At 11½ m. (rt. *Oakbank Oil Works*) the lines rt. to Glasgow (Rte. 21) and l. to Carstairs diverge. The Pentlands stand out well l. as we pass

15¼ m. **Harburn Stat.,** and 18½ m. **Cobbinshaw Stat.,** whose large reservoir l. supplies the Union Canal with water.

21½ m. **Auchengray Stat.** [Branch rt. to 2 m. *Haywood Stat.* and 3½ m. *Wilsontown Stat.*, where are iron works on the E. border of the Lanarkshire coalfield.]

Cowthally Castle, now a gloomy ruin, where James IV., James V., and James VI. were entertained by the Somervilles, lies rt. 1 m. before reaching

26 m. **Carnwath Stat.,** *i.e.* "the ford of the cairn," a large mound l. The church here includes a small fragment of Third Pointed Gothic—a window with tracery—and contains monumental effigies.

27½ m. **Carstairs Junc. Stat.,** see p. 16.

ROUTE 10.

Symington Junc. to Peebles by Biggar and Broughton. Cal. Rly.

19 m., 5 trains daily in 45 min.

This is the shortest route to Peebles from Glasgow and the S. (see Rte. 3), and from Edinburgh (see Rtes. 9 and 3), to Biggar, &c., but from Edinburgh to Peebles itself Rte. 6 is much shorter.

2 m. **Coulter Stat.,** where the Clyde is crossed.

"A singular feature of the Clyde's course is that it approaches within 7 miles of the Tweed. . . . Between the rivers is the broad flat valley of Biggar, so little above the level of the Clyde that it would not cost much labour to send that river across into the Tweed. . . . That it once took that course, thus entering the sea at Berwick instead of at Dumbarton, is possible, and . . . it might do so again."—Sir A. GEIKIE.

1 m. rt. beyond the conspicuous mansion of *Cornhill* lies the village at the foot of the *Culter Fell* (2454 ft.) range. There are traces of several Roman camps in the neighbourhood.

3¼ m. **Biggar Stat.** ✲, a country town of one wide street. The *Church*, built 1545, was a beautiful cruciform Gothic structure; but all its internal beauty has been purposely destroyed. It has a square central tower: E. end, a semi-hexagon. In the churchyard are gravestones of the family of Gledstanes or Gladstone, ancestors of the statesman and scholar, whose grandfather, Thomas, left Biggar about 1756 for Leith. At the end of the town is a large mound, 300 ft. in circumference and 36 ft. in height, supposed to have been used as a law-court or moothill. Of *Boghall Castle*, once a seat of the Earls of Winton, there is only left one small tower. Biggar was the birthplace of Dr. John Brown (1810-82), author of "Rab and his Friends," etc. From Biggar the rly. keeps parallel with the stream called Biggar Water, to

8 m. **Broughton Stat.** ✲, 1½ m. l. of which is the British fort of *Langlaw Hill*, consisting of five concentric rings. 1 m. S. of the stat. is *Rachan* (J. Tweedie, Esq.)

[16 m. S. of this is the Source of the Tweed, 1500 ft. above sea-level, reached by what was formerly the great highroad between Edin. and Dumfries. At 6 m. stands *Crook Inn*★, once a famous posting-house. From it *Broad Law* (2754 ft.), after Merrick (2764 ft.) [pp. 108, 122] the highest hill on the mainland S. of the Forth, may be ascended easily in 2 hours by following up the *Hearthstane Burn*. The "broad" moor at the top is very remarkable. Near the ch. of Tweedsmuir (7½ m.) is a standing stone, 5 ft. high, in the midst of a bog. From the church a cart road leads in 12 m. up the glen of the *Talla* and down the *Megget Water* to Rodono on St. Mary's Loch (p. 32), through a district peculiarly interesting to geologists because of the evidences of glacier action.]

The valley of the Tweed is entered 1½ m. farther on below *Drummelzier*, in the churchyard of which Merlin's grave is pointed out. On the W. side is the Tweed, and on the E. is the *Powsail* burn. An old prophecy attributed to Thomas the Rhymer says—

"When Tweed and Pausayl join at Merlin's grave,
England and Scotland shall one monarch have";

and it is said that on the day of James VI.'s coronation the Tweed overflowed its banks, and its waters ran into the Powsail. It must have been a great inundation, as the churchyard is about 10 ft. above the level of either stream. The castle of *Drummelzier*, now in ruins, was formerly the fortress of the Tweedie family, a powerful and very quarrelsome faction in the 16th cent. The ruins of *Tinnis* (*i.e.* Thane's) *Castle* are conspicuous on a height near Drummelzier.

12½ m. **Stobo Stat.**, to the left of which is *Stobo Castle*, the beautiful seat of Sir Graham Montgomery, Bt., built 1805, and *Stobo Kirk* (restored), with a square tower, an E. E. nave, and Norm. chancel. The "*jougs*," or iron collar for the neck of offenders, is attached to the porch. On the rt. is *Dalwick* or *New Posso* (Sir J. Naesmyth, Bt.), noted for its fine timber and rhododendrons. The trees are of large growth, especially an avenue of silver firs, and the larches, which are reported to have been first planted here in 1725.

16 m. **Lyne Stat.**, N. of this, occupying a strong position on the left bank of the Lyne, is a Roman castrum stativum, originally a parallelogram of 850 ft. by 750. The N. side has been destroyed by agricultural operations, although the entrances at the remaining sides are still visible. *Lyne Church* is one of the smallest in Scotland, and has some curious carving. At *Sheriffmuir*, between the rly. and the Lyne, there are 2 erect stones, known as the *standing stones*. 4 m. up the Lyne, overlooking the river, is *Drochil Castle*, a fine old mansion, partaking of a mixture of the fortress and the manor-house. It consists of 2 square blocks of building, with a cleft between, formerly connected by an arch. At the extreme angles of the double square are 2 round towers, each with a semi-turret, uniting it with the square mass. It was commenced by the Regent Morton, but the building was abruptly checked by his execution in 1581, for his participation in the murder of Darnley.

[A wild lonely road between the *Meldon Hills* (1400 ft.) leads N. in 5½ m. to *Eddleston Stat.* (p. 78).]

On the S. bank of the Tweed, opposite Lyne, is the old ivy-covered tower of *Barns* (Earl of Wemyss), the residence in the 16th cent. of William Burnett, who for his propensity for marauding expeditions at night was nicknamed "the Howlet." rt. is the *Vale of Manor* (p. 92), and l. is *Neidpath Cas.* (p. 91) before reaching

19 m. **PEEBLES Stat.** ✲

[There is another station across the river on the N.B. Rly. for Edinburgh, Innerleithen, and Galashiels (Rte. 6), but there is no rly. communication between them except for goods.]

This old county town is agreeably situated on the left bank of the

Tweed (at its junction with the Eddleston Water) 25 m. from its source and 1000 ft. below it.

The river is here crossed by an old stone bridge of 5 arches, and on the S. side is a pleasant residential quarter. The town was a favourite residence of the Scottish monarchs, particularly of Alexander III., who (1261) built the *Crosskirk*, of which the shell of the tower and an ivy-covered gable are still standing near the N. B. Rly. stat. It was noted for its fair or feast of Beltane, which James I. made the subject of his poem "Peblis to the Play." The facetious saying—"For real pleasure give me Peebles"—marks it as being now a particularly sleepy place. It is noted for its anglers.

St. Andrew's Church was founded in 1195; but Cromwell's troopers converted it into a stable, and very little is now left save a venerable old tower, the restoration of which was in 1883 undertaken by the late Dr. W. Chambers,[1] of Glenormiston, the publisher. Of the *Castle* of Peebles nothing is left, but a small portion of the town walls may be seen near the E. port. The town was burnt in 1544 by the Earl of Hertford. A conspicuous building is the *Chambers Institute*, presented to the town by the late Dr. W. Chambers. The building in which the library is placed dates from the 16th cent., and once formed the residence of the Queensberry family. In the centre of the quadrangle is the shaft of the old *Town Cross,* given to the burgh by Sir Adam Hay. Mungo Park, the African traveller, once practised as a medical man in Peebles, and had his surgery in the High Street. The inn of the Cross Keys, formerly known as the Yett, was the town mansion of the family of Williamson of Cardrona, and dates from the 17th cent. It is the reputed original of the "Cleikum" in "St. Ronan's Well." Some of the houses have vaulted floors level with the street, and are remnants of the bastel houses erected for security against Border invaders. There are many good country residences in the neighbourhood. *e.g.* *Rosetta,* *Venlaw* (Admiral Erskine), *Kerfield, Kingsmeadows,* and *Haystoun* (Sir J. A. Hay, Bt.), *Kailzie* (W. C. Black, Esq.) The surrounding country is very pretty, and there is excellent angling in the Tweed and its tributaries.

[1] See the very complete and interesting "History of Peeblesshire," by Wm. Chambers, 1864.

[EXCURSIONS :—

(1) To the ruins of **Neidpath Castle**, 1 m. up the Tweed, charmingly situated, overlooking the river.

It formerly consisted of 2 castles united, the original Border tower having attached to it an imposing building of vast strength, "which now constitutes the castle visited by strangers."—CHAMBERS.

On a gateway in the courtyard is the crest of the Earls of Tweeddale—a goat's head over a coronet—and a bunch of strawberries, a rebus on the name of Fraser, the family from whom it had passed to the Hays of Yester. The 2nd Earl of Tweeddale held it for Charles II., but the old tower, the weakest part, was battered by the cannon of Cromwell, and it was taken after an obstinate resistance. It was afterwards purchased by the 1st Duke of Queensberry. "Old Q.," the 4th and last Duke, cut down the fine timber, hence Wordsworth's sonnet, "Composed at —— Castle"—

"Degenerate Douglas! oh, the unworthy Lord!
Whom mere despite of heart could so far please,
And love of havoc (for with such disease
Fame taxes him), that he could send forth word
To level with the dust a noble horde,
A brotherhood of venerable Trees,
Leaving an ancient dome, and towers like these,
Beggared and outraged!"

At the death of "Old Q." (1810) the castle passed to the Earl of Wemyss.

(2) To **Innerleithen,** 6½ m. Drive down the l. bank of the Tweed, returning by the rt. bank past **Traquair Ho.** (p. 78), 15 m.

(3) To the **Manor Valley,** approached by *Hundleshope* or by the bridge over the Tweed above Neidpath (opened 1882). Here, about 5 m. from Peebles, is the cottage occupied by David Ritchie, "The Black Dwarf," where he was visited by Scott (1797), then the visitor of Prof. Adam Ferguson at *Hallyards,* now the residence of Dr. Wm. Anderson. *Manorhead* is 6 m. farther, from which pedestrians can cross in 6 m. by the Megget Water to St. Mary's Loch. The Manor valley lends itself to innumerable walking expeditions, and the neighbourhood abounds in ancient forts and camps.

(4) Pedestrians may ascend **Venlaw** (1066 ft.), 1 m. N., and penetrate into the recesses of the **Moorfoot Range.**]

ROUTE 11.

Carstairs Junc. to Lanark (Falls of Clyde) and Ayr.

From Glasgow, the N., and the S., to Carstairs, see Rte. 2, and from Edin. Rte. 9. Trains from Glasgow go by loop to Lanark, from Cleghorn, without entering Carstairs. Several trains daily to Lanark, but only about 2 through to Ayr, which is generally reached by Rte. 18.

The train runs W. from Carstairs (2¼ m.); then S. to

4¾ m. **Lanark Stat.** ✲, an uninteresting town on a cold upland, nearly 700 ft. above the sea-level. Little evidence now exists of the antiquity of which it boasts. In a central market-place, from which five streets diverge, stands an ungainly Parish *Church* (date 1777), indented in its front with a niche to contain a huge statue of the patriot Wm. Wallace, who commenced his exploits of arms here, 1297, by overpowering the English garrison and slaying their leader, Wm. Hazelrigg, in revenge, it is alleged, for the murder of his wife. Not far from the rly. station is a Gothic Rom. Cath. Church. Beyond it, in the *Parish Burial Ground,* several pointed arches are preserved of the old Parish *Ch. of St. Kentigern.*

The ** **Falls of Clyde**[1] above Lanark — *Corra Linn* and *Bonnington* —are most easily seen from the N. side of the river. Allow 2-3 hrs. The road zigzags steeply down to the settlement of *New Lanark* (abt. 2½ m.), founded in 1784 by David Dale, and his son-in-law, the visionary socialist, Robert Owen, now the property of a Manchester firm. It is a street of mills and tall houses on the right bank of the Clyde. ½ m. farther is the Lodge of *Bonnington Ho.* (Sir C. Ross, Bt.)—reached more directly by a footpath. Here carriages must be left and tickets (3d. each) obtained.

It is a very pleasant walk from the Lodge to the Falls of 1½ m. through well-wooded grounds along the right bank of the Clyde, here bordered by cliff and rock alternating with fine hanging woods. About ½ m. from the lodge a view is obtained of *Corra Linn,* the finest of the Falls, descending 86 ft., and visible in its full extent from the path. It is situated in a magnificent amphitheatre of rock and exceeds any fall in Britain in the body of water.

The mansion of *Corehouse*[2] (once the seat of the Scotch Judge Cranstoun, Lord Corehouse, now of C. J. E. Cranstoun, Esq.) stands on the left bank slightly back from the Fall, while the old "time-cemented tower," called *Wallace's Tower,*[3] in

[1] *Coach* daily in summer from the stat. to these Falls, proceeding afterwards to Cartland Crags, Stonebyres Falls, and Tillietudlem, pp. 148, 149, where the train may be joined.

[2] Here are some good pictures: Group of Cupids, *Rubens;* Madonna, *Titian;* Portrait of an Elector Palatine, *Vandyck,* etc.

[3] It may be reached (3 m. from Lanark) by crossing the Clyde at *Kirkfieldbank* (p. 148), and entering the grounds of Corehouse (adm. 3d.) at the N. or W. lodge.

sight of which Wordsworth wrote his poem

"Lord of the Vale, astounding Flood,"

overhangs the verge of the cliff.

About ¾ m. farther on we come to *Bonnington Linn*, the uppermost of the Falls. The banks of the Clyde have here risen into high cliffs, and a bend in the channel causes it to sweep round a sharp turn dividing into two branches. Between them is left a rocky island, to which a light iron bridge gives access. The height is not much more than 30 ft., but the surrounding rocks add a picturesque effect.

The *Fall of Stonebyres* is 2½ m. below Lanark, close to the road to *Tillietudlem* and Hamilton (p. 148).

The **Cartland Crags**, precipitous cliffs, 200-400 ft. high, bordering a remarkable chasm (¾ m. long) on the *Mouse Water*, 1 m. W. of Lanark, deserve a visit. On the edge of the cliffs is *Castle Quaw*, a fragment of wall, connected with caves in the cliff, said to have been a portion of Wallace's stronghold when he made his first raid upon the English. The defile near its upper end is crossed by one of Telford's elegant *Bridges* of 3 arches, on piers 120 ft. above the water. A low bridge crosses near its mouth close to a very old narrow *Bridge* said to be Roman.

From Lanark the train runs back 1 m., and then trends S.W., crossing the Clyde, and passing (7 m.) *Sandilands Stat.* and (9 m.) *Ponfeigh Stat.*—with l. *Tinto Hill* (2335 ft.) very conspicuous (p. 16)—to

11 m. **Douglas Stat.** ✡ An omnibus drives by the fine parks—through which the Douglas Water flows—of *Douglas Cas.* (Earl of Hume), a modern house, to the quaint and irregular little town 2½ m. distant.

"Of the redoubted *Castle* [Sir Walter's '*Castle Dangerous*'] itself there remains but a small detached fragment, covered with ivy, close to the present mansion; but Scott hung over it long, or rather sat beside it [19th July 1831] drawing outlines on the turf, and arranging in his fancy the sweep of the old precincts."—LOCKHART.

The town contains a partially ruined *Church of St. Bride*, of the pointed transition style. In the choir, which is the only part in preservation, may be seen

"the very extraordinary *Monuments* of the house of Douglas, one of the most heroic and powerful families in the annals of Scotland. That works of sculpture, equal to any of the 14th century in Westminster Abbey (for such they certainly were, though much mutilated by Cromwell's soldiery), should be found in so remote an inland place, attests strikingly the boundless resources of those haughty lords, 'whose coronet,' as Scott says, 'so often counterpoised the crown.'

"The effigy of the best friend of Bruce is among the number, and represents him cross-legged, as having fallen in battle with the Saracen, when on the way to Jerusalem with the heart of his king. . . . Sir Walter Scott examined by torchlight these silent witnesses of past greatness. It was a strange and melancholy scene. . . .

"The appearance of the village, too, is most truly transferred to the novel; and I may say the same of the surrounding landscape. We descended into a sort of crypt, in which the Douglases were buried until about a century ago, when there was room for no more; the leaden coffins around the wall being piled on each other until the lower ones had been pressed flat as sheets of pasteboard, while the floor itself was entirely paved with others of comparatively modern date, on which coronets and inscriptions might still be traced. Here the silver case that once held the noble heart of the good Lord James himself is still pointed out. It is in the form of a heart, which, in memory of his glorious mission and fate, occupies ever since the chief place in the blazon of his posterity:—

"'The bloody heart blazed in the van,
Announcing Douglas' dreaded name.'"
LOCKHART'S *Life of Scott*.

[4 m. N. of Douglas Stat. is *Lesmahagow* (p. 149).]

Following the line of the Douglas Water and passing (17¼ m.) *Inches*

Stat. and (19¾ m.) *Glenbuck Stat.*—with ironworks, a small loch and a reservoir—we cross the watershed to

23½ m. **Muirkirk Stat.**, an Ayrshire town with the large *Ironworks* of W. Baird & Co., Lim.

To the S. lies *Cairntable*, 1942 ft., and to the N.E. *Priesthill* farm on which is a monument to John Brown, the Covenanter, here shot in presence of his wife and family by Claverhouse, May 1, 1685.

The line skirts *Aird's Moss* (rt.) a wild dreary swamp, marked by scattered pits and ironstone mines, but also known as the scene of a skirmish between the Royalists and Covenanters, in which Richard Cameron, their leader, was slain, 1680, "leaving his name to a religious sect and a renowned regiment in the British army" (BURTON). An obelisk at the E. extremity commemorates the event.

30 m. **Cronberry Stat.** [*Branch* rt. by *Lugar Stat.* (with *Ironworks*, W. Baird & Co., Lim.), situated on the N. bank of the *Lugar Water*, here very picturesque, to *Auchinleck Stat.* [4 m.] (p. 102).]

The line crosses the G. and S.W. Rly. (Rte. 12) to

33 m. **Cumnock Stat.** ✲, ½ m. S. of the town (p. 102).

35¼ m. **Dumfries House Stat.** In the grounds of the *House* (Marquis of Bute) [¾ m. N.], on the l. bank of the Lugar, are the ruins of *Terringzean Cas.*

37 m. **Ochiltree Stat.** The village lies 1½ m. N.

The line turns N., passing

41½ m. **Drongan Stat.** to

46½ m. **Annbank Stat.**, where the line from Mauchline to Ayr (p. 103) is joined.

51¼ m. **AYR** ✲, see p. 119.

ROUTE 12.

Carlisle to Glasgow by Annan, Dumfries, Sanquhar, and Kilmarnock. Glasgow and S.W. Railway.

About 11 trains daily in 2½-5 hrs. 115½ m. This is the route by which the Midland trains from England reach Glasgow (or Greenock).

This line leaves Rte. 2 at Gretna Junc., and runs W. to

9½ m. **Gretna Green Stat.** The neighbouring village was formerly the haven of runaway couples from England, who took advantage at this, the first place across the border, of the Scotch law, by which a simple declaration before 2 witnesses makes a man and woman husband and wife. The ceremony was generally performed by the *Blacksmith*, and here Lord Chancellor Erskine married his 2nd wife (cf. *Coldstream*, p. 86). An Act of Parliament in 1856, requiring residence in Scotland for 21 days by at least one of the parties, put an end to the custom. The view from Gretna Hill, though only 200 ft. high, is pleasing, as it commands the Solway, the long viaducts over it, and the distant mountains.

11¼ m. the rly. crosses the Kirtle Water, a tributary of the Esk, with the estuary of which it runs parallel through a somewhat dreary country, to

14½ m. **Dornock Stat.**, and

17½ m. **Annan Stat.** ✲

[There is another rly. stat. on the line between *Kirtlebridge* (p. 9) and *Maryport*, carried across the Solway by a long viaduct.]

This is a neat little town—a royal and parl. burgh—on the l. bank of the river of the same name, 2 m. from its mouth. It possesses a cotton mill, some bacon-curing establishments, etc., and has an export trade by sea with England.

In 1332, after the death of King

Robert, Edward Balliol, having been crowned at Scone, summoned the barons hither to swear fealty to him. He was surprised by Archibald Douglas and 1000 cavalry, and barely escaped to Carlisle on horseback, without saddle, bridle, or a single attendant.

Annan was the birthplace of Edward Irving in 1792, and the scene of his deposition from the Scotch Church by the Presbytery of Annan in 1833. Hugh Clapperton, the African traveller, was also a native of Annan (1788).

The line crosses the river, and the scenery improves as the rly. reaches

21 m. **Cummertrees Stat.**, a pretty village situated on the small stream of the Pow Water. About 1 m. N. is *Kinmount House*, the fine seat of the Marquis of Queensberry, and 3½ m. N. is *Hoddam Castle* (p. 10). Much of the scenery of "Redgauntlet" is taken from this neighbourhood.

At 23¼ m. the train passes l. *Ruthwell Ch.*, in the apse (N. end) of which is the remarkable **Ruthwell Cross**,[1] 18 ft. high, covered on its principal faces with rude carvings relating to the life of Christ, and bearing inscriptions in Latin, chiefly from the Vulgate, easily translated; on its sides it has interlacing vinework with birds and beasts devouring the fruit, and *Runic* inscriptions, first deciphered, in 1840, by John M. Kemble, who discovered that the language was Early English. He afterwards found, in an Anglo-Saxon MS. of the 7th or 8th century in the Library at Vercelli, a poem on "The Holy Rood" (supposed to be by the great Northumbrian bard Cædmon), from which the inscription was an extract. These lines are the earliest English that we possess just as it was written. The arms of the Cross are modern. A brass tablet behind the cross bears the following inscription:—

"The *Ruthwell Cross:* Dates from Anglo-Saxon times: Destroyed during the conflicts which followed the Reformation: Lay in the earthen floor of this church 1642-1790: Erected in the Manse Garden in 1823: Sheltered here and declared a monument under the Ancient Monuments Act in 1887."

½ m. beyond the ch. is the village.

25 m. **Ruthwell Stat.**, ¾ m. S.W., is the tower of *Comlongon Castle*, in good preservation, on the edge of an extensive wood. It belongs to the Earl of Mansfield, and was once the residence of the Warden of the Western Marches.

The line now trends inland through a moorland district, skirting l. *Lochar Moss*, which is 10 m. in length, and passes

29¼ m. **Racks Stat.** to

33 m. **Dumfries Stat.**

[*Branches* (1) E. to *Lockerbie* (p. 11); (2) W. to *Kirkcudbright* and *Wigtown*, Rtes. 13, 14.]

DUMFRIES✲, a royal and parl. burgh, the chief town of the S.W. Border Counties, addressed by Burns as—

"Maggie, by the banks o' Nith,
A dame wi' pride eneuch"—

is well situated on rising ground on the left bank of the Nith, about 9 m. from its mouth. The old castle, of which not a vestige remains, was built by Edward I., and stood on the spot now occupied by the new *Greyfriars Church*, a handsome red building with a tall spire, standing at the upper end of the High Street or Market Place, in the middle of which rises the picturesque tower of the *Town Hall* or *Mid Steeple*, built by Tobias Bachup of Alloa. S. and W. of the fortress stood the monastery of the Greyfriars, in the old ch. of which Robert Bruce, flying from the Court of Edward I., in 1306, encountered

[1] Key of ch. can be got at the manse which is close at hand.

John, the Red Comyn, and finding him loyal to the English, got to high words, and stabbed him before the altar. Rushing from the scene of blood and sacrilege, and meeting his partisan, Roger Kirkpatrick, he said, "I doubt I have slain Comyn." "You doubt?" said Kirkpatrick, "I mak sicker" (make sure), and went in and finished the deed.

> "Vain Kirkpatrick's bloody dirk
> Making sure of murder's work."—SCOTT.

The next act of the murderers was to expel the English judges, then sitting in the town. Edward I. swore by the "Vow of the Swan" to avenge on Scotland the murder of Comyn, and proceeded to reconquer the country, though carried in a litter.

A neat Doric pillar is erected in Queensberry Square to the third Duke of Queensberry. On Prince Charlie's return from Derby, in 1745, he occupied Dumfries, and his council-chamber is still shown in the Commercial Hotel. He levied a tax on the inhabitants of £2000 in money, and 1000 pair of shoes, but a false alarm of the Duke of Cumberland's approach started him off at short notice, having received only £1100 of the levy.

The *Old Bridge* connecting the town with the suburb of Maxwelltown, on the right bank of the Nith, was built by Devorguilla, wife of John Balliol, and founder of the Greyfriars monastery and of *Sweetheart Abbey* (p. 99) in the reign of Alexander III. At that time it had 13 arches, 6 only of which are now standing. In 1795 the new bridge was built, and the traffic over the old one is that of foot-passengers only. In 1876 a third (foot) bridge was built.

Burns's House is in Burns St., a narrow lane on left as you go to St. Michael's Ch. In this he lived for 3 years, and in this he died on July 21, 1796, aged 37. It was afterwards rented by his widow, who survived him for 38 years. It is now occupied by the master of the Industrial School, who is kind enough to allow any stranger to see it, and keeps the rooms as much as possible in the same state as they were when inhabited by the poet. In December 1791, when Robert Burns gave up his farm at *Ellisland*, and became an exciseman, he lived for 18 months in a house at the foot of Bank Street. In 1882 a *Statue of Burns* (by Mrs. D. O. Hill) was erected in Dumfries.

Burns was first buried in the N. corner of St. Michael's burying-ground, but was removed to the E. corner on 19th September 1815, when the *Mausoleum* was erected. It is a mean Grecian temple, containing a poor sculpture by Turnerelli, representing the genius of Coila finding her favourite son at the plough, and casting her inspiring mantle over him. The open temple was utterly unsuited to the climate, and so the intervals between the pillars have been filled with glass. The churchyard of St. Michael's is remarkable for the number of monuments and tombstones, altogether amounting to more than 2600. Near Burns's mausoleum, marked by a granite obelisk, lie two Covenanters, who suffered death 1667.

Sir John Richardson, the Arctic voyager, and companion of Franklin, was born at Nith Place, Dumfries, in 1787.

The *Town Council Chamber* contains portraits of William of Orange and Mary, also of the third Duke of Queensberry. There is still preserved amongst the civic treasures the silver gun presented by James VI., for the purpose of encouraging the use of firearms amongst the inhabitants of the town.

The large building on the left bank of the Nith, a little below the town, is the *Crichton Institution*, a lunatic asylum, founded by Dr. Crichton of Friar's Carse, at a cost of £100,000, and originally designed as a university.

Dumfries is celebrated as a mart of sheep, bred in the adjacent districts, and brought hither for sale or exportation to England. It has a considerable manufacture of tweeds and woollens, the Nithsdale and Kingholm mills, below the Bridge, employing a large number of hands.

The town of **Maxwelltown** across the Nith, called *Bridgend* before 1810, is an independent burgh of barony in the county of Kirkcudbright, but is included within the burgh of Dumfries for Parliamentary purposes. It contains handsome *Estab.* and *Free Churches*, a large *R. C. Nunnery*, *Tweed Mills*, and a combined *Observatory and Museum*.

EXCURSIONS from Dumfries :

(1) N.E. to ***Lincluden Abbey** ($1\frac{1}{2}$ m.) and **Irongray Ch.**, 5 m.

Cross the bridge to Maxwelltown, and take the first turn to the right.

The Abbey was founded in the 12th cent. by Uhtred, Lord of Galloway, as a priory for Benedictine nuns, but late in the 14th it was closed by Archibald the Grim, Earl of Bothwell.

The buildings are very prettily situated on a promontory, surrounded on two sides by the Cluden, and on the third by the Nith, into which the former stream flows at the S.E. angle of the grounds.

The remains consist of a small but beautiful *Church* in the Middle Pointed style, of which the nave is quite gone. The choir, walled off by a screen, is entered by a flat archway, surmounted by sculptures of the Life of Christ, supported by a row of Angels. Part of the transepts are also preserved. The tracery of the windows is almost wholly gone. There is a handsome canopied monument on the N. side, with inscription, to Margaret, Countess of Douglas, daughter of King Robert III. (d. *circ.* 1430). The effigy has long since disappeared. Close by the tomb is a doorway, beautifully carved and surmounted by the heart and chalice. On the opposite side are three fine sedilia, each with a canopy and crocket, and cusps in the interior, and a piscina of like design.

Beside the ch. are the ruins of a massive square Peel Tower, probably a part of the Provost's house. Lincluden was a favourite haunt of Burns, and here it was that he saw the "Vision."

The abbey stands within ancient *Earthworks*, and at the side of the ch. rises a mound or *Moot-hill*.

The return to Dumfries may be by the river-side, a very picturesque walk,—that is, should the tourist not feel inclined to extend his ramble up the Cluden Water to **Irongray Ch.**, where the "Recreations of a Country Parson" were written, and in whose ch.-yd. is a stone erected, 1831,

"by the author of 'Waverley' to the memory of Helen Walker, who d. 1791. This humble individual practised in real life the virtues with which fiction has invested the imaginary character of Jeanie Deans . . . "

On a shaded knoll about $\frac{1}{4}$ m. off is the grave of two Covenanters, named Gordon and M'Cubbin (1685). Upon the tombstone are the following lines :—

"By Lagg and Bloodie Bruce commands
We were hung up by hellish hands;
And so, their furious wrath to stay,
We died near Kirk of Irongray;
And boundless peace we now partake,
For freedom's and religion's sake."

The hilly road to the S. may be taken to Dumfries, passing *Terregles House* (H. Maxwell Stuart, Esq.). It is a handsome mansion (1789) of red stone. In a former one Queen Mary found rest and refuge for a few days after her flight of 80 miles from the fight of Langside (1568), its owner being the 4th Lord Herries, her staunch supporter. Hence she wended her way to England.

Among the family portraits is one of the Countess of Nithsdale, who so heroically rescued her husband from the Tower by taking his place, 1716. Here are preserved her cloak in which she disguised him, and Queen Mary's prayer-book. Thereafter all the then combined titles of Lord Maxwell, Lord Herries (restored 1848), and Earl of Nithsdale were forfeited.

(2) To * **Caerlaverock Castle**, which stands on the l. bank of the river 8 m. S. of Dumfries, on the flat marshy shore of the Solway, between the Nith and the Lochar. It was a place of great strength, flanked by the Solway in front, and by Lochar Moss behind, so as to be virtually the key to S. W. Scotland. The upper road, generally taken going, is somewhat uninteresting, but at 5½ m. is *Caerlaverock Ch.* and *Churchyard* where Robert Paterson, "*Old Mortality*" (d. 1801), is buried, and where a monument to him was erected in 1869 by Messrs. A. and C. Black, publishers.

The Castle, a very interesting and picturesque building, is situated at a spot identified by antiquaries as the Carbantorigium of Ptolemy. As far back as the days of Malcolm Canmore it belonged to the Maxwells, afterwards and for long Earls of Nithsdale, ancestors of its present proprietor. It was besieged and taken in 1300 by Edward I. in person, after being bravely defended by a garrison of only 60 men against an army furnished with all the war engines then known. A minute account of the siege exists in Norman French.[1] It was afterwards retaken by Bruce in 1313, to be again recaptured by the English. Not until 1355 was it recaptured from the English by Roger Kirkpatrick. A large part of the exterior of the castle dates from the 14th cent. It was dismantled after a siege by the Earl of Essex, 1570, in revenge for the part Lord Herries had taken in defending Queen Mary. The interior was rebuilt, and the banqueting-hall, 90 ft. long by 26 broad, with 2 turrets, was erected by Maxwell, 1st Earl of Nithsdale, 1638, but war approached its walls in 1640, when it was besieged by the Covenanters under Col. Home, and capitulated after 13 weeks. Since then it has been a ruin.

The castle, in ground plan a triangle with round towers at the angles, is well built, and protected by a double moat.

> "I believe there never was seen a castle so beautifully situated, for at once could be seen the Irish Sea towards the W., and to the N. a fine country surrounded by a arm of the sea."—NICOLAS.

The great gateway, over which is the Maxwell crest, and the motto "I bid ye fair," pierces a narrow curtain between two machicolated round towers of old baronial architecture, and one of the round towers at the other angles of the triangle still remains. It is called Murdoch's Tower, because Murdoch, Duke of Albany, was confined there by order of James I., previous to his execution at Stirling, 1426. "The buildings in the courtyard have the canopied and sculptured window-cases of the domestic architecture of James VI., and remind one of Linlithgow Palace and Heriot's Hospital." On the lower storey are heraldic devices, the stag, hedgehog, spread eagle, etc.; on the second are illustrated legends; and on the third are fables from the "Metamorphoses" of Ovid.

Sir W. Scott in "Guy Mannering," acknowledges that the general outline of his description of Ellangowan resembles Caerlaverock, but see p. 115.

The return drive is up the l. bank of the Nith passing (3½ m.) *Glencaple* ✲, a port and bathing place frequented by the Dumfries folk,

[1] Supposed to be the work of Walter of Exeter, a Franciscan friar. Edited and published by Sir Harris Nicolas.

—the *Portanferry* of Guy Mannering—with a ferry to *Maxwellbank* and *Kirkconnell.* By it the pedestrian can reach *Sweetheart Abbey* (below) after a pleasant walk, on the other side, of 3 m.

(3) To **New** or ** **Sweetheart Abbey** (7½ m.) and **Criffel** (1866 ft.) 10 m.

Travellers not pressed for time, and desirous of seeing a part of Scotland seldom explored, but full of beauty, are recommended to take the road from Dumfries to Dalbeattie Stat. (26 m.) round Criffel, and near the sea, by Kirkbean, an easy day's drive, as follows:—The road crosses Dumfries bridge, and descends the valley of the Nith, at some distance from the river. 3½ m. is *Cargen.* At 5½ m. from *Whinnyhill* is a beautiful view of Dumfries, with the valley of the Nith, its luxuriant cornfields pleasantly varied by plantations.

7 m. (l.) *Kirkconnell* is a fine ancient mansion, surrounded by old trees (R. M. Witham, Esq.). In front rises the bulky mass of *Criffel*, 1866 ft. above the sea, at the foot of which, in a most picturesque secluded valley, watered by the Abbey stream, is the Cistercian ruin of New Abbey.

New or **Sweetheart Abbey** was founded in 1275 by Devorguilla[1] Balliol, one of the founders of Balliol College, Oxford, who was herself buried here, and ordered the casket containing the heart of John Balliol, her husband (which she had treasured after his death), to be placed in her tomb. From this circumstance the abbey obtained the name of Doux Cœur, Dulce Cor, or Sweetheart Abbey, but both tomb and heart have disappeared.

The *Church* is cruciform, consisting of nave of 6 bays, with all the main arches perfect, and part of the clerestory; transepts having E. aisles or chapels, one retaining its vaulting; choir without aisles; and central tower 90 ft. high. The style is, generally speaking, E. Pointed, though the building appears to have been finished, or perhaps altered, in the Decorated period. The W. entrance is of very simple character, but above it is a triplet window surmounted by an elegant rose within an enclosing arch. There is a fine Middle Pointed window in the N. transept. The E. window is of 5 lights, and its tracery remains; and is surmounted by a window similar to the one in the transept. The S. transept wall, partly built up, retains part of a wheel window of original character. Of the roof nothing remains, except that of the aisle of the S. transept, which is groined with shields at the intersections. Upon one of these are two pastoral staves in saltire, surmounted by a heart, probably the coat of arms belonging to the abbey. There is also an inscription, "Chus tim of nid" (choose time of need)—a sort of punning motto adopted by this fraternity of Nithside. The abbey seems to have figured but little in history. Its last abbot, Gilbert Brown, is said to have been the original of Scott's Abbot of St. Mary's.

The abbey ruins stand close to the village of *New Abbey* ✲, where there is a R. C. Chap. erected by Lord Herries. An ugly kirk has been planted close to the ruin, obstructing the view of it. About 1 m. S. W. is a *Waterloo Monument,* 50 ft. high.

[The return may be made to Dumfries by proceeding up the valley of the Abbey water to its source in Loch Arthur, and joining the rly. at Killywhan Stat. (p. 105) about 5½ m. distant.]

In pursuing the road to Dalbeattie the driver should be directed to follow the road to the E. of **Criffel** (which is a very picturesque object from all points) by Kirkbean (12½ m.), and by the shore road through Colvend (21 m.) At 16½ m. *Southwick Ho.* (Sir Mark J. Stewart, Bt., M.P.) is passed rt., and at 19½ m. l. *Douglas Hall.* The country is beautifully wooded, the road almost an avenue, at other times a sort of "cornice" along the seashore, with constant variety of views—seaward over Solway to the Cumberland mountains and landwards towards Criffel, and up a succession of pretty glens. It ascends the small valley of the Urr, passing granite quarries to (26 m.) Dalbeattie (p. 105).

From Dumfries the rly. to Glasgow runs N.W. up the valley of the Nith, which in this, its lower portion, is broad and well cultivated, to

[1] See *Shairp's* poem of "Devorguilla."

36½ m. **Holywood Stat.**, where formerly a Premonstratensian abbey, founded by Devorguilla Balliol, 13th cent., stood. The last remains were taken down in 1778, and the parish ch. built of the materials. The old bells are still preserved.

Crossing the Nith, on right is *Dalswinton*, the seat of W. M'Alpine Leny, Esq. This estate formerly belonged to the Millers; Patrick Miller was the first to experiment, 1788, upon steam as a locomotive power on water, in a little vessel launched on the lake, which still forms the chief ornament of the park.[1]

On the opposite bank of the river is *Ellisland*, the farm which Burns rented of Mr. Miller of Dalswinton, and where he resided previous to taking up his abode in Dumfries. Here he wrote "Tam O'Shanter," and the touching verses, "To Mary in Heaven." On a window in the house may still be seen, scratched by Burns upon the glass, "An honest man's the noblest work of God." A road from Holywood Stat. leads direct to Ellisland (2½ m.) A little farther is *Friar's Carse*, a house once belonging to the Riddles, where the poet spent much of his time. Overlooking the river, close to it, are a camp and a Druidical circle, 240 ft. in diameter.

40¾ m. **Auldgirth Stat.**, close to a handsome bridge over the Nith—perhaps the prettiest spot in its whole course.

[2 m. W. are the ruins of *Lag*, the seat of the once powerful family of Grierson, one of whom shares with Claverhouse the reputation of being the persecutor of the Covenanters; while 8 m. beyond is the Farm of *Craigenputtock*, once the residence (1828-34) of Thomas Carlyle (d. 1881), and bequeathed by him to the University of Edinburgh.]

Here the valley begins to contract. The scenery becomes more broken, and the Permian sandstones, which have formed the bottom of the valley of the Nith from the sea upwards, cease. The river here winds through a defile in the Silurian rocks.

44½ m. **Closeburn Stat.** A little beyond it, on right, is *Closeburn Hall*, in whose grounds is *Closeburn Cas.*, an old seat of the Kirkpatrick family, from whom Eugénie, ex-Empress of the French, derives her Scottish descent. It is a square tower, with vaulted rooms.

At 45½ m. the Cample Water is crossed, upon a trib. of which (1 m. rt.) is *Crichhope Linn*, where the cliffs rise 40 or 50 ft. above the stream, yet so little separated that it is possible to leap across the fissure. Of this fact Sir Walter Scott, who knew the spot and had it "ever present to his fancy," has taken advantage in the scene in "Old Mortality," between Morton and Balfour.

47¼ m. **Thornhill Stat.** ✲ The town, abt. 1 m. W. beyond *Morton Parish Ch.*, is neat and well built, having in the centre a *Cross* surmounted by the Queensberry Arms. There is an interesting *Museum*, founded by T. B. Grierson, Esq. It contains a good geological, antiquarian, and natural history collection, including stone, bronze, and iron implements found in Nithsdale, numerous historic relics of the Covenanters and of Burns, etc.

3 m. N., on the right bank of the Nith, is **Drumlanrig**,[1] a seat of the Duke of Buccleuch. The situation of the castle is high and open, overlooks the tall woods and undulating hills, and commands a view over terraced gardens tapestried with flowers, down to the brawling Nith and its wooded banks. During the rebellion of 1745, the young Chevalier halted here, and the castle suffered

[1] Burns was a passenger on this trip, and Brougham witnessed it from the bank. For a full account of the incident, see James Nasmyth's Autobiography.

[1] The interior of the Castle may be seen Tuesdays and Fridays, or in absence of the family.

much at the hands of his followers. The park was devastated by its former owner, old Q——, but, since 1811, when it came to the Buccleuch family, is once more restored, and boasts of noble forest scenery. The castle was built 1675-1688 by William, first Duke of Queensberry, minister of James II. It is a quadrangular building of red stone. It has the character of a stately château, somewhat like Heriot's Hospital, retaining parts of an old castle, including a grim dungeon, now a wine-cellar. The paintings are chiefly family portraits. In the park is a ruin called *Tibber's Castle*, which was destroyed by Bruce in 1311. It is thought to have been Roman (? Tiberii Castellum). In the *Church of Durisdeer* (4 m. N.E.) are the sculptured monuments in marble of the Queensberry family, including James Douglas, 2nd Duke (1622-1711), and his Lady.

3 m. N.E. of Thornhill is *Morton Castle*, said to have been founded about 1080 by a De Morville, grandfather of the founder of Kilwinning and Dryburgh Abbeys. It was afterwards bestowed by Robert Bruce (being then part of the confiscated property of Balliol), upon Randolph, Earl of Moray, who lived here as Regent of the kingdom to David II. It then passed into the hands of the Douglas family, to whom it gave the title of Earl, and now belongs to the Duke of Buccleuch. It stands on the margin of a deep glen, and was at one time nearly surrounded by water, which has drained away.

[Coach twice daily to **Penpont** (2 m.) and **Moniaive** ✲, 7 m. S. W. There are some sculptured upright *stones* (prob. 11th cent.) between Thornhill and Penpont, a pretty village on the Scarr Water, on whose rt. bank is *Capenoch Ho.* (Mrs. Field Gladstone). *Moniaive* lies in quiet pastoral scenery at the junction of 3 waters, which together make the *Cairn*, on whose l. bank, 3 m. down, is *Maxwellton* (Rev. Sir E. Laurie), the locale of the favourite song of "Annie Laurie," commencing

> "Maxwellton braes are bonnie."

The *old* version was written about 1700 by Wm. Douglas of Fingland in honour of Miss Laurie ; the prettier and *more refined* version is by Lady John Scott (1835).

A fine moorland road leads S.W. from Moniaive to *Dalry* (12½ m.) or *New Galloway*, 14 m. (p. 107). At 3 m. *Loch Urr* lies 1 m. left. On its island are the traces of an ancient Caledonian town and of a fortress of later date.]

At 49 m. *Carronbridge* village is past l., and the *Carron Water* is crossed by a noble viaduct just before

50½ m. **Carronbridge Stat.**

[Here an excellent road runs rt. up the *Carron* past *Durisdeer* (above), and through the grand *Dalveen Pass* to Elvanfoot, 12½ m. (p. 16).]

Passing through a tunnel 4200 ft. long the rly. keeps the high ground on the l. bank of the Nith, crossing (53 m.) the *Enterkin Burn* and (57 m.) the *Menoch Water* (p. 16). Here across the Nith is *Eliock* (Rev. H. G. J. Veitch), where the "Admirable Crichton" is said to have been born in 1560, although the Cas. of Clunie. Perthshire (p. 287), also claims that honour.

59¼ m. **Sanquhar Stat.** ✲, a parl. burgh, and once a place of importance, in a dreary situation, surrounded by round-backed hills. Some of the inhab. are employed in the mines of glance coal. A party of armed Covenanters under Richard Cameron in 1680 attached to the town-cross a Declaration renouncing allegiance to the Stuarts, and declaring war against them. A little to the S. of the town is the ruin of its castle—one of the strongholds of the S.W. of Scotland. Near it is a *Moothill*.

Nearly 2 m. to the W. are remains of an earthwork running parallel with the Nith, and called the *Devil's Dyke*.

[From Sanquhar the excursion by *Menoch Pass* to *Wanlockhead* and *Leadhills*, 10 m. may be made (p. 16).]

62½ m. **Kirkconnel Stat.** The same earthwork is to be traced to the S. of this station. As the rly. approaches the source of the Nith the scenery becomes more wild and dreary, although relieved by (rt.) *Cairntable* (1942 ft.) and (l.) *Blackcraig* (2298 ft.) We now pass into Ayrshire, and reach

70 m. **New Cumnock Stat.**, situated at the confluence of the Nith with Burns' "*Sweet Afton.*"

Soon thereafter the watershed is reached. The line from Lanark *via* Muirkirk to Ayr (Rte. 11) is crossed before

75¼ m. **Old Cumnock Stat.**, where the Lugar is crossed by a viaduct 756 ft. long and 150 ft. high. **Cumnock**✲, ½ m. W.—at the junc. of the *Lugar* and the *Glaisnock*—is now chiefly dependent on the Lugar *Iron Works* 1½ m. E. See p. 94.

77¼ m. **Auchinleck Stat.**

[*Branch* rt. by *Lugar* to *Cronberry* (4 m.) and *Muirkirk*, 10 m. p. 94.]

3 m. W. is *Auchinleck House*, residence of the family of which Boswell, the friend and companion of Johnson, was a member. His father, a Judge of Session, under the title of Lord Auchinleck, resided here, and was visited by Johnson, who praised the sullen dignity of the old castle. James Boswell, Johnson's biographer, who alone of his family has made the name distinguished, is buried here.

At 81 m. the river *Ayr* is spanned by a lofty viaduct (180 ft.) whose breadth (175 ft.) and extreme lightness are very striking as seen from below. 1¼ m. l. there is another remarkable viaduct for the road erected at the end of the 18th cent. by Lord President Sir T. Miller near his seat *Barskimming Ho.* (now Sir W. F. Miller, Bt.) rt. is *Catrine Ho.*, once the residence of Prof. Dugald Stewart, with whom Burns dined before going to Edinburgh; and beyond it **Catrine**,[1] a village of Cotton Mills, and *Ballochmyle Ho.* (Gen. Sir Claud Alexander, Bt.) This is the scene of Burns's two songs—"The Braes o' Ballochmyle," commencing—

"The Catrine woods were yellow seen,
The flowers decay'd on Catrine lee,"

written to express the sorrow of Miss Whitefoord when her father, Sir John Whitefoord, was obliged to part with the old family place; and the "Lass o' Ballochmyle" in honour of Miss Alexander, whose father purchased the property. The park is well wooded, and very picturesque, the ground sloping rather abruptly to the Ayr.

1½ m. farther up the river is the castle of *Sorn*, an old baronial seat of the Earls of Loudoun and Winton, now of James Somervell, Esq.

82 m. **Mauchline Stat.**✲ The town stands ½ m. rt. on a commanding height, and is well known as the place where Burns spent much time while living with his mother and brother at *Mossgiel*, 1½ m. N. (1784-86). At that farm he wrote most of his first volume of poems; and thence, after their publication, and the abandonment, at the solicitation of his friends, of the passage to the W. Indies his follies had forced him to contemplate, he set out on his celebrated first visit to Edinburgh. The *church*, the main feature in the town, is a heavy Gothic building, very different from that which stood in its place at the end of the 18th century. The churchyard was the scene of "The Holy Fair."

[1] Coach to Mauchline.

Opposite to it is the cottage of Ann Gibson, better known as "Poosie Nansie," in whose kitchen the "Jolly Beggars"

"held the splore
To drink their orra duddies."

Next house to this, but separated by a lane, was the Whitefoord Arms Inn. It now bears the sign of the Cross Keys, but has ceased to be a public-house. One John Dove was landlord of it in Burns's time, and upon him the poet wrote the epitaph beginning—

"Here lies Johnnie Pigeon."

A little way up the lane lived Jean Armour before she was publicly acknowledged as Burns's wife. On the other side of the ch.-yd. is "Nanse Tinnock's," and close by, between the ch.-yd. and the remains of Old Mauchline Castle, was Gavin Hamilton's house, in which Burns was married.

Mauchline is well known for its manufacture of wood ware, snuff-boxes, etc., painted with tartan and other patterns.

There is a *Covenanters' Monument* on the Green with the usual rhyming inscription.

[*Branch to Ayr* 11½ m.

4¼ m. **Tarbolton Stat.**

1 m. N. are *Montgomerie Cas.* (R. P. Paterson, Esq.) and its woods, addressed in Burns's touching farewell to "Highland Mary." There are some well-preserved *Roman trenches* quite near, and an ancient burying-place with the supposed grave of Kyle, King of the Britons. Beyond is the village of Tarbolton, and at *Lochlea* in this parish Burns lived before his father's death (1777-84). *Spittalside Farm* was the abode of David Sillar his friend and correspondent.

Passing 6½ m. **Annbank Stat.**, where the Muirkirk line (p. 94) comes in l. we reach

8½ m. **Auchincruive Stat.** In the grounds of the *House* (R. A. Oswald, Esq.) 1 m. E. on the Ayr is *Laighland Wood*, where it is said Wallace hid before burning the Barns of Ayr.

11½ m. **Ayr** (p. 119).

The drive to Ayr is also interesting (p. 121).]

89½ m. **Hurlford Stat.** on the *Irvine.*

[*Branch to Galston and Newmilns.*

3½ m. **Galston Stat.**, dependent principally on the coal trade.

1 m. N. is *Loudoun Castle*, an old castle with an ugly modern front, of 1811, purchased 1868 for £300,000 from the Marq. of Hastings by Lord Bute, but now the property of Lord Donington, father of the Earl of Loudoun. It contains one of the best libraries in Scotland. The grounds are charming, and there is a pleasant walk through them from Galston to

5½ m. **Newmilns Stat.**, a small manufacturing town, noted for its fine muslins. 4 m. to the E. of Newmilns, on the Strathavon road, is *Loudoun Hill*, where in 1307 Bruce defeated the Earl of Pembroke, and laid the foundation of his ultimate success. On the farm of **Drumclog**, 2 m. N.E. of Loudoun Hill, the famous engagement took place on Sunday, 1st June 1679, when Claverhouse, with a troop of life-guards and some dragoons, marching to disperse an armed Conventicle, was met and charged by 200 fighting men, commanded by Hackston of Rathillet, Balfour of Burley, and others, all experienced officers, and was signally routed by them. 36 of the soldiers were left dead on the field: only 3 Covenanters being slain. A monument now crowns the hill, and a commemorative service used to be annually held here.]

---

91 m. **Kilmarnock Stat.**

[*Branches* (1) E. to *Newmilns* (above).

(2) S.W. by *Gatehead*, *Drybridge*, and *Barassie* to *Troon*, *Prestwick*, and *Ayr* (cf. Rte. 18).

(3) W. by *Crosshouse*, *Springside*, and

Dreghorn to *Irvine*, *Kilwinning*, and *Ardrossan*.

(4) N. W. by *Crosshouse*, *Cunninghamhead*, and *Montgrennan* to *Dalry* (p. 124). Through carriages to Greenock go this way.]

Kilmarnock ✫ a parl. burgh and place of considerable importance in the manufacturing world, producing carpets, shawls, bonnets, boots, and (prior to the introduction of the hat) the "Kilmarnock cowl." It stands on a small stream of the same name that falls into the Irvine. The older part of the town is narrow and irregularly built. In the *Laigh Parish Ch.-yd.* are several Covenanters' monuments and an Epitaph, by *Burns*, over "Tam Samson."

At the cross, in King Street, is a statue of Sir James Shaw, a native of this town, and the first Scottish Lord Mayor of London (1806).

In 1866 Mr. Kay, a rich native of Kilmarnock, bequeathed a sum of £16,000 to the city, £9000 of which was laid out in the purchase of about 40 acres of land near the station, which now form the *Kay Park*. Here in 1879 was erected the *Burns Monument* (Railton, archt.). It consists of a sort of temple of red sandstone on a raised platform, and surmounted by a tower 80 ft. high. Under a canopy is a marble statue by W. Grant Stevenson, A.R.S.A. The structure comprises a room fitted up as a *Museum*, in which are a complete set of Burns's Works, his dambrod or draught-board, and many other relics.

From the press of this town Burns's poems first issued (1786); and among its inhabitants were included many of his most generous friends.

[There is a pretty walk up the Fenwick Water to *Dean Castle*, 1 m., the ancient fort of the Boyds, Barons and Earls of Kilmarnock, the last of whom was beheaded in 1746. The castle was destroyed by fire 11 years before. 2 m. is the ruined castle of *Craufordland*, and 4 m. is *Fenwick* village, the ch.-yd. of which place contains a number of Covenanters' tombs.

1 m. S. of Kilmarnock, across the Irvine, is the village of *Riccarton*, where Wallace is said to have spent many of his younger days at the farm of an uncle.

3½ m. N.W. is *Rowallan Cas.* (below).]

93¼ m. **Kilmaurs Stat.**, an old burgh formerly belonging to the Earls of Glencairn. In the burial-place of the family, near the church, is the monument of the 9th Earl, Chancellor of Scotland *temp.* Charles II. Elephant remains have been found here in beds below the boulder clay. About 1½ m. E. is *Rowallan Castle* (Earl of Loudoun), once the baronial residence of the Mures of Rowallan, a member of which family, Elizabeth Mure, was wife of King Robert II. of Scotland. Sir William Mure, who flourished in the 17th cent., was an author of no mean repute, and, amongst other works, wrote the history of his family. The castle is a place of great antiquity, the more modern portions of which were built in 1560. It is charmingly situated, but hidden from view by plantations.

96½ m. **Stewarton Stat.**, with woollen manufactures and the remains of Border towers which belonged to the Cunninghams. ¾ m. l. is *Lainshaw Ho.* (J. W. H. Cuninghame, Esq.)

98¾ m. **Dunlop Stat.** This district is famous for its *Cheeses*.

101 m. **Lugton Stat.**

See Rte. 72 for stats. between this and

113½ m. **Strathbungo Stat.**, where the line diverges to

115½ m. **St. Enoch's Stat., Glasgow.**

For **Glasgow** ✫ see p. 132.

ROUTE 13.

Dumfries to Portpatrick by Castle-Douglas (for Kirkcudbright), Newton-Stewart (for Wigtown and Whithorn) and Stranraer.

G. and S.W. Rly. and Portpatrick and Wigtownshire Rly.

3 trains to Portpatrick daily, 80½ m., in abt. 3½ hrs.

5 trains to Stranraer, 73 m.—express (in connection with steamer to Ireland) 2 hrs. 10 min.

6 trains to Kirkcudbright daily, 30 m., in 1 hr. 20 min.

This rly. leads to some of the finest, most varied and least known scenery in Scotland. The *Stewartry of Kirkcudbright* and *Wigtownshire* together make **Galloway,** which is famous for dairy farming. The black Galloway cattle are bred for stock; they are similar to the polled Angus cattle but rather coarser in the skin. In some farms the stock cattle are grazed out of doors all the year round. Galloway also gives the title of Earl to a branch of the Stewart family.

Quitting Dumfries the line curves N. and W. crossing the Nith into Kirkcudbrightshire or the "Stewartry" as it is still called.[1]

1¾ m. **Maxwelltown Stat.**, ½ m. W. of that town (p. 97). 1½ m. rt. is *Terregles* (p. 97).

At 4½ m. *Goldielea Ho.* (Balfour Browne, Esq.) is passed (l.) in a dell before reaching

6 m. **Lochanhead Stat.** where moorland begins. From

8¼ m. **Killywhan Stat.** a road leads S.W. by Loch Arthur to New Abbey (5½ m.) [p. 99].

10½ m. **Kirkgunzeon Stat.** (pron. *Kirkgunnion = Ch. of St. Finan*, cf. Kilwinning, p. 124). In the neighbourhood are the ruined towers of *Drumcoltran* and *Corra*, the latter an old seat of the Maxwells. The hills on the left begin to assume a more formidable height, the principal ones being Cuil Hill, 1377 ft., and Hard Hill, 1335 ft., leading up to the main elevation of Criffel, 1866 ft.

12½ m. **Southwick Stat.**, ½ m. S. of which is *Barclosh*, an old seat of the Herries family, overlooking the stream of Kirkgunzeon Lane. 6 m. S.W. is *Southwick Ho.* (Sir Mark J. Stewart, Bt., M.P.). (Cf. p. 99).

14½ m. **Dalbeattie Stat.** ✲, a prettily situated thriving town in the valley of the *Urr*, navigable to its mouth (4 m.) by small vessels at high tide. The population, employed in various works and mills, are principally dependent on the *Granite Quarries*, from which most of the houses are built, and which are in good repute with engineers, having furnished stones for the Thames Embankment, and many of the largest docks in the kingdom. Messrs. Newall and Co. have extensive works, in which monuments, pillars, window frames, etc., are polished and turned out quite as good as those from Aberdeen.

2 m. to the S., on the right bank of the Urr, is *Munches* (W. H. Maxwell, Esq.), a fine granite mansion, re-built after having been struck by lightning and burnt down in 1868, in a beautiful park beside the winding Urr. The grounds abound with fine trees, pines, etc. The name probably originated with the *Monks*, its former owners.

[*Excursions*.—(1) From Dalbeattie it is a pleasant drive of 13 m. to **Dundrennan Abbey** (p. 113), passing 2 m. (l.) *Munches*, 2½ m. (l.) *Kirkennan Ho.* (Wellwood Maxwell, Esq.), and rt. the "*Lion's Face*" and 3½ m. *Palnackie Village*. At 4½ m. the curious *round tower* of *Orchardton* lies 1 m. l. and **Castle-Douglas** (p. 106) 5 m. rt. At 6½ m. *Orchardton Ho.* (W. D. R. Douglas, Esq.), beautifully situated at the head of a bay of the same name, is passed l.; and at 8 m. we drive through **Auchencairn**

[1] When the possessions of the Balliols and their vassals were forfeited, the whole district fell into the possession of the Crown, and was put under the authority of a royal steward.

village from which a charming road l. overlooking the sea should be taken going or returning.

(2) Another fine drive is *up the Urr valley* to **Moniaive,** 22 m. (p. 101).

At 2½ m. (l.) is the remarkable earthwork the **Moot of Urr,** a very perfect circular mound surrounded by a deep trench, and standing on a wide platform also enclosed within a fosse. In Celtic days it was probably used as a seat of justice and place of council: we pass l. (6 m.) the *Old Bridge of Urr*, cross the river (11 m.) close to *Corsock* (Mrs. E. E. Murray Dunlop) and pass rt. (18 m.) *Loch Urr* (p. 101).]

From Dalbeattie the line turns northward, crossing the Urr, and ½ m. S. of the *Moot* (above) trends W. to

19¾ m. **Castle-Douglas Stat.** ✲

[*Branch* S. to *Kirkcudbright*, 10¼ m., Rte. 14.]

This is a busy country town (with a good market) well situated to the N. of *Carlingwark Loch*,[1] ¾ m. long by ¼ m. broad, which has a number of small wooded islands upon it. Formerly a causeway led from the shore to one of these islands, whence Castle - Douglas was once called Causeway-End. At the S. end of the loch is a place called the Gallows Plot, from the executions that used to take place there when the district belonged to the Douglas family. Ancient canoes and various antiquities, now in the national museum at Edinburgh, were recovered from this loch.

About 2½ m. S. is *Gelston Cas.* (Major W. F. M. Kirwan).

1½ m. to the W., on an island of the Dee, is **Thrieve Castle,** long the headquarters of the Douglas family; afterwards of the Earls of Nithsdale.

It consists of one large gloomy tower, with a small courtyard in front, and entrance guarded by small turrets. Over the doorway is a projecting block of granite, called the "hanging stone," or "gallows knob," which the Douglas used to boast "never wanted its tassel." Thrieve witnessed some bloody scenes, and none more so than the murder (1452) of Maclellan, guardian of Lord Bombie, by William, 8th Earl of Douglas, who captured him by bribing his warder with the promise of a ladleful of gold. When the traitor claimed his reward, the Earl, with a grim humour, caused the gold to be melted and poured down his throat. James II. sent Sir Patrick Gray to claim Maclellan's release; while Sir Patrick dined and before opening the King's letter Douglas slew his prisoner. He shortly afterwards finished his career by being stabbed by the King in Stirling Castle. Some say "Mons Meg" was forged here, see p. 39.

"From Castle-Douglas to Newton-Stewart is by far the wildest portion of the whole rly. route. Indeed for rugged desolation it is hardly equalled by any piece of rly. in the Highlands."—*Sir A. Geikie.*

The line now makes a wide circuit. At first it keeps N.W. up the l. bank of the Dee, passing (rt.) *Greenlaw*, (l.) *Danevale* (W. Duncan, Esq.), and (rt.)—very conspicuous, commanding a splendid view—*Culgruff* (R. Stewart, Esq.), to

23½ m. **Crossmichael Stat.** There is a ch. here dedicated to the Archangel, but no traces, traditional or material, of his cross. On the opposite side of the river, which here expands into a series of lakes, is Balmaghie Ch. *Balmaghie Ho.* (Graham Hutchison, Esq.) is 2½ m. S.

26½ m. **Parton Stat.,** a charming spot before the wild scenery begins. The rly. turning W. here crosses the S. end of narrow *Loch Ken* (4½ m. long) just above its junc. with the Dee. There is a carriage ferry here.

[Coach twice daily by the E. side of the loch to Dalry ✲ 8½ m. (p. 107).]

We pass l. *Hensol Ho.* (R. D. B. Cunninghame, Esq.) to

28¾ m. **New Galloway Stat.** [*Coach* to the town, 5 m. distant twice or thrice daily, the road thither keeping the W. bank of Loch Ken, under the picturesquely wooded slopes of *Cairn Edward*, 1066 ft. Overlooking the head of

---

[1] Pleasure boats for hire.

the lake is **Kenmure Castle** (Mrs. Maitland Gordon, niece of the last Viscount Kenmure, d. 1847), on a lofty mound, and approached by a splendid avenue. The older parts of it belong to the 15th cent., and the modern, which may be 2 centuries later, are well adapted to them. The title of Kenmure, first granted by Charles I. to Sir John Gordon, was forfeited in 1716, when the 7th Viscount was beheaded for high treason. It was revived in favour of his grandson, but has again become extinct.

New Galloway✲, with a pop. of only 391—a royal but no longer a parl. burgh—is a village on the right bank of the *Ken* crossed higher up by a bridge of 5 arches.

This is an interesting centre for

EXCURSIONS:—

(1) N. E. to **Moniaive,** 14 m. (p. 101).

(2) S. W. to **Newton Stewart,** 19 m. (p. 108).

(3) To **Dee Bridge** (7 m.) thence on foot N. W. to **Loch Dee** (15 m.), and **Loch Trool**, 20 m. (p. 108).

(4) N. to **Dalmellington**✲ (p. 122) through the fine district of the *Glen Kens*, 22 m.

As far as **Dalry**✶ (3½ m.) there is a road on both sides of the Ken, that on the W. passing *Glenlee*, the prettily-wooded park of G. Maxwell, Esq.; that on the E. passing *The Holme* (A. F. M. Spalding, Esq.)

The valley above Dalry assumes more of a Highland character as the road approaches, 12 m., the village of **Carsphairn**✶.

[From this the pedestrian may ascend rt. *Cairnsmore* (2612 ft.) [below], in whose range the Ken, Nith, and Afton rise; *or* may cross the hills l. to the head of *Loch Doon* and the wild mountainous country beyond (p. 122).]

At 17½ m. a bay of Loch Doon, N. of its centre, is only 1 m. l.]

Leaving New Galloway Stat. and crossing the end of *Loch Stroan*, through which the Dee flows and N. of which is *Cairnsmore of Dee*, by another viaduct the rly. traverses a very desolate and bare tract, passing, right, *Loch Skerrow*. Beyond, viaducts cross the *Little* and then the *Big Water of Fleet*, down which there is a good view towards *Gatehouse* at its mouth (p. 114), to which a coach runs twice daily (descending 500 ft. in 6 m.), fare 1s. from

38¾ m. **Dromore Stat.** Rt. is *Cairnsmore of Fleet* (2331 ft.), one of the loftiest mountains in Galloway:

"There's Cairnsmore of Fleet,
There's Cairnsmore of Dee,
But Cairnsmore of Carsphairn
Is the highest of a' three."

43¼ m. **Creetown Stat.**, on a height, built of a mosaic of boulder stones—granites, slates, greywacke. Its walls are quite a geological study.

Below (1 m. l.) is the town, a small port at the mouth of the Cree on Wigtown Bay, across which there is a fine view of Wigtown itself.

In the manse of *Kirkmabreck* was born, 1778, Dr. Thomas Brown, the distinguished Professor of Moral Philosophy in Edinburgh, 1810-20. He is buried in the old ch.-yd. There are large *Granite Quarries* on the E. shore of Wigtown Bay, about 1 m. S. of Creetown, which have supplied some of the stone of which the Liverpool docks are built.

For the fine coast scenery between this and Gatehouse described in "Guy Mannering" see pp. 114, 115.

The rly. sweeps N. to

46½ m. **Palnure Stat.,** where the line crosses the Palnure water. Rt. is *Cairnsmore Ho.* (Major Stewart).

[There is a pleasant road up the Palnure Water past *Bargaly Ho.* (J. M'Kie, Esq.), to the New Galloway road (3¼ m.), and thence in 4¼ m. to Newton Stewart, below.]

The line runs W. crossing the Cree into Wigtownshire and up its rt. bank to

49¾ m. **Newton-Stewart Stat.**✲ [Branch S. to Wigtown, etc. (p. 108)] commanding a grand view N., and standing above the town which consists of a street nearly 1 m. long. At its S. end is the *Macmillan Hall* erected 1886 at a cost of £4000 with funds left by a lady of that name. In its centre is a *Bridge* over the Cree—an artist's view point—with a monument to the 9th Earl of Galloway (d. 1873) at the W. end. W. of the bridge is the modern *Parish Ch. of Penninghame*, with a lofty spire. Beside it is the *Ewart Institute* and at the N. end of the town the *Douglas Institute*, both educational foundations. Important cattle markets are held here.

[EXCURSIONS :—

(1) Up the Cree, immortalised by Burns in his beautiful little poem "The Banks of Cree," to **Loch Trool**, 13 m. This is one of the loveliest drives in Scotland—especially if the charming but "switchback" road along the *left* bank of the Cree be taken going.

Having crossed Cree Bridge we cross (½ m.) the *Penkill Burn*—up which, among very rich woods, is *Cumloden* (one of the properties given by the Bruce to three widows' sons), a shooting-box of the Earl of Galloway, with the ivied ruins of *Garlies Castle* in the woods beyond—and pass *Minnigaff Ch.*, beautifully situated, with a *Moot hill* adjoining.

At 3 m. the road runs close beside the river, across which an excellent view of *Penninghame Ho.* (Mrs. Maxwell Blair) is obtained. At 7½ m. the *Minnoch Water* is crossed, and again at 10 m. where the other road is joined. **Loch Trool** (1½ m. long)—where Lord Galloway has another shooting-box in the midst of the moors, surrounded by a pretty garden, with hedges of fuchsias and other delicate plants, which testify to the mildness of the climate—is a narrow sheet of water, beautifully broken by wooded promontories, and lying embosomed in lofty hills, which rise precipitously towards the N.E., presenting some of the highest and most rugged ground in the S. of Scotland. At the N. end the English force was nearly destroyed (1306) by Robert Bruce and his men rolling down huge stones on the enemy as they marched along the bank of the lake below. At the S. end are some Covenanters' graves, marking the site of a skirmish which took place 1685. [The pedestrian may (*a*) walk over the hills W. to **Loch Dee** (5 m.), and thence (after a night's lodging in *Black Laggan*, the Shepherd's Cottage) to **Loch Doon** and **Dalmellington** (p. 122), or to New Galloway (p. 107); or he may (*b*) by the *Buchan Burn* ascend **Merrick** (2764 ft.), the highest mountain on the mainland of Scotland S. of the Forth and Clyde, 5 m. N. (cf. p. 90).] Returning, after crossing the Minnoch, we pass rt. *Glencaird Ho.* (J. M'Kie, Esq., of Bargaly), and cross the Cree in 5 m. at *Bargrennan Ch.* (see p. 115). We keep its rt. bank and beyond the ruins of *Castle Stewart* (rt.) pass *Challoch Epis. Ch.*, an elegant little Gothic building, erected by the late Mr. Blair of Penninghame, 2 m. from Newton-Stewart.

(2) To **New Galloway** (p. 107) 19 m. N.E., a grand moorland drive.

Having crossed the Cree we keep rt., passing l. *Kirroughtrie Ho.* (Major Armitage), and leaving (1 m.) the Creetown road ascend l. At 4¼ m. the road down Palnure Glen goes rt. (p. 107). At 6 m. (rt.) is a *Rocking stone*, and at 7½ m. l. the *Murray Monument*, a granite obelisk erected in a commanding position by Mr. Stewart of Cairnsmore in memory of Dr. Alexander Murray (1775-1813), a celebrated linguist and Professor of Oriental languages in the University of Edinburgh. He was the son of a shepherd at a farm near, and was educated at Minnigaff parish school. Just beyond is the *Grey Mare's Tail* waterfall, and at 12 m. the Dee, rushing over slabs of rock, is crossed.]

[*Branch S. to Wigtown* and *Whithorn*. This rly. traverses the promontory known as **"The Machers"** of Wigtownshire. At first the line runs through a cultivated but uninteresting country past the old hamlet of *Penninghame*, where are a deserted church and burial-ground, and S. of which once stood the Palace of the Bishops of Galloway.

7 m. **Wigtown** ✫—a royal burgh, 1469—is a pleasant and picturesque little seaport town, having in the middle of its broad main street a well-shaded *Bowling-green* with the old and new (1816) *Burgh Crosses*. The handsome *Town-hall* and *County Buildings* form a picturesque group at the N. end. An obelisk stands on high ground behind the town, commemorating the Wigtownshire Covenanters, including Margaret M'Lauchlan (an old woman) and

Margaret Wilson (a girl of 18), who were tied to a stake and drowned by the rising tide of the Bladenoch river in 1685. They are buried in the parish churchyard below, where a slab with a lengthy rhyming inscription marks their resting place.

Drowning was an old mode of punishment in Scotland, and especially in Galloway, where the right of pit and gallows (in Latin *fossâ et furcâ*), that is, of inflicting death either by drowning of women or hanging of men,—subsisted longer than in other counties.

[By following a road on the N. bank of the Bladenoch for about 3 m., the antiquary will find, at *Torhouse*, rt. of the road, 3 *rude stones*, the highest 4 ft. 6 in. high. Left of the road, in a field, is a complete *circle* of 19 stones of 60 ft. diameter, the 2 largest about 5 ft. 6 in. and 5 ft. high. In the centre of the circle are 2 blocks 5 ft. high.]

At 8 m. the *Bladenoch* is crossed at the village of the same name, noted for its whisky, having on the opposite bank the little quay of Baldoon, and the ruined castle of *Baldoon*, belonging to the Earl of Galloway.

9¼ m. **Kirkinner Stat.**, to the W. of which is *Barnbarroch* (R. Vans Agnew, Esq.) The rly. makes a sweep westward to

10¾ m. **Wauphill Stat.**, and again turns E. to

13¼ m. **Sorbie Stat.** 1½ m. rt., was *Dowalton Loch*, which has been drained, revealing lake dwellings similar to those in Switzerland. No less than 4 artificial islands were found, constructed with timber and hurdles weighted with heavy stones, and furnished with fireplaces; also a large quantity of bones of deer, boars, *Bos primogenius*, etc. Between Sorbie and Garlieston is the old *Place of Sorbie*, a former residence of the family of Hannay in James IV.'s reign.

15¼ m. **Millisle Stat.**

[A *Branch* runs E. (1 m.) to **Garliestown Stat.** ✲, a small seaport on a bay of the same name. S. of the town is *Galloway House*, the seat of the Earl of Galloway, with extensive woods surrounding it. The house and grounds command fine views of the Cumberland and Man mountains. On Eggerness Point, to the N. of the bay, are slight ruins of *Eggerness Castle*, and 2 m. S. are the scanty remains of *Cruggleton Castle* on the sea-coast, once an important fortress belonging to the Comyns.]

18¼ m. **Whithorn Stat.** ✲, the terminus. The town— a royal burgh since Bruce's days—consisting of one long street containing the Town-hall with its tower and bells, derives its name from A.S. *Hvit-aern* = *White House* (Lat. *Candida Casa*), because hereabouts St. Ninian [1] (356(?)-432) in 397 built the first church of *stone* in Scotland. That saint, otherwise called St. Ringan, was a Briton, and the first bishop of the Southern Picts. He dedicated his church to his master, St. Martin of Tours, from whom he had obtained masons to shape its walls after the Roman fashion.

"In this 'White House' the body of St. Ninian had its rest, with the bodies of many other saints, and for ages the place continued to be famous, not only in North Britain, but throughout the Anglo-Saxon kingdoms, and among the races of Ireland. Subsequently the ancient shrine was renowned as a pilgrimage, whither kings and princes, churchmen and warriors, with people from many realms, came by sea and land to make their devotions."—ROBERTSON.

James IV. of Scotland used to make annual pilgrimages to the shrine of St. Ninian, and sometimes twice in one year, undertaking the whole journey from Edinburgh on foot.

Whithorn and the **Isle of Whithorn**, a port 3½ m. S.E., contend for the honour of having the site of

[1] See monograph by R. W. Cochran Patrick, Esq. LL.D., in Church of Scotland Year Book for 1890; and "*Candida Casa*," by Sir Herbert Maxwell, Bart., in *Good Words* for 1891.

this church. Whithorn churchyard stands upon the vaults and cellars of an old 12th cent. Priory. In the middle is the remnant of the *Priory Ch.*, which was used as a parish ch. up to 1822, when the new one was built close by. This fragment is the chancel of a still older ch. On the N. of the high altar are two canopied tombs; these have been restored, and one of them is said to mark the last resting-place of St. Ninian. On the S.W. side is a Norman door, with handsome mouldings, and a ram's head on the keystone; and there is also a good S.E. door with carved imposts. The old vault is the burying-place of the Murrays of Cally, near Gatehouse. Two fine sculptured stones of the W. Highland type, found in the churchyard, have been set up in the ruin.

On the right side of the street is an *Archway* (which led to the Priory), supported by old pillars, with heads decorated with oak leaves, and bearing a shield; that on the right has a bar saltier, and that on the left the arms of Vans of Barnbarroch, one of which family was the Prior and a bishop about 1550.

A stone on the roadside near the town, with a *Chrisma* upon it, is supposed to date back almost, if not quite, to Ninian's time.

Whithorn was the birthplace of John Ramsay M'Culloch (1789-1864), author of the "Commercial Dictionary," and of many other valuable works on Political Economy, etc.

2¼ m. N. of the town is *Castle Wigg* (Col. Hathorn's Trs.), and 2 m. S.W. is *Glasserton* (R. H. J. Stewart, Esq.). 1 m. S. is a *Cave* called *St. Ninian's*, its rocky walls covered with interesting small crosses of various dates.

Burrow Head, nearly the most southern point of Scotland, lies E. between this and the Isle of Whithorn (p. 109), which the geologist will find interesting, as foot-tracks of extinct animals have been discovered in the Lower Silurian rocks.

8 m. W. of Whithorn is **Portwilliam**✲ (with a thriving little harbour), beyond *Monreith Ho.*, the seat of Sir H. E. Maxwell, Bt., M.P., within whose park is the *White* or *Myrton Loch* of which Boece writes as

"the Great Lake of Mirton, the one-half whereof doth freeze by naturall congelation as other pooles and plashes, but the other is never seene to bear anie yce at all, which unto me dooth seeme to be a greate wonder."

A *Moot hill* on its banks is crowned by the ruins of a castle once held by the powerful family of M'Culloch, who so harried the Isle of Man that its inhabitants used to pray

"Keep me, my good cows, my sheep and
 my bullocks,
From Satan, from sin, and those thievish
 M'Cullochs."

A road (not very interesting, *coach* twice a week) leads hence along the shore of Luce Bay to Glenluce 13½ m. (p. 111).]

Quitting Newton-Stewart, the rly. passes left *Merton Hall*, the seat of J. C. Boyd, Esq. (a descendant of the Earl of Kilmarnock, who suffered in the rising of 1745), and runs through an uninteresting country to

56 m. **Kirkcowan Stat.** 1¼ m. rt. is *Craighlaw* (W. M. F. Hamilton, Esq.). The railway gradually ascends into a treeless region of heath. This part of Wigtownshire is bleak and bare, and far from interesting.

At 62 m. rt. are the ruins of *Carscreuch*, the seat of Lord Pres. Dalrymple, 1619, whose daughter was the heroine of the story made classic by Sir W. Scott in the "Bride of Lammermoor."

64¼ m. **Glenluce Stat.** at the head of Luce Bay, 1½ m. from which, up the valley of the Luce, are the remains of **Luce Abbey**, founded by Roland, Lord of Galloway, in 1190.

When entire it must have been on a very extensive scale. A mass of prostrate masonry rises still upon the site, but a great part has been removed. The foundations of the nave, transepts, and choir remain, encumbered with rubbish and planted with trees. The gable of the S. transept (E.E.) stands erect, with the E. chapels attached to it. The cloister square still exists, with a range of apartments, including the chapter-house to the E. The latter is vaulted, and has a central pillar, with good bosses and some Dec. windows. Michael Scott, who resided here, is said to have locked up the plague in a vault; and his books are still buried in the ground.

[*Omnibus* twice a week to Port-William, 13½ m. (see p. 110)].

Crossing the Luce by a lofty viaduct, an extensive view is obtained of the bay, the Mull of Galloway, the lighthouse, the Isle of Man, and the Cumberland Mountains. l. of the rly. is *Castle of Park*, the former seat of the Hay family, built in 1590 from the spoils of Glenluce Abbey. It is a good type of the Scotch mansion of the period, and over the entrance we read, "Blessit be the name of the Lord—This verk was begun the first day of March 1590, be Thomas Hay of Park and Janet MacDouel, his spouse." It is now tenanted by farm-servants. There is a fine view of Glenluce Bay from it. The rly. from Glasgow, *viâ* Ayr, Maybole, and Girvan to Stranraer, opened in 1877 (Rte. 15), comes in rt. before reaching

67½ m. **Dunragit Stat.**, where there is a large *Creamery*. rt. is *Dunragit*, the seat of J. C. Cuninghame, Esq., and l. *Genoch* (J. M'Douall of Logan).

70½ m. **Castle Kennedy Stat.** Rt., within a mile of this stat., is **Loch Inch Cas.**, the noble residence of the Earl of Stair, erected 1870 by the 10th Earl, in the Scoto-French style, on a site commanding the picturesque loch which forms the chief feature of the domain. In front, on a peninsula, rise the ivy-clad ruins of

Castle Kennedy, built in the time of James VI., destroyed by fire 1715, long a seat of the Earls of Cassilis. It passed to the Stair family in the 17th cent. The gardens and grounds[1] are the most beautiful in this part of the country. The *Pinetum* especially is the finest in Scotland. This most successful example of landscape-gardening has been created since 1847. A curious range of terraces, part of a former garden, and the ivy-clad ruins of the castle, form interesting objects, around which all the newest and most elegant pines have been arranged in groups and groves and avenues with excellent effect. The result is that the *Araucaria*, *Deodar*, *Pinus nobilis*, *Insignis*, *Normanniana Webbiana*, and the *Cupressus macrocarpa*, and many more, grow here in full vigour and large masses, whereas in most other places they occur only as single specimens.

On the banks of Soulseat Loch, l. of the stat., are slight remains of the Abbey of *Soulseat*, or "Sedes Animæ," founded by Fergus, Lord of Galloway, in the 12th cent.

73 m. **Stranraer Stat.** ✡, an important seaport at the head of the expansive **Loch Ryan**, down which there is a fine view to **Ailsa Craig** (p. 115).

[There is a *Harbour Stat.* at the *Quay*, whence commodious steamers sail once daily (twice 11th July to 30th Sept.)—Sundays excepted—to Larne (for Belfast) in 2 hrs.]

In the heart of the town is a *Castle* or tower built by the Kennedys. A pretty view of the town and Loch Ryan may be obtained from the cemetery or from the heights above.

For *Castle Kennedy* see above.

Stranraer stands in the centre of the district known as the **"Rhinns of Galloway,"** which comprises the two promontories bounded on the E. respectively by Loch Ryan and Luce Bay, and on the W. by the Irish Channel. Both promontories are traversed by good roads.

[1] Open Wednesdays and Saturdays.

(1) In the northern one is **Lochnaw Castle** (5¾ m. N.W. of Stranraer), the ancient seat of the old family of Agnew, which held the office of Hereditary Sheriff of Galloway down to the abolition of heritable jurisdictions in 1747. The monument on the hill is to the memory of Sir Andrew Agnew. 6½ m. N. close to the village of Kirkcolm, is *Corsewall House* (J. Carrick Moore, Esq.), and 4 m. N.W. of Kirkcolm beyond the ruins of the ancient castle of Corsewall is *Corsewall Pt.* with a lighthouse. On the E. shore of the loch, opposite, is Cairn Ryan (p. 118).

(2) *Coach* daily to **Drummore** ✲ (17½ m.) in the southern promontory, which is terminated by the rugged headland of the **Mull of Galloway,** with a Lightho. (22½ m.), whence a good view may be obtained of the coasts of England and Ireland on the left and right, and the hills of the Isle of Man in front. The road passes 3½ m. *Garthland Tower*, once the seat of the M'Doualls, Lords of Galloway. At 5 m. in the parish of Stoneykirk, two stones, bearing inscriptions in Roman characters of the 4th cent., commemorating the death of 3 saints—Florentius, Majorius, and Viventius—now form the gateposts of the deserted ch.-yd. of *Kirkmadrine.* We pass 7½ m. *Balgreggan* (Mrs. Maitland) 10½ m. *Ardwell House* (Mrs. Ommaney M'Taggart), and 12½ m. *Logan Ho.* (J. M'Douall, Esq.), with (1½ m. beyond at *Port Logan*) a singular *sea-fish preserve* or pond accessible to the tides, and filled with great cod and other fish, some of them so tame as to come and receive food out of the hand.

Near *Drummore* the cliffs are 150-200 ft. high, and on the hill W. is *Kirkmaiden Ch.*, the most S. parish in Scotland, hence Burns's line—

"Frae Maiden Kirk to John o' Groats."

The line passes (77¼ m.) **Colbin Stat.** to

80½ m. **Portpatrick Terminus** ✲. The town is a poor little place, but is the nearest point on the Scottish coast to Ireland—only 21 m. distant. The harbour and pier were constructed (1843) by Rennie at a cost of £200,000, but, not proving convenient, the mail service between Portpatrick and Donaghadee has long been discontinued, and the sea is rapidly destroying Rennie's work. From Portpatrick the submarine telegraph wire is carried across the channel. 1 m. N. is *Dunskey Ho.*, and ½ m. S. the ruins of *Dunskey Castle*, standing on a rocky cliff pierced with many caves, which projects into the sea. There is fine rugged cliff-scenery along the coast-line near this.

ROUTE 14.

Dumfries via Castle-Douglas to Kirkcudbright (Dundrennan Abbey, Gatehouse-on-Fleet, and Anwoth). G. and S.W. Rly.

To **Castle-Douglas** (19¾ m.) see Rte. 13.

The rly. trending S. passes rt. *Thrieve Cas.* (p. 106), crosses the Dee at a picturesque spot with an island, to

22½ m. **Bridge of Dee Stat.**, and leaving the river reaches

26½ m. **Tarff Stat.** with *Tarff Water* rt. At 28½ m. there is another picturesque crossing of the Dee. Rt. there is the road bridge, 1 arch of 112 ft. span—built of Arran freestone (1804-8) from plans by Telford—beyond it the confluence with the Tarff, *Compstone Ho.* (D. Maitland, Esq.), and the old *Castle* of *Compstone*, where the poet Montgomery (1771-1854) once resided. ½ m. up the Dee (at Tongueland) is an old bridge (1737) of 2 arches, and there, near the Church, is the site of an *Abbey* founded by Fergus, Lord of Galloway (12th cent.). Farther up is the site of *Queen Mary's Bridge*, by which she crossed the Dee on her way from Langside to Dundrennan. From the hill behind a charming view is obtained of Kirkcudbright, its peninsula and bay, the island of Little Ross, and the sea beyond.

30. m. **KIRKCUDBRIGHT Stat.** ✲ (pron. Kir-cóo-bry), a royal and parl. burgh and clean town of wide streets, with an iron bridge (1866) across the Dee, and a harbour for vessels of some size. The "*Kirk of Cuthbert*," so called because that saint's bones reposed here for a time during their wanderings, is a pleasant little town, and the head of the Stewartry. The kirk from which it takes its name was founded in the 8th cent. At the end of the principal street are the ivy-covered ruins of the old *Castle* of the M'Lellans of Bombie, barons of Kirkcudbright, built in 1582. The *Established Ch.* (1838) is a handsome building. The old ch. was pulled down, with the exception of a fragment that contains a monument to a Lord Kirkcudbright, a title extinct since 1832. The *County Buildings*, with excellent Court room, were erected 1868. Opposite them is the quaint old Court House. The *Town Hall Buildings* contain a large public hall and an excellent museum. There is a fine *Free Ch.*, and also a large *U.P. Ch.*, an *Epis. Chap.*, and a *Life-Boat Station*. A tall granite *Cross*—after the Scottish type—erected by his widow to the memory of the late Earl of Selkirk (1809-85), occupies a conspicuous position.

About 1½ m. to the S. is **St. Mary's Isle** (Capt. John Hope, R.N.), now no longer an island, but a peninsula, stretching into the estuary of the Dee, and occupied by the grounds and dark woods which belonged to the late Earl of Selkirk (title extinct since 1885). Through green vistas of beech-trees fine views of the sea appear. Here is an old *Heronry* containing many hundred birds, which are carefully guarded from intrusion. Paul Jones' Point, at the end of the tongue of land, commemorates a raid made by that daring pirate, 1778, in the hope of carrying off the Earl, who was, luckily for himself, away from home. The pirate, however, looted the plate; and a silver teapot, which was returned by him on the remonstrance of Benjamin Franklin, is still in possession of the family. His father was gardener at the Isle. A nunnery was founded here in the reign of David I., and some portions of it are embodied in the plain sash-windowed modern house. The grounds contain a cut-leaved alder, the finest in the country, and good conifers. In the neighbourhood of Kirkcudbright are remains of several forts — Caledonian and Roman — especially at Spyland and Bombie.

[EXCURSIONS:—

(1) To ***Dundrennan Abbey**, 6 m. E., and about 2 m. from the coast. One road thither passes a Roman camp, and the site of *Bombie Castle*, the early residence of the M'Lellans. A part of the way is lined by hawthorn hedges, which grew most luxuriantly here, and gave to the place the name of *Dun-nan-draighnean* (*Hill of the Thorn Bushes*). The Abbey stands at the head of a pretty valley running down to the sea from the village of Dundrennan ✲, which has a Gothic Ch. (1865).

The abbey was built in 1142 by King David, or, as some say, by Fergus, Lord of Galloway, for Cistercian monks, brought from Rievaulx, in Yorkshire.

On entering the W. door, which is Early Pointed, it will be seen that the whole of the nave and choir (E. wall) have disappeared, together with the tower, the cloisters, and almost all the chapter-house. The materials have been removed to build the village, and several of the stones may be recognised in the houses. Further dilapidations are now arrested by the Commissioners of Woods. On the W. are the cellars, and the garden entrance. The present remains of the church, built of picturesque gray stone, consist of the N. and S. transepts, each with a roofless aisle on the E. side, and the N. and S. walls of the chancel. The arches of the S. transept stand perfect, and are pointed, while the windows of the chancel, and those of the clerestory in the transept, are circular. The most beautiful fragment is upon the S. side of the ch. This was the entrance to the chapter-house, and consists of a pointed Gothic doorway, flanked on each side by a double window. Within this entrance are the stumps of 4 pillars which supported the roof.

In the aisle of the N. transept is the monument of Alan, Lord of Galloway, grandson of the reputed founder, and Constable of Scotland in 1233. The figure is clothed in mail; the legs have long ago disappeared.

From the high ground above the Abbey a fine view is obtained. N. is a range of hills, the highest peak of which is *Bengairn*, 1280 feet; across the water is seen the coast of Cumberland, with Skiddaw and Helvellyn in the background; and on the extreme right are the dark-blue hills of the Isle of Man. Dundrennan Abbey was the last place where Mary Queen of Scots slept before embarking for England, and from here she wrote a letter to Queen Elizabeth, 15th May 1568. In returning drive down the Abbey Burn to *Burnside;* E. is *Port Mary*, where the very rock is shown from which Queen Mary stepped on board the boat; N.W. a lovely wooded road leads up the Netherlaw Burn to the high road.

(2) To **Gatehouse-on-Fleet** ✡ (8 m.) and **Creetown**, 20 m.

[*Coach* twice daily to Gatehouse.]

The road crosses the Dee and ascends for 3½ m., thence *Earlston Ho.* (Sir W. Gordon, Bart., one of the Balaclava "Six Hundred") with fine parks, lies 1 m., and *Borgue* village 2 m. S. Approaching Gatehouse l. is **Cally**[1] (H. G. Murray Stewart, Esq.), a stately mansion of granite, with a portico of columns, each a single shaft. The lofty *Hall*, lined with precious marbles, cost £50,000 alone. Cally is approached through shady groves and avenues of lofty beech, and is backed by gardens and grounds of great beauty, with many rare pines, *e.g. C. Lambertiana*, 40 ft. high. It is one of the finest places in these parts. The manse of *Girthon*, as the parish is called, stands rt. ¾ m. before entering the town, which is pleasantly situated on the *Fleet*.

[*Coach* twice daily up this river to *Dromore Stat.* 6 m.; fare, 1s. (see p. 107).]

Crossing the river we pass (9 m.) rt. the ruins of *Cardoness Cas.*, but it is better to make a slight detour inland by the ivy-covered ruins of **Anwoth Ch.**, where the saintly Samuel Rutherford (1600-61) ministered, where in his favourite "Walk" the memorable interview with Archbishop Usher (1580-1656), who came from Ireland to see him, took place, where on the hill a granite obelisk was erected to his memory 1842, and where there is an interesting Covenanter's tombstone in the ch.-yd. Beyond, *Cairnharrow* (1497 ft.) is a prominent feature in the landscape. 10 m. (l.) is *Ardwell* (A. Jameson, Esq.), and beyond (l.) *Cardoness Ho.* (Sir W. F. Maxwell, Bart.) At 14 m. we pass *Ravenshall Point* with a fine sea view including E. the *Islands of Fleet.* On the shore are several caves, the largest being "*Dirk Hatteraick's.*"[2] rt. is *Kirkslaugh*, and beyond, the old *Castle of Barholm*—well placed —before the *Kirkdale Burn* is crossed at a lovely turn of the road. Up

1 Grounds open Tuesdays and Thursdays.

2 The original of Sir Walter's Hatteraick was one Yawkins, a Dutch smuggler, who used to land cargoes between the mouths of the Cree and the Dee.

this glen is *Cairnholly*, with a giant grave, said to be that of Galgacus, who gave his name to Galloway. Here Meg Merrilees' gipsies had their encampment. l. is *Kirkdale Ho.* (Colonel R. W. R. Hannay), —totally destroyed by fire 4th May 1893,—and at 17 m. (l.) the ruin of *Carsluith.* This and Barholm both claim to be "Ellangowan," or at least its site (see p. 98). The whole district breathes of "Guy Mannering" — Gatehouse being "*Kippletringan.*" Passing (rt.) large granite quarries and *Cassencary Ho.* (J. A. Caird, Esq.), we reach

20 m. **Creetown** (see p. 107), with the stat. 1 m. beyond.]

ROUTE 15.

Stranraer to Ayr by Girvan and Maybole. G. and S. W. Rly.

$58\frac{1}{2}$ m., about 5 trains in $2\frac{1}{2}$-3 hrs.

To $5\frac{1}{2}$ m. **Dunragit Stat.**, see p. 111.

1 m. beyond, at *Challoch Junc.*, the line turns due N. up the valley of the Luce, passing rt. the ruins of Luce Abbey (p. 110). Near

12 m. **New Luce Stat.** is an old rocking-stone called the *Laggan Gun*, and here the *Main Water of Luce* and the *Cross Water of Luce* join. The former is soon crossed by a high bridge, commanding pretty views, and the latter is approached at

$16\frac{1}{2}$ m. **Glenwhilly Stat.**, and ascended to the borders of Ayrshire, where we reach the summit level (nearly 700 ft.) and traverse a dreary plateau to

$24\frac{3}{4}$ m. **Barrhill Stat.** The village lies below on rt.

[There is a road hence up the valley of the Lavery, and between Lochs Dormal and Maberry to Newton-Stewart, 19 m. (occasional *coach*), *or* keeping W. and crossing the Lavery one may drive down the Cree by Bargrennan Ch. (p. 108).]

We now descend the valley of the Duisk till, passing close by the picturesque ruin of *Pinwherry Castle*, we arrive at

29 m. **Pinwherry Stat.**, situated at the confluence of the Stinchar and Duisk.

[Coach twice daily S.W. down the *Stinchar* valley, *via* Colmonell to Ballantrae p. 118) 10 m.]

Passing l. the house of *Daljarroch*, we now ascend the valley of the Stinchar as far as Kinclaer Viaduct.

32 m. **Pinmore Stat.** *Pinmore House* (Capt. Hamilton) was rebuilt in 1877, after a fire. The summit level is passed in Dinvin tunnel (33 m.), from which we descend rapidly traversing the land of *Glendoune House* (J. G. K. Young, Esq.) to

37 m. **Girvan Stat.** ✲, a dull but neat town, at the mouth of the Girvan Water, consisting of one long street. It is situated on the edge of a small detached coalfield, which gives occupation to the people.

Girvan is a good centre for the geologist who will find fossiliferous rocks of lower Silurian as well as of Carboniferous age in the neighbourhood.

It is also the most suitable place for making a water excursion to **Ailsa Craig,** which rises grandly about 10 m. out at sea and gives the title of *Marquis of Ailsa* to the Earl of Cassilis. It is 1114 ft. in height, 2 m. in circumference at the base, and has a *Lighthouse.* From this side it appears to be dome-shaped, but from N. and S. it takes the form of a pyramid, and from the W. seems to be rectangular. It is in reality shaped like a wedge, and is perpendicular towards the W., while it slopes gradually away to the E., on which side alone it is accessible. When the wind is favourable a landing is easy, but the narrow path up winds at places round the edge of the precipice. The rock is a syenitic greenstone, rising on the E. in terraces. About ¼ of the way up are the ruins of a tower. Ailsa Craig is inhabited by great quantities of sea-fowl. The cliffs fronting the W. rise to a height of 400 ft. in columns from 6 ft. to 9 ft. in diameter, which differ from those of Staffa in being of gray syenite, not of basalt.

A *Coach* runs daily in summer from Girvan to Ballantrae by the shore road, returning by Colmonell (see Rte. 16).

The *Railway* from Girvan to Ayr (21½ m.) takes an inland course by Maybole so that the tourist is shut out from the places of interest on the coast. Some may prefer, therefore, to follow the coast road, although hilly, by *Turnberry Cas.* (6 m.), *Culzean Cas.* (9 m.), and *Dunure Cas.* (15 m.) [p. 117] to Ayr 22 m.

The Rly. follows the course of the Girvan river through a valley of pleasing character in places, especially in the neighbourhood of

39¾ m. **Killochan Stat.** Near here is *Killochan Castle* (Sir R. Cathcart, Bt.), and across the river is *Bargany* (Earl of Stair) in a pretty park. On a hill near Killochan is the *Baron's Stone*, a giant boulder of granite weighing abt. 37 tons which, like thousands of others, has been brought by ice from the source or "Eye" of the Girvan, a "great cauldron between the heights of the Kells and Merrick."

42¼ m. **Dailly Stat.** In the ch.-yard is the grave of J. B. Collis, who was buried 23 days in a coal-pit, was dug out alive, but survived only 3 days. 1¼ m. N. is *Dalquharran Castle* (Trs. of F. T. R. Kennedy, Esq.)

45 m. **Kilkerran Stat.** On the slopes of the opposite bank of the Girvan is *Kilkerran*, the seat of the Right Hon. Sir James Fergusson, Bt.

47½ m. **Maybole Stat.** ✠, now principally known for its *Boot and Shoe Factories* and also for the manufacture of agricultural implements, is a place of some historical importance as the capital of the lonely, hilly, cattle-feeding district called **Carrick** (see p. 119), the domain of the Bruces. Here Lord Cassilis, the hereditary bailie, and other local magnates, had their town mansions, and held their courts in the olden times.

Maybole still retains two ancient buildings of interest—the *Tolbooth*, which has some Gothic details, and was the old town residence of the Kennedys, and the *Tower* or *Castle* (now restored, and the abode of Lord Ailsa's factor), which was the residence of the Bailie of Carrick. This was the scene of the ballad of "Johnnie Faa," the gipsy, who, according to the story (which is proved to be untrue), eloped with the lady of the 6th Earl of Cassilis.

Within the ruins of the *Old Church* is the burying-place of the Ailsa family. In the old Red Lion Inn took place the memorable theological contest in 1561, of 3 days' duration, between John Knox and the Abbot of Crossraguel, Quentin Kennedy.

Maybole was the residence of Kennedy of Cullayne, who was murdered by Mure of Auchendrane, one of the most dangerous and bloodthirsty men of his time, scrupling not to assassinate anybody whom he had reason to envy or fear. For this last offence, however, he was with his son brought to trial and executed in 1611. The story has been dramatised by Sir. W. Scott in his "Ayrshire Tragedy."

[EXCURSIONS :—

(1) To **Crossraguel Abbey** 2 m. S.

It was founded previous to 1240 by Duncan, Earl of Carrick, for Cluniac monks from Paisley, and is approached beneath a grand turreted gatehouse to the W. of the Abbey. A large portion of the buildings is still standing, and forms a curious mixture of "the half baronial, half ecclesiastical construction." The ch. consisted of a nave, without aisle or transept, and a choir, divided by a rood-screen and loft, and terminated at the E. by an apse of 3 sides. At the S.E. is a fine altar tomb with 4 canopied arches. The *chapter-house*, retaining its vaulted roof supported on light piers, has very handsome windows, and is evidently the most modern part of the whole. To the W. of the chapter-house is a square, in which the cloisters can easily be traced, and beyond this was the refectory. At the S.E. corner of the ch., built upon an arch spanning a stream that runs through the gardens, was the Abbot's house.

(2) To **Dunure,** 6 m. N.W., a little fishing and bathing place which had a harbour cut out of the solid rock (1811) by Abercrombie, the engineer, at an expense of £50,000. It proved, however, too small for any practical purpose. Here, overlooking the sea, is the solitary fragment of *Dunure Castle*, the seat of the Kennedys, but dismantled in the middle of the 17th cent.

(3) To **Culzean Cas.** 4 m. W., and **Turnberry Cas.,** 7 m. S.W.

Overlooking the coast is *Culzean Castle*, the modern Gothic castle of the Marquis of Ailsa, built 1777 by David, 10th Earl of Cassilis (Adam, archt.) It contains a fine *Armoury*. It is not open to visitors, and no view can be obtained of it from this side; but it is a beautiful object from the sea, on the very edge of which it stands. On the land side are the terrace-gardens of the old house, removed to make way for its grand successor. At the foot of the rock on which the castle stands are the coves of Culzean, three caves hewn in the rock, which were used as hiding-places during the civil wars, and afforded refuge to Sir Archibald Kennedy after the Revolution. Here, according to Burns, the fairies gather on "Hallowe'en."

Culzean has been, ever since the 15th cent., in the hands of the Kennedys, Earls of Cassilis, who played an important part in the history of the times, and had such power that it gave rise to the popular rhyme—

"'Twixt Wigtown and the town of Ayr,
Portpatrick and the Cruives of Cree,
No man may think for to bide there,
Unless he court Saint Kennedie."

3 m. S. are the ruins of *Turnberry Castle*. The principal portion now standing consists of a piece of masonry about 30 ft. above the sea, to which there was a subterranean passage from the castle. There is also a little masonry among the rocks which formed the foundation of the castle, but so built into the crevices that it is difficult to distinguish between art and nature.

Turnberry was in former times the seat of the Earls of Carrick, and was occupied by Martha, Countess of Carrick, who married, in 1274, Robert Bruce, Earl of Annandale. The eldest son of this marriage was the great Robert Bruce, who was probably born in it (cf. p. 111), and who is represented in the "Lord of the Isles" as seizing the castle in his first descent from Arran. It is more probable, however, that it did not fall into his hands till after the battle of Bannockburn.

To the S. of the castle is the *Weary Nuik*, a little romantic green hill where Bruce and his party are said to have rested after assaulting the castle.

1 m. E. is the farm of *Shanter*, once the residence of Douglas Graham, original of "Tam o' Shanter."

The tourist can return to Maybole inland by *Kirkoswald* village and Crossraguel, about 6 m. In the ch.-yd. of Kirkoswald is the grave of Tam and his "ain wife Kate," with the epitaph—

"She tauld thee weel thou wast a skellum,
A bleth'ring, blust'ring, drunken blellum."

"Souter Johnnie" (John Davidson) is also buried here.]

Continuing by rail from Maybole, 52 m. **Cassilis Stat.** 1 m. rt., is *Cassilis House*, another seat of the Marquis of Ailsa. In the grounds are the "Cassilis Downans," mentioned by Burns in his "Hallowe'en." The rly. crosses the *Doon* between this and

54 m. **Dalrymple Stat.**, with the village 1 m. rt. on that river. 1 m. beyond the Stat. the Dalmellington line (Rte. 17) strikes off rt.

58½ m. **Ayr** ✲ see p. 119.

ROUTE 16.

Stranraer to Girvan by Road—by Glen App and Ballantrae.

This road (30 m.) keeps near the coast, the scenery of which at Glen App, and between Ballantrae and Girvan, is very fine, and will repay a visit.

For the first 9 m. the road skirts the eastern shores of **Loch Ryan**, running at the foot of a plateau of bleak moors. It was the Rericonius Sinus of the Romans, the presumed [1] station of Rericonium being passed at 3 m. from Stranraer. Earthworks visible at this spot are called the *Mote*. On the bank overlooking it is *Craigcaffie Castle*, the fortress of the Neilsons in the 13th cent. The foundation-stones are said to have been laid on bags of wool on account of the boggy nature of the ground.

6 m. Opposite Kirkcolm (p. 112) we reach Cairn Ryan, whose shales yield graptolites, close to which is *Loch Ryan Ho.* (J. Wallace, Esq.) At 8 m. the Galloway Burn is crossed, and the traveller enters Ayrshire.

9 m. At **Finnart Bay**, which is nearly opposite Milleur Point, the N. end of the *Rhinns of Galloway*, the road leaves the sea-coast and turns up the picturesque and finely wooded **Glen App**, quitting it (13 m.) at the base of Carlock hill, 1054 ft. It then takes a direction due N. past *Glen App Ho.* (Bryce, archt., 1870), in a fine position overlooking the sea, to

17½ m. **Ballantrae** ✲ a small fishing port, with *Golf Links*, at the mouth of the Stinchar, a considerable stream crossed by a bridge. Above it is the shell of *Castle Ardstinchar*, which once commanded the pass out of Galloway. The scenery is very pretty up the *Stinchar* N. to Colmonell village (5½ m.), beyond *Knockdolian* the seat of W. M'Connel, Esq., and N.E. into *Glen Tig*.

[*Coach* twice daily to *Pinwherry Stat.*, 10 m. (p. 115), and in summer a coach comes from Girvan daily by the shore road returning by Colmonell.]

The road from Ballantrae to Girvan closely hugs the coast, which in many parts is exceedingly bold, with romantic cliffs, particularly at **Bennane Head** (20 m.). The tourist obtains a succession of grand sea-views, in which **Ailsa Craig** (p. 115), is a prominent object.

23½ m. At **Lendalfoot** the cliffs are fine and bold—the trap rock assuming fantastic shapes—and are covered with creeping vegetation, especially at *Gamesloup* where the marine spleenwort grows. The neighbouring ruined tower of *Carleton Castle* is the scene of the ballad of "May Cullean."

Here lived a baron who had a habit of frequently marrying and becoming tired of his wives, whom he despatched by pushing them from the top of the cliffs. Seven had already gone this way, when May Cullean, the eighth wife, appeared on the scene, and was led out on to the rocks to perform the same ceremony. Requesting the baron to turn away his head while she took off her apparel, she adroitly managed to push him over instead.

Passing 27 m. *Ardmillan Ho.*, we reach

30 m. **Girvan** ✲ see p. 115.

---

[1] See Skene's *Celtic Scotland*, I. 72.

ROUTE 17.

Ayr to Dalmellington (Loch Doon), G. and S.W. Rly.

Rlys. from Ayr (1) N. to Troon, Kilwinning and Glasgow, 41½ m. (Rte. 18).
(2) N.E. to Troon and Kilmarnock, 15½ m.
(3) E. *via* Tarbolton to Mauchline, 11½ m. (p. 103).
(4) N.E. *via* Cumnock and Muirkirk to Lanark, 47½ m. (Rte. 11).
(5) S.E. to Dalmellington, 15 m. (p. 121).
(6) S. to Girvan and Stranraer, 58½ m. (Rte. 15).

Ayrshire is divided into 3 portions —*Cunningham* in the N., *Kyle* in the centre, and *Carrick* in the S.

' Kyle for a man, Carrick for a coo (cow),
Cunningham for butter and cheese, and
Galloway for 'oo (wool)."

AYR✲, with a large rly. stat. built 1882, is a pleasant seaport and a royal and parl. burgh situated in the central division on the coast, at the embouchure of the *River Ayr*, which is crossed by a couple of bridges connecting the town with the suburbs of Newtown and Wallacetown. Although it dates its rise as far back as 1205, when it was made a burgh by William the Lion, it has kept pace with the improvements of the times, and exhibits well-built broad streets, and pleasant surburban roads fringed with villas and country houses.

The harbour was greatly improved in 1878 at a cost of £200,000, and a dock added in 1883, so that Ayr, though inferior to Kilmarnock in manufactures, now ranks with Ardrossan and Troon in shipping prosperity. It has also undisputed claims to importance from its position as a provincial capital of considerable social standing and attractions, and a favourite hunting centre, besides its associations with the two national celebrities, Wallace and Burns, the latter of whom describes it as

"Auld Ayr, wham ne'er a toun surpasses
For honest men and bonnie lasses."

There was an old castle here on the left bank of the Ayr, a little way below the New Bridge, of which nothing remains, but the site is believed to be the same as that on which Oliver Cromwell built one of his 5 forts or bastilles to overawe the West Country, 1652. The *Old Church* was partly built by Cromwell, in lieu of that of St. John the Baptist, a large pile near the shore, which he seized upon and converted into an armoury at the same time that he included it within the fort. The tower of that ch. (now turned into a dwelling house), with part of the magazine, is still standing. It was in the Dominican convent which occupied the site of this ch. that the Parliament which settled the succession upon Robert Bruce and his heirs assembled in 1315.

The *Wallace Tower* in the High Street is one of the most conspicuous, if not the most tasteful, objects in Ayr, being 133 ft. in height. It was built in 1832 upon the site of a very old tower, in which Wallace is said to have been confined, and over the walls of which he was let down by his friends to escape from the Southrons. It contains the old "drowsy dungeon clock" removed from a demolished tower, and, in a niche in front, a statue of Wallace by James Thom, an artist of local fame. The lower story is a coffee shop.

In Wellington Square is a *Statue*, by Noble, of the Indian *Gen. Neill*, who was a native of Ayr. The pedestal of Dalbeattie granite bears an inscription describing him as "a brave, resolute, self-reliant soldier, universally acknowledged as the first who stemmed the tide of rebellion in Bengal," and a representation of his death at the relief of Lucknow, 25th Sept. 1857.

The same square contains the *County Buildings*, designed after the model of the Temple of Isis, Rome. The *Town Buildings and Assembly*

Rooms at the corner of High St. and Sandgate, are surmounted by a conspicuous spire 226 ft. high; and adjoining them is the *Public Hall*, erected 1881.

Thanks to Robert Burns's facetious "Dialogue," no public buildings are more celebrated than the **Twa Brigs** of Ayr, of which the *Auld Brig*, now used only as a footway from the High Street, was built in the latter part of the 13th cent. by two old maids of the name of Lowe. For 500 years the "Auld Vandal" satisfied the wants of Ayr, though but a

"... poor, narrow footpath of a street,
Where twa wheelbarrows tremble when they meet."

The *New Bridge*, lower down, nearer the harbour, was built in 1788, from designs by Adam. The abutments of the arches, adorned with allegorical figures, roused the ire of the "Auld Brig," whose "prophecy" that the New Bridge would not last has come strangely true. It was replaced in 1877, at a cost of £16,000, by a newer structure of 5 arches, which had to be repaired in 1879 and again in 1882.

The fashionable *Western* (Race) *Meeting* is held here annually in September. Near the Race Course are several of the best residential villas.

EXCURSIONS:—

(1) To **Burns's Cottage, Alloway Kirk, Burns's Monument,** and the **Brig o' Doon,** $2\frac{3}{4}$ m. These—the main attractions of the neighbourhood—are visited annually by thousands of tourists.

At the top of High-street or Townhead, take the road which runs alongside of the rly. on the S. and keep straight on. This is the direction in which "Tam o' Shanter" proceeded after he had left the public-house in Ayr. It is not exactly the same road, for it has been somewhat straightened, and some localities mentioned in his ride are now at some distance from it.

At $1\frac{1}{2}$ m. just before arriving at (l.) *Rozelle* (J. Houldsworth, Esq.), the road crosses a stream, over which, a little distance from the bridge, was

"... the ford,
Whare in the snaw the chapman smoor'd."

Rt. is the cottage in the garden of which stood

"... the meikle stane,
Whare drucken Charlie brak's neck-bane."

and beyond is *Belleisle* (G. Coats, Esq.)

At 2 m. (rt.) is a row of cottages, in one of which Burns was born on the 25th Jan. 1759. It was originally a "clay biggin'," rebuilt by the poet's father with his own hands. On the night of his birth a storm came on, part of his mother's cottage fell in, and she and her child were forced to take shelter in that of a neighbour until their own had been repaired. This interesting structure, long used as a public-house, was in 1880 purchased for £4000, to be converted into a *Burns Museum.* Admission 2d.

Well to the rt. lies *Cambusdoon* (Mrs. James Baird, whose husband d. 1876, leaving £500,000 to the Church of Scotland), prettily situated on the Doon. In its park stood

"... the cairn
Whare hunters fand the murder'd bairn."

At $2\frac{1}{2}$ m., right opposite *Alloway Church* (1858), a flight of steps, worn by the feet of pilgrims by the thousand, leads over a wall to

"Alloway's auld haunted kirk,"

a ruin long before Burns's day, and now reduced to 4 bare walls with gables and a bell-cote. Here Tam o' Shanter witnessed the witches' hellish orgies. Within the ch.-yd., amongst a crowd of other forefathers of the hamlet, Burns's father is buried. A new stone was erected over his grave in 1881, the old one having been carried off piecemeal by relic hunters.

Beyond, in a garden overlooking the Doon, is **Burns's Monument,** built in 1820, at a cost of £3350. It is a circular temple, supported by 9 fluted Corinthian columns, emblematic of the 9 Muses. In the interior are preserved a copy of the best edition of the poet's works, a bust and copy of the portrait of him by Nasmyth (the best ever painted), and a Bible said to be the one presented by him to "Highland Mary" at their last interview. A staircase leads to the temple, whence a pretty view is obtained of the surrounding scenery. In a grotto at the end of the garden are the figures of "Tam o' Shanter" and "Souter Johnnie,"—specimens of caricature of little value as works of art—by James Thom, the sculptor of Wallace's statue. There is much bad taste in all this cockneyfied homage to the poet: the real interest lies in the beauty of the spot, the *Banks of the Doon* contrasting pleasantly with the rather monotonous country around Ayr. The tourist should descend to the Doon, just above the two bridges, one, comparatively new, the other the "Auld Brig," of one slim arch, to "win the keystone" of which was the utmost effort of Meg in her flight from the witches, for as Tam well knew,

"A running stream they darena cross."

By the side of a small tributary of the Doon, in the garden of *Doonbrae Cottage,* is

the thorn aboon the well,
"Whare Mungo's mither hanged hersel."

There is an *Inn* between the two bridges, the garden of which runs down to the river, and contains a shell grotto.

Above the bridge on the rt. bank of the Doon is *Doonholm* (Lord Blackburn); across the river are *Newark Cas.*, almost rebuilt by the Marq. of Ailsa, and *Doonside* (W. H. Dunlop, Esq.); and 1½ m. up the l. bank is *Auchendrane* (James Coats, Esq.), the fine seat of the late Sir Peter Coats, containing the site of the old castle, the scene of Scott's "*Ayrshire Tragedy*" (see p. 116).

To the E. on the other side of the Doon, lie *Mount Oliphant* farm, once rented by Burns's father, and where the poet received his early education, and **Dalrymple Stat.** (p. 118), whence the pedestrian may return to Ayr.

(2) To **Mauchline** (*a*) by rly. (or road), keeping the north side of the river Ayr, 11 m., see p. 103; (*b*) by road 13 m., keeping the S. side of the river. The second road passes several charming residences. At 5 m., after crossing the picturesque trib. of the *Coyle*, rt. is *Sundrum*, the very ancient seat of Lieut.-Col. Hamilton, and l. *Gadgirth* (Major-Gen. Burnett). At 7½ m. l. is the ch. and old house of *Stair*, from which the Earl takes his title. *Barskimming Ho.* (p. 102) lies l. of the bridge over the Ayr (11½ m.), which we cross before ascending to Mauchline, p. 102.

(3) By **Greenan Cas.** 3 m. and the **Heads of Ayr** 5 m. to **Dunure** (p. 117) 8 m.

(4) Rly. to **Dalmellington** 15 m.

This branch leaves the Girvan line (Rte. 15) at 4 m., and trends l. to

6¼ m. **Hollybush Stat.** 1½ m. N. is *Loch Martnaham*, 2 m. long, with an island crowned by an old castle.

[At 8 m. a *Branch* strikes l. to **Rankinston** (3½ m.), a mining village on the Coyle].

Our line approaches the Doon (rt.) whose course it now follows. At

9½ m. **Patna Stat.**, the hills begin to close in, and ironworks and pits show themselves.

11¾ m. **Waterside Stat.** To the rt., extending for several miles, is the dreary moorland plateau of Keir's Hill, 1005 ft.

15 m. **Dalmellington Stat.** ✲, where the population is employed in the Dalmellington Iron Co. (Messrs. Houldsworth), who have 5 furnaces here. It is a neat and compact village, situated about ¾ m. from the Doon, and overhung by a lofty Mote hill.

The only attraction in the neighbourhood is the scenery of the romantic narrow glen called the *Ness*, through which the river Doon flows from its issue out of *Loch Doon*, 3 m. to the S. (driving road 4 m.). The owner of the beautiful grounds in which the Ness lies permits visitors (except on Sunday) to skirt the river for the whole distance.

Loch Doon is one of the largest lochs in the south of Scotland. From the head of Ness Glen to the loch head, where the *Gala Lane* flows into it, it is 5½ m. in length, though seldom above ½ m. in breadth. The scenery is pleasing near the head of the loch, where the Hill of Craigmulloch, 1381 ft., and the Black Craig, 1730 ft., rise up directly from the water's edge. On an islet underneath Craigmulloch are the ruins of *Loch Doon Castle*, which appears to have been of some importance in the 14th cent.

In the loch—open to the public —there is tolerable trout *fishing*. The fish, however, are small, only averaging about 4 or 5 to the pound. The pedestrian will find a path skirting the loch the whole distance to the head on the W. side, and geologists should notice the striated rocks and boulders on its shores, exhibiting the effects of glacial action.

The country to the S. of Loch Doon is exceedingly wild and almost untrodden save by the shepherd or the sportsman. Two lofty and rugged ranges of mountains run nearly due S. towards the coast of Kirkcudbright,—viz. the **Rhinns of Kell**, of which *Corscrine* (2668 ft.) and *Meikle Millyea* (2446 ft.), with *Loch Dungeon* on their east side, are the highest points, to the E., and the range of **Merrick** (2764 ft., the highest mt. on the mainland S. of the Forth and Clyde) to the W. They give rise to the northern rivers, *Stinchar*, *Girvan*, and *Doon*, and to the southern rivers, *Cree*, *Minnoch*, and *Dee*.

E. of the stern and savage escarpments of Merrick lie *Loch Enoch* (at an elevation of 1650 ft.), and several smaller lochs and tarns encompassed by a wild *entourage* of mountains and rocks which will well repay the scenery-loving pedestrian who is hardy enough to explore these recesses.

From the S. end of Loch Doon (abt. 10 m. from Dalmellington) follow up the stream of *Gala Lane* for 5 m.; thence (1) keep rt. up *Pulskaig Burn* (2 m.) to Loch Enoch, [ascend Merrick], and descend S.W. by the *Buchan Burn* in abt. 6 m. to *Glen Trool Lodge* (p. 108), to which a carriage may be ordered from Newton Stewart; *or* (2) keep up the Gala Lane to its source (2 m.), descend the *Cooran Lane* to **Loch Dee** (4 m.), and find quarters at the Shepherd's Cottage (*Black Laggan*) on the S. side of the loch (p. 108). Newton Stewart (p. 107), New Galloway (p. 107), and Carsphairn (p. 107), are also starting-points, but the whole district is necessarily very inaccessible.

ROUTE 18.

Ayr to Glasgow by Troon, Kilwinning, and Paisley. G. and S.W. Rly.

41½ m. abt. 13 trains daily in 1 hr.—1¾ hrs.

For **AYR** ✲, see p. 119.

The line crosses the river and passes rt. *Craigie Ho.* (J. A. Campbell, Esq.), to

1 m. **Newton-on-Ayr Stat.**

3 m. **Prestwick Stat.** This town, once the property of the Abbey of Paisley, contains a curious old market cross, remains of an ancient ch., and the ruins of *Kingswell*, a hospital founded for lepers by Robert Bruce, who is said to have been cured of leprosy by drinking the waters. Golf is keenly pursued on the extensive *links* here—one of the finest courses in Scotland. (Introduction by a member of the club necessary.) Rt. on a knoll are the walls of the ancient

parish ch. which had an old bell now in the schoolhouse.

The line winds along the shore of Ayr Bay, allowing good views of the opposite coast of Arran, with Holy Island and Goatfell.

4 m. **Monkton Stat.** Here too are ruins of an early church and an inscribed bell. *Fullarton House*, a seat of the Duke of Portland, and in 1801 the residence of Louis Philippe, King of the French, is seen ($\frac{3}{4}$ m. rt.) as we reach

$6\frac{1}{2}$ m. **Troon Stat.** ✲ one of the 3 leading ports of Ayrshire, standing on a neck of land. N. and S. are sands which render it a favourite sea-side resort, while W. is the harbour, with extensive quays (connected with the rly.), from which a very large quantity of Scotch coal is shipped—especially to Ireland. At the end of the pier is a lighthouse. S. of the town are *Golf Links* (private), and 4 m. inland is

Dundonald Castle, now a mass of uncouth masonry, all the wrought stones having been taken out from the doorways and windows, and even the corners of the buildings carried away. The ruins stand in a prominent position, occupying the summit of a hill.

Robert Stewart lived here before he came to the throne under the title of Robert II., and here he died in 1390. The property was afterwards granted by James V. to a member of the Wallace family, who in 1638 sold it to Sir W. Cochrane. The surrounding land passed, in 1726, to the Eglinton family, and now belongs to Lady Sophie Allenby, d. of the 14th Earl, but the castle and its hill are still the property of the E. of Dundonald. Boswell, who with Johnson visited the ruins, says,—"Dr. Johnson, to irritate my old Scottish enthusiasm, was very jocular on the homely accommodation of King Bob, and roared and laughed till the ruins echoed."

To the N. of the hill is *Auchans Ho.* and $\frac{1}{2}$ m. W. *Auchans Castle* a castellated manor-house of 1644, remarkable architecturally for its crow-stepped gables. The castle has massive walls like Dundonald, and was built principally of materials taken from there. In the adjoining orchard was raised the celebrated "Auchans" pear.

$7\frac{1}{2}$ m. **Barassie Stat.**

[*Branch* rt. in 8 m. to Kilmarnock (p. 104) by **Drybridge**—close to which is *Shewalton Ho.*, formerly the seat of the Boyle family, and the nearest stat. ($1\frac{1}{4}$ m.) to *Dundonald* (above)—and **Gatehead** with *Caprington Cas.* (W. C. S. Cunningham, Esq.) $\frac{3}{4}$ m. E.]

$9\frac{1}{2}$ m. **Gailes Stat.**, for a *Golf Course* (private) and a *Militia Camping Ground.*

$11\frac{1}{4}$ m. **Irvine Stat.** ✲

[*Branch* rt. in $7\frac{1}{2}$ m. to Kilmarnock by *Dreghorn* and *Crosshouse.*]

Another Stat. $\frac{1}{2}$ m. N.E. is a terminus of the Cal. Rly., see Rte. 72.

The town — a royal and parl. burgh—situated on the *Irvine* river has large *Chemical Works*, and its *Moor* is in summer a huge *Militia Camp*, with a long land range for artillery practice. In the neighbourhood are numerous coal mines, and coals are shipped from its harbour, but it has of late years declined as a seaport. The "*Seagate*" contains the lines of a *Castle* (14th cent.) with a later Norman doorway—belonging to the Montgomeries, Earls of Eglinton. In the broad High Street is a *Statue* to David Boyle of Shewalton (1772-1853), Lord President of the Court of Session, who was born here, as were James Montgomery the poet (1771-1854) and Galt the novelist (1779-1839). Burns was a flax-dresser here (1781-83) until his shop was burnt down.

We are now in one of the busiest districts of the Ayrshire coalfield with numerous pits in the neighbourhood; on the rt. are the woods of *Eglinton Cas.* (below). Having passed (l.) the *Bogside Race-course*, we notice the blazing furnaces—best seen at night —of *Ardeer* (Messrs. Merry and Cunninghame) and *Nobel and Co.'s Dynamite Works* to the left and close at hand (l.) the large *Eglinton Iron-*

works of W. Baird and Co. Lim., before reaching

14½ m. **Kilwinning Stat.** ✲

[*Branch* l. to *Ardrossan* and *Largs* (Rte. 73).]

There is another stat. upon the Cal. Rly. line, see Rte. 72.

The archæologist should visit the ruins of **Kilwinning Priory**.

It was founded in 1140 for Tironensian monks, by Hugh de Moreville, to whom also Dryburgh Abbey is attributed. The remains are reduced to the W. doorway, with a door of the S. aisle, the south transept, a fine S. gable with an early pointed 3-light window, a circular window in the gable above, and an arch of the S. transept aisle. Outside the transept was the Chapter-house, entered by a circular door, and flanked by a window on each side. A modern bell-tower, erected in 1815, stands within the enclosure.

St. Winnin, Finan, or Inan, the patron saint of the ch. (cf. Kirkgunzeon, p. 105), was of Irish extraction, and landed on the coast of *Cunningham*, as this N. district of Ayrshire is called (see p. 119). Finding starvation rather near at hand, he went to fish in the Garnock, the river on which Kilwinning stands, and being unable to catch anything, cursed the stream, and forbade fish ever to enter it—a fate which it only escaped by diverting its course.

Freemasonry was introduced into Scotland by the builders of Kilwinning Priory, and Mother Kilwinning was for some centuries the parent lodge of the society in Scotland.

Kilwinning was noted for the excellence of its archers; and the shooting at the popinjay, as described in "Old Mortality," used until late years to be an annual custom here. The Kilwinning Company of Archers claims an antiquity of about 400 years, but the practice of archery has now fallen considerably into disuse. The shaft of the *Town Cross* probably dates from the 15th cent., but the upper part has been restored.

1½ m. S.E. of the town is **Eglinton Castle**, the seat of the Earl of Eglinton.

[The principal gateway is on the Irvine Road. The grounds are open on Sats. The drive round the *Deer Park* is recommended as charmingly wild, and then exit should be made by the long S. avenue leading to the picturesque ruins of *Stanes Cas.* outside its gate and 1 m. N.E. of Irvine.]

The house of Montgomerie has for upwards of 600 years held a prominent position in the history of Scotland. Robert de Montgomerie, descended from the great Norman house of that name in England, died about 1180. A descendant of his, Sir John, married the heiress of Eglinton, who was also a niece of Robert III.; and Hugh, the fifth Lord Montgomerie, was created Earl of Eglinton in 1503. In 1612 the title passed over to the Earl of Winton, whereby the two became united.

In the castle (built 1798) an attempt is made to combine the style of the feudal fortress with the light and conveniences of a modern dwelling-house, but the appearance of its bold round towers is spoilt by the rows of sash windows.

In 1839 the *Eglinton Tournament*, held in the park, which is traversed by the river Lugton, and contains some fine forest trees, was an attempt to reproduce on a large scale the chivalrous forms and ceremonies of the olden times. Among the knights was Prince Louis, afterwards Emperor Napoleon III. The banners carried by the different knights are hung in the castle.

Leaving Kilwinning, at 16 m. the *Dusk Water* is crossed, up which is a stalactite cave called *Elf House* (180 ft. long and 12 ft. high), said to have been a hiding-place of the Covenanters. At 16½ m.—where a line from Kilmarnock comes in—rt. is *Blair Ho.* (W. F. Blair, Esq.). This house, picturesquely situated, is, in part, the oldest inhabited house in Ayrshire.

18 m. **Dalry Stat.** ✲, with the *Blair Ironworks* rt. The geologist will find on the *Dusk* (above) and on the *Rye Water* (N.W.) good sections of carboniferous rocks.

20¾ m. **Kilbirnie Stat.** The village, 1 m. l. beyond the *Glengarnock Ironworks*, overlooks Kilbirnie Loch, a rather fine sheet of water, 1¼ m.

long. To the W. stand the ruins of *Kilbirnie Place* (14th cent.) a seat of the Earls of Crawford, which was burnt down in the 18th cent. The *Church*, between the stat. and the village, built after the Reformation, has a gallery which belonged to the Crawford family, containing some good carved woodwork in Renaissance style. In the ch.-yd. is the monument, with effigies, of Thomas Crawford, who scaled and took Dumbarton Castle, 1571. It is enclosed in a sort of stone case, and is visible through loopholes.

22¾ m. **Beith Stat.** ✲ is at the other end of the loch, and 1 m. from the town, which is connected E. with the Caledonian Rly. by a branch to Lugton (p. 324). It has large furniture factories, and a great horse fair is held every year in August, on a day called "Tenants," a corruption of St. Inan's Day.

We enter Renfrewshire, shortly before reaching

24¾ m. **Lochwinnoch Stat.** ¾ m. l. is a large village, engaged in the bleaching of linen for the Paisley manufactories. It stands at the S. end of *Castle Semple Loch*, which, when frozen, is a favourite resort of devotees to the Scottish game of *Curling*. Here many of the principal matches or *Bonspiels* are played.[1]

S. of the loch is *Barr Castle*, which, with the exception of its roof, is tolerably complete. It is a loopholed tower of great height, and consists of 4 stories, on the 2nd of which is a fine hall. Between the rly. and the loch are the ruins of *Peel Castle* (16th cent.) formerly on an island. At the N. end of the loch is *Castle Semple*, now the seat of H. Lee-Harvey, Esq., and near it are the remains of a Dec. collegiate ch. founded by Lord Semple (1504), whose original seat was *Elliotson Tower*, ¾ m. E., which is passed rt. before reaching

27½ m. **Howwood** (or Hollowwood) **Stat.**, at the W. foot of the Fereneze Hills (p. 324). 1½ m. N.W. near Clochoderick farm is an enormous drift boulder, called the *Druids' Stone.*

29 m. **Milliken Park Stat.**, 1 m. l. is *Kilbarchan*, a small town (with cotton factories), whose ch. steeple is adorned with a statue of Habbie Simpson, the famous piper (d. 17th cent.)

"'Weel hae ye play'd your part,' quo' Meg,
'Your cheeks are like the crimson;
There's nane in Scotland plays so weel
Since we lost Habbie Simpson.'"

E. of the town is *Milliken Ho.* (A. M'Kenzie, Esq.).

30½ m. **Johnstone Stat.**, a busy town, with a considerable reputation for its flax and cotton manufactories and engineering works. It has a handsome ch., built in 1793, with a light and elegant spire. Here is the terminus of the Glasgow, Paisley, and Johnstone Canal, opened in 1811, and intended to be extended to Ardrossan, but never completed. 1 m. S. is *Johnstone Castle* (A. Galbraith, Esq.)

A line strikes l. to Bridge of Weir and Greenock (Rte. 70) between this and

21¾ m. **Elderslie Stat.**, see p. 322.

33¾ m. **Paisley Stat.** ✲, see p. 318.

See pp. 322, 321 for route hence to

41½ m. **St. Enoch's Stat., Glasgow.**

For **GLASGOW** ✲, see p. 132.

[1] See the late Principal Shairp's spirited poem of *The Bonspiel.*

SECTION II.

WESTERN MIDLANDS—GLASGOW—HAMILTON—LOCH LOMOND—STIRLING—LOCH KATRINE—THE TROSSACHS—CALLANDER AND OBAN RAILWAY.

§ 1. GENERAL INFORMATION.

THIS section contains the routes between Edinburgh and Glasgow, a description of the great commercial Metropolis of the West and its surroundings—other than the Clyde Estuary—the routes from Edinburgh and Glasgow to Stirling, and that most generally attractive district of Scotland comprising The Trossachs, Loch Katrine, and Loch Lomond.

The approach to Oban by railway from Callander (opened 1880), including Loch Awe and Loch Etive, is also given in this section, leaving the ways of getting to and from Oban by the West Coast, and the excursions from that "Charing Cross of the Highlands" to Section VI.

So greatly have the facilities of locomotion increased that those perfunctory tourists, whose ambition is to "do" everything in the shortest possible space of time, can not only accomplish the round of the Trossachs and Loch Lomond from either Edinburgh or Glasgow after a very late breakfast, or before afternoon tea; but from Glasgow may take train to Loch Awe, steamer up the loch, coach to Oban, and be back in Glasgow the same day!

Circular tickets are available for the season, and the journey may be broken anywhere on the route.

Up the Clyde from Glasgow is "Bothwell Brig," a historic site, Bothwell Castle, a grand ruin, close to the modern house in which are preserved some of Lord Chancellor Clarendon's finest Vandycks, and Hamilton Palace with its noble park. Between Hamilton and Lanark the Vale of Clyde is exceedingly pleasing, with fine country seats, while in a side valley are the ruins of Craignethan Castle, the prototype of Tillietudlem.

Hamilton borders on the "*Black Country*" of Scotland, situated to the East of Glasgow. Those who take an interest in other things besides grand scenery should visit this coalfield, where the *Manufacture of Iron* has been developed to a wonderful extent. It is one of the most extraordinary scenes of industry in the world; the "Black Diamond" having produced more genuine wealth than the brilliant of Golconda, and the "Black Band" vieing in rich results with the silver veins of Potosi. The principal *Iron Works* in this district are at Govan (William Dixon, Lim.), Gartsherrie (Wm. Baird and Co., Lim.), Coltness, Coatbridge, Omoa, Shotts, etc., while there are *Steel Works* at Hallside, Mossend, etc., and large *Oil Works* at West Calder, Bathgate, Airdrie, Uphall, Broxburn, etc. Most of these grimy but busy fields of industry are reached by Rtes. 20–22, while the Govan Ironworks are close to Glasgow. It should, however, be borne in mind that, although more concentrated here, some of the largest *Iron Works* in Scotland are to be found in Ayrshire —*e.g.* at Muirkirk, Lugar, Dalmellington, Kilwinning, Dalry, Glengarnock, etc. (cf. Rtes. 11, 17, and 18).

§ 2. PRINCIPAL CENTRES.

1. **Glasgow** for its immediate Environs and the neighbouring "Black Country."
   Loch Lomond, Loch Katrine, and The Trossachs, described in this section, can be visited in one day; as can also Ayr, Lanark and the Falls of Clyde, and other places described in Section I., and much of the Estuary of the Clyde described in Section V.
2. **Stirling** or **Bridge of Allan** for Stirling Castle, Bannockburn, the upper part of the Forth, the Lake of Menteith, and Loch Ard; also for Dunblane Cathedral, and the Glens in the Ochils described in Section III.
3. **Callander** for The Trossachs, Loch Katrine, Doune Castle, Braes of Balquhidder, etc.
4. **Dalmally** or **Loch Awe** for Glen Orchy, Loch Awe, Ben Cruachan, Loch Etive, etc.

ROUTES.

ROUTE 19.

Edinburgh to Glasgow [Balloch, Helensburgh and Stirling], by Linlithgow and Falkirk. N.B. Rly.

This is the most interesting route between Edin. and Glasgow, 47½ m. About 18 trains daily. 1¼ hr. by express.

The Cal. Rly. trains for Stirling, Perth and Aberdeen, *via* Larbert (Rtes. 25, 38, and 47) run over the N.B. Rly. line from beyond the Haymarket to Polmont, but start from Princes St. Stat.

For Edinburgh see Rte. 4.

Leaving the Waverley Stat. the line passes through the Princes St. Gardens (once the *Nor' Loch*) which, after much opposition, were encroached upon in 1894 for an additional set of double rails. l. under the Castle Rock are the remains of the *Wellhouse Tower*, supposed to be a fragment of the first city wall of 1450. Rt. there is good view of Princes St. At ¾ m. a long tunnel (doubled in breadth 1894) is passed through to

1½ m. **Haymarket Stat.** for the W. End. Beyond, rt. is *Donaldson's Hospital* (p. 60), then *Murrayfield*, with large suburban residences; l. we pass the juncs. with the suburban line (N.B.R.) and with the Cal. Rly., and *Saughton* (a lunatic asylum), while in the distance are the *Pentland Hills*.

3½ m. **Corstorphine Stat.**

[*Junction* for the line across the *Forth Bridge* (Rtes. 30-35).]

The *Church* is an interesting specimen of Dec. style, built in the form of an irregular cross. At the S.W. stands a belfry-tower, with a foreign-looking octagonal spire. In the interior are some monuments of the Forrester family (now represented by Lord Verulam), who founded this as a collegiate ch. in 1429. The figures in the niche in the chancel are supposed to represent Sir John Forrester and his wife.

E. of the village is the *Convalescent Hosp.* in connection with the Edinburgh Royal Infirmary; behind rises *Corstorphine Hill*, with a *Scott Centenary* (1871) *Tower* on the summit.

5½ m. **Gogar Stat.** with several pleasant country houses in the neighbourhood.

8¼ m. **Ratho Stat.**

[*Junction* for lines—(1) l. to Glasgow by Bathgate (Rte. 20);

(2) rt. to Kirkliston and Dalmeny; but the *direct* line from Edin. to Dalmeny is Rte. 30. On *this* route the *Almond* is crossed before

1½ m. **Kirkliston Stat.** Here is a fine *Romanesque Ch.* much disfigured by modern alterations. Field-Marshal the 2nd Earl of Stair (1673-1747), who lived at Newliston (below), is buried here.

½ m. further E. across the Almond is an inscribed stone called the "Catstane."

At 3 m. *Dundas Cas.* (p. 202) is 1½ m. l.

4 m. **Dalmeny Stat.** (p. 178).]

Beyond Ratho a *Viaduct* of 36 arches—the longest in Scotland—carries the line across the *Almond Water*, which separates Linlithgowshire or West Lothian from Edinburghshire or Midlothian. On the right is *Newliston* (S. B. Hog, Esq.), formerly the residence of the 2nd Earl of Stair (1673-1747) who had a hobby for arboriculture, and was said to have arranged his trees to represent the grouping of regiments in certain battles.

The rly. now passes through cuttings, a break in which (rt.) affords a glimpse of the ruined castle of *Niddry*, where Queen Mary passed her first night after her escape from Lochleven. It then belonged to Lord Seton. Passing through a tunnel we reach

12 m., **Winchburgh Stat.** after which the Union Canal appears l. and runs parallel with the line. 3 m. rt. are *Hopetoun House* (Earl of Hopetoun) and the village of Abercorn (p. 202).

14½ m. **Philipstoun Stat.**, rt. is an obelisk on Bonnington Hill in memory of General Hope, who fell in the Indian Mutiny.

17½ m. **LINLITHGOW Stat.** ✫ Linlithgow or Lithgow, "the lake of the winding stream," long a royal residence and place of importance, was made a royal burgh by David I., and is the capital of the county. The town is old and irregular, with high-roofed houses, occasionally adorned with traces of sculpture. Its loch, 1 m. long, is a great ornament, and the best sheet of water for skating in the E. of Scotland. No town in Scotland has so many fountains, and a local rhyme speaks of "Lithgow for wells, Glasgow for bells, Peebles for clashes and lees, and Falkirk for beans and peas."

The *Fountain of St. Michael*, with the figure of the archangel upon it, and the inscription, "St Michael is kinde to strangers," is passed (l.) on the way from the stat. to the palace, 10 min. walk. Farther on is the

Cross Well, the facsimile of an older one, restored 1807.

Passing up the hill between this well and the *Townhouse* we reach the **Precincts of the Palace and Church**, which are entered by a fine embattled **Gateway,** built by James V. It is flanked by octagonal towers, and over the entrance are the coats of arms of the 4 orders of knighthood to which that king belonged. They consist of—1st, 3 lions (Garter of England); 2nd, 1 lion (St. Andrew of Scotland); 3rd, castles and lions (Golden Fleece of Spain); 4th, Fleur de Lis (of France).

The **Church,** founded by David I. (12th cent.), and dedicated to St. Michael, whose image may be seen at the S.W. angle, "is one of the finest in Scotland, and is of the so-called Scottish Decorative, in which French architectural influence is marked." It owed much of its grandeur to Crichton, Bp. of Dunkeld (16th cent.). At its W. end is a tall pinnacled tower, formerly surmounted by a crown of crossed arches, beneath which is a fine doorway, and there is a 2nd door on the S. side under a very elegant *Porch*, having a watch-room above it. The tracery of the windows is very varied and elegant, especially that of the S. transept. The interior consists of 8 bays, with pointed arches, resting on clustered piers carved with shields of arms. It is hideously white-washed, and is divided by an ugly partition wall, only the chancel being used for service, but is (1894) in course of restoration. At the E. end is a 3-sided apse of tall windows. The nave is stately and unusually wide. Notice the restored Flamboyant window in the S. transept, called St. Catherine's Chapel. It was in this chapel that an apparition warned James IV. not to go to war with England.[1] The pointed roof, the clerestory of round arches (date 1424), each enclosing two pointed lights, and the bosses of the vault, deserve attention. In the vestry is a well-sculptured stone altar-piece representing the Passion and Betrayal of our Saviour. "In the tower are 3 ancient bells, still used. The largest bears date 1490, the smallest was recast 1718."

Edward I. halted at Linlithgow the night before the battle of Falkirk, in 1298; and, while he was sleeping on the ground by the side of his charger, the horse put its foot upon the king and broke two of his ribs. Three years afterwards Edward wintered here, and built a fort, on the site of which arose one of the favourite palaces of the later Stuarts. Though much altered in appearance by additions, it has in a great measure retained its original character, and is a good specimen of a fortified palace.

Although the ***Palace** is generally said to have grown out of the fort built by Edward I., there seems no doubt that there was a royal castle here in the time of David I.

The situation of the palace is pleasant; it stands on a promontory of some elevation, which advances almost into the midst of the loch.

> "Of all the palaces so fair,
> Built for the royal dwelling,
> In Scotland, far beyond compare,
> Linlithgow is excelling."
> *Marmion*, Canto iv.

A low portal flanked with turrets, stone vaulted and ribbed across, leads into the *Courtyard*.

The first appearance of the interior of the quadrangle reminds those who have seen the ruins of Heidelberg of that castellated palace, which was in part built under the eye of one who had spent much of her earlier life in Linlithgow—Elizabeth, daughter of James VI., and Electress Palatine.

This quadrangle is furnished with a round tower in each corner, and a fifth in the N. front opposite, each containing a corkscrew stair. The

[1] Described in "Marmion."

peel or S.W. corner tower was erected by Edward I. in 1302, and the buildings which had grown up round it, with the Parish Ch., were destroyed by fire in 1424. In the following year the building of a new palace was begun, and actively carried on till 1451. The S. side appears, from the Lord Treasurer's accounts, to have been built between 1488-96.

On the E. side was the original entrance, approached from without by a drawbridge (now removed) over the deep moat, which is still flanked below by the drums of 3 towers. This gateway, on the side towards the courtyard, is faced with some rich niches and Gothic work. Beneath it yawns a deep dungeon. On the first floor is the great hall, 94 ft. long, lighted by 5 windows on each side, while one end is entirely occupied by a fireplace and ornamented mantelpiece; at the other end it communicates with the kitchen, furnished with a fireplace nearly as wide. The hall communicated with the *Chapel* in the S. wing, lighted by 6 lancet windows. The Royal Pew opened from a gallery above.

On the W. side of the quadrangle were the private apartments, fitted up most probably, if not built, by James IV., the bower of whose queen, Margaret, is at the top of the tower staircase. This room has a groined roof, and a slab commemorates its former occupant, in Sir W. Scott's lines :—

"His own Queen Margaret, who in Lithgow's bower
All lonely sat, and wept the weary hour."

Here is the gloomy chamber where Queen Mary was born, 1542. Her father, James V., lying sick at *Falkland*, died immediately after (see p. 182). Communicating with these rooms is a small private chapel and oriel window looking down upon the loch. Galleries run round two sides of the building, partly formed in the thickness of the walls, for the passage of servants and retainers, and another runs round the top. At the W. end is the antechapel, and at the E. is the robing-room for the priests. The lower story was devoted entirely to offices and stabling. The ruined *Fountain* in the centre of the quadrangle is richly and boldly sculptured. The palace continued in a perfect state until 1746, when it was occupied by General Hawley's dragoons the night of the battle of Falkirk (in which they were routed by Prince Charles Stuart), and was burnt by them.

In the town of Linlithgow the Regent Murray was shot, in 1570, by James Hamilton of Bothwellhaugh, from a house belonging to the Archbishop of St. Andrews, who, suspected of having been accessory to the crime, was put to death in consequence. Bothwellhaugh's wife had become mad, in consequence of being ejected from her house (see p. 77) by Patrick Home, an adherent of the Regent, on whom the forfeited property had been bestowed. The assassin slipped out in the rear of the house, the site of which is occupied by the present *County Buildings*, and a fleet horse, ready saddled, soon carried him out of reach.[1]

Linlithgow produces shoes and whisky, but is not a flourishing town. It has a somewhat obtrusive *Jubilee Town Hall*.

1½ m. W. of Linlithgow Stat. the Avon, up which the scenery is pleasing, is crossed, and Stirlingshire entered. *Linlithgow Bridge*, rt., was in 1526 the scene of a battle between the Earls of Angus and Lennox.

19¾ m. **Manuel Junc. Stat.**

[*Branch* runs rt. in 4 m. to *Bo'ness* (p. 202), and l. *via Blackston*, *Slamannan*, and *Coatbridge* to *Glasgow*.]

---

[1] See Scott's ballad of *Cadyow Castle*.

Near this are the scanty ruins of the *Priory of Emmanuel*, founded by Malcolm in 1156.

22¼ m. **Polmont Junc. Stat.**

[*Branch* rt. *via Grahamston* (3¼ m.) to (1) *Grangemouth* (6¼ m.) [p. 203] and (2), crossing the *Forth and Clyde Canal* on a single set of rails, to *Larbert* (6¼ m.) for Stirling and Perth (see Rte. 25).]

Beyond Polmont l. are *Blair Lodge*, an excellent Boys' Boarding School, and Nobel's *Explosive Works*. Rt. (across the other line) is *West Quarter* (J. N. E. F. Livingstone, Esq.), and between the lines *Callendar* (W. Forbes, Esq.), formerly a seat of the Earls of Callendar, whose title was forfeited in 1716, and the grounds of which contain the best-preserved portions of the *Roman Wall* of Antoninus. A tunnel is passed through before

25½ m. **Falkirk Stat.** The town, a parl. burgh, lies ½ m. N., and beyond is the suburb and stat. of **Grahamston** (above).

Falkirk ✲ is a busy town, consisting chiefly of one long street, and has of late years acquired importance from its situation on the coalfield, as testified by the number of blazing ironworks and collieries, but it is chiefly celebrated for its "*Trysts*" or fairs held monthly, except Dec. to Mar., on *Stenhouse Muir*, about 3 m. N.W. of the town. Large quantities of cattle brought great distances—ponies from Shetland, sheep from Ross and Sutherland, and horned cattle from the western islands—are then sold, but weekly local market auctions are rapidly reducing the number.

History gives account of two *Battles* of Falkirk—

1. Fought on the 22nd of July 1298, between Edward I. and Wallace, in which the latter was defeated. The suburb of Grahamston now occupies part of the field.

2. The battle of Falkirk Muir, between Prince Charles Stuart and General Hawley, on the 17th January 1746, in which Charles was victorious.

In the ch.-yd. lie Sir John Graham and Sir John Stewart, killed in the first battle on the side of the Scotch; and Sir Robert Munro, and his brother Dr. Munro, killed in the second on the side of the English.

1½ m. N., on the Carron Water, are the blazing furnaces of the *Carron Ironworks*, founded 1760, and among the oldest in Scotland; the old-fashioned piece of ordnance, "a Carronade," was first made here, and hence derived its name.

On quitting Falkirk most pleasing views are obtained N. in clear weather of the *Ochil Hills*, the *Wallace Monument* at Stirling, and the rich vale of the Forth, with *Ben Ledi*, and *Ben Voirlich* behind.

The line now crosses the *Union Canal* and begins to run parallel with the **Forth and Clyde Canal** (rt.) [see p. 150]. Beyond

28¾ m. **Bonnybridge Stat.** rt. is *Greenhill Junc.* on the Cal. Rly. (Rte. 25), where N.B.R. trains from Glasgow to Larbert, Alloa, Stirling, etc., begin (under running powers) to use the Cal. Rly. rails.

The line of the rly. for a time becomes identical with the **Roman Wall** of Antoninus, commonly known in Scotland as *Graham's* or *Grime's Dyke*.[1] This wall was built during the Roman occupation by Lollius Urbicus (139 A.D.) with the intention of shutting off the Lowlands from the wild tribes to the north, and extended from the Forth at Kinneil (p. 203) to the Clyde at Bowling (p. 150), a distance of 36 m., in which it was guarded and strengthened by forts every 2 miles. We know the names of three of the

[1] Perhaps *Grim* is a Teutonic word for the Devil: Grim's Dyke is a common name in England for ancient earthworks.

legions employed on the work—II. "Augusta"; VI. "Victrix"; and XX. "Valens Victrix." An inscribed stone, now in Glasgow College, preserves the name of Lollius Urbicus.

31¾ m. **Castlecary Stat.**, named from one of the forts on the line of the Roman wall. Here we obtain views on the rt. of the *Kilsyth Hills*, the highest point of which is *Meiklebin*, 1870 ft.

34½ m. **Dullatur Stat.**

35¾ m. **Croy Stat.** On *Bar Hill* and *Croy Hill* the remains of the *Wall* are well marked. 2 m. rt. across the Canal is **Kilsyth** ✲ (p. 155).

At 40 m. rt. the long Gothic edifice with chapel and clock-tower, facing the railway, is the *Barony* or *Woodlee Lunatic Asylum*, erected 1874, but largely increased since.

40¾ m. **Lenzie Junc. Stat.**

[*Branch* rt. *via Killearn* and *Buchlyvie* to *Aberfoyle* (Rte. 24).]

Lenzie is a growing place of residential villas. Beyond, Lanarkshire is entered, and before

44 m. **Bishopbriggs Stat.**, the peak of Ben Lomond is visible on the right in clear weather.

The direct line from Edinburgh to *Balloch* and *Helensburgh via Maryhill*—joining the line from Glasgow before *Drumchapel Stat.* (Rtes. 23, 67)—turns off rt. before

45¾ m. **Cowlairs Stat.** A suburb of Glasgow, deriving its name from the days when cattle were driven by the road, and rested here for the market. Here are the workshops of the N.B. Rly. Company. The engine is removed and brake trucks are attached for a very steep decline. Ascending, a wire rope is attached to the engine. Having passed l. *Sighthill Cemetery*, the train goes through a long tunnel to

47¼ m. **Glasgow, Queen St. Stat.** (*High Level*).

GLASGOW ✲, the commercial metropolis and the most important seaport of Scotland, stands on the Clyde, 22 m. above Greenock where the Firth begins. It yields to London and Liverpool only in its shipping; approaches Manchester in its cotton-spinning, Newcastle in its coal; exceeds the Thames and the Tyne in its iron shipbuilding, and equals Merthyr and Wolverhampton with its iron furnaces. The once shallow Clyde has been deepened, widened, and straightened, so that the largest vessels afloat navigate it in safety, while at Glasgow it has been converted into a Harbour upwards of 2 m. long by from 400 ft. to 500 ft. wide, lined with Quays and Wharves, extending on the N. side continuously from Victoria Bridge opposite Stockwell St. to Govan Ferry, and on the S. side from Glasgow Bridge to the Burgh of Govan, where they terminate at the entrance to Cessnock Dock (p. 141). Glasgow was the birthplace of the steam-engine, James Watt's invention having been perfected here, and in 1812 Henry Bell launched the "Comet" on the Clyde—the first steamboat in Europe.

Although, after the romantic position of Edinburgh, that of Glasgow must seem flat and monotonous, it is in reality very advantageously, and, to a certain extent, picturesquely situated on both banks of the Clyde; the southern suburbs, known as Gorbals, Hutchesontown, Laurieston, and Tradeston, bearing the same relation to the city as Southwark does to London. The northern portion is laid out in long and regular streets crossing at right angles, and rises up a considerable slope, with ranges of hills stretching away to the N.W., at a few miles' distance, in the background. Glasgow suffers from the misfortune of an atmosphere almost always, even in summer, tainted with dense smoke, and a very rainy climate, to compensate which it enjoys a supply of the purest water in Europe, brought direct from Loch Katrine, 1859. See pp. 150, 165.

Historical Notes.—The origin of the name of Glasgow is uncertain; but the most probable derivations (either "Claishdhu," the dark glen, or "Glas-coed," dark wood) evidently point to the secluded position of a monastery. Tradition, too, agrees in attributing the origin of Glasgow to an ecclesiastical source; for St. Kentigern (or, as he is commonly called, *St. Mungo*, "Dear friend") is said to have founded a bishopric here in 560 A.D., and to have worked miracles. One of these was the restoration, in the mouth of a fish caught in the Clyde, of a ring lost by the wife of the local chieftain. A salmon with a ring in its mouth is still part of the arms of Glasgow. The other parts, also traditionally associated with St. Mungo, being a tree, a bird, and a bell, with the motto "Let Glasgow Flourish." In 1450 William Turnbull, the bishop of the see, obtained a charter from James II. by which all the property of the neighbourhood was held by the bishops. In 1556, when the royal burghs were taxed by Queen Mary, Glasgow had a pop. of 45,000, and appears to have been only the 11th city in the kingdom in wealth and population. Indeed it was not raised to the dignity of a Royal Burgh until the reign of Charles I. In 1650 Oliver Cromwell took up his abode in *Silvercraigs Land*, and went to hear divine service in the Cathedral (see p. 136).

Few cities can boast greater improvement in the general character and sanitary condition of its buildings than Glasgow. Since 1866, when an Improvement Trust was instituted, more than £3,000,000 has been most effectively laid out in opening up new streets, removing squalid and pestiferous "rookeries," and generally amending the state of the city.

Trade and Commerce.—There is scarcely an industry in the United Kingdom which is not represented in Glasgow. Foremost is its *Shipbuilding*, for which the *Yards* on the Clyde between Glasgow and Greenock (see Rte. 68) are renowned all over the globe. In 1893, 253 vessels, chiefly iron, representing 280,160 tons, were built on the Clyde and its tributaries (cf. p. 142).

Next to the ship-yards in prominence are the *Chemical Works*. Those of the Tennants, at St. Rollox (a little to the N. of the cathedral), cover an area of 16 acres, and are conspicuous for *the lofty Chimney*, 435 ft. in height, that carries off the deleterious fumes from more than 100 retorts and furnaces. They supply sulphuric acid, chloride of lime, soda, and other chemicals used in manufactures. Still higher is the *Chimney* in Port-Dundas, belonging to Townsend's Chemical artificial manure works, which is 454 ft. high, and 50 ft. diameter at the base—one of the highest buildings in the world. Its oscillation on a stormy night is perceptible.

The West Indian trade, which was formerly the staple of Glasgow, has given place to that of *Cotton-spinning* and *Calico-printing*, which is carried on to a great extent in the suburbs and neighbouring towns.

Turkey-red dyeing was commenced in Glasgow 1816, and is one of the most successful branches of the calico-printing trade, but it has been largely transferred to Levenside, Dumbartonshire (p. 152). From its proximity to the coal-fields, *Iron* has long been an important feature in Glasgow commerce. Strangers who have never seen great iron furnaces in work should repair to the *Govan Ironwork*, on the S. side of Glasgow, where they will see one on a large scale in full operation.

There are also large *Engineering Works*, *Glass Manufactories* and *Potteries*, while the *Hyde Park Locomotive Works* (Messrs Neilson and Co.'s) at Springburn, founded in 1837, are the largest in Europe employed in the manufacture of locomotive engines. 2500 men are employed, and the annual output is 200 engines.

"The rapidity of the progress of the city may be inferred from the following facts. In 1735, though the Glasgow merchants owned half the entire tonnage of Scotland, it amounted to only 5650 tons. In that year the whole shipping of Scotland was only one-fortieth part of that of England; it is now about one-fifth. In point of value of exports, Glasgow ranks fourth among the ports of the United Kingdom, and Greenock now takes precedence of Bristol."—SMILES.

For the *Clyde* and the *Docks* see p. 141.

The tourist will do well to start from the lower part of **Buchanan St.** which is near the principal rly. stats., contains the best shops in the city, and is close to most of the tramway lines, which, however, do not run along it. On its W. side are the *Western Club*—the leading club,—the *Stock Exchange* in Moorish architecture, and *St. George's Parish Ch.* (in St. George's Place). Through an archway on its E. side is the **Royal Exchange**, in Exchange Sq. (1829, archt. D. Hamilton), a well-proportioned building in a rather confined situation. The portico of Corinthian columns supports frieze and pediment. It cost £60,000. The reading-room is open to strangers, introduced by a subscriber, 30 days *free*, and afterwards 5s. a month. The *Equestrian Statue* in front, of the Duke of Wellington, by Marochetti, cost £10,000. The *Royal Bank* beside the Exchange, the *Union Bank* in Ingram St., the *Scottish Legal Life Assurance Soc. Offices* in Wilson St., the *National Bank* in Queen St., and the *Clydesdale Bank* in St. Vincent Place (all in this neighbourhood) are good specimens of modern street architecture. The town may be conveniently described under the following routes:—

(1) **E., from Buchanan St. to the Cathedral, returning by the High Street, Cross, and Trongate.**

Passing along *St. Vincent Place*, lined with well-designed buildings, we enter the spacious

George Square, a busy thoroughfare. In the centre stands the *Scott Monument* (1837), a Doric column, 80 ft. high, surmounted by a colossal statue (by Ritchie). On either side are equestrian statues by Marochetti of *H.M. Queen Victoria* (1854) and *Prince Albert* (1866). Facing the W. side are *Sir Robert Peel* (1858), *Livingstone* (1879), both by Mossman, and *James Watt*, by Chantrey (1832). Facing the S. side are *Sir John Moore* (a native), by Flaxman (1819); *Lord Clyde* (a native), by Foley (1866); *Burns*, by Ewing (1877), and *Thos. Campbell*, by Mossman (1877). Facing the E. side are *Dr. T. Graham*, Master of the Mint, by Brodie (1872), and *James Oswald*, M.P., by Marochetti (1865).

The W. side of the Square is occupied by the *Bank of Scotland Buildings* and the *Merchants' House*, in whose Hall, adorned by portraits of leading citizens, the Chamber of Commerce meets. On the N. side are the *N.B. Rly. Stat.* and *Hotels*.

The **General Post Office,** erected 1876-78, in the Italian style, is on the S. side, while the whole of the E. side is taken up by the

****Municipal Buildings**[1] (1889, archt. Wm. Young). The exterior is somewhat disappointing, but the interior is hardly surpassed in magnificence by any modern building in Europe. They are esti-

[1] Open to the public, 10.30 to 11.30, and 3 to 4; by order of a member of the Town Council, 2 to 3. Sats. 10.30 to 11.30.

mated to have cost over half a million. Almost every quarter of the globe has contributed something. Colossal statues of "Knowledge" and "Power" guard the Council staircase, of "Purity" and "Honour" the main staircase. These staircases are of marble, with alabaster balustrades, and pillars from Italy and Derbyshire. The vistas obtained of and from the staircases are striking. There are 3000 yds. of mosaics, those in the vestibule being from Venice, while the lamps are copied from St. Mark's. The ground floor is laid with Numidian and Irish (black) marble. The tapestry in the Library and in the Lord Provost's room is worth noticing. The Committee Rooms lobby has its walls and roof of majolica from Staffordshire, and one of the Committee Rooms contains portraits of the Lord Provosts of Glasgow since 1832. The *Council Chamber* is lined with St. Domingo mahogany. There is a suite of *Reception Rooms* furnished with satin-wood from Ceylon, amber-wood from S. America, and mahogany from Cuba. The *Ball* or *Dining Room* is 120 ft. long by 50 ft. broad, and has 3 large candelabra of hammered work, each weighing 16 cwts. The whole building is lit with electric light.

Passing along George St. and up High St., with *Duke St. Prison* to the rt., we have l. the large ugly new *Barony Ch.* (1888), with a statue (G. Mossman) of *Dr. Norman Macleod* (1812-72) opposite, near the site of the old ch., of which he was minister 1851-72. Before us is the **Royal Infirmary** on the site of the old archiepiscopal palace—founded 1792, and the largest general hospital outside of London. In front of it is a statue (by Mossman) of *Lord Provost Lumsden* (1776-1856), and near it one (by Leslie) of *James White* of Overtoun (1812-1884), father of Lord Overtoun, while to the E. in a commanding position rises

****The Cathedral**,[1] dedicated to St. Mungo (p. 133), the finest unmutilated Gothic edifice in Scotland. It is indeed a venerable and beautiful building—

"a brave kirk—nane o' yer whigmaleeries and curliewurlies and opensteek hems about it—a' solid, weel-jointed mason-wark, that will stand as lang as the warld, keep hands and gunpowther aff it."—*Andrew Fairservice in "Rob Roy."*

The bishopric was first restored, and the original cathedral built, by David I. in 1136. It was burnt down in 1192, but restored, and reconsecrated, in 1197, by Bishop Jocelyn. The present building probably dates from about 1240-1260. In 1492 the See of Glasgow was declared metropolitan, and the building of the cathedral went regularly forward, although even up to the time of the Reformation it was still unfinished. After that time the fortunes of the building were on the wane, and it became more and more neglected until 1829, when public attention was strongly drawn to its dilapidated state, and repairs under Mr. E. Blore were carried out. Since then, public and private generosity, aided by grants from the Crown, to which the cathedral belongs, have contributed to restore it. The Cathedral, as it at present stands, consists of a nave with aisles, transepts, choir, and central tower with spire 219 ft. high, the transepts being so short that the external outline is scarcely broken at all by their projection. Some years ago there were a N.W. belfry-tower and a consistory house on S.W., which were taken down for the sake of symmetry. The roof throughout is high-pitched, and the general character of the windows is Early Pointed, particularly on the N. side; while on the S. they are more recent, and are trefoil-headed.

"The crypt and the whole choir belong to the latter part of the 13th cent., the nave

[1] Open 1st Nov. to 1st Mar. 10-4; rest of the year 10-6. Tues. and Thurs, 2d.; other days, *Free.*

to the 14th. The central aisle never having been intended to be vaulted, the architect has been enabled to dispense with all pinnacles, flying buttresses, and such expedients, and thus to give the whole outline a degree of solidity and repose which is extremely beautiful." Ferguson's *Architecture.*

From the S. transept projects a low basement story, forming a continuation of the crypt.

The Cathedral, which is entered by a door in the S. aisle, is 319 ft. long by 63 ft. broad.

The Nave—155 ft. long by $62\frac{1}{2}$ ft. broad—is stately and well proportioned, 90 ft. high, with a triforium of 2 arches to each bay, and a clerestory. A Rood screen and loft separates the nave from the choir, which is entered by a low elliptic-arched doorway. On both sides are steps leading down to the crypt. The Choir, 97 ft. long, still used as a parish ch., is an exquisite example of Early Pointed; it is attributed to Bishop Jocelyn, and to the date 1175, although it more probably belongs to the latter part of the 13th cent. It is separated from the aisles by pointed arches springing from clustered pillars with flowered capitals, while those of the nave and Lady Chapel are plain. The fine *Organ* is a memorial to his daughter presented by Dr. Burns, minister of the Cathedral. The choir, like the nave, is lighted by a clerestory of lancet windows. To the E. is the *Lady Chapel*, with double aisle, supported on 3 piers, and opening into the choir through 2 graceful arches behind the altar. Adjoining it on the N.E. is the Chapter-house (founded by Bp. Lauder, 1408), a square, with one central shaft supporting the roof.

The 13th-cent. * *Crypt* is the pride and boast of the Cathedral; and certainly its peculiarities are unique. As the ground falls rapidly towards the E., the architect could give it all the height and light that he required, while it served, at the same time, as a basement story to the choir, beneath which it extends for 125 ft.

"There is a solidity in its architecture, a richness in its vaulting, and a variety of perspective in the spacing of its pillars, which make it one of the most perfect pieces of architecture in these islands."

At the S.E. corner is *St. Mungo's Well*, now covered up.

On the N. side of the crypt is interred the pious but eccentric Rev. Edw. Irving, who d. at Glasgow, Dec. 1834. His grave is marked by a brass plate, and the window above it is occupied by the figure of John the Baptist, of austere character, by Bertini of Milan.

After the Reformation the Cathedral was divided among three congregations. One met in the choir, another (now in St. Paul's, John St.) in the nave, and the third in the crypt.

In the nave Cromwell sat, Oct. 1650, to hear himself railed at and called "Sectary and Blasphemer" by the celebrated Dr. Zachary Boyd, in a discourse 2 hours long. Mr. Secretary Thurlow proposed to pull him forth by the ears and have him shot. Cromwell's only answer was, "He's a fool, and you're another, I'll pay him out in his own fashion." So he asked Dr. Boyd to dinner, and concluded the entertainment with a prayer that lasted 3 hours.

The Crypt or Laigh Kirk (Low Ch.), as it was called, was used as a place of worship by the parishioners of the Barony down to 1820.

"Conceive an extensive range of low-browed, dark, and twilight vaults, such as are used for sepulchres in other countries, and had long been dedicated to the same purpose in this, a portion of which was seated with pews, and used as a church. The part of the vaults thus occupied, though capable of containing a congregation of many hundreds, bore a small proportion to the darker and more extensive caverns which yawned around what may be termed the inhabited space."—*Rob Roy.*

The modern *Stained Glass* in the

Cathedral is unworthy of notice, except as a monument of the liberality of the citizens of Glasgow. The cost of it was about £100,000.

The churchyard around the Cathedral is literally paved with acres of stone slabs, memorials of the forefathers of the city.

On the hill E. of the Cathedral, reached by a handsome bridge, erected by the Merchants' House 1833, which spans the valley of the *Molendinar Burn*, now entirely covered over, is the **Necropolis.** The most conspicuous monument is a statue of *John Knox* (1505-72) surmounting a Doric column, erected 1825 to the memory of the Reformers. There are also monuments to *Ed. Irving* (1792-1834), buried in the Cathedral, *Rev. Principal Macfarlane* (1771 - 1857), *Michael Scott*, author of "Tom Cringle's Log" (1789-1835), *Motherwell* the poet (1798-1835), *Charles Tennant* of St. Rollox (1767-1838) (with sitting statue by *Park*), *Major Monteith* of Carstairs — a curious octagon building to the S.W. without inscription, etc.

The *Jews' Burial Ground* is an interesting corner, and the *View* of the city from the summit of the hill is fairly extensive.

Nearly 1 m. beyond the Necropolis is **Alexandra Park,** opened 1873, commanding a view of Ben Lomond, etc.

Returning from the Cathedral down the High Street, in which Thomas Campbell the poet was born 1777, we pass (beyond George St.) l. *College Stat.*, occupying the site of the Old University Buildings, every trace of which has disappeared, and reach the site of the **City Cross,** from which the *Gallowgate* leads E. and the *Trongate* leads W. At the corner is the *Cross Steeple*, a tower containing a chime of 28 bells—the sole remnant of the Old Tolbooth (the prison described in "Rob Roy")—which projects across the pavement, and dates from 1637. Hard by is an equestrian *Statue* of *Wm. III.* Here the Glasgow tobacco merchants, whose dealings far surpassed those of any other city, and who have left a record of their calling in the names of *Virginia St.* and *Jamaica St.*, used to congregate.

Keeping S. we pass down the **Saltmarket**, crossed by a viaduct of the Union Rly., long the fashionable part of the city, then degraded to a sort of rag fair, but greatly improved by recent (1894) changes carried out by the Corporation. Here dwelt Bailie Nicol Jarvie, the Lowland cousin of Rob Roy. James Duke of York also lodged here, and the great printers of the day, Robert and Andrew Foulis, had here their book auctions.

Rt., before the *Albert Bridge* across the Clyde is reached, are the **Justiciary Courts,** where the Circuit Courts or Assizes are held 6 times a year.

Opposite them is **The Green,** a park of 136 acres,—a public recreation ground since the 15th cent.,—much used for open-air demonstrations, with an *Obelisk* to Nelson (1806), and a large *Terra Cotta Fountain*, in the style of Francis I., built for the Glasgow Exhibition of 1888, and presented to the city by Sir H. Doulton, Lambeth (1890), in the centre. The Green will ever be memorable as the place where Watt was walking one Sunday when the idea of the separate condenser, involving the principle of his steam-engine, occurred to him.

Returning to the Cross, we turn W. along the **Trongate,** in which General Sir John Moore (1761-1809) was born. We pass (l.) the *Tron Steeple*, in the church behind which Dr. Chalmers preached for many years. The *Tron* was a public weighing machine, to which the owners of false weights were nailed by the ears. Across the street are the *Tontine Buildings*, which have incorporated the *Old Town Hall*.

Opening N. off the Trongate are the *Candleriggs*, with the *City Hall*, used for large meetings, and capable of holding 2500-3000 people, *Hutcheson St.*, *Glassford St.*, and *Miller St.*

Turning up *Hutcheson St.* we pass rt. the **County Buildings**, an extensive block with a Corinthian Portico, and have in front **Hutcheson's Hospital**, founded (1641) by two brothers of that name, whose statues appear upon the building, erected 1805, with a tower and spire 150 ft. high behind. Its income now amounts to £7000 per annum, which is spent in pensions to decayed burgesses, and in educating their children.

In *Glassford St.* is the **Savings Bank** and the **Trades House** (1791), which contains a list (since 1604) of the Deacon Conveners of the *Trades* or *Guilds*, now 14 in number, but existing only as Charity Organisations with (1893) a capital of £561,143, a revenue of £22,000, and an expenditure of £18,645.

In *Miller St.* are the **Mitchell Free Library** (No. 21), established by a bequest of £70,000 by Mr. Stephen Mitchell, and the Glasgow **Public Library** (No. 48), incorporated with *Stirling's Library*.

The Trongate forms the E. part of **Argyle St.**, a thoroughfare which with its continuations extends some 4 m., and is the most crowded in the city. It crosses the foot of Buchanan St., S. of which is **St. Enoch's Sq.** (the name a corruption of *Thanew*, mother of St. Mungo), with a parish ch. and the large *G. and S. W. Rly. Stat.* and *Hotel*.

---

(2) **Sauchiehall St. to the W. End Park, University Buildings, and Hillhead.**

Sauchiehall St., (from *Saugh* = a willow) runs W. from the upper part of Buchanan St. On its S. side (No. 175) is the **Art Gallery**, a fine building where there is an Exhibition by living artists held annually during the spring months. It is now the principal exhibition of the kind in Scotland, and usually contains good examples of those rising impressionist painters known as the Glasgow School. On its N. side farther W. (No. 270) are the **Corporation Galleries of Art**[1] which originated in a collection of pictures formed by Archibald M'Lellan, a coachmaker (d. 1854), and purchased for the town by the magistrates of Glasgow from his creditors. To these were added, partly by gift and partly by purchase, the pictures of Mr. Wm. Euing, and in 1877 Mrs. John Graham Gilbert bequeathed her husband's valuable collection to these Galleries.

The best pictures are—*The Woman taken in Adultery—*Giorgione*. Christ's Entry into Jerusalem—*Alb. Cuyp*. Saviour Asleep, watched by the Virgin—*Murillo*. Town of Katwyk—*J. Ruysdael*, an admirable work. Landscape with figures—*Wynants*. Sea-piece—*W. Vandervelde*. Milking time, and Peasants before a Fire—*Teniers*. Landscape with Rocks, *Wouverman*. Landscape—*Hobbema*. St. George and a man, portraits, part of an altar-piece—*Mabuse*. The Virgin Enthroned, with St. Sebastian and other Saints; a fine landscape background, a very large picture, attributed to *Mantegna*. The Holy Family—*Palma Vecchio*. Adoration of the Magi—*Antonello da Messina*. Annunciation—*Botticelli*.

The Graham Gilbert Collection comprises a good sea-piece, with a large man-of-war in foreground—*Wm. Vandervelde*. View near Tivoli—*Berghem*. A Holy Family—*Paris Bordone*. A few portraits by *Raeburn*, etc. etc., besides works by the late *Graham Gilbert* himself.

The Euing Collection includes some Dutch pictures—a Sea-beach Scene by *Creswick*. The Quack Doctor—*Cuyp*, etc. There are also a series of portraits of English kings by *Ramsay*, which were formerly in the old Town-hall, and some *Sculpture*, including a statue of Wm. Pitt by *Flaxman*, bust of the same by *Nollekins*, and busts of Sir W. Scott and D. of Wellington by *Chantrey*.

There are 2 pictures by *Turner*, lent by the National Gallery, London, and a series of water-colours of Old Buildings, etc., in Glasgow, 1844-50.

S. of **Charing Cross**, towards the W. end of Sauchiehall St., are a

[1] Open daily, 10 to dusk—free.

convenient underground Rly. Stat. and the **St. Andrew's Halls,** with large Concert Room, accommodating 3000, Ball Room above, etc. N. is *Woodside Crescent* leading to the *Free Ch. College* and to some of the finest residences. Farther W. are the *Queen's Rooms* for smaller balls, etc., at the entrance to

Kelvin Grove or the **West End Park** on the banks of the Kelvin, originally laid out by Sir Joseph Paxton in 1853 at a cost of £100,000. It contains a piece of animal statuary presented by Mr. J. S. Kennedy of New York, a native of Glasgow, the Stewart memorial fountain, and the *City Industrial Museum* [open daily—free]. On a commanding site across the Kelvin, called *Gilmorehill*, stands

The University, from which an excellent view is obtained in clear weather. This imposing Gothic building (archt. Sir G. Scott), begun 1866, was first occupied in 1870, when the University was transferred from the Old College in High Street. It has a frontage of 532 ft., with a *Central Tower* 200 ft. high (surmounted by a spire), in which there is a fine peal of bells.

The buildings in the rear form 2 quadrangles divided by a *Central Hall*, raised on open cloisters with granite columns, named after the Marquis of Bute, to whose munificent gift of £45,000 its completion is due. This Hall is 110 ft. long, 72 ft. wide, and 74 ft. high. There is also a smaller hall, separated from the other by an ornamental screen of walnut wood, approached by a magnificent staircase and known as the *Randolph Hall*, in honour of one of the most munificent of the recent benefactors of the University.

The total cost of the site and buildings was, first and last, upwards of £400,000, of which sum £117,500 was realised in connection with the sale of the Old College; £120,000 was granted by Parliament, and £165,000 has been subscribed by individuals, chiefly in the city of Glasgow, not reckoning £30,000 allocated to the **Western Infirmary** (opened 1874 at a cost of over £100,000), which adjoins and is intimately associated with the University.

At the N.E. entrance to the University Grounds stands the *Old Lodge*, removed from the High St. and re-erected at the expense of the late Sir Wm. Pearce, Bt., M.P. The N.W. entrance is through an arch flanking the *Students' Union* erected 1888 (Frank Burnet, Archt.) by an old alumnus Dr. MacIntyre.

The General Library occupies 2 long galleries on the 1st and 2nd floors in the north front. It includes the Library of Sir Wm. Hamilton, purchased and presented to the University by citizens of Glasgow; also a unique Collection of Bibles and other rare books, amounting to about 15,000 volumes, bequeathed to the University by the late Mr. Wm. Euing. The Treasury makes an annual grant of £707 in lieu of the copyright privilege formerly enjoyed in common with the Advocates' Library (p. 46), etc.

Observe 1st edition of "Paradise Lost," many good Caxtons and Aldines; a set, tolerably complete, of the 1st and 2nd editions of Shakespeare's Plays; the MS. Collections of Robt. Wodrow; the unpublished works, 13 vols. 4to, of Zachary Boyd (1590-1653), and many costly and valuable books in English and foreign modern literature.

In 1783 Dr. Wm. Hunter bequeathed to the University his very valuable collection of *Pictures*, *Antiquities*, *Books*, *MSS.*, *Coins*, and *Geological* and *Zoological Specimens*. These may now be seen to great advantage in the **Hunterian Library and Museum,**[1] which is situated in

[1] Admission daily, 12 to 3, 6d. each; but the Coins are not open to public inspection.

the eastern half of the north front of the University.

The Collection of Greek and Roman *Coins* is especially good. It cost £23,000 a hundred years ago, but is now probably second in value only to that of the British Museum.

The Zoological cases are noteworthy for their construction. The minerals are a fine series formed by Dr. W. Hunter and Dr. W. Brown.

Obs. also a model of Newcomen's steam-engine, in repairing which James Watt discovered the principle of the separate condenser.

Among the Pictures are: A fine Dutch Landscape, by *P. de Konninck;* The Entombment of Lazarus, and an Old Man at Study, by *Rembrandt;* Study of a Female Head, by *Rubens;* The Good Shepherd, by *Murillo;* Detection of Laomedon, by *Salvator Rosa;* Vesalius, the Anatomist, by *Titian*, and a large number of portraits, including Lady Maynard, Dr. Hunter, and himself, by *Sir J. Reynolds;* Dr. Arbuthnot, Dr. Radcliffe, and Sir I. Newton, by *Sir G. Kneller*, and several *Raeburns*.

Observe also Statues of James Watt, by *Sir F. Chantrey*, and of Adam Smith, by *Gasser;* also busts of Zachary Boyd, removed from tower of Old College, and of Thomas Campbell the poet, Maquorne Rankine, and Professor Lushington.

Glasgow University was founded through the exertions of Bishop Turnbull, its first principal, confirmed by a bull of Pope Nicholas V. in 1451. For a long time it seems to have been almost destitute of endowments, though a building was erected on a site in the High Street as early as 1460; and at the time of the Reformation its condition was far from flourishing. In 1560 Queen Mary endowed it with a moiety of the confiscated church property in the city. This was increased by the corporation, and added to by succeeding monarchs.

An impulse was given to its fame and efficiency by the advent, 1574, of Andrew Melville, the friend of Knox, as a teacher, but the buildings remained mean and incomplete until about 1632, from which time the chief part of the old college dated. As a seat of learning it reached the height of its fame during the 18th cent., when it numbered among its teachers Cullen and Black in medicine and chemistry, and Reid in mental philosophy. "Here Adam Smith taught doctrines which have changed the policy of nations, and Watt perfected discoveries that have subdued the elements to be the ministers of mankind." Thos. Campbell, Francis Jeffrey, Sir Wm. Hamilton, John Gibson Lockhart, and Archbishop Tait were students here.

The University is governed by a Chancellor—elected for life by the General Council, composed of graduates, who, along with those of Aberdeen, also return a member of Parliament—a Rector elected every 3 years, a University Court, and a Senate. The Chancellor and the Rector are invariably men of mark in the political or literary world. The latter is elected by the Students, who vote by *Nationes*—the *Natio Glottiana*, including those born in Lanarkshire; *Transforthana*, those born N. of the Forth; *Rothseiana*, those from the counties of Renfrew, Bute, and Ayr; and *Loudoniana*, those not already included. If the Nationes are equally divided the majority of individual votes decides. In 1893 the General Council numbered 4990, and the matriculated students 2050.

The other principal educational establishments of Glasgow are—*St. Mungo's College* on the S. side; *Queen Margaret's College* for ladies (established 1883, and incorporated with the University 1893); the *Andersonian College*, 204 George St., founded by Prof. John Anderson in 1797, and principally devoted to the study of medicine and physics; the *High School*, which, though now under the jurisdiction of the School Board, dates from the 12th cent.; the *Glasgow Academy* at Kelvinbridge; the *Kelvinside Academy*, etc.

W. of the University is **Hillhead,** with the **Observatory,** N. of which are the **Royal Botanic Gardens,** occupying $6\frac{1}{2}$ acres on the banks of the Kelvin, originally laid out by Sir J. Hooker, and containing the *Kibble Crystal Palace*, opened 1872 (admission free). From this point terraces of large houses extend for more than 2 miles to the W.

Return may now be made to the city from **Hyndland Stat.** (p. 149), or by tramway along the *Great Western Road*—a broad thoroughfare — and the dingy *Cowcaddens*, once a grazing pasture !

---

(3) **The Clyde, Broomielaw, and Docks.**

By keeping S. along *Buchanan St.*, crossing *Argyle St.*, and turning down *Jamaica St.*, we come to **Glasgow Bridge,** rebuilt 1835, and again (1894) about to be rebuilt, with the Cal. Rly. viaduct immediately below it ; and above it 6 other bridges and the G. and S.W. Rly. viaduct.

The **Clyde,** from the noisy cataract of Corra Linn (p. 92), has become a sedate and sober stream. West of the bridge is the bustling quay of the **Broomielaw,** once overgrown with *Broom*, now crowded with vessels and bristling with steamers' funnels —one of the most remarkable sights in Glasgow.

The river is almost entirely an artificial canal, it having been originally a broad shallow stream which only continual dredging (a work still carried on, see p. 313) has made capable of floating the largest vessels, thus affording a strong contrast to its shallowness in 1651, when it was fordable at the Broomielaw, and "when no vessel of any burden could come up nearer the town than 14 miles, where they must unlade and send up their timber on rafts." One result of modern "improvement" has been to convert the Clyde at low tide in summer into somewhat of an offensive and muddy sewer, thus confirming the forebodings of Tom Campbell, who thus writes :—

"And call they this improvement?—to have changed,
My native Clyde, thy once romantic shore,
Where Nature's face is banished and estranged,
And Heaven reflected in thy wave no more ;
. . . . . .
And for the daisied greensward, down thy stream,
Unsightly brick lanes smoke and clanking engines gleam."

(For the various Loading Sheds and Ship-building Yards see Rte. 68.)

DOCKS.—**Kingston Dock** is situated on the S. side of the river, a little to the W. of Bridge St. Stat. and has an area of $5\frac{1}{3}$ acres. The **Queen's Dock** (1872-80) at Stobcross on the N. side, close to Finnieston Stat. (p. 149), is a very fine piece of engineering work, carried out by Mr. Jas. Deas, C.E. It includes a water area of $33\frac{3}{4}$ acres, and 3334 lineal yds. of quayage. Entrance is afforded by a huge swing bridge, adjoining which is the engine-house, surmounted by a clock tower. The bridge and the hydraulic machinery for opening it were constructed by Sir Wm. Armstrong. The basins, three in number, are tidal, with a depth of 20 ft. at low water. The enclosing walls, 42 ft. high and 18 ft. broad at their base, rest for the most part on concrete cylinders, of which 600 triple groups were sunk ; the boulder clay on which many of them rest was found to be so hard that it had to be blasted with dynamite. Each cylinder rests on an iron shoe, weighing $4\frac{1}{2}$ tons, and the total weight of artificial foundation laid was nearly 365,000 tons. These works cost over $1\frac{1}{2}$ million, and the docks are brought into communication with the rlys. by goods' lines.

The **Cessnock Dock** at Govan on the S. side, also constructed (1894) by Mr. Deas, and the largest in Scotland, has $34\frac{2}{3}$ acres water space and 3760 lineal yds. of quayage. Immediately to the W. of it are 3 large *Graving Docks* belonging to the Clyde Trs. (1893-95), one of them capable of taking in the largest war vessels ever likely to be built.

The total water area of Glasgow Harbour including Kingston, Queen's, and Cessnock Docks, is more than 175 acres, and the total length of quayage 7 m.

The Board of Trade statistics for the year 1891 show Glasgow to be the third largest ship-owning port of the Kingdom, with 1576 vessels of an aggregate tonnage of 1,316,809 as compared with Liverpool with 2307 vessels of 1,994,903 tons, and London with 2685 vessels of 1,500,572 tons. Glasgow in regard to entrances and clearances of vessels to and from foreign countries and British possessions stands sixth in the list of British ports with 2303 vessels of 2,657,057 tons, being surpassed by London, Cardiff, the Tyne ports, and Hull, while in regard to the coasting traffic it stands fifth with 16,271 vessels of 3,110,211 tons.

---

(4) **The S. Side of the Clyde** has few attractions for the tourist except the **Queen's Park,** nearly 2 m. from the river, reached by tramway from St. Vincent St., or train from Central Stat. It is a pleasant place for recreation of 80 acres, laid out by Sir Joseph Paxton and opened 1862.

Contiguous to it on the S.E. side is the **Battlefield of Langside,** fatal to Queen Mary's cause, where, 11 days after her escape from Lochleven, her adherents, 6000 strong, desirous of conveying her from Hamilton to Dumbarton as a place of security, May 13, 1568, ventured to attack the forces of Regent Murray, numbering only 4000, but by his superior tactics were utterly defeated, leaving 300 dead and 400 prisoners. The houses of the village through which the road ran were occupied by Kirkaldy of Grange for the Regent; the efforts to take it were ineffectual: the skirmish lasted only ¾ hour, but it settled the fate of Scotland. A *Memorial Column,* whose foundation stone was laid 1887 on the 319th anniversary of the battle, marks its site. At *Queen's Knowe,* in the village of Cathcart, S. of the park, is a memorial stone marking the spot from which Mary is said to have witnessed the battle.

On the W. side of the park is *Camp Hill,* from which a good view is obtained N. of Glasgow, and S. to the valley of the Cart and the Battlefield of Langside. On the other side of the park is the *Deaf and Dumb Institution.*

---

(5) **Excursions** from Glasgow are endless; the following may be suggested:—

(*a*) Up the Clyde to Bothwell, Hamilton, Lanark and the Falls of Clyde (Rtes. 22 and 11).

(*b*) To Loch Lomond and the Trossachs (Rtes. 23 and 26).

(*c*) To Campsie Glen and Aberfoyle (Rtes. 24 and 28).

(*d*) To Milngavie and the Whangie (pp. 150 and 155).

(*e*) Some of the Excursions down the Clyde (Rtes. 67-76).

ROUTE 20.

Glasgow to Edinburgh by Airdrie and Bathgate. N.B.R.

This is really the shortest route between Glasgow and Edinburgh (44¼ m.); but it is a slow one (about 1 hr. 50 min.). By it, however, the G. and S.W. Rly. through carriages from Greenock and Ayrshire (Rte. 18) run to Edinburgh.

It is not an attractive route, but will interest many by carrying them through a considerable portion of the *Black Country* of Scotland, with its coal, iron, and oil industries.

Trains start from the W. end stat. of *Hyndland* and run E. by *Partick,* etc., in 3½ m. to *Queen St. Low Level Stat.* See beginning of Rte. 23.

Leaving **Queen St. Low Level Stat.** the train runs underground to ½ m. **College Stat.,** the site of the old University Buildings.

$1\frac{1}{4}$ m. **Bellgrove Stat.**

[*District Circular Rly.* round Glasgow turns off here l., and the *Union Rly.*, connecting with the G. and S.W. Rly., branches rt.]

We pass $2\frac{1}{2}$ m. **Parkhead,** and 3 m. **Carntyne,** to $3\frac{3}{4}$ m. **Shettleston,** whence a line strikes rt. to *Hamilton* (Rte. 22).

Passing 6 m. **Easterhouse,** 7 m. **Cuilhill,** $8\frac{1}{2}$ m. **Drumpellier,** with (rt.) *Drumpellier Ho.* (Col. Buchanan), we reach 9 m. **Coatbridge (Sunnyside) Stat.** (see p. 17).

[*Branch* (l.) by Slamannan to Manuel (p. 130).]

11 m. **Airdrie (South) Stat.**

[There is another *N.B.R. Stat.*, **Commonhead**, on the Slamannan and Manuel line; and a *Cal. Rly. Terminus* with lines—

(1) W. to **Whifflet**, etc., and

(2) S.E. to **Chapelhall** (near which are the *Monkland Iron and Steel Works*) and **Newhouse.**]

Airdrie is a busy mining town, dependent on the *Collieries* in the vicinity, and on some *Cotton Works.* It is tolerably well built, and has a handsome *Town Hall* with a spire.

Since 1850 the Airdrie coal district has become covered with works for refining *paraffin oil*, produced from the shales of the coal-beds, which are similar to, though perhaps not so rich as, those of Bathgate.

$12\frac{1}{2}$ m. **Clarkston Stat.** The line approaches the *North Calder*, and runs parallel with it, through hilly country of some 600 ft. above sea level, past $13\frac{1}{2}$ m. **Plains Stat.** to

$15\frac{1}{4}$ m. **Caldercruix Stat.,** where the Calder takes its rise in a large sheet of water called Hill End Reservoir. At the E. end of it is

$17\frac{1}{2}$ m. **Forrestfield Stat.**

$20\frac{1}{4}$ m. **Westcraigs Stat.**

[A mineral line runs rt. to *Shotts Iron Works* (p. 144).]

$23\frac{1}{2}$ m. **Armadale Stat.** in Linlithgowshire. 2 m. S. is *Polkemmet*, seat of the late Sir W. Baillie, Bt.

$25\frac{1}{2}$ m. **Bathgate Stat.**

[Branch i. (l.) to *Blackston* on Glasgow, Slamannan, and Manuel line.

ii. (rt.) across *Fauldhouse* (p. 144) *Moor* to *Morningside* (p. 144).]

Bathgate is an important centre of the coal district, and by no means unpicturesquely situated at the foot of the *Bathgate Hills.* The modern portion of the town is neat, and boasts of an excellent *Academy*, founded by Mr. John Newlands (1737-99), a native of Bathgate, who made his fortune in Jamaica, and left £14,500 for the purpose.

Adjoining the town on the N. are the policies of *Balbardie.*

Both antiquary and geologist will find the neighbourhood more than commonly interesting. The district within a few miles to the N., between Bathgate and Linlithgow, contains several cromlechs, camps, and earthworks, denoting that the early inhabitants considered this country to be of importance, perhaps on account of its proximity to the Firth of Forth.

There is a camp at *Torphichen* ($2\frac{1}{2}$ m. N.W.), as also slight remains of the Preceptory Ch. and Hospital of the Knights of St. John of Jerusalem, who had here their principal Scottish resort; and in some sandhills, about 100 yards from one of the boundary stones of the Hospital, stone coffins containing skeletons have been found. Torphichen gives the title of Baron to a member of the family of Sandilands whose seat is *Calder Ho.* (p. 88), and was the birthplace (1767) of Henry Bell (p. 151). Adjoining the village is *Wallhouse*, the seat of the Gillon family. At the mouth of the Brunton Burn, which near this joins the river Avon, is a cave traditionally said to have been occupied by Wallace.

Beyond *Torphichen Hills* (777 ft.) are the *Kipps* mentioned by Camden as "an ancient altar of great stones unpolished, so placed as each of them does support another and no one could stand without leaning upon another."

2 m. S. of Bathgate is *Torbanehill*, rendered famous by a mineral—held in a great law-suit in 1853 to be included in a lease of coal, but peculiarly valuable for the naphtha or paraffin oil distilled from it. This district has been gradually covered by oil retorts and refineries.

28½ m. **Livingston Stat.** The village (1 m. rt.) contains the remains of an old *Peel*, and gave the title of Baron to the Livingstones, Earls of Linlithgow, attainted 1716.

31½ m. **Uphall Stat.**, with a mining village, 1 m. N.W. of which is *Houston Ho.* (16th cent.), with crow-stepped gables. It has always belonged to the Shairp family. Behind the village is *Uphall Ch.*—partially Pre-Reformation—in which Lord Chancellor Erskine (1750-1823), Hon. Harry Erskine (1746-1817), and Principal Shairp of St. Andrews (1819-1885) are buried.

¾ m. S. of the station are the *Pumpherston Oil Works*, covering 23 acres, where the daily output of shale is 600 tons, where 424 of Young and Beilby's retorts, each capable of dealing with 30 cwt. of shale per day, are used, and where 700 men are employed.

33 m. **Drumshoreland Stat.** for **Broxburn,** which is 1 m. N., and has the *largest Oil Works* in Scotland, being twice as large as those of Pumpherston (above); 1 m. S. is *Almondell* (Earl of Buchan). Crossing the Union Canal, and, close beyond it, the river Almond, which is crossed by the other N.B.R. line on a viaduct of 36 arches, well seen l., we enter Midlothian before reaching

36 m. **Ratho Stat.** For line to

44¼ m. **Edinburgh,** see pp. 128, 127.

For **EDINBURGH** ✲ see p. 36.

ROUTE 21.

Edinburgh to Glasgow by Midcalder and Holytown. Cal. Rly.

Slightly quicker and pleasanter (no tunnels), but less interesting than Route 19. 46¼ m., abt. 14 trains daily. 65 min. by express train.

Several paraffin oil works are passed and glimpses caught of the *Black Country*.

From **Princes St. Stat.** to

10 m. **Midcalder Stat.**, see p. 88.

1½ m. beyond, the line to Carstairs and Carlisle (Rte. 9) trends l., and rt. are the *Oakbank Paraffin Oil Works.*

14 m. **Newpark Stat.**

16 m. **West Calder Stat.** The small town (l.) has grown rapidly in consequence of *Young's* large *Paraffin Oil Works* (rt.), passed just before

17½ m. **Addiewell Stat.** Before

20¼ m. **Breich Stat.,** a bleak country is entered. Beyond, the Bathgate and Morningside line (with *Crofthead Stat.* and *Village* rt.) is crossed; also a corner of Linlithgowshire. Beyond

22½ m. **Fauldhouse Stat.**, Lanarkshire is entered.

25¾ m. **Shotts Stat.** with Ironworks l., and the village of *Dykehead* rt.

27½ m. **Hartwood Stat.,** l. is a pretty hollow through which the Edinburgh and Ayr road runs, and in the distance the chimneys of the *Coltness Iron Works* (below) and of numerous furnaces about Wishaw. Beyond, *Tinto* (p. 16) can be seen on a clear day as we descend the hill.

30½ m. **Omoa Stat.,** beyond which (l.) are *Neilson's Ironworks. Carfin Hall*, a modern mansion, is conspicuous (l.) as we approach

33 m. **Holytown Junc. Stat.,** for the "Black Country" to the S.E. and N.

[*Branches:*—i. E. *via* **Cleland** [near which are *Cleland Ho.* and *Coltness* (J. Houldsworth Esq.)] and **Newmains** to **Morningside,** beside which are the *Coltness Iron Works.*

ii. *Via* **Mossend** and **Whifflet** to **Coatbridge.**

iii. S.E. *via* **Wishaw** to **Law Junc.** on the Cal. Rly. Main line.
iv. S. *via* **Motherwell** to **Hamilton** and **Lesmahagow.]**

35¼ m. **Bellshill Stat.** Beyond, a huge red sandstone quarry, on both sides, is passed and the main line (l.) [Rte. 2] is joined before

37¾ m. **Uddingston Stat.** Beyond, the *Clyde* is crossed and a glimpse of the ruins of *Bothwell Castle* (below) is caught l. Then *Rotten Calder Water* (p. 149) is crossed.

39½ m. **Newton Stat. [**Branch S.E. *via* Blantyre to *Hamilton* (p. 146).**]** l. are the *Hallside Works* belonging to the Steel Co. of Scotland, Lim., which supplied most of the steel for the Forth Bridge. See p. 146 for line hence by **Cambuslang, Rutherglen, Gushetfaulds, Eglinton St.,** and **Bridge St.,** across the Clyde to

46¼ m. **Glasgow Central Stat.,**

For **GLASGOW**✲ see p. 132.

ROUTE 22.

Glasgow to Bothwell and Hamilton.

The N.B. Rly. runs *via* Bothwell to Hamilton; the Cal. Rly. has separate lines to Bothwell (a terminus) and Hamilton.

(A) By N.B. Rly. from **Queen St. (Low Level) Stat.** as in Rte. 20, to 3¾ m. **Shettleston Stat.** Thence rt. by **Mount Vernon Stat., Broomhouse Stat.** (beyond which, passing l. *Calder Park*, and rt. *Daldowie*, the N. Calder is crossed), **Maryville Stat.,** and **Uddingston W. Stat.** to

7½ m. **Uddingston Stat.,** composed almost entirely of villas.

9¼ m. **Bothwell Stat.**✲ on a height above the Clyde.

The *Parish Church* is a red stone edifice, with tall tower, chiefly modern, but including part of an ancient church, deserving the architect's notice for its peculiar stone barrel-vault and roof without timber. It was built in 1398 by Archibald "the Grim," Earl of Douglas. In this ch. his daughter was married to David, Duke of Rothesay, heir-apparent to the throne, who was afterwards starved to death in Falkland Palace (p. 182).

The manse of Bothwell was the birthplace of Joanna Baillie the poetess, 11th Sept. 1762.

W. is **Bothwell Castle** (Earl of Home) in the midst of beautiful woods and grounds stretching down to the Clyde, on whose lofty right bank rise the picturesque red ruins of *Old Bothwell Castle.*[1] The castle, an admirable specimen of the baronial fortress, has a grand and imposing front of two round towers, connected by a lofty and massive curtain of red sandstone. It has the style and appearance of an Edwardian Castle, and was probably built by the English, but was taken from them 1337; it owes its preservation to the thickness of its walls. Besides its front there is the chapel on the S.E. side. The castle belonged originally to the Murrays, and was inhabited by Sir William Wallace during the term of his governorship. From that family it passed by marriage to that of Douglas, was confiscated by James III. and restored by James IV. in exchange for the Castle of Hermitage, which he took from them.

The *modern house* contains a gallery of pictures possessing much interest, because they include half the collection of the great Lord Chancellor Clarendon, formerly at Amesbury in Wilts, the other half of the collection being now at Lord Clarendon's seat "The Grove," Herts. Of this part of it Walpole remarked, "Not one original, I think—at least not one fine one." Walpole was not quite right. The whole-lengths of Lord Lindsay, Lord Binning, Lady Paulett, and Mrs. Howard are by *Van Dyck*, and fine works; Nell Gwynn and others are by *Lely;* Cromwell and Sir

[1] Admission, Tues. and Frid. 10-3.

Thomas More by *Holbein;* Raleigh by *Van Somer;* Margaret Duchess of Douglas, etc., by *Reynolds.*

A *Foot-Bridge* across the Clyde leads to *Blantyre Stat.* (below).

¾ m. S.E. of Bothwell is **Bothwell Bridge** (2 m. from Hamilton), celebrated for the battle, June 22, 1679, described in "Old Mortality," between the royal troops, commanded by Monmouth and Claverhouse, who approached from the N., and the Covenanters strongly posted on the S. bank, but commanded by nobody at all, for they were squabbling about the election of their officers when attacked. Their position was well chosen, the only access to it being by the bridge, which was held by a small force under Hackston of Rathillet, until his ammunition was exhausted. When this force was withdrawn the Duke's army crossed the bridge, and his artillery sufficed to put the insurgents to rout. The bridge was rebuilt in 1826; formerly it had a steep rise in its centre, where it was crossed by a gate, and was only 12 ft. wide, its approaches also being much steeper than at present.

Leaving Bothwell the line crosses the Clyde and, sweeping round, crosses the Cal. Rly. (below), passes **Greenfield Stat.** and **Peacock Cross Stat.** and enters

11¾ m. **Hamilton Stat.** ✲ (see below).

(**B**) By Cal. Rly from **Central Stat.** The Clyde is crossed to

½ m. **Bridge St. Stat.**, and

1 m. **Eglinton St. Stat.** where, on a different level, the line to Ayrshire (Rt. 72) strikes rt. Beyond

1¼ m. **Gushetfaulds Stat.** is

3 m. **Rutherglen** (pron. *Rúg-len*) **Stat.**

[*Branches*—i. N. to *Bridgeton* and *London Road Stats.*

ii. N.W. by *Carmyle* (with l. the *Clyde Iron Works*), *Mt. Vernon*, *Baillieston*, and *Langloan*, to *Coatbridge*.]

Rutherglen was a town before Glasgow, of which it is now a suburb. The topheavy tower of the *Town-Hall* is conspicuous. A bridge crosses the Clyde ½ m. N., and on May 29, 1679, a body of 86 armed Covenanters rode into the town, and fixed on the cross a seditious "Declaration," which led to the skirmish of Drumclog, and the battle of Bothwell Brig.

The battle of *Langside* (1568) [p. 142] was fought 2 m. W.

5 m. **Cambuslang Stat.** Near this is a natural amphitheatre, used in 1742 for religious meetings—hence the phrase "*Cambuslang Wark*," as applied to a revival.

6½ m. **Newton Stat.** Here the line for Hamilton trends rt. leaving the Cal. Main line (Rtes. 2, 21).

[The line to 10¾ m. **Bothwell** (p. 145) *passes* **Uddingston** and branches rt. from the main line at **Fallside Stat.**]

9 m. **Blantyre Stat.**, a workmen's village, dependent on large cotton mills and dye-works established here since the 18th cent. The illustrious traveller and missionary, David Livingstone, was born here 1815, and from that circumstance the Mission Station of *Blantyre* in E. Central Africa is named after this village. Livingstone commenced life, as he tells us himself, "as a piecer in Mr. Monteith's Works." ¾ m. down the Clyde a very small fragment of the *Priory of Blantyre*, founded by Alexander II., hangs on the edge of the bank.

A *Suspension Foot-Bridge* crosses the Clyde to *Bothwell*, ¾ m. (p. 145).

10¾ m. **Hamilton West Stat.**, about 1 m. from the town.

11½ m. **Hamilton Central Stat.**

[Junc. for i. W. to *East Kilbride* (p. 324).
ii. S. to *Strathaven* (p. 148).
iii. N.E. to *Motherwell* and *Holytown*.
iv. S.E. to *Stonehouse*, *Lesmahagow*, etc.]

HAMILTON ✲, a good starting-point for exploring an interesting neighbourhood, is a cheerful and prosperous town on a slope (the old and dirtier quarter below), about 1 m. from the Clyde, here joined by its pretty tributary the Avon. The town, though tolerably free from smoke, is surrounded, at a distance of 3 or 4 m., by collieries and iron furnaces, which light up the horizon at night. It was the birthplace of the eminent physician Dr. Cullen, 1712.

The stately **Palace** of the Duke of Hamilton stands in the bottom of the valley, close to the old town—so close that about 1826 a whole street was purchased and thrown into the park. The fronts of the houses only remain, and with their doors and windows walled up still serve as a boundary wall. At the same time the *Old Tolbooth*, a picturesque building with a tower, was cut off from the town, and now stands within the grounds of the Palace.

Queen Mary, on escaping from Lochleven Castle, made Hamilton Palace her rallying-point, here collecting around her all her adherents and partisans, 1568. "Queenzie Neuk," her residence at the time, is shown in the old town.

The old Palace was rebuilt in 1695-6, but the building was augmented by nearly one-half, and a new front added, by Duke Alexander in 1828-29 (Hamilton, archt.). It is a stately and imposing piece of architecture, with an extent of 264 ft. and a portico of monolith Corinthian columns, copied from those of the Temple of Vespasian at Rome. Each of these is 30 ft. high, 3 ft. in diameter, and cut out of a single stone from Dalserf Quarry. The interior evinces that its owners have combined with a love of splendour a true knowledge and appreciation of art.

The *Grand Staircase* is entirely of black marble. The entrance-hall extends through 3 stories.

The unique collection of pictures and art treasures—of world-wide fame—was sold 1882. The pictures that remain are chiefly family portraits; among them are portraits of Alderman Beckford by *Romney* and *Sir J. Reynolds;* Mrs. Peter Beckford and Miss Gunning by *Reynolds;* 1st Duke of Hamilton and the Earl of Newport, by *Van Dyck.*

The *Grounds*[1] abound in noble trees, and are traversed by a stately avenue stretching from the Palace up to and beyond Chatelherault. Within them are shown a Runic Cross, and the Mote Hill, or ancient place of assembly.

Near to the palace is the *Mausoleum*, a square building, surmounted by a round tower and a stone cupola (D. Bryce, archt.), reminding one of the tomb of Cecilia Metella near Rome. The interior is an octagonal chapel, underneath which are the vaults. The terrace front is adorned by colossal lions, by *Ritchie.* On the basement are representations of Life, Death, and Eternity. It was erected at a cost of £130,000 by Alexander, the 10th Duke, whose remains lie within the sarcophagus of an Egyptian queen. The building within has a truly sepulchral character, and the *echo* produced by the arrangements of the interior is remarkable, since the wind as it passes over it seems to moan a perpetual requiem for him who sleeps below. The bronze gates are copied from those of the Baptistery at Florence.

EXCURSIONS:—

(1) ½ m. S.E. close to the rly. viaduct over the *Avon* is *Barncluith*, noted for its old-fashioned Dutch gardens laid out in 1583.

(2) 1 m. higher up the Avon, on the l. bank is the ruined **Cadzow Cas.**, the cradle of the Hamilton family, built on a crag above the Avon, now a shapeless ruin overgrown with trees and briars, among which may be traced dark vaults and foundations of towers.

[1] Open Tues. and Frid.

A few old stagheaded oaks, several of which measure upwards of 24 ft. in circumference, are all that remain of the great *Caledonian Forest* which once extended from sea to sea through the whole S. of Scotland. Here too is a herd (numbering about 60) of the *wild cattle* identical with the breed still preserved at Chillingham, in Northumberland. They are very handsome and are perfectly white, except that the muzzle and tips of the ears are brown. Sir Walter Scott alludes to them in his ballad of "Cadyow Castle."

On the rt. bank, approached by a bridge, is the toy **Castle of Chatelherault,**[1] copied, 1732, from the Château in France, from which the Duke takes his French title. It stands in a commanding position, conspicuous with its four towers, on the open hillside, and is connected by a double avenue of trees with Hamilton Palace below, and has a splendid view over Clydesdale. One wing is fitted up as a summer pavilion in the Louis XIV. style for picnic parties; the rest is occupied by gamekeepers and dog-kennels. The terraced garden behind, with its formal yew hedges, looks into the winding and wooded Avondale.

(3) N. **Bothwell Bridge** and **Castle** (p. 145), 3 m.

(4) S.E. by road **up the Clyde to Lanark,** 14 m.

This is a charming drive up the l. bank of the river past handsome houses and smiling orchards, which cannot be seen from any rly.; at first numerous iron furnaces are much in evidence.

At 2 m. *Dalzell* (pron. Dée-el) *Ho.* (Lord Hamilton) is one m. N. across the Clyde. At 4½ m. the road approaches the river, across which is *Cambusnethan Ho.* (Major-Gen. Lockhart, C.B.).

[1] Admission by order from the Duke's factor.

At *Garrion Br.* (6 m.) the river is crossed by the Edinburgh and Ayr Road and above by private bridges leading to *Mauldslie Cas.* (Sir Wm. Hozier)—on an estate which, till 1817, belonged to the Earls of Hyndford—and *Milton Lockhart* (Major-Gen. D. B. Lockhart), designed by Burn.

Before *Crossford* village (9½ m.) the *Nethan* is crossed. ½ m. up this glen to the right stands *Craignethan Cas.*,[1] the original of **Tillietudlem** in "Old Mortality."

Scott visited the spot in 1799 and expressed such rapture with the scenery that Lord Douglas offered him the farmhouse for life. The castle was a fortified manor-house of the great Evandale branch of the Hamilton family, but is now reduced to two towers, with portions of the walls and of a stone vaulted hall, but its situation, embowered in foliage, overlooking the Nethan and defended by a ditch, is highly picturesque. The enthusiast may discover the window out of which the hot broth was soused over Cuddie Headrigg by Jenny.

On the rt. bank of the Clyde are *Carfin*, and (1 m. behind) *Halbar Tower*, a square peel tower 52 ft. high.

About 2½ m. from Lanark a gate at the roadside leads through a wood down to **Stonebyres Fall** (admission 3d.)—the farthest down of the *Falls of Clyde.* The *Fall* is more than 60 ft. high over a double ledge of rock. On the S. side of the road is *Stonebyres Ho.*, in part as old as the 15th cent.

At 13 m. *Kirkfieldbank*, a village occupied by weavers, the road to Lanark crosses the Clyde by a bridge of 3 arches and ascends steeply, with l. the *Cartland Crags.* The road straight on leads in 2 m. to *Corehouse* and *Corra Linn*, p. 92.

For **Lanark, Cartland Crags,** and **Falls of Clyde,** see p. 92.

(5) S. by Rly. to **Strathaven** (pron. *Straven*), 11 m. [By road 7 m.]

[1] May be reached from *Tillietudlem Stat.* (p. 149), ¾ m. higher up the Nethan, or by Coach from Lanark, p. 92.

The line runs W. by ¾ m. **W. Hamilton Stat.** to

3½ m. **High Blantyre Stat.** near which, on the *Calder*, are *Crossbasket Ho.*, *Craigneith Cas.* and *Calderwood Cas.* (with fine woods), W. of which is *Long Calderwood*, the birthplace of Drs. William and John Hunter, the famous 18th-cent. anatomists.[1]

We now turn S.E. by 6¼ m. **Meikle Earnock,** 7¾ m. **Quarter Road,** and 10¼ m. **Glassford,** to 11 m. **Strathaven.**

This is a small town with an old quarter in which are situated the ruins of *Avondale* (or *Evandale*) *Cas.* built 15th cent. by a member of the Albany family.

(6) S.E. by rly. to **Lesmahagow,** 13 m.

This line passes 2 m. *Ferniegair;* 4 m. *Larkhall;* and 5 m. *Ayr Road* for Garrion Bridge (p. 148).

[Branch rt. in 3½ m. to *Stonehouse* on the Avon.]

7½ m. *Netherburn.*

8¾ m. **Tillietudlem Stat.** for *Craignethan Cas.* (p. 148).

[Branch rt. in 1¾ m. to *Blackwood.*]

A high viaduct over the Nethan is crossed on the way to

10¼ m. *Auchenheath Stat.*

13 m. **Lesmahagow Stat.** beyond which is, 16¾ m., *Coalburn*, the terminus for passenger traffic. Coals, etc., are taken from Lesmahagow in 4½ m. to *Douglas Stat.* on the Carstairs and Muirkirk line (p. 93).

The mining town of Lesmahagow (from Machute or Mahego, a Culdee Saint)—also called *Abbey Green*, from an abbey founded here 1140—stands on the Nethan, and is interesting to geologists, many remarkable fossils (*Crustaceæ*—pterygotus, stylonurus, etc.) having been discovered in the black slabs of Silurian rock.

ROUTE 23.

Glasgow to Ardlui (Loch Lomond) by Dumbarton and Balloch. N.B. Rly. and Steamer.

A circular tour by Balloch, Loch Lomond, Loch Katrine, The Trossachs, and Stirling can be made daily in summer from Edinburgh or Glasgow in abt. 10 hours (Rtes. 19, 23, 26, 25).

Leaving **Queen St. (Low Level) Stat.,** the train runs W. underground to

¾ m. **Charing Cross Stat.,** for the Crescents and the West-End Park (p. 138), and

1¼ m. **Finnieston Stat.,** which is above ground, close to *Queen's Dock* (p. 141), seen l.

2 m. **Yorkhill Stat.,** for Ferry to **Govan** (p. 313). The line crosses the *Kelvin*, just above its mouth, to

2½ m. **Partick Stat.,** an important suburb.

[Beyond, rt., is 3½ m. **Hyndland Terminus** (pp. 141) for *Dowanhill* and the fashionable W. End mansions.]

[At 3½ m. a line turns l. to 3¾ m. **Jordanhill Stat.** (near *Jordanhill Ho.* the seat of the late James Smith, Esq., geologist, etc., 1782-1867);

4¾ m. **Scotstounhill Stat.**;

6 m. **Yoker Stat.** (with *Shipbuilding Yd.* and large *Distillery*); and

6¾ m. **Clydebank Stat.** (p. 314).]

The train passes (rt.) *Gartnavel Lunatic Asylum* before

4 m. **Gt. Western Rd. Stat.,** for residences in the extreme W. End.

[Here the *Glasgow City and District* (*Circular*) *Rly.* trends rt. to 5 m. **Maryhill Stat.** (with Military Barracks); 6 m. **Lochburn**; 6¾ m. **Possilpark**; 8¼ m. **Springburn**; 8½ m. **Barnhill,** 9 m. **Garngad**; 9¾ m. **Alexandra Park**; 10 m. **Duke St.**; 10½ m. **Bellgrove**; 11¼ m. **College**; and

11¾ m. **Queen St.** (**Low Level**).]

The line now passes under the *Forth and Clyde Canal* and at 5 m. the direct line from Edin. falls in;

---

[1] See *Two Great Scotsmen—William and John Hunter*, by G. Mather, M.D. (J. Maclehose and Sons, 1893), with interesting illustrations.

rt. lies *Garscube Ho.* (Sir A. S. L. Campbell, Bt.), erected in 1827 on an estate which has belonged to the Campbells of Succoth since the middle of the 17th cent. It stands in picturesque grounds and contains a good collection of paintings.

[At 5½ m. a line strikes rt. to

6 m. **Bearsden Stat.** (for New Kilpatrick and a well-marked portion of the Roman Wall), and

8 m. **Milngavie** (pron. *Milgúy*) **Stat.** ✲, E. of which is *Dougalston Ho.* (T. Ripley Ker, Esq.), and beyond, *Bardowie Cas.*

1 m. N. is **Mugdock Reservoir** of the Glasgow and Loch Katrine Waterworks (see p. 165), 311 ft. above sea-level, 70 acres in area, and holding 500 million gallons of water, which is here stored and hence conveyed to Glasgow in pipes. Adjoining is **Craigmaddie Reservoir** (1894), with a water surface of 86¼ acres. It is capable of containing 700 million gallons, being a supply to the city of 40 million gallons per day for 17½ days, in addition to the 12½ days' supply which the Mugdock Reservoir contains.

½ m. E. of these reservoirs is *Craigmaddie Ho.* (Mr. and Mrs. Higginbotham), with an old moated tower in the grounds, and ½ N. is *Mugdock Cas.* (Duke of Montrose), with an ancient tower, formerly the principal seat of the Montrose family. Slightly farther N. is *Craigend Cas.* (Sir J. Buchanan, Bt.).

There is a pleasant drive from Milngavie N.E. to *Killearn*, 10 m. (p. 156), or *Drymen*, 10½ m. (p. 166), with rt. the *Campsie Fells*, and l. the *Kilpatrick Hills*. At 4½ m. we pass (l.) the entrance to *Auchineden Ho.* (J. J. Pollock, Esq.), 3 m. W. of *Blanefield Stat.* (p. 155). Pedestrians should ascend *Auchineden Hill* (abt. 1½ m. W.), with a remarkable chasm called **"The Whangie"** on the far side running parallel with the face of the cliff for some 350 ft. The rock is greenstone overlying the old red sandstone and from the summit there is one of the best views near Glasgow, comprising Loch Lomond, Strath Endrick, the Lake of Menteith, Ben Ledi, etc.

At 7 m. we cross the *Carnock Burn*, which has cut out in the sandstone beds *Finnich Glen* (l.), a very interesting narrow gorge with steep sides. In one part is a large tabular mass of sandstone called *The Devil's Pulpit.* Beyond the burn the road to Killearn strikes rt.]

The train runs W., keeping alongside the Canal.

6½ m. **Drumchapel Stat.**; rt. lies *Garscadden Ho.* (Rev. J. E. Campbell Colquhoun, whose family have had the estate since 1664).

8 m. **Kilbowie Stat.** (for Clydebank, p. 314) with *Singer's* large *Sewing Machine Works* (l.).

9 m. **Dalmuir Stat.** 1 m. N. is *Duntocher*, where there is a large establishment of spinning mills, and near which many of the Roman Remains in Glasgow University Museum were found.

10½ m. **Old Kilpatrick Stat.** St. Patrick was probably born here abt. 387 A.D., his father having care of part of the Roman Wall. l. is *Erskine Ferry*, and across the Clyde *Erskine Ho.* (Lord Blantyre) [p. 314] is well seen.

The rly. begins to run very near the river as we approach

12¾ m. **Bowling Stat.** ✲, a cheerful and busy-looking village with landing stages, wharves, and a large enclosed *Dock* where Clyde steamers are laid up during the winter.

The **Forth and Clyde Canal,** which leaves the Forth at Grangemouth, (p. 203), and here enters the Clyde, was opened 1790. It follows nearly the line of the *Roman Wall* (p. 131), which here terminates, is 38 m. in length and includes 39 locks, with a rise of 156 ft. from the sea to the summit level. It was one of Smeaton's works, and was for those days a triumph of engineering skill, the country through which it was carried abounding in deep valleys and dells. It was in 1867 purchased by the Caledonian Rly. Co.

On the hill immediately above Bowling is *Auchentorlie*, the beautiful residence of Mr. Fergusson-Buchanan, and N.W. are *Milton Print Works*, backed by the wooded hill of *Dumbuck*, an outlier of the Kilpatrick Hills, with the modern Scottish mansion of *Overtoun* (Lord Overtoun) on its western slopes.

Just beyond Bowling (l.) is *Dunglass Point*, with the ivy-covered ruins of a *Cas.*; in front of it may be seen an obelisk to the memory of Henry Bell, originally a mason, who in 1812 launched the "Comet" (with an engine of 3 horse-power) on the Clyde—the first *Steam*boat in Europe.

$15\frac{1}{4}$ m. **DUMBARTON Stat.** ✲, a thriving but rather dirty town, with large shipbuilding yards on the l. bank of the *Leven*, which enters the Clyde to the W. of the castle rock, having once flowed on both sides of it. Turning down *Church St.*, we pass (l.) the **County Buildings**, the **Wm. Denny Institute**, and the **Academy**, burnt in 1883, but rebuilt with an imposing sq. *Tower* attached.

Opposite the Academy stands "one of the tower arches of St. Patrick's Collegiate Ch., founded MCCCL. . . . The rly. caused the removal of the arch, the sole remnant of a once extensive pile, to its present site, MDCCCL."

Just beyond, we turn l. along *Castle St.* and *Ter.*, then rt. down *Leven St.*, skirting the high enclosing wall of **Denny's Shipbuilding Yard**, and reach, in nearly 1 m., **The **Castle.**

It consists of a group of modern barracks, with an ancient dungeon, which occupy the hollow near the summit of the picturesque bifid rock of basalt which rises abruptly from the water's edge. The garrison, which guards a powder magazine and three batteries, now consists usually of only 1 sergeant and 3 gunners, who live in what was the Governor-General's house, 1735-1832, situated near the shore. From it a flight of 365 steps within the cleft which divides the 2 peaks of rock leads to the top through an ancient pointed *Gothic Archway* (12th cent.), grooved for a portcullis, the gate of which is in Paisley Museum. This was always the access to the sea, and is now the only approach, the principal entrance, from the land side, having been removed. From the summit, 326 ft. above the Clyde, a beautiful view is obtained—N. to the Mts. around Loch Lomond, S. and W. over the Clyde Estuary.

The name *Dun Breton* ("The Hill of the Britons") marks its antiquity, although there are scanty remains of ancient days. It was a frontier stronghold of the British Kingdom of Strathclyde; Bede calls it Alcluyth, and it is probably the Balclutha of Ossian. Sir John Menteith, the captor of Wallace (1305), was governor of the castle, but it is doubtful if Wallace was ever here, as he was taken near Glasgow and sent off at once to London. In later days the castle commanded an important Pass into the Highlands, and preserved an opening by sea with France and other foreign lands. From it the infant Mary was smuggled on board the French fleet, which, to elude the English cruisers of Henry VIII., had sailed round by the Pentland Firth to receive her, and landed her safely at Brest, 1548. The *Sun-dial* at the foot of the rock was presented to the Castle by Queen Mary.

Steep and inaccessible as Dumbarton rock may appear, it was, nevertheless, scaled in 1571 by 100 men under Crawford of Jordanhill, led by a guide who had been a sentry. They approached the foot of the rock at dead of night, furnished with scaling ladders, ropes, and iron crampons; hauling one another up, and gaining a precarious footing on ledges and in cracks, they succeeded in surprising the garrison, turned their guns against them, and killing only four, won the castle for James VI. John Hamilton, Archbp. of St. Andrews, a partisan of Queen Mary, who was living here at the time, was taken, and hung at Stirling 4 days later for alleged complicity in the murders of Darnley and the Regent Murray.

The Treaty of Union (1707) undertook to maintain the castle as one of the chief national fortresses of Scotland.

The Queen visited the castle and ascended the rock in 1847.

A long *Steamboat Pier* was thrown out into the Clyde from the foot of the castle rock in 1874, and in 1884 a *Public Park*, on the rt. bank of the Leven, was presented to the town by Mr. Peter Denny and Mr. John Macmillan, both shipbuilders.

The line crosses the Leven to

$15\frac{3}{4}$ m. **Dalreoch Stat.**, where the line forks—W. to Helensburgh (Rte. 67), N. up the *Vale of Leven* to

$17\frac{1}{2}$ m. **Renton Stat.**, a flourishing town occupied by *Print and Bleach-*

ing Works and by the colossal *Dye Works* of Stirling and Buchanan, established 1728.

In front of the School stands a Monument with a Latin inscription (partly by Dr. Johnson) to Tobias Smollett, the novelist (1721 - 71), who was born at the old house of *Dalquharn* (pron. Dalwhan), ½ m. S. Some say Renton was named after a lady in "Humphrey Clinker." Smollett's "Ode to the Leven,"

"Pure stream, in whose transparent wave,"

is strangely inapplicable to the river in its present polluted state. Across the river is *Strathleven Ho.*, with splendid parks.

18½ m. **Alexandria Stat.**—one of several towns that have risen on the banks of the Leven since 1728-1768—has a large trade in bleaching, dyeing, and printing. It was named by the Smollett family, who have for 200 yrs. owned the neighbouring lands of Bonhill, after *Alexander* Telfer Smollett. From its once having consisted of only one grocer's shop, it is still known locally as "the grocery." The pastoral vale of Smollett is now teeming with an immense industry in bleaching, dyeing (Turkey red), and printing calico, carried on by the Stirlings and the Orr-Ewings.

A *Suspension Bridge* over the Leven (erected by Capt. Smollett, 1836) connects Alexandria with the manufacturing village of *Bonhill.* At 19¼ m. l. is *Tullichewan Castle* (James Campbell, Esq.), a modern edifice, and rt. the line from Stirling comes in.

19¾ m. **Balloch Stat.** ✡ Here is the junc. with the Forth and Clyde Rly. to Stirling (Rte. 27).

20¼ m. **Balloch Pier Stat.**

Steamers 3 or 4 times a day up Loch Lomond in summer to Ardlui. There is a restaurant on board, at which a fair breakfast or dinner can be obtained. Pier dues on landing, 2d.

"**Loch Lomond** is unquestionably the pride of our lakes—incomparable in its beauty as in its dimensions, exceeding all others in variety as it does in extent and splendour, and uniting in itself every style of scenery which is found in the other lakes of the Highlands. . . . Nor do I think that I overrate its richness in scenery when I say that if Loch Achray and Loch Katrine be omitted, it presents numerically more pictures than all the lakes of the Highlands united."—MACCULLOCH.

It is the largest fresh-water lake in Britain. From Balloch to Ardlui its extreme length is 24 m., and its greatest breadth, at the south end from Glenfruin to Endrick Water, 5 m. It contains 24 islands, some of which are of considerable size, and by their craggy and wooded features add greatly to the scenic beauty; three belong to Sir G. Leith-Buchanan, Bt. of Ross Priory, and the rest to Sir James Colquhoun of Luss,[1] or the Duke of Montrose. The lower portion of the lake freezes in very hard winters, but never above Tarbet, between which and Ben Lomond the depth is upwards of 100 fathoms.

The lower end of the loch, which is beautifully wooded, is ornamented with some picturesque residences. On the rt. is *Balloch Castle* (A. J. Dennistoun-Brown, Esq.), with the remains of the old castle of *Balloch*, once the property of the Earls of Lennox. Higher up is *Boturich Castle* (R. E. Findlay, Esq.), occupying the site of the old seat of the Lennox family, with *Mt. Misery* (576 ft.) behind—visible for a long distance. On the W. side are *Cameron House* (P. B. Smollett, Esq.), *Auchindennan* (J. M. Martin, Esq.), and *Arden* (James Lumsden, Esq.). A good view is obtained of the forked rock of Dumbarton, nearly due S. To the E. is the valley of the *Endrick*, in which Napier of Merchiston, the inventor of logarithms (1550-1617), passed a

[1] See Fraser's *Chiefs of Colquhoun and their Country*.

great part of his life. To the S. of the embouchure of the river, which falls into the loch, is *Ross Priory* (Sir G. Leith-Buchanan, Bt.), where Sir W. Scott used to stay when in this neighbourhood, and to the N. of it the striking *Conic Hill* (1175 ft.).

In the middle of the loch about this point is *Inch Murrin* ("Grassy Island"), the largest and most southerly island, belonging to the Duke of Montrose, who keeps a herd of fallow deer on it. At the S. extremity are the ruins of *Lennox Castle*, to which the Duchess of Albany retired from Doune Castle after her husband had been executed in 1424. It used to be the practice to confine insane persons, and those addicted to drunkenness, on this island, and on *Inch Lonaig*.

Glen Fruin, a fine though triste-looking glen, runs from the S.W. corner of the loch parallel to the Gareloch (Rte. 67).

It acquired a sad notoriety in the annals of the **Lennox**, as this district is called, from the battle (1603) near the head of the glen, in which the M'Gregors encountered the clan of Colquhoun, who suffered sorely, leaving 200 dead upon the field. A number of the sons of the principal families in the Lennox came to look on at the battle, and were shut up in a barn by the Colquhouns, where they were all treacherously murdered by the M'Gregors. The latter accusation was, however, denied by the M'Gregors, who in the end suffered for their triumph. Sixty widows of the clan Colquhoun appeared before James VI. at Stirling, each having in her hand the bloody shirt of her husband, by which the king was so moved that he proscribed the M'Gregors, who from this time forth were hunted mercilessly down (pp. 164, 165). *Bannachra Castle*, 1½ m. up the Fruin, is a ruined stronghold of the Colquhouns.

On the E. bank is

† **Balmaha**, where some of the steamers call. Opposite the pier is *Inch Cailliach* ("Island of Old Women"), so called because a nunnery formerly existed there. It is celebrated as being the burying-place of the M'Gregors, who often swore "upon the Halidome of him that sleeps beneath the gray stone at Inch Cailliach." Numerous monuments belonging to that family still remain, but the island is so wooded with yew and fir that they are not to be seen from the water.

"The shaft and limbs were rods of yew,
Whose parents in Inch Cailliach wave
Their shadows o'er Clan Alpine's grave,
And, answering Lomond's breezes deep,
Soothe many a chieftain's endless sleep."
Lady of the Lake, c. iii.

The steamer now steers through a group of islands, the principal of which are *Inch Fad* ("Long Island"), cultivated and farmed; *Inchruim*, *Inch Moan*, *Inch Tavannach*, *Inch Connachan*, and *Inch Lonaig*.

Luss ✲ is a small village picturesquely situated close to what, taking the loch as a whole, is the most lovely portion of it. Coleridge, Wordsworth, and Wordsworth's sister Dorothy slept in the inn here, 24th August 1803.[1] There are *Slate Quarries* behind, but they now only give employment to 5 men. 2 m. S. is *Rossdhu*, the beautiful seat of Sir J. Colquhoun, Bt., the owner of most of this side of the loch. His predecessor was drowned in the lake by the upsetting of a boat overladen with dead deer, 1873. W. of Rossdhu is *Glenfinlas* and behind Luss *Glen Luss*, both parallel to Glen Fruin (above).

The privilege was obtained of cutting from the woods of Luss the timber for the erection of Glasgow Cathedral.

[There is a good *Road* from Luss to Helensburgh, 9 m., crossing the opening of Glen Fruin; it continues N. from Luss along the shores of the loch to Tarbet, 8½ m. (thence 2 m. W. is Arrochar), and Ardlui, 16½ m.]

rt. † **Rowardennan** ✲, whence the *Ascent of Ben Lomond*, 4 m., can be made in a little more than 2 hours (3 hrs., with ladies), the path being so gentle that those who choose can ride up the whole way. Ponies are kept at the *Hotel*.

[1] See Dorothy Wordsworth's most interesting "Tour in Scotland."

The beauty of **Ben Lomond** (3192 ft.), which is covered with grass to the top, is much enhanced by contrast with *Ben Arthur* ("The Cobbler") and the mountains of Arrochar to the W. of the loch, which have steep declivities and bare rocky summits, nearly of the same elevation. On a very clear day the view from the summit is magnificent, and it presents the spectator with a wide panorama. On the N. the view is limited by the jealous barrier of the Grampians—a view in themselves—Ben Nevis being occasionally visible; S. the view extends from Arran to the Pentlands and Edinburgh Castle, with the windings of the Clyde and Dumbarton Rock in the foreground; E. are Loch Ard, the valley of the Forth, and Stirling Castle.

See Map, p. 168.

[There is a good *pedestrian excursion* from Rowardennan to Aberfoyle (about 5 hours). Cross the S. shoulder of Ben Lomond, and follow down a tributary of Duchray Water until that stream is crossed by a wooden bridge; go over this, cross the Glasgow Waterworks conduit, and strike the high road at the W. end of Loch Ard.

There is a *Ferry* from Rowardennan to *Inverbeg Inn* on the W. shore, whence there is a pleasant walk up Glen Douglas.]

On the W. shore, 5 m. higher up, is

† **Tarbet** ✲ [with a Rly. Stat. ¾ m. W. on the W. Highland Rly. (p. 347)] 8 m. from the head of the loch in a charming situation. W. appears the fantastic top of Ben Arthur ("*The Cobbler*"). The view of Ben Lomond is magnificent.

The *Ascent* from the opposite side (2½ hours), although frequently made, and by no means difficult, is not quite so easy as that from Rowardennan. When once over the loch, do not keep straight up, but strike through the woods in a slanting direction to the right hand, until the first plateau is gained, from which the way lies pretty direct to the summit.

Only 2 m. W. of Tarbet[1]—a pleasant road with a very slight ascent—is **Arrochar** ✲ at the head of Loch Long, where a Glasgow steamer calls (Rte. 76).

For route to Inveraray by Glen Croe see Rte. 77.

Continuing up the loch, which is here 100 fathoms deep, the steamer passes rt. *Rob Roy's Prison*, where he is said to have kept his prisoners till he had extorted sufficient ransom. The views looking N. through the vista of Glenfalloch are very beautiful, although the principal objects, Ben Lomond and the Cobbler, are now left behind. The W. Highland Rly. is seen running along the W. side. (Cf. p. 347.)

rt. † **Inversnaid** ✲, where the river Arklet forms a pretty *Waterfall*, alluded to by Wordsworth in his poem, "The Highland Girl," whom he met here.

[Here the routes from the Trossachs and Loch Katrine (Rte. 26), and from Aberfoyle (Rte. 28) fall in. *Coaches* convey passengers between Inversnaid and Stronachlachar on Loch Katrine, corresponding with the steamers on the two lochs.]

Opposite Inversnaid is *Inveruglas Water* (reached by a ferry), up which a walk of 4 m. leads to *Loch Sloy*.

Higher up the loch (rt.) is *Rob Roy's Cave*, marked by R. R. painted on the face of the rock.

1¾ m. farther up is a small island, *Eilean Vow*, on which are ruins of a *Castle* called M'Farlane's.

The upper part of the loch is shallow, from the river deposits.

† **Ardlui Pier** ✲ (8 miles from Tarbet) is the highest point to which the steamers go, although a canal (not used now) was cut by the Marquis of Breadalbane, to (2 m.) Inverarnan.

At Ardlui is a stat. on the W. Highland Rly. (p. 347), but it is a pleasant drive (coaches twice daily)

[1] *Tarbet* or *Tarbert*, a very commonplace name in Scotland (Gael. *Tarruin bád*=*Draw-boat*), signifies a neck of land across which a boat may be drawn from one sheet of water to another. Cf. pp. 335, 340.

up Glen Falloch past (2 m.) *Glenfalloch Ho.*, and ($4\frac{1}{2}$ m.) the *Falls of Falloch*, to

$8\frac{3}{4}$ **Crianlarich** ✲, pp. 170, 347.

ROUTE 24.

Glasgow to Aberfoyle by Campsie Glen and Buchlyvie. N.B.R.

From **Queen St. (High Level) Stat.** to

$6\frac{1}{2}$ m. **Lenzie Junc.,** see p. 132. The line trends N., passing rt. the *Barony Asylum*, to

8 m. **Kirkintilloch Stat.** an ancient little town on the banks of the Luggie, near its confluence with the Kelvin, traversed by the Forth and Clyde Canal. There are traces here of a Roman fort, in the shape of a mound and ditch, whence there is a beautiful view of the *Campsie Fells* (below).

[*Branch* rt. via *Gavell* to **Kilsyth Stat.** ✲, $\frac{1}{2}$ m. N. of which are the remains of the old *Castle*, and, behind, the *Kilsyth Hills*.

S. of Kilsyth are well-marked portions of the *Roman Wall*.

Here, 15th August 1645, Montrose gained a most complete victory over the Covenanters, under General Baillie, putting 6000 of them to the sword.

From Kilsyth a line runs E. by *Bonnybridge* to *Larbert* (p. 156), and W. down the Kelvin Valley by *Gavell*, *Torrance*, *Balmore*, *Summerston*, and *Maryhill* to *Queen St. Low Level Stat.*]

The line crosses the *Kelvin*, and keeps W. up the *Glazert Water*.

$9\frac{3}{4}$ m. **Milton Stat.** Here are the large Kincaid printworks. rt. is *Antermony Ho.* (Mrs. Peareth Lennox), and l. is *Kincaid Ho.* (Hon. C. S. B. H. Kincaid Lennox).

$11\frac{1}{2}$ m. **Lennoxtown Stat.**, a small town, dependent on various print, bleaching, and alum works, with the handsome *Parish Ch. of Campsie* rt. In its ch.-yd. Norman Macleod is buried, his father having been minister here. 1 m. E. is *Glorat Ho.* (Sir C. E. J. Stirling, Bt.).

$12\frac{1}{2}$ m. **Campsie Glen Stat.** is $\frac{3}{4}$ m. S. of the village of *Campsie* ✲, with the ruins of an old ch. at the entrance of *Campsie Glen*, one of the most charming little glens in Scotland. There is a path up both sides. From the rt. bank, beyond the wooded part, you can get behind one of the waterfalls, and look through the fall. There are also pretty bits in the steep-sided *Fin Glen* to the W.

The **Campsie Fells**, a fine range of hills with *Earl's Seat* (1894 ft.) as the highest pt., give much variety to the scenery around Glasgow, to which they afford a favourite holiday resort.

They consist of igneous rocks, "along the S. flank of which the successive sheets of lava may be traced by the eye from a distance of several miles, rising above each other in successive bands of dark rock and grassy slope."—GEIKIE.

Turning W., and skirting l. the grounds of the imposing *Lennox Castle* (Mrs. Peareth Lennox), we pass l. the *Devil's Craig*, a striking isolated trap boss, and reach

$15\frac{3}{4}$ m. **Strathblane Stat.** This village is very prettily situated on the *Blane*, which rises on the adjoining heights of Earl's Seat and flows into the *Endrick*. 1 m. N.E. is the *Spout of Ballagan*, a series of cascades, where a very fine geological section of strata known as the *Ballagan Beds* is exposed. They consist of thin bedded limestones, sandstones, clays, and shales, of the Lower Carboniferous age, the whole being overlaid by trap.

A road S. leads to *Mugdock* and *Milngavie* (p. 150).

$16\frac{3}{4}$ m. **Blanefield Stat.**, $4\frac{1}{2}$ m. W. of which is the *Whangie* (p. 150).

Beyond, we pass (rt.) *Duntreath Castle* (Sir Arch. Edmonstone, Bart.), 15th cent.

"The possessor of the barony of Duntreath enjoyed the fullest feudal powers, and the dungeons and stocks still remaining attest the extent of the authority once exercised by the nobility and higher gentry of Scotland."—BURKE.

Rt., *Dungoyn* and *Dunfoyn*, outliers of the Campsie Hills, are remarkably bold and picturesque.

19¾ m. **Killearn (old) Stat.**

21¼ **Killearn (new) Stat.** 2 m. W. is the interesting *Finnich Glen* (p. 150). *Killearn Village* ✲, 1 m. E., was the birthplace (1582) of Geo. Buchanan the historian—buried in Greyfriars ch.-yd., Edin.—and has an obelisk to his memory. The public hall was formerly a ch., built in 1826.

In 1882 the line was continued from this point to Aberfoyle by adding 2 new sections at a cost of £62,000. The first section, crossing the Endrick on an iron girder bridge, joins the Forth and Clyde Rly. beyond Gartness Stat. (p. 166).

We traverse this line past

24¼ m. **Balfron Stat.** as far as

28½ m. **Buchlyvie Stat.** ✲, where we leave the Forth and Clyde rly. and enter on the second new section, which proved a very difficult engineering work, as it traverses *Flanders Moss*, in parts 20 to 30 ft. deep, and very shifting.

The Forth is crossed on an iron bridge before reaching

32½ m. **Gartmore Stat.** on the borders of Perthshire. 1 m. S. is *Gartmore Village* and *Ho.* (R. B. Cunninghame-Graham, Esq. The *Lake of Menteith* (p. 167) lies 2 m. E.

34¼ m. **Aberfoyle Stat.** ✲ (see p. 167).

ROUTE 25.

Glasgow [or Edinburgh] to Stirling by Larbert and Bannockburn. Cal. Rly.

There are through trains over this line to *Callander* and *Oban* (Rte. 29), to *Crieff* and *Comrie* (Rte. 39), to *Perth*, *Dundee*, and *Aberdeen* (Rtes. 38, 46, 47).

The *Edinburgh* line falls in at Larbert, see Rte. 19.

Leaving **Buchanan St. Stat.**, the line passes

1 m. **St. Rollox Stat.**,

4½ m. **Steps Road Stat.**, and

6 m. **Garnkirk Stat.**, to

7¼ m. **Gartcosh Stat.** [Line rt. to *Gartsherrie* and *Coatbridge* (p. 18).] The rly. trends N. to

9 m. **Glenboig Stat.**, with celebrated *Brick Works*. Here trains from Carlisle to the N. *via* Carstairs and Coatbridge (Rte. 2) come in rt.

13 m. **Cumbernauld Stat.** *Cumbernauld Ho.* (J. W. Burns, Esq.) and *Village* are 1½ m. farther on (l.) The N.B.R. is passed under close to Castlecary Stat. (Rte. 19), and the Forth and Clyde Canal is seen l. before

18½ m. **Greenhill Stat.** The Canal is crossed to

22 m. **Larbert Stat.**, an important Junction with a long-needed new stat. (1892).

[*Lines*—i. E. to *Edinburgh* by Polmont (Rte. 19).

ii. To *Grangemouth* (p. 203), 5¾ m., by Grahamston.

iii. W. to *Denny*, 3¾ m., a small manufacturing town on the Carron.

iv. To *Kilsyth* (p. 155), 10 m., by *Bonnybridge Central*, *Dennyloanhead*, *Banknock*, and *Colzium*. Between the two last stations the watershed which separates the *Carron* and the *Kelvin* is crossed. *Colzium Ho.* is a seat of the Edmonstones.

v. N. to *Alloa* (p. 198), 8¾ m., by Airth. Through carriages run over this line from Glasgow (Queen St., N.B.R.) to Perth *via* Alloa Bridge and Glen Farg.]

At 23 m. l. is *Glenbervie Ho.*, and 11½ m. rt. *Kinnaird Ho.* (Lord Thurlow), formerly the residence of Bruce the Abyssinian traveller (1730-94), who, after going through unheard-of dangers in distant lands, came to his death at the door of his own house by falling when in the act of handing a lady to her carriage. He was buried in Larbert churchyard, where an iron pillar was put up to his memory.

At 24 m. l. is *Carbrook Ho.* (J. C. Bolton, Esq.), and rt. the line to Alloa.

There is a good view rt. of the *Ochils* and of *Wallace's Monument* at Stirling as we approach

$27\frac{3}{4}$ m. **Bannockburn Stat.** The village (with a brisk trade in tartans) is $\frac{1}{2}$ m. W., and 1 m. beyond it lies the scene of the battle fought on June 24, 1314, between the English army under Edward II., and the Scots under King Robert Bruce, in a plain watered by the *Bannock.*

The English army, amounting to 100,000 men, were advancing to the relief of Stirling, which Bruce was then besieging. His force amounted to no more than 30,000, and was very deficient in cavalry, a weak point which he counterbalanced by a judicious selection of the field of battle.

The *Borestone* (now protected by an iron grating) with a tall flagstaff, is said to have been the spot where Bruce's standard was planted during the battle, and to have marked the position of his left wing, while his right was protected by the *Bannock Burn.* Bruce further strengthened his position by digging pits across the tongue of land between the lower end of Milton bog and the burn, and covering them over with boughs and earth. The English, although defeated, stood their ground until the Scottish camp followers, like a fresh army, suddenly appeared over the *Gillies' Hill* on the N.W.—now planted with fir trees—when a rout ensued. The English lost abt. 10,000 men, the Scots abt. 4000.

About $1\frac{1}{2}$ m. S. of Bannockburn is *Sauchieburn*, the scene of a battle, in 1488, between James III. and his insurgent nobles, headed by his son, afterwards James IV., by whose forces — far superior in point of numbers — the king was defeated. He fled from the field wounded; but was thrown from his horse after crossing Bannock Burn, and conveyed to a small old house called *Beaton's Mill*, still existing but no longer a mill. Here he was stabbed by a man pretending to be a priest, who then vanished, and could never be found. To the E. of Sauchieburn is *Bannockburn House*, the temporary headquarters of Charles Edward in 1746.

[From the field of Bannockburn the visitor can proceed to Stirling through the village of *St. Ninian's*, or St. Ringan's, as it is popularly called. The greater part of the old ch. was destroyed by sheer clumsiness in 1746, when the Highlanders fired the neighbouring powder magazine upon their retreat from Stirling. The steeple stands at one end, with part of the chancel at the other, and a new ch. has been built at the edge of the churchyard. The village, which possesses a manufacture of nails, consists of one long street, through which the main road passes. *Omnibus* from Stirling to Bannockburn about 7 times a day, passes through St. Ninian's.]

30 m. **Stirling Stat.**

[Junc. for i. W. *Forth and Clyde Rly.* to Buchlyvie, Aberfoyle, Balloch, etc. (Rtes. 24, 27, 28).

ii. E. to *Dunfermline* by Alloa (Rte. 35.)

iii. N.E. to Kinross and Ladybank, by Dollar, etc. (Rte. 36).]

STIRLING✲ stands nobly on rising ground, overlooking the river Forth, "that bridles the wild Highlander." The town is built on the slope of the hill, whose top, a projecting rock of trap, 340 ft. above the plain, descends on the N.W. side in a black precipice, and is occupied by the Castle, resembling in this respect the situation of Edinburgh.

As the "gray bulwark of the North," the key of the main passage between the N. and S. of Scotland, at no period of Scottish history can it be said that Stirling was not an object of the highest interest, and in no war was it not one of contention.

It was the last place in all Scotland that held out against Edward I., who laid siege to it in person, 1304, when 65 years old. He was repeatedly hit by the engines from within; and when the garrison, which under Oliphant had resisted obstinately the whole force of England, surrendered, they amounted to only 140 men. The king, who was prouder of its capture than of any other success in the war, treated them with unusual leniency. It was in order to raise the siege of Stirling 10 years later that his successor hazarded the fatal fight of Bannockburn. In the time of the Stuarts it became one of the king's residences. James II. (1430) and James V. (1512) were born within its walls. But, as at Holyrood, it was not till the reign of James V. that any separate building was set apart for the Royal family. The Castle was taken by Gen. Monk (1651), and was unsuccessfully besieged by Prince Charlie in 1646.

Leaving the stat. turn rt. and ascend the steep Friars St., Baker St., and Bow St. to *Broad St.* On its W. side is the old **Town House**, built 1701 in place of that in front of which John, last R.C. Archbp. of St. Andrews, was hanged 1571 (p. 151). In the centre of the street is the *City Cross*, of which the shaft is modern. A small pillar on the pavement is said to be a portion of the old shaft.

At the N. end of Broad St. and the S. end of Castle Hill, is **Mar's Work**, a singular fragment of Scottish domestic architecture (1570) never finished. Over the main entrance are the Royal Arms, flanked by those of Mar and his Countess. It is said that the building was erected with the materials of Cambuskenneth Abbey, but of this the architect finds slight evidence, the masonry and the mouldings being all of later style. The architecture is an uncouth sort of Renaissance, with enriched pediments and scrolls over the windows and doors, and statues or pilasters projecting from the walls. W. of Mar's Work stands ***Greyfriars Church**,[1] a fine Gothic building, with a high pitched roof. It measures 200 ft. long, and 55 ft. wide inside. At its W. end is a plain square battlemented *Tower* 90 ft. high—a prominent object for miles around—on which the shot marks made by the guns during Monk's siege (1651) are still visible. The *Nave* with massive round pillars and 5 bays is said to date from 1270, but the windows—mid-pointed—and the roof, low and vaulted throughout, are 15th cent.

The elegant *Choir* built by James IV. in 1494 is loftier than the nave and comprises 3 bays with aisles. The E. end (an appendage attributed to Cardinal Beaton) is apsidal with a notable roof. The fine E. window should be noticed, in which "the long thin shafts, extending through the whole length instead of diverging into wavy or geometrical figures, and the transoms crossing them at right angles, are certainly types of the latest age of Gothic Perpendicular." In this ch. Mary was crowned (1543) at the age of 8 months; here, too, in the same year, the Earl of Arran, Regent of the kingdom, renounced the Reformed religion, and here in 1567 James VI. was crowned when a year old—John Knox preaching the sermon. Since 1656 it has been divided into two—the W. and the E. parish churches.

W. of the Church is the *Military Prison*, in which all soldiers in Scotland sentenced to imprisonment for more than 14 days and less than 2 years are confined, and the *Guild Hall* (1638) which contains a museum of curiosities.

E. of Mar's Work is **Argyll's Lodging** (now a military hospital),

[1] Admission 2d. each.

where the Duke of York, afterwards James VII., stayed in 1681. It is "probably the finest specimen of an old town residence remaining in Scotland." It was built about 1630 by the 1st Earl of Stirling, and passed at his death (1640) to the Argyll family.

Beyond it is the **Castle Esplanade** with a colossal *Statue*, in the N.E. corner, of Bruce, executed in freestone by Mr. Currie of Darnick and erected in 1877. The king is represented as sheathing his sword after Bannockburn. To the W. is a *Pyramid* to the Covenanters. At the N. end of the Esplanade is

The **Castle[1] in a commanding position, but it has been sadly neglected and its historical buildings sacrificed to the necessary (?) requirements of a modern barrack.

The *Outworks* at the first moat only date from the time of Queen Anne (1709). The second moat is now used as the officers' tennis lawn. The *Entrance Gateway* had originally 4 *Drum Towers*, which remain, but in a more or less stunted condition. They were probably erected by James III. (1460-88), who also built the square *Baronial Tower* (l.) in which James VI. was educated. Entering the outer court we have (l.) the **Palace** (now used as officers' quarters) begun 1540 by James V. and finished by his widow, Mary of Guise. It is a fantastic building with curious pillars and emblematic figures. Among those on the S. side are examples of Scottish soldiers of the 14th cent.; among those on the E., grotesque representations of a King, a Queen, a Chamberlain, a Cook, Lust, Venus, etc. Upon the N.E. corner of the roof is a statue of James V. Some of the oak carvings of the kings and queens called the "Stirling Heads," which formed part of the internal decorations, but were taken down in 1777, are preserved in the Smith Institute.

Facing us is the gable end, with 2 of the original windows entire though built up, of the **Parliament Hall**, 125 ft. long, a fine Gothic building of the time of James III., but now divided into flats, and converted into soldiers' dormitories and store rooms. It and the Palace form respectively the S. and the E. sides of the Inner Quadrangle, on whose N. side is the *Chapel Royal* in which James VI. was christened (1566), and afterwards crowned, and which was rebuilt by him in 1594. Long an *Armoury*, it is now roofed across and used for stores or as a shelter hall for picnic parties! On the W. side is a building said to have been an older palace.

By a passage in the N.W. corner of this quadrangle, access is gained to a small garden and thence by a flight of steps to the **Douglas Room,** partially rebuilt after a fire in 1856, and filled with a few historical relics. In this room William, Earl of Douglas, was foully murdered by James II., 1452, and then thrown out of the window. It is believed that he was buried where he fell, and a skeleton, supposed to be his, was in 1797 found in the garden. From this room a subterranean passage is said to have led into *Ballangeich* ("windy pass"), a narrow path to the W. of the castle much used by James V. when he went out in disguise seeking adventures, several of which are given in Scott's *Tales of a Grandfather*. From this exit he took the assumed name of the "Guidman of Ballangeich."

The *View* from "*Queen Victoria's Look-out*" (340 ft. above the plain, and 420 ft. above the sea) at the N.W. corner of the ramparts is magnificent:—W. are the Campsie Fells; from W. to N. Ben Lomond, Ben Venue, Ben Ledi, and Ben Voir-

[1] Guides, appointed by the commanding officer, are in attendance to conduct visitors at fixed charges.

lich; N.E. the Ochils, below which are the "Links of Forth" (p. 204), with Wallace's Monument and Cambuskenneth Abbey; and S. the Field of Bannockburn. In the foreground N.W. is the rich "Carse of Stirling" and across it Doune Cas. Below, to the N.E. across Ballangeich is the "*Heading Hill*,"

> "The sad and fatal mound
> That oft has heard the death-axe sound."
> SCOTT.

On it Prince Charlie in 1746, to oblige the citizens and spare the town, planted his fortifications, which were speedily destroyed by the Castle guns.

Between the Castle and Greyfriars is a *Valley*, in old days the *Tilting Ground*, now a **Cemetery**, laid out as a *Public Garden*, and embellished with various statues by *Ritchie* of Scottish people famous in the annals of religion. These include a representation of the Wigtown Martyrs (p. 108) enclosed by glass, close to which is

The *Ladies' Rock*, once the chief place for viewing the games. It commands almost as good a view as that from the Castle Ramparts, and is furnished with an ingenious Compass-dial, presented (1890) by W. Connal, Esq. of Solsgirth, Dollar, on which are shown the various objects of interest that can be seen, and their direction.

In the lower valley to the W. the outline of the ancient *King's Gardens* and the Round Hill called the *King's Knot*, can still be traced in the grass. Beyond them is the *King's Park*, now a public recreation ground. To these Lindsay of the Mount, friend of James V., alludes in the lines—

> "Adieu, fair Snawdon,[1] with thy towers high,
> Thy Chapel Royal, Park, and Table Round."

---

[1] "For Stirling's tower
Of yore the name of Snowdoun claims."
SCOTT.

Beside the *High School*, near Greyfriars Ch., is an old house with date 1530, a pair of tailor's scissors, and the following inscription:—

> Erected in honour of Robert Spettal, Taylor to King James the Fourth, Donor of the Hospital in this Burgh for relief of decayed Tradesmen. "The liberal man deviseth liberal things."

At the foot of Baker St., and at the N. end of the Square are the **Corporation Buildings**, with a spire, and a large figure of Wallace over the entrance. The **County Buildings** (1874-75) are near the station; and the *Public Halls* (1881-83) are behind the Castle Rock.

The *Old Bridge* of Stirling, long the only access to the N. from the S., is of great antiquity, but the *Battle of Stirling Bridge*, 1297, was fought at a wooden bridge, situated 1 m. farther up the river, all trace of which has disappeared. The river is now crossed also by a modern bridge of 5 arches, and by 2 railway bridges side by side.

Stirling is a good starting-point for innumerable **Excursions** (see Rtes. 26-28 and 35-39), but **Bridge of Allan** ✲ (p. 205), 3 m. N., reached by railway or tramway, is a pleasanter place to stay.

ROUTE 26.

Stirling to Loch Lomond by Callander, the Trossachs, and Loch Katrine.

This rte. may be done daily in summer as a circular tour from Glasgow in about 10 hours, or from Edinburgh in about 12 hours (Rtes. 19, 25, 26, 23). From Edinburgh the round is more quickly done the reverse way.

From Stirling to **Dunblane** (in Perthshire) see Rte. 38.

The line becomes single at Dunblane, turns W. and crosses the Ardoch Burn to

8¾ m. **Doune Stat.** ✲, a town noted for its *Fairs* of cattle and sheep, driven from the western Highlands.

The **Castle** (visible on the l. just before arrival at the stat.) is one of the grandest relics of Scottish baronial architecture. Whatever the date of its foundation, it owes its present plan and strength to Murdoch Duke of Albany. After his execution (1424) it was forfeited to the Crown, and James IV. settled it upon his wife Margaret. She married thirdly Lord Methven, a descendant of the Dukes of Albany, and appointed the younger brother of her husband constable of it for life. The office then became hereditary, and now belongs to his descendant, the Earl of Moray. In 1745-6 the castle was held for Prince Charlie by Macgregor of Glengyle, to whom were confided the prisoners taken at Falkirk, including a number of the Edinburgh University Volunteers (among them Home, the author of *Douglas*), who escaped by letting themselves down the walls by twisting their bedclothes into ropes. The situation of the castle is admirably chosen, on a triangular piece of ground, washed on 2 sides by the Teith and Ardoch, while the 3rd is protected by a deep moat. It is in form an oblong, enclosing a large court, and with towers at the external angles. The buildings are of various dates, but no architectural details of beauty or importance remain. The walls of the great tower are 10 ft. thick, and built with cement. The most modern part is the interior tower, containing the kitchen and dining-hall. In 1883 a partial restoration of the building was carried out.

The reader of "Waverley" will remember that it was in this fortress that the hero of the tale was confined by the Highlanders.

The *Bridge of Doune* was built in 1535, as its inscription informs us, by Robert Spittal, tailor to Margaret, queen of James IV., the same who founded Spittal's Hospital in Stirling. (See p. 160.)

Blair Drummond, 1¾ m. S., is the seat of Col. Home-Drummond.

1 m. S.W. of Doune are *Deanston Ho.* (Sir John Muir, Bt.) and *Village*, where, since 1785, cotton mills have been established. James Smith of Deanston, long manager of the works (d. 1850), is well known for the system of "Thorough Drainage," which he contributed to introduce. Water-wheels of great power are turned by the Teith.

Leaving Doune, the rly. passes the Braes of Doune on the rt., having for their highest point **Uam Var** (2179 ft.), which the stag in the "Lady of the Lake" crossed.

10 m. rt. *Doune Lodge* (Earl of Moray).

11 m. l. *Lanrick Castle*, the seat of R. Jardine, Esq., succeeded at 14 m. by *Cambusmore* (J. B. Baillie Hamilton, Esq.), where Prince Charlie once slept a night, and where Sir W. Scott often resided as a youth, the guest of the Buchanan family, gathering lore for the "Lady of the Lake." The rly. here crosses the *Keltie*, the very name of which is sufficient to remind the traveller that he is on the borders of the Highlands. Straight in front rises the giant peak of **Ben Ledi** ("the Hill of God)" to the height of 2875 ft.

16 m. **CALLANDER Stat.** ✲ Callander is an overgrown village, with numerous villas and lodgings for visitors, near the junction of the Leny from Loch Lubnaig with the Teith from Loch Vennachar. It has of late years become of importance as the nearest rly. stat. to the Trossachs, Lochs Vennachar, Achray, and Katrine, and to the most beautiful scenery in this part of Scotland, so that it is animated and bustling enough in summer.

The situation is far from commonplace; to appreciate it stand on the bridge over the Teith and face upstream. Above (rt.) rises the *Craig* of Callander, a well-wooded hill; and in front is the grand outline of *Ben Ledi*, which is nowhere seen to greater advantage.

The "Lady of the Lake" is an almost essential companion in all the

EXCURSIONS:—

See Map, p. 168.

(1) Walk to "*Bracklinn's thundering wave*," a fall on the Keltie, 1½ m. N.E. above the village.

[A track up the Keltie (striking l. ¼ m. before the fall) leads in 8 m. to *Auchinner Lo.*, where a carriage can be met to drive down by "*lone Glen Artney's hazel shade*" to Comrie or Crieff (pp. 209, 213).]

(2) Ascent of **Ben Ledi**, 2875 ft.

The easiest point to start from is *Coilantogle*, 2½ m. (below), whence the summit is about 3 m. N.W. The descent may be made to the Pass of Leny or to Glen Finlas and Brig of Turk (p. 163).

(3) Drive W. to **The Trossachs** and **Loch Katrine** (p. 163).

(4) Drive S. to **Lake of Menteith** (p. 167) 7 m. and **Aberfoyle** 11 m., whence visit **Loch Ard** (p. 168). Return by private hill road (with fine views) to the *Trossachs Hotel* 16¼ m., and *Callander*, 24½ m.

(5) Drive E. to **Doune** (p. 161) by the l. bank of the Teith (8 m.); return by rt. bank, 17 m.

(6) Drive W. to the gate of *Invertrossachs Ho.* (G. A. Cox, Esq.) [see below], by the rt. bank of the Teith, the Hydro. Estab., and the S. side of Loch Vennachar, 5 m.

(7) Drive N.W. by the **Pass of Leny,** the E. side of **Loch Lubnaig, Strathyre** (9 m.), and *Kingshouse Inn* to **Balquhidder** (with *Rob Roy's Grave*) and **Loch Voil**, 13 m. (see p. 169). Returning, cross the *Balvaig* as it issues from Loch Voil, and keep the hilly road on its rt. bank to Strathyre (p. 169).

In summer there are about 6 coaches daily to, and 4 coaches from **The Trossachs.**

The booking-office is at the stat.

The coach leaves the village at its W. end, approaches rt. the grounds of *Leny Ho.* (J. Buchanan Hamilton, Esq.), and turns left at 1 m. *Kilmahog*, where the Loch Earn road falls in from Loch Lubnaig and the Pass of Leny, which is only 1 m. distant. Having crossed the Leny, on l. is the old farmhouse of *Bochastle*, and conspicuous on the opposite side of the Teith valley is the *Hydro. Estab.*, burnt down 7th Nov. 1893. At 2½ m. is **Coilantogle Ford**—"Clan Alpine's outmost guard"—at the outlet of Loch Vennachar, where the combat took place between Fitz-James and Roderick Dhu. The ford is now superseded by a bridge.

At the end of Loch Vennachar are the *Great Sluices* of the Glasgow Waterworks (p. 165), erected so that a regular flow of water may be maintained in the River Teith in dry as well as wet seasons.

The amount of compensation water which the Glasgow Water Commissioners are bound, by Act of Parliament, to send down the river daily is 40,000,000 gallons.

Loch Vennachar, "the Loch of the Fair Valley," so well described in the "Lady of the Lake," is 4 m. in length and ¾ m. in breadth, and serves as a fitting introduction to the superior beauties of Loch Achray.

On the opposite shore is the house of *Invertrossachs* (G. A. Cox, Esq., Dundee), the residence of Queen Victoria, Sept. 1869, for 10 days. Pearls of considerable beauty and value have been fished up from the shallows of this loch, chiefly near its outlets.

Passing on rt. (6 m.) the waterfall of Miltown, the road strays away from the loch, leaving *Lanrick Mead* between it and the water. This was the trysting-place of the Clan Alpine, summoned by "the fiery cross."

"The muster-place be Lanrick mead."

Ben Venue now becomes more and more visible in front.

At 7 m. is the clachan of **Duncraggan,** where Angus had to leave his father's funeral and his widowed mother to carry on the fiery cross. In front rises Ben A'an.

[Rt. is the opening of *Glen Finlas*, the subject of one of Sir W. Scott's earliest contributions to the Border Minstrelsy. 1 m. up the glen is the cataract (referred to in the "Lady of the Lake"):—

"Whose waters their wild tumult toss,
Adown the black and craggy boss
Of that huge cliff, whose ample verge
Tradition calls the Hero's Targe."

By following the Finlas the *pedestrian* will find a choice of 3 valleys, viz. Glen Finlas to the W., leading over high hills to Loch Doine and Loch Voil; Glen Main, up which a track leads by Glen Buckie to Balquhidder 11 m. (p. 169); and Glen Casaig (rt.) over *Ben Vane* (2685 ft.) to Strathyre (p. 169).]

There is a rough road S. from here to Aberfoyle, 4½ m., joining the driving road (p. 167), in 2 m.

Just beyond Duncraggan the *Finlas* is crossed by the **Brig of Turk.** Here Fitz-James had outdistanced all his fellow huntsmen :—

"And when the Brigg of Turk was won,
The headmost horseman rode alone."

The road, made entirely since Sir Walter first visited the district, now passes through a wood of oaks upon the N. shore of **Loch Achray,** a very lovely piece of water 1¼ m. long by ¼ m. broad, its shores clothed with copse to the water's edge. Upon its N. shore stands the *Trossachs Church*, a modern Gothic building, and beyond (rt.) is

8¼ m. **Trossachs Hotel** ✲, a large gloomy château-like building with pinnacled turrets. It was erected in 1852 by Lady Willoughby d'Eresby, in place of an inn called in Gaelic *Ardcheanochrochan = head height of the knoll.*

Fine views of Loch Achray, Ben A'an, and Ben Venue are to be obtained by ascending the hill behind the hotel and by taking the private road (*Coach twice daily*) which runs round the W. end of the loch and over to Aberfoyle 5¼ m. (p. 167).

It must have been in one of the dells near the head of Loch Achray, in full view of Ben Venue, that Fitz-James's chase ended, by the death of the "gallant grey."

The *Ascent* of *Ben A'an* (1800 ft.) may be made from the Trossachs, the path commencing close to the hotel.

The road to Loch Katrine (1¼ m.), on quitting the hotel, soon enters the gorge of **The Trossachs** ("Rugged country"). This gorge extends from Loch Achray to Loch Katrine, between the mountains of Ben A'an (1800 ft.) on rt. and Ben Venue (2393 ft.) on l. It is a rugged labyrinth of mounds and rocks, covered with the richest vegetation of oaks and pensile birch and rowans, among which the road winds in and out, up and down, and at each turn presents a fresh view of the grand crags of the two mountains above mentioned. The road runs out of sight of the *Achray Water*, which escapes from Loch Katrine and up which there is a capital walk to *Bealach-nam-Bo* ("Pass of the Cattle"), lying nearly 1 m. W. of the steamboat pier.

["No visitor to the Trossachs should omit to visit this Pass, within an hour's walk of the hotel, and offering by far the grandest scenery in this district. To visit it, the tourist on foot may pass from the hotel round the head of Loch Achray, cross the Achray Water by a bridge, then turn to the rt., and pass (by sufferance only) through Achray farm, where a bridge will carry him over the stream which descends from Ben Venue, after which he will find a pleasant path along the elevated bank of the Achray Water, followed by a somewhat marshy way through stony meadows, and thus he will reach the *sluice* at the E. end of Loch Katrine. From the sluice the walk must be continued parallel to the lake side, but separated from it by rocky swells (some of the 'rocks, mounds, and knolls, confusedly hurled,' which Fitz-James saw); in fact it is impossible to walk by the side of the lake. The dell of the Bealach-nam-bo is now before the tourist, with the great cliffs of Ben Venue to the l., the rocky swells to the rt., and the narrow cleft, 'which yawns like a gash on warrior's breast,' high in front. The ascent to the cleft is steep, but not very troublesome. On the ground there are numerous blocks which have fallen from the cliffs, some of large dimensions. The whole scene is very grand. Of the birch-trees, which Scott particularly mentions, very few remain. After passing through the cleft, a shoulder of Ben Venue is reached, about 1000 ft. above the lake. . . . The utility of the Bealach-nam-bo as a cattle-pass is thus explained. Suppose cattle to be driven from the S. end of Loch Lomond to Inversnaid and Stronachlachar. They could not then proceed to Loch Achray by the lake side of Loch Katrine, because there is no possibility of passing the cliffs. . . . By rising to the head of the Bealach-nam-bo, and descending to the Achray water, all difficulties were avoided."—Sir G. B. AIRY.

The top of **Ben Venue** (2393 ft.), which may be ascended from Bealach-nam-bo, commands Ben Lomond, Ben More of Glen Dochart, and other mountains of Breadalbane.]

The first view of Loch Katrine is only of a contracted reach, a projecting crag concealing the main basin.

A rough cart-road, not passable for carriages, runs along the N. side of the lake to *Glengyle* at the W. end, whence a track continues to Inverarnan, at the head of Loch Lomond (17 m.). No one has seen the real beauties of the loch and shore who has not traversed this road for a mile to the **"Silver Strand,"** the scene of the meeting of Fitz-James and the fair Ellen. The steamer does not go near it.

A Steamer, the "*Rob Roy*," with the Macgregors' motto, *S'rioghail mo dhream* ("Royal is my clan"), round the wheel, plies between the E. end and Stronachlachar (6 m.) 4 times daily in summer. A Coach runs twice daily from this steamboat pier to Aberfoyle, 6½ m. (p. 167).

Embarking at a curious rustic pier, the traveller finds himself upon **Loch Katrine,** a sheet of water 8 m. long, by 1 m. broad at its widest part and deriving its name according to Scott from the *Caterans* or freebooters who frequented its shores in olden times. The E. end, forming a little basin by itself, is lovely in the extreme, but after 1 m. the loch becomes tame. There is a charming view as the steamer makes its way through a narrow channel into the open:—

"Where, gleaming with the setting sun,
One burnished sheet of living gold,
Loch Katrine lay beneath him rolled,
In all her length far winding lay,
With promontory, creek, and bay,
And islands that, empurpled bright,
Floated amid the livelier light,
And mountains, that like giants stand,
To sentinel enchanted land.
High on the south huge Ben Venue
Down on the lake in masses threw
Crags, knolls, and mounds confusedly hurl'd,
The fragments of an earlier world;
A wildering forest feather'd o'er
His ruined sides and summit hoar,
While, on the north, through middle air,
Ben A'an heaved high his forehead bare."

At **Ellen's Isle** the loch widens out. It was once the cattle-pen, shambles, and larder of the Clan Macgregor, who hid here their stolen booty of flocks and herds, and guarded it by a flotilla of boats against all comers.

On the N. side is the **Silver Strand**; on the S., at the base of Ben Venue, is Coir-nan-Uriskan or *The Goblin's Cave*, where Douglas hid his daughter when he took her from Roderick Dhu's island. Still higher on the mountain side is the Bealach-nam-bo, or Pass of the Cattle—the gap through which the Macgregors drove their stolen herds (above).

Such a local habitation and a name have all these spots, that it is hard to persuade oneself that they have attained their celebrity from the creations of one man. It is interesting, however, to remember that Wordsworth's poems and his sister Dorothy's most graphic journal, descriptive of their adventurous visits to this neighbourhood, were written years before the appearance of the "Lady of the Lake."

As the steamer advances, the peak of Ben Lomond comes into sight on the l., and soon afterwards a row of shafts rising one behind the other from the water's edge over the hill marks the commencement of the aqueduct of the **Glasgow Waterworks.** By means of them 40,000,000 gallons of pure bright water are daily conveyed to Glasgow by tunnels or aqueducts, through the mountains in the first instance, then parallel to Loch Chon, the distance being 34 m. The number of tunnels on the route is 70, of varying lengths up to 2650 yards, and the total cost of this public-spirited scheme was about £1,500,000. Loch Katrine, in addition to its beauty, may thus boast of forming one of the finest reservoirs in the world. The surface of the lake has been raised about 5 ft. by penning up the outlet of its waters. Lochs Vennachar and Drunkie share indirectly in the water contribution, for they supply the Teith, as compensation for the water taken away for Glasgow. The works were the masterpiece of J. F. Bateman, Esq., C.E., and were partially opened by the Queen and Prince Albert in 1859. Owing to the purity and softness of the water, an immense saving has been effected in the domestic economy of the city of Glasgow. As this aqueduct was found insufficient for the water-supply of the rapidly increasing city of Glasgow, a duplicate aqueduct was constructed (1893-5) at the cost of £1,000,000. It follows a line, somewhat parallel to the other, is about 23½ m. long, and is of sufficient size to discharge 70,000,000 gallons per day. This, in addition to the 40,000,000 gallons discharged by the original aqueduct, makes a total of 110,000,000 gallons per day (cf. p. 150).

There is a splendid view W. of the Mts. across Loch Lomond before the steamer reaches

Stronachlachar ("Point of the mason") **Pier** ✲, 2½ m. from the head of the loch.

[At the head of the loch is *Glengyle*, once a stronghold of the Macgregors; and on the *Black Island*, between that and Stronachlachar, is their ancient burying ground, in which Sir Chas. Macgregor, who fell in Burmah, was buried. The clan was proscribed by an Act of Privy Council, April 3, 1603. The Act of outlawry was reversed by Charles II., 1663, in consideration of the services they had rendered to Montrose, but was renewed by William III., 1693. Their legal rights were finally restored by George II., 1755.]

Coaches are in waiting to convey passengers to Inversnaid on Loch Lomond, 5 m., to meet the steamer on that loch (Rte. 23). The road is highly picturesque, and very good, with the exception of a somewhat breakneck zigzag descent before Inversnaid. Loch Katrine is 364 ft. above sea-level, while Loch Lomond is only 23 ft.

½ m. l., the road (rough) from Aberfoyle, by Lochs Ard and Chon (p. 168), falls in. Beyond, l. is *Loch Arklet*, 1 m. long.

At 4 m. (rt.) in the descent down Glen Arklet stood the cottage where Helen Macgregor, Rob Roy's wife, is said to have been born. The ruins of a *fort* built to overawe the clan still remain.

5 m. **Inversnaid Pier** ✲ and *Waterfall*, abt. 3 m. from Tarbet and 4½ m. from the head of Loch Lomond (see p. 154).

ROUTE 27.

Stirling to Balloch (Loch Lomond) by Forth and Clyde Rly. N.B.R.

30¾ m. 4 trains daily in 1½-2 hrs.

The *Forth and Clyde Rly.* connects the two great central rivers of Scotland, and runs in the wide strath between the Gargunnock, Fintry, and Campsie Hills on the S., and the advanced posts of the Highland ranges on the N. Leaving Stirling, the line turns sharply round to the l., underneath the Castle rock, and follows the rt. bank of the Forth, passing rt. the isolated *Craigforth Hill* (of ironstone), and l. *Touch*, the seat of Sir Alan H. Seton-Steuart, Bt.

6 m. **Gargunnock Stat.** This name (*Caerguineach*) means a conical fort, and relates to the Peel of Gargunnock, long since swept away, which was held by the English for some time against the attacks of Wallace, who was encamped on Keir Hill. Beyond

9 m. **Kippen Stat.** are seen l. the *Fintry Hills,* a picturesque series of trap hills, of the same geological age as the Campsie Fells, and separated from them by the *Endrick Water.*

13 m. **Port of Menteith Stat.** This is the nearest stat. to the *Lake of Menteith,* the only "Lake" in Scotland, 3 m. N. (Rte. 28). 1 m. N. is *Cardross* (Capt. H. D. Erskine).

15¾ m. **Buchlyvie Stat.** ✲ [The rly. to Aberfoyle (Rte. 24), opened in 1882, here branches off rt.] The line, which has been gradually ascending, soon reaches the highest point between the Forth and Clyde. The country all round is uninteresting, and rather barren, but the distant peaks of the Highlands are frequently seen. At

19¾ m. **Balfron Stat.** the line of the Glasgow Waterworks is crossed on its way from Loch Katrine. The village (1½ m. l.) is prettily situated on the Endrick Water, a considerable stream rising in the Fintry Hills, and flowing into Loch Lomond.

The line to *Killearn, Campsie,* etc., strikes off l. (Rte. 24) before we reach

22 m. **Gartness Stat.** The Endrick Water is crossed to

23½ m. **Drymen Stat.** The village is 1½ m. N., and 1 m. W. of it is *Buchanan Cas.,* seat of the Duke of Montrose, a modern house amid fine grounds and woods. It contains 2 portraits of the great Marquis of Montrose, respectively by Jamesone and Dobson (cf. pp. 254, 270).

1¾ m. W. of the stat. is *Kilmaronock Ch.,* near which is the site of "*Maronnan's Cell*" (mentioned in the "Lady of the Lake"), where the Culdee St. Maronoch dwelt. A pleasant driving road leads S.E. to Milngavie, see p. 150.

26½ m. **Caldarvan Stat.** 1 m. N. is *Caldarvan Ho.* (R. D. Mackenzie, Esq.).

29½ m. **Jamestown,** where are some of the largest printworks in Scotland.

30¼ m. **Balloch Stat.** ✲, the junc. with the line from Glasgow and Dumbarton (Rte. 23).

30¾ m. **Balloch Pier Stat.,** on Loch Lomond (see p. 152).

ROUTE 28.

Stirling to Inversnaid (Loch Lomond) by the Lake of Menteith, Aberfoyle, and Loch Ard.

Omitting the *Lake of Menteith*—the only sheet of water in Scotland called a "*Lake*"—Aberfoyle can be reached by rail *via Buchlyvie* (Rtes. 27 and 24), 21½ m., in ¾ hr.

The Port and Lake of Menteith, Aberfoyle, and Loch Ard are all in Perthshire.

Stirling to Aberfoyle by road is 19 m., Aberfoyle to Inversnaid 15½ m. No coach. *There is a coach between Aberfoyle and Loch Katrine.*

The **Port of Menteith** ✲, on the N. shore of the lake, with a Church, beside which is the burial vault of the Grahams of Gartmore, and a hotel, from which boats can be hired for visiting the islands, is 4 m. N. of the station of that name (above). Accordingly a carriage must be ordered from the hotel to be at the station, or the tourist may drive from Stirling.

The road from Stirling runs N.W. up the rt. bank of the Forth, which it crosses (2½ m.) beyond *Craigforth Hill.* It then keeps up the Teith valley, passing rt. (4½ m.) *Ochtertyre* (C. M. Dundas, Esq., R.N.), formerly the residence of Mr. John Ramsay, the friend of Burns and Scott, to (6 m.) *Blair Drummond* (Col. Home Drummond), and *Kincardine Ch.* [Here a road leads N. in 2 m. to *Doune* (p. 161).] The Teith is now left. The road goes through the village of *Thornhill* (9 m.), and passes l. *Blairhoyle Ho.* and *Rednock Ho.* (Rev. H. A. G. Sheppard), with the fragment of an old castle, before reaching the Port of Menteith, 15 m.

[At Rednock a road leads N. by *Loch Rusky* in 6 m. to *Callander* (p. 161).]

The **Lake of Menteith** is $1\frac{1}{2}$ m. long by 1 m. broad and has 3 islands, on the largest of which are the picturesque Gothic ruins of the *Priory of Inchmahome*, "Isle of St. Colmoc," also called the "Island of Rest," founded for Austin Canons Regular in 1238 by Walter Comyn of Badenoch. He acquired this property and was made Earl of Menteith upon marrying (1230) Isabella, elder daughter of the 3rd earl; on his death (1258) the earldom passed to Walter Stewart (brother of the High Steward of Scotland), who had married Mary the younger daughter.[1]

In the Ch. David II. was married in 1363 to his second wife, Margaret, daughter of Sir John Logie. The style of the building is Early Pointed. The remains consist of part of the choir, the Tower arch, and 2 arches of the nave. There appears to have been an aisle on this side which has disappeared, though the light and graceful arches which separated it from the nave are still standing. The mouldings of the W. Entrance, which is deeply recessed, are exceedingly beautiful. The chancel contains 2 tombs, one with effigies in full relief of Walter Stewart (d. 1295), in complete armour, with crossed legs and triangular shield, bearing the Stewart arms, and of his Countess (d. 1286) by his side, with her arm round his neck; the other with an effigy of Sir John Drummond (d. 1300), a liberal benefactor of the Priory—both in tolerable preservation.

After the battle of Pinkie, Sept. 1547, and in consequence of the English invasion, Mary Queen of Scots, then aged 5, was sent to this island as to a place of inaccessible security, and stayed here until July 1548. She was then stealthily removed to Dumbarton, where she embarked for France. A little garden is shown on the island, called "Queen Mary's Bower," said to have been tended by herself, and to have remained as she left it.[2] Noble old planes and Spanish chestnut trees form an avenue over a terrace called "The Nun's Walk."

[1] See "The Red Book of Menteith," by Sir Wm. Fraser, C.B. (1880).

[2] Read "Queen Mary's Child Garden," by Dr. John Brown ("Rab").

The ruined Castle on *Tulla Island* was the principal residence of the Grahams, Earls of Menteith, 1427-1694. The date of its erection is unknown. It is much overgrown with rubbish and underwood. The third or *Dog Island* was used for kennels.

Skirting the base of a craggy line of hills the traveller reaches in 4 m.

19 m. **Aberfoyle** ✡ (cf. Rte. 24). The "clachan," where Frank Osbaldistone and Bailie Nicol Jarvie repaired to meet Rob Roy, has been levelled with the ground. In its place a tidy village of châlet-like houses with red tile roofs—a favourite country resort of summer visitors from Glasgow—has grown up. Through the village flows the Laggan, which is formed by the joint streams of the Duchray and the Avondhu ("Black Water"), and which a little lower down becomes the Forth. The scenery of the clachan, without being grand, is highly broken and romantic, and cannot fail to give delight, especially when invested with the interest of Scott's well-known novel of "Rob Roy."

[There is a splendid drive N. over the hill to the Trossachs Hotel, $5\frac{1}{4}$ m., with fine views as we ascend of Loch Ard and Ben Lomond, and as we descend of Lochs Drunkie, Vennachar, and Achray.

This is a private road open to carriages upon payment of toll, but, since an accident occurred to the coach, cyclists are not admitted. There are 2 coaches each way daily in summer to Loch Katrine pier. It is a steep zigzag ascent. At the top of the hill ($1\frac{1}{2}$ m.) l. are the Aberfoyle Slate Quarries. From above Loch Drunkie (rt.) the pedestrian may descend direct to Duncraggan (p. 163). The road keeps round the W. end of Loch Achray, and joins the Trossachs and Callander road just at the Hotel (p. 163).]

For a walk of about 5 hours to

Rowardennan on Loch Lomond, see p. 154.

2 m. S. is *Gartmore*, the family seat of the *Grahams*.

$2\frac{1}{2}$ m. S.W. is *Duchray Castle* (Rev. H. A. G. Sheppard). This neighbourhood is also referred to in the "Lady of the Lake":—

"In Rednoch courts no horsemen wait,
No banner waved on Cardross gate,
On Duchray's towers no beacon shone,
Nor scared the herons from Loch Con."

$1\frac{1}{2}$ m. W. of Aberfoyle is the lovely **Loch Ard.**

It is a bright and placid basin imbedded in surrounding woods, over which l. rises the graceful form of Ben Lomond, and to the rt. that of Benochrie. The best view is the first that is obtained, where a small portion only of the loch, nearly separated from the main body of the water by a wooded promontory, is seen. From beneath a perpendicular rock over the road a remarkable echo is given off.

The road goes round the E. end and along the N. side through the **Pass of Aberfoyle**, where Helen Macgregor discomfited the king's troops. It then leaves the loch for $\frac{3}{4}$ m., where the contraction takes place, and rejoins it where the loch proper opens out; then for 2 m. it keeps beside the water's edge, passing several pleasing country residences. On a tiny island on the S. side are the foundations of a castle inhabited by Murdac, the 2nd Duke of Albany, beheaded 1425. *St. Malloch's* is another small island in the S.W. corner, which once had a chapel. *Lobelia dortmanni* flourishes in this loch. Towards the W. end (rt.) are

The *Falls of Ledard*, 2 picturesque cataracts some little way above the road — the first, about 12 feet in height and the second 50 ft. From them Sir Walter took his description of the *Waterfall* in "Waverley," beside which Flora M'Ivor sang to her harp.

At the W. end of Loch Ard ($4\frac{1}{2}$ m. from Aberfoyle) the path to Rowardennan strikes l. (p. 154). A line of towers on the S. side of the valley marks the course of the Glasgow Water Supply. The road becomes very rough for a few miles.

6 m. **Loch Chon,** with its little companion *Loch Dhu*, is more rocky and wild than Loch Ard, and beautifully wooded with birch, ash, and other forest trees. A precipitous hill rises on the S.W., one of the outliers of the Ben Lomond range. Beyond the N. end the road (9 m.) crosses the culvert of the Glasgow waterworks, *Loch Arklet* is seen in front, and at 11 m. the road from Stronachlachar ($\frac{1}{2}$ m. rt.) is joined. See p. 165 for road (l.) to

$15\frac{1}{2}$ m. **Inversnaid** ✲ (cf. p. 154).

ROUTE 29.

Callander to Oban by Killin Junc. (for Loch Tay) Tyndrum, Loch Awe, and Loch Etive.

This is a single line worked upon the tablet system. 71 m. in about $2\frac{3}{4}$ hours. There are through carriages from Glasgow and Edinburgh *via* Stirling. (See Rtes. 25 and 26.)

The *Callander and Oban Rly.* (Cal. Rly.), completed 1881, leads through some of the most beautiful scenery in Scotland, in variety only rivalled by that on the West Highland Rly. (Rte. 81).

Leaving Callander the Leny is crossed. Left is the meeting of the Leny and the Teith, and (across the Teith) the *Hydro. Estab.*; rt. are the *Leny Feus* and *Leny Ho.* (J. Buchanan Hamilton, Esq.).

At $2\frac{1}{2}$ m. the line threads the romantic **Pass of Leny**, through which river and railway and road have barely room to pass, between the roots of Ben Ledi on the l., and a lower range on the rt. The scenery of this neighbourhood is described in "The Legend of Montrose," and in the fiery-cross scene of "The Lady of the Lake." $\frac{3}{4}$ m. beyond the Pass rt. is a tiny ch.-yd., the site of *St. Bride's Chapel*, mentioned in "The Lady of the Lake," which lies near the S. end of *Loch Lubnaig*—"the crooked loch," so called from an obtuse angle at the middle—4 m. long by $\frac{1}{2}$ m. broad.

The rly. is carried along the W. and pathless shore of the loch under a rock which has to be constantly watched for falls of stones. The high road runs along the E. side.

Half-way up across the loch is *Ardchullarie*, where Bruce, the Abyssinian traveller (p. 156), wrote part of his book.

[Up the Glen behind and down *Glen Ample* with *Ben Each* (2660 ft.) *Stuc-a-Chroin* (3189 ft.) and *Ben Voirlich* (3224 ft.) rt. to Lochearnhead is a pleasant walk of 8 m.]

1 m. beyond the head of the loch is

$8\frac{3}{4}$ m. **Strathyre Stat.** ✲, a place of summer resort, whither young Angus carried the fiery signal.

"Ben Ledi saw the cross of fire
It glanced like lightning up Strathyre."

There is a fountain here, as a memorial of Dugald Buchânan, the Gaelic poet and evangelist, who was a native. (See p. 240.)

[On l. a (carriage) bridge crosses the river, offering a short and picturesque route for those who intend to make an excursion to Loch Voil and Balquhidder, 4 m. (see below).]

$10\frac{3}{4}$ m. **King's House Inn** ✲. The train stops on notice being given previously. It is situated at the opening of the valley of *Balquhidder*.

[2 m. up the valley of the *Balvaig* (l.) is the neat village of **Balquhidder**, and the modern parish ch. on a knoll commanding a lovely view of *The Braes of Balquhidder*—the subject of Tannahill's pretty song — and of *Loch Voil*, with the ornamental seat and woods of *Stronvar* (J. Carnegie, Esq.). In the well-kept ch.-yd., shaded by yews and planes, in front of the roofless ivy-clad *Old Ch.*, is **"Rob Roy's" Grave** (1660-1734).

"His tombstone is only distinguished by a rude attempt at the figure of a broad-sword."—SCOTT.

A stone on the rt. purports to be, as the inscription says, the gravestone of his son Colin; one on the l. belongs to his son Hamish, or James. It is a rough slab of slate, carved with a rude cross, on one side of it a sword, on the other a man in a kilt, bearing a shield, with a dog at his feet. On Colin's grave are the arms of the Macgregors—viz. a pine tree torn up by its roots, crossed by a sword piercing a crown, in allusion to the claims of royalty made by the chiefs of the clan. There is also in this burial-ground a rude old font, a stone with the sculptured figure of a Culdee priest. Here (1589) the clan Macgregor gathered round the head of the king's forester, which they had cut off, and swore to protect the murderers. (See Introd. to "Legend of Montrose.")

Balquhidder stands at the E. end of *Loch Voil*, a piece of water $3\frac{1}{2}$ m. long, and separated only by a small neck of land from the smaller picturesque *Loch Doine* to the W. From the bridge at the E. end of Loch Voil a fine view may be had in both directions, Ben Voirlich (3224 ft.) being conspicuous to the E.

From the bridge a road runs l. up the charming little valley of *Glen Buckie*, for about 3 m., to some farmhouses, and from it, at *Bailemore* ($2\frac{1}{2}$ m.), a *footpath* branches rt. to Glenfinlas and Brigg of Turk (p. 163), a very beautiful walk of about 4 hours in dry weather, but one which at other times had better not be attempted. The Pedestrian may also follow the driving road to Loch Doine, keeping on through the hills to the head of Loch Lomond (18 m., 6 hours' walk), or to the head of Loch Katrine at Glengyle (p. 164).]

$11\frac{3}{4}$ m. **Lochearnhead Stat.** (2 m. from the hamlet, hotel, and loch, p. 211).

Coach to Comrie (15 m.) daily. See Rte. 40.

The train winds round the hill-side, passing rt. *Edinchip* (Lady H. L. Macgregor). On the same side looking back *Stuc-a-Chroin* (3169 ft.) and *Ben Voirlich* (3224 ft.) are seen towering up. Below is seen the whole length of **Loch Earn** (6 m.)—with *St. Fillans* (p. 210) at its E. end, and the *Melville Monument* above Comrie in the distance—before we enter **Glen Ogle,** a wild glen ascended by a very steep incline, with rushing streams and threatening rocks l. Across the valley 2 roads older than the present excellent driving road may be traced along the hill side.

At 17 m. the watershed (950 ft.) is crossed. Beyond l. is a lonely tarn, and rt. the *Old Killin Stat.*, occasionally used, as there is no road from

19 m. **Killin Junc. Stat.**

[*Branch* rt. to

4 m. **Killin Stat.** ✲, and

5 m. *Steamer Pier* on Loch Tay (Rte. 43). This is a light line—the rails being laid without "chairs"—on a steep gradient.]

Looking back rt. a glimpse is caught of Loch Tay, with Ben Lawers range on its N. bank; in front up *Glen Dochart* are the twin peaks of **Ben More** (3843 ft.) and **Stobinian** (3827 ft.).

$22\frac{3}{4}$ m. **Luib Stat.** ✲

In the Inn here Wordsworth and his sister Dorothy spent the night of 5th Sept. 1803. "The servant was uncivil, because, forsooth! we had no wine."—D. W.

[The *Ascent of Ben More* may be made in about 2 hrs. from a point $1\frac{1}{2}$ m. W. of Luib or (steeper) from a point 2 m. E. of Crianlarich. From its central position this mountain commands one of the finest views in Scotland. Stobinian separated by a heavy dip rises behind it.]

The rly. continues up Glen Dochart, the scene of Hogg's "Spectre of the Glen." It skirts l. the foot of Ben More; while rt. is *Loch Dochart Ho.* (E. S. Place, Esq.), picturesquely situated across the river just after it has left *Loch Tubhair*, the E. portion of *Loch Dochart*, which is altogether $2\frac{1}{2}$ m. long, and has in its W. portion "one grove-like island" with a ruined *castle*.

"This building, which, on that beautiful evening, seemed to be wrapped up in religious quiet, we were informed had been raised for defence by some Highland chieftain. All traces of strength, or war, or danger are passed away, and in the mood in which we were we could only look upon it as a place of retirement and peace."—DOROTHY WORDSWORTH.

Beyond the loch the stream is called the *Fillan Water* and *Strathfillan* is entered at

29 m. **Crianlarich Stat.** ✲

[*Coaches* start twice daily for *Ardlui* (Loch Lomond), $8\frac{3}{4}$ m. S., by *Glen Falloch* (p. 154).]

Here the West High. Rly. from Glasgow to Fort-William has a stat. (p. 347) before it crosses this line and the river on 2 lofty viaducts.

The country now becomes very bleak. 2 m. farther on were the clachan and "Holy Pool" of *St. Fillan*—not to be confounded with St. Fillans on Loch Earn—in which epileptics and lunatics were ducked and left bound all night in the open air:—

"Saint Fillan's blessed well,
Whose spring can frenzied dreams dispel,
And the crazed brain restore."—SCOTT.

If found loosened in the morning they were considered curable. This mode of treatment is mentioned by Pennant as being practised as late as 1790. He adds that the patients were generally found in the morning relieved of all their troubles—by death.

At $32\frac{1}{2}$ m. (rt.), after passing the *Parish Ch.*, is the tiny *Free Ch.*, and between it and the rly is *Dalry* (*Dal-Righ*, "the King's Field"), celebrated for Robert Bruce's escape (1306).

After being defeated at Methven by Lord Pembroke, he was attacked here by John of Lorn (grandson of the Red Comyn, whom Bruce murdered at Dumfries), at the head of a swarm of Highlanders. One of these seized Bruce's mantle, and though mortally wounded held it so fast that Bruce was compelled to abandon it. The buckle which fastened it remains a trophy at Dunolly. Bruce skilfully withdrew his mailed warriors, whose armour baffled the assault of the wild Highlanders.

Left, we get a good view of the grand *Ben Laoigh* (Lui), "The hill of the calf," 3708 ft., on the slopes of which are the *Sources of the Tay*.

The Ascent from this side is very steep but is easily made from Dalmally (below).

34 m. **Tyndrum Stat.** ✲

There is another Stat. ½ m. N. on the West High. Rly. In the neighbourhood are lead mines belonging to the Marquis of Breadalbane, no longer worked.

[An excellent driving road strikes N. to *Bridge of Orchy*, 7 m., following the line of the W. High. Rly. (p. 347). There it leaves the railway, passes **Inveroran** ✲ 9½ m., at the S. end of *Loch Tulla*, and crosses the *Black Mount*, one of the finest deer forests in Scotland (Marquis of Breadalbane), and the dreary *Moor of Rannoch* at the height of 1500 ft. to **Kingshouse Inn** ✲, 19 m., whence one can go W. down *Glen Coe* to *Ballachulish*, 17 m. (p. 364); or S.W. in 14 m. to *Loch Etive Head* (pp. 364, 174); or E. (on foot) to *Loch Rannoch Stat.* (p. 348); or N. (on foot) by the *Devil's Staircase* to the head of Loch Leven 9 m. and Fort-William 22 m.]

Leaving Tyndrum we cross the border of Perthshire and enter Argyllshire. Passing the watershed 850 ft. and the little *Loch-an-Bhe* (l.), the train hurries down Glen Lochy. The giant steps on Ben Lui are soon seen l.; rt. we get a view up Glen Orchy; in front is the "Horseshoe" of **Ben Cruachan**, over which the highest point (3689 ft.) is just visible, but lost before we reach

46¼ m. **DALMALLY Stat.** ✲

The *Hotel* and the *Parish Ch.*, with apsidal end and square tower, picturesquely situated beside the river, are ¾ m. E. There are a P.O. and a couple of shops close to the stat. and numerous scattered houses and cottages but no village. This is a good halting-place for the following

EXCURSIONS :—

(1) To the **Monument** to Duncan Ban MacIntyre, the Gaelic poet (1724-1812),—1½ m. up the Inveraray road,—which commands a splendid view of Loch Awe, Kilchurn Castle, and the neighbouring mountains.

(2) Up **Glenorchy** to **Inveroran** (above) 15 m. (lovely but rough road), passing, 7 m., the **Falls of Orchy**.

(3) **Ascent of Ben Lui** (3708 ft.), 8 m., in 3½-4½ hrs.

Walk or drive to Socach farm 4 m. E. Thence an easy ascent, crossing over Ben Chleibh (3000 ft.). The view—N. over the Black Mount to Ben Nevis and the Cairngorms; W. to the Paps of Jura and Mull; S. to Ben Lomond, the Clyde, and Arran, and E. to Ben More, Ben Lawers, etc.—is not easily surpassed in Scotland.

(4) Coach daily by *Loch Awe*, to **Inveraray** (Loch Fyne), and **Tarbet** (Loch Lomond). [Rte. 77.]

Quitting Dalmally the rly. descends upon Loch Awe, and crosses the joint streams of the *Strae* and the *Orchy*. Rt. may be seen a handsome *Celtic Cross*, erected 1889 (Sydney Mitchell, archt.) to Duncan M'Laren (1800-86), Lord Provost of Edinburgh 1851-54, and M.P. for Edinburgh 1865-81. It occupies the site of the cottage in which he lived, "during his short school life," and has a medallion by D. W. Stevenson, R.S.A. Left is

Kilchurn Castle, a majestic ruin situated on a peninsula, and consisting of an oblong building, with a square keep, flanked by bartizans. It was spontaneously addressed in 1803 by Wordsworth in the lines :—

"Child of loud-throated war! the mountain stream
Roars in thy hearing; but thy hour of rest
Is come, and thou art silent in thy age."

It is best visited by boat from Loch Awe. The oldest part, including the dungeon, was built in 1440 by Sir John Campbell, Knight of Rhodes, ancestor of the Breadalbane family, or, according to legend, by his wife Lady Margaret during his absence in the East. The S. side is assigned to the 16th cent. The stair bears date 1621. The N. side (used as a barrack by the Hanoverian troops 1746) was erected by Ian Earl of Breadalbane 1693, and over the gateway are his arms with those of his wife. The property of his descendant the Marquis of Breadalbane now extends from the sea to beyond Aberfeldy, a distance of something like 100 miles. The top of one of the towers was blown down by the Tay Bridge gale (Dec. 1879), and turned completely over without being broken.

Many of these glens were in former times the property of the Macgregors, until dispossessed by the Campbells.

"Glenorchy's proud mountains, Kilchurn and her towers,
Glenstrae and Glenlyon no longer are ours."—*Macgregor's Gathering*, SCOTT.

Beyond the bridge a goods line leads rt. (1 m.) to the *Cruachan Granite Quarries* (Marquis of Breadalbane).

49 m. **Loch Awe Stat.** ✲, with a pier for the steamers on the loch to Portsonachan (7 m.), several times daily, and to Ford (22 m.) at the S. end.

[**Loch Awe** is one of the largest and most beautiful of the Scottish lochs, although the characteristic of most lochs of possessing the finest scenery at the head is here reversed, the head being comparatively tame and the foot magnificently grand. The researches of geologists, however, tell us that these positions have been changed, and that the S. end was once the foot.

"No one can ascend from the Sound of Jura to Kilmartin, and thence up the terraced valley of Loch Awe, without being convinced that this must have been the old outlet of the great valley of that loch." —GEIKIE.

Its length is 23 miles. The road from Dalmally to Ford ($25\frac{1}{2}$ m.) along its E. side, although hilly for 8 m., is excellent in every way. The view northwards from the steamer, between Loch Awe Stat. and Portsonachan, of the islands[1] in the foreground, and the enormous mass of Ben Cruachan in the background, constitutes one of the most striking scenes in the Highlands.

Sailing S. the steamer passes rt. *Innis Chonain* (Isle of Dogs), with a house erected by the Campbells of Blythswood, *Fraoch Eilean*, with the ruins of a castle of the Macnaughtons, the entrance to the *Pass of Brander* (p. 173), *Innishail*, with old ecclesiastical ruins and cemetery, and *Ardaneiseig Ho.* (J. S. Ainsworth, Esq.), well placed on a promontory.

Left are seen *Duncan MacIntyre's Monument* (p. 171), *Innistrynich Ho.* (W. C. Muir, Esq.), and, beyond, *Cladich Ho.* (J. C. Kay, Esq.), behind which the road to Inveraray ascends (Rte. 77), and *Ardvrecknish Ho.* (J. Thorpe, Esq.), with a little *Epis. Chapel* above it, before we reach

7 m. (rt.) †**Taychreggan** ✲ [Coach to *Kilchrenan, Glen Nant*, and *Taynuilt* (p. 173)], and (l.) †**Portsonachan** ✲ [Coach to *Blairgour Falls* 6 m.] Both places are favourite angling quarters, and there is a *ferry* here. The loch now becomes tamer though Ben Cruachan still remains in sight for a time.

At 13 m. l. are *Blairgour Falls*, the spray from which may be seen a long way off in wet weather; rt. is the mouth of the *River Avich* (p. 353).

At 15 m. l. is *Innis Chonell*, with the picturesque ruins of a castle which belonged to the Lords of Loch Awe. The proverb "It's a far cry to Loch Ow" was first used by a Campbell in trouble far from home, or by one in the security of home in defiance of his enemies, or to signify the extent of the Campbells' possessions. Beyond is †**Port-in-Sherrich** ✲, in front of which lies *Innis Sherrich* with an old chapel and cemetery.

The last reach of the loch is now

1 See Mr. P. G. Hamerton's "Isles of Loch Awe."

entered upon. l. is *Eredine Ho.* (Col. J. W. Malcolm, of Poltalloch), rt. *Innis Struire*, in the S.E. corner the shell of the old castle of *Finchairn*, and in the S.W. corner

22 m. **Ford**✲, whence coaches run to Oban (30 m.), p. 352, and to Ardrishaig (13½ m.) p. 350.]

The line keeps close to the shore of the loch. In ½ m. a beautiful little chapel—St. Conan's (Ch. of Scotland)—built by the Campbells of *Innis Chonain*, is passed rt. (scarcely seen), and beyond (l.), their island mansion. The loch and its islands are well seen before reaching

52 m. **Falls of Cruachan Stat.**, at which one or two trains stop. The Falls are close at hand rt. This is the best starting-point for the

Ascent of Ben Cruachan,[1] 3689 ft., abt. 3 hrs.

Keep up the W. side of the Cruachan Burn and do not leave it until the saddle between the peak and an outlier *Meall Cuanail*, 3004 ft., is quite open l. Then make for the saddle (2750 ft.), which has a tiny tarn, and thence up a rocky staircase to the top. There are grand precipices and corries on the N. side, and the *View*, especially W. to Oban, the Sea, and Mull, and N. up Loch Etive to the Glencoe giants, is particularly fine. The sharp W. peak (3611 ft.) may be visited if the descent is to be to Taynuilt. If to Dalmally the 3272 ft. E. peak—there are 7 peaks in all—may be visited, and a steep descent made to a glen leading to the Quarries (p. 172).

The solid walls of masonry and the viaduct beyond the station show the difficulties the engineers had to overcome as they approched the grand **Pass of Awe** or **Brander,** through which Loch Awe finds its sole exit. But though

"Ben Cruachan stands as fast as ever
Still downward foams the Awe's fierce
river" (SCOTT),

geologists say that

"the present outflow of the lake through the deep narrow gorge of the Pass of Brander is, comparatively speaking, recent."—GEIKIE.

The screes on the S. side rise with startling abruptness, casting a shade over the deep dark waters below. The most beautiful effects are produced in sunshine after rain, when numerous waterfalls and their reflections present a wonderful picture. To the N. rise the steep but less precipitous sides of Ben Cruachan. This locality is thus referred to by Scott in the "Highland Widow":—

"The tremendous mountain, Ben Cruachan, rushes down in all the majesty of rocks and wilderness to the lake, leaving only a pass in which, notwithstanding its extreme strength, the warlike clan of MacDougal of Lorn was almost destroyed by the sagacious Robert Bruce (1308)."

At 56 m. both road and rail cross the foaming Awe. Up the first burn E. is the best way to the W. peak of Ben Cruachan (3611 ft.), which soon comes into view looking back. The highest peak is not visible, and the whole mountain is best seen from the steamer on Loch Awe or Loch Etive. Passing rt. *Inverawe Ho.* (Mrs. Campbell of Dunstaffnage), we reach

58 m. **Taynuilt Stat.**✲, a growing little place for summer quarters. 1 m. N. at *Bonawe* where the Awe enters Loch Etive, which here contracts, there is a ferry across the loch to large *Granite Quarries*, and a *Pier* where the Loch Etive steamer (p. 174) calls. There a furnace for smelting ore brought from England, by means of charcoal fuel, was established 1753, but is now disused. Conspicuous on a hill l. of the stat. is a "stone erected to the memory of Lord Nelson by the Lorn Furnace workmen 1805"—the first Nelson monument.

EXCURSIONS :—

(1) A coach runs twice daily S.E. up the charming *Glen Nant* and over the

[1] For a particularly interesting description of "*Ben Cruachan*" (with illustrations) by William Douglas, see "Scottish Mountaineering Club Journal" for Jan. 1893.

hills—splendid view of Ben Cruachan—to 8 m. *Taychreggan*★ on Loch Awe opposite *Portsonachan* to which there is a *ferry.* At 6½ m. in *Kilchrenan* ch.-yd. is a block of red granite with a large claymore raised upon it, erected by the Duke of Argyll (1866) to "Cailean More, slain on the sreang of Lorne, A.D. 1294," his ancestor, from whom the chief of the clan is called MacCallum More (Son of great Colin). Behind it is an older defaced slab built into the ch. wall.

(2) The *Ascent of Ben Cruachan* (Taynuilt Peak) is made in abt. 3 hrs. by keeping up the *Cruiniche Burn*, which is 3 m. E. (cf. p. 173).

(3) A rough pleasing road (just driveable) leads S.W. by *Glen Lonan* and *Loch Nell* to *Loch Feochan* 12 m. and Oban 15 m. (p. 353).

(4) There is a good *walking* excursion, about 25 m., to Ballachulish. Cross the ferry and strike N.W. up Glen Salach, at the end of which, passing *Barcaldine House* (Mrs. Ogilvie), you reach Loch Creran; follow its S. shore to the loch head, and then keep the line of Glen Creran as far as Salachail, where you bear to the left; *or* crossing Loch Creran at Creagan ferry, keeping W. along its N. shore, recrossing at Shian ferry, and turning S. to Connel ferry (below) you may rejoin the train after a capital walk of fully 20 m.]

The rly. skirts (rt.) the grounds of *Aird's Bay House*, and reaches the S. shore of L. Etive, along which it runs as far as Connel Ferry. At

61½ m. **Ach-na-Cloich Stat.**, is a *ferry* across the loch to the ivy-covered *Ardchattan Priory*, so called from Caton, a follower of St. Columba, founded 1231 by the Macdougalls for Benedictine monks of the order of Valliscaulium, a reformed branch of the Cistercians, and destroyed in the 17th cent. by Colkitto. Robert Bruce held a Parliament here, one of the last at which the business was conducted in the Gaelic language. The ch. is E. Eng., and consists of a simple nave, without piers. In the interior are the tombs of Duncan and Dugald, former priors, with some curious sculptured figures, including one of Death, with a toad beneath the knees.

[Here the steamer (twice daily) sails for *Loch Etive Head* in connection with coaches (once each way) to Glen Coe and Ballachulish—one of the best expeditions in Scotland on a clear day.

Loch Etive is one of the longest of those fiords that indent the W. coast of Scotland—running inland some 16 m. in the direction of Glencoe. Before reaching Bonawe (p. 173) there is a fine view back of *Ben More* in Mull.

"Above Bonawe it is not like the same loch. For a couple of miles it is not wide, and it is so darkened by shadows, that it looks less like a strait than a gulf; huge overhanging rocks on each side ascending high."—J. WILSON.

The upper part of the loch in addition to Ben Cruachan, whose peaks and glens by looking back are seen to perfection, is girdled by (rt.) *Ben Starav* [3541 ft.], (l.) *Ben Trilleachan* (2752 ft.), *Ben Sguliard* (2807 ft.), and (in front), the imposing "*Shepherds of Etive*" and *Bidean-nam-Bian* (3756 ft.), the highest mountain in Argyllshire. (For road from *Loch Etive Head* to *Kingshouse Inn*✡, 14 m. and through *Glencoe* to *Ballachulish*, 29 m., see pp. 363, 364.)]

Skirting the shores of the loch, which are here low and flat, we reach

64¾ m. **Connel Ferry Stat.**✡, situated at the mouth or sea-opening of Loch Etive, which is not only contracted by the approximation of the opposite shores, but is also obstructed by a reef of rocks stretching two-thirds across, and at spring tides, during ebb, presents the phenomenon of a *Sea Cataract*, called the Ossianic *Falls of Lora*, pouring over the obstructive wall of rock 5 or 6 ft. high, with a tremendous roar.

"The greatest depth of the loch above these falls is 420 ft. At the falls themselves there is a depth of only 6 ft. at low water, while outside this barrier the soundings reach, at a distance of 2 m., 168 ft."—GEIKIE.

[Below the falls is the *ferry* by which *Ballachulish* (23 m.) is reached by carriage.

On the other side the road skirts Ardmucknish Bay, and in 2 m. passes a little rocky eminence called *Dun Macsniochan*, or the Fort of the Sons of Usnoth, surmounted by the remains of a vitrified fort. This is believed by some antiquaries to be the site of *Beregonium*, the old Pictish capital of this district, before it was occupied by the Scots. The rock has two peaks each surmounted by a vitrified wall; and a raised way, called Straidmhargaidh, "the market street," said to have been the principal street of the city, but which was more probably the work of Christian times, and connected with the small cemetery at the base of the cliff. The "Selma" of Ossian also claims a position on this spot. On the opposite promontory is *Lochnell Ho.*, the seat of A. A. L. Campbell, Esq. of Loch Nell.

At 3½ m. (rt.) is the ruined *Barcaldine Cas.*, built in 15th cent. by Sir Duncan Campbell of Glenorchy. A modern *Barcaldine Cas.* (A. G. Cameron, Esq., to whom the old castle belongs) stands near it. At *Shian Ferry*, 5 m., where the inlet of Loch Creran is crossed, the traveller leaves the district of Lorn and enters that of Appin. From the foot of Strath Appin the road keeps near the coast the greater part of the way to Ballachulish (cf. p. 363).]

We now come in sight (rt.) of *Dunstaffnage House*, the modern mansion of Sir Donald Campbell, and beyond it of the ruined **Dunstaffnage Castle** commanding the entry into the loch, —the seat of government of the Scots from about 500 A.D., till, after their union with the Picts under Kenneth Macalpin in 843, they found it necessary to have a capital in a more central situation. The *Coronation Stone*, now in Westminster Abbey, was used here before it was carried to Scone (p. 197). The belief that this stone, the "Lia Fail," carried sovereignty with it was at one time very strong, both in England and Scotland.

The castle afterwards became the stronghold of the Lords of Lorn, and was taken by Robert Bruce soon after his victory in the Pass of Awe. It stands upon a natural pedestal of pudding-stone or conglomerate rock, and the entrance is reached by a narrow staircase. The building is said to belong to the 13th cent., but, as it now stands, exhibits slight evidence of construction older than the 15th; it is of coarse masonry, and not picturesque. It is an irregular 4-sided structure, with a round tower at 3 of the angles, the remaining angle being also rounded. The circumference of the whole is about 400 ft., and the walls are in some places 66 ft. high and 10 ft. in thickness. On the castle wall are some of the brass guns which were fished up from one of the ships of the Spanish Armada sunk off Mull. The castle is the property of the Crown. The magnificent *View* from it of Ben Cruachan and other hills, including Ben Nevis, gives an interest to the spot not possessed by the ruins. There is an old chapel close by, which seems to date about a century later than the castle. It is the burial-place of Campbell of Dunstaffnage.

The rly. here separates from the old post road (which keeps nearer the coast), descends rapidly, makes a wide sweep to the S.W. and then suddenly turns N. Rt. the unsightly ruin-like walls of an unfinished Hydro-Estab. are painfully conspicuous, but a fine view is obtained (l.) of Oban Bay, the Island of Kerrera, and the Mts. of Mull, etc., as we approach

70¾ m. **Oban Stat.**

For **OBAN** ✡ and its numerous excursions see p. 352.

SECTION III.

EASTERN MIDLANDS AND CENTRAL HIGHLANDS—FORTH BRIDGE —FIFE—ST. ANDREWS—TAY BRIDGE—KINROSS—CLACKMANNAN—PERTHSHIRE—HIGHLAND RLY.

§ 1. GENERAL INFORMATION.

THE first route in this section describes the Forth and Tay Bridges, those triumphs of engineering skill which have done so much to bring the important cities of Perth, Dundee, and Aberdeen nearer the capital. Towards the end of the section the traveller is taken along the famous Highland line which has opened up the mountains and moors of the North to the tourist and the sportsman.

Fife and Kinross would be more explored if their numerous attractions were better known. Besides being counties of the highest agricultural cultivation (especially at the "Howe of Fife") they are full of picturesque beauty, and abound in fine seats and parks—Broomhall, Donibristle, Raith, Dysart, Wemyss Castle, Balcarres, Leslie House, Melville, etc. The country bordering on the estuaries of the Forth and Tay commands most inviting prospects; it is also unrivalled in the number and variety of its *Golfing Links.* It has hills of respectable height, such as the Two Lomonds in Fife and the rolling round-backed Ochils, which give little indication at a distance of the deep gorges and narrow chasms, threaded by bright burns and waterfalls, which intersect them—such as those of Glen Farg, of the Rumbling Bridge on Burns's "Crystal Devon, winding Devon," of Castle Campbell, and of Glen Alva—all easily reached from Perth or Stirling. These fine glens are a prelude to the magnificent scenery of Perthshire—a grand county, extending from the fertile Carse of Gowrie and Strath Earn to the mountain passes of Glen Lyon and Killiecrankie. The upper valley of the Earn from Crieff to Loch Earn is scarcely to be surpassed for beauty in Scotland. In this county, too, the traveller has the full enjoyment of the finest Highland scenery in the midst of mountains such as Ben Voirlich, Ben More, Ben Lawers, and Schiehallion. Perthshire also includes those noble parks and seats—Scone, Dupplin, Kinfauns, Rossie, Ochtertyre, Drummond Castle, Dunira, Dunkeld, Castle Menzies,

Taymouth, Blair, etc., while the city of Perth is remarkable for the beauty of its situation.

The historic sights and antiquities of this section include Dunfermline Abbey, Falkland Palace, the popular city of St. Andrews (which may also be styled a Gothic Pompeii from the number of its ruins), Lochleven Castle (a fragment of shapeless wall, which yet attracts pilgrims for the sake of Queen Mary), the Roman Camp at Ardoch, the Romanesque Church of Leuchars, the Gothic Cathedrals of Dunblane and Dunkeld, Culloden Moor, and the Stones of Clava.

§ 2. Principal Centres.

1. **Edinburgh** for the Forth Bridge, Dunfermline, Loch Leven, Falkland, etc. Cf. Section I.
2. **St. Andrews** for its Architectural Remains and its Golf Course.
3. **Dunfermline** for its Abbey, but it is best visited from Edinburgh, Stirling, or Perth.
4. **Stirling, Bridge of Allan,** or **Dunblane** for the Rumbling Bridge, Castle Campbell, the Windings of the Forth, Dunblane Cathedral, etc. Cf. Section II.
5. **Perth** for its pleasing neighbourhood, Loch Leven by Glen Farg, Falkland, the lower portions of Strath Tay, Strath Earn, and Glen Isla, etc. Cf. Section IV.
6. **Crieff** for the beauties of upper Strath Earn, Ardoch Camp, Glen Almond, etc.
7. **Dunkeld** for its Cathedral and lovely surroundings.
8. **Pitlochrie** for the Pass of Killiecrankie, Falls of Tummel, and Loch Tummel.
9. **Aberfeldy** or **Kenmore** for Loch Tay and Glen Lyon.
10. **Killin** for Loch Tay and the upper valley of the Tay.
11. **Kinloch-Rannoch** for Loch Rannoch, Schiehallion, and Upper Strath Tummel.
12. **Blair Atholl** for Blair Castle and Glen Tilt.
13. **Kingussie** for Glen Tromie, Glen Feshie, the upper part of Strathspey, and Loch Laggan.
14. **Grantown** for Strathspey and the grand scenery of the Cairn Gorm Mountains.
15. **Forres** for the Findhorn.
16. **Nairn** for Sea-Bathing and Golf.

ROUTES.

ROUTE 30.

Edinburgh (Waverley Stat.) to Dundee and Aberdeen by the Forth Bridge, Thornton, Ladybank, and the Tay Bridge. N.B.R.

This is the shortest route to Dundee (59¼ m.) and Aberdeen (130½ m.).

Ordinary express trains go to Dundee in about 1¾ hrs., and to Aberdeen in about 4 hrs.

The night train from London reaches these towns from Edinburgh in 1 hr. 15 min. and 3 hrs. 13 min. respectively.

3½ m. **Corstorphine Stat.** [see Rte. 19]. Here the line trends N. passing l. *Gogar Ho.*, a curious old castellated building of the 16th or 17th cent., and crossing the Almond at 6½ m., with l. *Carlowrie Cas.* famous for its conifers. A rich shale pit is passed rt. before reaching

9½ m. **Dalmeny Stat.** for **So. Queensferry**. Dalmeny, a neat well-kept little village, arranged round a green, is ½ m. S. Its **Romanesque Church,**[1] built probably at the beginning of the 12th cent. (restored in 1866), is, next to Leuchars, the most perfect specimen of this style of architecture in Scotland, though the chancel and its apse alone remain in their original state.

The windows are round-headed, with dog-tooth mouldings. The S. doorway has a circular arch of double mouldings, one a row of monstrous heads, very singular, but much worn. Above the door is an interlaced romanesque arcade of 5 arches.

In the interior the nave has been wretchedly modernised, but in the stone-vaulted *chancel* there are 2 richly-sculptured circular arches, one at the entrance to the chancel and another at the junction of the apse. "An ugly modern excrescence has been added to the N. side, to furnish space for the Rosebery pew [and burial vault] and the outer wall is flanked by 2 black tall stove-tubes!" The pilasters supporting the chancel arches inside have been ruthlessly hewn away to make room for pew backs. The church was attached to the Abbey of Jedburgh. In the churchyard are several old tombstones.

Leaving the station, rt. are the policies of **Dalmeny Park** (E. of Rosebery) [p. 65], while the *Hawes Inn* (see p. 65), where the coaches from Edin. to the Forth Bridge stop, and **So. Queensferry** (p. 202), are seen far below (l.) as the train advances along the approach to

The ****Forth Bridge,** begun in Jan. 1883, and opened by the Prince of Wales, March 4, 1890,—one of the engineering wonders of the world. The engineer was Sir John Fowler, Bart., assisted by Sir Benjamin Baker, with Sir William Arrol as contractor, who all received their titles in recognition of this great achievement. Now that the bridge is a *fait accompli* it is difficult to realise the tremendous difficulties that had to be contended with and the enormous size of the structure. The Firth of Forth is here 1¼ m. wide, with water 200 ft. deep in the channel, and only the small island of **Inch Garvie** as a stepping-stone. The principle of construction of the bridge is that of the cantilever or bracket. There are three towers, 360 ft. high above high-water mark, each of which extends an arm on both sides to meet the neighbouring arm, or the viaduct from the land, as the case may be. These towers are made of tubes of steel 12 ft. in diameter. Each of their foundations consists of 4 caissons filled with cement, one set being sunk in comparatively shallow water on the N. side, another set beside Inch Garvie, while the third set, on the S. side, is 71-89 ft. below high water. The centre tower is nearly double the breadth (N. and S.) of the other two, being 260 ft. as compared with 145 ft. The two central spans are

1 Key at one of the cottages opposite.

1710 ft. each and the spans between the br. and the land are 689 ft. 9 in. each. Thus the total length of the br. proper is 5349½ ft. or more than a mile. The S. viaduct with 11 stone piers is 1680 ft. long; the N. viaduct with 6 piers 1069 ft., giving a total length of 8098½ ft. or rather more than 1½ m. The height of the bridge above high water is 150 ft. 54,000 tons of iron and steel were used; there are 250,000 tons of solid masonry in the piers; 8 million rivets were used, and the surface painted represents 20 acres. 5000 workmen were employed during the busiest period. 57 men were killed and 378 injured. The bridge cost about 2¾ millions to build, of which more than one million went to wages and salaries.

The train takes abt. 2½ min. to cross the bridge. Looking out about the middle the traveller finds himself in a network of huge tubes and girders, the guardship and training ship below appearing little bigger than models. Up and down the firth the view on a clear day is very pleasing. At the north end of the bridge is

11¼ m. **No. Queensferry Stat.** with rt. a *Golf Course* (private) belonging to the Dunfermline Club. After passing through some very deep rock cuttings a curious isthmus is crossed. l. *St. Margaret's Hope* (called after *Queen* Margaret who gives her name to the ferry) is a safe anchorage in E. winds, overlooked by the square keep of *Rosyth Cas.* (15th cent.) [see Scott's "Abbot"].

rt. a good view of Edin. Cas. and Arthur's Seat is obtained.

13¼ m. **Inverkeithing Stat.** ✲ [Branch line l. to Dunfermline, Perth, etc. (Rtes. 34, 35)], an ancient royal and parl. burgh, on a hill sloping down to a small bay, in which some shipbuilding is carried on. It was the residence of David I., and a house is still pointed out in which Arabella Drummond, Queen of Robert III., is said to have lived. The belfry of the *Tower-house* is Palladian. The *Church*, except the Middle-pointed Tower, is modern, but contains an *old font*, almost the only one in Scotland.

The *County* or "*Kingdom of Fife*,"[1] as it is sometimes called, was a place of great importance when the king lived at Dunfermline and hunted at Falkland. This is proved by the fact that it has no less than 17 royal burghs, viz. E. and W. Anstruther, Auchtermuchty, Burntisland, Crail, Cupar, Dunfermline, Dysart, Earlsferry, Falkland, Inverkeithing, Kilrenny, Kinghorn, Kirkcaldy, Newburgh, Pittenweem, and St. Andrews. It is one of the richest and most productive of all the Scottish counties, having a fertile soil, great wealth of coal, and large manufactures.

For 5 m. not much can be seen for cuttings, although rt. are *Donibristle* (E. of Moray), *Dalgetty Ch.*, and *Inchcolm* (see pp. 201 and 202).

17½ m. **Aberdour Stat.** ✲, with the ruins of Decor. church and of a castle (17th cent.) in a wooded ravine. It is a favourite seaside resort for "trippers" from Edinburgh, steamers plying almost hourly from Leith in summer. *Inchcolm* (p. 201) is conveniently visited from here by boat (1½ m.). The line runs close by the sea before reaching

20¼ m. **Burntisland Stat.** ✲, one of the Kirkcaldy group of parl. burghs, with a small golf course. Behind is the *Binn Hill* (652 ft.), being half of an old crater, and W. is *Dunearn Hill*, with pleasant walks. The distillery and large sandstone quarry 1 m. N. of the town are on the estate of *Grange*, which belonged to Sir Wm. Kirkaldy (beheaded 1573), the partisan of Mary Queen of Scots. Nearer the town is the ruined ch. of Kirkton, formerly the parish ch.

When besieged by Cromwell,

[1] See Sheriff Mackay's interesting monograph "Fife and Kinross."

Burntisland is said to have opened her gates to him on condition of his paving the streets and repairing the harbour.

The harbour, to which a new dock was added in 1876, is one of the best on the E. coast of Scotland.

rt. overlooking the harbour is *Rossend Castle*, a house grafted on a 15th-cent. castle, associated with the story of the ill-fated Chastelard. Steamers still ply between Burntisland and Granton, but the through traffic is now all by the Forth Bridge.

At 21¾ m. a monument erected 1886 near the spot where Alex. III. was killed by a fall from his horse, 12th March 1286, is passed l. and then the promontory of *Pettycur* is crossed to

22½ m. **Kinghorn Stat.** If the day is clear, the views over the opposite coast of Haddington, embracing North Berwick Law and the Bass Rock, are very charming. In 1878 a strong battery was established here in connection with the forts on Inchkeith. There are *Shipbuilding Yards* here which are being (1894) re-arranged and largely extended.

26 m. **Kirkcaldy Stat.** ✲, called the "Lang Toun," because, with *Linktown* to the W., and *Pathhead*, *Sinclairtown*, and *Gallatown* to the E., it extends for quite 3 m. Its principal industries are cloth, floorcloth, and linoleum factories, iron works, engineering works, and pottery works.

An old religious establishment belonging to the Abbey of Dunfermline existed here, the head of which resided at a place still called "Abbotshall," the position of the old house being marked by a venerable yew tree which stood close by.

In 1644 Charles I. made Kirkcaldy a free port, with additional privileges, and it now possesses a large shipping business in coals, etc. It was the birthplace of Adam Smith (1723), and the house in High St. is still shown in which he wrote his *Wealth of Nations*. Opposite Adam Smith's house is Old Dunnikier House, a good specimen of 17th-cent. architecture, and formerly the town residence of the Oswalds. It is now converted into shops. At Pathhead, on the shore, are the ruins of *Ravenscraig Castle* (abt. 1440), commemorated in the tragic ballad of "Rosabelle."

"Moor, moor the barge, ye gallant crew,
  And, gentle lady, deign to stay!
Rest thee in Castle Ravensheugh,
  Nor tempt the stormy Firth to-day."

The castle was granted by James III. to William Sinclair, Earl of Orkney, on his resignation of that title. It was inhabited till the Restoration, but is now a picturesque ruin overhanging the sea. The same family have handed down their name to the suburb—*Sinclairtown*.

1½ m. W. are the ruins of a tower called *Balwearie* which has walls 7 ft. thick. In the 13th cent. Michael Scott the wizard was born, and resided at Balwearie. In the limestone *quarries* near Kirkcaldy are found many minerals, calcite, steatite, augite, apophyllite, etc.

Overlooking Kirkcaldy are the beautiful grounds and woods of *Raith* (R. C. Munro Ferguson, Esq., M.P.), which are embellished with an artificial lake of 20 acres, and a tower commanding a magnificent view of the Forth and distant Edinburgh. The house was built in 1694; subsequently two wings and an inner portico were added. It contains many portraits by *Raeburn*. Noble pine trees here. Between this and the town is the *Public Park* presented by Mr. Munro Ferguson.

It is a pleasant walk of 3 m. to Dunnikier Den, in the grounds of *Dunnikier House*, the family seat of the Oswalds, 1 m. N. of

27¼ m. **Sinclairtown Stat.** Adjoining to the S., is Pathhead.

28 m. **Dysart Stat.**, a dull town with one or two cotton mills. Adjoining is *Dysart House* (Earl of Rosslyn). The old ch. of Dysart, standing close by the sea, was a venerable and stately edifice, but is now a ruin. One of the windows bears the date 1570, but a great deal of it is far older. The tower is peculiar in its little staircase turret,

and the decorations above the corbel gable. On the shore are several caves, the largest of which was excavated in the rock as a hermitage, or *Desertum* (whence the town's name), by St. Serf, who preached the gospel on the shores of the Firth, and had a ch. at Culross, 680-700.

"Along the shore from Dysart to Fife Ness there is a range of caves which present evidence of human occupation. These caves are thickly studded with incised sculpturings, principally crosses. There are also four-footed beasts, serpents, and birds."—ANDERSON.

1 m. to the E. are the "*Red Rocks,*" where witches were burnt in former times.

The rly. now trends inland to

30¾ m. **Thornton Junc. Stat.**

[BRANCH LINES—(1) W. via *Cardenden Stat.* (6 m.), with Auchterderran to the N., and *Lochgelly Stat.* (8 m.) through the colliery country to *Cowdenbeath* (old) *Stat.* (10 m.); *Crossgates Stat.* (11¾ m.); *Halbeath Stat.* (13¼ m.), and **Dunfermline Upper Stat.** (15¾ m.) [pp. 192 and 198].

(2) [Rte. 32] E., *via* Leven, Anstruther, etc., to **St. Andrews.**

(3) S.E. to (1 m.) **West Wemyss Stat.** The village, which gets its name from the numerous "*weems*" or caves in the neighbourhood, is 1 m. S.; 2¾ m. **Wemyss Castle Stat.** for E. Wemyss, close to which rise the ruins of *Macduff's Castle. Wemyss Cas.* (R. G. E. Wemyss, Esq.) is a sumptuous mansion (Peddie and Kinnear, archts., 1876), with a terrace close to the sea. At the old Cas. Queen Mary in Feb. 1565 met Darnley, to whom she was married in the July following. 4 m. **Buckhaven Stat.** 5¼ m. **Methil Stat.** with a good harbour, only 1 m. S.W. of Leven (p. 188).]

Proceeding N. from Thornton Junc. the main line crosses the Leven to

33¼ m. **Markinch Stat.** [Junc. for *Leslie* (below)]. 1 m. S.E. are the ruins of *Balgonie Castle*, a work of great strength, probably built in the 12th cent. The approach, through a grove of walnut-trees, is very picturesque. The ruins consist of a large courtyard, with a tower 80 feet high rising on the N. side. In *Balgonie Ch.* rests David Leslie (Lord Newark), General of the Kirk and Estates army, who withstood Wallenstein at Stralsund, and was defeated by Cromwell at Dunbar (d. 1682).

[*Branch to Leslie Stat.*, 4¼ m. W. **Leslie** is a populous and busy place, dependent on its flax and bleaching-mills, and, like many of the Fife towns, contains some interesting remains of street architecture. To the E. is *Leslie House* (Hon. G. Waldegrave Leslie), a fine old place. Adam Smith, when a child, was kidnapped from Strathendry by gipsies, and carried into these woods. "The Green" is one of the many places where the scene of King James I.'s poem, "Christ's Kirk on the Green," is supposed to be laid.

The views from above the old ruins of *Strathendry Castle*, 1½ m. W., embrace Loch Leven, and the straight channel of the Leven issuing from it, with Kinross on the opposite shore.]

36¼ m. **Falkland Road Stat.**

Falkland ✲, 2½ m. W., a quiet village, but an ancient royal burgh, lying at the head of the plain called "*The Howe of Fife*"[1] consists largely of modern houses with a Gothic clock-tower, and several spinning-mills for linen. In former days, as its name "*Falcon-land*" indicates, it was resorted to by the Stuart kings for purposes of the chase. It is charmingly situated at the foot of the **East Lomond** (1471 ft.), while the **West Lomond** (1713 ft.) is 3 m. W. These twin hills are seen from a great distance. On a raised platform, overlooking the plain, stands the * **Palace**, built from the materials of an older *Castle* of which the foundations to the N.

1 Omnibuses meet most of the trains, or a conveyance may be ordered beforehand from the town.

A good way to get to Falkland is to take train to Ladybank Stat. and post 5 m. Posting estab. close to Ladybank Stat.

alone remain. That castle was built by the Macduffs, the powerful Thanes or Earls of Fife. Their descendant, Robert Stuart, who became also Duke of Albany, here in 1402 starved to death his nephew, David, Duke of Rothesay, son of Robert III., and heir to the throne. For some days the young man's life was preserved by a woman, who through a reed gave him milk from her own breast, but was discovered, and it is said put to death (cf. Sir W. Scott's "Fair Maid of Perth"). On the attainder and execution of Albany's grandsons (1424), the castle became the property of the Crown. The palace is entered from the street by a very picturesque gateway flanked by 2 loopholed round towers, and shows on this side a late Gothic front. It was built by James V., who frequently repaired hither to hunt, as did also his daughter, Queen Mary, and her son James VI. Within its walls, James V. died of a broken heart (1542), after the defeat of Solway Moss, having just heard of the birth of his daughter Mary, afterwards Queen of Scots, news which he received, remembering that his family had got the kingdom by marriage, with the words, "God's will be done: it cam wi' a lass and it'll gang wi' a lass." It was partially burned in the time of Charles II., who lived in it ten days, 1650. It was never adapted for a place of defence, but has much of the character of one of those sunny châteaux of Touraine, Blois, Amboise, or Chambord, in which Mary of Guise may have passed her youth. The S. side, which turns to the main street an elegant façade of narrow mullioned windows, alone is tolerably perfect, and is in part inhabited. The façade towards the courtyard, now a garden (1530-40), is more Italian in character. It is divided by buttresses, faced with Renaissance columns and entablatures, its upper windows being flanked by medallion heads of kings and queens. In this courtyard is a monument with statues of two of the Tyndall Bruce family, long owners of Falkland House (see below). The most interesting part is a large hall, now proved to have been the *Chapel*, 75 ft. long, with a flat roof of oak, ribbed and panelled in artistic patterns. It has been restored by the Marquis of Bute, hereditary keeper, who purchased the Falkland Estates in 1887, and is still (1894) excavating and restoring in a most praiseworthy manner. *Falkland House* (Marq. of Bute), a modern Gothic mansion (Burn and Bryce, arch. 1840), on the edge of a shady glen running up into the Lomond, about 1 m. W. of the town, is noted for the beauty of its grounds.

38¼ m. **Kingskettle Stat.** The line here crosses the Eden to

39 m. **Ladybank Junc. Stat.** ✲ (see p. 189).

[Junc. for lines (1) W., *via* Auchtermuchty (4½ m.), "the place of the wild boar," from ancient hunting days, Strathmiglo (6½ m.), and Gateside (8½ m.) to Mawcarse (11 m.) and Kinross (15 m.).

(2) N.W., *via* Newburgh and Abernethy to Perth (18¾ m.) (Rte. 33).]

The line now runs through a wooded country, passing l. *Nether Rankeillour* (M. B. Nairn, Esq.), to

42¼ m. **Springfield Stat.**, on rt. of which is *Crawford Priory*, a fine modern Gothic mansion (Lady Gertrude Cochrane). On the hill 2 m. S.E. is the old ruined tower of *Scotstarvit*, once the residence of Sir John Scott, the quaint author of "The Staggering State of Scots Statesmen," 1652.

[*Cults Church*, 1 m. S., contains a medallion by Chantrey of the father and mother of Sir David Wilkie, who was born (1785) in the *manse*, which is backed by what he called "my own blue Lomonds." His first picture was Pitlessie Fair, now in the National Gallery, Edin., a subject of 140 figures.]

44½ m. **Cupar Stat.** ✲ (pronounced Cooper), the county town of Fife, a parl. burgh and one of the royal burghs of David II. Notwithstanding its antiquity it has a modern appearance, the castle having been long superseded by the Madras Academy, which is built on its site. There is, however, a slight fragment of the old Dominican monastery, and the parish church is of the 15th cent., although modernised. The neighbourhood is adorned with pleasant villas and seats, as *Eden Park, Kingask, Tarvit*, etc.

Lord-Chancellor Campbell was born here, 1779, in the house next to the Bell Inn, his father having been minister of Cupar.

1¾ m. N.W. is *Kilmaron* (Rt. Hon. W. E. Baxter), and 1½ m. W. of it, on an eminence formerly known as *The Mount*, which commands a large extent of country, the property and patrimonial seat of Sir David Lindsay, the poet and Lyon King of Arms, is an *Obelisk* erected to the memory of the 4th Earl of Hopetoun.

[At *Dura Den*, 2½ m. E. of Cupar (now closed) Hugh Miller, Murchison, Anderson, and others found in the old red sandstone a remarkable number of fossils in a fair state of preservation, principally consisting of fishes. The most abundant were the *Holoptychius Andersoni*, an armour-plated fish, together with the *Pamphractus*, a fossil resembling the *Ptericthys*, also found there (*P. hydrophilus*).]

47½ m. **Dairsie Stat.** The ruins of *Dairsie Castle* stand on an eminence overhanging the river Eden, which is here crossed by a *Bridge* of 3 arches supposed to date from 1522. David II. lived here, as in a place of retreat and security, during a great part of his minority; and here, in the early part of the 17th cent., Archbishop Spottiswood wrote his "History of the Church and State of Scotland."

The little *Church* of Dairsie was built in 1621 by the same dignitary, as part of his great scheme for bringing Scotland into religious conformity with England, and is alluded to as "one of the beautifullest little pieces of church work that is left to this unhappy country." The ch. had at one time a handsome rood-screen, or, as it was called, "a glorious partition-wall of timber," which the Provincial Assembly of Fife, in 1641, ordered to be cut down to the level of the pews.

50¾ m. **Leuchars Junc. Stat.**

[*Branch lines* (1) E. to St. Andrews (Rte. 31); (2) *via* Tayport to Dundee (p. 184).]

The village, ¾ m. N., is celebrated for its * **Church** (supposed early 12th cent.) containing the most beautiful fragment of Romanesque work to be found in Scotland. This fragment is not used as part of the present Parish Ch., and is not now so large as Dalmeny Church, but from the richness of what remains it is evident that it must have been a much finer building. The mouldings of the arch at the entrance of the apse are very rich.

½ m. to the E. is *Earl's Hall*, formerly a seat of the Bruce family, begun in 1546, and finished in 1607. It has been restored by the present proprietor, R. W. R. Mackenzie, Esq. It stands in a small park, surrounded by a belt of trees, and in construction is a development of the L plan with a large tower in the N.E. corner, and the main staircase in a tower in the internal angle. In the drawing-room is a mantelpiece, with a coat-of-arms, on which are the initials A. B. (Alexander Bruce) and E. L. (Elizabeth Lindsay, his wife). On the next floor is the hall, 50 ft. long, 18 ft. broad, and 13 ft. high, with a ceiling painted to represent various coats-of-arms of different ages, such as "Hector Prince of Troy," "David King of Israel," "Emperor of Judea," and so forth, with others of less illustrious families, though derived probably from more authentic sources.

[*Branch via Tayport to Dundee.* ½ m. **Leuchars Old Stat.** (near the village); thence across the solitary *Tents Moor* to 5½ m. **Tayport Stat.**, from which there is a ferry steamer several times daily to Broughty Ferry (p. 261). Here the line turns W. (with, 1 m. l., *Scotscraig*, Mrs. Maitland Dougall) to 8 m. **East Newport Stat.**, and 8¾ m. **W. Newport Stat.** Between these stat. is **Newport**, a watering-place (with ferry communication to Dundee), and *Tayfield House.* 10¼ m. **Wormit Stat.**, immediately after which the direct line is rejoined and the Tay Bridge crossed to 13 m. **Dundee.**]

From Leuchars Junc. the line trends N.W. to

54½ m. **St. Fort Stat.** 2 m. W. is *Naughton* (Mrs. Morison Duncan), and 1½ m. beyond, near the Tay, are the ruins of *Balmerino* (pron. Bamérnie) *Abbey*, founded in 1229 by Alex. II. and his mother Ermengard (buried in the ch.), widow of William the Lion, for a Cistercian colony from Melrose. Only the beautiful cloistral entrance to the chapter house and the roofless sacristy remain. At the E. end is a very ancient Spanish chestnut, over 17 ft. in girth.

At 56½ m. the train reaches

The ****Tay Bridge**, principally remarkable for its great length of 2 m. The chief danger to be guarded against in the construction of a bridge so high and so long, was the stress of wind upon it, which had proved fatal in the case of its predecessor, which, with a train and its occupants, was blown over and destroyed, 28th December 1879. In this case it was possible to build piers in the bed of the river, which could not be done in the centre of the Forth. The first Tay Bridge was begun 1871, was opened June 1878, and cost nearly £400,000. It had 85 spans with a clear headway in the centre of 88 ft. above high-water mark, and was broad enough for only a single line of rails. The present structure (Messrs. Barlow, C.E., London, Engineers, and Messrs. Tancred, Arrol and Co., Contractors) is 20 yards W. of the old one, has 73 pairs of piers built of brick, faced with granite and iron, carries a double set of rails and has a clear headway of 77 ft. It was begun in 1883, was opened 1888, and cost £650,000.

58½ m. **Esplanade Stat.** at the W. end of Dundee.

59¼ m. **DUNDEE Tay Bridge Stat.**

For Dundee ✡ see p. 248.

For line on to Aberdeen see Rte. 48.

ROUTE 31.

Edinburgh to St. Andrews by Leuchars. N.B.R.

From Edinburgh by Forth Bridge to 50¾ m. **Leuchars**, see Rte. 30.

Thence the line strikes S. through a well-cultivated district to

52 m. **Guard Bridge Stat.**, with *Paper Works*, where the Eden is crossed. The narrow carriage bridge rt., originally built by Bp. Wardlaw about 1420, was repaired by Archbp. Beaton 1520. Note the arms on the central arch. The line now runs S.E., the Links and Golf Course being well seen l. before the train reaches

56 m. **St. Andrews Stat.** [For line *via* Anstruther, etc., to Thornton see Rte. 32.]

ST. ANDREWS ✡, standing on a rocky and exposed promontory jutting into the North Sea, is a strange combination of an ancient Cathedral and University town and a fashionable resort of golfers, whose Mecca it is universally admitted to be. The Autumn Golf Meeting at the end of September is here the principal event of the year.

The *Golf Course* (nearly 5 m. round) is over the *Links* W. of the town. There are also Ladies' Links and a Children's Course. The *Club-*

house (built 1853) is available for limited periods for strangers properly introduced.

Behind it on the *Scores* is the **Martyrs' Monument**, an obelisk, erected 1843, to the memory of Hamilton, Forrest, and Wishart, burned 1528-1546.

Farther E. on a rock rising abruptly from the sea is the Episcopal **Castle**, founded by Bp. Roger in 1200, but wholly rebuilt by Bp. Traill in the end of the 14th cent. It is now an empty but very picturesque shell. A drawbridge led over the moat to the part of the castle from which Cardinal Beaton watched Wishart burning, 1st Mar. 1546. In the centre of the courtyard is a well, and in the sea tower a curious *Bottle-shaped Dungeon*. Upon 29th May 1546, the castle was entered by Norman Leslie, son of the Earl of Rothes, James Melville, the young laird of Grange, and 15 soldiers, who slew the Cardinal, and being reinforced and supplied with provisions, stood a siege for 14 months, during which they were joined by John Knox. Upon the capture of the castle by a French fleet, Knox along with the rest of the garrison was sent to the galleys at Nantes.

At the E. end of the town, to which the Scores and the 3 principal streets —*North St.*, *Market St.*, and *South St.*—converge, are the ruins of the **Cathedral.**

In 736, the *Relics of St. Andrew*, who henceforth became the *Patron Saint* of Scotland, were brought hither, and the See of St. Andrews — the oldest in Scotland — was founded. Beside the Culdee *Monastery of Kirkheugh* then erected, and the site of which is between the Cathedral and the harbour, the town grew. Picts and Scots having been united in 844, St. Andrews in 908 succeeded Iona, Dunkeld, and Abernethy in the Primacy of the Scottish Church, an honour it held until the Reformation. In 1471, Pope Sixtus VI. raised the Bishopric of St. Andrews to an Archbishopric —the first instituted in Scotland.

Bishop Robert (1121-59) built a *Priory*, which has almost disappeared, for Augustinian Canons from Scone, and possibly the Ch. and Tower of St. Regulus (p. 186).

The **Cathedral**, N. of the Priory, begun by Bp. Arnold, 1160, was only finished and consecrated (in presence of King Robert Bruce) in 1318. When perfect it was no less than 358 ft. long, and the only great ch. in Britain directly overhanging the sea. The only remains are part of the S. wall of the Nave (which consisted of 12 bays), pierced with windows, of which 2 to the E. are round-headed, and all are at least 18 ft. above the ground, and part of the W. and E. ends which stand isolated, marking the vast extent of the ch. The portion of the W. front still standing has a picturesque pointed and deeply-recessed central doorway, surmounted by a blank early-pointed arcade, and flanked by a turret still propped by a flying buttress. The E. end wall stands perfect, with its flanking turrets, 3 narrow windows with round heads below, and a pointed window above rising into the gable, 1202-20. Adjoining the S. transept was the *Chapter House*, of which an arcaded wall and part of a vestibule with 3 pointed entrance arches of great elegance, now walled up, remain. Here are preserved many old gravestones chiefly of 15th and 16th cent.

John Knox's sermons for 4 consecutive days on the "Cleansing of the Temple" (June 1559) may have led to the first acts of demolition, subsequently accelerated by the greed of builders of houses and dykes.

Adjoining the ruins, now well protected and cared for, is, as heretofore, a *Churchyard*, where Samuel Rutherford (see p. 114), who was

Prof. of Divinity in the University (d. 1661), is buried, and where there is a monument of questionable taste to young Tom Morris, the golf champion (d. 1875).

Within the ch.-yd. close to the S. E. corner of the Cathedral, is the small *Church* or *Basilica* of *St. Rule* or *Regulus*, surmounted by a square tower 108 ft. high, remarkably perfect, though of rude masonry, and with a fine view from the top. It is a Romanesque building, erected 1127-44, though legend asserts it was erected in the 4th cent., in honour of St. Regulus, who then drifted here from Greece in a boat without sail or oars, but freighted with the relics of St. Andrew. This small ch. consists of a choir, very narrow in proportion to its height, with its chancel arch built up. Whether it ever had a nave is a disputed point. Some think that the tower is older than the ch. and was originally intended for a place of refuge.

E. of the Cathedral is the small *Harbour*.

At the E. end of South St. near the S.W. corner of the Cathedral is the *Priory Gateway* or **Pends**, which consist of 2 stately Gothic arches finely groined. Above the outer one is a row of niches. There was formerly a third and lower arch situated between the other two. The road through this gateway passes l. "The Priory," and rt. *St. Leonard's College*, and *St. Leonard's School*, the Infirmary of which occupies the site of the *Teinds Barn*. These are all enclosed by the old **Abbey Wall**, built by Prior Hepburn in the 16th cent., 20 ft. high, nearly 1 m. long, loopholed and flanked with turrets for defence, and still very perfect.

St. Leonard's College was founded in 1511 by Archbp. Alex. Stewart, natural son of James IV., with whom he died at Flodden (1513), aged 21! Here the youthful Reformers studied, so that "to have drunk of St. Leonard's Well" meant to have become imbibed with Protestant doctrines. By Act of Parliament 1747, its foundation was transferred to St. Salvator (below). Its roofless chapel contains several interesting monuments, but has been sadly neglected. The College is now used as part of

St. Leonard's School, a Ladies' School, which has achieved for itself a high reputation, and includes among its buildings *The Bishop's Hall*, once the residence of the Bishop of the diocese.

The 2nd house W. of the Pends on the S. of South St., is said to have been occupied by Mary Queen of Scots when she visited St. Andrews.

The **University of St. Andrews**[1] —the oldest but smallest in Scotland —was founded by Bp. Henry Wardlaw in 1413. It comprised the Colleges of St. Salvator (below) founded 1456, and St. Leonard (above)—which, since 1747, have together formed "The United College"—for courses in Arts and Medicine, with St. Mary's College (p. 187) as a Divinity Hall. To it University College, Dundee (founded 1883) [see p. 250], was united, 1890. Each College has its own Principal, and staff of Professors, but these all form one Senate. The General Council of St. Andrews—composed of graduates—along with that of Edinburgh University returns a Member of Parliament.

"The United College" buildings are on the N. side of North St. There are class rooms, an exam. hall, with portraits of eminent professors, and a small but interesting museum, containing Knox's pulpit, *Dura Den* fossils, a fine collection of fishes, Dean Stanley's collection of Eastern curios, etc. They occupy the site of **St. Salvator's College**, founded in 1456 by Bishop Kennedy (1440-66), who also built the *College Church*, which

[1] See "The Earliest Scottish University," by Principal Shairp.

still remains, and who is buried in an apsidal tomb within its walls. When his tomb was opened in 1683, six very beautiful maces were found —one made in Paris in 1461 by the Dauphin's goldsmith. 3 of them were retained, and the remaining 3 were presented to the other Universities of Scotland. This Ch. has some good modern stained-glass windows, especially one to the memory of Principal Shairp (1819-85). The *Tower* over the College gateway dates from 1411.

St. Mary's College, on the S. side of South St.—devoted to Theology—was founded by Bp. Stuart in 1512, and by Papal Bulls of 1537 and 1552. It contains the *University Library* of about 55,000 vols. (including some valuable MSS.), and portraits of Knox, of Lord Melville by *Wilkie,* of Principal Tulloch by *Herdman,* etc. Attached to it is the residence of its Principal, and a garden in which grows *Queen Mary's Thorn.*

Nearly opposite St. Mary's is the **Town Church**, originally built in 1112. It was "restored"(?) in 1798, and galleries added, so as to seat 2500 people; but some of the seats, where it was almost impossible to hear or even see the minister, were afterwards removed. It is an interesting example of a huge, ugly, old-fashioned Scottish ch. It contains a heavy and elaborate marble monument, executed in Holland, to Archbishop Sharpe, erected by his son, representing his murder on Magus Moor (below). Examples of the "*branks,*" or "*scold's bridle,*" and of the "*cutty-stool,*" on which any one undergoing church discipline had to stand, are preserved here.

Farther W. on the S. side of South St. are the picturesque ivy-clad ruins of the N. transept of the ch. of the *Blackfriars Monastery* founded (1274) by Bp. Wishart, and behind them is

Madras College, erected 1833 at a cost of £18,000 (part a bequest by Dr. And. Bell) as a school for boys and girls. At the S. end of South St. is the **"West Port,"** a gateway originally erected in 15th or 16th cent., but greatly altered in 1843.

In the centre of Market St. is a *Memorial Fountain* to Major Whyte-Melville (1821-78) the novelist; and close by a cross in the causeway marks the site of the *Market Cross* where executions took place.

The *Epis. Church* is in Queen's Terrace, S. of South St.

The geologist and lover of coast scenery should visit the cliffs for 3 or 4 m. E. The strata visible at low water are much bent and contorted. Between the Castle and the harbour is the Cave

> "Where good St. Rule his holy lay
> From midnight to the dawn of day
> Sang to the billows' sound."—SCOTT.

The *Spindle Rock* (3 m.) is a curious example of marine denudation.

Numerous caves between this and Dysart (p. 180) are believed to have sheltered the early missionaries.

3½ m. S.W. passing l. *Mount Melville* (J. Balfour-Melville, Esq.), and then turning rt., one reaches a plantation, within which a cairn marks the spot on **Magus Muir** at which, upon the night of 3rd May 1679, Archbp. Sharpe was waylaid, dragged from his coach and butchered in the arms of his daughter, who vainly strove to protect him, by a party of Covenanters commanded by Balfour of Burley and Hackston of Rathillet. Five of the Bothwell Bridge prisoners were here executed and hung in chains. A stone with an inscription in the field adjoining marks where they were subsequently buried.

For Excursions to *Crail, Anstruther, Elie,* etc., see Rte. 32.

ROUTE 32.

Thornton to St. Andrews — by Leven, Anstruther, and the East Neuk of Fife. N.B.R.

To Thornton from Edinburgh or Dundee, see Rte. 30.

The line is carried through a pretty glen alongside the small river *Ore*, falling into the *Leven*, which is crossed before

3¾ m. **Cameron Bridge Stat.**, close to which are Distilleries, and followed to

5¾ m. **Leven Stat.** ✲, a small seaport at its mouth with good *Golfing Links* stretching E. to Largo. 1½ m. N. is *Durie Ho.* (R. Christie, Esq.).

7¾ m. **Lundin Links Stat.**, as the E. portion of the Leven golf course is called. In a field behind the station are 3 large *Standing Stones*, and beyond, l., houses let to summer visitors. 4 m. inland is *Montrave*, the seat of John Gilmour, Esq., to whom the Links and much of the land in its neighbourhood belong.

8¾ m. **Largo Stat.**, a considerable fishing village, and the birthplace, in 1675, of Alexander Selkirk, the original of Robinson Crusoe, of whom there is a bronze Statue near the harbour. Behind are the romantic glen called "Kiels Den," the village of Kirkton of Largo, and (1½ m.) **Largo Law** (965 ft.), a conspicuous conical hill with a fine view. 1½ m. farther N. is *Norrie's Law*, a tumulus in which a large number of silver ornaments were found.

12½ m. **Kilconquhar Stat.** It is locally pronounced Kinew′-cher, and means the Ch. of St. Conacher. The village beside a loch is ¾ m. E. In *Kilconquhar Ho.* (E. of Lindsay) are some good pictures. 2 m. N. is the village of **Colinsburgh**, in the neighbourhood of which are the estates of *Charlton* (J. Anstruther Thomson, Esq.), *Balcarres* (E. of Crawford), and *Pitcorthie*. At Balcarres, with lovely grounds, Lady Anne Lindsay (1750-1825) wrote the ballad of "Auld Robin Gray."

14 m. **Elie Stat.** ✲. The village runs W. to its suburb **Earlsferry**, and the *Golf Course*, which, with the sands, makes it a favourite summer resort. N. of the stat. is *Elie Ho.* (W. Baird, Esq.). The ruins of *Newark Cas.* (17th cent.), formerly the seat of Lord Newark, a title now extinct, are conspicuous (rt.) just before *St. Monan's Ch.* and

16¼ m. **St. Monan's Stat.** The Church, built by David II. abt. 1362 in gratitude for his recovery at St. Monan's shrine from a wound received by a barbed arrow, was originally cruciform. It now retains only the short square tower, surmounted by an octagonal steeple, the little belfry windows on which give a foreign effect, the transept, and the choir, which serves as the Parish Church. The interior, which is lighted by beautiful mid-pointed windows, has a fine groined roof, and a sq. recess with ogee-headed compartments for sedilia.

17¾ m. **Pittenweem Stat.** The village (rt.) is a poor place although a royal burgh. Near the Town Hall are the remains of the Dormitory and Refectory of the *Priory of Pittenweem*, which before the Reformation owned large territories in Fife (including the Isle of May) and in other counties of Scotland. 1½ m. N.W. is *Balcaskie* (Sir Ralph W. Anstruther, Bt.), a Scoto-French mansion, with gardens interesting for their hanging terraces and clipped hedges.

18¾ m. **Anstruther Stat.** ✲, a small seaport town, the birthplace, in 1780, of the Rev. Thomas Chalmers, D.D. Efforts have been made to improve its harbour, and abt. £80,000 has been laid out in piers and breakwater, under the direction of Sir John Hawkshaw, C.E. *Anstruther*, *W. Anstruther*, and *Kil-*

renny, which practically form one town, are 3 distinct royal burghs.

[6 m. S.E. is the **Isle of May** with a *Lighthouse*—the only one in Scotland lighted by electricity. On the island are the ruins of a Chapel of St. Adrian, an early missionary from Hungary, who was murdered by the Danes. His stone coffin is said to have floated across to W. Anstruther, where it is still shown!

St. Andrews is 9 m. N. from Anstruther by road.]

23 m. **Crail Stat.** ✲, another royal burgh, has an interesting old Ch. with finely-carved seats, and, "of all the country ch.-yds in Fife that of Crail [1] is by far the richest in quaint old tombstones"; among them is that of Miss Cunningham (discovered 1893), who was betrothed to Drummond of Hawthornden, but died abt. 1619, aged 19.

Here Knox began the preaching of the Reformation, and Archbp. Sharpe was parish minister here before he became an Episcopalian. In the *Town Hall* are Bulls granted by Popes Julius II. and Leo X.

This is the last of the seaboard towns on the Fife shores of the Firth of Forth. The red tile roofs of the fishermen's houses, though less numerous than formerly, are very picturesque as seen from the sea.

2 m. N.E. is *Fife Ness*, the eastmost promontory of this corner or "East Neuk" of Fife.

1 m. W. of the headland is *Balcomie Cas.*, where Mary of Guise was entertained upon her landing to marry James V. (1538), and 1 m. N. is the dangerous *Carr* reef, now marked by a light-ship.

The line turns N.W. to

26 m. **Kingsbarns Stat.** The village is 1 m. E.

27½ m. **Boarhills Stat.** These names recall the times when kings hunted here.

1 See "The Churchyard Memorials of Crail," by Erskine Beveridge (T. and A. Constable, 1893), a handsome large volume with numerous illustrations.

29¾ m. **Stravithie Stat.** 1¾ m. N. is *Kinkell Ness* and *Cas.*, near which is the *Spindle Rock*, and from which it is a pleasant cliff walk of abt. 3 m. to St. Andrews.

32 m. **Mount Melville Stat.** with *Mount Melville* (p. 187) 1 m. W.

34 m. **St. Andrews** (p. 184).

[To Edinburgh or Dundee *via* Leuchars, see Rtes. 31 and 30.]

ROUTE 33.

Ladybank to Perth by Newburgh and Abernethy. N.B.R.

To Ladybank from Edinburgh or Dundee, see Rte. 30.

2½ m. **Collessie Stat.** 1 m. rt. is *Melville* (Miss Leslie Melville Cartwright), formerly the seat of the Earl of Leven and Melville. The principal approach (1 m. long) is at first charmingly wild, and ends in a fine avenue of beeches. The Ho., a large square Elizabethan building erected 1702, stands in an extensive park in which are many noble trees. It contains portraits of the Leven family, an interesting full-length of Gustavus Adolphus, and a quarter-length of Claverhouse. In the old-fashioned garden is a *Tower* which formed part of the country residence of the Archbishop of St. Andrews, and was inhabited by Cardinal Beaton 1560.

At 4½ m. the line skirts the S. bank of *Lindores Loch*, across which is *Inchrye Abbey*, a modern mansion, and at its far end the *Parish Ch. of Abdie* and the ruins of a Gothic Ch. The line creeps under the steep *Craig of Clatchard*, crowned with the remains of a *Hill Fort*, and reaches the Tay at

7½ m. **Newburgh Stat.**, an uninteresting town of one street, but prettily situated as seen from the train. ¾ m. E. are the scanty remains of **Lindores Abbey.**

It was founded in 1178 by David Earl of Huntingdon (brother of Wm. the Lion, and grandfather of Robert Bruce), the Sir Kenneth of Scott's "Talisman," on his return from Palestine, and was a place of note until it passed into secular hands after the Reformation. John Knox records his visit to Lindores and the burning of the Mass Books of the black monks.

The remains cover a considerable area, and the ground plan can still be easily traced. The groined arch of the principal entrance and a portion of the W. tower are the only important features standing, this having been thought an excellent quarry.

N. of the Stat. is *Mugdrum Ho.* with an old *Cross* in the park. In the Tay is *Mugdrum Island*, 1 m. long, and W. of which is the mouth of the Earn. Perthshire is entered before

10¼ **Abernethy Stat.** ✲, a straggling village. Here was the old Pictish capital, but the only monument of its early greatness is its celebrated **Round Tower**, one of three in Scotland—the others being Brechin (p. 270), and Egilsay (p. 431).

It is 74 ft. in height, and in circumference 48 ft. at the bottom and 32 ft. at the top. It was probably built as a place of refuge, and the door has only been brought near the ground by an accumulation of soil. The somewhat Norman-looking upper windows, and the very perfect, even masonry, resembling that of St. Rule's Tower at St. Andrews, deserve notice. Dr. Petrie thinks it was built "between 712 and 727, and by the Northumbrian architects of the monastery of Jarrow," thus assigning to it a date much earlier than that of Brechin. Dr. Joseph Anderson, however, thinks it is of the same age (abt. 983) or slightly more recent.

About 6 ft. from the ground hang the "jougs," an iron pillory collar (see p. 62).

Leaving Abernethy the plain of Strath Earn is crossed with l. the entrance to *Glen Farg*, and the rly. S. to Kinross, etc. (Rte. 34).

15¼ m. **Bridge of Earn Stat.** ✲ See p. 194 for this and for line to

18¾ m. **Perth Stat.** ✲

ROUTE 34.

Edinburgh to Perth by the Forth Bridge, Dunfermline, Loch Leven, and Glen Farg. N.B.R.

This route, opened in the summer of 1890, has greatly shortened the journey to Perth, now reached in 1¼ hr. It is the old coaching route with the bridge for the ferry. Tourists are recommended to choose the rt. side of the carriage for the views.

From Edinburgh to 13¼ m. **Inverkeithing Stat.,** see Rte. 30.

Just beyond Inverkeithing the line trends N.W.; rt. is the line to Dundee (Rte. 30). Dunfermline Abbey is well seen l., towering above the houses of the town, which is built on the steep sides of a hill 300 ft. above the sea, before reaching

16¾ m. **Dunfermline Lower Stat.** [There is an *Upper Stat.* (p. 198) for (E.) Alloa and Stirling and (W.) Thornton (p. 181).]

DUNFERMLINE ✲, a royal and parl. burgh, is the seat of the Sheriff Court for the W. division of the county, and famous for its *Manufactures* chiefly of fine table linen. Its distinguishing features are the *Abbey* and the *Ruins of the Palace*. Among modern structures St. Leonard's Works are the handsomest though not the largest of the weaving mills. At the corner of Kirkgate and Bridge St. stand the *Corporation Buildings*, a fair modern imitation of Scottish civic Gothic architecture, surmounted by a tower (Walker, arch., 1878). Cost £19,000.

The *Public Hall*, in Margaret St., was built in 1878; adjoining it is a Free Library, which, together with the Public Baths in Schoolend St., was the result of a munificent gift of £13,000 by Mr. A. Carnegie.

The ****Abbey,** "The Westminster of Scotland," was founded for Benedictine monks from Canterbury by the Saint-Queen Margaret, sister of the refugee Edgar Atheling, and Malcolm Canmore, whom she married 1070. Of their church nothing remains. It was replaced by David I. by one of which fortunately the pure and simple Romanesque *Nave* (1150), perhaps the best of the style in Scotland, remains. Externally it is somewhat marred by the great size and massiveness of the buttresses, added in the 16th cent. On each side of the round-headed W. doorway rises a narrow square tower, lighted with Gothic windows. The N. aisle is entered by a porch whose inner doorway is very rich Romanesque, presenting a contrast to the groined roof which is of later date. The nave is 106 ft. long, and 54 ft. high; and is supported by tall cylinder piers and round arches, forming 6 bays. The arch next the door was rebuilt by James VI. in the early-pointed style. The piers are grooved in zigzags and spirals not unlike those of Durham—possibly the masons were the same—and Lindisfarne. One of the piers, really straight, by a strange optical illusion appears to taper upwards when looked at from one side, and downwards when looked at from the other. The triforium, with large spaces behind, is very perfect.

An elegant pointed *Choir* and *Transepts* were added to David I.'s nave in 1250, but ruined by the Reformers 1560, and finally swept away 1818, to make room for the present tasteless edifice, which is separated from the nave by a hideous partition wall. It is constructed in entire ignorance of the true principles of Gothic, but serves as a commodious *Parish Church*.

Below the space between the two eastmost piers, once the site of the high altar, *Robert Bruce* is buried—a spot now marked by a brass over which stands the present handsome wooden pulpit—under the central *Tower*, the outer balustrade of which is in consequence wrought into the words "King Robert the Bruce." Bruce's remains were disinterred in 1818 (see Scott's "Tales of a Grandfather"). They were found wrapped in a shroud interwoven with threads of gold and encased in two coverings of sheet lead. They were placed in a new coffin and re-interred. A cast of the king's skull was taken by the Phrenological Society of Edinburgh.

In the *S. Transept* are marble monuments to Lady Augusta Bruce, wife of Dean Stanley, and to General Bruce, Tutor to the Prince of Wales.

Dunfermline Abbey succeeded Iona as a place of sepulture of the Scottish kings. Duncan I. or Macbeth was the last buried at Iona. Malcolm Canmore was killed at Alnwick, and his Queen Margaret died in Edinburgh Cas. 1093. They lie to the E. of the church, in ground once covered by the Lady Chapel. Their sons, Edgar, Alex. I., and David I., and their descendants, Malcolm IV., Alex. III., and Robert I. are buried beneath the church.

The *N. W. Tower* commands an extensive view.

Of the rest of the Abbey nothing is to be seen but the *Abbey Gatehouse* and "Fratry," or *Refectory*, standing in the S.W. corner of the ch.-yard, the most striking portion of which is the W. window, still perfect, of 7 lights, the upper part filled with quatrefoils. It was probably put up at the end of the 16th cent. The remains appear to date from the 14th cent. Edward I. wintered in the Abbey in 1303, and had no sooner quitted it than it was burned by his soldiers, along with the town.

Across the road, which passes through a massive Gothic vaulted *Gateway*, the scanty ruins of

The Palace, long the residence of the Scottish Kings, and still the property of the Crown, stand on a projecting rock above the wooded glen of *Pittencrieff* (J. A. Hunt, Esq.). Through the glen winds a burn, and beyond the palace is a mound marking the site of an ancient fort, from which Dunfermline, "the fort of the crooked linn," derives its name.

In the original palace, built by Malcolm Canmore, were born Maud, wife of Henry I. of England, and her brothers (afterwards kings) Edgar, Alexander, and David I., ancestor of Robert Bruce.

King Edward I., in his second invasion of Scotland, 1303, held his Court here, and at that time the palace was burned, it is supposed by accident. It was rebuilt by James IV., 1500.

Mary Queen of Scots lived here in 1561. Her son, James VI., subscribed the Covenant here; and here his children, Charles I. and Elizabeth, were born. Charles II. also inhabited the palace before his march to Worcester, and was forced by the Covenanters to sign "the terrible act" known as the *Dunfermline Declaration*, in which his parents are condemned in sufficiently strong language.

A *Cave*, reached by a path near the Volunteers' Hall, is said to have been used by Queen Margaret as an oratory.

The bulky *Unit. Presbyt. Ch.* in Queen Anne St. was one of the earliest churches of the Secession (below). That movement had its origin here. Monuments to its chief leaders, Ralph Erskine and Thomas Gillespie, were erected in the Abbey in 1876.

[3 m. from Dunfermline on the Firth of Forth is *Broomhall*, seat of the Earl of Elgin. In it are preserved the sword (and helmet?) of Robert the Bruce, and the bed of Anne of Denmark, in which Charles I. was born, brought from Dunfermline.

Here are also some valuable paintings by *Seb. del Piombo*—A Sibyl. *Leon. da Vinci*—St. Sebastian. *An. Caracci*—St. Francis before the Crucifix. *Velasquez*—Duke of Olivarez. *Moroni*—A blacksmith. *Teniers*—A game of skittles, etc.]

---

19 m. **Halbeath Stat.**, beyond which l. is the *Hill of Beath*.

20½ m. **Crossgates Stat.** (rt. to Thornton, p. 181).

22½ m. **Cowdenbeath New Stat.**—a colliery centre.

24¾ m. **Kelty Stat.** Beyond this l. is *Blairadam*, the seat of the late Rt. Hon. W. P. Adam, the Liberal Whip, who d. 1881 while governor of Madras. His grandfather was the lifelong friend of Sir Walter Scott, and his son Sir C. E. Adam, Bt., now owns the property. Here "The Abbot" was concocted (1819), and many scenes in the beautiful grounds, *e.g. the Kiery Craigs* from which Lochleven Cas. is visible, are described in the novel. The *Kirk of Cleish*(*botham*) is 3 m. N.W.

26¾ m. **Blairadam Stat.**, rt. is *Benarty Hill* (1131 ft.), and 3 m. l. the *Cleish Hills* (1241 ft.). At 28 m. an *Obelisk* is seen l. (at Gairney Bridge), marking where the first *Secession Presbytery* was formed 1733. The line now runs alongside of Loch Leven. rt. on a promontory is *Kinross Ho.* (now uninhabited), built 1685 for the Duke of York by Sir W. Bruce, the architect of much of Holyrood. It belongs to Sir G. Graham Montgomery, Bart., who also owns the loch.

29¾ m. **Lochleven Stat.** ✲, one of the stats. of Kinross, situated close to the loch, and to mills for the manufacture of coarse linen and woollen goods.

Loch Leven is a sheet of water fully 3½ m. long by about 2 m. broad, famous for its pink trout and its historical castle. On the S. shore rises the picturesque hill of *Benarty*, and to the N.E. are **The Lomonds.**[1]

1 "Both 'Lomond' and 'Leven' are derived from the Gaelic *Leaman*=(wych)elm trees. The conjunction of the same names in the W. where another *Leven* flows out of Loch *Lomond* is noteworthy."—Sir H. MAXWELL, Bt.

The fishing season is from Feb. 5 to Aug. 31, but the number of fish caught varies considerably: in 1892 it was 12,735, weighing 11,744 lbs.; in 1893, 22,825, weighing 19,168 lbs.

The loch is rented by the *Lochleven Angling Association* whose office is in Kinross. They charge 2s. 6d. an hour for a boat, and fishers have to pay 4s. a day for one boatman, and provide food for two—the second one being paid by the association.

There are several islands, on the nearest of which, ½ m. from the shore, is **Lochleven Castle**, a fortress of considerable antiquity, belonging to the Douglas family. Here Queen Mary was imprisoned after her surrender at Carberry Hill, 1567, and remained 11 months in the custody of Lady Douglas of Lochleven, a woman adapted by temper, and still more by circumstances, for a gaoler, having been the mistress (she said wife) of James V., and mother of the Earl of Murray, who, if legitimate, would have been King of Scotland.

A picturesque object at a distance, the castle on a nearer approach is seen to be a rough square Peel Tower, standing in a court, surrounded by a rampart wall, which once included various offices now pulled down. The tower was entered at a round-headed low door, halfway up the wall, by a draw-stair or platform. It comprised two vaulted chambers below, a storehouse and kitchen, with trap-doors in the floors, and above three stories, of which the wooden floors are gone. In this tower dwelt Lady Douglas. Her prisoner was secured in a round turret in the angle of the rampart, where she occupied a room only 15 ft. in diameter, furnished with a fireplace and one window, and entered by a stair from the courtyard. Within these walls, on the 23rd July 1567, by persuasion or compulsion of Lord Lindsay and Robert Melville, Queen Mary signed a deed of abdication of the crown in favour of her son, and another appointing her brother, Murray, Regent. Many attempts were made by Mary's friends for her deliverance, but in vain. She was more successful with her personal fascinations, by which she succeeded in captivating the heart of George Douglas, the son of her gaoler, whose devotion to her caused him to be expelled from the castle. He left behind, however, a confederate, Willie Douglas, a lad of 18, who, on the night of the 2nd May 1568, while the inmates of the castle were at prayers, secured the keys, placed the queen in a boat belonging to the castle, having locked the gates behind him, threw the keys overboard, and conveyed her to the mainland, where she was received by Lord Seton, George Douglas, and Sir James Hamilton, and taken to Niddry Castle (p. 128).

Owing to the drainage of the lake, by which 1400 acres of land have been added to its margin, the area of the island has been enlarged, and boats can no longer land, as in Mary's time, close under the castle walls. Queen Mary's escape forms one of the principal scenes in Sir W. Scott's "Abbot." On the 15th of May 1568 (13 days after her escape), Mary was defeated at Langside by her brother, and fled to England.

Upon *St. Serf's Isle* are the ruins of an old priory, said to have been founded for the Culdees by Eocha, King of the Picts. David I. transferred the building and property to Augustinian canons, and ordered the Culdees to conform to the rules of that order, or to leave the priory. Andrew Wyntoun, one of the earliest of the Scotch chroniclers, was prior of this place.

30½ m. **Kinross Junc. Stat.**

[*Branch* W. to Stirling, Rte. 36.]

Kinross✲, ½ m. rt., is the capital of the county of the same name. The whole of this district, including the 3 counties of Kinross, Fife, and Clackmannan, used to be called the Ross (*i.e.* the peninsula), and Kinross means the "head of the peninsula"; just as Culross on the Firth of Forth means the "bottom of the peninsula," and so on. It is a sleepy little town, but with mills near the loch [see Lochleven (above)].

31½ m. **Milnathort Stat.** has also woollen manufactories.

The line bends rt. allowing another excellent view of Lochleven and its castle.

34¼ m. **Mawcarse Junc. Stat.**

[*Branch* E. to Ladybank, p. 182.]

A pleasing view is obtained of the "Howe of Fife" and the *Hopetoun Monument* (p. 183) before the line turns N. ascending to

37½ m. **Glen Farg Stat.**, beyond which is a lovely Norwegian-like defile 4 m. long, which gave great difficulty to the rly. engineers.

Both road and stream had to be diverted at different places. Three tunnels were necessary, and the line finally is carried high up on the l. bank of the stream. Charming peeps are caught rt. between the tunnels, but the glen should be visited by road, especially as the lowest part is completely lost. An older road l. led over the *Wicks of Baiglie*, and it is from this road or a point near it, that Sir Walter Scott's description of Perth in the "Fair Maid" is taken.

Upon issuing from the last tunnel a fine view is obtained (rt.) down the Carse of Gowrie to the Tay Bridge at Dundee; and (l.) up Strathearn. At 42 m. rt. is *Balmanno*, one of the most perfect examples of the old Scottish mansion. Close by it is the pretty waterfall of *Dron*, a noted place for the breeding of water-ousels, the nests of which are placed between the waterfall and the rock, so as to be almost inaccessible. There is a charming walk, turning off to the l. at Dron, and following the road to Forteviot.

44¼ m. **Bridge of Earn Stat.** ✲

[*Branch* rt. to Newburgh and Ladybank, Rte. 33.]

Behind the hotel are the ivy-covered remains of an old bridge over the Earn, introduced into *Millais's* "Sir Isumbras at the Ford."

l. is *Kilgraston Ho.* (J. P. Grant, Esq.), the birthplace of the late Gen. Sir Hope Grant, and Sir Francis Grant, Pres. of the Royal Acad. 1 m. W. are the *Mineral Wells* of Pitcaithley; rt. is *Moncrieffe Hill* (p. 196). The Earn is crossed, and the Cal. Rly. to Stirling is joined just before the tunnel is entered, at the N. end of which

A fine view is obtained (rt.) of *Kinnoull Hill*, across the Tay. The *General Convict Prison* is passed rt. before reaching

47¾ m. **Perth Stat.**

[Lines run (1) S. to Edinburgh by the Forth Bridge (Rte. 34, N.B.R.).

(2) S. to Edinburgh and S.W. to Glasgow by Stirling (Rtes. 38 and 25, C.R.).

(3) S.W. to Glasgow by Alloa (Rtes. 34, 36, and 25, N.B.R.).

(4) S.E. to Ladybank (Rte. 33, N.B.R.).

(5) E. to Dundee (Rte. 46, C.R.).

(6) W. to Crieff and Comrie (Rtes. 41 and 39, C.R.).

(7) N.E. to Forfar and Aberdeen (Rte. 47, C.R.).

(8) N. to Inverness (Rte. 42, High. Rly.).]

PERTH ✲ is charmingly situated upon the rt. bank of the Tay, and is a place of great antiquity.

There is a story that the Roman soldiers of Agricola, when they came in sight of the Tay and the South Inch, exclaimed, "Ecce Tiberis! ecce Campus Martius!"—a compliment which Sir Walter Scott has turned as follows—

"'Behold the Tiber!' the vain Roman cried,
Viewing the ample Tay from Baiglie's side;
But where's the Scot that would the vaunt repay,
And hail the puny Tiber for the Tay?"

Considering that it is an old historic city, long a residence of Scottish kings, it may surprise a stranger that it should possess no remains of antiquity, until he calls to mind that this was the place where Knox, in 1559, preached his first sermon, inciting to "the purging of the churches from idolatry." The immediate pulling down of the religious houses, the Black and Grey Friars and Carthusian convents, by the hands of the "rascal multitude," as Knox styles them, was the consequence of his eloquence.

South St. and *High St.*, long, busy, but poor, with the quieter *Victoria St.*, *Canal St.*, and *Mill St.*, run from W. to E. towards the Tay, along the rt. bank of which is the handsome boulevard of *Tay St.*, with the principal public buildings.

Parallel to it, and almost in one continuous line, are *George St.*, *St. John St.*, and *Princes St.*, containing the leading banks and shops.

Near the S. end of Tay St. is the **Museum of the Perthshire Society of Natural Science,**[1] containing an excellently-arranged collection typical of the botany, geology, and

[1] Open free Wed., Thur., Fri., and Sat., 10-1 and 2-5.

zoology of the County, also reading-room and lecture-room.

Behind it is *Greyfriars Ch.-yd.*, on the site of an ancient Franciscan Monastery.

At the corner of South St. and Tay St. are the **County Buildings** erected 1808-20 on the site of the *Gowrie Ho.*, built 1520, taken down 1807. It was the scene in 1600 of the mysterious Gowrie conspiracy by the Earl of Gowrie and his brother to seize and carry off James VI., which failed, the conspirators being slain on the spot.

In Tay St. there are also the **Savings Bank, Post Office**, the **City Chambers,** at whose erection in 1880, portions of the old city wall were discovered, the *Police Office*, the *New Club*, and two *Free Churches*, one with a fine spire 215 ft. high. At the W. end of South St. is **James VI. Hospital,** founded 1569, erected 1750 on the site of the old Carthusian Monastery, and formerly used as a school. In *Parliament Close*, High St., was the building, removed 1818, in which the Scottish Parliaments met until the days of James II. (1437-1460).

A tablet in **Curfew Row,** near Pullar's Dye Works, marks the house of Simon Glover, father of the "Fair Maid of Perth." In a niche at the corner of the street an image of St. Bartholomew, patron saint of the Glovers' Corporation, used to stand. Close at hand was the *Blackfriars Monastery* (founded 1231, destroyed 1559), in which James I., the poet king, so long a prisoner in Windsor Castle, and author of the "King's Quhair," was assassinated in 1437 by Sir Robert Graham, in presence of the Queen, after Catherine Douglas had in vain barred the door with her arm, which was broken. This brave lady afterwards married Richard Lovel of Ballumbie (p. 267).

Perth was held as a centre for military operations by the Marquis of Montrose in 1644; was taken by Cromwell after one day's siege in 1651, and was occupied by the Jacobite insurgents in 1715, and again in 1745.

The principal **Church** in the town is **St. John's** in St. John St., which was founded before the 10th cent., although nothing of that age remains.[1]

The existing building is cruciform, with a central square tower surmounted by a low spire dating, along with the transepts, from the 14th cent. The basement of an older tower (1125) may be seen on the N. side of the nave, which is the oldest part of the church. The present choir was built 1440. Over forty altars dedicated to as many saints were erected in the church, and endowed. In this ch. Knox preached his famous sermon of 11th May 1559, after which, every article within the building was destroyed. Seats were erected 1582, galleries in 1590, while in 1598 the interior was divided into two parts. In the W. ch. sat the Assembly of 1618, which passed the famous "Five Articles of Perth." In 1650 Charles II. attended service here, and Prince Charlie in 1745. In 1773 another partition was put up, making three churches which still remain. In 1893 the E. ch., in which is a monument to Lord Gowrie and another to the officers of the 90th Regiment (Perthshire Light Infantry) killed before Sebastopol, was restored, its galleries being removed. The bells are rung every day at 5.30 A.M., and 10 P.M.

From this Church, dedicated to John the Baptist, Perth was known as "St. John's Town" (see p. 251), and is so called in a despatch of Cromwell. Its war-cry was "St. Johnston's hunt is up."

St. Ninian's Cathedral[2] in Athole Street, close to the *Barracks*, is the Epis. Cath. for the Diocese of St. Andrews, Dunkeld, and Dunblane. The choir and transepts were finished 1850, the nave was added 1890 (Butterfield, archt.). The style is transition from Early Eng. to Decorated. The church is 200 ft. long and 72 ft. high; and

1 See "The Historic Church of St. John," a Lecture by Rev. W. Stevenson, M.A., F.S.A. Scot., published (1893) by Cowan & Co. Limited, Perth.

2 Open daily 9 A.M. to 6 P.M. Sunday Services 8 A.M., 11 A.M., 7 P.M.

the interior is fine, but the exterior lacks the W. spire.

There is another small Epis. Ch. (*St. John's*) in Princes St.

A *Grecian Temple*, erected in George St. to the memory of E. T. Marshall, one of the city's provosts, contains a (neglected) *Antiquarian Museum* [1] and a *Library*.

The **North and South Inches** are two wide meadows, situated on either side of the town, and left open for the enjoyment of the inhabitants. The South Inch is surrounded and intersected by avenues of noble sycamore and other trees; upon it is a *Monument to Sir Walter Scott*. Facing it is a Free Ch., with a crown tower—a poor imitation of St. Giles's, Edinburgh. At its S. end is the **General** (Convict) **Prison for Scotland**—erected in 1812 to contain the French prisoners of war—converted into a prison 1841, and enlarged 1858 and 1881.

On the N. Inch, which is the larger of the two, the memorable judicial combat between the Clan Chattan and the Clan Quhele (Kay), so admirably described in Scott's "Fair Maid of Perth," was fought in 1396, in the presence of the king, by 30 champions on each side. A man was wanting on the side of the Clan Chattan, but his place was filled by Hal o' the Wynd, a bandy-legged smith of Perth, who fought well, and contributed to the victory without knowing why or on which side he was fighting. Upon this Inch is an insignificant *Statue of the Prince Consort*, by Brodie. Facing the Inch is the *Royal Golf Club*, also the **Perth Academy** with a classic front. Upon it is an excellent *Golf Course*, and here too the *County Cricket Club* has its ground.

The principal industries are *Pullar's Dye Works* (founded abt. 1820, and now the largest in the world, employing 1700 hands, and containing 40 steam engines, 130 sewing machines, and 1400 dye vessels), *Campbell's Dye Works*, and *Coates Brothers' Jute Works*.

[1] Open daily 12-5. Adm. 3d.

The Tay *Salmon* (*Net*) *Fishings* yield a rental of about £16,460 a year, of which the city of Perth gets about £565. The Salmon *Rod* Fishings on the Tay and its tributaries and on Loch Tay which are let are valued at about £5300, but much of the best water is kept in the proprietors' own hands.

At the N. end of the town, the Tay is crossed by a handsome **Bridge** of 9 arches, built by Smeaton 1766-71, and widened 1869. It commands a charming view N. of the river, the North Inch, and the hills above Dunkeld and Pitlochrie. Across the bridge is the suburb of **Bridgend** and the villa-covered slopes of **Kinnoull Hill.**

WALKS:—

(1) S.E.—Up **Kinnoull Hill,** the S.W. spur of the *Sidlaw Range*, rising abruptly from the l. bank of the Tay, and commanding a fine view of the *Carse of Gowrie, the Tay Bridge*, the *Lomonds* in Fife, the *Ochils*, and the *Highland Mts.*, 1½ m.

Cross the bridge and turn rt. Then the first road l. will lead, passing rt. a *R.C. Retreat*, to the lodge from which a path (rt.) takes to the summit (729 ft.), crowned by a ruined tower. The cliffs of porphyrite are almost sheer. The geologist will note that the hill forms an anticlinal arch with the Ochils. *Kinfauns Cas.* (p. 247) lies below (E.).

(2) S.—up **Moncrieffe Hill** (725 ft.), according to Pennant, "the glory of Scotland," 3 m.

From the top of the hill, before reaching the 2nd milestone on the Edinburgh road, a path leads l. to the summit, which commands the best view of the town and surrounding country.

(3) N.—up the rt. bank of the Tay to the *Woody Island*, 2 m.

DRIVES:—

(1) **Round Kinnoull Hill** (return-

ing by the Dundee road), 9 m., or (by the Moor of Durdie), 11 m.

Cross the bridge, keep str. up, and then the 1st road rt. will lead past l. *Lunatic Asylum* (1 m.) above *Kinfauns Cas.* rt. (2¾ m.), with charming views over the Carse of Gowrie, to a steep hill (4 m.). This is descended to the foot if the Dundee road is to be reached; otherwise take 1st turn l., passing rt. *Balthayock Ho.* (4¼ m.). At 5½ m. turn l., and again (7 m.) take 1st turn l.—passing l. *Murray's Hall* (Major Murray Graham) and *Bonhard* (Alex. Macduff, Esq.)—to the Scone road.

(2) N.E.—**To Dunsinane Hill** (1012 ft.), 8 m.

It is crowned by a hill fort of several successive ramparts of loose stones, is the site of the castle celebrated in "Macbeth," and overlooks the country to and far beyond Birnam Hill (p. 218). The ascent from the driving road is short and easy.

(3) **Round Moncrieffe Hill**, 11 m.

Go by Rhynd Ch. (4 m.), ½ m. N. of which on the rt. bank of the Tay is *Elcho Cas.* (p. 247), and return by *Moncrieffe* (Sir R. D. Moncrieffe, Bart.).

(4) N.E. to **St. Martin's Abbey**, by New Scone and Balbeggie (6 m.); returning by *Newmiln* (J. M. Matthew, Jun., Esq.) and *Scone Palace*, 12 m.

Scone Palace (2½ m. from Perth Bridge) is the seat of the Earl of Mansfield. No admittance is granted except by special order. A modern castellated mansion, built 1803-8, occupies the site of an Augustine Abbey founded in 1114, and sacked by the Perth mob after Knox's sermon, 1559. It has a charming situation among parks upon the l. bank of the Tay.

This is one of the most famous historical places in Scotland. Its *Mote-hill*, to the N. of the Abbey, was a place of solemn meeting in the 8th century. It became the capital of Kenneth Macalpin, who united Picts and Scots 843, and is said to have brought hither the "*Stone of Destiny*" from Dunstaffnage (p. 175). That stone was removed from Scone to England by Edward I. 1296, and is under the seat of the Coronation Chair in Westminster Abbey. At Scone the Scottish kings—including Robert Bruce—were crowned until the days of James IV., and here Charles II. was crowned 1651. The Chevalier James Stuart lived here in January 1716, Prince Charlie visited Scone 1745, and the Queen and Prince Consort slept in the palace 6th Sept. 1842. Upon the Mote-hill, a parish ch. was erected 1624, of which only an aisle remains—used as a family mausoleum.

In the interior of the palace, among other ancient furniture, are some bed hangings, said to have been worked by Mary Queen of Scots while a prisoner in Lochleven Castle.

The Abbey Grounds are converted into beautiful shrubberies, gardens, and groves, 15 acres in area, part being planted with choice conifers; within them stands the old cross of Old Scone Market Place. On one side an avenue of limes leads up to the house, planted 1816, on another an avenue of sycamores 300 yrs. old. The garden contains many choice trees of great size and beauty, as the sycamore on the lawn planted by Q. Mary, a lime 76 ft. high, and an oak 70 ft., planted by the present Earl, who has planted more than a million oaks on his estates. Here are specimens of *Pinus Douglasii*, the first planted in Scotland, 1826-27, 75 ft. high. Douglas, who lost his life in a bison-trap, was gardener here.

William Murray (1705-93), first Earl of Mansfield, the illustrious Chief-Justice of England, was born here.

(5) N.—To **Campsie Linn** and **Stobhall** (cf. p. 251), passing through *Guildtown* (5½ m.)—founded 1818, and with a curious masonic device, dated 1835, upon a cottage (l.)—7½ m. 4 m. farther on is **Meikleour** and its famous *Beech Hedge* (p. 251).

Stobhall (Earl of Ancaster), an old mansion in a strong and picturesque site overlooking the Tay, was the seat of Sir John Drummond, whose daughter m. Robert III. (1390-1406). The house bears date 1578, but part of it is supposed to be 400 years older. The roof of the banqueting hall contains curious representations of the kings of the principal countries in Europe and Africa. The garden with trimmed hedges should be visited, and the tower, where the Duke of Perth was concealed, 1745, ascended.

(6) S.E.—To **Glen Farg** (cf. p. 193), 9 m.

The road leads through *Bridge of Earn*, p. 194 (3 m.), and across Strath Earn. Horses can be baited at *Bein Inn* (7½ m.).

ROUTE 35

Edinburgh to Stirling by Dunfermline, Clackmannan, and Alloa. N.B.R.

Except for variety or for the purpose of crossing the Forth Bridge, this route is inferior as a means of reaching Stirling to that (from Princes St. Stat.) described in Rtes. 19 and 25.

Leaving Waverley Stat. we proceed as in Rte. 30 to

16¾ m. **Dunfermline Lower Stat.** ✲, then sweep E. round the town, passing the junc. where through trains from Thornton (p. 181) come in, to

19¼ m. **Dunfermline Upper Stat.** whence the line strikes W. through an uninteresting country (not well seen) with a few coal-pits, to

23¾ m. **Oakley Stat.**, 1 m. S. of which is *Inzievar* (Trs. of A. V. Smith-Sligo, Esq.[1]).

25¼ m. **East Grange Stat.**, *Coach* 3 or 4 times daily to **Culross** ✲, 2 m. S. (p. 203).

[1] At Inzievar is a good collection of pictures :—portraits of Sir W. Scott by *Sir J. W. Gordon;* Landscape by *Cuyp;* Mary Queen of Scots as a Girl (?), *Holbein;* S. Sebastian, *P. Veronese;* A Doge of Venice, *L. da Vinci.*

27¼ m. **Bogside Stat.**

29¾ m. **Kennet Stat.**

30¾ m. **Clackmannan Stat.** ✲. The town stands on high ground to the S. of the rly., but, though the capital of its little county, it is a dull place, and so out-of-the-way as almost to justify one of Aytoun's characters alleging that no one (!) had ever been there. In a field W. of the town is a strong *Tower* 79 feet high, said to have been built by Robert Bruce, and now the property of the Marquis of Zetland. It is not older than the 15th cent., but it may have had a predecessor.

1 m. S.E. of the town is *Kennet*, a beautifully-situated mansion in a domain which has belonged since the days of King Robert I. to a branch of the family of Bruce, now represented by Lord Balfour of Burleigh.

33 m. **Alloa Stat.** (see p. 204).

[Lines run (1) N. to *Dollar, Rumbling Bridge, Kinross, Perth*, etc. [Rte. 36].

(2) S. across the Forth (p. 156) to Larbert, Glasgow, etc.

(3) S.E. by Clackmannan to Kincardine (p. 203), 6 m.]

Alloa ✲ is a thriving and increasing town with a small harbour and dock formed 1879-81. Abundance of coal in its neighbourhood renders it alive with numerous manufactories of woollen tartans, notably that of Paton and Co., Kilncraigs, while it is particularly distinguished for its extensive whisky distilleries and breweries of ale, iron foundries, and copper works.

The Episcopal *Church of St. John*, Broad Street, was built by the Earl of Mar and Kellie, 1869, at a cost of £5000, and is a commodious building, with a peal of 6 bells.

The Gothic Parish Church was built 1819. In the old churchyard stands the tower of an older ch.

In the Glebe Park, near the Masonic Hall, is the *Museum* of Nat. Hist. and Antiquities. In Bank Street are the *Municipal*

Buildings, built 1865. In 1882 the handsome new Post-Office, adjoining the Crown Hotel, was opened.

Eleanor Syme, Lord Brougham's mother, was born here.

On the E. side of the town, within the Park, not far from the mansion of the Earl of Mar and Kellie, rises the *Tower of Alloa*, 89 ft. high, with walls 11 ft. thick, built in the 13th cent., and long a stronghold of the Earls of Mar. It formed part of their mansion, destroyed by fire 1800. Queen Mary spent some years here when a child, and two nights with Darnley in 1566. James VI., when a boy, was birched by George Buchanan within its walls, having been educated here; and Prince Henry, the King's eldest son, was also partly brought up at this place.

Alloa House, the modern mansion of the Earl of Mar and Kellie, built in 1838 and 1868, contains family portraits and relics, and extensive gardens have been laid out.

Castle Campbell, near Dollar, a quarter of an hour by rail from Alloa, is well worth a visit (p. 200). See Rte. 36 for the rest of the journey by *Cambus* and *Causewayhead* to

39¾ m. **Stirling Stat.** ✲ (p. 157).

ROUTE 36.

Stirling to Kinross and Ladybank by Alloa, Dollar, and the Rumbling Bridge. N.B.R.

Trains from Glasgow to Perth by Alloa Bridge and Glen Farg traverse this line between Alloa and Kinross.

This—*The Devon Valley Railway*—crosses the Forth, and keeps along the S. base of the Ochil Hills, a striking range "formed by a broad anticlinal fold of the volcanic rocks of the Old Red Sandstone."

1¼ m. **Causewayhead Stat.** under the picturesque **Abbey Craig** (362 ft.)—a limestone and greenstone rock—held by Wallace on the eve of the Battle of Stirling 1297, and now crowned by a much-criticised Monument to that hero (erected 1861-69, at a cost of over £16,000), which commands a splendid view. **Bridge of Allan** (p. 205) is 1½ m. W., and between is the beautiful estate of *Airthrey Cas.* (p. 205). 2½ m. N. (beyond *Logie Ch.*) rises **Dunmyat** (1375 ft.), from which one of the finest low ascent views in Scotland may be obtained.

The line turns sharply E., having the "*Links of Forth*" and *Cambuskenneth Abbey* (p. 204) rt., and crosses the Devon—whose junction with the Forth, after a curious course of 33 m., is not 6 m. from its source—just before

4½ m. **Cambus Stat.**

[*Branch* l. across the Devon to

2 m. **Menstrie Stat.**, close to *Glen Ochil Distillery*, a seat of the woollen cloth, tartan, etc. manufacture, and the birthplace (1734) of Sir Ralph Abercromby.

3½ m. **Alva Stat.**, a thriving town, abounding in woollen mills, but from which the picturesque glens of the Ochils can be best visited. Behind the town is the striking gorge of *Glen Alva* (with a pretty waterfall at its head), called the "Silver Glen" from the former silver mines. 1½ m. E. is *Alva Ho.* (Miss C. E. M. Johnstone), which the Johnstones bought from the Erskines, Earls of Mar. It was built in the reign of Charles I., but was subsequently much altered. It has lovely grounds and a fine avenue of oaks.

Ben Cleuch (2363 ft.), the highest of the Ochils, is 3 m. N., and may be reached by the horse path which leads to Blackford, 8 m. (p. 207). The view from the top is most extensive, and has been excellently engraved in Knipe's "Panorama" (from a drawing by the Ordnance Survey Officers) published at Stirling.]

Beyond Cambus (rt.) on the Forth is *Tullibody Ho.* (p. 204).

6½ m. **Alloa Stat.** ✲ (p. 198), whence the line trends N. to

8 m. **Sauchie Stat.**, and, crossing the Devon,

10 m. **Tillicoultry Stat.** ✲, another important seat of woollen manufactures, with a very handsome ch. on its outskirts (E.). **Alva** (p. 199) is only 2½ m. W.

Beyond Tillicoultry *Harvieston Ho.* (James Orr, Esq.), with a square ch.-like tower, is well seen l. It was sung of by Burns, and in the grounds is *Tait's Tomb*, the family burial-place of the late Archbp. of Canterbury, whose father built the present mansion.

Macculloch calls "this portion of Clackmannan one of the most delicious in Scotland . . . bounded on the one hand by a lofty and continuous wall of green cultivated and wooded mountains, and on the other looking over a wide and open expanse of country, which dazzles the eye by its richness."

12¾ m. **Dollar Stat.** ✲ (from "*Dalard*" = the Steep Valley) is a village celebrated for its large *Academy*, a Doric building and excellent school, founded by a wealthy sea captain, John M'Nab (d. 1802), who left this, his native place, a poor boy. Conspicuous on the l. above the village are the ruins of ***Castle Campbell**, occupying an isolated position on the steep hill-side, and guarded by deep gorges which meet 300 yds. below the fortress.

It is reached by a pleasant walk of rather over 1 m., following the l. bank of the burn from the Stat. After crossing a field the glen[1] is reached. When the glen forks, keep rt. up the E. gorge or "Burn of Care" to the Castle. The origin of this castle, or how it came into the hands of the Argyll family, is unknown, but it was originally called the Castle of Gloom, situated in the parish of Dolour (Dollar) beside the waters of Grief (Griff), and surrounded by the Glen of Care. In 1489 the first Earl of Argyll obtained an Act of Parliament to change its name to Castle Campbell. In 1556 John Knox preached here a short time prior to his going to Geneva; and in 1645 Montrose, on his way to Kilsyth, sacked and burnt it in revenge for the destruction of Airlie (p. 266), and it has never since been inhabited save by a keeper. It remained in the possession of the Argyll family from 1465 to 1805, when it was sold. It now belongs to Harvieston estate.

It is approached through an outer court or Barmekin, and has, as its chief feature, a square keep tower probably of the 12th cent., to which a more modern wing with an open arcade is attached. On the first floor of the tower is the great hall (now roofed across), and adjoining it was the trap door into the pit or dungeon. The hall's ancient and remarkable cradle roof of stone, ribbed, can be seen from the next story. The *View* from the top of the tower is extensive and pleasing, but not specially interesting. A more picturesque view is got from a point above the castle, as it then forms a striking foreground.

Descend by the other stream—the "Burn of Sorrow"—which flows through a gorge called the *Windy Pass*, resembling that of Pfeffers in miniature.

It is an extraordinary and romantic chasm, in one place not 3 yds. wide, with steep walls of bare rock some 80 ft. high, and but for the bridges, clamped with iron stanchions to the rock, it would be impassable.

From Dollar the *Ascent of Ben Cleuch*, the highest of the Ochils (p. 199), is a walk of 5 m. N.W., passing Castle Campbell.

Just beyond Dollar the rly. is carried over the Devon on a viaduct of 6 arches, 110 ft. high, and makes a wide sweep, affording good views of this striking valley.

It crosses a burn by another high viaduct on its way to

17 m. **Rumbling Bridge Stat.** ✲, about 100 yds. from the famous **Bridge* over the Devon. Like the Pont du Diable on the Pass of St. Gothard, it is double, consisting of an old narrow arch, built by a local mason 1713, surmounted by a more modern and loftier one, 120 feet above the stream which *rumbles* beneath. Access[1] to the river banks

---

[1] Admission (including the Castle) 6d. each.

[1] Apply at the Hotel 200 yds. farther on. Admission free to persons dining in the hotel. Other persons 6d. each. Persons picnicking in the grounds 1s. each.

is obtained through doors in the walls. The channel of the river above the bridge is particularly striking and picturesque, especially at the *Devil's Mill*, a waterfall so called because of the strangely marked sound it makes, resembling a mill wheel, and because it never rests on Sunday. The path on the l. bank down the river is very pretty. It leads in 1¼ m. to the *Cauldron Linn*, a beautiful spot with a double cascade well worth seeing, especially after rain.

[There is an excellent driving road hence across the Ochils to Blackford (p. 207), 12 m., or Crieff (p. 211), 20 m. It ascends the pleasing *Glen Devon*, and descends the wilder *Glen Eagles.*]

1½ m. S.E. of the Rumbling Bridge is *Aldie*, the seat of the Mercers of Aldie, now represented by the Marchioness of Lansdowne.

18½ m. **Crook of Devon Stat.**, so called from the doubling back here of the Devon. Near it is *Tullibole Cas.* (Lord Moncreiff).

21½ m. **Balado Stat.**

23½ m. **Kinross Junc. Stat.** ✲ (p. 193).

See p. 182 for rest of the line by *Mawcarse* to

38½ m. **Ladybank** ✲.

ROUTE 37.

Stirling from Leith by Queensferry, Alloa, and the Windings of the Forth—Steamer.

A charming sail of abt. 4 hrs. Steamer daily in summer, if and when the tide permits, the difficulty being the shallow banks in the river on which the steamer occasionally grounds.

Leaving Leith with its 2 long piers, the island of **Inchkeith** is seen 4 m. off N. in the middle of the channel. Dr. Johnson who landed there with Boswell (1773) found "very good grass but rather a profusion of thistles." In 1547 the English planted a fort and garrison to command the harbour of Leith and the Firth, to the disgust of the Scots. The French held and garrisoned it 1549-67 in accordance with the Treaty of Edinburgh, and Brantôme calls it "L'île des Chevaux," but it was dismantled 1567. The remains of a fort inscribed "Maria Ré 1564" were pulled down to furnish materials for the *Lighthouse* (1803) which has now a revolving light. In 1878-81 three batteries (mounting four 18-ton guns) were erected and connected by a military road.

Turning W. fine views are obtained of Arthur's Seat, Edin. Castle, etc., and, after passing **Newhaven** and **Granton** (p. 63), at 5 m. **Cramond** with its island, which may be reached over the sands at low tide, is seen, l. E. of it is *Laurieston Cas.* once the residence of John Law (1671-1929) the Mississippi financier, and W. *Barnbougle Cas.* (E. of Rosebery) in the grounds of **Dalmeny Park** (p. 65). rt., beyond a smaller island and some rocks, is **Inchcolm**, ¾ m. from the Fife coast, alluded to by Rosse in his account of the victory over Sweno, King of Norway.

"Nor would we deign him burial of his men,
Till he disbursed, at St. Colme's Inch,
Ten thousand dollars to our general use."
Macbeth, Act i. sc. 2.

"Inchcolm is the only island on the E. coast of Scotland which derives its distinctive derivation from St. Columba," though the name is comparatively common in the West.

Upon the island are the ruins of a *Monastery* founded in 1123 by Alexander I., who had been driven on the island by stress of weather, and fed by a poor hermit there, whom in gratitude he made the first Prior. In the time of Edward III. it had become so wealthy as to excite the cupidity of the English fleet lying in the Firth. It was accordingly plundered, but the fleet was soon after overtaken by a storm, in which many of the ships foundered, and the rest were only too glad to return and make restitution. The ruins consist of a small church and some conventual buildings, and an octagonal *Chapter-house*, 22 ft. diameter, with stone roof (date 1263). W. of the church is a very ancient *Cell* or *Oratory* of rudest masonry, with a slit window at the E.; a doorway on the S. side; and a rude attempt at a stone vault, of the same primitive style as those on the W. coast of Ireland, and probably as old as the 9th cent.

N.W. of Inchcolm are seen the ruined *Ch. of Dalgetty*, with a chapel at the W. end, in which Chancellor Seton (1555-1622) lies buried, and the old *Cas. of Donibristle*, humble at the best, once the residence of the Abbot of Inchcolm, and near which "the bonnie Earl of Moray," sung of in the old ballad, was slain in 1592, by the Earl of Huntly; the modern mansion of *Donibristle* (Earl of Moray) lies W. near the shore.

At 9 m. the steamer passes under the **Forth Bridge** (p. 178), which is best seen from the water. *Inch Garvie*; once a fortified rock and a State prison, whose castle surrendered to Cromwell 1651, now supports the central pier. Above lie the guardship and a training ship.

9½ m. the steamer calls l. at **So. Queensferry** (p. 178), a royal burgh, but a small though quaint place. It derives its name from Queen Margaret, wife of Malcolm Canmore (pp. 190, 40), who constantly travelled from Dunfermline to Edinburgh. The tolls of this ferry belonged at the Reformation to the Abbey of Dunfermline. In later days this was the coach route to the N., and a steam ferry-boat still crosses abt. 7 times daily, though much less used since the opening of the bridge. A *Carmelite Priory*, founded by Dundas of Dundas, 1330, was restored in 1890 as an Epis. Ch. 1 m. behind the town is *Dundas Castle* (James Russel, Esq.), held by the Dundas family from early in the 12th cent. until 1875. The old square keep is attached to the modern mansion.

12 m. (l.) are the Park and Grounds of **Hopetoun House**,[1] the seat of the Earl of Hopetoun, a fine 17th-cent. Italian house (renovated by Adam).

The grounds contain some remarkably fine specimens of cedar and abies, and the views from the green terrace walk parallel to the Forth are superb, embracing the whole sweep of the Firth of Forth and the Ochil Hills. It is a most stately domain, and the giant trees, the long umbrageous avenues, and the sunny *Garden* (shown when the family are absent), are hardly to be matched. Here are an *Abies morinda*, 80 ft. high, and large cedars of Lebanon.

In the interior, which is not shown to the public, are paintings by *Rubens* (Adorations of Shepherds, one of his very finest works); *A. Cuyp*, Landscape with figures on horseback; *Vandyck*, Ecce Homo; *Teniers*, The Painter, his Wife and Child, in a landscape, etc.

Adjoining the park on the W. is the village of **Abercorn** from which the Duke of Abercorn takes his title. It was the seat of an English bishop of the Picts in the 7th cent. The *Church*, originally very ancient, retains only one semicircular chancel arch and a doorway, the rest being hideously modernised. Still farther W. inland is *Binns*, for centuries the family seat of the Dalyells, and on the shore *Blackness Cas.*, long a State prison, and one of the 4 fortresses which by the Articles of Union were to be left fortified—now a powder magazine.

Opposite Hopetoun rt. is *Rosyth Cas.* alluded to in "The Abbot." It was formerly a castle of the Stuarts, and has over the gateway "M.R. 1561." W. of it is *Limekilns* and *Charleston*, celebrated for their lime works. Between them is *Broomhall Ho.* (p. 192).

At 19 m. l. is the town of **Bo'ness** (shortened from *Borrowstounness*), whence there is a short rly. line in 4¼ m. to Manuel (p. 130). It is a

[1] Grounds open to the public Wed. and Sat.

busy seaport and possesses considerable docks, constructed in 1879. Shipbuilding, coal-mining, and iron-working are the chief industries. S.W. of the town are *Kinneil Ho.* (D. of Hamilton), once the residence of Dugald Stewart, and traces of *Graham's Dyke* (p. 131).

4 m. higher up, on the same side, is the port of **Grangemouth,** situated at the E. end of the Forth and Clyde Canal (p. 150), and at the mouth of the *Carron* river. The celebrated *Carron Ironworks* are about 3 m. W. and a rly. runs S. in 3 m. to Grahamston (p. 131).

Opposite Bo'ness is *Torry Bay*, with **Torryburn, Torry,** and **Culross** ✲ (pron. *Coo'ross*), a decayed royal burgh, containing many old houses [*Coach* to E. Grange station 2 m. (p. 198)]. It was better known in Scotland for its manufacture of girdles for oat-cakes than for its ecclesiastical reputation, though St. Mungo, patron saint of Glasgow, is said to have been cast ashore here as an infant, and educated by St. Serf in the 6th cent. This peculiarity is alluded to in the "Heart of Midlothian"—"The hammermen of Edinburgh are na' that bad at girdles for carcakes neither, though the Cu'ross hammermen have the gree for that." On a terrace above the sea, a little to the E. of the town, is the fine mansion of *Culross Abbey* (Hon. R. Bruce), originally built, 1590, by Sir Wm. Bruce of Kinross, the renovator of Holyrood Palace, afterwards repaired by Sir Robert Preston of Valleyfield. It contains a room with a panelled roof, each panel decorated by a painting of one of the Virtues, and some inscriptions in Latin and English. James VI. came here to visit the coal and salt pits in the neighbourhood, which were then extensive, but are now exhausted.

Culross Abbey was founded in 1217 by Malcolm, Earl of Fife, for Cistercian monks. The tower remains, and the Gothic choir is partly used as the *Parish Ch.*, and contains numerous incised monumental slabs. In the N. aisle is a marble monument to Sir Geo. Bruce (d. 1625), with effigies of him, his lady, and 7 children. Within the masonry is inserted the heart of Edward, 2nd Lord Bruce of Kinloss, killed in a duel with Sir Edw. Sackville at Bergen-op-Zoom, 1614.

½ m. W. of the town on the hill-side facing the Firth of Forth and surrounded by woods is *Dunimarle*, a modern castellated building, the residence of the late Mrs. Erskine.

It has a *Museum* of antiquities and curiosities collected by that lady and, by her will, open to the public, containing a collection of arms, mostly of the 18th cent., some family portraits, 3 pictures by *Wouverman*, a *Hobbema*, a *Teniers*, and a *Corregio* of 12 Cupids; also some good old Venetian, German, Flemish, and French glass, point lace, Nürnberg silver plate, and a draped torso said to be of the age of Pericles.

Mrs. Erskine was sister of Sir James Erskine, A.D.C. to the Duke of Wellington at Waterloo, whose collection of pictures formed the nucleus of the National Gallery in Edinburgh.

Below is the little *Epis. Ch.* of St. Serf, and a short distance W. is the gate of *Blair Castle* (R. Millar, Esq.).

21 m. rt. **Kincardine,** a small sea-port, with a rly. (1893) to Alloa, p. 198, and a steam ferry across the Forth (½ m.)

1 m. to the N. is *Tulliallan Castle*, the modern seat of Lady Osborne Elphinstone, built by Adm. Lord Keith, 1820, in a beautiful Park. There are some remains of an older castle near it.

Here the Firth may be said to stop and the river to begin.

On left is *Airth Castle* (T. P. Graham, Esq.), finely situated on a hill overlooking the Firth. A somewhat modernised house, with a strong tower, called Wallace's Tower, dating probably from the battle of Falkirk, 1298. This tower has the distinctive features of a covered turret and a battlemented bartizan, added in the 16th cent.

Dunmore House, l. farther on, but nearer the shore, is the seat of the Earl of Dunmore.

It contains a collection of pictures, the most important being:—Portrait of Admiral Capello, *Tintoretto;* Orpheus and Eurydice bitten by the Asp, *N. Poussin;* Charles I. and Henrietta Maria, *D. Mytens;* Landscape, *Holbein;* Soldiers maltreating Peasants, *Rubens;* Altarpiece, *A. Dürer;* The Visitation, *L. Caracci;* Perseus and Andromeda, *Vandyck;* Martyrdom of St. Catherine, *P. Veronese;* Peasants with Garlands, *Velasquez.*

As the river narrows, the beauty of the scenery is increased by the near approach to the Ochil Hills (rt.) (cf. Rte. 36).

23 m. **Clackmannan Pier.** The town, the capital of the county, is 2 m. N., with a rly. stat. on the Dunfermline to Stirling line (p. 198). Between is *Kennet*, the seat of Lord Balfour of Burleigh (p. 198).

25 m. **Alloa**✲, see p. 198.

There is a ferry between N. and S. Alloa, above which is *Alloa Inch* (island) and then the swing rly. bridge of 17 spans (opened 1885, at a cost of abt. £40,000) which carries a line to Larbert (p. 156), giving Alloa unbroken rly. communication with the South.

The river now winds along **"The Links of Forth,"** so celebrated for their fertility that it is a popular saying in the district that

"A crook o' the Forth
Is worth an earldom o' the North."

As the crow flies it is 5½ m. from Alloa to Stirling, while by the river the distance is 12½ m.

Passing Tullibody Inch there is seen on right *Tullibody House* (Lord Abercromby), the family seat but not the birthplace of Sir Ralph. There is a monument to him and others of the family in the *Church*, of which John Knox records that the French troops sent to aid Mary of Guise, "expert enough in such feats, tuke down the roof to make ane brig over the Devon," and so they escaped to Stirling. Beyond it is the mouth of the Devon, foul with mill-refuse, whose upper course is famous for its romantic scenery (Rte. 36).

2 m. farther, on the S. bank, is *Polmaise* (Col. Murray), just beyond which the celebrated *Bannock Burn* falls into the Forth. The turns of the river now become more abrupt than ever, and the steamer is compelled to slacken speed to get round them.

In front rt. is the **Abbey Craig** (362 ft. high) with *Wallace's Monument* (p. 199).

On right, a conspicuous object on the plain is **Cambuskenneth Abbey,** founded by David I. in 1147, and at one time perhaps the richest abbey in Scotland.

It consists now only of a very noble detached tower, the W. doorway of the ch., and the foundations of walls. The staircase is sufficiently preserved to enable the visitor to ascend the tower, the view from which is very fine, embracing the windings of the Forth for many miles, with the noble rock and castle of Stirling close by, the Grampian Mountains, and the Ochil Hills. The abbey and its estates were given at the Reformation to the Earl of Mar, who is said to have pulled the greater part of the building down to erect his house at Stirling (p. 158). The unfortunate James III. (d. 1488) and his Queen, Margaret of Denmark, were buried at Cambuskenneth. Their remains having been discovered in 1864, a monument was put up to their memory by Queen Victoria as a "restoration of the tomb of her ancestors."

At the S. end of the last long "Link" the steamer stops at the pier close to

Stirling✲, see p. 157.

ROUTE 38.

Stirling to Perth by Dunblane and Auchterarder. Cal. Rly.

Through carriages from Glasgow to Perth (see Rte. 25); and from Edinburgh to Perth (see Rtes. 19 and 25).

Leaving Stirling the line crosses the Forth and traverses the plain, with l. fine views of Stirling Cas., the Campsie Fells, Ben Lomond, Ben Venue, and Ben Ledi, and rt. Abbey Craig (p. 199), to

3 m. **Bridge of Allan Stat.** ✲, a watering-place, very popular, especially in spring, in consequence of its sheltered situation, and its saline waters (antiscorbutic and aperient). These waters, which have their source on Westerton Hill on the N. E., are collected in the reservoir of an old copper-mine, and then raised to the "Well-House" on the shoulder of the hill, and drunk warm. Attached to it are baths, reading and billiard rooms. The village, a collection of lodging-houses and neat detached villas, stretches in terraces along the wooded slope of Westerton Hill, overlooking the Allan Water, which below this spot joins the Forth, after a picturesque and beautiful course through Strathallan. There are mills and bleaching works on the river.

The views, walks, and drives around are charming, and render this superior to Stirling as a centre for the tourist.

Near the village on the Stirling road is *Airthrey Castle*[1] (Donald Graham, Esq.). *Keir*[2] (a corruption of "Caer," it being the site of a Celtic fort), formerly the seat of the late Sir W. Stirling Maxwell, and now the property of Arch. Stirling, Esq., stands ½ m. N.W. on the road to Doune.

[1] Admission on Thursdays to the grounds. Enter at the lodge; leave by the gate near the old ch. of Logie.

[2] The beautiful gardens and park are open to visitors from 2-6 p.m. on Fridays.

It contains some good *pictures*, principally by Spanish masters. The most important are an altar-piece, *Murillo*—the Virgin and Child—formerly in the convent of La Madre de Dios at Seville, in which Murillo's daughter took the veil; Philip IV. of Spain, by *Rubens*, "animated, warm, and clear in colour"; Virgin lamenting over Christ's body, *Morales;* Portrait of his first wife, *Rubens;* Landscape with two friars, *G. Poussin*, "beautiful and poetical"; Finding of Moses, *N. Poussin;* Christ and His Disciples going to Emmaus, *C. Lorraine;* Landscape, *Teniers;* Baptism of Christ, *P. Veronese;* the Virgin, *Zurbaran;* Portrait of Cromwell, *Walker;* Miss Stirling, *Raeburn*. The library is a magnificent lofty room, lined throughout with fragrant cedar-wood. Upon the cornice are mottoes in various European languages.

In the prettily-situated *Ch. of Lecropt*, on the S. outskirts of Keir, are monuments to Sir Wm. Stirling-Maxwell, his two wives, and other members of the family.

½ m. N.E. on rt. of rly. is *Westerton*, the seat of Sir J. Alexander, and farther on is *Kippenross*[1] (P. Stirling, Esq.).

EXCURSIONS:—

(1) *Stirling* (tram or rly.) (p. 157).

(2) *Abbey Craig*, 1½ m. E. (p. 199), and *Cambuskenneth Abbey*, 1 m. beyond (p. 204).

(3) *Dunblane Cathedral*, 3 m. N. (p. 206).

(4) *Dunmyat Hill*, 4 m. E. (p. 199).

(5) *Castle Campbell, Rumbling Bridge, etc.* (Rte. 36).

(6) *Ardoch Camp*, 10 m. N. (p. 207).

(7) *Doune Castle*, 5 m. N.W. (p. 161).

(8) *Callander and Trossachs* (Rte. 26).

(9) *Lake of Menteith and Aberfoyle* (Rte. 28).

The rly. now enters Perthshire, ascends the Allan Water, crosses it, and passes through a tunnel to

5 m. **Dunblane Stat.** [Branch to *Callander* and *Oban*, Rtes. 26 and 29].

[1] Grounds open Weds. and Sats.

Beside the stat. rt. is a *Victoria* (Jubilee) *Hall*.

Dunblane ✲ (Fort of St. Blane) stands on the l. bank of the river Allan. It was originally a Culdee cell, and was made a bishopric by David I., by whom also the **Cathedral**[1] was founded about 1140. Of his Cathedral nothing remains but the 4 lower stages of the fine Romanesque *Tower*, which was originally a detached campanile, but is now attached to the S. aisle of the nave. The existing edifice erected 13th cent. through the instrumentality of Bp. Clemens, of a pure and masculine Gothic, consists of a noble nave of 8 bays, surmounted by a fine double mullioned clerestory, and of a choir. The W. front, a good specimen of the purest pointed style, comprises a deeply-recessed *Portal*, surmounted by a triplet of 3 tall lancet windows of 2 lights, with a cinquefoil in the head.

The Choir was carefully repaired (1873) by the late Sir W. S. Maxwell, and served as the Parish Ch. until the judicious restoration of the roofless Nave (Rowand Anderson, archt.), completed by public subscription 1893. The whole building is now used. An elegant wooden *Rood-Screen* and a *Pulpit* were erected 1893.

In the N. wall of the choir is the monument of Bp. Finlay Dermot, consecrated to this See in 1406. Remains of the old prebendal stalls of black oak, elaborately carved, some with canopies and some without, are also seen. A staircase leads to an upper chapel now occupied by the organ.

In the N. aisle of the Nave are the recumbent effigies of Malise, 5th Earl of Strathearn, and his countess, 1271, and in the S. aisle is that of Bp. Ochiltree, d. about 1447.

S.W. of the cathedral, near the river, are scanty remains of the *Bishop's Palace*.

Dunblane is honoured by having had Leighton as its bishop, who held this diocese from 1662 to 1669, when he was translated to the archbishopric of Glasgow. Finding, however, that all attempts to reconcile the people of Scotland to the episcopal form of church government were futile, he resigned his See and returned to England, where he died, and was buried in the small village churchyard of Horsted Keynes, in Sussex. He left his *Library* of 3000 vols. to Dunblane, a great part of which is still preserved in a house marked with the episcopal mitre near the gate of the churchyard.

There is a pleasant walk by the side of the river, passing the W. end of the cathedral.

The visitor will recall the fact that here lived the subject of Tannahill's ballad, "Jessie, the flower o' Dunblane."

[3 m. E. is **Sheriffmuir**, celebrated for the undecided battle fought there in 1715, between the Earl of Mar, who commanded the Pretender's forces, and the Duke of Argyll, at the head of the royal troops, which were inferior in number. Mar's object was to cross the Forth and join his friends in the S., and to prevent this, Argyll gave him battle. The rt. wing on each side was completely victorious, and pushed its successes so far as not to have noticed that its left was irretrievably routed. Both sides claimed the victory, but the fruits of it were with Argyll, for the Earl retreated. An old song says :—

"There's some say that we wan,
And some say that they wan,
And some say that nane wan at a', man ;
But of one thing I'm sure,
That at Sheriffmuir,
A battle there was, which I saw, man ;
And we ran, and they ran,
And they ran, and we ran,
And we ran, and they ran awa', man."

[1] Admission 3d. each. Hours :—1st Apr. to 30th Sept. 10-5, 1st Oct. to 31st Mar. 10-3, but Sat. 10-5.

The *Gathering Stone of the Clans* (renewed 1840), upon which the Highlanders are said to have sharpened their dirks before the action, as well as the mound where the slain were buried, are still to be seen.]

A good view is obtained of the cathedral (rt.) as the train leaves Dunblane. The line keeps N.E. up the valley of the Allan, to

7½ m. **Kinbuck Stat.**

10¾ m. **Greenloaning Stat.**

1½ m. N. are *Braco Village* ✱, and, across the *Knaik*, *Ardoch House* (Col. Home-Drummond), in whose park close to the road the archæologist will find the most perfect **Roman Camp** in Great Britain, a series of green turfed banks and ditches, one within the other, arranged in the form of squares. The space within one set of entrenchments is oblong, and measures 420 ft. by 375, with its four sides nearly facing the cardinal points of the compass. The prætorium is a regular square of 60 ft. in the centre of the camp, and stands upon slightly rising ground. Upon the N. side of this, the smallest camp, is the Procastrum, 1060 ft. by 900 ft., where the baggage was placed; and N.W. of that is the Great Camp, 2800 ft. by 1950 ft., which is considered to have been able to contain 26,000 men. The form of this camp is oblong, but not a regular parallelogram. Gen. Wade's road enters it by its S. gate, and has thus destroyed part of the vallum. The N. gate is a little E. of the road, and covered by a straight traverse, and another gate on the W. is protected in a similar manner. The 3rd stands on the W. of the great one, apparently within it, its ramparts crossing those of the larger one, which was evidently the older, and seems by its superior state of preservation to have been occupied at a subsequent period, when a part of the original force was withdrawn. It is probable that they were all constructed by Agricola.

A covered way is supposed to have led to *Kaims Castle*, about 1½ m. farther N., on the road to Crieff. W. is *Braco Castle* (Sir Renny Watson), and N.E. is *Orchill* (Sam. Smith, Esq., M.P.). For roads to Crieff see p. 213.

15 m. **Blackford Stat.**, beyond which (rt.) are the *Sources of the Allan*, the remains of *Ogilvie Cas.*, once a place of great strength, and *Gleneagles* (Earl of Camperdown), a modern mansion at the mouth of a fine Pass leading through the Ochils to the Rumbling Bridge (p. 201). The watershed is crossed before reaching

17¼ m. **Crieff Junc.** [Branch l. to *Crieff* and *Comrie* (Rte. 39).]

In the park of *Kincardine Castle* (J. Johnston, Esq.) (modern) rt. is a beautiful glen, 3 m. long, crossed by the railway on a viaduct of eight arches.

19¼ m. **Auchterarder Stat.**, rt. is *Cloanden* (R. B. Haldane, Esq., M.P.).

Auchterarder ✲, ¾ m. l., consisting principally of a street a mile long, is of little importance in itself, but was of considerable notoriety as the scene of one of the events which led to the disruption of the Church of Scotland in 1843. Auchterarder, with Dunning and other places in the neighbourhood, was burnt by the Earl of Mar in 1715, to impede the progress of the royal troops, for which compensation was promised to the sufferers in a proclamation from the palace of Scone.

Beyond the stat. a fine view may be obtained (l.) of Ben Ledi, Ben Voirlich, Crieff, and Glen Turret. At 22 m. l. is **Aberruthven**, with the ruins of *St. Kattan's Chap.*, beside which is the *Mausoleum* of the Dukes of Montrose.

23½ m. **Dunning Stat.**, between which and the village (2 m. rt.) is *Duncrub*, the seat of Lord Rollo.

The rly. now approaches and keeps parallel with the Earn to

26¼ m. **Forteviot Stat.** In the *Manse* here Lord Robertson, the present Lord Justice - General of Scotland, was b. 1845, and on *Holy Hill*, near the ch., are remains of a royal residence of very early times.

It was the favourite summer quarters of Kenneth MacAlpin who d. here 860. It was probably taken by him from the Pictish kings, of whose country—*Fortrenn*—it was the capital. Duncan and Macbeth spent much of their time here, as did also Malcolm Canmore and his son Alex. I., whose charters are dated from this place. In and after Malcolm's days, however, the more southerly residence of Dunfermline became preferable, and Forteviot was allowed to go to ruin.

1½ m. S. of the station is *Invermay* (Hon. C. J. Trefusis, formerly the seat of the Belshes), celebrated in Mallet's ballad "The Birks of Invermay," near which the river May rushes down from the Ochils in a wild and broken stream; in one place it is called Humble-Bumble, from the deep booming sound kept up by the water between narrow walls of rock.

At 27½ m. l. on the N. side of the Earn is *Dupplin Cas.* (Earl of Kinnoull)—4 m. by road from Perth—a modern house in Elizabethan style, completed at a cost of £30,000 in 1832 (its predecessor having been burnt down 1827), and visited by the Queen 1842.

Dupplin is one of the finest-timbered estates in Scotland. The house is approached on all sides by magnificent avenues—8 in number—of beech, oak, limes, and araucaria. In the park and grounds, which command lovely views over Strathearn, and the walks in which extend through dells planted with rhododendrons, are many rare conifers. The *Salmon Breeding-Ponds*, formerly at Stormontfield, are now here. Dupplin was the scene of a battle, in which Edward Baliol and his English auxiliaries defeated the Regent Mar in a night attack in 1332. Here too is preserved a wrought stone cross.

29 m. **Forgandenny Stat.**, 1 m. S. are the Ch., *Rossie* (Mr. Bell's Trs.), and *Freeland* (C. L. Wood, Esq.), with fine limes. W. is *Condie* (Col. L. J. Oliphant), and E. *Dunbarney*.

The rly. now crosses the Earn and joining the N. B. Rly. from Fife (Rtes. 33 and 34), passes through a long tunnel, at the end of which there is a fine view rt. of *Kinnoull Hill*, across the Tay. Passing the *General Convict Prison* and the *South Inch* (p. 196) rt., the train enters

33 m. **Perth Stat.** ✲ see p. 194.

ROUTE 39.

Stirling to Crieff and Comrie. Cal. Rly.

It is an exceedingly pleasant round from Edinburgh or Glasgow to go to Comrie by train, thence by coach to Lochearnhead Stat. (Rte. 40), returning by Callander.

For the route from Stirling to

17¼ m. **Crieff Junc.** see Rte. 38.

From Crieff Junc. Stat. the line diverges N. W. to

19¾ m. **Tullibardine Stat.**, adjoining which (l.) is the site of *Tullibardine Castle*, once the seat of the earls of that name, before receiving the title of Duke of Atholl, and which gives the courtesy title of Marquis to the Duke's eldest son. There is a small Gothic chapel (1440), where the Dukes of Atholl were formerly interred, and now used as the Mausoleum of the Strathallan family. rt. is *Strathallan Castle*, the seat of Viscount Strathallan.

22¼ m. **Muthill Stat.** The village, 1½ m. l., has a Gothic Parish Church, erected in 1828, and the ruins of a 15th-cent. church,—a square tower, with Pius I. wall,—containing effigies of the lords of Strathearn; also Free and Epis. Chs. The road thither passes (l.) *Culdees Castle* (R. T. N. Spiers, Esq.), containing a small collection of Spanish pictures. 1½ m. N. W. of the village is *Drummond Castle* (p. 212).

After leaving the stat. there is a magnificent view l. (W.) of *Ben Voirlich* and *Stuc-a-Chroin*. The rly. crosses the Earn near a Roman Camp (there are a very large number in this neighbourhood), from which an ancient Roman road, with stations, stretches in a direct line to Perth.

24¾ m. **Highlandman Stat.**, l. are some very interesting old river terraces. Soon after passing this stat., the rly. from Crieff to Perth direct (Rte. 41) comes alongside rt. The line sweeps round to the l.; a fine view of Crieff climbing up the hill rt. is obtained, and the train stops at

26¼ m. **Crieff Stat.** ✲, see p. 211. The line onwards from Crieff was opened in 1893. After passing under two of the streets in a deep cutting, it crosses the *Turret*, and keeps close along the l. bank of the *Earn* parallel to *Lady Mary's Walk* (p. 211), allowing pleasant views of the river.

At 28 m. rt. is *Tomachastle Hill*, with a granite Monument to Sir David Baird of Seringapatam fame (1757 - 1829) which cost £4000, was curiously rent by lightning in May 1878, and was restored in 1890 ; l. across the river is *Strowan Ho.* (T. J. Graham Stirling, Esq.). A tunnel is now passed through, beyond which, looking back rt., a glimpse may be caught of *Ochtertyre Ho.* (Sir Patrick Keith Murray, Bt.) (p. 212).

At 30¾ m. an excellent view is obtained (rt.) across the parks and through a grand avenue of trees of *Lawers*, the handsome seat of Col. Williamson.

32 m. **Comrie Stat.** ✲, on the outskirts of the village, which is not interesting in itself, but a favourite summer resort, beautifully situated, at the junc. of the lateral Glens Artney (S.) and Lednock (N.) with the central Earn valley, under the picturesque Aberuchill Hills to the W. The *Parish Ch.* is a barn-like structure, but there is an exceedingly handsome *Free Ch.* (with a graceful spire), the gift of a lady ; also *U.P.* and *Epis. Chs.*

The best idea of the surrounding country will be obtained by ascending *Dunmore*—a commanding hill N. (837 ft.), marked by an obelisk of granite from Glen Lednock, set up as a *Monument* to Henry Dundas of Dunira, 1st Lord Melville (1740-1811). The way to it lies through the picturesque wooded *Glen Lednock*, by a path commencing behind the town, running through the grounds of *Comrie House*. About 20 mins.' walk brings the tourist to the *Falls of the Lednock*, which, though not of great volume, will repay the visit of the artist and lover of nature by the picturesque grandeur of the remarkable chasm in the rock called the Devil's Cauldron, through which they worm their way.

A winding path is carried in zig-zags from this up l. crossing the carriage road to the *Melville Monument* (above). A circuitous carriage road leads in 1½ m. from Comrie to within a short distance of the falls.

[It is a good walk of about 12 m. from Comrie up Glen Lednock to Ardeonaig, on Loch Tay (see p. 238). The first 4½ m. as far as *Innergeldie Lo.* can be driven. (Behind Innergeldie is a tiny granite quarry out of which the stones for the monument (above) came). Up *Innergeldie Burn* is a good way to ascend *Ben Chonzie* (3048 ft.) 4 m., descending to Loch Turret (see pp. 213, 238). At 5 m. l. is the waterfall of *Sput Rollo*. At *Bovaine* farm (6½ m.), keep a track well up the hill rt. The view of the Ben Lawers range in the descent of *Fin Glen* is very fine.]

For many years Comrie, which is situated on the line of the great geological fault between the Highlands and the Midland Valley, has been subject, from to time, to slight shocks of *Earthquake*, so slight as only to cause glasses or vessels to rattle on the shelves in the houses, accompanied by a slight rumbling sound. In October 1839, at least 70 shocks were felt, in some instances accompanied by a loud report and sulphureous smells. Again in Jan. 16, 1876, 3 distinct shocks were felt—sufficiently strong to awaken sleepers.

A road crosses the Earn to the hamlet of *Dalginross*, where there are the remains of a Roman camp, then l. to Crieff, 7 m., or rt. up Glen Artney to *Auchinner Lo.* 7 m. (see pp. 162, 213).

For Drive to St. Fillans and Loch Earn see next route ; for Drive to Ochtertyre and Crieff see p. 212.

ROUTE 40.

Comrie to St. Fillans and Lochearnhead Stat.—Coach.

Coach once daily each way in connection with trains from and to Edinburgh and Glasgow—15 m. in 4 hrs. allowing time for dinner at St. Fillans or Lochearnhead.

Just beyond Comrie a road—recommended for those in private carriages, and only ½ m. longer—crosses the Earn, passes *Aberuchill Cas.* (Captain Robert Dewhurst), well situated under the *Aberuchill Hills*, and *Dalchonzie Ho.*, and rejoins the main road before it passes (rt.)

3 m. *Dunira* (Sir Sydney J. Dundas, Bt.). This handsome modern mansion (Bryce, archt.), which has succeeded the cottage to which Henry Dundas, 1st Lord Melville, the friend of William Pitt, retired, stands at a spot where the valley is most smiling, the river most picturesque, and the mountains grandest.

Ascending the l. bank of the river Earn, we pass (rt.) a rock curiously resembling an enormous crocodile and (l.) on the other side of the river, the green conical hill of *Dunfillan*, 600 ft. high, on the top of which St. Fillan, the patron saint of Robert Bruce, used to say his prayers so assiduously that he has left the marks of his knees in the rock!

½ m. before reaching St. Fillans, the road along the S. side of Loch Earn crosses a bridge l.

6 m. **St. Fillans**✲. This pretty village lies at the E. end of the loch on the N. shore surrounded by hills and facing *Dundurn* (2011 ft.), amidst scenery far finer than that at Lochearnhead.

Loch Earn is a lovely Highland loch, stretching 7 m. from St. Fillans to Lochearnhead; near the E. end is a small islet, covered with trees, and made up of stone heaps, said to be the remains of a stronghold of the Neishes, destroyed by the M'Nabs.

There is a good road on both sides of the loch, and it is a very pleasant drive from St. Fillans to go by the one and return by the other (16 m.). The coach road along the N. shore is the more level, and commands a better view of Ben Voirlich, but the other has far more variety, and is the better one for enjoying the loch. At the distance of 4 m., looking across the loch S., the House of *Ardvoirlich* is barely seen (Col. John Stewart), where the Macgregors committed the atrocity of displaying to his widow in a dish the head of the Stewart, whom they had murdered, with a crust between the teeth. (See Scott's "Legend of Montrose.")

Near Ardvoirlich, by the side of the road, stands a stone informing passers-by that the bodies of six Macdonalds of Glencoe lie buried there. They were killed in an attempt to "harry" Ardvoirlich.

At the head of the valley opening behind the house rises the peak of **Ben Voirlich** (3224 ft.), and from Ardvoirlich the *Ascent* can be most easily made in abt. 2½ hrs.

The *View* is extensive—S. to Ben Ledi and Stirling Cas. and across the plain between Glasgow and Edinburgh; W. to Ben More; N. to the Ben Lawers range, and N.W. to Ben Nevis. From the summit descent may be made into Glen Artney, or Glen Ample; or *Stuc-a-Chroin* (3189 ft.) may be first climbed in 1½ hrs. with a dip of 700 ft. and a steep "chimney" ascent.

To the E. of Ardvoirlich is *Ardvoirlich Cottage*, a picturesque little habitation, which, along with the mansion house, has been in the possession of the family for several centuries. Still farther E., also on the S. side of the loch, is *Edinample*, an old castellated house at the mouth of *Glen Ample*, belonging to the Marq. of Breadalbane. The *Ample Burn* here forms a pretty cascade and rushes through a picturesque rocky rent. Not far off at the S.W. corner of the loch stand the ruins of *St. Blane's Chapel*.

13 m. **Lochearnhead** ✲, abt. ¼ m. from the loch, stands at the foot of *Glen Ogle* (p. 170), and 7 m. from *Killin* (p. 239). Visitors staying here should drive to the *Braes of Balquhidder* and *Rob Roy's Grave*, 5 m. S.W. (p. 169), on the way to which we pass

15 m. **Lochearnhead Stat.** (p. 169), where, however, the coach stops.

ROUTE 41.

Crieff to Perth via Methven. Cal. Rly.

CRIEFF ✲ is a thriving town built on the side of a hill, with numerous churches, several hotels, an old-established Hydro. Estab., banks, good shops, and large villas for summer visitors.

It has a *Bowling Green* and *Golf Course*, and *Morrison's Academy* (an endowed school for boys and girls) has a considerable reputation. Although a town, its commanding situation overlooking Strath Earn and Strath Allan and its innumerable walks and drives make it a most attractive centre. The liberal opening of the surrounding properties to the public lends an additional charm to the neighbourhood, while its position close to the great fault, which marks the line between the Midland Sandstones and the Highland Schists, renders it peculiarly interesting to the geologist.

The *Square* in the centre of the town with its small artificially levelled boulevard is picturesque. E. of it are the *Town Hall*, where "Jougs" (see p. 62) still hang, and a venerable *Cross* carved with Runic knots but without inscriptions—prob. of the 12th cent. Farther east is an old *Market Cross*. It is a steep descent S. to the stat., beyond which is the *Gallows Hill* where the "Kind Gallows of Crieff" (see "Waverley," Note H) stood. Here many Highland caterans and thieves were hanged by the Stewarts of Strath Earn, who held their courts on a circular mound (on the lands of *Broich*), ½ m. to the E., which no longer exists. In return for this the Highlanders bore a grudge against the town, burnt it in 1715, and nearly did so again in 1745.

WALKS :—

(1) **The Knock** (1 m.), **Barvick Falls** (2½ m.), and **Turret Falls** (3 m.).

For a delightful round of 8 m. keep N. up the W. side of the grounds of the Hydro. Estab. From its W. gate keep l. along a path round the *Knock* with charming views—*Ben Voirlich* and *Ben More* in the distance—descending behind *Aberturret Ho.* and crossing the *Shaggie Burn* to the Turret. Keeping up its l. bank one comes in a mile to the *Barvick Glen* in a wood rt. after crossing its stream. (Exit may be made l. from the top of the glen.) ½ m. farther along the road—which passes through a gate and ascends steeply—are the *Turret Falls* in a wood l. Descend to the stream, cross a stone bridge and return by rt. bank and through Ochtertyre grounds.

(2) Ascend **The Knock** (911 ft.)—charming view. On the E. side is *Ferntower* (Lord Abercromby), where Sir David Baird, of Seringapatam fame, resided for many years, and where he died. In the interior is the sword of Tippoo Sahib, and Wilkie's picture of the finding of his body.

(3) **Lady Mary's Walk, Strowan Bridge,** and **Tomachastle Hill,** 3 m. W. on the N. side of the Earn.

Cross the Turret by the lowest bridge, keep l. along rt. bank of the Turret and l. bank of the Earn for 1½ m., when the path joins a good cart road. Keep l. for a mile when a high road is joined. 300 yds. l. is *Strowan Bridge*—picturesque, with lovely bit of water—across which is *Strowan Ho.* (p. 209), and the enclosed ivy-covered ruin of an old church; 50 yds. rt. a gate rt. leads up to *Tomachastle Hill*, with Sir D. Baird's *Monument* (p. 209), commanding a good view W.

The first path rt. beyond this gate, leading along the wooded ridge between the Earn and the Comrie road, is a pleasant way to return to Crieff.

DRIVES :—

(1) **Drummond Castle,**[1] with its beautiful *Gardens.* 3 m. S.

Crossing the Earn below the station (½ m.) the Muthil Road (l.)—a beautiful avenue of beeches and limes, sadly thinned by the gale of 17th Nov. 1893—is followed for 1½ m. passing l. an imposing section of the large trap dyke which can be traced across Scotland, and here forms a protection to rifle butts. From a high massive gate rt. the avenue (1 m. long) leads up a rocky ridge to the castle.

This is perhaps the most interesting object in the neighbourhood. Founded in 1491 by the first Lord Drummond, whose descendants became Earls of Perth, it passed through the female line to the present proprietor the 1st Earl of Ancaster, who is the 23rd Lord Willoughby D'Eresby. It was well battered by Cromwell and only the square tower (containing a small armoury and commanding an extensive and pleasing view) is old, but it has all been rebuilt in the old style. It contains interesting family and historical portraits including James Drummond, Earl and titular Duke of Perth (attainted in 1746), James V. and VI., Queen Mary, Charles I. and II., etc. etc. Queen Victoria and Prince Albert stayed here in Sept. 1842.

Behind, it looks down upon the beautiful old-fashioned *Garden* laid out in a series of natural terraces formed on the rock itself, as it descends step-wise. The flower-beds are most tastefully arranged, so as to resemble a rich Persian carpet, the whole set off and relieved by evergreens, box and yew hedges, cut and carved in quaint fashion, and by fine specimens of cypress, cedars, and rare conifers. Statuary, and fountains, with stately staircases, give great effect to the whole. The multiplex *Sun-dial* was designed by John, 2nd E. of Perth, who laid out the gardens 1662.

N.W. of the Castle rises the formerly wooded hill of **Torleum** (1291 ft.); but terrible havoc was wrought among its trees, among those in the castle avenue, and indeed among all the woods of the neighbourhood by the gale of 17th Nov. 1893.

[1] Grounds open Tues., Thurs., and Sat.

(2) W. through *Ochtertyre Grounds* to **Comrie** (7 m.), **St. Fillans** (12½ m.), and **Lochearnhead,** 19½ m.

Although not wild this is one of the most charming drives in Scotland. 1½ m. W. of the town is the entrance to **Ochtertyre**[1] (Sir Patrick Keith Murray, Bt.). A lady of the Murray family was immortalised by Burns as "The Flower of Strathmore." Drive up the avenue, passing l. the *Mausoleum* on the site of the *Old Ch.* of *Monzievaird*, in which a large number of Murrays with their wives and families were (1511) burned by their enemies the Drummonds and Campbells. On a peninsula in the loch are the remains of *Cas. Cluggy*, a very old fort. Beyond the house avoid the 1st road l., keep straight on behind *Monzievaird Ch.*, and rejoin the public road 4 m. from Crieff.

At the old house of Monzievaird (now destroyed) Gen. Sir George Murray, the faithful lieutenant of "The Duke" in Spain and at Waterloo, was born 1772.

[From Monzievaird a pretty road, crossing the Earn and passing *Strowan Ho.* (T. J. Graham Stirling, Esq.), leads to the road on the S. side of the river. This makes a pleasant round of 10½ m. from Crieff.]

Passing rt. *Clathick* (Capt. Campbell Colquhoun) and *Lawers* (Col. Williamson) we reach Comrie, p. 209. Hence to Lochearnhead see Rte. 40. Return from Comrie may be made by the S. side of the Earn, see p. 209.

[1] The grounds are at all times (Sundays excepted) open to the public, for whom boats are kept on the loch. Cycles are excluded.

(3) N.W. up **Glen Turret** to **Loch Turret** (1200 ft.), passing *Barvick* and *Turret Falls* (p. 211), 7 m.

A fine moorland drive with magnificent views back, but a very steep road. Horses need to walk about 3 m.

Burns wrote "Lines on Scaring some Water-fowl in Loch Turret." The transition from sandstones and conglomerates to schists, and the moraines beyond the N. end of the loch, will interest geologists. *Glen Turret Lo.* (Sir P. K. Murray, Bt.) at the N. end of the loch is the nearest point from which to ascend *Ben Chonzie* (3048 ft.), abt. 3 m.

(4) E. through the Grounds of **Inchbrakie** [1] (for 300 years the seat of the Græmes—house now removed) and **Abercairney** [1]—noble mansion with fine parks and lake—(both Capt. Home-Drummond Moray) to **Fowlis-Wester** ✲—a quaint little village consisting of a church, manse, inn, school-house, ancient Celtic Cross, with *jougs* (see p. 62) attached, and a few picturesque cottages ($6\frac{1}{2}$ m.). Return by Gilmerton (3 m.) and round the back of the *Knock*, passing (l.) *Monzie* (pron. Monee') *Cas.* (G. Johnston, Esq. of Lathrisk, Fife) —house not seen for trees, amongst which are some of the oldest larches in Scotland, one of them, at 3 ft. from the ground, being 20 ft. in girth—and *Monzie Ch.* (rt.); 14 m. in all.

From Fowlis-Wester a road leads over the hill N. in 3 m. to *Buchanty*★ on the Almond, with a pretty linn, whence the *Sma' Glen* is 2 m. W., *Glen Almond College* 3 m. E., and *Glen Almond Ho.* (Mrs. Malcolm Patton) $\frac{1}{2}$ N. across the river [cf. Drive (8)].

(5) S.W. up S. side of the Earn for nearly 4 m., then (oppos. *Strowan Ho.*) sharp l. up a very pretty road to *Mill of Fortune* (6 m.), l. over the moor by *Blair-in-roar* to *Tighnablair* (9 m.), and down the *Knaik Water* to *Braco* ✲ (15 m.), where the famous **Ardoch Camp** is (see p. 207). Return by *Orchill* (2 m.) rt. (Samuel Smith, Esq.), crossing *Machany Water* ($4\frac{1}{2}$ m.), and passing through *Muthill* (6 m.) (p. 208) to Crieff (9 m.)—24 m. in all.

(6) S.W. to *Auchinner Lodge* (Earl of Ancaster) at the head of **Glen Artney**, abt. $13\frac{1}{2}$ m., whether the glen be reached by the *Mill of Fortune* or by *Comrie.*

It was "in lone Glen Artney's hazel shade," through which the Ruchill Water flows, that the stag in the "Lady of the Lake" made "deep his midnight lair" on the eve of "The Chase."

A cart track continues up the Ruchill Water, crosses it $1\frac{1}{2}$ m. above the Lodge, and then crosses the moor and descends the *Keltie Water* to Callander, 8 m. The Keltie Burn should not be left without visiting the *Bracklinn Falls* (see p. 162), $\frac{1}{2}$ m. l. of the direct path.

Either *Ben Voirlich* (3224 ft.) or *Stuc-a-Chroin* (3189 ft.) can be conveniently ascended in abt. 6 m. from Auchinner Lo. by following up the Ruchill Water to its source.

(7) E. to **Perth** by *Millearn*, $6\frac{1}{2}$ m. (Drummond Forbes, Esq.), *Trinity Gask Ch.* $8\frac{1}{2}$ m., *Gask Ho.* $10\frac{1}{2}$ m. (T. L. K. Oliphant, Esq.)—in the grounds of which stand the ruins of "*The Auld House*" of Lady Nairne's song —and the *Roman Road.* $19\frac{1}{2}$ m.

This is a far more interesting road than the other two more direct ones (17 m.), which practically follow the same line as the rly. (p. 214).

Kinkell Bridge over the Earn beside Millearn should be visited for the lovely view up the river. On the other side, $\frac{1}{2}$ m. down the rt. bank, is the site of the Ch. of St. Bean who, acc. to Dr. Skene, dwelt here in the first half of the 10th cent. Between Millearn and Gask there are beautiful views across to the Ochils. The road passing Gask Ho., for the 3 m. during which it follows the old Roman road, might have been laid down by a ruler, but being through wood and broken country it is by no means tedious.

(8) To **Amulree** by the **Sma' Glen,** 12 m.

At Gilmerton (2 m.) the road turns l. and in $\frac{1}{4}$ m. trends rt., up a steep hill from which *Monzie Cas.* (above) can be seen below, and a

[1] Grounds open Mon., Wed., and Frid. by order procurable at the hotels and coaching establishments.

magnificent view up Strathearn to Ben Voirlich obtained.

At 6 m. a charming view of the Almond bursts upon the tourist and the road bifurcates—rt. to *Buchanty* ✲ 2 m. (p. 213) and *Trinity College* (below), 5 m.—l. into the **Sma' Glen,** an interesting Highland pass.

The road is carried for about 2 m. through a narrow rocky defile, one of the gates into the Highlands. In its jaws, near its upper end, is the reputed tomb of Ossian, a rude flat stone, removed from off the bones it was meant to cover, when the road was made in 1746 :—

" In this still place, remote from men,
Sleeps Ossian in the narrow glen :
In this still place, where murmurs on
But one meek streamlet—only one."
WORDSWORTH.

At *Newton Bridge* the Almond is crossed (8¼ m.) and, over a bleak moor, we come to *Corriemuckloch* where the road to *Loch Freuchie* (see p. 237) strikes l. and soon after reach

12 m. **Amulree** ✲, a small hamlet, in the midst of moorland, with ch., manse, school, hotel, and post office, situated on the Braan, which issues out of *Loch Freuchie*, 2 m. W.

Amulree is 9¾ m. from Dunkeld by Strathbraan (see p. 219); 11 m. from Aberfeldy by Glen Cochill (see p. 236); and 12¼ m. from Kenmore by Glen Quaich (see p. 237).

(9) S.E. to *Innerpeffray Chap.*, *Library*, and *Cas.* (below), 4 m.

The rly. from Crieff—with through carriages from Comrie, p. 209—to Perth runs E. through a rich agricultural country.

2¼ m. **Innerpeffray Stat.**, ¾ m. N. is *Dollerie* (Anthony Murray, Esq.), and 1½ m. S., on the l. bank of the Earn, are the ruins of *Innerpeffray Chap.*, the burying-place of the Drummonds.

Close by it is an endowed school, which contains a *Library* founded in 1691 with a bequest of David, 3rd Lord Maderty. It has between 2000 and 3000 vols., among them some black-letter works, and a small French Bible of 1632, bearing the autograph of the Great Marquis of Montrose. ¼ m. farther down the river are the ruins of *Innerpeffray Cas.*, built by the 1st Lord Maderty.

We pass l. *Abercairney* and its Parks (p. 213) before

4¼ m. **Abercairney Stat.**

6½ m. **Madderty Stat.,** close to which (l.) are the fragmentary ruins of *Inchaffray Abbey*.

It was founded in 1200 and largely endowed by Alex. III. Maurice, the Abbot of the time, attended Bruce to Bannockburn with the arm of St. Fillan in a silver casket, a relic to which great importance was attached in those days. The Abbey was called "Insula Missarum" (Island of the Masses). The ground is now the property of the Earl of Kinnoull.

8¾ m. **Balgowan Stat.,** with l. *Balgowan Ho.* (Capt. Black), the birthplace of Lord Lynedoch, 1750.

11½ m. **Methven Junc. Stat.**

[*Branch* runs N. in 1¼ m. to

Methven ✲ (pron. Meff'en), a small village with a fragment of its old 15th-cent. church, which serves as a burial-place for the Methven family. In the ch.-yd. Lord Lynedoch and his wife are buried (see p. 215). *Methven Cas.* (Col. D. M. Smythe), 1½ m. E., is a fine estate abounding in old timber, the *Pepperwell Oak* being 18 ft. in girth.

Near the village (N.) is the battlefield where Robert Bruce was defeated in 1306 by the English under Aymer de Valence, Earl of Pembroke and Viceroy of Scotland.

Glen Almond to the N. is of a very picturesque character. Of it Wordsworth wrote

" A convent, even a hermit's cell
Would break the silence of this dell;
It is not quiet, it is not ease,
But something deeper far than these."

In this glen, 4 m. from Methven, is situated **Trinity College**, founded in 1841 as a Public School, principally for the sons of members of the Episcopal Church. It consists of a fine pile of buildings (John Henderson, archt.) which, including the ground, cost £90,000. The elegant Gothic *Chapel* was subsequently added by Bp. Wordsworth at a cost of £5500. In Oct. 1891 the Jubilee of its foundation was celebrated—Mr. Gladstone, one of the Founders, the late Rev. Chas. Wordsworth, Bp. of St. Andrews, the first Warden, and the Marquis of Lothian, the first boy who entered, being present.

3 m. down the Almond (abt. 6 m. drive from Methven), on its N. bank, stands old *Logie Ho.* (Earl of Mansfield)—uninhabited—in a pretty glen down which a walk of fully 1 m. will lead to the site of the *Bower* (marked by a heap of stones) l., and the *Grave* (surrounded by a railing) rt.—not easily found—of "Bessie Bell and Mary Gray," who died of the Plague in 1666.

"They were two bonnie lasses;
They biggit a house in yonder lea
And theekit it ower wi' rashes."

Just below are the *Lynedoch Woods*, now used by the E. of Mansfield as a rabbit warren. They were largely planted with choice trees by General Thomas Graham, Lord Lynedoch (1750-1843), one of the Peninsular heroes who took his title from this place where he had a charming cottage, now removed. He did not enter the army until he was 45 years old, a step taken in consequence of the loss of his beautiful wife whom he survived for 50 years.]

12¾ m. **Tibbermuir Stat.**

To the rt. is *Lamerkin Muir*, where the Marquis of Montrose, with 1100 half-clad Irish, and 1300 half-armed Highlanders, defeated a tumultuous mob of about 6000 Covenanters, Citizens of Perth, and others, hastily gathered together to oppose him under Lord Elcho. The *Battle* was fought on 1st Sept. 1644, and the Town of Perth was the prize of the victory.

14 m. **Almondbank Stat.** The village, with *Bleaching Works*, is ¾ m. N.

The precipitous banks of the Almond, just beyond the village, are interesting, and yield large numbers of Old Red Sandstone fossils to the geologist. *Pitcairn Green*, ¾ m. farther, with its large *Green*, bordered by high tree hedges cut to resemble festoons, is one of the most picturesque little villages in Scotland.

15 m. **Ruthven Road Stat.**, with large *Print Works*. The ruins of *Huntingtower Cas.* (3 m. from Perth)—called *Ruthven* until the Gowrie plot 1600—stand ¼ m. rt.

It consists of two massive towers (the W. one double) joined by a screen. It is not particularly interesting and in sad disrepair. The towers, however, can still be ascended, and there is an old fireplace in the E. one. Part of the ground floor, where the key may be got, is occupied by humble families.

Here, in 1582, took place the so-called "Raid of Ruthven." King James VI., when a youth of 16, returning from Blair Castle to Edinburgh, was invited by the Earl of Gowrie to his hunting seat of Ruthven. He accepted the invitation, but, on arriving, found himself a prisoner in the hands of certain nobles banded together against him. A list of demands was presented to him, the chief being that he should dismiss his favourites, the Duke of Lennox and the Earl of Arran. James endeavoured to leave the room, when the Master of Glamis put his back against the door, at which outrage the king burst into tears, and was told roughly, "Better bairns greet than bearded men." In this way the Ruthven confederates obtained control of the realm for some months.

17¾ m. **Perth Stat.** ✲, see p. 194.

ROUTE 42.

Perth to Inverness via Dunkeld, Blair Atholl, and Forres. High. Rly.

The Highland Rly. is a single line (except for seven miles approaching Inverness) from *Stanley Junc. to Wick* (298 m.) with branches—(1) *Ballinluig to Aberfeldy*, 8½ m.; (2) *Aviemore to Carr Bridge*, 7 m., to be continued as the main line to Inverness; (3) *Muir of Ord to Fortrose*, 13½ m.; (4) *Dingwall to Strome Ferry* (for Skye), 53 m., to be continued to Kyle Akin; (5) *Dingwall to Strathpeffer*, 5 m.; (6) *Georgemas to Thurso*, 6¾ m. There is a junc. with the Great N. of Scotland Rly. at Boat of Garten.

The line is described on p. 251 as far as

7¼ m. **Stanley Junc. Stat.**, where the Cal. Rly. going N.E. and the Highland Rly. going N.W. diverge.

$10\frac{1}{2}$ m. **Murthly Stat.** To the rt. is the large County Lunatic Asylum. Visible on the opposite side of the Tay, and reached by a bridge opened in 1889, are the ch. and village of *Caputh* (p. 219).

The train soon reaches the woods of *Murthly Castle* (W. T. J. Steuart Fothringham, Esq.), which is not visible, but glimpses are caught of the shell of the new castle, a very large square Elizabethan château (Gillespie Graham, architect), begun on a vast scale abt. 1826, but never completed. On the river side stands a small chapel, built by Sir W. D. Stewart, a former owner, and dedicated to St. Anthony. The gardens, in the old Dutch style, are quaint. The grounds are very beautiful, and adorned with rare pine-trees of new kinds, hardly to be matched elsewhere for size, but are closed to the public.

Near *Birnam Hall* (rt.) is an old oak, called the hangman's tree, where Highland marauders, etc., were suspended. This custom was common when what were known as the "Heritable Jurisdictions" prevailed in Scotland, when the superior of the land tried and condemned criminals without the intervention of the King's Courts.

The scenery is only partially revealed through the screen of thick fir-trees, which form the outskirts of Birnam Woods, rapidly passed by the train. Emerging from a tunnel, the traveller is all at once introduced to a most exquisite view, which combines the charms of Highland mountain and river with the rich foliage of Lowland plantation. The rly. skirts l. the base of

Birnam Hill (see p. 218), which is said by Macculloch never to have recovered the march of its wood to Dunsinane. Now, however, a young and vigorous plantation covers the sides, which is the more necessary, as the hill has been much broken into for its slate. At its foot lies

$15\frac{3}{4}$ m. **Dunkeld Stat.**, on the S. bank of the Tay, about 1 m. from the town.

Adjoining the stat. is the village of **Birnam** ✲, a most charming and popular summer resort, composed chiefly of country-houses, among them *St. Mary's Tower* (Duke of Rutland) and *Erigmore* (C. B. Logan, Esq.), villas, lodging-houses, and shops. The *Parish Church of Little Dunkeld* and *Recreation Grounds* are also on the S. side of the river, equi-distant from Birnam and Dunkeld. Highland Games are held annually at Birnam in August.

DUNKELD ✲ (the "Fort of the Wood") lies in a beautiful situation on the l. bank of the Tay, here hemmed in between grand wooded mountains, and crossed by a handsome bridge of seven arches, erected by Telford in 1809, at a cost of £42,000, and widened in 1880.

Beyond the N. end of the main street, abt. $\frac{1}{2}$ m. from the bridge, is the *Lodge Gate* to the *Duke of Atholl's Grounds.*[1] Some distance from the entrance are the foundations of a *Palace*, designed by Hopper and begun by John, 4th Duke of Atholl, but abandoned at the Duke's death (1830), having cost £30,000. The actual ducal residence, occupied by the present Dowager-Duchess, is a modest cottage on a smooth lawn near the river bank. Here, in 1842, Queen Victoria and Prince Albert were entertained and welcomed by the late Duke, then Lord Glenlyon, at the head of 900 Highlanders, 500 of them being from the Atholl estates. A palatial-looking building on a hillock at the back of the town is the Duke of Atholl's dog-kennels.

Near the house stands the venerable and picturesque ***Cathedral,** the choir of which is fitted up as the

[1] Visitors are admitted under the conduct of a guide, and the charge is 1s. each; a single person 2s.

parish church, the nave being a ruin, and open to the sky.

[The Cathedral may be visited by itself from *High St.*, through a square in which is a *Memorial Fountain* to the 6th Duke, b. 1814, d. 1864.]

It is a Gothic edifice, apparently of the 15th cent., though portions of it may date as far back as the 12th cent., when a ch. was erected here, and we know that it stands on the site of one of the oldest churches in Scotland, founded by Culdee missionaries, who, in the 9th cent., were driven from Iona by the roving Northern pirates and settled here, bringing with them the relics of St. Columba. The main arches of the nave, which are pointed, and rest on plain round pillars, are surmounted by an awkward round-headed triforium, and that by a clerestory.

In the chapter-house is a monument to John, 4th Duke of Atholl, (d. 1830), with all the armorial bearings.

The W. front of the ch. is pierced with a large window, which is placed awry, its canopied moulding being twisted away from the line of the gable. It is flanked by a massive projecting tower (1469-1501). In the S. aisle of the nave is the monument of Bp. Robert Cardney, who laid the foundation of the nave (1406). The choir is now used as the parish church. In its vestibule are the remains of a statue of Bp. Sinclair, "a brave and patriotic man, whose war-cry at Donibristle against the English invaders is historical—'All ye that love Scotland's honour, follow me,'" and who, in 1318, commenced the building of the choir. Here, too, is a recumbent effigy of Alexander Stewart, Earl of Buchan, natural son of Robert II., better known as "The Wolf of Badenoch" (see pp. 225, 240, 303), whose greatest exploit was the destruction of Elgin Cathedral. After a career of unparalleled cruelty and vice he died, and was buried here in 1394. Against the E. wall is a monument to the 42nd Highlanders (Black Watch) who fell in the Crimean war,—a bas-relief by Steell, erected by the surviving officers in 1872; opposite is a mural tablet to a minister of this parish who was drowned in the "Forfarshire," 1838. The poet, Gavin Douglas, was Bp. of Dunkeld (died 1522).

Close to the ch. tower rise two of the oldest and finest *larches* in Britain, brought from Tyrol in 1738, 14 ft. 8 in. in girth at 3 ft. from the ground, 99 ft. high, but maimed in the leading shoot. Between 1774 and 1830 John, Duke of Atholl, planted 16,500 acres with nearly 28,000,000 trees. In the "Tay Bridge" gale (Dec. 1879), 80,000 trees are said to have been blown down on the Duke of Atholl's estates.

In 1689 a regiment of 1200 Lowlanders took up a position in and around the cathedral, and was attacked by the Highland army, fresh from its victory at Killiecrankie. After a most obstinate fight the Highlanders were beaten off, with great loss, and soon afterwards dispersed. The regiment has since been known as the 26th Cameronians. The grave of Col. Cleland, who commanded them and was killed, is to be seen in the churchyard.

Nothing can be lovelier than the broad *Terrace-walks* of velvet turf stretching up the l. bank of the Tay, commanding the brisk river, the bridge, and the noble mountains, and shaded by trees of magnificent growth (silver fir 150 ft. high and 16 ft. in circumference, Scotch firs and vigorous deodars). Near the bridge is a fine cedar of Lebanon, and a hemlock spruce 80 ft. high.

The Tay is crossed by a ferry-boat to reach the fine woods of the **Hermitage**, a charming spot on the river Braan, which here forms a picturesque fall over the slate strata turned on edge. A summer-house, called *Ossian's Hall*, which stood here, was blown up and destroyed by some malicious person, much to the loss of visitors, 1869. The miscreant was never found out, but the summer-house has been rebuilt.

Higher up the stream is the **Rumbling Bridge**, a favourite resort of tourists, below which the Braan, falling into a deep chasm, growls among the rocks, and if there has been much rain this is of itself worth a visit.

Visitors *from* the Duke's grounds can get out at a small gate ¼ m. below the Rumbling Bridge, but there is *no entrance by this gate* which is locked.

[WALKS—(1) **Birnam Hill** (1325 ft.), a short hr.'s ascent from Birnam, richly rewarded.

Opposite the hotel take the road up the rt. bank of the *Inchewan Burn*, but *before* passing under the rly. step through a gap in the paling and enter the path, which also goes under the rly., then leaves the burn, keeps straight on, *crossing* a back road, and zigzags, as a cart road (gradually narrowing to a path), up the hill. From a flagstaff, there is a lovely view of Dunkeld and its surroundings, the lochs and river forming specially pleasing features. The highest pt. is 10 min. farther back, and commands a magnificent wide view, comprising *Ben Lawers*, *Glen Lyon Hills*, *Schiehallion* (particularly imposing), *Farragon*, *Pitlochrie*, and *Ben Vrackie*, *Glen Shee* and *Forfarshire Hills*, *Strathmore* and the *Sidlaws* (including *Dunsinane*), *Perth*, the *Lomonds*, *Strath Earn*, the *Ochils*, and the *Campsie Hills*.

(2) **Birnam Falls**, a pretty walk, 1½ m. from Birnam.

Follow the road up the rt. bank of the *Inchewan Burn* to the semicircle of stone seats called the *Seven Sisters*. Beyond, a *narrow* path *beside* the stream leads to the falls, small but picturesque.

(3) *Duke's Grounds*, *Hermitage*, and *Rumbling Bridge* (see p. 216).

(4) **Rumbling Bridge** and **Inver Village**—a round of 6 m.

Drive or walk W. 2½ m. along Amulree Road, when the Rumbling Br. is 300 yds. down a road rt. 2 m. from Dunkeld, high up l., is *Inverbraan Ho.* (W. Steuart Fothringham, Esq.). The chasm below the br. and the falls above are well seen from the br., but a guide opens gates leading to better view-points. *If walking*, cross the br. and take the first (cart) road *rt.* It leads past the gate from the Hermitage (*no admittance, see above*) and, through woods, to the high road on the S. side of the Tay. Turning rt. one passes through *Inver*, a hamlet 1 m. from Dunkeld, in which Neil Gow, the famous fiddler (1727-1807), whose grave is in Little Dunkeld Ch.-yd., lived, and crosses the Braan by one of General Wade's bridges.

(5) The *Terrace-Walk*, down rt. bank of the Tay. Here may be seen the finest *Sycamore* in Britain, and an oak nearly its equal, said to be the sole survivors of the Forest of Birnam.

The walk which extends for fully 1 m. is reached through Birnam Hotel grounds or by path l. off the road to St. Mary's Tower.

(6) The Walks up and around *Craig-y-barns*,[1] on the N. of the Tay (1106 ft.), command fine views of the river above and below Dunkeld.

At ¼ m. beyond the N. end of Dunkeld, go rt. 150 yds. up the Blairgowrie Road, pass through *Calley Lo.* gate and go 300 yds. up the avenue. At a gate l. cross the wall by a stile, and, after going 50 yds. along a grass road, diverge by a path to rt., which takes along the base of the E. portion of the hill across a small ravine (the "*Cave Pass*") and leads by zigzags to the top, passing rhododendron bushes on the way. Near the summit, on the bare N. shoulder, is a curious large *perched boulder*, resting upon 3 stones.

(7) Other pleasant walks may be made by *Newtyle Hill* to *Dungarthill* and *Stenton;* to the slate quarries on both sides of the river; and to *Craigvinean*, the wooded hill to the N.W. of *Inver*.

LONGER EXCURSIONS :—

(*a*) To **Blairgowrie**, 12 m., and **Braemar**, 47 m. (Rte. 58). Coach daily in summer.

[1] An amusing story is told in James Nasmyth's autobiography of the manner in which this hill was "planted by artillery."
When the Duke of Atholl was at a loss how to carry out his design of planting Craig-y-barns, owing to its inaccessible steepness, he, at the suggestion of Alex. Nasmyth, the artist, caused some small cannon to be loaded with canisters of seed and fired at the crags. This ingenious device met with complete success.

(*b*) By Blairgowrie road to *Loch of the Lowes* (2 m.) and along its south bank. At 4½ m. *Kincairney* (Lord Kincairney) is on the left hand and *Snaigow* (W. Cox, Esq.) on the right. Turning S. *Glendelvine* (Sir Alex. Muir Mackenzie, Bart.) is passed l. (5¾ m.). At 6¼ m. the road to Bridge of Isla (5 m. E., see p. 251) is reached ; and from this point *Delvine* (Sir A. M. Mackenzie), approached through the tidy English-like village of *Spittalfields*, is 1¾ m. left. Turning rt. *Caputh Ch.* (7 m.) is reached, behind which in the village is a fountain erected (1890) by the late T. G. Murray, Esq. of Stenton and his wife. The road continues pretty along the l. side of the river passing (8½ m.) *Stenton* (A. Graham Murray, Esq.). A lovely surprise view, 1¼ m. from Dunkeld, and a piece of road close to the river, bring a capital round of 11½ m. to an end.

(*c*) Drive along Blairgowrie road 4 m. and just before Butterston P.O. turn l. up rt. side of *Buckny Burn*—a steep hill. *Riechip Shooting Lo.* (900 ft.) is seen across the burn (5½ m.), with *Ben-a-Chally* (1594 ft.) behind. Keep straight on, not crossing the burn, until a gate into the woods is reached (7 m.)—*Riemore Shooting Lo.* (1000 ft.) is seen rt. From this point ¼ m. walk will take to **Loch Ordie**, a beautiful sheet of water in the heart of pine woods.

(*d*) W. to **Amulree**✲ by *Strathbraan*, 9¾ m.

At 2½ m. the *Rumbling Bridge* (see p. 218) is 300 yds. rt. 4 m. *Strathbraan Free Ch.* and the hamlet of *Trochrie* are passed. 4½ m. the road crosses the river—a fine bit, with *Dromour Ho.* (W. Steuart Fothringham, Esq.) on a commanding site high up on l. bank. The country becomes barer and less interesting. 6 m. (rt.) *Tomnagrew* (James Macduff, Esq.); 7¾ m. (rt.) *Kinloch Ho.* (Marquis of Breadalbane). Here, immediately after crossing the *Cochill Burn*, a road (ascending to 1143 ft.) leads rt. in 9 m. to Aberfeldy. The Braan is again crossed just before *Amulree* is reached. For Amulree and distances therefrom (see p. 214).

After leaving Dunkeld Stat., when the leaves are not out, a glimpse is caught rt. of the cathedral and town. Presently *Inver* village (see p. 218) is passed rt., the Braan is crossed, and a tunnel at the base of Craigvinean is entered. After emerging lovely stretches of the river are seen rt.

20¼ m. **Dalguise Stat.** l. is *Dalguise Ho.* (J. Nairne Durrant Steuart, Esq.), and high up rt. across the river is *St. Colme's*, the Dowager-Duchess of Atholl's farm. The line now crosses the Tay to

21½ m. **Guay Stat.**

[A high-level road with extensive views begins to ascend here rt. Traversing the *Braes of Tullymet* it passes *Tullymet Village*, with a disused R.C. ch. built by the late proprietor of *Tullymet Lo.* (now the Duke of Atholl), and, farther on (keeping rt.), a Baptist chap., rejoining in 6 m. the low level road 2 m. N. of Ballinluig.]

The old river terraces are very well marked here. Across the river is *Kinnaird Ho.* (D. of Atholl). A fine view opens up l. up the Tay, with *Schiehallion* (3547 ft.) at the end and the round-topped *Farragon* (2559 ft.) in the centre, just before reaching

24 m. **Ballinluig Junc. Stat.** ✲

[*Branch line to Aberfeldy* 8½ m. See Rte. 43.] l. across the *Tummel*—here spanned by both a carriage suspension br. (opened 1889) and a rly. br.—on an eminence is a Celtic Cross Monument to the 6th D. of Atholl (d. 1864), with devices taken from his favourite out-door pursuits.

Quitting Ballinluig the railway ascends the valley of the Tummel, passing rt. the hamlet of *Moulinearn*, *Easthaugh* (D. of Atholl), and *Croftinloan* (Mrs. Murray)—high up—and l. *Dunfallandy* (Miss Fergusson), and reaches

28½ m. **Pitlochrie Stat.**

PITLOCHRIE ✲, charmingly situated above the Tummel, surrounded by woods and backed by the grand mass of *Ben Vrackie* (2757 ft.), has long been a favourite summer resort, and of late years has grown considerably. The old Parish Ch. is at *Moulin* (¾ m. N.), but a neat little church was erected in 1885 on a central site above the village for evening service. There are also Free, Baptist, and Epis. Chs. In the centre of the village is a *memorial fountain* to "Lieut.-Col. Arch. Butter, Younger of Faskally, b. 1836, d. 1880."

The excursions that may be made from Pitlochrie are very numerous.

WALKS :—

(1) To the *Black Spout*, returning by **Moulin** ✲, 3½ m.

Follow the Dunkeld road for ¾ m., and after crossing a burn turn l., pass under the rly., and follow the l. bank of the stream. The waterfall will be passed (1¼ m.) and *Kinnaird* reached (2 m.). Turn l. to *Moulin* (2¾ m.), a picturesque tiny village, near which in a field are the ruins of *Castle Dhu*, once a stronghold of the Campbell family. Behind Moulin are *Balnakeilly* (A. Blair Stewart, Esq.) and *Baledmund* (T. Grant Ferguson, Esq.).

(2) To *Port-na-Craig Ferry*, along N. bank of Tummel and back by *Clunie Bridge*, 2½ m.

(3) To *Port-na-Craig Ferry*, and over the hill to *Grandtully Stat.* 4 m.

(4) To the **Pass of Killiecrankie**, **Falls of Tummel**, *Bonskeid Ho.*, **Queen's View**, **Loch Tummel**, and back by the *S. side of the Tummel*, 14 m.

This is one of the most charming Highland walks in Scotland.

Take the train to *Killiecrankie* and walk (1 m.) down the *Pass* (see p. 221). [*or*, Walk 2½ m. along the Blair road, pass through a narrow opening in the wall, and cross the rly. by a ft.-br. whence a path leads down to Garry Bridge]. Cross the *Garry Br.*, turn l. through a gate into a path which leads in ¾ m., to the *Falls of Tummel*, where a small granite monument records the Queen's visit upon 27th Sept. 1844. Follow the l. bank of the Tummel, a lovely walk (private, but no objection is made), to *Bonskeid Ho.* 3½ m., behind which the public road is rejoined and followed to the *Queen's View* (see below), 6½ m. The ferry across the Tummel, ½ m. farther on (7 m.), conveys carriages, but the road—commanding beautiful views of the river—to the Falls of Tummel (11 m.) is almost too steep and rough except for a dogcart. Pitlochrie may be reached by *Clunie Bridge* or *Port-na-Craig Ferry*, 14 m.

(5) **Ascent of Ben Vrackie** (*Ben Bhreac* = the brindled hill), 2757 ft., 2-2½ hrs.

The direct path goes behind the hotel at Moulin, but it is better to keep along the road ½ m. beyond Moulin, then follow a track by the side of a little burn and ascend by the E. shoulder. Descend direct to Moulin, *or* (easy) to Killiecrankie Stat. 3 m. The *View* includes *Ben Nevis*, *Shepherds of Etive*, *Ben Lawers*, *Schiehallion*, *Ben-y-Gloe*, and the *Lomonds*.

(6) From *Port-na-Craig Ferry to Ballinluig* by the S. side of the Tummel — charming views of the river—5 m. By going round by *Clunie Bridge* this road can be driven, but it is very hilly and sometimes very rough.

(7) *Ascent of Craigour* (1300 ft.), from which a lovely view is obtained of Loch Tummel, Schiehallion, and the Shepherds of Etive. Abt. 1 hr.

Cross the rly. by a stile rt. where the road down to Clunie Bridge leaves the main road. Keep between the 2nd house and one next it on rt. A track trending rt. and then keeping steadily l. leads to the top. The path may also be joined from Moulin.

DRIVES : [1]—

(*a*) To **Queen's View**, **Tummel Bridge**, and **Kinloch Rannoch**, 20¾ m.

Garry Bridge is crossed in 3 m. From it there is a fine view of the *Pass of Killiecrankie*, with *Cairn Liath* (3193 ft.) in the background. Upon the oppos. side a path l. leads to the *Falls of Tummel* (¾ m.) [see above]. 4½ m. *Bonskeid Ho.* (Trs. of late Rev. R. W. Barbour)—beautifully situated —is passed l. 5½ m. *Fincastle Burn* is

[1] For Coaches and Mail-gigs, see Index and Directory under heading Pitlochrie.

crossed [road rt. up *Strath Fincastle*, from the head of which *Tulach Hill* (see p. 222) might be reached on foot and a descent made to Blair Atholl], and the road bends l., passing *Fincastle* post office. At 6¾ m. *Allean Ho.* (F. A. S. Colquhoun, Esq.) stands l., and at 7¼ m. a rocky eminence, beside the road l. and reached through a wicket gate, called *The Queen's View*, commands a magnificent prospect of *Loch Tummel* (3 m. long), *Schiehallion*, and the *Shepherds of Etive*, near Glencoe. The river leaves the loch by a fine sweep round a bold wooded promontory, and flows immediately below the precipitous sides of the crag from which the view is obtained.

At 7¾ m. there is a carriage ferry across the river (see p. 220). The road keeps going up and down along the N. side of the loch, passing (10 m.) *Loch Tummel Inn*✱ rt., *Portnellan Ho.* l. and reaches *Tummel Bridge*✱ (13¼ m.), 3 m. beyond the W. end of the loch.

[From here a road runs N. (ascending to 1089 ft.) to *Trinafour* (5 m.), and thence E. down *Glen Erichdie* to *Struan* (11 m.) [see p. 223]. Another runs S. (ascending to 1262 ft.) by *Loch Kinardochy* and *Keltney Burn* to Aberfeldy (13½ m.) see p. 240.]

The N. side of the Tummel which becomes wild and rocky with rapids, is kept. *Dun-Alastair*, a fine property (17 m.) and *Lochgarry Ho.* (both J. C. Bunten, Esq.) are passed l., and *Kinloch-Rannoch* (20¾ m.) is reached (see p. 240).

(*b*) To **Kirkmichael**✲[1] (12¼ m.) **and Braemar** ✲ (40¼ m.). See Rte. 58.

(*c*) To **Falls of Tummel** (S. side) (3 m.) by *Clunie Bridge* (see p. 220). The best view of *Faskally* is obtained from this road.

(*d*) Drives may also be taken to *Killiecrankie* (4 m.), *Blair Atholl* (7 m.), *Forest Lo.*, *Glen Tilt* (15 m.), *Falls of Bruar* (10 m.), *Aberfeldy* (15 m.), *Kenmore* (21 m.), and *Dunkeld* (13 m.)

From Pitlochrie the rly. ascends the valley of the Tummel in cuttings and through the woods behind *Faskally* (A. Butter, Esq.), which is scarcely seen, situated l. in the midst of a sunny haugh, just below the junction of the Garry with the Tummel, surrounded by charming scenery. Through the ***Pass of Killiecrankie** (below), 1 m. farther on, the rly. and the road run side by side, but from neither can the defile through which the *Garry* rushes be well seen in summer. At the N. end, however, the rly. is conveyed over a small burn on a noble *Viaduct* of 10 arches, bending l. before a tunnel is entered, and from this viaduct the whole Pass can be seen by looking back. Close at hand are the *Soldier's Leap*, and *Killiecrankie Cottage* (Miss Alston Stewart) picturesquely perched upon the opposite bank. Emerging from the tunnel the train reaches

32¼ m. **Killiecrankie Stat.**, from which the *Pass* is best visited.

Entrance is obtained at a gate ¼ m. along the Pitlochrie road rt. The *Queen's View*, overlooking the *Soldier's Leap*, should be visited, and then the path down the glen should be taken to Garry Bridge (1 m.), following the line of the old road by which Gen. Mackay marched his army to encounter Dundee. Return may be made by crossing the br., taking the 1st road rt. past *Tenandry Ch.*, and recrossing by the br. (fine bit of river) at Killiecrankie Stat.—a pleasant round of 3½ m.

It must be remembered that the battle of Killiecrankie (graphically described by Lord Macaulay and Sir W. Scott), fought on 17th June 1689, between Gen. Mackay, who commanded for William III., and Claverhouse (Viscount Dundee) on the side of James II., in which Dundee was mortally wounded, did not begin in the Pass, but to the N. of Killiecrankie Stat. Mackay's troops had emerged from the Pass, and were trying to form in the opening of the valley when the Highlanders received the signal to charge.

"It was past 7 o'clock. Dundee gave the word. The Highlanders dropped their plaids. The few who were so luxurious as to wear rude socks of untanned hide spurned them away. It was long remembered in Lochaber that Lochiel took off what possibly was the only pair of shoes in his clan, and charged barefoot at the head of his men. . . . In two minutes

[1] Mail-gig daily (Coach in summer) at 9 A.M.; leaving Kirkmichael 1.45 P.M.

the battle was lost and won . . . and the mingled torrent of red coats and tartans went raving down the valley to the gorge of Killiecrankie."—Macaulay.

" Like a tempest down the ridges
Swept a hurricane of steel,
Rose the slogan of Macdonald—
Flashed the broadsword of Lochiel!
. . . .
Horse and man went down like drift-wood
When the floods are black at Yule,
And their carcases are whirling
In the Garry's deepest pool."
Aytoun.

32¾ m. rt. is *Urrard Ho.* (Mrs. Alston Stewart), into which Dundee is said to have been taken after he had received his fatal wound. An upright stone in a field below the house (traditionally) marks the spot where he fell.

33¾ m. l. upon rt. bank is *Strathgarry Ho.* (A. D. Stewart, Esq.).

34¼ m. *Lude* (W. M'Inroy, Esq.) is seen high up rt., finely situated in a grass park with woods behind; the Tilt is crossed, and

35¼ m. **Blair Atholl Stat.** ✲ reached. Across the road and close at hand is the entrance to **Blair Castle**,[1] a large plain white-washed mansion in the Scottish baronial style, rather destitute of architectural features, the principal residence of the Duke of Atholl. It was dismantled in 1690, to prevent its being garrisoned by the rebels, but was restored with towers and re-embattled 1870. It was built by John of Strathbogie, one of the Comyns, who became Earl of Atholl by marriage. In 1644 it was garrisoned by Montrose; in 1653 stormed by Cromwell. Claverhouse occupied it in 1689, and in 1745 it was besieged by the rebels. The site and the grounds are charming. They include fine trees, especially a row of grand *Larches*—rivals in size of those at Dunkeld, but not so old.

1 Strangers are admitted to the park and grounds between 9 A.M. and 6 P.M., but must be attended by a guide, who receives 1s. from each person.

In the ruined *Ch.* behind the house is buried the valiant Dundee, the hero of Killiecrankie. The family of Murray ranks high in antiquity and importance in the annals of Scotland, and the motto now borne by them, "Furth fortune, and fill the fetters," was granted to an ancestor by James I., who sent him in command of his troops against a rebellious Lord of the Isles. The Marquis of Tullibardine and two brothers were "out" with Mar in 1715, on the side of the Old Pretender, and after many years' exile, two of them (the third being dead) returned with Charles Edward in 1745. The Marquis unfurled the Prince's banner at Glenfinnan, and Lord G. Murray was the ablest and most devoted officer in his army—the first to advance, the last to retreat. He finally escaped to Rome; but his elder brother was captured, and died in the Tower. The Castle, occupied as an outpost of the Duke of Cumberland, was besieged by Lord George, and defended by a garrison under Sir Andrew Agnew, just before the battle of Culloden.

A Highland gathering is held annually in Sept. in a field beautifully situated, not far from the Castle. The Duke of Atholl marches from the Castle to the ground at the head of his men.

Excursions:—

(1) *Killiecrankie and Pitlochrie* (see pp. 220, 221).

(2) *Tulach Hill* (1541 ft.) lies 1 m. to the S. It is approached by a footbridge across the Garry, behind the village, and commands a fine view, which was greatly admired by H.M. Queen Victoria when she ascended the hill with the Prince Consort in 1844.

(3) *The Falls of Bruar* (3 m. W.) well deserve to be visited, but

they are nearer *Struan Stat.* (see below).

(4) **Glen Tilt.** Carriages from the hotels can drive to the Forest Lo. (8 m.), crossing the old Bridge of Tilt, and entering the 1st gate rt. Pedestrians must apply to the factor for an order, or make a detour, losing the first and finest 3 m. of the river.

For description of Glen Tilt and pedestrian route to Braemar (29 m.), see Rte. 59.

(5) *Falls of Fender.*

Cross the Tilt, ½ m. E., pass immediately through wicket gate l. and up l. bank. The path joins the driving road just above the *York Fall.* Keep rt. up l. bank of Fender Burn. ¼ m. up is *Fender Bridge* l. and the falls. Across the br., up rt. bank, and then through a gate l. is the public right of way to Glen Tilt.

(6) **Ascent of Ben-y-Gloe.** This is a group of mts.—*Cairn Liath* (3193 ft.), a *Peak* (3505 ft.), and *Cairn Gabhar* (*Gour*) 3671 ft.—occupying a somewhat inaccessible isolated central position, well worth mastering. The highest point is about 8 m. from Blair Atholl.

The nearest point to which to drive is probably the Forest Lo.; but the whole range can be done on foot, without fatigue, by a pedestrian in good training in 8-9 hrs., about 21 m. Go to *Fender Bridge;* don't cross, but keep rt. to N. end of *Loch Moraig* (3 m.). If *Cairn Liath* is to be omitted, go to *Monzie farm* (½ m. l.), and keep round W. side of Cairn Liath; otherwise, keep on the road for 1½ m. until the top of Cairn Liath is seen quite clearly without any rising ground in front, and ascend (at first by the side of a wall) straight to the top—a steep, but easy ascent, 1¾ m. The higher tops and the screes and corries look very fine from here, and the retrospect view towards Schiehallion is extensive. ¾ hr. (2 m.), with a dip of 700 ft., takes to the next cairn (3505 ft.), from which there is a magnificent view—near at hand *Glen Tilt* (including *Loch Tilt*), in the distance *Cairn Toul, Braeriach, Ben Muich-dhui, Lochnagar, Ben Lawers, the Black Mt. Hills,* and *Ben Nevis.* Another ¾ hr. (2 m.), with another dip of 700 ft., takes to *Cairn Gabhar* (3671 ft.), commanding the Forfarshire and Aberdeenshire mountains. Keep S. along the ridge (very stony), and descend to the burn on the W. (2 m. from top), follow its course for 2½ m., and then take track rt., back by *Loch Moraig* to Blair in 6½ m., *or,* continue down *Glen Girnaig* for 4½ m. to *Killiecrankie* Stat.

At 38½ m. the line, which here runs nearly due E. and W., crosses the Bruar a little above its junction with the Garry and below the Falls. The Garry is crossed—fine view up and down the river—just before reaching

40 m. **Struan Stat.** ✡

To see the *Falls of Garry* and *Salmon Leap* cross the river, and take path rt. down l. bank as far as a summer house. The ***Falls of Bruar** are also most easily visited from here.

Follow high road 1½ m. towards Blair, then path runs l. up rt. bank of the *Bruar.* The Falls consist of 3 romantic cascades, each differing from the others, and afford fine studies for the artist of rock and water. There is a br. across the burn between the 1st and 2nd falls and another above the 3rd fall (a good mile from the road), which can be reached by either side from the 1st br. The fir plantations in which the falls are situated were made by the 4th D. of Atholl, in consequence of a visit from Robert Burns (in 1787), who after seeing the falls wrote the "*Humble Petition of Bruar Water*"—

"Would then my noble master please
 To grant my highest wishes,
He'll shade my banks wi' towering trees
 And bonnie spreading bushes."

One may stroll 2½ m. above the 3rd fall on the rt. bank, and return to Struan by the road coming down from *Bruar Lodge.*

[*Coach route* from Struan to **Kinloch-Rannoch,** 13 m.

[Coach *daily* at 11 A.M., from K.-R. 7 A.M.]

This road runs up *Glen Erichdie,* passing (5 m.) rt. *Auchleeks Ho.* (Edgar W. Robertson, Esq.), to *Trinafour* (6 m.) where there is a neat little ch. [Here a road strikes due N. in 5 m. to *Dalnacardoch Lo.* (p. 224), 6 m. above Struan—rising on the way to 1409 ft.] Turning sharp l. we cross the *Erichdie Water,* pass *Trinafour Ho.,* formerly an inn, and farther on a tiny village, and ascend rapidly to 1089 ft. at 7 m. After a mile of moorland the road forks left to *Tummel Bridge,* 3 m., and rt. to Rannoch. The latter road was made privately by General Macdonald, lately proprietor of Dunalastair, and has a toll upon it. Schiehallion stands boldly out in front. The road descends steadily and at 10½ m. joins that from Pitlochrie and Tummel Br. (see p. 221). The l. bank of the Tummel is then followed through a broad and pleasing but tame valley to

Kinloch-Rannoch ✲, 13 m., see p. 240.]

Leaving Struan the rly. begins to ascend, more slowly at first, rapidly afterwards, more than 800 ft. being ascended in 12 m. The first 2 m. are through a birch plantation—*Clunes* rt.; then the country becomes much wilder and more desolate, and trees are not seen again until Glen Truim and Strathspey. The Garry tumbles over the tilted quartzite schists of reddish hue which form its channel. *Dalnamein* is passed rt., and (46 m.) *Dalnacardoch,* in coaching days a well-known inn, now also a shooting lodge; both belong to the Duke of Atholl).

[Hence a road runs S. to *Trinafour*, *Glen Erichdie*, *Strath Tummel*, and *Rannoch* (see pp. 223, 221), and ½ m. farther on one strikes N. to *Edendon Lo.* and (by path) *Gaick Lo.* and *Kingussie* (see p. 225).]

The Garry is crossed; snow posts and strong palisade screens for the rly. against snow-drifts testify to the severity of the winter in these parts, and well-marked moraines are seen.

51 m. **Dalnaspidal Stat.**

"To the W. lies Loch Garry—a lake held back by moraine stuff, which is there cut into a succession of terraces, marking former levels of the water. The glacier of L. Garry split upon the summit of the pass and sent one branch into Glen Garry, the other into Glen Truim." —Sir A. GEIKIE.

At 53 m. "the summit, 1484 ft." is passed and the train hastens down the *Pass of Drumouchter*, "by far the wildest scene through which any rly. passes in this country" (*Geikie*), crossing from Perthshire into Inverness-shire with the *Boar of Badenoch* backed by the *Sow of Atholl* on the left. *Drumouchter Lo.* stands rt. The head of Loch Ericht is visible from the rly. l. before reaching

59 m. **Dalwhinnie Stat.** ✲, at the head of Glen Truim, a desolate and solitary spot, protected by a few fir-trees from the cold winds.

[On l. lies **Loch Ericht** or **Errochd,** good fishing and boats (no road except to *Locherícht Lo.* 6 m.)—a long (15 m.) dreary loch famous for *salmo ferox*, and surrounded on all sides by the mountains of the forest of Drumouchter and those of the forest of Ben Alder, of which *Ben Alder* (3757 ft.) is the highest point. The water of this loch is never known to freeze. It discharges its water at its S. end by the *Ericht* into L. Rannoch (see p. 241). In a cave on Ben Alder Prince Charlie lay concealed along with Cluny Macpherson.

A road runs N. from Dalwhinnie to Laggan, 7 m., to join that between Kingussie and Fort-William, p. 226.]

Near the hotel on the rt. is Gen. Wade's stone, with the date 1729 upon it. This marks the spot where the troops, who made the roads from Inverness, met those who were working up from Dunkeld. The wild country here has on more than one occasion been a favourite rendezvous and stronghold of the Highlanders, who have here held their own against a far more numerous force of disciplined troops. In this neighbourhood even Cromwell's Ironsides received a check from the men of Atholl; and from here Gen. Cope declined to encounter the Highlanders descending from the *Pass of Corrieyairack* (p. 226), and retired to Inverness, leaving open the Lowlands and the road to Edinburgh, 26th Aug. 1745.

Beyond Dalwhinnie the *Truim Water* is crossed. At 64½ m. l. are *Etteridge Bridge*, where the road crosses the river, and the *Falls of*

Truim. The river flows through birches and the country becomes more smiling, with fine views of isolated mountains in front. *Glentruim Ho.* (Col. Lachlan Macpherson) is passed, l. just above the junc. of the *Truim* with the *Spey.* Just below the junc. (l.) is the site of the Battle of *Invernahavon,* fought in 1386 between the clans Cameron and Mackintosh. 3 m. up the Spey is *Cluny Cas.*, the seat of Cluny Macpherson (p. 226).

The rly. descends the valley for some way parallel with the Spey, which it crosses before reaching

69 m. **Newtonmore Stat.** ✲, where the country becomes more picturesque, producing a short turf that forms excellent pasture for the Badenoch sheep. The Spey soon swells into a broad stream, its banks fringed with corn crops, and finally backed by the outline of the Grampian chain on rt.

72 m. **KINGUSSIE Stat.** ✲[1], (740 ft.), pronounced Kinyew'sie — a large village annually growing in size and in favour with summer visitors. Together with the greater part of the surrounding district, it is the property of J. E. B. Baillie, Esq. of Dochfour, whose grandfather purchased it from the last Duke of Gordon. It serves as a sort of capital to this wild country of **Badenoch,** which formerly belonged to the Comyns, though, upon their annihilation by Bruce's party, some of it was bestowed upon Randolph, Earl of Murray. Part of it was retained in the royal power, and was subsequently granted to the natural son of Robert II., better known as the Wolf of Badenoch. One of the fortresses by which his power was maintained was on the opposite side of the Spey, on a spot now occupied by the ruins of the *Ruthven Barracks,* which were built in 1718 to keep the Highlanders in check, and were destroyed by them 1745.

This place was the closing scene of the rebellion, for here the Highlanders assembled after the rout at Culloden, to the number of 7000, several clans having joined who were too late for the battle, in hopes that Prince Charlie would take the field again. He, however, saw the uselessness of another attempt, and, bidding them farewell, commanded them to disperse.

[EXCURSIONS :—

(1) A charming walk N.—up the burn which comes down past the station—to *Loch Guinach* (2 m.) and the neighbouring heights.

(2) Drive S. across the Spey to Ruthven Barracks (1 m.), E. across *Tromie Bridge* (3 m.), up rt. bank of the stream, past *Glen Tromie Lo.* (5 m.) to *Loch Seilich* (11 m.), 1500 ft., and along its N. bank to *Gaick Lo.* (Sir G. Macpherson Grant, Bart.), 13 m.

Pedestrians may save 2 m. by going over the hill to above Glen Tromie Lo., but they lose a pretty bit of the Tromie. The walk (5½ m.) from Gaick Lo. by the E. side of *Loch Vrotten* and the W. side of *Loch-an-Duin*—a miniature Wastwater—to *Edendon Lo.* is very fine. Thence road to *Dalnacardoch* (5 m.), and *Struan* or *Dalnaspidal,* 11 m. (27½ or 29½ m. in all; but carriage may be ordered from Struan or Blair Atholl to Edendon Lo.).

(3) Drive by *Tromie Bridge* (3 m.) and the village of *Insh* (5 m.), and the E. side of Loch Insh to **Kincraig** (8 m.), and return by W. side of Spey, 14 m. The drive (very beautiful) may be continued beyond Kincraig along E. side of the Spey, crossing the *Feshie* behind *Invereshie Ho.* (Sir G. Macpherson - Grant, Bart.) to **Aviemore,** by the *Doune of Rothiemurchus* (14 m.), returning by W. side, 26 m.

(4) Drive (rough road) across the hills to **Glen Feshie** (7 m.), up the

[1] See "Glimpses of Church and Social Life in the Highlands in Olden Times," by Alex. Macpherson (of Kingussie), F.S.A. Scot. (W. Blackwood & Sons, 1893).

glen rt. to the *Huts* (11 m.), back, and down to Kincraig (20 m.), then to Kingussie, 26 m.

[From the Huts (rt.-of-way path) up the Feshie and down the Geldie to the junc. with the road to Bynach Lo. (see p. 288) is 12 m.; thence to Braemar 11 m. The Queen took this route from *Balmoral to Grantown*, 4th Sept. 1860, and from *Balmoral to Kingussie*, 8th Oct. 1861.]

(5) Drive S.W. by *Cluny Cas.* (8½ m.) and *Laggan Bridge* (10½ m.) to **Loch Laggan** (17½ m.).

Keep alongside the rly. to 3 m. **Newtonmore** ✱ (p. 225), a long village. At its far end we leave the road to Perth, and trending W. cross the *Calder* and pass rt. the tiny old ch.-yd. of *Beallidbeg*. We now ascend a narrow valley—one of the prettiest parts of the drive. The *Spey* and two lovely little lochs are l.; on the rt. rise the precipitous cliffs of *Craigdhu*, among which is a *Cave* where Prince Charlie hid with Cluny Macpherson, and on the hill-top in front is a cairn to the memory of Mrs. Cluny Macpherson (d. 1886).

At 6½ m. is *Craigdhu Ho.* (Mrs. Fitzroy) —charmingly situated. In a spot below, the late proprietor, Capt. Fitzroy, is buried. Beyond, the valley suddenly opens out, affording an extensive view over broad meadow land, with *Ben Alder* and other mts. in the distance.

At 8½ m. we reach a beautiful little ch.-yd., beside a burn, in which Cluny Macpherson, C.B., "Chief of the Clan Chattan" (1804-85), his wife, and his eldest son (1833-86) are buried. Just beyond is the principal *Entrance* to **Cluny Cas.** (not seen from the road), the seat of Cluny Macpherson. Here are preserved the bagpipes which are said to have been played at the famous battle, fought in 1396 on the N. Inch at Perth, between Clan Chattan and Clan Quhele, so well described in Scott's "Fair Maid of Perth."

At 10½ m. are **Laggan** ✱ hamlet and ch. Mrs. Grant (1755-1838) who wrote "Letters from the Mountains," was wife of the minister here.

[An old military road made by General Wade, 1735, turns off rt. up the l. bank of the Spey to *Meallgarbha*, 10½ m., beyond which carriages cannot go (4 m. W. is *Loch Spey* and beyond, *Glen Roy*, see p. 349). It then crosses the **Pass of Corrieyairack** (2507 ft.) 15 m.—commanding "a view of every mountain head from Moray Firth to the Peaks of Skye, nothing I ever saw like it" (SHAIRP)—and descends 16 extraordinary zigzags to *Glen Tarff* and **Fort-Augustus**✱, 24 m. It was before the Highanders descending by this road that Gen. Cope retired in 1745.]

We now cross the Spey by an iron bridge of a single span—on the hill in front is a cairn to Cluny Macpherson,—and turn rt. up *Strath Mashie*. At 12 m. rt. in the angle between this glen and the Spey, towers "*The Dun*," upon which is a *Fort* (*Dun-da-lamh*) 60 ft. above the valley, 420 ft. long, 250 ft. broad at the W. end, and 75 ft. broad at the E. end with walls 2-13 ft. high, and 14-25 ft. thick, having no cement, earth, or sand. It is said to be "the most perfect relic of a British stronghold of that class in Britain." Beyond a bridge over the Mashie Water, the watershed (848 ft.) is imperceptibly crossed, but soon the *Pattack*, which flows into the Atlantic, comes rushing down a picturesque gorge l. from *Ben Alder* (3757 ft.) away to the S. The road—here very fine—follows the rt. bank of the Pattack. The Ben Nevis range comes into view before reaching Loch Laggan.

17½ m. *Loch Laggan Hotel* ✱ stands on the N. shore near its E. end.

Loch Laggan, 7 m. long and ½ m. broad, has 2 small islands; upon one of them are the ruins of a castle said to have been built by Fergus II. On the S. side of the loch is *Ardverikie*, the imposing shooting lodge of Sir J. W. Ramsden, Bt. The Queen and Prince Consort occupied this house for some weeks in 1848, when it belonged to Lord Abercorn. On the walls are some admirable sketches of deer-stalking by *Sir Edwin Landseer, R.A.*

(6) Drive round by *Laggan Bridge*, 10½ m., and *Dalwhinnie*, 17½ m., to *Kingussie*, 31½ m.

To Laggan Bridge see (5). After crossing the bridge, turn l. past the Free Ch. A wild moorland road leads to Dalwhinnie (p. 224).

(7) Drive by *Loch Laggan* to **Fort-William**, 49 m.

To Loch Laggan see (5). The road keeps along the S. shore to the E. end (24 m.) where *Moy Lodge* (Sir J. W. Ramsden, Bt.) stands. After this a bleak moor is crossed. At *Roughburn* (28½ m.), the old *lake terraces* begin to be very well marked, and the road descends steeply to 31 m. *Inverlair Stat.* where the W. Highland Rly. comes in l. from Loch Treig, see p. 349.

From this point the road and rly. run practically side by side, and the route by 36¼ m. *Roy Bridge*✱, whence the famous *Parallel Roads* (see p. 349) should be visited, and 39½ m. *Spean Bridge*✱ to 49 m. **Fort-William** ✱ is described in Rte. 81.

A *Coach* in July, Aug., and Sept., and a *Mail-gig* the rest of the year, runs daily between Fort-William and Kingussie, but now that the W. Highland Rly. is open, it may possibly not run between Fort-William and Inverlair.]

Leaving Kingussie the rly. pursuing a N.E. direction next passes l. *Belleville* (C. J. B. Macpherson, Esq.), beautifully situated on high ground. There is an obelisk lower down (l.) of which a glimpse may be caught, to the memory of Macpherson (1738-96), the translator or writer of Ossian, who built the house from designs of Robert Adair. Sir David Brewster lived here, having married Macpherson's only child and heiress. The Castle of *Raits*, upon the site of which Belleville stands, was the scene of the slaughter of the Comyns by the clan Mackintosh. Comyn had asked his opponents to dinner, and placed each of them at table next to one of his own clan. At the appearance of the boar's head on a dish, each Comyn was to slay a Mackintosh. But the guests, having been warned of the plot, were too quick for their opponents, and when the boar's head appeared each Mackintosh slew a Comyn. At the W. of the castle is a large gray stone called the Listening Stone, at which the plot was revealed.

The valley of the Spey is here very subject to serious flooding. Soon the river loses itself in *Loch Insh*, lying in a scene of beauty and variety, at the foot of which is

77½ m. **Kincraig Stat.**

To the S. opens out the picturesque wild vale of Glen Feshie, where the late Duchess of Bedford built a rustic colony of wood huts, on whose rough walls Sir Edwin Landseer, R.A., left traces of his pencil.

[At Kincraig a dogcart may be got to drive up Glen Feshie. *Achlean* l. (5½ m.) is a good starting-pt. for climbing *Cairn Ban* (3443 ft.), 2 hrs., and thence on to *Cairn Toul* (4241 ft.), 2 hrs., or *Braeriach* (4248 ft.), 2 hrs. At the *Huts* (9 m.) the path to Braemar (32 m. from Kincraig) begins (p. 288).]

On rt. is *Kinrara* (Duke of Richmond). Birch-woods abound here and continue with little alteration as far as *Rothiemurchus*, where the woods and walks of *The Doune* (J. P. Grant, Esq. of Rothiemurchus), on the rt. bank of the Spey, are especially beautiful. To the N.W. extends the range of the *Monadhliath* (= *The gray moor*) *Mts.*

81 m. on l. is *Loch Alvie*, and on rt. the *Tor of Alvie*, upon which are a cairn to the memory of those who fell at Waterloo, and a monument to the last Duke of Gordon, to whom this property belonged.

Close to the rly., near Loch Alvie, is *Lynwilg Inn* ✲, the only one between Kingussie and Boat of Garten. It is 2½ m. from

83½ **Aviemore Stat.** ✲, which will be a most important junc. when the line N.W. direct to Inverness, reducing the distance from 60 m. to 35 m., is finished. This line passing l. *Kinveachy Lo.* (Dowager-Countess of Seafield) was opened in 1892 as far as **Carr Bridge** ✲, 6½ m. (see pp. 231, 232).

A magnificent view of the *Cairngorms* is obtained from the stat., and for some miles north, but their length and mass prevent realisation of their great height.

Behind the stat. (l.) is *Craigellachie Rock*, in olden times the trysting-place of the Clan *Grant*, and hence their war cry "Stand fast, Craigellachie."[1] There is another Craigellachie 37 m. down the Spey (p. 309), and "between the two Craigellachies" is the *Seafield Country*.

[EXCURSIONS :—

See Map, p. 232.

Aviemore is the nearest rly. station for the following :—

(1) *The charming little* **Loch-an-Eilean** (Loch of the Island), 3 m.

1 See the late Principal Shairp's poem, "A Cry from Craigellachie," written (1867) shortly after the opening of the Highland Railway.

Cross the Spey and keep along l. bank of the *Druie*. At *Inverdruie* (1 m.) take first road rt. until the *Doune* of Rothiemurchus (J. P. Grant, Esq.), and its park are seen rt. At a garden gate (2 m.) take road l. leading past *Polchar Cott.* and the *Manse*, and along a lovely birch avenue to the N. end of the loch. ¼ m. along the loch is a shed where horses may be put up; upon a picturesque island are the ruins of a cas. with an osprey's nest; and rt. is *Ord Ban* (1250 ft.), with path to the top, whence there is a very fine view of the mountains and of numerous little lochs. Round the loch is a walk of 3 m. In returning from the N. end keep straight on to the *Free Ch.* (1½ m.), thence l. to the Station (1½ m.). In this loch Gen. Rice was drowned, while skating, 26th Dec. 1892.

(2) *To* **Braemar** *by the Larig Ghru* (30 m.), through probably the grandest Pass in Scotland. [Gael. *Lairig*=a *Pass*, and *Gruamach*= *Gloomy*.] (Described in the reverse way in Rte. 56.)

This is a splendid but fatiguing route, for which ample time should be allowed. For more than 20 m. there is no house. Ponies cannot be taken. Cross the Spey; pass the Free Ch., and before reaching *Coylum Bridge* (2 m.), go over a stile rt. For the next 4 m., notwithstanding right-of-way sign-posts, the path is not easy to find. Keep along road for ¾ m., then behind a cottage l. get beside the stream, and follow its l. bank 1¼ m. until a bridge which must be crossed is reached just below where the stream forks E. and W. of the Watch Hill. Keep along rt. bank. [The other stream comes from *Loch Eunach* (see below).] After crossing a grass field the path keeps l. high above the stream, until at 6 m. the last of the Rothiemurchus pines is left. The route is now quite open—Braeriach to rt., Cairngorm l., while a well-marked moraine guards the pass. At the highest pt. (2750 ft.), 10 m., Aberdeenshire is entered. The next mile—over boulders—is the roughest walking possible. The ground continues very uneven past the *Wells of Dee* (11 m.), 3 clear tarns connected by streams underground. [From here a path up *Braeriach* (4248 ft.), immediately above on rt., may be seen, and the top reached by an hour's climb. This is the *only route* always open.] 13 m. rt. is the truly magnificent corrie into which the *Garrachorry Burn*—the highest Source of the Dee—leaps from its springs 4000 ft. up on Braeriach, which flanks the corrie rt., while Cairn Toul (4241 ft.) flanks it left. The *Devil's Point* (3303 ft.) stands bodily out in front. When it is reached (15 m.) the Dee may be followed to the Linn of Dee 23½ m. [see p. 283] (or by keeping high up along l. bank, and bearing E. round *Cairn Maim*, the Luibeg Burn may be struck and followed, passing *Derry Lo.*, to *Linn of Dee*, 21½ m.). Thence to Braemar is 6½ m. (see p. 281).

(3) **Ascent of Braeriach** (4248 ft.), far more interesting than Cairngorm or even than Ben Muich-dhui. [*Ascent of Cairn Toul*, 4241 ft., may be added.]

(*a*) The best and easiest way, if consent can be obtained, or the gate at Coylum Bridge found open, is to drive through Rothiemurchus forest to N. end of *Loch Eunach* (9 m.), a fine wild lonely loch, 1 m. long, with a splendid corrie at S. end, and thence climb l. up a deer road in 1½ hr. or 2 hrs. to the top. Even walking you may be turned in the stalking season. Return to the road 2 m. N. of the loch at the bothy (where a horse can sometimes be put up) by one of the N. shoulders of Braeriach, and down the burn at the foot of the N. corries. This, indeed, is the *shortest* way up from the bothy, but misses the loch.

(*b*) To *Wells of Dee* (11 m.), and thence an hr.'s steep climb by path rt. (see above). The 4000-ft. plateau (clothed in July and August with *Silene acaulis* and watered with the innumerable bubbling infant Sources of the Dee), the corries, and the *Views* E. across the Larig Ghru to Ben Muich-dhui, Deeside, and Lochnagar, S. to Cairn Toul and Ben-y-Gloe, W. to Ben Nevis, and N. to Strathspey, Ben Rinnes, and Ben Wyvis, are the distinguishing features of this too little known mt.

(*c*) From Achlean in *Glen Feshie* (p. 227).

[**Cairn Toul** (4241 ft.) is even more inaccessible, for it is best reached from Braeriach by a 2 hrs.' walk round the Garrachorry corrie, 4 m., without descending below 4000 ft. The final climb is up a staircase of enormous boulders (cf. p. 227).]

(4) *To* **Loch Morlich, Cairngorm** (4084 ft.), and **Ben Muich-dhui** (4296 ft.) [or **Loch A'an**].

Cairngorm, except for the view N. and W., is in itself uninteresting, but is useful as a stepping-stone to better things beyond. Either expedition will take fully 9 hours from Glenmore Lo. as a starting-place.

Cross *Coylum Br.* (2 m.), and go straight on [l. is road to Nethy Br., 9½ m., and Grantown, 15 m.]. 5 m. Loch Morlich is reached [l. is road over Sluggan Pass to Grantown road], and 6 m. *Glenmore Lo.* (Duke of Richmond), where they are generally willing to put up horses. [Straight on is road to

Nethy Br. (11 m.) by Rebhoan Pass.] A foot-br. leads across the stream in the meadows below the Lo. Take the path (no objection usually made) up l. bank of a stream which comes down from Cairngorm, immediately opposite, through a wood of Scotch firs. At end of the wood (2 m.) cross the stream. The path leads you well up the mountain. The way to the top, which is reached after an exceedingly easy walk of 2 or 3 hrs., is just straight on. There is a fine view W. to Ben Nevis and N. down Strathspey, with the Ross-shire Hills in the distance, but S. it is blocked by the neighbouring giants. The *Summit* of *Ben Muich-dhui* lies 4 m. due S., and can be reached with hardly any dip in about 2 hrs. From Ben Muich-dhui a steep descent may be made by the side of a burn in ¾ hr. to the Larig Ghru, 1 m. below the Wells of Dee (see pp. 228, 283). [For descent to Braemar, see Rte. 57.] For *Loch A'an* descend 500 ft. from Cairngorm in a S. direction, when a stream will be struck which, if followed, will lead down by a steep but the only feasible descent to the loch side in less than 1 hr. from the top. The loch, 1½ m. long, lies N.E. and S.W., 2400 ft. above the sea, in a wild and most inaccessible hollow. The cliffs are precipitous, although not sheer, and there are the most lovely beaches of red granite ground to sand. The *Shelter Stone* lies abt. ¼ mile from the S.W. end upon the S. side of the main feeder of the loch, and among a large number of fallen rocks, of which it is the largest. In the chamber below it 15 or 20 persons could stand upright. This is entered by a low roofed passage. [For the way to reach Loch A'an from Braemar, see Rte. 57.] For the return down *Glen Nethy*—a rough wearisome walk, although the cliffs are fine—keep the N.W. side of the loch until near the N. end; then ascend 300 ft. l., and descend the Nethy 5 m. until the ruins of a wooden house are reached, whence there is a road l. (leaving the Nethy) to Glen More by Rebhoan (3 m.). [The Avon or A'an which flows out of the loch runs N.E., then N. by Tomintoul and Ballindalloch to the Spey. The purity of its water has given rise to the doggrel:—

"The water o' A'an, it rins sae clear,
'Twould beguile a man o' a hunder year."

It will take good 4 hrs. from the Shelter Stone to Glen More, as the walking is very rough.]

The view of the Cairngorm Range will fully occupy the tourist until 88½ m. **Boat of Garten Junc. Stat.** ✲ —a somewhat bleak and exposed place.

[Here the Great North of Scotland Rly. down the Spey to Elgin and Keith by Nethy Bridge and Craigellachie goes off (see Rtes. 66 and 65).]

There is a carriage ferry here across the Spey, by which *Abernethy Forest* and *Loch Garten* (2½ m.) may be visited.

At 91 m. on rt. is *Tullochgorum*, renowned for its "Reel," composed by Hamish Dallasach, a famous musician of Strathspey, in the 18th cent. The song was written by the Rev. J. Skinner (1721-1807), minister of the Epis. Ch. of Langside, Aberdeenshire. ½ m. farther on the G.N.S. Rly. (Rte. 66) crosses the Spey rt.

92¼ m. **Broomhill Stat.** Here is a timber carriage br. over the Spey to (1½ m.) **Nethy Bridge** ✲, seen rt. (see pp. 231, 309).

At 93½ m. the *Dulnain* is crossed—a pretty wooded stream—1 m. up which is the old tower of *Muckerach*, built 1598.

96 m. **GRANTOWN Stat.** ✲ There is another rly. stat. on the G.N.S. Rly. on the farther side of the Spey, 1¼ m. S.E. of the town.

This is a well-kept growing little town of granite cottages and villas. It is ½ m. from the station, and consists of one long street and a large square at the N. end, with trees. True to its name it is a hive of the Clan Grant. There are good shops, a *Public Hall*, an *Orphanage*, a *Cottage Hospital*, a *Court Ho.*, a *Parish Ch.* (the gift of the Countess Dowager of Seafield, in memory of her husband, the 7th Earl, d. 1881, and her only son, the 8th Earl of Seafield, d. 1884, containing a beautiful black oak pulpit and old oak panelling taken out of Castle Grant), *Epis.*, *Free*, and *Baptist Chs.* The view of the town from the Highland Rly. across the meadow land to the N.W. is not prepossessing, but the charms, especially the pine woods and the swift-flowing Spey on the E., are not visible. It stands 700 ft. above sea-level, the air is very bracing, and year by year it is growing in favour as a summer health resort. As a tourist centre it well deserves a visit. The expeditions are innumerable.

[WALKS :—

(1) Numerous paths through the *Pine Woods*, which can only be mastered by frequent visits.

(2) S. Down to the Spey and up its l. bank, passing *Inverallan Ho.* (the Countess's factor) and *Church-yd.* to *Ballyfirth ferry* (3 m.). Cross over and return (4 m.) by Spey Br. 7 m.

(3) N. Into the grounds of **Castle Grant** (1½ m.)—a plain house like a factory—the seat of the Earls of Seafield, but presently (1894) belonging to the Countess Dowager, widow of the 7th earl. The house contains many very curious family portraits, and one of the most remarkable collections of old Highland arms in existence. Close to the house is a fine lime avenue, and in the grounds are some splendid specimens of Scotch firs.

The main entrance is ½ mile N. of the town. Keep another mile along the Forres road, and enter by the next gate opposite a rly. arch. As you near the Cas. keep rt., then l., passing behind it on the S. side, and then straight on, passing l. "The Earl's Tree," to a road 2 m. from Grantown.

(4) E. Before reaching Cas. Grant main entrance take road rt. At 3 m. turn down to the river and cross by suspension foot-bridge to *Cromdale Ch.* and rly. stat.; return (4 m.) by road or rly. on the other side of the Spey.

(5) A fine walk may be taken along the **Cromdale Hills**, which are 9 m. long, and are best reached from a point 5 m. or 6 m. along the Tomintoul road, or from Cromdale, or from Advie. The highest point (2329 ft.) is 6 m. from Cromdale.

(6) To *Dreggie Farm* (with fine view), 1¼ m.

Pass under the rly. arch behind the town, and go straight up. Proceed over the moor behind to *Glen Beg* and return down the glen, 5 m.

(7) N.W. To **Loch-in-Dorb** and **Dava**, 10½ m.

The pedestrian should ascend to Dreggie (see above) and proceed on into Glen Beg, trending, however, slightly rt. Up the glen keep along the path high up rt. Never descend to or cross the stream, and if the path disappears look ahead for it. Approaching the watershed the path bears l., not rt. The highest pt. (4 m.) is 1252 ft. Thence the path keeps rt. of a little loch, and at 5 m. *Loch-in-Dorb* is seen below. It is fully 2 m. long, and has an island with a ruined castle upon it, once a mere hunting seat of the Comyns, but taken and occupied by Edward I. in person, 1303, and then strengthened. In 1342 it was a state prison. In 1372 it became the stronghold of the Wolf of Badenoch (see pp. 217, 303). It was destroyed by orders of James II. It passed from the Earls of Moray to the Cawdor family, 1606, and by them was sold to the Earl of Seafield, 1750. The Lodge near the S. end of the loch is 7 m., and thence to Dava Stat. 3½ m.

(8) For the *Ascent* of *Cairngorm* and *Ben Muich-dhui* drive to Glenmore Lodge (see pp. 231, 228); for the *Larig Ghru* and *Braeriach* drive to Coylum Bridge, or take train to Aviemore (see pp. 231, 228).

DRIVES :—

(1) S. *Round by* **Nethy Bridge**, 12 m.

Go by W. side of the Spey. Cross at Broomhill and return by the E. side. 100 yds. N. of Abernethy Parish Ch. is *Castle Roy*, a quadrangular fortress of the Comyns. Here there is a fine retrospective view of the Cairngorm range.

(2) S. *To* **Loch Garten** *and round* **Abernethy Forest,** 22 m.

This is the same drive as (1) with the addition of the forest—a charming combination of heather, pine, moorland, and loch.

(3) S. To **Nethy Bridge** (5½ m.), **Abernethy Forest, Rebhoan** (pron. *Revoan*) **Pass** (14 m.), and **Loch Morlich** (16½ m.); returning by the *Sluggan Pass* (19½ m.) to Grantown, 33 m. This is undoubtedly the finest drive in the neighbourhood—perhaps in Scotland. It embraces almost every variety of Highland scenery.

At Nethy Bridge (5½ m.) turn l. up l. bank of the river. At 6½ m. the forest is entered. At 8½ m. the road makes a detour l., passing *Lynemacgilbert Lo.*, and becomes very heavy and steep. A path straight on joins the carriage road well up the hill. At 11 m. the road goes into a field, which it descends l., then turns rt. The mountains, of which magnificent views are obtained in front, begin to look exceedingly near. At 13½ m. the road descends rapidly through *Rebhoan Pass*, a narrow gorge of pines with a lovely tarn l. At 16½ m. *Glenmore Lo.* (Duke of Richmond) is reached. Here horses can generally be put up. [For Ascent of Cairngorm, etc., see p. 228.] For the next mile the road runs alongside of *Loch Morlich*, and at 17½ m. turns rt. [From here Coylum Bridge is 3 m. and Aviemore 5 m. (see p. 228).] Having crossed the *Sluggan Pass*—very fine—the high road is joined just before *Kincardine Ch.* is reached standing rt.; l. is a lovely reach on the Spey. [From here Coylum Bridge is 3½ m. S., and half-way is *Loch Pityoulish.*] At 24½ m. l. is the ferry across to Boat of Garten, and at 25 m. rt. a road to Loch Garten. At 27½ m. Nethy Bridge is again reached.

(4) Across Spey Bridge, down the Spey by Cromdale to **Advie** (10 m.), across *Tulchan Bridge*, past *Tulchan Lo.*, and along W. bank of the Spey to Grantown, 18 m.

(5) Round by **Dava** (7½ m.), **Loch-in-Dorb** (10 m.) [see p. 230], and **Duthil** (19 m.), to Grantown, 27 m.

At 3½ m. rt. is a ravine—reached by a path crossing a stile and the rly.—with *Huntly's Cave* (where the Marquis of Huntly hid himself in 1645 during Montrose's campaign) in it. Beyond this the road crosses a bleak and exposed moor (1050 ft.), and ½ m. before Dava Stat., oppos. a house which was once an inn, the road turns l. At the S. end of Loch-in-Dorb it turns rt., and at 12 m. joins the Forres and Carr Bridge road, and ascends l. to 1229 ft., where there is a Pass. It descends to Duthil [whence Carr Bridge is 1½ m. rt.], and turns l. Beside Duthil Ch. is the *Mausoleum* where the 7th and 8th Earls of Seafield are buried.

(6) S. To **Loch-an-Eilean**, 17 m., see p. 227.

Drive by Aviemore (14 m.); return by Coylum Bridge and Nethy Bridge. 3½ m. N. of Aviemore on E. side of the road and only 50 yds. away, but quite hidden by the bank, is the lovely *Loch Vaa.*

(7) N.E. round by *Craig Beg* and *Dellifure*, 9½ m.

2½ m. along the Forres Road the road turns rt. and descends into a hollow; then crosses a stream (up which *Huntly's Cave* (see above) may be visited on foot), ascends steeply and keeps—somewhat rough—over the wood towards the Spey.

(8) S.E. To **Tomintoul**, 13½ m. Thence N. by *Glen Livet* to **Ballindalloch**, 29 m., and S. to Grantown, 42½ m.

The road crosses Spey Bridge, turns l., and then takes the 1st turn rt. [At 6 m. is a road rt. to Abernethy Ch. and Nethy Bridge, 6 m.] At 10 m. *Bridge of Brown* is crossed, the road descending and ascending by "devil's elbow" zigzags. At 12 m. the *Avon* (coming from Loch A'an, see p. 229) is crossed. Its banks are very pretty. **Tomintoul** ✱—described by the Queen in 1860 as the "most tumble-down, poor-looking place I ever saw"—is the highest village in the Highlands, being 1160 ft. It has a Parish Ch. and R.C. Ch. It is bare and uninteresting, but 2 m S. on the *Altnack* burn there is a fine, little-known chasm—interesting to geologists. [For the roads to Braemar see p. 282; and for the road to Strath Don, etc. see pp. 297, 278.] The road leaves the town l. at rt. angles to the main st., and crosses the *Conglass Water*. At 20 m. the *Livet* is crossed (see p. 308). There is a picturesque old br. of General Wade's on the Livet. At 21½ m. the *Glen Livet Distillery* is seen l. across the stream. At 28 m. is *Dalnashaugh Inn*✱. At 28½ m. is the entrance to *Ballindalloch Cas.* (see p. 309). At 29½ m. is Ballindalloch Stat. The rt. bank of the Spey may be kept to Spey Bridge, or the river crossed at Advie (see above).

(9) N.W. To **Inverness** by **Carr Bridge** (9½ m.), *Freeburn Inn* (19 m.), and *Moy Hall* (23 m.), 34 m. Return by **Culloden Moor** (5½ m.), *Cawdor Cas.* (14 m.), *Dulsie Bridge* (22 m.), *New Inn* (27 m.), and Dava (33½ m.), to Grantown 40 m. [*or*, going from Cawdor Cas. to New Inn by Ferness Bridge, 36½ m.]

At *Dulnain Bridge* (3 m.) keep rt. up l. bank of the Dulnain, passing Duthil (8 m.) to **Carr Bridge** ✲ (9½ m.), a village 6½ m. by rly. from Aviemore, which is rapidly becoming a favourite summer resort. Beside the present bridge there is the picturesque arch of the old br., while 2 m. up the river is *Sluggan Bridge*, one of General Wade's bridges. At the br., which is not crossed, the old mail-coach route from the S. to Inverness is joined, and for the next 17 m. the line of the rly. to Inverness from Aviemore, in course of construction (1894), is followed.

After leaving Carr Bridge the road keeps away from the Dulnain, and at 17½ m. crosses the Findhorn (see p. 306). At 19 m. is *Freeburn Inn* ✲. At 22½ m. are *Moy Ch., Inn* ✲, and *Loch*, 1 m. long (very pretty), with an island. At 23 m. rt. *Moy Hall*, the seat of The Mackintosh. At 25 m. is a splendid *View*—back, of the *Cairngorm Range*, and forward, of the *Ben Wyvis Range* beyond the Moray Firth. At 27½ m. the *Nairn* is crossed, and *Daviot Ch.* passed rt.; charming view before descending to Inverness. [For Inverness see p. 375.]

From Inverness to *Culloden Moor* (5½ m.) the road keeps high, affording fine views of the Moray Firth and the mountains beyond. It passes close beside the memorial monument (marking the site of the battle) and the headstones showing where the different clans are buried (see p. 234). At 10½ m. is the entrance to *Kilravock Cas.* (see p. 233). For Cawdor Cas. (14 m.), see p. 233. At *Little Urchany farm* (16 m.) the road forks l. by *Rehaurie* and *Ferness Bridge* to *New Inn* ✲ (23½ m.), *or*, (*much finer*) rt. passing (21 m.) *Glenferness Ho.* (Earl of Leven and Melville), seen l. beautifully situated across the Findhorn, to *Dulsie Bridge*, 23 m. (see p. 306).

The road crosses the br. to *Dunearn Lo.* (23½ m.), the avenue of which the traveller is kindly permitted to make use of, as the public road is only fit for carts, and joins the Forres and Carr Bridge road. Left takes to New Inn, 27 m., and thence rt. over the moor to Dava, 33½ m.; rt. (worse road) takes by *Loch-in-Dorb*, 27½ m. (turn off l. at 26½ m.), to Dava 31½ m. (see p. 231). (New Inn is 10 m. from Nairn; 11 m. from Forres; 13 m. from Grantown; and 15½ m. from Carr Bridge.)]

Continuing the main route from Grantown Stat. the line keeps ½ m. W. of the town, leaves Strathspey, across which the heathery *Cromdale Hills* stand well out, and passes rt. 98½ m. *Cas. Grant* (Countess Dowager of Seafield), and 100½ m. rt. *Huntly's Cave* (see p. 231). The woods are then left, and a bleak moor with snow palisades crossed at a height of 1050 ft. to

104½ m. **Dava Stat.**

[Here roads run S.W. to Loch-in-Dorb; and N.W. to Nairn by Dulsie Bridge or Ferness Bridge (see above).]

The rly. descends, crossing at 109½ m. a lofty viaduct over the *Divie*, a trib. of the Findhorn—close to which (l.) is *Edenkillie Ch.*—to

111 m. **Dunphail Stat.** l. is *Dunphail Ho.*, the seat of Lord Thurlow.

[From here the junc. of the *Divie* and the *Findhorn*, one of the prettiest spots on the latter river, is only 2½ m. Above it is *Randolph's Leap;* below it the path leads in 2½ m. by the rt. bank of the Findhorn to *Sluie*, from which Forres is 5 m. by road (see p. 306).]

The rly. traverses the fine firwoods of *Altyre* (Sir William Gordon Cumming, Bart.), passes rt. *Sanquhar Ho.* (Mrs. W. F. Fraser-Tytler), and *Cluny Hydro. Estab.*, and reaches

119¼ m. **Forres Stat.** ✲

[*Junc.* for the *Branch* of the High. Rly. which runs E. to *Elgin* and *Keith.* At these Stats. the G.N.S. Rly. system to Strathspey and to Banffshire and Aberdeenshire is joined (see Rtes. 58-61).]

For *Forres*, *Darnaway Cas.*, and the beautiful scenery up the *Findhorn*, see pp. 306, 307.

Beyond Forres the line crosses the Findhorn, which is one of the most rapid and dangerous streams in Scotland, by an iron plate bridge closed at the sides.

The mouth of the Findhorn is bounded on N.W. by the *Sands of Culbin*, a broad range of moving hills and sand-drifts, which, since the latter part of the 17th century, have overwhelmed and destroyed a tract of 3600 acres, once known as the Garden of Moray. In these sands have been and continue to be found an extraordinary number of primitive and mediæval relics, evidences of former habitation. The rly. passes rt. *Dalvey*, famous for its gardens (the finest in Morayshire).

122¾ m. **Brodie Stat.**, to rt. of which is the House of *Brodie*, of which a glimpse may be caught through an alley ¼ m. beyond the stat., one of the stateliest in Morayshire, in the midst of well-grown fir-woods, seat of the ancient family of Brodie. In the park is a sculptured stone with singular interlaced work.

We next pass (l.) *Hardmoor*, now partly cultivated and partly wooded, but supposed to have been the heath on which Macbeth and Banquo met the witches. At 125¾ m. l. are the ruins of *Inshoch Tower*, once the seat of the Hays of Lochloy.

A mile farther on, but 1 m. S., are *Boath House* (Sir A. J. Dunbar, Bart.), and the village of **Auldearn**—the scene of one of Montrose's most brilliant victories, gained on the 9th May 1645, in which, with 1500 foot and 200 horse, he routed the Covenanters, with 3500 foot and 400 horse, under General Urry, with great slaughter. There is a magnificent view of the cliffs across the Moray Firth and of the entrance to the Cromarty Firth as we approach

128¾ m. **NAIRN Stat.**✲, a parl. burgh and favourite watering-place, having good sands, easily accessible, with bathing machines. There is a large *swimming bath*, roofed with glass, near the shore, into which sea-water is pumped. Swimming lessons are given. There is also a good *Golf Course* of 18 holes.

[5¼ m. S.W. are **Cawdor** ✱ and, overlooking the Nairn river, *Cawdor Castle* (Earl of Cawdor), a well-preserved and picturesque castellated building of gray stone, from one corner of which springs a great square tower, with small turrets at the angles. It is approached by a drawbridge over the fosse, and is shown 2 days a week.[1] Its chief interest lies in the belief that Macbeth, who, it will be remembered, was Thane of Cawdor, murdered Duncan in this castle. In reality, however, no part of the castle is older than the 15th century. It contains some family portraits and fine tapestry, representing among other subjects the adventures of Don Quixote. In a dungeon is an old hawthorn-tree which grew on that spot. According to the legend, the founder of the castle was advised by a hermit to build wherever his ass, with a chest of gold on its back, stopped. It stopped at this very tree, which he enclosed in the fabric. It was here that Lord Lovat concealed himself after the battle of Culloden.

Around the castle are some noble old trees: *obs.* a walnut and chestnut especially. There are fine walks in the woods.

2¼ m. higher up the river Nairn, on its l. bank, is *Kilravock Castle* (Major Rose). It consists of an old square tower, built in 1460, with lower buildings of a later date, and has always been in the Rose family. There is a good collection of armour and family pictures, and the gardens are beautifully laid out. An excursion coach from Inverness is allowed to drive through the grounds. The 14th April 1746 Prince Charles Edward spent at Kilravock, where he praised everything, and made himself exceedingly agreeable. The next day was the Duke of Cumberland's birthday, which he spent at Kilravock, remarking to Mr. Rose, the then proprietor, "You had my cousin here yesterday." On the 3rd day the cousins met at Culloden.]

134½ m. **Fort-George Stat.** The fort, which is 3½ m. N., is an irregular polygon, with 6 bastions, and was built soon after the Rebellion of 1745, to keep the Highlanders in check. It is large enough to hold 3000 men. Johnson and Boswell were entertained here by Sir Eyre Coote, who was governor at the time. It was made one of the military centres and depôts 1872.

Beside the fort is a ferry (1 m.) across the Moray Firth to the "Black Isle" (see Rte. 99).

137¼ m. **Dalcross Stat.** (pron. *Dacus*), to the l. of which, 2 m. off, is *Dalcross Castle*, where the royal troops were put in array just before the battle of Culloden.

The castle consists of 2 blocks of buildings, joining one another at right angles.

[1] Apply at the Inn. Tickets 1s. each.

The windows are stanchioned with iron, and the original massive oaken door, studded with huge nails, still swings at the entrance. The hall is perfect, and has the dais or raised part at one end for the lord and his guests. The ceiling is of carved oak, partly painted. It was built by Lord Lovat in 1621, and in 1702 was purchased by the Mackintosh family. The Mackintosh is about to restore it (1894).

Rt. about halfway between Dalcross and Culloden Stats., overlooking the Moray Firth, is *Castle Stewart*, a fine example of the turreted house. It seems to have been built by the Earl of Moray early in the 17th cent. In 1624 it was taken by the Mackintoshes and rendered uninhabitable, though in later years it has been repaired.

140¾ m. **Culloden Stat.** On l., close at hand but not visible, is *Culloden House* (D. Forbes, Esq.), built on the site of the old mansion, which in 1745 belonged to Duncan Forbes, President of the Court of Session, and a staunch supporter of the Hanoverian cause. Here are preserved Prince Charlie's walking-stick and some books of Thomson the poet. It was for some days before the battle the headquarters of Prince Charlie. About 3 m. from the stat. is *Drummossie Moor*, the ground on which the *Battle of Culloden* was fought, 16th April 1746. It was then a wide open swampy heath, extending southwards from the Moray Firth, but a great part of it has since been converted into arable land, and covered with luxuriant crops of grain.

"By the road from Inverness it is 6 m. to the large boulder stone upon which the Duke of Cumberland is said to have breakfasted that morning. The ground, it will be seen, was admirably adapted for the Royalists—strong in horse and artillery—and everything else appears, as if by a fatality, to have conduced to their success. Prince Charles was obliged to fight to protect Inverness, but he might have chosen better ground than this. In spite of his previous successes his army was demoralised as though by a succession of defeats. The pay of the men had been long in arrear, and among the officers there was jealousy and distrust of one another. The whole of the previous day the army had but one biscuit per man, and it had been marching all night with the vain intention of surprising the Duke. At the last moment arose that ever-recurring difficulty about the position on the right wing. The Macdonalds claimed it as their right from time immemorial. The Stewarts and Camerons were placed there, and the Macdonalds on the left. The armies had been about equal in numbers, but, pressed by hunger and fatigue, nearly one-half the rebels had straggled into Inverness, or fallen asleep on the line of march. The Duke of Cumberland drew up his forces in 3 lines, and began the battle with his artillery. The French gunners in Prince Charles' service feebly replied. The Highlanders waxed impatient and began to waver. Lord George Murray, seeing no time was to be lost, led forward the clans on the right, who, charging with their usual impetuosity, broke the Duke's first line. But the second, drawn up 3 deep, front rank kneeling, reserved their fire till the enemy were almost on their bayonet-points, and then poured in so murderous a volley as to make the Highlanders recoil. The chief of M'Lachlan was killed, while Lochiel was carried off badly wounded. Now was the time for the Macdonalds to have proved the justice of the claim they held so tenaciously, and, like the Macphersons on a similar occasion, to have retrieved the fortunes of the day; but in vain the Duke of Perth rode up and implored them to advance. In vain Macdonald of Keppoch charged at the head of a few of his kinsmen, and fell, exclaiming, "My God! do the children of my clan forsake me?" Still one chance remained, and all might yet be well. Lord Elcho galloped up to the Prince, and begged him to put himself at their head and lead the charge in person. The Prince hesitated, and declined. Lord Elcho turned away with a bitter execration, and swore he would never see his face again. A few minutes afterwards Charles suffered himself to be led from the field—the Macdonalds marched off without striking a blow, but with pipes playing and colours flying—the battle of Culloden was lost, and with it the hopes of the Stuarts. The insurgents lost 1000 men killed and wounded, the royalists 300. The Duke of Cumberland was accused of cruelty after the battle, but without proof. He certainly was most strict in punishing plunderers and deserters. On the other hand, an order issued before the battle on the authority of Charles Edward, signed by Murray, gave no quarter to the Elector's troops."—LORD STANHOPE.

A large monument in the form of a cairn, ¼ m. to the W. of the great boulder, shows where the contest was fiercest, and rough headstones, with their names upon them, mark the burial-places of the several clans engaged.

[1 m. to the S.E. of Culloden Moor, and 4 m. from the station on the S. (rt.) bank of the river Nairn, stand the **Stones of Clava**, one of the most extensive remains of the kind in the kingdom. A good road leads S. from Cumberland's boulder stone, past a farm-house, to the edge of the river Nairn, which is crossed by a wooden bridge. On the S. side of the river are several cairns, but it is probable that originally they were scattered about on both sides of the stream, for on the N. there are upright stones here and there in the cornfields, and the little tributary of the Nairn is choked with stones of all sizes which have been cleared off the fields.

The monuments on the S. side extend rather more than 1 m. They consist entirely of cairns surrounded by circles of stones, and of many detached upright stones, either marking the spot where a cairn has stood, or part of an avenue leading to and from the centre. The cultivation of the valley, and still more the erection of cottages and farm-buildings close by, have played sad havoc with this curious monument of antiquity—here detached stones have been heaped together, there the cairns have been scattered. The valley extends N.E. and S.W., and the uncultivated part of it is so covered with gorse and juniper as to prevent one's comprehending the general ground-plan of the whole. The principal object is a line of 4 cairns, more or less perfect. When undisturbed they were 16 ft. high and 50 ft. in diameter. A ring of upright stones confines the base of each, and the whole is surrounded by a circle of detached slabs, some 50 yds. in diameter. The 3rd from the E. seems to be the most important, and the slabs are larger and flatter. With the exception of the last, which has fallen in, the cairns have all been opened, the easternmost very scientifically, by the order of Mrs. Campbell of Kilravock; it was found to contain a chamber 12 ft. in diameter, with a passage 2 ft. wide opening towards the S. In the chamber was an urn, in which were ashes. The fields to the W. are full of blocks which show how far the cairns extended. The largest of all is nearly a mile to the W. Round this cairn was a circle of moderate-sized stones, and beyond that a ring of very large ones, of the latter of which a single specimen is standing, 12 ft. high by 9 ft. broad in its widest point. There can be little doubt, from all these indications, that the plain of Clava was at some prehistoric time a cemetery for the great and noble Caledonians in the N. But whether all the interments took place at once, or whether, as in Iona, these sepulchral monuments must be attributed to the history of several centuries, is a matter of conjecture. Fergusson ("Rude Stone Monuments") supposes Clava to have been the burial-place of Brud, King of the Picts, who was converted to Christianity by St. Columba.]

The flat shores of the Moray Firth are carefully cultivated, as are also those of the "Black Isle" opposite. With the entrance to the Beauly Firth rt., there is a beautiful approach to

144 m. **INVERNESS Stat.** ✲ (see p. 375).

ROUTE 43.

Perth to Killin by Aberfeldy, Kenmore, and Loch Tay.

See Map, p. 224.

From **Perth** to 24 m. **Ballinluig Junc.**, see Rte. 42.

At Ballinluig Junc. the line turns W., crosses the Tummel, and passes below the Monument erected to the late Duke of Atholl (see p. 219). At 24¾ m. the hamlet of **Logierait** ✲ is seen rt.

The Tay (ferry for carriages) is then crossed, and the rt. bank kept. Logierait *Ch.* and *Manse*, the district *Poorhouse*, *Eastertyre*, *Ballechin* (John Stewart, Esq.), and *Pitnacree* (Dr. J. A. Menzies) are seen on the left bank.

28 m. **Grandtully Stat.** ✲ This is a pretty wooded little place composed of a variety of modern villa residences. A driving suspension bridge crosses the river, here rapid and rocky.

[The *Ascent of Farragon* (2559 ft.) may perhaps best be made from here, and well repays the slight exertion required. It will take abt. 3 hrs.

Cross the river and walk or drive 2 m. towards Aberfeldy. Then follow the cart track up the l. bank of *Derculich Burn* to *Loch Derculich*. From the N. end the top looks quite near, but it will take nearly an hour. Keep the slope to the rt. The *View* comprises *Ben Nevis*, the *Shepherds of Etive*, *Ben More*, *Ben Lawers*, *Schiehallion*, *Ben-y-*

Gloe, the *Cairngorms*, and the *Lomonds*. The descent may be made to Aberfeldy in 2 hrs. by *Loch Glassie* (1 hr.), thence by a cart road to the *Weem* road.

Another pleasant walk with fine views is up the *Tullypowrie Burn*, and over the hill by cart track to *Port-na-Craig Ferry* at Pitlochrie, 4 m.]

After Grandtully the river scenery, rt., becomes finer. *Findynate* (D. M'Pherson, Esq.), *Derculich* (D. F. Dempster, Esq.)—a large white-washed mansion with turrets—and *Edradynate* (J. Stewart Robertson, Esq.), all occupy commanding sites on the l. bank.

30 m. l. is *Grandtully Cas.* (not visible from the rly.), one of the rival claimants to be Tullyveolan in "Waverley." It bears the date 1626, but the oldest part is said to date from 1550. In 1893 it was restored and greatly enlarged for the widow of the late Sir A. Douglas Stewart, Bart. of Murthly.

31 m. on l. bank *Killiechassie* (Mrs. E. O. Douglas).

32½ m. **Aberfeldy Stat.** ✲, a large village, uninteresting in itself, but a favourite summer resort, pleasantly situated near the S. bank of the Tay, ½ m. above the influx of the little river *Urlar*.

Overlooking the village is *Moness Ho.* (Marquis of Breadalbane), and upon the Urlar are the **Falls of Moness.** The entrance[1] to the glen is beside the bridge in the village. The glen, abt. 1½ m. long, is pretty, but owes much to the description of Burns, who visited it 29th Aug. 1787:—

"The braes ascend like lofty wa's,
The foaming stream deep roaring fa's,
O'erhung wi' fragrant spreading shaws,
The birks of Aberfeldy.
The hoary cliffs are crown'd wi' flowers,
White o'er the linns the burnie pours,
And, rising, weets wi' misty showers
The birks of Aberfeldy."

[1] Admission 6d. each for 4 persons or less, and 3d. each above 4.

There are 3 different *Falls*, all picturesque, but none of any great size. The tourist in search of a comprehensive and beautiful view cannot do better than ascend *Farrachel Hill*, 1 m. l., on the Kenmore Road.

For a description of the *Black Watch Memorial Cairn*, the old *Tay Bridge* and *Weem*, *Castle Menzies*, *Dull*, and the road to *Tummel Bridge*✱, and *Kinloch-Rannoch*✱, see Rte. 45.

For the road to *Glen Lyon* see Rte. 44. Excursion Coaches make the circuit of *Drummond Hill*, going by Kenmore to the Pass of Lyon, and returning by Fortingal and Weem. [Cf. Drive (4) from Kenmore (p. 238).]

The road S. to *Amulree* (11 m.) turns l. at the W. end of the village, passes the Estab. Ch., and ascends very steeply in 4 m. to *Loch-na-Craig*. It crosses the watershed at 1250 ft., and descends *Glen Cochill* to the Dunkeld and Amulree road (see p. 219), 2 m. before *Amulree* ✱ (p. 214) is reached.

For the scenery down the Tay and for the Ascent of *Farragon* see above, and p. 235.

The road up the Tay W. to Kenmore[1] passes through the village and keeps straight on by the S. bank. It is shaded by trees almost the whole way. A prettier continuous 6 m. of road it would be difficult to find.

1 m. View across the valley rt. to *Weem* (p. 239).

2½ m. l. *Bolfracks Shooting Lo.*, formerly the residence of the Marquis's factor; rt. across the valley is *Farleyer* (Sir Robert Menzies, Bart.). Only a glimpse of the roof of *Castle Menzies* can be obtained.

3 m. View across the valley to *Dull*, and first view of *Schiehallion*.

3½ m. Rt. is an entrance to *Taymouth Cas.* (Marquis of Breadalbane).

3¾ m. l. School for the children on the Marquis's estates, and behind, the village of *Stix* (not visible).

4 m. l. in a field is a *Druidical Circle*, and (not visible) another estate village *Kilmaronaig* (St. Mary's).

[1] Abt. 4 coaches daily in summer, 2 in winter.

4½ m. Rt. is the principal entrance to Taymouth Cas. from Aberfeldy. After ½ m. ascent, and just before 5 m. rt. is a *Bird Museum*, and the *Fort Lodge*, from which the best view is obtained of the castle and park.

Upon the 3rd October 1865 the Queen, while driving from Dunkeld *incognita*, visited the Fort, and thus pathetically records her impressions :—

"We got out and looked from this height down upon the house below, the mist having cleared away sufficiently to show us everything, and then, unknown, quite in private, I gazed—not without deep emotion—on the scene of our reception twenty-four years ago, by dear Lord Breadalbane, in a princely style, not to be equalled in grandeur and poetic effect. Albert and I were only twenty-three, young and happy. How many are gone that were with us then! I was very thankful to have seen it again. It seemed unaltered."

[A road, with splendid views back of *Ben Lawers*, the *Glen Lyon Range*, and *Schiehallion*, ascends steeply here l. for 3 m. to 1672 ft., and after a mile more or less level, descends very steeply to the *River Quaich*, which at 5 m. is crossed by a bridge. At 7 m. *Loch Freuchie* (2 m. long) is reached. The S. side is kept, passing *Glen Quaich Lo.* (Marquis of Breadalbane) and a little *Free Ch.* At 10 m. the road forks rt. to Sma' Glen and Crieff (11 m.), and l. in 1 m. to *Amulree* ✱ (see p. 214).]

5¼ m. A capital view of the Cas. is obtained rt., and a stream is crossed upon which (l.) are the *Falls of Aldavalloch*. Here Roy, whose wife is famed in song, was a miller.

6 m. The road turns rt. (the road straight on keeps along the S. side of Loch Tay) and enters

6¼ m. **Kenmore** ✲, a neat, picturesque village in the form of a square. At the W. end is the *Parish Ch.* on a promontory overlooking the loch, on the N. side the *Hotel* and the village *Institute*, on the S. side are cottages, the general store (with post-office), and the *Estates Offices*, and at the E. end the chief entrance to Taymouth Cas. There is also a *Free Ch.*, an *Orphanage* maintained by the Marchioness, and (1 m. off on the N. side of the Tay) an *Epis. Ch.* Behind the village the Tay is crossed by a bridge just after it has left the loch a full-grown river. Close to the village is the *Pier* for the loch steamers.

[EXCURSIONS :—

(1) **Taymouth Castle Grounds.** A guide is necessary, who expects a gratuity.

Strangers are restricted to the road leading to the Castle and back, not being allowed to diverge to other parts of the grounds.

The Castle (not shown) is a large gray structure of slate, with round towers at the angles, surmounted by a central block, while 2 wings, that on S.W. being a remnant of the old castle restored, project from the main building. There is a magnificent hall, grand staircase, library, and a suite of apartments occupied by Her Majesty and the Prince Consort on their first visit to Scotland in 1842. "The Gothic staircase is of stone, and very fine."

The Castle was originally founded by Sir Colin Campbell of Glenorchy, scion of the house of Argyll, *circa* 1573. The present edifice, built early in the present cent. and added to in 1879, though large and stately, is of inferior style, and stands in the bottom of the valley, but its surroundings are lovely.

There is some magnificent timber in the park: oak, ash, beech, lime, and chestnut trees line the walks that lead to the house, occasionally diversified by some light and elegant larch of great height and age.

On both sides of the Tay there is a grand *Beech Walk*.

(2) To the **Falls of Acharn,** 2 m. along the S. side of the loch.

(3) Ascend **Drummond Hill,** which

lies behind Kenmore to the N. It is more than 2 m. long, and is the highest wooded hill in Scotland. The E. end is 1250 ft.; the W. end 1500 ft. From both there is a lovely view. It is a deer forest belonging to the Marquis of Breadalbane.

(4) **Drive round Drummond Hill,** 12 m.

Cross the Tay and keep along the N. side of the loch, passing an island on which are the ruins of a *Priory* built in 1122 by Alexander I. over the grave of his wife Sybilla, daughter of Henry I. of England. At 3 m. keep rt. above *Fearnan.* At 4½ m. keep along the S. bank of the Lyon *or* cross the *Bridge of Lyon* to Fortingal (see p. 241). If the latter route is adopted the Lyon will have to be crossed again at the ford at *Comrie Cas.* (see p. 240). In either case Kenmore is approached by the N. bank of the Tay.

(5) Drive S. by the *Fort Lodge* and *Glen Quaich* (see p. 237) to *Amulree* (12½ m.), returning by *Glen Cochill* and *Aberfeldy* (23½ m.)—29¾ m.]

Loch Tay[1] is 14½ m. long, and 1⅛ m. broad at the widest part. Its "surface is 346 ft. above the sea, and its depth varies up to more than 500 ft. Its bottom is thus upwards of 150 ft. below the level of the sea." Its chief feeders are the Dochart and the Lochay at its W. end; at its E. end issues the full-grown Tay. The road to Killin along the N. side is the shorter one (16 m.), but that along the S. side (18 m.) keeps nearer the loch and commands finer views—especially of Ben Lawers.

Embarking at Kenmore the first stopping-place is

3½ m. rt. **Fearnan**✲, whence a coach road strikes N. to Fortingal and Glen Lyon (see above and p. 242). The steamer crosses to

7 m. l. †**Ardtalnaig.** 1 m. W. copper is found.

[From here a Pedestrian can walk up the *Alt Chilleine* to *Dunan* (4½ m.); thence he can descend the *Almond* to Newton Bridge in the *Sma' Glen* (14½ m.) and so reach Crieff 22½ m., *or* from Dunan he can ascend *Ben Chonzie* rt. (3048 ft.), and reach Crieff by *Glen Turret*, abt. 18 m.]

Almost opposite Ardtalnaig is †**Lawers**✲ the best point from which to ascend **Ben Lawers** (3984 ft.), the richest in its botany of all the mountains of Scotland, perhaps of Britain. Nowhere is such an abundance of alpine plants to be found. Here occur the curious *Cherleria* or mossy cyphel, the fragrant *Myosotis alpestris*, and the *Gentiana nivalis.*

The Ascent and return will occupy about 5 hours. Guides can be obtained at the hotel, and ponies can be taken the greater part of the way.

"This wide-based, broad-shouldered mountain rises from the valley of Loch Tay on one side, and sinks into Glen Lyon on the other. It forms thus a huge dome-shaped mass between 2 deep valleys. But instead of owing this form to an upward curving of the schists, it actually lies in a basin of these rocks which dip underneath the mountain on the banks of Loch Tay, and rise up again from its farther skirts in Glen Lyon. Thus Ben Lawers is in reality formed of a trough of schists, while the valley of Loch Tay runs along the top of an anticlinal arch."—Sir A. GEIKIE.

The steamer again crosses the Loch to

10 l. †**Ardeonaig**✲.

[From here there is a delightful walk up the *Finglen Burn* and down *Glen Lednock* past *Sput Rollo* and *Innergeldie Lodge* to Comrie, 12 m. The top of the pass is 1750 ft. When it is reached do not join the stream on the other side at once, but keep a track high up l. The last 4½ m. can be driven. See p. 209.]

Soon after leaving Ardeonaig the twin peaks of *Stobinian* and *Ben More* come into view, forming a very striking background to the W. end of the loch. From *Edramuckie* rt.—4½ m. from Killin—a steep carriage road, ascending to 1750 ft., leads over to Bridge of Balgie in *Glen Lyon,* 9 m. (see p. 242).

14 m. rt., †**Killin Pier,** where the train meets the steamer. It passes *Finlarig*, a picturesque ruined castle and cemetery, ancient seat and burial

---

[1] 3 steamers each way in summer but the mid-day one does not call at intermediate ports; 2 steamers each way in winter.

place of the Breadalbane family, beautifully situated in some fine wood, and reaches in 1 m.

Killin Stat. Thence it runs up the *Dochart*, as the Tay before it reaches Loch Tay is called, for 4 m. to **Killin Junc. Stat.** on the Callander to Oban Rly. (see p. 170).

Killin ✲, or *Kil Fin*, signifies the Cell of Fingal, whose grave is marked by an upright stone in a neighbouring field. It is a considerable village lying between the mouths of the *Dochart* and the *Lochay*—the two principal feeders of Loch Tay. Above the village the Dochart is crossed by a bridge, the scene from which has possibly been more painted by artists than any other in Scotland. The Dochart here divides into two or three rapidly flowing branches, forcing their way over and between masses of bare projecting rock. It encloses 2 islands; on the lower of them, surrounded by a belt of fine firs, is the burial-place of the M'Nabs, a clan which once owned all the surrounding district, now absorbed in the Breadalbane domain. The M'Nabs emigrated to North America, but this cemetery still remains their possession. It was Sir Allan M'Nab, the head of this clan, who aided in repulsing American marauders from Canada, and who avenged the invasion of British territory by sending the rebel steamer *Caroline* in flames over the Falls of Niagara.

1½ m. E. of Killin is *Auchmore* (Marq. of Breadalbane).

Killin lies somewhat in a hollow, but is a good centre for mountaineers exploring the long range of hills to the N. Pleasant walks may be taken up the Lochay passing in 4 m. some falls or rapids. The upper part of Glen Lyon (Rte. 45) may be reached in this way.

ROUTE 44.

Aberfeldy to Kinloch-Rannoch.

See Map, p. 224.

This is a fine Highland drive, but there is no coach. At the W. end of the village the road turns rt., passing the Free Ch., to the Tay. In an enclosure (l.) on the rt. bank is a large *Jubilee Cairn*, erected 1887 in commemoration of the raising of the "Black Watch," afterwards the 42nd Highlanders, "whose first muster took place in May 1740 near Tay Bridge." Upon the different sides of the cairn are the Queen's Head, suitable inscriptions in Gaelic and English, and a list of the regiment's engagements.

The river is crossed by a handsome example (1733) of General Wade's bridges—having 4 obelisks on the parapet in the centre, and a tablet with crown, crossed swords, and "G.R." on the central arch.

At 1 m. is the little village of **Weem** ✲, with *Parish Ch.* and *Epis. Chap.* The small old ivy-grown church still standing is the Menzies (pron. Ming'is) family vault, and behind it is the private burying-ground of the Douglases of Killiechassie, containing a beautiful Celtic cross over the grave of the late Bp. Douglas of Bombay, d. 1875. Behind rises *Weem Crag*, and in the village is the entrance to *Castle Menzies* (Sir Robert Menzies, Bart.), the grounds of which the road skirts for the next mile. The Castle, of which a peep may be caught rt., was built 1571, and is a fine example of a strong old Scottish mansion, with small door and walls of immense thickness. It has been slept in by Mary Queen of Scots, by General Mackay (after Killiecrankie), and by Prince Charlie. The Park contains timber of remarkable girth and beauty.

2 m. the W. entrance to the Castle is passed, and above the road rt. is

Farleyer, where Sir Robert Menzies lives. It is a new house on the site of one set on fire by the sun (1889) and burnt to the ground.

2½ m. rt. *Camsernay*—the residence of Sir Robert's factor—with a clachan of the same name a few hundred yds. off. A good view is obtained across the valley of *Bolfracks Shooting Lo.* (p. 236).

3½ m. rt., upon the hillside, are the ch., manse, and village of *Dull*, which still possesses an ancient market cross. An Abbey stood here in the 11th century. A story goes that a loop (Gael. *dull*), by which St. Andrew's relics were being carried broke here, and so led to the founding of a Culdee settlement, which developed later into St. Andrews University.

At 4½ m. the road passes through a pretty bit of wood, in the middle of which are a ford and passenger ferry over the *Lyon* ½ m. above its junc. with the Tay. (Across the ferry are the ruins of *Comrie Cas.*, a small square keep of 3 stories, completely enveloped in ivy. Hence to Kenmore is 2½ m., passing *Epis. Ch.* (1½ m.) on the way.)

5¼ m. *Coshieville Inn* ✲. [At 5½ m. a road strikes l. across the Keltney Burn to *Fortingal*, 3 m., and *Glen Lyon* (see Rte. 45).] The road ascends rapidly up l. bank of the *Keltney Burn*, which flows in a deep wooded ravine. At 6¼ m. a peep is got l. across the burn of the ruins of *Garth Cas.* (on a well-chosen site at the junc. of 2 streams, reached from the other side of the glen), built and inhabited by the "Wolf of Badenoch" (d. 1394), who is buried in Dunkeld Cath. (see pp. 217, 303).

Schiehallion (3547 ft.)—henceforth and for more than 20 m. the feature of the landscape—comes into view l., and for ½ m. the road is comparatively level. *Glengoulandie Farm* (7¾ m.) is passed l. and the road again ascends steeply, crossing the *White Bridge* to the 9th milestone where the road divides.

[The road straight on, slightly rt., reaches (9¾ m.) its highest pt. (1262 ft.) upon the E. side of *Loch Kinardochy*, and then descends. [At 11½ m. a road strikes rt. to ½ m. *Foss Ch.* and 1 m. *Foss Ho.* (Sir R. Menzies), and along the S. side of Loch Tummel to a *Ferry* across the Tummel 5 m.—not crossed—*Falls of Tummel*, 9 m., and *Pitlochrie*, 12 m. (see p. 220).]

At 12½ m. the road begins to run alongside of the *Tummel*, and at 13¼ **Tummel Bridge** ✱ is reached (see p. 221).]

The road to Rannoch trends l. passing the S.W. corner of little *Loch Kinardochy*, and at 10 m. the highest pt. (1223 ft.) is reached. A splendid view is obtained rt. of *Loch Tummel*, *Ben-y-Gloe*, and *Glen Tilt*, before reaching *Braes of Foss Farm* (11½ m.) from which *Schiehallion*—here seen as a massive ridge—is *most easily* ascended, keeping the shoulder all the way (2½-3 hrs.). The road keeps across the Moor with ups and down to 14 m., where Loch Rannoch comes into view with the *Glencoe Mts.* in the background. It now descends rapidly for 1 m. passing rt. the entrance to *Crossmount Ho.* (J. C. Bunten, Esq.), and then traverses a pleasant broad valley, through which the Tummel flows (p. 221).

At 16 m. *Tempar Burn* is crossed, and by a stone bridge over the Tummel we reach

18 m. **Kinloch-Rannoch** ✲, a neat little village situated near the foot or E. end of **Loch Rannoch**, a beautiful piece of water 10 m. in length and 1 m. in breadth, and abounding with large trout. In the centre of the village is a granite obelisk erected 1875 "in memory of *Dugald Buchanan*, the Rannoch Schoolmaster, Evangelist, and Sacred Poet, who died 2nd June 1768" (cf. p. 169).

Schiehallion "appears as a perfect cone, raising its gleaming peak of snowy quartzite to a height of 3547 ft. Seen from the S.E. it appears as a long rocky ridge, mounting slowly from the E. and descending abruptly at its W. end. It is a noble instance of a cone not yet freed from its parent ridge" (GEIKIE). It is also interesting as the Mt. with which Dr. Maskelyne, the Astronomer-Royal, made his experiments in 1774 for ascertaining the specific gravity and weight of the earth. It may be ascended most shortly, directly, and steeply (in 2-3 hrs.) up the *Tempar Burn*, or more easily along the ridge from the *Braes of Foss Farm*, 6½ m. from *Kinloch-Rannoch* (see p. 240).

EXCURSIONS :—

(1) **Ascent of Schiehallion** (p. 240).

(2) By Coach to **Struan Stat.** (p. 223), 13 m.

(3) By **Loch Tummel** to **Pitlochrie** (p. 220), 20¾ m.

(4) **Round Loch Rannoch,** 24 m.

(5) By the N. side of *Loch Rannoch* to **Rannoch Stat.** (below), 16 m.; and (for pedestrians) to *Kingshouse* (Glencoe), 31 m.

There is a good road on both sides of the loch which exhibits a pleasing combination of cultivation and wood.

That on the N. side is rather shorter and offers better views. It keeps close to the loch, and is pleasantly shaded by birches.

At 5 m. across the loch is *Dall Ho.* (T. V. Wentworth, Esq.); at 8 m. the hamlet of *Killichonan* with an old ch.-yd. is passed, and the country becomes more open; and at 9¼ m. we cross the *Bridge of Ericht* ✲, a brawling river some 5 m. long, issuing from *Loch Ericht*, a desolate dreary loch, 15 m., in length, lying under *Ben Alder* (see p. 224).

At 10 m. we pass l. *Rannoch Lo.* (Sir R. Menzies), and keep up the l. bank of the *Gauer River*, which is crossed near the head of the loch (11¼ m.), if return is to be made by the other side. The *Glen Lyon Mts.* (Rte. 45) are now conspicuous to the S. Passing (13 m.) *Dunan Shooting Lo.*, we traverse the excellent road beside the rushing Gauer, made 1892-94 in connection with the W. Highland Rly. It crosses (15 m.) the *Alt Eigheach*, up the l. bank of which leads to *Corrour Lo.* (p. 348), to

16 m. **Rannoch Stat.** ✲ (p. 348).

For track to *Kingshouse* (15 m.) and *Glencoe* see pp. 348, 364.

ROUTE 45.

Aberfeldy to Tyndrum (44 m.) or Inveroran (46½ m.) by Fortingal and Glen Lyon. Last part for pedestrians only.

A *mail cart*, with room for 3 passengers, leaves Aberfeldy *daily* for Fortingal and Bridge of Balgie upon arrival of the morning train, and Bridge of Balgie daily at 9.15 A.M.

Excursion Coaches run daily in summer from Aberfeldy to the *Pass of Lyon* by Kenmore and Fearnan, returning by Fortingal and Weem—thus making the circuit of Drummond Hill.

A *Coach* also runs some miles up Glen Lyon from Fearnan in connection with the steamer from and to Killin.

* **Glen Lyon** is a grand glen more than 30 m. long, running between and parallel to Loch Rannoch and Loch Tay, at the back (N. side) of Ben Lawers. The narrow *Pass* 1 m. above Fortingal is exceedingly fine, but throughout its entire length the glen never becomes monotonous, and exhibits a wonderful variety of Highland scenery. Exit from the W. end, however, can only be made by walking 7½ m., and the only resting place for the night is a small Temp. Hotel (to be opened 1895) beside Innerwick Ch. 19 m., or lodgings at Bridge of Balgie, 20 m., generally full in summer.

To *Coshieville Inn* (5¼ m.) the road is the same as described in Rte. 44.

Beyond the inn the road turns l. across the Keltney Burn, and follows l. bank of the Lyon, passing

7 m. *Garth House* (Sir Donald Currie, K.C.M.G.), which was the birthplace of Gen. David Stewart, author of "A History of the Highlanders."

8½ m. **Fortingal** ✲, a neat little

hamlet. Within a railing in the parish churchyard are the remains of a *Yew*, more than 2000 yrs. old, and, therefore, the oldest known tree in Great Britain. 100 yrs. ago, according to Pennant, the trunk measured 56 ft. in circumference. W. of the village there is a Roman camp, of which the Prætorium is well marked. According to Skene this was an outpost of the *Emp. Severus* (208 A.D.).

Leaving the hotel a burn is crossed and *Glen Lyon Ho.*, formerly the residence of the Campbells of Glen Lyon, one of whom was a chief agent in the massacre of Glencoe, is seen rt.

9¼ m. A splendid view of the ***Pass of Lyon** is obtained.

9¾ m. "*Macgregor's Leap*," where the Aberfeldy coaches turn. The glen opens slightly more on the rt. for ½ m., and l. there is a peep of Meall Gruadh, one of the Ben Lawers range.

11 m. Fine rock scenery under the "Black (foot) bridge" across the Lyon.

11¼ m. The river becomes quieter with the road alongside.

11½ m. *Chesthill Ho.* (J. B. Stewart Menzies, Esq.). Waterfalls l. with an old br. crossing the burn. The valley begins to open out rt. with well-marked river terraces.

13 m. Road ascends rt. leaving the river for a mile. Ruins of *Carnbane Cas.*, an old stronghold of the Macnaughtons, are upon a hillock rt. as the ascent begins. At the top there is an extensive view up the valley.

13¾ m. *Invervar Ho.* (J. B. S. Menzies, Esq.) rt., after which a burn, coming down from a fine corrie, is crossed.

14½ m. *Invervane Farm* on oppos. side with ravine and cascades behind. The valley then becomes very open for 2 m. with few trees.

16¾ m. Avenue of beeches, Free Church and Manse, and a pretty bend in the river. An iron br. crosses the Lyon to the farms on the other side. There is a splendid view up a side valley l. of Ben Lawers and its companion Meall Garbh. In the river there is a large grassy island ; then the valley opens out again until

19 m. *Innerwick* ✲ *Ch.* with clachan below.

[Track rt. to Loch Rannoch (7 m.).]

After crossing a burn the road becomes exceedingly pretty. Rapids surround a rocky woody island in the river.

20 m. **Bridge of Balgie,** a charming spot with the surrounding country broken up and diversified.

[Carriage road (steep) across the br. l. (ascending to 1600 ft.) to Edramuckie (9 m.) on Loch Tay and Killin 13½ m.]

Just past the bridge is the gate into *Meggernie Cas.*, the house being 2 m. beyond. There is a broad pretty cascade l. upon the burn which the Killin road follows.

21 m. The road forks. Keep l. if walking, or if driving only to see Meggernie Cas., but rt. if driving farther, so as to avoid a bad bit before the roads re-unite.

22 m. **Meggernie Cas.** (Trs. of the late J. Bullough, Esq.) is a white-washed square house with turrets, approached by an avenue of beeches and limes ½ m. long, and delightfully situated in the midst of grass. Originally erected in 1579 the house was restored and repaired in 1673, and enlarged and improved by recent proprietors.

22½ m. The scenery becomes wilder, with numerous Scotch firs. The glen divides, the Lyon coming from the left and a large tributary, out of 2 lochs (respectively 2 m. and 4 m. distant), from the rt. through a pretty birchen ravine.

24¼ m. Lovely bit of calm water. Remains of *Pictish Towers*, one on each side of the road. The glen then becomes bare, the hills l. standing out in isolated ridges.

27 m. *Cashlie Farm.* Br. across the Lyon. Well-marked moraines begin on the other side. Rt. is a sharp conical peak.

29 m. *Pubill Burn* with clearly-defined encampment upon its l. bank. Also (rt.) Pubill farm with waterfalls behind. The country becomes less interesting, but soon *Ben Vannoch* (3125 ft.) comes into view, and at

32¼ m. there is a fine view back, while Loch Lyon lies in front backed by Ben-a-Chaisteil (2897 ft.), Ben Fhuaran (2632 ft.), and Ben Doran (3523 ft.). At

33 m. *Invermeran Shooting Lo.* (a poor house) the driving road ends. Cross the Meran Burn by a foot-br. behind the house, whence a well-marked cart track leads past two small plantations of firs to

Loch Lyon, a pleasing sheet of water 2 m. long and ¼ m. wide. The cart road leads along the N. shore, but when the loch is at all high a path above, very boggy in places, must be taken.

35 m. *Ardvannoch*, a shepherd's cottage. Beyond this the track going N. of Ben Fhuaran is well marked for 1 m., when the highest pt. (1250 ft.) is reached. It then becomes intermittent, but 1½ m. farther on leads to another shepherd's cottage, where there is a foot-br. Thence the route is S.W., between Ben-a-Chaisteil and Ben Doran, and the l. bank of the burn should be kept (path *very* boggy in wet weather). A West Highland Rly. Viaduct is passed under (p. 348), and at

40½ m. the Ballachulish Road is reached. 3½ m. S. is

44 m. **Tyndrum**✲ (see p. 171), or 6 m. N. is

46½ m. **Inveroran**✲ (see p. 348).

SECTION IV.

NORTH-EAST OF SCOTLAND—DUNDEE—FORFARSHIRE—ABERDEENSHIRE—DEESIDE—BRAEMAR—BANFFSHIRE—ELGIN.

§ 1. GENERAL INFORMATION.

THE country traversed by the following Routes contains the important towns of Dundee, Forfar, Aberdeen, Peterhead, Fraserburgh, and Banff, and the Cairngorm range of mountains, containing some of the highest peaks, and some of the wildest and most impressive scenery in Great Britain. Ben Muich-Dhui is the monarch of the group, surrounded by the almost equally lofty Braeriach, Cairn Toul, Cairn Gorm, Ben-na-Buird, and Ben A'an. The first three of these granite giants hang over the "Wells of Dee," sources of that grand river on whose banks our Queen has fixed her quiet and sunny residence, where, backed by another giant, most alpine of peaks—Lochnagar—and surrounded by a circle of mountains, she enjoys a retirement more complete than any other part of her dominions could afford.

Braemar may be reached by carriage from Pitlochrie, and a coach runs thither daily in summer from Dunkeld, by the Spital of Glenshee, passing over the ridge of the Grampians ; while from Aberdeen a railway will carry travellers to Ballater, whence it is a drive of 16½ m. to Braemar. It (or Aviemore or Grantown-on-Spey, cf. Rte. 42) is the headquarters for exploring this region, but it is distant from 18 m. to 20 m. from the mountain summits mentioned above, and as there is no Inn or place of refuge nearer than the vale of the Spey—15 m. farther—it is a feat not unworthy a member of the Alpine Club to visit their summits and recesses.

To hardy pedestrians the excursions to the Wells of Dee in the Larig Ghru (from which Braeriach (4248 ft.) with a 4000 ft. plateau containing the *true* wells of Dee—highest river source in Britain—may be ascended), through that Pass to Aviemore, to the summits of Ben Muich-dhui and Cairn Gorm, to Loch A'an, and to the top of Lochnagar, are specially recommended. They will nowhere find valleys or gorges narrower, corries deeper, or precipices loftier. If more convenient, they may begin their walks on the S., from Blair Atholl by Glen Tilt, or from Forfarshire by the romantic Glen

Clova or Glen Isla—paradise of plants and flowers; or, on the N.W. boundary of the district, from Strathspey.

Strathspey, a glorious valley, skirting the N.W. roots of the Grampian range, and commanding most attractive views of their (even in summer) snow-dotted peaks, presents many modes of access to their recesses (cf. Rte. 42). Parallel with this chain, W. of the Spey, are the Monadhliath Mountains, from whose sides springs the Findhorn—dear to salmon-fishers and artists—studded with lovely seats, Darnaway, Altyre, Relugas, Dunphail, Glen Ferness, etc.

On the S. outskirts of this range, besides the lovely valleys of the North and South Esk and Glen Isla, with the *Den of Airlie* and its two waterfalls—a most attractive country—attention must be called to the very grand Cliff Scenery on the sea-shore from Arbroath northward—including Red Head, Dunnottar Castle, and the Bullers of Buchan.

The district is by no means barren in **Antiquities**, such as the primitive but huge Stone Forts on the *Caterthuns* (p. 270).

Ecclesiastical Remains of high interest occur at Brechin, whose Round Tower resembles those of Ireland; in the Church and College of Aberdeen; in the magnificent ruins of Elgin Cathedral and Chapter-House; and in the less extensive remains of Pluscardine.

This is the country of the *Sculptured Stones*—rude monuments, but deftly carved in relief—with figures of men and animals, and patterns of interlacing knots, mixed with strange symbols, the meaning of which has never been explained. Some of the carvings are like the letter Z, with two circles resembling a pair of spectacles; some bear the Christian cross, combined with figures of dragons and other monsters, resembling the elephant or walrus, and similar to the peculiar figures on early Irish illuminated MSS. The date assigned to them is the 8th or 9th cent. They occur most frequently in the country between the mouth of the Tay and the shores of the Moray Firth. Among the chief examples, the Stones of Meigle, of Aberlemno, and of Forres (Sweno's) may be specified.

In no part of the United Kingdom are there so many grand *inhabited Castles* as in Forfar, Aberdeen, and Nairn shires, built in a peculiar and very picturesque style—partly as defensible houses, sometimes with drawbridge and portcullis, and always with bracketed angle-turrets, and in some few instances with bartizans. Among the finest of these are Glamis, Drum, Castle Fraser, Craigievar, Midmar, Crathes, Fyvie, and Cawdor.

There is no lack of more modern mansions and seats—the princely Gordon Castle, Haddo, Aboyne, Invercauld, Castle

Forbes, Cortachy, and, at the head of all, the regal Balmoral—an admirable specimen of the French-Scottish style of architecture revived.

Aberdeenshire is divided into several districts—*Mar* in the S., *Buchan* in the N.E., *Garioch* (pronounced Gherry), traversed by the Urie, and *Formartine* in the centre, and *Strath Bogie* in the N.W. Though once possessed by a great Celtic population, Gaelic is not at all spoken, except in the Braemar district. The present inhabitants are partly of Saxon or Flemish, and partly of Norwegian and Danish origin, and speak a *patois* peculiar to themselves. It is somewhat like the dialect spoken in the lowlands, but much sharper : for example, *what* is always *fat ; boots*, *beets*, etc. Diminutives are also used very freely. For several excellent anecdotes illustrating the dialect, see Dean Ramsay's "Reminiscences of Scottish Character," a most excellent and entertaining work, and the amusing local classic "Johnny Gibb of Gushetneuk," to which a glossary of the dialect is appended. In no portion of Scotland have greater industry and skill been exhibited, or more capital invested, in agricultural pursuits, than here, and that with a soil naturally wet and cold, and a climate so unpropitious that it has been described as divided into two seasons—"nine months winter, and three months bad weather." Consequently wheat is seldom sown here, and 100,000 acres of arable land are devoted to oats and turnips. From skilful management of the turnip crop, this district has become one of the chief meat-producers in Britain, and sends copious supplies both of live cattle and dead meat to the London market. On the week preceding Christmas more than 2000 head of cattle, besides sheep, have been sent up to London from the markets of Aberdeenshire, Banff, etc.

The *Hotel* accommodation is good. Many of the landlords can give or let fishing to their visitors. (See "Sportsman's Guide.")

§ 2. PRINCIPAL CENTRES.

POINTS OF INTEREST.

1. **Perth.** The Carse of Gowrie, etc. Cf. Section III. Airlie Castle and the striking scenery on the lower Isla can be easily visited in one day.

2. **Kirkton of Isla.** The wild upper part of Glen Isla.

3. **Dundee.** Its trade and manufactures. The Tay Bridge. (Dundee is best visited, by rail or steamer, from Perth.)

4. **Carnoustie.** The Golf Course. Arbroath Abbey and the cliff scenery N. of Arbroath.

5. **Kirkton of Clova.** Glen Clova and Glen Prosen, and the grand recesses of Glen Doll, Glen Fee, and Glen Esk.

6. **Brechin** or **Edzell.** Brechin Cathedral and Round Tower, the Caterthuns, West Water, and the picturesque scenery on the N. Esk.

7. **Aberdeen.** The "Granite City" itself and Old Aberdeen.

8. **Banchory** or **Aboyne.** Lower Deeside, Glen Dye, the Feugh Water, and Glen Tana.

9. **Ballater.** Glen Muick and the Royal Domain.

10. **Braemar.** Lochnagar and the grand Mts. at the head of the Dee.

11. **Alford.** Strath Don.

12. **Elgin.** Its Cathedral, Pluscarden Abbey, and the pleasing coast scenery to the E.

13. **Forres.** The Findhorn (cf. Rte. 42).

ROUTES.

ROUTE 46.

Perth to Dundee. Cal. Rly.

There are about a dozen trains daily each way—expresses take 30 min., slow trains 50 min.—and in summer a Steamer sails daily from Perth to Dundee calling at Newburgh. The hour depends upon the tide.

For **Perth** ✲ see p. 194.

After skirting the S. Inch the line crosses the Tay on a long low iron and stone bridge, and follows the l. bank of the river to Dundee, traversing the low flat alluvial **Carse of Gowrie**, which is bounded on the N.W. by the *Sidlaw Hills.* We pass a lovely reach of the Tay (rt.), and (l.), situated on the side of *Kinnoull Hill* (p. 196), **Kinfauns Cas.** (E. A. Stuart Gray, Esq.).

The land originally belonged to the Charteris family, but no trace remains of the old castle described in the "Fair Maid of Perth." The present castle was built in 1822 by Smirke, and contains a fine library and some good pictures:—*Guercino*, Peter denying Christ; *F. Francia*, Virgin and Child; *A. del Sarto*, Male portrait; *Titian*, Head of a female; *Rembrandt*, The Banished Lord; *Rubens*, Male head.

$3\frac{3}{4}$ m. **Kinfauns Stat.** rt. is a backwater of the Tay, the scene of *Millais's* "Chill October." $\frac{1}{2}$ m. beyond l. is *Seggieden* (Col. Drummond Hay, a leading ornithologist), and across the river the ruins of *Elcho Cas.* (16th cent.), from which the E. of Wemyss derives his 2nd title. At 6 m. l. is *Inchyra Ho.*, and rt. *Pitfour Cas.* (Sir J. Richardson, Bt.).

$6\frac{1}{2}$ m. **Glencarse Stat.** rt. are *St. Madoes Ch.* and *Manse*, picturesquely situated; l. is the village with an *Epis. Chap.*, and $\frac{1}{2}$ m. N. *Glencarse Ho.* (T. W. Greig, Esq.). *Megginch Cas.* (Capt. Malcolm Drummond)—16th cent.—stands l. before reaching

10½ m. **Errol Stat.** The village, with a Parish Ch. rebuilt in Romanesque style 1832 (Gillespie Graham, archt.), and *Errol Park* (W. Ogilvy Dalgleish, Esq.) are 1 m. rt. 3 m. l. is *Fingask Cas.* (W. Murray Thriepland, Esq.), which contains an interesting collection of Jacobite Relics, the House of Thriepland having been one of the most devoted to the cause of the Stuarts. The gardens are good examples of Dutch gardening.

13 m. **Inchture Stat.** The village, to which there is a horse tramcar, is 1½ m. N., and 1½ m. beyond is **Rossie Priory** (Lord Kinnaird), built in 1817.

"It contains a valuable Collection of pictures; amongst them are—*Vandyck*, Portrait of a Lady, painted in his Genoese manner; *Gainsborough*, Portrait of a Man, delicately executed in a cool tone; *Guido Reni*, The Repentant Magdalen; *L. da Vinci*, Beautiful Portrait of a lady, called La Columbine; *Sassoferrato*, Virgin and Child, a particularly fine example; *P. Veronese*, Kneeling Woman at Altar; *L. Caracci*, Repentant Magdalen; *A. del Sarto*, Portrait of a Man, one of his finest pieces; *Michael Angelo*, or more probably *Marcello Venusti*, The Crucifixion; *Rubens*, Portrait of a Man, of great freshness of conception; *Rembrandt*, Portrait of a Man, signed and dated 1666; *Tintoretto*, Conversion of St. Paul, spirited; *Sir J. Reynolds*, a good replica of The Banished Lord, in the National Gallery."—W. There are some fine pieces of sculpture and interesting antiquities. The Grounds of Rossie are very pretty, having some fine conifers dispersed through them, *Ab. menzesii*, 60 ft., Atlantic cedar, 50 ft. high. Within the Park is a Campanile Tower, with a very sweet peal of bells. The old keep of *Kinnaird Cas.* (12th cent., restored 1855), and the village of *Kinnaird* are situated 3 m. W.

15½ m. **Longforgan Stat.** The village is 1 m. N. 1 m. N.W. is *Castle Huntly* (C. J. G. Paterson, Esq.), standing on a high rock, perpendicular to the S.W., but sloping off to the E. The great tower, to which some very tasteless additions have been made, was built on the foundations of a still older one by Lord Gray, Master of the Household to James II., in 1452, and the present mansion comprises, besides the Castle Huntly of 1452, additions made by the 1st Earl of Strathmore (d. 1695), who called it Castle Lyon, and wings added by Mr. Paterson, who bought it in 1777 and restored its original name.

For the rest of the way the rly. skirts the edge of the Tay; it is carried on huge substructures through the deserted stone quarries of Kingoodie, near

17½ m. **Invergowrie Stat.** Here the line enters the county of Forfar. At the head of the bay is the small mouldering ruin of *Invergowrie Ch.*, an old building chiefly of 15th cent., but founded in the 12th cent. The **Tay Bridge** (p. 184) is well seen rt.

At 18 m. a line strikes l. to *Newtyle* and *Alyth Junc.* (Rte. 49).

19¾ m. **Magdalen Green Stat.** for the W. end of Dundee.

21 m. **Dundee West Stat.**

DUNDEE ✲ occupies a favourable position on the N. side of the Firth of Tay, not far from its mouth, on two hills, sloping gently to the water. It is a flourishing seaport and parl. burgh, ranking third in all Scotland for population and shipping, and second only to Glasgow in respect of its manufactures. It was made a Royal Burgh by William the Lion, *circa* 1160, and was created a City by Royal Charter, dated 26th Jan. 1889. Its Chief Magistrate is styled Lord Provost by virtue of a Royal Warrant, dated 10th Feb. 1892. Dundee returns 2 Members of Parliament, and is the only town in Scotland which does so undivided into electoral areas.

It bristles with tall chimneys and abounds in great steam-loom shops and mills, the latter all built with freestone. In these the spinning and weaving of *jute* and *flax* is carried on. Jute—from which the town has been nicknamed *Jute-*

opolis—is the fibre of a Bengal annual plant (*Corchorus capsularis*) 8-10 ft. high, with the stem no thicker than a finger. It is imported direct from Calcutta, and is made into carpets and sacking. It was first introduced during the Crimean War when Russian hemp became scarce and dear. Now about one and a quarter million of bales, each weighing 400 lbs., are imported annually at about £14 a ton. The *Camperdown Jute Works* of Cox Bros., Lim., at *Lochee*, N.W. of the town, occupying 28 acres, containing 20,000 spindles and 1000 power looms, producing 30-40 million yds. of cloth annually and employing 5000 hands, are the largest in the world, while those of Messrs. Gilroy in Lochee Road, with fewer hands, are 5 stories high and have nearly 60 windows in a row. The value of the annual export of linen from Dundee is about £3,000,000. The *Flax Mills* of Baxter Bros. and Co., Lim., alone employ about 4000 hands.

Dundee enjoys a curious specialty in its manufacture of *jams* and *marmalade*, of which about 4000 tons are turned out annually by James Keiller and Son, Lim., in their two factories, requiring abt. 15,000 half-chests of oranges and 2500 tons of sugar. They are also manufacturers on a large scale of confectionery, peels, chocolate, etc. As an instance of the collateral requirements of the trade, 3 million packages (jars, etc.) are furnished from Newcastle annually for this firm.

Before the general introduction of iron and steel ships, wooden shipbuilding was a large industry in Dundee, and was also carried on at Tayport. Since then iron and steel steamships of large tonnage are turned out by several builders, among whom are Gourlay Brothers and Co. and W. B. Thomson, Limited, while Messrs. Stephen and Son are builders chiefly of sailing ships and whalers. Besides shipbuilders Messrs. Stephen are tanners and furriers, confining this branch of their business to the preparation of the sealskins and furs procured by their own ships in the Arctic Seas.

At the waterside, between the West and East Rly. Stats., are the **Docks**, named after Earl Grey, King William IV., Queen Victoria, and Lord Camperdown, occupying an area of 35½ acres, and upon which more than £700,000 have been spent. An **Archway**, singular rather than beautiful, and called *Royal* because built in honour of Queen Victoria's visit, 1844, stands between Earl Grey and King William Docks.

Union St. leads up from the W. Stat. into the broad *High St.*, in which is the steepled **Town House**, built 1734 from designs by John Adam.

Opposite to it is *Reform St.*, the chief thoroughfare in the town.

At the W. end of High St. is an irregular modern Gothic edifice containing three Parish Churches, and adjoining is the **Old Steeple** (St. Mary's), one of the finest Gothic towers in Scotland. It dates from the 15th cent., though attributed to a vow made, when in danger of shipwreck, by David, Earl of Huntingdon (12th cent.), brother of King William the Lion, to build a ch. to the Virgin on the spot where he should first step on shore. It is a massive structure, 156 ft. high. In 1651, when General Monk assaulted Dundee—at that time a place of refuge for the Royalists—this tower was occupied by the garrison, and held out until burning straw was applied below. The tower was restored in 1872 by Sir Gilbert Scott.

The only other bit of antiquity is the *Old Port*, in Cowgate, not far from Baxter's mills. George Wishart, the Reformer, having heard that the plague was raging in Dundee, came to give the consolations of religion to the stricken, and is traditionally said to have chosen this building whence he might preach to the sick outside the gate, and to the sound within. Not long after (1545) Wishart was burned at St. Andrews by order of Cardinal Beaton.

Reform St. leads into an irregular open space, in the middle of which is the **Albert Institute**, a Gothic building surmounted by a spire, designed 1867-69 by Sir Gilbert Scott, and containing *Free Library, Hall, Assembly Rooms, Museum*, and *Picture Gallery;* a curved or horse-shoe staircase, on the model of that of Versailles, leads up to the entrance. In the grounds are *Statues* of James Carmichael, a native engineer and inventor, and of Robert Burns, the latter a replica of the New York Statue by Sir John Steell. W. is the Post Office, divided by Meadowside Road from the *Houff*, or old burial-ground, a very remarkable place, containing monuments of the older Dundee families, with many curious epitaphs. It was originally the orchard connected with the Franciscan Monastery founded by Devorguilla Balliol (cf. p. 99). The ground was given to Dundee by Queen Mary in 1565 as a burial-place when the ecclesiastical property was secularised. N.W. is *Euclid Crescent*, in which is the **High School**, with a Greek portico; N. is the Gothic *Exchange*, with square tower and newsrooms; and S. is the *Eastern Club*.

In Bank Street is the **Kinnaird Hall**, capable of holding 2000 people. Here concerts and large gatherings are held.

St. Paul's Episcopal Ch., at the corner of Commercial St. and High St., built 1855 by the exertions of Dr. Forbes, Bp. of Brechin (d. 1875), is one of the most successful of Sir Gilbert Scott's Gothic Churches, and has an elegant tower and spire, 210 ft. high. It occupies the site of the Castle of Dundee.

The **Sheriff Court Buildings** (with Prison behind), a large classical pile in Ward Road, were erected 1836, and enlarged 1854. Close beside them is the Constitution Road *Cemetery*. Proceeding N.W. we come upon the *Royal Infirmary*, built 1852-55; and *Dudhope Castle*, which was leased by the Government as a barrack in 1792, but not used for that purpose after 1868. In 1893, upon the expiry of the lease, the town acquired Dudhope Park and Castle as a recreation ground.

The oldest portion of the Castle was built by Sir Alex. Scrymgeour in 1296, and extended by his descendant in 1600. It was the seat of the Scrymgeours, Earls of Dundee (title extinct since 1660). The Castle was the residence of Graham of Claverhouse, who set out from it to Killiecrankie. It is referred to in "Waverley."

W. of the Queen's Hotel are the **University College Buildings.** This college, built and endowed by the late Miss Baxter (d. 1884) and her cousin the late Dr. J. B. Baxter, was opened in October 1883. The buildings cost £50,000, and £100,000 was given as an endowment. A notable feature is the evening classes. There are now (1894) 9 professors, 8 lecturers, and about 300 students. It was united to the University of St. Andrews in 1890.

Morgan's Hospital in the E. of the town was built and endowed with £80,000 (1868) by a native, for the maintenance and instruction of 100 boys, but is now a School Board school.

There are two *People's Parks*, viz. the **Baxter Park** to the E. (with no special attractions), the gift of the late Sir David Baxter, Bt., a millionaire, and the **Balgay Park** to the W., with charming walks and fine trees, and containing a new *Cemetery*.

To the N. rises **Dundee Law** (571 ft.), from which a good view of the town, the Tay Bridge, the river and firth, the Bell Rock Lighthouse, and St. Andrews, can be obtained without fatigue. The cone of the Law has been acquired by the Police Commissioners for a Public Park, but is not yet (1894) fully laid out.

Hector Boece, the most untrustworthy of Scottish annalists, was born in Dundee in the middle of the 15th cent.; also Admiral Viscount Duncan of Camperdown (1731-1804).

Steam or horse tramway cars traverse the principal streets, and run to the suburbs. A ferry steamer plies to *Newport*, 1¾ m. S. (p. 184), abt. every 45 min.

A Steamer sails daily in summer up the Tay to Newburgh and Perth, according to the tide—a capital sail of abt. 1½ hrs.

Large well-appointed Steamers sail to Leith, Newcastle, London, Hamburg, New York, the Baltic, etc. etc.

ROUTE 47.

Perth to Aberdeen by Coupar-Angus (Blairgowrie), Alyth Junc., Forfar, and Stonehaven. Cal. Rly.

Express trains run in 2-2½ hours.

Through carriages from Edinburgh, Glasgow, and the South, by the Cal. and L. and N.-W. Rlys. follow this route.

For **Perth** ✲ see p. 194.

2 m. rt. on the opposite side of the Tay is **Scone Palace** (see p. 197); l. a fine view over Strath Earn.

Crossing the Almond river, the line reaches

4¼ m. **Luncarty Stat.** In a field upon the l. Kenneth III., about 985, defeated the Northmen. It was in this battle that the Scots were rallied by a peasant of the name of Hay; and the victory being gained, Hay became a great man and founded the Tweeddale family. This, like many other picturesque traditions, is said to be apocryphal; indeed the De la Hayes appear among the Norman settlers both in England and Scotland. Several families, however, bearing the name of Hay still have a peasant with a yoke over his arm as one of the supporters of their coat of arms. Before

5 m. **Strathord Stat.** we cross the streams *Shochie* and *Ordie* immediately above where they unite before running into the Tay. An old rhyme runs—

Says the Shochie to the Ordie, "Where shall we meet?"
"At the Cross o' St. Johnston, when a' are fast asleep."

The Cross of St. Johnston stood in the higher part of the city of Perth, and the story runs that the inhabitants, to avoid the flood which this rhyme was supposed to foretell, removed the cross and built it into the middle arch of the bridge over the Tay.

7¼ m. **Stanley Junc. Stat.** Here the Highland Rly. (Rte. 42) turns off l.

The village was named in the beginning of the 18th cent. after Lady Emily Stanley, dau. of the Earl of Derby, who was beheaded by the rebels 1651, and mother of the first Marquis of Atholl. 1 m. S.W. is *Stanley Ho.* (Col. F. Stewart Sandeman), and ½ m. N.E. *Taymount* (E. of Mansfield), overlooking the **Linn of Campsie**, the only cataract of the Tay, and the scene of Eachan MacIan's death in the "Fair Maid of Perth." It is best seen from the other side. Cross the ferry and walk up the river to **Stobhall** (see p. 198), passing the Linn.

The line trends N.E., passing rt. *Ballathie* (Col. Edmund R. S. Richardson) just before crossing the Tay to

11¼ m. **Cargill Stat.** 1 m. N. is *Bridge of Isla*, above that river's junc. with the Tay, which Skene favours as the site of the much-disputed battle of *Mons Grampius*, won by Agricola, 86 A.D. Across the bridge is *Meikleour* (Dowager Marchioness of Lansdowne), a noble mansion built by Bryce 1873, but chiefly remarkable for a magnificent *Beech Hedge* bordering the public road, ¼ mile long and 80 ft. high. In *Meikleour Village* is a curious *Cross* with crosses and stars upon it and date 1698. In the neighbourhood are the remains of an important Roman Camp.

13¾ m. **Woodside Stat.**, with another Camp, 1 m. E. Rt. is a fine view of the **Sidlaw Range**, including *Dunsinane* (p. 197) and *King's Seat* (1235 feet), the highest pt. N. of this it is largely wooded to the top.

15¾ m. **Coupar-Angus Stat.**

[BRANCHES—(1) S.E. by *Ardler* and *Newtyle* to *Dundee* (22 m.) [cf. Rte. 49].

(2) N.W. to *Blairgowrie* (4¾ m.) [see p. 287], whence a *Coach* runs by the Spital of Glen Shee to *Braemar* (Rte. 58).]

Coupar-Angus✲, distinguished from Cupar in Fife by the addition of Angus, the old name for the county of Forfar. The town stands on the borders of Perthshire and Forfarshire, and on the bank of the Isla, and possesses some factories for the coarser kinds of linen.

An *Abbey* was founded here in 1164 by Malcolm IV. for Cistercian monks, but it had been getting out of repair before the Reformation, and its ruin was completed at that time. The only vestiges of this once magnificent structure are in the N. angle of the present *Churchyard*, on the side of the road to Dundee.

2 m. E. of the town, passing the village and church of *Kettins*, is *Hallyburton* (W. D. Graham Menzies, Esq.). 18¼ m. **Ardler Stat.**

20½ m. **Alyth Junc.**, for **Meigle**✲ and **Alyth**✲, see Rte. 49.

Beyond, rt. is a conspicuous ruined tower on the summit of *Kilpurney Hill*, 1134 feet.

24¾ m. **Eassie Stat.** *Lindertis* (Sir T. Munro, Bart.) is well seen 2½ m. l. on the slope of a hill backed by woods.

26¾ m. **Glamis Stat.**, 1 m. from which on rt. is **Glamis Castle** (Earl of Strathmore). Admission to castle and gardens granted only by special order.

This "magnificent old baronial castle" is one of the finest and most picturesque of the Scottish castles now inhabited, and at the same time one of the most cheerful and habitable. It owes its present aspect, clustered with turrets, bartizans, and extinguisher roofs, to the first Earl of Strathmore, 1675-1687, but it has much older portions included in the square tower with walls 15 feet thick which overlooks the whole. The lower wings were originally built in the 17th cent., but the roof of the greater part of them has been taken off in modern times and a battlement added. Fordoun and other chroniclers say that Malcolm II., grandfather of Duncan, was murdered at Glamis in 1034. Now Macbeth was Thane of Glamis, and perhaps lived there, and he was said to have murdered a king. So, by a conjunction of tradition and fiction, the scene immortalised by Shakespeare has been transferred hither, and the room in which Duncan breathed his last is even pointed out.

"It contains a curious monument of feudal times, being a *secret chamber*, the entrance of which by the law or custom of the family must only be known to 3 persons at once, the Earl, his heir-apparent, and any third person they may take into confidence."—Sir W. SCOTT.

At the burning of Lady Glamis in 1537 for witchcraft, and for conspiring to poison King James V., the castle was forfeited to the Crown; but when her innocence had been established it was restored to her son, whose descendant, Patrick, became Earl of Strathmore in 1672. In 1715 the Old Chevalier lodged for some time here, and held a sort of court. Sir Walter Scott writes—

"A disciple of Kent had the cruelty to render this splendid old mansion more parkish, as he was pleased to call it, to raze all the exterior defences, and to bring his mean and paltry gravel walk up to the very door from which, deluded by the name, we might have imagined Lady Macbeth (with the form and features of Siddons) issuing forth to receive King Duncan."

The house is entered by a low door surmounted by shields of the bearings of the noble family of Lyon; also by the arms of the royal family, in allusion to the time when James V. lived here during the forfeiture. A winding stair in the circular tower, set in an angle of the building, leads to a low vaulted hall decorated with armour and the buff coat of Claverhouse. This occupies nearly the whole space of the tall square central tower, which seems to be the oldest part of the castle. The drawing-room (once the hall) is embellished with a finely-carved and cradle-vaulted ceiling and noble fire-place. In addition to family portraits are some pictures of the Stuarts and their ministers, of Claverhouse the Duke of Lauderdale, and James Thomson the poet. There are also some handsome cabinets, and tapestry representing scenes in the life of Nebuchadnezzar. Opening off the drawing-room is a small dark-panelled chapel, one of the oldest portions, consecrated before the Reformation. The kitchen is old. The visitor should not omit to see the view from the top of the castle, over Strathmore and 12 counties; the range of the Grampians; the towns of Alyth, Blairgowrie, and Forfar; Mount Blair, and the Craigs of Clova.

In front of the house is a curious sundial, with an extraordinary number of faces to the sun. Amongst the curiosities of the place is the "lion-cup" of Glamis, the original from which Sir W. Scott took the idea of the "Blessed Bear of Bradwardine" in "Waverley." The park of 1000 acres is traversed by the Dean Water; it abounds in fine trees. The pinetum and gardens are modern.

In front of the manse, in the village of Glamis, is a sculptured stone, called King Malcolm's gravestone.

Soon after passing Glamis Stat. **Kirriemuir** (Barrie's "*Thrums*") is seen l. 3 m. off, and a fine view N. of it into the recesses of Glen Clova (Rte. 50) is obtained before reaching

32½ m. **Forfar Stat.**

[BRANCHES—(1) W. to Kirriemuir, 6 m. See Rte. 50.

(2) S. to Dundee, 21½ m. See Rte. 50.

(3) N.E. to Brechin, 11 m. (opened 1894). See Rte. 51.]

FORFAR ✲, a royal and parl. burgh, and capital of the county of the same name, nearly ½ m. S. of the stat., is situated at the E. end of a small loch, on the shores of which were fought the last battles between the Scots and Picts. Bristling with chimneys, it is by no means an attractive town; but possesses handsome **County Buildings** (1873) and a **Public Hall** (1871), for which it is indebted to a liberal townsman, Peter Reid, confectioner. It contains eight or nine large mills, which employ many of the inhabitants in weaving coarse linens.

An octagon turret, formerly the Town Cross (time of Charles I.), now marks the site of the Castle, which was a royal residence in the days of Malcolm Canmore. Queen Margaret had a retreat upon the Inch in Forfar Loch, now partly drained.

The town acquired an infamous notoriety from the number of old women executed here under a charge of witchcraft. A hollow on the north of the town is still called "The Witches' Howe," and the Forfar "Bridle," which was used as a gag, is still preserved in the **Town Hall**, where are also portraits of Admiral Lord Duncan, by *Opie*, and of Henry Dundas, Lord Melville, by *Raeburn*.

The hill above the town is converted into a public burial-ground, planted with coniferous trees, and laid out in walks.

[5 m. N. at the back of *Finhaven Hill* (751 ft.), with a vitrified fort, and commanding a fine view, is *Finhaven* or *Finavon* (Col. Gardyne), near which is the old *Castle*, a ruined stronghold of the Earls of Crawford, with which many of that family's traditions are associated. According to the rhyme—

"When Finhaven Castle rins to sand
The warld's end is near at hand."]

1¼ m. beyond Forfar, rt., are the remains of *Restennet Priory*, of the 13th cent., although an earlier church is supposed to have existed here, founded by St. Boniface in the 7th cent. The square tower, surmounted by an octagonal spire, is the principal portion that remains.

34¾ m. **Clocksbriggs Stat.** ½ m. beyond (l.) is *Rescobie Loch*, in which *Lastræa thelypteris* is found. The *Lunan* flows out at the E. end.

37½ m. **Auldbar Road Stat.** ½ m. l. is *Balgavies* (pronounced Beguys) *Ho.* (Geo. Lowson, Esq.), a modern building engrafted on the old castle.

[3 m. N. is **Aberlemno** Ch. and village, with 2 *Celtic Stones* strangely sculptured with combats. 1½ m. E. of it is *Melgund Cas.* (Earl of Minto, Viscount Melgund), a fine old ruin, said to have been built by Cardinal Beaton.

Auldbar (Patrick Chalmers, Esq.) is a castellated mansion between Melgund and Brechin, part of which was built by Sir T. Lyon, Treasurer of Scotland, whose arms, impaling those of his wife, daughter of the Regent Morton, are cut below the bartizan. The castle is built on the edge of a ravine of great depth. The grounds are very picturesque, and contain a charming terrace garden.]

Guthrie Cas., the seat of the family of the same name, a sq. tower built 1468, but much added to of late years, is well seen l. just before

39½ m. **Guthrie Stat.**

[BRANCH RLY. S.E. TO ARBROATH.

1¼ m. **Friockheim Stat.**

3 m. **Leysmill Stat.** A glimpse is caught rt. of *Colliston Ho.*, said to have been built by Cardinal Beaton, before reaching

4¼ m. **Colliston Stat.** The *Brothock Water* is crossed and recrossed; on its banks are screens belonging to the neighbouring mills for drying the yarn.

At 6½ m. **St. Vigeans**, a curious little *Ch.* originally of the 11th cent. and dedicated to St. Vigean or Fechin (d. 664), is passed rt. In the ch.-yd. are many *Celtic Sculptured Stones*, and portions of many more have been used at various times in the repair of the fabric of the ch., where they may now be seen.

7¾ m. **Arbroath**✱, see p. 261.]

The rly. now turns N.E. to

41½ m. **Glasterlaw Stat.**

44¾ m. **Farnell Road Stat.** A little farther on l. is seen *Kinnaird Cas.*, on the banks of the S. Esk, the stately seat of the Earl of Southesk. This title, after being long attainted, was restored in 1855. The house contains a fine library and an interesting collection of paintings, including a portrait of the great Marq. of Montrose, *æt.* 17, by *Jamesone* (cf. pp. 166, 270).

The *S. Esk* is crossed before

48 m. **Bridge of Dun Junc.** [*Branch* W. to Brechin (p. 270), 4 m.].

2 m. N.W. is *Dun's Dish*, a little loch; on the way thither are *Dun Ho.* (A. J. W. H. K. Erskine, Esq.) and *Ch.* A good view is obtained rt. across the estuary of the S. Esk, or *Montrose Basin*, of the town of Montrose (p. 264).

50½ m. **Dubton Junc.**

[Branch rt. to Montrose 3 m.]

1¼ m. beyond is Kinnaber Junc. (Rte. 48), where the E. and W. Coast Rtes. from London to Aberdeen unite.

The line now takes a sharp turn N.W. passing l. *Sunnyside Lunatic Asylum*, one of the largest and best in Scotland, and *Craigo Ho.* (Miss Carnegy), to

54 m. **Craigo Stat.** Beyond, it crosses the *N. Esk*, passes rt. *Marykirk Ch.* and village, and begins to traverse the *Howe of the Mearns*[1] at

56 m. **Marykirk Stat.**

59¼ m. **Laurencekirk Stat.** ✲ was founded by Francis Garden, Lord Gardenstone, in 1779, on the estate of Johnston, which he had then recently purchased. Dr. Beattie (1735-1803), author of "The Minstrel," was born close to the town on a farm of which his father was tenant. The town was once famous for its manufacture of snuff-boxes. E. are the *Garvock Hills*, on which *Johnston Tower*, which commands a fine view, is conspicuous. 4½ m. N.W. is *Fettercairn* ✲ (p. 272).

62½ m. **Fordoun Stat.**

The village, called **Auchinblae**✱, beside the *Ch.* of **Fordoun**, is 2½ m. N.W., prettily situated on the steep banks of the *Luther Water*. It is supposed to have been the birthplace of John of Fordoun (14th cent.), author of the "Scoto-Chronicon," and the oldest authority on the subject of Scottish History. Dr. Beattie was parish schoolmaster here, and describes the scenery in his "Minstrel." Near it is annually held *Paldy's Fair*, a corruption from St. Palladius, who is supposed to have come over with the early missionaries to Iona, and who d. 452. The modern ch. has a fine tower; in the ch.-yd. there is a portion of the old ch. remaining.

Between the stat. and the village (rt.) is *Monboddo* (Capt. Burnett), the seat of the judge Lord Monboddo (1714-99), who was celebrated for holding remarkable opinions about men having tails. Dr. Johnson and Boswell dined here, and the latter says it was then "a wretched place, wild and naked, with a few old houses, though, if I recollect aright, there are two turrets which mark an old baron's residence." The house has been much improved and enlarged.

---

[1] *Mearns* is another name for *Kincardineshire.*

The rly. crosses the *Bervie Water*, with *Glenbervie Ho.* (J. B. Nicolson, Esq.) 1 m. l. before reaching

66½ m. **Drumlithie Stat.**, a little manufacturing village. It then descends the valley of the Carron Water, having *Fetteresso Castle* (Rt. Hon. Sir R. W. Duff) on the l., and *Dunnottar Ho.* rt., before reaching

73¾ m. **Stonehaven Stat.** ✲, a flourishing little port, and the county town of Kincardineshire. It is situated very near the mouth of two streams, the Carron and the Cowie, and is considerably in repute as a bathing place.

rt. 1½ m. S. of the town are the ruins of ***Dunnottar Castle,** seat of the Keiths, Earls Marischal of Scotland. It stands on a projecting rock, separated from the mainland by a deep chasm, which in former days must have made it impregnable. The great square tower, which is still the most complete part, and the chapel, are said to have been built by the Crawfords, Earls of Lindsay. The modern part consists of 3 sides of a quadrangle, and is more like a barrack than a castle. The Castle was taken from the English by Wallace in 1296. During the wars of the Commonwealth the Scottish Regalia were kept here, and, when the Castle was besieged (1652), the governor, George Ogilvie of Barras, held out strenuously, and did not surrender until they had been conveyed away through the midst of the besieging force by Mrs. Grainger, the minister's wife — the crown in her lap, the sceptre disguised as a distaff. The English General is said to have helped her into her saddle himself, quite unconscious of the treasure she had about her. She buried them behind the pulpit of *Kinneff Church* [1] until the Restoration. At the Union the regalia were conveyed to Edinburgh, and almost forgotten till their discovery in 1818. Dunnottar was used in 1685 as a place of imprisonment for the Covenanters, and the "Whigs' Vault," in which they were confined, still remains. The Witch of Dunnottar figures in the Early French poem, "Fergus," by William the Clerk of Normandy. One of the labours imposed on Fergus, before he could be admitted a Knight of the Round Table, was to secure the sword guarded by the Witch.

The Cliffs here are bold and rocky, and rise to 200 ft. a little farther S., at Fowlsheugh on the way to *Bervie* (p. 265). In the churchyard of Dunnottar Walter Scott met for the first and last time Robert Paterson (cf. p. 98), the original of "Old Mortality," cleaning the headstones of the graves of the Covenanters who died in Dunnottar Castle.

[1] At Kinneff Kirk, on the coast, about 7 m. S. of Stonehaven may be seen the spot behind the pulpit where the regalia were concealed, and the monument to Mrs. Grainger. In the manse a room still bears the name of the regalia room.

Leaving Stonehaven Stat. the rly. crosses the *Cowie Water*, 1 m. up which is *Urie* (Alex. Baird, Esq.), and approaches the coast. Looking back there is a good view of Stonehaven, and Dunnottar Castle is also seen. The line skirts the edge of the cliffs, commanding fine sea views, to

78¼ m. **Muchalls Stat.,** near which is the small but quaint-looking house of *Muchalls*, begun, as an inscribed slab tells us, in 1619, and finished in 1627, by the Burnetts of Leys. A low courtyard wall in front supports a row of formidable-looking bartizans, a fashion which has outlived the necessities of the times.

79½ m. **Newtonhill Stat.** The line now leaves the cliffs for some miles. In the distance l. is seen a *Monument* to the late Mr. Irvine-Boswell of Kingcausie on Deeside (1785-1860).

81¾ m. **Portlethen Stat.** The village is 1 m. S.E. on the coast, while 1 m. N.E. is the village of *Findon*, or Finnan, well known for the production of smoked haddocks.

The rly. again keeps close to the coast, which is bold and rocky, affording many a beautiful peep down the gullies, before

85 m. **Cove Stat.**

At 87½ m. the rly. curves inland with rt. *Girdleness Lightho.*, and, crossing the Dee, enters the suburb of *Ferryhill*, where the Deeside line comes in l. On rt. is a good view of Aberdeen with the *Dee*, the *Wellington Suspension Bridge* and *Victoria Bridge* in the foreground, and the imposing *Municipal Buildings* in the background.

90 m. **Aberdeen Stat.**

ABERDEEN ✲ is one of the oldest and most important towns in Scotland, possessing charters of privilege —older than those of any other Scottish city—from William the Lion, Alex. I. and II., and Robert Bruce. The Town-Council Registers begin 1398. At the invasion of Edward III. 1337, Sir Thomas Roscelyn, one of his lieutenants, landed a body of troops at Dunethan, and marched upon Old Aberdeen; whereupon the citizens mustered their forces and gave Sir Thomas battle on the Green. The English were defeated with great slaughter, and Sir Thomas being killed, the English in revenge burnt Aberdeen to the ground. The city was then rebuilt at the mouth of the Dee, and called New Aberdeen. Robert II. assembled a parliament here to concert measures for an invasion of England.

In the minority of James I. the citizens marched out under their Provost, Robert Davidson, and fought with the Earl of Mar against Donald of the Isles at *Harlaw* (p. 297), 1411. Davidson was killed, and a rule was then made that the Provost should not leave the city during his term of office. In 1569 Aberdeen was entered by a body of Reformers, who, after some opposition from the inhabitants, succeeded in destroying the ecclesiastical buildings; but the town itself soon gave in its adhesion to the new creed. One hand of the Marq. of Montrose was sticking on the top of the Tolbooth until the visit of Charles II. in 1650, when it was taken down at the request of Montrose's son, and sent to Edinburgh to be buried.

Aberdeen is now a handsome town, situated at the mouth of the Dee on its N. bank, and ranks fourth in Scotland in point of population and trade. It is chiefly built of granite (the local stone valued all over the world), and is accordingly called the **"Granite City."**

The *Municipal Buildings* (p. 257), the adjoining *N. of Scotland Bank*, with its Corinthian portico of four columns, the offices of the *Northern Assurance Co.* in Union St., the *Grammar School* (p. 259), and the *Free Library*, are all good examples of finely-wrought granite buildings.

The Docks of Sebastopol were built of Aberdeen granite, in connection with the artistic and commercial value of which the visitor should inspect Messrs. Macdonald, Field, and Co.'s granite-works. The art of working granite with the axe, instead of the pick, and the invention of patent axing or chiselling tools with a number of cutting surfaces combined, as well as that of polishing by machinery, is due to the late Alexander Macdonald. There are also numerous other granite-polishing yards and important manufactures and industries, in combs, paper, linen, wool, and iron.

Aberdeen has some shipbuilding-yards, and is the chief seaport of the N. of Scotland. Great difficulties were experienced in the formation of the harbour, owing to the shifting nature of the soil at its mouth. Under Smeaton and Telford more than £300,000 was expended upon it. New and expensive works were begun

1871 — including a *S. Breakwater* of concreted blocks, 1050 ft. long. The "diversion" of the Dee by the straightening of its course, cutting off a great bend just below the Wellington and Railway Bridges, was achieved in 1872.

A fine *N. Pier* 2000 ft. long, having on the pier-head a fixed red light, was thrown out 1848-76.

The **Bridge of Dee,** 2 m. up the river, is a structure of 7 arches, built in the early part of the 16th cent. by Bishop Dunbar. It is one of the oldest bridges in this part of the world, having survived the floods of 1829. It was restored in the 18th cent. and almost doubled in width 1842. It was the scene of the first of Montrose's victories,—the passage of the bridge having been won by him on June 19, 1639, after a battle of two days, one of the many fluctuating struggles of the Scottish Civil War, in which Aberdeen constantly changed hands, passing from Cavalier to Covenanter, and back again. At this date Montrose belonged to the latter party.

Below it are the *Rly. Bridge* (1848) and the *Wellington Suspension Bridge* (1831) while, farther down, is *Victoria Bridge* (completed 1881, Dyce Cay, Engr.) connecting Aberdeen with the suburb of Torry.

Leaving the Rly. Stat., ascend Bridge St. or Market St. to Union St., and proceed along it rt. to *Castle St.*, a central open space, the N. side of which is occupied by the imposing **Municipal and County Buildings,** modern Gothic, 1873, of picturesque design (Peddie and Kinnear, archts.), with a very effective belfry tower 200 ft. high. They cost £80,000 and contain Alex. Brodie's excellent marble statue of the Queen (1866) removed from Union St. where it was being affected by the weather; also some good portraits—Queen Victoria, by *H. L. Smith;* Prince Consort, by *John Phillip;* Queen Anne, by *Kneller,* etc. Incorporated in this building, but almost hidden by it, is the good old *Tower* of the *Tolbooth.*

The Town Council possesses some interesting Charters and Autographs and the Blade of the *Aberdeen Maiden,* a rude sort of guillotine used for executions in 16th. cent.

Near this stands the **Cross,** a structure in the Renaissance style, with hexagon base, the panels ornamented with medallion heads of Scottish Kings, from James I. to James VII., surmounted by a pillar bearing the royal unicorn rampant. It was the work of a mason, John Montgomery, of Auld Rayne, 1686.

Here also is a *Statue* of the Marquis of Huntly, 5th and last Duke of Gordon (1770-1836), "1st Col. of the 92nd Gordon Highlanders," which he raised. Having been transferred to the 42nd, Scott addressed him in 1822:—

> "Cock of the North, my Huntly braw,
> Where are you with the Forty-twa?
> Ah! wae's my heart that ye're awa'—
> Carle, now the King's come!"

On the W. side of the Municipal Buildings is *Broad St.,* the reverse of its name. Byron when a boy lived at No. 64 with his mother.

A narrow entrance in Broad Street leads (rt.) to **Marischal College** (now an integral portion of the University, see p. 260), named from its founder, George Keith, Earl Marischal, in 1593. The present building, forming 3 sides of a quadrangle, with a tower 100 ft. high, of modern Gothic, was completed in 1841, at a cost of £38,000.

[A large extension of these buildings is now (1894) in progress, and a frontage to Broad Street is to be provided. Towards this scheme a large sum has been raised, Dr. Mitchell, Newcastle, an alumnus of the University, having given the handsome donation of £20,000.]

In the centre of the court is an *Obelisk* to Sir James M'Grigor, head of the medical staff in the Egyptian, Walcheren, and Peninsular campaigns. A flight of stairs leads to the *Hall*, containing some good portraits by *Jamesone*, a pupil of Vandyck, born at Aberdeen 1587. The *Library* contains *Sir Joshua Reynolds's* "Triumph of Truth," a portrait of Beattie, and *Sir G. Reid's* portrait of Dr. Bain.

This College has had among its *Eminent Students:—Gilbert Burnet*, Bishop of Salisbury (1643-1715); *Dr. Arbuthnott*, the friend of Pope (1675-1735); *Dr. Beattie* (1735-1803), author of "The Minstrel," and Prof. of Moral Philosophy in this College; *Jas. Gregory*, the mathematician (1638-75); *Colin Maclaurin*, the mathematician (1698-1746); *Dr. Reid*, the metaphysician (1709-96); *Robert Hall*, the divine (1764-1831); *Sir James Mackintosh* (1766-1832); *Dr. Neil Arnott* (1788-1874), etc. etc.

In addition to many other famous men Aberdeen may well be proud of her *Artist* Sons. Besides *Jamesone*, portrait-painter (1587-1644), and *Gibbs* (1674-1754), architect of St. Martin's-in-the-Fields and of the Radcliffe Library, she boasts in recent times of the eminent artists *John Phillip* (1817-1867), son of a shoemaker and apprenticed to a house-painter, and *Wm. Dyce* (1806-1864); also *Sir John Steell*, sculptor, (1804-91).

To the E. of Castle St. are *Castle Brae* with the *Children's Hospital* and the *Barracks*. On this hill once stood the old Castle of Aberdeen, which in the time of Edward I. was garrisoned by the English, and is said to have been captured from them by a night attack of the citizens, whose watchword "Bon Accord," has ever since been the motto of the city. From the N.E. corner of the square a street leads down to the *Links*, upon which Montrose encamped on three different occasions.

We now retrace our steps along **Union St.**, a fine avenue of granite houses, with many good shops, banks, hotels, etc., stretching nearly 1 m. W. from Castle St. At the corner of *Market Street* l. is the **Market**, which is worth a visit. It was opened 1842 and burned down 1882, but restored and enlarged 1883. At the foot of Market St. is the *General Post-Office*. Rt., at the corner of *St. Nicholas St.*, is a *Bronze Statue* of the Queen (Birch, sculp.), erected 1893 by the Royal Tradesmen, to replace Brodie's Statue (p. 257). Beyond (rt.), an open Grecian colonnade discloses to view the *E.* and *W. Churches*, forming a continuous building and standing in a large ch.-yd. in which Dr. Beattie is buried.

St. Nicholas' Ch. before the Reformation was the largest Parish Ch. in Scotland. After that it was divided into the *W.* (Nave) and *E.* (Transepts and Choir) *Churches*. The W., rebuilt 1753, was designed by Gibbs—his last work. In the vestibule are several handsome monuments, a fine *Brass* (1613), and some large **Tapestries*, representing the Finding of Moses, the Return of Jephthah, and the Intercession of Esther, attributed to a daughter of the painter Jamesone. The East Ch., after being rebuilt, was burnt 1874, but has since been restored. Fortunately the *Old *Transepts* which form its vestibule, and the "*Lower Church*," or **Crypt*, remain.

The *N. Transept* or *Colison's Aisle* is an interesting little example of transitional architecture (1153-1520), having specimens of pure Norman and of early and late Gothic. It contains an effigy of Provost Davidson (p. 256) killed at Harlaw 1411, and a tablet to the wife of the first Protestant minister of Aberdeen (Heriot, Canon of St. Andrews), who d. 1568. Daily week-day service has been held here in summer since 1883; in winter it is held in St. Mary's Chapel.

In the *S. Transept* or *Drum's Aisle* are effigies of Forbes of Drum and his wife Lady Elizabeth Keith, who had been engaged to his brother killed at Harlaw 1411. A *Brass* here is the oldest in Scotland.

The *Crypt* or **St. Mary's Chapel**, "vaulted throughout in stone, and the only ancient example of ecclesiastical stone vaulting in Aberdeenshire, consists of a nave with N. and S. aisles, of one bay each, the nave being prolonged E. by a semi-octagonal apse, from which it is separated by a strong, low, round arch. The other arches are pointed." It was founded and endowed about 1420 by Elizabeth Gordon, whose father fought at Chevy Chase (1388), and who m. Alex. Seton and became the ancestress of all the Earls and Marquises of Huntly, all the Dukes of Gordon, 2 Dukes of Richmond, and 4 Dukes of Sutherland. She died 1432, and is buried in the central aisle before the altar of Our Lady. In 1562 her descendant Sir John Gordon, suitor of Mary Q. of Scots, having been defeated (see p. 275), captured, and executed by the E. of Moray, was also buried here. In the 17th cent. it was a prison for witches, in the 18th cent. a plumber's shop, and in the beginning of the 19th cent. a soup kitchen.

It contains fragments of old *Gothic Stalls*, made 1506, and a large number of fine panels and seats, dating 1613-1706. Every Thursday the weekly sermon, which dates in Aberdeen from 1562, is preached in it, and here daily week-day service is held in winter. A scheme for its proper restoration was set on foot in 1893.

The **Trades' Hall**, containing some portraits by Jamesone, and some curiously carved chairs, lies l. before we cross the fine granite *Union Bridge*, erected by Telford (1803), with a span of 132 ft. across the Denburn valley, now occupied by the railway. At its W. end (rt.) is a seated *Statue of the Prince Consort* (by Marochetti), at the uncovering of which (1863) the Queen attended. He is in a field-marshal's uniform, with the robe of the Thistle over it, and holds in his hand a scroll. It is not a successful work. Here are the handsome *Northern Assurance Co. Offices*, and rt. facing Union Terrace, in which is a granite *Statue of Burns* (erected 1892), are *Union Terrace Gardens*, at whose N. extremity is a granite *Statue of William Wallace* (erected 1888). At the extreme W. end of Union St. is the *Free Ch. Theological College* (founded 1843, erected here 1850). On **Schoolhill**, behind the W. and E. Churches, and reached by Union Terrace Gardens or St. Nicholas St., are the handsome granite buildings of the *Free Library*, the *North Ch.* and *Rosemount Viaduct.* Facing Schoolhill is the *Art Gallery and Museum*, a fine building, erected 1885, in which Loan Exhibitions are held, and behind it is *Gordon's College*, an educational establishment founded 1730 by the bequest of Robert Gordon. In front of it is a granite *Statue of General Gordon* (1833-85) erected 1888.

W. of this, in Skene St., is the handsome *Grammar School*, the predecessor of which in Schoolhill was Byron's first place of education. [Read his admirable Reminiscences of Aberdeen in Moore's "Life of Byron."]

N. of the Grammar School, in Rosemount, adjoining Low Stocket Road, is the **Victoria Park** (open daily to the public).

On the N. bank of the Dee, adjoining Ferryhill and the Allanvale Cemetery, is **Duthie Park**, a pleasant recreation ground, ornamentally laid out, for which the city is indebted to the liberality of Miss Duthie, an Aberdonian.

Little more than 1 m. N. of the crowded streets and bustle of Aberdeen a singular contrast is presented in the silent ways of **Old Aberdeen**,[1] or "The Auld Town," near the river Don, a collection of old detached houses, with some large and handsome modern mansions, amidst trees and gardens, much more like a village than a city. It is said to have been deserted for the new site after the inroad of the English, *temp.* Edward III.

The ***Cathedral**, dedicated to St. Machar, a companion of St. Columba, was founded about 1136, but the earliest extant work (1356-82) consists of only two piers at the crossing of the transepts, a portion of the transepts, and a window in the E. bay of the S. aisle of the nave

[1] Frequent omnibuses from Market St.

which are all of gray sandstone. The Cathedral as it stands is practically the work of Bishop Lichtoun (1424-40) and is of red granite—the only granite Cathedral in the world. It consists of a nave of 7 bays with pointed arches resting on round piers and two W. towers. These towers (112 ft. high) were completed with octagonal steeples of sandstone by Bp. Gavin Dunbar (1518-30) who in 1520 added the noteworthy flat ceiling of panelled oak, with its 48 shields, glittering with the blazonries of the Pope, the Emperor, St. Margaret, the kings and princes of Christendom, and the bishops and nobles of Scotland. The Central Tower, completed about 1500, fell in 1688 owing to Cromwell's soldiers having 30 years earlier removed the stones from the choir to build a fort. In the ruined S. Transept is the handsome canopied tomb of Bp. Dunbar. In the N. Transept a damaged arched recess covers the effigy of Bp. Lichtoun; in the S. Aisle is what is supposed to be the memorial of Barbour (1330-96), author of "The Bruce," and Archdeacon of Aberdeen, while the largest monument of all is that of Bp. Scougal (1685). The Cathedral was well restored 1871, when much whitewash and heavy galleries were removed. After that 5 stained-glass windows were inserted, one of which commemorates the painters Jamesone, Dyce, and Phillip.

A little S. of the Cathedral is **King's College**, founded in 1494, in accordance with a bull of Pope Alexander VI., by Bp. Elphinstone, to whose zeal and liberality it owes its existence, and the patronage it received from James IV. At the Reformation it was possessed of very considerable revenues, but was deprived of a great part of its wealth in the general scramble. In 1641 Charles I. granted it a charter, incorporating it with the Marischal College as a part of the "Caroline" University. But after the Restoration the two colleges were again disunited, and it is only since 1860 that they have been finally merged as the University of Aberdeen—King's College being devoted to Arts and Divinity, and Marischal College to Law and Medicine.

The building was completed 1870-1874, and now forms a square, on one side of which, the only part remaining of the original, is the *Chapel*, begun 1500, and the massive tower attached to it, surmounted by a crown on flying arches, similar to St. Giles's, Edinburgh, and St Nicholas', Newcastle. The chapel has a good round-headed Flamboyant W. window, and contains some very elaborate beautiful carved woodwork, consisting of a double row of canopied stalls, with miserere seats and a lofty open screen. The carving throughout is gorgeous and delicate, and the tracery differs in every panel. Bp. Stuart's pulpit was brought here from the Cathedral; upon it are heads in relief of the Scottish monarchs (as on the city cross) from James I. to James VII.

In the pavement is a monumental slab to Bp. Elphinstone, the founder, and one to Hector Boece (d. 1536), the first Principal, which has been completely renovated. The *New Library*, opposite the chapel, contains over 100,000 volumes and several fine old MSS. (among them the Salisbury missal, a bequest of Bp. Gilbert Burnet) and missals. In one of the class-rooms are pictures of the Ten Sibyls, and of Principal Middleton, attributed to Jamesone, but showing small trace of his hand. The *Senate Room* contains a curious contemporary portrait of Bp. Elphinstone on a panel, also a portrait of his successor Bp. Dunbar, and a picture of King's Coll. in 1670. The General Council of the University, composed of graduates, elects the Chancellor for life, and along with that of Glasgow returns a Member of Parliament. In the triennial election of Lord Rector by the Students the vote as in Glasgow (cf. p. 140) is by "Nations," viz., *Mar*, *Buchan*, *Moray*, and *Angus*. In 1893 the General Council numbered 3448, the Matriculated Students 900. Facing the College is the strange Oriental gateway of *Powis House*.

Nearly 2 m. from Aberdeen and ½ m. from Old Aberdeen is *The Old Bridge of Don* or **Brig o' Balgownie**, a very picturesque single pointed arch, 62 ft. wide, erected 1320 by Bp. Cheyne, spanning a deep black pool of the river, backed by fine woods, and quite worthy of the artist's pencil. Old as it is, it withstood the floods of 1829, which swept away almost all the modern bridges in this part of Scotland. In 1605 Sir Alex. Hay devoted a small property to the maintenance of the bridge, but the value so greatly increased that from the proceeds, a modern bridge of 5 arches was built lower down the Don.

The Old Bridge has been made famous by Lord Byron, who remembered it, and the superstition connected with it, many years after he had left Aberdeen. The poetic legend runs thus :—

"Brig o' Balgownie, wight's your wa';
Wi' a wife's ae son, an' a mear's ae foal,
Down ye shall fa'."

Byron, who had crossed it as a boy nine years old, alludes to it in "Don Juan," and recalls to mind its "one arch, and its black deep salmon stream is in my memory as yesterday. I still remember, though I may misquote, the awful proverb which made me pause to cross it, yet lean over with a childish delight, being an only son."

ROUTE 48.

Dundee to Aberdeen by Arbroath and Montrose. N.B.R.

This is the line over which trains from Edinburgh and the South to Aberdeen by the Forth and Tay Bridges (Rte. 30) run.

Express trains from Dundee to Aberdeen in abt. 2 hrs.

Cal. Rly. trains to Forfar (Rte. 50) and to Arbroath run over this line starting from the E. Stat.

Leaving **Tay Bridge Stat.**, we pass E. through a tunnel to

3½ m. **West Ferry Stat.**, and

4 m. **Broughty Ferry Stat.**

[A Steamer crosses the Tay abt. nine times a day in 10 min. to *Tayport* (p. 184).

Branch (Cal. Rly.) N. to *Forfar* and *Kirriemuir* (Rte. 50).]

This is a colony of villa residences of Dundee merchants. On rt. are the ruins of *Broughty Castle*, occupied by the English in 1547, after the victory of Musselburgh. It was stormed by the French auxiliaries in the Scotch service, in 1550, and dismantled. Of late years, however, it has been repaired and fortified to guard the entrance of the Tay, which it commands.

6¼ m. **Monifieth Stat.** On rt. across *Barry Links*, one of the principal camping grounds in Scotland, with rifle ranges, is the promontory called *Buddon Ness*, conspicuous by the Tay Lighthouse.

9¼ m. **Barry Stat.**

10¾ m. **Carnoustie Stat.** ✲, a seaside resort with an excellent *Golf Course*.

12¾ m. **East Haven Stat.** 3 m. l. is *Panmure* (Earl of Dalhousie), a modern Scottish castle by Bryce, which replaces the old 12th-cent. castle destroyed in 1651 by General Monk. Of recent years large sums have been expended in planting the estate and in building a magnificent range of greenhouses and conservatories. The pillar upon a hill in front is a monument to the 1st Lord Panmure.

15½ m. **Elliot Junc.**

[There is a mineral line from here 6 m. N.W., to *Carmylie*, where are extensive flag-stone quarries. At Carmylie Manse the reaping-machine was invented by the Rev. Patrick Bell, 1826.]

17 m. **ARBROATH Stat.** ✲ [Branch (Cal. Rly.) N. to *Guthrie* (p. 254)], a busy town and

a parliamentary burgh, bristling with chimneys of large factories, where coarse linen and canvas are woven. It stands on a height above the sea, where a dirty stream pours itself into a harbour of small account, to which a dock was added in 1877. Flagstones of Old Red Sandstone are exported under the name of "Arbroath Pavement." It is the Fairport of Sir Walter Scott's "Antiquary." Its unabbreviated name is Aberbrothock, from its situation at the mouth of the Brothock river. It was made a royal burgh by William the Lion (1165-1214), to whom the town is also indebted for its Abbey.

At the end of the long High St., abt. 10 min. walk from the stat., is

The *Abbey,[1] founded 1175 for Tyronensian monks from Kelso, and dedicated (1178) to St. Thomas of Canterbury. Its remains (visited by Dr. Johnson in 1773, by Burns 1787, and by Scott 1814) are very disjointed and fragmentary, but they are grand in position, and picturesque in outline and in the colour of the dark red sandstone. "I should scarcely have regretted my journey," wrote Dr. Johnson, "had it afforded nothing more than the sight of Aberbrothock." It seems to have been very spacious, and enclosed a large portion of the present town, though its community consisted only of an abbot and 24 monks. The *Church* (completed 1233) was 270 ft. long — 6 ft. longer than the Cathedral of Elgin—and consisted of nave of 8 bays, with aisles, transept with aisles, and choir. It was burnt in 1216, in 1232, and finally in 1559. It is a very fine example of the first pointed style, and even though the grand and deeply moulded *W. Doorway* is circular, its mouldings are of that style. Above the W. Porch is an *Arcade* of 6 pointed arches opening into the nave, but the fine W. rose window has perished. The entire N. wall of the ch. is gone, along with piers and pier-arches.

The windows at the E. end consisted of 3 rows, each of 3 lancets, deeply embayed; of these the 2 upper rows and the gable have perished.

The grave of William the Lion is pointed out in front of the high altar.

The S. wall of the nave is still standing, also the bases of 2 towers and a part of the S. transept. The S. window is called the O of Arbroath. It still acts as a guide to ships at sea. In former days it was lighted up as a beacon. Attached to this transept is a tower-like structure, probably either the *Sacristy* or *Chapter House*, still perfect in walls and roof. It is surrounded with sedilia; and a stone-closet adjoining (miscalled "The Confessional") was probably a strong room for ch. plate and title-deeds. Among the monuments preserved in it is part of a sculptured figure, with feet resting on a lion, supposed, on this slight foundation, to be the effigy of the founder.

A massive machicolated square tower at the corner of the street served as a *Dungeon*, as well as to flank the *Abbey Gatehouse*, which, though a decorated building, shows, by the grooves for a portcullis, that the monks often found it necessary to resist their neighbours the townsfolk. There are considerable remains of vaulted crypts, etc., in a large modern house adjoining the Gateway.

King John granted leave to the monks and burgesses of Aberbrothock to trade without molestation or tax with any place in England, except the city of London. In 1320 a general assembly of the Estates of Scotland was held in the abbey, when a spirited declaration was drawn up of the independence

[1] Its Grounds—a public *Cemetery* with seats—are always open. Key of the *Sacristy* from the keeper, who is generally in attendance and lives near.

of the Scottish Kingdom of the English Crown, and a protest against any interference by the Pope or his legates.

The Abbot of Arbroath had the custody of the *Brechbannach* or sacred banner of St. Columba, for which the lands of Forglen in Banffshire were given to the abbey. As, however, the banner required to be followed to the field of battle, it remained really in the hands of laymen who held it of the abbot. Amongst the abbots of Aberbrothock were the three Beatons, the Cardinal David, and two Archbishops James, one the uncle and the other the nephew of the Cardinal; also Gavin Douglas, the translator of Virgil. Of the Abbot's house the kitchen is still visible on the S. side of the church.

For many years the municipal authorities were in the habit of selling the materials (without giving any account of the proceeds), which is the cause of the disappearance of so much of the building. This nefarious practice was stopped in 1815, by order of the Barons of the Exchequer, who, by seasonable repairs, saved the remainder.

11 m. S.E. is the **"Bell Rock,"** probably so called from its shape, but the legend of the name is given in Southey's fine ballad:—

"The Abbot of Aberbrothock
Had placed that bell on the Inchcape rock;
. . . .
When the rock was hid by the surge's swell
The mariners heard the warning bell;
And then they knew the perilous rock,
And blessed the Abbot of Aberbrothock."

A *Lighthouse* was erected upon it in 1810, at an expense of £60,000 under the superintendence of Rennie assisted by Robert Stevenson, founder of the present well-known firm of D. and T. Stevenson, C.E.

[The best **Excursions** are northwards along the coast, where the red sandstone cliff scenery is remarkably fine and hardly surpassed on the E. coast of Scotland. It is best visited in 3 sections.

(1) Follow the *excellent path* which continues for fully 2 m. along the cliffs to the *Pint Stoup*, an isolated stack. From this path many charming peeps are caught down the rocks and into the chasms, of which the most singular is called *The Pot.*

(2) Drive to **Auchmithie**★, 3½ m., an interesting fishing village, picturesquely placed on the top of the cliffs and having a neat little harbour with breakwater below. It is the *Mussel Crag* of Scott's "Antiquary." Here hire a boat and visit the caves towards the S. The *Lady's Cave* obtains its name in consequence of the light falling in such a way as to resemble a veiled figure. Another is the *Mason's Cave*, from the appearance of the rocks at the entrance, which look as if they had been built up artificially; while another is the *Green Cave*, on account of the luxuriance of the hart's-tongue fern (*Scolopendrium vulgare*). *Asplenium marinum* also grows here.

(3) Drive 3½ m. beyond Auchmithie, passing *Ethie Ho.* (E. of Northesk), to the E. Mains; *or* walk there in 2½ m. from Inverkeillor Stat. Thence walk 1 m. to the grand cliffs at *Red Head*. An additional interest is imparted by their being the scene of the escape of Sir Arthur and Miss Wardour in the "Antiquary." From this point the coast N. trends inward, forming the graceful curve of *Lunan Bay.*

There is a kind of path all along the cliffs from Arbroath (abt. 8 m.), but after 3 m. it is often exceedingly unpleasant walking.]

Leaving Arbroath the line passes l. *St. Vigeans* (p. 254) to

20 m. **Letham Grange Stat.**, and

22 m. **Cauldcots Stat.**

23¼ m. **Inverkeillor Stat.**, from which the cliffs at *Red Head* (above) may be reached in 3½ m. The rly. crosses the *Lunan Water*. 1 m. rt. is *Red Castle*, an old fortress of William the Lion, of which but a fragment remains, picturesquely situated on the shore at the centre of *Lunan Bay*. Passing rt. *Lunan Ch.* and *Ho.* (Col. Blair Imrie), the train reaches

25¾ m. **Lunan Bay Stat.**

2 m. beyond Lunan we pass (rt.) the disused lime-kilns of *Boddam*, and 1 m. farther catch (rt.) a glimpse of the curious trap *Rock of St. Skeagh*, jutting sharply out from the old red sandstone. It is perforated with natural archways so as to present the appearance of an elephant. Close

to it is the fishing-village of *Usan*, with an ancient burying-ground. Beyond, in a field by the rocks, another small burial-ground of the families of Williamson and Scott is seen rt. before we traverse a deep cutting close to the fishing-village of *Ferryden* rt. (with a ferry to Montrose), on quitting which we come upon a fine view of the picturesque town and basin of Montrose. This basin, formed at the mouth of the S. Esk, and having only a narrow outlet to the sea, constitutes a commodious tidal harbour. The mouth of the river is divided by the little island of *Inchbrayock* or *Rossie* into 2 channels, which are crossed by the railway on 2 viaducts.

30¾ m. **Montrose Stat.** is built on land reclaimed from the lagoon. [Branch to *Bervie* (below). There is another (Cal. Rly.) Stat. on the E. side of the town for trains to *Dubton Junc.* (p. 254).]

Montrose ✲ stands on a tongue of flat land stretching S., flanked on the W. by a large tidal *Basin* formed by the estuary of the S. Esk river, and on the E. by the North Sea. It is a parl. burgh, grouped with Arbroath, Bervie, Brechin, and Forfar for the election of a Member of Parliament. It has some trade, which, however, is not increasing. The principal industries are Messrs. Millar's extensive wood-yards, and Messrs. J. and G. Paton's large manufactories of linen yarns. There is also a little shipbuilding.

The town, which is well built, has one of the broadest *High Streets* in Scotland, furnished with excellent shops, and containing an interesting *Town Hall* and *Statues* of Joseph Hume (b. here 1777 and long M.P. for the burgh) and of Sir R. Peel. The *Parish Ch.* is a handsome building with a peculiarly graceful spire. Montrose was the birthplace (1805) of Sir Alexander Burnes, the traveller nd Eastern diplomatist, murdered 1) at Cabul; and of Robert Brown, the botanist (1773-1858). At the end of the High Street is a portion of the town-house in which the celebrated Marquis of Montrose is said to have been born, 1612.

In the Castle of Montrose John Baliol surrendered the insignia of Scottish royalty to King Edward I., 1296, after the disastrous battle of Dunbar, and here Sir James Douglas embarked for the Holy Land with the heart of Bruce. Here also ended the Rebellion of 1715-16 by the secret embarkation of Prince James Stuart, accompanied by Mar, on board a French vessel, leaving his army in the lurch, Feb. 4, 1716.

The mouth of the S. Esk is spanned not only by the rly. viaduct, but also by a suspension bridge, built, 1829, by Sir Samuel Brown, who saw in the little island of Inchbrayock a useful ally. On the S. bank of the basin are the beautiful braes of *Craig*, and *Rossie*. The visitor should cross the ferry, ascend the hill above Ferryden for the sake of the view, and return by the suspension bridge. The *Links of Montrose* are one of the finest golf-grounds in Scotland.

[A BRANCH RLY. TO BERVIE strikes due N. along the coast, skirting the cliffs, to

3¼ m. **North Water Bridge Stat.**, close to which the N. Esk is crossed below the Pounage Pool, where John o' Arnha encountered the Water Kelpie, according to the old ballad composed by George Beattie, who sleeps in the ch.-yard of St. Cyrus, at the foot of the rocks.

5¼ m. **St. Cyrus Stat.**, beyond which rt., by the sea, is the *Kaim of Mathers*, built by Barclay (1421) to escape the vengeance of James I., for having slain and afterwards "suppit in bree," the body of the Sheriff of the Mearns.[1] At

6¼ m. **Lauriston Stat.** the traveller should stop to visit *Den Finella*, one

[1] *Mearns* is another name for *Kincardineshire*.

of the most romantic dens in the county, in the grounds of *Lauriston Cas.* (D. S. Porteous, Esq.), crossed by the rly. on a bridge of 4 arches.

8½ m. **Johnshaven Stat.**

12 m. **Gourdon Stat.**, a small fishing-village, with a harbour.

13 m. **Bervie,** made a royal burgh by David II., 1342, was the birthplace (1735) of Coutts, the banker. *Hallgreen Castle* (J. Farquhar, Esq.) was the residence of the father of Dr. Arbuthnott, the friend of Pope; he was probably born here. 2 m. N. is *Kinneff Ch.*, to which the regalia were conveyed from Dunottar in 1652 (see p. 255).

Coach to Stonehaven, 10 m., 5 times a week.]

Skirting the Basin and trending inland we reach

32¾ m. **Hillside Stat.,** beyond which, at *Kinnaber Junc.*, the Cal. Rly. from Perth to Aberdeen is joined. See Rte. 47 for the line from here by **Stonehaven** to

71¼ m. **Aberdeen Stat.**

For **ABERDEEN** ✲ see p. 256.

ROUTE 49.

Perth or Dundee to Meigle and Alyth (for Glen Isla). Cal. Rly.

From Perth direct to Alyth Junc. 20½ m., see p. 251.

From Dundee West Stat. the line runs W., passing

1 m. **Magdalen Green Stat.,** and at 3 m. trends N. to 4¼ m. **Liff Stat.** Liff village is 1½ m. N.W. Between it and the Stat. is *Gray Ho.* (E. A. Stuart Gray, Esq. of Kinfauns), and 1 m. W. of Liff is **Fowlis Easter,** with *Ch.* of the 15th cent. (restored 1888) having a most singular arrangement of windows, and containing a fragment of the original *Rood Screen*, with painted panels representing the crucifixion and other Bible subjects. Near the S.W. door hang the "jougs" (see p. 62).

The line now runs due E. passing

5¼ m. **Camperdown Stat.,** 1 m. N. of which is Camperdown House (Earl of Camperdown) to

6 m. **Lochee Stat.** the N.W. suburb of Dundee—with which it is connected by tramway—a busy centre of textile manufactures. The line again bends first N., and then N.W., through a not very interesting country, to the *Sidlaw Hills* which it crosses, passing on the way

7¾ m. **Baldovan Stat.,** 2 m. E. of which are *Claverhouse* village (with bleachfields) and the ruins of *Claverhouse Cas.*, the family seat of Viscount Dundee (1643-89), the hero of Killiecrankie; 8¾ m. **Baldragon,** 11 m. **Dronley,** and 12½ m. **Auchterhouse**. The line is carried through the *Glack of Newtyle*, a narrow pass overlooked (rt.) by the ruins of *Hatton Cas.* (16th cent.), before reaching

16¾ m. **Newtyle Stat.** [Branch l. by 3 m. Ardler and 5½ m. Coupar-Angus to 10 m. Blairgowrie (p. 287).]

18 m. **Alyth Junc.** (p. 252), where the main Cal. line to Aberdeen is crossed and Perthshire entered.

19¼ m. **Meigle Stat.** ✲. In the ch.-yd. is a group of upwards of 20 *Sculptured Stones*.

These represent (*inter alia*) the story of Prince Arthur's wife, Vanora (or Guinevere?), who was captured by the Picts. Her husband some time afterwards rescued her, but finding that she had been seduced sentenced her to be torn in pieces by wild beasts. This is supposed to be depicted on the stones; but some regard them as hunting scenes.

½ m. S. of Meigle is *Belmont Cas.* (Rt. Hon. H. Campbell-Bannerman, M.P.), and 2 m. W. *Kinloch* (Sir John Kinloch, Bt., M.P.). Continuing N.W. the line crosses the *Isla*.

21½ m. **Jordanstone Stat.** *Ruthven Ho.* (Col. Ogilvy), 1½ m. rt. (in

Forfarshire), on an estate which long belonged to the Crichtons, is a modern mansion situated near the Isla and close to the site of the ancient castle.

23¼ m. **Alyth Stat.** ✲, a small town with some coarse linen factories, lies pleasantly at the base of outliers of the Grampians.

EXCURSIONS :—

(1) Drive N.E. to **Airlie Cas.**, 5 m., visit the **Slug of Auchrannie.* Return by *Loch Lintrathen* (8½ m.) and the *Reekie Linn* (11½ m.), 16 m.

Airlie Castle is picturesquely situated on a cliff overlooking the junc. of the Melgam and the Isla. It is the residence of the Dowager Countess of Airlie, the Earl's principal seat being Cortachy (p. 268). Some remains of the old castle have been incorporated into the present building, the E. wall, with its portcullis-entry, being still entire.

In 1639 the Earl of Airlie was a strong royalist, and left Scotland to avoid signing the Covenant. During his absence the castle was burnt by the Earl of Argyll acting under the authority of the Committee of Estates. This is the subject of the song "The Bonnie House o' Airlie." The injury was afterwards avenged by Montrose, by the destruction (1645) of Castle Campbell (p. 200).

The grounds are open Tues. and Sat., but carriages must be left at the *Mains of Airlie*, near which is a "weem" or cave the roof of which is rudely sculptured, and the castle approached by a path leading into the main avenue.

Below the castle cross the Melgam and follow the l. bank of the Isla for nearly 2 m. The path, although not always close to the water, allows views of the extraordinary gorge or cañon which the river has cut out of the old red sandstone, and which is unsurpassed in Scotland. At the **Slug of Auchrannie**, where the path terminates, and where there is a waterfall 60 ft. high, the scenery culminates. On the return drive the Isla is crossed some 3 m. higher up by the *Bridge of Craig* (4½ m. from Alyth). A private path, always open to visitors, here leads down the rt. bank of the river for 100 yds. to

The Reekie Linn; a fine fall so named from the "reek" or "smoke"-like vapour which rises from it in certain states of the atmosphere.

(2) Drive N. up **Glen Isla**, an open glen which gets wilder as one penetrates into its recesses.

The road passes the *Reekie Linn*, crosses the *Bridge of Craig* (4½ m.), then turns l., ascending more steeply.

At 7½ m. the road to Kirriemuir strikes off rt.

At 10½ m. is the hamlet or **Kirkton of Glenisla** ✶. [1]

The driving road continues up the glen for 10 miles, passing in 4 m. *Forter*, with a ruined castle, burnt (1640) while occupied by Lady Ogilvie at the same time as Airlie Castle. Here a driving road leads l. in 3 m. over the shoulder of Mt. Blair into Glen Shee, 5 m. below the Spital (p. 285).

Continuing up Glen Isla from *Tulchan*, a Shooting Lodge of the Earl of Airlie (10 m.), where the road stops, the pedestrian reaches in 2½ m. the grand *Ceanlochan Glen* (l.) on the E. slope of *Glas Maol* (3502 ft.), where amid precipitous cliffs the Isla has its source. The *Corrie of Ceanlochan* is unrivalled on this side of Scotland for the beauty and number of its rare plants (see Prof. MacGillivray's *Natural History of Deeside*).

Two courses are now open—either ascend this glen and after a rough walk of some 5 m., having crossed the shoulder of Glas Maol, join the Spital of Glenshee road at Cairnwell, its highest point (p. 285); or cross the mouth of the glen, keep straight on and rt. and reach the head of *Glen Doll* (p. 268) in 4 or 5 m.

(3) Drive N.W. into **Glen Shee.**

The road ascends the *Alyth Burn*, passes (3 m.) *Bamff* (Sir J. H. Ramsay, Bt.), traverses moorland, and after crossing the *Blackwater* joins the Blairgowrie road in 9½ m. at a point 4 m. N. of *Bridge of Cally* and 10 m. S. of the *Spital of Glen Shee* (see Rte. 58).

---

[1] *Coach* twice daily to and from Alyth, July to Sept.; once daily in June and Oct. Coach from Kirriemuir (13 m.) on Thurs., July to Sept.

ROUTE 50.

Perth or Dundee to Kirriemuir. Cal. Rly.

Kirriemuir by Glen Clova to Braemar (or Ballater). Latter part for Pedestrians.

From **Perth** to Forfar (32½ m.) direct, see pp. 251-253.

From **Dundee East Stat.** the train runs E. to

3½ m. **Broughty Ferry Stat.** (see p. 261), and then turns N.

4¾ m. **Barnhill Stat.,** beyond which the *Dighty Water* is crossed and the *Panmure Bleaching Works* passed l.

7 m. **Kingennie Stat.**, 1½ m. l. of which, past *Murroes Ch.* and village, are the ruins of *Ballumbie Cas.*, formerly the seat of the Lovels (p. 195).

11½ m. **Monikie Stat.** 2 m. rt. is *Panmure Ho.*, a seat of the E. of Dalhousie. Crossing the E. end of the Sidlaw Hills we reach

15½ m. **Kirkbuddo Stat.** Passing l. *Fothringham Hill* (761 ft.), to the S. of which lie *Fothringham Ho.* (W. T. J. S. Steuart Fothringham, Esq.), and *Inverarity Ch.* and village, we come to

18½ m. **Kingsmuir Stat.** 1½ m. E. are *Dunnichen* village, Ch., and *Ho.* (Lady K. H. D. Metcalfe), and the site of the *Battle of Nechtansmere* in which Ecgfrith of Northumbria was killed by the Picts 685 A.D.

21½ m. **Forfar Stat.** ✲ (p. 253). Passing 3 m. W. along the Perth line and then 3 m. N. we reach

27½ m. **Kirriemuir Stat.** ✲ A brisk little manufacturing town with a trade in brown linen. Like Alyth it is pleasantly situated on the S. slopes of the Braes of Angus. It has been brought into notice by Mr. Barrie in his novels under the name of "Thrums." The streets are narrow except the Square or High St., off which runs Bank St. where the *Auld Licht Kirk* was situated. Its gable has been preserved in the new Kirk for "Auld Lichts" (with shops below), of which Mr. Barrie laid the foundation-stone in 1893. A red sandstone quarry behind the town supplies building materials for the neighbourhood. In the ch.-yd. are some *Sculptured Stones.*

1½ m. N.W. is *Kinnordy,* the seat of Sir Leonard Lyell, Bt., M.P., nephew of the famous geologist Sir Charles Lyell, Bt. (1797-1875), who was born here.

EXCURSIONS :—

(1) To **Airlie Cas.**, 6 m. W., and the fine river scenery on the Isla, see p. 266.

(2) Up **Glen Isla.**

Coach runs on Thurs. July-Sept. to *Kirkton of Glen Isla*✱, 13 m. (see p. 266).

(3) Up **Glen Prosen** (see pp. 268, 274).

Coach runs Wed. and Sat. July-Sept. to *Inchmill*✱, 11 m.

(4) Up **Glen Clova** (see p. 268).

Coach runs Tues. and Sat. July-Sept. to *Kirkton of Clova*✱, 15½ m.

This Glen is interesting to the student of botany, but its scenery, although pleasing, is not remarkable until the grand recesses at the top are reached. Those, however, will be well rewarded who take the next excursion.

(5) By *Glen Clova* and *Glen Doll* to **Braemar,** 34½ m.; *or* by *Glen Clova* and *Glen Muick* to **Ballater,** 36½ m.

One can drive 18½ m. at the Kirriemuir end, 5 m. at the Braemar end, and 9 m. at the Ballater end.

The road ascends steeply N. out of Kirriemuir, and at

1 m. bends l. [Straight on to *Glen Ogil* is 7½ m.]. There is a capital view of the mts. to be crossed. At

1½ m. at the corner of a wood the road turns rt., and for 2 m. is dull.

At 3 m. rt. (½ m.) is the well-preserved strong 4-storied fortalice of *Inverquharity Cas.* (15th cent.), the seat of a branch of the Ogilvies, one of whom fought for James VII. at the Battle of the Boyne (1690), and wrote the song "It was a' for our rightful King."

3½ m., *Prosen Bridge*, where the water of that name is crossed: for the next mile the road skirts the policies of **Cortachy Cas.** (Earl of Airlie) rt. (not visible), a lovely domain. Here is kept the Earl's famous herd of polled Angus cattle.

At 4 m. a *Well* l., with a coronet and inscription, "Sep. 23, A. B., 1854," is passed, and

At 4½ m. the road strikes l. [The road straight on passes the pretty little village of Cortachy, the red stone ch. of which has a good Perp. window, and the N. entrance to Cortachy Castle, crosses the S. Esk, and leads in 14 m. to Brechin (see p. 271).]

5½ m. *Dykehead*✲.

[A road l. leads up **Glen Prosen**, *Inchmill*✱ being 5½ m. up, and 1 m. farther *Balnaboth* (Mrs. Ogilvy), in the grounds of which are the ruins of a R.C. Chap., prob. built by the Kinlochs in the 16th cent. Here the driving road ends. This glen is very different from Clova, the hills being much lower and wooded nearly to the summit (cf. p. 274).]

At 6 m. rt. there is another "coronet" well, dated "Sep. 23, A. B., 1860."

At 8 m. there is an extensive view back over the flat strath, with Forfar in the distance. Passing a little wood l., the Esk is seen more distinctly rt., and the road reaches Glen Clova.

At 8½ m. there is a bridge over the Esk, and either side of the river may be taken.

At 10 m. upon rt. bank is *Tarrabuckle*, and at 12 m. upon l. bank is *Rottal*, both shooting lodges of the E. of Airlie.

15½ m. The **Kirkton** or village of **Clova** ✲ consists of a small ch., a manse, an inn, and some farms. This is a good place for exploring the Braes of Angus.

Overlooking the village is a single fragment of *Clova Castle*, concerning which there is but little account; indeed, the only historical interest of Clova is associated (rather strangely) with Charles II. When this sovereign in early life (1650) was established at Perth amongst the zealous Presbyterians, he formed a design to escape from their hands, and take refuge with the Highland and other Royalists. He got as far as Clova, but there finding none of his expected supporters, he put himself into the hands of Colonel Montgomery, with whom he returned to Perth. This incident is known in Scottish history by the name of *The Start*.

[A steep ascent of ¾ hour, path faintly marked, at the back of the inn following the burn which runs out of the loch, leads up the hill to 1½ m. *Loch Brandy*, a picturesque tarn embosomed in a deep hollow of precipitous cliffs.

About 2 m. farther E. is *Loch Wharral*, a similar tarn, though not so well worth visiting; and to the W. of Loch Brandy is the *Corrie of Clova*, apparently the bed of a loch drained away. The sharp ridge between the two is called the *Snub of Clova*, and is marked by a very curious gap or indentation in the rock. This fissure is gradually widening, and must eventually separate a huge mass of rock which will fall into Loch Brandy. On the opposite line of hills is a depression known as the *Sneck of Barns*, over which lies the shortest way to Glen Prosen (see p. 274).]

From Clova to the head of the glen the scenery is incomparably finer. The hills draw nearer and are rugged in the extreme.

18½ m. is the farm of *Braedownie* where the public driving road stops and the Glen forks—l. up Glen Doll, rt. up the Esk to Braemar by *Bachnagairn* and *Cairn Bannoch* (see p. 269), or to Ballater by Glen Muick (see p. 271).

The right of way up **Glen Doll** was only established in 1888, after a lawsuit keenly contested, in the Court of Session and in the House of Lords, between the Scottish Rights of Way Association and Duncan Macpherson, Esq. of Glen Doll.

Just above *Braedownie* the path crosses a bridge over the Esk, and leads, as indicated by signposts, through the fields below *Acharn Shooting Lo.*, and up the l. bank of the *White Water*. Across this stream is the fine jagged peak of the *Sgur of Doll*, and behind it the Mts. of *Dreish* (3105 ft.) and *Mayar* (3043 ft.).

20 m. l. is the wild glen down which comes the *Fee Burn*, out of a striking corrie, whose loch has been drained.

[By ascending this corrie and crossing the moor a good mountaineer may get down the *Glencally Burn*, into *Glen Isla*, abt. 3½ m. above Forter, cf. p. 266.]

Glens Clova, Doll, and Fee are celebrated for their Alpine flowers, and for a number of rare plants and ferns. This is the only habitat of *Oxytropis campestris*, DC., in the British Isles. The region is peculiarly rich in its moss flora. The scenery is now very grand, on both sides are high rocky cliffs, and in front is an imposing crag, l. of which the stream falls in a series of cascades, and rt. of which is *Jock's Road*, a steep and stony pass, resembling those in the English Lake District.

At 21¾ m. the real climb begins, and 750 ft. are ascended in ¾ m. From the summit (2250 ft.) the view back and down is very fine. An upper valley—much less interesting and bleaker—is now entered. The track practically disappears, but its line—very uneven walking—is marked along the hillside rt. by stakes and small perched cairns. The *Tolmount* (3143 ft.) is right ahead at the top of the glen. The point to be made for is ½ m. rt. of it, but the ridge rt. should be kept so as to avoid the bogs as much as possible, to get a peep down into *Loch Esk* (see below).

The 3 m. from the top of Jock's Road to the watershed at the *Knaps of Fafernie* (3000 ft.), 25½ m., are very fatiguing. Here a magnificent view in front of the whole Ben Muich-dhui range is obtained, and then a steep descent to *Loch Callater* (1600 ft.) lying in the hollow below must be made and its N. side kept to

29½ m. *Loch Callater Lo.* (see p. 282), which is 5 m. from

34½ m. **Braemar✲.**

Going from Braemar to Clova, when Loch Callater is reached, the depression to the l. of the *Tolmount* should be made for, by the N. shore, and from the watershed the stream rt. should be kept *in view*, remembering however to remain on the l. ridge along the upper valley.

The route from Clova to Braemar by *Bachnagairn*, a variation of that just described, and about the same length—not recommended unless Glen Doll has already been visited—is as follows:—

Instead of turning off at *Braedownie* up Glen Doll, keep straight on to the head of Glen Clova as far as *Bachnagairn* (Sir A. R. Mackenzie, Bart. of Glenmuick), a shooting-lodge, 7 m. from Clova. Half way up the Esk has to be forded, but the pedestrian may avoid it by crossing the bridge near Acharn, and following a footpath on the W. bank of the river. *Bachnagairn* is splendidly situated amongst the rocks at the head of the glen, and deeply embosomed amidst firs. The *South Esk* which rises in *Loch Esk*, about 1½ m. higher up, *falls* in one grand leap of 70 or 80 ft. in height, the cliffs on each side bounding it like a wall. Unfortunately it is so shrouded by the forest that the visitor must approach close to it before he can see it, and thus some of the effect is lost. From Bachnagairn cross the stream by a footbridge and follow the path to the rt., which winds right round the crest of the hill. (Do not attempt to follow the river, for the ground is uneven and very boggy.) The path keeps to the N. of *Broad Cairn*, from which there is a view of *Loch Muick*, to the W. of *Dhu Loch*, and close to the side of *Cairn Bannoch*, from whence on a clear day the Ochil and Lomond Hills may be seen. From thence it descends and joins the path from Braemar to Lochnagar on the side of Cairn Taggart (p. 282).

ROUTE 51.

Forfar to Brechin. Cal. Rly.

From N. of Forfar the junc. for Brechin is *Bridge of Dun* (p. 254).

This line, opened 1894, runs N. to

4½ m. **Justinhaugh Stat.**, with the village of *Oathlaw* 1 m. rt. It then trends N.E., crossing the So. Esk with *Tannadice* village l. before reaching

6½ m. **Tannadice Stat.** *Tannadice Ho.* (Trs. of the late W. Neish, Esq.) is ½ m. rt., and 1 m. beyond, across the river, is *Finhaven* (p. 253). We cross the *Noran Water*, which comes from *Glen Ogil*, and pass rt. the extensive policies of *Careston Cas.* (J. Adamson, Esq.) before

10 m. **Careston Stat.**; thence E. to

13½ m. **Brechin Stat.** ✲—with another stat. for Bridge of Dun, etc., ½ m. S.—a flourishing and increasing town with paper and large linen manufactures, lying on the side of a hill overhanging the S. Esk. The modern quarter occupies the high ground. The principal objects of interest are the **Cathedral**, and especially the ***Round Tower** at its S.W. corner.

A Bishopric was founded here by David I. abt. 1150, and some of the remains of the ch. date from then. The nave and transepts have been barbarously supplanted by a modern sash-windowed church, but at the W. end the ancient middle pointed window and portal remain, together with a broad M. pointed projecting Tower (commanding a good *View*) surmounted by a low spire; while the Choir, a graceful example of pure lancet work, remains ruined and roofless at the E. end.

The *Round Tower*, which is thought to date from the 10th or 11th cent., is 87 ft. high, 25 ft. in diameter at the base, and 12½ ft. at the top, surmounted by a conical roof of the 15th cent. It differs from Abernethy (p. 190) in being attached to the church, and in being of irregular but solid masonry. Its chief architectural feature is a narrow doorway on the W. side, 6 ft. above the ground, with jambs inclining inwards, surrounded by a beaded moulding, and surmounted by a crucifix carved in low relief. The two figures at the sides were evidently intended to represent saints. It is certain, therefore, that it was built after the conversion of the country to Christianity. It perfectly resembles the round towers of Ireland, and reminds one of Kilkenny, as regards its proximity to the cathedral; of Cloyne, in its type and manner of building; and of Donaghmore, in its ornamentation over the door. These towers partly served as belfries, and partly to protect sacred property and vessels.

Also picturesquely situated in the ravine of the S. Esk, and separated from the Cathedral by its moat, is *Brechin Cas.*, the seat of the E. of Dalhousie, the head of the Maule family.

During the invasion by Edward I. (1303) Brechin Cas. held out under Sir Thomas Maule for 3 weeks, and only surrendered after the Governor had been killed. It has been much modernised, and is a comfortable mansion, containing some interesting portraits, *e.g.* the great Marq. of Montrose (æt. 37) by *Gerard Honthorst* (cf. pp. 166, 254), Charles Fox, and Neil Gow, the famous fiddler.

EXCURSIONS:—

(1) N.W. to the **Caterthuns**, 5½ m.

The *White Caterthun* (976 ft.) and the *Brown Caterthun* (943 ft.) are 2 round-backed hills, lying respectively S. and N. of the road to Lethnot Ch., and are both capped with a Caledonian or *British Fort.* That on the White Caterthun is an oval fortification of concentric rings of loose whitish stones, measuring 25 ft. across at the top and 200 ft. at the base. It seems to have been a castle of dry mortarless masonry of rude stones raised in a wall, perhaps 25 to 30 ft. thick, and of uncertain height. The whole having been overthrown by violence has poured down the hillside in a cataract of stones, confounded with a lower outer wall or rampart. The fort is entered by one opening at the E. The platform on which it stands projects, as a great bastion, in front of the Grampian Range which it commands to the N. and W., and it overlooks the plain of *Strathmore*, which is studded with Roman camps. That on the Brown Caterthun is a series of concentric entrenchments, nearly circular. There is a splendid view looking S. over Brechin, and the flat country to the N. of Arbroath and Dundee, and northwards over the Forfarshire hills, in which the *Hill of Wirren* (2220 ft.) is a very conspicuous feature.

(2) N. by *Edzell*, *Fettercairn*, and the *Cairn o' Mount* to **Banchory** (Rte. 52).

(3) N.W. by *Glen Esk* and *Glen Mark* to **Ballater**—Latter part for pedestrians (Rte. 53).

(4) By *West Water*, *Glen Clova*, and *Glen Prosen* to **Glen Isla**—For Pedestrians (Rte. 54).

(5) By *Glen Clova* to **Ballater** (43 m.) [or to **Braemar** 46 m.]—Latter part for Pedestrians.

28 m. can be driven from Brechin ; 9 m. at the Ballater end ; and 5 m. at the Braemar end. This road keeps the l. bank of the S. Esk by *Tannadice* (p. 270) to *Cortachy Castle* and *Ch.* (p. 268), where at 14 m. the river is crossed.

The road from Kirriemuir is now joined, and from this point up Glen Clova to

28 m. *Braedownie Farm* is described in Rte. 50. [Here the path by Glen Doll to Braemar (p. 268) strikes off l.] Keep up the l. bank of the Esk for 1 m., when a zigzag bridle path is seen rt., ascending the *Capel Mt.* [Across the Esk is the way to Braemar by Bachnagairn (p. 269).] As we climb a splendid view is obtained in front up the Esk, and, looking back, of *Dreish* (3105 ft.), *Mayar* (3043 ft.), and *Glen Fee.* Follow the path (marked by posts) along the N. shoulder of the *Capel Mt.* to the E. of the *Dog Hillock*, and crossing the watershed at 2250 ft., descend to *Loch Muick.* A peep is obtained W. of the savage *Dhu Loch* and the waterfall that issues from it. It is 6 m. from Braedownie to the foot of Loch Muick, for which and the road thence in 9 m. to 43 m. Ballater, see pp. 277, 278.

ROUTE 52.

Brechin to Banchory by Edzell, Fettercairn, and Cairn o' Mount.

Coach to Edzell several times daily. The construction of a rly. from Brechin to Edzell was begun in June 1894.

This is a very pretty route by which a cross-cut may be made with a carriage into Deeside without going round by Aberdeen ; it also affords an excellent opportunity of seeing the Forfarshire hills more closely.

Follow the Aberdeen road for 2 m., then turn off l. crossing the *Cruik* and *West Water.* E. near their junc. with the N. Esk is *Stracathro* (J. A. Campbell, Esq., M.P.), and beyond, across that river, is the Gothic castle of Inglismaldie (E. of Kintore). The road passes through an *Arch*, erected 1888 to the memory of the 13th E. of Dalhousie and his wife, who d. respectively on 25th and 24th Nov. 1887, before

6 m. **Edzell** ✲, a neat little village, suitable for staying at, with a golf course and near pretty scenery on the N. Esk.

[1 m. W. on the road to Lethnot are the ruins of *Edzell Castle* surrounded by trees.

This fortress in old times commanded the entrance to the Lowlands in this direction, and the tall tower of Glenmark (p. 273) was its outpost. Its first possessors were the Stirlings, from whom it passed to the Lindsays, and it is now the property of the Earl of Dalhousie. As in many other Scottish castles, the oldest part, the square tower at the S., built by the Stirlings, is still the most perfect. This was connected with a round tower (much dilapidated) by a lower range, containing the state apartments, built by the Lindsays, now a mere shell, though comparatively modern. The keep tower and Lindsay buildings overlook a square enclosure, once the flower garden or *Viridarium* of Sir David Lindsay, whose arms and the date 1604 appear over a doorway in the N.E. corner. The walls have this peculiarity: not only are they decorated all round with emblematical figures in bas-relief of the Cardinal Virtues, the Sciences, Planets, etc. etc., but at intervals they are indented with large square holes, like pigeon holes, intended to hold flowers and creeping plants, but which, viewed at a distance, formed in combination with the mullets surmounting them the Lindsay coat of arms —the fesse chequée. In the angle of this court is an elegant turreted *Garden-house* or lodge of the same date, where pic-nic parties may make their tea by leave of the owner.

In the Stirling Tower is the Ladies' Bower, the window of which overlooks a noble prospect. Here Queen Mary sat when she visited Edzell.]

At 7 m. the N. Esk, here flowing through a fine glen cut in the old red sandstone, is crossed by *Gannochy Bridge,* beyond which is a long and pleasant avenue.

The road up Glen Esk (Rte. 53) strikes off l.; rt. is the road to Montrose (12 m. distant) so remarkable for its direct line of 4 m. that it is called "*The Lang Straight.*"

The country is now very open rt. and Sunnyside Asylum (p. 254) 9 m. off may be seen.

At 9¾ m. l. is *Balbegno,* an old tower built abt. 1567.

10½ m. **Fettercairn** ✲ is entered by a handsome Tudor *Arch,* erected to commemorate the "Visit of Victoria and Albert, Sept. 1861," who stayed *incog.* at the "Eagle." It is a picturesque village with a *Cross* brought from the extinct town of Kincardine, a *Public Hall* (1890), and a *Fountain,* erected 1869, in memory of Sir J. H. S. Forbes, Bt., of Pitsligo and Fettercairn.

The road now passes rt. *Fettercairn Ho.* (Hon. C. F. Trefusis) and l. *Fasque,* the seat of Sir John Gladstone, Bt., built 1809.

At 13 m. the ruins of *Kincardine Castle* are ½ m. rt. in a wood. There in 994 Kenneth III., enticed into this stronghold by Finella, wife of the Mormaer of the Mearns, was slain; and there the helpless King John Baliol signed his abdication in favour of Edward I. who visited the castle in 1296. The road here trends N. Before

14½ m. *Clattering Brig,* a foot bridge over the *Slack Burn,* we turn sharp l. and begin a long ascent of 2½ m., at first exceedingly rough and steep.

[The geologist should pay a visit to *Birnie Slack,* up the Slack Burn, where the stream issues from a deep corrie in the hills and flows for some distance underground, or rather under a tremendous accumulation of debris of quartz and felspar.

The road straight on, fording this burn, keeps round *Finella Hill* (rt.), and passes in 2½ m. (l.) *Drumtochty Cas.,* the beautiful seat of the Rev. J. S. Gammell, to

4½ m. **Auchinblae** ✱ (see p. 254), beside the Ch. of **Fordoun** and 2½ m. from **Fordoun Stat.**]

17 m. The view from the summit of the **Cairn o' Mount** (abt. 1450 ft.) on a clear day is very extensive. The road descends more gradually on the other side to the valley of the *Dye,* which rises in *Mt. Battock* (2555 ft.) and flows under *Clochnaben* (1944 ft.), the striking top of which is conspicuous l. The Water of Dye is crossed at

21 m. **Bridge of Dye** with (l.) *Glen Dye Lodge* (Sir J. Gladstone). After 2 m. the road forks [l. in 3 m. to *Whitestanes Inn,* pp. 275, 276]; keeping rt., through woods, we again cross the Dye at 24½ m. *Bridge of Broggendrip,* and turn l. to

26 m. **Strachan** village, where the *Feugh Water* (see pp. 273, 275) is crossed. At the manse here the learned Dr. Thomas Reid, author of "An Enquiry into the Human Mind," was born 1710. The l. bank of the Feugh is followed and the *Dee* crossed to

30 m. **Banchory** ✲, see p. 275.

ROUTE 53.

Brechin to Ballater by Edzell, Glen Esk, and Glen Mark. Latter part for Pedestrians.

This is a fine but long route of 35 m., of which the first 22 m. can be driven.

It is well to make the start from Edzell; there is no inn between there and Ballater.

From Brechin through Edzell to

7 m. *Gannochy Bridge* is described in Rte. 52. A little beyond Gannochy Br. the road strikes off l. up the l. bank of the N. Esk, passing round *The Burn* (Col. M'Inroy), built by Lord Adam Gordon 1791.

Visitors should, however, apply at the Lodge for leave (which is always kindly given) to walk along the river side through the grounds. The N. Esk here flows through a gorge of old red sandstone, forming a succession of romantic views not to be excelled of their kind in Scotland. The narrowness and depth of the ravine, the great body of clear brown water, the curious tilted arrangement of the rocks, and the Alpine character of the woods, make up altogether a perfect picture. One of the finest bits is where a suspension bridge is flung across the chasm, and where the geologist will observe some very remarkable masses of conglomerate as large as a house. Near the top of the gorge the arrangement of the rocks is different—serpentine and jasper occur.

The botanist will find, amongst other plants, *Galium anglicum*, *Saxifraga aizoides*, *Asplenium Adiantum-nigrum*, *Alchemilla alpina*, etc. The tourist will discover that by the time he has exhausted the beauties of the glen, he has escaped 1½ m. of a tedious road, which he can rejoin at the end of the grounds.

Above *The Burn* the valley of the North Esk becomes open, and although very pretty and pastoral, is not of any grandeur or wildness. *Mt. Battock* (2555 ft.) is a conspicuous feature due N.

10 m. At *Auchmull Castle* there is a pretty view across the Esk up Mooran and Forbie glens.

18 m. At **Tarffside,** the *Water of Tarff*, coming in from the N., is crossed.

[A track leads up this water and over the hills to the *Forest of Birse* and *Birse Cas.* (8 m.) on the *Water of Feugh.* There it bifurcates, leading N. in 7 m. to Aboyne and E. down the Feugh (p. 275).]

Beyond Tarffside the road passes at the foot of *Migvie Hill*, and a beautiful view opens up of *Glen Effock* (l.) across the Esk.

22 m. At **Lochlee Ch.**, the *Lee* joins the Esk after passing through *Loch Lee*, a wild loch 1 m. long, almost surrounded by mountains, lying 1 m. l. At its W. end is the farmhouse where the late Rev. Dr. Guthrie spent his summers, and at the E. a ruined Ch. on a Culdee site dedicated to St. Drostan. The Earl of Dalhousie has a pretty shooting lodge here called *Invermark*, and close at hand are the ruins of *Invermark Cas.*, the old residence of the Stirlings, and the first great barrier opposed to the Highland forces. We keep up the l. bank of the Esk. The glen, now called *Glen Mark*, narrows considerably, and the road becomes a mere bridle path.

24 m. Here Fox Maule, 11th Earl of Dalhousie, enclosed within a conspicuous structure of stone arches a clear spring called the *Queen's Well.* An inscription records the visit of the Queen and Prince Consort, Sept. 20, 1861. Just beyond is a keeper's cottage, at the foot of the Ladder Burn, which the path ascends and crosses; farther on it keeps up the rt. bank. It then trends l., and by a zigzag called "*The Ladder*" ascends the W. shoulder of *Mt. Keen* (3077 ft.), a singular conical-shaped hill. From the summit (about 2500 ft.) a descent is made in 2 m. to

29 m. **Glen Tana** (p. 276), the water of which is crossed at 1235 ft. An ascent of 500 ft. is then made rt. round the *East* shoulder of *Cairn Leughan* (2293 feet), and finally a descent W. to *Bridge of Muick*, 1 m. from

35 m. **Ballater** ✲, p. 277.

ROUTE 54.

Brechin by West Water, Glen Clova, and Glen Prosen to Glen Isla. For Pedestrians (2 days).

This is a good cross-country expedition, allowing a peep into several of the Forfarshire glens.

Drive or walk 7 m. N.W., passing between the *Caterthuns* (p. 270) to *Lethnot Ch.* Thence keep up the rt. bank of the *West Water* to

10 m. **Stonyford Bridge**, a charming bit of landscape at the foot of *Wirren* (2220 ft.). The glen becomes very pretty, although the hills are by no means of broken or romantic outline. They are, however, purple with heather to the summits in autumn.

About 3 m. above Stonyford is *Hunthill*, a shooting lodge of Lord Dalhousie near the junc.—a particularly fine bit—of the *Water of Saughs* and the *Corscarie Burn*, which united form the West Water. Cross the former and keep up the latter to its source (16 m.). Now keep due W., having *Ruragh* (2410 ft.) rt. and *Dog Hillock* (2369 ft.) l., to the *Kennet Burn*, which will be struck in about 2½ m. Follow it down to

20½ m. *Rottal Lodge* in Glen Clova, and keep up that Glen to

24 m. **Kirkton of Clova** ✱, p. 268. Next day ascend the hill exactly opposite the hotel by what is called the *Sneck of Barns*, and descend the other side by *Glen Logie* to *Balnaboth Ho.* (see p. 268), and

30 m. **Inchmill** ✱ in **Glen Prosen.** Cross the bridge, keep up the rt. bank of the Prosen Water for 1½ m., then trend l. to

35 m. *Glenhead Lodge*, where a road strikes l. to Alyth, and on to

37½ m. *Glenmarkie Lodge*. Here turn l., cross the *Newton Burn* and keep its rt. bank, and then trend rt. to

40 m. **Kirkton of Glenisla** ✱. For the various courses open from this point see p. 266.

ROUTE 55.

Aberdeen to Braemar by Deeside Rly., Ballater, and Balmoral. Gt. N. Scot. Rly. and Coach.

Abt. 5 trains daily to Ballater, 43½ m., in 1 hr. 50 min., and an express extra each way when the Queen is at Balmoral.

Coach, Ballater to Braemar, 16½ m., in 2½ hrs., once daily; thrice in summer.

The line keeps the l. bank of the Dee and for the greater part comparatively near the river. The **Dee,** which drains the S. half of Aberdeenshire, rises among the wilds of *Braeriach* and *Ben Muich-dhui* (p. 283), and has a total course of about 90 m. From the *Linn of Dee* (p. 281) the country watered by it is diversified by plantations and natural woods of fir and birch. Since even Braemar stands so high the current is often extremely rapid. As compared with the northern part of the county watered by the Don, it used to be said—

"Ae fit o' Don 's worth twa o' Dee,
Unless it be for fish or tree."

Quitting the stat. at Aberdeen, the rly. leaves the Perth line at Ferryhill, close to the Wellington Bridge, and turns due W. Left are *Duthie Park* and *Allanvale Cemetery*. S.E. across the river is Nigg Ch., on a hill.

2 m. **Ruthrieston Stat.**, and (3 m.) across the river *Banchory Ho.*, where the Prince Consort stayed in 1859, when he came to Aberdeen to preside at the British Association Meeting.

4 m. **Cults Stat.** Close by, rt., is *Cults Ho.*, and on the opposite side of the river the Kirk of Banchory-Devenick, *Ardoe Ho.* and *Heathcot*, the *Deeside Hydropathic Estab.*

5½ m. **Murtle Stat.** On the opposite side of the Dee is *Blairs College*, endowed 1829 by John Menzies, Esq. of Pitfodels, for the education of candidates for the Roman Catholic priesthood. The college contains portraits of Mary Queen of Scots, Cardinal Beaton, Prince Charlie and his father.

6½ m. **Milltimber Stat.** Amongst the residences in this neighbourhood are, across the Dee, *Kingcausie Ho.* (J. Fortescue, Esq.), and on rt. *Culter Ho.*

7½ m. **Culter Stat.** Near this rt. are paper-mills, and l. the ch. and manse of *Peterculter*. Across the Dee is *Maryculter Ho.*, and 1 m. beyond, *Maryculter Ch.* Near it is the **Corbie Pot**, or **Linn**, a little picturesque rent, with a brook, and cascade, abounding in botanical specimens which are usually to be found only on high mountains. Between the line and the river are the remains of a fortified Roman encampment, called *Normandykes.* The rly. ascends a steep incline to

10 m. **Drum Stat.** 1¼ m. rt. is *Drum Cas.* (F. H. F. Irvine, Esq.). The house consists of a 16th-cent. mansion attached to a square peel-tower (some 600 years old), with

bartizan, turrets, and walls 12 ft. to 15 ft. thick. The hall on the 1st floor has been converted into a library, the groined ceiling of which is adorned with armorial bearings. The lower story is called the dungeon. The family of Irvine of Drum is of great antiquity, and played a conspicuous part in the battles of the 15th cent., and particularly in that of Harlaw (see p. 258).

11 m. **Park Stat.**, on l. is a Bridge over the Dee to ($1\frac{1}{2}$ m.) *Durris Ho.*, beyond which is a tower, built upon an eminence, in honour of the last Duke of Gordon. At 12 m. l. is *Park Ho.*

[6 m. N. is the village of *Echt*, and 1 m. beyond that is the *Barmekine* (a corruption of Barbican) of Dunecht. It is a conical hill covered with fir-trees, but having on it 5 concentric lines of fortification, 2 of which are still of considerable height. These ramparts are built of rubble stones, without mortar, yet with a regularity approaching to a face of masonry, and not mere heaps of stones; it is the most perfect ancient fort in the N. of Scotland. Near the fortress are several stone cairns. *Dunecht*, $1\frac{1}{4}$ m. N., the chief seat in Scotland of the Earl of Crawford and Balcarres (Lindsay), is a handsome modern mansion grafted on to an older house, with a fine *library*, *chapel*, and *observatory*, established by the late Lord Crawford (d. 1880), the theft of whose body in 1881, from the mausoleum, caused a widespread sensation. Lord Crawford presented his valuable astronomical instruments to Edinburgh (1888), and an observatory is being erected, 1894, on Blackford Hill (p. 64) for their reception. 2 m. W. of Echt is the picturesque turreted mansion of *Midmar* (Sir R. and Lady Gordon Cathcart). *Coach* daily from Echt to Aberdeen 12 m.]

14 m. **Crathes Stat.** with a bridge across the Dee. At 15 m. rt. is *Crathes Cas.* (Colonel Sir T. Burnett of Leys), on the slope of a wooded hill.

The original portion is the old double square tower, to which additions have been made at various times. Its top is surmounted by conical turrets, and has a number of dormer windows; but the lower stories exhibit the old precautionary style of building, plain and dark. It contains a fine vaulted hall, and a room with ancient decorations as well as some good oak carving, and some family portraits, including the 1st Bart. by Jamesone, 1626. A branch of the house of Burnett produced Gilbert Burnet, Bp. of Sarum, author of the "History of His Own Times."

On l. about $2\frac{1}{2}$ m. S.W. is *Tilquhillie Cas.* (J. W. E. J. Douglass, Esq.), backed up in the distance by the mountains at the head of Glen Dye, conspicuous amongst which is *Clochnaben* (1944 ft.).

17 m. **Banchory Stat.** opposite the junc. of the Feugh with the Dee. *Bridge of Feugh*, $\frac{1}{4}$ m. up stream, is a picturesque spot. $\frac{1}{2}$ m. W. is

BANCHORY ✲, a long neat village, with many villas, well situated above the Dee, here crossed by a bridge. The *Burnett Park Recreation Ground* was presented to the village by the late Sir R. Burnett of Leys in 1887.

[EXCURSIONS :—

(1) Drive S. by *Glen Dye* and *Cairn o' Mount* to *Brechin* (Rte. 52).

(2) Drive up the *Feugh* to *Whitestanes Inn*✱, 6 m., and at 8 m. turn rt. by *Finzean Ho.* (Dr. R. Farquharson, M.P.), *Ballogie Ho.* (W. E. Nicol, Esq.), and *Birse Ch.* to *Aboyne*, 16 m.

(3) Walk up the Feugh 8 m. beyond Whitestanes Inn to *Birse Cas.* in the *Forest of Birse*, 14 m.; thence N. in 6 m. to *Aboyne* 20 m., or S. in 8 m. to *Tarfside, Glen Esk* (p. 273), 22 m.]

The line leaves the river for a time, missing the pretty scenery passed by the road to Aboyne. At 19 m. l. is *Inchmarlo Ho.*, beyond which are the reservoirs of the Aberdeen Water Works, and across the river *Blackhall* (J. T. Hay, Esq.), prettily placed among woods.

$21\frac{1}{2}$ m. **Glassel Stat.** On rt. is the *Hill of Fare*, 1545 ft., in a hollow of which to the S.E., at *Corrichie*, a fight took place 28th Oct. 1562 between the Earl of Huntly and his son, Sir John Gordon (p. 259), and the Earl of Moray (in the presence of his sister, Mary Queen of Scots), in which Huntly, the great potentate of N.E. Scotland, was defeated and slain, and the power of the House of Gordon broken. A well near the place is still called Queen Mary's Well. On the S. slope of the Hill of Fare is *Campfield* (A. H. Hall, Esq.); *Craigmyle* (J. Gordon, Esq.) is rt. before reaching

24 m. **Torphins Stat.** ✲ 2 m. rt., finely situated, is *Learney* (Col. Innes); 2 m. l. is the village of **Kincardine-O'Neil** ✲ on the Dee, a favourite resort of those who wish pure and bracing air. 2 m. farther down the river is *Potarch Bridge* ✲, where the scenery is very picturesque, and whence a road runs S.E. in 4 m. to *Whitestanes Inn*, and thence N.E. to Banchory (p. 275), or S. to Brechin (Rte. 52). Beyond Torphins the line crosses the pretty dingle of the Beltie Burn, having on l. *Pitmurchie* (J. H. Bowers, Esq.), and 1 m. up the stream, *Findrack* (W. N. Fraser, Esq.).

27 m. **Lumphanan Stat.** ✲, to the rt. of which, and close to the line, is the "*Peel Bog*," a circular earthwork, about 120 ft. in diameter and 18 ft. high, surrounded by a moat. It was probably constructed about the 10th cent., and Lord Hailes supposes that Macbeth made his last stand here. Farther on is *Macbeth's Cairn*, supposed to mark the place where Macbeth, fleeing from his castle at Dunsinane, met his death at the hands of Macduff.

[Road N. to *Alford* on the Don 8½ m. (p. 294).]

The line now runs southward to

29½ m. **Dess Stat.** on the Dess Burn. High up on l. is *Desswood* (A. Davidson, Esq.), in a beautiful situation, commanding views over 3 m. of the Dee's course. Across the river is *Carlogie* (W. E. Nicol, Esq.). Kincardine-O'Neil (above) is 2 m. E. from this stat.

32½ m. **Aboyne Stat.** ✲, sometimes called Charlestown of Aboyne—from its founder the Marquis of Huntly (Earl of Aboyne)—a neat village, arranged around a Green where monthly sheep and cattle markets are held, and surrounded by distant hills. Close to the stat. is the Lodge of *Aboyne Cas.* (Marq. of Huntly), a building of ancient foundation, but, as it stands, chiefly modern (1671-1801). By entering the gate opposite the Rom. Cath. Chapel you may obtain a distant view of the house, and turning l. into the wood may see an ancient *Circle* of 5 stones, and near it a carved granite *Cross* with vermicular ornaments. The bridge over the Dee at Aboyne was swept away by the floods in 1829, and is replaced by a handsome *suspension bridge*, from which a good view up and down the Dee is obtained.

[On rt. is a road to *Tarland* and *Strathdon* (p. 294); on l. routes cross the Dee to *Banchory*, *Glen Dye*, and *Glen Esk* (see Banchory).]

Glentana, running S.W. from Aboyne, is highly picturesque, and stretches up to Mt. Keen. Up the glen, 5 m. from Aboyne, a shooting-lodge has been converted into a residence by Sir W. Cunliffe Brooks, Bt., who has there rebuilt, with heather-thatched roof and rustic woodwork, the *Ch. of St. Lemno*[1] (Episcopal), containing fragments of an ancient oratory.

From Aboyne the rly. runs across the *Moor of Dinnet*—a bleak unpromising tract of country—to

37 m. **Dinnet Stat.** ✲. 1½ m. rt. is *Loch Cean-ord* (or *Ceander*), a very pretty lake, fringed with wood, and a good place for finding aquatic plants. On one of its islands is a small fort, once a stronghold of the Celtic princes of the district, and occupied also in the Middle Ages.

[Beyond the loch is seen the fine range of **Culblean**, which was the scene of a battle in 1335 between David Bruce and the Earl of Atholl. The cairns in the neighbourhood are said to cover the slain.

1 *Service on Sundays—open to all—when family at home.*

2½ m. N.W. of the stat., across the moor, is the **Burn of the Vat**, a singular fissure at the base of Culblean, out of which a small burn issues not far from the road. The entrance is so narrow and concealed by fallen blocks that it is hard to find, except by following up the stream to a scar on the hillside, where it issues out by one narrow aperture, and the explorer may enter by another. A few yards beyond this its rocky walls, of a large-grained easily-disintegrated granite, 40 ft. to 50 ft. high, expand into a circular cauldron, in the shape of a dome, formed, no doubt, by the burn, when augmented by floods and impeded in its course by the narrowness of its outlet, forming a sort of whirlpool and turning round in its vortex the boulders and pebbles which it had brought down. It is a rough but not difficult walk of about 1 m. up the burn to the head of the glen, whence it is 5 m. across the hill to Ballater.]

39½ m. **Cambus o' May Stat.**

On rt. behind Culblean may be seen the grand mountain mass of **Morven** (2862 ft.).

At *Ballatrich*, upon the opposite side of the Dee, Byron spent some weeks of his boyhood, hence the lines:—

"When I see some dark hill point its crest to the sky,
I think of the rocks that o'ershadow Culblean."

The line now passes an obelisk memorial to Farquharson of Monaltrie, and the *Pannanich Wells Hotel*, a long white building on the other side of the river, near mineral wells strongly impregnated with iron. The scenery now improves as the tourist nears Ballater, the bleak moorland giving place to mountain scenery of a picturesque description.

43½ m. **BALLATER Stat.** ✲ is finely placed on the l. bank of the Dee, just below the junction of the *River Muick*, which descends through a grand glen from the E. flanks of Lochnagar. It is surrounded by wooded hills and distant mountains. A granite bridge (opened 1885 by the Queen) crosses the Dee, a substitute for the wooden successsor to the fine old granite bridge which was swept away by the flood of 1829. A building with a tower, close to the stat., serves the purpose of a town-hall and post-office, along with that of a memorial to Prince Albert.

In summer Ballater is very full of visitors, who resort to it for the purity of its air and the beauty of its situation. The mountain excursions are numerous, but towards the stalking season the hills are jealously watched by keepers, in order that the deer may not be disturbed.

1½ m. S. of Ballater is *Glenmuick House*, the modern residence of Sir A. R. Mackenzie, Bt., whose father built an *Episcopal Chapel*. On the N. of the village rises the wooded **Craig-an-Darroch** (1250 ft.). At its foot is *Monaltrie House* (A. H. Farquharson, Esq. of Invercauld). There is a fine view from the summit, which is easy of access, a path running up from about ¼ m. along the Braemar road. It seems to have been split off from the mass of Culblean, for behind it runs a precipitous wooded ravine, called the *Pass of Ballater*. In the distance behind rises *Morven* (2862 ft.), remarkable for having scarcely any heather upon its sides, though the lower portions are thickly clad with juniper.

EXCURSIONS :—

(1) *Walk* N. by *Pass of Ballater* round **Craig-an-Darroch** (1250 ft.), 5 m.; also ascend to the top for the excellent view.

(2) *Drive* E. to **Pannanich Wells**, (2 m.), and **Ballatrich**, 5 m. (see above).

(3) *Walk* N.E. across the hill to the **Burn of the Vat**, 5 m.; or drive by *Loch Ceander* (see above, and p. 276).

(4) N. **Ascent of Morven**, 7 m.

(5) *Drive* S.W. by *Glen Muick* to **Loch Muick**—the Royal Domain, 11 m.

See Map, p. 282.

There are roads for 8½ m. up both sides of the Muick, and by fording a round can be made; but that on the l. bank is the *Queen's Drive*, and not always accessible to tourists. Having crossed the Dee, after a short mile we cross or pass the *Bridge of Muick*. At 2 m. on the W. bank are the beautiful woods of *Birkhall*, now the property of the Queen. At 5 m. is the *Linn of Muick* and *Falls of Muick*, where the scenery is very charming; above this the glen is rather monotonous and bare. At 8½ m. on the W. side of the glen, 1 m. short of the foot of the loch, is *Alt-na-giuthasach*, or "*The Hut*" (H.M. the Queen), in which the Queen and Prince Consort first stayed upon Aug. 30, 1849, and which was afterwards occupied by the Court when the Queen stayed at the *Glassalt Shiel*, 2½ m. farther on, on the N. side of **Loch Muick**, a beautiful sheet of water 2½ m. long, and hemmed in on all sides but one by steep mountains. The *Glassalt Shiel* was built by the Queen in 1868, and of it she says—"The sad thought struck me that it was the first *widow's house*, not built by him or hallowed by his memory. But I am sure his blessing does rest on it, and on those who live in it." Beyond, there are riding paths to *Dhu Loch* which is guarded by the precipices of Lochnagar on the N. and of Cairn Bannoch on the S.

(6) S.W. **Ascent of Lochnagar**—12 m. to the top—one of the most prominent features in Byron's Highland reminiscences, which neither time nor distance effaced from his memory—

"The infant rapture still survived the boy,
And Lochnagar with Ida looked o'er Troy."

The mountain is 3786 feet above the level of the sea (Ballater itself being 668 ft.). Drive up Glen Muick, 8½ m., as far as *Alt-na-giuthasach* (above). From this point there is a good path to the summit. Ponies and guides may be hired at Ballater. There is also a path from Crathie, near Balmoral (frequently closed to the public), and the ascent may also be made from Braemar (see p. 282, where the view from the top is described).

(7) S. by *Glen Muick* and *Capel Mount* to **Clova**, 18 m. (p. 271).

(8) S.E. by *Glen Mark* and *Glen Esk* to **Edzell**, 29 m. (Rte. 53).

(9) N.W. by *Glen Gairn* and *Glen Finzie* to **Cock Bridge** ✲, on the Don, 15½ m. (p. 296), and thence by **Tomintoul**, 25½ m. (p. 231), to **Grantown-on-Spey**, 40 m. (p. 229), through wild country all the way.

An exceedingly steep but driving road, ascending to 2048 ft. No change of horses is possible on the way, and it is advisable to order a carriage from Grantown to be in waiting at Tomintoul.

(10) To **Balmoral**, 8 m., and **Braemar**, 16½ m. (below).

Coach daily—3 times in summer.

See Map, p. 282.

The road to Braemar, ascending the l. bank of the Dee, winds round Craig-an-Darroch, passes Craig-an-Darroch Lodge, with the Dee brawling beneath, and the entrance to the Pass of Ballater.

At 1½ m. is *Bridge of Gairn*, where the Gairn is crossed, and the Strathdon road turns off rt. The road now lies through a district pleasantly diversified with wood and affording charming scenery. On l. is *Craig Youzie*, "Hill of Firs"; in front may now be seen the *Prince's Cairn*.

At 6 m., on the opposite bank, is **Abergeldie Castle**, an old turreted square tower, enlarged by modern additions, which used to be inhabited by the Duchess of Kent, now leased by the Queen. The river is crossed here by a wire suspension bridge. At 7 m. (rt.) is the modern *Parish Ch.* of **Crathie**, built of granite (A. M. Mackenzie, A.R.S.A., Aberdeen, architect), and of which the Queen laid the foundation stone on 11th September, 1893. It has superseded the ugly old ch. so often attended by Her Majesty, who presented it with stained glass windows commemorative of the Prince Consort and of Rev. Dr. Norman Macleod. In the ch.-yard is a gray granite monument erected by the Queen over the grave of her faithful attendant, John Brown, d. 1883. Beyond Crathie is the obelisk to the memory of the late Prince Consort, put up by his tenantry. Above this is the Cairn and monumental *Statue* of the Prince. A magnificent view is obtained of Lochnagar, rising behind and above two nearer and lower peaks. There is a suspension footbridge over the Dee at Crathie, leading to the Free Ch. and the Lochnagar Distillery. On the hill beyond is seen the pyramidal cairn raised to the memory of Prince Albert by his tenantry, and on other neighbouring heights are many other commemorative *cairns* to various members of the Queen's family.

[The *Ascent of Lochnagar* may be made from this point, but only at certain times; there is a good path to the foot of the mountain.

A public bridge crosses the Dee to Balmoral, but there is no public road *south* of the river from Balmoral to Braemar.]

At 8 m. on a plain, at the foot of the hill of *Craig-an-Gowan*, and bounded by a curve of the Dee, stands **Balmoral Castle**, the Queen's Scottish residence. The reversion of the lease of the property was acquired in 1848 by Prince Albert from the trustees of the late Sir Robert Gordon, and on its expiry the estate itself was purchased from the trustees of the Earl of Fife for £31,500. It is a castellated palatial mansion in the mixed Elizabethan and Scottish style, with a tall and picturesque tower at one end, flanked by turrets. The whole is of white Crathie granite, and was designed and planned by the Prince Consort, to occupy the place of an older building. Near the entrance is a bronze statue of the Prince. There is also a bronze *Jubilee Statue* of the Queen erected by the tenantry. The interior is not shown; nor, indeed, is there anything within to reward curiosity, the whole arrangement being simple in the extreme, but in perfect good taste, and suited to a Highland residence. The chief ornament is a statue (by Theed) of the Prince Consort, in his Highland dress, in the corridor, which is hung with stags' horns and other hunting decorations. The castle and grounds are seen from the high road, together with the model farm and schools built by Her Majesty. The ball-room, for occasional festivities of the Queen's retainers, occupies a detached wing to the N. The gardens and half-wild grounds, very picturesque, planted by the Prince with rare conifers and forest trees, stretch to the top of the fine wooded hill, Craig-an-Gowan.

Beyond, the road passes on rt. the remains of the old house of *Monaltrie*, burned in 1745; on l. is a cairn on a hill, to commemorate the marriage of the Princess Alice, and, farther on, one commemorating that of the Princess Royal. In the valley between them is the Home Farm of Balmoral. Good views of Lochnagar are obtained from the high road through the vista of *Glen Gelder*, up which is a private drive leading to a lodge. Just at the edge of the river is a small mound, on which is a group of firs. This is the *Cairn-na-cuimhne*, or Cairn of Remembrance, it having been the custom of the Farquharsons to assemble here previous to an expedition, and deposit each man a stone. On their return they each picked one off, and the number left on the cairn marked the loss of the clan.

At 10 m. is **Inver Inn** ✲. The hills now begin to close in.

Left is **Ballochbuie Deer Forest**, which, along with that of Balmoral, belongs to the Queen. The woods which fringe it are exceedingly beautiful.

[The walks and drives through them are private, but visitors on foot or in carriage are admitted at the lodge, close to Invercauld Bridge (below). The drive thence of 1 m., to the **Falls of Garrawalt**, is very pretty. They are not remarkable for depth or height, the stream descending by a number of small leaps, overhung by dark firs or graceful birches, yet the effects are very picturesque, and a fine retrospective view is obtained from the bridge thrown over the Falls. Tourists must keep the prescribed road. The Garra walt Falls are 4 m. from Braemar.]

At (14 m.) *Invercauld Bridge* the

road to Castleton of Braemar crosses the Dee, while that to the magnificent domain of Invercauld continues along the l. bank.

The country here is finely wooded, with abrupt bold hills, conspicuous among which is *Craig Cluny* (on l.), a towering cliff, fringed with pines, and overhanging the road. Not quite halfway up it are the remains of an old tower, which goes by the name of the "Laird of Cluny's Charter Chest," because there, in unsettled times and when pressed by enemies, the laird of Cluny used to hide his title-deeds. The valley here expands, and presently *Invercauld House*, the seat of A. H. Farquharson, Esq., comes in sight on the opposite (l.) bank of the Dee; it dates in part from the 15th cent., and received the addition of a tower on its old foundations, and other improvements in the Baronial style, 1874. On the rising of the Earl of Mar, 1715, he dated from this house his address calling out the clans, whose chiefs were assembled here.

At 15½ m. the road passes under a crag (l.) called "*The Lion's Face*," from a supposed resemblance, while (rt.) between the road and the river is **Braemar Castle**, a tall plain whitewashed building, of 1628, also belonging to the laird of Invercauld. It occupies a fine situation, and after 1715 was long used as a barrack, garrisoned by Hanoverians, to keep the Highlanders in check. The annual Highland games are generally held in front of it in August or September, and are attended not only by the Deeside clans, but also by those of Strathdon and Atholl, being frequently honoured by the Queen's presence. Opposite the castle, on the other side of the Dee, is a monument to the late Mr. Farquharson of Invercauld. Rounding a sharp turn and passing the little churchyard, the tourist reaches

16½ m. **CASTLETON OF BRAEMAR** ✲ on the *Clunie Water* above its junc. with the Dee. It is a scattered double village, that portion of it lying W. of the Clunie being called **Auchindryne.** It stands 1100 ft. above the sea, and is celebrated for the extreme purity and bracing character of its air. Although it has changed from a rough Highland hamlet to a tidy watering-place it is not overgrown, as building is largely restricted. There are *Estab.*, *Free*, *Epis.*, and *R.C. Churches*, and 2 *Public* (*Jubilee*) *Halls*—that in Auchindryne having been built by the Duke of Fife.

A fragment of wall in a clump of trees near the bridge over the Clunie, which dashes in leaps and falls through the midst of the village to join the Dee, marks the site of the ancient castle of Braemar, which is assigned to the age of Malcolm Canmore. The rock upon which the Earl of Mar raised the standard of rebellion in 1715 has been removed to make way for the coffee-room of the Invercauld Arms.

In the midst of the village are the scientific instruments belonging to the *meteorological* station established here by the Prince Consort.

From the advantages it possesses for enjoying the finest mountain scenery in Scotland, Braemar is a great centre of attraction, but the proximity of deer forests and of the Royal Domain greatly restricts freedom of rambling over the hills.

EXCURSIONS:—[1]

(1) *Walks* by the banks of the Clunie and the Dee.

(2) Ascend **Morrone,** 2819 ft., the hill on the S. side of Braemar, dividing the valleys of Dee and Clunie, 3 m.

Fine view—in some respects better even

[1] Guides may be engaged from 7s. 6d. to 12s. 6d. a day, according to the expedition, and ponies hired at about the same charge.

than that from Lochnagar, as the surrounding country is more open.

(3) **Falls of Garrawalt**, 4 m. E. (see p. 279).

Walking, a grassy road—the "*Queen's Drive*"—round the S. of the "*Lion's face*," may be taken instead of the first 1½ m. of the high road.

(4) W. up the Dee to the **Fall of Corriemulzie**, 3 m., and the **Linn of Dee**, 6½ m.

As the road runs up the Dee valley the scenery is varied and interesting. It is a beautiful terrace drive, overlooking the Dee. About a mile from Braemar there is a ford across the river a little below the opening of *Glen Quoich*, which is marked by the rubbish it discharges into the Dee. As you proceed you may discern, if the weather is clear, above intervening hills, in succession the summits of the flat-topped mountains *Ben-a-Buird*, 3924 ft., *Cairngorm of Derry*, 3788 ft., and *Ben Muichdhui*, 4296 ft.

3 m. l. near the road but scarcely seen is **Mar Lodge** (Duke of Fife). Before reaching the lodge the road crosses a small bridge just above the * **Fall of Corriemulzie.** In order to see it you must enter a wicket gate on rt., and descend the glen. The pretty stream falls over a precipice about 30 ft. high, the ravine being of considerable depth, and charmingly shrouded with foliage.

On the other side of the Dee, which is crossed by the Victoria wooden bridge (closed to the public), is *Old Mar Lodge*, a seat of the Duke of Fife.

At 4½ m. the road passes the hamlet of *Inverey*, at the junction of the Ey with the Dee. It is worth while to follow that stream up for a little distance, for the sake of the views of the Ben Muichdhui range.

[½ m. up the glen the Ey receives rt. a tributary from Glen Connie. Follow the path which crosses the Ey and keeps up its l. bank. It leads to a deep chasm in the rock called the "*Colonel's Bed*," from a tradition that a Col. John Farquharson, who had been out with Claverhouse at Killiecrankie (1689), found refuge in a narrow ledge or groove in the rock a few feet above the torrent. It is a remarkable scene, the cliffs rising 50 ft. or 60 ft. above the water, and descending 20 ft. below its surface, and forming a pool as black as ink.]

6½ m. The * **Linn of Dee** is a narrow fissure between rocks of mica slate, through which the river has to struggle, fretting against the sharp sides, and tumbling down some 4 or 5 small cascades. The rocks on either side project over the water to within 4 ft. of one another, and in flood-times, when the chasm is nearly filled up by the torrent, it is very grand. To watch the salmon in crowds after a spate trying to rush up this tearing race, and leaping in sheer effort out of the foam, to be dashed against the rocks, is a sight worth seeing. Lord Byron, when a boy, had a narrow escape here, by his foot catching in some heather. He fell, and was rolling downwards, when an attendant seized hold of him and saved his life.

A bridge of white Aberdeen granite over the Linn "erected by James, 5th Earl of Fife, was opened on 8th Sept. 1857 by H.M. Queen Victoria."

Return may be made by the Linn of Quoich [see (5)].

(5) W. to **Linn of Quoich**, 4 m. (direct), *or* by the Linn of Dee, 11 m.

The *Quoich Water*, which rises between Ben-na-Buird and Ben Avon, and joins the Dee about 1½ m. above Braemar, here rushes, amid picturesque surroundings, over a succession of rocky ledges, and in its fretted course, whirling the loose stones along with it, has scooped out several hollows in the micaceous schist, which have earned for it the name of "*Quoich*" (cup).

In order to reach it the Dee must be crossed. There is a ford about 1 m. above Braemar practicable for carriages, except when the Dee is high, and there is a private ferry-boat lower down, sometimes available for foot-passengers. Access may also be got driving by Invercauld Bridge and the l. bank of the Dee (9 m.), but the gates on this road are not always open. Failing these one must, and in any case going should drive round by the Linn of Dee (p. 281), keep the l. bank of the Dee to the mouth of Glen Quoich, and then up the rt. bank of the Quoich.

(6) S.E. to **Lochnagar** (3786 ft.), "The Jewel of the Mountains," as the Queen has styled it.—abt. 12 m.

Drive 2 m. up the *Clunie*, and then l. along a very rough road, up the *Callater Burn*—crossing a bridge not always very safe—to (5 m.) a small shooting lodge at the N. end of *Loch Callater* (1 m. long), where the horse can be put up.

A well-marked path, practicable for ponies and not easily missed except in case of mist, clouds, or snow, leads up the hill l. from behind the lodge, the ascent requiring from 2½-3 hrs. It is carried along the hillside, rough and stony above the loch, but on leaving it behind, turns l. up a shallow glen. Striking across the head of it you keep rt., along the slope of *Cairn Taggart* (Priest's Hill) round the shoulder of which the path makes a semi-circle, before descending to cross a small burn which separates Cairn Taggart from *Cairn of Corbreach*. [Good climbers, however, are recommended to keep up the side of the railing from the shallow glen, and cross the summit of Cairn Taggart (3430 ft.), which otherwise obstructs the view to the N. during the ascent.] This is the Muick Water, which rising in some springs high up on the l. passes through Dhu Loch, on the S. side of the Cairn of Corbreach, and thence into Loch Muick. Toiling up the slopes of the Cairn of Corbreach a plateau is soon reached, and the highest peaks of Lochnagar come into view in front. Keep l. and look down the precipices into the *N. Dhu Loch* ("Black Loch"), beyond which is the *Loch-an-Eoin* ("Bird's Loch"), in which the Garrawalt takes its rise. The central summit (3768 ft.) is exceeded in height by the N. point—*Cac Carn Beag* (3786 ft.). To the N.E. of these peaks is *Loch-na-Gar* (Loch of the goat), which gives its name to the mountain. Nestling at the foot of precipices about 1000 ft. perpendicular, which nearly enclose it, it affords a scene of sublimity and desolation not to be forgotten. Lochnagar, with its corries and precipices, is of granite,—"a rock which, from its usual decomposing character, and its abundant vertical joints, combines in its decay a grandeur of lofty cliff with a smoothness of mountain top, such as none of the other Highland rocks can boast."—Sir A. GEIKIE.

The grand view comprises the low ground of the *Balmoral Forest* and *Ballater*, and the following mountains:—N.W. the magnificent range of *Ben Avon*, *Ben-a-Buird*, *Ben Muich-dhui*, *Braeriach*, and *Cairn Toul;* W. *Ben Nevis* (more easily identified from Cairn Taggart); S.W. *Glas Maol*, *Ben-y-Gloe*, *Schiehallion*, *Ben Lawers*, *Ben More*, and *Ben Cruachan;* S. the *Forfarshire Hills* and the *Lomonds* in Fife; N.E. *Morven* and *Bennachie*; N. *Ben Rinnes*, etc. You may descend direct to Ballater (p. 278), or by the Dhu Loch to Loch Muick, or, having recrossed the Muick Water, keep S. over the 3200 ft. plateau, and descend to Clova by Glen Doll or Glen Esk (p. 269).

(7) S.E. to **Clova**, 19 m., and **Kirriemuir**, 34½ m. (Rte. 50).

(8) N.W. to **Aviemore** by the *Larig Ghru*, 30 m. (Rte. 56).

(9) N.W. to **Ben Muich-dhui**, **Cairngorm**, and **Aviemore**, 32 m. (Rte. 57).

(10) S. by *Spital of Glenshee* to **Dunkeld**, 47 m. (*Coach* daily), or (no coach) to **Pitlochrie**, 40¼ m. (Rte. 58).

(11) S.W. to **Blair Atholl** by *Glen Tilt*, 29 m. (Rte. 59).

(12) W. to **Kingussie**, 34 m., or **Kincraig**, 32 m., by *Glen Feshie* (p. 288).

(13) N.E. by *Balmoral*, 8½ m., Rinloan Inn, 13 m., to **Cock Bridge**, 23½ m. (p. 296); thence to **Tomintoul**, 33½ m., and Grantown-on-Spey, 47½ m.—a *very* heavy road [cf. Ballater (9)]. *Or*, Drive to *Loch Builg* (ascending to fully 2000 ft.), 13 m. Walk in 3½ m. to Inchrory Lodge (p. 297), where, 7 m. from Tomintoul, carriages (from Grantown) can be met.

ROUTE 56.

See Maps, pp. 282, 232.

Braemar to Aviemore by the Larig Ghru—For Pedestrians —30 m.

[Described the reverse way at p. 228.]

This route leads over probably the wildest and grandest pass in Scotland (2750 ft.) and through the lofty range of the Cairngorm Mountains. But the distance from Braemar to the Spey at Aviemore is fully 30 m., and there is scarce a hut, and no inn or house of shelter on the way, therefore only robust pedestrians should attempt it. Take provisions and waterproof. The expedition from Braemar to Aviemore Stat. will occupy quite 12 hours. Remember that the path is exceedingly rough, and the consequences of not getting through Rothiemurchus Forest before darkness comes on may be very serious; also that at present (1894) the nearest inn to Aviemore is *Lynwilg*, 2½ m. beyond the station.

The first 9½ m. can be driven. The road as far as the Linn of Dee (6 m.) is described at p. 281.

The Dee is crossed and its left bank followed for 3 miles—rather monotonous—to 9½ m., where there is a wooden bridge over the river.

[Or the road from the *Linn of Dee* to *Derry Lodge* (see p. 284) may be taken, and thence by Glen Lui Beg into Glen Dee 8½ m. above the Linn.]

Across this bridge is the road to Bynach Lodge for *Glen Tilt* (see Rte. 59) and to *Glen Feshie* (see pp. 288, 226). At this bridge the right-of-way path begins, keeping up Glen Dee along the l. bank of the river.

Soon the most magnificent scenery of Glen Dee opens up, while looking back *Lochnagar* and *Ben-y-Gloe* can be seen. To the rt. is *Ben Muich-dhui*; to the l. *Ben Bhrotain*, and in front the imposing *Devil's Point* (3303 ft.)—the S.E. shoulder of *Cairn Toul* (4241 ft.)—which separates 2 tremendous corries or dark glens, each sending its tributary to the infant Dee. The S. one, the mouth of which is passed at 15 m., is *Glen Geusachan*, opposite which rt. is the depression leading to Glen Lui Beg and Derry Lodge (see p. 284). The N. one, the mouth of which is passed 3 m. farther on, is that down which the *Garrachorry Burn* leaps from its springs—the highest Sources of the Dee—4000 ft. up on *Braeriach* (see p. 228). This corrie, flanked on the N. by *Braeriach*, and on the S. by *Cairn Toul* (4241 ft.), and with *Ben Muich-dhui* (4296 ft.) opposite, is for solitary grandeur unsurpassed in Scotland. If there are mists rolling in it, as if boiling in a mighty cauldron, the majesty of the scene will be, if possible, enhanced.

At 19 m. are the (so-called) **Wells of Dee**, 3 lovely clear tarns out of which the Dee flows in subterraneous passages below the rocks. The walking, or rather climbing over boulders, is very fatiguing for a mile to

20 m. the summit (2750 ft.) of the **Larig Ghru**, as this Pass is called (see p. 228).

Aberdeenshire is now left and Inverness-shire entered.

About 2 m. on the other side of the crest the geologist will notice a great extent of glacier moraine. The path—better marked—keeps down the rt. bank of the stream, but by degrees diverges from it, entering the outskirts (24 m.) of *Rothiemurchus Forest*. It keeps through the heather for 2 miles more, when it turns l. to a grassy field close to the river. At the N. end of the field and just after a trib. has come in from the W. the stream is crossed by a foot-bridge. The l. bank of the united stream is kept for 2 m. to

28 m. *Coylum Bridge* (see p. 228, etc.), thence l. by carriage road to

30 m. **Aviemore Stat.** ✲, see p. 227.

ROUTE 57.

See Maps, pp. 282, 232.

Braemar to Aviemore across Ben Muich-dhui and Cairn Gorm. (After 10 m. for Pedestrians only)—33 m.

If walking all the way, allow 13-15 hours. Although the height ascended is much greater, this is probably (on a clear day) an easier route than that through the *Larig Ghru* (Rte. 56), as the ground is less rough. By those to whom both routes are too fatiguing the **Ascent of Ben Muich-Dhui** (18 m.) may be made from Braemar by starting early and driving to Glen Derry (called 12 m., really only 10 m.); the rest of the work may be got through on foot or pony-back, and a return made to Braemar by nightfall (guide and pony 25s.). Warm wraps should be taken, as the warmth of the weather on Deeside is no criterion whatever of what its severity may be 3000 ft. higher up.

As far as the *Linn of Dee* (6½ m.) the road is described at p. 281. Crossing the bridge the road leaves the Dee and strikes N. up *Glen Lui* to

10 m. *Derry Lodge* (D. of Fife), with a forester's cottage, beautifully situated near the junction of the *Derry* with the *Lui Beg* (which together form the *Lui Water*) and surrounded on all sides by mountains. Here carriages must be left.

[Up the *Lui Beg* for 2 m. then l. to the S. of *Cairn Maim* is one way (3½ m.) to *Glen Dee*, which is struck abt. 16 m. from Braemar (see Rte. 56).]

The path to Ben Muich-dhui keeps up Glen Derry. The top is 8 m. distant and it will take fully 3 hours to reach it. Cross the Derry by a foot-bridge, and keep alongside its rt. bank through an open wood of firs, which the wind and floods are rapidly thinning. At the end of this cross the Derry again; a naked glen succeeds, bounded on the N. by *Ben-na-Main* (3883 ft.) [distinguished by cairns on the summit], and behind which is Loch A'an or Avon. On the l. is *Cairngorm of Derry* (3788 ft.), through a deep corrie of which, on the N. side, the *Water of Etchachan*, as the upper part of the Derry is called, flows. About 4 m. from Derry Lodge, where the stream forks, keep the l. feeder, soon cross to its rt. bank, and climb W. up *Corrie Etchachan* to (16 m.) *Loch Etchachan*, which is passed on the rt., "lying like a drop of ink at the base of a huge, dark, mural precipice."

[By keeping to the E. side of Loch Etchachan and due N. till a stream is reached, and following down its l. bank, a steep descent may be made in 1 m. to the wildly grand **Loch A'an** and the "Clach Dhian," or "*Shelter Stone*," a huge rock of granite fallen from above upon smaller blocks which support it, forming a cave capable of holding more than half a dozen persons, the only refuge in case of a storm, and in some cases the only night's lodgings that the pedestrian can procure. It is situated ¼ m. from the S.W. end of the loch, among a number of fallen rocks of which it is the largest, between the stream by which the descent has been made and the main feeder of the loch. An easier but longer route to Loch A'an from Braemar, taken by the Queen, 28th Sept. 1861, is *not* to keep W. up Corrie Etchachan at 4 m. from Derry Lo., but to keep straight on N. to the E. of *Ben-na-Main* and to descend by the *Dhu Lochan* in other 4 m. to the N.E. end of the loch. For the approach from Cairn Gorm and the N. see p. 229.]

During the steep and long ascent splendid views are obtained of the table-land that separates Glen Derry and Glen Quoich, with the long flat outline and N. and S. summits of *Ben-a-Buird* (3924 ft.). The path is now pretty well defined, and by keeping to the l. turning nearly S. a gradual ascent leads in other 2 m. to the top of **Ben Muich-dhui** ("The mountain of the black sow") 4296 ft., a broad, level, but stony platform, marked by a cairn and the remains of the kitchen built by the Royal Engineers when surveying the district. It is the second highest mountain in Great Britain (Ben Nevis being higher by 108 ft.), is the centre of the Great Cairngorm group of the Grampians, and is flanked by 4 main outliers—to the W., across the *Larig Ghru*, *Braeriach* (4248 ft.), and *Cairn Toul* (4241 ft.), with the magnificent *Garrachorry Corrie* between; to the N. *Cairn Gorm* (4084 ft.); and to the N.E. *Ben-na-Main* (3883 ft.). Farther to the E. are *Ben-a-Buird* (3924 ft.) and *Ben Avon* (3843 ft.). All these mountains are composed of coarse-grained granite (cf. *Lochnagar*, p. 282). Transparent smoked quartz crystals are found on these mountains, often of large size, and adapted for cutting, though the particular brown crystals, known as "Cairngorms," are not limited to this district. The upper regions of these hills are bare and devoid of vegetation, but their sides are full of springs, as is usually the case in granite formations. The Lui, the Avon, and, to some extent, the Dee, spring from Ben Muich-dhui. The N.E. side of Ben Muich-dhui consists of a precipitous front from 1000 to 1500 ft. in height, beneath which lies Loch A'an, 1½ m. in length (see p. 284). The W. side also is grandly precipitous, the extraordinary character of the view consisting in the fact that it is separated from the adjoining mountains of Cairntoul and Braeriach by such narrow valleys that they may almost be called clefts.

"Standing on the western shoulder, you might almost imagine that you might throw a stone on to Braeriach. Yet between these two summits rolls the river Dee, and Braeriach presents, right opposite to the hill on which you stand, a mural precipice 2000 ft. high."—HILL BURTON.

This *knot* of giant mountains rises close upon the junction of the counties of Aberdeen, Banff, and Inverness.

Besides the view of the neighbouring heights the view down the *Dee Valley* backed by *Lochnagar*, and of the *Ben-y-Gloe* range, is very fine. The Queen describes the view which she saw after the rising of the mist upon October 7, 1859.

[A steep descent may be made down a stream W. into the Larig Ghru, 1 m. S. of the Wells of Dee (see Rte. 56).]

From Ben Muich-dhui it is a comparatively easy walk of 4 m. in about 2 hrs. along the ridge N. to

22 m. **Cairn Gorm**, 4084 ft., for which and route thence to

27 m. *Glenmore Lodge*, to which a carriage may be ordered from Nethy Bridge or Grantown, see p. 228.

33 m. **Aviemore Stat.**✲ (p. 227). *Lynwilg Inn*✲ is 2½ m. farther.

ROUTE 58.

Braemar to Dunkeld by Spital of Glenshee, Bridge of Cally, and Blairgowrie. 47 m.

A *Coach* runs every day in summer. One can drive to **Pitlochrie,** by *Spital of Glenshee* and *Kirkmichael,* 40¼ m., but there is no coach.

Between Braemar and the Spital of Glenshee the road crosses a high pass of the Grampian range, the ascent of which by horses from either side involves 4 miles at a walking pace. The road gradually ascends *Glen Clunie.*

2 m. *Achallater Farm,* where flows in on l. the Callater Burn, up which lies the road to Lochnagar (p. 282).

5 m. *Glen Baddoch* is reached on rt., and Glen Clunie makes a turn to the l. The road now becomes very steep, and by an uninterrupted ascent gains at 9 m. the summit of the pass, 2200 ft., at *Cairn Well,* and quits Aberdeenshire for Perthshire. **Glas Maol**, 3502 ft., is a fine object on the l., although it is not so broken and precipitous on the N. as on the S. side. The pedestrian who wishes for a fine scramble may cross the shoulder, and descend into Ceanlochan, and thence into Glen Isla (p. 266).

The descent from Cairn Well is much steeper than on the N. side, and at one place encounters an awkwardly made zigzag, popularly known as the **Devil's Elbow**. *Glen Beg* is followed down to the

15 m. **Spital** (*Hospital*) **of Glenshee**✲, placed at the junction of Glen Beg with Glen Lochy, the united rivers of which form the *Shee.* On the l. bank of the Shee below the junc. is a tumulus, with a clump of trees, known as Diarmid's Tomb. The church and two or three cottages form the only group of buildings between this and Braemar. Above this trees cease to grow.

[From the Spital the pedestrian who wishes to go to Pitlochrie (16 m.) takes a slanting path over the hill to the rt., striking on the other side, in 5¾ m., the Kirkmichael and Pitlochrie road below Dirnanean, 2 m. from Kirkmichael, and 10¼ m. from Pitlochrie (see below).]

As the road to Blairgowrie recedes from the Spital, the tourist gets fine views of the southern face of Glas Maol.

20 m. l. *Dalnaglar* (D. A. Paterson, Esq.), a picturesque modern house in the baronial style, sheltered by *Mt. Blair* (2441 ft.) and a forest of pines.

[A road on l. crosses the Shee, and runs to Glen Isla, over the shoulder of Mt. Blair, passing the square ruined castle of Forter. Distance to *Kirkton of Glen Isla*✱ 7 m. (p. 266).]

21 m. l., at *Cray*, the scenery is pleasing.

22½ m., we pass *Glenkilrie* (Trs. of Mr. P. A. Fraser) on rt., and across the river *Drumfork*.

23½ m., *Dalrulzian House* (J. Small, Esq.) on l.

[At 24 m., a carriage road is given off rt. to *Kirkmichael* 4 m., passing halfway (rt.) the entrance to *Ashintully Cas.* (Mrs. Rutherford Lindsay).

Kirkmichael✱ is a village on the l. side of the *Ardle*, 12¼ m. from *Pitlochrie*—to which there is mail-gig (coach in summer) daily—and 7 m. from *Bridge of Cally* (see below).

There is a faint track from here over the hills S.W. to *Tullymet* and *Ballinluig Stat.* (p. 219), 8 m.

To Pitlochrie the road keeps up the l. bank of the Ardle, passing (1 m.) rt. *Balvarran* (Miss Keir of Kindrogan), 2 m. rt., *Invercroskie* and *Dirnanean* (both J. Small, Esq.), charmingly placed on a burn, down the rt. bank of which comes the direct path from the Spital of Glenshee (see p. 285). At the bridge over this burn is *Enochdhu Post* and *Tel. Office.* Across the Ardle l. is *Kindrogan* (Miss Keir) backed by *Kindrogan Hill*, a fine wooded crag.

At 3¼ m. the glen forks rt. up *Glen Fernach*, and l. (to Pitlochrie) up *Glen Brerachan* past *Straloch Ch.* and *P.O.*

At 6¼ m., just beyond *Clunskea* and below *Stronhavie* (rt.), the road crosses the stream, and begins to ascend steadily.

[From this point a *footpath* on rt. follows the stream and turns up the Glen between *Ben Vrackie* and *Ben Vuroch.* It crosses the ridge and comes into the head of Glen Girnaig, which it descends to Killiecrankie, 8 m., or, crossing the Girnaig, joins a track keeping round the S. shoulder of *Cairn Liath*, by *Loch Moraig* (p. 223) and the *Fender Valley* to Blair Atholl, 11 m.]

For nearly 3 m. the road to Pitlochrie ascends the hill, facing Ben Vrackie, which is remarkably broken and fine. Higher up on rt. Ben-y-Gloe, with its tremendous precipices, becomes the prominent feature. From the summit of the hill (1224 ft.) 3½ m. above Pitlochrie there is a most superb view over the mountains of Perthshire, among which Schiehallion and Ben Lawers are conspicuous. The road then descends through *Moulin* to **Pitlochrie**✱ (p. 220).]

At 24½ m. a track leads rt. (in 3 m.) to *Balnabroch* on Strath Ardle, across an elevated moor with a rocking-stone and early remains well worth visiting by an antiquary. They consist of clusters of circular walls, one of which, known as the "Gray Cairn," is 90 ft. round. In the neighbourhood are other circles of nearly equal dimensions, showing that the district was one of importance in pre-Christian times. Calcined bones have also been found, together with stone tools.

Keeping down Glenshee at 25 m. a road strikes off l. crossing the *Blackwater*, as the Shee is now called, to Alyth (9½ m.), see p. 266.

26 m. **Persie Ch.**, built as a Chapel of Ease abt. 1785. In a field l. cattle auctions are sometimes held.

27½ m. l. across the river is *Ashmore* (J. Pattullo, Esq.), finely situated. A steep descent with *Strone Ho.* (G. Constable, Esq.) l. is made to

29 m. **Bridge of Cally**✲ over the Ardle. The view from the bridge is charming looking up the stream, which is also spanned by an old ruined bridge.

[A road runs up the l. bank of the Ardle to *Kirkmichael*, 7 m., passing at 1½ m. l. *Cally Ho.* (J. C. Constable, Esq.), and across the stream *Blackcraig* (Trs. of Mr. P. A. Fraser), a fine baronial seat where Mr. Gladstone spent his autumn holidays 1893. The scenery continues pleasing but not striking. For Kirkmichael and road thence to Pitlochrie in 12¼ m., see above.]

For the next 3 miles the road keeps the rt. bank of the *Ericht*, formed by the united waters of the

Ardle and the Blackwater. The country is smiling although somewhat tame; but the following 2 m. along the terrace above the ***Gorge of the Ericht** are picturesque in the extreme. The best *View* point is at the 3rd mile stone from Blairgowrie. The precipitous rocks, at least 200 ft. high, remind one of Hawthornden or Matlock. Sir Arch. Geikie compares it and the gorges on the Isla (p. 266) and N. Esk (p. 273), all gorges in the old red sandstone, to the cañons of the far West of America. Soon *Craighall* (Lieut.-Gen. C. Rattray, C.B.) is seen perched high up on a precipice on the oppos. side, so that a stone dropped out of one of the windows would fall into the stream.

The peculiarities of this house and its position are so exactly described by Sir Walter Scott in "Waverley," that its owner recognised it as being the original of *Tullyveolan*. Also on the l. bank but a little higher up than Craighall are the remains of a fortress known as *Lady Lindsay's Castle*.

The road crosses the Ericht close to the lodge of Craighall, and keeps the l. bank until, beyond the village of *Rattray*, it finally crosses the river to

35 m. **Blairgowrie**✡, an industrious town on the rt. bank of the Ericht, which sets in motion the wheels of several jute and flax spinning-mills, employing many hands. To the S. of it are *Blairgowrie House* and *Altamont*.

[RAILWAY, 4¾ m. to **Coupar-Angus** on the Caledonian main line from Perth to Aberdeen (p. 252), passing right the little loch of *Stormont*, with its island and castle, and then crossing the *Isla*. In this neighbourhood strawberries are cultivated in the open fields to the extent of many hundred acres. They chiefly go to fill the jam pots of Keiller of Dundee.]

The road to Dunkeld, 12 m., is rather picturesque, skirting the N. bank of a chain of lakes through which flows the *Lunan Burn*. Beyond the village of *Kinloch*✡ (2 m.) comes **Loch Marlie,** which is succeeded by (4 m.) **Loch Clunie** with an island on which is the ruined *Castle of Clunie*, built by Bp. Brown of Dunkeld about 1500, and said to have been the birthplace of the Admirable Crichton in 1560 (cf. p. 101). Between this loch and the road is *Forneth* (Miss Speid).

The road keeps to the N. of (8 m.) **Butterston Loch,** and to the W. of the beautiful **Loch of the Lowes** (p. 219), and of little **Loch Craiglush** which completes the series. *Craig-y-barns* is seen rt. as the road descends into

47 m. **DUNKELD**✡ see p. 216.

ROUTE 59.

Braemar to Blair Atholl, by Bynach Lodge and Glen Tilt.

This route (29 m. long), of which 9 m. are merely a bridle-path, is the only direct communication between Braemar and Blair Atholl. 12 m. at the N. end and 8 m. at the S. end may be done by a conveyance. A pony may go the whole way with a little care. Queen Victoria describes the route in her "Journal." There is no place of shelter or refreshment on the way, so it should not be attempted except in fine weather.

Between Bynach and Forest Lodges the rough path admits only of a foot-pace. It is quicker to walk than to ride.

A carriage may be ordered from Blair Atholl to meet the party at Forest Lodge, but it must be remembered that as soon as the deer season begins, Glen Tilt is often *closed* for carriages after noon, so that in such a case the ponies must be taken on. The right-of-way was established about 1850 after a keenly-contested lawsuit.

The first 9½ m. are the same as in Rte. 56.

At 9½ m. the Dee is crossed by a wooden bridge, Glen Dee, which stretches away to the rt., up to the Wells of Dee (Rte. 56), is left, and the l. bank of the Geldie is followed.

At 11 m. the *Geldie Burn* is forded —there is a foot-bridge 200 yds. rt.

[The path to Kingussie and Strathspey (the Queen's route) follows the l. bank of the *Geldie Burn* for some 6 m. farther, when it crosses the watershed into **Glenfeshie**, having on l. *An Sgarsoch* and *Cairn Eelar*. On the other side of the hill, cross the *Eidart* at its junction with the *Feshie*, and follow the rt. bank of the latter stream. In about 6 m. farther the *Feshie* is crossed near "The Huts," and the l. bank followed. 4 m. farther, nearly oppos. *Achlean*, at 7 m. from Kingussie the road runs straight on to Kincraig and l. to Kingussie, passing the outlet of Glen Tromie and Ruthven Barracks. The whole distance from Braemar to Kingussie is about 34 m., or to Kincraig 32 m., see p. 227.]

After crossing the Geldie the road crosses the Bynach, and reaches (12 m.) *Bynach Lodge* (Duke of Fife), where it becomes a bridle-path. The view here looking back is truly magnificent—the range of the giants *Cairntoul* (4241 ft.), *Braeriach* (4248 ft.), *Ben Muich-dhui* (4296 ft.), *Ben-a-Buird* (3924 ft.), and *Ben A'an* (3843 ft.), with the prominent *Devil's Point* (3303 ft.), guarding the upper part of Glen Dee, being imposing in the extreme. The path turns nearly due S. across an open moor, and for a mile or two is not very distinctly marked. Behind is the whole of the Ben Muich-dhui range, while in front are the steep slopes and precipices of Ben-y-Gloe. At 14 m. Perthshire is entered and soon afterwards the tiny *Tilt* comes down rt. from *Loch Tilt* (½ m. off) and is crossed. It flows through a glen

"so narrow as seldom to give room for more than the river, while in many places its channel is but a ravine through the solid rocks. This valley is distinguished by its extreme depth and narrowness, and by the wildness of its upper extremity. The ornamented beauty is confined to that part which approaches to Blair."

The peculiarity of the glen is its extreme straightness, which makes it appear in some parts almost like a gigantic canal-cutting, and the uniform steepness of the hills on both sides; in fact there are not in the whole of its course half-a-dozen places where it is possible to get out of it, except by somewhat arduous climbing.

At 15½ m. the first considerable trib. comes in l., up which a steep path leads in 1½ m. to *Falar Lodge* (Duke of Atholl).

At 16 m. the *Tarff*, a bigger stream than the Tilt, flows in from the W. in a succession of fine falls hemmed in by precipitous cliffs. The bridge over it was washed away many years ago, and until 1884 the ford through the Tarff (called the *Pil Tarff*) had to be waded—an undertaking by no means easy even in dry weather. In August 1879 Mr. Bedford, an English gentleman, was swept away and drowned while attempting to ford the Tilt, the Tarff being impassable. A suspension bridge over the Tarff in his memory, for which funds were raised by subscription, was erected in 1884. At 17 m. a stream comes in l. from *Loch Loch* behind *Cairn Gabhar*. At 18 m., above the path, there is a cairn commemorating the place where the Queen lunched on her excursion from Blair-Atholl, Oct. 9, 1861. Here there is a fine view in front of Ben-y-Gloe and Schiehallion.

At 19 m. is one of the grandest bits in the glen. The Tilt flows through a granite dyke; picturesque burns come down on both sides; striking peeps are obtained into the recesses of Ben-y-Gloe; and the old river terraces on the E. side are very marked. Across a shepherd's foot-br. the *Ascent of Ben-y-Gloe* (3671 ft.) may be made (cf. p. 223).

21 m. *Forest Lodge* is the principal shooting quarters of the Duke in the glen, or indeed in the whole of his extensive Forest of Atholl, which embraces more than 100,000 acres, and is computed to contain upwards of 15,000 head of red deer. 3000 deer were driven at once in sight of the Prince and Princess of Wales in Sept. 1872. Everything in the dis-

trict is subordinate to the breeding of deer, with which even sheep pasturing interferes. Glen Tilt was once inhabited by the clan M'Intosh, from whom it was purchased by the Earl of Atholl in 1532.

From Forest Lodge, where no accommodation or refreshment can be obtained, there is a good carriage road. At a picturesque foot-br. over the Tilt ($22\frac{1}{4}$ m.) observe the pink hue of the granite in the river bed. The view back of *Cairn Bhac*—12 m. off, 2 m. W. of Loch Tilt—with its white (quartzite) peak is very striking. Near this marble occurs, and at 24 m., just after crossing the river, a keeper's cottage, called the *Marble Lodge*, is passed. The glen, in the lower part of its course, is fringed with woods, while the river offers at every turn delicious combinations of rock and water. At 25 m. the public rt.-of-way keeps l. behind a wood, leaves the glen, ascends, keeps along the brow of the hill, and comes down to Blair-Atholl by the side of the Fender. Carriages keep straight on. At $25\frac{3}{4}$ m. a gate is passed through and at $26\frac{1}{2}$ m. the Tilt is again crossed. The river, much more rapid and very thickly wooded, becomes exceedingly fine, but to see it the carriage road must be left and paths at intervals l. to different view-points taken.

At 28 m. the Duke's grounds are left, and old Br. of Tilt is crossed l. From it is visible the *York Fall*, formed by a small trib., and above it the *Fender* joins the Tilt in a series of pretty cascades, the uppermost one being the finest. From here to the new *Br. of Tilt* the *path* by the l. side of the stream should be taken.

The *Geologist* will find Glen Tilt very interesting on account of the limestones which are associated with the rocks of the Highland Metamorphic Series. M'Culloch calls attention to its minerals, particularly those of Sahlite and Tremolite (both silicates of Magnesia). It was under the first bridge beyond the enclosure that Sir James Hall first observed the phenomenon of granite veins that proved the commencement of a most important era in geology.

29 m. **Blair-Atholl** ✲, see p. 222.

ROUTE 60

Aberdeen to Peterhead and Fraserburgh. G.N.S. Rly.

Abt. 5 trains daily in $1\frac{3}{4}$-$2\frac{1}{4}$ hrs. to Peterhead $44\frac{1}{4}$ m., and Fraserburgh $47\frac{1}{4}$ m.

This line, opened 1861, passes through the districts of *Formartine* and *Buchan*, a very characteristic portion of Aberdeenshire in a high state of cultivation, but, with some marked exceptions, somewhat treeless.

$1\frac{1}{2}$ m. **Kittybrewster Stat.**, to the rt. of which is a good view of Old Aberdeen with its two-towered Cathedral, and the crown-tower of King's College.

$2\frac{1}{4}$ m. **Woodside Stat.**

$4\frac{1}{4}$ m. **Buxburn Stat.** The vale of the Don is the scene of active industry—paper mills, woollen mills, granite quarries, etc., occurring in succession. Across the river is *Grandholm* (W. R. Paton, Esq.).

$6\frac{1}{4}$ m. **Dyce Junc. Stat.** The village lies rt. Here are extensive skating and curling ponds, large granite quarries for ornamental purposes, rly. creosote works for making "sleepers" impervious to wet, and artificial manure works. 2 m. W. is a *Stone Circle*; 1 m. N.W. is the Ch., and behind it, situated on a bend of the Don, is the *Old Pre-Reformation Ch.*, with two sculptured stones in the ch.-yd. wall. The line to Alford, Banff, and Inverness (see Rtes. 61-64) strikes off N.W.; we keep N., crossing the Don to

$7\frac{1}{2}$ m. **Parkhill Stat.**, with *Parkhill Ho.* (Alex. Gordon, Esq.) rt.

$11\frac{1}{2}$ m. **New Machar Stat.** 4 m. S.E. is *Belhelvie*, the seat of Sir H. B. Lumsden.

$14\frac{1}{2}$ m. **Udny Stat.** *Udny Castle* (J. H. Udny, Esq.), $2\frac{1}{2}$ m. N.W., is an interesting specimen of an old peel tower of 4 stories incorporated in a handsome modern house (Wardrop, Archt.). The two lower stories, one of which is entirely occupied by the hall, have groined ceilings.

$16\frac{1}{4}$ m. **Logierieve Stat.** 4 m. W. is *Tolquhon Cas.* (Earl of Aberdeen), an interesting ruined building of the baronial order. An inscription over the entrance says—"Al this warke, excep the auld tor, was begon by William Forbes, 15 Aprile 1584, and endit be him 20 Oct. 1589."

[5 m. E. is the little seaport town of **Newburgh**, at the mouth of the *Ythan*. N. of it across the river at *Forvie* are a large number of shell mounds, some of which have been opened and found to contain hearth stones, charcoal, and bones of the ox and deer.

4 m. N. along the coast is *Old Slains Cas.* (p. 292).]

$17\frac{3}{4}$ m. **Esslemont Stat.** *Esslemont Ho.* (H. Wolrige Gordon, Esq.) is seen l. among trees before we cross the *Ythan*, a considerable and good fishing stream, which rises in Strathbogie N. of the Hill of Foudland (p. 301), and drains a large portion of Buchan and Formartine. It is celebrated for its mussel pearls (*Mya margaritifera*), and is said to have furnished one of the jewels of the Crown of Scotland.

$19\frac{1}{2}$ m. **Ellon Stat.** ✲ In the town ($\frac{1}{2}$ m. rt.) is the *Earl's Mount*, an ancient moothill, where justice was administered in the open air by the Earls of Buchan, and where was the "doom-man's" place of execution. *Ellon Cas.* (A. J. L. Gordon, Esq.), situated in beautiful grounds, was built, 1852, near the site of an older mansion, of which one tower remains.

About 8 m. up the Ythan is *Haddo Ho.* (Earl of Aberdeen), a handsome house built in the 18th cent. by Adam. The present earl has enlarged it, and added a chapel. The park contains very fine trees, a long avenue of limes being a special feature, and 3 pretty lakes. The Haddo Ho. Games and Flower Show are held within the policies in August, and are attended by nearly 10,000 people. $3\frac{1}{2}$ m. N.W. of the house the ruins of the old *Cas. of Gight*, occupy a picturesque position overlooking the river. In 1644 it was taken and plundered by the Covenanters. Byron's mother (a Gordon) was heiress of the Cas., which was sold in 1787 to Lord Aberdeen to pay her husband's debts.

Beyond Ellon **Bennachie** (p. 300), now nearly 20 m. off, stands out conspicuously to S.W.

23 m. **Arnage Stat.** Rt. are *Arnage Ho.* (J. L. Ross, Esq.), and *Turnerhall*, the seat of Col. Turner.

27 m. **Auchnagatt Stat.**

$31\frac{1}{4}$ m. **Maud Junc. Stat.** Here the line forks—N. to Fraserburgh (p. 292), and E. to Peterhead. 3 m. l. is the village of *New Deer*, with a large monument to the late laird of Brucklay (p. 292). The scenery becomes more pleasing as we descend the *South Ugie Water*. The ruins of the **Abbey of Deer**, founded 1218 by Wm. Comyn, Earl of Buchan, for Cistercian monks, stand close to the rly. (l.) in the grounds of *Pitfour* (Col. Ferguson), which also contain a large sheet of water; a tablet has been placed to the memory of Wm. Pitt and Henry Dundas, Lord Melville.

$35\frac{1}{4}$ m. **Mintlaw Stat.** Rt. is *Aden Ho.* (Col. Russell), and beyond the village of *Old Deer*, with very pretty surroundings.

It once possessed an Abbey and Church of very ancient foundation (6th cent.), of which we have an early record in the M.S. *Book of Deer*, preserved at Cambridge, but all traces of this earlier abbey have been swept away.

$38\frac{1}{2}$ m. **Longside Stat.** Beyond, the *S. Ugie* is crossed just above its junc. with the *Strichen* or *N. Ugie Water* which together form the *Ugie*. The country again becomes bare.

$40\frac{3}{4}$ m. **Newseat Stat.** Before

$42\frac{1}{4}$ m. **Inverugie Stat.** the ruins of *Inverugie Cas.*, the residence of the Keiths, Earls Marischal of Scotland, until the property was forfeited at the rebellion 1715, are well seen l. The brother of the last earl, who became a field marshal in the Prussian service (see below), was born here, 1696. The Cas. had a splendid hall 50 ft. long, lighted by 4 deeply embayed windows. Beyond is the *Heading Hill*, where executions took place. Near this on the rt. bank of the Ugie is *Ravenscraig Cas.* It belongs to the 13th or 14th cent., and was probably built by the Cheynes, a family subsequently merged in the Keiths.

$44\frac{1}{4}$ m. **PETERHEAD Stat.** ✲, the chief town of Buchan, a parl. burgh, and a busy sea-port, is principally dependent on the herring fishery. *Port Henry*, the part of the town nearest the point, is exclusively occupied by fishermen and curing yards. In 1893 the fishing fleet numbered 577 boats, and 196,777 crans of herrings were cured here. Several of the boats, however, belonged to other ports. The townsfolk used to engage largely in the seal and whale fishery, long a nursery for the bravest and best seamen, and 1894 was the first year since 1788 that no vessel sailed from Peterhead.

The town was founded, 1593, by the Keiths, Earls Marischal, the former owners of the soil. When their estates were forfeited, the ground on which the town stands was sold, and in 1726 passed to the Edinburgh Merchant Co., who are still the superiors. The Pretender landed here in disguise, 1716. Field Marshal Keith, banished from Britain as a supporter of the Stuarts, became one of Frederick the Great's best generals, and was killed at Hochkirchen, 1758. His *Statue* in front of the *Town House* in Broad St., which dates from 1788, was "the gift of William I., King of Prussia, to the town of Peterhead, 23 Aug. 1868." A monument in the centre of the town, and a featureless tower conspicuous to the W. both commemorate the passing of the Reform Act, 1832. The *Public Library* and *Arbuthnot Museum*, in a handsome building with a tower in Queen St., erected 1893, deserve a visit. There is a harbour on both sides of the tongue of land on which the town stands, and these are connected by a canal, but a *Refuge Harbour*, which the severe storms and the exposed nature of the coast render most desirable, is (1894) in course of construction in the bay to the S. It is estimated that it will cost £750,000, and the work is being aided by convict labour from the large *Convict Prison* built beside the shore, 1 m. from the town.

The Bay of Peterhead is bounded (about 3 m. to the S.) by **Buchan Ness**, near which are the ruins of *Boddom Cas.*, built in the 14th cent. by the Keiths, upon the extreme end of a high rocky promontory. Near this, at *Sterling Hill*, the famous pink **Granite Quarries** begin, and extend at intervals for 2 or 3 miles.

7 m. S. of Peterhead are the **Bullers** (or *Roarers*, from Scot. "Buller" = to roar like a bull) **of Buchan.**

This is a tremendous hollow or crater in the rock, 200 ft. deep, and 50 ft. wide, into which the waves flow through a natural archway at the bottom. In rough weather and with a high wind the waves rush in with incredible violence, often dashing over the enclosing rocks. It is a fine sight, and has the advantage of being accessible to view from the land as well as by sea. Dr. Johnson calls it "a rock perpendicularly tubulated. He insisted on being rowed into the Pot. He also describes the *Dunbuy* or Yellow Rock, as "a yellow protuberance of stone, open to the main sea on one side, and parted from the land by a very narrow channel on the other, covered with sea birds."

½ m. S. of the Bullers there is an *Arch* in a headland, and ½ m. farther is **Slains Cas.**, the seat of the Earl of Erroll (Hered. High Constable of Scotland) finely situated on the very verge of a precipice above the sea, in a position which Dr. Johnson declared was "the noblest he had ever seen," but its complete exposure to the sea spray and briny winds absolutely prevents the growth of tree or shrub near it. The house, rebuilt in castellated style in 1836, contains family portraits by *Gainsborough*, and *Sir Joshua Reynolds.* Near it is the small fishing village of *Port Errol*, furnished with a commodious little harbour. Some 7 m. farther S. (14 m. from Peterhead) are the slight and shapeless ruins of *Old Slains Cas.* (cf. p. 290), destroyed by James VI. in 1594, see p. 308.

Branch Line to Fraserburgh.

From 31¼ m. Maud Junc. (p. 290) this line runs N.

33 m. **Brucklay Stat.** The large and handsome *Brucklay Cas.* (A. D. Fordyce, Esq.), visible above the woods for many miles round, is soon seen l. The woods of *Strichen Ho.* (Mrs. Baird) are passed rt. before

37 m. **Strichen Stat.**, where the *Strichen* or *N. Ugie Water* is crossed. The country now becomes very bare; l. is **Mormond Hill** (769 ft.), commanding wide views over Buchan. On its S. slope is the outline of a white horse executed 1700, and at its E. end is that of a stag (1870) just above

39½ m. **Mormond Stat.**

42 m. **Lonmay Stat.** 3 m. S.E. is *Crimond*, scene of the ballad "Logie o' Buchan," written by Geo. Halket, a schoolmaster, and author of several Jacobite songs.

44½ m. **Rathen Stat.**

45¾ m. **Philorth Stat.** Left is *Philorth Ho.*, the seat of Lord Saltoun, in a wooded demesne, in marked contrast to the bare country around. Rt. stands *Cairnbulg Cas.* a fort of the Comyns, forfeited 1308. Till the 18th cent. it was always a stronghold of the different families who held the earldom of Buchan.

47¼ m. **Fraserburgh Stat.** ✫, a town of considerable importance owing to the herring fisheries. In 1893 its fishing fleet numbered 805 boats, the largest fishing at any port in Scotland, and 252,790 crans of herrings were cured here.

The town was founded in the reign of Queen Mary by Lord Saltoun's ancestor, Sir Alex. Fraser. In Saltoun Square are the *Cross* (1736), the *Parish Ch.* (1802), and the *Town Hall* (1855), above the entrance of which is a statue of the 16th Lord Saltoun (d. 1853). The *Harbour*, naturally a very difficult one, has been much improved at various times.

On **Kinnaird Head**, just N. of the town, a slate rock, 60 ft. above the sea—the most N. point of Aberdeenshire, and the *Promontorium Taizalum* of Ptolemy—are the remains of a *Castle* built by Sir A. Fraser, 1574. It is a sq. battlemented tower of 4 stories, now surmounted by a *Lighthouse.*[1] Close at hand is the *Wine Tower*, built over a cave called *Sealch's Hole*, 100 ft. long.

It is 25 ft. high, and from the carvings on the stone pendents is conjectured to be of the 15th cent., but its origin is unknown. There is no outer entrance, and the only communication between the 2 stories was by a hole in the vaulted floor.

For road W. to **Macduff** and **Banff**, 22 m., see p. 300.

---

[1] Admission daily except Sat. and Sun. 11-3.

ROUTE 61.

Aberdeen to Alford and Strathdon by Kintore. G.N.S. Rly. and Coach.

Rly. to Alford 29¼ m.—4 trains daily in about 1½ hrs.

To 6¼ m. **Dyce Junc.**, see p. 289. The line continues up the S. side of the Don.

8¼ m. **Pitmedden Stat.** Close at hand (l.) is *Pitmedden Ho.*, and ½ m. farther on (rt. across the river) *Fintray Ho.* (Lord Sempill).

10½ m. **Kinaldie Stat.**

13¾ m. **Kintore Stat.**, a royal and parl. burgh, although its pop. in 1891 was only 686.

1½ m. S.W. are the ruins of *Hallforest Cas.*, an old building said to have been a hunting-lodge of the Earls of Mar before Bruce's time. It has only two stories with vaulted roofs, but each of these could be divided by a temporary floor into two rooms; there are no traces of staircase, which must have been at the outside. The castle was granted to Keith, Earl Marischal, for services at Bannockburn. It was inhabited as late as 1639, and the present Earl takes the title of Kintore from this property.

The train leaving the main line to Keith (Rte. 63), keeps W. passing l. the extensive *Kemnay Quarries*, of nearly white granite, which was largely used for the Thames Embankment and for the Forth Bridge, before

17¾ m. **Kemnay Stat.** ✲, a village built of granite. On l. is *Kemnay Ho.* (A. G. Burnett, Esq.). From the rly. bridge at the stat. a good view is obtained rt. of *Fetternear* (C. S. Leslie, Esq., of Balquhain), beautifully situated on the N. bank of the Don. It was once the country seat of the Bishops of Aberdeen, and was made over to William Leslie, the 9th Baron of Balquhain, by Bishop Gordon, in 1566, for the service performed by him in saving Aberdeen cathedral from destruction.

2 m. to the S. is *Castle Fraser* (Col. Fraser), which passed into the Fraser family in the year 1532. Its main feature is a double square tower, probably of the 15th cent., topped with conical roof and turrets of the early part of the 17th cent., the time when the turreted style had reached its highest development in Scotland. At that time a round tower was added, and from the angle, where this joins the square mass, there springs a light turret surmounted by a pavilion-shaped roof. A broad and handsome moulding runs round the building, which gives the upper part a peculiarly rich and pleasing effect, especially as it is contrasted with the singular plainness and almost studied absence of ornament of the lower stories. Internally the hall is worth notice from its elaborate ceiling.

20¾ m. **Monymusk Stat.** The village (rt.), which is of considerable antiquity, is neatly built, and is in the form of a square, with some fine old trees in the centre. Malcolm Canmore is said to have founded a priory on this spot in the 11th cent. A priory was subsequently founded here by Bruce, who, on his way to the battle of Inverurie, bivouacked in a meadow called the "Camp Field." The *Ch. of St. Mary* is Romanesque, but much defaced by alterations. It consists of nave, chancel, and W. tower.

Monymusk House (Sir A. H. Grant, Bt.), to the N., is beautifully situated on the banks of the Don. The principal tower is of the 15th cent., but modern additions have been made to it. The grounds are well wooded, and in a part called Paradise are some of the finest pines and larches in Scotland. Here is preserved the *Monymusk Reliquary*, a small box made of one piece of wood and plated with bronze and silver, jewelled and enamelled. It has been identified by antiquarians with the *Vexillum* or *Brecbennoch* of St. Columba, the hereditary custody of which was granted to the Monymusk family by the Abbey of Aberbrothock in 1315.[1] The Monymusk Stone has a well-carved cross upon it, and is supposed to have been at some time a landmark on the Priory property.

Higher up the Don are the ruins of *Pitfichie Castle*, once the property of General Urry, hanged at Montrose in 1650. He began as a Royalist, and then joined the Covenanters, whom he deserted after their defeat at Auldearn.

S. of the stat. is *Cluny Cas.* (Sir R. and Lady Gordon Cathcart), an imposing modern structure, built in 1836 on the site of an old stronghold of the Gordons.

24 m. **Tillyfourie Stat.**, to l. of which is the wooded *Corrennie Hill*, with red granite quarries.

26¼ m. **Whitehouse Stat.** 2½ m. N. is *Castle Forbes*, the seat of Lord Forbes, a modern castellated house in a beautiful situation.

29¼ m. **Alford Stat.** ✲, a pleasant little village, near which Montrose defeated the Covenanters under Generals Baillie and Urry in 1645. A cattle-market is held here every third Tuesday, when a large quantity of Aberdeen stock changes hands. There are also some *Granite Quarries* in the neighbouring hills, or "Howe of Alford."

¾ m. N. is *Haughton Ho.* (Miss Farquharson), and

¾ m. S. of Alford, on the Haughton estate, are the ruins of *Balfluig Castle*, built 1556, and formerly belonging to the Forbeses.

[EXCURSIONS :—

(1) N.W. to *Terpersie Cas.* (5 m.), a small fortified house, consisting originally of a quadrilateral building with a round tower (internally octagonal) at each alternate corner, and a later building added about 1600. In the original tower there are but three stories, with one room in each. On one of the window-sills is the date 1561, and above, the Gordon crest, a boar's head, beautifully cut.

(2) S. *To Craigievar, Corse, Aboyne, etc.*—The road passes 5 m. *Craigievar Cas.* (Sir W. Forbes, Lord Sempill). The estate belonged to the Mortimers, and was purchased in 1611 by Mr. Wm. Forbes, a rich merchant, son of the Laird of Craigievar. The building consists of three towers seven stories high, surmounted by turrets, high pitched roofs, dormer windows, and mouldings and sculpture. "Its uses as a fortress against the Highland reiver, rather than a mere dwelling-house, are recalled by all its attributes of sullen strength, and not less startlingly by the admonition round the shield, by which the adventurous intruder is warned against the temerity of waking sleeping dogs." The most interesting portion of the castle is the hall, which has a magnificent Renaissance ceiling with pendants. Over the fireplace are carved the British Royal Arms, quartered Scottish wise. The house is kept up in the original style, but seldom occupied by the family. At 6½ m. the high road from Aberdeen is joined, and *Lumphanan Stat.* (p. 276) is only 2 m. S. Turning W. we pass (8 m.) rt. *Corse Ho.* (The Hon. J. O. Forbes) and the ruins of *Corse Cas.* The old castle was built in 1581, and belonged at the beginning of the 17th cent. to Patrick Forbes, Bishop of Aberdeen, who was greatly respected for his learning and goodness. It is said that the devil paid him a visit here, and, being worsted in an argument, went away in a rage, carrying with him the whole front of the house. At Tarland (13 m.) the road turns sharp to the l. and leads by the ruins of Coul Castle to Aboyne, 19½ m. [3½ m. N.W. of Tarland, in *Migvie Ch.-yd.*, is a sculptured stone monument, and in the neighbourhood a *Weem* or Pict's House.] At the corner of the *Hill of Coul*, at a place called the Slack of Tilly Lodge, there is a magnificent view. On a rocky eminence near *Coul Ch.* (16 m.) are the remains of the old *Cas. of Coul*, a fortification of square form, with hexagonal towers at the corners. It belonged to the Durwards, a family of considerable note in the time of Alexander II., and it is said that the ch. bell still rings of its own accord whenever one of the name dies.]

There is an excellent driving road from Alford for 28 m. up Strathdon, which is well worth visiting. Rough driving roads lead from the head of the Strath to Ballater, Braemar, and Tomintoul.

A *Coach* runs twice a day up the strath—once at 11.20 a.m. for 19½ m., ret. at 6.10 a.m., and once at 4.35 p.m. for 15 m., ret. at 10.30 a.m.

The road up Strath Don crosses the river at *Bridge of Alford* (1½ m.),

[1] See Anderson's "Scotland in Early Christian Times."

and keeps up its l. bank. Across the river is *Breda Ho.* (N. M'Lean, Esq.), and farther on the woods of *Brux,* once the property of the Camerons. They being at feud with the Mowatts of Abergeldie, it was agreed that 12 horsemen on either side should meet and draw up articles of peace. The Camerons came to Drumgowdrum, the place of rendezvous, according to agreement. The Mowatts brought 12 horses, but 2 men on each, who immediately fell on the Camerons and slew them. The property devolved on an only daughter, who was then, or subsequently, wooed by a cadet of the house of Forbes. She declared her intention of marrying none save the avenger of her father's murder. Whereupon young Forbes challenged Mowatt and killed him in single combat, married the heiress, and established the family of Forbes of Brux. The last of his line, Jonathan Forbes, was proscribed in 1715, but concealed himself in the neighbourhood by working as a labourer. A dyke built by his own hands may be seen running up the hill. The road, having rt. *Littlewood House*, now enters a beautiful pass, after which it leaves the river for several miles.

At **Mossat Toll** (7½ m.) the road forks. N. leads to *Lumsden* 1½ m.—beyond which is the burn and old Cas. of *Craig*, a picturesque spot—*Tap o' Noth* (1851 ft.), with a vitrified fort, 6 m., and down *Strathbogie* to *Gartly Stat.* (p. 301) 9 m., and Huntly 14 m.

We keep S.W. up Strathdon.

"From Esset to Mosset,
From Bogie to Don,"

extended the original territory of the Forbes family. We cross the Mossat Burn and presently see l. (9 m.) the curiously shaped old *Kildrummie Ch.*, with a Norman wall and a vault, containing *Monuments* of the Elphinstone family and of the Earls of Mar. Across the Don is the conical hill of *Drumgowdrum;* in a glen behind took place the massacre of the Camerons by the Mowatts.

At 9½ m. is *Kildrummie Inn*✲, and at 10 m. (rt.) **Kildrummie Cas.**, the most picturesque object in the whole strath. Now a large and imposing ruin, it was a royal fortress in the days of Robert Bruce.

It is said to have been built in the reign of Alexander II. by Gilbert, Bishop of Caithness, and to have had 7 towers. The chapel with its triplet of lancet windows, in imitation apparently of Elgin, is very conspicuous among the remains. "Kildrummie may be pronounced the only castle in Scotland of which a chapel forms a conspicuous feature." Of the Snow Tower towards the W., which is said to have been 150 ft. high, there is but little trace. Bruce's wife and children were placed here for safety when he fled to Rathlin (1306), but, the castle being besieged by the Earls of Lancaster and Hereford, they fled to St. Duthac's sanctuary at Tain, where they were taken by the Earl of Ross and given up to Edward I. It was betrayed into the hands of the English, and, as for the garrison, the chronicler relates concisely:—"thai were all hangyt and drawyn." The ruin has been ruthlessly used as a quarry for building purposes. It commands a good view N. of *Tap o' Noth* (above).

The road now enters the *Den of Kildrummie*, a narrow picturesque pass, with steep wooded sides. Beyond, *Morven* (2862 ft.) appears to the S. and the road descends, passing *Glenkindie Arms Inn*✲, to

13 m. **Inverkindie Village.** ½ m. across the Don are the ch., hamlet, and ruined castle of **Towie.**

Of the castle only an insignificant square keep is left. In 1571 it belonged to Alexander Forbes, and in his absence was besieged by Adam Gordon, brother of the Earl of Huntly. On Forbes's wife refusing to surrender, Gordon set fire to the tower, and burnt her, her children, and servants, 27 in all. Upon this tragic incident is founded the ballad of "Edom o' Gordon," though the scene is there transferred to Berwickshire.

In the ch.-yard is an old *gravestone* with a sculptured cross. It has 8 branches with trefoiled ends, and a gilt chalice, implying that it covered the body of a priest.

14 m. rt. *Glenkindie* (A. N. Leith,

Esq.), and beyond it, in the second field on rt., is a very remarkable *Picts' house.* It has two chambers, communicating with each other by means of a small aperture, 3 ft. from the ground of the outer chamber, but on the floor level of the inner.

15 m. At **Bridge of Bucket** the *Water of Bucket* is crossed. On its rt. bank are the ruins of *Glenbucket Castle*, built about 1590. An inscription over the door tells the visitor that "no thing on arth remanis bot fame." The laird, a Gordon, took the part of the Stuarts in 1715 and in 1745.

[A road here strikes up the l. bank to *Glen Bucket Lodge*, 6 m.

Mowatt's Stone, 4 m. up the burn, marks the spot where the duel between Mowatt and young Forbes took place, which ended in the death of Mowatt. An old-fashioned dirk found near the place is now in the Banff museum.

A rough road N. passing under (rt.) the *Buck of Cabrach* (2368 ft.) leads to *Cabrach Ch.* (9 m.). 3 m. beyond it divides, one branch going rt. down the valley of the Deveron to Huntly (25 m.), and the other l. through Glen Fiddich to Dufftown (20 m.).]

Continuing up Strathdon, on rt. is *Ben Newe* (the Holy Hill), and at the *Farm of Buchaam* (rt.) there is another *Picts' house* in the garden.[1] It has one chamber, and winds considerably. An old "quaigh" or drinking-cup and some wood ashes were found at the farther end.

At the foot of Ben Newe is *Castle Newe* (17½ m.), the imposing seat of Sir Chas. Forbes, Bt., the great landowner of this district. An excellent view of it is obtained between the bridges by which the Don is crossed and recrossed.

At 18¾ m. rt. is **Colquhonny Inn** ✲, standing 1100 ft. above the sea. Beside it is the *Lonach Hall*, built 1845, and the scanty ruins of *Colquhonny Cas.*, begun (16th cent.) by one of the Forbeses of Towie, but never finished, because, as is said, three lairds fell from the top and were killed.

[1] Inquire at the house for the key and a candle.

At 19½ m. is **Bellabeg**, with large shop, bank, and P.O. Beside the P.O. is old *Bellabeg Ho.*, the original property and habitation of the Forbes family, now occupied by the factor. Across the river the spire of **Strathdon Ch.** is conspicuous.

Here the Alford coach stops; another coach runs daily to Gartly Stat. (p. 301) *via* Mossat and Lumsden, 21 m., but as it starts at 4.20 a.m. tourists had better come *from* Gartly, leaving at 9.25 a.m.

Having crossed the *Nochty*, rt. is the *Dune of Invernochty*, a natural elliptical mound, 40 ft. high and 970 ft. in circumference, once fortified. A little farther on (l.) is *Pooldullie Bridge*, built, as an inscription (now effaced) testified, by Black Jock Forbes of Inverernan, 1715.

At 20½ m. is the hamlet of **Parkvilla**, beyond which l. is *Candacraig* (Sir C. Forbes), and rt., after crossing the *Ernan*, *Inverernan* (Gen. Sir J. Forbes). Across the Don is *Glen Conrie*, where the Earls of Mar are said to have kept their hounds. The road now passes through a beautiful bit of scenery. Rt., opposite *Lonach Farm*, formerly an inn, is *Lonach Hill*, commanding a good view, and with a cairn commemorating the acquisition of the baronetcy by Sir Chas. Forbes's father. Beyond *Skellater Ho.* (rt.) the country becomes more open.

At 25 m. is *Tomnahaish Bridge*, crossing which a road leads in 12¼ m. to Balmoral, and in 12¾ m. to Ballater (see p. 278). 1½ m. beyond we cross the Don, and again at

27¾ m. **Cock Bridge** ✲ (1330 ft.). S. of it stand the ruins of *Corgarff Cas.*, supposed to have been a hunting seat of the earls of Mar, subsequently purchased by government and kept up as a small military station for the repression of smuggling; N. is *Allargue Ho.* (Capt. Wilson); 2 m. farther up the Don is *Dalnadamph*, Sir Chas. Forbes's shooting lodge.

A fine wild moorland road, available for carriages but very steep, ascending in 2 m. to 2048 ft., runs N.W. to *Tomintoul* (p. 231) 10 m.

S. to Ballater is 15½ m., and to Braemar (*via* Balmoral 15 m.) 23½ m.

A track leads W. by the *Sources of the Don* to *Inchrory Lo.* on the Avon (6 m.), whence a driving road leads down that river in 7 m. to Tomintoul.

ROUTE 62.

Aberdeen to Banff and Macduff, by Inveramsay Junc. and Turriff. G.N.S. Rly.

4 or 5 trains daily in 2-2¾ hrs.—50¼ m.

To 13¼ m. **Kintore Stat.**, see pp. 289, 293.

Just before Inverurie, having crossed the Don above its junc. with the *Urie*, we notice rt. the "*Bass*," a mound washed by the latter stream, partly an example of "drift," partly artificial. It is supposed once to have been the seat of justice; at its foot there is now a cemetery. A local prophecy says:—

"When Dee and Don run both in one,
And Tweed shall run in Tay,
The bonnie water of Urie
Shall bear the Basse away."

16¼ m. **Inverurie Stat.** ✲, a neat small town and a royal and parl. burgh on the Urie, with several churches and modern villas. Bruce is said to have made it a royal burgh in commemoration of a victory gained near here in 1308 over Comyn, Earl of Buchan, an adherent of Edward I. Rt., across the Urie, is *Keith Hall*, the seat of the Earl of Kintore. It once belonged to the Johnstones, and Arthur Johnstone, the Scottish Latin poet, was born there 1587. Left, **Bennachie** (1733 ft.) is a prominent object.

[*Branch* to 2¾ m. **Lethenty**, and 5¾ m. **Old Meldrum** ✱, on the high road from Aberdeen to Banff.

2 m. N. of Meldrum is *Meldrum Ho.* (B. C. Urquhart, Esq.); S. is *Barra Hill*, with a prehistoric fort, said also to mark the site of the battle between Bruce and Comyn.]

The line soon crosses the Urie twice. Between the bridges l. are the remains of *Balquhain*, a ruined tower (1530), belonging to the old family of Leslie of Balquhain.

Here Sir W. Leslie entertained Queen Mary for 2 days, 1562. The Duke of Cumberland on his way to Culloden (1746) ordered it to be burnt, but one of the tenants bribed the soldiers and damp straw was used. Here were born Walter, Count Leslie, who served with distinction in the Austrian army, and was created (1637) a Count of the Holy Roman Empire, and his nephew James, who succeeded him in his German estates, and was second in command at the siege of Vienna (1683).

W. of Balquhain is the village and Ch. of *Chapel of Garioch*, beyond which is the *Maiden Stone*, about 10 ft. high, sculptured on all 4 sides. On the E. side are 3 compartments—in the lowest a comb and mirror (common emblems on Scotch sculptured stones), in the middle an animal like an elephant, and in the top one a dog. This district of **Garioch** (pron. *Gherry*) is called from its fertility the "girnel" or meal press of Aberdeenshire.

Rt., across the river, is *Harlaw Ho.* and "*the sair field*" of **Harlaw**, where, on 24th July 1411, the Earl of Mar checked the advance of the Highlanders, under Donald of the Isles, with enormous loss on both sides. "The great battle of Harlaw . . . might be said to determine whether the Gaelic or the Saxon race should be predominant in Scotland," says Sir Walter, who has introduced a fine ballad referring to it into Chap. 40 of the "Antiquary."

20½ m. **Inveramsay Junc.** where the line to Keith, etc. (Rte. 63) turns off N.W. 2 m. N.E. is *Glack*, formerly a residence of the Elphinstones and subsequently of the Mackenzies, but in 1888 converted into a *Lunatic Asylum* for the city of Aberdeen. We once more cross the Urie and keep N. to

24¼ m. **Wartle Stat.**, beyond which l. is *Warthill Ho.* (G. A.

Leslie, Esq.), a handsome modern house built in the Scoto-French style, and containing some objects of Oriental art, and an interesting portrait of Prince Charles Edward, with a hawk. The house is surrounded by thriving woods, which hide it from the rly.

28 m. **Rothie-Norman Stat.** ✲, rt. of which is *Rothie-Norman House* (Mrs. Crawford Leslie). As we approach

31¼ m. **Fyvie Stat.**, a glimpse is caught rt. of the roofs and towers of **Fyvie Cas.**, overlooking the banks of the *Ythan*, one of the stateliest and best preserved castellated mansions in Scotland.

It is the seat of A. J. Forbes Leith, Esq., who has added a new wing and restored a great part of the castle in an admirable manner. It occupies a commanding site and is built in the form of the letter L, with 3 lofty square towers, crowned by extinguisher turrets, and named, after their founders, the Preston, Meldrum, and Gordon towers. In the middle of the S. front is the Seton tower, through which is the old entrance, flanked by round bastions, now closed, but retaining its massive iron cross-barred gate. The present entrance is at the back, and leads to a broad winding stair. The interior contains portraits of Monmouth, Claverhouse, Queen Mary, Montrose, and Cecil, Earl of Salisbury. The original Castle, probably a tall peel tower, dates from the 13th cent. Edward I. is said to have slept in it in 1297. The domain was part of the royal chase down to the time of Robert II., whose son received it as a gift from his father, but shortly gave it up to his cousin, Sir James Lindsay. In 1390 the estate of Fyvie, with the castle, passed from the Lindsays to Henry de Preston, by whom the Preston tower on the S.E. was built. In 1596 it was bought by Alexander Seton, created Lord Fyvie and Earl of Dunfermline, Lord Chancellor, and tutor to Charles I., a nobleman skilled in architecture. By him not only was the Seton tower added, and his arms sculptured on a tablet of freestone over the gateway, but the whole was remodelled and redecorated under his supervision. The tower on the N.W. was added by the Gordons, who bought the estate in 1726. In the S.W. tower is the charter-room, adorned with grotesque carvings, and underneath it is a chamber walled up. No one knows when or why it was closed, but a superstitious tradition that some great calamity would follow its opening has hitherto checked curiosity. In 1644 the park was occupied by the Marquis of Montrose, whose entrenchments may still be traced near the garden. He was defeated here by Argyll. On the Preston tower is a figure of the Trumpeter of Fyvie, the subject of a charming love-ballad.

5 m. lower down the Ythan is the *Tower of Gight* (p. 290).

34½ m. **Auchterless Stat.** On l. is *Towie*, now a farm house, but formerly *Tolly Castle*, the residence of the Barclay family. The old hall is still complete. It has a groined and ribbed roof, and is decorated with sacred emblems. In the recess at the farther end are 4 shields with representations of the Evangelists. An inscription on the exterior (partly illegible) says :—

"Sir Alexander Barclay de Tolly
Fundator, decessit
Anno Domini 1136
In time of valth al men
Semis frindly and frindis is not
Knavin bot in adversity. 1593.

In reality the date of the foundation must be about 1300. Of this family was Field Marshal Barclay de Tolly, who commanded the Russian troops at the battle of Smolensko, and on other occasions during the Napoleonic war.

At 36 m. rt. is *Hatton Cas.* (Garden Duff, Esq.), which still preserves part of the old tower of Balquholly, the seat of the Mowatts, sold by them in 1723.

38½ m. **Turriff Stat.** ✲, a thriving town, pleasantly situated (rt.) on a hill side, is a place of considerable antiquity, as shown by the remains of the old *Church*, once the property of the Knights Templars. It is 120 ft. long and 18 ft. broad, and has a handsome belfry, with a fine toned bell of the year 1557. There are monuments to the Lindsay and Leslie families. The town *Cross* is very old, and used to be the spot where the Sheriff's Court assembled. In 1639 the Master of Forbes, who had collected a body of Covenanters here, was ignominiously routed by a party of Royalists, and the skirmish was afterwards known as the "Trot of Turriff." Thus, in this remote village, the first blood was drawn in the civil war of Scotland.

2 m. farther on *Forglen* (Sir R. J. Abercromby, Bt.) is well seen l.—a handsome modern house beautifully situated on the banks of the *Deveron*, which the rly. approaches, and then trends rt. to

43 m. **Plaidy Stat.** 2 m. E. is *Craigston Cas.* (Major Pollard-Urquhart) built 1604-7—a plain copy of the principal tower of Fyvie.

We pass (l.) the remains of a castle on a rocky eminence, one of the Comyn's strongholds, on the way to

45¼ m. **King Edward Stat.**, a corruption of *Kin-edart* = head of valley.

50 m. **Banff Bridge Stat.**

BANFF✲ (pronounced *Bamff*), a parl. burgh and a small seaport, stands on an eminence ½ m. across the Deveron, here spanned by a bridge of Smeaton's (1779).

Omnibus to and from the town, which has another rly. stat. near the harbour for the lines to Portsoy, Elgin, Keith, Inverness, etc. (see Rte. 64).

On the shoulder of the hill next the sea stood the *Castle*, at times a royal residence, and occupied for a day or two by the invader Edward I. in 1296 and 1298. The castle, in which Archbishop Sharp (1618-79) was born, is now supplanted by a modern house; and a few lumpish walls and a ditch alone represent it. Beyond it is *Chalmers Hospital*. In the *old churchyard*, behind the Post-Office, is a fragment of a *Gothic Church*, with one or two monuments. On the height near the present church are the *Schools*, a handsome building with a Grecian portico, built from funds left by Jas. Wilson, a native of Banff. In this building is a *Museum*, where some relics are preserved of Ferguson the astronomer (b. at Rothiemay, 1710). Readers of Dr. Smiles's Life of Thomas Edward (1814-86), who resided in Banff, will be familiar with this museum.

In Low St., opposite the Fife Arms, are the *County Buildings*, and near the end of the street, close to the church, is the entrance lodge to

Duff House (Duke of Fife), a handsome Italian mansion on the Deveron, sheltered by trees, with towers at the four corners. It is a facsimile, though unfinished, of part of the Villa Borghese, was built about the middle of the 18th cent., and contains a fine collection of paintings, which can be seen, in the absence of the family, by an order from the factor.

Besides a number of family portraits of more than average merit, the following are the most noticeable old pictures:—Charles I. as Prince of Wales, *Velásquez*, a good picture, but not a favourable portrait—the expression is sinister, and reminds one of his son James II. Lady Mary Coke, *Sir J. Reynolds*, a lovely picture, face full of expression and softness of colouring; Hawking, *Wynants;* Sir W. Lenthall, Speaker of the House of Commons, 1640, *Mytens;* Infant Saviour feeling the sharpness of the Crown of Thorns, *Alonzo Cano;* Italian Landscape, *Zuccarelli;* Salvator Mundi astride upon the globe, *Luca Giordano*, a fine picture, with more expression than is generally found in this subject; Assumption, *Murillo* (?); Duke of Richmond, *Vandyck;* Duchess of Richmond, *same;* Charles I., *Vandyck;* Duchess of Richmond, *Lely*, a beautiful face and figure; Prince Henry, *Jansen;* Princess Elizabeth; 3 children of James I., stiff and disagreeable; 3 small heads by *Holbein;* an ecclesiastic, *J. van Eyck;* a philosopher with a skull, *Q. Matsys;* head of a girl, *Murillo;* Louis XIV., *Rigaud;* Queen Elizabeth, *Hilliard;* portraits of the English kings from Henry V. to George II., including a full length of Henry VIII. by *Holbein;* the Chevalier, and Cardinal York by *G. Hamilton*, etc. There is a handsome *library* 70 ft. long, and a good collection of arms and armour.

There is a charming walk straight through the park to *Alvah Bridge* (2 m.), where the rocks rise to the height of 50 ft., and are said to be as deep below the surface of the water. There is a Gothic *Mauso-*

leum in the park containing monuments to various members of the family.

Banff has a reputation for sea-bathing, and a bath-house was opened in 1872.

[5 m. W. of Banff on the road to Portsoy, passing the gable end of the old ruined ch. of *Boyndie*, are the remains of the *Castle of Boyne*, once the property of the Edmonstones and then of the Ogilvies. An older castle stood once upon the sea-shore, of which a few fragments remain. Boyne Castle overlooks a deep ravine, which served as a defence to the N.W. On the S. is the entrance by a raised causeway across the moat. The gateway is protected by 2 round towers, and the whole building consisted of a rectangle, defended by towers at the angles. The W. side, with its hall, 80 ft. long, was added in the latter part of the 16th cent.

3 m. S.W. of Banff is *Inchdrewer* Castle. Here, in 1713, Lord Banff was burnt under very suspicious circumstances.]

$50\frac{1}{4}$ m. **Macduff Stat.** Macduff✲, politically united to Banff, though otherwise independent, is devoted to herring-fishing and possesses a fair harbour, enlarged in 1877. It takes its name from the Fife family, whose property it is. From the hills above there is a charming view of the vale of Deveron, and the Caithness mountains in the distance.

[*From Macduff to Fraserburgh* there is a road, running in places near the coast, which affords some fine cliff scenery. Inland the country is monotonous.

10 m. *Pennan Bay*, beyond the promontory of Troup Head.

$13\frac{1}{2}$ m. *Aberdour Bay*. On a rock 65 ft. above the sea is *Dundargue Castle*, a mere stump of a tower joined by a narrow neck to the shore; near this are two large natural arches through which the sea flows at high water. $1\frac{1}{4}$ m. W. of Dundargue is the Cave of Cowshaven, on the shore, its entrance nearly choked with shingle. Here Alex. Forbes, last Lord Pitsligo, outlawed for his share in the '45 Rebellion, was concealed and protected by the fidelity of his neighbours, despite the large rewards offered.

$16\frac{1}{2}$ m. *Pitsligo*, 1 m. N. of which is *Rosehearty*, whence there is a coach to Fraserburgh.

21 m. **Fraserburgh**★ (p. 292).]

ROUTE 63.

Aberdeen to Inverness by Keith, Mulben, Elgin, and Forres.

About 7 trains daily in 4–5 hrs. $108\frac{1}{4}$ m.

Between Huntly and Elgin travellers by morning express have a choice of 3 routes—all interesting—with through carriages on each, re-uniting at Elgin, viz.—(1) By *Keith and Mulben* [Rte. 63]; (2) By *Grange Loop, Portsoy and Buckie* [Rte. 64—a coast route]; (3) By *Keith* and *Craigellachie Junc.* [Rte. 65]. By (2) and (3) the line is G.N.S. Rly. all the way; by (1) it is High. Rly. after Keith. Beyond Elgin the line is High. Rly.

To $20\frac{1}{2}$ m. **Inveramsay Junc.**, see pp. 289, 293, 297. The line turns W. up the Urie to

$21\frac{1}{4}$ m. **Pitcaple Stat.**, with rt. *Pitcaple Cas.* (Col. Lumsden). It was formerly a seat of the Leslie family. Queen Mary rested here a night and day, and planted a thorn-tree. In 1650 the Marq. of Montrose, on his way south as a prisoner, was allowed to rest here for a night, the lady of the house being his cousin. On l. are the ruins of *Harthill Cas.* built 1600 by Patrick Leith, and burnt soon after by the Covenanters. At $22\frac{1}{4}$ m. rt. is *Logie-Elphinstone* (Sir G. H. Horn-Elphinstone, Bt.). which contains family and other portraits—Bishop Elphinstone, Viscount Dundee, Count Leslie, etc.—and several by Raeburn. 1 m. l. is *Pittodrie* (H. W. Knight Erskine, Esq.).

$24\frac{1}{2}$ m. **Oyne Stat.**✲, on the *Gady Burn*, $4\frac{1}{2}$ m. up which is *Leslie Castle*, one of the most convenient of these ancient structures. It was built by the Forbes in 1661, and consists of three towers joined together and turreted. Rt. close to the stat. is *Petmathen* (Major T. Leith), built 1886 in Eng. Manor House style. To the S. rises the beautiful ridge of **Bennachie**, characterised by a number of granite peaks; it commands a charming and extensive view, and is best ascended from here. The highest peak is *Oxen Craig* (1733 ft.); on "*Mither Tap*" (1698 ft.) to the E. are the remains of a remarkable hill fort.

"O an I were where Gadie rins,
'Mang fragrant heath and yellow whins,
Or brawlin' down the bosky linns,
At the back o' Bennachie."

27½ m. **Insch. Stat.**, 1 m. beyond, rt. is the conical hill of *Dunnideer*, with an old fort on the summit, of the date of the 14th cent. Hector Boece says "that the sheep that gangs on this mountain are yellow, their teeth hewit like gold." "On the l. is the hill of *Christ's Kirk*, a suppressed parish, where a fair, called 'The Sleepy Market,' was at one time held during the night. It has been supposed that it is the scene of the old poem of 'Christ's Kirk on the Green,' ascribed to King James I."—OLIVER (cf. p. 181).

2½ m. from Insch Stat. at *Newton* (Alex. Gordon, Esq.) is an inscribed stone of great interest to archæologists.

Conspicuous on the N. are the *Foudland Hills*, on the old coach-road to Huntly, which, although of no great height, were in winter the terror of travellers on account of the snow.

31 m. **Wardhouse Stat.**

33 m. **Kennethmont Stat.**, rt. of which is *Leith Hall* (Colonel Leith-Hay). Beyond, the line enters the valley of **Strathbogie** and the country becomes wilder. Looking S.W. the traveller sees the peak of the *Buck of Cabrach* (2368 ft.) between Strathbogie and Strathdon; while to the W., near at hand, is the conical summit of the *Tap o' Noth* (1851 ft.), a conspicuous landmark from the German Ocean. The archæologist should visit it (from Gartly) for its *Vitrified Fort*, which is very perfect, enclosing a large area by a rampart some 15 ft. high, with a single opening at the S.E. corner. From the extent of the outworks it is plain that the fort must have been one of the greatest importance. 3 m. S. of Kennethmont is *Drumminor* (Trs. of the late R. Grant, Esq.), the ancient seat of the Lords Forbes, with curious 16th cent. architecture.

36 m. **Gartly Stat.** ✲

[For roads and coaches to Strathdon, see pp. 296, 295.]

41 m. **Huntly Stat.** ✲, a clean looking town in a good situation in Strathbogie, above the confluence of the Bogie with the Deveron, and consisting principally of 2 streets that cross one another at rt. angles, forming a spacious market-place, in which is a statue of the 5th and last Duke of Gordon, d. 1836. The visitor should notice the *Gordon Schools* erected in 1851 to his memory. The Gothic building with a tower in Gordon St. is the *Town Hall*. N. of the town are the ruins of *Huntly*, or *Strathbogie Castle*, as it was called till the year 1544, cradle and seat of the Earls of Huntly, the most powerful lords in the N. down to the middle of the 16th cent. An old fortress here belonged in early times to the Comyns, but very little is left but the vaults. The lands of Strathbogie were granted by Robert Bruce to Sir Adam Gordon, founder of the Huntly family, whose chief, in the time of Queen Mary, held three earldoms, and ruled more like a monarch than a subject from Deeside to the W. Ocean.

The later and more ornamental part of the castle was begun early in the 17th cent. by the 6th Earl and 1st Marq. of Huntly. In the middle of the 18th cent. the mansion ceased to be inhabited, and much of the material has been used for the building of *Huntly Lodge*, occupied by the late Duchess of Gordon, the gardens of which are very pretty. 3 m. N.E. of Huntly is *Lessendrum* (Mrs. Elrington Bisset), where are the family portraits of the

Peterborough (Mordaunt) family, including fine examples by *Zacchero*, *Vandyck*, *Hahneman*, etc.

The Deveron is crossed by a bridge of 5 arches before

45¼ m. **Rothiemay Stat.**

48¾ m. **Grange Stat.** [*Branch* N. to *Banff*, *Portsoy*, etc. (Rte. 64).] Here Banffshire is entered. The parish ch. occupies the site of an old castle of the abbots of Kinloss.

53¼ m. **Keith Stat.**

[A line (G.N.S.R.) runs S. to *Craigellachie Junc.* and *Speyside* (Rte. 65); another (High. Rly.) runs N. to *Buckie* and *Portessie* (below).]

Keith✲, ½ m. S., with mills, on the rt. bank of the Isla, consists of several straight streets crossed by others at right angles, and has 4 great cattle and horse fairs in the year. It commands a wide view of the surrounding country—with E. *The Balloch* (1199 ft.), W. *Ben Aigan* (1544 ft.), and S.W. *Ben Rinnes* (2755 ft.)—especially from behind the R. C. *Chapel*, which has an imposing front, with large statues of SS. Peter and Paul, and an altar-piece—the Incredulity of St. Thomas—presented by Charles X. of France. Beside it is a R. C. school. Across the river is *Fife-Keith*, once a separate town, and in the valley between is *Earlsmill Stat.* (p. 308).

[*Branch to Portessie* 12 m.

This line runs N. over the high ground of Altmore, ascending to 650 ft. and passing 2¾ m. *Forgie*, 7½ m. *Enzie*, 10½ m. *Rathven*, and 11¼ m. *Buckie*, and joins the Portsoy to Elgin line (Rte. 64) at Portessie.]

From Keith the line skirts the boundary of Banff and Moray shires. Beyond

58¼ m. **Mulben Stat.** it passes through a prettily wooded defile to the valley of the Spey, which is crossed not only by the rly. *Viaduct* of 6 arches, 230 ft. long with a single iron span over the river, but also by a driving suspension bridge, which has superseded the old ferry, from which the place is called the "*Boat o' Brig.*" The geologist will notice the sections of wealden-clay and drift on the banks of the Spey, which may be traced down below Fochabers.

62 m. **Orton Stat.** in Morayshire.

65 m. **Fochăbers Junc.** A *Branch*, opened 1893, runs (rt.) in 3 m. to

Fochăbers Bridge Stat. ½ m. across the bridge is **Fochăbers**✲, visible from the junc. with the *Bin of Cullen* (1050 ft.) prominent in the background. It is a neat little place, built upon a regular plan, with a handsome square in the centre. At the E. end is an *Educational Institution*, founded 1846 by Alexander Milne, a native of Fochabers, who made a large fortune as a merchant at New Orleans.

N. of the town is **Gordon Castle**, (Duke of Richmond and Gordon), standing in a spacious park of 1300 acres, which was formerly a marsh, called the Bog of Gight, but is now well covered with trees. The castle, which passed in 1836 to the Duke of Richmond—in whose favour the title of Duke of Gordon was revived 1876—is the largest mansion in this part of the country. Its exterior measures 600 ft. in length, and it has four stories, the whole being faced with freestone and surmounted by battlements. Behind the centre rises a ponderous square tower of the 15th cent., 90 ft. high. With the exception of this tower the whole is modern, and there is no grandeur about it except as regards size. The gardens are well laid out, and occupy an area of 12 acres. In the interior are good family portraits, some copies of the old masters, and some statuary. The Spey fishings, which are part of the property, have realised as much as £15,000 per annum.

68 m. **Lhanbryde Stat.**, beyond which, on a clear day, the traveller obtains a distant view across the Moray Firth of the Sutherland and

Caithness Mts., among which the peak of **Morven** (2313 ft.) is conspicuous. Left is *Coxton*, a good specimen of the old Peel tower. It is completely fire-proof, and has no access whatever to the entrance save by a ladder. The rly. now runs W. to

71¼ m. **Elgin Stat.**

[Lines go (1) N. to *Lossiemouth* (p. 305); (2) E. to *Buckie*, *Portsoy*, etc. (Rte. 64); (3) S. to *Rothes* and *Strathspey* (Rte. 66).]

ELGIN ✲ is a neat, pleasant, and somewhat busy town and royal and parl. burgh, with residential villas in the outskirts. N. of it winds the deep but sluggish *Lossie*. It is the capital of the shire of Elgin or Moray, and has a resident sheriff-substitute. Near the stat. is the modern *Town Hall* with conspicuous tower. In the middle of the town is a long and broad market-place, in the centre of which stands the *High Kirk*, faced with a Grecian portico. In front of it a fountain marks the site of the old *Tolbooth*. Behind it is "the *Muckle Cross* of Elgin, built abt. 1650, destroyed abt. 1792; rebuilt and presented to his native city by Wm. Macandrew of Westwood Ho., Little Horkesley, Essex, 1888." There are some quaint old houses in High St. At the W. end of the town is *Gray's Hospital* (Infirmary), built with money left by Dr. Alex. Gray (d. 1808), a native. At the E. end are the *County Buildings* and the *Museum* (a praiseworthy collection of local antiquities and geological specimens), beyond which (about ¾ m. from the stat.) are the ruins of

***Elgin Cathedral,**[1] one of the finest in Scotland. It was founded abt. 1224 by Bp. Andreas de Moravia, and dedicated to the Holy Trinity, but does not appear to have been completed, when, in 1270, it was burned down. Again it was given to the flames on the Feast of St. Botolph, 1390, by the Wolf of Badenoch, King Robert III.'s half-brother, at the head of a band of wild Highlanders. It was rebuilt with a steeple, which fell in 1506, was raised again in 1538 to a height of 198 ft., and again fell in 1711. A considerable part of the building was destroyed in consequence of an order of Privy Council (1568) to strip the roof of its lead to raise funds for paying the troops. A heavier blow was dealt (1640) by the General Assembly ordering the demolition of the interior, including a very perfect and beautiful rood-loft, richly adorned, painted with Bible subjects. This work was effectually carried out by the minister of Elgin (Gilbert Ross), and the Lairds Innes, Brodie, and others. Much of the existing remains, however, is antecedent to the catastrophe of 1390, including the 2 stately *W. Towers*, 84 ft. high, flanking a very handsome pointed portal, deeply recessed with vigorous and beautiful mouldings—indeed all the carved work is excellent although much defaced—surmounted inside by a pointed arcade, over which stands a large window, long since emptied of its tracery. From the top of the S. tower a good view is obtained over an extensive tract of low-lying country; to the N. *Morven* in Caithness may be seen, and E. rises the *Bin of Cullen*. Of the Nave, of 6 bays with double aisles, nothing remains but the stumps of some of the piers.

The total length of the building was 264 ft. The two best bits of the church date originally from the 13th and 14th cents., and escaped the conflagration by "the Wolf." They are the façade of the S. transept, showing a fine bold doorway, with a sort of toothed moulding, surmounted by a pointed oval, the round arch appearing in the upper

1 The keeper lives at the gate. The ruins are now well taken care of.

range of windows above the pointed; and the E. end of the choir. The *Choir* possessed an elegant clerestory of lancet windows in 2's and 3's. It was flanked by side chapels, has a *chancel* raised on 3 steps, and is terminated by what is virtually a great E. window, composed of 2 rows of 5 lancets each, with piers instead of mullions between the compartments, and surmounted by a rose-window in the gable, from which however the tracery has disappeared.

The best preserved part of the building is the octagonal *Chapter-house*, entered from the N. choir aisle, retaining still its elegant central pier and finely-groined roof, not unworthy to be compared with some of those of England. It dates from the first quarter of the 15th cent.

Of the *Monuments*, the best is an armed effigy of Hay of Lochloy (1421).

The S. choir aisle (*St. Mary's Aisle*) which retains its stone vault, was the burial-place for the Gordon family, and will not again be used. A stone erected 1890, by the Duke of Richmond and Gordon, records the burial here of the 4th Marq. of Gordon, created 1st Duke 1684, d. 1716; of Alex., 2nd Duke, d. 1728; of Cosmo George, 3rd Duke, d. 1752; of Alex., 4th Duke, d. 1827, aged 84; and of George, 5th and last Duke of Gordon, d. 28th May 1836. In the nave is placed an antique block of granite, carved on one side with a *Runic Cross*, on the arms of which are the symbols of 4 priests (or the 4 evangelists?); on the other side are figures of a knight carrying his hawk, the spectacle ornament, the broken mace (Z), and the half-moon. It dates probably from the 9th or 10th cent., and deserves notice. It was dug up in the town 1823.

On the N.W. of the cathedral, within the grounds of *Grant Lodge* (Dow. Countess of Seafield), the site of the college, are the remains of the *Bishop's Palace*. The *Greyfriars Church*, a long narrow building of the 15th cent., and the remains of the *Dean's House*, are also interesting.

½ m. E. of the town is *Anderson's Institution*, for the maintenance of 10 old people and the education of about 300 children. Its founder, General Anderson, H.E.I.C.S., was an orphan, who, according to the story, was reared in the lavatory of the Abbey chapter-house. The building has a Doric portico, supporting a pediment, on which are 3 sculptured figures representing the founder of the institution and its objects.

Upon *Lady Hill*, among the ruins of an old castle, is a monument to the last Duke of Gordon (d. 1836).

Pluscardine Abbey, 7 m. S.W., is well deserving of a visit.

Protected from the chilling blasts of the Northern Ocean by a long and high ridge of hills, now thickly planted with fir, the abbey stands at the narrowest point of a valley which expands towards the E. and W. in a long vista of luxuriant fertility. The very perfect remains have been enclosed together with some 10 acres of well-planted and well-kept garden. The nicely-shaven lawn and well-pruned trees convey a vivid impression of mediæval civilisation and monastic repose.

The Cistercian monastery of Pluscardine was founded by Alexander II. in 1230, and dedicated to St. Andrew.

Its church, chiefly First Pointed, though retaining the round arch in its doorways, was cruciform, with a square central tower. The nave, which was never completed, is gone, all but a fragment of wall; the aisleless choir of 3 bays is 56 ft. long.

The *Chapter-house*, about 30 ft. square, shows remarkably delicate mouldings, and, like that of Elgin, is supported by a single central pier. The N. transept is a fine composition, and has had a large round window in the gable. The old groined roof is still standing in the aisles of the transept, and also in a small chapel at the N. of the choir.

On the N. wall of the choir is a recess, above which 2 angels are represented as supporting a monstrance. A flight of steps leads from the ch. up to the dormitories, upon which a substantial roof has been set.

The refectory has been fitted up as a Free Ch., and the old pulpit of St. Giles Ch. Elgin (dated 1684) has been placed in it. The buildings are luxuriantly overgrown, and there are some fine old trees in the grounds.

The *Church of Birnie* on the Lossie, 3 m. S. of Elgin, the oldest bishop's ch. in the diocese of Moray, still preserves its nave and chancel entire. There is no E. window, the church being lighted by round-headed windows of Norman date. In the interior is a copper bell, called the "Ronnel Bell," and said to have been brought from Rome, but probably of Celtic origin. To be buried in Birnie kirkyard is the ambition of many of the country people, who consider its soil peculiarly sacred.

[*Branch to Lossiemouth Stat.*

At $2\frac{3}{4}$ m. l., are the ruins of *Spynie Castle*, the old residence of the Moray bishop, whose See (afterwards transferred to Elgin) was settled at Spynie by a Papal bull in 1203. In 1590 the temporalities of the Moray bishopric were granted to Alexander Lindsay, who was created Lord Spynie, and was afterwards killed in a street skirmish at Edinburgh. The castle originally consisted of a huge square tower of six stories, with turreted angles at the roof. A court was subsequently added, protected at the other 3 angles by towers, and on the S. and E. sides by a moat. Over the main entrance the crozier is still seen, and on the S. side the chapel can be identified.

Rt. are *Pitgaveny Ho.* (Capt. Brander) and all that remains of *Loch Spynie*, once very large, but drained by the Spynie Canal.

$5\frac{1}{2}$ m. **Lossiemouth** ✲, the N. part of which is called *Branderburgh*, serves as the port of Elgin. A harbour, built here in 1839, with 2 basins, was deepened in 1893-4 at very considerable expense.

4 m. W. of Lossiemouth along the coast, beyond *Covesea* (pron. Causea) *Lightho.*, are the *Covesea Caves.*]

Quitting Elgin, the line crosses the Lossie at *Palmer's Bridge*, a name betokening its association with Pluscardine and Elgin, to

$74\frac{1}{2}$ m. **Mosstowie Stat.** Rt. on a wooded hill is *York Tower.*

$76\frac{1}{2}$ m. **Alves Stat.**

[*Branch* runs N., passing

$2\frac{3}{4}$ m. **Coltfield Stat.** to

5 m. **Burghead Stat.** ✶, a watering-place and important fishing village. Traces of ramparts and earthworks across the promontory on which it is situated bear out the tradition that Burghead was a Danish fort, although some antiquaries have considered it to have been the site of the Roman "ultima Pteroton" (?). In 1864 some mounds were examined at Bennet Hill, when kists were found with complete skeletons and flint arrowheads. The line now turns E. along the coast, passing

6 m. **Cummingston Stat.** to

7 m. **Hopeman Stat.**, another fishing village. 2 m. E. is *Duffus Ho.* (Sir A. Dunbar, Bt.), and beyond, *Gordonston* (Sir W. Gordon Cumming, Bt.).]

A fine view W. across the Moray Firth of the Rosshire Mts., including *Ben Wyvis*, is obtained from

$80\frac{1}{2}$ m. **Kinloss Stat.**, close to which are the ruins of **Kinloss Abbey,** one of the magnificent Cistercian foundations of David I. (1150). The abbot was mitred and had a seat in Parliament. At the Reformation it was sold, and for centuries the building served as a quarry for all the houses and walls in the neighbourhood; now it is reduced to 2 fine round-headed archways and a few vaults. King Edward I. in 1303, and King Edward III. in 1336, lodged in the Abbey.

[*Branch to* **Findhorn**, a fishing-village 2 m. N.W. at the entrance of Findhorn Bay, the estuary of the *Findhorn*, which, owing to the devastations caused by the sea, is the third village of its name.

"The first stood about a mile W. of the bar, the point at which the river originally entered the Firth, before the eastward progress of the moving sand drove it into the channel it now occupies. The second village was planted a little to the N. of the present one, but it too has been swept away. Nor does it appear that the existing town is free from the risk of being overtaken, partially at least, by a similar catastrophe."—Sir A. GEIKIE.]

83½ m. **Forres Stat.**, where the High. Rly. main line from Perth to Inverness (Rte. 42) is joined.

FORRES ✲ is a clean little town, believed by some to have been a Roman station, and the Varis of Ptolemy. On an elevated platform, at the W. end of High St. nearest the station, stood the *Castle*, the site of which is marked by a tall granite *Obelisk* to the memory of Dr. Thomson, a native, whose devotion to the troops in the Crimea is gratefully remembered. S. of the town rises the wooded *Hill of Cluny;* its summit, crowned by a *Tower*,[1] raised (1807) as a monument to Nelson, and accessible by winding paths, may be reached by following the street at the side of the Town Hall. On the S. slope of this hill is *Cluny Hydro. Estab.*, one of the oldest in Scotland.

About a mile W. of Forres the Findhorn is crossed by a driving *Suspension Bridge* replacing a stone bridge swept away by the floods, 1829.

The most interesting antiquarian relic in the neighbourhood is **Sweno's Stone*, a narrow shaft of sandstone, standing in a field at the side of the road leading to Kinloss, 1 m. E. of the Town Hall. It is 23 ft. high, and is carved with figures of warriors and animals.

"These figures are arranged closely in five divisions, forming, as it were, so many passages of the story."—MUIR.

It is asserted that the stone was erected by Malcolm II. or Macbeth (?) to commemorate the expulsion of the Danes.

A short distance beyond Sweno's Stone, but almost concealed in a hedge is a mass of granite riveted with iron, which marks the spot where witches used to be burnt.

Forres is especially interesting as being the scene of a portion of "Macbeth."

EXCURSIONS :—

(1) S. **Up the Findhorn River.** The scenery of its high old red sandstone banks is almost unrivalled in Scotland. This excursion, at least as far as *Randolph's Leap*, should on no account be omitted.

Drive by the public road, or (*by order*) through the *Altyre Grounds* (Sir W. Gordon Cumming, Bt.) to *Sluie*, 5 m. Thence visitors are allowed to follow a beautiful path along the rt. bank of the river for 2½ m., passing l. *Logie Ho.* (Mrs. Smith Cumming), the carriage being sent round.

The bends and twists of the river, as it forces its way through grooves in the rock at the base of precipices of old red sandstone, are extraordinary. The path commands a new view of a fresh reach or bend at every 100 yards, as the water, brown as porter, settles in dark pools or eddies over shelving rocks.

The public road is joined at the bridge over the *Divie*—a tributary which has to be crossed. Left is *Relugas Ho.* (Mrs. Ernald Smith). 200 yds. farther on a path, crossing a stile and passing a stone which marks the extraordinary height the river attained during the terrible floods of August 1829, which devastated the grounds of Relugas, planted and laid out with so much care and taste by Sir Thomas Dick-Lauder[1] (1784-1848), their former owner, leads to **Randolph's Leap**, where the bed of the stream contracts, and down the river to its junc. with the Divie. [From here *Dunphail Stat.* is only 2½ m. distant, see p. 232.] The path also leads *up* the stream to *Daltulich Bridge* (1 m.) to which the carriage may be sent. [This bridge is crossed to reach *Darnaway Cas.* (p. 307)]. Driving 3 m. beyond this bridge up the rt. bank of the Findhorn we pass *New Inn.* (11 m. from Forres), and rt. (at 12¾ m.) *Glen Ferness Ho.* (Earl of Leven and Melville) to *Dunearn Lodge* and **Dulsie Bridge** 16 m.

At Dulsie Bridge the river runs through an extraordinary narrow granite gorge called the "*Streens.*" "What spot on earth can exceed in beauty the landscape comprising the Old Bridge of Dulsie,

---

[1] Key kept at the Cemetery Lodge.

[1] See Sir T. Dick-Lauder's "*Moray Floods,*" 3rd ed., 1873.

spanning with its lofty arch the deep dark pool, shut in by gray and fantastic rocks, surmounted with the greenest of greenswards, with clumps of ancient weeping birches, backed by the dark pine-trees!"—*St. John.*

For roads hence to **Grantown** and to **Inverness**, see p. 232.

The neighbourhood of the Findhorn has been rendered classic ground to the sportsman by the writings of Charles St. John, author of "Wild Sports in the Highlands," etc. etc.

(2) S.W. to **Darnaway Castle**[1] (Earl of Moray), 4 m.

Drive there direct, or visit it by returning from the last excursion *via* Daltulich Bridge. Part of an old castle is included in the modern Italian edifice. *Earl Randolph's Hall*, 100 ft. long, with roof of oak, carved with pendants, is very magnificent. The castle is embosomed in a forest of oak and pine, and the extensive walks through the woods on the banks of the Findhorn afford pretty views.

(3) E. to **Pluscarden Abbey** (p. 304), 9 m.

See p. 232 for the rest of the rly. journey from Forres *via* Nairn to

108¼ m. **INVERNESS**✲ (p.375).

ROUTE 64.

Aberdeen to Inverness and by Grange Loop, Portsoy, Elgin and Forres.

See *Note* beginning of Rte. 63.

Before 48¾ m. **Grange Stat.** (see Rte. 63) the line trends N., crosses the *Isla*, and ascends *Glen Barry* to

51½ m. **Knock Stat.**, and

52¾ m. **Glenbarry Stat.**, with l. *Knock Hill* (1409 ft.). Passing

56 m. **Cornhill Stat.** we reach

58¼ m. **Tillynaught Junc.**

[Branch N.E. by 1¼ m. *Ordens Stat.*, and 3½ m. *Lady Bridge Stat.*, to

6 m. **Banff Harbour Stat.**, p. 299.]

61 m. **Portsoy Stat.** a small seaport. The geologist will find in the rocks in the immediate neighbourhood a perfect storehouse of mineralogical specimens. *Portsoy marble*, a beautiful variety of serpentine, and a peculiar flesh-coloured granite are quarried here. The line now runs W. by 63 m. **Glassaugh Stat.** and 65¼ m. **Tochieneal Stat.**, with l. the *Bin of Cullen* (1050 ft.), to

66½ m. **Cullen Stat.**✲, a small modern fishing town, but an ancient royal and parl. burgh, sloping down to the bay, on which is the fishermen's quarter, and on the shore of which rise 3 rocks called the "*Three Kings of Cullen.*" In a castle, whose site is doubtful, Bruce's Queen died. ½ m. S. of the town is *Cullen House*[1] (Dow. Countess of Seafield), a very picturesque and handsome castellated mansion, which contains a Portrait of *George Jamesone* by himself, one of his best works. Near it is the cruciform *Cullen Ch.* (well restored), founded by Bruce and made collegiate 1543 by Ogilvy of Findlater, whose fine mural tomb it contains. The ruins of *Findlater Cas.* are 2 m. E. on a rock jutting into the sea. The Norman family of St. Clair obtained it by marriage with Joanna of Findlater in the reign of David II. and in the 15th cent. the Ogilvies also obtained it by marriage. An Ogilvy was created Earl of Findlater 1638, but on the death of the 7th and last earl, 1811, the estates passed to the Seafield family.

The rly. crosses the principal street on a bridge of 6 arches, afterwards traverses a lofty viaduct, commanding a good view of the bay, and keeps along the coast—a charming bit—passing

68½ m. **Portknockie Stat.**

69¾ m. **Findochty Stat.** and

71¼ **Portessie Stat.** (whence a line runs S. to Keith, p. 302) to

72½ m. **Buckie Stat.**✲, a fishing

[1] Grounds open Tues., Thurs., and Sat. House generally shown.

[1] Visitors are generally allowed the privilege of driving through the fine woods.

town of some importance, with a second stat. on the Keith line. A good harbour constructed at the cost of £60,000 by the late Mr. Gordon of Cluny, was opened 1880. Passing

73½ m. **Buckpool Stat.,** and

75 m. **Port-Gordon Stat.,** with a harbour formed by the Duke of Richmond and Gordon in 1874 at the cost of £15,000, we reach

77¼ m. **Fochăbers Stat.** from which the town (p. 302) is 3½ m. S. The mouth of the Spey is now crossed by a handsome long iron girder bridge to

78½ m. **Garmouth Stat.** The Spey like the Findhorn is notorious for its sudden floods or "spates." In consequence the river bed and delta at its mouth are constantly changing. Charles II. landed here 1650 and was at once compelled to sign the Solemn League and Covenant. In 1784 two Yorkshire men came here to purchase timber from the Duke of Gordon, and established 1 m. farther down the river a shipbuilding village which they named *Kingston*, after their own Kingston-on-Hull.

81¾ m. **Urquhart Stat.** 1½ m. N. is *Innes Ho.* (D. of Fife) a 17th cent. mansion, formerly a seat of the Innes family, which in 1812 succeeded to the ducal title of Roxburghe. Passing

84¼ m. **Calcots Stat.,** and turning S. we cross the *Lossie* twice and reach

87¼ m. **Elgin Stat.** ✲ See p. 303. See Rtes. 63 and 42 from Elgin to

124¼ m. **INVERNESS** ✲ (p. 375).

ROUTE 65.

Aberdeen to Inverness by Keith Craigellachie Junc., Elgin and Forres.

See *Note* beginning of Rte. 63.

To 53¼ m. **Keith Stat.** see Rte. 63.

The train now ascends (S.W.) the valley of the little river *Isla*.

54. m. **Earlsmill Stat.** close to Keith (p. 302).

56¾ m. **Auchindachy Stat.**

59½ m. **Drummuir Stat.,** just beyond (rt.) the handsome *Drummuir Cas.* (T. D. Gordon Duff, Esq.), and its park and gardens are well seen. Presently we keep along the E. bank of the beautiful narrow *Loch Park*, the steep W. bank of which is clothed with firs. Beyond the watershed we cross the *Fiddich* and pass l. the massive ruin of *Balvenie Cas.* (not older than 15th cent.), once the property of the Atholl family, whose motto is on the front of it, before

64 m. **Dufftown Stat.** ✲ The town, 1 m. S., was founded 1817 by James Duff, 4th Earl of Fife, at the confluence of the *Dullan* and *Fiddich Waters.* ½ m. S. of it, on the steep banks of the Dullan, is *Mortlach Ch.*, originally founded as a primitive Cathedral Ch. by Malcolm II. (1153-65), but hideously modernised. A few small lancet windows and some tombstones in the interior are the only parts really old.

[A driving road runs S.W. up *Glen Rinnes*, through which the Dullan flows. The limestone scenery in this glen contrasts well with the granite peaks of the *Convals* (1810 and 1867 ft.) and of *Ben Rinnes* (2755 ft.) to the W. The road, having crossed (7 m.) a high watershed (1022 ft.), joins the foot of *Glen Livet* (abt. 12 m.) near the celebrated distillery (pp. 231, 309).

By *Glen Fiddich*, also very pretty, and 2 m. up which l. is the *Tower of Auchindoun*, burnt by the Clan Mackintosh (16th cent.)—an event commemorated in an old ballad—the *head* waters of the Livet can be reached.

In Glen Livet James VI. in person defeated the rebel earls Huntly and Erroll Oct. 14, 1594, and afterwards destroyed their strongholds of Huntly and Slains Castles.]

The line now runs N.W. down Glen Fiddich, passes rt. the fine old turreted mansion of *Kininvie Ho.* (Col. A. Y. Leslie), and through a fine gorge to

68 m. **Craigellachie Junc.** ✲, sometimes called Lower Craigellachie to distinguish it from the rock and bridge at Aviemore (p. 227), where the Fiddich falls into the Spey. S. W. a line ascends Strath Spey (Rte. 66). We cross the Spey into Morayshire by Telford's elegant *iron bridge* of a single span (150 ft.), devised to allow ample waterway for floods, and descend its l. bank.

$68\frac{3}{4}$ m. **Dandaleith Stat.** Across the river is *Arndilly Ho.* (Mrs. Kinloch Grant).

71 m. **Rothes Stat.** ✲ This little town is picturesquely situated on the l. bank of the Spey and in full view of *Ben Aigan* (1544 ft.). From it the noble family of the Leslies takes the title of Earl. The ruined walls of their old *Castle* rise above it on the W. They sold this estate to the Earl of Seafield about 1700 and migrated to Fife. The line now quits the river and passes through the "*Glen of Rothes*" to

$77\frac{3}{4}$ m. **Longmorn Stat.**

$80\frac{3}{4}$ m. **Elgin Stat.** ✲, p. 303. See Rtes. 63 and 42 from Elgin to

$117\frac{3}{4}$ m. **INVERNESS** ✲ (p. 375).

ROUTE 66.

Elgin to Perth by Strathspey and Boat of Garten.

About 2 trains daily in $4\frac{1}{2}$-6 hrs. The most convenient route is *via* Forres, but this is a far finer route, the Strathspey portion of this line being pretty and interesting and keeping alongside the river.

The line is G. N. S. R. to Boat of Garten and thereafter High. Rly.

Strath Spey which this route traverses gives its name to the Scottish dance music "*The Strathspey.*"

To $12\frac{3}{4}$ m. **Craigellachie Junc.** ✲, see above.

Aberlour Ho. (J. R. Findlay, Esq.), a handsome modern mansion, is passed (l.) before

15 m. **Aberlour Stat.** ✲, a thriving little town. 1 m. up the *Lour* is a pretty fall called the *Lynn of Ruthrie.* **Ben Rinnes** (2755 ft.) is a conspicuous object l. *Carron Ho.* is seen rt. before crossing the river to

$18\frac{1}{4}$ m. **Carron Stat.** The *Windings of the Spey* are particularly fine between this and

23 m. **Blacksboat Stat.** The *Avon* falls in l. and the Spey is again crossed at

$24\frac{3}{4}$ m. **Ballindalloch Stat.** ✲ *Ballindalloch Cas.* (Sir G. Macpherson Grant, Bt.), on the rt. bank of the Avon, consists of an imposing old sq. tower with modern additions. In the park are some fine avenues leading towards the junc. of the two rivers. The Avon from Loch A'an (p. 229) is the largest trib. of the Spey. [2 m. up is *Dalnashaugh Inn* ✲; 5 m. up, the *Livet Water* from Glen Livet (pp. 231, 308) falls in, and at 15 m. is **Tomintoul** ✲, p. 231.]

28 m. **Advie Stat.**, with a driving bridge across the Spey. 1 m. farther on (rt.) is *Tulchan Lo.* (Countess Dow. of Seafield) charmingly situated, see p. 231.

$33\frac{3}{4}$ m. **Cromdale Stat.**, with a fine range of hills l., see p. 230. $\frac{1}{2}$ m. beyond, rt. a glimpse is caught of the top of *Castle Grant* (p. 230).

$36\frac{3}{4}$ m. **Grantown Stat.** ✲. The village lies 1 m. rt. and is a very favourite summer resort and excellent centre, see p. 229.

$41\frac{1}{4}$ m. **Nethybridge Stat.** ✲, a pleasant summer retreat with delightful pine and heather forest behind, see pp. 230, 231. The Spey is once more crossed to

46 m. **Boat of Garten Stat.** ✲ (see p. 229). Here the main High. Rly. line (Rte. 42) is joined and followed to

$134\frac{1}{2}$ m. **PERTH** ✲ (p. 194).

SECTION V.

WEST COAST (SOUTHERN PORTION)—ESTUARY OF THE CLYDE—BUTE—KYLES OF BUTE—ARRAN—LOCH FYNE—CAMPBELTOWN—ISLAY AND JURA.

§ 1. GENERAL INFORMATION.

IT may be truly said that few districts in Britain excel in beauty the Estuary of the Clyde and the numerous sea lochs or fiords which branch out of it, penetrating into the very heart of grand mountain chains. Thus there is the greatest variety of scenery, starting from the flat borders of Dumbartonshire and Renfrewshire, and ending in the wild glens of Argyll.

Every part of this district is now made accessible by *Steamboats*, and the Clyde river steamers are among the most comfortable and best adapted for their purpose to be met with anywhere. They combine great speed with the most commodious arrangements, and the newest of them are furnished with spacious lavatories, hair-dressing rooms, post office, and good restaurants, with prices on the whole moderate. One of the sights of Scotch travel is to see the tourist cargo sit down to breakfast and dinner.

Between Glasgow, Greenock, Gourock, Craigendoran, or Wemyss Bay, and Rothesay, the traffic somewhat resembles that of the cabs in the *Strand*, or the *Gondolas* in the Grand Canal of Venice.

During summer and autumn, Glasgow and its suburbs are emptied into seaside places of sojourn, and a vibrating crowd, morning and evening, of merchants, clerks, and shopmen rather tends to crush and elbow the traveller from a distance, who should also avoid, if possible, descending the Clyde on Saturday.

The shores of the Clyde from Glasgow to Greenock are interesting as a field of human activity and industry, while lower down, as far as the open sea, they are dotted with watering-places, and with the neat villas or stately mansions of Glasgow manufacturers and merchants.

The impressive Rock and Castle of Dumbarton alone in such a scene throw back the mind to ancient days.

A visit to Arran, a model on a small scale of Alpine scenery, and containing more variety of beauty than almost any island of the same size, is highly recommended. The numerous ways in which it and the other places of interest on the W. coast can be reached, are apparent from the number of routes in this section leading to the same place.

§ 2. PRINCIPAL CENTRES.

POINTS OF INTEREST.

1. **Glasgow.** The Estuary of the Clyde, cf. Section II.
2. **Paisley.** Its Abbey, its Threadmills, and the Braes of Gleniffer (all best visited from Glasgow).
3. **Rothesay.** The Island of Bute.
4. **Brodick.** The Island of Arran.
5. **Inveraray.** The Castle, the Beech Avenues, Loch Fyne, and Loch Awe by Glen Aray.
6. **Campbeltown** or **Machrihanish.** Golf Links and the Mull of Kintyre.
7. **Port Ellen** or **Bridgend.** Islay.
8. **Port Askaig** (in Islay). Islay and Jura.

ROUTES.

ROUTE 67.

Glasgow to Helensburgh and Gareloch [also to Rothesay, etc.] N.B.R.

Express trains run to Helensburgh in 45 min. There are through trains from Edinburgh to Helensburgh *via* Cowlairs (pp. 132 and 149).

We leave **Queen St. Low Level Stat.**, or one of the W. end stats.

This route is described as far as

15¼ m. **Dumbarton Stat.** ✲, the *Junc.* for *Loch Lomond*, etc., in Rte. 23.

The line crosses the *Leven* and passes through a sandstone tunnel above which is the site of *Cardross Cas.*, marked by a clump of trees, where King Robert the Bruce d. 1329.

19 m. **Cardross Stat.** The grandfather of Lord Macaulay was minister here 1774-89. On the hillside 1 m. above the stat. is the keep-tower of the *Castle of Kilmahew*, and near it the handsome modern house of *Kilmahew* (J. W. Burns, Esq.) in the old Scottish style of architecture. *Kilmahew Chapel* is a small Gothic building, consecrated May 10, 1467, to St. Mahew, a companion of St. Patrick.

Across the Clyde are Port-Glasgow and Greenock (p. 314); and passing the promontory of *Ardmore* a fine view of the Argyllshire Mts. opens out l. as the train approaches

22½ m. †**Craigendoran Pier Stat.**

[This is the **Junc.** for the *West High. Rly*, via *Garelochhead, Arrochar, Loch Lomond.*

and *Moor of Rannoch* to **Fort-William** (Rte. 81).

Steamers, mostly owned by the N.B. Rly., sail from here to *Dunoon* (40 min.)—where the "Ivanhoe" for Arran (Rte. 71), the "Lord of the Isles" for Inveraray (Rte. 74), and the "Columba" for Ardrishaig and Oban (Rte. 82) can be joined—*Rothesay* (1¼ hrs.), *Arrochar* at the head of *Loch Long* (2 hrs.), *Garelochhead* (45 min.), etc. (see below and Rtes. 68 and 76).]

23¾ m. **Helensburgh Stat.** ✲, with another stat. ½ m. N. on the W. High. Rly. (p. 347), acquired its name at the end of the 18th cent. from the wife of Sir James Colquhoun of Luss, on whose property it was built. It is situated at the mouth of the **Gareloch** (not to be confounded with *Gairloch* in Ross-shire) an arm of the sea running inland (N.) for about 8 m. amidst charming scenery, although not so wild as that of the neighbouring Loch Long (Rte. 76).

The town consists of a row of shops and lodging-houses facing the sea and stretching along the shore for nearly 1 m., and of a hill behind, covered with pleasant villas, with roads intersecting each other at right angles. A road crossing this hill leads in 5 m. to *Loch Lomond*.

Near the *Pier*, from which *Steamers* sail several times daily to *Greenock* on the opposite side of the Clyde, is a granite *Obelisk* in memory of Henry Bell (pp. 143 and 151).

[There is now a delightful moorland drive, commanding fine views of the Loch Long Hills, to the top of the hill behind the town (2 m.), up *Glen Fruin* [cf. p. 153] (8 m.), across the hill (steep) to *Faslane Bay* (10 m.), and along the side of the Gareloch to Helensburgh 16 m.

Another fine, but long, circular drive is that by the road through 7½ m. *Garelochhead*, 9 m. *Whistlefield* [below], and by the E. side of Loch Long to 18 m. *Arrochar*, returning by 20 m. *Tarbet*, and 28½ m. Luss to Helensburgh, 37½ m.]

Helensburgh to Garelochhead, 7½ m.

By *Road* (omnibus daily), *Rly.* from *Upper Helensburgh* (p. 347), commanding fine views; or *Steamer*, generally from *Craigendoran Pier*.

1 m. from Helensburgh is *Ardincaple Cas.* (Sir J. Colquhoun, Bt.), and the *Training Ship* "Empress" is seen lying off

2 m. †**Row** ✲ (pron. *Rue* from rugha = a headland), one of the most select of the Clyde watering-places. The houses here, and indeed all along the E. side of the loch to Garelochhead, are chiefly large villas—permanent residences not let as summer quarters—with beautifully kept gardens: the climate being peculiarly mild and favourable for horticulture.

The famous Rev. J. Macleod Campbell was parish minister here until deposed for heresy 1831, and in the ch.-yd. Henry Bell is buried.

There is a *Ferry* (½ m.) across to

†**Roseneath** ✲, a small hamlet with a pretty little modern Gothic Ch. Close to the *Old* Ch. is a shady grove of yews called the *Bishop's Walk*. 1 m. S. a gate on the public road flanked by 2 stone pillars leads in 100 yds. to a couple of *Silver Firs*, called "Adam and Eve," prodigies of growth hardly to be matched elsewhere. 2 m. S. on a promontory, beside *Old Roseneath Cas.*, is *Roseneath Ho.* (The Duke of Argyll), an Italian mansion begun in 1803.

4 m. (W. side) †**Barremman** for **Clynder**, both favourite watering-places.

4½ m. (E. side) †**Shandon** ✲, ½ m. from *W. Shandon Ho.*, a somewhat fantastic building erected by the late well-known R. Napier, engineer, and now a *Hydro. Estab.*

Opposite is †**Rahane Ferry**, and further up the W. side †**Mambeg**.

7½ m. †**Garelochhead** ✲, a considerable village, with numerous villas and a rly. stat. on the W. High. Rly., p. 347.

The road over the hill by *Whistlefield* ★ to 2 m. *Portincaple* (ferry) on Loch Long commands a fine view of both lochs, of

Argyll's Bowling Green (the hills separating Lochs Long and Goil), and of *Loch Goil* with *Carrick Cas.* near its mouth (Rte. 76).

Return from Garelochhead may be made by *Glen Fruin* (p. 312).

ROUTE 68.

Glasgow to Rothesay (Island of Bute). Steamboat all the way.

This sail takes 3¼ hrs. by fast steamer.

Tourists, if they have once sailed down the river and seen the extraordinary mass of shipping and the wonderful line, on both sides, of quays, docks, shipbuilding yards, and embankments, will probably prefer to take train to *Craigendoran* (Rte. 67), *Gourock* (Rte. 69), *Greenock* (Rte. 70), or *Wemyss Bay* (Rt. 71).

Moving off from the **Broomielaw** (see p. 141), the grand works for widening and deepening the channel of the Clyde will not fail to arrest the stranger's attention. Since the year 1770 about £14,200,000 have been expended on these operations, which have employed the skill of such engineers as Smeaton, Watt, Rennie, Telford, Golborne, Walker, and Deas. 4 m. below the town a trap-dyke, which crossed the stream, 900 ft. long by 300 ft. broad, was in 1852 blasted by gunpowder, so as to open a channel 14 ft. deep at low water, now more than 24 ft. Whole mountains of rock and earth have been and are constantly being raised from the bottom by dredging. The banks, formerly defended by dykes, now, for a long distance, rise above the level of high water, and need no protection but loose whinstone rubble. The result is that the largest ocean-going vessels can now moor alongside the quays at Glasgow.

Along the l. bank are the iron-roofed sheds of Clyde Place, Kingston Dock, and Windmillcroft, followed by Springfield Quay (for iron-ore traffic), General Terminus Quay (export coal trade), Mavisbank Quay, Finnieston Elevating Ferry (by which vehicles of all descriptions, up to 50 tons weight, can be taken across the river at all states of the tide on the level of the quays), Plantation Quay, Cessnock Dock (p. 141), and the Graving Docks.

Along the rt. bank, below the River Steamboat Wharf, with its iron-roofed sheds, waiting-rooms, and offices, is Robertson St. Quay, succeeded by a continuous line of sheds from York St. to the entrance to Queen's Dock (p. 141), with the exception of Finnieston and Stobcross Quays, which have some very large cranes — capable of lifting weights up to 130 tons. W. of Queen's Dock are Kelvinhaugh Wharf and Yorkhill Wharf (for discharging timber, and with extensive lairage slaughter houses and sale-room accommodation for American cattle).

The Quays and Docks end on both sides at Govan Ferry. To these succeed long lines of iron shipbuilding yards, the number and magnitude of which attest the pre-eminence that the Clyde has over all other rivers in this special and important trade.

l. The town of **Govan** [Rly. from St. Enoch's Station, Glasgow, in 15 min.], founded in very early times, has of recent years advanced immensely in importance, owing chiefly to the shipbuilding trade. Here are the far-famed yards of Messrs. Napier and Messrs. Elder, the latter—*Fairfield Works*—being the largest in the world. Opposite is †**Partick** [Rly. from Queen St., Glasgow, p. 149], where the Kelvin joins the Clyde near the *Shipbuilding Yard* and *Graving-Dock* of Messrs. D. and W. Henderson.

Behind, the *University Buildings* on Gilmore Hill (p. 139) are conspicuous. Passing *Whiteinch*, at 5 m. rt. is *Scotstoun Ho.*, and across the river

l. *Elderslie Ho.* (A. A. Speirs, Esq.), built abt. 1780, upon part of the lands which originally belonged to the Wallace family. Sir Wm. Wallace was born abt. 1270 in the village of Elderslie 6 m. S.W. (p. 321). Behind Elderslie Ho., amongst the trees, is

l. †**Renfrew** (rly. from St. Enoch's *via* Paisley, ½ hr.), the capital of the county, which gives the title of Baron to the Prince of Wales. It was made a royal burgh in 1396, and, although not now of great importance, is still a thriving place with shipbuilding yds.

To Renfrew succeed the woods and grounds of *Blythswood*, the seat of Lord Blythswood, whom the Queen visited in Aug. 1888. It is bounded W. by the *Cart*, formed by two streams, the Black and White Cart, which, rising in the Ayrshire hills, unite at Inchinnan, 1 m. S., and here join the Clyde.

It has been celebrated by Burns in his song of the Gallant Weaver —"Where Cart rins rowin' to the sea." Near *Inchinnan Bridge* the Earl of Argyll was arrested 1685 as a rebel.

rt. at **Clydebank,** with the large *Shipbuilding Yards* of Messrs. G. and J. Thomson, is a cut to the Forth and Clyde Canal.

The steamer now runs parallel with (rt.) the rly. between Glasgow and Loch Lomond (see Rte. 23).

l. is *Erskine Ho.*, the seat of Lord Blantyre, a tudor mansion built 1828, with an obelisk on a hill W. of it to the 11th Lord Blantyre, who, after passing through the Peninsular War, was accidentally shot during the riots in Brussels 1830.

The opening reach of the river is very fine, with the magnificent isolated *Rock of Dumbarton* standing in the distance as sentinel over the crowded waterway. In clear weather *Ben Lomond's* top may be discerned.

11 m. rt. †**Bowling** ✲ and *Dunglass Cas.* (p. 150).

14 m. rt. †**Dumbarton** ✲, nestling under the shadow of the two-peaked rock (p. 151).

Across the river from Dumbarton is the village and rly stat. of **Langbank** (p. 321), and 2 m. W. *Finlayston*, in former times the residence of Lord Glencairn, patron of Burns.

19 m. l. †**Port-Glasgow** ✲ was founded in 1668, to be, as its name indicates, the harbour of Glasgow, but since the river has been so much deepened it has declined in importance, and ships that do not stop at Greenock go right up to Glasgow. E. of the town, on a low peninsula, is *Newark Cas.*, a large quadrangular pile of the 16th cent., but much modernised. Over the doorway is the date, and an inscription, "The blessing of God be hereon." It belonged to the Dennistouns, and is now the property of the Shaw-Stewart family; it is inhabited by working men's families.

Rt. is **Cardross** (p. 311), and beyond it *Ardmore Point*.

On both banks may be seen the steam of the locomotive; that on rt. from the Glasgow and Helensburgh Rly. (Rte. 67), and on l. from the Greenock lines (Rtes. 69 and 70).

Looking N., the tourist sees the beautiful entrance to the Gareloch, backed by rugged mountains. To the rt. of it is **Craigendoran Pier** and **Helensburgh** (pp. 311, 312).

We now stop l. at the bustling

22 m. †**Greenock Custom House Quay**, with a sea frontage of more than 300 yds., and a *Custom House* in Grecian style.

GREENOCK ✲ is a busy seaport, where all passengers for Ireland, America, etc., join their steamers. It is important likewise for its trade and industries, its sugar refineries, woollen spinning, iron-works, shipbuilding yards, and docks.

"The prosperity of Greenock dates from the year 1707, shortly after the union with England, when the British Parliament granted what the Scottish Parliament had refused, viz. the privilege of constructing a harbour."—SMILES.

The town stretches for fully 4 m. along the sea margin, has quays and docks measuring 2 m., and boasts several shipbuilding yards, which rival those of Glasgow. The graving-dock was opened in 1874. The **James Watt Dock**, opened in 1886, is capable of holding the largest steamers afloat.

In front of Greenock is situated the "Tail of the Bank," the best anchorage in the Firth of Clyde.

The theatre, originally built by Kemble, adjoining the Cathcart St. Rly. Stat., is now the **Sugar Exchange.** The present theatre is ½ m. farther W.

The **Municipal Buildings** in the centre of the town, with a tower 245 feet high, were completed 1886, at a cost of more than £100,000.

In Greenock James Watt was born (1736), and is commemorated in the **Watt Monument,** a modern Gothic building in Union St., built by his son in 1837, to contain a *Statue* of the great engineer by *Sir Francis Chantrey*, subscribed for by the people of Greenock, and to afford accommodation for a *Scientific Library* founded by him, and for the *Greenock Library*, instituted in 1753, the second oldest subscription library in Scotland, that in Kelso being the oldest. Adjoining this building are a *Museum* and a *Lecture Hall*, erected in 1876 by Mr. J. M'Lean.

The town is well supplied with water from a **Reservoir** of 300 acres called *Loch Thom*, or "Shaw's Water," about 3 m. to the S. As it is situated at a height of 500 ft. above the sea, the water when nearing the town is turned to economical purposes for driving *wheels* of mills and manufactories, instead of steam. Water for drinking is now supplied from another large reservoir, in the valley of the Gryfe.

The streets in the business part of Greenock are narrow and unattractive, but in the west end the streets are broad, planted with trees, and lined with handsome villas and mansions. The extreme beauty of the situation must not be forgotten, on the broad expanse of the Clyde, gay with shipping, in every position and every variety of form.

The finest view is to be got from the **Esplanade**, which stretches from Princes Pier for 1¼ m. to the west.

The *Heights* behind the town are worth ascending for the sake of the romantic *Highland View* over sea and mountain, which may be advantageously commanded from the picturesque **Cemetery**, and still more advantageously from the *Lyle Road*, which winds over the hill to the west. Those who can walk should ascend the hill behind the paper mills of Brown and Stewart, and follow the "lead" or aqueduct of the Shaw's Water to the reservoir.

Admirers of the national poet Burns may feel disposed to visit the tomb of "Highland Mary," with a monument erected by the Greenock Burns Club, in the graveyard of the North Kirk.

Leaving the Custom Ho. Quay we have rt. *The Tail of the Bank* (above), as we approach

23 m. †**Princes Pier**, where passengers by the G. and S.W. Rly. (new stat. erected here 1894) join the Steamer (Rte. 70).

We now skirt the *Esplanade*, flanked by *Fort Matilda*, a puny battery of 7 guns, above which appears the *Wood Institution* for aged and infirm seamen, to

25 m. †**Gourock**✲, with a bay, largely used for laying up yachts in winter.

Since the extension of the Cal. Rly., and the erection of their large stat. and pier (Rte. 69) in 1889, Gourock rivals Princes Pier and Craigendoran as a place of embarkation for the Clyde excursion steamers.

The Darroch family have property here, and a mansion in the place of the *Old Castle.* Off Kempock Pt., the W. boundary of the bay, the steamer "Comet" (p. 151) was run down by the "Ayr" (1825) and 50 passengers drowned. 2 m. W. of the town, beyond the suburb of **Ashton,** stands the ruined tower of *Leven* Castle, and 1 m. further W. is the **Cloch Lighthouse,** where the open Firth (running N. and W.) may be said to begin.

Opposite Gourock (N.) is **Kilcreggan** (p. 334). W. of Kilcreggan open *Loch Long* (Rte. 76) and *Holy Loch* (Rte. 75), at the mouth (S. side) of which is

29 m. †**Hunter's Quay**✲ (called after the Hunters of *Hafton Ho.*, ¾ m. N.W.), at which a few steamers call. Here are the *Head Quarters* and Club Ho. of the *Clyde Yacht Club* and a *ferry* across the loch to Strone Pt. (Rte. 76). The steamer generally crosses from Gourock direct to

29¾ m. †**Kirn**✲, almost a prolongation of

31 m. †**Dunoon**✲, one of the most frequented of the Clyde watering-places, where numerous steamers call daily, and, from its position, commanding the whole sweep of the firth.

Above the Pier, between the E. and W. Bays, is a conical rock, which bears traces of the foundations of an ancient *Castle* which played a considerable part in the history of Scotland. It was early the seat of the Lord High Steward of Scotland, and in 1370 became a Royal Palace under the Hereditary Keepership of the Campbells of Lochow, ancestors of the Duke of Argyll, who still holds that office. Behind are the grounds of Castle Ho., now a *Public Park.*

[Here the *Coach* starts for the *Loch Eck* route to Inveraray (Rte. 75).]

Crossing the W. Bay with its pleasure boats, along and above which are numerous private residences, passing l. the *Gantock Rocks,* marked by a beacon, and keeping along the "*Bulwood*" we reach

35 m. †**Innellan**✲. Opposite is **Wemyss Bay** (p. 322), to which Rothesay steamers calling here cross.

37½ m. †**Toward**, at which a few steamers call. On *Toward Pt.*, one of the S. extremities of the District of **Cowall,** is a *Lighthouse.* 2 m. W. is *Castle Toward* (C. C. Findlay, Esq.), a modern mansion with well wooded policies, below which near the shore is an ivy covered *Tower*, the remains of a stronghold of the Lamonts (cf. p. 331).

The steamer now crosses to Bute, beyond which the Arran Mts. are visible.

The **Island of Bute**, although far inferior to Arran in grandeur of scenery, is too often underrated. It is hilly, though not mountainous, commands fine views, and contains some interesting antiquarian remains.[1] On its E. side is *Mount Stuart* (p. 317), the seat of the Marq. of Bute, to whom most of the island belongs. We call at

40 m. †**Craigmore,** with its pleasant villas, before reaching the busy town of

41 m. †**ROTHESAY**✲,[2] an ancient royal burgh, giving the title of Duke to the Prince of Wales, and the capital of the county, which embraces Arran and the Cumbraes.

Its Pier is, after Greenock, the most thronged with steamers on the

1 See "Bute in the Olden Time," by Rev. J. K. Hewison, F.S.A., Scot. (Wm. Blackwood and Sons, 1894).

2 See, for miscellaneous information, the useful "Buteman Guide to Rothesay and Bute," 1d.

Clyde, whilst Rothesay Bay is always crowded with pleasure boats of every variety. Here are the *Head Quarters* of the "*Royal Northern Yacht Club.*"

It has long been the resort of invalids on account of its mild climate, but in summer—especially at Glasgow Fair time in July—it is somewhat overrun with trippers, being the Margate of the Clyde.

The modern town stretches round the bay, the houses E. of the pier enjoying lovely views up *Loch Striven* (p. 323). W. stretches the **Esplanade.**

The older town mounts the hill behind the pier, from which after 3 min. walk we reach **Rothesay Cas.**[1] said to have been founded in the 11th cent., by Magnus Barfod, King of Norway (see p. 340). The existing castle, not older than the 14th cent., is circular in plan, but flanked with 4 round towers at equal distances, of which 2 have wholly and one has partially fallen, and with a sq. projecting gatehouse in which were the principal apartments. It was built for a Royal Palace, and here lived Robert III., whose ill-fated son David, murdered at Falkland (p. 182), was 1st Duke of Rothesay. Cromwell began the work of destruction here 1650, completed by the Earl of Argyll's brother 1685, and since then it has been a ruin. The Marquis of Bute, Hereditary Keeper, in 1874 removed several old houses which had encroached on the palace precincts, cleared out the moat, filled it with water, laid out a pleasant walk round it, restored the old drawbridge, and put the buildings into a thorough state of repair, in which they are still maintained.

E. of the castle are the **County Buildings,** with sq. tower. In the *Court Room* is a portrait of the late Marq. of Bute, by J. Graham, 1839.

N. of the castle is the *Norman Stewart Institute* (with library, reading and recreation rooms, and temp. restaurant), the gift of Mr. N. Stewart of America, and his nephews (all natives of Rothesay). Traversing the squalid *High St.* we reach in ½ m. the Parish Ch., beside which is the ruined *Chancel* (13th cent.) of the Old Gothic **Ch. of St. Mary,** containing 2 canopied tombs with 3 effigies—one said to be that of Walter, 8th Heredit. Grand Steward of Scotland, the 2nd that of Marjory, daughter of Robt. Bruce, and the 3rd that of William Cumming, Sheriff of Ayr in 1265.

On high ground abt. 2 m. N.W. of the town is a *Golf Course* commanding fine views.

EXCURSIONS :—

(1) *Walk* along the **Heights** E. of the town, which command magnificent views.

(2) *Ascend* **Barone Hill** (530 ft.) 2 m. S. which is wooded and has well-marked ice-worn rocks.

(3) *Drive* along the shore to **Mount Stuart,**[1] 5 m.

The road—frequent public conveyances—leads round *Bogany Pt.* past a succession of villas, extending to 2½ m. *Ascog* (T. Russell, Esq., D. L., and Convener of the County), opposite the gate of which is a little bay with a *Free Ch.* on the promontory, then by *Ascog Hall*, etc., to

4 m. *Kerrycroy*, a picturesque little hamlet on the seashore, at the entrance to *Mount Stuart.*

This seat of the Marq. of Bute was rebuilt in Gothic style, from designs by Dr. Rowand Anderson, after it had been burnt in 1876, and contains a good collection of pictures which were fortunately saved. The *Hall* is lined profusely with costly

[1] Open daily (free) 10 to 6.

[1] Grounds always open to pedestrians when family away from home. Special order from the factor necessary for driving or to see the house.

foreign marbles of great beauty, and one of the large apartments has a frieze, 5 ft. deep, of wall paintings executed by Mr. H. W. Lonsdale, illustrating the life of St. Margaret. In one of the parks there are a number of Kangaroos.

(5) *Drive* S. by **Loch Fad** (1½ m.) and **Kingarth** (6½ m.) to **Kilchattan Bay,** 8 m., returning by *Kerrycroy*.

This is a *circular coach tour* (numerous coaches daily) of 17 m. On the W. shore of the narrow inland *Loch Fad* (fully 2 m. long (*fada*=*long*), with pleasure boats upon it) is *Kean's Cottage*, built by the actor 1827, and subsequently occupied by Sheridan Knowles.

From **Kingarth**✶ *Parish Ch.*, near which is a *Golf Course* parallel to the shore, a rough driving road, passing the *Standing Stones of Lubas*, leads in 2 m. S. to the ruins of *St. Blane's Chapel*, consisting of a nave and chancel, the latter being built of rubble with 2 lancet windows at the E. end and having a Norman arch. N. of the chapel, are traces of a remarkable circular structure, about 32 ft. wide, called the *Devil's Cauldron*. ½ m. W. on the shore is the *Vitrified Fort of Dunagoil*. *Garroch Head* the southernmost point of Bute is 1 m. S.

† **Kilchattan Bay** ✶ (1½ m. S.E. of Kingarth), where steamers from Fairlie and Millport (p. 330) call, is a pleasant quiet watering-place. We return to Kingarth and ascend the broad "new road" made by the Marq. of Bute, enjoying a grand retrospective view of the Arran Mts. From the top of the hill the coach descends to Kerrycroy (above), or a hilly moor road inland passing the S. end of *Loch Ascog* may be taken by those in carriages.

(6) *Drive* N. round the bay to **Port Bannatyne** (2½ m.) and W. across the island to **Etterick Bay** 5 m.

There are frequent excursion coaches. †Port Bannatyne✶ (or *Kamesburgh*) is a large village on *Kames Bay*. At its head *Kames Cas.*, the picturesque old tower of which is said to date from the 14th cent., stands in a park of fine trees. Here John Sterling was born 1806. Beside it is *Wester-Kames Cas.* At 3½ m. l., across the road from N. Bute Church, are the remains of a *Fort;* further on rt. a *Standing Stone* with a cross on it marks the site of *St. Colmac's Chap.*, and l. are the remains of a *Stone Circle*. Opposite Etterick Bay is *Ardlamont Pt.* (p. 331). The drive may be prolonged 4 m. N. along the shore to *Kilmichael Ferry*, where the remains of a Church dedicated to St. Michael may be seen.

Return may be made from *Etterick Bay* in 6 m. by *St. Ninian's Bay*, and over the hill passing *Greenan Loch*.

(7) *Drive* N. by *Kames Bay* (above) and along the *Kyles of Bute* to **Colintraive Ferry** (p. 323), 8 m. This road keeps along the base of *Kames Hill* (911 ft.), the highest ground in the island.

(8) For Excursions by steamer see Rtes. 71, 74, 82, and local time bills.

ROUTE 69.

Glasgow to Rothesay by Gourock. Cal. Rly.

Abt. 26 trains daily in ¾ hr. to Gourock; and abt. 8 steamers thence in 1 hr. to Rothesay.

Leaving the **Central Stat.** the train crosses the Clyde to

½ m. **Bridge St. Stat.**, then trends W. to

1¼ m. **Pollokshields Stat.**, adjoining *Shields Road Stat.* on the G. and S.W. Rly. (Rte. 70). The same set of rails are used as far as

7¼ m. **Paisley (Gilmour St.) Stat.**, an important junc. situated upon a lofty viaduct and provided with commodious station buildings for both rly. companies. Approaching the stat. a glimpse may be caught l. of the *Abbey* (p. 319).

[Lines run (1) to *Greenock* and *Gourock* [Cal. Rly.] (Rte. 69); (2) to *Greenock* (*Princes Pier*) [G. and S.W. Rly.] (Rte. 70); (3) to *Wemyss Bay* [Cal. Rly.] (Rte. 71); (4) to *Ardrossan and Ayr* [G. and S.W. Rly.] (Rtes. 73 and 18).]

PAISLEY✲, a royal and parl. burgh, the 6th largest town in Scotland, is situated on the *White Cart*—not now of the purity suggested by its name—a trib. of the Clyde, navigable from that river by small vessels and in process (1894) of being deepened.

Historical Notes.—Paisley was first known to civilisation when the Romans came here in 84 A.D. and placed forts on various sites. One of these *Vanduara* gave its ancient name to the town, and traces of the Roman occupation remained until the 18th cent.

The lands of Renfrew were assigned to Walter Fitz Alan, who in 1163 founded the Abbey [see below], in recognition of his elevation to the office of Lord High Steward of Scotland. In 1488 Paisley, then a modest village, received the charter of a town from James IV. who frequently visited it as the guest of Abbot Schaw, being accompanied in 1507 by his queen, Margaret, daughter of Henry VII. of England. Queen Mary visited it in 1563 shortly after her return from France. After the Reformation the lands of the Abbey were settled on Lord Claud Hamilton (3rd son of James Duke of Chatelherault, better known as the Earl of Arran) who was created Baron of Paisley 1487, and Earl of Abercorn 1606. Anne of Denmark, wife of James VI., was his guest at Paisley on 24th July 1597. James VI. visited the Earl of Abercorn at the *Place* of Paisley 24th July 1617. The Lordship of Paisley subsequently passed to the Dundonald family, by whom part of it was sold, but what remained was in 1764 re-purchased by James Earl of Abercorn, and now belongs to the Duke of Abercorn. Queen Victoria visited Paisley while staying at Blythswood in September 1888.

Trade and Commerce. The trade of the town was paralysed by the spoliation of the Abbey, as the inhabitants derived their principal sustenance from such religious houses, but subsequently it improved, especially after the Union of the Parliaments in 1707, and several industries developed.

During the greater part of the 18th cent. Paisley was noted for its fine manufactures of silk gauzes, Bengal cloths, shawls and thread. The shawl industry has declined, but the manufacture of thread is one of the staple trades of the town.

The **Ferguslie Thread Mills** of Messrs. J. and P. Coats (now a limited company with a paid-up capital of £5,500,000) the largest in Great Britain, if not in the world, and employing 3000 hands, are situated at the W. end of the burgh; while the **Anchor Thread Works** of Messrs. Clark and Co., of nearly equal dimensions, are at the S.E. Both are well worthy of a visit.

Paisley also possesses *Engineering Works, Bleaching and Finishing Works*, Manufactories of *Starch and Cornflour*, and of *Fireclay and Sanitary Pottery*, and other industries.

Literary Men. — Although a manufacturing town Paisley can boast of many literary men, including *Alexander Wilson*, poet and ornithologist [1766-1813], *Robert Tannahill*, the weaver poet [1774-1810], whose birthplace and last residence are marked by mural tablets, and *Professor Wilson* (Christopher North) [1785-1854]. Paisley is peculiarly rich in gifts from its prosperous citizens (see p. 320).

The Abbey is situated at the E. end of the town and faces the Clark Town Hall (p. 320). The *Monastery of Pasletum* was founded in 1163 by Walter Fitz Alan (above) who brought 13 monks from Wenlock, Shropshire. Hither also were transferred the altar and relics of *St. Mirin*, henceforth the patron saint of Paisley, whose shrine soon became a place of pilgrimage. The Monastery was made an *Abbey* in 1219, and gradually through the favours of the Stewarts became a rich house. It was destroyed by the English under Pembroke in 1307, and was not rebuilt until the reign of James I. At the Reformation the Abbey was despoiled, with the exception of an endowment retained by James VI. for the Grammar School. The *Abbey Church* originally consisted of a Nave, a Choir without aisles, and Transepts. A central spire, built by John Hamilton, the last Abbot and also the last Primate of Scotland, said to have been 300 ft. high, fell in 1560, ruining the choir and the north transept. The *West Front* is a graceful composition — a deeply recessed early pointed doorway, flanked by two blank lancet arches, and surmounted by three traceried windows.

The *Nave*, used as a parish ch., is remarkable chiefly for a richly developed triforium of broad round arches, but mid-pointed in style, in front of which project a number of heavy brackets.

The *N. Transept* was partially restored in 1861 for the sake of its fine window.

In the *S. Transept* is *St. Mirin's Chapel*, the gift of two pious citizens in 1499. It has a remarkable *Echo*, and is hence commonly called the "Sounding Aisle." In it is the recumbent effigy of Marjory, daughter of Robert Bruce, the Queen Blearie of Scottish tradition, and the "lass" by whom the crown came to the Stewart line (see p. 182). She died from the effects of a fall from her horse while hunting near Paisley. The two wives of Robert II. (1316-90), who is buried at Scone, are also buried in the abbey.

Before the high altar at the E. end of the *Choir*, of which only the foundations remain, is the grave of Robert III. who died 1406. Over it was placed in 1888, by H.M. the Queen, a slab of Sicilian marble, upon which is carved a cross, with the shield and arms of Scotland on one side, and a representation of an ancient sword and belt—the symbol of kingly investiture—on the other. The inscription should be read.

In the *Grounds* of the Abbey are statues to Wilson and Tannahill.

Opposite the abbey is the **Clark Town Hall,** built 1879-82 at a cost of about £80,000. Mr. Geo. A. Clark of Newark, U.S.A., bequeathed £20,000 for this purpose, and his relatives, Messrs. Clark of the Anchor Thread Works (p. 319), contributed the rest. The large hall, capable of holding nearly 2000 people, and which can be emptied in four minutes, possesses a fine organ, and the building is fully equipped with smaller halls, chorus rooms, and reading-room.

In *County Square*, in front of the Prison (now disused), are the **Municipal Buildings,** erected 1821 in the castellated style, and the **General Post Office** (1893) harmonising in architectural design.

The **Sheriff Court** and **County Buildings** (1878-86), situated in *St. James St.*, are of imposing dimensions in the Italian style.

At the *Townhead, High St.*, are the **Free Public Library** and **Museum,** erected 1869 through the munificence of the late Sir Peter Coats (1808-90) at a cost of £15,000, the donor afterwards adding an endowment fund. The Museum is full of local antiquities and natural history collections, and an addition has had to be built to it.

Behind the museum, in *Oakshaw St.*, is an **Observatory** (where a daily meteorological record is kept) built and equipped in 1883 by the late Mr. Thomas Coats (1809-83).

The **Grammar School,** also in *Oakshaw St.*, has an ancient history.

The **John Neilson Educational Institute**, in the style of the Greek Cross, crowns *Oakshaw Hill*, said to be the site of the old fort of Vanduara.

The **Thomas Coats Memorial** (*Baptist*) **Church** in *High St.*, built by his family (1894), is a most magnificent erection. It is built of red stone in a freely decorated

Gothic style, is cruciform, has a tower resembling St. Giles's, Edinburgh, and is estimated to have cost £100,000 (H. J. Blanc, Archt.).

St. James U.P. Church (1884), in *Underwood Road* to the N., is also a handsome structure, and has a fine peal of bells.

Paisley possesses 3 **Public Parks,** viz. the *Fountain Gardens*, to the north, which cost £20,000, and were presented by Mr. Thomas Coats in 1868 ; *Brodie Park* to the south, bequeathed in 1871 by Mr. Robert Brodie, Banker ; and *St. James Park* to the north, where the annual *Race Meeting*, the best attended in Scotland, is held. Horse-racing, with silver bells for a prize, was established at Paisley in 1620 by the Earl of Abercorn and the Town Council, and has continued ever since.

[EXCURSIONS :—

(1) Drive to the ruins of **Crookston Cas.** (3½ m. E.), which stands on the *White Cart*, and belonged to the Darnley family. Queen Mary, however, was probably never there.

(2) Drive to the **Water Works' Reservoir** (2 m. S.W.) on the banks of which stands the old ruined fortress of *Stanley* at the foot of the **Braes of Gleniffer.**

"Keen blaws the wind o'er the braes o' Gleniffer,
The auld castle's turrets are cover'd wi' snaw;
How chang'd frae the time when I met wi' my lover
Amang the broom bushes by Stanley's green shaw."—TANNAHILL.

Continue along the braes—lovely views of the Highland hills over the Firth—and descend to Milliken Park Stat. (6½ m.) [p. 125]; then turn E. by *Elderslie* where Wallace was born—a traditional house is pointed out—to Paisley (4½ m.) 11 m.]

Just beyond Paisley Stat. the G. and S.W. Rly. (Rtes. 70 and 18) continues W. ; we trend N.W. to

8 m. **St James's Stat.** (Paisley). *The Black Cart* is crossed, with *Walkinshaw Ho.* rt., and then its trib. the *Gryfe Water*, before

10¼ m. **Houston Stat.**, the village and *House* (A. A. Speirs, Esq. of Elderslie) are 3 m. W.

12¼ m. **Bishopton Stat.** 1½ m. N.E. is *Erskine House* [p. 314]. Emerging from a tunnel an excellent view across the Clyde to Dumbarton Cas., Ben Lomond, etc., is obtained before

16¼ m. **Langbank Stat.** The railway now runs alongside the Clyde.

20¼ m. **Port-Glasgow Stat.** (p. 314), beyond which the Wemyss Bay line strikes off l. [Rte. 71]. Beyond

21¼ m. **Bogston Stat.** and 22 m. **Cartsdyke Stat.**, situated near the Greenock Docks, is

23 m. **GREENOCK**✲ **(Cathcart St. Stat.)** [see p. 314].

23½ m. **Greenock West Stat.**

25 m. **Fort Matilda Stat.**

26¼ m. **Gourock Stat.** with *Steamboat Pier* alongside.

For *Gourock* and route thence to *Rothesay* see Rte. 68.

ROUTE 70.

Glasgow to Rothesay by Greenock (Princes Pier). G. & S.W. Rly.

Abt. 24 trains daily in ¾ hr. to Greenock; and abt. 12 steamers thence in 70 minutes to Rothesay. This route is preferable to Rte. 69, on account of the more extensive view obtained above Greenock.

Leaving **St. Enoch's Stat.** the Clyde is crossed to

¾ m. **Main St. Stat.**, and

1¾ m. **Shields Road Stat.**, side by side with the *Cal. Rly. Stat. of Pollokshields* [Rte. 69].

[*Branch* l. to *Paisley* (Canal St.) *via Bellahouston* and *Crookston.*]

A good view is obtained rt. of the Glasgow University buildings.

3¼ m. **Ibrox Stat.** [*Branch* rt. in 1¾ m. to **Govan**, p. 313].

$4\frac{1}{4}$ m. **Cardonald Stat.** A line runs rt. to *Abercorn Stat.* (Paisley) and **Renfrew** (p. 314) before reaching

$7\frac{3}{4}$ m. **Paisley Gilmour St. Stat.** ✲ [see p. 318]. *Woodside Ho.* (Arch. Coats, Esq.) and *Ferguslie Ho.* (Mrs. T. Coats) are passed l.

$9\frac{3}{4}$ m. **Elderslie Stat.**, where William Wallace was born (1270 ?). The train leaves the Ayr line [Rte. 18] and turns N.W. to

$11\frac{3}{4}$ m. **Houston Stat.** The *Village* and *Ho.* (A. A. Speirs, Esq. of Elderslie) lie 2 m. N. Rt. in clear weather Ben Lomond is visible.

$13\frac{3}{4}$ m. **Bridge of Weir Stat.**, a small manufacturing village. Here are Mr. Quarrier's excellent *Orphan Homes*. After passing

$17\frac{1}{2}$ m. **Kilmalcolm Stat.** ✲, a wonderful prospect opens out on the rt. over the valley and estuary of the Clyde from Dumbarton downwards.

The rly. descends through a series of tunnels, partly running under the streets of Greenock, to

24 m. **Greenock Lynedoch St. Stat.**

For **Greenock** ✲ see p. 314.

$25\frac{1}{2}$ m. **Princes Pier**, where steamers for all the Clyde watering-places can be joined.

Thence to **Rothesay** ✲, see Rte. 68.

ROUTE 71.

Glasgow to Arran by Wemyss Bay, Rothesay, and the Kyles of Bute ("Ivanhoe" Route).

The *quickest* routes to Arran are *via* Ardrossan [Rtes. 72, 73], in abt. $1\frac{1}{4}$ hr., but this route (abt. $3\frac{1}{2}$ hrs.), through some of the finest scenery on the Clyde, is greatly preferable. The "*Ivanhoe*" can also be joined at Princes Pier, Greenock [Rte. 70], at Gourock [Rte. 69], or at Dunoon, *via* Craigendoran [Rte. 67], whence it crosses to Wemyss Bay. There are abt. 7 trains daily to Wemyss Bay in an hour (Cal. Rly.), and 6 steamers thence in 35 min. to Rothesay.

Leaving the **Central Stat.** the line is the same as that described in Rte. 69 as far as

$20\frac{1}{4}$ m. **Port-Glasgow Stat.**, thence it ascends to

23 **Upper Greenock Stat.**, with a magnificent view across the Firth.

$25\frac{1}{4}$ m. **Ravenscraig Stat.** Beyond, we pass (l.) the imposing *Greenock Poorhouse and Asylum*, and obtain views (rt.) of *Ardgowan*, the seat of Sir Michael Shaw-Stewart, Bt., one of the most beautiful places on the Clyde, and *Inverkip village* where Galt the novelist (1779 - 1839) is buried, before crossing a high viaduct to

$28\frac{1}{2}$ m. **Inverkip Stat.** A tunnel is passed through to

31 m. **Wemyss Bay Stat.** ✲ Rt. lies the bay, with large villas, and an *Epis. Church*. Its N. boundary is Wemyss Point with *Castle Wemyss*, designed by Billings, the seat of Sir John Burns, Bart., chairman of the Cunard Company.

W. of the Stat. are *Kelly Ho.* and grounds, formerly the residence of the late Mr. James Young, the founder of Young's Paraffin Oil Works and the faithful friend of David Livingstone.

1 m. S. is **Skelmorlie** ✲, a quiet but fashionable watering-place with handsome villas, and $\frac{1}{2}$ m. beyond it *Skelmorlie Cas.* (Earl of Eglinton), part of which dates from 1502. 4 m. farther along the coast is **Largs** ✲ (p. 331).

Steamers sail from Wemyss Bay Pier, adjoining the Station, to *Rothesay* (6 times); *Largs and Millport* [cf. Route 73] (5 times); and *Kilchattan Bay, Bute* [p. 318] once daily.

The "Ivanhoe" crosses to **Craigmore** and **Rothesay** (p. 316).

Leaving Rothesay it crosses the bay, passing l. † **Port Bannatyne** (or Kamesburgh) ✲, and Kames Bay with *Kames Cas.* (Marq. of Bute), at its head (see p. 318).

Rt. is the entrance to **Loch**

Striven with *Knockdow*, the seat of J. Lamont, Esq., the hunter of the sea-lion, author, and geologist, on its E. shore. Up this arm of the sea, which is 9 m. long, the rounded top of the Cowall Mts. may be seen. Upon the promontory that separates it from the Kyles of Bute is *South Hall* (Col. D. Campbell). The steamer now turns l. into the ****Kyles [1] of Bute,** a long strait going in a semicircle between the N. part of Bute and the mainland, with a very narrow channel and a sharp curve at its N. end.

Beyond † **Colintraive**✲ (rt.) is the *pièce de resistance* of this part of the sail—a group of islets, W. of which "The Narrows" have to be threaded; rt. is **Loch Riddon,** 3½ m. long, in front the picturesque mansion of *Glen Caladh*, and l. the continuation of the Kyles.

[Among the islets is *Eilean Dheirig*, upon which a fort was built in 1685, by the Earl of Argyll, in his unsuccessful invasion of Scotland. It was subsequently dismantled by an English fleet. This invasion was undertaken in conjunction with that of Monmouth in the W. of England, and had an equally disastrous termination, both leaders being beheaded, the one at Edinburgh and the other on Tower Hill. 1 m. up *Loch Riddon* is **Ormidale Pier** (steamer twice or thrice daily from Rothesay), and beyond the head of the loch in *Glen Daruel*✱ is *Ormidale Ho.* (Mrs. Burnley Campbell), whence a road runs W. to *Otter Ferry* on Loch Fyne (7 m.), and E. to Dunoon by the head of Loch Striven, 16 m.]

Rounding *Buttock Point* and turning southward, the steamer passes on the l. 2 pieces of rock in a green hollow, rudely painted, known as the "Maids of Bute."

At † **Tighnabruaich**✲ ("House on the Brae"), where the Kyles begin to widen, is a small colony of marine villas, which enjoy a distant view of the Arran mountains.

1½ m. farther (rt.) is †**Kames,** inland from which are extensive powder-mills.

[1] Kyles = Gael. *Caolas* = a strait.

The vessel now leaves **Ardlamont Point** (p. 331), the most southerly promontory of the Cowall district (rt.), crosses *Etterick Bay* (p. 318), and keeps along the W. side of Bute, passing *Inch Marnock* —with 8 m. W. *Skipness Point* and *Castle* (p. 336), on the Kintyre coast —and steering for Arran, whose majestic mountains loom in the distance.

As we approach nearer, having to the rt. the **Cock** (or N. end) **of Arran** (p. 327), and to the l. **Garroch Head**, the S. end of Bute, these mountains, with **Goatfell,** 2866 ft. in the centre, and many a fantastic peak, stand out magnificently.

Just beyond *Sannox Bay*, with a grand view up *Glen Sannox*, the steamer stops at

†**Corrie**✲, a row of picturesque, unpretentious cottages.

3 m. beyond, **Brodick Bay** in all its beauty, with *Brodick Castle* (D. of Hamilton) and its woods, opens out and we stop at

†**Brodick**✲ (see p. 325). Round *Clauchlands Point* is

†**Lamlash**✲ (see p. 329), and its bay, shut in by **Holy Island**, and having to the south

†**King's Cross Point,** where we enjoy splendid views of the mountains looking back.

At †**Whiting Bay**✲ the steamer turns.

On the return voyage the "Ivanhoe" sails direct from *Corrie* to *Rothesay* by the E. side of Bute.

Arran is fully described in Rte. 72.

ROUTE 72.

Glasgow to Arran by Ardrossan. Cal. Rly.

Twice daily. Saturdays 3 times. Abt. 1½ hr.

The train leaves the **Central Stat.**, crosses the Clyde, and passes

½ m. **Bridge St. Stat.**, 1 m. **Eglinton St. Stat.**, 1¾ m. **Strathbungo Stat.**, and 2¼ m. **Crossmyloof Stat.** to

3¼ m. **Pollokshaws Stat.** on the "White Cart." ½ m. W. is *Pollok Ho.*, seat of Sir John Stirling Maxwell, Bart., to whose family the estate has belonged since the 13th cent.

[BRANCH l. to 4¼ m. (from Glasgow) **Thornliebank Stat.**, where Messrs. Crum have large calico-printing and bleaching works.

5¼ m. **Giffnock Stat.** for the village of (3 m. S.) **Newton-Mearns**, 1 m. E. of which is *Mearns Cas.*, an ancient stronghold of the Maxwells, and 1 m. W., on a commanding site, *Pollok Cas.* the ancient seat of the Polloks, founded in the 12th cent., enlarged 1686-97, and burnt 1882, but afterwards restored and enlarged (C. S. S. Johnston, archt.).

6¼ m. **Clarkston Stat.** for (3¾ m. S.) **Eaglesham** village and *House* (Allan Gilmour, Esq.).

7¼ m. **Busby Stat.**, a manufacturing village on the "White Cart."

8¼ m. **Thornton Hall Stat.**

9¾ m. **Hairmyres Stat.**, and

11½ m. **East Kilbride Stat.**, a small town. 1½ m. S. is *Torrance Ho.* (Col. Stuart), on the Rotten Calder Water. A few trains run from East Kilbride by the *Calder Valley* (see pp. 146, 149) to

17½ m. **Hamilton**✱ (p. 146.)]

4¼ m. **Kennishead Stat.**

5¾ m. **Nitshill Stat.**

7¼ m. **Barrhead Stat.**, a busy manufacturing town on the *Levern Water* at the foot of the *Fereneze Hills* (500–700 ft.) rt. with still higher ground in the distance l.

9½ **Neilston Stat.** also stands among hills, and has manufactures. *Neilston Pad* (854 ft.) 2 m. S. commands a fine view. The line is very pretty as we approach

12½ m. **Caldwell Stat.** Beyond (rt.) is *Caldwell Ho.* (Wm. Mure, Esq.) well seen just before

14¼ m. **Lugton Junc. Stat.** where the train leaves the main line to Kilmarnock [Rte. 12] and turns W. The *Dalry Hills* now bound the horizon rt. A *Branch* from *Lugton* to 3 m. *Barrmill*, and 5½ m. *Beith* (p. 125) strikes off rt. before we reach

18 m. **Giffen Stat.** [*Branch* rt. to 3¼ m. *Glengarnock* and 4¼ m. *Kilbirnie* (p. 124)]. ¾ m. l. is *Giffen Castle*, formerly the headquarters of the Montgomerie family.

19¾ m. **Auchenmade Stat.** The Arran Mts. now come into view rt. The G. and S.W. Rly. from Dalry to Kilmarnock is crossed before reaching

24 m. **Kilwinning Stat.** (p. 124), [*Branch* S. to Irvine 3 m. (p. 123)], beyond which the G. and S.W. Rly. lines (Rtes. 12 and 73) are crossed, and a slightly more inland course than Rte. 73 is taken by

26¾ m. **Stevenston Stat.** and

28 m. **Saltcoats Stat.** (p. 329) to

29¼ m. **Ardrossan Stat.** ✲ (see p. 330), and

29½ m. **Ardrossan Pier,** N. of the Harbour.

[From this pier a steamer crosses daily in summer to Belfast (3½ hrs.) returning same day.]

The steamer crosses in 40 min. direct to **Brodick**✲, and thence to †**Lamlash**✲, †**King's Cross**, and †**Whiting Bay**✲ (p. 329), whence a coach runs S. to **Kildonan**✲, 4½ m., and **Lagg**✲, 9 m. (p. 328).

The **Island of Arran** is about 20 m. long by 11 m. broad, the interior consisting of wild uncultivated mountains, several of which exceed 2600 ft. in height. For many centuries it was a royal domain, well stocked with red deer and other beasts of chase, and was principally used as a hunting-ground. It figures largely in the "Lord of the Isles." The earldom of Arran was conferred for the first time (1467) upon Sir Thomas Boyd, who married the sister of James I., but the property and the lady were after Boyd's death given to Sir James Hamilton. Hogg's ballad makes Walter Hamilton win the princess and the island of Arran in a tournament—a poetical version of the circumstances. With the exception of *Kilmichael* up Glen Cloy (belonging to the Fullarton family, the oldest proprietors in Arran), and one or two farms, the whole island belongs to the Duke of Hamilton, who occasionally resides at Brodick Castle.

The *Geology* of Arran is a subject which has attracted much attention, and has been frequently described by the able pens of many eminent geologists, as Jameson, Sedgwick, Ramsay, Bryce,[1] Sir A. Geikie, etc. To those fond of this science the island is a unique field for study, embracing within its area an extraordinary variety of different phenomena,

"and so perfectly are all the phenomena exhibited, that it is difficult to imagine any space of the same limited extent more worthy of being studied for the purpose of understanding the mutual relations of pyrogeneous rocks."—Phillips.

"To the N. tower the granite peaks with their surrounding belt of schist; to the S. lie the rolling moorlands, formed of the old red sandstone and its igneous rocks. Many of the details of Arran scenery are full of instruction. Such, for instance, are the corries and the ballochs in the granite; the moraines; the erratics, especially on the E. shore from Clauchlands Point to Glen Sannox; the dykes which abound along the E. coast, but still more at the S. extremity of the island, and the raised beach, which forms the platform for the coast road from Brodick to Glen Sannox and runs interruptedly round the island."—Sir A. Geikie, *Scenery of Scotland*, p. 451.

† **Brodick** ✲, the name of the pier, parish, and P.O., but not of the village, is undoubtedly the best centre for exploring the island, and the place where most tourists disembark—at an *iron pier* of peculiar construction, with buffer-sides to protect the steamers in rough weather.

It must, however, be borne in mind that it is rarely of any use going to Arran without having secured accommodation beforehand, as in summer it is crammed with visitors. At Brodick especially the Duke of Hamilton discourages building, and even the smallest cottages are secured months in advance at high rents. There is only one fairly large hotel at the head of the pier. The old inn was near the Castle.

[1] See Bryce's *Arran and the Clyde Islands.*

Brodick Bay, with its sandy beach, its village of *Invercloy*, the *Castle*, the woods, the 3 glens of *Cloy*, *Shurig*, and *Rosa*, and the distant background of Mts.—*Goatfell* (2866 ft.), *Cir Mhor* (2618 ft.), *A' Chir* ("Lord Brougham's Nose"), *Ben-a-Chliabhain* (2141 ft.), *Ben Tarsuin* (2706 ft.), and *Ben Nuis* (2597 ft.)—possesses a combination of scenery difficult to surpass anywhere, especially when seen during the afterglow of sunset. Here Robert Bruce gathered his forces before descending on his own country of Carrick opposite, prior to meeting the English at Bannockburn:—

"'Twas bustle all in Brodick Bay.
The Bruce's followers crowd the shore."
Lord of the Isles.

Besides the steamers from Ardrossan [Rtes. 72 and 73], and from Wemyss Bay [Rte. 71], there are public conveyances once or twice a day from Brodick N. to *Corrie* (6 m.) and *Loch Ranza*, 14 m. (where the Campbeltown steamer [Rte. 78] calls), and W. across the island to *Shisken*, 9 m., and *Blackwater Foot*, 11 m. Also from *Whiting Bay*, the terminus of the steamers, to *Kildonan*, 4½ m., and *Lagg*, 9 m. An excursion steamer generally sails round the island weekly, and makes evening cruises along the coast or round *Holy Island*.

Excursions from Brodick:—

(1) **Ascent of Goatfell** (2866 ft.), or *Ben Gaoith*. Abt. 3 hrs.

"Ben Ghoil, the 'Mountain of the Wind.'"
Scott.

The first 2 m. round the bay may be driven [p. 326]. The path leaves the road at the old Inn, passes through the plantations behind the Castle, and emerges on the moor. The mountain stands out clearly in front, and the path is so well marked no guide is necessary; only any temptation not to keep the rt. shoulder, but to take a direct course, should be firmly resisted. The last 20 minutes, up a steep rocky staircase, are alone trying. The *View* on a clear day embraces the *Firth of Clyde* and *Ailsa Craig* to the E. and S., the *Coast of Ireland* to the S.W., *Islay*, and the *Paps of Jura* to the N.W., *Loch Fyne* and *Ben Cruachan* to the N., and *Ben Lomond* to the N.E. But even on a dull day, or by moonlight, the view W. into *Glen Rosa* and over to the neighbouring heights is exceedingly fine.

"Near the summit of Goatfell, and also on the S. shoulder, the granite suddenly arises in perpendicular cliffs, assuming the artificial appearance of huge Cyclopean walls. Large blocks are arranged one above another with the utmost nicety, thus frequently presenting a vertical face of rock of considerable height."—Ramsay.

A descent may be made to Corrie or (steep) into Glen Rosa, or, better still, to the *Saddle* between that glen and Glen Sannox, and thence down the latter glen to Corrie. This last alternative route will always be associated with the mysterious murder upon 15th July 1889, by J. W. Laurie of his companion Edwin Rose, whose body was, after a long search, found concealed under a rock in Glen Sannox, and afterwards buried in the small churchyard of that glen.

(2) **Up Glen Rosa,** as romantic a glen as any in the Highlands, which runs immediately beneath Goatfell, and is separated only by a ridge from Glen Sannox.

The lower part of the glen is easily accessible, there being a driving road to its entrance (2½ m.), and a footpath for another 1½ m.; but after the wooden bridge over a trib. stream (with pretty waterfall) is passed (4 m.), the path becomes excessively wet and boggy. For those who do not mind this, it is a fine walk to the head of the glen (7 m.), across the ridge and down Glen Sannox to Corrie 12 m. Return to Brodick (6 m.) by coach. If this route be reversed, remember the "Saddle" is l. at the head of Glen Sannox and *not* in front, otherwise the desolate *Glen Iorsa* leading to the W. coast will be entered.

(3) Mountaineers, by varying and extending route (2), may enjoy as grand a walk as any in Scotland.

At the wooden br. in Glen Rosa (1 hr.) keep l. up the side of the waterfall. Ascend *Ben Nuis* (pron. Noosh) 2597 ft., the S. end of the range in front (other 2 hrs.). Keep along the ridge N., with imposing precipices, to *Ben Tarsuin* (2706 ft.) 1 hr. Descend to the "*Archer's Pass*"; keep W. of *A' Chir* (pron. A Keer = The coxcomb-like ridge), called from the resemblance "Lord Brougham's Nose," and *Cir Mhor* (pron. Keer Vore = big ridge), cross the *Iorsa Saddle* at the head of Glen Sannox, and ascend *Casteal Abhail*, "The Castles" (2735 ft.) 1½ hr., with a charming view N. of Loch Ranza, etc. Descend behind the remarkable fissure called *Caim-na-Cailliach*, "The Witches' Leap," "which seems to have once been entirely filled with a trap dyke now decomposed" (Ramsay), ascend *Sui Feargas* to the E., and descend by the N. slopes of Glen Sannox and the mouth of that glen to **Corrie**★ (3 hrs.). The complete round will take fully 12 hrs., but the first 2½ m. and the last 6 m. may be driven.

(4) To **Lamlash**✫, 3½ m. S. (see p. 329).

It is a capital round to go by the driving-road direct 3½ m. and return on foot by the cliffs (fully 1 m. longer). If on foot, take a cart road behind Invercloy, commanding fine views, and join the driving road at the top of the hill—the telegraph posts will guide you. Returning keep N. along Lamlash Bay for 1 m. beyond the Coast Guard Station, then turn l. by a cart road, crossing Clauchlands Point by Clauchlands Farm and passing the old fort of *Dun Fionn*, with a fine breezy view, *Corrygills Farm*, and *Brodick Free Ch.*

(5) **Round the Island by the coast road,** abt. 55½ m. Driving N. the village of Invercloy is passed, and then the mouth of *Glen Cloy*, up which is a pleasant stroll, Glen Cloy House and Cottages, and the School Ho. In front of this is a statue of the late Duke of Hamilton, and across the road an old *stone monument*, or menhir, placed upright — probably the entrance to an avenue. Below the parish church the stream from *Glen Shurig*, up which is the direct road to the W. side, is crossed, *Glen Rosa* is seen l. and *Brodick Castle* is passed.

The *Castle* (Duke of Hamilton) was seized by Edw. I. and held by Sir John Hastings, from whom it was taken at the general liberation of Scotland from the English yoke. It was garrisoned by Oliver Cromwell; but his soldiers, having provoked the indignation of the islanders, were massacred. It has been rebuilt in the Scotch baronial style from designs by Mr. Gillespie Graham, and, though not a very large building, has, from its commanding position, a very good effect.

The road, passing the Duke's private landing stage, keeps along the shore upon a raised beach. There is a fine cascade abt. 250 ft. high before reaching

6 m. †**Corrie**✲, a picturesque collection of cottages.

Here steamers call daily (see Rte. 71).

At 7½ m. the stream from **Glen Sannox** is crossed.

The *View* up this glen, which is one of the grandest in Scotland, is exceedingly fine.

About ½ m. up is an ancient ch.-yd.—the scene of "*Graves of oor ain folk*," by J. Smart, R.S.A.

The road now quits the coast.

1½ m. farther N. along the shore is a large accumulation of *Fallen Rocks*.

N. Glen Sannox is crossed and after a steep ascent to 600 ft. *Glen Chalmadale* is descended to

14 m. †**Loch Ranza**✲, an inlet of the sea, abt. 1 m. long and ½ m. broad at high water, a celebrated herring station, situated 1½ m. W. of the N. end or **Cock of Arran** (*Norse* Kok = lump).

At the head of Loch Ranza rises the graceful form of *Torr-Nead-an-Eoin* (1057 ft.)—"bird's nest hill"—to the S. of which is the rugged top of *Caistail Abhail*, "The Castles."

The loch is divided by a promontory running out into it from the W. shore; and upon this stands a *Castle*, consisting of 2 square towers, the roofs of which are still tolerably perfect. It was erected as a royal hunting seat prior to the year 1380. A nunnery dedicated to St. Bride, in which, according to the "Lord of the Isles," Isabel, Bruce's sister, found refuge, formerly existed here, but there are no traces of it left.

This is altogether one of the most beautiful landscapes in Arran.

The Campbeltown Steamer (Rte. 78) calls daily at Loch Ranza.

Rounding *Coillemore Point* and turning southward, the traveller arrives at

16½ m. **Catacol**, where the geologist will notice curious examples of contorted schist.

At 19 m. is a lonely little *Free Ch.*, belonging to the hamlet of **North Tundergay**, 2 m. from which, inland, is the secluded and solitary lake of *Correin Lochain*, which looks as if it had been scooped out of the recesses of Ben Bharain (pron. Varen.) Its sides are almost wholly destitute of vegetation, and the lake has the appearance of having been the centre of an extinct volcano.

"Ben Varen itself is in form like a long house, with rounded roof, and on its summit are two of the Cyclopean walls meeting at right angles."—ANDERSON.

As the road progresses S. very fine views are obtained of the mountainous coast of Kintyre, from which *Ben-an-Tuirc* (1491 ft.) stands out pre-eminently.

20 m. **South Tundergay.**

21½ m. †**Pirnmill**, where the Campbeltown steamer calls daily.

22 m. **White Farland.**

23 m. **Imachar.** These are all merely small hamlets.

25½ m., at **Glen Iorsa**, the river of the same name enters the sea. On the rt. bank is *Dougrie*, a shooting-box belonging to the Duke of Hamilton, and behind it is the keeper's house, picturesquely situated.

At 28 m., the road crosses the *Machrie Water*, up which a road leads across to Brodick, abt. 8 m. Beyond, is **Tormore**, 1 m. E. from which are prehistoric remains in the shape of upright stones and circles.

Here are 2 upright stones upon 2 hills, commanding the entrance to what was evidently an avenue leading up to the great circles. At the beginning of this avenue there is a *dolmen*, formed of large slabs put together like a house of cards, so as to enclose a space. The interior when opened was found to contain some ashes.

1. The first monument consists of 2 concentric circles, the ground in the interior being somewhat raised.

The diameter of the largest of these two circles is about 55 ft., and the stones are granite boulders; the 2 largest in the interior circle point E. and W., in which direction all the circles lie, though not all in the same line. On the S. side of this one is a stone with a hole bored in it. The centre of this circle has been opened, and human bones or ashes were found in it.

2. A circle, composed of 5 boulder stones, one removed.

3. To the N. of the last is a single upright slab, about 12 ft. high from the ground, evidently one of a circle of similar stones.

4. Three upright slabs, 15 ft. high, belonging to a circle 60 ft. in diameter. There are, here and there, groups of stones, which may be the remnants of circles scattered about between this and the hills; but the surface has been removed constantly in search of peat, so that, doubtless, many more have disappeared.

[A little beyond Tormore where the road trends inland the tourist should quit the road, and turn rt. to the coast for the **King's Caves.**

The whole line of rock has been hollowed here into caves, some of which are fitted with doors and windows. The last and largest is called the *King's Cave*, and is said to have been inhabited by Fingal, Bruce, and several other Scottish heroes, fabulous and historical. The roof is partly supported by a natural pillar that rises from the floor and divides the upper part of the cave into 2 chambers. Upon its side is rudely carved a sword, and on the walls are rough sketches of the chase, ascribed to the leisure hours of Bruce and his companions, but from the softness of the stone and the continual damp they cannot be nearly so old.]

At 31 m. **Shisken**✲, or Shedog, across the *Black Water*, a road (coach daily) runs N.E. in 9 m. to Brodick, joining the one *via* Glen Machrie.

[1 m. up this road in an old cemetery St. Molus is said to be buried, but the Irish assert that Inishmurray off the coast of Sligo is his resting place.]

The road rejoins the coast for some miles near **Blackwater Foot**✲. In the sandstone cliffs N. of this, towards Tormore the geologist will notice the prevalence of dykes of pitchstone and trap porphyry.

36 m. rt. is *Tor Castle*, or, as it is commonly called, Castle Hill.

This is an oblong barrow running from N. to S., on the top of which are the remains of 2 circles, which may have been walls, or simply stones in position. The larger one is about 80 ft. in diameter, the smaller 54 ft. On the S. side are 3 fragments of stone of superior workmanship to the rest.

On the S. of the Castle Hill is a smaller barrow, with a very narrow ridge, upon which there seem to have been stones also, judging from the collection at its foot. The position of these remains being on the coast, and principally the W. coast, induces the antiquary to attribute them to a Norse origin.

At 37 m. the *Sliddery Water* is crossed.

[Beyond, a fine wild road strikes l. up *Glen Scorradale*, ascending to 900 ft., and down *Monamore Glen* to Lamlash, 9 m.]

38½ m. **Lagg Hotel**✲, very prettily situated in a wooded dell, through which the *Kilmory Water* flows. Up this stream is the *Church of Kilmory*, one of the two original parishes into which the island was divided.

41 m. rt. is **Bennan Head** (with the *Strucy Rocks*), on the face of which is the *Black Cave*, a large dark excavation abt. 80 ft. high.

42½ m. l. is *Essiemore*, or the Great Fall, in which the water descends 100 ft. in a long, thin stream into a pool from which it forces its way to the sea through a rocky channel of red sandstone.

At 43½ m. the hamlet of **Kildonan**✲ lies ½ m. rt. On the shore is *Kildonan Castle*, a sq. keep of 2 stories; the roof of the lower story still perfect, and a part of the upper one still left.

1 m. S. across the sound is the island of **Pladda,** with a lighthouse showing two fixed lights, one above the other.

There is a splendid line of cliffs, called the *Dippin Rocks*, extending northwards to **Dippin Head**, which the road crosses after passing *Dippin Lodge* (Duke of Hamilton).

At *Largybeg Point* (45½ m.) **Whiting Bay** begins, and after crossing 46¾ m. *Glen Kiscadale*, in which there is a good waterfall, the houses, scattered along the shore, and the pier of

47½ m. † **Whiting Bay** ✲ are reached. This is a favourite watering place, more bracing than Brodick or Lamlash, because lying open to the sea.

Here all the steamers, which have to be reached in boats, call and turn. A *Coach* runs to Kildonan and Lagg Hotel once or twice daily.

Beyond, † **King's Cross Point,** so called because Bruce is said to have embarked here for Carrick, and which separates Whiting Bay from Lamlash Bay, is crossed.

In the latter King Haco moored his shattered fleet after his defeat at Largs 1263, and it forms a well-known harbour for shelter, being admirably protected by the breakwater of

Holy Island, a picturesque island, nearly 2 m. long, and rising to a height of 1030 ft.

This island is supposed to have been the resort of St. Molus, a disciple of St. Columba. His *Cave* by the shore is marked by some curious inscriptions, in Runic characters, which have been interpreted as memorials of those who fell at the Battle of Largs. A projection on the side of the cave is called St. Molus's chair. The composition of the rocks is red sandstone overlaid by felstone, and the surface is covered with heath and the *Arbutus uva ursi*.

At the S. end is a *Lighthouse.*

51 m. *Monamore Glen* (p. 328) is crossed before reaching

52 m. † **Lamlash** ✲. This straggling village is the largest on the island.

The shore at low tide is very ugly with rocks and seaweed, but a long wooden pier enables travellers to disembark direct at all states of the tide. Here the Duke's Chamberlain has a house; there is a coastguard station, and houses and cottages for summer quarters are more numerous than at Brodick. The second original parish of Arran—*Kilbride*—has here its church. A barn-like structure has now been replaced by a red sandstone building.

It is 3½ m. over the hills to

55½ m. **Brodick.**

(6) Drive up *Glen Shurig*, across the island to **Shisken** ✲, 9 m., and **Blackwater Foot** ✲, 11 m., see p. 328. *Coach* daily.

ROUTE 73.

Glasgow to Arran by Ardrossan; and to Fairlie (for Millport) and Largs. G. & S.W. Rly.

This route to Arran competes with Rte. 72 for quickness, and has (1894) the finer steamer. Twice daily, Saturdays three times, in abt. 1½ hr.

To Millport 4 times daily, in abt. 1¾ hr.
To Largs 10 trains daily in abt. 1½ hr.

For the line from **St. Enoch's Stat.** to 26¾ m. **Kilwinning Stat.** see Rtes. 70 and 18.

At Kilwinning the line trends W., passing furnaces and coalmines to

29¼ m. **Stevenston Stat.,** 1 m. N. of which are the ruins of *Kerilaw Castle.* Close by are Messrs. Merry and Cunninghame's *Ardeer Iron Works,* on the estate of *Ardeer Ho.* (P. Warner, Esq.). 1½ m. S.E. are the nitro-glycerine and dynamite works of Messrs. Nobel and Co.

30½ m. **Saltcoats Stat.,** a dirty, straggling port and sea-bathing place, where salt-works were established by James V., and where magnesia was manufactured in 1802 in connection with the saltpans.

$31\frac{1}{4}$ m. **Ardrossan South Beach Stat.**, a pleasant suburb of

32 m. **Ardrossan Stat.**

[The *Cal. Rly.* has a *Stat.* and *Pier* to the N. (p. 324).]

Ardrossan✲ is a well-built but uninteresting town on a promontory, with a few broad streets at right angles to one another. It was founded 1806 by the Earl of Eglinton. Great sums of money have been expended upon the *Pier* and *Harbour;* and at one time it was hoped to make it the port of Glasgow, by connecting it with that city by means of a canal. This was completed as far as Johnstone, when the introduction of railways arrested the project. It is a sea-bathing place and a flourishing seaport, principally occupied in the shipping of pig-iron. On the height above the town are the foundations of a chapel, and some detached fragments of a strong castle, one piece of which has a vaulted roof, still perfect. It was reduced to its present state by Cromwell's troops. There are fine views of Arran from the obelisk and the *Pier head*, to which trains for the Arran boat run.

The Arran boat crosses in 40 min., and follows the same course as that of the Cal. Rly. steamer [Rte. 72].

The train leaving Ardrossan for Largs backs out of the station and runs N., passing *Horse Island.* There are capital views of Arran before reaching

$35\frac{3}{4}$ m. **West Kilbride Stat.**, an old village, and now somewhat of a summer resort, from which there is a pleasant walk (2 m.) W. to *Farland Head* and the ruins of *Portincross Cas.* (13th cent.).

At 38 m. *Hunterston Ho.* (Col. Hunter Webster) lies $\frac{1}{2}$ m. W.

40 m. **Fairlie Stat.**✲, a small watering place, which has greatly grown in importance since the rly. was opened in 1880. The extraordinary distance (fully 1 m.) to which the tide goes out here is unequalled on the W. coast. The train passes through a long tunnel to

$40\frac{1}{2}$ m. **Fairlie Pier Stat.**

A steamer crosses S.W. to †**Keppel Pier** (Cumbrae) (2 m.), and then rounds *Farland Point* to †**Millport**✲, a small town situated on a sheltered bay at the S. end of the **Great Cumbrae Island** (4 m. long by 2 m. broad), and looking over to the Little Cumbrae (below), $1\frac{1}{2}$ m. S.

There is no other village on the island. It is a pleasant place for a short stay, with a good *Pier* built by the late Lord Glasgow, and contains the Episcopalian Cathedral for the diocese of Argyll and the Isles, built from designs by Butterfield, in the style of the 13th cent. (1849, consec. 1875).

The *Garrison*, formerly a seat of the late Lord Glasgow, is built on the site of an old fort, and now belongs, with the island, to the Marquis of Bute.

An anecdote is told of a former minister of the parish of Cumbrae, who, with exalted notions of the little world in which he lived, used to pray for the island of Cumbrae, together with the "adjacent islands of Great Britain and Ireland."

The geologist will find on the E. shore of Millport harbour a whin dyke rising like a wall from the sea and stretching up the hill.

The **Little Cumbrae** ($1\frac{3}{4}$ m. long by $\frac{3}{4}$ m. broad) has no village. It once had a fort on it, until it was burnt by Cromwell's troops. The stump of a tower on the E. side is supposed to have been a defence against Norwegian pirates. On the W. side is a *Lighthouse*, which lights the entrance to the Clyde. An older one stood on the hilltop. To the N. are the remains of the chapel of St. Vey, with the tomb of the saint considerably mutilated. The views from both the islands over the shores of Bute and Arran are very fine.

From Millport the steamer sails to

†**Kilchattan Bay**✲ in Bute (p. 318), and thence to **Rothesay**✲ (p. 316).

Beyond Fairlie Pier the train passes rt. *Kelburn Cas.* (Earl of Glasgow), prettily situated on the banks of a stream, near a waterfall. In front of the house (16th cent.) is a curious and ingenious sundial.

43 m. †**Largs Stat.**✲, a clean town, with several large churches, including a Gothic *Episcopal Chapel*, built 1877 (Ross, archt.), containing painted windows and carved reredos, numerous houses for summer visitors, and comfortable residential villas in the neighbourhood. The railway was opened in 1885; there is now a *Golf Course*, and the shelter afforded by the *Great Cumbrae* makes it an excellent place for boating. Behind there is high country, into which run pretty glens.

Largs is celebrated for the victory gained here by Alexander III. over Hakon IV., King of Norway, Oct. 3rd, 1263, the date being fixed by the calculation of the eclipse that occurred just before. Hakon fled north, and died at Kirkwall (see pp. 429, 430). The result of the victory was the cession of the Hebrides and Man to Scotland, after they had been for 400 years occupied by the Norwegians. The Northmen buried their slain in a *mound*, still existing, which was opened 1873, and found to contain burnt human bones.

In the aisle of the *Old Church*, near the mound, is a monument to Sir Robert Montgomery.

Brisbane Ho. (C. T. Brisbane, Esq.) stands inland 1½ m. N.E.; 2 m. N. along the coast is *Knock Castle;* and beyond that, past **Skelmorlie**✲, is **Wemyss Bay**✲, 5½ m. (see p. 322), to which steamers ply about 5 times daily in ½ hr.

ROUTE 74.

Glasgow to Inveraray by Rothesay, the Kyles of Bute, and Loch Fyne. 5 hrs.

("Lord of the Isles" Route.)

This steamer may be joined at Princes Pier, Greenock [Rte. 70], at Gourock [Rte. 69], or at Dunoon *via* Craigendoran [Rte. 67].

A pleasant round (circular ticket 11s. 6d.) may be made by going or returning by Rte. 75.

The Clyde to Rothesay is described in Rte. 68.

Rothesay through the Kyles of Bute to Ardlamont Point in Rte. 71.

The steamer rounds *Ardlamont Point* and passes rt. *Ardlamont Bay* and *House*, formerly the seat of the Lamonts, the oldest family in Argyllshire. The wood adjoining was the scene of the mysterious death of Lieutenant Hambrough from a gunshot wound, 10th August 1893, followed by the famous trial for murder Dec. 12th-22nd of Mr. A. J. Monson, in which the Scotch verdict of "Not Proven" (see p. 46) was returned. We now sail up

Loch Fyne, one of the largest sea-lochs in Scotland—being some 40 miles long—famous for its herrings. Only those who have tasted that fish cooked immediately after being caught know what a delicacy it is.

Beyond l. **Loch Tarbert** (p. 340), *Ardmarnock Ho.* (D. N. Nicol, Esq.) is passed rt. and then *Kilfinnan Bay*, church, and village with *Otter Ho.* (Gaven Rankin, Esq.). **Loch**

Gilp with *Ardrishaig* and *Lochgilphead* (pp. 350, 351) is seen l. and the narrower part of Loch Fyne is entered rt.

Rt. is *Ballimore Ho.* (Col. Burnley Campbell) finely situated near the shore with woods behind. Beyond it is *Otter Ferry* (where the slow steamer calls) from which a road runs E. to Dunoon (22 m.). *Loch Gair* with *Loch Gair Ho.* (Col. J. D. M'Iver Campbell) and *Minard Castle* (T. Lloyd, Esq.) are passed l. and the steamer stops l. at

†**Crarae** with large *Granite Quarries*—the scene, Sept. 25, 1886, of an extraordinary accident to a number of excursionists, who were suffocated by entering the quarries too soon after a "monster blast" which they had gone to witness.

Opposite (rt.) is *Castle Lachlan* (Maclachlan of Maclachan), and 3 m. beyond l. is **Furnace,** so called from an iron smelting work no longer used, granite quarries being now the great local industry.

3 m. farther (rt.) is †**Strachur** ✲, with *Strachur Ho.*, where those who have come by *Loch Eck* [Rte. 75] join the steamer. The loch is again crossed, and after 4 m. we reach

†**INVERARAY** ✲ (6 m. from the head of the loch), a very small (pop. 743), sleepy, and isolated county town (with resident sheriff-substitute) finely placed on a bay of the W. shore into which pour two small streams, the *Aray* and *Shira;* between them rises the grand wooded conical **Hill of Duniquoich.**

It is a royal burgh (1648), its arms being herrings in a net, and, although the constituency numbers only 113, it joins with the burghs of Ayr, Campbeltown, Irvine, and Oban in returning a member of parliament.

The town consists of a row of whitewashed houses, and a broad street running from it, in the middle of which the ch. is planted. At the end of this, on the shore, stands a small but very elegant *Iona Cross*, richly sculptured with foliage, animals, and the worm ornament. It is thought to have come from a neighbouring old cemetery called Kilmallen. On the edge is a commemorative Latin inscription for Duncan, Patrick, and Maelmore MacGillycomghan. Near the top a florid Gothic arch is represented, proving the date of this monument not to be earlier than the 13th cent.

Inveraray Castle, the residence of the Duke of Argyll, ¼ m. from the town, stands on a level green meadow beside the Aray, thick-set with ancestral trees—beech, lime, Scotch and silver fir, and ash of great age and growth—to make way for which the original town was moved to its present site. It is neither an attractive nor imposing edifice, having been erected in the castellated style before that style was understood, about 1750, by Adam, for Duke Archibald. In 1877 the castle was partially destroyed by fire, and underwent a thorough restoration. The *old* castle, to which the exciting scenes in the "Legend of Montrose" belong, stood nearer the sea, and is quite swept away. The present castle is a spacious quadrangular moated structure of greenish gray slate or soap-stone, which in rainy weather becomes almost black, with round towers at the angles, and surmounted by a central tower. The drawing-room and gallery are decorated with tapestry, paintings, and family portraits. Lord Frederick Campbell, by *Gainsborough*, John the Red (1678-1743)—"Jeanie Deans's" Duke—etc., deserve notice.

At the side of the Argyll Arms hotel a noble avenue of beech trees, many of them 16 to 18 ft. in girth, planted *circa* 1654, leads into woods behind the town. These avenues—

there are more than one—are the principal features in the scenery, and indeed few, if any, places in Scotland are more beautifully timbered than the policies of Inveraray Castle. Boswell had great pride in pointing them out to Johnson.

[The conical hill of *Duniquoich* (900 ft.) forms the terminating buttress of the range of hills between Glens Aray and Shira, and should certainly be ascended, by winding paths, for its charming, if somewhat restricted, outlook. There is also a beautiful walk up the *Aray* by the public road to the *Miller's Linn* (2 m.), returning by the Castle Grounds.]

Coach daily N. to Dalmally (16 m.) and E. to Tarbet (24 m.) [Rte. 77].

Slow *steamer* daily all the year round to Glasgow, besides the "Lord of the Isles" in summer.

Steam ferry twice daily to *St. Catherine's*✱ (2 m.) in connection with coach (once daily) to *Hell's Glen* and *Lochgoilhead* ✱ [Rte. 76].

ROUTE 75.

Glasgow to Inveraray by Dunoon, Holy Loch, Loch Eck, and Strachur. 5 hrs.

To Dunoon *via* Gourock (Rte. 69), or *via* Greenock (Rte. 70), 1 hr.

Coach Dunoon to Inverchapel, 1½ hr.

Steamer up Loch Eck, 40 min.

Coach Loch Eck head to Strachur, 1 hr.

Steamer to Inveraray, ½ hr.

A pleasant round (circular ticket, 11s. 6d.) is made by going or returning by Rte. 74.

Leaving Dunoon [p. 316], the coach keeps N. along the seashore to *Kirn* and *Hunter's Quay* [p. 316]; and thence along the S. shore of **Holy Loch** passing *Hafton Ho.* (Miss Hunter), **†Ardnadam** and **Sandbank** (4 m.) to *Cothouse Inn* (6 m.) at the head of the loch, where the *Eachaig*, a very pretty stream issuing from Loch Eck, is crossed.

[At 5 m. a fine road runs W. up the *Little Eachaig*, across *Glen Tarsan*, round the head of *Lochs Striven* and *Riddon*, and across *Glen Daruel*✱ and the hills to *Otter Ferry* on Loch Fyne, 18 m. (p. 332).]

1½ m. S. of the bridge, but on the N. side of Holy Loch and opposite Sandbank, is **†Kilmun**✲ ("The *Ch. of St. Mun*"), from which probably the loch took its name of "Holy."

There has been a church here since the 6th cent. In 1442 Sir Duncan Campbell of Lochawe founded a collegiate church of which the *Tower* alone remains. In the burial vault repose several of the mighty family of Argyll, including the founder of the ch., and the great Marquis, beheaded 1661.

Steamers from Greenock, Gourock, and Craigendoran call at *Ardnadam* and *Kilmun*.

Turning l. beyond Cothouse Inn, and keeping up the l. bank of the stream, the mouth of **Glen Massan,** praised in one of the oldest Gaelic poems, and *Benmore Ho.* (D. J. Younger, Esq.) are passed left before reaching

8½ m. *Inverchapel Pier*, where we join the little steamer on

Loch Eck, 6 m. long, but not much more than ¼ m. broad. Its beauty consists in the abrupt rise of the hills from the water's edge, and in its wild loneliness although so near favourite watering-places. There is a good road along the E. bank.

Half way up it (rt.) is **Whistlefield**✲.

[A driving road runs hence in 5 m. by Glen Finart to *Ardentinny* on Loch Long, where steamers call (p. 334).]

From the head of the loch, where we leave the steamer and again take to a *coach*, the road ascends, crosses the watershed, and descends to

5 m. **Strachur**✲, on the E. bank of Loch Fyne. Here we join the "Lord of the Isles" and cross the loch to **Inveraray** (4 m. farther on). See Rte. 74.

ROUTE 76.

Glasgow to Inveraray by Loch Long, Loch Goil, Hell's Glen, and St. Catherine's [also to Arrochar (Loch Long)].

Train to Princes Pier, Greenock [Rte. 70], or Gourock [Rte. 69], ¾ hr.
Steamer to Lochgoilhead, 2 hrs.
Coach to St. Catherine's, 2 hrs.
Ferry to Inveraray, ¼ hr.
This round *cannot* be combined in one day with either Rte. 74 or Rte. 75.

Leaving Gourock the steamer steers N., having the entrance to the Gareloch (Rte. 67) rt., to

† **Kilcreggan**, a row of florid villas along the shore, continued W. without interruption for 2 m. There is an excellent road with good views, over the hill to *Roseneath* (p. 312), 3 m. The steamer passes rt. *Craigrownie Cas.* as it rounds the point to

†**Cove,** 2 m. W., and a continuation of Kilcreggan, situated on the margin of Loch Long. It then crosses the loch to

†**Strone,** with *Dunselma* (James Coats, Esq.), high above *Strone Point*, commanding a grand view, and †**Blairmore.**

Sailing up Loch Long we notice conspicuous on the rt. *Knockderry Cas.* which replaces and stands upon the dungeons of an old castle called in the "Heart of Midlothian" *Knock Dunder*.

1½ m. farther up rt. are *Ardpeatôn* and *Peaton House*, behind which a pleasant road E. (1½ m.) leads over the hill to **Rahane** on the Gareloch [p. 312]. N. is *Coulport*, where the road along the E. shore stops, and where there is a *ferry* to

l. †**Ardentinny** ✲ at the mouth of **Glen Finart**—with *Glenfinart Ho.* (C. J. C. Douglas, Esq.)—up which a road leads to Loch Eck [p. 333]. Here lived Tannahill's

"Sweet lass o' Arranteenie."

4 m. beyond, **Loch Goil,**[1] an arm of Loch Long, is entered l. and

† **Carrick Castle,** on its W. shore, with the ruins of a stronghold of the Argylls, is visited.

[Crossing the mouth of Loch Goil, opposite which rt. is †**Portincaple** with a ferry, and passing l. the rough and lofty tops of "**Argyll's Bowling Green,**" separating it from **Loch Long,** the steamer for Arrochar keeps straight up the latter loch, one of the longest, deepest, and most beautiful *fjords* of Scotland. 2 m. up rt. the road from Garelochhead [p. 312] comes down to the loch side, while high up runs the West Highland Rly. [Rte. 81]. 2 m. from the head of the loch l. is the entrance to **Glen Croe** [Rte. 77], and rt. is *Ardmay House*.

†**Arrochar** ✲, the heart of the Macfarlane country, at the head of the loch, is abt. 19 m. N. of Gourock, and 2 m. W. of Tarbet on Loch Lomond. Between Arrochar and Tarbet is a *Stat.* on the W. High. Rly. (p. 347). The feature of the landscape is *Ben Arthur* (2891 ft.) to the W., better known as "**The Cobbler**" from its fantastic resemblance to a shoemaker bending over his last. The adjoining summit is the cobbler's wife.

Here the steamer waits 1½ hr. before returning.
Omnibus to Tarbet✱ (Loch Lomond).]

---

† **Lochgoilhead** ✲, 6 m. from the entrance of the loch, is not easily surpassed for beauty of situation and fine scenery, while the severity of the mountains, splendidly grouped round the head of the loch, is relieved by the woods and grounds of *Drimsynie* (Trs. of Mr. H. Neilson). The *Coach* follows the side of the stream flowing into the loch, and crosses it (for the second time) at

[1] Often erroneously supposed to be the scene of Campbell's "Lord Ullin's daughter." See *Loch-na-Keal*, Mull (p. 357).

Monevechadan Bridge ($2\frac{1}{2}$ m.), whence a road leads rt. in 3 m. to "*Rest-and-be-Thankful*" [below], then climbs up the wild **"Hell's Glen"** to 719 ft., and descends in steep zigzags to the shores of Loch Fyne, along which it runs 3 m. S. to

$8\frac{1}{2}$ m. **St. Catherine's** ✲, whence a ferry steamer crosses (2 m.) to † **Inveraray** ✲ [p. 332].

ROUTE 77.

Tarbet (Loch Lomond) to Inveraray, Loch Awe, and Dalmally by Arrochar and Glen Croe.

For Tarbet and Loch Lomond see Rtes. 23 and 81. Coach daily in summer, 40 m. $6\frac{1}{4}$ hrs.

A narrow isthmus of moderate elevation, barely 2 m. broad, divides Loch Lomond from the sea—Loch Long. Over this pass the Norwegian ships of Haco were dragged,[1] and launched in Loch Lomond to ravage its islands and shores. An avenue of oaks lines the pretty road to Arrochar upon Loch Long. Between Tarbet and Arrochar is a Stat. on the W. High. Rly. (p. 347).

2 m. †**Arrochar** ✲, see p. 334.

From Arrochar the road winds round the head of Loch Long, commanding a fine view of Ben Lomond, keeps along the W. side of the loch for $1\frac{1}{2}$ m., and then turns into **Glen Croe.** This must not be confused with the more celebrated Pass of Glencoe, near Ballachulish. It is a green but treeless valley, with black rocks projecting through the greensward, and ranks high among the wild and desolate mountain valleys of the South Highlands. The summit of the pass, which is about $4\frac{1}{2}$ m. from Loch Long, reached by a long ascent in zigzags, is marked by a well-known rude stone seat inscribed "Rest-and-be-Thankful.—Military Road repaired by 93rd Regiment 1768; transferred to commissioners for Highland Roads and Bridges in the year 1841."

"Doubling and doubling with laborious
 walk,
Who that has gained at length the
 wished-for height,
This brief, this simple wayside call can
 slight,
And rest not thankful?"—WORDSWORTH.

The zigzags are continued l. by a road leading in $5\frac{1}{2}$ m. to Lochgoilhead (p. 334). Our road keeps straight on, descending steeply past *Loch Restil* (l.) into the pastoral valley of *Glen Kinglas*, and reaches Loch Fyne.

14 m. **Cairndow** ✲. To the S., overlooking Loch Fyne, is *Ardkinglas House* (G. F. W. Callendar, Esq.). At Cairndow is a ferry to the opposite bank, by which the pedestrian will save nearly 3 m.

[The shortest road to Inveraray turns S. and follows the E. shore of Loch Fyne to

†*St. Catherine's* ✱ where the Loch, 2 m. wide, may be crossed at any time by row-boat, and twice a day by steamer ferry in 10 min.]

The coach road from Arrochar bends round the head of the loch; crosses the valley of *Glen Fyne*, which runs up to the borders of Perthshire; and is carried down the W. shore of the loch, in the course of which we obtain charming views of Inveraray and the Castle.

At 20 m. is the ruined tower of *Dunderawe*, a fortress of the M'Naughtons, on the gate of which is the date 1596, and an inscription. The road makes another circuit, by the little bay and glen of Shira, before reaching

24 m. † **Inveraray** ✲ [see p. 332]. The road to Oban is carried through the Duke's domain, and up the picturesque vale of *Glen Aray*, at the mouth of which Inveraray is situated. Within the first 3 m. there are 3 *waterfalls* on the Aray, the last, called Linnhe-ghlutain,

[1] Cf. *Tarbert* (Loch Fyne), p. 340.

being the finest. Arrived at the summit level of Glen Aray, 673 ft., there is a magnificent view of Loch Awe, with Ben Cruachan flinging its mighty shadows over it. A series of steep descents leads to

34 m., *Cladich House* (J. C. Kay, Esq.) and Cladich post office.

[Here the road to *Portsonachan*✱, 3 m., and to *Ford* ✱, 19½ m. [p. 172] turns l.]

The next 3 m. by the loch side past *Innishail Ch.* and *Innistrynich Ho.* (W. C. Muir, Esq.) are very pretty. Then another steep ascent has to be made to a *Monument* in the form of a small *Grecian Temple*, erected to the memory of *Duncan Macintyre*, the Gaelic poet (1724-1812), commanding a magnificent view of Loch Awe, Kilchurn Castle, Ben Cruachan, Dalmally, Ben Lui, etc., before descending to

39½ m. **Dalmally Stat.** ✲, and
40 m. **Dalmally** ✲ [p. 171].

ROUTE 78.

Glasgow to Campbeltown and the Mull of Kintyre.[1]

A steamer sails daily to Campbeltown—from Wemyss Bay on Mondays, and on other days from Glasgow, Greenock, and Gourock. 5-6 hrs. from Glasgow (railway and boat).

In July and August there are 2 daily boats from *Gourock*, one in the morning and the other in the afternoon, and the same from Campbeltown. To Greenock or Gourock see Rtes. 68-70; to Wemyss Bay see Rte. 71.

The steamer keeps due S. until **Garroch Head,** the S. end of Bute, is passed, when it steers W. to the **Cock of Arran** (p. 327), the N. end of that island.

Approaching the promontory magnificent views are obtained of the Arran mountains; rounding it the steamer calls at the beautiful inlet of **Loch Ranza** (p. 327). The strait between the W. coast of Arran and that of Kintyre is called **Kilbrannan Sound.** Down this the steamer sails, passing on l. the solitary little Free Church of *North Tundergay*, and calling at †**Pirn Mill** (p. 327). It then crosses obliquely over to Kintyre, touching first at the little fishing harbour of †**Carradale** ✲. Near Carradale House, overlooking the sea, are the ruins of *Aird Castle;* also a vitrified fort on a promontory.

[From this point there is a road along the coast running N. to 14 m. **Clunaig**✱, and 16½ m. **Skipness**✱, at the entrance of Loch Fyne, and also one running south through Saddell to Campbeltown, 15 m.

Skipness Castle is somewhat dilapidated. Its outer walls are 7 ft. in thickness, and it has 2 projecting towers, one of which was evidently the keep of the Castle, and goes by the name of the "Tur-an-tsagairt" or Priest's Tower. One of its former owners, a Campbell, called "The Captain of Skipness," studied the art of war under Gustavus Adolphus, and fought against Charles I. and Montrose. At Skipness is also the ruined ch. of St. Columba, "which in its entirety was the largest ch. in Kintyre, except that of Saddell."—C. BEDE.]

Carradale is a good place for ascending **Ben-an-Tuirc,** "The Mountain of the Boar" (1491 ft.), which is the highest mountain in Kintyre. The hills throughout the whole peninsula are noways remarkable for their picturesque features, as they consist rather of a succession of swelling uplands than of rugged or precipitous heights. Nevertheless, the view from Ben-an-Tuirc will repay the ascent, as it includes Ayrshire and Wigtownshire to the E.; Ireland, the Giant's Causeway, and Rathlin Island to the S.; Islay, Gigha, and Jura, with the broad Atlantic to the W.; and northward, as far as Ben Cruachan and Ben Lomond.

1½ m. S. of Carradale is the pretty

[1] "Kintyre = Gael. *Ceann tír*, at the head of the land, land's end."—Sir HERBERT MAXWELL, Bt.

Torrisdale, at the entrance to which is *Torrisdale Castle* (Col. Carrick Buchanan). About 4 m. to the S. is the Glen and Castle of **Saddell,** one of the most picturesque bits on the eastern coast of Kintyre. The castle is a plain quadrangular tower, with a machicolated embattlement. There are also some remains of the *Monastery of Saddell,* founded in 1163 for Cistercian monks, by Reginald, the son of Somerled, Lord of Kintyre and the Isles. In the old churchyard are some very ancient sculptured stones, also monuments of the Macdonalds, the former possessors of Saddell, concerning whom there are many singular stories in the district. A little to the S. of Saddell is **Ugadale,** a small property of the Macneals of Ugadale, one of whose ancestors, a peasant named Mackay, received it in consideration of kindness offered by him to Robert Bruce, while on his flight to Ireland. An upright stone on a shoulder of Ben-an-Tuirc is said to mark the place where he parted from the royal fugitive, after having guided him within sight of the western shore of Kintyre and the coast of Ireland. A brooch, presented by him, is still preserved as an heirloom in the family, at Lossit Park, near Machrihanish, the seat of the Macneals.

At Ardnacross is the romantic **Glen Lussa,** through which the *Stradaigh Water* runs down to the sea. Presently the picturesque island of **Davaar,** on which there is a revolving light, points out the entrance to the harbour of Campbeltown, in whose landlocked waters the navy of Great Britain might ride safely. At the head of it, pleasantly sheltered from the rough winds of the Atlantic, is Campbeltown.

†CAMPBELTOWN ✲ was made a Royal Burgh by William III. in 1700, but the charter narrates that this was in fulfilment of an unexecuted design by James VI. It is the headquarters of the malt distillery trade, was formerly a somewhat dirty town, but is now much improved, and possesses a park of about 30 acres, recently reclaimed from the sea. It is of great antiquity, having been the capital of the early Dalriadan monarchy about the 6th or 7th cent. The principal object of interest in the town is the **Cross,** which stands on a pedestal in the centre of the main street—date about 1500. The one side is covered with elaborate ornamentation, similar to that on the cross at Inveraray, and the other contains an inscription in Lombardic characters, together with a few figures of men and animals.

Although Campbeltown is well sheltered from all directions but the west, it has no very picturesque scenery, except towards the Isle of Arran and the Sound. The population depends principally on the whisky distillation and the herring fishery. Of *Distilleries* there are upwards of 20, which turn out about 1,250,000 gallons of whisky a year. This trade has nearly superseded the fishery.

Excursions :—

(1) **W. to Machrihanish ✲,** 5¼ m. The road traverses the "*Laggan*" or "Hollow" of Kintyre, the largest stretch of agricultural land in Argyllshire, which produces the earliest potatoes in Scotland. It belongs for the most part to the Duke of Argyll.

At 4 m. the road passes through **Drumlemble,** where *Coal* (of an inferior quality) is worked to supply the neighbourhood and the Campbeltown Distilleries. A little beyond Drumlemble is the village of *Kil Coivin,* where the ruins of the Ch. or oratory of St. Coivin are still visible. In the burial ground are some curious old sculptured tombstones.

N. of Machrihanish spreads for 4 m. a long open Bay, at the lower end of which is the now famous *Golf Course* of the Machrihanish Golf Club.

(2) **N. to Tarbert**✲, 38 m., by the W. side of Kintyre (Rte. 79).

(3) **S. to the Mull of Kintyre.** To Southend it is 13 m. by the coast road, and 10 m. by the direct inland road; thence to the lighthouse is 8 m., of which the last 1½ m. must be walked.

We drive along the E. coast, skirting Campbeltown Loch, and passing (1 m.) *Kilkerran*, the site of the cell of the Irish St. Kieran (6th cent.), the first missionary to the W. of Scotland. Of the church of Kilkerran, once annexed to the Abbey of Paisley, nothing remains, though the burial ground is still used. There is here a portion of the shaft of a 15th cent. *Cross*, carved with Christian symbols. Between the church and the sea is the old ruined *Castle*, garrisoned by James VI. to overawe the Macdonalds, who, however, thought so little of it that they captured it, and hung the governor from the walls before the king was well out of sight.

To the S. is *Ben Ghuilean* (1154 ft.), which commands a good view. At 3½ m. is *Kildalloig*, the seat of the late Sir Norman Campbell, Bt., and now belonging to his niece; and at 4½ m., *Achinhoan Head*, is St. Kieran's cave, of which Pennant speaks in high terms.

At 8½ m. *Glen Hervie* is crossed, and at 10½ m. *Macharioch*, a shooting lodge of the Duke of Argyll, where the climate is peculiarly mild.

At 12½ m. *Conie Glen* is crossed (up which runs the *direct* road to Campbeltown, 10 m.) before

13 m. **Southend**✲, a neat little village, with a *Golf Course* between it and the sea.

About 2 m. off the coast is the island of **Sanda** (D. J. K. M'Donald, Esq.), containing a *Lighthouse.*

At 14 m. we pass *Keil House.* There is another large cave here, to which is attached the legend of the piper who ventured in with his dog; the latter eventually coming out, but the piper lost his way for ever.

Near it is the site of *Dunaverty Castle*, a stronghold of the Macdonalds, the Lords of Kintyre, where Edward Bruce once lay in hiding.

The castle was situated on the summit of a very precipitous rock, only accessible from the land side by a narrow approach, and obtained its name of Dunaverty from Dunamortaich, or "Rock of Blood," on account of the scenes of warfare which it witnessed. At the close of Montrose's Royalist War, 1647, a remnant of his forces, chiefly Irish, under Alastair M'Collkeitoch, being defeated by the Marquis of Argyll, took refuge in Dunaverty and from there "Colkitto" sailed to Ireland, leaving 300 men as garrison. During his absence the Covenanter General Leslie besieged the place with a force of 3000 men, and the castle, which was naturally impregnable, was forced to yield at last from the stoppage of the supplies of water. The unfortunate garrison were all most cruelly put to death.

The pedestrian may keep W. along the coast and visit the Danish fort at *Balemacumra*, situated at the top of a perpendicular rock overlooking the sea, and surrounded by 3 walls.

The road crosses *Glen Breakerie*, passes *Carskey Ho.* (Col. Mackay), and ascends to high ground, from which a fierce descent of 1200 ft. in 1½ m., which tourists always walk, leads to the *Lighthouse.*

The **Mull of Kintyre** (supposed by some to be the Epidium Promontorium of the Romans), although of no great height, is attractive from its wild and precipitous rocks and the tremendous currents and tides that beat against them, and which in rough weather are fearful to behold. At the summit of a rock on the W. side is the *Light-*

house, built by Peter Stuart in 1788, and afterwards remodelled by Robert Stevenson; the tower is sheathed with copper, and contains a light visible for 22 nautical miles. The view from it is remarkably fine, extending over the N. coast of Ireland, as far as the cliffs of Donegal, the island of Rathlin, Islay, and a vast extent of the Atlantic. The geological composition of the rocks is that of the metamorphic sandstones of the Lower Silurian series.

There is no road or even a path along the W. coast from the Mull, but it is a grand walk of about 7 m. along the cliffs under *Cnoc Moy* (1462 ft.) and "*The Slate*" (1263 ft.) to *Earadale Point*, and thence in 4 m. to **Machrihanish**✲, p. 337.

ROUTE 79.

Campbeltown to Tarbert (Loch Fyne).

A *Coach* leaves Campbeltown at 6 A.M. every week-day morning for Tarbert (38 m.), catching the steamer thence to Glasgow, or to Ardrishaig and Oban (Rte. 82).

This route skirts the western coast of Kintyre, offering on a fine day a beautiful excursion, by what Macculloch calls "a very amusing road."

The road begins by striking N.W. across the peninsula (6 m.), skirting the northern edge of the *Laggan* (p. 337) with the hills on the right hand. At 4 m. is the ancient cemetery of *Kilchenzie*, still in use. As the road ascends the hill, the traveller gains on l. a distant view of the cliffs at the south end of Machrihanish Bay.

At 7 m. is a picturesque glimpse of *Tangy Glen*.

At $9\frac{1}{2}$ m. is *Ballochantuy*✲.

At $12\frac{1}{2}$ m. *Barr Village*✲ and *Glenbarr Abbey* (Major C. B. Macalister), on the Barr Water, abt. 1 m. from the coast, are passed. The house, though ancient, has been considerably modernised, and is beautifully situated amidst rich timber.

The road now regains the coast, and very fine views are obtained at *Glencreggan* (Col. Eddington) rt.

"The portion of the Irish coast seen from Glencreggan is that of Fair Head and the Giant's Causeway, in the front of which Rathlin Island is plainly visible. Then come Islay and Jura, their rugged outlines forming one long bold line against the sky, the Paps of Jura being the most conspicuous feature. Between us and them lie the pretty islets of Cara and Gigha. . . . From the moors on the hills behind Glencreggan we can "sight" another portion of the Hebridean group—the islands of Colonsay and Oronsay; and still farther to the rt. the island of Scarba, with the Gulf of Corryvrechan, while shadowy Mull fills in the background."—*Glencreggan*, by C. BEDE.

From Glencreggan the road winds down a steep hill to the seaside, where there is a cave with the unpronounceable name of Beallachaghaochean, and then keeps close to the shore to $15\frac{1}{2}$ m. *Muasdale*.

$16\frac{1}{2}$ m. *Killean Ch.*, near which are the ruins of the old kirk, very rude and primitive, though containing a double window with tooth moulding. *Killean Ho.* (J. Macalister Hall, Esq.) is passed before reaching

19 m. **Tayinloan Village**✲. Beyond, the road passes *Largie Castle*, (J. R. M. MacDonald, Esq.), a fine modernised building of the Scotch baronial style, in a prettily-wooded park, through which flows the stream that rises in Loch Ulagadale. The Macdonalds of Largie were in former times the most considerable proprietors in Kintyre.

[From Tayinloan there is a *ferry* to the island of **Gigha** (pron. **Geea**), 6 m. long by $1\frac{1}{2}$ m. broad, and about 4 m. distant from the mainland; between it and the smaller island of **Cara** to the S. is the still smaller islet of **Gigulum**. They belong to W. J. Yorke Scarlett, Esq. The only village of

Gigha is **Ardminish✱** on the E. coast, which boasts of a ch. and a manse, but there is not much to see in the island save a fortification in the middle of the islet called Dun Chifie, and a blow-hole, called in Gaelic Slocan-leim, or the Squirting Cave, from which the sea in rough weather throws up high jets.

Near Ardminish Ch. are a few remains of an older one, with some monumental relics. Cara also has an old ruined chapel.]

At 23 m. *Ballochroy* the road crosses another picturesque stream, that has its source in Loch Garisdale.

At 25½ m. is *Ronachan*, and 1½ m. farther on is the village of **Clachan✱**, prettily situated in the bottom of a dell, to which several streams converge. It is sheltered by the woods and grounds of *Ballinakill* (John Mackinnon, Esq.)

An island in *Loch-an-Dughaill* (now drained) on this estate contains a *Lake Dwelling*, with a construction of logs hitherto unknown in Scotland. Excavated by the late Sir W. Mackinnon, Bt., the proprietor (1892), it yielded several interesting antiquities, including a flint scraper of the stone age type, half a ring bracelet of cannel coal, well made and polished, the fragments of a wheel-made pottery vessel, 6½ in. high 7½ in. diam., 6½ in. across the mouth, etc.

The hill of *Dunskeig*, overlooking the property, is marked by a vitrified fort and some intrenchments, and is worth ascending for the sake of the lovely view over **West Loch Tarbert**, a long narrow arm of the sea that runs inland for about 10 m., and separates the districts of *Kintyre* and *Knapdale.*

On the wooded shores of Knapdale across Loch Tarbert are situated several fine residences, *e.g. Ardpatrick Ho.* (Capt. J. C. Campbell), and *Dunmore Ho.* (A. G. Fraser, Esq.), which the traveller sees as he surmounts the steep hill beyond Clachan.

32½ m. **Whitehouse✱**. ½ m. beyond, a road is given off rt. to *Skipness*, 7 m. (p. 336), and the E. coast of Kintyre.

†37 m. **West Tarbert**, at the head of the loch, thence across the isthmus to

†38 m. **Tarbert✱**,[1] a busy and important village, the chief centre of the herring-fishery of Loch Fyne, most picturesquely situated at the head of **East Loch Tarbert**, which is about 1 m. in length, and in its rugged rocks and landlocked waters widely differs from the softer beauties of West Loch Tarbert. The East Loch is overlooked by a 14th cent. *Castle*, which, though now crumbling, was once the stronghold of Kintyre, and for a time the residence of Robert Bruce and King James II. It "is said to have been supplied with water from the other side of the loch, conveyed under the harbour by pipes." The visitor will be interested in all the busy preparations for herring fishing, and the loading of the steamers, if the smell of the fish is not too much for him.

Steamers (1) "Columba" or "Iona," twice daily to Glasgow and Ardrishaig (Rte. 82).
(2) Daily to Islay from W. Tarbert (Rte. 80).
Coach daily to Campbeltown (Rte. 79).

ROUTE 80.

Glasgow to Islay and Jura.

Steamer twice weekly to *Port Ellen* in the S. of Islay, going on once a week to *Bruichladdich* on the E. coast of the *Rhinns of Islay*, as the W. part of the island is called, and once a week to *Port Askaig* in the N.E.,

---

1 The meaning of *Tarbert* (Gael. *Tarruin, bad* = Draw-boat) a neck of land across which a boat may be drawn, is well illustrated here. Magnus Barfod is said to have been actually dragged (abt. 1100) in his ship across this isthmus, because by treaty he was to keep all the land he could circumnavigate, cf. pp. 154, 335. The suggestion of cutting a canal here has been made more than once.

whence there is a ferry (½ m.) to *Jura*. This steamer sails round the Mull of Kintyre, and a pleasanter way is to go to *Tarbert* by the "Columba" or "Iona" (Rte. 82), thence coach (1 m.) to *W. Tarbert*, whence a steamer sails daily in 3 hrs. to Islay—4 days to *Port Ellen*, and 2 days to *Port Askaig*. Circular tour combining the 2 routes, 19s.

Sailing down W. Loch Tarbert, which is 10 m. long, we call rt. at *Dunmore* and *Ardpatrick*, then touch at **Gigha** (p. 339).

From Gigha we steer due west, and in fine weather can descry **Rathlin Island,** whence Bruce started on his expedition in 1314.

ISLAY is seldom visited by tourists, but, although it does not possess scenery of the highest order, and is inferior in this respect to Jura, there is much to interest the traveller. It is the most westerly as well as the largest island of the Southern Hebrides, being 25 m. long by 20 broad, and containing in its 3 parishes of *Kilchoman*, *Killarrow*, and *Kildalton*, a pop. of about 7375. It closely adjoins the **Island of Jura,** separated only by the **Sound of Islay,** a narrow strait, lined by precipitous cliffs. They correspond so nearly with those of the opposite coast that the imagination is perforce carried back to the time when not only Islay and Jura were contiguous with each other, but also with the mainland, and even with Rathlin Island and the N. coast of Ireland. A very strong and unpleasant current runs through the sound, rendering the navigation rather intricate. The outline of the coast is irregular on the S. and N., the largest portion of the island being separated by an isthmus from the western prolongation called **The Rhinns.** The deep indentations thus formed are *Loch Indaal* on the S. and *Loch Gruinaird* on the N. The interior is by no means lofty; the highest point, *Ben Bheigeir* in the S.E. being only 1609 ft. The finest coast scenery is to be found at *Rhinns Point*, and from Laggan Bay round **"The Oa,"** the most southern part of the island, to the E. side.

The geological formation of Islay is that of the Lower Silurian slates, varied with occasional bands of thin limestone, and on the E. coast, near Port Ellen, with interbedded greenstones.

†**Port Ellen** ✲ in the S. is a modern village named in honour of Lady Eleanor Campbell of Islay, and has large distilleries, which, with horses and black cattle, are the source of the principal riches of the island.

Roads run (1) N. to **Bowmore** ✲ (10 m.), and **Port Askaig** ✲ (18 m.) [p. 342].

(2) N.W. to **Machri** ✲ (4 m.), on **Laggan Bay,** where there is a *Golf Course*.

(3) S.W. for 6 m. across "The Oa" to within about 2 m. of the **Mull of Oa.**

A promontory near the Mull is occupied by the ruins of an old entrenchment called Dun Aidh. In the N.W. of "The Oa" are *Caves*, including *Slochd - mhaol - doraidh*, accessible only by boat.

(4) E. along the coast to **Claggan Bay,** 9 m.

The road winds under the hill of Cnoc, where two upright stones mark the supposed resting-place of a Danish princess named Yula, whence Islay may have derived its name. Off the coast are numerous rocky islets. l. is *Sgur Voucharan* (1157 ft.).

At 2½ m. overlooking *Lagavulin Bay*, are the remains of a strongly-built round tower called Dun Naomhaig, supposed to be one of the fortresses of the powerful Macdonalds, Lords of the Isles.

At 4½ m. *Kildalton Ho.* (Trs. of the late J. Ramsay, Esq.), is passed rt., and at 7½ m. near *Ardmore* (rt.) is the burying-place of **Kildalton** (one of the island parishes), containing a couple of *Sculptured Crosses*, among the best existing specimens of Celtic art.

Into Claggan Bay flows the *River Claggan*, which has its source in **Ben Bheigeir** (1609 ft.) to the N.W., the highest hill in the island. From Claggan Bay a walk N. of about 5 m. will lead to **McArthur's Head** with a *Lighthouse* at the entrance to the Sound of Islay.

---

† **Port Askaig** ✲ in the N.E., tolerably well sheltered by woods and plantations, is situated on the narrowest part of the Sound, which separates Islay from Jura, here only ½ m. wide and traversed by a *ferry*. To the N.W. of the town lead was formerly worked, and the proprietor of the estate used silver plate from his own mines.

Taking the road S.W., at 2 m. *Loch Finlaggan* lies 1 m. rt. On its Island are the remains of the principal *Castle* of the Macdonalds, Lords of the Isles, who here held their court.

At 3 m. the direct road to Port Ellen strikes off l.; at 3½ m. we pass *Kilmeny Ch.*, and then keep down the river Sorn to 8 m. **Bridgend** ✲ near the centre of the island, adjoining the pretty grounds and woods of *Islay House* (Chas. Morrison, Esq.), formerly the residence of the Campbells of Islay, for 2 generations owners of the island, which formerly belonged to the Macdonalds.

Near Bridgend is an *Episcopal Chap.*, close to which is a *Monument* to the late John Campbell, Esq., of Islay.

We skirt **Loch Indaal,** the scene of the rifling exploits of an American privateer in 1813, S. to

11 m. **Bowmore** ✲, the chief village of Islay, but Bridgend is a much better place at which to stay.

From Bridgend an excursion can be made to the **Rhinns of Islay,** the road keeping W. close to the head of Loch Indaal, then S. along the shore past 6 m. **Bruichladdich** ✲, with a *Pier* and *Distillery*, and 8 m. *Port Charlotte* to the little village of 15 m. **Portnahaven,** at the S. end of the Rhinns. On **Orsay Island** just off *Rhinns Point* is a *Lighthouse*, showing a flashing light every 5 seconds.

"The promontory of the Rhinns is noted for the extreme violence and rapidity of the tides that run past it—scarcely less violent and fearful than the stream of Corryvrechan, and attended with currents even more difficult to explain."—MACCULLOCH.

From Bridgend the tourist may also drive N.W. in 6 m. to the head of **Loch Gruinard,** which indents the N. coast for 5 m.

A fierce battle was fought here in 1598 between the Macdonalds of Islay and the M'Leans of Mull, who had invaded the island. The latter were driven back with the loss of their chief. On hearing of M'Lean's death, King James VI. made a grant of the island to the Earl of Argyll and the Campbells.

Crossing the portion of Islay W. of this loch the pedestrian will reach an extremely fine piece of coast scenery containing numerous caves. Of these the principal one is *Sanaigmore* visited by Pennant, who describes it as "a perfect subterranean labyrinth."

This spot is noted for a terrible shipwreck in 1847, when the *Exmouth*, with her freight of 240 emigrants, was lost with all hands.

Turning S.W. from the head of Loch Gruinard we pass (rt.) *Loch Gorm*, with an island containing the ruins of a *Castle*, another stronghold of the Macdonalds, and reach in 5 m. **Kilchoman Ch.** where there is a very fine *Sculptured Celtic Cross*.

By direct road we can return to Bridgend in 9 m.

JURA.

Jura may be reached (1) by occasional *Steamer* from Glasgow; (2) by *Ferry* from Port Askaig in Islay (above) to Faolin, ½ m.; (3) by *Ferry* from Craignish on the mainland (p. 352) to Kinuachdrach at the N. end, 3½ m.; (4) From Keills on Loch Sween (p. 352) to Lagg on the E. side, 6 m.

To the N.E. of Islay, separated only by the narrow sound, is the long tapering island of **Jura**, 28 m. long by ¾ m. to 8 m. broad, containing some very fine scenery, but seldom visited on account of the scantiness of accommodation. Considering its size, Jura has a small population (724), the cultivation being extremely limited, since the whole area is filled with mountains of a sterile character. There are a few scattered hamlets along the S. and E. coasts, which are provided with a road; the W. coast is utterly uninhabited, and the centre of the island is deeply indented by *Loch Tarbert*, which nearly cuts it in two.

The most romantic scenery is found in the S. division, and consists principally of the **Paps of Jura**, three mammillary eminences which are conspicuous from long distances both on land and sea, viz., *Beinn-an-oir* (Mountain of Gold), 2571 ft., *Beinn Siantaidh* (Hallowed Mt.), 2477 ft., and *Beinn-Chaolais* (Mt. of the Firth), 2407 ft. There is no difficulty whatever in the ascent, which is worth making for the sake of the magnificent views over the Atlantic and the coast of Mull, but it must be remembered that they are in *Jura Deer Forest*.

The N. portion of the island, with *Beinn-Bhreac* (1527 ft.), and *Ben Garrisdale* (1194 ft.), forms another (*Ardlussa*) *Deer Forest* (Walter Macfarlane, Esq.)

The *Antiquities* of Jura are few, consisting of a singular line of stones running down seawards from Beinn-an-oir, and traces of a triple entrenchment on the N. side of the bay overlooking the Small Isles.

The road from the ferry at Faolin runs round the S. coast to *Ardfin* (4½ m.), near which is *Jura House* (James Campbell, Esq., in whose family the lordship of Jura has been retained since 1666), thence it skirts the E. coast to

8 m. †**Craighouse** ✲, at the S. end of *Small Isles Bay*, near which is *Jura Church*.

Passing 17 m. **Lagg** ✲, 19 m. *Tarbert Bay*, where the island is only 1 m. broad, and 23 m. *Ardlussa*, we reach 34 m. *Kinuachdrach*, near the N. extremity of the island, and the usual landing-place from the mainland.

To the N. of Jura is the small island of **Scarba**, separated by the terrible gulf—

"Where Corryvrechan's surges driven,
Meet, mount, and lash the breast of heaven."

Corryvrechan or Coire-bhreacain, "The Speckled Whirlpool," is the terror of light craft sailing these seas, although, as in all cases of so-called whirlpool, the effects of it are immensely exaggerated.

"Through the channel, about ¾ m. in breadth, the sea rushes with a velocity (as ascertained by the Admiralty surveyors) of 9½ miles an hour. By the pilots of the district the speed is reputed to be 17 or 18 miles an hour."—Sir G. B. AIRY.

In rough weather, at the flood-tide, which curiously sets to the W. out to sea, it is a very awful-looking place, which no mariner in his senses would care to attempt; but in smooth weather even rowing boats can sail over it without danger. The poet Campbell

"Often listened with great delight to the sound of this vortex . . . like the sound of many chariots."

Scarba consists almost entirely of a conical hill 1470 ft. high.

Lunga Island is separated from it by a narrow and striking strait, easier of access than Corryvrechan.

"We have seen, at the distance of 30 ft. from our boat, a rapid conical whirl, of perhaps 40 or 50 ft. in diameter, force itself, like a huge corkscrew, towards the bottom of the sea. This passage is called in Gaelic 'Bealach-Chonglais, Pass of the Gray Dog, but the sailors call it the Little Gulf."—Sir G. B. Airy.

About 9 m. to the W. of Jura are the isles of **Oronsay** and **Colonsay,** almost touching each other—indeed connected for three hours at low water. (*Steamer* twice a week from Glasgow.)

Oronsay (of a curious shape, 3 m. E. to W., 2 m. N. to S.) contains some of the most interesting ecclesiastical ruins, next to Iona, in the W. of Scotland, consisting of a monastery founded in the 14th cent. by the Lords of the Isles. The *Church,* which is roofless, is about 60 ft. in length, and almost entirely without decoration, and adjoining it is the cloister, the arches of which, resting on square wall piers, are straight-sided, like those of Saxon buildings in England. In the churchyard is a fine sculptured **Cross,* the head of which is adorned with a relief of the Crucifixion. The inscription at the base is to the memory of Colin, Prior of Oronsay, who died in 1510. Both of these islands are associated with and took their respective names from St. Columba, and St. Oran his companion.

An Abbey existed also in **Colonsay**✲, but all traces of it are gone, save the foundations. This island is much larger than Oronsay, being 8 m. long by 3½ m. broad, and is remarkable for the richness of its pasture, in which it forms a marked contrast to Jura. At *Scalasaig* on the E. side is good sea-bathing ; N. of it is *Colonsay Ho.*, the seat of Gen. Sir J. C. M'Neill, V.C., K.C.B., the owner of both islands, whose uncle, the late Rt. Hon. Duncan M'Neill (1794-1874), after being Lord President of the Court of Session, was raised to the peerage by the title of Lord Colonsay. The granite *Obelisk* on a conspicuous headland was raised to his memory 1876.

SECTION VI.

WEST COAST (CENTRAL PORTION)—WEST HIGHLAND RAILWAY (GLASGOW TO FORT-WILLIAM)—ARDRISHAIG—CRINAN CANAL—OBAN—MULL—STAFFA—IONA—LOCH LINNHE—GLEN COE—FORT-WILLIAM—BEN NEVIS—CALEDONIAN CANAL.

§ 1. GENERAL INFORMATION.

THIS section, although short, contains routes of unrivalled interest, uniting the finest and best-known scenery on the W. Coast with some of the wildest and least accessible. The traveller, who has breakfasted amid the smoke of Glasgow, may take the interesting West Highland Rly. route to Fort-William, lunch there, and view the sunset from the summit of Ben Nevis; or he may spend a pleasant day on board the well-equipped "Columba" and "Chevalier" sailing down the Clyde, threading the Kyles of Bute, passing through the Crinan Canal, and coasting along the shores of Argyll—a land-locked passage all the way—and reach Oban in time for dinner, or even the base of Ben Nevis for supper.

At Oban several days may with advantage be occupied in excursions. The cruise round Mull to Staffa and Iona should not be omitted, nor the circular tours by Loch Etive and Glen Coe and by the Pass of Melfort and Loch Awe.

Loch Sunart can be visited in one day from Oban, and by staying at Shiel Bridge the Wilds of Ardnamurchan or of Glen Moidart can be explored.

The drive from Fort-William to Arisaig is strongly recommended, whilst those bound for Inverness follow the favourite route by the Caledonian Canal.

From Invergarry, on Loch Oich, the inhospitable Loch Hourn may be reached by Glen Quoich, or the picturesque Loch Duich by the grand defile of Glen Shiel.

A few days may well be spent at Foyers on Loch Ness, enjoying the sylvan surroundings of the Falls.

Drumnadrochit, at the foot of Glen Urquhart and near the banks of Loch Ness, is another charming halting-place, and within driving distance of Glen Affric.

Coaches or steamers visit all the more important places described in this section, and carriages can be easily obtained to visit most of the more isolated spots, while, at the leading centres, the hotel accommodation is excellent.

§ 2. PRINCIPAL CENTRES.

POINTS OF INTEREST.

1. **Oban.** The bay. Staffa and Iona. Loch Feochan and Pass of Melfort. Loch Awe and Loch Etive, etc. (cf. Rte. 29).
2. **Salen** or **Tobermory.** The Island of Mull.
3. **Shiel Bridge.** Loch Sunart. Loch Shiel. Loch Moidart.
4. **Ballachulish.** Loch Leven. Glen Coe.
5. **Fort-William** or **Banavie.** Ben Nevis. Glen Nevis. Glenfinnan and Arisaig. Glen Spean and the Parallel Roads of Glen Roy.
6. **Invergarry.** Loch Oich. Glen Garry. Loch Hourn. Glen Shiel and Loch Duich (cf. Rte. 96).
7. **Foyers.** Loch Ness. Falls of Foyers.
8. **Drumnadrochit.** Glen Urquhart. Glen Affric (cf. Rte. 92).

ROUTES.

ROUTE 81.

Glasgow to Fort-William by Gareloch, Loch Long, Loch Lomond, Glen Falloch, the Moor of Rannoch, and Glen Spean (West Highland Rly.). N.B.R.

This line, opened from Craigendoran in 1894 (Messrs. Formans and M'Call, Engineers; Messrs. Lucas and Aird, Contractors) is in itself an object of interest.

Its construction, through some of the most desolate and uninhabited parts of Scotland, was no light undertaking; and its deep and difficult cuttings (with but one short tunnel), its numerous lofty viaducts, its artificial foundations over miles of bog, and its innumerable culverts across mountain torrent-beds, all triumphs of engineering skill.

Beginning on the banks of the Clyde and ending under the shadow of Ben Nevis, it traverses a greater variety of scenery than probably any other railway in Scotland, embracing grand views of the Clyde sea-lochs, of the Upper reach of Loch Lomond, of the wild and solitary Moor of Rannoch, and of the lonely Loch Treig.

It also affords an excellent means of reaching Loch Rannoch, Kingussie, Oban, and the Caledonian Canal.

The finest views, with the exception of those of Loch Lomond, are all to the left as we travel North.

The line from **Queen St. (Low Level) Stat.** to

$22\frac{1}{2}$ m. **Craigendoran Stat.** (p. 311) is described in Rtes. 23 and 67. There it turns N. and sweeps, on a steep gradient, round the outskirts of Helensburgh, with fine views of the Clyde estuary l., and through a deep cutting in the geological series of the old red sandstone to

24½ m. **Upper Helensburgh Stat.** ✲ (p. 312). *Roseneath Cas.* (p. 312), is seen across the mouth of Gareloch, and the training-ship "Empress" lying off Row.

26½ m. **Row Stat.** ✲ (p. 312). The Gareloch now opens up with the Loch Long hills in the background.

29¼ m. **Shandon Stat.** ✲ (p. 312). The train sweeps inland round *Faslane Bay*, then rising, overlooks the loch and stops at

31½ m. **Garelochead Stat.** ✲ (p. 312), just above the village of that name.

33 m. **Whistlefield Stat.** ✲ (p. 312). Just beyond, a glimpse may be obtained l. of the entrance to *Loch Goil* and *Carrick Cas.* (p. 334). "*The Cobbler*" comes into view in front; the scenery becomes wilder; l., across **Loch Long,** are the mountains called **"Argyll's Bowling - Green"**; *Ardarroch* (C. B. White, Esq.), pleasantly situated on the loch side, and *Finart Ho.* (Mrs. Marryat), surrounded by fir trees, are seen below. The line keeps high above, and then leaving the loch traverses the dreary *Glen Mallin* to

37 m. the summit level (560 ft. above the loch). Beyond, *Glen Douglas* (p. 154), strikes off rt. to Loch Lomond. Presently the entrance to **Glen Croe** (p. 335) comes in view across Loch Long. Above *Ardmay*, where the hillside is very steep, we catch sight of *Arrochar* ✲ (p. 334), and the head of the loch—one of the finest views on the whole route.

42 m. **Arrochar and Tarbet Stat.,** situated midway between Loch Long and Loch Lomond, here only 1½ m. apart.

Ben Lomond (3192 ft.) on the rt. is well seen from here. After leaving the stat. we look down (rt.) upon

Tarbet ✲ (p. 154), and proceed along the hillside to the W. of **Loch Lomond.** Looking back we can see *Mt. Misery* (576 ft.) 15 m. off at the S. end of the loch.

At 47 m., almost opposite **Inversnaid** ✲ and its *Waterfall* (p. 154), we cross *Craigenarden Viaduct* of 8 arches, then traverse one of the most difficult cuttings on the line, with high retaining-walls on the loch side, and pass through a short tunnel—the only one on the route.

1½ m. beyond we pass rt. the *Pulpit Rock*, utilised for preaching in olden days.

50 m. **Ardlui Stat.** ✲ (p. 154).

The line now begins to ascend the wild and romantic **Glen Falloch,** and 2 m. farther passes from Dumbartonshire into Perthshire; rt. is *Glenfalloch Ho.*, the old mansion of the branch of the Campbells now represented by the Marq. of Breadalbane.

53 m. The dell of the *Dubh Eas* is crossed by a viaduct of 8 spans, of which the central arch is 118 ft. long and 140 ft.— almost the height of the Forth Br.—above the stream. A height of 700 ft. is attained at the head of the glen, and descent made to Strathfillan.

59¼ m. **Crianlarich Stat.** ✲ (cf. p. 170), where travellers may join the *Callander and Oban Rly.* (Rte. 29), crossed by a viaduct of 3 spans, followed by one of 6 spans over the *Dochart*. The line turns W. along the N. side of *Strath Fillan* (p. 170), commanding a view back of the twin peaks of *Ben More* (3843 ft.), and *Stobinian* (3827 ft.), and of the *Glen Falloch Mts.*, and l. across the Strath into the recesses of *Ben Lui* (3708 ft.), where spring the *Sources of the Tay*.

63¾ m. **Tyndrum Stat.** ✲ (There is another stat. ½ m. S., see p. 171.) From here the railway strikes due N. and in 2 m., at another watershed (1043 ft.), crosses into Argyllshire. Down the valley (l.) the *Black Mount Mts.* come into view: in front (rt.) is *Ben Doran* (3523 ft.), sung of by Duncan MacIntyre[1] (1724-1812), called the Burns of the Highlands, who was born near Inveroran.

Before its base is reached the train makes a horse-shoe sweep round the foot of *Ben Odhar* (pron. *Or*) and *Ben-a-Chaisteil* crossing 2 glens, up the second of which runs the path to *Loch Lyon* (Rte. 45). A large boulder called "*Rob Roy's Putting-Stone,*" is passed l. before reaching

71¼ m. **Bridge of Orchy Stat.** ✲

[A rough driving-road strikes S.W. down *Glen Orchy* to **Dalmally** (p. 171) 12 m.; and a good road leads N. to **Inveroran** ✱ 3 m., at the W. end of *Loch Tulla*, and ascending to 1449 ft., across the *Black Mount* (the Marq. of Breadalbane's famous Deer Forest) to **Kingshouse Inn** ✱, at the head of *Glen Coe*. 12 m. (see pp. 174, 364).]

The line now keeps to the E. of *Loch Tulla*, 2 m. long, well-wooded with pines at its W. end. Across the loch is the Marq. of Breadalbane's Shooting Lodge.

Quitting the loch we obtain a view (l.) of the precipitous sides of *Clachlet* (3602 ft.), and ascend the valley of the Tulla, passing (l.) the ruins of *Achallader Cas.*, an old stronghold of the Fletchers, which passed afterwards into the hands of the Glen Lyon Campbells; here the plot for the Massacre of Glencoe was hatched. Beyond is *Crannach*, where there are to be seen some of the finest remains of the old Caledonian Forest. We now re-enter Perthshire and traverse the **Moor of Rannoch,** the largest and dreariest moor in Scotland, "lying in great measure on granite, while the range of mountains that bounds its S.E. margin consists of quartz rock" (Sir A. GEIKIE). Across this moor huge bundles of faggots had to be used in making a foundation for the line. Wild, bleak, and dreadfully exposed in bad weather, on a clear day this part of the route is exceedingly interesting, the panorama of mountains, especially to the W., being very fine. Looking back from the summit of the moor, at the watershed of the Tulla, *Ben Cruachan* may be seen to the S.W.; N.W. is *Ben Nevis*, and in front *Ben Alder*. Halfway across, the *Glencoe Mts.* are visible on the l., behind is *Ben Lawers*, while *Schiehallion* stands out conspicuously to the E. before we cross the *Gauer* and reach

[1] See the late Principal Shairp's "Modern Gaelic Bards and Duncan MacIntyre" in *Aspects of Poetry* (1881).

86¾ m. **Rannoch Stat.** ✲

[An excellent road runs E. to 6 m. *Loch Rannoch* and along its N. bank to 16 m. **Kinloch Rannoch**✱ (p. 240).

A track, difficult to follow, leads W. to 15 m. **Kingshouse Inn**✱ at the head of Glencoe (see pp. 174, 364). Keep well up on the high ground to the N. of the narrow *Loch Laidon* (some 6 m. long) and of the smaller sheets of water which succeed it. The conical mts. at the head of Glen Etive, called "*The Shepherds of Etive,*" immediately to the W. of Kingshouse, are conspicuous landmarks on a clear day. A *Shooting Lodge* is reached 3 m. before the inn.]

Beyond Rannoch Stat. is a handsome viaduct. In the deep cuttings beyond boulders of all sizes were found resting on the granite.

In 2 m. beyond Rannoch we pass (l.) little *Loch Chlaidheimh* (pron. *Cly*). Here the 3 counties of Perth, Argyll, and Inverness meet.

This loch is said to derive its name, which means "*a sword,*" from the story of Lochiel and an Atholl chief who agreed to meet here in conference, unarmed. One of them, getting angry, drew a sword which he had concealed about his person, when the other promptly produced his sword. Finding that each had failed to outwit the other, they, by mutual consent, hurled their weapons into the loch.

A grand view is obtained l. down the valley of the *Black Water* of the *Ballachulish* Mts. and farther S. of the *Glen Coe* Mts. We here enter Inverness-shire, and presently notice on the hillside rt. *Corrour Lodge* (Sir John Stirling Maxwell, Bt.), 1723 ft. above the sea.

At 94 m., the highest point of the route (1350 ft.), little *Loch*

Siolaig is passed, and beyond a view is obtained (rt.) of lonely **Loch Ossian** (3 m. long) as the train hurries down the incline. Looking l. towards Glen Nevis the *Observatory* on the summit of Ben Nevis may be distinguished in clear weather before we reach **Loch Treig**, at the head of which stands Lord Abinger's *Shooting Lodge*, approached only by boat. This straight almost treeless loch ($5\frac{1}{2}$ m. long by $\frac{1}{2}$ m. broad), running N. and S. with steep grassy sides, is most interesting, and so many mountain streams fall into it that the train has to cross more than 150 large and small bridges as it keeps along the hillside on the E. Moraines and old lake terraces begin to appear W. and N. (see below). At the N. end of the loch we keep the rt. bank of the rushing *Treig*. There are fine rapids just before it joins the Spean, which we cross by a 3-span viaduct. Turning W. we reach

104 m. **Inverlair Stat.**, p. 226.

E. runs the coach road by *Loch Laggan* to *Kingussie*, 31 m. (see p. 226).

Beyond the stat. l. are the *Spean Rapids*, and across the valley *Inverlair Ho.* (Lord Abinger); rt. one of the famous parallel roads (below) is well marked. The line now descends *Glen Spean*, and, after traversing meadow land penetrates the grand **Gorge of Achluachrach**, perhaps the most striking bit of scenery on the route. The salmon, for which the Spean is famous, are unable to surmount the fall in this gorge. Above it rt., but not seen, is *Glen Spean Lodge* (The Mackintosh), and further on a *R.C. Chapel*.

$109\frac{3}{4}$ m. **Roy Bridge Stat.** ✲, where the *Roy* falls into the Spean, and where every geologist will alight in order to visit the famous **Parallel Roads of Glen Roy.**

[A rough driving road leads N. 9 m. up the glen to The Mackintosh's Shooting Lo., but an excellent view of "the roads" can be obtained at 4 m., whence 3 distinct parallel terraces are seen extending along both sides of the valley at corresponding heights.

"Each of them is a shelf or terrace cut by the shore-waters of a lake that once filled Glen Roy. The highest is of course the oldest, and those beneath it were formed in succession as the waters of the lake sank. They are seen not only in Glen Roy . . . the old lake not only filled up Glen Roy, but also some of the other valleys to the west. Until Agassiz suggested the idea of a dam of glacier-ice the great difficulty in the way of understanding how a lake could ever have filled those valleys was the entire absence of any relic of the barrier that must have kept back the water."—See Sir A. Geikie's *Scenery of Scotland*, p. 267.

At 8 m. the pedestrian may turn (1) l. up the *Turrit*, cross the ridge and join the Caledonian Canal in 6 m. at *Laggan Locks* (p. 368). Or, (2) he may walk to the head of *Glen Roy* (12 m. from Roy Bridge), cross the *col* N.E. to *Loch Spey* (14 m.), the cradle of the river of that name, and descend the Spey to *Meallgarbha*, 18 m. (p. 226). Thence he can turn rt. to *Laggan*✱, 29 m., or l. over the *Pass of Corrieyairack* to *Fort Augustus*✱, $31\frac{1}{2}$ m. (p. 369).]

Leaving Roy Bridge Stat. we cross the *Roy*; l. is a range of mts. of which **Ben Nevis** (4404 ft.) is the most westerly.

113 m. **Spean Bridge Stat.** ✲ The lovely bit of river below the bridge is unfortunately not seen from the rly.

[A road runs W. along the rt. bank of the Spean to *Gairlochy Lock* on the Caled. Canal, 3 m. (p. 368). At *Highbridge*, 1 m. W., the Spean is crossed by a picturesque old bridge of 3 arches, built by Gen. Wade, and here the campaign of the '45 opened, Capt. Scott and a detachment from Fort Augustus being surprised and made prisoners by the Macdonalds of Keppoch.]

The line from Spean Bridge affords magnificent views of Ben Nevis and of the Glenfinnan Mts. at the head of Loch Eil. 3 m. from Fort William (rt.) is new *Inverlochy Cas.* (Lord Abinger); beyond (rt.) are the *Suspension Br.* across the *Lochy* to Banavie, the old *Long John Distillery*, and the ruins of old *Inverlochy Cas.*, a quadrangular building flanked by round towers at the four corners.

It is possible that this castle was erected by Edward I. for the same purpose of checking the unruly mountaineers as Fort William was built about 4 centuries later. Under its walls, on 2nd Feb. 1645, the Covenanters under Argyll were surprised by Montrose and defeated with the loss of 1500 men. Argyll himself retired on board ship at the beginning of the action.—See Scott's "*Legend of Montrose.*"

Crossing the stream from Glen Nevis, the line runs through the new distillery and past (rt.) the remains of the *Fort*.

122¼ m. **Fort-William Stat.**, ✲ see p. 364.

A *Branch* line runs N. in 2 m. to **Banavie** ✱ on the Caledonian Canal (p. 368).

ROUTE 82.

Glasgow to Oban by Kyles of Bute, Ardrishaig, and Crinan Canal [or Loch Awe].—"Columba" Route.

This is deservedly a favourite route, for the whole voyage is land-locked, or otherwise so sheltered as seldom to cause disquiet to the traveller unaccustomed to the sea. Moreover, the "Columba" and "Iona," which convey the tourist as far as Ardrishaig, are superb boats both in speed and fittings. The saloons are splendidly furnished, and there is a hurricane deck for fine weather. Newspapers, books, and a post-office are provided, together with lavatories and every convenience for passengers; the cuisine too is admirable. The first chapter of Lockhart's novel "Fair to See" graphically describes the fellow-passengers one is likely to meet.

The following is the usual time-table:—

The "Columba" leaves Glasgow at 7 A.M. but can be joined at Princes Pier, Greenock [Rte. 70], at Gourock [Rte. 69], at Dunoon *via* Craigendoran [Rte. 67], or at Rothesay *via* Wemyss Bay [Rte. 71], by trains leaving 1 hr. or 1½ hr. later. She also calls at Innellan, Rothesay, Colintraive, Tighnabruaich, and Tarbert, and reaches Ardrishaig about 12.40 P.M.

At Ardrishaig passengers change into the Crinan Canal boat, which reaches Crinan about 3 P.M., or join the coach for Loch Awe.

At Crinan another steamer is in waiting which, touching at Craignish, Luing, and Easdale, arrives at Oban about 5 P.M. and, calling at Appin, Ballachulish, Corran, and Fort-William, reaches Corpach (for Banavie) [Rte. 85] abt. 8.30 P.M.

Going by Loch Awe one reaches Oban 6.15 P.M.

The "Iona" leaves Glasgow at 1.30 P.M. and reaches Ardrishaig 7.15 P.M.

For the Clyde from Glasgow to Rothesay see Rte. 68.

From Rothesay through the Kyles of Bute to Ardlamont Pt. see Rte. 71.

Rounding *Ardlamont Point* (p. 331) the steamer steers diagonally across **Loch Fyne** [Rte. 74]—fine views S. of the Arran mountains—to

†**Tarbert** ✲ (see p. 340) on the Kintyre coast.

[Coach daily to Campbeltown (38 m.) arriving abt. 9 P.M. (Rte. 79).

Omnibus to W. Tarbert (1. m.) whence steamer daily to Islay (Rte. 80).]

The steamer now passes on l. *Barmore*, a handsome modern mansion, and, beyond, *Stonefield* (both belonging to Trs. of C. G. Campbell, Esq.). The long ridge of *Sliabh Goil*, generally supposed to be the scene of the death, from a wild boar, of Ossian's "Diarmid," lies l. The old (disused) *Ch. of Inverneil*, and behind it *Inverneil Ho.* (Capt. D. Campbell) are passed l. before entering **Loch Gilp** and reaching

†**Ardrishaig** ✲, where the traveller leaves the "Columba," to be transferred by the Crinan Canal to the Oban boat. The heavy baggage is at once taken out and put into large vans, which are driven across the isthmus by a road alongside of the Canal. The distance to the Canal boat is about a quarter of a mile, which the tourist has to walk.

[A *Coach* starts from the pier for Ford on Loch Awe (13½ m.); whence Oban is reached by steamer down the loch and then train. This is an excellent route, but it is better to go to Oban by the Crinan Canal and make the circular tour by Loch Awe (p. 353) from there. The road keeps alongside of the Crinan Canal (below) for 3½ m., then, before reaching *Cairnbaan Inn* turns rt. and passes *Bridgend* (5 m.), N. of which is the village of *Kilmichael Glassary*, whose old *Cross* has been removed to the grounds of *Portalloch*. There in 1814 a small bell in an ornamented brass shrine (now in the Antiquarian Museum, Edinburgh) was discovered. Near Kilmichael is Kirnan, of which the last occupant was Archibald Campbell, grandfather of the poet, who over its ruins wrote the lines—

"At the silence of twilight's contemplative hour
I have gazed, in a sorrowful mood,
On the wind-shaken weeds that embosom the bower
Where the home of my forefathers stood,
All ruined and wild is their roofless abode,
And lonely the dark raven's sheltering tree."

Poltalloch Ho. (Col. J. W. Malcolm, C. B.) lies l. before we reach

10 m. **Kilmartin** ✶, a pretty village, with the spire of the *Ch.* crowning the hill, and the shell of an old tower. In the churchyard are several old monumental crosses. 1 m. farther on l. are the ruins of *Carnassarie Cas.*, built in the 16th cent. by the Bp. of the Isles. Here the road to Oban (27½ m.) is left and we turn rt. up the *Pass of Craigenterrive* (cf. p. 354) to **Ford** ✶, 13½ m.

The road from Ford to Oban is described p. 353.

Loch Awe is described pp. 172, 173.]

The **Crinan Canal**, by which passengers are conveyed across the isthmus from Ardrishaig on Loch Fyne to Crinan on the W. ocean, is 9 m. long, and was cut in 1793-1801 to obviate the necessity of the long and dangerous voyage round the Mull of Kintyre, for which purpose it is broad enough to receive ships and steamers of considerable burden. It is supplied with water from natural reservoirs in the hills.

Passengers are conveyed in a tiny but neat steamer, whose deck-house, when crowded with tourists, presents a curious appearance. The distance is completed in 2 hours, 1 hr. being entirely taken up by the delays at the 9 locks (out of a total number of 15) through which we pass. During these stoppages most people get out and walk, rejoining the boat at the last lock. The scenery along the canal is peculiar, and in many places exceedingly picturesque, the bed of the canal having been deeply excavated out of the mica schist, from which great thickets of underwood and bramble spring up, mingled with flowers and ferns.

For the first 1½ m. the boat skirts the bay of Loch Gilp, on the other side of which is the mansion and beautifully wooded estate of *Kilmory* (Sir J. W. P. Campbell Orde, Bt.), and a carved *Stone Cross.* At its head is **Lochgilphead** ✡, a watering place, behind which is a large *Poors' House* and *Lunatic Asylum.* l. of the canal are the grounds of *Auchindarroch* (A. Campbell, Esq.). In ½ hr. we reach *Cairnbaan Inn* (4 m.) where the coach road to Loch Awe strikes N. In this neighbourhood several rude stone monuments have been found. Locks now occur in rapid succession: those who prefer to walk can do so, and rejoin the steamer at lock No. 8. Having passed the summit level (5 m.) we descend to the Atlantic.

Near *Bellanoch* (7½ m.) the river *Add* (rt.) approaches the canal, flowing through a wide and open moorland. An enormous quantity was reclaimed, at a very great expense, by the late John Malcolm, Esq. of *Poltalloch*, a beautiful house now belonging to his son Col. J. Wingfield Malcolm, C.B., seen on the N., overlooking the estate, backed by rising woods and craggy ridges of hill. Model farming has been largely carried on here.

[From Bellanoch a very pretty road runs S. to *Loch Sween*, a beautiful and characteristic fiord, 10 m. long. The tourist should proceed due S. for 1 m., when the road diverges rt. to *Tayvallich*, 6 m., and *Keills*, 12 m., on the W. side, and l. to *Kilmichael Lussa*, 5 m., on the E. side, where a boat may be obtained. About 6 m. beyond Kilmichael is *Castle Sween* or *Sweno*, a strong square fortress. At the very mouth of the loch, is the island of *Eilean Mor*, which contains the ruins of an early oratory and chapel of St. Cormac, with the tombstone of a priest, represented in his robes, with some grotesque figures. There is also a *Chapel* with many old sculptured monuments at *Kilmory*, on the promontory dividing Loch Sween from *Loch Killisport*, across which is *Ormsary Ho.* (Walter Campbell, Esq.). Kilmory is 14 m. by direct road from Ardrishaig and Ormsary House 12 m. From *Keills*, on the W. coast of Loch Sween the pedestrian can obtain a *ferry-boat* to Jura 6 m. (see p. 343).]

At **Crinan**✲, with a *Lighthouse*, where the canal terminates in the Sound of Jura, travellers betake themselves to the steamer for Oban, a voyage of 2 hrs. The accommodation on board the "Chevalier," is nearly as good as that on the "Columba." On this side, if the weather is rough, a taste may be got of the Atlantic swell, but the number of islands breasting the sea generally secures an easy passage inshore.

On the moss of Crinan is *Dunadd*, the ancient capital of Dalriada (Skene). As the steamer leaves *Loch Crinan*, through the "Dorusmor," or "great gate," it passes on rt. *Duntroon* (Col. Malcolm), an old fortress modernised, and then (also on rt.) the entrance to *Loch Craignish*, another of the characteristic W. coast arms, with a string of islands dotting it. Round Craignish Pt. is †**Craignish**, with *Craignish Cas.* beyond.

[There is a *ferry* from Craignish to Jura, 3½ m. (see p. 342).]

To the l. is seen the island of **Jura** with its long line of dark hills, forming a bold skyline. The 3 dome-shaped mountains to the S. are the *Paps of Jura*, behind which lies **Islay**. To the N. of Jura, separating it from Scarba, is the needlessly dreaded *Whirlpool of Corryvrechan*, left by the steamer about 2 m. on the W. Beyond it are the islands of **Colonsay** and **Oronsay** [see p. 344].

The vessel now steers up the *Sound of Luing*, between the islands of †**Luing** rt. and **Scarba** and **Lunga** l. Rt. of Luing, at the mouth of *Loch Melfort* (p. 353), is the island of **Shuna**, bequeathed to the city of Glasgow, for benevolent purposes, by Mr. Yeates. At †**Black Mill Bay** (rt.), on the W. coast of Luing, is *Ardlarich Ho.*, and near this are the *Cobblers of Lorn*, 3 isolated rocks. Passing (l.) *Fladda Lighthouse*, and the little island of **Belnahua** (where are slate quarries), we emerge into the open Atlantic. In front is **Mull** with its *Cliffs* (p. 361). Away to the left are the **Isles of the Sea** (p. 361), and on rt. is the *Sound of Cuan*, between Luing and Seil, through which a tremendous current flows. The island of **Seil** is separated from the mainland by a narrow strait, across which is a bridge of 70 ft. span. Both on it and on the little island of †**Easdale**, which lies close to its W. coast, are large slate quarries. (*Coach* from Easdale to Oban, 15 m.) Beyond Seil on rt. is **Loch Feochan** (p. 353), above which the tourist occasionally gets a distant view of Ben Cruachan. The steamer soon after enters the *Sound of Kerrera*, E. of the island of **Kerrera**, which makes an excellent natural breakwater for the harbour of Oban. At its S. end is the ruined castle of *Gylen*, an old Norwegian fortress, in which Alexander II. died in 1249, having come to the W. with the intention of recovering the Hebrides.

On the rt. is *Gallanach House* (J. Patten M'Dougall, Esq.) At the N. portion of the Sound the steamer rounds a point, and enters the harbour of Oban.

[For rly. from Oban see Rte. 29.]

OBAN✲ ("Obe-an = the little bay"), pleasantly situated on a landlocked bay, spreads along the shore, and climbs the heights behind. It is a bustling place in summer, a focus of travellers constantly arriving and departing by rail, coach, steamer, or yacht, and has been aptly described as the "Charing Cross of the Highlands." It contains good shops, several banks, and some eight churches. Sometimes during the tourist season it is difficult to obtain even a bed in the town, although there are more than 20 hotels, beside numerous lodgings.

The beautiful bay, shut out from the ocean by the low island of Kerrera, above which rise the grand mountains of Mull, is constantly enlivened by shipping, and presents in fine weather a most attractive scene. Good views may be obtained from the hills behind the town, or from the rising ground which forms the S. boundary of the bay. The finest view, however, is from *Dunolly Castle*[1] at the N. end of the bay, now reduced to a square tower and dungeon with part of the enclosing wall, but magnificently situated on a steep knoll, terminating in precipitous cliffs.

This ancient stronghold was originally (12th cent.) protected landward by a moat, and was the property of the Macdougalls, Lords of Lorn; it now belongs to their descendant, Col. C. A. M'Dougall, whose modern house occupies a sheltered nook below it. The "Brooch of Lorn," torn from Bruce in the battle of *Dalrigh*, 1306 (p. 170), is here preserved.

Between Dunolly and Oban stands the *Clach-a'-Choin*, or Dog Stone, an upright stone with a hole in it, to which it is said Fingal used to tie his dog Bran.

EXCURSIONS :—[2]

(1) To **Dunstaffnage Castle** 3 m., (p. 175), which commands a magnificent view. Going by small steamer and returning by road or rail from Connel Ferry, 2s.

(2) Circular tour by **Loch Etive, Glen Coe,** and **Ballachulish** (pp. 174, 363), or *vice versa*, 10½ hrs., 21s. One of the grandest tours in the Highlands.

(3) Circular tour by **Loch Awe Stat., Taychreggan, Glen Nant,** and **Taynuilt** (pp. 172, 173), 4½ hrs., or *vice versa* 5¾ hrs., 9s. and 7s. 6d. A very pretty short round.

(4) Circular tour by **Loch Awe Stat., Ford, Ardrishaig,** and **Crinan** (pp. 172, 173, 350), 8½ hrs., or *vice versa* 10 hrs., 15s.

(5) Circular tour by **Loch Feochan, Pass of Melfort, Ford,** and **Loch Awe,** 8½ hrs., 19s. 6d. and 17s. 6d. Another very fine round.

The Coach runs S.E. 3 m. to the head of *Loch Feochan*.

[Thence a road strikes l. by the *Serpent's Mound* to (1 m.) *Loch Nell*, and thence N. to *Connel Ferry* 6 m., or N. and E. by *Glen Lonan* to *Taynuilt* 15 m., p. 174.]

The road keeps along the S. side of Loch Feochan to 8 m. **Kilninver.**

[Here a road is given off rt. to *Seil Island* and *Easdale* 7 m. (p. 352).]

The road turns inland, and ascends (crossing the *Euchar*, up which lies *Loch Scalladale*) for 3 m., then over moorland and down the fine **Pass of Melfort** (13½ m.) to 15 m. the village of **Kilmelfort★,** near *Loch Melfort*, at the head of which rt. is *Melfort Ho.* and *Powder Mills*.

[A road strikes l. in 5 m. to *Loch Avich*, 3 m. long, the "Loch Launa" of Ossian, which drains into Loch Awe by a river with fine falls and deep pools.]

The road now keeps round the coast, with fine views seawards to the outlying islands of *Shuna*, *Luing*, and *Scarba*, then across another high isthmus to the head of *Loch Craignish* (23 m.), where the *Barbreck River* is crossed with l. *Barbreck Ho.* (J. A. Campbell, Esq.). Loch Craignish is one of the most beautiful inlets on the coast from the number of wooded islands that are dotted about. A zigzag climb, overlooking the loch, with the *Paps of Jura* conspicuous to the W., is quickly followed by a steep descent, and at 27½ m. we turn l. off the road, which leads to Ardrishaig (p. 350), ascend the

[1] The public are admitted, at the lodge on the Dunstaffnage Road, on Mon., Wed., and Fri.

[2] Boyd's local "Timetable and Guide," 1d., published monthly, gives full particulars of routes and hours.

pretty *Pass of Craigenterrive*, pass rt. *Ederline Loch* and *Ho.* (H. Bruce, Esq.), and reach **Ford**✱ 30 m. For Steamer route down **Loch Awe** see pp. 172, 173.

(6) *Steamer* to **Staffa** and **Iona**, sailing round **Mull** (Rte. 83).

(7) Circular tour by *Steamer* to **Strontian** (head of Loch Sunart), *Coach* to **Ardgour**, Steamer to Oban (see Rte. 84).

Steamers [1] also sail from Oban :—

i. Daily to **Glasgow**, *via* **Crinan Canal** (Rte. 82).

ii. Twice weekly to **Glasgow**, round the **Mull of Kintyre**, 15 hrs.

iii. Daily to **Inverness**, *via* **Ballachulish**, **Fort-William**, and **Caledonian Canal** (Rtes. 85 and 87).

iv. Daily (twice) to **Tobermory** (Mull) 2½ hrs. (cf. Rte. 83).

v. To **Kilchoan** (Ardnamurchan), 4½ hrs. (p. 362), **Coll**, 6 hrs (p. 357), **Tiree**, 8 hrs. (p. 357), and **Bunessan** (Mull), 11 hrs. (p. 361), 3 days a week, returning the following day.

vi. By *swift Steamer*, *via* **Tobermory**, **Eigg**, **Arisaig**, [2] **Loch Scavaig** [2] (for Loch Coruisk), **Armadale**, **Glenelg**, **Balmacara**, **Kyleakin**, and **Broadford** [2] to **Portree**, [2] 9 hrs. (pp. 392-396), and **Gairloch**, [2] 11½ hrs. (p. 384), 3 days a week, returning the following day (see Rtes. 83, 98, and 97).

vii. To **Portree**, 13 hrs., **Gairloch**, [3] 22 hrs., **Ullapool**, [3] 22 hrs. (p. 382), **Lochinver**, [3] 27 hrs. (p. 413), and **Stornoway**, 30 hrs. [4] (p. 397). Twice a week.

1 See Macbrayne's "Timetable and Tourist Programme."

2 Once a week going N. it calls at *Loch Scavaig*, taking 2 hrs. longer. On that day it does not call at *Arisaig* or *Broadford*.

3 Once a week.

4 As the intermediate ports vary, and are not always visited in the same order, careful inquiries should be made as to them before sailing.

viii. By "*The Island Route*," *via* **Rum**, [1] 5 hrs. (p. 393), **Canna**, [1] 6½ hrs. (p. 393), **Loch Bracadale**, **Loch Pooltiel**, and **Dunvegan** [2] (W. Skye), 11 hrs., to **Loch Maddy** [2] (N. Uist), 15 hrs., 3 times a week, returning during the night reversing ix.

ix. By "*The Island Route*," *via* **Castlebay** (Barra), 7½ hrs., **Loch Boisdale** (S. Uist), 10½ hrs., and **Loch Maddy**, [2] 14 hrs., to **Dunvegan**, [2] 17 hrs., 3 times a week, returning during the night reversing viii.

ROUTE 83.

Oban to Staffa and Iona—a Cruise round the Island of Mull.

Daily in summer a *Steamer* makes this most interesting excursion ; tourists, especially ladies, had better not attempt the trip when the weather is at all bad—for with a rough sea it is impossible to land at Staffa, and they are sure to get a good tossing off the Mull coast. In fine weather nothing can be more delightful. The fare is 15s., including the landing expenses at Staffa and Iona.

The time employed is 10 hrs., including abt. 1 hr's. stay at Staffa and the same at Iona. Dinner and refreshments on board at moderate rates.

The steamer in this excursion makes the circuit of the Island of Mull, going by the Sound of Mull 3 days a week, and on the other days returning by it.

Leaving Oban Bay by the N. channel the points to be noticed are rt. *Dunolly Castle*, while farther on and more inland is *Dunstaffnage*. On l. is the N. end of *Kerrara*, with a *Monument* to the late David Hutcheson, founder of Macbrayne's line of steamers. In fine weather as the steamer crosses the mouth of Loch Linnhe a grand view is obtained to the N. and E. of mountain

1 Twice a week each way.

2 There is thus a steamer to *Dunvegan* and *Loch Maddy* daily.

ranges from *Ben Nevis* to *Ben Cruachan*. Lying in the very centre of Loch Linnhe is (rt.) the **Island of Lismore,** "the great garden," a long, low mass of limestone, 9½ m. long by 1½ m. broad, with a *Lighthouse* at the lower extremity (see p. 364).

The steamer next passes l. the *Lady Rock*, visible only at low water, but marked by a beacon. One of the Macleans of Duart, about 1530, having married a sister of the Earl of Argyll, and wishing to be rid of her, placed her upon the Lady Rock, that she might be drowned by the rising tide. She was found and rescued by some of her own people, and Maclean was eventually assassinated by her brother. This story is the subject of Joanna Baillie's "Family Legend," and Campbell's poem of "Glenara." On the mainland of **Mull** (l.) are the tolerably preserved ruins of *Duart* Castle, formerly the property of the Macleans, standing on the brink of a high cliff, at the extremity of a long and elevated peninsula. The main building is a large and nearly square tower, with walls 12 ft. thick. Across the bay is *Duart Ho.*, now called *Torosay Cas.* (A. C. Guthrie, Esq.), charmingly situated and protected by trees. The vessel now enters the "melancholy" **Sound of Mull,** a sea channel, varying in breadth from 1 m. to 3 m., and having on rt. the high grounds and cliffs of *Morven* on the mainland, and on l. the still more picturesque mountains of *Mull*.

The **Island of Mull,** "a mass of hill," round which the tourist is about to coast, is some 30 m. long, while its greatest breadth is 20 m. The indentations of the bays and creeks, however, are so deep and irregular, especially on the W., that while the coast-line measures some 300 m., it is only 3 m. from sea to sea between *Salen Bay* and the Atlantic at *Loch-na-Keal*, a long, broad, and deep fiord that nearly cuts the island in two. To the S. of it is *Loch Scridain*, beyond which projects a long granitic promontory called the Ross of Mull. Though the island contains some lofty mountains, it cannot be said, as a whole, to be picturesque, consisting, with the exception of occasional patches of arable land, of a vast moor, devoted to the pasturage of cattle and horses.

The cliff scenery on the S. is certainly grand, and contains several caves; and considering that very fair accommodation is to be got, and the roads, few as they are, are good, it is surprising that Mull is not visited oftener than it is. *Salen* is the best place to stop at, from its central position, but the accommodation at *Tobermory* is better.

To the S. of Salen is the great range of mountains that fills up the interior, and ranks in height and abruptness of outline with the principal ranges in the W. of the mainland. *Ben More* rises to 3169 ft.; *Dun-da-Gu* to 2512 ft.; *Ben Talla* to 2496 ft.; and *Ben Buie* to 2354 ft. The result of the proximity of such high peaks to the moisture-laden breezes of the Atlantic is, that Mull is one of the rainiest parts of Scotland. *Dr. Johnson* said it was a dreary country, much worse than Skye.

The voyage we are now describing will, however, enable the traveller to pronounce the coast scenery and cliffs of Mull exceedingly grand. Both to the artist and geologist the *Carsaig Arches* (p. 361) on the S. coast, and the display of basaltic columnar cliffs are full of interest.

Some of the localities in Mull are very interesting to the geologist. Nine-tenths of the island consist of trap rocks of the tertiary age, and peculiar terraces characteristic of those igneous overflows. Along the E. and S. coasts in the neighbourhood of Loch Buy is a thin strip of oolite—and again on the W. coast of Gribun, facing Staffa. The promontory of the Ross, as far as *Bunessan*, consists of granite, the red colouring of which imparts a picturesque warmth to the rocks. At *Ardtun* to the N. of Bunessan, are some basaltic pillars, together with tertiary beds, containing leaf impressions associated with volcanic ash, discovered by the Duke of Argyll, and described by the late Professor Forbes in the "Geological Journal."

The first point we touch at in Mull is †**Craignure.** On the N. side of the bay is *Java Lodge* (Miss Maclaine). Beyond, Mull becomes bare and uninteresting. We now cross the sound to the Morven coast, and on l. is visible a cascade, the spray from which is often taken at a distance for smoke, the water being hidden by a projection till the steamer is abreast of it.

Rt. are the ruins of **Ardtornish Castle** in a wild and picturesque situation on a chain of rocks overhanging the sea, backed by basaltic cliffs, over which pour 2 graceful waterfalls, and at the base of which are copsewoods of birch and alder.

Ardtornish was, during the latter part of the 14th and the whole of the 15th cent. the headquarters of the "Lords of the Isles." The ruins are not large: the square keep, with its thick walls, and the broken rampart of the courtyard, give one but a faint notion of the grandeur of the "Ardtornish Halls" of Sir Walter Scott. But the introduction of Ardtornish at the date of the poem is an anachronism, for the residence of the Lord of the Isles at that time was Islay, the castle of Ardtornish being built about 1340. The Lord of the Isles, in the time of Robert Bruce, was in reality Angus Og, but his name has been converted by Scott into the more euphonious title of Ronald.

Just beyond Ardtornish is the narrow entrance to †**Loch Aline,** and, as we cross it, a brief glimpse can be caught of the handsome modern residence of T. V. Smith, Esq. of Ardtornish, at the head of the loch. In the village at the foot of the loch is a *Cross* brought from Iona. 4 m. along the coast is *Fiunarie*, where lived Norman Macleod's grandfather and uncle, both parish ministers of Morven.

A grand view of the Mull Mts., with *Ben More* in front and *Ben Talla* conspicuous to the S., is enjoyed as the steamer crosses to

†**Salen**✲, a good place whence to make excursions either to Loch-na-Keal or to the summit of Ben More. The latter is easily reached by the road from Salen to Loch Scridain, which leads to its base, passing *Loch Ba*, 3 m. S. of Salen, and worthy of a visit on account of the surrounding scenery. To the N. of Salen Bay on a high rocky peninsula at the mouth of the Aros are the ruins of

Aros Castle, at one time a stronghold of the Lords of the Isles. It was probably more a fortress than a habitation, being 90 ft. long, with walls 40 ft. high.

As the vessel proceeds through the sound, the rugged *Ben Hiant* (1729 ft.), and the other high ground in Ardnamurchan, form a magnificent background.

l. †**Tobermory**✲

[There is a *steamer* from here every morning, carrying the mails to Oban in connection with the rly.]

The name of this place means "*St Mary's Well.*" It was built in 1788 by the Society for the Encouragement of British Fisheries, is the only town in Mull, and stands on the shore of a well-sheltered bay, having in front the small island *Calve*. It is rapidly increasing in popularity as a summer resort.

The town faces the S.E., and, with high ground behind, has a somewhat gloomy appearance, although on a fine summer day the thick woods are deliciously shady. Here Mrs. Bishop (Miss Bird), the celebrated traveller, has a house. There is a pretty waterfall in the stream at the back of the town, and also several cascades in the woods around, which after rainy weather fall directly over the cliffs into the bay with a peculiarly beautiful appearance. 1¼ m. S. of Tobermory is *Aros House* (Alex. Allan, Esq. of Aros). On the banks of a picturesque lake in the grounds is *Aros Fall*, which after rain is very fine.

Good fishing in Loch Mishnish, with leave from the proprietor.

There is a road from Tobermory W. to, 6 m., *Dervaig* ✲, at the head of *Loch Cuin*, an inlet of the sea. From Dervaig a road runs W. of Loch Frisa to Salen, 12 m.

On the Morven coast opposite Tobermory is *Drimnin Ho.* (J. C. Gordon, Esq.) with a R.C. Chap.

Leaving Tobermory Bay the steamer passes a *Lightho.* l.—rt. is the entrance to **Loch Sunart**, and N. *Ben Hiant*, *Mingary Cas.*, and **Kilchoan** (Rte. 84)—then rounds *Ardmore Point*, and steering S. gains the Atlantic, the effects of whose rolling swell, except on a calm day, are sure to be experienced here. To the N. is the *Lighthouse* on **Ardnamurchan Point**, beyond which the precipitous **Scuir of Eigg** is seen, together with the lofty peaks of **Rum**; and, if the day is clear, the magnificent outline of the **Coolins** in Skye. In the distance, straight in front, are the islands of **Coll** (pop. 522) and **Tiree**, both composed of Laurentian gneiss. [Steamers 3 times a week from Oban.] Tiree (pop. 2450) yields a beautiful pink marble spotted with green. 10 m. S.-W. of Tiree is *Skerryvore* (Great Rock) *Lighthouse*, a tower of granite 138 ft. high, built 1844, on a rock barely rising out of the sea at low water, by Alan Stevenson, C.E., at a cost of £86,977.

On Mull l. is *Glengorm Cas.* (James Cowan, Esq.), and in front *Caliach Point*, near which the poet Campbell lived as a private tutor, and where he composed "The Exile of Erin," and much of "The Pleasures of Hope." Having rounded this point we see S. the **Treshnish Islands**, a picturesque group of basaltic trap rocks rising into terraces about 300 ft. in height. The one seen most to the rt. is, from its curious shape, called "The Dutchman's Cap." On the most northern, *Cairnburg*, pierced by a natural arch, are the remains of a stronghold of the Norwegian kings mentioned in the sagas under the name of Bjornarborg. The existing parts are ascribed to the Macleans, who defended the island against Cromwell. The 2 largest, *Fladda* and *Lunga*, are used for pasturing cattle. Passing these islands rt. we cross l. the mouth of *Loch Tua* bounded on the S. by the islands of *Gometra* (with basaltic columns), and "*Ulva dark*," with lofty cliffs also of basalt.

S. of **Ulva** ✲ (Norse *Ulf-ey*=wolf's isle), the property of F. W. Clark, Esq., **Loch-na-Keal** (the *Loch Gyle* of Campbell's poem of "Lord Ullin's Daughter"), runs far into Mull. At its entrance lies the small green islet of *Inch Kenneth*, where Johnson and Boswell were so hospitably entertained by Sir Alan Maclean, and which Johnson has commemorated in a Latin Ode. It contains the ruins of a modern mansion-house and of a very old church, 60 ft. long, which belonged to the nuns of Iona. Having passed Gometra, we get a good view of *Ben More* over **Little Colonsay** l. and reach rt.

****STAFFA** (Stafa-ey=the island of staves or columns), a small uncultivated island, used for grazing cattle, and rented by the Steamboat Co., who have a large boat, with boatmen who come from Gometra, 4 m. off, awaiting the arrival of the steamer. It is little more than 1½ m. round, with a perpendicular face towards the S. and W., and a more gradual slope to the sea on the N.E.

Staffa was unknown to the world before an accidental visit paid to it in 1772 by Sir Joseph Bankes, who, on his way to Iceland, had been driven into the Sound of Mull, and heard by chance from some inhabitants of the district of this real wonder of the world. The earliest account of it is to be found in Pennant's Tour in Scotland, 1774.

In order to comprehend its formation, it must be remembered that the N.W. coast of Scotland was once the scene of violent volcanic action, and that the subterranean disturbances found vent along a line from Skye to Ireland, the effects of which may be traced through Staffa, Mull, Islay, Rathlin, and the Giant's Causeway. By this means a great quantity of liquid basalt was ejected to the surface, which, when beginning to cool, formed a number of nuclei, equidistant from each other, which gradually absorbed the intervening mass into as many equal spheres. The pressure of the spheres one upon the other caused them to assume a prismatic shape, and if we could take off the top of the island, we should find that the pillars in the centre are regular hexagons, while those on the outside are more inclined to form irregularly-sided pentagons.

The island, moreover, consists of 3 distinct strata of trap—the lower of conglomerate, or trap-tuff; the middle of columnar basalt, in which most of the caves have been formed by the action of the sea and the weather working out portions of the pillars; and an upper bed of confused basalt and fragments of pillars.

The usual landing-stage is at the mouth of the **Clam Shell Cave,** of no great dimensions, but interesting from the curious curvature of the basaltic columns, which gives it its name. We walk W., holding on, if necessary, to the railing supported by iron stanchions driven into the rock, across the **Great Causeway,** similar to the Giant's Causeway in Ireland, and as interesting as anything in the island. Left is an islet, about 30 ft. high, called "*The Buachaille*" or *Herdsman,* with the basement columns, visible only at low water, distorted so as in many cases to become horizontal and even inverted; rt. the convex curvature of the columns, due to the superincumbent weight, should be noticed before we come to

Fingal's Cave, the most famous of all the caverns. Its length is 227 ft., and the height from the water at mean tide, 66 ft., the depth of the sea within being about the same. The sides of the aperture are vertical, and nearly parallel. The whole of the sides, ground, and roof is composed of black pentangular or hexagon pillars, not consisting of one solid mass from top to bottom, but divided transversely by joints at nearly uniform distances of 2 ft. A good path with a stout hand-rail has been made along the interior, and in calm weather visitors are taken in by boat. Sir Walter Scott thus describes the scene:—

"Where, as to shame the temples decked
By skill of earthly architect,
Nature herself, it seemed, would raise
A Minster to her Maker's praise!
Not for a meaner use ascend
Her columns, or her arches bend;
Nor of a theme less solemn tells
That mighty surge that ebbs and swells,
And still, between each awful pause,
From the high vault an answer draws,
In varied tone, prolonged and high,
That mocks the organ's melody.
Nor doth its entrance point in vain
To old Iona's holy fane,
That Nature's voice might seem to say,
'Well hast thou done, frail child of clay!
Thy humble powers that stately shrine
Task'd high and hard — but witness mine.'"

Sir Robert Peel made it his boast that he

"had seen the temple not made with hands, had felt the majestic swell of the ocean—the pulsation of the great Atlantic—beating in its inmost sanctuary, and swelling a note of praise nobler far than any that ever pealed from human organ."

Beyond Fingal's Cave, not visited but seen as the steamer sails S., is the **Boat Cave**, accessible only by sea, and cut out of the volcanic tuff *below the columnar stratum.* It is 12 ft. wide, 16 ft. high, and 150 ft. long. Further W., also not visited, is **Mackinnon's** or The Cormorant's **Cave**, 48 ft. wide, 50 ft. high, and 220 ft. long.

After visiting Staffa in the mixed society of a crowded steamboat, most persons will agree with Wordsworth,—

"We saw, but surely, in the motley crowd,
Not one of us has felt the far-famed sight;
How *could* we feel it? each the other's blight,
Hurried and hurrying, volatile and loud.
. . . . *One* votary . . . . at will might stand
Gazing, and take into his mind and heart,
With undistracted reverence, the effect
Of those proportions where the Almighty hand
That made the worlds, the Sovereign Architect,
Had deigned to work as if with human Art."

6 m. from Staffa to the S. is the island of **Iona**, separated from Mull by a strait only 1 m. broad, across which there is a *Ferry*. Passengers are conveyed from the steamer in boats to a jetty on the E. side. Those who wish to see the island properly should remain at least one night.

IONA ✲ is a rather barren treeless island, 3 m. long by 1½ m. broad, belonging to the Duke of Argyll, and owes its interest entirely to its associations.

"That man is little to be envied whose patriotism would not gain force upon the plain of Marathon, or whose piety would not grow warmer among the ruins of Iona."—Dr. JOHNSON.

St. Columba, b. 521 in Ireland, which he left in 563, for some reason not fully known, with 12 companions, landed at Iona as being the first land from which he could no longer see his native land. Here he founded a monastery, but none of the existing buildings are nearly so old as his days. Hence he set out on those journeys, which resulted in the conversion of the Northern Picts, and in the extension of Christianity far and wide over Scotland and even over Orkney, Shetland, and Iceland. Here too he died 597, shortly after St. Augustine had landed in Kent to convert the English, and here he was buried. A hundred years later his remains were taken to Ireland, but all subsequent trace of them has disappeared.

The Danish and Norwegian pirates pillaged the island over and over again, especially in 807 when they burnt and destroyed the monastery and all belonging to it.

The original name of Iona was "I" or "Hy" (Island) afterwards *I-Colm-Kill* (the *Island of Columba of the Church*). Its present form is probably from a Latin adjective I-*oua* (qualifying *insula*) and is due to a transcriber's error.

The island is studded with ruins, carefully preserved by the Duke, and in a great measure restored by Dr. Rowand Anderson (archt.), over which a *guide* appointed by the Duke conducts visitors. Among them the square tower of the Cathedral is a prominent feature.

The highest ground is **Dun-I.**, 332 ft., at the N. end, commanding a fine panorama. On the way thither a *Cross*, erected 1879 by the Duke to the memory of his first wife, on her favourite view point, is conspicuous.

Upon landing the visitor is surrounded by children offering strings of shells for sale.

Behind the irregular street or row of cottages, which lines the shore, we arrive first at the ruins of the *Romanesque Church* of the **Priory for Austin Nuns**, founded 1203, which measures 58 ft. by 20 ft., comprising nave, with aisle and chancel, adjoining which is a little chapel still retaining some of its vaulting. The tomb in the wall is that of the last Prioress (d. 1543), whose effigy in hood and cloak occupies one half of the slab, the rest being broken away. To the S. of the Ch. are the remains of the *Cloister Court* and *Dormitory*.

Following an ancient paved causeway, called the "*Street of the Dead*," we pass **Maclean's Cross,** a single shaft 11 ft. high, carved with great force and excellence of design, said to date from the 6th cent. It and the better known Iona Cross (below) alone remain of 360 crosses on the island before the Reformation. We next enter **St. Oran's Cemetery,** the oldest Christian burial-place in Scotland, and where kings were interred until 1040, the last being Duncan, murdered, according to Shakespeare, by Macbeth—

"Where is Duncan's body?
Carried to Colme's Kill,
The sacred storehouse of his predecessors
And guardian of their bones."

Here 48 Scottish, 8 Norwegian, and 4 Irish kings are said to rest. They were originally buried in 3 chapels, all of which have disappeared; their remains, covered with interesting slabs curiously carved, being now in an enclosure surrounded by a railing.

Another enclosure contains the tombs of such chiefs as the Macleans of Mull; the last 4 priors of Iona and Dr. John Beaton of Mull (d. 1657), physician to James VI., being also buried here. Within the cemetery is **St. Oran's Chapel,** a small roofless chamber of *Romanesque* architecture, said to have been built by Queen Margaret, 1080, and therefore the oldest building on the island. It is entered by a low doorway, deeply recessed, with chevron mouldings. Within is the tomb of Scott's "Lord of the Isles," the friend of Bruce, and an effigy of an armed knight, Macquarrie of Ulva. Leaving "this awful ground," to use Johnson's words, we proceed N. to the ruins of the **Cathedral** (*St. Mary's*), the principal building on the island, dating from 1203 A.D. Before its W. end stands *the* **Iona Cross** or *St. Martin's Cross* of granite, 14 ft. high, picturesque and curious, boldly carved with Runic ornaments and figures.

The Cathedral consists of a nave, central tower (70 ft. high), transepts, choir, S. aisle of choir, and sacristy on N. side of choir. The interior length is 148 ft., and the width across the transepts 71 ft. The walls of the nave are about 12 ft. high, but the remainder of the ch. retains nearly its original height. Adjoining the ch. on the E. are some remains of the monks' dwelling-rooms, and the *Chapter-house*, which is nearly complete, has a double Norman doorway, and retains its vault. At the N.W. angle, outside the nave, are foundations of a cell or chamber, in which it is said the shrine and bones of St. Columba were placed. The *Tower*, at the crossing, 70 ft. high, rests on pointed arches. Remark the 4 square windows, openings to emit the sound of the bells, each filled with different tracery of elegant design and late date. On the N. side of the altar is the monument of Abbot Mackinnon (d. 1500), on the S. of Abbot K. Mackenzie, and in the centre that of Macleod of Macleod, with effigy in armour. On the S. side are 3 elegant sedilia, which, together with the fine E. window, are in the Decorated Gothic of the 14th cent.

To the N.E. of the abbey is a small quadrangular chapel, of which the dedication is unknown; also a single gable representing the *Bishop's House*. To the S.E. lies *St. Mary's Chapel*.

Those who have some time to spend on the island should visit *Port a Currach* to the S., where St. Columba is supposed to have first landed, and the circle of stones which marks the site of the first place of Christian worship. On the W. there is a *Spouting Cave*.

There is no corn-mill in Iona; grain is carried over to Bunessan, in Mull, to be ground. Failing this "*the quern*," or hand-mill, mentioned in the Bible, is still resorted to.

Across the *Sound of Iona* is the **Ross of Mull**, the W. end of which is composed of granite, with *Quarries* worthy of notice.

"The Rev. Thomas M'Lachlan has traced for a distance of 7 m. a series of granite monoliths in Mull, each about 6 ft. in height, at intervals of about half-a-mile, the one within sight of the next, extending eastwards and along the shore of Loch Scridain from the first nearest the shore, which stands in a conspicuous place within sight of the Cathedral."—ANDERSON.

A road leads from the E. side of the *Ferry* to **Bunessan**✲, 6 m., at the head of Loch Lathaich, and not far from *Ardtun*, where the geologist will find the tertiary leaf beds before alluded to.

N.E. of Bunessan *Loch Scridain* runs inland for about 10 m.

S. of Bunessan a strip of schistose rocks separates the granite of the Ross from the basalt of the rest of the island.

[15 m. S.W. of Iona is the solitary rock of **Dhu Heartach**, or St. John's Rock, a solitary trap rock, 220 ft. long, rising 30 ft. out of deep water, in the midst of dangerous reefs occupying some square miles —long a source of danger to mariners—but since 1867-72 surmounted by a *Lighthouse* 100 ft. high, erected by the Messrs. Stevenson, engineers to the Commissioners of the Northern Lighthouses. The difficulties in approaching the rock were very great. On an average this was possible on only 50 days in the year. The stones and other materials were prepared at Erraid granite quarries in the Ross of Mull. On one occasion 14 stones, each of 2 tons, fixed by joggles and cement into the masonry, 37 ft. above high water, were torn out by the waves and swept off the rocks.]

Leaving Iona the steamer steers through an archipelago of granite islets and turns E. along the S. coast of Mull.

Rt. are the *Torrin Rocks*, a reef extending to *Dhu Heartach Lighthouse* (above); l. the cliff scenery, where the granite has given place to basalt, is extraordinarily fine, especially at the **Carsaig Arches**, beyond which is *Carsaig Bay*. The cliffs here are abt. 1000 ft. high, and exceed in height all others in Scotland, except those of Hoy and Foula.

At †**Carsaig** is *Carsaig Ho.* (Col. Cheape), with a picturesque waterfall near it.

We now cross the mouth of **Loch Buy**, the property around which has for centuries belonged to the Maclaines of Lochbuie.

Lochbuie's modern seat is at the head of the loch, near the ruins of *Moy Cas.* and the old mansion-house where Johnson stayed, and was so offended at getting cold sheep's head for supper. There are grand basaltic cliffs inland between Loch Buy and *Loch Spelvie* (a curiously shaped sea loch with a narrow entrance) as well as along the sea coast; behind rise *Ben Buie* (2345 ft.) and *Ben Creach* (2289 ft.)

As we cross to the mainland we enjoy grand views rt. of the **Garvelloch Islands** (or *Islands of the Sea*, with hermits' "beehive" retreats older than any on Iona), of **Scarba**, and, in the distance, of the **Paps of Jura**, **Islay**, and **Colonsay**. Presently a splendid view N. of *Ben Cruachan* is obtained in clear weather, before reaching the **Sound of Kerrera** (p. 352), through which we regain Oban.

ROUTE 84.

Oban to Loch Sunart (Loch Shiel and Loch Moidart), Strontian, and Ardgour.

Excursion Steamer Mon., Wed., and Frid. to Strontian; *Coach* to Ardgour; thence *Steamer* back to Oban. Also *Steamer* Tues.,

Frid., and Sat. to Salen, and every 2nd Tues. to Strontian.[1]

From Oban to Tobermory see Rte. 83.

From Tobermory the steamer crosses the Sound of Mull N.E. to the entrance of **Loch Sunart** which runs E. into the mainland for more than 20 m., with fine scenery. N. rises the bold *Ben Hiant* (1729 ft.), l. of which are the imposing ruins of *Mingary Cas.*, which belonged to the M'Ians, a younger branch of the Macdonalds, Lords of the Isles. Here, in 1495, James IV. held his court to receive the submission of the insular chieftains. In 1644 it was taken by Alister Macdonald (Colkitto) for Montrose, and subsequently besieged by the Marq. of Argyll, but relieved. W. of it is **Kilchoan ✱**, where the steamer from Oban to Tiree calls 3 times a week.

[From Kilchoan a rough driving road leads 7 m. N.W. to within ¼ m. of *Ardnamurchan Point*, with a *Lighthouse* 180 ft. above the sea, showing a fixed light visible for 18 nautical miles; a good road leads E. up Loch Sunart to *Salen*, 17 m., and *Strontian*, 26 m.]

The steamer calls first at **†Salen✱**.

[A driving road strikes N. to

4 m. **Shiel Bridge✱** at the S.W. end of **Loch Shiel** (see p. 366), and across which Inverness-shire is entered. A very pretty road leads down the *Shiel*, along its rt. bank, to 2½ m. *Dorlin Cas.*, a modern house (Lord Howard of Glossop) at the mouth of **Loch Moidart**, where it stops. Opposite Dorlin on a steep peninsula—an island at high water—is the curious old ruined fortress of **Castle Tirrim**, a pentagon in shape, supposed to have been built in the 14th cent. by the wife of John, Lord of the Isles, and set fire to by its proprietor 1745, before he joined Prince Charlie. It still belongs to Clanranald and, with the small neighbouring island of *Riska*, is the only property now belonging to the representative of that branch of the Macdonalds, who formerly owned most of this district.[2]

From Shiel Bridge a road leads N.E. to

5 m. **Kinloch Moidart** (no inn), at the head of Loch Moidart, which is almost dry at low tide. *Kinloch-Moidart Ho.* (R. Stewart, Esq.) is a handsome, modern mansion with an *Epis. Chap.* in the grounds. A former house was burnt down by George II.'s troops in revenge for its owner's partiality to the Stuart cause. In it Prince Charlie spent 24 days collecting his followers, before setting out to raise his standard at Glenfinnan (p. 366), the first to join him being "the seven men of Moidart," gentlemen of the clan Macdonald. It was long the seat of the Macdonalds, now represented by the Robertson-Macdonalds, descended maternally from the historian, one of whom, Mrs. Macdonald MacVicar, still owns the island of *Shona Beag* at the mouth of the loch.

A charming path leads from Kinloch Moidart by the N. side of the loch, *Glen Uig*, and *Roshven* to

Kinloch Ailort✱, 14 m. (see p. 367).]

Above Salen the steamer passes through some fine "Narrows" before reaching

†Strontian✱ (pronounced *Stronteé-an*), on a bay near the head of Loch Sunart. At the mouth of *Glen Strontian*, is *Strontian Ho.* (Sir Rodney-Stuart Riddell, Bt.), and up the glen are some lead mines, now disused. Beside the lead ore a greater number of rare minerals has been found here than perhaps in any spot in Britain, including Calcite, Apophyllite, Harmotone, Sphene, Staurolite, Brewsterite, and especially *Strontianite* (discovered 1790), from which the element *Strontium* is derived and which gets its name from this locality.

The *Coach* road from Strontian runs E. by the head of the loch, ascending for 5½ m. (326 ft.), with fine views back, then descends the wild *Glen Tarbert* to

9 m. *Inversanda Bay*, and strikes N. by the shore of *Loch Linnhe* to

15 m. **†Ardgour✱** (or **Corran**), p. 364.

ROUTE 85.

Oban to Ballachulish (Glen Coe), Fort-William (Ben Nevis), and Banavie.

Steamer 3 times a day to *Corpach* in 3 hrs., thence *omnibus* to *Banavie* (1 m.), the starting-point for the *Caledonian Canal* (Rte. 87), through which one steamer sails to *Inverness* daily in July, Aug., and Sept., and 3 times a week in June.

By leaving Oban at 6 a.m. Inverness can be reached at 6.30 p.m., but it is more comfortable to start for the Canal from Fort-William or Banavie.

By taking this early steamer *Glencoe* can be visited from Ballachulish and return made the same day to Oban or Banavie; but *far better*, make the splendid (daily) circular tour by *Loch Etive* (p. 174), *Glen Coe*, and *Ballachulish*, leaving Oban by train 8.20 a.m.

---

[1] The Season's Time-tables must be consulted.

[2] *Among the Clanranalds*, by the Rev. Charles Macdonald, late R.C. priest in Moidart, gives an interesting account of this neighbourhood.

This sail up Loch Linnhe is very beautiful. Leaving Oban by the N. Channel we pass rt. *Dunollie Cas.* and, in the distance, *Dunstaffnage Cas.* at the entrance to *Loch Etive*, with *Ben Cruachan* conspicuous in the background. As we enter the *Lynn of Lorne* we have rt. *Ardmucknish Bay*[1], with *Loch Nell Ho.* (A. A. L. Campbell, Esq.) on a promontory, and l. the verdantly green **Lismore** ("*Great Garden*"), a long, low, narrow island, composed of limestone, lying at the mouth of **Loch Linnhe.**

Lismore once contained an important ecclesiastical establishment and the cathedral of the diocese of Argyll, now modernised and used as a Parish Ch.

"The Cathedral of St. Moluac, the seat of the bishops of a diocese, which was dismembered from Dunkeld in the beginning of the 13th cent., is perhaps the humblest in Britain. The High Ch. of Argyll is less than 60 ft. in length by 30 ft. in breadth. It has no aisles, and seems to have had neither transepts nor nave."—ROBERTSON.

On the W. coast, on a high rock, are the ruins of *Auchindown Cas.*, the ancient seat of the Bps. of Argyll, from which they acquired the title of "Episcopi Lismorenses," just as the Bps. of Sodor and Man obtained their title from the *Sudreys*, Sodorenses or S. Hebrides, which formed part of the diocese of *Ebudæ*, of which *Hebrides* is a corruption.

At the S. end of the island is a *Lighthouse;* at the N. end a short *ferry* to *Port Appin.*

Passing rt. *Eriska* island at the mouth of *Loch Creran* (pp. 174, 175), and *Aird's Bay*, at the head of which is *Aird's Ho.* (R. Macfie, Esq.), we call at

† **Port Appin** ✲ (Gael. *Abthain* = Abbey lands), where the scenery is particularly pleasing. The Mts. of Appin tower to the rt. ; l. over Lismore (above) rise the Mts. of Morven and Mull. Beyond, we pass rt. *Cas. Stalker*, long the residence of the Stewarts of Appin, with the royal arms over the door, because built for James IV., on a rock in Loch Laich, from the head of which runs the fairly wooded *Strath Appin.* Except at high tide we keep outside the island of **Shuna,** with remains of a castle ; behind on the mainland is *Appin Ho.* Ben Nevis now comes into view in front ; l. are the bold Mts. of *Ardgour*, into which runs *Glen Tarbert* (Rte. 84), and after passing rt. *Ardsheal Ho.* (G. W. Anderson, Esq.) we enter the mouth of *Loch Leven* and touch at

†**Ballachulish** ✲. 1 m. E. is a *ferry* across the "Narrows" of Loch Leven, which runs some 9 m. farther inland. On each side of the ferry is a hotel. Behind that on the S. side, in a beautiful glen, is *Ballachulish Ho.* (Trs. of Sir. G. de la Poer Beresford, Bt.). 2 m. beyond the hotel are extensive *Slate Quarries* and a straggling village, principally occupied by the quarrymen. There are Estab., Free, 2 Epis., and R.C. Chs. on the S. side of the loch, and an Epis. Ch. on the N. side, at which the present Bp. of Argyll and the Isles, who lives near it, frequently officiates. It was while staying with him that the well-known Rev. Mr. Mackonochie of St. Alban's, Holborn, lost his way and was found dead in the snow, 17th Dec. 1887.

On a little island in the loch are ancient burial-places—one for the inhabitants of Glencoe and the other for those of Lochaber. In the former repose the bones of M'Ian, the chief who was shot in the massacre of Glencoe. About 3 m. above the hotel where the loch again narrows, is the *Dog ferry* (boat uncertain).

[EXCURSIONS :—

(1) Through **Glencoe** to **Kingshouse,** 17 m. and **Loch Etivehead,** 29 m.

The road runs by the S. shore of Loch Leven, past the village to 5 m. *Bridge of Coe.* On a wooded eminence l. stands *Invercoe Ho.* (Trs. of Mrs. B. Macdonald). A portion of the old house of Macdonald, the head of the clan, where the officers of the king's regiment were

[1] For road from Oban, by Ardmucknish Bay to Ballachulish 28 m. see pp. 174-175.

quartered before the massacre, and where the massacre began—now a ruin—may be seen above the trees. Behind rises the picturesque conical mountain, called the *Pap of Glencoe* (2430 ft.), a bare peak with steep rifted gullies, dangerous to ascend. The road now turns (rt.) up the rt. bank of the Coe and enters **Glen Coe**. This glen will for ever be memorable for the *Massacre* here carried out, under the orders of William III., upon the 13th Feb. 1692, by Campbell of Glen Lyon and 128 soldiers after living for 12 days upon friendly terms with the inhabitants. The cause of it was the failure of Macdonald of Glen Coe to take the oath of allegiance to the king at the time specified. That he had taken the oath required, although by unavoidable detentions a few days too late, was suppressed by the Secretary of State for Scotland, and the extirpation of his clan was decreed at the instigation of the Earl of Breadalbane, whose lands the Glen Coe men had plundered. Out of 200 occupants of the glen at least 40 were slain, several died from exposure, and more would have perished had not the severity of the weather prevented the royal troops occupying the passes in time.

"In the Gaelic tongue Glencoe signifies the Glen of Weeping; and in truth, that pass is the most dreary and melancholy of all the Scottish passes, — the very Valley of the Shadow of Death. Mists and storms brood over it through the greater part of the finest summer; and even on those rare days when the sun is bright, and when there is no cloud in the sky, the impression made by the landscape is sad and awful."—LORD MACAULAY.

It is hard to say under which aspect Glencoe is finest—whether with the shifting lights of cloud and sunshine, or when the storm is breaking over its precipitous black jagged rocks. In the latter case the innumerable torrents that tumble down the rifted walls form not the least remarkable feature of the scene.

At 7½ m. is *Clachaig*✶, and beyond it about the middle of the glen is the tarn or small loch of *Triochatan*, through which flows the Cona, of which Ossian sang, and on whose banks Ossian was born.

On the rt. the imposing *Aonach Dhu*, *Gearr Aonach*, and *Ben Fhada*, the N.E. spurs of **Bidean-nam-Bian** (3766 ft.)—the highest mountain in Argyllshire—stand out conspicuously. At 11½ m. (850 ft.) a path strikes rt. to Loch Etivehead, but tourists are recommended to make the detour with the coach.

In another mile the watershed is crossed at 1011 ft., and at 14 m. *Altnafedh* an old steep road, called the *Devil's Staircase*, ascending by zigzags to 1754 ft., leads l. to the head of Loch Leven (6 m.) and *Fort-william* (19 m.). At 16 m.—1 m. short of **Kingshouse** ✶ (see pp. 174, 348)—the road turns rt. round "*The Shepherds of Etive*," and down *Glen Etive*, through *Dalness Deer Forest* (Mrs. D. Stewart), to 29 m. **Loch Etivehead**, where the steamer for *Taynuilt* and *Achnacloich* (p. 174) is joined.

(2) **Along the N. side of Loch Leven** to its head, 10 m.

This is a most beautiful drive, with lovely views. (There is no road along the upper part of the S. side, which is very steep.) In 3 m. we pass *Callart Ho.*, the residence of Mrs. Cameron Campbell of Monzie, who also owns the extensive *Mamore Deer Forest* to the N.E.; the shooting lodge is *Kinlochmore* at the head of the loch, where there is a fine waterfall. Thence the old road over the *Devil's Staircase* (above) strikes S. The river *Leven*, in its upper part called the *Black Water*, which passes through a long succession of small lochs, may be followed for about 16 m.—but the ground is very soft—to its source in *Loch Chlaidheimh* (pron. *Cly*), about 2 m. from *Rannoch Stat.* (see p. 348).

(3) By driving road to **Fort-William**, 12 m.

We cross the ferry, pass through the village of *Onich* (3 m.), with slate quarries, and keep the E. shore of Loch Linnhe parallel to the course of the steamer.

(4) By driving road to **Oban**, 28 m. (see p. 175).]

Leaving Ballachulish the steamer crosses the mouth of Loch Linnhe to †**Onich**✲, a favourite place for summer quarters, then rounds the point and enters the *Corran Narrows*, less than ¼ m. broad, with a strong tideway, and stops l. at †**Corran**✲ (or **Ardgour**), with a *ferry*. Behind is *Ardgour Ho.* (Trs. of the late A. T. Maclean, Esq.) and *Ardgour Towel*, a waterfall presumably so named from its whiteness.

[For Excursion to *Loch Sunart* and *Loch Moidart* see Rte. 84.]

3½ m. beyond, (l.) is *Cona Glen* and *Conaglen Ho.* (Earl of Morton); then a fine view is obtained of Ben Nevis before reaching (rt.)

† **FORT-WILLIAM**✲, so called from a fort at the N. end of the town, built by General Monk, and afterwards enlarged by *William* III. chiefly with the view of keeping in check the turbulent Clan Cameron. It was sold by Government to Mrs. Cameron Campbell of Monzie; by her it was sold to the W. Highland Rly. Co., and it has now been largely pulled down to make way for that railway. The town, which it was originally intended to call *Maryburgh*, after William III.'s queen, consists of one long narrow street, and is not attractive, although pleasantly situated. It contains a very handsome Gothic *Epis. Church* built in 1880. There is a *Fountain* and other *Memorial Monuments* to leading townsmen, and on the N. outskirts is *Belford Hospital*, erected and endowed by Mr. and Mrs. Belford of Glenfintaig.

At the S. end is the *Low Level Observatory*, built 1890, and connected by telegraph with that on the summit of Ben Nevis. They are worked as one observatory, are 4¾ m. apart, and their heights above sea-level are respectively 42 ft. and 4407 ft. Here the instruments are self-recording, but those at the High Level Observatory have to be read hourly.[1]

[Excursions :—

See Map, p. 349.

(1) **Ascent of Ben Nevis**,[2] 4404 ft., 7¼ m. (3-4 hrs.). The four facts that this is the highest mountain in the British Isles, that there is an *Observatory* on the summit (no admittance except by introduction), erected by the Scottish Meteorological Society in 1883, with a resident staff who take hourly observations day and night; the fact that an excellent pony track (toll for tourist on foot, 1s.; on horseback, 3s.) leads to the very top, and that there is a *Temp. Inn* close to the observatory, where food and shelter can be obtained, and where the night may be passed in fair comfort (bed and breakfast 10s.)—not to mention the *View* on a clear day—cause Ben Nevis to be more frequently ascended than probably any other mountain in Great Britain, except perhaps Snowdon. The ascent was made by the Empress Eugénie in Aug. 1872.

The first impression of Ben Nevis is disappointing; it is not a graceful mountain, and, from the absence of peak or cone, it takes some time to realise its great height and gigantic mass. Its leading features are the deep Glen Nevis (composed of Silurian crystalline schist) to the S., the tremendous precipices to the N., in which snow is almost always found, even in the hottest summer, and the scarcely less bold cliffs facing the corrie to the E., round which a ridge—"so narrow in some places that a single block of granite might split into two parts, of which one would roll crashing down the steep slope into the valley on the left hand, while the other would leap to the bottom of the glen on the right"—leads to the (pink granite) spur of *Cairn Mor Dearg* ("the big red cairn"). "The lower three-fourths of Ben Nevis are composed of a coarsely crystalline pink granite . . . the upper fourth of a dark porphyry. . . . The silurian crystalline schists through which the granite rises are well seen where the road to the mountain leaves the highway." The long neighbouring ridge of *Aonach Mor* (3999 ft.) and *Aonach Beag* (4060 ft.) to the E. is also schist, not granite.

A road leads up the *rt.* bank of the *Nevis* burn to 2¼ m. *Achintee Farm*, where the path, 5 m. long, strikes l. up the mountain. At 2200 ft. beyond a small lake, by which the path to *Banavie* descends, is the road-keeper's hut. Behind it a direct line (not recommended) may be taken to the summit. From here the path, now steeper and rougher, leads to the top in 6 long zigzags. Telegrams are taken in at the Observatory for despatch at an extra charge of 6d.

The *View* on a clear day is very extensive, but not so pleasing as from many other more isolated mountains. It com-

[1] For a most interesting account of these observatories and of Ben Nevis see *Guide to Ben Nevis*, prepared by R. T. Omond, Esq., superintendent, printed for the directors, and published by John Menzies & Co., Edinburgh and Glasgow, 2nd ed., 1893, 1s. See also Sir A. Geikie's *Scenery of Scotland*, 2nd ed., pp. 128, 129, 161-164, etc.

[2] Guide, 6s. Guide and pony, 21s.

mands a radius of nearly 100 m., except to the N.E., where the *Cairngorm Mountains* bound the horizon, but it is rarely clear in all directions at the same time. To the S. *Loch Linnhe*, the *Glencoe Mountains*, *Ben More* (Mull), *Ben Cruachan*, and the *Paps of Jura* are visible, and, in an exceptionally clear atmosphere, the N.E. coast of Ireland; to the S.E. *Ben More*, *Ben Voirlich*, *Ben Lawers*, and (very marked) *Schiehallion;* N.E. a glimpse is caught of *Loch Laggan* and (occasionally) of *Ben Muich-dhui;* N. runs the line of the *Caledonian Canal*, while *Inverness* can sometimes be seen; N.W. is a sea of mountains, among which *Mamsoul* and *Scour Ouran* may be identified, and further W. the ragged peaks of the *Coolins* (Skye), the hills of *Rum*, and the north end of *Eigg*, towards which runs Loch Eil.

(2) Drive up **Glen Nevis,** 8 m.

This is one of the grandest glens in Scotland. The road keeps up the *left* bank of the stream, passing rt. a *Rocking Stone* (now off its balance), *Dunjardil*—a good vitrified fort 1500 ft. above the road and commanding a magnificent view—and a waterfall. Beyond where the road stops is another fine waterfall.

(3) To the **Parallel Roads of Glen Roy**, p. 349.

(4) N.E. by **Loch Laggan** to **Kingussie**, 49 m. See p. 226.

(5) W. to **Arisaig** (*Coach* daily), 38 m. (Rte. 86).

(6) S.E. to the **Head of Loch Leven,** 13 m., and over the **Devil's Staircase** to **Kingshouse** (Glen Coe) (for pedestrians), 22 m., see p. 364.]

From Fort-William the steamer crosses the head of Loch Linnhe, passing rt. the mouth of the *Lochy*, *Inverlochy Cas.* (p. 349), and *Neptune's Staircase*, as the series of locks between Corpach and Banavie is called, to

† **Corpach** ✲, p. 368, whence omnibuses convey tourists in 1 m. to

Banavie ✲, where the steamer on the Caledonian Canal lies.

ROUTE 86.

Fort-William to Arisaig passing Glenfinnan and Loch Shiel.

Mail Waggonette (daily, July - Sept.; 3 times a week the rest of the year) to Arisaig, 38 m., fare 11s.

Tourists can visit *Prince Charlie's Monument* at Glenfinnan, 17½ m., and catch the return coach, fare 8s. 6d.

There is a *Steam Launch* in summer, in connection with the coaches, from Glenfinnan down Loch Shiel to Shiel Bridge (p. 362).

This is a very fine drive, the scenery for the last 10 m. especially being difficult to surpass.

After leaving Fort-William we pass l. the ruins of *Inverlochy Cas.* (p. 349), and cross (2 m.) the *Lochy* by a Suspension Br., and (3 m.) the *Caledonian Canal* at Banavie to

4 m. †**Corpach**✱, (above). Rt., in *Kilmallie Ch.-yd.*, is an obelisk to Col. John Cameron of the 92nd Highlanders, shot at Waterloo, with an inscription by Sir W. Scott. Byron's famous lines in "Childe Harold," form an even more lasting epitaph. There is a grand view looking backwards of Ben Nevis. The road now skirts the N. shore of **Loch Eil** (9 m. long), which forms a right angle with Loch Linnhe. It is somewhat uninteresting, but the mts. to the W. make a pleasing background.

At 9 m. we pass *Fassifern*, the residence of the late Sir Duncan Cameron, whose father Sir Ewen was created a baronet for his son's eminent services in Holland, Egypt, and the Peninsula.

Passing *Lochiel Ho.* (now a farmhouse), the head of the loch, and a Shooting Lodge of Lord Morton, we reach

17½ m. **Prince Charlie's Monument** at the mouth of *Glenfinnan*, and the head of *Loch Shiel*. It stands in a beautiful situation close to the road, at the junction of 4 glens, and consists of an ordinary *Pillar*, built of the common stone of the country, surmounted by a statue of the Prince in the act of addressing his followers. It is erected on the very spot where in the presence of about 700 Camerons, and 300 Macdonalds, the Prince's standard was unfurled by the Marq. of Tullibardine, 19th Aug. 1745; it also serves to commemorate the Prince's final flight from the same district, 20th Sept. 1746.

[**Loch Shiel** [1] is a freshwater loch, 18 m. long, but nowhere more than 1 m. broad, separating Ardgour and Sunart in Argyllshire from Moidart in Inverness-shire. At its head and for two-thirds of

[1] Steam launch generally twice weekly to *Shiel Bridge* but inquire at Shiel Bridge Hotel.

its length it is wild, with rocky sides clothed with Scotch firs and birches, and bounded by mountains of considerable height.

At 6 m. down (rt.) is *Glen Aladale*, for generations the property of the Macdonalds. In this neighbourhood Prince Charlie lay hid for several months.

At 12 m. are "Narrows" with an island —*Eilean Fhionain*—containing a ruined *chapel*, with an old *bell*, and a *burying ground*, filled with graves of the ancient families of Moidart.

Beyond this there are enormous peat mosses on both sides of the loch; a river, 2 m. long, issuing out of the loch at *Shiel Bridge* (p. 362) connects it with the sea.]

Near the Monument is a handsome *R.C. Chapel*. Beyond, among trees, and commanding grand views of Ben Nevis and Loch Shiel stands *Glenfinnan Ho.*, the seat of J. A. Macdonald, Esq. of Glenaladale. Climbing a steep hill we reach

18½ m. **Stagehouse Inn**✱, where the coach stops for lunch.

[Excellent walks may be taken from here through glens running N. into a mountainous district; up Glenfinnan and over the *col* (1586 ft.) will lead in abt. 10 m. to the foot of *Glen Dessary*, p. 371.]

The road now becomes wilder and more picturesque.

At 22 m. we reach *Loch Eilt*, and skirt its N. shore for 4 m.; we then descend the river *Ailort* to

28 m. **Kinloch Ailort**✱.

[A track leads N. in 7 m. to *Loch Morar*, across which a boat may be got to within 1 m. of *Tarbet*✱, on *Loch Nevis*, p. 371.

A driving road leads S. in 1 m. to *Inverailort Ho.* (Mrs. Head), turning into a charming path along the E. side of **Loch Ailort**, by *Roshven* (Prof. Blackburn), 4½ m. to *Glen Uig Bay*, 8½ m. It then strikes S. up the glen, and over the hill through pleasant woods, descending on *Loch Moidart* and *Kinloch Moidart*, 14 m. (cf. p. 362).]

We now enter upon the finest part of the drive. After crossing, by a somewhat breakneck road, the high ground between *Loch Ailort* and *Loch-nan-Uamh* (Loch of the Caves), we keep along the wild sea-shore for 2 m., then strike slightly inland, and for the last 4 m. pass through beautiful woods.

At 35 m. we cross the *Borrodale Burn*, close to *Arisaig Ho.* (Mrs. Nicholson). At the head of Loch-nan-Uamh Prince Charlie disembarked from the *Doutelle*, July 25, 1745, and found shelter in *Borrodale* farmhouse, then held by one Angus Macdonald. Here too he re-embarked 14 months later, having been a wanderer for 5 months—ever since Culloden.

38 m. **Arisaig**✱ is a hamlet overlooking a bay, with *Estab.*, *Free*, and *R.C. Churches* and a *Hall* presented by Miss Astley. It commands fine sea views W., especially of **Eigg** and its famous *Scuir*, p. 393.

The landing place, where steamers call about 4 times a week, going both N. and S., is unfortunately 4 m. distant, but a driving road leads to it. Even there, however, the coast is so rocky, that in a high wind it cannot be visited.

In *Loch-nan-Eala*, near Arisaig, a "crannog" or lake dwelling has been discovered about 250 yds. distant from the land, formed of layers of trunks of trees, making a strong and firmly built rectangular house.

N.E. of Arisaig are the bold hills of S. Morar, behind which lies Loch Morar.

2½ m. N. along the coast is a *Golf Course*.

EXCURSIONS:—

(1) To **Loch Morar** 6 m., and **Mallaig** on Loch Nevis, 10 m.

This is a delightful drive N. along the shore, passing rt. (3 m.) *Trahimore Ho.* (Mrs. Nicholson), where it trends inland. At 6 m. it crosses the short river *Morar* above its fine rapids, and just where it leaves the loch.

Loch Morar, 12 m. long by fully 1 m. broad, is studded with islands at its W. end, reminding one of Loch Maree. It is only 40 ft. above the sea, and is remarkable for its extraordinary depth of 175 fathoms, "the deepest known hollow on any part of the European plateau except the submarine valley, which skirts the S. part of Scandinavia."—Sir A. GEIKIE.

[A bridle track leads along its N. shore, and across a low isthmus to *Tarbet*✱ on Loch Nevis, 8 m. (p. 371).]

We notice on its N. bank a handsome R.C. Chap.

The road strikes N. to **Mallaig**, at the mouth of Loch Nevis, to which it is proposed to continue the W. Highland Rly.

(2) By sailing boat or steamer to the **Island of Eigg**✱, 12 m. W. p. 393.

(3) By sailing boat from Arisaig or Borrodale S. across the Sound of Arisaig to *Glen Uig Bay* (above), or Dorlin on Loch Moidart, p. 362.

ROUTE 87.

Banavie to Inverness by the Caledonian Canal.

A steamer starts 3 times a week in June, and daily in July-Sept., at 9.30 A.M. on the arrival of the steamer from Oban, reaching Inverness about 6.30 P.M. The steamer from Inverness leaves at 7 A.M. and reaches Banavie abt. 3.45 in time to catch the steamer to Oban. Breakfast, dinner, and tea are comfortably served. A halt of ¾ hr. allows a hasty visit to the lower and finer of the Falls of Foyers.

The **Caledonian Canal** runs N.E. and S.W. through the **Great Glen,** which appears to coincide with the line of a great geological fault, and must, Sir A. Geikie says, be as old as the Lower Old Red Sandstone. It connects Loch Linnhe, an arm of the Atlantic, with the Beauly Firth, an arm of the German Ocean. The total length of waterway from sea to sea is 60½ m., but of that only 22 m. are canal, the remainder consisting of the natural *Lochs Lochy, Oich* and *Ness.* There are 29 *locks*—11 at the S.W. or Corpach end, 12 through which the tourist steamer passes, spending 10 minutes in each, and 6 at the N.E. or Clachnaharry end. The medium width of the Canal is 40 ft. at the bottom and 110 ft. at the surface, with a depth of 18 ft. The locks are 170 ft. long and 40 ft. wide, with an average lift of 8 ft.

Watt made the survey in 1773, and *Telford* began its construction in 1803, but it was not finally opened for traffic until 1847, having then cost £1,256,000. It presented great advantages to sailing vessels by saving them the long voyage round Cape Wrath, ships of 500-600 tons being able to pass through the Canal, but it is less needed now that steam is so universally employed.

There are 3 locks close to the sea at Corpach, followed by a succession of 8 locks called *Neptune's Staircase,* which was Telford's greatest difficulty, leading up, with a total rise of 80 ft., to

1½ m. **Banavie**✲,[1] where the steamer starts. Ben Nevis is probably best seen from this point and the whole view rt. over *Lochaber* (= the district at the *mouth of the lochs*) is very fine, including both *Old* and *New Inverlochy Cas.* (p. 349). As we steam along, the canal's embankment to the rt. deserves notice. Soon the *Lochy* is parallel with the canal and we see rt. *Tor Castle,* beautifully situated close to a ruined stronghold of the Mackintoshes, on a cliff. Beyond we get a good view in front up the *Great Glen,* pass l. the entrance to *Glen Loy,* which is well wooded and reach

8 m. †**Gairlochy**✲.

[A road leads E. to *Spean Bridge,* 3½ m. (see p. 349). The view across the wooded entrance of *Glen Spean* to the mountains beyond is very fine.]

We pass through 2 locks into **Loch Lochy,** 10 m. long, ½ m.-1 m. broad, and 90 ft. above sea-level. There is a driving road along its E. side: that on its W. side stops at 4 m. beyond *Achnacarry House* (Cameron of Lochiel), (see p. 371)—scarcely visible—on the rt. bank of the *Arkaig,* a short rapid river issuing from *Loch Arkaig* (Rte. 88). In front l. the sharp *Ben Tee* (2956 ft.)—facetiously called "*Glengarry's Bowling Green*"—is conspicuous and remains so for 20 m. An old ch.-yd.—the burial ground of the MacDonnells of Glengarry—with a sq. tower, in which the chiefs lie, is seen l. as we approach

18 m. †**Laggan Locks.**

[Here, or at *Cullochy Lock,* those for *Invergarry*✱ (p. 369) must disembark, a conveyance being ordered beforehand. *Pedestrians* may from here visit the *Parallel Roads of Glen Roy,* and join the train for Fort-William at *Roy Bridge,* 14 m. (see p. 349). Only those, however, who have passed along the rest of the Canal should leave it here.]

After 2 locks we pass for 1½ m. through a lovely avenue of firs, at the end of which is a drawbridge, and enter the narrow **Loch Oich,** a beautiful Highland loch, nearly 4 m. long and 100 ft. above sea-level. We are now at the summit level of the canal. At 20 m. (l.) there is a singular monument by the loch side called *Tober-*

[1] See Map, p. 349.

nan-Ceann ("Well of the Heads") erected in 1812 by the late Col. MacDonnell of Glengarry.

On the top of the Monument is a group of 7 human heads carved in stone; beneath is a well. Early in the 16th cent. Keppoch, head of a branch of the MacDonnells, having sent his two sons to France for education, died leaving his affairs to the management of his seven brothers, who murdered the boys on their return. The bard of the family never rested until he got assistance and put the murderers to death. He then presented their heads to the chief of the clan at Glengarry, having first washed them in this well. An inscription in Gaelic, English, French, and Latin records this "ample and summary vengeance."

The middle portion of this loch, with the foot of *Glen Garry* l., graceful islets in the centre, and steep banks rt., is the finest part of this route; l. on a rock called "*Craig-an-Fhithich*" (Rock of the raven"), which became the war cry of the clan, stands the picturesque ruins of the five-storied castle of *Invergarry*, the ancient seat of the MacDonnells of Glengarry, burnt by the Duke of Cumberland, 1748. Col. MacDonnell, who d. 1828, was a thorough Highlander, admiring everything Celtic with dogged enthusiasm, and despising everything from the South, and is supposed to have been the original of Fergus MacIvor in "Waverley." His son sold the estates, afterwards bought for £120,000 by the late Rt. Hon. Edward Ellice, M.P. who built (1869) the handsome modern *Invergarry Ho.* (Mrs. Ellice), which stands in the midst of charming richly wooded scenery on the rt. bank of the *Garry* and ½ m. from **Invergarry Hotel**✲, the starting-point for a delightful route through Glen Garry to the W. Coast (Rte 89).

23½ m. †**Cullochy Bridge,** at the N. end of the loch, where passengers from Inverness for Invergarry disembark. (Conveyance must be ordered beforehand.) Rt. is *Aberchalder Lo.* at the foot of a grand ravine. Here Prince Charlie's forces assembled before marching S. A *Suspension Br.* l. crosses the *Oich*, which flows out of the loch. Passing through *Cullochy Lock* we begin to descend.

2 m. farther on is *Kyltra Lock*, where passengers may get out and walk to

29 m. †**Fort-Augustus**✲, as 5 locks have there to be descended.

This fort at the S. end of Loch Ness, commanding the *Pass of Corrieyairick* (pp. 226, 349), was built by Gen. Wade, 1729, and captured by the Highlanders in '45, but, after Culloden, fell into the hands of the Royal troops. It was visited in 1773 by Dr. Johnson, who in 1778 wrote to Boswell, "The best night I have had these 20 years was at Fort-Augustus." In 1867 it was sold for £5000 to Lord Lovat, who in 1876 presented it and some surrounding land to the Benedictine Order for the erection of a monastery, raised in 1882 to the dignity of an *Abbey*. The buildings are very handsome and consist of a college, monastery, hospice, and scriptorium, ranged round a quadrangle in E. E. style (Pugin, Archt.), and cost about £80,000. The *Church* in course of erection (1894) is estimated to cost another £80,000. Part of the *old Fort* is still preserved in the N.W. corner, but strangers are not admitted even into the grounds. The village is clean and attractive looking; a local industry is the manufacture of "Crook" walking sticks.

Loch Ness, the last of the chain of lochs, is nearly 24 m. long, has an average breadth of fully 1 m., is very deep, and has never been known to freeze. The retrospective view of Fort-Augustus with "Glengarry's Bowling Green" in the background is very fine. The hills on both sides of the loch rise to a considerable height, and are well clothed with trees, but the scenery is somewhat monotonous.

34 m. †**Invermoriston** ✲ (l.), the starting-point for the W. coast by *Glen Moriston* (Rte. 90). The *Falls of Moriston* are ½ m. from the pier. The mouth of the glen is surrounded by a semicircle of well wooded hills in front of which is *Glenmoriston Ho.* (J. M. Grant, Esq.).

40 m. **Foyers** ✲ (rt.), near the mouth of the river Foyers, and the pretty wood and meadows round *Foyers Ho.* (J. C. Cuninghame, Esq.), where the steamer stops (pier dues 4d.) to allow a hurried visit to the famous lower **Fall of Foyers**[1] (90 ft. high), nearly 1 m. distant. The *River Foyers*, with its sources in mountain lochs to the S.E., here descends through a deep and tortuous gash or glen in the hill side, rocky but shrouded within thick woods of birch, which greatly enhance the beauty of the scene, but render the fall invisible from the loch. The post of vantage is a promontory overlooking the pool.

"Among the heathy hills and rugged woods
The roaring Foyers pours his massy floods."
BURNS.

"It cannot be disputed that Foyers is the first in order of all our cascades; but it is as vain to attempt to compare it, in respect of beauty, with that of Tummel or those of the Clyde, as it would be to compare a landscape of Cuyp with one of Rubens, or the Bay of Naples with Glencoe."—MACULLOCH.

The *Upper Fall* (30 ft. high) is nearly 1 m. farther up and can be seen from a stone br. which crosses the river above it. To reach it the glen is temporarily left; but tourists from the steamer have not time to visit it, and may console themselves with the fact that it is in no way comparable to the lower one.

For those staying at Foyers there is a pleasant drive S. through the woods above the Falls, and a good round N. to *Inverfarigaig* (below) taking the high road going and returning along the shore road. There is a *ferry* across the loch.

Opposite Foyers rises **Mealfourvonie** (2284 ft.), a fine mt. of old red conglomerate, the last of the range separating Glen Moriston from Glens Urquhart and Affric, very conspicuous from the N.

42 m. †**Inverfarigaig** (rt.) under a precipitous hill surmounted by the vitrified fort of *Duniardd.* Near its mouth the river Farigaig passes through a narrow gorge called the *Pass of Farigaig.* Here, in July 1877, Dr. James Bryce, the geologist, was killed by a fall of stones while in pursuit of his favourite science. At 45 m. we round a rocky promontory (l.) crowned with the extensive ruins of **Castle Urquhart,** built by the engineers of Edward I., after they had (1303) destroyed an older cas. built in the 12th cent. It afterwards belonged to the Chisholms, and passed in 1509 into the hands of the Clan Grant, whose property it still is.

Crossing *Urquhart Bay* we stop at †**Temple Pier,** beautifully situated at the mouth of *Glen Urquhart.*[1] In the lovely woods l. is *Balmacaan Ho.* (Countess Dowager of Seafield, see p. 229). 1¾ m. up the glen is **Drumnadrochit** ✲.

[From Drumnadrochit a pretty driving road leads W. up *Glen Urquhart*, passing 5½ m. a quaint thatched *Epis. Chap.* on the N. shore of *Loch Meikle*, to *Invercannich* ✲ (p. 380), 12½ m. Another road rising to 750 ft. leads N. through *Glen Convinth* to *Beauly*, (p. 376) 13 m.]

49½ m. l. is the solitary pier of †**Abriachan,** under a fine hillside of red screes clothed with birches. Passing rt. *Aldourie Cas.* (E. G. Fraser-Tytler, Esq.), a handsome yellow house overgrown with ivy, where Sir James Mackintosh was b. 1765, we leave Loch Ness and, through a channel charmingly wooded rt., enter the small narrow *Loch Dochfour*, on the l. bank of which is *Dochfour* (J. E. B. Baillie, Esq.), a modern Italian mansion, beautifully situated. There are now woods on both sides; a chain

[1] Waggonette, fare 1s. each, takes visitors to within ¼ m. of the fall. A climb is saved, but pedestrians can go as quickly by the shorter paths.

[1] See "*Urquhart and Glenmoriston—Olden Times in a Highland Parish,*" by William Mackay (1893).

carriage ferry crosses the loch; the *River Ness* flows away rt., and we enter the last stretch of Canal proper, passing through *Dochgarroch Lock*. We pass rt. *Ness Cas.* (C. Fountaine Walker, Esq.), and then *Tomnahurich* ("Hill of the fairies"), with its *Cemetery*, before reaching

59 m. †**Muirtown**, beyond which 6 locks lead to sea, but where omnibuses from the various hotels are waiting to convey passengers in $1\frac{1}{2}$ m. to

INVERNESS✲, see p. 375.

ROUTE 88.

Banavie to Loch Nevis by Loch Arkaig and Glen Desseray.

Drive to Glen Desseray, 26 m.—thence walk. There is no inn between Gairlochy, 6 m., and Inverie, 42 m., but accommodation can generally be obtained in one of the houses in Glen Desseray.

This road keeps N. alongside of the Caledonian Canal for 10 m. (p. 368).

At $8\frac{1}{2}$ m. it crosses the river *Arkaig*, $\frac{1}{2}$ m. up which on the rt. bank is *Achnacarry Ho.*, the modern residence of Cameron of Lochiel. Only a fragment remains of the *old castle* burnt by the Duke of Cumberland in 1746. The grounds have some magnificent and remarkable timber. In the Park is the famous *Beech Avenue*, planted by Lochiel, before setting out to join Prince Charlie, and the subject of Lady Middleton's "Ballad of the Beeches."

At 10 m. we turn W., approach **Loch Arkaig** by a fine avenue called "The *Dark Mile*," and keep along its N. bank for 13 m., when we enter

24 m. **Glen Desseray**.[1] At its W. end (29 m.) is the fine pass of *Mam-Cloich-Airde* (1000 ft.), from which a steep descent is made to

33 m. **Sourlies**, a farm at the head of **Loch Nevis**, and at the base of *Sgur-na-Ciche* (3410 ft.), where a boat may sometimes be got to *Kyles Morar* ($4\frac{1}{2}$ m.), 1 m. from *Tarbet*✶ (p. 367).

The chief features of Loch Nevis ("*Loch of Heaven*"), are the outlines and grandeur of the hills, which rise immediately from the shore, though there is a lack of wood or any softening contrast for the eye to rest upon.

The track now strikes N. away from the loch, then W. behind *Ben Bhuidhe* (2803 ft.), and down *Glen Meadail*, from which a road crossing the *Inverie River*, and passing *Inverie House* (E. S. Bowlby, Esq.), leads to

42 m. **Inverie**✶, on a bay of the same name at the entrance to Loch Nevis.

Inverie may be left in one of the following ways:—

(1) By steamer N. or S. (once a week) [Rte. 98.]

(2) By boat across the loch to *Mallaig* (p. 367), 5 m., or to *Tarbet*✶ (above, and p. 367), 5 m., 8s. to 10s. either place.

(3) By boat to *Sourlies* (above), 10 m. about 15s.

(4) By walking to *Kyles Knoydart*, 5 m., and getting boat across the Narrows to *Kylesmorar* and *Tarbet*.

(5) By a delightful bridle path up Glen Dulochan to *Barrisdale* on Loch Hourn, 10 m., and along the shore to *Loch Hournhead* 16 m. (p. 372).

1 For description of surrounding scenery, and its associations with Prince Charlie, see the late Principal Shairp's Poem of "*Glen Desseray*."

ROUTE 89.

Invergarry (Caledonian Canal) by Glen Garry and Glen Shiel to Loch Duich (West Coast) [also to Loch Hourn].

This is an excellent carriage route from the Caledonian Canal to the W. Coast—much grander (ascending to 1424 ft.) than the easier although slightly longer one from Invermoriston, described in Rte. 90. Carriages can be hired at Invergarry, Tomdown Inn, Clunie Inn, and Shiel Inn.

From Banavie or Inverness to Invergarry, see Rte. 87.

From Invergarry (p. 369) the road, keeping the l. bank of the stream, ascends the pretty **Glengarry**, through pensile woods of birch, and emerges in 3 m. upon **Loch Garry**, a smiling sheet of water. It runs along the N. shore for 5 m., and then up the river to

11 m. **Tomdown Inn**✶, where it turns N.

[From Tomdown a good road keeps W. up Glen Garry through *Glen Quoich Deer Forest* (where Lord Burton in 1893 shot a stag with 20 points), and along *Loch Quoich* ($6\frac{1}{2}$ m. long) for 4 m. It then strikes N.W., having rt. *Sgur Mhoraire* (3365 ft.)—it was here Prince Charlie had to run the gauntlet of the sentries[1]—and descends to **Loch Hourn** head, 16½ m., near which is the attractive-looking *Kinlochourn Shooting Lo.* (Robert Birkbeck, Esq.).

"In Great Britain I know no better illustration of ice action than is to be seen on the road leading down from Glen Quoich to Loch Hourn, one of the most striking examples of desolate and savage scenery in Scotland. Its name in Celtic is said to mean the Lake of Hell."—Sir J. LUBBOCK.

The road stops here, but a charming path leads by the S. side of the loch to 6 m. *Barrisdale*, and thence over the hill to *Inverie* (p. 371), 16 m. 2 m. along this path is *Skiary*✱, a clachan where a boat may be obtained down the loch to *Corran* (p. 395). A path away from the loch climbing W. behind the Shooting Lo. leads to Glenelg (p. 395), abt. 16 m.; from it (at 4 m.) one can strike S. down *Glen Arnisdale* to *Corran*, 9 m., or N. over the *Pass of Corryvarlingen* (2500 ft.)—very rough—to *Glen Shiel Inn*✱ (p. 385), 13 m.]

From Tomdown the road ascends N., crosses *Glen Loyne*—where *Loch Loyne* narrows to a river and where we enter Ross-shire—reaches at 18½ m. 1424 ft., and descends steeply to

22 m. **Clunie Bridge Inn** ✱ (728 ft.). See Rte. 90 for road up *Glen Clunie*, and down *Glen Shiel* to

34 m. **Glen Shiel Inn**✱ on **Loch Duich** (p. 385).

ROUTE 90.

Invermoriston (Caledonian Canal) by Glen Moriston and Glen Shiel to Loch Duich (West Coast).

From Banavie or Inverness to **Invermoriston,** see Rte. 87.

This route to Clunie Bridge Inn (25 m.) is 3 m. longer than that from Invergarry (Rte. 89), but much easier—consequently not so wild.

The road keeps up **Glen Moriston** through deer forests belonging to Mr. Grant of Invermoriston, passes (8½ m.) *Torgyle Inn*✱, beside which is a R.C. Chapel, and at 18 m. reaches *Loch Clunie.* It keeps along the N. bank for 4½ m., entering Ross-shire, and then up the river Clunie to

25 m. **Clunie Bridge Inn**✱, where the road from Glen Garry (Rte. 89) falls in.

From Clunie Bridge we continue the ascent for 2½ m., when we commence an almost continuous descent into **Glen Shiel,** through a magnificent defile, deep and narrow, yielding in grandeur only to Glencoe, overhung by preponderating mountains, with peaked sugar-loaf heads, serrated ridges, and mysterious corries. Few trees or houses.

This **Pass of Strachel** was in 1719 the scene of a skirmish between a small force of regular troops and a body of Highlanders, chiefly Macraes and Mackenzies under the Earl of Seaforth, who had joined the rising of the Earl of Mar, backed by a Spanish fleet despatched from Cadiz in support of the Stuart cause. Only 2 vessels out of 30, however, reached Loch Duich, where they landed 300 Spaniards and 2000 stand of arms. They were encountered in this glen by Gen. Wightman. The Highlanders fought fiercely, and inflicted severe loss on the troops, but were routed; the Spaniards laid down their arms; Lord Seaforth was badly wounded, and the rebellion was crushed.

Glen Shiel is interesting as having inspired Dr. Johnson with the idea of writing his "Journey to the Western Isles."

As to its natural attractions Sir A. Geikie thus writes:—

"Perhaps the defile of Glen Shiel, with its encirling group of lofty naked hills, may be taken as one of the best examples of the more savage and rugged forms which these rocks (mica schists and fine gneisses) assume. Dark masses of bare rock piled upon each other, give a corrugated outline to the steep acclivities that mount up into an array of broken serrated ridges and deep corries, over which frown the peaks of Glenelg."—*Scenery of Scotland*, p. 209.

At the foot of the glen and at the E. end of **Loch Duich** is

37 m. **Glen Shiel Inn**✱, an excellent halting place (see p. 385).

---

[1] See Shairp's "*Glen Desseray,*" p. 34.

SECTION VII.

North-West Highlands—Inverness—Glen Affric—Dingwall—Strathpeffer—Ullapool—Loch Maree—Gairloch—Strome Ferry—Loch Duich—Skye—Outer Hebrides.

§ 1. General Information.

This section commences at Inverness and the pretty country about Beauly, Dingwall, and Strathpeffer, and then proceeds to describe the wilder scenery of W. Ross-shire, Skye, and the Outer Hebrides.

The **Vale of Beauly,** in its upper portions called Strath Glass and Glen Affric, deserves to be explored to its farthest extremity; pedestrians can pass through it to Kintail and the W. Coast. Those in carriages can easily visit the *Falls of Kilmorack* and the lovely gorge of the *Dhruim* (Dream), but should without fail penetrate to the *Chisholm's Pass* and *Loch Affric* through scenery unrivalled in Scotland for its combination of beauty and grandeur.

Coaches run from the railway at Achnasheen in Strath Bran to *Loch Maree* (on which there is a steamer) and *Gairloch*—excellent accommodation at both places. From Kinlochewe the traveller, especially if he be a geologist, should visit *Glen Torridon*, with its mountains of Torridon Sandstone.

Tourists can cross over to Skye from Gairloch three times a week, and daily from Strome Ferry, the present terminus of the Dingwall and Skye Railway, to be superseded by Kyle Akin. No one should leave Strome Ferry or Kyle Akin without seeing Loch Alsh, and the picturesque *Loch Duich* at its head.

Skye is fully described in Rte. 97. Its climate is variable and damp, the annual rainfall averaging 65 inches; but it is not so bad as it has been described. June and July are generally pleasant months, and although in August and September the weather is often very broken, the traveller, well prepared, will find here no more serious impediments to his movements than in other parts of the Highlands.

Its rocky peaks and crags—many inaccessible—render its mountain scenery unique in Scotland. It is the favourite haunt of the adventurous climber, while by carriage, boat, or pony the ordinary traveller can visit such outstanding scenes of savage grandeur as the *Quiraing*, *Loch Coruisk*, and *Glen Sligachan*.

The "**Long Island,**" as the Outer Hebrides—stretching from the Butt of Lewis to Barra Head in Berneray—are called, in most parts a dreary and boggy country, is worth a visit as something by itself. It is intensely interesting to geologists as being almost entirely composed of Archæan gneiss, the oldest geological formation in the world, and affords excellent means of sport to the angler, as it contains nearly as much water as land.

In **Lewis** are the famous *Standing Stones of Callernish*, which may be visited from Stornoway, where the most comfortable quarters in the Outer Hebrides are to be found.

§ 2. PRINCIPAL CENTRES.

POINTS OF INTEREST.

1. **Inverness.** The Islands in the Ness. Culloden Moor. Cawdor Castle. Caledonian Canal. Black Isle. Cf. Rtes. 42, 87, 99.
2. **Beauly.** Falls of Kilmorack. The Dhruim (Dream).
3. **Invercannich.** Glen Cannich. Chisholm's Pass. Loch Affric.
4. **Strathpeffer.** The Wells. Castle Leod. · Falls of Rogie. Ben Wyvis.
5. **Ullapool.** Gorge of Corrie Halloch. Loch Broom. Summer Isles. Drive to Lochinver (cf. Rte. 102).
6. **Dundonnell.** Falls of Ardessie. An Teallach Mts.
7. **Kinlochewe.** Glen Torridon. Loch Maree. Slioch.
8. **Talladale.** Loch Maree.
9. **Gairloch.** Flowerdale. Coast scenery by Poolewe and Gruinard Bay to Dundonnell.
10. **Balmacara.** Loch Alsh. Loch Duich. Falls of Glomach.
11. **Glen Shiel Inn.** Loch Duich. Glen Shiel. Scour Ouran. Falls of Glomach. Glen Elg.
12. **Portree** (Skye). Loch Coruisk. Quiraing. Dunvegan.
13. **Stornoway.** Stornoway Castle. Stones of Callernish.

ROUTES.

ROUTE 91.

Inverness to Strome Ferry by Beauly, Dingwall, and Achnasheen. High. Rly.

Trains, S. to Perth (Rte. 42); E. to Elgin, Banff, and Aberdeen (Rtes. 63-65); N. to Wick and Thurso (Rte. 100); W. to Strome Ferry (Rte. 91).

Steamer—from Muirtown (1½ m.)—by Caledonian Canal to Oban (Rtes. 87 and 85); daily in July, Aug., and Sept. at 7 a.m., and daily to Fort-Augustus at 3 p.m.

INVERNESS✲, the capital of the Highlands, stands near the mouth of the river Ness, chiefly on its rt. bank. The river, whose course is only 6 m. long between Loch Ness and the sea, is crossed by a footbridge above the cathedral, by a suspension bridge just below the castle, by a third bridge close to the quay, and finally by the rly. bridge of the Highland Rly. to Dingwall and the N. Inverness is a well-built and prettily-situated town; but it is a dull one except on market-days and county meetings, and at the Highland Gathering in September, when it is much too full. There is not much to be be seen in the town itself.

The *Rly. Stat.* which, together with the adjoining hotel, was built in 1876, in the place of a smaller station, is in Academy St. In front of the station is a monument erected in 1893 to commemorate the Cameron Highlanders who fell in the Egyptian war, 1882-87, and opposite the stat. runs *Union St.*, where are some of the best shops. At the junction of *High St.* and *Bridge St.* stands the **Town Hall,** a handsome Gothic building, erected 1877-80. In front of it is an ornamental *Fountain*, the gift of the late Dr. Forbes, in which is incorporated a rude untrimmed stone, called *Clach-na-Cudainn* ("Stone of the tubs"), because the water-carriers used to rest their tubs on it. Close at hand is the *Old Cross.* By following *Bridge St.* we reach the *Suspension Bridge*, from which we see l., on the height, the **City Jail** and **County Courts,** imitating in a humble way the feudal and royal castle which once occupied this grand site and commanded the passage between the N. and S. of Scotland. There is a pleasing view from the terrace. The town was occupied by the Jacobites during the '45, and the old castle was blown up by Prince Charlie, 1746. Crossing the river and turning l., we come to the

Episcopal Cathedral (St. Andrew's) of the See of Moray and Ross, the bishop of which resides in Inverness. It is a handsome modern Gothic building, erected 1866-71 (Alex. Ross, archt.), at a cost of about £20,000, and conspicuous for its twin *Towers*, intended to be crowned with spires when money comes in. It is a cross Ch., in style Dec., with aisles ending in an apse. The *Nave*, of 5 bays, has granite piers; the roof is of timber. The *Font*, of white marble and supported by an angel, is copied from one by Thorwaldsen at Copenhagen (cf. p. 45).

The Estab., Free, and United Presbyterian churches are also Gothic in style.

Oliver Cromwell appreciated the strategic importance of Inverness, and built a strong fort on the rt. bank of the river, below the town, to command its passage and bridle the wild Highlanders. It was pulled down at the Restoration to please the clans and their chiefs.

The *Academy* is a school where about 200 pupils are educated, to which is attached a bequest of a Captain Mackintosh for boys of his name. Here is also one of the schools endowed by the late Dr. Bell of St. Andrews.

The country in the neighbourhood is exceedingly pretty, with every charm of wood and cultivation in profusion. The landscape is flanked on the one side by the Firths of Moray and Beauly, and on the other by the freshwater Lochs of Dochfour and Ness.

The dialect of the Inverness people is much more pleasant and less broad than that of the lowland or Aberdeenshire Scotch. Some account for this by the fact that the English troops of Cromwell were garrisoned here, and taught the people (who then spoke nothing but Gaelic) a better English than they would otherwise have acquired. Certain it is that English spoken more "trippingly on the tongue" is not to be met with in Great Britain.

About a mile above the town the Ness is divided by several **Islands,** covered by trees, intersected by agreeable paths, and joined by foot bridges.

EXCURSIONS :—

(1) S.W. to **Tom-na-hurich** (*Hill of the Fairies*), resembling in shape an inverted boat, 1½ m.

This hill, lying between the river and the Caledonian Canal, is prettily wooded, commands pleasant views, and has a beautifully laid out *Cemetery* on the top.

(2) W. to **Craig Phadrick** (*Patrick's Rock*) an isolated conical hill 550 ft. high, 2 m.

It forms the extremity of the hills W. of the Caledonian Canal, and commands a large expanse of flat country. Its summit is traversed by two walls or ramparts of large stones, partly vitrified on the surface. This hill fort was the chief stronghold of the Northern Picts in the 6th cent. St. Columba came hither from Iona to convert and baptise Brud, King of the Picts.

(3) Drive (Coach daily in summer) E. to **Culloden Moor,** 6 m. (p. 234), and **Cawdor Castle,** 14 m. (p. 233).

(4) **Clava Plain,** 1 m. S.E. of Culloden Moor, is strewn with a number of stone circles and cairns (p. 235).

(5) The **Falls of Foyers** on Loch Ness by *Steamer* (pp. 370-371).

The morning canal steamer reaches Foyers abt. 9.50 a.m., and the return steamer leaves abt. 4.15 p.m.

(6) For Drives to the *Findhorn*, *Grantown*, etc., see pp. 231, 232.

Rly. to Strome Ferry, 71½ m. 3 trains daily in 3¼-4½ hrs.

Quitting the station at Inverness the train runs W., crossing the Ness and a promontory, at the N. end of which is *Kessock Ferry*, to the **Black Isle** (Rte. 99).

The mouth of the *Caledonian Canal* is crossed just before

1¾ m. **Clachnaharry Stat.,** the "Watchman's Stone," whence the citizens of Inverness in olden time looked anxiously out for the predatory bands who came from N. and W. to plunder and destroy. The line now skirts the S. side of the *Beauly Firth*.

3½ m. **Bunchrew Stat.** *Bunchrew House* was a residence of Lord-President Forbes of Culloden (1685-1747).

5¾ m. **Lentran Stat.**

On the opposite side of the Firth is *Redcastle* (J. E. B. Baillie, Esq.), the old fort of the Mackenzies. The Firth is left before

7½ m. **Clunes Stat.,** beyond which the *Beauly River* is crossed.

10 m. **Beauly Stat.** ✲ The village, (½ m. rt.) pleasantly situated near the mouth of the Beauly river, derives its name from the *Priory* "de *bello* loco," the ruins of which still remain, surrounded by some venerable trees, at the end of the broad street. It was founded by Sir John Bisset

of Lovat in 1230 for monks of the house of Val des Choux or Vallis Caulium,[1] in Burgundy. At the Reformation the then prior gave it in trust to Lord Lovat, and his descendants have retained its revenues. The Ch. is of pointed Gothic, consisting of nave and choir without aisles, rather plain, if not rude, in style; in the S. wall are 3 windows in shape of large trefoils. It contains several monuments, chiefly to the Mackenzie family. Adjoining is a large modern *R.C. Church*.

[EXCURSIONS:—

The beauties of the Valley of the Beauly can hardly be exaggerated. No stranger should omit to visit the *Falls of Kilmorack* (2½ m.) and the gorge of *The Druim* [pron. Dream] (3½ m.-6 m.); if possible he should penetrate to the still grander *Chisholm's Pass* (23 m.), and *Loch Affric* (29 m.), amid scenery unrivalled in Great Britain, see Rte. 92.

4 m. S. of Beauly, on the S. side of the open valley, beyond the river, are *Belladrum* (A. W. Merry, Esq.), on a tributary stream, and, still nearer, *Beaufort Castle* (Lord Lovat), long the seat of the Bissets, now of the Frasers. The old tower was besieged by Edward I., and was nearly razed to the ground after Culloden. The old house is now replaced by an imposing structure in the Scottish baronial style. A charming drive of 8 m. or 10 m. may be taken by *Belladrum* and through the parks and woods of *Beaufort Cas.*, returning by the timber bridge crossing the Beauly below the *Falls of Kilmorack*, 2½ m. from the village.]

The line now turns due N. to

13 m. **Muir of Ord Stat.** ✲, on the borders of Ross and Inverness.

[Branch E. (opened Feb. 1894) across the **Black Isle**, by 3¾ m. *Redcastle Stat.*; 5½ m. *Allangrange Stat.*; 8 m. *Munlochy Stat.*; and 11¼ m. *Avoch Stat.*, to 13½ m. **Fortrose Stat.** ✶ (see p. 402).]

Large sheep and cattle fairs are held in an enclosed space upon the *Moor* once a month during winter and spring, and twice a month during the remainder of the year. Passing l. *Highfield* (J. Gillanders, Esq.), where is a neat *Episcopal Chapel*, and *Conon House*, the property of Sir Kenneth Mackenzie, Bart., of Gairloch, a lovely view is obtained on l. of *Strathconon*, a picturesque and fertile valley backed by a range of mountains of moderate height. Over it in the distance towers *Ben Wyvis* (3429 ft.), while *Castle Brahan*, the seat of the Seaforth family, stands across the valley on the lower slopes of a ridge, surrounded by thick masses of trees. It is an old castle, but so cropped and modernised outside as to look like a factory.

16¼ m. **Conon Stat.** The river of that name is crossed just before it flows into the *Cromarty Firth*. About 2 m. rt. on the E. bank of the firth is *Ferintosh*, once greatly celebrated for its whisky. The privilege of distilling it free from duty was originally granted in 1689 to Duncan Forbes, father of the President of the Court of Session, as a recompense to him for the losses he had incurred from the soldiers of Buchan and Carron at the Revolution. It was redeemed in 1786 for a payment of £20,000 to the family.

18½ m. **Dingwall Junc. Stat.**

[RAILWAYS.—(1) The main line (Rte. 100) runs N. to Wick and Thurso; (2) a short line runs W. to Strathpeffer (Rte. 93); (3) the Strome Ferry line (below) also runs W.]

Dingwall ✲, a royal burgh (1226) and one of the Wick group of parl. burghs, is still called in Gaelic *Innerffeoran*, because of its situation at the mouth of the Peffery, near the head of the Cromarty Firth. *Dingwall* is a Norse name derived from Thingvöllr, "Field of the Thing," or Parliament, or Place of general assembly (cf. *Tingwall*, p. 438).

There is one long street, with an old tower, once a jail, in the centre. At its E. end is the Rly. Stat., close

[1] The three houses of this order in Scotland were Beauly, Ardchattan, and Pluscardine. In Gaelic Beauly is called *A Mhanachuinn = The Priory*.

to which is a Gothic *Free Ch.* with a graceful granite column (and medallion) to the *Rev. Dr. Kennedy* (1819-84), and across the rly. the *County Buildings.* N. of the town in a field adjoining the *Parish Ch.* is an *Obelisk*, 57 ft. high, "Erected by George, 1st Earl of Cromartie . . . who d. 1714, and is buried 3 ft. 6 in. to the S. thereof."

The Strome Ferry line—opened 1870—now turns W. at rt. angles to the main line N. and ascends *Strathpeffer.* At 21 m. the line to Strathpeffer Spa (Rte. 93) strikes off l. It is a steep incline to

23 m. **Achterneed Stat.** Left is the old ivy-covered *Castle Leod*, with pretty grounds (see p. 381), (open to the public at times), the seat of the late Earl of Cromartie (d. 1893), a title revived in 1861 in favour of his mother, the Duchess of Sutherland, Countess of Cromartie, descending to her 2nd son. Beyond it is seen *Strathpeffer Village* (Rte. 93).

After 1 m. the scenery becomes very fine. The line—blasted through slate and gneiss rocks—traverses a ravine having l. *Craig-an-Fhithich* (the Raven's Rock), and rt. the shoulders of *Ben Wyvis*; it then descends steeply.

At 28 m. the line crosses the E. end of *Loch Garve* (1¾ m. long) and keeps along its S. bank to

30¼ m. **Garve Stat.** ✲, a small hamlet on a pretty green plain.

[Here a road (*Coach* daily) strikes N.W. to 32 m. **Ullapool** on *Loch Broom* (Rte. 94).]

Across the *Black Water* (rt.) is Mr. Hanbury's Shooting Lo. of *Strathgarve.* Leaving the stat. we obtain a good view rt. of *Ben Wyvis*, look up *Strath Garve* and ascend some miles of moorland before descending into scenery affording an agreeable contrast; a wood of birch and larch is traversed, on the shores of the crescent-shaped *Loch Luichart*, of which pleasing but partial glimpses are caught through the branches l. It is 5 m. long, but the rly. touches merely its upper extremity, passing (rt.—not seen) the Italian villa and grounds of *Kinloch Luichart* (Dowager Lady Ashburton).

35½ m. **Loch Luichart Stat.**

A lattice girder bridge carries the line over the *Bran* below its junc. with the *Fannich* from *Loch Fannich*, which is 6½ m. long and lies 4 m. to the N.W., backed by a magnificent range of mts. We have now a brawling stream rt., and keeping up its rt. bank, along the S. side of *Loch Culen*, and passing between that loch and *Loch Achanalt*, we reach

39¾ m. **Achanalt Stat.** The scenery is now bare and monotonous as we again ascend, but l. towers the grand *Scuir Vuillin* with its three peaks, dividing Strath Bran from Strath Conan.

46¼ m. **Achnasheen Stat.** ✲, the starting point (*Coach* daily) for *Loch Maree*, *Gairloch*, etc. (Rte. 95).

Leaving behind Achnasheen, the train passes rt. *Loch Gown*, and attains the summit-level, 634 ft. The melancholy *Loch Scaven*, with two wooded islets, sends its waters W. into Loch Carron.

54½ m. *Glencarron Platform. Glencarron Lodge* (rt.), a fishing-lodge which, together with the surrounding Deer Forest, belongs to Lord Wimborne. The scenery now becomes very impressive; l. is a fine gorge and beyond are the magnificent corries of *Moruisg* (3026 ft.).

58¾ m. **Achnashellach Stat.** *Achnashellach Deer Forest* also belongs to Lord Wimborne.

[A path leads N. through the hills by *Loch Coulin* to 11 m. *Kinlochewe* (p. 383).]

64¼ m. **Strathcarron Stat.** ✲, at the N.E. extremity of the grand sea-loch *Carron*, of which a fine view opens as far as Strome Ferry, the mountains of Skye rising in the far distance to the W.

[EXCURSIONS:—(1) To **Shieldaig** on Loch Torridon 19½ m.; (2) **Applecross** 22 m.

(1) A Mail-gig runs 3 times a week to Shieldaig. It passes (3½ m.) through **Jeantown** or **Lochcarron**✱, a fishing village on the N. shore of the loch. The road then leaves the loch, ascends steeply to 400 ft., crosses the promontory, and descends by the romantic *Pass of Kishorn* to the sea-loch of that name. There is a magnificent view W., over the mouth of Loch Carron and an archipelago of islands, to the Skye mountains, and N. to *Ben Bhan* (2936 ft.), on which the *Torridon Sandstone Formation* is well seen. Beside the loch is

9½ m. *Kishorn* P.O. and Tel. Office, and beyond, *Courthill* (C. J. Murray, Esq. of Loch Carron). The road from the head of the loch (10½ m.) up the river Kishorn and down Glen Shieldaig is very wild, but the approach is exceedingly pretty to **Shieldaig**✱, a quiet little village circling round the bay, inhabited by fishermen, with ch. and manse. Its secluded situation on the shores of *Loch Shieldaig*—as the middle portion of **Loch Torridon** is called—backed by *Ben Shieldaig* reminds one of a Norwegian village.

An excellent track passing round *Ben Damph Lo.* (Earl of Lovelace)—a fine place—leads E. in 9 m. to the head of Loch Torridon (p. 383), or one may go by boat. Here a carriage, ordered beforehand from Kinlochewe, may be met.

By crossing Loch Shieldaig to *Doireaonar* or (better although farther) to *Inverbane*, one can walk S.W. across the hill, ascending only to 1213 ft., and reach in 10 m. *Applecross*, the driving road to which is 21 m. (see below).

(2) **Strathcarron** to **Applecross** (*Mail-gig* 3 times a week). The road is the same as to Shieldaig so far as the head of *Loch Kishorn* (10½ m.), when it turns l. and winds in a series of slants up the truly alpine *Pass of Bealach-nam-Bo*, to a height of 2054 ft.—the highest driving road in Scotland. Splendid views are obtained from this road S. over the mouth of *Loch Carron* to the *Mts.* between *Loch Duich* and *Loch Hourn*, S.W. of the *Coolins* in Skye, and N.W. of the *Quiraing* in Skye, and of the *Outer Hebrides.* We descend to

22 m. **Applecross**✱ on the sea, inland from which is Lord Middleton's *Deer Forest*. One would scarcely expect to find any architectural remains in such an out of the way district as this, but in former times Applecross was selected as one of the earliest sites for a religious home by the brethren of Iona, and *St. Malrube's Ch.* was founded here in 673. A slab carved with a cross is still standing near the modern Ch. Other crosses once existing have disappeared. It is said that the name *Applecross* is derived from a belief that every apple in the monks' garden was marked with the sign of the cross. The Gael. name for Applecross is *A Chomraich = The Sanctuary.*

The course followed by the rly. along the S.E. shore of Loch Carron is perhaps the most picturesque and interesting of the whole route. Very winding, it follows, in rapid curves and some cuttings, the ins and outs of the rocks, which frequently descend vertically into the sea, being carried only a few feet above the level of high tide.

66¾ m. **Attadale Stat.**

71½ m. **Strome Ferry Stat.** ✲ On the opposite side of the loch, here crossed by a *Ferry* ¾ m. wide, are the remains of *Strome Castle.*

4 m. W., on the S. shore of outer Loch Carron, rises *Duncraig Castle*, the modern seat of Sir K. J. Matheson, Bt., in a lovely situation, and beyond, to the W., is the village of *Plockton*, 6 m.

No one should leave Strome Ferry without visiting Loch Alsh and Loch Duich (see Rte. 96).

Steamer sails daily to *Portree, Skye*, in 3 hrs., and to *Stornoway* in 7 hrs. (Rtes. 97, 98). *Skye* may also be reached by *Kyle Akin Ferry* (pp. 385, 395), to which (8 m.) a continuation of the rly. is in course of construction (1894).

ROUTE 92.

Beauly by Strath Glass and Glen Affric to Loch Duich (West Coast).—Latter part for Pedestrians—48 m.

This route leads through scenery unrivalled in Great Britain. The first 6 m. up the *Beauly* are exceedingly fine; the next 14 m. called *Strath Glass*, not remarkable, but the following 10 m. up *Glen Affric* include truly magnificent Highland scenery. There is a driving road for 29 m. but the only hotel the whole way is a Temp. one (with conveyances) at *Invercannich* (17 m.)—a good centre. A comfortable parlour and large bedroom may also be had at the P.O. there.

A Mail-gig, conveying passengers, runs from Beauly to *Tomich* (21 m.) every afternoon.

From **Beauly** ✱ (p. 376) we drive S.W.

At 2½ m. we reach *Kilmorack Ch.* By crossing the field beyond the ch.-yd. (l.) a good view is obtained of the rapids or **Falls of Kilmorack.** There is a beautiful walk up the *rt.* bank from the bridge below the falls.

At 3½ m. the road keeps beside the river and the grand defile of **The Dhruim** (pron. *Dream*) begins. The detached "stacks" of old red sandstone, rising out of the middle of the river, are very remarkable—the surrounding foliage, chiefly of birch, is beautiful. At the upper end of the *Pass* (5¼ m.) a footpath should be taken to the side of the river, here divided by *Eilean* (island) *Aigas*, with a small house (reached from the other side), the refuge of Lord Lovat 1697, and occupied as a summer retreat by Sir R. Peel before his death.

The valley now becomes tamer. We pass rt. *Aigas Ho.* and l. (6½ m.) *Aigas Ferry*, by which the pedestrian may gain the other side and return to Beauly.

At 9 m. l. is **Erchless Cas.**, the seat of Mrs. Chisholm, whose son, "*The Chisholm*" (d. 1887) was the last acknowledged chief of a clan which has possessed this valley since the 14th cent. It is an unpretentious modernised old mansion house, hid from the road by trees, with large parks stretching down to the river. Presently we pass a picturesque group of cottages with a pretty little *Estab. Ch.* and *Manse.*

At 10 m. we cross the *Farrar.*

[A driving road runs up *Strath Farrar* for some 20 m. to the W. end of *Loch Monar* (5 m. long), passing 2 smaller lochs and several Shooting Lodges. Thence exit may be made in some 18 m. by track to *Attadale Stat.* (p. 379).]

Beyond the Farrar the Beauly is crossed by *Struy Bridge* by which we may drive back to Beauly. Continuing up the l. bank of the river, now called the *Glass*, we pass rt. 14 m. the *Well of St. Ignatius*, with various R.C. inscriptions. By an iron girder br. of a single span, replacing a br. washed away by the autumn floods of 1892, like so many others in the Highlands, we cross the mountain torrent of the *Cannich* to the tiny hamlet of

17 m. **Invercannich** ✱, with a large *R.C. Ch.*

[An excellent road leads E. by *Glen Urquhart* to

Drumnadrochit✱ (p. 370), 12½ m.

The scenery W. up **Glen Cannich,** beginning with a pretty *Waterfall* (1½ m.), is very striking. The glen becomes wild and extremely grand. The S. side is densely wooded with Scotch fir and birch. A carriage road leads past a succession of smaller lochs to the W. end of *Loch Mullardoch* (5 m. long), 14 m. Exit may be made by pedestrians in abt. 12 m., passing *Loch Lungard* to *Loch-na-Leitreach* in *Glen Elchaig* (p. 385); thence to

Glen Shiel Inn or **Dornie**, see pp. 386, 385.]

---

2 m. beyond Invercannich is a *Free Ch.* where the road forks. That crossing the river leads in 2 m. up the rt. bank of a trib. the *Dhiag* (pron. Gee-ag), to the model village of **Tomich,** at the end of which is the entrance to *Guisachan*, a luxurious modern mansion belonging to Lord Tweedmouth, who kindly allows visitors access to the well-wooded park surrounding it. A public path leads S. from Tomich into *Glen Moriston.*

The road up Glen Affric, keeping rt. of the ch., begins to ascend steeply behind *Fasnakyle Ho.*, up the l. bank of the river, now called the *Affric*, and for 2 m. away from the stream. As we ascend, the river is heard thundering to the l. through a forest of birches in which lie the *Badger Falls*, reached by path from Fasnakyle.

At 20½ m. the **Chisholm's Pass** is entered. This defile, 3 m. long, surpasses any other in Scotland by its combination of sylvan beauty and mountain grandeur.

At 21½ m. are the *Dog Falls*, and 1 m. beyond the end of the Pass the road strikes **Loch Beneveian** (3½ m. long) and keeps along the N. shore.

At 28½ m. the beautiful **Loch Affric** (3½ m. long) begins, with (29 m.) *Loch Affric Lo.* (Mrs. Chisholm) most picturesquely placed on a promontory on its N. bank—a situation probably unsurpassed by that of any other Shooting Lo. in the Highlands. In front (rt.) tower **Scuir-na-Lapaich** (3401 ft.) and **Mam Soul** (3862 ft.).

Here the driving road ends; a track leads along the N. side of the loch to

33½ m. *Coulavie*, a shepherd's hut. Across the stream is *Ardnamulloch.* The *Pass of Ardnamulloch* was defended by Col. Donald Murchison, ancestor of the geologist, for his chief, the Earl of Seaforth, against the soldiers of George II. From Coulavie a wild path leads up this Pass by the l. bank of the Affric to

37 m. *Alltbeath*, another shepherd's cottage, where shelter for the night can sometimes be obtained. From this point the track decomes very rough, but is quite distinct. **Ben Attow** (3383 ft.) is in front. The path keeps to the *rt.* of it up what is now called *Glen Grivie*, to

40 m. *Loch Bhealaich*, the source of the *Glomach* (p. 386). Leaving it rt. we cross 41 m. the **Bealach** or **Pass of Kintail**, whence a rough descent leads into the glen at the mouth of which is

45 m. *Croe Bridge*, where the driving road along **Loch Duich** is joined. Crossing the bridge we reach

48 m. **Glen Shiel Inn***, see p. 385.

ROUTE 93.

See Map, p. 377.

Dingwall to Strathpeffer. High. Rly.

This short line of 5 m. was opened in 1886. For half the distance the train runs over the rails of the Dingwall and Skye line (Rte. 91), then keeps the valley up the rt. bank of the *Peffery*, having l. the ridge of *Druim Chat* (the Cat's Back), which separates Strathpeffer from Strathconan, and on which is the large and very perfect vitrified fort of *Knockfarrel*.

5 m. **Strathpeffer Stat.**

[*Achterneed Stat.* (p. 378) on the Skye line is 1¼ m. N.]

STRATHPEFFER*, a watering-place of increasing repute, is resorted to for its mineral waters. These are strongly impregnated with sulphuretted hydrogen gas—far more so than those of Harrogate—and contain some saline ingredients which add much to their medicinal properties; a new sulphur spring was opened in 1892. The sulphur waters are specially suitable for gout, and for rheumatism proceeding from gout. An *Iron Spring* gives additional medicinal advantages to the place, cases of anæmia frequently deriving great benefit from these waters. There is a pump room, built in 1829, to which a suite of public rooms was added in 1881. In the neighbourhood are pleasant walks around the Wells, and many large houses, in a well-cultivated valley, which was at one time the property of the Earl of Cromartie, but now belongs to a number of persons, who hold it as a speculation.

The ivy-covered **Castle Leod** (with pretty grounds), 1 m. N., built abt. 1600, was the seat of the late Countess of Cromartie, a title revived in 1861 in favour of the Duchess of Sutherland, which descended in 1888 to her 2nd son as Earl of Cromartie (d. 1893).

Strathpeffer was in 1478 the scene of a bloody fight between the M'Donalds and M'Kenzies, and subsequently between the latter and the Monros, in both of which the M'Kenzies were victorious. Near the pump-room a stone pillar, with a rude sculpture of an eagle, marks the spot where the tide of battle turned, and the Monros fled.

EXCURSIONS :—

The chief ones are—(1) N. The **Ascent of Ben Wyvis** (*Ben Uabhais*, Mountain of Awe), which rises to the height of 3429 ft., though from its enormous bulk it does not seem so lofty (10 m. walk). It is held from the Crown by the tenure of producing a snowball from its ravines on any day of the year—no very difficult task.

"On the ascent, the pedestrian will be annoyed at the immense extent of mossy broken ground at the base; but after passing the first snow-wreaths in Aultcunire, which we recommend as the easiest track, he will find the whole upper acclivites deeply covered with a fine elastic moss, and from the corrie on the top he may approach and look down the cliffs of Coire-na-Feola or the Flesh Corrie. Ben Wyvis is composed of slaty gneiss, with numerous large veins of hornblende and granite, and intermixed with garnets."

(2) The **Falls of Rogie**, formed by the *Black Water* that issues from Loch Garve, and situated in a fine birch forest on the estate of Coul, are picturesque but of no great volume—a drive of 5 m. passing *Coul Ho.* (Sir A. G. R. Mackenzie, Bt.), *Contin Ch.*, and *Achilty Inn*, to the W. of which is *Loch Achilty*.

There are numerous other Walks and Drives through beautiful country, and there are good *Golfing Links*.

ROUTE 94.

Dingwall by Garve to Ullapool.

Rly. from Dingwall to Garve, 12 m. (p. 378).
Coach (every afternoon) Garve to Ullapool, 32 m.

The first 20 m. from Garve are on the whole monotonous and uninteresting. The road ascends **Strath Garve** N. for 8½ m., by the side of the *Black Water*, with *Ben Wyvis* (3429 ft.) rt. It then runs W. through bleak country, passing

10 m. **Alguish Inn**✱, up the rt. bank of the *Glasgarnoch River*. At 15 m. it is crossed, just before the *Watershed* (900 ft.) is reached.

Keeping along the N. bank of *Loch Droma* for 1 m. we descend the even drearier **Dirrie More** (*i.e.* "*Long Steppe*").

At 20 m. the scenery suddenly and completely changes. Rt. is the entrance to **Braemore**, the handsome mansion of Sir John Fowler, Bt., the well known C.E.—a singular creation of art and wealth in this wilderness, the bare hill side being planted for 3 m. or 4 m. with woods.

[A road called "*Destitution Road*," because made during the famine of 1851, chiefly at the expense of Mackenzie of Dundonnell, strikes l. to **Dundonnell**✱, 13 m. (below).]

We now descend rapidly through fir woods passing l. the picturesque *Falls of Measach*, and keeping alongside of the extraordinary deep gorge of ***Corrie Halloch**, well seen from the suspension bridge which spans it, and is reached by a footpath. It is one of the finest cañons in Scotland, and, unlike those of the Beauly, Findhorn, Ericht, Isla, etc., is eroded not in the Old Red Sandstone but in Schist.

At 22 m. we pass the *Gardens* and *Offices* of *Braemore*. The *Ho.* may be seen from the field behind perched up on the cliff. It is reached in ¾ m. by a path, but the carriage has to ascend for 3½ m. by a well engineered road to the front door! At 25 m. a br. (not crossed) leads to *Inverbroom Ho.* and *Loch Broom Ch.* This parish will always be remembered in connection with Robertson, who was minister here in 1746. Himself faithful to the Government, he helped to check the Rebellion in these parts, acquired influence with the Duke of Cumberland, and was able to mitigate the sufferings of those who had been induced to join the Stuart cause.

At 26 m. we reach *Inverlael* at the S. end of **Loch Broom**, whose E. shore we keep. Up the glen rt., in which is a ruined chapel and burial ground, we get a good view of *Ben Dearg* (3547 ft.); in the distance in front is *Ben More Coigach* (2438 ft.).

At 27½ m. the road skirts a cliff disclosing an excellent view of

32 m. **Ullapool**✱, established by the British Fisheries Association in 1788, a large dreary fishing village, in spite of its row of well-built houses fringing the beach. It stands on a promontory, and is almost treeless. The houses have a strange variety of roofs—thatch, slate, tile, and zinc! The scenery is uninteresting except for its being somehow utterly unlike anything the traveller has yet seen. A conspicuous feature is the patchwork of *Crofts* to the N. Ullapool has, however, a good harbour, where one of the Steamers from Glasgow to Stornoway calls weekly on its outward journey, is a capital bathing-place, and is within reach of grand scenery—the district lying N. between this and *Loch Inver*, being one of the most interesting in Scotland to the geologist.

EXCURSIONS:—

(1) **S.E. to Garve** 32 m. (above).

(2) N.W. to the **Summer Isles**, at the mouth of Loch Broom (by boat).

(3) **N. to Lochinver**✱ (p. 413).
There are 2 driving roads—(*a*) To *Drumruinie Lo.*, 10 m., thence W. through fine scenery, but over a bad road, to *Enard Bay*, and N. to, 32 m. *Lochinver*; (*b*) To *Drumruinie Lo.*, 10 m., thence N. by *Ledmore*, 19 m. (see p. 412) to 37 m. *Lochinver*.

(4) N.E. by road up *Glen Achallt*, and thence by track to 20 m. **Oykell Bridge** (see p. 412).

(5) S.W. to **Poolewe**, 32 m.—a most interesting route. Cross Loch Broom by ferry, and take a carriage (previously ordered from there) to 6 m. *Dundonnell Inn*✱, at the head of **Little Loch Broom.** [It is 25 m. by road from Ullapool to Dundonnell by Braemore, above.] From the ferry the road ascends 500 ft. in 1 m.! A magnificent view S. of the *An Teallach Mts.* (3483 ft.) is obtained as we descend to the loch.

From Dundonnell we keep its S. side, passing (in 2 m.) the very fine **Ardessie Falls*, cross the promontory (530 ft.), and descend to **Gruinard Bay**. Traversing 16 m. a *Grand Pass* we cross *Gruinard River*, skirt the head of the Bay, again ascend by a fine road, cut out of the face of the cliff, and descend upon the W. portion of the Bay through an interesting "clachan" of wretched looking hovels. Curious "stacks" are now passed (rt.) on the sea-shore, and again high land, commanding fine mountain views N., is crossed to

25 m. **Aultbea**✱ on **Loch Ewe,** where one of the Glasgow Steamers to Stornoway calls weekly on its outward journey. The road, with fine sea views extending N.W. to the mts. in *Harris,* again ascends to 300 ft., and passes *Inverewe Ho.* (Osgood H. Mackenzie, Esq.), before reaching

32 m. **Poolewe**✱ (p. 385), at the head of the loch.

ROUTE 95.

Achnasheen to Loch Maree and Gairloch.

A coach leaves Achnasheen daily for Gairloch, 30 m. upon arrival of the train from Inverness and Dingwall at 12.10 P.M. see Rte. 91 ; a mail-gig runs on to Poolewe 36 m. Carriages can also be hired at Achnasheen hotel.

The drive is very beautiful, embracing some of the finest scenery in Ross-shire, and may be pleasantly varied by taking steamer down Loch Maree.

The road from Achnasheen, passing l. *Ledgown* (John Ross, Esq.), and rt. *Lochrosque Lo.* (Arthur Bignold, Esq., runs W. alongside of *Loch Rosque,* a long melancholy lake, with bare treeless sides. At the foot of the lake, near Achnasheen, the geologist will observe interesting examples of alluvial Lake-Terraces, similar in character to the famous "Parallel Roads" of Glen Roy (p. 349), through which the river has cut its way. Beyond its head the road trends N. W., crosses the watershed (800 ft.), and passes down the narrow *Glen Docharty,* affording a vista of **Loch Maree,** which suddenly comes into view, flanked on the E. by the grand mass of **Slioch,** 3217 ft., and intersected by promontories.

10 m. **Kinlochewe** ✲ is a scattered hamlet (with a large shooting-lodge belonging to Sir Kenneth Mackenzie), 2 m. from the head of Loch Maree, near the junction of three streams, which unite to form the Kinlochewe river, and flow into the loch, which was originally called *Loch Ewe.* The scenery around is grand. The white quartzite peaks of **Ben Eighe** (3309 ft.) tower up to W. "It is literally powdered with its own dust. Except from snow I never saw a whitish hill before" (Lord Cockburn). Birches and alders on the banks of the streams add further charms to the landscape.

[There is a rough track S. over the hills to *Achnashellach Stat.*, p. 378, 11 m.

Kinlochewe to Torridon, 10 m.

A good carriage-road turns S.W. from Kinlochewe up the *Garry,* under the white quartzite crags of *Ben Eighe.* At 3½ m. (l.) the *Garry* flows out of *Lochs Clair* and *Coulin,* beyond which is *Coulin Ho.* (W. Ogilvie Dalgleish, Esq.) surrounded by every variety of Highland scenery. Now looms into view the grand form of **Leagach** (3456 ft.), whose strange mural terraces are skirted (rt.) as we descend to **Glen Torridon.** It forms the grand predominant feature of this journey, and is typical of the "*Torridon*" *Sandstones.* Its sandstone strata at a height of 3000 ft. are strangely capped with quartzite. "As these overlying patches are light gray or white in colour the contrasting hues of the two rocks give rise to some of the most unexpected features in the scenery."—Sir A. GEIKIE'S "*Scenery of Scotland,*" pp. 116 and 204.

At the head of Loch Torridon (10 m.) is a fishing hamlet, where boat for Shieldaig might be got, but without proper inn. 1½ m. farther, on the N. shore, is *Torridon Ho.,* the handsome modern seat of Duncan Darroch, Esq., behind which rises *Ben Alligin,* 3232 ft., another of the Torridon giants. For path thence to Gairloch see p. 284.

Loch Torridon, though very little visited, is better worth seeing than most of the Scottish sea-lochs, and it is to be regretted that the country is so wild, and the accommodation so scanty, as to preclude many tourists from approaching it. It consists really of three inlets, the outer or lower loch, and the upper loch, between which branches Loch Shieldaig, separated from the others by narrow channels.

Shieldaig✱, near the head of that loch may be reached from Torridon in 9 m. by an excellent path passing behind the well laid out grounds of *Ben Damph Lodge* (Earl of Lovelace) on the S. shore of the loch, but the approach by water is finer. For *Shieldaig* and routes thence to *Applecross* and (by mail-gig) to *Strathcarron Stat.* see pp. 378, 379.]

At 12 m. the road begins to run along the S. side of

Loch Maree (St. Malrube's or St. Maree's Loch) which is 12 m. long and 2¼ m. broad in the middle. While possessing many of the ordinary features of the Scottish lochs, it has some very distinguishing ones, such as the abrupt way in which **Slioch** (3217 ft.) rises on the N. side—in such an uninterrupted mass, that the tourist can scan its great rifts and gullies from base to summit at a glance—the striking *Ben Lair* (2817 ft.), farther W., the beautiful vegetation which for the first 4 m. on the S. side festoons the rocks, and the cluster of islands —more than a dozen—in the centre. At 12½ m. is **Ru Noa Pier** where *Steamer* may be taken to *Talladale* (below), or *Tollie* at the W. end of the loch (p. 385). The sail, especially among the islands, is very fine and affords better views than the road. On the road the scenery is particularly striking at 16 m. *Bridge of Grudie.*

20 m. **Talladale** ✲, commanding a grand view of loch and mountain. The hotel here was occupied by Queen Victoria for a week in the autumn of 1877, as the inscription on a *Stone*, erected by Sir Kenneth Mackenzie, testifies.

Ascend the hill in front for the view; *Slioch* and *Ben Lair* may also be ascended from here by taking boat across the loch. The road passes through thick hanging woods of birch and pine to

22 m. **Slattadale.** The loch, now increased to its greatest breadth, is here crowded with picturesque islands covered with Scotch firs and heather. Upon the little **Eilean Maree,** close to the opposite shore and crowned with woods and thickets, *St. Maree* is said to have lived as an anchorite. It has a burial ground, still used by some of the families in the neighbourhood.

E. of it on the mainland is *Letterewe* (Mrs. Meyrick Bankes), where ironworks were carried on a century ago.

4 m. W. of Letterewe is *Ardlair*, a modern house very conspicuous above the loch, also belonging to Mrs. Bankes.

[A path runs alongside of Loch Maree from Slattadale to Poolewe, 7 m.]

The road to Gairloch now leaves the loch, ascending 400 ft. in 2 m., with a magnificent retrospective view, and descends a narrow and romantic glen, traversed by the river *Kerrie*, passing *Loch Balnaskalloch.* A little farther on the river falls in a series of grand and picturesque *Cascades. Kerrisdale* is a charming glen, in its lower course completely grown up with firs and pines.

29 m. **Gairloch** ✲ is a pretty hamlet situated at the head of a sea-loch of the same name, which must not be confounded with the *Gareloch* in Dumbartonshire. [*Steamer* 3 times a week to and from Portree and Oban.] A little way up the picturesque glen of *Flowerdale* is an old-fashioned but comfortable house, built in the 18th century, in a nook surrounded by thriving plantations. It is a seat of Sir Kenneth Mackenzie, Bt. of Gairloch, the possessor of an immense tract of country in this district, and is well protected on the N. by a bank of rock covered by trees. We enjoy a magnificent view S. of Mts., among which *Ben Alligin* (3232 ft.) is conspicuous, before we reach *Gairloch Hotel*, 1 m. farther N., beyond the *Parish* and *Free Churches.*

[A magnificent *walk* to **Torridon** (p. 383) without going back to Kinlochewe is to skirt the bay S. to (3½ m.) *Shieldaig Gairloch;* then turning l. follow a path leading (*a*) to (10 m.) *Loch Vallich,* the last of a succession of lochs. From its head (13 m.) the route is between *Ben Alligin* (rt.) and *Ben Dearg* (l.) to Torridon House, 17½ m., and 19 m. **Torridon hamlet.** Possibly some difficulty may arise from keepers, at least in the deerstalking season. (*b*) Turning rt. at the first of the series of lochs, and making for *Tombuie* (1563 ft.), which must be crossed, *Loch Diabaig* might be struck, and boat got for *Shieldaig* (p. 379).]

The road to Poolewe, passing Gairloch Hotel, commands fine views W., over a wide expanse of sea, of the northernmost promontory of Skye, and the island of Lewis. It soon turns E., crossing a ridge (456 ft.), and descends, passing *Loch Tollie* and allowing a view of the W. end of Loch Maree, with **Tollie Pier** (2½ m. from Poolewe), from which a steamer sails daily in connection with coach from Gairloch. The short river *Ewe*, famous for its salmon fishing, is followed for nearly 2 m. to

36 m. **Poolewe** ✫, at the head of *Loch Ewe*, with a curious "*Pool*," where the river enters the sea.

Glasgow steamer calls once a week. For grand coast route to *Ullapool* see p. 382.

ROUTE 96.

Strome Ferry to Loch Alsh and Loch Duich.

No one should leave Strome Ferry without taking this drive—one of the most beautiful and varied in the Highlands.

Waggonette every afternoon to Balmacara and thence *Mail-gig*, conveying passengers, to Loch Duich.

Tourists on arriving at Strome Ferry would do well to proceed the same afternoon to *Balmacara* (below), and there hire a carriage next day for the rest of the drive.

The road ascends nearly due S., attaining 683 ft. in 4 m., and affording excellent views back over Loch Carron. Descending we see (rt.) across Loch Alsh to the Coolins in Skye and (l.) up Loch Duich.

Loch Alsh, although an arm of the sea (lying E. and W.), is almost completely land-locked, having S. the narrow strait of **Kyle Rhea**, and W. that of **Kyle Akin**, (p. 395). The Highland Rly. is being (1894) continued to *Kyle Akin Ferry*, by which it is only ½ m. across to Skye.

8 m. from its mouth Loch Alsh divides into 2 arms—the exceedingly narrow fiord of **Loch Long** running 5 m. N.E., and the beautiful **Loch Duich** running 6½ m. S.E.

At 7 m. near a *School Ho.* the road forks —leading W. past *Loch Alsh Parish Ch.*, to

8½ m. **Balmacara Hotel**✶, beautifully situated; 1½ m. beyond are *Balmacara Village, House*, and *Landing Stage* (p. 395), where the Oban and Skye steamers call 4 or 5 times a week, both going N. and S.

We turn E. at the Schoolhouse through pleasantly diversified country, but behind hillocks which hide the loch, to

9 m. *Ardelvie P.O. and Tel. Office.*

[Here a driving road strikes l. leading up the W. side of *Loch Long*, and reaching in 6½ m. *Killilan* beyond the head of the loch; thence it runs for 7 m. up *Glen Elchaig* to Carnach at the head of *Loch-na-Leitreach*, whence the **Falls of the Glomach** (cf. p. 386) may be visited in about 2½ m.—rough walking.]

1 m. beyond *Ardelvie* we reach the loch side and cross by ferry the narrow mouth of *Loch Long* to

Dornie✶, a considerable village with a *R.C. Convent and Ch.*, founded by the late Duchess of Leeds.

At the entrance to Loch Long on **Eilean Donan** are the picturesque ivy-covered ruins of a stronghold of the Mackenzies, Earls of Seaforth, which was battered by a war-ship 1719, after the fight in Glen Shiel (p. 372).

From Dornie the road ascends steeply for 2 m. to 500 ft., where a magnificent view of **Loch Duich**, with the conspicuous **Scour Ouran** (3505 ft.) at its head, is obtained.

After descending we pass 13½ m. the hamlet of *Inverinate*—opposite which on the S. shore is *Glen Shiel Parish Ch.*—then through woods which hide Sir Kenneth Matheson's charming little villa on the banks of the loch, and, beyond *Kintail Parish Ch.*, we make a wide circuit l. to cross 17 m. *Croe Bridge.* In front, here, rises **Ben Attow** (3383 ft.), to the N. of which runs the path to *Loch Affric*, etc. (Rte. 92). Turning rt., in 3 m. we cross *Shiel Bridge*, just above where the Shiel falls into Loch Duich, and reach

20 m. **Glen Shiel Inn**✶, in a beautiful spot overshadowed by grand mts. 1½ m. from the Inn is a remarkable subterranean "*Pict's House.*"

EXCURSIONS :—

(1) N.W. to **Balmacara** 14½ m., and **Strome Ferry** 20 m. (above).

(2) **Ascent of Scour Ouran**, 3505 ft., 2-3 hrs. up. Cross the br., keep up the rt. bank of the river—path rather boggy—for 2 m. After crossing the mouth of a ravine, climb straight up the nose of the mt.—steep but easy. A most magnificent view may be enjoyed of the whole *Outer Hebrides* from the Mts. of *Harris* to *Barra*, including the *Coolins* in Skye and the *Scuir of Eigg;* N. the Mts. around and beyond Loch Maree are visible; S. *Ben Nevis*, the *Glen Coe Mts.*, and *Ben Alder* are seen, and beyond, *Ben More* (Mull), *Ben Cruachan*, and

probably the *Paps of Jura;* E. the view is chiefly of neighbouring Mts.; N.E. rise the long ridges of *Ben Attow* and *Mamsoul*, while a glimpse can be caught of *Loch Affric*.

(3) N.E. to the **Falls of Glomach**, 10 m. Carriage road to (3½ m.) *Linassie* up the valley rt. after crossing *Croe Bridge*. Thence it is a very rough walk over a pass 2000 ft. above the sea. The glen to be followed is *W.* of *Glasven* (3006 ft.)—that to the *S.* of Glasven, between that mt. and *Ben Attow*, leads to Glen Affric, and on its *E.* side are the lochs which are the *Sources of the Glomach*. Crossing the pass over the *N.* end of Glasven and descending 900 ft., we strike the *Glomach* near the *Falls*, which are in a narrow gully, amid a scene of perfect solitude. The volume of water is not large, but the pure white foaming cascade falling over black precipices of inverted strata, and the depth of the chasm are very impressive.

Return may be made (1) by following the Glomach to *Loch Bheulaich* (5 m.), and thence in 5 m. to *Croe Bridge*, over the *Pass of Kintail* (p. 381); or (2) down *Glen Elchaig*, p. 385.

(4) Drive W. over the **Pass of Mam Rattachan** to **Glenelg**✶, 8½ m.

An excellent road, much improved since Johnson and Boswell rode on horseback over it—"a terrible steep to climb, notwithstanding the road is formed slanting along it"—ascends 1072 ft. in 3 m., allowing fine views back of Loch Duich and the mts. at its head. From the summit there is a good view S., in which the singular peak of **Ben Screel** (3196 ft.) is conspicuous.

The sea, and the road beyond in Skye, are visible as we descend to **Glenelg** (p. 395).

(5) N.E. by **Glen Affric**, etc., to **Beauly** (Rte. 92).

(6) Walk S. over the *Pass of Corryvarlingen* (Coire Mhalagain) 2500 ft., which crosses the E. end of **The Saddle** (3317 ft.) to

Loch Hourn Head (p. 372), abt. 13 m., but will take nearly 5 hrs. Keep 4 m. up Glen Shiel, sighting the *Mhalagain Burn* before leaving the road.

ROUTE 97.

Strome Ferry to Skye.

A steamer sails daily at 3 p.m. (upon arrival of the night mail from London which leaves Edinburgh 4.45 a.m., Glasgow 5.10 a.m., Perth 7 a.m., and Inverness 11.25) and reaches Portree (Skye) at 6 p.m. and Stornoway (Lewis) at 10 p.m. The steamer leaves Stornoway at 1 a.m. Portree at 6.45 a.m., and reaches Strome at 9.30 a.m. in connection with train to the South.

Quitting Loch Carron through the narrow strait at Strome Ferry, the steamer traverses outer Loch Carron, in view rt. of the grand mountains of Applecross, and l. of Sir K. J. Matheson's modern *Castle of Duncraig*, while in front appear the picturesque mountains of Skye. We first touch at † **Plockton**, whence there is a road to Balmacara (p. 395). Leaving to the S. the Strait of Kyle Akin, the shore is coasted along until abreast of

† **Broadford** ✲ which is overshadowed by *Ben-na-Cailliach* (2403 ft.).

It is but a fishing village, with an ugly church and a small pier.

[Broadford is 8 m. from *Kyle Akin* ferry and 11 m. from *Kyle Rhea* ferry, both leading to the mainland.]

[*Excursion from Broadford* to **Loch Coruisk** and **Sligachan** by **Torrin** and **Elgol** [or **Camasunary**]. The hotel proprietor will furnish a carriage and bespeak a boat. Those who do not mean to return to Broadford can telegraph to Sligachan for ponies to meet them at Camasunary or, better still, on the hill above Coruisk. The journey may be made thus:—By carriage or on foot to Torrin by a good road, passing the small lake and ruined ch. of Kilchrist, in full view of the wonderful mountain of **Blaven** (3042 ft.).

6 m. **Torrin**, a poor hamlet near the head of *Loch Slapin*.

The tourist may proceed from Torrin either (1) by road to Elgol on the W. side of the peninsula which separates Loch Slapin from Loch Scavaig, and take a boat thence to the head of L. Scavaig; or (2) by boat, which may be hired for 25s. for one or two persons, or 10s. a head for more, to Coruisk and back, including a visit to the Spar Cave. The distance is 14 m., requiring from 2½ hrs. to 3 hrs., according to wind and tide. This approach, though fine, is tedious, and when the S.W. wind blows is exposed round the point to heavy seas.

(1) A carriage can drive from Broadford through Torrin and round the head of Loch Slapin, where on the rt. the bold form of *Blaven* towers up into the mist, to

12 m. *Kilmaree*, where are the Shooting Lo. and Kennels belonging to the Trs. of the late Sir Wm. Mackinnon, Bt.

[There is a footpath from Kilmaree leading in 3 m. to Camasunary, commanding fine views from the top of the peninsula, but beyond Camasunary the path to Loch Coruisk is difficult, if not dangerous,—in one place, called "*The Bad Step*," a ledge along the cliff 6 in. wide,—and is not recommended.

Camasunary is a solitary white farmhouse, the only one on the savage shores of Loch Scavaig. Here a boat may sometimes be hired to row to Loch Coruisk, and here ponies from Sligachan may be met.

(The path to Sligachan (9 m.) runs due N. past 2 lochs, having first *Blaven* (3042 ft.) and afterwards *Marsco* (2414 ft.) to the rt., but a hill overlooking Coruisk may be ascended from that loch, ponies met there, and descent made thence into Glen Sligachan.)]

Driving 3 m. beyond Kilmaree we reach

15 m. **Elgol**, a poor village on the top of the peninsula, commanding the mouth of Loch Scavaig and fine views out at sea to the island **Rum**, towering and mountainous ; **Canna**, flat and fertile ; and **Eigg**, distinguished by the lofty *Scuir*. On the opposite side of the loch rise the pinnacles of "The Coolins"[1] whose sides slope down into ocean with shelf and precipice. To the S.E. the eye travels along the coast of the Island to the Sound of Sleat, to the hills of Knoydart, and to the long point of Ardnamurchan, dim in the distance.

A steep path from Elgol leads in about 1 m. to the rocky beach, where the tourist must embark, the boat having been, if possible, bespoke beforehand. It takes fully 1 hr. to row to the head of Loch Scavaig. For the approach to it and Loch Coruisk see description below.

[1] Gael., *A Chuilionn* = *The Coolin*, cf. "*The Caucasus*" — only of recent years, and erroneously, written *Cuchullin*. Although there was an Ossianic hero of that name, they were *not* called after him. —Nicolson.

(2) Having reached Torrin from Broadford by carriage or on foot, the tourist must proceed *by water*. The boatmen keep pretty close to the coast of the rocky peninsula of **Strathaird**, which is interesting from its geological features. Halfway along its shore is *Kilmaree* (above), and before reaching *Strathaird Point* we pass the **Spar Cave** —directly opposite *Loch Eishort*— an enlarged example of a cavern worked out of the calcareous Jurassic sandstone, smaller examples of which are visible all along the coast. The entrance is strikingly picturesque, through a narrow rift bounded by very high cliffs, rocks of which strew the ground in wild confusion. After proceeding some little distance into the interior the stalagmite floor of the cave suddenly rises steeply up, like a Montagne Russe, beyond which a steep descent leads to a deep pool.

The boat soon rounds the Point, passing between the rocks of Strathaird Point, which are much frequented by seals, and a small island tenanted by rats. Once the corner is turned, and the boat is fairly within ****Loch Scavaig**, a view faces the tourist not to be surpassed in Britain. A huge amphitheatre of peaked hills girdles the blue sea, the centre being formed by a serrated line of jagged peaks, which, if the weather is clear—a rare thing in this district—cut the sky like so many lancets. Below is a deep dark mass of purple colour, often relieved by drifting wreaths of vapour. As the boat nears the land, the hills grow upon the sight until we imagine that we are entering a huge hall, and we land at the head of Loch Scavaig.

(The swift Oban steamer, once a week, on her voyage N., weather permitting, touches here and lands passengers to see the loch.)

Rt. and l. rise up directly from the water's edge the rough peaks of *Trodhu* or *Sgor-na-Strigh* (Peak of Strife), 1623 ft., and *Gairsbheinn*, 2934 ft., down which the *Mad Cataract* comes dashing with a loud roar. The visitor lands on the spot where the Bruce is said to have landed, and after a short climb up the l. bank of the stream, which discharges the waters of Loch Coruisk into the sea after a course of 300 yds., he stands on a rocky dam, from which he looks upon the marvellous wilderness of ****Loch Coruisk**, or Coiruisge, *i.e.* the water cauldron, from *Coire* (Gael.), a cauldron or dell, and *uisge*, water. A small boat might easily be carried across and launched on the lake, which contains quantities of small trout. It is not deep except in one place, 20 fathoms, and seems to be filled with gravel.

"Picking your steps carefully over huge boulders and stepping-stones, you come upon the most savage scene of desolation in Britain. Conceive a large lake filled with dark-green water, girt with torn and shattered precipices, the bases of which are strewn with ruin, and whose summits jag the sky with grisly splinter and peak. There is no motion here save the white vapour steaming from the abyss."

Loch Coruisk is nearly 2 m. long but narrow, and the little valley at its upper end is bounded by a barrier of perpendicular rocks, composed of hypersthene. An awful silence reigns in this Avernus of the North, where all is hard, dark, and motionless. The geologist will notice the frequent occurrence of glacial striations and perched boulders.

It will be remembered that upon the shores of this lake Bruce met Cormac Doil and his companions. The description of the scene given by Scott in "The Lord of the Isles" is wonderfully spirited, but somewhat highly coloured.

Instead of returning the way he came, the stout pedestrian, by keeping a short distance along the E. side of Loch Coruisk as far as a tumbling torrent, may clamber up its precipitous rocky bed till he reaches the source of the burn, a small tarn in the lap of the mountain. Thence by climbing l. he will get a grand view of the loch from *Drumhain*, whence he may descend by *Harta Corrie* (p. 392) to Glen Sligachan, or climbing rt. he will find a pony (if ordered) at the top of the ridge from which a path leads to Sligachan, joining that from Camasunary before the watershed is reached. By Sligachan to Portree see pp. 391, 392.

There is a circuitous road along the coast from Broadford by the head of *Loch Ainort* to Sligachan, 16 m., but, unless Coruisk be visited, it is best reached in 9½ m. from Portree.]

Leaving Broadford and skirting l. the Island of **Scalpa**, on which is a chapel marking the site of an ancient Culdee cell, we turn l. into the Kyle Mhor, or big strait, which divides Scalpa from the Island of **Raasay**. Left, behind Scalpa is *Loch Ainort*, whose shores are the resort of the heron and of herds of red deer, and W. between it and *Loch Sligachan* is the grand and picturesque syenite pyramid of *Ben Glamaig* (2537 ft.) backed by the more romantic peaks of **Scuir-na-Gillean** (3167 ft.).

Next the *Narrows of Raasay* are threaded, and we skirt the W. shore of the island of **Raasay**, in view rt. of *Raasay Ho.*, the modern mansion of the proprietrix of the island, Mrs. Wood, which has succeeded that of Macleod of Raasay (the former laird) where Johnson and Boswell were so hospitably entertained. At †Raasay the steamer calls. The island is 14 m. long and has the picturesque ruin of *Brochel Castle* upon a rocky slope on its E. side. On Raasay the young Chevalier was some time sheltered by the laird in a miserable hut, all the houses having been burned down by the soldiery.

As the Sound of Raasay widens out the steamer turns l. into the harbour of

†**Portree**✲ the capital of Skye. It is built on a platform of rock, which presents towards the harbour a cliff 60 or 80 ft. high. Its name, "King's Haven," was given to it after a visit of King James V. It has several churches and banks, and a Sheriff Court-house. Behind the U.P. Ch. is a pretty *Walk* among the trees, overlooking the sheltered harbour. From this, and other commanding points, views may be had N. of *Storr Rock*, and S. of the *Coolins*. On the outskirts of the town is a cloth (tweed) mill, employing some hundred persons.

Steamer daily to Strome Ferry, 3 hrs.; 3 times a week by swift steamer to Oban in 9 hrs., and to Gairloch in 2½ hrs.; twice a week to Stornoway, and by slower steamer to Oban, and once a week to Gairloch, Ullapool, and Lochinver; to Tarbert (Harris), 5 hrs., Lochmaddy (North Uist), 8 hrs., and Dunvegan (Skye), 10½ hrs., 3 times a week, returning next day.

Coaches (*Waggonettes*) daily in summer to *The Quiraing*, to *Sligachan* (for Coruisk), and to *Dunvegan*, returning in the evening.

Distances.—Prince Charlie's Cave, 4 m.; Storr Rock, 8 m.; Uig, 15 m.; Quiraing, 21½ m.; Stenscholl, 24 m.; Duntulm, 23 m.; Dunvegan, 23 m.; Sligachan, 9½ m.; Broadford, 25½ m.; Loch Coruisk, 18 m.; Kyle Akin, 33½ m.

EXCURSIONS:—

(1) **To Prince Charlie's Cave,** 4 m. N., on the seashore. It is best approached by boat (abt. 10s.). Its mouth is screened by a fringe of stalactites. It is pretty, but is scarcely worth the trouble of a visit, and its connection with the Prince is not established. The hill between it and Portree (1286 ft.), however, is well worth ascending on a clear day for the view. 2 m. beyond the cave, near the shore and opposite a small green island, is the singular *Holm Waterfall*, bursting over a shelf of hard basalt, which, having resisted the water's action in washing out the oolitic bed below, has formed a cave, so hollowed out that you can get *behind* the cascade and see the sea-view through it. 1 m. inland the track may be joined leading from Portree to the Storr.

(2) **To the Storr** (2360 ft.), the highest of a remarkable range of black basaltic cliffs running N. and S. through *Trotternish* as the N. portion of Skye is called. It stands nearly at their S. end while the *Quiraing* (below) is at the N. end. Its summit commands a grand and extensive sea view. At the base of this range is a broad terrace of moorland, from which a succession of precipitous descents (in fact, an *Undercliff*) leads down to the sea.

The *Old Man of Storr* is an isolated black obelisk of trap, rising to a height of 160 ft. on the E. side of the mountain.

The tracks from Portree (8 m.) -only fo pedestrians and somewhat indistinct and marshy—lead N. past two small *lochs*, *Fada* and *Leathan*. One keeps to the W. of the *Chracaig Valley* and of both lochs, the other up the valley and between them.

An experienced Skye traveller, the late Sheriff Nicolson,[1] a native of Skye, suggested as an alternative to returning to Portree "to ascend the Storr, and follow the mountain ridge the whole way till you come to the high road near Quiraing. I have no doubt it is one of the grandest promenades in Skye, commanding wide views in all directions." In that case the night would probably need to be passed at *Stenscholl Inn* (p. 390).

(3) **N. to The Quiraing,** 21½ m. *Coach* (waggonette) every morning in summer; returning at night. A good road, traversing first a monotonous undulating moor of peat land, with few patches of cultivation. Glimpses S. of the *Coolins;* W. of *Macleod's Tables.*

[1] Born 1827, d. 1893; see "Verses by A. N.," which include two excellent poems on Skye.

At 4 m. the road to Dunvegan (p. 391) strikes off l., and at

7 m. we reach *Snizort Ch.*, at the head of an arm of the sea loch of that name.

[Path rt. up *Glen Haultin* to the Storr (p. 389), 6½ m.]

At 10 m. (l.) is *Kingsburgh House*, from which—as the former seat of his ancestors — the present Lord Justice-Clerk has taken his title. The old mansion in which Prince Charlie found refuge 1746, and where Johnson and Boswell were entertained by the laird and his wife, Flora Macdonald, 1773, has been pulled down.

After surmounting a long ascent, the eye is relieved by a view down into the cheerful *Uig Bay*, shut in by high hills, and so sheltered as to enjoy a climate like that of Devon. It is bordered by neat houses, two churches, and well-to-do-cottages, constituting

15 m. **Uig**✲. Near the centre of the bay is the comfortable house of Captain Fraser, whose well-managed estate extends from this to Stenscholl.

From Uig Bay the road ascends in a sweeping zigzag, which the pedestrian may abridge by a short cut.

[3 m. N. of Uig at *Monkstadt*—once a seat of the Macdonalds, and previously of the "Monks," — Prince Charlie landed, 1746, from the Long Island, disguised as a female servant accompanying Flora Macdonald. The situation is very fine, backed as it is by basaltic cliffs.

3 m. beyond, in **Kilmuir** ch-yd., is the *Grave of the brave Flora Macdonald*, long neglected and undistinguished, until in 1871 an *Iona Cross* of gray granite, 21 ft. high, was placed over it by a public subscription. There are 6 *duns* or old forts in Kilmuir parish.

2 m. farther, on the top of a cliff above the sea, rise the ruins of *Duntulm Castle*, the original seat of the Macdonalds, grandly placed on the edge of a precipice of basaltic columns.

From the top of the cliffs, which extend around the N. of Skye to Loch Staffin, noble views are presented of the indented coast of Skye, and of Lewis and Harris on the N W. horizon.]

About 5 m. from Uig, just where the road begins to descend E. to the sea, a well-marked footpath strikes l. across the grassy slope, which a little way on is crested by a range of black rocks. Skirting these, and constantly rising, at the end of about 2 m. a massive detached rock, resembling a *Castle*, is passed. And now the black cliffs become split into projecting towers, spires, and pinnacles, which together form **The Quiraing**. One of these, the *Needle Rock*, forms a natural obelisk 120 ft. high. A steep scramble leads to a nook surrounded by these colossal skittles, but allowing peeps of the deep precipice through the interstices, and down to the sea 1500 feet below. Above this rises the *Table*, a large cylinder of rock, with vertical sides, like a great plumcake. It is difficult to climb, but on surmounting it is found to be a circular turfed platform. From this there is a magnificent view down on the sea below, and across it to Lewis on the N., and the mountains of Ross-shire on the E.

About 2½ m. from Quiraing on the shore, is **Stenscholl**✲, near the landing-place on Loch Staffin. Boats may be hired here. The shore is of the softest sand, admirable for bathing; the sea abounds with marine animals.

The *Sea Cliffs* around *Staffin Bay* are grand in the extreme, and peculiar from the clustered columnar arrangement of the basalt. Though not so exactly formed as in Staffa, their effect at a distance is equally grand. The name — like that of Staffa — comes from their resemblance to *Staves*. They ought to be seen from the sea.

A road runs N. round the coast to Uig.

2½ m. S.E. a remarkable though small *waterfall* dashes over the cliffs 300 ft. clear height into the sea. It is the outlet of *Loch Mealt*. A projecting mass nearly opposite is called the *Kilt Rock* (Creag-na-Feile), from the resemblance of the strata to the bars of tartan, curiously banded and folded. It is a very striking object, and is best seen from a boat. Hence to the *Storr* is a rough and boggy walk of some 8 m., not recommended, but see p. 389.

(4) **W. to †Dunvegan,** 22 m.

Dunvegan Castle is an interesting historic residence of a Highland chief — Macleod of Macleod — but few ordinary travellers will find it worth while to make a journey expressly to visit it, through a country for the most part dreary. The road from Portree to Uig is followed for 4 m.; we then turn l. by *Carbost* and *Skeabost* to

6 m. the head of **Loch Snizort,** the W. side of which is kept for 4 m.

At 10 m. **Tayinlone Inn** the promontory is crossed to 14 m. the head of *Loch Greshornish*, and the road continues W. to

18½ m. *Fairy Bridge.*

[Hence a road strikes N. through the district of **Vaternish,** passing 3½ m. **Stein** on *Loch Bay*, once a station of the British Fishery Company. The **Isle of Isa** (Iosa, Jesus), at the mouth of this loch, was offered by Macleod to Dr. Johnson, provided he would live in it for three months every year.]

We turn S. and then W. to 22 m. *Duirinish Ch.* (in whose ch.-yd. is a monument to the father of Simon, Lord Lovat), and **Dunvegan** ✲.

1 m. farther on is **Dunvegan Castle** (Macleod of Macleod), which has for centuries been the residence of the chief of the clan, a picturesque building, partly old, partly modern, on a rock surrounded on 3 sides by the sea, backed by well-grown plantations. Formerly it was accessible only from the sea by a boat and a subterranean staircase, now by a modern bridge crossing the chasm. It forms 2 sides of a small square. It is said to be the oldest inhabited castle in Scotland, and contains some antique family relics — a square Irish cup of wood, beautifully carved and mounted in silver, which belonged to John Macguire, chief of Fermanagh, and his wife, Catherine O'Neill, bearing the date 1493; the fairy banner, supposed to be associated with the destiny of the family; the claymore of Rory More (Sir Roderick Macleod), and his horn carved and ornamented with silver, holding perhaps 2 quarts, which, filled with claret, the heir of Macleod, as a proof of manhood, was expected to empty at a draught. (See notes to Scott's "Lord of the Isles.")

Here Johnson and Boswell were hospitably entertained to their hearts' content for many days (1773). Here Sir Walter Scott was a welcome guest, and composed "MacCrimmon's Lament." The country around is comparatively barren; but the neighbourhood of the castle is adorned with plantations. Behind the castle is a waterfall.

[*Steamer* from Dunvegan to Oban 3 times a week, to Lochmaddy 3 times a week, and to Glasgow twice a week. From Oban *daily.*]

[There is a good road direct from Dunvegan to **Sligachan** (24 m.) abounding in fine scenery. At *Caroy* (5½ m.) is an *Epis. Chap.*, and at 11 m. is **Bracadale**✱, at the head of **†Loch Bracadale**, where the Oban steamer calls 3 times a week. From its shores inexpressibly fine views are commanded of the *Coolins*, while on the W., off the S. point of *Duirinish*, as the N.W. portion of Skye is called, are seen **Macleod's Maidens**—3 stacks of basaltic rock resembling "*The Needles*," compared by Sir Walter Scott to the Norwegian "Riders of the Storm"—rising sheer above the waves, and backed by cliffs 600 ft. or 700 ft. high.

At *Ulinish*, 2 m. W. of Bracadale, is a well-preserved example of the Celtic burg or dune, which is described by Dr. Johnson in his "Tour to the Western Islands."

The road from Bracadale skirts the shores of *Loch Harport*, at the head of which (19 m.) a road branches off W. to **Carbost,** 3 m. distant, celebrated for its *Talisker Distillery*, and thence over the hill to **Talisker,** 5 m. farther, on the W. coast at the foot of a rich valley, overlooked and sheltered by the bold basaltic hill, *Preshal.*]

(5) **S. to Sligachan** and **Loch Coruisk.** *Coach* daily in summer to Sligachan, 9½ m., and back.

See Map, p. 387.

Except for the views of the *Coolins*, it is a dreary and uninteresting drive due S. to **Sligachan Inn** ✲, standing near the head of *Loch Sligachan*—on the S. shore of which is *Sconcer*, a poor scattered hamlet, and, beyond, Lord Macdonald's *Shooting Lo.*—at the junc. of roads from Portree, Broadford, and Dunvegan, and at the mouth of *Glen Sligachan*, up which runs the rugged path to Coruisk (9 m.).

The view from the Inn is backed

by the grand form of **Scuir-na-Gillean** (*Peak of the Youths*), most picturesque of the Coolin range, surmounted by 3 peaks. Its summit, 3167 feet high, was first attained by the late Prof. James Forbes, 1836. It may be reached, with a guide, in 3 hrs. from the *Inn*, not less. It is somewhat difficult, and requires a steady head. There is no beaten path. It is not suited for ladies ; and, when mists arise, is dangerous for strangers to the mountain. The "*Pinnacle Route*," along the peaks, should only be attempted by members of the Alpine Club, to whom it offers attractions in the way of rock work unsurpassed in Great Britain.

Ponies and guides, *Sligachan* to *Coruisk*, 9s. each. It is a walk or ride of 3 hrs. We cross the bridge and turn rt., along a path as rough as any in Scotland, intersected by frequent water-courses, but the guides are careful and the ponies hardy. It skirts at first the base of *Marsco* (2414 ft.), a conical hill (l.), but *Scuir-na-Gillean* (rt.) is still the grand feature of the view. As soon as it is passed, the deep mysterious glen called *Harta Corrie* is seen rt., surrounded by jagged peaks at the base of which rises the Sligachan river.

By this corrie *Drumhain*, with its striking view of Loch Coruisk, may be reached (cf. p. 388).

Passing this corrie (rt.) the watershed is crossed, and soon the path is seen across the stream, going (rt.) up to the ridge from which **Loch Coruisk** may be viewed. Below is the loch, shut in all round by an abrupt wall of mountains, black as ink, and herbless, cutting the sky with their fantastic jagged outline. The view out to sea extends over *Loch Scavaig* to the Islands of *Eigg*, *Rum*, and *Canna*.

Here ponies must be left if it is desired to descend to the loch, for the description and surroundings of which see p. 388.

If **Camasunary** (p. 387) is to be reached it will be necesssary to retrace our steps to the glen, and keep S. down the stream, unless a boat has been ordered, as the path by the cliffs is somewhat dangerous (p. 387).

ROUTE 98.

Glasgow or Oban up the West Coast and to the Outer Hebrides.

Steamer communication has so developed of late years that **Lochmaddy** (N. Uist) can be reached daily from Oban, and **Stornoway** (Lewis) daily from Strome Ferry ; while mail steamers sail regularly from Oban to *all* the important ports on the Outer Islands 3 times a week, besides other steamers. A week's cruise to and among these islands may be enjoyed for £3 (including meals), by the "Hebridean," which leaves Glasgow (or Greenock) on Mondays, or by the "Dunara Castle," leaving on Thursdays,—for ports of call see advertisements.

Better still, take Macbrayne's large and well-appointed "Clansman" on Monday, or "Claymore" on Thursday, up the W. coast by Oban and Skye to Stornoway. Ret. fare (including meals) £4. These are in addition to his mail steamers from Oban, and his swift tourist boat 3 times a week from Oban to Portree and Gairloch. For further particulars consult Macbrayne's "Summer Tours."

The scenery on the voyage round the Mull of Kintyre and up the Sound of Jura to Oban, passing (l.) Islay, Jura, and Scarba, is described in Rtes. 78, 80, and 82, but great part of it is lost, as the boat leaves Greenock in the evening.

See Rte. 83 for the voyage from Oban through the **Sound of Mull** to **Ardnamurchan Point** with a conspicuous *Lighthouse* (p. 362). To the S.W. are seen the islands of **Coll** and **Tiree** (p. 357). [Steamer 3 times a week from Oban.] After rounding the Point a magnificent view opens up on a clear day. Left are the *Mts. of Rum* with the low island of *Canna* to the W. ; in front are *Muck* and *Eigg* with its towering *Scuir*. Between Rum and Eigg the range of the *Coolins* in Skye stands out clearly in the distance. Rt. on the mainland are the *Mts. of Moidart.*

Muck ("Insula Porcorum," the Isle of Sea Swine, *i.e.* Porpoises) is only 2 m. broad, and contains nothing of interest. Its geological constituents are mainly trap and basalt. To the N. is

†**Eigg** ✲ (Professor Macpherson), 5 m. long by fully 3 m. broad. [Steamer 3 or 4 times a week from and to Oban.] The landing is difficult, and there is no anchorage. It is distinguished by a peculiarly shaped hill at the S. end, terminating in a very remarkable peak 1289 ft. in height, called the **Scuir of Eigg.**

"The Scuir of Eigg is a veritable Giant's Causeway, like that on the coast of Antrim, taken and magnified rather more than 20 times its height, and then placed on the ridge of a hill nearly 900 ft. high. This strange causeway is columnar from end to end; but the columns from their great altitude and deficient breadth, seem mere rodded shafts in the Gothic style—they rather resemble bundles of rods than well-proportioned pillars. Under the old foundations of this large wall we find the remains of a pine forest, that, long ere a single bed of the porphyry had burst from beneath, had sprung up and decayed on hill and beside stream in some nameless land—had then been swept to the sea—had been entombed deep at the bottom in a sand of the oolite—had been heaved up to the surface and high over it by volcanic agencies working from beneath—and had finally been built upon, as arches are built upon piles, by the architect that had laid down the masonry of the gigantic Scuir in one fiery layer after another."—HUGH MILLER, "Cruise of the Betsy."

The tree which formed this fossil wood has been long known to geologists by the name of the *Pinites Eiggensis.*

Hugh Miller mentions that in the Bay of Laig, which is to the N.W. of the island, is an oolitic sand, which on being struck emits a distinct musical sound—a metallic ring like that described as existing in the mountains of Jebel Nakous, near the Isthmus of Suez.

A cave (*Uamh Fhraing*) in the S.W. of the island, 250 ft. long and 25 ft. high, was at the end of the 16th cent. the scene of a terrible tragedy referred to in the "Lord of the Isles." Some Macleods of Skye, having been thrown ashore upon Eigg, were hospitably treated by the Macdonalds; but in consequence of their offering an insult to some young women, they were bound hand and foot, and turned adrift in an open boat. They were picked up by some friends, and Macleod landed at Eigg with a large force to avenge their injuries. The inhabitants took refuge in the cave, and could not be found, and Macleod, after two days' search, was on the point of re-embarking his warriors, when a man was discerned on the shore. Landing again, they tracked him by his footsteps (there being a light snow on the ground) to the mouth of this cave. There they lit a fire and stifled the whole population of about 200 souls.

Some 4 m. to the N.W. of Eigg is the island of **Rum** (George Bullough, Esq.), called by Sir Walter Scott "Rona," the magnificent peaks of which appear to rise immediately from the water's edge. [Steamer 3 times a week from and to Oban.] It is seldom visited save by the geologist, and has no inn.

"The geology of Rum is simple but curious. Let the reader take from 12 to 15 trap hills, varying from 1000 to 2300 ft. in height; let him pack them closely and squarely together, like bottles in a case-basket; let him surround them with a frame of old red sandstone, measuring rather more than 7 m. on the side, in the way the basket surrounds the bottles; then let him set them down in the sea a dozen miles off the land, and he will have produced a second island of Rum, similar in structure to the existing one."—MACCULLOCH.

On the E. coast of Rum is the inlet of *Loch Scresort*, at the head of which is the mansion-house, whence a glen of red sandstone can be followed across the island to *Scuir More*, 1272 ft., which contains the blood-stones or heliotropes for which Rum is celebrated. The most lofty summits are to be found in the S.E. in the peaks of *Askival* (2659 ft.), and *Allival* (2368 ft.), *Ashval* (2552 ft.), and *Scuir-na-Gillean* (2503 ft.).

[About 2 m. N.W. of Rum is the much smaller island of **Canna.** [Steamer 3 times a week from and to Oban.]

It is celebrated for its "*Compass Hill*" on the N.E., so called from the variation in the compass experienced by vessels which pass it. This phenomenon, Macculloch says, is by no means confined to Canna, but is frequent through all the basaltic islands of the coast owing to the quantity of iron present in the rock. In a pretty bay opening towards the E. there is a lofty and slender rock, detached from the shore. Upon the summit are the ruins of a very small tower, accessible only by a steep and precipitous path. Here it is said that one of the Lords of the Isles confined his wife, a beautiful foreigner, of whose fidelity he entertained suspicions—a legend also referred to in the "Lord of the Isles."]

Due E. of Eigg is †**Arisaig** ✲ on the mainland (p. 367). The landing stage, nearly 4 m. from the village, is approached by a narrow channel bounded by numerous reefs, and inaccessible in rough weather.

[Steamer 3 or 4 times a week from and to Oban, but the same boat does not always call at both Eigg and Arisaig.]

The mountains on the mainland and the Coolins in Skye continue to arrest and delight the eye, and make this sail on a clear day one of the most enjoyable in the British Isles.

Once a week the swift steamer from Oban proceeds W. of the *Point of Sleat* to †**Loch Scavaig** (l. of which is the island of **Soa,** inhabited by a few fishermen). At the head of the loch it remains for an hour to enable passengers to explore the gloomy solitude of *Loch Coruisk* (cf. p. 387).

Rt., at the entrance to the **Sound of Sleat,** is †**Inverie** ✲ (visited about once a week) on the N. shore near the mouth of **Loch Nevis** ("*Loch of Heaven*"), a fine wild fiord running inland for 12 m., separating **Morar** from **Knoydart.** See p. 371.

Left, up the Sound, on the S. part of Skye called **Sleat,** is †**Armadale** ✲.

[Steamer from and to Oban 4 or 5 times a week.]

Here is *Armadale Castle,* the seat of Lord Macdonald, the lineal descendant of the Macdonalds of Sleat, and a competitor with the Glengarry family for the chieftainship of the great clan Macdonald. The modern Gothic castle is pleasantly situated amongst woods and conifers round the house and garden, in which standard fuchsias attain unusual size, with a background of hills. It was built about 1815, and is not, therefore, "the small house on the shore" in which Johnson and Boswell were entertained so inhospitably in 1773. "Instead of finding the Lord of the Macdonalds surrounded with his clan and a festive entertainment, we found a small company, and cannot boast of our cheer" (BOSWELL). The present house is ornamented with a window of stained glass, representing Somerled, Lord of the Isles, and founder of the family. To the clan Macdonald Napoleon was indebted for one of his best marshals. There is a good road from Armadale to Broadford, 16 m.

The steamer now passes on l. *Sleat Ch.* and the gray and ruined *Castle of Knock,* and then calls at †**Isle Ornsay** (St. Oran's Isle) on the mainland of Skye. [Steamer twice a week from or to Oban.] It takes its name from an island lying across the bay, on which are the ruins of a small chapel, formerly belonging to a nunnery, and a lighthouse. Beyond is *Duisdale,* a handsome modern seat of Miss Mackinnon, with gardens. Opposite this is the opening of Loch Hourn, which separates the district of Knoydart from that of Glenelg.

Loch Hourn ("*Loch of Hell*") is a sea arm extending 11 m. inland, very narrow, and particularly grand in its upper reach. See p. 372. On its N. shore is *Ben Screel* (3196 ft.); on its S. *Ladhar Bheinn* [pron. *Lairven*] ("Hoof Hill"), 3343 ft.

"Examples of savage scenery may be found along the gneissoic shores of Loch Hourn and Loch Nevis. The height and the angular forms of the mountain ridges, the steep and deeply-rifted slopes, and the ruggedness and sterility of the whole landscape, distinguish these two sea-lochs from the rest of the fiords on the W. coast."—Sir A. GEIKIE.

The Sound begins to contract, and the steamer stops rt. at †**Glenelg** ✲, a pleasant neat village grouped around the bay, but one of the most rainy places in all Scotland. [Steamer from and to Oban 4 or 5 times a week.] *Glenelg* (Glen of the Roe), which gives its name to the district, consists mainly of two subordinate glens, Glen More and Glenbeg. At the foot of the former are the ruins of *Barracks* erected in 1745; the latter has some very fine scenery at *Ellanreoch* near the mouth of the river, where the Master of Blantyre has a house pleasantly situated.

[EXCURSIONS:—

(1) A walk of about 3 m. from Glenelg up Glenbeg leads to two ruined *Pictish Towers* at the roadside. In both cases only half of the tower remains, exhibiting an instructive section, to show how it was constructed, about 25 ft. high, and 30 ft. diameter. The whole of this district once belonged to the Macraes.

(2) A track leads to Loch Hourn Head, about 16 m. (p. 372).

(3) A rough driving road leads round the shore to *Corran*✱ (about 11 m.), on the N. shore of Loch Hourn, where a boat may be hired to visit the fine upper reach of that Loch.

(4) A good driving road leads up Glen More and over the *Pass of Mam Rattachan*, 1072 ft., to **Glen Shiel Inn,** 8½ m. (p. 385).

(5) *Ascent of Ben Screel*, 3196 ft.

(6) By *Kyle Rhea Ferry* (2 m. N.) across to Skye (scarcely ½ m.), thence to **Broadford** (11 m.), but by steamer is *very* much finer.]

We now enter the narrow Straits of **Kyle Rhea,** bordered on the Skye side by *Scuir-nan-Coinnich* (2401 ft.), and *Ben-na-Cailliach* (2396 ft.), and on the mainland by the mountains of Glenelg. There is a *ferry* here across the straits (above).

Emerging from Kyle Rhea, the tourist will be puzzled to make out in which direction can be the exit from the landlocked sheet of water now before him. In front, and stretching to the rt. is **Loch Alsh,** which at its eastern extremity is divided into 2 narrow arms, N.E. *Loch Long*, and S.E. *Loch Duich* (Rte. 96). Right opposite the mouth of Kyle Rhea, on the N. shore of Loch Alsh, is

†**Balmacara** ✲ (cf. p. 385), charmingly situated. Rt. is *Balmacara Ho.* (Sir K. J. Matheson, Bt.) and l. a *Monument* on the shore, erected by Sir Roderick Murchison, the geologist, to his ancestor Donald Murchison, the faithful but ill-requited factor of Mackenzie of Kintail, Earl of Seaforth, who, during the troublous times after 1745, collected and transmitted the rents of the confiscated estates to his master in exile.

The steamer now turns sharp to the W. through the straits of *Kyle Akin*, which owe their name to Hakon, King of Norway, who sailed through the strait in 1263 on his way to and from Largs, to

†**Kyle Akin** ✲, the neatest village in Skye.

[From this there is a *ferry* (½ m. across) to the mainland; and a driving road leads in 8 m. to *Broadford*.]

Upon a rock, near the village, are the ruins of *Castle Maoil*, a small keep, said to have been built and furnished with a chain across the strait, by the daughter of a Norwegian king, wife of a Macdonald, and usually called "Saucy Mary," for the purpose of enforcing a toll from every ship that passed.

The steamer, passing the *Lighthouse* at the N. mouth of the Kyle, now comes more into the open, although it hugs the shore pretty closely as it passes to the inner side of the curiously green island of **Pabba**, interesting to the geologist as belonging to the Upper

Lias, and "whose shores would furnish a museum with fossils." We stop at

†**Broadford**✲, for which and for voyage hence to

†**Portree**✲, see Rte. 97.

We now cross the **Minch** to the **Outer Hebrides.**

The mail steamer from Strome Ferry sails daily *direct* to Stornoway in about 7 hours.

The "Clansman" and "Claymore" call at one or more of the following ports on the mainland:—*Gairloch, Poolewe, Aultbea, Ullapool,* and *Lochinver*, before reaching Stornoway.

The **Outer Hebrides,** commonly called "*The Long Island,*" extend from the **Butt of Lewis,** the most northerly extremity of that island to **Barra Head,** a distance of 130 m., and are separated from the mainland by the Minch. They include *Lewis, Harris, N. Uist, Benbecula, S. Uist, Barra,* etc. To the N.W. part of Scotland they form a sort of breakwater. By the tourist these islands are seldom visited, although the accommoda-tion is much improved. There are good hotels at Stornoway, and fair ones at Barvas and Garry-na-hine in Lewis, at Tarbert in Harris, at Lochmaddy in N. Uist, at Loch Boisdale in S. Uist, and at Castlebay in Barra. There are good roads, but the scenery is monotonous, from the comparative absence of bold features, except for the picturesque ranges in Harris and Barra, and the number of little lakes and sea-arms that intersect the country at every turn. To the geologist the islands are interest-ing as being entirely composed of archæan gneiss, the oldest forma-mation known. The archæologist will find special interest in the *Stones of Callernish* and the *Ch. of Rowardill.*

Lewis (called *The Lews*), the N. part of the principal island, belongs to the county of Ross, and the S. por-tion, which is called Harris, to that of Inverness. The climate is mild but humid; annual rainfall 30 inches; average temperature 40° to 46° 5″, but liable to violent storms. The surface is flat, and is remarkable for the extraordinary large proportion of water to land. The soil is extremely poor, and, though great efforts were made by the late proprietor, Sir James Matheson, to improve its powers of production, they have as yet been attended with but little success. The peat is so soft and spongy that it is only by continual repair that the drains can be kept from closing up. The division between Harris and Lewis is partly arbitrary and partly decided by the approach of two fiords—*Loch Seaforth* and *Loch Resort.* The W. coast-line from the latter to *Gallon Head* consists of groups of mountains of considerable height, and frequently approaching the sea in rugged precipices. To the N.E. of Gallon Head are a number of winding fiords, all form-ing part of the large bay of **Loch Roag.**

"The loch is hollowed into bays, and interrupted by passages of such variety and intricacy that it requires no ordinary de-gree of attention and readiness to effect its circumnavigation. With the chart it is sufficiently difficult, without that it would be almost impracticable. The entrance by *Loch Roag* in particular is so obscure that a boat may pass within a few hundred yds. of the entrance without perceiving it. The cliffs which bound most of the islands and shores are rugged, without beauty, and with little elevation. One or two detached rocks may, perhaps, be exempt from this general remark, and of these, Gariveilan, placed at the mouth of the loch, is the most interesting, displaying a detached arch of great height, with considerable simplicity and grandeur of effect."—MACCULLOCH'S "Western Islands."

The cattle on *Great Bernera Is-land* in Loch Roag pass to the main island by swimming across the sea straits at certain seasons in search of pasture.

In the reign of James VI. an extra-ordinary project was started by some Fife lairds to colonise Lewis, as we in our time have colonised Nova Scotia and New Zealand. It proved eminently unsuccessful.

The only town in Lewis is

†**STORNOWAY** ✲, on the E. coast, originally founded by James VI. Separated from it by a narrow channel of the bay is *Stornoway Castle*, the seat of Lady Matheson, widow of Sir James Matheson, who, in 1844, purchased the Lewis from Mackenzie of Seaforth for £190,000. Here he used to reside during a portion of every year, managing and improving this domain of 406,090 acres, and laying out, first and last, on education and other works, a sum of £200,000. Stornoway Castle is a large turreted building in the Tudor style, principally of granite, with extensive conservatories. Great skill and much money have been expended on the garden, which, by artificial soil, glass, and other contrivances, is as productive as any in the S. of England. The grounds, which are liberally shown to the public, have been planted with suitable trees, but they have a hard struggle to grow.

Stornoway is situated at the neck of the Eye Peninsula, which projects far out into the Minch, and forms a commodious and well-sheltered harbour. The town is a cheerful small town of slate-roofed white-washed houses, well supplied with water and gas. There are a commodious *Pier*, 3 *Banks*, several *Presbyterian Churches*, and an *Episcopal Chapel*. A *Lighthouse* marks the entrance to the harbour, which, in the autumn, is thronged with herring boats from all quarters; there is a patent slip. In 1893 the herring fleet numbered 721, and 20,726 crans of herrings were cured here, but in 1891, with only 652 boats, 95,297 crans were landed and cured. There is a *Court-House* and *Prison*, and a resident *Sheriff-Substitute*. Mr. Black's novels, especially "A Princess of Thule," have served to cast a halo of romance over this somewhat desolate region.

Steamers.—In addition to those mentioned in this Route, there is regular communication with Aberdeen, Dundee, and Leith, *via* Stromness in Orkney, and with Liverpool.

The **Standing Stones of Callernish,** next to Stennis in Orkney the most remarkable relic of the kind in Scotland, form the principal object of interest to antiquaries. They are situated near the head of **Loch Roag** (above) on the W. side of the island, 16 m. from Stornoway by a good road. 2 m. before reaching them is *Garry-na-hine* ✲.

These stones, planted on a high table-land above the sea, are arranged in the plan of a cross, with a circle in the centre, 42 ft. in diameter, and a tall stone in the centre, 18 ft. high. The circle consists of 13 stones from 8 ft. to 13 ft. in height, great boulders of gneiss, which have been moved to the top of the eminence. The N. extremity of the cross is an avenue of 19 stones, the highest of which is 12 ft. Excavations were made in the peat of 6 ft. deep, and a stone chamber was discovered in the centre of the circle—probably the grave of the individual in whose honour the whole was erected.—*Proc. Scot. Ant. Soc.*, vol. iii.

There are also, ½ m. distant, 2 more circles, one within the other, and scattered about the island there are a great number of single stones or pairs, probably erected over the graves of Celtic or Norse warriors. Cairns, too, are frequently met with, some of which have been opened and found to contain bones.

Numerous specimens of the old *Dunes* or *Burghs* occur in Lewis. That of *Bragair*, 5 m. W. of **Barvas** ✲, which is 13 m. N. of Stornoway, constructed of unhewn stone, is 3 stories high, and tapers towards the summit. It has a double wall, bound by large flags, which encloses a winding staircase round the building. A similar fort at *Carloway*, about 7 m. S. of Bragair and 7 m. N. of Callernish, is still more perfect. There are also ruins of very early Christian churches, hermits' cells, and religious houses.

The extreme north point of the island, the **Butt of Lewis,** abt. 23 m. N. of Stornoway (Road by Barvas abt. 30 m.), is a wild spot with precipitous cliffs surmounted by a *Lighthouse*, and surrounded by detached rocks and pinnacles worn by the sea. A natural arch above the sea is said to have been made by the Devil, to attach a chain by which he meant to drag Lewis out to sea !

The lower or S. half of the island is called

Harris, which consists almost entirely of high sterile hills covered with stones, with a slight sprinkling of stunted heather. The N.W. part rises into a scattered group of grandly peaked mts., attaining a height of 2229 ft., called the (*Deer*) *Forest of Harris*, striking for weirdness and sublimity.

The principal village is †**Tarbert**✲, 32 m. by road S.W. of Stornoway, situated, as its name implies (see p. 154), on a narrow isthmus between two sea lochs of the same name, which divide N. Harris, belonging to Lady Scott, from S. Harris, belonging to the Earl of Dunmore.

21 m. farther is †**Obbe**✲, and 3 m. beyond that, keeping along the base of *Roneval* (1506 ft.), is †**Rodel,** at the S. end of the island.

[Steamer 3 times a week from Tarbert and Rodel to Dunvegan (Skye); 3 times a week to Portree and once a week from Tarbert and Obbe to Glasgow.]

At Rodel there is a house formerly inhabited by Macleod of Harris, and ½ m. from a glen with a thriving plantation of trees.

"Above the house are the ruins of the ancient *Church of Rowardill*, unfortunately burnt down some years ago by accident. It is in the form of a cross, with a rude tower at the E. end. Upon this are certain pieces of sculpture of a kind, the last which one would have expected to find on a building dedicated to religious purposes."—Sir W. SCOTT's *Diary*.

"The sculptures present some peculiarities which are well worthy the notice of an antiquary, and, from their analogy to certain allusions in oriental worship, are objects of much curiosity."—MACCULLOCH.

Inside are two monuments of the Macleods of Dunvegan, described by Sir Walter Scott, one of them an effigy in armour, 1428. Macculloch describes the extreme violence of the wind as instanced around the mountain of Roneval, where the ground has been ploughed up by its action as though in great dykes.

Southwards, and separated from Harris by the *Sound of Harris*, is **North Uist**, the property of Sir John Orde, Bt., succeeded by **Benbecula, South Uist**, and **Barra** (all belonging to Sir Reginald and Lady Cathcart). The three first named are really only separated from each other at flood-water. In the ebb, traffic can be carried on across the sounds which intervene.

In the N. E. of **North Uist** is †**Lochmaddy**✲, a settlement rather than a village, at the head of a loch of that name, consisting of the *Pier House*, a *Hotel*, the *Post Office*, the *County Buildings*, the *House* of the resident *Sheriff-Substitute*, the *Poor-House*, a *Bank*, a *Schoolhouse*, the *Factor's House*, and the *General Merchant's !*

[*Steamer* daily to and from Oban and to and from Dunvegan (Skye); 3 times a week to Portree; once a week to Glasgow.]

The entrance to Loch Maddy, which is a good harbour, is flanked by the projecting basalt islet crags of the Big and Little Maddy ("Madadh," a dog). This island is such an intricate network of lochs, rivers, and bogs as to be almost impassable even in summer. A road runs round it keeping near the coast.

Benbecula is reached by boat from the S. point of N. Uist, or by the "*North Ford*" at low tide. Here Prince Charlie met Flora Macdonald. In the N. is *Gramisdale*✲ ; in the S. *Greagorry*✲, from which the "*South Ford*" leads to

S. Uist, more mountainous than the two foregoing islands. From

†**Loch Boisdale** ✲ in the S.E. there is a *Steamer* 3 times a week to and from Oban; also twice a week to and from Glasgow. On the E. coast is a cave in which Prince Charlie was sheltered for a month after Culloden by Clanranald.

†**Barra,** which supplies the earliest herrings in Great Britain, and those first sent abroad, brings up the rear. It was once the property of the Macneils, whose old *Castle* of *Kisamul* still stands on an isolated rock in †**Castle Bay** ✲, ½ m. from the shore. [Steamer 3 times a week to and from Oban.] It is certainly the grandest and most picturesque ruin in the West Islands. The walls are about 60 ft. high, and enclose an irregular area, within which are a strong square keep and other buildings.

South of Barra is a group of smaller islands, one of which is **Mingulay,** a strange rocky island, with cliffs 700-900 ft. high. The inhabitants climb the rocks like monkeys after birds and eggs. The rocks are fissured by whin dykes, which the sea has in part washed out, so that boats pass between their vertical walls. In one instance a fragment of a dyke left *in situ* forms a na ıral bridge 550 ft. above the water.

Beyond Mingulay is **Berneray,** upon whose S. point of **Barra Head,** 580 ft., is a *Lighthouse.*

The westernmost of the Scottish islands is **St. Kilda,**[1] 40 m. W. of North Uist, and the property from time immemorial of Macleod of Macleod—sold in 1779 but re-purchased 1871. It is 3¼ m. long by 1¼ m. broad, surrounded on all sides with magnificent cliffs, swarming with sea-fowl. It is dangerous to approach save in moderate weather, and has no regular means of communication with the mainland. The "Hebridean" from Glasgow makes occasional voyages there in summer. The settlement, numbering abt. 80 persons, is lodged in abt. 20 cottages with zinc roofs, which replace the ancient low hovels where the people sat and slept alongside of the accumulated offal of birds and fish, which in summer they spread over their fields. They have a *Free Ch.* and a *School,* and are now better housed than the average of Highland peasants, but the general health and vitality of infants has hardly advanced. The inhabitants live almost entirely upon fish and sea-fowl, which they catch for exportation of the oil and feathers. A breed of small dun sheep is peculiar to the island. The flock amounts to 300.

Habit and hardships have given these poor people a nerve which appears to strangers unaccountable, and they are devotedly attached to their dreary home. Bird-catching is a dangerous occupation, but is followed with much hardihood by men who have been fowlers from time immemorial. A good rope is one of the most valuable possessions of a St. Kildan, and is even regarded is an heirloom. They used to be made of horse-hair wrapped in plaits of salted cow-hide, now they are usually made of manilla hemp, and are protected by a sheath, to run in, made of leather, raw cow-hide, or sheepskin.

The flocks of sea-birds which breed amongst the cliffs are practically inexhaustible; the most characteristic species is the *Fulmar petrel,* somewhat resembling a sea-gull. When attacked it ejects a bad-smelling oil from its nostrils at the face of its assailant, who thrusts the head into the dried stomach of a solan goose, which serves as a bag to contain the oil.

The only point in the island accessible by boat is a little bay on the E. side. At times it is not possible to land for a week together, and strangers have by a sudden shift of the wind been detained several days, the vessel which brought them having drifted to a distance. In spite of certain primitive habits and customs, as the use to this day of spindle and distaff to spin the wool with which they make their own clothes, and of the quern to grind grain, they have acquired from the sight of casual visitors an inveterate habit of begging. Warm clothing such as mittens, also needles, scissors, and knives, are very acceptable, and should be sent to the minister for distribution.

In 1724 the pop. was reduced by small-pox to 4 adults and 26 children.

In 1732 a judge of the Court of Session, Erskine, Lord Grange, found it expedient to get rid of his wife. She was carried away from Edinburgh by some followers of Lord Lovat, conveyed to St. Kilda, and put under the care of the chief of Macleod. She died, May 1745, and, on her death, was buried at Trumpan, in Skye.

---

1 For a good account of the island, see G. Seton's "St. Kilda Past and Present" (1878), and R. Connell's "St. Kilda and the St. Kildans" (1887).

SECTION VIII.

North of Scotland—Black Isle—Cromarty—Sutherland—Loch Inver—Caithness—John o' Groat's—Cape Wrath.

§ 1. General Information.

This section, after taking the traveller across the "Black Isle" to Cromarty, situated in an interesting position at the narrow entrance of the Cromarty Firth, conducts him through the wild and varied scenery of the two most northern counties of Scotland, Sutherland and Caithness, which possess peculiar attractions for the angler and the geologist.

The Highland Rly. passes the imposing and well-situated Dunrobin Castle, principal seat of the Duke of Sutherland, to Wick, an important centre of the herring fishery, and to Thurso, both towns within easy distance of much striking cliff scenery, and not very far from John o' Groat's House, the extreme N.E. corner of Scotland. In order to visit the most characteristic scenery of Sutherlandshire, however, it is necessary to drive long distances, but coaches run along the leading routes. The Inns (with fishings attached), chiefly frequented by anglers, are small but comfortable, but there are large hotels at Lochinver, a most attractive halting-place.

Sutherland received its seemingly inappropriate name from the Norwegians, who lived much farther N. in Orkney and Shetland. It has an area of 2126 sq. m., of which only 2.9 per cent is under cultivation, notwithstanding the liberal expenditure on reclamation of the Dukes of Sutherland. On three sides it touches the sea; the interior is an elevated plateau, in many parts covered with heather, and including vast tracts of peat intersected by straths of some fertility, and containing numerous lochs, weird and desolate, and solitary mountain peaks. The mountain scenery to the W. in Assynt is unique in the British Isles. Great part of the county is entirely uninhabited.

The principal landowner is the Duke of Sutherland. The original possessions of the Sutherland family form only a small portion of their now vast domain. The district of *Assynt*, long possessed by a branch of the Macleods of Lewis, was acquired by the Earl of Sutherland, towards the middle of the 18th cent., from the Mackenzies who had dispossessed the Macleods. The *Reay Country*, some 80 m. in length and 18 m. in breadth, extending from the border of Caithness to Kyle Sku, which divides it from Assynt, and separated from Sutherland proper by Ben Griam, Ben Clibreck, and Ben Hee, was the original home of the great Clan Mackay, who are known to have been flourishing there in the time of William the Lion. Various portions of it fell into the hands of the Sutherland family at different dates, but the great bulk was purchased only in the early part of the 19th cent. by the Marquis of Stafford, who married the daughter and heiress of William, seventeenth Earl of Sutherland, and who added to the family possessions some other small estates.

Caithness also consists of an elevated table-land—a large part of it barren heath although much has been reclaimed by the farmer. Owing, however, to its exposure to sea blasts and brine it is almost quite destitute of trees, except in the chinks of a few valleys, such as Berriedale, Castletown, etc. Only towards the S. is it varied by the mountain groups of *Morven* and *Scaraben*, visible far and wide. On the other hand its cliff scenery, as already stated, is very fine, and probably unrivalled on the mainland of Scotland.

§ 2. PRINCIPAL CENTRES.

POINTS OF INTEREST.

1. **Cromarty.** The Sutors. Black Isle. Alt Graat (from Novar).
2. **Dornoch.** Cathedral. Golfing Links.
3. **Golspie.** Dunrobin Castle. Strath Brora.
4. **Inchnadamph.** Loch Assynt. Mts. of Assynt.
5. **Lochinver.** Fine surroundings. Drive to Ullapool (cf. Rte. 94).
6. **Scourie.** Coast scenery. Eas-coul-aulin Waterfall. Mts. of N.W. of Sutherland.
7. **Altnaharra.** Strathnaver. Dun Dornadilla.
8. **Wick.** Cliff scenery. Herring curing.
9. **John o' Groat's.** Duncansbay Head.
10. **Thurso.** Holburn Head. Dunnet Head.
11. **Tongue.** Kyle of Tongue. Ben Loyal.
12. **Durness.** Cave of Smoo. Cape Wrath.

ROUTES.

ROUTE 99.

Inverness across the Black Isle to Cromarty.

The **"Black Isle,"** so called from snow not lying there in winter, and its being black, while the surrounding country is white, is the broad promontory between Moray and Beauly Firths to the S., and Cromarty Firth to the N. Its central ridge is *Ardmanach*, the "Monks' Height," from its religious establishments. Mary Queen of Scots on her marriage with Darnley created him Duke of Albany, Earl of Ross, and Lord of Ardmanach. At the N.E. extremity of the "Isle" stands Cromarty.

Cromarty is most quickly reached by taking train to Invergordon (p. 404), and thence by steam launch. It may also be reached by taking train to *Fortrose* (p. 377), and mail gig ($9\frac{1}{2}$ m.); or by steamer (once a week) from Inverness.

For **INVERNESS** ✱ see p. 375.

Cross *Kessock Ferry*, 1 m. N.W. of Inverness, to *North Kessock Inn*, across the Beauly Firth ($\frac{1}{2}$ m.), where carriages may be hired. Behind is a conical hill, wooded to the top, with the remains of a vitrified fort.

[Road l. up the Firth passes at 5 m. the old tower of *Redcastle* (J. E. B. Baillie, Esq.), once the principal house of the promontory, which, on the forfeiture of the earldom of Ross, became a royal castle, and then the property of the Mackenzies; it then reaches

8 m. *Muir of Ord Stat.* (p. 377).]

By the road N. through the Black Isle we reach in 4 m. *Munlochy Village* (whence a road runs N. to Invergordon ferry) and turn rt.

At 7 m. *Rosehaugh Ho.*, the seat of J. D. Fletcher, Esq., lies $\frac{1}{2}$ m. l. It was formerly the property of Sir George Mackenzie, Lord Adv. to Charles II., called from his severity to the Covenanters "Bluidy Mackenzie."

8 m. **Avoch** (pron. *Auch*) **Village** ✱ is occupied, it is said, by the descendants of a Danish colony, who have preserved many Norse words and expressions in their Saxon tongue. $\frac{1}{2}$ m. N. *Avoch Ho.* (J. D. Fletcher, Esq.).

10 m. **Fortrose** ✱, a somewhat lifeless seaport, although a royal and parl. burgh, was formerly the seat of the Bishops of Ross, whose palace has utterly disappeared.

[*Fortrose* is most conveniently reached by train from *Muir of Ord;* also by ferry ($1\frac{1}{2}$ m. E., and 1 m. across) from *Fort-George* (p. 233); or by *Steamer from Inverness*, 6 days a week in summer, 3 in winter.]

The lane on the rt., at the broken shaft of the old *Cross*, leads to the **Cathedral**, standing in a green close.

It is a mere fragment of a large cross ch., and consists of the S. aisles of nave and choir of elegant 2nd middle-pointed, in red sandstone, the sharp mouldings testifying, as usual, to the skill of Scottish masons. It was only completed in 1485, by Abbot Fraser, who came from Melrose, and the ch. retains portions of his work in the perp. style of that southern abbey. The ruin of the ch. is attributed to Cromwell, who used its stones to build the fort at Inverness. Against the wall of the chancel is the canopied tomb, much mutilated, of a Countess of Ross, said to be founder of the ch., 1330; and there is a later and poorer monument of a bishop. One arched compartment under the tower is walled off as the burial-place of the Mackenzies of Seaforth. A curious old bell, formerly rung at funerals, is kept here.

Near the N.E. corner is the *Chapter-house*, a detached building of 2 stories; the upper one is used as a school, and the lower—a crypt, in which there are some sedilia—as a granary or coal hole.

11 m. **Rosemarkie,** included in the burgh of Fortrose, is much

frequented for sea-bathing. In the churchyard of the Parish Church there is an old stone *Cross* of very considerable interest to antiquarians. "The high boulder-clay cliffs at Rosemarkie are conspicuous from almost all parts of the Moray Firth" (Sir A. GEIKIE).

The road to Cromarty is very uninteresting, but the walk along the edge of the cliffs is a favourite resort of geologists, and has been much illustrated by the writings of Hugh Miller. If the weather be fine, it is a good plan to hire a boat and sail to Cromarty, passing the *Caves* noticed by him.

At 12½ m. the road forks; that running N.W. leads in 5½ m. to Invergordon Ferry, passing rt. *Poyntzfield* (G. M. G. Munro, Esq.), *Braelangwell House* (Major Lyon Mackenzie), and l. *Newhall Ho.* (C. F. H. Shaw Mackenzie, Esq.).

We keep N.E. to

19½ m. **Cromarty** ✲ (from *Crombaigh*, "Bend of the bay"), which was in former days a place of some importance, but has been reduced to its present insignificance principally by the failure of its herring-fishery. Cromarty Bay, at the N.E. end of Cromarty Firth which is 18 m. long, is well known as one of the safest anchorage grounds in the north. This is due to the entrance to the firth being protected by two precipitous headlands called **"The Sutors,"** with a channel between, 170 ft. deep, and less than 1 m. wide.

"One who approaches from the E. is at once struck with the narrow chasm-like entrance of the Cromarty Firth, cut through a long lofty range of red sandstone precipices. It is wholly unlike the mouth of any other firth in the country, for it is not the seaward expansion of a land valley, but seems in some abnormal fashion to have been broken through a high barrier of hard rock; and, in actual fact, it is an abnormal opening, and not the original mouth of the firth."—Sir A. GEIKIE's "Scenery," p. 187.

Cromarty House (Capt. Ross) stands upon the site of the old castle of the Earls of Ross. Sir Thomas Urquhart, the translator of "Rabelais," was born here. On a hill above the town rises a pillar *Statue* of red sandstone to the memory of Hugh Miller (1802-56), born in a humble cottage close to the churchyard, which contains several tombstones cut by him while a mason. *Tarradale*, at the other extremity of the Black Isle, was the paternal estate of Sir Roderick Murchison the geologist.

[There is a ferry to the N. From the other side it is 2 m. to *Nigg* Ch. (p. 404), 5 m. to *Nigg Stat.*, and 9 m. to **Tain.**]

ROUTE 100.

Inverness to Wick and Thurso by Bonar Bridge, Lairg, and Helmsdale. High. Rly.

2 or 3 trains daily in 6-9½ hrs. to and from *Wick*, 161 m. (*Thurso* is 148 m.).

6 or 7 trains daily in 1½-2¾ hrs. to and from *Tain*, 44 m.

This line leads to within 20 m. of *John o' Groat's House.* The portion of the line traversing the east of Ross-shire passes through one of the most fertile and best-farmed districts in the Highlands, while in Caithness it traverses some of the most dreary country in Scotland.

See Rte. 91 for the line from **Inverness** to 18½ m. **Dingwall** ✲.

The railway from Dingwall keeps N.E. close to the shore of the Cromarty Firth, having on l. the hill and woods of *Tulloch Castle.*

23 m. **Fowlis Stat.**; l. is *Fowlis Castle*, the seat of Sir Hector Munro, Bt. The clan of that name has been seated in this country for many centuries.

At 24½ m. l. is the village of *Evanton.* On the rt. is *Balconie House*, built on the site of an old fortress of the Earls of Ross.

25 m. **Novar Stat.** 1½ m. from the stat. is the extraordinary ravine

of the **Alt Graat** ("Ugly Burn"), which flows out of *Loch Glass* (4 m. long) on the northern flanks of Ben Wyvis. Its deep and tortuous channel, nearly 2 m. long, is in one place only 17 feet wide, between Old Red Conglomerate cliffs, 110 ft. high.

"This remarkable gorge is fully 5 times deeper than it is broad—a ratio very unusual among the river ravines of this country."—Sir A. GEIKIE's "Scenery of Scotland," p. 174.

"The precipices are green, with some moss or byssus, that, like the miner, chooses a subterranean habitat—for here the rays of the sun never fall; the trees, fast anchored in the rock, shoot out their branches across the opening, to form a thick tangled roof at the height of 150 ft. overhead—while from the recesses within, where the eyes fail to penetrate, there issues a combination of the strangest and wildest sounds ever yet produced by water—there is the deafening rush of the torrent blent as if with the clang of hammers, the roar of vast bellows, and the confused gabble of 1000 voices."—HUGH MILLER.

Then succeed the beautiful beech and fir woods which surround *Novar Ho.* (R. C. Munro Ferguson, Esq., M.P.), at the back of which is the *Hill of Fyrish* (1483 ft.).

28½ m. **Alness Stat.**, a village of considerable size, at the mouth of the valley. 5 m. up the Alness river is *Ardross*, a grand modern castle, the seat of Sir K. J. Matheson, Bt., built by his father. The rly. crosses the Alness by a singular *Viaduct* consisting of a skew bridge built on a curve, to

31½ m. **Invergordon Stat.** ✲, a flourishing little port with a good harbour, situated on the W. side of *Cromarty Bay* (cf. p. 402).

[*Ferry* across the Cromarty Firth to the "**Black Isle,**" Rte. 99.]

Invergordon Castle, a short distance to the W., is the property of Capt. Macleod of Cadboll: it was burnt down in 1804. The views in the neighbourhood are varied and pretty, embracing seaward the whole of Cromarty Firth and the Black Isle, while Ben Wyvis is a conspicuous and magnificent inland feature.

34¾ m. **Delny Stat.** 2 m. rt. on Nigg Bay is *Tarbat House*, a seat of the late Earl of Cromartie, Viscount Tarbat, a title restored in 1861 (cf. p. 381). It was built by Lord M'Leod on the site of one of the old castles of the Mackenzies, Earls of Cromartie, forfeited after the rebellion of 1745, but subsequently restored. It is surrounded by some venerable yews and elms, and old gardens.

36¾ m. **Kildary Stat.** On rt. is *Shandwick Ho.*, the seat of the ancient family of the Rosses of Shandwick; on l. is *Balnagown House* (Sir Charles Ross, Bt.), a very handsome mansion consisting of an old tower with a pointed roof, numerous turrets—one of the grandest specimens of the Scottish architecture of the 16th cent. It has beautiful gardens and grounds, communicating with a picturesque rocky glen.

39¼ m. **Nigg Stat.** 3 m. S.E. is the village of *Nigg*.

Attached to the S.E. corner of the Parish Ch. is a very curious *Sculptured Stone* It has been broken, but is riveted together again. Upon the top are 2 figures in an attitude of supplication, and below their outstretched hands are 2 dogs, while between the two descends the Holy Dove, with the wafer in its mouth. Underneath is a cross composed of rectangular figures.

40¾ m. **Fearn Stat.**, l. is *Calrossie House*. The high farming of this district is celebrated.

[The ecclesiologist should visit the old **Abbey Ch. of Fearn.**

This *Abbey* was originally founded at Edderton, 12 m. to the N.W., but was subsequently placed here, on account of the fertility of the soil. It was built by Farquhar, 1st Earl of Ross, about the year 1230, and inhabited by Augustinian monks. Patrick Hamilton, the earliest martyr of the Scottish Reformation, who was burnt at St. Andrews in 1528, was Abbot of Fearn, and at his death the abbey was annexed to the bishopric of Ross. The chapel was used for Divine worship till the year 1742, when the roof fell in on a Sunday and killed 44 persons. The ch.

was subsequently repaired, without the slightest regard to architectural propriety.

The style is mixed, the doors being round and the windows pointed. The entrance was on the N. side by a Dec. door. Both on the N. and S. sides are small chapels, which at first sight bear the appearance of transepts. The chapel was roofed with 5 arches or ribs, 2 of which are still standing. In the S. chapel, now the Shandwick burial-ground, is a recumbent figure, under a handsomely-carved canopy, long supposed to be that of an abbot, but ascertained to represent a lady of the clan Mackenzie, with a veil over her face. One-half of the chancel is set apart as the burial-place of the Ross family.

3 m. E. on the coast is the *Cross* at **Shandwick**, even more handsome and curious than that at Nigg (p. 404). The stone is about 9 ft. high, and has on it a large cross formed of a number of bosses, which, being covered with lichen, look like so many brass-headed nails. Below the horizontal shaft are 2 representations of St. Andrew's martyrdom, and below that again an elephant and a dog. These stones, which with a few exceptions are peculiar to the N.E. counties of Scotland, are sepulchral monuments, as has been proved by excavating near them.

N. of Shandwick are *Cadboll* (Capt. R. W. Macleod) and *Geanies Ho.* (W. H. E. Murray, Esq.), while at the N. end of the peninsula is **Tarbat Ness**, with a *Lighthouse* (10 m. from Fearn Stat.). In the ch.-yd. of *Tarbat Ch.* are some curious stones, both plain and sculptured, and in the neighbourhood a fragment of the old castle of *Balone*, an outpost of the Earls of Ross, allowed to fall into decay after the strength and aggressive power of Denmark and its settlements had ceased to be formidable.]

The rly. now turns N.W. and descends slightly to *Dornoch Firth.*

44¼ m. **Tain Stat.** ✲, an antique town of gradually decreasing importance. Its name is evidently a corruption of "Thing," the Norse for "Court," the town having been the capital of the district lying between the Firths of Dornoch and Cromarty. It was made a royal burgh by Malcolm Canmore, and is still a picturesque old-fashioned place, which will well repay a halt. In the centre of it stands the original *Tower* of the Sheriff's Court, recased, but retaining its quaint old shape and its conical spire, with small pointed turrets at each angle.

Below the town, that is, between it and the Dornoch Firth, is a large flat, partly covered by the drifting sand. Here stands an old rough *Chapel* in ruins, dedicated in the early part of the 13th cent. to St. Duthus, a Bishop of Ross. Probably there was some restoration at that time, for it will be seen that the E. end is of later date than the rest. The masonry of the body of the ch. is excessively rude, and must be as old as the 11th cent. To this ch. the queen and daughter of Robert Bruce fled from *Kildrummie Castle*, and from it they were taken by the Earl of Ross and given up to Edward I. In 1429 the church was burnt by the M'Neills during the prosecution of a feud with Mowat of Freswick, who with some followers had taken refuge here, and it was never rebuilt. King James V. made a pilgrimage to it in 1527, at the instigation of Cardinal Beaton, who wished to get him out of the way during the martyrdom of Patrick Hamilton.

In 1471 the *Church* of St. Duthus (now restored but not used for service) was founded in the centre of the town. It is a fine specimen of the Dec. style, with an E. window of 5 lights, surmounted by a six-foiled circle supported by 2 trefoils. At the W. end a heavy porch has been erected in modern times, above which is the figure of a bishop, probably St. Duthus himself. Beyond this ch. stands the *Academy*, a school of some reputation. On the S. side of the town is the present *Parish Ch.* which many people mistake for a jail. It is a square battlemented building, with formidable towers in front. N. across the firth may be seen the *Cathedral of Dornoch* (p. 411).

Mound Stat. (p. 406) is only 10 m. N. of Tain, but the train runs 36 m. before reaching it, striking N.W. up Dornoch Firth—crossing the *Carron*, the *Oykell*, and the *Shin*—to Lairg. The entrance to the mouth of the firth is much impeded by a long sandbank called the *Gizzing* or *Geysen Briggs* — a term evidently of Norse origin—and in stormy weather the breaking of the waves upon it may be heard at a considerable distance.

At 46½ m. *Tarlogie Ho.* is l.; 1½ m. rt. is *Meikle Ferry* (¾ m.) for **Dornoch** (p. 411), and across the firth *Skibo Cas.* (E. C. Sutherland, Esq.).

49¾ m. **Edderton Stat.** Near the *Church*, built 1793, are 2 sculptured Scandinavian monuments. Passing under (l.) *Struie Hill*, 1082 ft., we reach

57¾ m. **Bonar Bridge Stat.** ✲, situated on the borders of Ross and Sutherland, and named from a bridge which the rly. leaves on the rt. and which spans the Kyle river between Dornoch Firth and its inner reach the "*Kyle of Sutherland.*" It was built by Telford in 1812 at a cost of £14,000, and after withstanding many floods was washed away in autumn 1892. It was rebuilt in 1893, Messrs. Crouch and Hogg, Engineers, Sir Wm. Arrol, Contractor.

[A road leads across the bridge (1) N.E. *via* Loch Buie, Strath Carnach, and Mound Stat. (15 m.) to *Golspie*, 19 m.
(2) E. to *Dornoch*, 14½ m., cf. Rte. 101.]

60¾ m. **Culrain Stat.** ½ m. N. Montrose made his final stand on behalf of Charles I., 1650. He was defeated and driven a fugitive into the wilds of Assynt where he was soon captured (p. 413). The rly. crosses the *Oykell* above the *Kyle of Sutherland* on a lattice girder bridge to

61¼ m. **Invershin Stat.** ✲ in Sutherlandshire. Keeping the l. bank of the Shin, a good and early salmon river, we pass l. *Achany Ho.*, belonging to Lady Matheson of Lews (Stornoway), who owns much land hereabout, and reach

66¾ m. **Lairg Stat.**, 2 m. S. of *Lairg Village* ✲, situated near the foot of **Loch Shin**, a tame narrow loch, 16½ m. long, abounding in fish. The late Duke of Sutherland carried out extensive and enterprising agricultural operations along this loch.

[The position of Lairg at the meeting of 5 roads makes it a place of importance in Sutherland communications.
(1) S. to Inverness (Rte. 100).
(2) W. to Ullapool, 46½ m., and Lochinver, 45½ m. (Rte. 102).
(3) N.W. to Scourie, 44 m., and Durness, 56 m. (Rte. 103).
(4) N. to Tongue, 36½ m. (Rte. 104).
(5) E. to Golspie, etc. (below).]

From Lairg the rly. turns sharp to the E., and surmounting a steep rise attains the headwaters of *Strath Fleet*, which, wild and moory at first, improves in appearance and value as we approach the coast. The farm-houses are comfortable and substantial buildings and the land, not long since uncultivated moor, is now fertile in corn crops, the result of the most improved scientific husbandry.

76¾ m. **Rogart Stat.** From this a road runs northward to *Strath Brora* (p. 408).

80¾ m. **The Mound Stat.** The *Mound of Fleet* (rt.) is an artificial embankment 1000 yards long, raised in 1815, at the cost of £9600, across *Loch Fleet*, an arm of the sea. It was the means of recovering from the sea a fine tract of alluvial land.

[*Coach* to Dornoch twice daily., 7 m., p. 411. Road S.W. to Bonar Bridge Stat., 15 m.]

To the l. is a line of hills, including *Ben Lundie* (1462 ft.), and *Ben-na-Braghie* (1256 ft.), upon which is a colossal statue, by Chantrey, of the 1st Duke of Sutherland.

84¼ m. **Golspie Stat.** ✲

Golspie consists of one long and cheerful street, at the N. end of which is the *Hotel.* A pleasant walk of about a mile up the pretty glen at the back of the hotel, through the beautiful park, leads to **Dunrobin Castle** (Duke of Sutherland), the most magnificent residence N. of Inverness.[1] Its oldest part was built by Robert, 2nd Earl of Sutherland, abt. 1275, and called

[1] Admission is given to the house when the family are not there, and to the beautiful gardens, even when they are resident, at certain fixed hours.

after him Dun Robin. It stands on a natural terrace close to the sea, which here permits free growth of trees and foliage nearly to its margin, and consists of a rather plain square old castle, with bartizan turrets at the angles, to which were added in 1856 (archt., Wm. Leslie) a new wing and front, with towers and turrets and extinguisher roofs, producing on the whole a picturesque effect, and preserving the national character of a Scottish chieftain's castellated mansion. Through the entrance-hall a noble staircase is reached, lined with white marbles, hung with banners, etc.

On the side next the sea are the Queen's Apartments, prepared for her from the first, but which she was prevented occupying until 1872.

There are some curious portraits of the Sutherland family; among them one of Lady Jean Gordon, wife of James, Earl of Bothwell, but divorced by him to enable him to marry Mary Queen of Scots. She afterwards married the 11th Earl of Sutherland.

The Earldom dates from about 1228, when Caithness and Sutherland were wrested from the Norwegian Jarls by Alexander II. The 9th Earl left an only daughter and heiress, who married Adam Gordon, 2nd son of George, 2nd Earl of Huntly; again William, the 17th Earl, left an only daughter and heiress, who married the 2nd Marquis of Stafford, created Duke of Sutherland, 1833, the great-grandfather of the present Duke (see pp. 400, 401).

Within the grounds is a *Museum* built by the late Duke to contain a very interesting collection of local antiquities, and objects found in Picts' houses, etc. Obs. several querns or hand corn-mills, stone implements, silver brooch, and other relics, partly the result of the many important excavations and interesting discoveries made in E. Sutherland by the Rev. J. M. Joass, LL.D., of Golspie.

The *Burn of Golspie* is very picturesque, with many pretty walks made through the glen to the waterfall.

On the Bridge over the little stream at the end of the town of Golspie is a Gaelic inscription concerning the exploits of "Morphear Chatt," which is the name borne by the head of the Sutherlands amongst the Gaelic population of these parts. Some say that the name "Chatt" is derived from the "Catti," a Teutonic tribe that settled in these parts, and left their name in "Caithness."[1] The crest of the family is a wild cat.

The rly. between Golspie and Helmsdale—constructed chiefly by the late Duke of Sutherland, 1870-1871—keeps mainly along the seashore. Leaving Golspie it crosses the burn on a high bridge, and traverses the domain of Dunrobin Castle, of which it commands fine views (rt.).

86 m. **Dunrobin Private Stat.** at the crossing of the Grand Avenue and the Old North Road. On l. beside the stat. is a bronze statue of the 2nd Duke of Sutherland. At the spot where the line emerges on the sea rt. is what looks like a deserted lime-kiln: it is a ruined *Pict's Castle*, the contents of which are partly in the Dunrobin Museum and partly in the Museum of Antiquities, Edinburgh.

[1] It is suggested, however, that the first syllable of Caithness is a relic of a Euskarian or pre-Celtic occupation, the word Ketje in Lapp meaning end or extremity. The population of the N.E. of Caithness are of Scandinavian descent. They bear marks of their origin not only in their features but in their names, and do not speak Gaelic. A line drawn from *Brims Ness*, 5 m. W. of Thurso, to *Clyth Ness*, 10 m. S. of Wick, would divide the county into 2 nearly equal parts with a Gaelic-speaking population to the S.W., and a non-Gaelic-speaking population to the N.E.

The *Brora* — well stocked with salmon — a turbulent river in its upper course, which passes through *Loch Brora*, 3 m. W., is crossed at

90¼ m. **Brora Stat.** ✻, picturesquely situated on the edge of a high bank.

Brora seems to have been a place of importance in early days, and was made a burgh of barony by David II. in 1345. It is a busy but scattered village, where the late Duke of Sutherland established several industries, such as a manufactory of pottery and tiles, a stone quarry, etc.; but its chief occupation is derived from the *Coal Mines*.

In the 16th cent. coal was worked here under the skilful estate management of the Countess, Lady Jean Gordon, and a shaft was long ago sunk to the depth of 300 ft. below the bed of the river. The works, after having been long discontinued, were renewed 1872. A steam-engine was then erected at Strath Stephen on the sea-shore, and a fresh shaft sunk. The coal is not bituminous, but is a brown coal or lignite of unusually good quality. It occurs in beds of the Lower Oolite, and bears a very strong resemblance to the coal of the E. moorlands of Yorkshire.

"It affords the thickest stratum of pure vegetable matter hitherto detected in any secondary rock in England."—LYELL.

A narrow border of oolite runs all along the sea-shore from Golspie to Helmsdale, and from the abundance of its oolitic fossils Brora offers a very tempting field of exploration to the geologist.

[The upper part of the *Strath Brora* has wild scenery, and includes a loch 4 m. long, round which a good road runs. Towards the upper end, on a wooded slope, is *Kilcolmkil*, a name indicating an early Christian ch. (St. Columba) and settlement, where there are curious traces of cairns or huts in a circle. Above Kilcolmkil is a fine succession of waterfalls, and the road continues up to *Cole Castle*, a Pict's house standing on a rock overhanging the river; its walls are 11 ft. high and 54 ft. in circumference. On the opposite (W.) side of the loch rises the picturesque Crag of *Carril Rock*, a precipitous cliff 684 ft. high (4 m. from Brora), and on the slope of the hill S. of it, 200 yds. above the road, is another Pict's house. The fishing in the Brora and loch, which is let, is excellent.]

At *Kintradwell*, 3 m. beyond Brora, and on rt. of rly., is a large *Pict's house* called *Cinn Troilla Burgh* (circumference 60 ft.), with an outer passage, and inner cells or domed storehouses. We cross the *Loth*, in whose glen the last Scotch wolf was killed abt. 1700 before

95¾ m. **Loth Stat.**, ch., and village. Passing

100 m. *Port Gower*, a neat little village, we reach

101¼ m. **Helmsdale Stat.** ✻, a busy fishing village with a small harbour, situated at the foot of a long strath through which the river *Ullie* or *Helmsdale* carries off the waters of a few small lochs in the interior. On the shore are the ruins of a castle, built by a Countess of Sutherland about the year 1488, and for many years the residence of the Earls of Sutherland.

The rly. from Helmsdale to Thurso and Wick was opened 1873, the late Duke of Sutherland contributing about half the cost of making it.

To avoid the *Ord of Caithness*, by which a fine road leads N. to Wick (Rte. 105), it strikes inland (N.W.), following a very circuitous course up *Strath Helmsdale*, a fine, wild, though somewhat bare glen.

The lowest part of the glen is exceedingly picturesque. Then follows one of the dreariest tracts of country in Scotland. Beyond

110¾ m. **Kildonan Stat.**, a burn falls into the river, on whose banks some particles of *gold* were found, which caused a rush to "the Sutherland gold-diggings" in 1868. After 600 ounces had been washed from the drift, the diggings were put a stop to by the late Duke on account of complaints by his pastoral tenants, but were resumed in 1894.

Passing the private stat. of

113¾ m. **Borrobol**, 118 m. **Kinbrace Stat.**, and the *Watershed* (575 ft.) we reach

125½ m. **Forsinard Stat.** ✻, at the head of *Strath Halladale*—

formerly the boundary between the Mackays' territory and that of the E. of Sutherland—and trend N.E.

[The *Road* up Helmsdale continues due N. for 15 m., descending Strath Halladale to the N. coast of Scotland, see p. 421.]

The rly. again ascends slightly and enters **Caithness**[1] in 3½ m. at a height of 650 ft. above the sea. There is a fine view rt. of the Mts. in the S. of Caithness among which *Morven* (2313 ft.) is conspicuous.

Beyond 133¾ m. **Altnabreac**, and 143 m. **Scotscalder Stats.** is

145¼ m. **Halkirk Stat.**, a village on the *Thurso*, one of the best fishing rivers in the north.

Brawl Castle (Sir J. G. Tollemache Sinclair, Bt. of Ulbster), an old feudal tower beyond the village, 3 stories high, with more modern buildings attached to each, has been fitted up as a residence for the lessees of the fishings, who are a club of gentlemen.

147¼ m. **Georgemas Junc. Stat.**

[*Branch* N. in 6¾ m.—passing in 1 m. *Hoy Stat.*—to **Thurso** ✲, p. 419. Capital view approaching the town.]

The main line turns S.E. passing (l.) *Loch Scarmclate* or *Stemster*. Beyond 150 m. **Bower Stat.**, it runs through a finely-cultivated country, passing along the N. side of *Loch Watten*, 3 m. long by ½ m. broad, abounding in trout, out of which flows a feeder of the *Wick Water*. Near its E. end is

153¾ m. **Watten Stat.**

156¼ m. **Bilbster Stat.**, 3 m. beyond which the river is crossed. *Stirkoke Ho.* (E. W. Horne, Esq.) lies 1 m. rt. The country here exhibits signs of great agricultural improvement.

161¼ m. †**WICK** ✲ (from *Vik*= (Norw.) *a Bay*), a royal and parl. burgh, is the capital of Caithness and an important seat of the Herring-fishery. It stands at the mouth of the *Wick Water* and at the head of *Wick Bay*. It is a busy thriving town, but not attractive to the tourist unless anxious for a lesson in gutting and curing herrings. The suburb of **Pulteneytown** to the S.E. was built in 1808 by the British Fisheries Association, and derives its name from Sir William Pulteney, president of that body.

Enormous sums of money have been expended on the *Harbour*, which was begun by Telford, and which can now be entered at high water by large steamers. At low tide passengers are conveyed to shore in boats, but with a strong S.E. wind blowing a landing can only be effected at *Ackergill*, 2½ m. N.

The season of the *Herring Fishery*, upon which the town is so dependent, and which brings a large influx of fishermen, fish curers, and gutters, begins about the middle of July and lasts until the middle of September. In 1893 there were 314 boats fishing at Wick, and 52,897 crans of herrings were landed and cured—each cran weighing about 3½ cwts. (cf. pp. 291, 292).

During the season the harbour is surrounded by some 20 wooden erections containing gutting troughs presided over by rows of women in strangely-shaped canvas garments the reverse of graceful, but appropriate to their somewhat unfeminine work, for which, however, they show marvellous aptitude. The herrings are brought from the boats direct to the troughs to be gutted, before being thrown into the salting boxes, and the rapidity with which the women perform this task is almost incredible.

The town is otherwise rather devoid of interest, but the vicinity is remarkable for several old ruined castles, the history of which is exceedingly meagre, and for the striking character of the cliff scenery.

"At some places, in particular to the south of Wick, the waves have quarried out masses of flagstone and piled them up

[1] See note on p. 407.

in huge heaps on the top of the cliffs, 60 or 100 ft. above high-water mark. . . . The largest disturbed mass contains more than 500 tons, and is known as *Charlie's Stone*. Others varying in bulk from 100 to 5 tons or less lie in hundreds, piled up in all positions in high and low ridges, which, before the march of improvement began in the district, extended far into the field above the cliff."—Sir A. GEIKIE'S "Scenery of Scotland," p. 63.

About 1 m. S. of Wick is "*The Castle of Old Wick*," or "*The Old Man of Wick*," otherwise called "*Castle Oliphant*," dating from the 12th cent. In the 14th it belonged to Sir Reginald le Cheyne, and afterwards to the Oliphants. It is a primitive square tower without window or other opening. A little beyond it is a stack, only connected with the mainland by a surviving natural arch called "*The Brig o' Trams*," and farther S., rising out of the sea, is a tall isolated Stack called "*The Brough*," with a tunnel extending from the one end to the other.

3 m. N. of Wick is the promontory of **Noss Head** with fine cliff scenery and a Lighthouse. It forms the S. side of *Sinclairs Bay*. ½ m. W. of the head are the ruins of *Castle Girnigo*, and beside it those of *Castle Sinclair*.

In 1672 the Earl of Caithness sold his estates to Lord Glenorchy, but George Sinclair of Keiss disputed the sale. In consequence Lord Glenorchy, at the head of the Campbells, invaded this territory and, after a fight which took place 1 m. W. of Wick, laid siege to Castle Girnigo. The well-known song of "*The Campbells are coming*" is said to be a reminiscence of this incident.

Still farther W. (2½ m. from Wick) is *Ackergill Tower* (Duff Dunbar, Esq. of Hempriggs), an old tower restored and added to in modern times. It is 65 ft. high and has square turrets at the angles. Its appearance from the sea is imposing, but on the land side it is rather tame.

The **Hill of Harland**, 3 m. N.W. of Wick, though only 200 ft. high commands a most extensive *View* seawards and landwards.

Steamers weekly to Aberdeen, Leith, Thurso, Orkney, and Shetland.

Coaches every afternoon (1) S.W. to Lybster, 13 m., and Dunbeath, 21 m. (Rte. 105).

(2) N. to Mey, 21 m. (cf. Rte. 106).

(3) N. (*Mail-gig*) to John o' Groat's House, 20 m. (Rte. 106).

ROUTE 101.

Bonar Bridge to Dornoch and Golspie.

The *quickest* route to **Dornoch** is to drive from Tain (p. 405) to *Meikle Ferry* (4 m.), cross in ¾ m., and be met by carriage from Dornoch, 4½ m.

The *most convenient* route is probably by coach from *Mound Stat.* (p. 406) in 7 m., twice daily.

By the route now described we hire at Bonar Bridge Stat. (p. 406), and in 1 m. cross the Bridge.

If Dornoch is not to be visited we may proceed N. and E. by Loch Buie direct to Mound Stat., 14 m.

Turning E. we keep along the N. shore of Dornoch Firth, passing 4 m. **Creich**, where is a sculptured obelisk, and on the promontory (rt.) *Creich Ho.* and *Dun Creich*, a vitrified fort. At 9½ m. (l.) is *Ospisdale* (J. R. Gilchrist, Esq.), where a large slab, 9 ft. high, is said to commemorate the death in battle of a Danish chief named Ospis. Beyond, rt. is *Skibo Castle* (E. C. Sutherland, Esq.), long the seat of the Dempsters, sold 1872 to Mr. Sutherland Walker of Aberarder for £130,000. The castle of *Skibo* was in former times the abode of the Bishops of Caithness, and after them passed to the Mackays. It is still remarkable for its excellent gardens and orchard.

$11\frac{1}{2}$ m. **Clashmore Inn**✲, from which *Meikle Ferry* is $2\frac{1}{2}$ m. S.

At 13 m. the road forks—straight on to Mound and Little Ferry (below) —rt. to

$14\frac{1}{2}$ m. **DORNOCH**✲, which, notwithstanding its insignificance (pop. 514 !) and inaccessibility, is the *Capital* of Sutherland, and was in times past the *Cathedral* city of the Diocese of Caithness. It still has the prim look of a miniature cathedral town, and much has been done of late years to improve it.

The old **Castle,** of which the high tower is alone standing, was a large and formidable building, destroyed in 1570 by the Master of Caithness and Mackay of Strathnaver, who, taking advantage of the minority of Alexander, Earl of Sutherland, plundered the city at the same time. Adjoining are the **County Buildings.**

The **Cathedral,** conspicuous by its high roof, low tower, and stunted spire, was built about 1230 by Gilbert de Moravia, most probably the uncle of Andrew de Moravia, the founder of the cathedral of Elgin. Though much damaged in 1570, and neglected afterwards, a great portion of it was standing till 1847, when it was restored by the then Duke of Sutherland. The work, however, was not trusted to competent hands ; and, though a capacious church is the result, no sort of resemblance can be traced in the interior to the cathedral of old days.

The church consists of chancel, nave, and transept, with single lancet windows, except at the W. end, where there is an interesting window of 5 lights, so common in this part of Scotland. In the chancel is a statue of the first Duke of Sutherland by *Chantrey*, with a long epitaph in praise of him and his Duchess-Countess. 16 Earls of Sutherland are said to have been buried in this ch. Under the chancel was found the effigy of Sir Richard de Moravia, brother of the founder. He was killed in battle against the Danes at *Embo*, between Dornoch and Little Ferry, where stands a large stone, supposed to commemorate the event.

There are excellent *Golfing Links* at Dornoch.

[It is 4 m. N. direct to *Little Ferry* ($\frac{1}{4}$ m. broad), across the narrow entrance of *Loch Fleet*, and 3 m. on the other side to Golspie. This is the best route for pedestrians or for those who order a carriage from Golspie.]

Striking N.W. in $2\frac{1}{2}$ m. the road from Bonar Bridge, which we left to visit Dornoch, is regained. *Skelbo*, an old house of the Earls of Sutherland, situated near Little Ferry, lies to the rt. as we proceed. It is now a ruin, and close by has been built a fine castellated farmhouse inhabited by the Duke's grieve.

Cambusmore House (D. of Sutherland) is passed l. before we cross *Loch Fleet* by "*The Mound*" (p. 406), which is 7 m. from Dornoch, 19 m. from Bonar Bridge by this route, and 4 m. from Golspie.

We keep beside the rly. line to

23 m. **Golspie,** p. 406.

ROUTE 102.

Lairg to Lochinver by Inchnadamph (Loch Assynt), $45\frac{1}{2}$ m.

Coach from Lairg (p. 406) daily, at 10.40 A.M., reaching Lochinver 6.40 P.M., and from Lochinver daily at 8 A.M., reaching Lairg 4 P.M.

The road leaves Lairg in a S.W. direction ; the river Shin is crossed, and a dreary moor is traversed.

At 9 m. the river *Cassley* is crossed, 1 m. above its junction with the *Oykell*. When full of water it is fairly supplied with fish below the

Falls of Glenmuick (9 m. up), which no fish can pass. Rt. of the bridge are the ruins of *Achness Castle* and *Pictish Towers;* l. is *Rosehall* (R. Tennant, Esq.).

11½ m. **Tuitumtarvach** ("*Effectual overthrow*") was in 1400 the scene of a battle between the M'Leods of Assynt and Lewis and the men of Sutherland, in which the M'Leods were defeated. Only one of their side returned to Lewis, and he died of his wounds. The road ascends the l. bank of the Oykell, which forms the boundary between Ross-shire and Sutherland. This is the prettiest part of *Strath Oykell.* The slopes on each side of the road are beautifully wooded with birch, oak, and wych elm, and at the bottom is a slip of cultivated land or pasture, watered by the Oykell.

15½ m. **Oykell Bridge** ✡. In the inn garden is an erect slab about 10 ft. high, set up to imitate an old stone monument, and scratched with *modern Runes!* Close by is a pretty waterfall.

The river is crossed here.

[A hill track l. ascends *Glen Einig* to Loch-na-Daimh; then crosses the watershed to (12 m.) *Rhidorroch Shooting Lo.* (Trs. of late Earl of Cromartie), near the head of *Glen Achallt*, down which a road leads to **Ullapool**, 20 m. (p. 382).]

We now ascend the rt. bank of the Oykell, passing,

17½ m., the shooting lodge of *Loubcroy* (Sir Ch. Ross, Bt.), an oasis in the desert, above which the strath is bleak and uninteresting.

26 m. **Aultnacallagach Inn** ✡ is on the N.E. side of *Loch Borrolan.* This name, which means the "*Cheat's Burn*," is said to have arisen from a dispute which took place here as to the boundary of the two counties, some witnesses having sworn that they were standing on Ross-shire ground because they had filled their shoes with earth from Balnagown in that county. The road, which ever since leaving Oykell Bridge has been in Ross-shire, now re-enters Sutherland. Here the singular and picturesque mountains of Assynt come into view. Rt. is *Ben More* (3273 ft.); l. are typical examples of Torridon sandstones rising above a platform of Archæan gneiss—*Canisp* (2786 ft.), *Suilven* (2399 ft.), *Coulmore* (2786 ft.), and *Coulbeg* (2523 ft.).

27½ m. *Ledmore.*

[Here a road branches off l. to *Elphin* (2½ m.) and **Ullapool**, 19 m., having rt. the wild desolate hills of *Coulmore*, *Coulbeg*, and *Ben More Coigach* (2438 ft.), crossing *Strath Kanaird*, and striking on the sea coast at *Loch Kanaird* (15 m.).]

A little farther on is the farmhouse of *Ledbeg*, near which the marble quarries of the Ben More district, now abandoned, were worked some years ago.

The road passes along the base of Ben More too closely to allow it to be seen to advantage.

At 29½ m. on l. is the little *Loch Awe*, with a number of small wooded islets, upon one of which are the ruins of a fort. The road now descends by the side of the *Loanan* to

33½ m. **Inchnadamph** ✡, standing in a well-sheltered corner, at the E. extremity of **Loch Assynt**. N. and E. rise the massive heights of *Quinaig* (2653 ft.), *Glasven* (2541 ft.), and *Ben More*, while away to the S.W. are seen *Canisp, Coulmore*, with its two heads, and *Coulbeg.* Beside the hotel is *Assynt Parish Ch.* Loch Assynt contains good brown and sea trout, and an occasional salmon. The rocks in the neighbourhood of Loch Assynt belong to the Cambrian and Torridonian age, resting on the oldest or granitoid gneiss. Loch Assynt is a fine sheet of water, 7 m. long; the scenery is considerably diversified by the nature of the rocks in which it is set. The upper end is terminated by the mural limestone cliffs of *Stron Chrubie*, backed by the majestic *Ben More* of Assynt and other mountains.

To geologists this is a classic region, and one about which more has been written than perhaps any part of Great Britain. The geological structure of Ben More and its immediate neighbours is extremely complicated, the various members of the Cambrian quartzite and limestone series being repeated again and again by thrust planes, while an outlier of the lowest Archæan gneiss, brought up by a powerful thrust, forms the highest part of *Glasven*. The botanist may gather many rare plants and ferns on these limestones. North of Loch Assynt the eye is arrested by precipitous Quinaig, formed of chocolate-coloured Torridon sandstone, upon which rests unconformably a capping of white Cambrian quartzite; while turning W. we see the rugged cliffs of Archæan gneiss.

Behind the hotel is the *Traligill Burn*, which rises in Ben More and for some distance passes underground through caves in the limestone.

1 m. beyond Inchnadamph on the margin of the loch are the ruins of *Ardvreck Castle*, consisting of part of the old keep and turret, with a square top. It has 3 stories, the lowest one vaulted, and was built about 1490 by the M'Leods, who in the middle of the 13th cent. obtained Assynt by marriage. It is remarkable as having been the prison of the Marquis of Montrose, who was captured after his defeat of Craigchoynachan (1650) by Neil M'Leod of Assynt, and confined here till he was taken to Edinburgh and put to death. Near it are the ruins of *Calda* or *Edderachalda House*, a capacious mansion built by the Mackenzies in the 18th cent., but destroyed by fire.

At 35½ m. the road crosses the *Skiag Burn* (p. 415).

[Here a road branches off rt. via *Unapool* and *Kyle Sku* ferry (7 m.) to **Scourie** 18 m. (see p. 414).]

The traveller now gets a good view of *Quinaig*, with its long jagged edge, looking very much like a saw. The road for the remaining distance runs

"through the district of Assynt, 97,000 acres, an alternation of patches of verdure, rocks, hills, mountains, and lakes. Nowhere, perhaps, within the same area will you see so many lakes as here. Every hollow cradles a sheet of water, nearly all tenanted by trout. To the S. of the road are seen the two heads of *Suilven* or "Sugar Loaf," 2396 ft. high. As seen from Loch Inver these two heads merge into one, and the mountain from that point of view acquired its name. From its sudden rise and vertical sides it has also been called 'the little Matterhorn.'" — SYMONDS's "Records of the Rocks."

Its regular horizontal strata were once continuous with those of Canisp, the intervening portions having been removed by erosion. The **Ascent of Suilven** (made from Inchnadamph or—shorter—from Lochinver) is difficult, but by no means impossible.

The road following the bend of the loch towards its W. end turns (39½ m.) S.W., and presently keeps down the bank of the roaring turbulent *River Inver*, which has a considerable fall to the sea.

[A little before reaching Loch Inver, a road on rt. branches off to *Drumbeg Inn*✱, 14 m. (passing (5 m.) Stoer and (13 m.) Oldany), where a boat may be obtained to cross (6 m.) Edderachillis Bay to Badcall, whence to **Scourie**✱ (p. 414) is 3 m.]

45½ m. †**Lochinver**✫ stands on the S. side of the river, and on the margin of the sea-loch of that name, with fine views of Lewis on the W. horizon, while inland rise the strangely-formed mountains already mentioned, which give a grand character to the scenery wherever they appear. The village—stretched round the head of the loch—consists of a few cottages, a church, and one or two shops, and is one of those places "which you see with delight, remain at with pleasure, and leave with regret." In the summer not only are the hotels full, but every available cottage where a bed can be procured. *Glencanisp Ho.* (D. of Sutherland), the shooting lodge for the deer forest of that name, is 2 m. inland.

6 m. S. of Lochinver, on the *Kirkaig* river, near Loch Fionn, are

the *Falls of Kirkaig*, 60 ft. high, and well worth visiting. The walk there is exceedingly interesting.

Steamer once a week to Stornoway, Oban, and Glasgow. Lochinver to Scourie by road via *Kyle Sku* ferry (p. 415) is 28 m.; also by boat from Drumbeg, 14 m. (p. 413).

For Roads from *Lochinver* to *Ullapool* see p. 382.

ROUTE 103.

Lairg by Loch Shin to Scourie, 44 m., and Durness, 56 m.

Coaches daily from **Lairg** (p. 406) at 6.30 A.M., reaching **Scourie** 2.10 P.M., and **Durness** 4 P.M.; and from Durness 6.30 A.M., and Scourie 8.50 A.M., reaching Lairg 4.30 P.M.

From Lairg the road keeps in a N.W. direction by the side of **Loch Shin**, which is 16½ m. long. As the hills which surround it are low, the scenery is not grand, but towards the upper end it becomes wilder, and views are obtained of (W.) *Ben More* (3273 ft.), in front *Ben Leod* (2864 ft.), and (N.) *Ben Hee* (2804 ft.)

The brown moors N. of Loch Shin were one of the scenes of the experimental efforts of the late D. of Sutherland to convert a wilderness into arable land by the aid of the steam-plough. The huge ploughshare, attached by wire-rope to two engines, turned up peat to a depth of 8 or 10 ft., and where large blocks of stone intervened they were shattered to pieces by dynamite. The Duke's attempts, however, resulted in a return of barely 3 per cent upon his outlay.

15½ m. **Overskaig Inn**✲. Beyond the end of the loch (17 m.) the road, which is delightfully fringed with wood of dwarf birch, is carried in succession along the banks of *Lochs Griam*, *Merkland*, *More*, and *Stack*. On the W. side of L. Stack (32 m.), in which sea trout abound, **Ben Stack** rises suddenly to the height of 2367 ft., composed of Archæan gneiss, capped with Cambrian quartzite. To the N. is *Arkle*, 2582 ft., and beyond it *Foinaven*, 2980 ft., one of the loftiest of the Sutherland mountains. N.W. from Loch Stack runs the *Laxford*, a river which received its name, meaning "Salmon Fiord," in Scandinavian times, from the abundance of its fish, which reputation it maintains to this day. The district through which we are now passing is called the **Reay Forest** (Duke of Sutherland). One of the lodges is on *Loch More*, a second on *Loch Stack*, a third at *Kyle Strome*, and a fourth at *Gobernuisgach*, at the head of Strathmore (p. 423).

37 m. **Laxford Bridge**.

Here the road strikes S.W. to

44 m. **Scourie**✲, a considerable village, with *Scourie Ho.* (Duke of Sutherland), on the edge of a bay backed by *Loch Baddidarroch*. It was the family property of General Hugh Mackay, who was defeated by Dundee at Killiecrankie.

The great attraction of Scourie is the **Island of Handa** (2 m. N.), which is worth a visit, for its own grandeur, and for the immense number of wildfowl that breed on it. The island is formed of red Torridon sandstone, and on the N.W. side of it is a range of precipitous cliffs, rising to the height of 400 ft. above the sea, and varied with every degree of indentation and irregularity, while in other places the rock descends to the water like a wall. The emerald water in the caves contrasts beautifully with the warm red cliffs. When the sea is smooth, a small boat may be taken close in.

The best landing-place in the island is at the S. On the narrow ledges of these cliffs, and upon every peak and point, during the breeding season from May to July, are myriads of guillemots, puffins, and razorbills sitting on their eggs; they are remarkably tame and apathetic, and though they are disturbed by the report of a gun, they will soon resume their places. The smell from the birds is strong.

Handa is sufficiently far from the coast to obtain magnificent views of the panorama of mountains.

"The most striking looking from this quarter is *Stack* (p. 414), the terminal aspect of which is that of an enormous pyramid, rising to a perfect point. *Suilven* (p. 413), appears under quite a new character, the two summits being far removed, and it shows itself to be in reality a long mountain, instead of the sugar-loaf figure from which it is so well known. To the S. a detached pillar of rock, at a point of Rhu Stoer, from 200 to 300 ft. high, looks in the distance exactly like a large ship under studding-sails."—ANDERSON.

Scourie to Lochinver, 28 m.

At 1 m. l. a good view is obtained of the sugar-loaf cone of *Ben Stack*, and at 2½ m. the kirk of *Edderachillis* is passed, and the village of *Badcall* comes in sight rt. At Badcall, where *salmon*, the product of the sea fishery, is packed in quantities, fish may often be purchased.

Presently there is a charming prospect (rt.) over Edderachillis bay, and its 24 islets, bounded on the S.W. by the distant line of coast, which ends in the Stoer Point. [For route across the bay to Lochinver, see p. 413.] At 8 m. the road ascends a steep hill, commanding views of some of the more distant mountains. *Quinaig* (2653 ft.) is prominent on rt., and *Glasven* (2541) on l. The general character of the country remains the same, the chief features being gneiss eminences, partially covered with heather and common grass. These stand among a number of small lochs, whose dark still waters give them, perhaps untruly, the appearance of great depth. A long hill leads down to *Kyle Strome* and

11 m. **Kyle Sku** ferry (¼ m.) across the upper part of *Loch Cairnbawn* which above the ferry divides into two branches —*Loch Glendhu* to the E. and *Loch Glencoul* to the S.E. On the S. side of the latter, near its head, is a fine, but little-known waterfall, *Eas-coul-aulin*, 300 ft. high. The scenery in both is wild and gloomy. Near the ferry on a little promontory, which at high water is an island, are the remains of an old dune, about 8 ft. high, composed of uncemented masonry. Mixed with the stones have been found human bones of rather small size. How or why they got into such a position is a question which has puzzled antiquaries. S. of the ferry is

Kylesku Inn✱.

The road now ascends, passing between Glasven on l. and Quinaig on rt. A fine view of these mountains is obtained from the road, the country on both sides being boggy peat moss, of a flat and tame character.

16½ m. From the top of the hill a view is obtained of *Loch Assynt* (p. 412), and at *Skiag Bridge*, on the shore of Loch Assynt (18 m.), the tourist joins the road from Lairg to Lochinver (Rte. 102).

The road to **Durness** from **Laxford Bridge** crosses the bridge, touches the head of *Loch Laxford*, a salt-water loch, and turns due N. through an exceedingly rough country, too much encumbered by ponderous masses of gneiss to afford many views of the more distant parts. It winds continually, however, and at every turn discloses some fresh feature. On the rt. is *Arkle* (2582 ft.), with its finely tapering form and independent position; and farther on is *Foinaven* (2980 ft.), a more bulky and less picturesque mountain.

At the head of the fiord of *Loch Inchard* is

41½ m. **Rhiconich Inn**✲.

The *Achriesgill Water* is soon joined and followed, although the stream itself is sometimes invisible from the immense fragments of rock which have closed it up. Near the summit of the road (45½ m.), 596 ft., is *Gualin Ho.*, originally built by the Duke of Sutherland as a house of refuge for the safety of travellers (cf. p. 423). Upon the gable end is a slab with inscription, but this, owing to its exposure, is nearly illegible, and the house has now been converted into a shooting-lodge. In the neighbourhood is a pretty waterfall on l., a pleasant relief amidst the desolate scenery around. 3 m. farther on is a small reservoir, with a stone put over it in 1832, to commemorate the kindness shown to Mr. Lawson, the engineer of these roads, by the inhabitants of Durness and Edderachillis. The *Gualin* ("shoulder") through which the road is carried, is a wide valley, producing nothing but peat and heather, and supporting only a few sheep. It is bounded on each side by mountains; those on the W. are of no great height, but those on the E. are very imposing, and the view of *Ben Spionnu* (2537 ft.) is the best that can be got anywhere of that mountain. It has two heads, and throws out a spur towards the W. When nearly opposite a small *Glasven* (1085 ft.) the road crosses (50 m.) the Grudie or Dionard, and descends by its side to the *Kyle of Durness*, crossing the promontory to the village of

56 m. **Durness**✲, for which and routes thence W. to Cape Wrath and E. to Tongue, see Rte. 108.

ROUTE 104.

Lairg to Tongue, 36½ m.

Coach from **Lairg** (p. 406) Tues., Thurs., and Sat. at 6.30 A.M., reaching **Tongue** 12.45; and from Tongue Mon., Wed., and Fri. at 8.25 A.M., reaching Lairg 1.20.

The road branches off (rt.) from the Scourie road on the shores of *Loch Shin*, about 2 m. from Lairg, ascending the desolate *Strath Tirry*.

At (12 m.) the foot of the flat-topped hill, named *Lord Reay's Green Table*, we cross the river, and 1 m. farther the watershed (830 ft.) called **"The Crask."**

We descend *Strath Bagastie*, having rt. *Ben Clibreck* (3164 ft.) to

20 m. **Altnaharra Inn**✱, at the W. end of **Loch Naver,** 6 m. long.

Altnaharra is in itself a rather desolate spot, but is much frequented during the season as an excellent fishing station.

[4 roads meet here:—(1) S. to **Lairg** (above); (2) N. to **Tongue** (below); (3) N.W. by *Strathmore* to **Heilim Inn** (*a*) by *Eriboll*, 22 m., or (*b*) by *Hope Ferry*, 23 m., passing (at 11 m.) a remarkable Pictish Tower (see p. 423); (4) E. and N. to **Bettyhill**✱, 24 m. This road skirts the N. shore of *Loch Naver*, where the scenery is very attractive, to its E. end, 7 m., where it strikes due N. down *Strath Naver*. The road from this point is rough, and many streams have to be forded. Shortly before reaching *Rhifail* (16 m.) is a considerable *Circle* of upright stones, and, 1½ m. beyond, near the mouth of a burn, a *Pict's house*, in good preservation. 19 m. we pass *Loch-ma-Naire*, the waters of which are believed to have wonderful healing powers. *Strath Naver* becomes narrower towards its mouth, and at 23 m. *Invernaver* the river is crossed. 24 m. *Bettyhill*, see p. 422.]

From Altnaharra the direct road to Tongue traverses a dreary moorland (732 ft.) to *Loch Coulside*, and then (27 m.) crossing the stream, keeps along the W. shore of *Loch Laoghal* or *Loyal*, a beautiful piece of water, which (with *Loch Creagach*, its continuation) is 7 m. long, situated at the foot of the bulky granite mt. *Ben Loyal* (l.), 2504 ft.

"Seen from the crumbling battlements of Castle Varich (p. 422), buttressed against the tempestuous North Sea by a chain of rocky islands, constituting a great natural breakwater, *Ben Laoghal* (or *Loyal*), with its magnificent precipices, well merits the title of the Queen of the Sutherland mountains. This noble mass occupies the centre of the great mountain amphitheatre, and rises in a series of precipices to the height of 2504 ft. terminating in 4 colossal splintered peaks, like gigantic cathedral spires. To the W. is *Ben Hope*, a grand dome-shaped mass, rising to the height of 3040 ft., and contrasting in stern sublimity with the battlemented precipices of Ben Laoghal."—Weld.

The loch is dotted with islands, and abounds with lake trout and char. The black and red throated divers are also found here.

36½ m. **Tongue**✱, see p. 422.

ROUTE 105.

Helmsdale to Wick by the Ord of Caithness.

This is the old mail-coach road. On leaving Helmsdale it enters the district of *Navidale* and ascends a long hill, winding round ravine after ravine. On the rt. an older and more precipitous road may still be traced. In 4 m. and at the height of 850 ft. the traveller reaches a mountain plateau, which ends E. towards the sea in the bold rocky promontory called the **Ord of Caithness**, the end of a bleak mountain range separating Caithness from Sutherland, and commanding a fine view seaward. By the roadside will be observed the black posts which direct the driver when the ground is covered with snow. It is considered unlucky for a Sinclair to cross the Ord on a Monday, because on that day a large party of the clan passed it on their way to Flodden, whence they never returned. A picturesque ruin of uncertain date under the Ord was, in 1567, the scene of the murder of the Earl of Sutherland and his wife by their hostess Isabel Sinclair, who mixed poison with their food.

The plateau is kept with a gradual decline for nearly 5 m., when the road descends abruptly to

9½ m. **Berriedale** ✱. Descending the traveller will be surprised and delighted with the sight of two little valleys, *Langwell* and *Berriedale*, both of which are closely wooded — a rare sight in this county — and watered by a small stream. These streams unite before falling into the sea. On an elevated height between the two valleys, picturesquely situated, stands *Langwell House*, purchased in 1857, as a shooting-lodge, by the Duke of Portland, with 81,600 acres, partly converted into a deer forest. Separating these valleys 4 m. W. is *Scaraben* (2054 ft.) and 4 m. farther *Morven* (2313 ft.). Upon a rock on the sea-shore nearly surrounded by water, stand the ruins of *Berriedale Castle*, an old fortress of the Earls of Caithness, from which the eldest son of that family derives his title.

Again a long hill is ascended, commanding extensive views to the summit of that flat, bare, treeless table-land, which is the main feature of the county of Caithness.

16 m. **Dunbeath**✱, 1 m. S. of which, on the coast, is situated *Dunbeath Castle* (E. S. Alexander-Sinclair, Esq.). The present building dates from the year 1633, but was greatly enlarged about 1870. The oldest part, which includes a 15th-century keep, was besieged and captured for Montrose in 1650. *Dunbeath Water* is a stream of some size, and affords fair trout fishing with an occasional salmon.

A road leads W. over the hill to *Braemore Lo.* (D. of Portland), on the Berriedale Water at the foot of *Maiden Pap* (1587 ft.), with *Morven* behind, from both of which extensive views can be obtained.

Coach daily to Wick *via* Lybster.

20 m. **Latheron** ✱. In front of the village is an upright slab, and near it is an old tower, in which the bells of the ch. formerly hung.

[From Latheron a road runs due N. to Thurso, 22 m., passing (16 m.) *Georgemas Stat.* (p. 409). At 5 m. (rt.) is a *Circle of old stones*, overlooking the waters of a small loch; l. is *L. Rangag*, a good fishing loch.]

Passing *Swiney* (=Sweyn's) *Village*, which has an upright stone, the tourist reaches the village of

24 m. **Lybster** ✱, one of the seats of the herring-fishery.

The road from Lybster keeps a little distance from the rocky coast line, passing through one or two highly cultivated farms, but traversing chiefly a crofting district.

34½ m., on l., is *Hempriggs Loch*, and on rt. is *Hempriggs House* (Duff Dunbar, Esq.), well situated, with fairly wooded grounds. Near this, the eye looking N. can discern the promontory of Duncansbay Head and the distant Orkneys, with the lofty cliffs of Hoy. Passing rt. the small remains of the "Castle of Old Wick" or "Old Man of Wick," the traveller reaches, through the suburb of *Pulteneytown*, the fishing town of

37 m. **Wick**✱, see p. 409.

ROUTE 106.

Wick to Thurso, by John o' Groat's House.

There is an afternoon *Coach* in summer to 21 m. Mey, passing within 4 m. of John o' Groat's House.

A *Mail-gig* (conveying passengers) runs every afternoon to 20 m. John o' Groat's House.

About 3 or 4 *trains* daily between Wick and Thurso in 1 hr.

For **Wick**✱ see p. 409.

We take the northern road from Wick to *Sinclairs Bay*, but away from the shore, traversing a district which in former days was the scene of much barbarity and quarrelling. The 4 principal families who have possessed it, or fought for it, are the Sinclairs, Sutherlands, Keiths, and Gunns; and of them there is an old rhyme:—

> "Sinclair, Sutherland, Keith, and Clan Gunn,
> There never was peace when they four were on."

The last was finally exterminated as a clan, and was broken up into smaller families, dependent on the larger clans. At 3 m. the direct road to Thurso strikes N.W.

6 m. *Wester Water* is crossed by a high-backed, old-fashioned bridge of 2 arches, $\frac{3}{4}$ m. above its mouth.

After traversing a wide, open, and barren moor bordering on the shore, we reach 8 m. **Keiss**✲. 1 m. beyond (rt.) is the modern *Keiss Castle* (F. T. Barry, Esq.), and, on a rock jutting out into the sea, the ruins of an old castle.

A number of mounds on the coast at Keiss were the subject of exploration by the late Mr. Samuel Laing and Dr. Joseph Anderson, who, following in the steps of Mr. A. H. Rhind, the pioneer of such researches in this district, discovered many kists enclosing skeletons, urns, pottery, etc. Mr. Laing considered that this district was the burial-place of the surrounding population. The "Harbour-mound" exhibited traces of buildings which Mr. Laing believed to be identical with the "burgh" or circular tower.

12 m. The road passes rt. the ruins of *Bucholy Cas.*, built 1155. It belonged to the *Mowats*, who claim descent from the Montebellos, and is perhaps the oldest and most interesting of the Caithness castles.

$13\frac{1}{2}$ m. *Freswick*, with *Freswick Bay* and *House* (E. S. Alexander-Sinclair, Esq.) rt.

At $16\frac{1}{2}$ m. the road forks. Straight on leads in $4\frac{1}{2}$ m. to **Mey**✲ (p. 419); we strike rt. to

$18\frac{1}{2}$ m. *Huna Inn*✲, built by 14th Earl of Caithness, and nearly equi-distant from Wick and Thurso. $1\frac{1}{2}$ m. E. is

20 m. **John o' Groat's House**✲. A hotel stands on the sandy beach, close to a mound marked by a flagstaff, on which stood the original *Octagon House*. That such a person as John o' Groat actually existed is proved by 2 deeds (dated 1678-1699) in possession of the landlord. His house had for a century and a half ceased to exist, when in 1876 the hotel was built to keep up the tradition.

The story is that John o' Groat was the descendant of one De Groot, a Dutchman, who, in the reign of James IV., settled in these parts. Every year John and 7 relatives, who were joint-owners of the land, and all bore the name of Groat, used to assemble for the purpose of celebrating the memory of their ancestor. A dispute, however, arose as to who should be president on the occasion, and sit at the head of the table. On each occasion this unseasonable contention disturbed the harmony of the evening. John o' Groat settled the dispute by building an octagon house, furnished with an octagon table and 8 doors, so that each man entered at his own door and sat at the head of the table.

The story may admit of this explanation —John o' Groat rented the ferry to Orkney, and to shelter his clients while waiting on the shore for the boat, built a round house with 8 screens or divisions adapted to shelter wayfarers from the storm, whichever way the wind might blow.

Near this, in 1650, the Marquis of Montrose landed with a forlorn hope of 2000 men, chiefly raised in Orkney, to redeem the cause of his king. He met with no support, and marching S. was soon defeated.

The view from this across the island of **Stroma** ($2\frac{1}{2}$ m. long by 1 m. broad) and the **Pentland Firth** to **S. Ronaldshay** and the **Cliffs of Hoy** in **Orkney**, and N.E. to the *Pentland Skerries* with their *Two Lighthouses*, is magnificent.

A pleasant walk of 2 m. E. over turf leads to

Duncansbay Head, the N.E. promontory of Scotland, the Vervedrum Prom. of *Ptolemy*, whence a fine view is obtained of the Orkneys, the Skerries, the open sea in front, and the projecting headlands of the E. coast. N. of the headland at the entrance to the Pentland Firth are the "*Boars of Duncansbay,*" so called from the force with which the sea runs and the fierceness of the waves. In a bay, a little to S., are the **Stacks of Duncansbay**, 3 pointed and insulated rocks, like obelisks, with precipitous sides, rising stately out of the sea. The cliffs, which are here composed of old red sandstone ("Caithness Flags") are severed by tremendous gashes (locally known as "*Geos,*" from the Norse *gja*, a chasm or rift) running up into the land, and exhibiting on each side a clean fracture of the horizontal strata. The view looking down into the sea boiling beneath is very grand. One of these *geos* is particularly striking, and is bridged over by a natural arch.

From John o' Groat's W. to Thurso (19 m.) the road passes Huna Inn and Canisbay Ch. to

7 m. **Mey**✲, whence there are coaches daily to Wick (21 m.) and Thurso (12 m.), returning the same day.

[½ m. N. *Barrogill Castle* (Heathcote Sinclair, Esq. of Mey) occupies a conspicuous position, from the absence of any enclosed park. Round the house some bushes have been coaxed to form a sort of avenue. The castle consists of a square tower, with heavy battlemented turrets at the angles and in the centre, and a lower building of 4 stories attached to it, also turreted at the corners. It is probably not older than the 17th cent.

Between *Stroma Island* and the shore, off *St. John's Point* (2 m. N.E.), a line of breakers marks the deadly reef of rocks called the "*Merry Men of Mey.*" When the ebb tide meets a W. wind the surface is ruffled and covered with foam, though all around is still and clear.]

At 9 m. *Rattar Ho.* (J. C. Traill, Esq.) lies off the road rt.

11 m. **Dunnet** Village✲, Church, and Loch.

3½ m. N. is **Dunnet Head,** a bold promontory of old red sandstone surmounted by a *Lighthouse*, and the most northerly point of the mainland of Great Britain.

The great tidal wave, rushing E. from the Atlantic round the N. of Scotland into the German Ocean through the *Pentland Firth*, renders the navigation of the latter dangerous owing to its tremendous and arbitrary currents. These do not run in one even flow, but in well-defined streams, at the rate of 8 or 9 knots, forming the well-known *Roosts* or Races. The little *Isle of Swona*, one of the Orkneys, set in the full brunt of one of these currents, causes by its opposition a whirlpool called the "Well of Swona," dangerous to sailing vessels, which are liable to be caught, and twisted round and round into its vortex, and have often difficulty in extricating themselves. At spring-tides the flood runs at the rate of 10 m. an hour, but the currents vary in different parts of the channel, according to the state of the tide.

The road keeps round *Dunnet Bay* to

14 m. **Castletown**✲, a village of considerable size, consisting of one long street, and possessing quarries of a slaty stone (Caithness flags), used for paving, which are prepared by steam-power. The works were established by Mr. Traill of Rattar, 1824. To this the village is indebted for its prosperity.

5 Coaches daily to and from Thurso; once daily to Wick. Here the direct road from Wick to Thurso (20 m.) is joined.

Rt. is *Castlehill* (J. C. Traill, Esq. of Rattar), with thriving shrubberies. We pass (rt.) *Harold's Tower* (p. 420) and *Thurso Castle* before crossing the river to

19 m. †**THURSO**✲. It is pleasantly situated on the Thurso river as it enters Thurso Bay, and can boast of considerable antiquity. It was formerly the chief place of trade between Scotland and Scandinavia, whence its name—Thor's river—and in the 14th cent. was of such importance that the weights and measures of Thurso were adopted for the whole country. The rly. station stands at the head of the modern town, which, as it descends the hill, contracts from broad streets into narrow, intricate, and dirty lanes, ending in the harbour, which is usually filled with vessels loading with *Caithness paving-stones*, produced from quarries in the neighbouring hills, worked in a particularly fissile stratum of the lower part of the old red sandstone, and known as "Caithness flags." The splitting, sawing, and trimming of these stones constitutes the chief industry of the place, and

they are exported to the extent of thousands of tons annually, and have furnished many of the *trottoirs* of Paris. One side of the harbour is occupied by the mills and works of the Caithness Flagstone Co. In the lower and dirtiest part of the town, close to the harbour, are the ruins of the Gothic Ch. of St. Peter, apparently 14th cent. In the handsome modern Gothic **Town Hall** is a *Museum*, containing the remarkable collection of plants and coral fossils bequeathed by the late Mr. Dick[1] (1811-66), to whom there is a *Monument* in the new cemetery. Opposite the church is a statue by *Chantrey* of Sir John Sinclair, famed for agriculture and longevity. About ½ m. to the N.W. are the scanty ruins of the old **Bishop's Palace,** where, in 1222, Adam, Bp. of Caithness, was burnt, along with his house, by the populace on account of his enforcement of tithes. A little above the harbour, on the E. side of the Bay, is the modern mansion of *Thurso Castle*, rebuilt 1874-6, the seat of Sir J. G. Tollemache Sinclair of Ulbster, Bt. E. of it, on the summit of the hill, is *Harold's Tower*, erected by Sir John Sinclair over the grave of Harold, Earl of Caithness, slain in battle on this spot, 1190. It serves as a burial-place for the Sinclair family.

The Bay of Thurso, embraced by the bold headlands and tall cliffs of Dunnet Head (E.), and Holburn Head (W.), is a roadstead open to the N., and therefore not a secure harbour. On the W. side of the bay, 1½ m. from Thurso, is *Scrabster Pier*, the starting-point of the Orkney mail steamer (Omnibus from the town).

Railway.—About 3 trains daily to Inverness (in 6½-9½ hrs.) and the S. (see Rte. 100); also 3 or 4 daily in 1 hr. to Wick.

Steamers.—*Every evening* (except Sunday) to Orkney upon arrival of mail train —to Scapa (for Kirkwall), 3 hrs., and to Stromness 4½ hrs. (see Rte. 109).

Weekly to Wick, Aberdeen, and Leith, and occasionally in summer to Stornoway, Oban, and Glasgow.

Coaches.—*Daily* to Castletown, Dunnet, and Mey (p. 419), and to Tongue (Rte. 107).

EXCURSION to **Holburn Head** :—

The road to it skirts Thurso Bay towards the N.W., passing rt. the remains of the Bp. of Caithness's *Palace.* The estate of *Scrabster* belonged to the Crown ; hence "Laird of Scrabster" was a title locally given to the Sovereign of Great Britain. It now belongs to John Miller, Esq. of Scrabster, Convener of the County. The carriage road ends at Scrabster Pier, 1½ m. ; from thence a walk of 20 mins. will bring the traveller to *Holburn Head.* The footpath follows the shore, passing between the lighthouse and the sea, and ascending to the end of the promontory. The flagstone rock of Holburn Head appears to be riven in many places from top to bottom, and in some places the sea has entered below through some of the numerous caves. The largest of these chasms is open on one side almost entirely to the sea, and is only spanned by two natural arches of rock. As the spectator peers over the precipice he may think of the fate of Captain Slater, who, in a fit of mental aberration, madly spurred his horse to the edge, but the animal, shying in terror on the very verge, threw over his rider and escaped, leaving the dents of his hoofs in the sward. An obelisk marks the spot.

"A short distance from Holburn Head, a tower-like detached mass of the flagstone rock (called the *Clett*) rises vertically from the sea to the height of about 150 ft., and during the breeding season is covered with sea-birds. Between this isolated rock and the land a terrific sea rages at times, violently plunging into the gloomy caves with thunder-like roar, and sending clouds of spray high into the air, which streams

[1] See "Robert Dick, Geologist and Botanist," by Smiles, which contains interesting illustrations of this neighbourhood.

down the cliffs in multitudinous waterfalls."

The geologist will find in the cliffs of *Thurso Bay* a fine example of the Caithness flags, one of the divisions of the old red sandstone system peculiar to the north of Scotland. These rocks were, by the labours of Robert Dick, a baker of Thurso (p. 420), discovered to be profusely charged with the fossil remains of fish, including the Holoptychius, which occur by thousands. The best place for the fossil-hunter is on the E. side of the bay, near Thurso Castle.

ROUTE 107.

Thurso to Tongue.

Coach daily, 44 m. in 9 hrs.

For 3½ m. after leaving Thurso the road ascends, with rt. *Holburn Head*, passing through one of the largest and most highly cultivated farms in Scotland, belonging to John Miller, Esq. of Scrabster, Convener of the County. The cliffs of Hoy in Orkney are conspicuous for many miles (see Rte. 109).

4 m. Rt. is *Brims Ness* (see p. 407, note).

5½ m. At the village of *Forss*, which is pleasantly sheltered from the E. by a thriving plantation, the road crosses *Forss Water*, and near a foaming waterfall passes rt. *Forss House* (Trs. of late J. Sinclair, Esq.), entering the *Parish of* **Reay,** from which Lord Reay, the chief of the clan Mackay, takes his title. It then traverses a cultivated district, on which large improvements have been made of late years.

At 9½ m. are the ruins of *Dun Reay*, one of the ancient seats of the Mackays of Reay.

10½ m. We pass l. *Achvarasdal Lo.*, the Caithness seat of Sir R. C. Sinclair, Bt. of Stevenston, before crossing *Reay Bridge* to

12 m. **Reay Village ✲,** near the head of *Sandside Bay*. It is said that a large village formerly existed between the present one and the sea, and that some of the buildings were discovered in 1751 by means of a waterspout. There are some caves in the cliffs, one of which is called by the natives *Gling-gling*, from the reverberation of the waves.

After leaving Reay rt. is *Sandside Ho.* (T. Pilkington, Esq.), in a charming situation well protected by trees. Then a long ascent has to be effected to the tableland, called *Drum-holliston*, the N. extremity of the mountain range, at S. end of which is the *Ord of Caithness* (Rte. 105). Here, as upon the E. coast, it forms the boundary between the county of Caithness and that of Sutherland, which the tourist now enters.

16 m. Rt. is *Bighouse* (Duke of Sutherland), formerly the seat of the Mackays of Bighouse, a branch of the Reay family.

At 17 m. a handsome Bridge crosses the *Halladale River*.

[A pretty road runs due S. on the E. side of the river up *Strath Halladale* to **Forsinard Stat.,** 15 m. (p. 408).]

18 m. **Melvich ✲.** A dull and uninteresting moor, bare even of heather, succeeds to this, beyond which *Strathy Head* may be seen stretching out into the North Sea. It is a pleasant relief to reach the edge of this tableland, and allow the eye to rest upon the village of

21 m. **Strathy ✲,** which occupies a pleasantly sheltered valley, well watered by a river of the same name. At its mouth a good number of salmon are netted every year, but the stream is too small for first-rate fly-fishing. After a flood of some

duration, however, grilse and sea-trout do find their way up, and may be caught with the fly.

Coach to Thurso daily, returning in the evening.

Another bare ridge lies between this glen and the next, that of 24½ m. **Armadale,** with *Armadale Village* and *Ho.* (D. of Sutherland), in which there is little cultivation, but some good rich pasture, and the sheep of the district have considerable repute in consequence.

At 28 m. the *Kirtomy Burn* is crossed and 2 m. N. is a promontory called the *Aird of Kirtomy*, where there is a long tunnel by which boats pass under the rocks, and which Pennant describes as the most curious cavern in the world.

32 m. **Bettyhill** ✲, at the entrance of **Strath Naver,** by far the most beautiful valley in Sutherland, and the only one to excite much admiration in this district (see Rte. 104). There is a fine *Sculptured Stone* in the ch.-yd. here.

The road now strikes due S., crossing the *Naver* in 1 m. and keeping up its l. bank for 1½ m., when it turns W., and at 37½ m. crosses the *Borgie River*, which comes out of *Loch Loyal* (Rte. 104). At the mouth of the river stands the old castle of Borgie, one of the strongholds of the clan Mackay.

Upon the top of the long ascent beyond, a fresh range of mountains comes in sight. Due S. is *Ben Clibreck*, 20 m. away, overlooking Loch Naver, and nearer, but rather more to the W., are *Ben Loyal* with its four jagged peaks, and *Ben Hope*. Across *Tongue Bay* are the *Rabbit Islands*, and at its mouth *Roan Isle*, with its S., face rising perpendicularly from the water.

At 43 m. is *Tongue House*, formerly the residence of the Lords Reay, the country around being known as "*Lord Reay's Country*," or in Gaelic "*Duthaich Mhic-Caoidh*" (Mackay's Country) before it was sold to the Duke of Sutherland. The house is beautifully situated, at the foot of a high hill, upon the E. side of a narrow arm of the sea known as the **Kyle of Tongue,** across which there is a ferry. It is irregularly built, and has no architectural beauty, but the plantations which surround it are as ornamental as they are necessary, and under this protection the gardens flourish with a success scarcely to be expected in so high and stormy a latitude. Between the House and the ferry the Duke has erected a picturesque *Shooting Lo.* of wood and concrete.

1 m. farther up the Kyle is

44 m. **Tongue** ✲, a charming place, with beautiful sea-views, and, to the S., a grand outline of the four-headed *Ben Laoghal* or *Loyal* (2504 ft.) in sight (see p. 416). On an eminence near the shore are the remains of *Castle Varich*, consisting of 2 stories enclosed by massive walls.

For *coach* road S. to Lairg, 36½ m., see Rte. 104.

ROUTE 108.

Tongue to Cape Wrath by Durness.

Durness, the nearest inn to Cape Wrath, distant 14½ m., is 20 m. from Tongue for pedestrians, who cross 3 ferries. A carriage from Durness has to drive 30 m. to the W. side of Tongue Ferry, across which it can sometimes be taken. It is 10 m. by road from one side of the ferry to the other round by the head of the Kyle.

1¾ m. N. of Tongue and below Tongue House is *Tongue Ferry* (¾ m.) across the **Kyle of Tongue.**

The **Moin** (=a *peat moss*) a highly elevated boggy moorland (740 ft.), which stretches from the bases of Ben Hope and Ben Laoghal to the sea, and between the Kyle of Tongue and Loch Hope, has to be crossed in 7 m. Its passage used to be a serious undertaking, but, since a good road has been made across it by the Duke of Sutherland, it can now be accomplished with comparative ease. The construction of this road was a work that entailed great expense and labour, it being necessary to construct an artificial foundation with turf and faggots. Half-way is the *Moin House*, erected as a refuge for travellers overtaken by storms. On one of the gables is a large slab with an inscription engraved upon it, stating the nature of the hill, by whom the road was made, and who were the managers of the Duke's property at the time. A long hill is descended to

9½ m. **Hope Ferry,** a *chain ferry* over the *River Hope* as it emerges from Loch Hope.

[**Loch Hope** is 6 m. long. Along its E. shore a road passing (¾ m.) *Hope Lo.* (D. of Sutherland) leads to 22 m. *Altnaharra Inn* (p. 416), joining at 7½ m. the road from Eriboll (below).]

Beyond the ferry a steep ridge has to be ascended, from which a good view is obtained of *Ben Hope* (3040 ft.). Rounding a corner Loch Eriboll comes in sight, and the little promontory of Ardneachdie, upon which stands

11½ m. **Heilim Inn** ✲, beside *Heilim Ferry.*

Loch Eriboll is a fiord running nearly due N. and S., and about 10 m. in length. There is a good road round it, and a *Ferry* (1½ m.) across it from Heilim *Inn* to *Portnan-con,* by using which the pedestrian will save 10 m., though carriages and horses have to go round (abt. 12 m.). This loch is an excellent harbour of refuge in N.E. gales, and, with its calm clear water nestling in the hills, is one of the most beautiful inlets along the coast.

On the E. side of its mouth is **Kennageal** or **Whiten Head,** a splendid perpendicular cliff, in which, towards the E. is a fine series of caves.

[From **Heilim Inn** to **Altnaharra,** 22 m. (p. 416), there is no public conveyance, but the road is charming, offering excellent views, and an opportunity of visiting *Dun Dornadilla,* one of the most curious relics of antiquity in Scotland.

3 m. is **Eriboll,** a hamlet on the side of the loch. The road then climbs the hill, from which a magnificent view is obtained of the whole expanse of Loch Eriboll ; and a little farther on of Loch Hope and *Ben Hope* (3040 ft.). At *Cashel Dhu,* 8 m., is one of the most distinct and comprehensive mountain prospects in Scotland. The W. front of *Ben Hope* has 2 terraces or divisions, one above the other. The lower range has upon its face a number of horizontal terraces clothed with dwarf birch. The upper one is scarred by numerous water-courses.

On Ben Hope, alone in Great Britain, grows the Alpine plant *Alsine rubella ; Betula nana* and *Astragalus alpinus* also occur in crevices of the rocks. Its summit is famous for ptarmigan. In 1872 a golden eagle and wild cat were shot on the mountain, and may be seen stuffed in Kinloch shooting-lodge. The river, which N. of the loch is called the *Hope,* is here called the *Strathmore Water.* Beyond the ferry the road enters *Strathmore,* a beautiful valley, with a lawn of smooth velvety turf at the bottom. On each side is a continuous wall of steep hill, covered with short turf, and surmounted by a perpendicular parapet of barren rock.

The glen is bounded on the S. by the conical form of *Ben Hee* (2804 ft.).

10½ m. The *Allt-na-Cailliach* (Old Women's Burn) is crossed. A little farther on is **Dun Dornadilla,** an old Pictish broch, built probably in the 7th cent. to afford the inhabitants shelter from hostile attacks. The idea that these brochs were erected by the Danes is now generally abandoned.

The circumference of the dun is about 150 feet. The wall next the road, which is propped up behind, is probably the original height, about 25 ft. The entrance is very low, and could only have been used on hands and knees. Of any opening in the walls for light or ventilation there is no trace, but these duns were open at the top

It is 11 m. from Altnaharra.

Up to the beginning of the present cent Strathmore was cultivated and contained a numerous population.

13 m. A road here strikes rt. passing *Gobernuisgach Lo.,* and leads in 9 m. by the W. side of *Ben Hee* to the Lairg and Durness road (Rte. 103), which it joins at the N. end of Loch Merkland.

The road to Altnaharra trends W., ascends to 507 ft., and then descends to the Inn at the W. end of *Loch Naver* (see p. 416)..

After crossing *Heilim Ferry* the road ascends the hill and turns N. down Loch Eriboll to

16½ m. *Rispond*, situated in a small creek, and surrounded by bare rocks. It was once the earliest station for the herring-fishery. But since the Minch fishery has been established (cf. pp. 397, 399) the supply of fish has diminished.

The road here turns to the W., passing 19 m. rt. the **Cave of Smoo,** on the shore below, of which Sir W. Scott in his Diary has given a most glowing account (perhaps a little exaggerated). On the opposite side of the road is seen the burn descending into the inner cave by a natural opening.

The cave consists of 3 chambers, and opens at the extremity of a deep cove, hollowed out of the limestone rock, which rises in lofty cliffs. The outer chamber is 33 ft. high, and 203 ft. long by 120 ft. broad, but has probably at one time extended farther out to sea. It is perfectly light, and at low water easily accessible, though neither the roof nor ground is dry. On a sunny day the light upon the seaside rocks when seen from the back of the cave is very picturesque, though the effect is somewhat marred by an irregular-shaped hole in the roof.

On the W. side there is a pool of water at the foot of an arch 15 ft. high, the passage through which is obstructed by a barrier of 3 ft. For those who wish to see the cataract and the inner cave, a boat must be lifted over this ledge, a tough job for 4 men, with whom a bargain had better be made before starting.

The length of the inner cavern is 70 ft. by 30 broad, the floor being entirely under water. The visitor is pushed into a niche in the rocks, from whence the view by torchlight is very striking. At the back is the cataract descending perpendicularly through the roof, a height of 80 ft. Beyond this is the third chamber, or rather passage, also containing a pool of great depth. In old times it was supposed that these caverns were tenanted by spirits, and formed the entrance to another world.

Dryas octopetala is to be found on the slope at the upper end of the cavern.

The *Durness Eriboll Limestones* of this district—of Upper Cambrian age—are particularly interesting to the geologist.

20 m. **Durness** ✲ stands on the E. side of the **Kyle of Durness** (across which there is a *Ferry*), and is a large and straggling village, with Parish and Free Chs.

Coach daily to Lairg, 56 m. (Rte. 103).

To the N.W. *Farrid* or *Farout Head* [corrupted from the *Gael.* for *Turning*, cf. *Cape Wrath* (p. 425)] juts 3 m. out to sea, and at its extremity rises to a height of 330 ft. N. the view extends to the cliffs of Hoy in Orkney.

Gold was found in the 16th cent. in the protozoic rocks of Durness, and was coined into money.

Balnakill, ¾ m. N.W., was once the summer abode of the Bishops of Caithness, afterwards of the Lords Reay; but the present house was built by a Master of Reay in the early part of the 18th cent. It is now converted into a farm-house, and has lost all appearance of antiquity. Beyond it is the old *Church* of Durness, formerly a cell connected with the Augustine monastery at Dornoch. It has been unroofed many years, but its burial-ground is still used. In the centre is a granite *Obelisk* to the memory of Rob Don, *alias* Calder, *alias* M'Kay, the Gaelic poet, who died in 1777. Upon the sides of the pedestal are inscriptions in Greek, Latin, English, and Gaelic. In the 5 Latin hexameters, which, being on the S. side, are most easily read, there are no less than 5 false quantities.

Durness to Cape Wrath, 14½ m.

The distance to the ferry across the Kyle of Durness is 2½ m., the strait is about 1 m. broad, and Cape Wrath is 11 m. beyond, making the journey there and back a good day's work.

Those who wish to drive to Cape Wrath must send their horses 2 m. farther up the Kyle, where they can cross at low water, there being no horse-boat, but a dog-cart can be taken by the ordinary ferry-boat.

The whole road to Cape Wrath is

very uninteresting, passing from the Kyle of Durness over a bleak moorish tract known as **The Parph,** without an inch of cultivated ground. 2 m. beyond the ferry there is a shepherd's hut at the mouth of a glen. The road then leaves the Kyle, turns W., and ascends a long hill, commanding a retrospect view of *Ben Spionnu* (2537 ft.), with the tops of Ben Hope and Ben Laoghal behind it. In front (l.) is *Fashven* (1498 ft.), with its broad, bare, and peaked summit, and presently *Scrishven* (1216 ft.) appears upon the rt., sloping gradually to the E., but with a bare precipitous face of red granite upon its W. side.

11 m. At the bottom of this hill a road on rt. leads to the small harbour and *Quarries* of *Clashcarnach.* At the top of the next hill the Minch comes in sight, and round the corner stands the

14½ m. *Lighthouse of Cape Wrath,* which, with its regular and turreted walls, looks like a small fort. It was built in 1828 at a cost of £14,000, is 70 ft. high, and is provided with 20 revolving lights, displaying alternately a red and a white light every minute. The stone of which it is composed was dug from the quarries of Clashcarnach, but all the other materials had to be brought from a great distance.

There is no admission to the lighthouse on Sundays. Permission to sleep there can only be obtained from the Sec. of the Commissioners of Northern Lights at Edinburgh, as the lighthouse-keepers are forbidden to take in any but storm-bound travellers.

Cape Wrath (which is really a corruption of *Hvarf* = (Norweg.) *Turning Point*), the N.W. extremity of Scotland, is 370 ft. high. The whole shore is very precipitous, and the cliffs, which afford striking examples of the action of the waves, present a gneiss wall, interspersed so abundantly by rich pink veins, that the face of the cliff glows with a roseate hue.

"Its huge veins of pink pegmatite seem to writhe up the face of the dark cliffs like the sinews of some antique statue."—Sir A. GEIKIE'S "Scenery of Scotland," p. 113.

On the rt., separated by a narrow gulf, in which vain endeavours have been made to keep up a staircase to the water's edge, is the highest point, a mass of rock rising above the sea, with a fine arch at its base. *Primula Scotica* grows in abundance about the Cape, and *Pinguicula lusitanica* in the neighbouring bogs.

To the E. lies the sandy, well-sheltered bay of *Kearvaig*, and farther on the Kyle of Durness, bounded by *Farout Head*, while in the distant E. and slightly N. the *Cliffs of Hoy* in Orkney may be seen. On a clear day, the *Stack Rock*, 37 m. to the N.E., the island of *North Rona*, 40 m. to the N.W., and the *Butt of Lewis*, 40 m. to the W., are visible; while to the S. are the island of *Bulgie* and the solitary peaked rock known as the *Herd*, as grand a pinnacle as the *Storr* in *Skye*.

SECTION IX.

THE ORKNEY AND SHETLAND ISLANDS.[1]

ROUTES.

ROUTE 109.

The Orkney Islands.

How to reach Orkney : see Index under "Orkney."

How to see Orkney. A day or two at Kirkwall, a tour by steamer to the North Isles returning the next day ; a drive to Stromness (seeing Maeshowe and the Stones of Stenness by the way), and a couple of days there for the purpose of seeing the rock scenery in the neighbourhood and of visiting Hoy, will give the tourist an excellent idea of these islands, which, though almost treeless, have a quiet charm of their own, especially if visited at the practically nightless midsummer.

The Orkneys are separated from Caithness, the extreme N.E. portion of Scotland, by the Pentland Firth, 6½ miles broad at its narrowest part. Of the whole group of 90 islands, 28 are inhabited, the rest being pasture holms or *skerries* — reefs of rock nearly awash at high water. The largest island is named the **Mainland** by the natives, and *Pomona* by geographers and mapmakers, probably from a mistranslation of Solinus, as such a misnomer has never obtained local currency with Pict, Northman, or Scot. The only ground more than 1000 ft. above sea level is in Hoy, and very little attains half that height. The average rainfall is 34 inches. In all the islands the climate is much milder than the latitude would indicate ; the Gulf Stream not only encircling them, but winding like an arterial system of tepid waters through every sound and inlet. There is therefore less frost and snow in Orkney than in most parts of Britain. The mean temperature is 45°, that of winter being seldom very low, while that of summer rarely exceeds 70°. At midsummer there is hardly any darkness. Cultivation is spreading more rapidly than in most counties of Britain, and the large steadings and broad squares of systematic and continuous husbandry entitle many of the islands to the description of "a slice of the Lothians surrounded by the sea." The pop. of the islands in 1891 was 30,453. Together with Shetland they return a member of parl., but Kirkwall is a parl. burgh associated with Wick, etc. There is a resident Sheriff-Substitute and a County Council for each group. These islands, unlike the rest of Scotland, still retain in part *Udal* or allodial tenure of land, which acknowledges no *feudal* superior (see p. 436).

The Orkney and Shetland Islands, already largely colonised by Northern rovers, were conquered in 875 by

[1] Those who wish for an exhaustive and interesting account of these islands should read the late Mr. J. R. Tudor's book, "The Orkneys and Shetlands : their past and present state." London, 1883.

Harold Haarfagr, first king of all Norway. They were given by him to Sigurd, brother of Rognwald the father of Rollo of Normandy, and were governed by their own Jarls, with more or less dependence on the crown of Norway, till 1468, when the sovereignty, and *Skatt* or land-tax payable by Udal proprietors, were mortgaged by Christian of Denmark to James III. of Scotland for his wife's dowry. Her father paid 2000 crowns, gave Orkney in security for 50,000, and Shetland in security for the remaining 8000. James, although he made him a landowner in Fife, practically confiscated from William Sinclair, the last Orkneyar Jarl, the lands of his Scandinavian fathers, thereafter called the Earldom Estate, and Queen Mary, in the middle of the 16th cent., gave them to her bastard brother, Robert Stewart, Earl of Orkney and Lord of Zetland. His son, Earl Patrick, grossly abused his powers as proprietor of the Earldom Estate, Tacksman of the Church Lands, Donatory of the Skatts, and Governor of the Islands. Rents and taxes being payable in kind, he doubled the burdens of the people, by tampering with their weights and measures; but in attempting to overreach Bp. Law he overreached himself. The astute Churchman, taking seven years to frame his case, gathered the complaints of the other proprietors, feudal, udal, and clerical, with the result that Earl Patrick was beheaded (1615). Before this time, the Earldom lands and the Bishopric lands were very much mixed. Law now marked off 7½ parishes as bishopric, the rest being earldom. The scattered relics of the earldom estate were mortgaged to James, Earl of Morton (1707), and, the mortgage having been declared irredeemable (1742), were sold to Sir Lawrence Dundas (1765), whose descendant, the present Marquis of Zetland, still owns a considerable amount of land in Orkney, but, strangely enough, very little in Shetland. Though the matter is now perhaps of no practical importance, yet in theory the King of Norway might perhaps claim restitution of the Orkney and Shetland Islands to his crown on payment of Queen Margaret's dowry into the British Exchequer.

The Approach to Orkney. The steamer from Leith and Aberdeen after passing *Wick* (p. 409), at which it calls abt. once a week, rounds the bold *Noss*[1] headland (the Berubium of Ptolemy), with its lighthouse and the ruined castles of *Sinclair* and *Girnigo* (l.), ancient strongholds of the Earls of Caithness, and passes *Ackergill Tower* (Duff Dunbar, Esq.), *Keiss Castle* (F. T. Barry, Esq.), and *Freswick* (E. S. Alexander-Sinclair, Esq.), near the older Castle of Freswick, the Lambaborg of the Sagas. From Freswick the steamer stands out to sea, to avoid the restless current of the Pentland Firth, and passing Duncansbay Head with Dunnet Head in the distance, we see the *Ward Hill* of *Hoy* (1564 ft.), the highest hill in Orkney, over the island of *Stroma*. We then pass the *Pentland Skerries*, with their twin lighthouses, and skirt the E. cliffs of the fertile island of **South Ronaldsay**, the most southern of the Orkneys.

[The mail steamer from *Thurso* after rounding Dunnet Head (3 m. E.) keeps N. along the W. side of this island.]

At its N. end the clustering masts of the fishing-fleet mark the little town of †**St. Margaret's Hope** ✲, where the ship on which Queen Margaret, the Maid of Norway, had died while on her way to Scotland, put in and received Bp. Dolgfimur on board before returning to Norway.

1 Old Norse, *nös* means a nose; *vik*, a small creek or bay; *gja*, a chasm or rift; *ey*, an island. The Norse is the source of all nomenclature in Orkney and Shetland, and of much of that of Caithness.

This (1290) was the sad prelude of the long wars of Scottish independence.

[The steamer from Leith calls here abt. once a fortnight, and a boat goes out daily from Hoxa Head (3 m. W.) to the mail steamer to Thurso.]

The sandy island to the N.—**Burray** (*Borgar-ey*)—owes its name to a very curious *Brough* which has been opened. Passing (l.) the entrance of *Holm Sound*, where there is an excellent anchorage near *Graemeshall* (A. S. Graeme, Esq.), the steamer runs between the E. shore of the peninsula of *Deerness* (the Kaupaneda-ness of the Sagas), fertile and cultivated to the beach, and the strangely-shaped island of **Copinsay** (Samuel Reid, Esq.), whose green W. slopes contrast strongly with its E. precipice, the noisy nest of myriads of sea-birds. N. of it is the curious islet called the *Horse of Copinsay*. In the *Bay of Sandside* (with *Deerness Ch.*) Torfin-Jarl defeated "the gracious Duncan," nicknamed by the Norsemen Carl-King, and in its ruined burg Thorkel Foster executed wild justice on the tyrant Einar-Jarl II. Rounding the *Mull of Deerness* (l.), we have a distant view (rt.) of the N. Isles of **Stronsay, Sanday, Eday**, and **Rousay**, and nearer of **Auskerry**, with its lighthouse, and of **Shapinsay**. The fine natural harbour of *Deer Sound* (the ancient Rörvaag) (l.) is full of legendary interest. Here Olaf Tryggveson of Norway surprised Sigurd-Jarl II., and forced on him Christian baptism (995). At the head of the Sound rises the sepulchral barrow called *Dinguy's* (Ninian's) *Howe*, where that saint drove out the evil spirit, which had for weeks reanimated the corpse of Amund to unnatural strife with his devoted brother, who had in his love entered and shared his grave. Farther down on the W. shore stands *Tankerness* (W. D. Baikie, Esq.), where Sir James Sinclair of Sanda, the Wallace of Orkney, lived, and whence his daughter, the greatest heiress of Orkney, eloped on her bridal morning with young Halcro of Brough, to escape a forced marriage with the old and ugly Tulloch of Sound. Tradition affirms that Mary of Guise dismissed Tulloch's appeal, with sympathetic approval of the young bride's choice. At the mouth of the Sound is the curious chasm called the *Gloup of Linksness*. The steamer next passes the mouth of the still finer anchorage of Inganess Bay, on whose W. shore is *Birstane House* (Col. Balfour), and through "The String" — between *Helliar Holm* (with a *Lighthouse* erected 1894) and the *Head of Work*—the narrow part of Shapinsay Sound which Sir Walter might well call "beautiful."

Behind Helliar Holm is the fine harbour of *Ell Wick*, the rendezvous of Hakon's fleet before his fatal raid to Largs (1263), overlooked by the imposing *Balfour Castle* on **Shapinsay,** the seat of Col. Balfour, whose predecessor, Col. David Balfour, not only redeemed this island from waste, but largely contributed to the prosperity of the other islands by encouraging agricultural improvements, mills, harbours, piers, etc. The gallery of Balfour Castle contains an original portrait of Mary Queen of Scots, historical and family portraits by *Vandyck, Kneller, Gainsborough, Walker, Dobson, Raeburn*, etc., some good works of old masters, and a fine collection of engravings. The ancestors of Washington Irving occupied the humble cottage of *Quholme* in the N.E. of the island, but he himself was born on board an American ship on its passage from here to New York.

The noble Bay of Kirkwall now opens before us on the left, and the massive Cathedral of St. Magnus looms grandly over the quaint little capital of the Orkneys. At the excellent deep-water pier the steamer moors long enough to allow even the tourist bound for Shetland time to visit the town and cathedral.

†**KIRKWALL**✲ (prob. = *Kirkevaag* = Church Bay), a royal and parl. burgh, stands upon "**The Mainland,**" which here narrows to an isthmus 2 m. wide between Kirkwall Bay (N.) and Scapa Bay (S.). It is a picturesque old-fashioned little town, the gables of the houses being turned to the long irregular narrow main street, which has wide pavements but only 4 ft. of a causeway. Of the interesting houses not yet swept away by modern improvements, that of the Baikies of Tankerness, opposite the W. end of the Cathedral, deserves particular notice.

Kirkwall was made a royal burgh by James III. (1486), and was visited by James V., who held various meetings with the island magnates in the "Parliament Close," a curious building, removed to make way for the handsome Commercial Bank. He lodged in the Bishop's House, still standing. In Poor-House Close is an elegant arched doorway, the sole remains of the original parochial church of St. Olaf, burnt by the English fleet of Henry VIII. in his rude courtship of the infant Queen Mary as a bride for his son (1544).

Castle Street passes over the site of the old *Castle of Kirkwall*, once so strong that its builder, Earl Henry, was believed to have been helped by the devil. This stronghold was held against the fugitive Earl of Bothwell by Balfour, Governor of Orkney (1567), but on the suppression of the Orkney Rebellion (1614) was so thoroughly demolished that only a fragment remained to be removed at the formation of the street in 1865. Near the S. end of the town stands the useful but unpretending *Balfour Hospital* for the sick.

The Romanesque * **Cathedral of St. Magnus** [1] is built of red and white freestone, and is perfect, with the exception of the spire. It is cruciform, comprising a choir of 6 bays and a nave of 8, both aisled and about 45 ft. broad, a central tower 133 ft. high, and transepts. The good Magnus-Jarl of Orkney was sacrilegiously murdered in the island of Egilsay (1115) by his cousin Hakon-Jarl, in one of those strifes of succession to which Odal-ret was so liable. Rognvald-Jarl III., the nephew and heir of St. Magnus, vowed that if ever he recovered his rights he would build a church in honour of his martyred uncle, and accordingly, in 1138, he began the original building of the cathedral, probably with a rounded apse (of which traces still remain), and two parallel aisles on each side of the nave, as indicated by the arches (of which two are built up) in the E. wall of what afterwards became the transept. Bishop Stewart inserted the E. window (circ. 1511). Bishop Maxwell (1525) built the central tower, which rests on First Pointed arches, and furnished it with three fine bells, cast by Robert Borthwick, the master gunner who tried so hard to save his master, James IV., from his own folly at Flodden. Bishop Reid (circ. 1550) added the westernmost portion, comprising 3 Romanesque bays. The extreme internal length is 218 ft., but the narrowness of the choir and nave adds to their apparent height, and considering that 400 years elapsed from the original foundation to the completion of the building, its uniformity of style is remarkable. The steeple was used sometimes as a prison and sometimes as a fortress, and the Cromwellian soldiers made a barrack and a stable of the nave. The carving has suffered as much from violence as from time and the softness of the stone.

The body of King Hakon rested here after the battle of Largs until a more permanent tomb was prepared for him in Trondhjem. A huge

[1] See the "Church of St. Magnus in Orkney" by Sir Henry Dryden, Bart., Daventry, 1871.

slab of white marble covers the bones of Earl Robert, and repairs in the choir brought to light fragments of the finely-crocketed tomb of Bishop Tulloch (p. 431) in the S. aisle, which bore his name. In the N. transept stands a handsome monument to William Balfour Baikie, the explorer of the Niger, and translator of the Bible into many African languages, and in the N. external aisle is a mural slab in memory of another distinguished native of Kirkwall, the historian Malcolm Laing (1762-1818), whose residence of *Papdale* looks down from the hill N.E. of the town. The cathedral was saved from Reformation violence by the affectionate zeal of the townsmen, and Kirkwall continued to be an Episcopal See under a succession of 7 Protestant bishops till the Revolution. The cathedral was partially restored under Government direction in 1845; and in 1883 some further restorations were undertaken with money left by Mr. Meason, the 5 windows on the S. side of the nave being cleared out and rebuilt; but it still awaits its Wm. Chambers. It is sadly neglected and galleries fill up the arches of the choir, which is used as the Parish Church.

S. of the cathedral stands the ruined **Bishop's Palace**, in an upper chamber of which the unfortunate King Hakon died heart-broken after his disaster at Largs (1263). The principal feature of the palace is a massive *Tower*, round without and square within, supported by very strong buttresses, and ornamented with a small statue, probably of some saint, but vulgarly attributed to the distinguished scholar, lawyer, and diplomatist, Bishop Robert Reid (d. 1558).

To the E. of the Bishop's Palace stands the ruined **Earl's Palace**, built by Earl Patrick Stewart (1600), a good specimen of the baronial style, when the castellated form came to be used more for ornament than defence. The main body of the building is rectangular, with turrets thrown out from the angles. The dining-hall is very handsome, with a three-light window to the S., and 2 bays to the E. The fireplace is a fine example of the straight arch, its pillars bearing the initials P. E. O. (Patrick Earl of Orkney). In this ruined dining-hall Sir Walter Scott places the scene of Cleveland's interview with Bunce in "The Pirate."

Between the two Palaces are the plain, modern, but commodious **Sheriff Court Buildings** (1876), and in 1883 a handsome **Town Hall** was erected in Broad Street.

Mr. J. W. Cursitor, F.S.A., Albert Street, has a good collection of local antiquities, etc., which he kindly allows visitors interested in such matters to see.

There is a *Golf Course* here, and a better one at Birsay (p. 434).

EXCURSIONS:[1]—

(1) **Wideford Hill.**

No tourist should fail to climb the easy ascent of *Wideford Hill*, to enjoy its splendid bird's-eye view of the Orkneys, the Pentland Firth, and the distant peaks of Caithness and Sutherland. The road to Stromness runs W. between the bay and the *Peerie Sea* (a salt-water lagoon) by one of those natural causeways called Ayres, which are so striking a feature of Orcadian scenery, and crossing a bridge winds to the right. A by-road strikes off (l.) directly from the bridge up the hill, passing (l.) *Grainbank* (Marquis of Zetland's factor), and (rt.) a Pict's house, in which was found a silver armlet. An easy walk of little more than a mile leads to the summit. The tourist is now in the centre of the Orcadian scenes of "The Pirate," and will probably, remembering the

[1] Peace's Monthly Diary and Time Table, 1d., gives hours of steamers and coaches.

changes the greater magician Time has wrought, do homage to the genius which could hit off such a likeness at one sitting, so brief and unsatisfactory as Scott's visit in 1814.

"From the top of Wideford Hill (740 ft.) nearly all the islands may be seen; and no one who goes there on a clear day will hesitate to admit that the scene before him, looking seaward, is one of exquisite beauty . . . a most lovely picture, in which the additional ornament of trees is not missed."—J. KERR.

(2) To the islands of **Rousay**✲ and **Egilsay**✲.

Rousay, 10 m. N., belongs to General Burroughs, C.B., whose fine seat of *Trumland House* is seen from Kirkwall. Its high ground of *Blotchinfield* (811 ft.) and *Knitchenfield* (732 ft.) commands extensive views, and its W. coast rock scenery is bold. E. of it is **Egilsay** with an old church, of 11th or early 12th cent. There is nothing in its architecture to fix its age. It is said to have been built upon the spot where St. Magnus was murdered (1115), and therefore dedicated to him. The building, however, is much older than the crime, which may have been committed within its walls. The most remarkable part is the **Round Tower** (like those at Brechin and Abernethy and in Norfolk), now reduced to 48 ft. in height (it probably was 60 ft). The building is roofless, and now only used as the mausoleum of the Baikies.

(3) To the **North Isles**✲.

These include **Eday, Stronsay, Sanday,** and **Westray,** but the tourist need only land on the last named. The route of the steamer varies. In its longest tour it goes due N. to the W. of **Shapinsay** (p. 428), then steers N.E. to Eday. To the N. Egilsay Ch. and Tower (above) are conspicuous. From the pier at the S. end of †**Eday**✲ the steamer sails E. to the flat "lobster-shaped" †**Stronsay**✲, whose *Well of Kildinguie* had once a great and widespread reputation for its healing powers in cases of leprosy. It is a strong spring of beautiful fresh water below high-water mark.

"Water from the Well of Kildinguie and dulse from Geo-Odin can cure anything but the Black Death," says Norna, in "The Pirate."

The course is now N. to †**Sanday**✲, with *Start Point* Lighthouse on its N.E. promontory. Farther N. is **N. Ronaldsay** (with a lighthouse), to which the only communication is a weekly post boat from Sanday.

The steamer now passes through the most picturesque part of the whole sail—***Calf Sound**—between Eday and the Calf of Eday, with the grand promontories of *Grey Head* to the E., and *Red Head* to the W. Here the *historical* "Pirate" Gow was wrecked and captured 1725. Having called at **Papa**[1] **Westray** we reach our destination at *Pierowall Bay*, **Westray**✲, on which are the extensive ruins of *Noltland Castle* (1 m. W.) founded by Thomas Tulloch, Bishop of Orkney, in 1422. The initials T. T., with the figure of a bishop kneeling, are upon the capital of the pillar supporting the staircase. The castle remained the residence of the bishops until 1560, when it was conveyed by Adam Bothwell, the last bishop, to his brother-in-law, Gilbert Balfour of Westray. Upon his representative espousing the cause of Charles Edward Stuart in 1745, the castle of Noltland was burnt by the Government troops. The castle is still the property of Colonel Balfour.

***Noup Head** (3½ m. W.), swarming with sea-fowl, and with overhanging cliffs more impressive than those of Hoy, although not so high, is one of the grandest bits of scenery in Orkney. Here is the "*Gentleman's*

[1] Several smaller islands with this name had originally hermits' cells. *Papa*=Pope=Father.

Cave," where Balfour, Stewart, Traill of Elsness, and others hid for a whole winter after their flight from Culloden.

(4) To **Stromness,** 15 m. *Coaches daily.*

Passing the Ayre and bridge, the road winds W. between Wideford Hill and the sea-coast, affording many pretty bits of landscape. On the N. face of the hill stands the remarkable *Pict's House* at *Quanterness* (2½ m.) described and pictured in Barry's "History of Orkney."

As we drive round the *Bay of Firth* rt. lies the pretty green islet of *Damsay* (St. Adamnan's-ey) and its ruined brough, so often named in the stirring legends of the Sagas.

The Kirk of Firth is l. as we enter

6½ m. **Finstown** Village ✲, whence a road strikes rt. to the N. mainland. We now actually come upon a plantation, and above a picturesquely-wooded pass stands *Binscarth* (R. Scarth, Esq.), which commands a magnificent view.

[A little farther on a branch road (rt.) leads northward to **Harray** and **Birsay**★, and one (l.) leads through the hills to the valley of *Bigswell* or *Sommerdale*, the Bannockburn of Orkney, where (1529) the Orcadians, under Sir James Sinclair, gained a great victory over their Scottish invaders under John, Earl of Caithness, in a field still marked by many a battle mound.]

At 9½ m. (rt.) stands one of the most remarkable ancient monuments of Orkney, the sepulchral mound of ***Maeshowe**[1] (*Mestr*, greatest; *Haugr*, mound or cairn). Many a legend still lingers around Maeshowe and its strong but stupid Hog-boy (*Haug Bue*, larva sepulchri), the guardian of its treasures and its secrets. His treasure has been stolen long ago, but he still keeps his secret. Perhaps, like Lady Percy—

"He will not utter what he does not know."

Its sculptured dragons may point to serpent-worship, and the Runes which cover its walls may long exercise the ingenuity of Scandinavian scholars; but as they were not written till the tomb had been ruined, they can throw no light on its origin, objects, or date. The mysteries of Maeshowe and Stenness will probably be solved with those of Stonehenge, Avebury, Karnac, and Gavr-ynis, and not sooner.

Maeshowe is about 92 ft. in diameter, 36 ft. high, and about 300 ft. in circumference, surrounded by a trench 40 ft. wide, and about 6 ft. deep. It had undoubtedly been rifled by the Northmen, who opened every place likely to repay their trouble. Whether they found it a ruin or not, it is evident that the Runes were not inscribed till the roof was uncovered, and probably not till ages of exposure had decayed the surface of the stone. They evidently showed little respect to the dead, for the stones which once closed the cells were torn out and buried in the ruins of the fallen roof. A passage, opening from the W., 26 feet long, 3¼ ft. wide, and 4⅓ ft. high, leads to the central chamber, which is a cube of nearly 15 ft., having sepulchral cells on three of the sides, the cells being respectively 6 ft. 10 in., 5 ft. 7 in., and 5 ft. 8 in. in length. The roof, floor, and walls of each cell are formed of a single stone, and the stones that formed the doors were found on the ground in front of them. The four walls of the central chamber are formed of immense slabs of stone or flag, 15 ft. long, and about 6 ft. above the floor they commence to converge towards the centre in the manner of a Pictish arch. But the present roof is composed of brick for lightness and protection, as it was found that a roof of the original material was too heavy for the time-wasted walls. In each angle is a large buttress of a single stone about 10 ft. high, the face of which, as well as the edge of those composing the walls, is covered with Runic characters (about 935 in all), besides a dragon of very lively action, and a knot of serpents, probably of a different hand and age from the Runes. The whole structure is without mortar, of undressed stones of huge size, of the same kind and quarry as the monoliths of Stenness, which, it is not impossible, may have been taken for the purpose, and may thus account for some blanks in the circles; and the whole is covered by an immense cone of earth, which is well entitled to the distinction of the *Mestr Haugr*, or "biggest barrow." The monument is well taken care of by Col. Balfour.

[1] The key is kept at the neighbouring farmhouse of Turmiston.

Beyond the Kirk of Stenness (rt.) are the ruins of the *House of Stenness*, the ancient Bu, where Havard-Jarl was murdered by his wicked wife, Ragnhild (circ. 980), and the imaginary site of some of the most stirring scenes of the "Pirate" (in which, however, Scott seems to have confused his topographical memoranda of Stenness with those of Clestrain on the other side of the Orphir Hills).

At 10½ m. a by-road rt. leads directly to the Stonehenge of Orkney.

Following this road a few hundred yards, we reach (rt.) the small **Circle of Stenness**, composed of 12 stones about 15 ft. high, of which only two are standing and two prostrate. The radius of this stone-circle, when complete, was about 50 ft., and that of the surrounding embankment about 120 ft. The plough has effaced nearly half of the once circular *vallum*—a sacrilege probably committed by the same farmer who destroyed the interesting *Stone of Odin*, which stood (till 1814) a few yards to the E. of this group.

It has a hole through it, is mentioned in Scott's "Pirate," and until recent times an oath taken with hands joined through this hole was deemed more binding than any other oath.

A little farther on stands the *Watch Stone*, the highest of all the standing stones, immediately before entering the narrow causeway—between the freshwater *Loch of Harray* (rt.) and the tidal *Loch of Stenness* (l.)—called the Bridge of Brogarth, which leads direct, past many tumuli and monoliths, to the great circle or * **Ring of Brogarth** or **Brogar**.

This is a deeply-entrenched circular space of about 2½ acres, with a diameter of 366 ft. The trench which surrounds it is 29 ft. broad and 6 ft. deep, crossed by two narrow earth banks. The erect stones in the circle stand about 18 ft. apart, and about 13 ft. from the trench, of various sizes from 6 to 13 ft., totally unhewn, and all of old red sandstone. The probable number when complete was about 60, but only 13 remain standing, 10 prostrate, and the broken stumps of a few others. Independent of its antiquarian interest, the situation of the Ring of Brogarth, standing on a narrow peninsula, sloping on both sides to the Lochs of Stenness and Harray, and with pleasing views from it in every direction, is strikingly beautiful. The neighbourhood seems to have been the Orcadian *Campo Santo;* for within a short distance there are two circles of standing-stones, 4 separate monoliths, 2 other circles, of which all the stones are prostrate, and scores of tumuli, in one of which were found various antiquities, including a very fine urn of micaceous schist.

Returning to the main road we soon cross at 12½ m. the shallow entrance of the Loch of Stenness by the *Bridge of Waith* ✲ (*Vaedr*, a shallow stream), a handsome stone bridge, which has replaced the ancient and dangerous structure of wood.

[Before the bridge a road strikes l. to Kirkwall in 14½ m., which should be taken by the tourist if returning. It skirts the *Ward Hill* (l.) 880 ft. to 5½ m. **Orphir,** where are traces of a circular church, supposed to have been erected by Hakon-Jarl, after his Pilgrimage to Jerusalem made on account of the murder of his cousin St. Magnus—the only specimen of a circular church in Scotland. The road passes l. the loch of *Kirbuster*, and 1½ m. from Kirkwall *Lingrow Farm*, where are "the remains of a broch, which in the perfect network of its buildings, of its E., S., and S.W. sides, affords one of the best specimens in connection with these structures of secondary occupation."]

Beyond the bridge the carriage road makes a detour, and the shorter though rough track l. over the hill, commanding good views of the lochs behind, the Sound in front, and the Islands of Graemsay and Hoy, should be taken to

15 m. †**STROMNESS** ✲.

This is a busy little town of one very narrow street, with steep branches running directly up the granite hill, which shelters it from the Atlantic, and down to the many jetties of its fine and important harbour. There is still considerable activity from the concourse of shipping, shipbuilding, and fisheries. It used to be the northern port of call for the Hudson's Bay whaling fleets The *Cemetery* is remarkable for the savage and lonely grandeur of its situation, and for the view of the opposite cliff of Hoy, which presents a remarkable profile likeness of Sir Walter Scott. On the high authority of Hugh Miller, this district is to the geologist not only the most interesting in Orkney, but surpassed by few in the N. of Scotland, yielding among its Ichthyolites the Asterolepis or star scale fish. There is a *Museum* here containing some good fossils, but it is neglected.

EXCURSIONS :—

(1) *Walk by the Cliffs to* **Bay of Skaill.** Abt. 8 m.

We see many interesting natural curiosities and pass *Black Craig,* in whose quarry many fossil fishes have been found, and two isolated pillars or "stacks," called *North Gaulton Castle* and the *Castle of Yeskenaby.* 1 m. from the bay is *Beacon Hill,* with a grand view back of Hoy, and at its base a natural pavement showing curious geometrical patterns caused by weathering, but long thought to be due to art. At the S. of the bay is the *Hole of Row,* a natural arch formed by two whin dykes, the material between them having been washed out by the sea. The rude ancient Picts' houses, which have been disinterred and exposed on the shore of the bay, are of the highest antiquarian interest.

To the N. of the bay is *Sandwick Church.*

(2) N. to **Birsay** ✲, by road 13 m. (from Kirkwall 19 m.).

We pass, beyond the N. end of Loch Stenness, (at 5 m.) *Loch Clumly,* and "an overthrown cromlech called the *Stones of Via.*" At 8 m. *Skaill Bay* (above) is about 1½ m. W. *Birsay Palace,* though now in a deplorable state of ruin, was once a fine residence, rebuilt by Earl Robert Stewart in imitation of Falkland, viz. a quadrangle, with a well in the middle.

The Latin inscription over the gate (now gone) — "Dominus Robertus Stewartus filius Jacobi V., *Rex* Scotorum, hoc opus instruxit," constituted one of the charges against his son when tried for high treason, though most likely it was only a grammatical error.

There is an excellent natural *Golf Course* here.

W. on the *Brough of Birsay,* an island except for a few hours daily, are the ruins of an interesting old ch. (abt. 1100), which consisted of nave, chancel, and apse, and possibly was twin-towered. S. is *Marwick Head* (263 ft.), and E. the most northern point of the mainland, *Costa Head* (478 ft.), with splendid cliff scenery.

(3) S. to **Hoy** (Norse *Há-ey* = *High island*), by boat 4 m.

This is the finest of the Orkney Islands. The *Ward Hill* (1564 ft.) is celebrated for its *Views* and its botanical treasures.

To the S.E. of it is the **"Dwarfie Stone,"** 2 m. from the landing-stage. This stone is 20 ft. long by 44 ft. wide and 7 ft. deep, and has an aperture scooped out in it, with a bed on each side. It is said to have been a heathen altar originally, and subsequently the abode of a Christian hermit; but in the mythology of the country it was the favourite residence of a Trold—the generic name for the dwarfs who were supposed to inhabit the hills.

It plays an important part in "The Pirate," and Hugh Miller has left his initials chiselled upon it!

The pedestrian should ascend the *Meadow of the Kaim* in the N. corner, and keep along the W. cliffs by *Braebrough* or *St. John's Head* (1140 ft.) to the "Old Man"; thence S. to *Rora Head* and *Rackwick,* up *Berriedale,* E. to the *Dwarfie Stone,* and back to the boat. This magnificent round of 16 or 17 m. will take abt. 8 hrs., but nearly a couple may be saved by going at once E. from the "Old Man." Climbing the Ward Hill is not included.

On a suitable day the W. cliffs

—after *Foula* (p. 440) the most glorious sea front in the British Isles—should be surveyed from a boat. The **"Old Man of Hoy"** is an insulated pillar, which is a prominent feature from the N. of Scotland.

"The groundwork of that wonderful column is composed of flagstones and shales, and across their denuded edges there stretches the band of amygdaloidal lava, which is capped by the red sandstones to a height of 450 ft."—PEACH.

Berry Head, at the S.W. corner of the island, is worth a visit on account of its height (595 ft.) and outline, but still more because of the beautiful colour of the rock composing it.

2 m. E. of it is *Melsetter Ho.* (with beautiful gardens), the seat of J. G. M. Heddle, Esq., the proprietor of Hoy.

ROUTE 110.

The Shetland Islands.[1]

How to reach Shetland: see Index under "Shetland."

How to see Shetland. A few days at Lerwick for the purpose of visiting the Noup of Noss, Scalloway, Mousa, etc., a tour by steamer to the N. Islands, returning by the same or the next boat, and a sail from Scalloway up the W. side to Hillswick (stopping there if possible a couple of days and returning to Lerwick by road), will show the tourist the best of the scenery, although by no means exhausting it.

These islands have the same bleak and treeless appearance as the Orkneys, but the cliff scenery is even more remarkable, and the long sea lochs or "voes" are peculiarly interesting, although far inferior to the fjords of Norway. No spot is more than 3 m. from the sea. Except at Lerwick there are hardly any inns, but comfortable though plain lodgings can sometimes be obtained.

[1] Besides Tudor's "Orkneys and Shetlands," see Sheriff Rampini's "Shetland and the Shetlanders," 1s.

The voyage from Kirkwall to Lerwick (116 m.) occupies in fine weather about 8 hrs., the steamer passing half-way **Fair Isle** (properly speaking *Faröe*=sheep isle), 24 m. from any other land, with 214 inhab. In 1588, after the defeat of the Spanish Armada, its admiral, the Duke of Medina Sidonia, retreated northwards, pursued by the English squadron, and was wrecked here, but escaped with some of his crew. From the Spaniards the islanders probably learned those Moorish patterns which are characteristic of their knitted hosiery. There are now 2 lighthouses on the island, which is 3 m. long by 1½ m. broad, and telegraphic communication was established in 1892. The Church of Scotland has a Mission here.

As soon as Fair Isle is lost to sight, **Sumburgh Head**, the most southerly point of Shetland, comes into view, with its bare top and naked sides, guarded by a lighthouse. This promontory (300 ft.), near which the reader of the "The Pirate" will remember dwelt the father of Mordaunt Merton, is constantly exposed to the current of a strong and furious tide, which, setting in between the Orkney and Shetland Isles, and running with force only inferior to that of the Pentland Firth, takes its name from the headland, and is called the Roost of Sumburgh. On a neck of land in the West Voe are the ruins of *Jarlshof*, near which is the modern residence of Mr. Bruce, the proprietor of Sumburgh. The cleft in the rock by which the inhabitants descend from the cliff above to the foot is called *Eric's Steps.* To the W. is the grander promontory of **Fitful Head** (928 ft.) (Old Norse, *Feitr-Fjall*, White Mountain), the abode of Norna, the Shetland prophetess. The tourist who wishes to explore the southern part of Mainland can land at *Dunrossness* (if arrangements have been made for a boat coming out), and work his way along the coast (about 24 m.) to Lerwick.

The name of Shetland or Zetland is a corruption of the old "Hjaltland," by which name these islands were known to the earliest chroniclers. The group consists of about 100 islands, but only 29 are inhabited, the population (1891) being 28,711. The climate is very variable, damp, and stormy. To strangers its incessant moisture is very depressing, though the inhabitants do not find it unwholesome. In winter the cold is not great, and, although the days are very short, owing to the wide horizon the actual difference in length of daylight as contrasted with such places as Edinburgh or Aberdeen is hardly perceptible. Spring can scarcely be said to commence till April, and little general warmth is experienced before the middle of June. Summer ends again with August. In the middle of summer it is sufficiently light at midnight to read. It is a sort of twilight, the northern heavens remaining so bright that frequently the rosy tints of the sunset only lose themselves in the dawn.

The traveller who makes his way to these parts in hopes of sport runs a great risk of disappointment. No doubt, of mere sea-fowl, every variety, some very rare, may be found among the less-frequented islands; but of geese, ducks, curlew, teal, snipe, etc., he will find no more than may be met with on many parts of the coast of England and Scotland. There is excellent fishing in the streams that run into the fiords, the sea-trout sometimes weighing as much as 15 lbs., and of ordinary sea-fish the supply is unlimited. Seal are rarely caught or even seen, except about certain spots, such as Papa Stour, to the recesses of whose porphyry caves they retire to breed.

The inhabitants are of Scandinavian origin, those islands like the Orkneys having belonged to Norway or Denmark until 1468 (see p. 427). In the olden days the "Thing" or Parliament met in the open air at a place still called "Tingwall," 4 m. N.W. of Lerwick. The tenure was originally and in a few instances still is Udal, acknowledging no superior. "Of whom, then," asked a southern judge, accustomed to feudal right, "does the Shetlander hold?" "Of God Almighty," replied the advocate.

At the death of a holder the land belonged equally to his children, male and female.

The Shetlands were, in the 16th cent., entrusted to stewards appointed by the Crown, but as they farmed the revenues, and it was their interest to make what surplus they could, the islanders suffered greatly from their exactions, and the memory of Earl Patrick Stewart (p. 427) is still the subject of execration. The land now belongs to several proprietors, of whom the Marquis of Zetland—who holds the Lordship of Zetland by grant from the Crown—is one, but the amount he holds is inconsiderable.

The fisheries are the principal employment of the people,—ling, cod, tusk, haddock, and herrings. Many of the young men are sailors in the mercantile marine, and some join the Greenland whalers which generally call at Lerwick to complete their crews. Farming in a primitive manner is carried on chiefly by crofters, and a peculiar breed of sheep, said to be identical with the wild sheep of Siberia, is reared. Their wool is prepared and knitted by the natives into various articles of clothing and especially into those beautifully soft shawls so well known.

Shetland ponies are bred and exported, and the manufacture of kelp is still carried on to some extent. In June Lerwick harbour is frequently full of Dutch fishing-boats which put in from time to time to obtain stores, and present a very gay appearance. In the end of July and beginning of August the harbour is full of fishing boats from all parts, including the Isle of Man, and the herring stations are crowded with women cleaning and salting the fish for exportation.

†**LERWICK** ✲, the capital of the Shetland Isles, is the most northerly town in the British Isles. It stands pleasantly on the E. side of "**The Mainland,**" facing the island of Bressay. Its houses are most irregularly placed, and some even built into the water of the harbour, or *Bressay Sound*, one of the finest natural harbours in the world.

Here may be seen, though in fewer numbers than formerly, the "sixerns," a build of boat which has come down from Scandinavian days. Every Shetlander is a born seaman, and the women can manage the boats almost as well as the men. All the steamers can now lie alongside of the excellent pier, opened June 1886 (Cay, archt.).

The town of Lerwick possesses little attraction to the tourist. It has one street—*Commercial Street*—running parallel with and close to the harbour edge. This street is a flagged causeway, wide in some places, but so narrow in others that carts can with difficulty pass. It was formed at a time before wheeled vehicles were used in Shetland. From Commercial Street there run at right angles to it up the hillside numerous lanes which end in the second largest thoroughfare, called the *Hill Head*. At the north end of the town is **Fort Charlotte,** built by Cromwell, and repaired by Charles II. in 1665. After being destroyed by the Dutch at the beginning of the 18th century, it was repaired and garrisoned during the French wars. Now it is used as a drill ground by the Naval Reserve, who meet there yearly—a fine body of men, the flower of Shetland. The *Anderson Institute* stands on a commanding site in the south part of Lerwick, erected 1862 by Arthur Anderson, as a good school for the Lerwegians. The *Widows' Asylum* is also situated at the south end, and was built by the same gentleman. It consists of tenements for 21 widows, of Shetland sailors by preference. In 1881 a **Town Hall** was built, to which was presented in 1883, by the inhabitants of Hamburg, a large stained glass window bearing a Latin inscription, in recognition of the good services rendered to Hamburg seamen and fishermen by the Shetlanders.

EXCURSIONS :—

(1) To **Clickimin Loch** 1 m. W., only separated by a narrow beach from the sea, and containing on a small island a Pict's *brough* second only in preservation to that of Mousa (p. 438). Beyond is the typical Shetland village of **Sound,** practically unchanged for centuries.

(2) E. to **Bressay**, the **Noup of Noss**, and the **Orkneyman's Cave.** This is *the* excursion of the neighbourhood. Cross the Sound to Bressay, and that island to (2 m.) Noss Sound, a narrow strait with a strong current, but across which is a ferry to *Noss Island* on whose E. side is the *Noup*, a grand headland (592 ft.) S. of it is an island —the *Holm of Noss*—separated by a fine chasm over which a cradle used to be slung, but many years ago it broke, and the sea birds (which swarm there in countless numbers during the breeding season) and their eggs are now left in peace.

The island of Noss and a farm in Bressay are occupied by the Marquis of Londonderry's establishment for the breeding of Shetland ponies. The *Ward Hill* on Bressay (742 ft.) commands a magnificent view, and at the S. end of the Island are *Bard Head,* an arch called the *Giant's Leg,* and the *Orkneyman's Cave.* The cave must be visited by boat and torches should be taken. A calm day is necessary and what wind there is should be N.E., and then Noup Head should be surveyed from the sea. There is another fine archway under *Bressay Lighthouse.*

(3) W. to †**Scalloway**✲ 6 m., the former capital of Shetland, which can be reached by either the N. or S. road. We advise the tourist to go by one road and return by the other. The town of Scalloway is old, but in itself uninteresting. The bay is very beautiful, and the tourist fond of boating can have a fine sail about the islands of *Trondra,* etc., lying to the south. *Cliff Sound* is a narrow sea way, along which small boats can sail S. between the islands of Trondra, Burra, and Havera, and the mainland for 10 m. The ruins of *Scalloway Castle* are an attraction. It was built by Earl Patrick Stewart in 1600. On one of the chimneys is an iron ring on which he used to hang his victims, and a small chamber is pointed out as the place of his concealment from the officers charged with his apprehension. He is said to have been discovered by the smoke from his pipe.

Gallow Hill overhangs the W. end of Scalloway. It was the Tyburn of Shetland, where criminals and witches met their death. Barbara Tulloch and her daughter were the last recorded victims, and were burned at the stake on this hill in the beginning of the 18th cent. for witchcraft. The tourist should ascend the hill for the fine view it affords of the isles, rocks, hills, capes, voes, and bays of the W. coast of the mainland, which he may not care to visit, though there is pretty scenery and good trout-fishing in Walls parish. Scalloway is the headquarters of the Faröe cod-fishery, also of the extensive trade with Spain in salted fish.

Tingwall Valley and Trout Lochs. This beautiful valley stretches N.E. from Scalloway, ending at (5 m.) *Laxfirth Voe.* It contains a chain of excellent trout lochs, two of fresh water (*Asta* and *Tingwall*), and a third, *Loch of Strand,* which is salt water, and connected with Laxfirth Voe. Leave to fish must be obtained at Lerwick.

The **Ting of Tingwall** was the old open-air Parliament of Shetland, which was held on a small island in the Loch of Tingwall, near the present manse. Stepping-stones lead to it.

Dale Valley is passed through on the return to Lerwick by the N. road, and is separated from Tingwall Valley by high hills. It is penetrated by *Dale's Voe,* is very picturesque, and a pleasant walk of 3 m. from Lerwick by the N. road. After passing this valley coming towards Lerwick, a good level piece of road is traversed through dark brown heath, and the Lerwick peat-hills are passed. Here are generally to be seen the peat-carriers, mostly women, who are generally knitting. On sighting Lerwick a fine view is obtained of the N. entry to the harbour, Whalsay Island, and Out Skerries.

(4) S. To ***Mousa Island, Sumburgh Head,** and **Fitful Head.** The scenery at Quarff, Cunningsburgh, and Sandwick is pretty. From Sandwick (14 m.) Mousa is reached by boat. The channel is 1 m. wide. On the island is the most perfect Picts' Castle in existence. It is 42 ft. high, swelling out below, and expanding again at the top. The

centre was an open shaft, admitting air and light to the galleries. Torfæus says that to this fortress Erland, son of Harold the Fair-spoken, carried off (abt. 1150) the mother of Harold the Norwegian jarl, a famous beauty; and that the jarl, unable to take it by force or famine, was glad to assent to terms by which the lady became the wife of her captor. At *Dunrossness* (20 m.) Fitful Head is 3 m. W., and Sumburgh Head, where is the mansion of Mr. Bruce, the proprietor of a great part of Shetland, is 4 m. S.

(5) **To the North Isles**✲.

The steamer passes (rt.) †**Whalsay Island**, 12 m. N. of Lerwick, a famous fishing station.

To the N.E. are the *Skerries*, with a lighthouse built 1852. We cross (l.) Yell Sound, call at *Burravoe* in the S. of **Yell**, pass up the E. coast to *Mid Yell Sound*, a fine fjord, with **Fetlar** (which has a castellated mansion occupying a picturesque situation, and belonging to Sir Arthur Nicolson) rt., visit *Uya Sound*, another important fjord and fishing station, in the S., and go on to †**Balta Sound**✲ in the E. of **Unst**, the most northerly of Her Majesty's home dominions, and a most interesting island to the tourist. It is 12 m. long by 4 m. broad, and contains good lochs and excellent trout-fishing.

Good rabbit-shooting may be obtained on **Balta Island**, by permission. Golden plover and snipe abound on the hills at Balta Sound. Pictish and Norse remains may be seen. The Unst Lighthouse is built on a rock called **Muckle Flugga**. This awfully wild situation and its surroundings are well worth a visit in calm weather.

Walk 4 m. from Balta Sound to the head of *Burrafjord*, where the lighthouse keepers live when on shore. The boatmen will row you 3 m. down the fjord and 1 m. out to the island in abt. an hour. Returning, visit the grand caves at the Noup. From Burrafjord return by *Loch of Cliff*, an inland loch 2 m. long, down which you may be rowed.

(6) **To the N.W. of the Mainland. Northmaven** is the most northerly parish on the mainland. It contains the highest hill in these islands, *i.e.* **Ronas Hill** (1475 ft.), which commands a splendid view. It is almost an island, for in the S. near †*Brae*, a neck of land called **Mavis Grind**, separating the long *Sullom Voe* to the E. from the sea on the W., is not 60 yards broad. Its W. promontory of *Eshaness* is perhaps the most interesting locality in Shetland.

Here is **Stenness**, one of the headquarters of the deep-sea fishing, with a row of typical Shetland fishermen's cottages—a boat's crew in each. On the face of the porphyry cliffs is the most wonderful giant staircase ever chiselled by the sea — the * **Grind of the Navir** (= *Gate of the Giants*)—and nowhere in the world can the force of the waves be better illustrated than in this neighbourhood. Near the Grind in the downs are the **Holes of Scraada** (once 2) now *one* enormous cauldron communicating with the sea by a passage 100 ft. long, and which must have originally begun with a blow-hole in the roof. Into it a small burn falls from a height of 60 ft. There is such a blow-hole called the "*Cannon*," close at hand. To the S. are *Eshaness Skerry* and the rock of **Dore Holm**, with a huge natural arch, and to the S.W. numerous stacks, including the **Drongs**, which take various fantastic shapes (*e.g.* a ship in full sail, a monk with a cowl, etc.), as seen from different points.

In the old ch.-yd. of *Tangwick* here is the following extraordinary epitaph:—

"He was a peaceable, quiet man, and, to all appearance, a sincere Christian. His death, which was much regretted, was caused by the stupidity of . . . who sold him nitre instead of Epsom salts, by which he was killed in the space of 3 hours after taking a dose of it."

The coast should be visited by boat. †**Hillswick** ✲ is the best centre. It is 34 m. by road—which crosses Mavis Grind(p. 439)—from Lerwick and 9 m. from Brae, where the local steamer calls once a week.

Foula, a solitary island 3½ m. long by 2½ m. broad (pop. abt. 267), 16 m. from the nearest land, viz. *Walls*, and 27 m. W. of Scalloway—with the grandest cliffs (1220 ft.) in the British Isles—can only be reached by the fortnightly mail smack from Reawick or by hiring a sailing-boat. Sea-fowl are very abundant, and it is the breeding-place of the rare bonxie or Skua Gull. Landing is by no means a certainty. There is a Congregational Chapel, which most of the islanders attend, but the Church of Scotland also has a reader here. The island is in the parish of Walls.

INDEX AND DIRECTORY

Note.—After the names of all places likely to be visited by tourists a ^{t} is inserted if there is a telegraph office there.

For the benefit of travellers from England, wherever there is an Episcopal Church, this is stated.

The numbers of the pages are arranged in the order thought to be the most convenient for reference.

An asterisk before any name is a special mark of recommendation.

Abbreviations: — Br. = Bridge; Cas. = Castle; Ch. = Church (Epis. = Episcopal; U.P. = United Presbyterian; R.C. = Roman Catholic); E. = East; Ho. = House; Lo. = (Shooting) Lodge; m. = mile; Mont. = Monument; Mt. = Mountain; N. = North; Rly. = Railway; S. = South; St. = Street; Stat. = Station; ^{t} = Telegraph Office; W. = West; C.R. = Caledonian Railway; G. & S.W.R. = Glasgow and South-Western Railway; N.B.R. = North British Railway.

Hotels: *Balmoral, Royal, Palace, Central* (smaller, good cooking), *Bedford* (quiet), *Edinburgh, Clarendon, Windsor, Douglas, Rutland*—all in Princes St.; *Waterloo* (handsome saloon for public entertainments), Waterloo Pl.

Private: * *Roxburghe*, Charlotte Sq.; *Veitch's*, 127 George St.; *Queen's*, 1 St. Colme Street (all good).

Temperance: *Old Waverley*, 43 Princes St.; *Cockburn*, 1 Cockburn St. facing Princes St.; *Darling's Regent*, 20 Waterloo Pl. (all comfortable).

Lodgings: *Anderson's*, 6, 46, 58, and 60 Melville St., and 6 Melville Cres.; *Black's*, 39 and 41 Melville St.; *Kerr's*, 13 and 17 Melville Cres.; *Mrs. Lunn's*, 43 Melville St.

Aurist: *P. M'Bride.*

Bakers, Confectioners, etc.: *Edinburgh Café*, 70 Princes St. (luncheon and teas); *Mackie*, 108 Princes St. (ices and teas); *Blair*, 37 George St. (luncheon); *M'Dowell*, 60 George St. (famed for shortbread and Chester biscuits); *West End Café*, 129 Princes St. (luncheon and teas); *M'Vitie*, 23 Queensferry St. (for cakes and Vienna bread); *Ferguson*, Geo. IV. Bridge (Edinburgh rock and sweets).

Banks: *Bank of Scotland*, top of the Mound; *Royal, National*, and *British Linen*, St. Andrew Sq.; *Commercial, Union*, and *Clydesdale*, George St.; also numerous branches.

Booksellers: *Douglas and Foulis*, 9 Castle St.; *R. Grant and Son*, 107 Princes St. (Ch. of Eng. publications); *A. Elliot*, 17 Princes St.; *Macniven and Wallace*, 138 Princes St.; *Religious Tract Soc.*, 99 George St.

Cab fares: *By distance*, according to table which driver is bound to produce. Generally, 1s. for $1\frac{1}{2}$ m. or part thereof for 1 or 2 persons; 1s. for 1 m. or part thereof for 3 or 4 persons; and 6d. for every additional $\frac{1}{2}$ m. in both cases.

By time: for shopping and calling in town 2s. for 1st hour or part thereof, and 6d. for every additional $\frac{1}{4}$ hr.; for "airing" in the country within 8 m. of the Cross, at not less than 6 m. an hr., unless otherwise desired, 3s. for 1st hr. or part thereof, and 1s. for every additional 20 min. thereafter.

Chemists: *Duncan and Flockhart*, 139 Princes St.; *Robertson*, 35 George St.

Churches: ESTABLISHED *St. Giles's*, High St.; *St. Cuthbert's*, Princes St.; *St. George's*, Charlotte Sq.; *St. Andrew's*, George St.

EPISCOPAL—*St. Mary's Cathedral*, Palmerston Pl.; *St. John's*, W. end of Princes St.; *St. Paul's*, York Pl.; *Trinity*, Dean Bridge; *All Saints*, Brougham St.

FREE—*St. George's*, Shandwick Pl.; *St. Andrew's*, Drumsheugh Gardens; *Barclay*, Bruntsfield Links.

U.P.—*Palmerston Pl. Ch.*, *Broughton Pl. Ch.*

R.C.—*Cathedral*, Broughton St.; *Sacred Heart*, Lauriston St.

Clubs: *New, Liberal, Conservative, University*, Nos. 85, 109, 112, and 127 Princes St. respectively; *United Service*, 14 Queen St.; *Northern*, 91 George St.

Dentists: *Amoore, Macleod, Matthew, Orphoot, Smith, Watson.*

Fishing Tackle Makers: *R. Anderson and Sons*, 67 Princes St.; *Phin*, 5 S. St. David St.; *Turnbull*, 60 Princes St.

Gunmakers: *J. Harkom and Son*, 30 George St.; *Henry*, 12 S. St. Andrew St.; *Mortimer and Son*, 86 George St.; *Macnaughton*, 26 Hanover St.

Hairdressers: *Pass*, 103 Princes St.; *Sturrock*, 33 Princes St.

Hosiers: *Cruickshank*, 57 George St.; *New Shetland Warehouse*, 144 George St.; and *White*, 10 Frederick St. (both for Shetland woollen goods).

Jewellers: * *Hamilton and Inches*, 88 Princes St.; *Brook and Son*, 87 George St.; *Aitchison*, 80 Princes St. (Scottish Jewellery).

Oculists: *Berry, Argyll Robertson.*

Photographers: *Crooke*, 103 Princes St.; *Moffat*, 125 Princes St.; *Marshall Wane*, 82 George St.

Physicians: *Affleck, G. W. Balfour, Brakenridge, Foulis, Maclaren, Muirhead, Simpson, Sir T. Grainger Stewart, Underhill, Heron Watson.*

Surgeons: *Annandale, Bell, Chiene, Cotterill, Duncan, Heron Watson.*

Tailors: *J. Christie and Son*, 11 St. Andrew Sq.; *Holtum and Welsh*, 6 George St. (Riding Breeches, etc.); *J. Stewart*, 88 George St.

For ladies, same as above; also *Durrant*, 4 Castle St.; *Redfern*, 31 Princes St.; *Romanes and Paterson* (Clan Tartan Warehouse), 62 Princes St.

Theatres: *Lyceum*, Grindlay St. (W. end); *Royal*, Broughton St. (E. end); *Empire* (Varieties), Nicolson St. (S. side).

Tramways: *Horse-cars* to the *West End, Leith*, and the *S. side* pass along Princes St. (Tourists recommended to go on the top of a car round the circular rte. by Morningside.

Cable-cars run from corner of Hanover St. and Princes St. to *Botanic Gardens* and *N. side*; and from corner of Frederick St. and Princes St. to *Stockbridge* and *Fettes College.*

Turkish Baths: 90 Princes St.; 12 Stafford St.

Edinchip, 169.

Edinshall, 80.

Edmonstone Ho., 72.

Ednam, 85.

Edradynate, 236.

Edramuckie, 238, 242.

Edrom, 80.

EDZELL.[t] *Panmure Arms* (very comfortable), 271.

Eggerness, 109.

EGILSAY, ISLAND OF. No *Inn.* Take boat from Rousay or Kirkwall, 431.

Eglinton Cas., 124.

Eidart Water, 288.

EIGG, ISLAND OF. *Scoor Inn*

Confectioners: * *A. Fenwick and Son*, 27 St. John St.; * *Miss Dick*, 45 George St.; *C. G. Kennaway*, 49 South St. and 29 High St.
Dentists: *A. P. Kelt; J. and J. Stewart.*
Fishing-Tackle Maker: ** *P. D. Malloch*, 209 High St.
General Post Office: corner of Tay St. and High St.
Gunsmiths: *D. Crockhart*, 44 George St.; *R. Lees*, 63 George St.
Hairdressers: *Hardie*, 39 George St.; *Muego*, 71 S. Methven St.
Jeweller: **D. MacGregor* 40 George St.
Museums: *Perthshire Natural History*, Tay St., excellently arranged; *Antiquarian*, George St. (neglected).
Physicians: *D. H. Stirling, R. Stirling, Ferguson.*
Restaurants: * *R. Wilson*, 38 St. John St.; *Mrs. Laidlaw* (Temperance), 18 Leonard St.; *Waverley* (Temperance), 38 Caledonian Road.
Peterculter, 274.
PETERHEAD[t] (Pop. 12,226), 291. *North Eastern, Royal, Laing's Temp.* (all good). Epis. Ch.
Pettycur, 180.
Phantassie, 8.
Philiphaugh, 31.
Philipstoun, 128.
Philorth, 292.
Picts' Ditch (Catrail), 21, 30.
,, Houses, see *Brochs.*
Pierowall Bay, 431.
Piershill, 66.
Pinkie Ho., 67.
,, Battle of, 68.
Pinmore, 115.
Pinwherry Stat., 115.
Pirn Hill (Fort), 78.
Pirnmill, 327, 336.
Pitcairn Green, 215.
Pitcaithley Wells, 194.
Pitcaple, 300.
Pitcorthie, 188.
Pitfichie Cas., 294.
Pitfour (Aberdeenshire), 290.
,, Cas. (Perthshire), 247.
Pitgaveny Ho., 305.
PITLOCHRIE[t] (Pop. 1136), 220.
Hotels: **Fisher's* (excellent), close to stat.; *Atholl Hydro. Estab.* (good) ½ m. from stat., omnibus meets trains; *Moulin Hotel* (very comfortable) ¾ m. N., no omnibus; *Pitlochrie Hydro. Estab.; Scotland's Hotel; Craigower Hotel* (all very fair). Numerous *Lodgings.*
Banks: *Bk. of Scotland; Commercial; Union.*
Churches: *Estab., Epis., Free, Baptist.*
Coaches: Mail-gig daily (coach in summer) to *Kirkmichael* at 9 A.M., returning at 1.45 P.M.; Mail-gig daily to *Tummel Bridge* at 8.30 A.M., ret. at 2 P.M.
Excursion Coaches from Fisher's Hotel to *Queen's View, Killiecrankie, Falls of Bruar, Dunkeld and Rumbling Bridge, Kinloch-Rannoch*, etc. *See* Time Bill. A daily coach is expected to run in 1894 to *Kinloch-Rannoch*, and on to *Rannoch Stat.* on the West High. Railway.
Doctor: *Beattie.*
Pitmedden, 293.
Pitmurchie, 276.
Pitnacree, 235.
Pitsligo, 300.
Pittencrieff, 192.
PITTENWEEM,[t] 188.
Pittodrie, 300.
Pladda, Island of, 328.
Plaidy Stat., 299.
Plains Stat., 143.
Plockton, 379, 386.
Pluscardine Abbey, 304, 307.
Polkemmet, 143.
Pollok Cas., 324.
,, Ho., 324.
Pollokshaws, 324.
Pollokshields, 318.
Polmaise, 204.
Polmont Junc., 131.
Poltalloch Ho., 351.
Polton, 76.
Polwarth Ch., 80.
Pomathorn Stat., 77.
Ponfeigh Stat., 93.
Pooldullie Bridge, 296.
POOLEWE.[t] *Inn* (comfortable), 385, 383.
PORT APPIN.[t] *Inn* (Temp., comfortable), 363.
,, ASKAIG.[t] *Hotel* (small, comfortable), 342.
,, BANNATYNE.[t] *Hydro. Estab.* (good), 318.
,, Charlotte (Islay), 342.
,, ELLEN.[t] *White Hart* (very good), 341.
Port Errol, 292.
Portessie Stat., 302, 307.
PORT-GLASGOW.[t] *Star*, 314 321.
,, Gordon, 308.
,, Gower, 408.
Portincaple Ferry, 334, 312.
Portincross Cas., 330.
Port-in-Sherrich. *Inn*, 172.
Portknockie Stat., 307.
Portlethen, 255.
Port-Logan, 112.
,, Mary, 114.
Portmore Ho., 78.
,, Loch, 78.
Port-na-Craig Ferry, 220, 236.
Portnahaven, 342.
Port-nan-con, 423.
Portnellan Ho., 221.
PORTOBELLO,[t] 66, 36.
PORTPATRICK.[t] *Downshire; Crown*, 112.
PORTREE.[t] *Marine, Royal* (both good). Epis. Ch., 389.
PORTSONACHAN.[t] *Hotel* (good; favourite angling quarters), 172, 174.
Portsoy, 307.
Port-William[t] (*Monreith Arms*), 110.
Possilpark Stat., 149.
Posso, New, 90.
Potarch Bridge. *Inn*, 276.
Potburn, 33.
Powsail Burn, 90.
Powtrail, 15, 16.
Poyntzfield, 403.
Preshal (Hill), 391.
Prestonfield, 62.
Preston Grange, 68.
,, Hall, 67.
,, Tower, 68.
Prestonkirk,[t] 8.
PRESTONPANS,[t] 68.
Prestwick,[t] 122.
Priesthill, 94.
Priestlaw, 80.
Prince Charlie's Cave, 389.
,, ,, Mont., 366.
Princes Pier, 315, 322.
Prosen Bridge, 268.
Pubill Burn, 243.
Pulpit Rock, 347.
Pulskaig Burn, 122.
Pulteneytown, 409.
Pumpherston Oil Works, 144.
Purvis Hill (camp), 78.

Quanterness, 432.
Quarff, 438.
Quarter Road Stat., 149.
QUEEN MARGARET. Cave (Dunfermline), 192; Chapel (Edinburgh), 40; (Iona), 360; Ferry, 179, 202; Hope, 179.
QUEEN MARY. Alloa, 199;

THE END

NEW MAP OF SCOTLAND.

Reduced from Ordnance Survey to Scale of 10 Miles to an Inch.

INDEX TO SECTIONS.

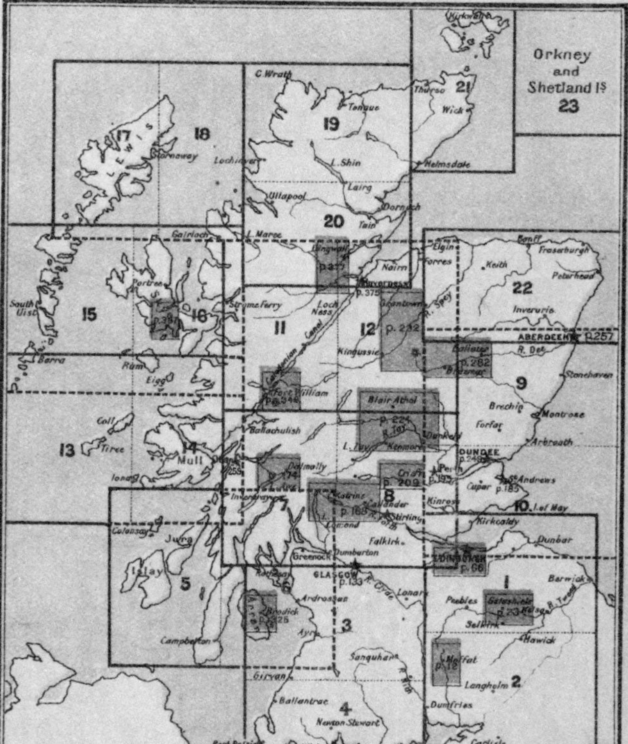

J. Bartholomew, Edinr.

The limits of the 23 Section Maps are shown above. They are designed to show all the Routes and Places described in the Handbook. For the areas coloured brown there are special maps on a larger scale; they will be found in the book at pages referred to.

Towns with Plans marked thus ★ The small figures thus p. 325 refer to the page numbers.

Continued on Section 10

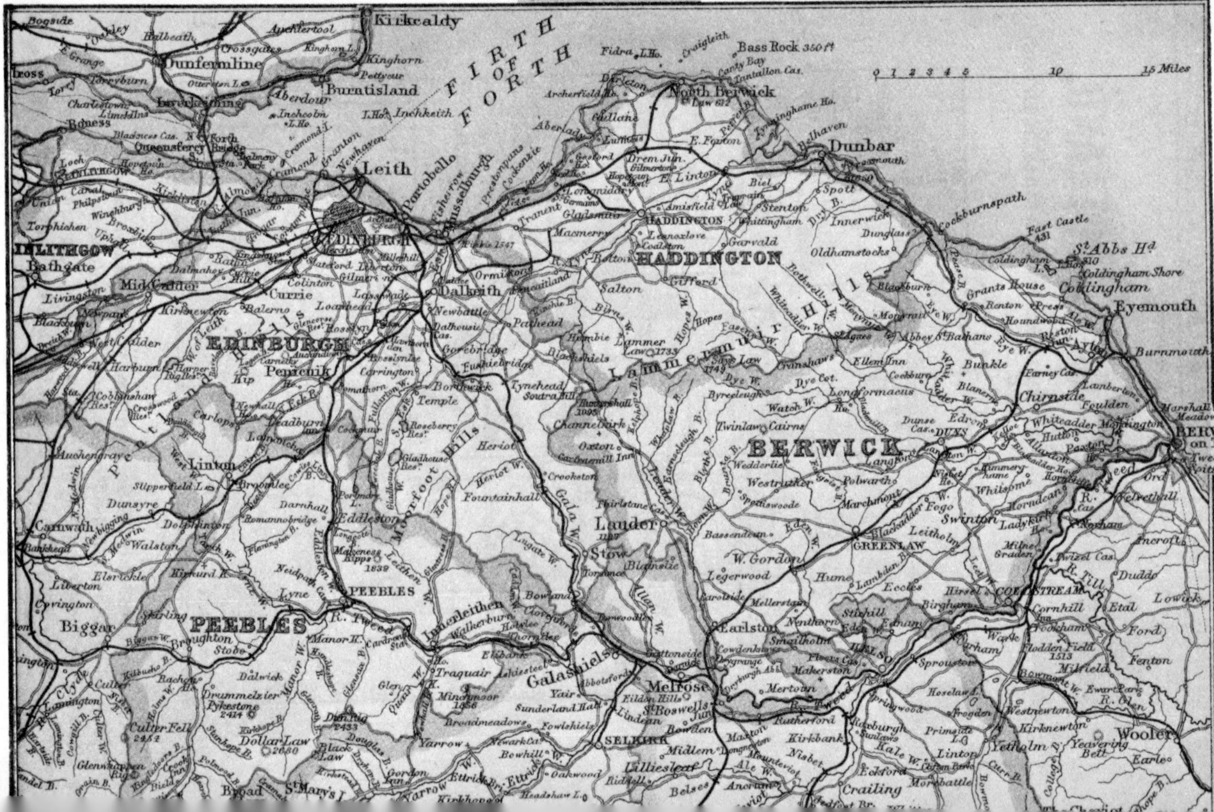

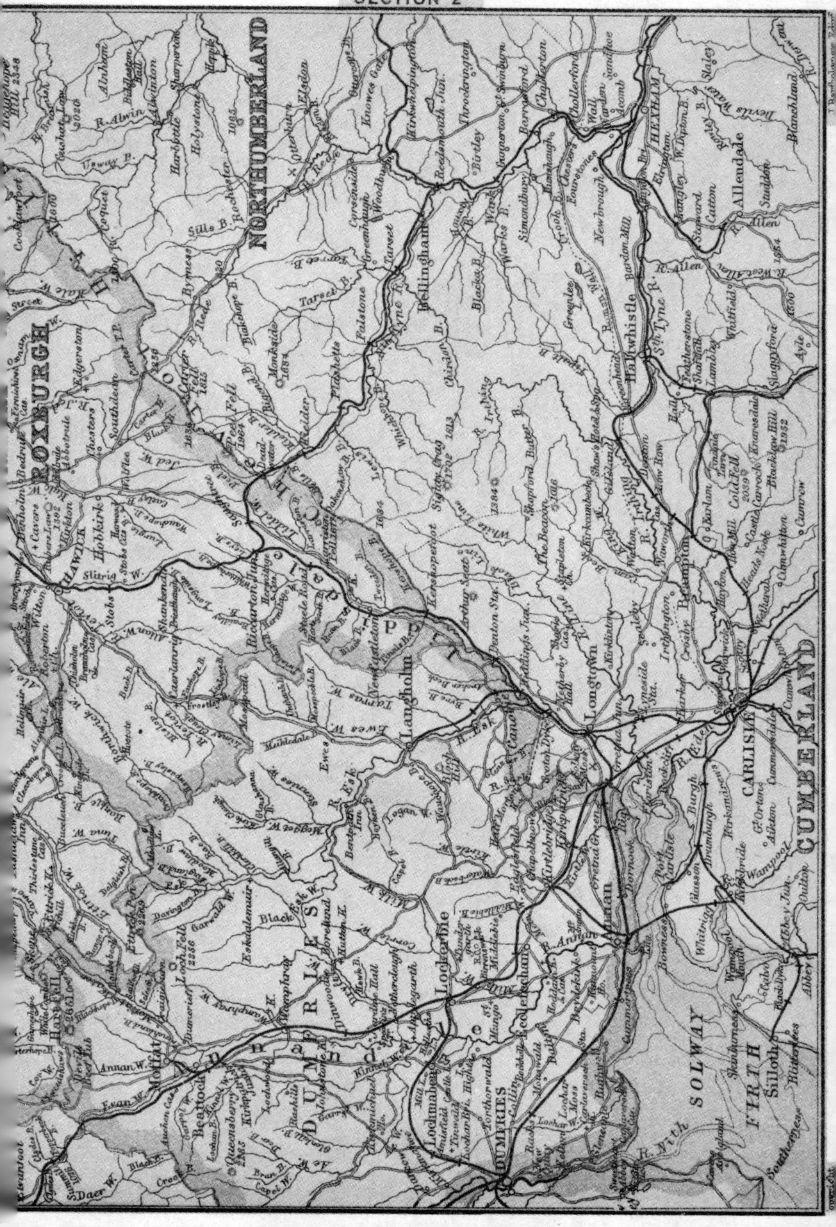
NORTHUMBERLAND
ROXBURGH
CUMBERLAND
DUMFRIES
SOLWAY
FIRTH
CARLISLE
HEXHAM
HAWICK
Langholm
Lockerbie
Moffat
Annan
Longtown
Bellingham
Haltwhistle
Brampton
Silloth
Allendale

Continued o

Continued on Sections 7 & 8

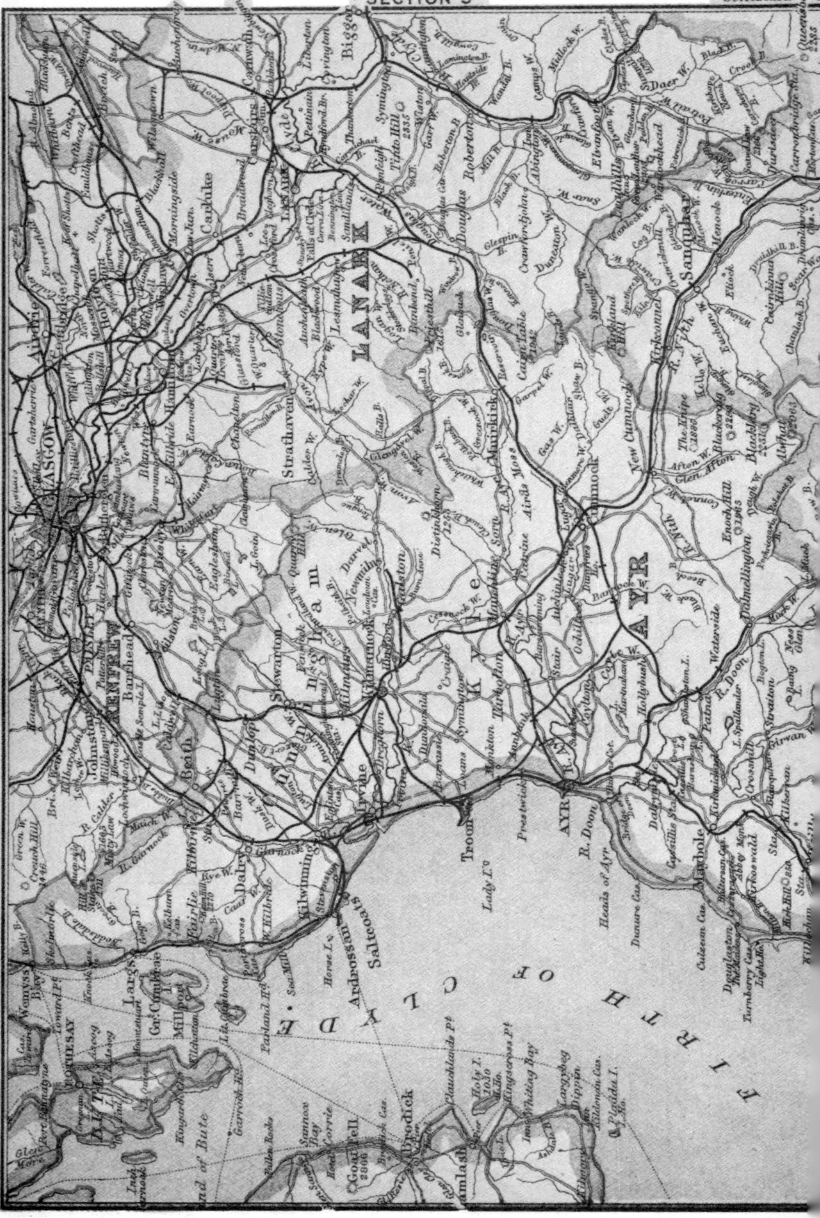

Sections 1 & 2
SECTION 4
DUMFRIES
Southerness
DUMFRIES
KIRKCUDBRIGHT
WIGTOWN
Carrick
Thornhill
Penpont
Moniaive
Closeburn
Carsphairn
Dalry
New Galloway
Kells Range
Merrick
2764
Barr
Ballantrae
Lendalfoot
Colmonell
Stranraer
Port Patrick
Loch Ryan
Glenluce
New Luce
Newton Stewart
Creetown
Wigtown
Gatehouse of Fleet
Castle Douglas
Dalbeattie
New Abbey
Criffell
1866
Kirkcudbright
Kirkcudbright Bay
Wigtown Bay
Luce Bay
Whithorn
Isle of Whithorn
Burrow Head
Port William
Mull of Galloway
SOLWAY FIRTH
Workington
0 1 2 3 4 5 10 15 Miles

Continued on

Sections 7, 8 & 14.

BUTE County, includes the Islands of Bute, Arran & the Cumbraes.

Continued on Sections 3 & 8

Continued on

tions 11 & 12

Continued on Sections 1 9 & 10

Continued on Section 22

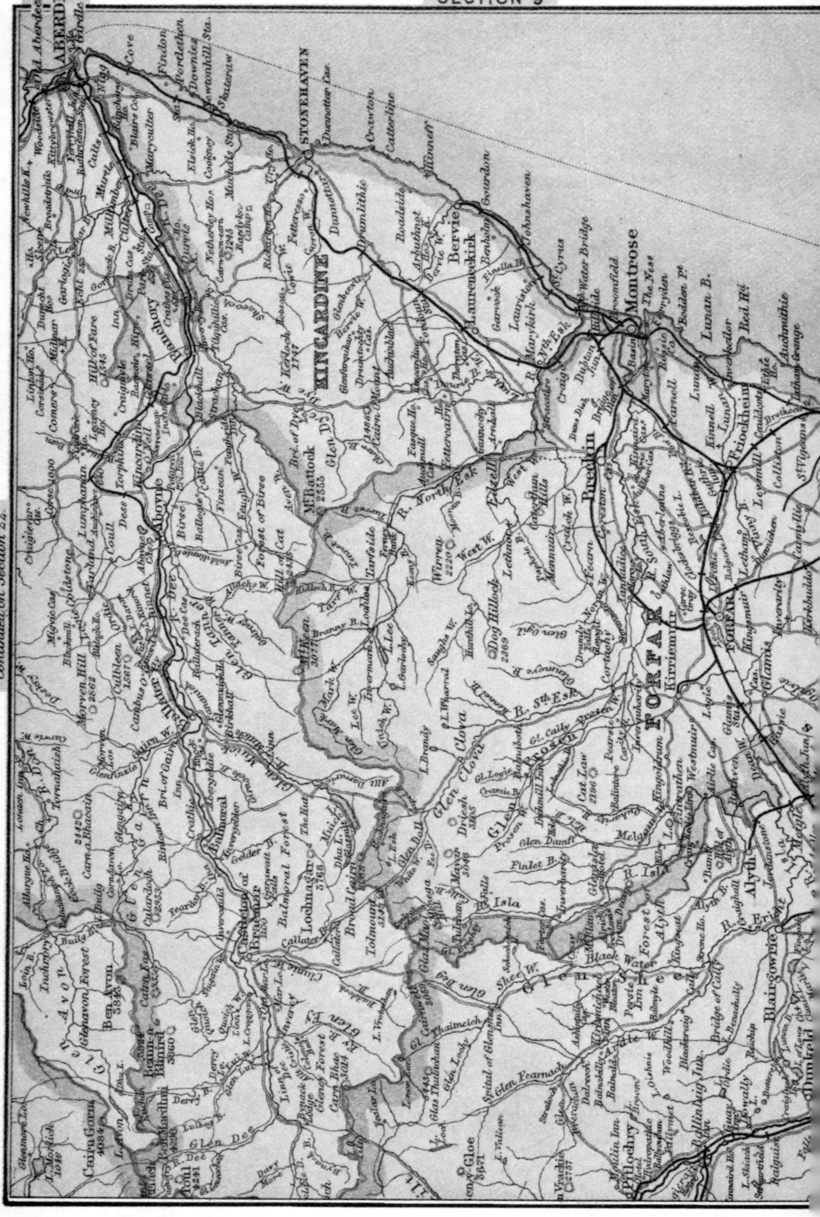

DUNDEE
PERTH
CUPAR
FIFE
KIRKCALDY
KINROSS
Dunfermline
St Andrews
St Andrews Bay
Carnoustie
Buddon Ness
Broughty Ferry
Tayport
Firth of Tay
Firth of Forth
Fife Ness
Isle of May
Crail
Anstruther
Elie
Largo Bay
Leven
Burntisland
Leith
Portobello
Musselburgh
North Berwick
Dunbar
HADDINGTON
LINLITHGOW
Bathgate
Bo'ness
Culross
Kincardine
Dollar
Methven
Dunning
Milnathort
Falkland
Newburgh
Abernethy
Auchtermuchty
Leslie
Dysart
Bass Rock 350 ft
(Inchcape) Bell Rock Light House
St Abbs Hd
0 1 2 3 4 5 10 15 Miles
J. Bartholomew, Edin.
Copyright
Continued on Section 1

Continued o

Continued on Section 16

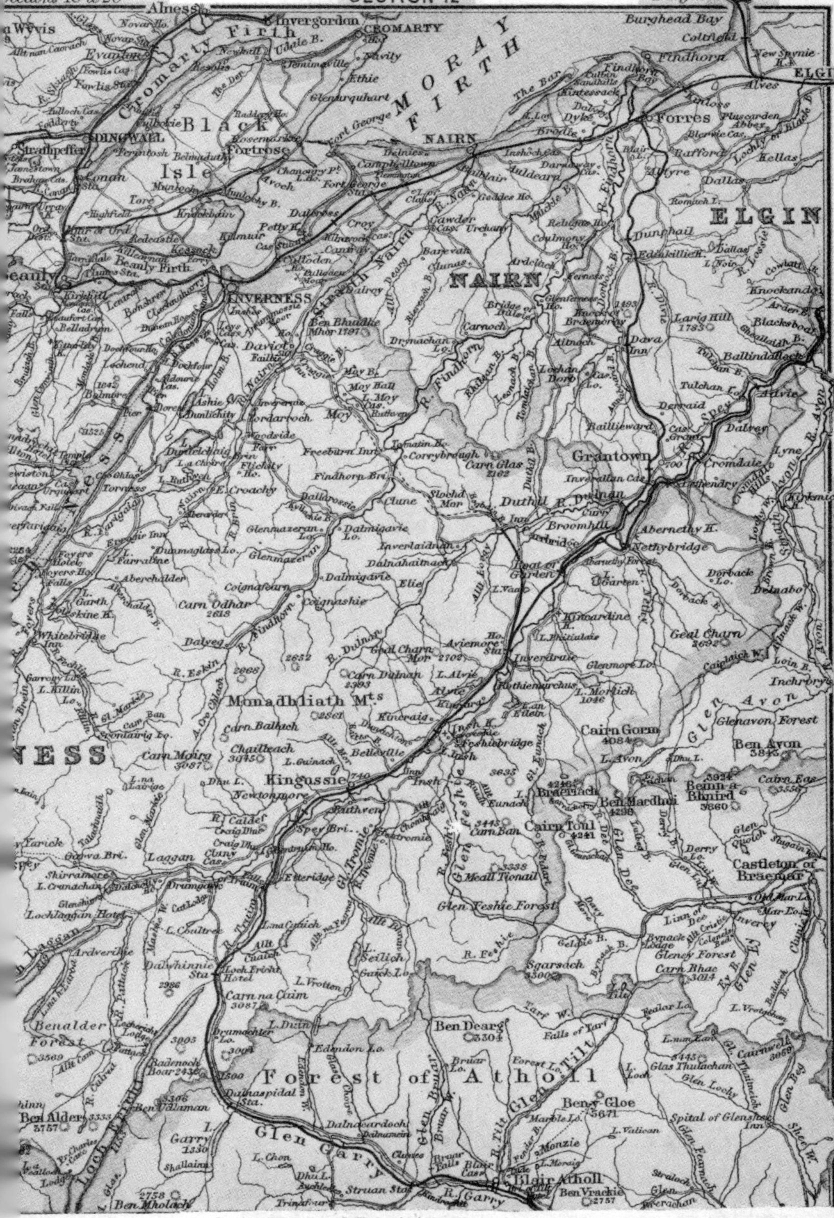
Alness
Invergordon
CROMARTY
Cromarty Firth
MORAY FIRTH
Burghead Bay
Findhorn
ELGIN
Alves
Kinloss
Forres
NAIRN
Black Isle
DINGWALL
Strathpeffer
Fortrose
Fort George
Conan
Evanton
Beauly Firth
INVERNESS
Culloden
Croy
Cawdor
Auldearn
Nairn
Dunphail
Carnoch
Moy
Tomatin
Corrybrough
Carn Glas
Grantown
Cromdale
Broomhill
Duthil
Nethybridge
Abernethy
Boat of Garten
Kincardine
Aviemore Sta.
Inverdruie
Rothiemurchus
L. Morlich
Glenmore Lo.
Cairn Gorm 4084
Glen Avon
Ben Avon 3843
Ben Macdhui 4296
Braeriach 4248
Cairn Toul 4241
Castleton of Braemar
Glen Dee
Kingussie
Newtonmore
Ruthven
Insh
Feshiebridge
Glen Feshie Forest
Monadhliath Mts
Carn Odhar 2618
Foyers
Whitebridge Inn
Fort Augustus
Laggan
Dalwhinnie Sta.
Loch Ericht
Ben Alder 3757
Benalder Forest
Forest of Atholl
Ben Dearg 3304
Glen Tilt
Beny Gloe 3671
Blair Atholl
Struan Sta.
R. Garry
Glen Garry
Dalnaspidal Sta.
Carn na Caim 3087
Spital of Glenshee Inn
Glas Thulachan
Cairnwell 3059
Sgarsach 3300
Carn Bhac 3014
Ben Vrackie 2757
Ben Mholach
NESS

Continued on

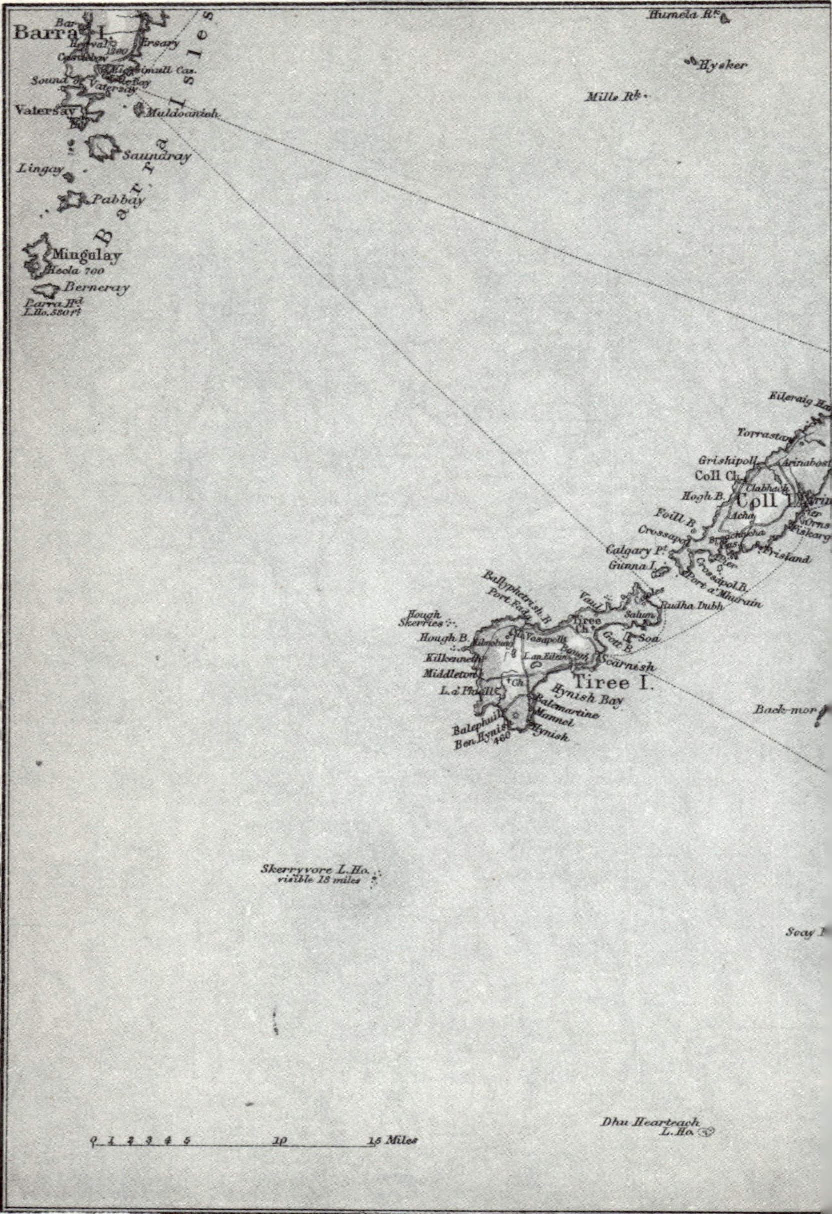

Continued on Sections 7 & 11

Continued o

Killegray
Berneray
Boreray
Rodel
Ru Renish
Groay
Gilsay
Lingay
Vallay
Griminish Pt.
Scalpeg
Harmetray
Steamer Weekly
Hougary
Hougary Pt.
Balranald
North Uist
L. Scatavagh
L. nan-Ian
Loch Maddy
LITTLE
MINCH
Vaternish Pt.
Loch Eport
Monach Is.
Baleshare
Ben Eval 1133
Gramisdale Inn
Ronay
Benbecula
L. Uskevagh
Benbecula Sound
Wiay I.
L. Carnan
L. Skiport
Howmore
L. Aultibrig
Hekla
1988
Ru Ushinish
South Uist
Hollay
Ben More 2035
Ardvula Pt.
L. Kildonan
Loch Eynort
L. Leanamore
Askernish Ho.
L. Allan
Loch Boisdale
L. Duine Kel
Pollachar Inn
Sound of Barra
Lingay
Ben Scrien 609
Eriskay
Fiaray
Scurrival Pt.
Fuday
Eoligarry
Stack Is.
Gighay
Hellisay
Grean Hd.
Barra I.
Ersary
Vatersay
Muldoanish
Saundray
Lingay
Pabbay
Mingulay
Barra Isles
Dunvegan Hd.
Loch Dunvegan
Trumpan
Ardmore
Geary
L. Pooltiel
Oisgill B.
Eist
Moonen B.
Ramasaig
Hoe Pt.
Duirinish
McLeods Tables
Ollisdal
McLeods Maidens
Idrigill Pt.
Loch Bracadale
ISLE OF
SKY
Canna I.
Compass Hill
Garrisdale Pt.
Tarbert
Humela Rk.
Hysker
Mills Rk.
0 1 2 3 4 5 10 Miles

Sections 17 & 18

Continued on Section 11

0 1 2 3 4 5 10 15 Miles
Butt of Lewis
Erropie
Aird Dhail
Cross
Dail
Galson
Borgh
Shader
Barvas
L. Barvas
Arnol
L. Sheabost
Brugar
Dalbeg Inn
Carloway
L. Carloway
Lit. Bernera
Loch Bernera or W. L. Roag
Gallon Hd
L. Roag
Great Bernera
Valtos
Uig
Uig B.
Breasclet
Callernish
L E W I S
Ben Barvas 900
Monach 800
R. Gress
Gress
Back
R. Coll
Coll
Vatsker
Tong
Broad Bay
Sandwick
Arnish
Stornoway Harb.
Luirbost
Ranish
Chicken Rock
Suainabhal 1250
Aird Bhreidhuis
Mealasbhal 1750
Criomabhal 1500
Malistay
L. Hamanaway
Resort
Scarpay
Gas Keir
Forest of Harris
Balallan
L. Erisort
Cromor
Park
L. Odairn
Kebock Hd
Loch Shell
Ben Mhor 1750
Crionaig 1500
Loch Seaforth
Loch Claidh
W. L. Tarbert
Tarbert
Hotel
Taransay
Aird Vanish
Luskentyre
Scalpa I.
E. L. Tarbert
Skeir-inoe
Toe Hd
Sound of Harris
C. Difficulty
Shillay
Pabbay
Ensay
Killegray
Berneray
Boreray
HARRIS
Obbe Inn
Rodel
Ru Renish
Finsbay
L. Stockinish
L. Gheosabhaigh
Skeir Graitich
Skeir na Mule
Fladdachuan
Eilean Mhuire
Shiant Is
Rudha Hunish
The Aird
Trodday I.
Groday
Gilsay
Lingay
Ant Iasgair
Steamer (alternate weeks)
Steamer Weekly

Continued on Sections 19 & 20

Continued

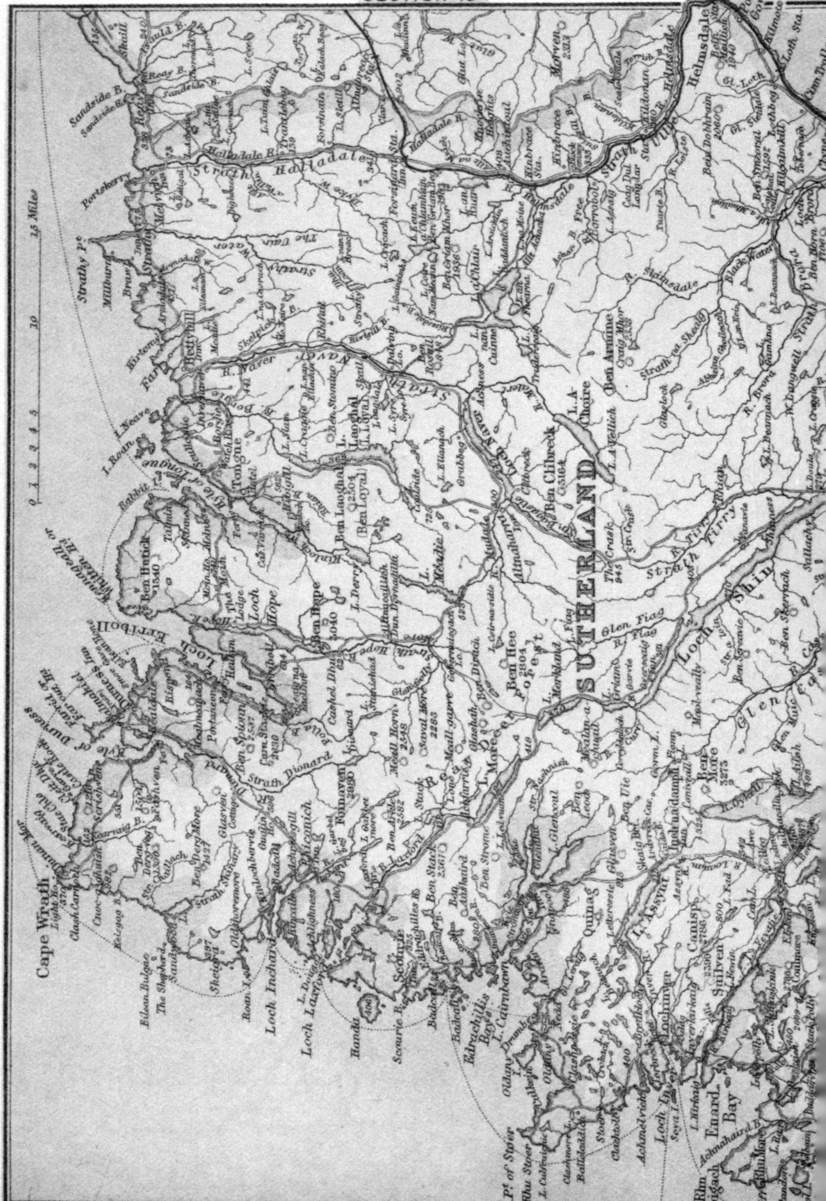
Cape Wrath
SUTHERLAND
0 1 2 3 4 5 10 15 Miles
Strathy Pt.
Portskerry
Melvich
Strath Halladale
Forsinard
Kinbrace
Kildonan
Helmsdale
Ben Griam Mhor
Strathy
Armadale
Kirtomy
Farr
Bettyhill
Strath Naver
R. Naver
Loch Naver
Ben Klibreck
Ben Armine
Kyle of Tongue
Tongue
Rabbit I.
Ben Hutick 1540
Ben Loyal
Loch Hope
Ben Hope 3040
Loch Eriboll
Ben Spionn
Durness
Foinaven 2980
Strath Dionard
Loch Inchard
Loch Laxford
Scourie
Handa
Ben Stack 2361
Ben Hee
Reay Forest
L. More
Loch Shin
Glen Fiag
Strath Tirry
Eddrachillis Bay
L. Cairnbawn
Quinag
L. Assynt
Ben More 3273
Canisp
Suilven
Lochinver
Loch Inver
Enard Bay
Pt. of Stoer
Rhu Stoer
Brora
Strath Brora

... Sections 12 & 21

Continued on Sections 11 & 12

J. Bartholomew, Edin

Continued on Section 23

Continued on Section 19

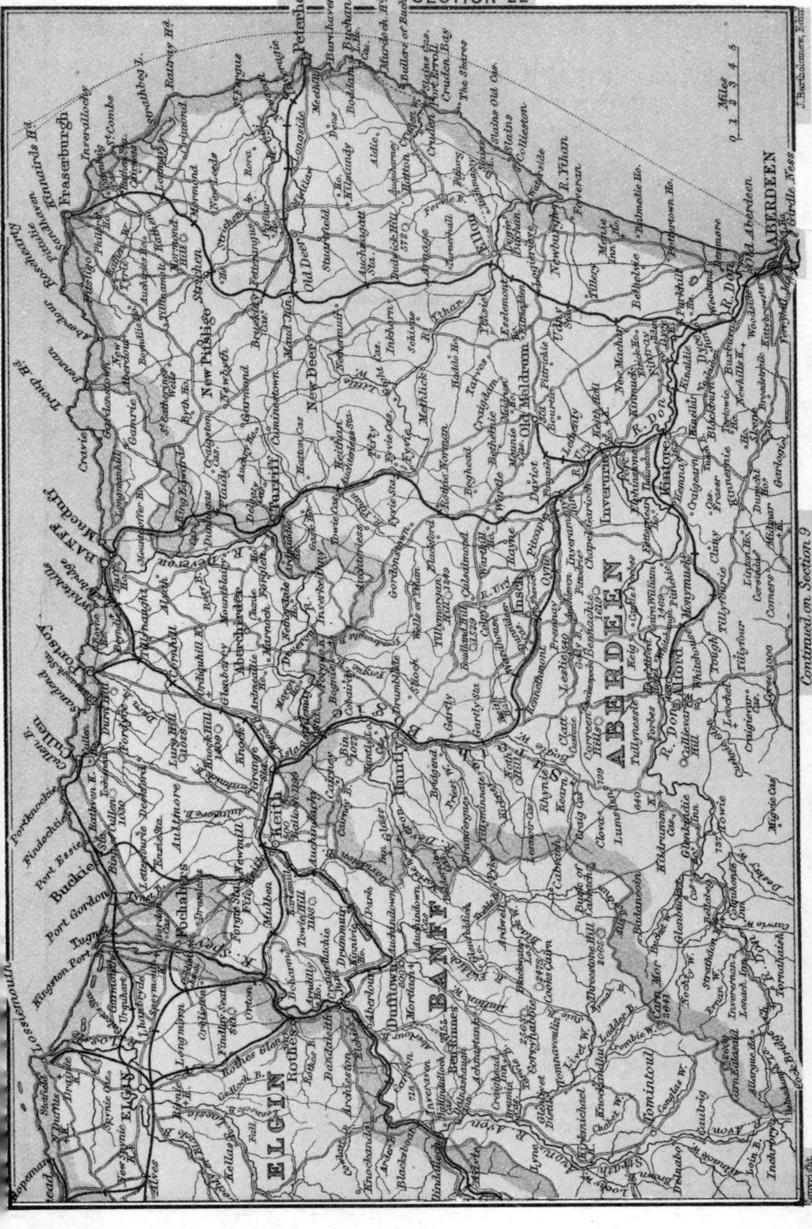

Continued on Section 9

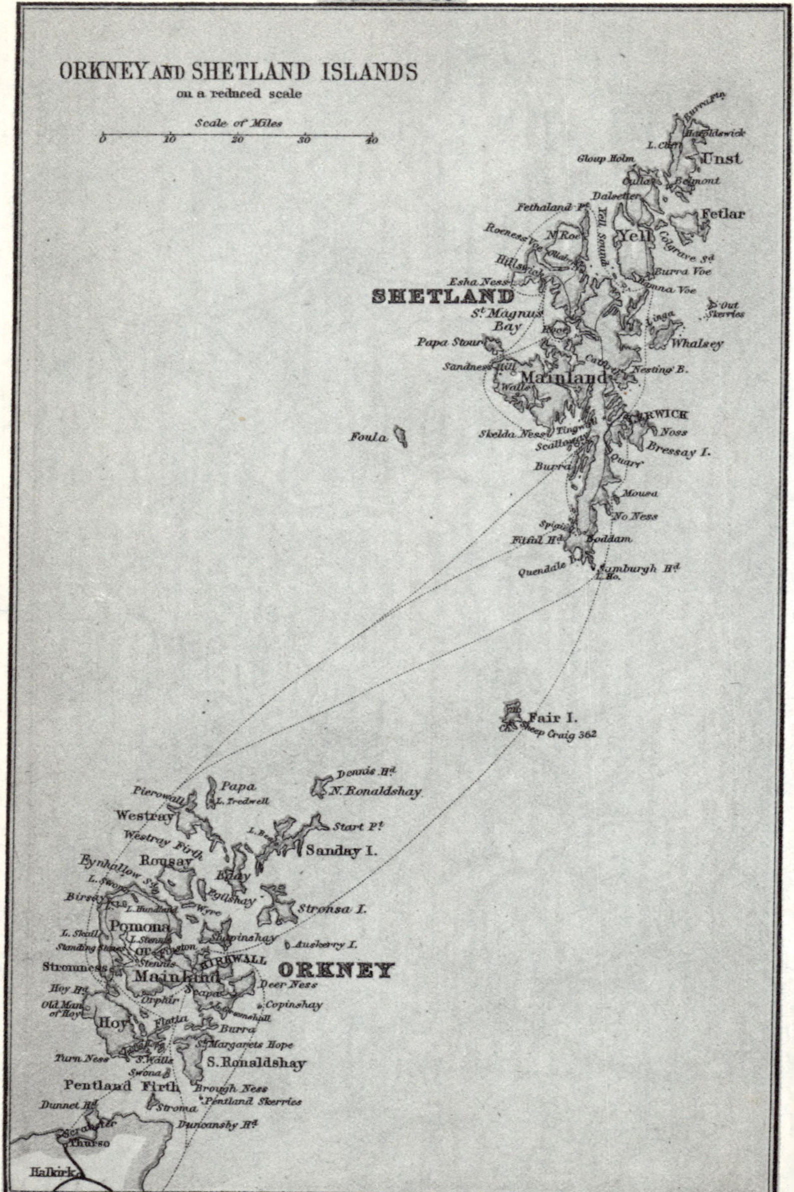
ORKNEY AND SHETLAND ISLANDS
on a reduced scale
Scale of Miles
0 10 20 30 40
SHETLAND
Unst
Gloup Holm
Belmont
Daleetter
Fethaland Pt
Fetlar
Roeness Voe
Yell
Yell Sound
Colgrave Sd
Hillswick
Burra Voe
Esha Ness
St. Magnus Bay
Out Skerries
Linga
Whalsey
Papa Stour
Sandness Hill
Mainland
Nesting B.
Walls
Noss
Bressay I.
Foula
Skelda Ness
Tingwall
Scalloway
Quarr
Burra
Mousa
No Ness
Fitful Hd.
Boddam
Quendale B.
Sumburgh Hd.
Fair I.
Sheep Craig 362
ORKNEY
Dennis Hd.
Papa
N. Ronaldshay
Pierowall
L. Tredwell
Westray
Start Pt.
Westray Firth
Sanday I.
Rousay
Eynhallow Sd.
Eday
Birsay
Egilshay
Stronsa I.
Wyre
Pomona
L. Hundland
L. Skaill
Standing Stones
Shapinshay
Auskerry I.
L. Stennis
Stennis
KIRKWALL
Stromness
Mainland
Hoy Hd.
Scapa
Deer Ness
Old Man of Hoy
Orphir
Copinshay
Hoy
Flotta
Burra
St. Margarets Hope
Turn Ness
S. Walls
S. Ronaldshay
Swona
Pentland Firth
Brough Ness
Pentland Skerries
Dunnet Hd.
Stroma
Duncansby Hd.
Thurso
Halkirk